Special Edition

Using

Using

MICROSOFT®

Project 98

New Edition

Special Edition

Using

MICROSOFT®
Project 98

Tim Pyron

Special Edition Using Microsoft Project 98, New Edition

Library of Congress Catalog No.: 97-68695

ISBN: 0-7897-1252-0

99 98   6 5 4

Interpretation of the printing code: the rightmost double-digit number is the year of the book's printing; the rightmost single-digit number, the number of the book's printing. For example, a printing code of 97-1 shows that the first printing of the book occurred in 1997.

Screen reproductions in this book were created using Collage Plus from Inner Media, Inc., Hollis, NH.

Contents at a Glance

I | **Getting Started with Microsoft Project 98**

1. The Power of Microsoft Project 98   15
2. Learning the Basics of Microsoft Project   27
3. Setting Up a New Project Document   61
4. Working with Project Files   91

II | **Scheduling Tasks**

5. Creating a Task List   125
6. Entering Scheduling Requirements   171
7. Working with the Major Task Views   215

III | **Assigning Resources and Costs**

8. Defining Resources and Costs   251
9. Understanding Resource Scheduling in Microsoft Project 98   283
10. Assigning Resources and Costs to Tasks   307
11. Resolving Resource Allocation Problems   345

IV | **Reviewing and Publishing the Project**

12. Reviewing the Project Plan   391
13. Printing Views and Reports   413
14. Publishing Projects on the Web   439

V | **Tracking and Analyzing Progress**

15. Tracking Work on the Project   473
16. Analyzing Progress and Revising the Schedule   507

VI | **Coordinating Projects and Sharing Data**

17. Working with Multiple Projects   543
18. Using Microsoft Project in Workgroups   565
19. Exchanging Project Data with Other Applications   593

VII | **Working with Views and Reports**

   20. Using the Standard Views, Tables, and Filters   659

   21. Formatting Views   695

   22. Customizing Views, Tables, and Filters   741

   23. Using the Standard Reports   767

   24. Customizing Reports   793

VIII | **Programming and Controlling Microsoft Project 98**

   25. Using Macros in Microsoft Project   833

   26. Using Visual Basic for Applications   849

   27. Customizing Toolbars, Menus, and Forms   871

IX | **Appendixes**

   A. Microsoft Project 98 Shortcut Keys   913

   B. Glossary   919

   C. Companion Products for Microsoft Project 98   927

   Index   945

Table of Contents

Introduction   1

Why You Should Use This Book   2

Why You Should Use Microsoft Project   2

What's New in Microsoft Project 98   3

How This Book Is Organized   6

Special Features in This Book   10

I │ Getting Started with Microsoft Project 98

1 The Power of Microsoft Project 98   15

Exploring What Makes Project Management Different   16

How Does Microsoft Project 98 Help with All This?   17

Some General, Commonsense Guidelines
for Project Managers   18

A Checklist for Using Microsoft Project   20
　Preliminaries   21
　Planning   21
　Managing the Project   22

Project Management Scheduling Techniques   23
　You Must Provide the Raw Data   23
　The Calendar Used for Scheduling   23
　How Project Calculates the Schedule   24
　How Resource Assignments Affect the Schedule   25

From Here...   26

2 Learning the Basics of Microsoft Project   27

Starting and Exiting Microsoft Project   28

Exploring the Microsoft Project Window   29
　The Menu Bar   33
　The Toolbars   33
　The Entry Bar   34
　The View Bar   34
　The Status Bar   35

Using the Online Learning Aids   36
    Accessing Online Help   36
    Using the Office Assistant   37
    Using Contents and Index   39
    Getting Started   43
    Microsoft on the Web   45
    Working with the Planning Wizard   48

Introducing the Gantt Chart View   50
    The Active Split Bar   52
    The Split Bar and the Split Box   54

Changing Views   54

Scrolling and Selecting Data Fields   56
    Using the Scroll Bars   56
    Scrolling the Timescale with the Keyboard   56
    Locating a Task Bar on the Timescale   57
    Finding Tasks or Resources by Name   57
    Selecting Data Fields in Tables   57
    Scrolling and Selecting Fields in Forms   58

From Here…   58

3   Setting Up a New Project Document   61

Supplying Information for a New Project   62
    Using the Project Information Dialog Box   62
    Using the Properties Sheet   66

Selecting the Environment Options   70
    Reviewing Critical Options   72
    Setting Other Useful Options   76

Defining a Calendar of Working Time   78
    Scheduling with Calendars   79
    Editing the Standard Calendar   79
    Creating a New Calendar   82
    Saving or Canceling Your Changes   85
    Working with Calendars   85

Working with the Organizer   85
    Copying Calendars to the Global Template   86
    Copying a Calendar from One Project to Another   87

Using Calendars from Microsoft Project 3.0   88

Printing the Base Calendars   88

From Here...   90

4 Working with Project Files   91

Starting and Opening Project Files   92
Creating a New Project Document   92
Opening an Existing File   92
Virus Protection   100

Locating Files   101
Specifying Search Criteria for Finding Files   102
Searching for Files of a Certain Type   102
Searching for Files by the Characters in Their File Names   103
Searching for Files that Contain Specific Text   103
Searching for Files by the Date Saved   104
Using the Advanced Find Dialog Box   104
Using the ODBC File Open Option   107

Saving and Protecting Files   107
Saving a File   107
Providing Security for Saved Files   109
Saving Files in HTML Format   111
Saving the Workspace   111

Templates   112
Opening Template Files   112
The GLOBAL.MPT   113
Using the Microsoft Project Sample Templates   113
Creating a New Template   114
Modifying Template Files   114

Using the Organizer   114
Using the Organizer to Modify the GLOBAL.MPT   116
Copying Objects with the Organizer   116
Renaming an Object with the Organizer   118
Deleting an Object with the Organizer   118

Displaying and Closing Files   119
Using the Window Command   119
Closing Files   120

From Here...   121

II | Scheduling Tasks

5   Creating a Task List   125

Approaching the Planning Process   126

Entering Tasks in the Gantt Chart   127
    Creating Tasks in the Gantt Chart   128
    Entering Task Durations   134
    Locating the Current Task Bar on the Gantt Chart   139
    Entering Milestones   140
    Entering Recurring Tasks   142
    Using the Task Information Dialog Box   147

Using Other Views to Enter Tasks   149
    Using the PERT Chart   150
    Using the Task Entry View   151
    Using the Task Details View   154
    Using the Task Sheet View   154
    Creating Tasks with the Mouse   155

Editing the Task List   156
    Undoing Changes in the Task List   156
    Inserting, Clearing, and Deleting Tasks   156
    Moving and Copying Tasks   157
    Editing Recurring Tasks   160

Outlining the Task List   160
    Indenting and Outdenting Tasks   162
    Collapsing and Expanding the Outline   162
    Editing Outlined Projects   164
    Selecting the Display Options for Outlining   164

Printing the Project Task List   166
    Printing the Task Views   166
    Printing the Standard Task Reports   167

From Here...   169

6   Entering Scheduling Requirements   171

Establishing Dependency Links   173
    Understanding Dependency Links   173
    Allowing for Delays and Overlaps   174
    Using the Term *Successor*   175
    Selecting the Dependent Task   175
    Defining Types of Dependency Link Relationships   176

Entering Dependency Links   179
    Creating Links Using the Menu or Toolbar   180
    Creating Links Using the Task Information Dialog Box   181
    Creating Links Using the Task Form View   183
    Creating Links Using the Entry Table   185
    Creating Links Using the Mouse   187
    Working with the Automatic Linking Option   189

Modifying, Reviewing, and Removing Dependency Links   191
    Entering Lags and Leads   191
    Removing Links   193
    Linking Outlined Task Lists   195
    Auditing the Task Links   197

Task Splitting   199

Working with Task Constraints   202
    Understanding the Types of Constraints   203
    Entering Task Constraints   205
    Removing Task Constraints   207

Resolving Conflicts Caused by Constraints   208
    Using the Adjust Dates Macro   212

From Here...   214

7 Working with the Major Task Views   215

Working with the Calendar View   216
    Understanding the Calendar View   216
    Moving Around in Calendar View   217
    Editing a Project in Calendar View   222

Working with the PERT Chart View   225
    Understanding the PERT Chart View   226
    Zooming the PERT Chart View   227
    Scrolling and Selecting in the PERT Chart   228
    Editing a Project in the PERT Chart   229
    Customizing the PERT Chart with the Layout Dialog Box   235

Adding Graphics and Text to Gantt Charts   237
    Introducing the Drawing Toolbar   237
    Descriptions of the Drawing Buttons   238
    Working with Drawing Objects in the Gantt Chart View   240
    Placing Free Text on the Gantt Chart   246

From Here...   248

III | Assigning Resources and Costs

8 Defining Resources and Costs 251

Understanding How Project Uses Resources and Costs 252

Understanding Resources and Costs 253
Defining Resources 253
Defining Costs 253
Understanding the Resource Fields 255
Defining Fixed and Total Cost 262

Defining the Resource Pool 263
Using the Resource Sheet 264
Using the Resource Form 265
Setting the Automatically Add New Resources Option 267
Filling in the Resource Fields 268
Using the Resource Information Dialog Box 270

Changing Working Times for Resources 273
Understanding Resource Calendars 273
Changing the Resource Calendar 273

Sorting Resources 276

Filtering Resources 278

Creating a Resource Template 280

Printing the Resource List 280

From Here... 282

9 Understanding Resource Scheduling in Microsoft Project 98 283

Reviewing the Essential Components of
Resource Assignments 284

Understanding the Resource Assignment Fields 285
Assigning a Resource Name 285
Assigning the Units 285
Assigning the Work 287

Understanding the Work Formula 287
Applying the Work Formula in New Assignments 288
Applying the Work Formula to Changes in Existing
Assignments 289
Understanding the Driver Resource Concept 290

Choosing the Task Type   291

Understanding Effort Driven Tasks   294

Understanding Duration with Multiple Resources Assigned   296

Modifying Resource Assignments   296
    Contouring Resource Usage   297
    Using Overtime to Shorten a Task   300
    Splitting a Task Assignment   301
    Scheduling a Late Start for an Assignment   303

From Here...   305

10 Assigning Resources and Costs to Tasks   307

Selecting the Appropriate Task Type   308

Assigning Resources to Tasks   311
    Using the Assign Resources Dialog Box   312
    Assigning Resources with the Task Information Dialog Box   318
    Assigning Resources with the Task and Task Details Forms   320
    Assigning Resources with the Task Usage View   324
    Using the Assignment Information Dialog Box   327
    Assigning Resources on a Task Table   331

Assigning Overtime Work   332
    Understanding How Microsoft Project Schedules and Charges for Overtime   332
    Entering Overtime Work   334
    Using the Task Form to Enter Overtime   334
    Using the Resource Form to Enter Overtime   336
    Viewing Scheduled Overtime   337

Assigning Fixed Costs and Fixed Contract Fees   337

Using Alternate Views of Resources and Resource Assignments   340
    Understanding the Enhanced Usage Views   340
    Understanding the Resource Allocation View   341
    Understanding the Resource Graph View   342

Printing Resource Work and Cost Reports   343

From Here...   344

11 Resolving Resource Allocation Problems 345

Understanding How Resource Overallocations Occur 346

Identifying Resource Overallocations 348
Viewing Resource Overallocations 351
Filtering Overallocated Resources 351
Working with the Resource Usage View 352

Strategies for Eliminating Resource Overallocations:
an Overview 357
Increasing the Availability of the Overallocated Resource 357
Reducing the Workload for the Overallocated Resource 359

Eliminating Resource Overallocations Yourself 360
Increasing the Availability of the Overallocated Resource 360
Reducing the Workload of the Overallocated Resource 365
Resolving Overallocations by Delaying Assignments 371
Splitting a Task 374
Delaying Individual Assignments 375
Splitting Individual Assignments 378

Project Can Level Overallocated Assignments for You 381
Configuring the Settings in the Resource Leveling Dialog
Box 381
Using the Level Now Command 385
Clearing the Effects of Leveling 387
Understanding the Pitfalls of Automatic Leveling 387

From Here... 388

IV | Reviewing and Publishing the Project

12 Reviewing the Project Plan 391

Looking at the Big Picture 392
Compressing the Timescale 393
Collapsing the Task List Outline 394

Filtering the Task or Resource List 395
Using Filters 397
Viewing the Costs 398

Sorting the Task and Resource Lists 399

Checking for Spelling Errors   402
  Using the Spelling Command   403
  Setting the Spelling Options   404

Shortening the Critical Path   405
  Identifying the Critical Path   406
  Strategies for Crashing the Schedule   407

Reducing Costs   408
  Reviewing the Cost Schedule   408
  Strategies for Reducing Costs   409

Printing Summary Reports   409

From Here...   411

13 Printing Views and Reports   413

Using the Print Commands   414

Changing the Printer Setup   415

Printing Views   416
  Preparing the View for Printing   417
  Changing the Page Setup   420
  Using Print Preview   430
  Using the Print Command   434

Printing Standard Reports   436

From Here...   437

14 Publishing Projects on the Web   439

Overview of Project 98's Internet Features   440

Navigating with Hyperlinks   441

Exporting Project Data to Web Pages   442
  Saving Your Project as an HTML Document   442
  Viewing Your Project as an HTML Document   447

Defining Import/Export Map HTML Options   448

Modifying Project's Standard HTML Template   450
  Changing the Background Color of Your Web Page   451
  Defining a Background Graphic for the Template   454
  Displaying a Graphic Image on Your Project Template   455
  Changing the Title Bar Text   456
  Formatting Text in Your Project HTML Template   457
  Adding Hyperlinks to Your Project HTML Template   460

Adding, Modifying, and Deleting Hyperlinks in Your Project   463

Creating Web Pages from MPD Files   466

Updating Your Project Web Pages   466

Publishing Your Web Documents   467

From Here...   468

V | Tracking and Analyzing Progress

15 Tracking Work on the Project   473

Setting the Baseline or Plan   474
Capturing the Baseline   475
Viewing the Baseline   476
Correcting the Baseline   477
Saving Interim Schedules   479
Comparing the Baseline with the Current Schedule   480
Printing the Views That Show Baseline Comparisons   486

Tracking Actual Performance and Costs   486
Establishing a Procedure for Updating Tasks   488
Understanding the Fields Used in Updating   489
Using the Facilities Provided for Updating Tasks   495

From Here...   505

16 Analyzing Progress and Revising the Schedule   507

Analyzing Variances and Revising the Schedule   508

Analyzing Progress   508
Definitions   509
Reviewing Summary Progress Information   510
Reviewing Progress Information at the Task Level   514
Reviewing Progress Information at the Resource Level   521
Analyzing Time-Scaled Data in Excel   530
Capturing and Reviewing Week-to-Week Trends   532

Updating the Schedule   533
Rescheduling Remaining Work   533
Rescheduling Tasks that Haven't Started   535

Revising the Schedule to Complete on Time and on Budget   536

Reducing Scope   538

Reducing Schedule   538

From Here...   539

VI | Coordinating Projects and Sharing Data

17 Working with Multiple Projects   543

Using the Window Commands   544

Viewing All the File Windows at the Same Time   545

Hiding and Unhiding Open Windows   546

Combining Tasks from Different Files into One Window   546

Using the Window, New Window Command   546

Combining Projects into One File   548

Working with Inserted Projects   549

Breaking a Large Project Apart Using Inserted Projects   551

Maintaining Inserted Projects   552

Identifying Tasks That Are Inserted Projects   553

Deleting Inserted Projects   554

Creating Links Between Tasks in Separate Projects   554

Sharing Resources Among Projects   558

Creating the Resource Pool   558

Using the Resource Pool   559

Saving Multiple Files in a Workspace   560

Discontinuing Resource Sharing   561

Identifying Resource Pool Links   562

From Here...   563

18 Using Microsoft Project in Workgroups   565

Exploring Project's Workgroup Features   566

Deciding on E-Mail, Intranet, or Internet Workgroup Communications   567

Communicating with a Workgroup by E-Mail   567

Communicating with a Workgroup on an Intranet   567

Communicating with a Workgroup on the Internet   575

Circulating the Project Schedule for Review   575
    Using the Send Command   576
    Using a Routing Slip   579

Sending Task Requests with TeamAssign   582
    Composing the TeamAssign Form   582
    Responding to TeamAssign Requests   583
    Workgroup Manager Feedback to Resources   584

Requesting and Submitting Status Reports with TeamStatus   586

Sending Task Updates with TeamUpdate   587

Setting Task Reminders   587

Sending Schedule Notes   588

From Here...   590

19   Exchanging Project Data with Other Applications   593

File Formats Supported by Microsoft Project 98   594

Exporting Project 98 Data to Older Releases of
Microsoft Project   598

Saving the Entire Project in a Database   599
    Using the Microsoft Project Database Format   599
    Saving Projects in Microsoft Access Format   604
    Saving Projects in a Microsoft ODBC Data Source   606

Exchanging Selected Parts of a Project with Other Formats   608
    Working with Import/Export Maps   608
    Reviewing the Predefined Import/Export Maps   609
    Creating Import/Export Maps for Access and
    ODBC Sources   611
    Working with Microsoft Excel Formats   620
    Exporting Project Data to the Internet or an Intranet   634
    Working with Text File Formats   637

Copying Selected Data Between Applications   639
    Copying Data from Other Applications   641
    Copying Microsoft Project Data into Other Applications   642

Linking Selected Data Between Applications   642
    Linking Microsoft Project Data Fields to Other Sources   643
    Refreshing Linked Data in Microsoft Project   645
    Deleting Links to Other Sources   646
    Identifying Tasks or Resources with Links Attached   647

Working with Objects   648
Pasting Objects into Another Application   649
Embedding Objects   654

From Here...   656

VII | Working with Views and Reports

20   Using the Standard Views, Tables, and Filters   659

Exploring the Standard Views   660
The Calendar   660
The Gantt Chart   661
The Rollup Views   662
The Leveling Gantt   665
The Detail Gantt   666
The Tracking Gantt   667
PERT Analysis Gantt Charts   668
The PERT Chart   668
The Task PERT Chart   669
The Task Sheet   670
Task Usage   670
The Task Form   672
The Task Details Form   672
The Task Name Form   673
The Resource Graph   673
Resource Usage   675
The Resource Sheet   676
The Resource Form   677
The Resource Name Form   677
The Task Entry   678
Resource Allocation   679

Exploring the Standard Tables   679
The Task Tables   681
The Resource Tables   683

Exploring the Standard Filters   685
Using the Standard Filters   686
Describing the Standard Filters   687
Applying a Filter to the Current View   690
Using the AutoFilter   692

From Here...   693

21 Formatting Views   695

Using the Format Options in the Standard Views   696
Sorting the Tasks or Resources in a View   696
Formatting Text Displays for Categories of
Tasks and Resources   697
Formatting Selected Text   700
Formatting Gridlines   701
Using the Outline Options   702
Formatting Timescales   704
Using Page Breaks   708

Formatting the Gantt Chart   709
Reviewing the Format Options for the Gantt Chart   709
Using the Bar Styles Options   709
Using the Gantt Chart Wizard   714

Formatting the Calendar   716
Formatting the Timescale for the Calendar   716
Selecting Calendar Bar Styles Options   717
Setting the Layout Options for the Calendar View   719

Formatting the PERT Chart   719
Reviewing the Format Options for the PERT Chart   719
Using the Box Styles Options   720
Using the Boxes Tab in the Border Styles Dialog Box   721
Using the Zoom Command   724
Selecting Layout Options   724
Redrawing the PERT Chart with the
Layout Now Command   727

Formatting the Task and Resource Forms   727
Reviewing the Format Options for the Form Views   727
Using the Entry Field Options   727

Formatting the Resource Graph   730
Reviewing the Format Options for the Resource Graph   732
Selecting the Values To Display   732
Using the Bar Styles Dialog Box   734

Formatting the Resource Usage View   736
Choosing the Details   736
Formatting the Detail Styles   738

Formatting the Task Usage View   738

Formatting the Sheet Views 738

From Here… 740

22 Customizing Views, Tables, and Filters 741

Creating New Views 742

Entering the Name of the View 744

Selecting the Screen 744

Selecting the Table for the View 745

Selecting the Filter for the View 745

Displaying the View Name in the Menu 746

Saving the View Definition 746

Creating a Combination View 746

Using and Creating Tables 748

Entering a Table Name 749

Adding and Changing the Columns in the Table 749

Completing the Definition of the Table 750

Changing Table Features from the View Screen 751

Creating Custom Filters 754

Naming the Filter 755

Defining the Filter Criteria 756

Using More Filter Criterion Tests 758

Using Interactive Filters 759

Creating Calculated Filters 761

Creating Multiple Criteria Filters 762

Creating Custom Filters with AutoFilter 763

Organizing Views in Project Files 764

From Here… 766

23 Using the Standard Reports 767

Accessing the Standard Reports 768

The Overview Reports Category 769

The Project Summary Report 769

The Top-Level Tasks Report 770

The Critical Tasks Report 771

The Milestones Report 772

The Working Days Report 772

The Current Activity Reports Category   774
    The Unstarted Tasks Report   774
    The Tasks Starting Soon Report   775
    The Tasks In Progress Report   776
    The Completed Tasks Report   776
    The Should Have Started Tasks Report   777
    The Slipping Tasks Report   777

The Cost Reports Category   779
    The Cash Flow Report   780
    The Budget Report   780
    The Overbudget Tasks Report   781
    The Overbudget Resources Report   782
    The Earned Value Report   782

The Assignment Reports Category   784
    The Who Does What Report   784
    The Who Does What When Report   785
    The To-Do List Report   786
    The Overallocated Resources Report   787

The Workload Reports Category   788
    The Task Usage Report   788
    The Resource Usage Report   789

From Here...   791

24 Customizing Reports   793

Understanding Report Customization in Microsoft Project   794
    Customizing the Existing Reports   794
    Using the Custom Category of Reports   796

Creating Reports   797
    Creating a New Report Based on an Existing Report   797
    Designing a New Report   798

Using the Common Customization Controls   799
    Controlling Page Breaks in a Report   799
    Formatting Text in a Report   800
    Choosing the Page Setup Options for a Report   801
    Changing the Sort Order for a Report   801
    Collapsing Task Detail in a Report   802

Customizing Specific Report Types   802
    Customizing the Project Summary Report   803
    Customizing the Calendar Type Reports   804
    Customizing Task Type Reports   805
    Customizing Resource Type Reports   814
    Customizing Crosstab Type Reports   821
    Customizing the Monthly Calendar Type Report   826

Saving and Sharing Your Custom Reports   827

From Here...   829

VIII | Programming and Controlling Microsoft Project 98

25   Using Macros in Microsoft Project   833

Planning Your Macro   834
    Adding Special Formatting   834
    Adding Heading or Outline Numbering   836

Creating a Macro   836
    Capturing the Summary Task Format Macro   839
    Capturing the Special Formatting Macro   840
    Capturing the Outline Numbering Macro   841

Running the Macro   842
    Running the Special Formatting Macro   843
    Running the Outline Numbering Macro   844

Editing the Macro   844
    Open the Visual Basic Editor   844
    Understanding The Project Explorer   844
    Understanding the Properties Window   846
    Understanding the Code Window   846

From Here...   848

26   Using Visual Basic for Applications   849

The Project Object Model   850
    The *Application* Object   850
    The *Project* Object   852
    The *Resource* Object   853
    The *List* Object   853

The *Task* Object   854
The *Calendar* Object   856

Understanding VBA   857
Understanding Procedures   857
Understanding Variables and Constants   858
Understanding Program Control Mechanisms   860
Understanding Error Handling   862

Correcting the Problem with the Outline Macro   862

Correcting the Problem with the Special
Formatting Macro   865

Exploring Macro Possibilities   867
Automating Summary Reporting Tasks   867

From Here...   869

27 Customizing Toolbars, Menus, and Forms   871

Creating and Customizing Toolbars   872
Reviewing the Built-In Toolbars   873
Displaying Toolbars   874
Using the Customize Dialog Box   875
Customizing Toolbars   876
Creating New Toolbars   880
Restoring the Built-In Toolbars   883

Customizing Command Buttons   884
Using the Modify Selections Button   884
Managing Toolbars with the Organizer   888

Customizing the Menu Bar   891
Adding a New Command to the Menu Bar   892
Using the Modify Selections Button   895

Using Custom Forms   899
Reviewing the Forms Supplied with Microsoft Project   899
Using Custom Forms   900
Creating a New Custom Form   902
Placing Items on the Form   905
Renaming, Editing, and Copying Custom Forms   908
Managing Forms with the Organizer   909

From Here...   909

IX | Appendixes

A **Microsoft Project 98 Shortcut Keys** 913

B **Glossary** 919

C **Companion Products for Microsoft Project 98** 927

Index 945

Credits

PRESIDENT
Roland Elgey

SENIOR VICE PRESIDENT/PUBLISHING
Don Fowley

PUBLISHER
Joseph B. Wikert

GENERAL MANAGER
Joe Muldoon

MANAGER OF PUBLISHING OPERATIONS
Linda H. Buehler

PUBLISHING DIRECTOR
Karen Reinisch

EDITORIAL SERVICES DIRECTOR
Carla Hall

MANAGING EDITOR
Thomas F. Hayes

ACQUISITIONS MANAGER
Cheryl D. Willoughby

ACQUISITIONS EDITOR
Jill Byus

PRODUCT DIRECTORS
Dana Coe
Rick Kughen

PRODUCTION EDITOR
Rebecca Mounts

EDITORS
Paige Force
Kate Givens
Tom Stevens

COORDINATOR OF EDITORIAL SERVICES
Maureen A. McDaniel

WEBMASTER
Thomas H. Bennett

PRODUCT MARKETING MANAGER
Kourtnaye Sturgeon

ASSISTANT PRODUCT MARKETING MANAGER
Gretchen Schlesinger

TECHNICAL EDITORS
Rob Houck
Brad Lindass
Vicky Quinn
Jim Spiller
Henry Staples

SOFTWARE SPECIALIST
David Garratt

ACQUISITIONS COORDINATOR
Travis Bartlett

SOFTWARE RELATIONS COORDINATOR
Susan D. Gallagher

EDITORIAL ASSISTANTS
Jennifer L. Chisholm
Jeff Chandler

BOOK DESIGNERS
Ruth Harvey
Kim Scott

COVER DESIGNER
Sandra Schroeder

PRODUCTION TEAM
Julie Geeting
Kay Hoskin
Laura A. Knox
Darlena Murray
Anjy Perry

INDEXER
Becky Hornyak

Composed in *Century Old Style* and *ITC Franklin Gothic* by Que Corporation.

Since the first edition I have dedicated and rededicated this book to Gerlinde Katharina Pyron. For this edition, I want to recognize the woman who gave us Gerlinde, her mother Katharina Söldner. In spite of the horrors and heartbreak of the war sweeping over her farm in Bavaria, Katie had the will and the courage to keep her farm going, to protect those escaping an unthinkable persecution, and to teach her daughter both courage and compassion. And she is today my own lovable, youthful, ever adventurous mother-in-law. I salute you, and I honor you, our beloved Katie.

Die früheren Ausgaben dieses Buches habe ich meiner Frau Gerlinde Katharina Pyron gewidmet. Diese Ausgabe möchte ich der Frau widmen die die Mutter von Gerlinde ist, nämlich Katharina Söldner. Trotz des Krieges und dem Herzeleid das sie auf ihrem Bauernhof in Bayern erlebte, hatte sie die Kraft und den Willen andere zu beschützen und ihrer Tochter Mut und Empathie zu lehren. Kathie ist für mich die liebevolle, jugendliche, und noch immer zu Abenteuernbereite Schwiegermutter. Ich ehre unsere geliebte Kathie.

About the Authors

Tim Pyron is the Information Systems Manager for the Texas operations of Productivity Point International, Inc. and lives in San Antonio, Texas. He is the author of three other Que books and has been contributing author for still more. You can contact Tim on the Internet at **tpyron@txdirect.net**.

Tim's undergraduate degree is in Music, but his Masters and Ph.D. are in Economics. He provides consulting services and conducts training classes in Microsoft Project and in spreadsheet and database applications.

Ira Brown is an independent consultant based in Philadelphia, Pennsylvania, specializing in developing automated business solutions for Microsoft Project. He is a leading authority in integrating Microsoft Office applications with Microsoft Project using Visual Basic and VBA. In addition, Ira has many years of experience developing and implementing automated methodologies centered around Microsoft Project.

He is available for training and consulting in the use and customization of Microsoft Project, as well as providing training in Microsoft Project's Visual Basic for Applications programming language.

To contact Ira, call (215) 535-7515, or he can be reached via e-mail at **ibrown@netaxs.com**.

Gus Cicala is the president of Project Assistants, Inc. in Wilmington, Delaware. Project Assistants is a full-service project management, software development, consulting, and training company. Project Assistants is the developer of ProjectCommander, the premier Microsoft Project companion product. Gus graduated Cum Laude from The Wharton School of the University of Pennsylvania, with dual majors in Operations Research and Management. He is a published author and contributing editor for the monthly publication *Inside Microsoft Planning Tools*. He is an expert in project management and the use of Microsoft Project as a project management tool, and regularly delivers consulting and training on project management, Microsoft Project, contract administration, and custom methodologies for organizations across North America and Europe.

For more information on consulting, training, or the purchase of ProjectCommander, you can reach Project Assistants at (800) 642-9259 or **http://www.projectassistants.com**. Gus can be reached at (302) 529-7075, fax: (302) 529-7035, or e-mail: **gcicala@projectassistants.com**.

Helen Feddema grew up in New York City. She was ready for computers when she was 12, but computers were not ready for her yet, so she got a B.S. in Philosophy from Columbia and an M.T.S. in Theological Studies from Harvard Divinity School, while working at various office jobs. It was at HDS that she got her first computer, an Osborne, and soon computers were her primary interest. She started with word processing and spreadsheets, went on to learn dBASE, and did dBASE development for six years, part of this time as a corporate developer. After being laid off in a flurry of corporate downsizing, she started doing independent consulting and development, using dBASE, ObjectVision, WordPerfect, and Paradox.

Always looking for something new and better, Helen beta tested Access 1.0, and soon recognized that this was the database she had been looking for ever since Windows 3.0 was introduced, and she saw the gap waiting to be filled by a great Windows database. She concentrated on Access development and writing for several years, and in 1994 joined Information Management Services, a Microsoft Solution Provider, as an Access and MS Office developer. In 1997 she joined Plato Software, where she does custom Access development. Helen lives in the mid-Hudson area of New York state, with three cats and two computers.

Laura Monsen is a senior instructor and consultant with Productivity Point International in San Antonio, Texas where she teaches a variety of presentation graphic, spreadsheet, project management, and database applications. Laura has designed a diverse number of PowerPoint presentations for her classes to graphically illustrate complex topics. Additionally, she frequently creates business presentations as part of Productivity Point International's consulting services. Laura contributed to Que's *Special Edition Using Microsoft Project for Windows 95* book. She has a B.A. in Economics from the University of South, Sewanee.

Pamela Palmer is an independent consultant specializing in software development. She assists businesses and organizations with the design and development of Windows-based applications. Pam has developed systems using Visual Basic, Visual Basic for Applications, Access, and Fox Pro. When not developing applications, she instructs as a Microsoft Certified Trainer. Pam also served as one of the co-authors of Que's *Using Visual Basic 3*. She can be contacted via Internet at: **74170.1526@compuserve.com**.

Jo Ellen Shires is an independent consultant and trainer who has been specializing in Microsoft applications since 1984. She owns Common Sense Computing, and has been designated by Microsoft as Project Champion for the Portland, Oregon area and for small businesses regionally. Construction and information systems are her areas of project management experience. Her firm writes and delivers customized training and programmed solutions to Project users at all levels in a wide variety of industries. She holds a BS in Economics and an MS in Biometry.

Kathryne Valentine is an independent computer trainer/consultant based in Annapolis, MD. Her degree is in Psychology and Education. She also graduated from New York University's special program in Construction Project Management program. In addition to teaching and writing in the Washington/Baltimore metropolitan area, she has extensive practical experience with planning and managing projects in a variety of industries: banking, construction, software development, government, and with law firms to manage large, complex litigation. You can contact her on the Internet at **kvalgra@ibm.net**.

Sam Dutkin has been working in the computer field for over 10 years, and at sixteen is the youngest contributor to this book. Sam is currently an Internet Programmer for DESIGNfx Interactive, L.L.C. (**www.designfx.com**), where he develops applications and designs web sites for companies who are looking to develop a web presence. Sam is Webmaster for several businesses in the Philadelphia area, including Project Assistants, Inc. (**http://www.projectassistants.com**) and Dutkins' Collectables (**http://www.dutkins.com**).

Acknowledgments

I think it's not until you write a book that you develop a true respect for the Acknowledgments page—the writer's ideas would remain meandering scribblings were it not for the hard work and improvements that are so rightfully to be credited to others. You also learn firsthand how impossible it is to adequately convey, in this short space, the debt the reader and author owe to the rest of the people who fill, polish, and convey the book to the reader. The familiar phrases "couldn't have done it without…" and "…made it all possible" often sound like social niceties—but they should be taken literally. Successfully publishing a book is entirely a team project, and the author-link is just one of many links in the chain that stretches from supportive families through the publishing house to the book stores to the readers.

There were several consultants and writers who contributed their expertise and insight to this revision. I encourage you to read about each of them in the section "About the Authors" in the preceding pages. You will probably be hearing more good things about these capable folks in the future. My thanks to each of them for their fine work. They bridged the gaps in my own imperfect understanding or struggled through the long, late hours of revisions.

Special thanks are due to Rebecca Mounts, the Production Editor at Que, who clarified and improved the text with her careful editing, and Jill Byus who, as Acquisitions Editor, not only found writers and reviewers, managed all the deadlines, and successfully herded us all to safety, but did not once shout or throw things while I was still on the phone.

I also want to express my appreciation to Mary Weaver, my long time colleague and friend for her support and encouragement.

Finally, I want to thank the Microsoft Project 98 Team for taking on so successfully the awesome task of this very radical and extensive revision of an already complex product. I am especially indebted to Adrian Jenkins, the Microsoft Project Beta Test Team Coordinator, who researched questions and provided answers to a wide range of questions for all of us. Congratulations to all of you on a job very well done.

We'd Like to Hear from You!

QUE Corporation has a long-standing reputation for high-quality books and products. To ensure your continued satisfaction, we also understand the importance of customer service and support.

Tech Support

If you need assistance with the information in this book or with a CD/disk accompanying the book, please access Macmillan Computer Publishing's online Knowledge Base at **http://www.superlibrary.com/general/support**. If you do not find the answer to your questions on our Web site, you may contact Macmillan Technical Support by phone at **317/581-3833** or via e-mail at **support@mcp.com**.

Also be sure to visit Que's Web resource center for all the latest information, enhancements, errata, downloads, and more. It's located at **http://www.quecorp.com/**.

Orders, Catalogs, and Customer Service

To order other QUE or Macmillan Computer Publishing books, catalogs, or products, please contact our Customer Service Department at **800/ 858-7674** or fax us at **800/ 882-8583** (International Fax: 317/228-4400). Or visit our online bookstore at **http://www.mcp.com/**.

Comments and Suggestions

We want you to let us know what you like or dislike most about this book or other QUE products. Your comments will help us to continue publishing the best books available on computer topics in today's market.

Rick Kughen
Product Director
QUE Corporation
201 West 103rd Street, 4B
Indianapolis, Indiana 46290 USA
Fax: 317/581-4663 E-mail: **rkughen@mcp.que.com**

Please be sure to include the book's title and author as well as your name and phone or fax number. We will carefully review your comments and share them with the author. Please note that due to the high volume of mail we receive, we may not be able to reply to every message.

Thank you for choosing QUE!

Introduction

Microsoft Project 98 is a gangbuster new release of the best-selling and most widely used project management software product in the world. There are, of course, lots of exciting new tools in Project 98, some of which are just plain fun to use. More importantly, however, Microsoft has made a number of fundamental technical changes that significantly extend the effectiveness and power of Microsoft Project. ■

Why You Should Use This Book

Almost anyone in the workplace can make good use of Microsoft Project at one time or another, but for project managers, it's a life support system. Microsoft Project is adaptable to both large and small projects. Managers of large, decade-long projects rely heavily on project management software to keep track of all the interrelated tasks and phases of their projects. On a much smaller scale, I have relied on Project to plan and coordinate software installations and upgrades over multiple corporate sites. And yes, I rely on it to keep me on track while writing this book. Quick as a wink, Project could tell that the publisher's deadlines were impossible. I then changed the scheduling calendar to include evenings, weekends, and holidays, and the goal became possible (assuming no hours need to be appropriated for family counseling).

This book gives you direct answers about how to put a project schedule together with Microsoft Project 98. It's organized to follow the cycle of developing a plan, implementing the plan, tracking progress and adjusting to changes, and preparing the final reports. You'll find step-by-step procedures for using Project's features plus help with common problems. Special Edition books from Que offer comprehensive coverage of software. You can be sure you will find what you need in this book to make Project work for you.

Why You Should Use Microsoft Project

Managing projects is a specialized field within management—there are professional associations, journals, professional certifications, and university courses for project managers. A project manager oversees all stages of a project, from planning through the completion and drafting of final summary reports.

ON THE WEB

One of the best Web sites for project management information is maintained by the Project Management Institute at **http://www.pmi.org**. Here you can find valuable references to publications, discussion forums on the Internet, other relevant Web sites, project management special interest groups (SIGs) in your area, educational opportunities, employment opportunities, Institute chapters in your area, and membership information. You can also download a free copy of the Institute's White Paper, covering the most up-to-date theory and best practices in project management.

At its core, Microsoft Project is a scheduling and planning tool for project managers, providing easy-to-use tools for putting together a project plan and assigning responsibilities, but it also gives you powerful tools to carry you through to the end of the project.

Once you have defined the goals for your project, you can start putting Microsoft Project 98 to use. Project is an invaluable planning tool for:

- Organizing the plan and thinking through the details of what must be done
- Scheduling deadlines that must be met
- Scheduling the tasks in the appropriate sequence

- Assigning resources and costs to tasks and scheduling tasks around resource availability
- Fine-tuning the plan to satisfy time and budget constraints or to accommodate changes
- Preparing professional-looking reports to explain the project to owners, top management, supervisors, workers, subcontractors, and the public

Once work begins on the project, you can use Microsoft Project to:

- Track progress and analyze the evolving "real" schedule to see if it looks like you will finish on time and within budget
- Revise the schedule to accommodate changes and unforeseen circumstances
- Try out different what-if scenarios before modifying the plan
- Communicate with team members about changes in the schedule (even automatically notify those who are affected by changes!) and solicit feedback about their progress
- Post automatically updated progress reports on an Internet Web site or a company intranet
- Produce final reports on the success of the project and evaluate problem areas for consideration in future projects

What's New in Microsoft Project 98

In terms of enhanced functionality, this is without question the most significant new release of Microsoft Project. If you are new to project management you will not be able to appreciate some of the items listed in this review of new features, but seasoned users of Microsoft Project will be excited by these improvements.

Scheduling Is Much More Flexible and Realistic

The major objective in this release was to provide a new scheduling engine to give you more control over exactly how tasks and resources are scheduled. You can now split tasks into multiple small segments to accommodate the interrupted work schedule of the people who must do the work, and you can schedule resource assignments precisely by assigning specific amounts of work, both regular and overtime, on specific days. Micromanagers will think they have died and gone to heaven.

A new Task Usage view offers you the option to show under each task an indented list of all the resources assigned to that task. To the right of the task and resource list is a time-scaled grid that displays the amount of work assigned during each unit of time. Similarly, an improved Resource Usage view can show for each resource an indented list of all the task assignments and the amount of work scheduled during each time unit.

In both views you can use the grid to edit work assignments during each time period, thus allowing you to develop precise schedules that can be downloaded into the resource's calendar in Microsoft Outlook. You can display more than just the work for each assignment. You can simultaneously display rows for up to 22 different scheduled, baseline, actual, and earned-value fields in the grid for each assignment under the task or resource list.

In addition to the Task Information dialog box and the Resource Information dialog box, there is now an Assignment Information dialog box that can be accessed when you select one of the assignment rows in the Task or Resource Usage views. This dialog box can be used to change the assignment details, including amount of work and units and the cost rate table. You can also set the start date or finish date for the resource to work on this task. You can now attach notes to individual assignments with this dialog box, and you can track actual work on the dialog box also.

You can define resources and costs now with much greater precision. You can limit resource availability to the project by defining starting and ending dates for the resource. Each resource can be given not just one, but up to five cost and overtime rates to choose from when assigning the resource to different tasks. Thus you can charge more for the resource on some tasks than on others. Furthermore, each of the five cost rates is actually a table where you can add up to 25 dates for future rate changes. Project will use the increased rates when work falls after the rate increases. When assigning resources, you can choose to view assignment units in percent instead of the traditional decimal value. Thus a worker assigned half-time to a task can be displayed as .5 units or as 50 percent.

In Microsoft Project 98 there are now three task types: Fixed Duration, Fixed Unit (formerly called Resource Driven), and a new type: Fixed Work. With Fixed Work tasks, you can let Project calculate the resource units you will need if duration changes. Project now uses Effort Driven scheduling as its default. That means that when you assign a second named resource to work on a task, the second resource takes half the work load and the task duration will be reduced (unless it is a Fixed Duration task). You can remove Effort Driven scheduling from any task to make it behave like earlier releases of Project.

Resource leveling has been improved significantly. It is now possible for leveling to reschedule resources to work around fixed commitments. And leveling can now be constrained to limited time periods, and to affect only the resources with an overallocation problem, leaving other resource schedules undisturbed. Leveling now works for projects scheduled with a fixed finish date, not just for projects with fixed start dates, because Project can now add negative delays that force tasks to start earlier. You can now change the leveling alert "granularity." This means that if you increase the granularity from a minute (the old standard) to a day, overallocations during a short time period within a day won't trigger the leveling flag so long as the resource can do all the work within a day. There is a new Leveling Gantt view that compares preleveling task bars with the post-leveling task bars.

Project 98 enables you to choose between hard and soft constraints (constraints are deadline dates for individual tasks). Soft constraints allow the constrained task to be delayed until all preconditions for the task are satisfied, even if that means the constraint will not be honored. This is more realistic than hard constraints, which require that Project always honor the constraint even if it means the task must start before necessary preconditions are satisfied. A new indicator alerts you to constraints that are missed.

Tracking and Tracking Analysis Is More Sophisticated

There is a new graphic element for Gantt Charts called a Progress Line that indicates visually the tasks that are slipping. There is now a true Status Date for Earned Value reports, and the Earned Value fields now have time-scaled values. The tracking and Earned Value fields can also be exported to Excel with the new Analysis toolbar for automatic graphing.

You can now enter Actual Costs instead of relying on calculated Actual Costs, and you can enter actual overtime work in the specific time slots in which the work was done.

Project Is Ready for the Web

Now you can save a Project screen view in HTML for Internet display and publish it on the Web. You can also create templates that take the most current data from your project and display updated views of your project without requiring you to create each new page. You can use your Web site to display up-to-the-minute project summaries for managers or for the public, or you can use the Internet or an intranet to ask for updates from project team members!

Furthermore, you can embed hyperlinks in tasks and resources in your project in order to jump directly to Web sites, locations in other applications, other project files, or other tasks or resources in the same file.

Exchanging Data with Other Applications Is Easier

Projects can now be saved directly in the new Microsoft Project Database format (with the new MPD file name extension), which includes all view and formatting settings, and the resulting file can be opened directly as a project file or as an Access file. This makes it possible to modify project data in Access or any product that reads the Access format, and then update the project in Microsoft Project by opening the changes and letting Project use smart analysis to incorporate changes that are consistent and to flag those that are not.

Complete projects (including formatting, calendars, and so on) can also be saved to an ODBC database. Access 8.0, Oracle 7.3, and MSD SQL Server 6.5 also support saving complete projects.

Exchanging data with other applications can now be controlled by a new field Mapping feature that lets you specify which Project fields will exchange with which data locations in the other application.

Programming in Visual Basic Is Fully Supported

Now that Microsoft Project has completed the conversion to the Microsoft Office standard programming language, Microsoft Visual Basic for Applications, you can develop applications that fully integrate Project with the other products in the Office family using Visual Basic. You can build Project-Excel applications to enhance the calculating and analysis power of Project, or automate PowerPoint presentations from within Project.

Links Between Projects Is Much More Advanced

You can now link tasks between projects just like you do with tasks in the same project, using all dependency link types. And you can embed subprojects in the master project at any outline level and treat them like they are part of the master project, linking tasks between master project and subproject.

The Interface Is Much More Effective

A view bar, similar to the one in Microsoft Outlook, lets you choose views with a single click and indicates which view is currently active. There are now more indicators in the Gantt Chart to the left of each task or resource row, showing not only attached Notes, but also constraint types, missed constraints, completed tasks, recurring tasks, hyperlinks to other files, inserted projects, overallocated resources, and more. A ScreenTip provides an explanation when the mouse pointer hovers over the indicator. Inplace controls are provided in many fields. Numeric fields have spin controls to change values; the date fields control lets you pick dates off a calendar. Fields with pick lists have controls to show the acceptable values for that field.

The AutoFilter introduced in Excel is now available in Project; but Project goes a step further and lets you save a set of AutoFilter specifications as a named, custom filter. There is an additional level of grouping in filters with Boolean operators. The Find command has been extended to include Find and Replace, which makes editing much easier and provides more consistency with other Office products.

Printed projects can now be made to fit the page by scaling to nonpostscript printers as well as postscript printers. And you can include formatted text and graphics in report headers and footers.

Capacities and Scale Match Enterprise-Wide Needs

Microsoft Project 98 can handle the heavy demands of enterprise-wide solutions. You can have up to a million tasks in a project now, or a thousand subprojects, and you can have up to 50 windows open, each with projects containing subprojects for a total of a thousand projects open at once. Of course, your machine's memory may keep you from reaching these limits. Resource pool information is now stored in all projects sharing the same pool, so each project can be updated and can update the pool even if one user has the pool open for editing. The number of custom fields has been tripled, giving you more text, number, date, cost, and flag fields to use for special data. And, you can assign an alias to a custom field that will appear instead of Text1 or Text2 when that field is used.

How This Book Is Organized

This book is divided into nine parts, which take you from an overview of project management and Microsoft Project through programming and customizing Microsoft Project to suit your needs. The following is a brief review of these parts and the chapters you'll find in each part.

Part I: Getting Started with Microsoft Project 98

Part I introduces you to Microsoft Project 98 and shows you how to set up a new project document.

Chapter 1, "The Power of Microsoft Project 98," introduces you to project management concepts and the major phases of managing a project with Microsoft Project.

Chapter 2, "Learning the Basics of Microsoft Project," introduces you to the Microsoft Project workspace. In this chapter, you learn to navigate the screen display, scroll and select data, and select different views of the project.

In Chapter 3, "Setting Up a New Project Document," you review the preliminary steps to take when creating a project. You learn how to specify the calendar of working days and hours, how to enter basic information about the project, and how to specify the planned date for starting or finishing the project. You also learn how to adjust the most critical of the default values that govern how Microsoft Project displays and calculates a project.

Chapter 4, "Working with Project Files," presents the information you need to work with project files. Included is a comprehensive discussion of the Global Project Template file and how to use it.

Part II: Scheduling Tasks

Part II shows you how to build the skeleton of the project plan.

Chapter 5, "Creating a Task List," explains how to define and enter the tasks, milestones, and recurring tasks that must be completed to successfully finish the project. You also learn how to enter the task list in outline form in accordance with top-down planning principles. You learn how to edit the data in a project and how to use different forms for editing the task data.

Chapter 6, "Entering Scheduling Requirements," shows you how to define the special conditions that govern the scheduling of tasks in your project: specific deadlines and sequencing requirements for the tasks.

Chapter 7, "Working with the Major Task Views," explains and compares the most popular views you can use in Microsoft Project to display the task list. The views covered are the Calendar view, the PERT Chart, and the special graphics capabilities of the Gantt Chart.

Part III: Assigning Resources and Costs

Part III shows you how to define and assign resources and costs to the tasks in your project.

Chapter 8, "Defining Resources and Costs," shows you how to define the resource pool that you plan to use in the project and how to define the working and nonworking times for those resources. You learn how to sort, filter, and print the resource list. You learn also how to save the resource pool as a template for use in other project documents.

Chapter 9, "Understanding Resource Scheduling in Microsoft Project 98," gives you an understanding of how Project calculates a schedule when resources are assigned to tasks, both when you first assign resources and when you change resource assignments. The detailed instructions for assigning resources are covered in the next chapter.

Chapter 10, "Assigning Resources and Costs to Tasks," shows you how to associate resources and costs with specific tasks. You also learn how to assign overtime for resources and how to assign fixed costs to parts of the project. Finally, you learn how to view the resources, costs, and task assignments in useful ways for auditing the project plan and how to print the standard views and reports.

Chapter 11, "Resolving Resource Allocation Problems," is a guide for troubleshooting problems in the schedule for assigned resources. Typically, some resources are scheduled for more work than they can possibly do in the time allowed; here you learn ways to resolve the conflict.

Part IV: Reviewing and Publishing the Project

Part IV covers that part of the project cycle where you have completed the initial planning and need to review the schedule and refine it to make sure it meets the objectives of the project. Then you will want to publish the final plan in printed reports or on an intranet or the Internet.

Chapter 12, "Reviewing the Project Plan," introduces features that help you review your task schedule for completeness and accuracy. You learn how to get an overview of the project to see if you can complete the project plan in a timely fashion and at an acceptable cost. You also learn how to view the task list through filters that focus on important aspects of the project and to sort and print the task list. You learn how to spell check the schedule and how to view the summary statistics for the project.

In Chapter 13, "Printing Views and Reports," you learn how to use the standard views and reports to publish your plan for the project.

Chapter 14, "Publishing Projects on the Web," covers the new capability of Project to prepare its views for HTML display on Web sites and intranets.

Part V: Tracking and Analyzing Progress

This part shows you how to keep track of actual work on the project and how to understand what is going on, with special emphasis on catching problems early so that corrective measures can be taken.

Chapter 15, "Tracking Work on the Project," deals with your role as project manager after work on the project begins. You learn how to save a copy of the finalized project plan to use as a baseline for comparisons. This chapter teaches you how to track the actual beginning and ending dates for tasks, the actual work amounts, and the actual costs.

Chapter 16, "Analyzing Progress and Revising the Schedule," is an important presentation of ways to look at the tracking information to see how well the project is meeting its objectives. Project offers many techniques and reports that you will learn to use in this chapter.

Part VI: Coordinating Projects and Sharing Data

The chapters in Part VI discuss more advanced topics that beginning users usually do not encounter; therefore, they are separated from the earlier Parts covering the basic steps of developing and tracking a project schedule.

Chapter 17, "Working with Multiple Projects," explains how to link one or more subprojects to a master or summary project and how to link an individual task in one project to a task in another. You also learn how to consolidate multiple projects and how to manage multiple projects that share a common resource pool.

Chapter 18, "Using Microsoft Project in Workgroups," will show you how to use Project's network workgroup features for communicating and coordinating the details of the project.

Chapter 19, "Exchanging Project Data with Other Applications," shows you how to export and import task, resource, and cost data with other applications and file formats, including the ODBC database format. You learn how to establish dynamic links with other Windows applications, so that changing a value in another application can change this same value in Microsoft Project.

Part VII: Working with Views and Reports

The chapters in Part VII teach you how to take advantage of the extensive options that Microsoft Project provides for displaying the data in your project. Some of the views and reports are mentioned in earlier chapters as the need arises. This section provides a comprehensive reference to all the major views and reports.

Chapter 20, "Using the Standard Views, Tables, and Filters," explains the many options for using tables, forms, graphic images, and filters to display your project in a view.

Chapter 21, "Formatting Views," provides all you need to know about the formatting options for all of the major views. You'll also find procedures, including tips and techniques, for changing the appearance of graphic elements and text display for categories of items and individual items.

Chapter 22, "Customizing Views, Tables, and Filters," shows you how to create your own views, with custom tables and filters, to display just the detail that you want for your projects.

Chapter 23, "Using the Standard Reports," explains how to use the standard reports to supplement the printed views.

Chapter 24, "Customizing Reports," explains how you can change the display elements in reports.

Part VIII: Programming and Controlling Microsoft Project 98

The chapters in Part VIII cover programming and customizing the Microsoft Project interface.

Chapter 25, "Using Macros in Microsoft Project," is a basic guide for nonprogrammers who want to record and use simple macros.

Chapter 26, "Using Visual Basic for Applications," is for programmers who know Visual Basic but want help in identifying the methods and properties available in Microsoft Project.

Chapter 27, "Customizing Toolbars, Menus, and Forms," is placed after the programming chapters only because you will typically customize a toolbar or menu to run your macros or Visual Basic procedures. This chapter explains the options for customizing the way Microsoft Project works. You learn how to change the standard toolbar buttons and how to attach commands and macros to a button. You learn also how to customize menus and how to create your own forms for data entry and review.

Part IX: Appendixes

The three appendixes provide reference materials that apply to more than one chapter or section of the book.

Appendix A, "Microsoft Project 98 Shortcut Keys," is a partial listing of the most commonly used special keys and key combinations in Microsoft Project.

Appendix B, "Glossary," lists some of the most commonly used terms found in this book and is especially helpful to those who are new to project management.

Appendix C, "Companion Products for Microsoft Project 98," describes some of the software products that you can buy to enhance Microsoft Project. The products are grouped by vendor, and each is described briefly.

Special Features in This Book

This book contains a variety of special features to help you find the information you need—fast. Formatting conventions are used to make important keywords or special text obvious. Specific language is used in order to make keyboard and mouse actions clear. And a variety of visual elements are used to make important and useful information stand out. The following sections describe the special features used in this book.

Chapter Roadmaps

Each chapter begins with a brief introduction and a list of the topics you'll find covered in that chapter. You know what you'll be reading about before you start.

Visual Aids

Notes, Tips, Cautions, and other visual aids give you useful information, and icons in the margin draw your attention to topics of special interest. The following are descriptions of each element.

New features that are introduced in Microsoft Project 98 are flagged with an icon in the margin.

N O T E Notes provide useful information that isn't essential to the discussion. They usually contain more technical information, but can also contain interesting, but less critical, information.

T I P Tips enhance your experience with Project 98 by providing hints and tricks you won't find elsewhere.

CAUTION

Cautions warn you that a particular action can cause severe harm to your project schedule. Given the many not-so-obvious calculations that Project processes at every turn, you shouldn't skip the Cautions in this book.

ON THE WEB

On the Web listings tell you about Web sites where you can find additional information and always include the Web address. For example, go to **http://www.mcp.com** for information about other Que books and post-publication information about this book.

◆ TROUBLESHOOTING

Do you have a vexing problem? Troubleshooting elements anticipate the problems you might have and provide a solution. The problem is stated in bold type, and the answer or solution follows.

Cross references point you to specific sections within other chapters so that you can get more information that's related to the topic you're reading about. Here is what a cross reference looks like:

▶ **See** "Starting and Exiting Microsoft Project," **p. 28**

Sidebars Are Interesting Nuggets of Information

Sidebars are detours from the main text. They usually provide background or interesting information that is relevant but not essential reading. You might find information that's a bit more technical than the surrounding text, or you might find a brief diversion into the historical aspects of the text.

Keyboard Conventions

In addition to the special features that help you find what you need, this book uses some special conventions to make it easier to read:

Feature	Convention
Hot keys	Hot keys are underlined in this book, just as they appear in Windows 95 menus. To use a hot key, press Alt and the underlined key. For example, the F in File is a hot key that represents the File menu.
Key combinations	Key combinations are joined with the plus sign (+). Alt+F, for example, means hold down the Alt key, press the F key, and then release both keys.
Menu commands	A comma is used to separate the parts of a pull-down menu command. For example, choosing File, New means to open the File menu and select the New option.

In most cases, special-purpose keys are referred to by the text that actually appears on them on a standard 101-key keyboard. For example, press Esc, press F1, or press Enter. Some of the keys on your keyboard don't actually have words on them. So here are the conventions used in this book for those keys:

- The Backspace key, which is labeled with a left arrow, usually is located directly above the Enter key. The Tab key usually is labeled with two arrows pointing to lines, with one arrow pointing right and the other arrow pointing left.

- The cursor keys, labeled on most keyboards with arrows pointing up, down, right, and left, are called the up-arrow key, down-arrow key, right-arrow key, and left-arrow key.

- Case is not important unless explicitly stated. So "Press A" and "press a" mean the same thing.

Formatting Conventions

This book also uses some special typeface conventions to help you understand what you're reading:

Convention	Description
Italic	Italics indicate new terms. They also indicate placeholders in commands and addresses.
Bold	Bold indicates text you type. It also indicates addresses on the Internet.
`Monospace`	This typeface is used for on-screen messages and commands that you type.
Myfile.doc	Windows file names and folders are capitalized to help you distinguish them from regular text.

Getting Started with
Microsoft Project 98

1 The Power of Microsoft Project 98 15

2 Learning the Basics of Microsoft Project 27

3 Setting Up a New Project Document 61

4 Working with Project Files 91

The Power of Microsoft Project 98

Y**ou** were anxious to try out the Microsoft Project software; to get your hands on keyboard and mouse and to see how it all works. So, you dove right in…and now you're looking for additional help. That's perfectly understandable, because becoming a confident user of Microsoft Project is not easy, especially if you don't have a project management background. There are many special terms to learn (like *critical path*, *task dependencies*, and *leveling resources*), and most of the screens in Project are unlike any you've seen in Word or Excel. You will learn faster if you start with some understanding of the special requirements of project management. So, unless you're an old hand at project management, take the time to browse through this chapter. ■

What Microsoft Project 98 can do for you

Microsoft Project has solutions for small and large projects. This chapter addresses the question "How can Microsoft Project 98 help you?"

Some guidelines for project managers—and a to-do list for using Microsoft Project 98

Review the most used steps and guidelines for successful project managers.

How *does* Microsoft Project figure out the project schedule dates?

You need to understand the basics of project scheduling and how schedules are calculated to interpret what Microsoft Project does with your data.

The essential vocabulary of project scheduling

You can't get far without knowing the language. The most basic terms are explained here.

Exploring What Makes Project Management Different

Project management differs from conventional management in that managing a *project* is more limited and narrowly focused than being a CEO or even managing a small department within an organization. Traditional management functions are concerned with managing the ongoing operations of an organization to assure its long-run success and survival. Project management is concerned with *temporary* goals of the organization.

■ *Projects are temporary.* A project is a temporary assignment relative to the life of the organization, lasting only until the project's stated objectives are achieved. A project involves a one-time goal, produces a *unique* product or outcome, and has a defined start and finish date.

Managing a department or division is an ongoing assignment that extends into the future, perhaps for the life of the organization and the manager. Problems and challenges come and go; providing continuity is an inherent aspect of departmental management.

For example, selecting and installing a new word processor is a project; ongoing management of the word processing pool is not a project.

Defining projects and project management by the terms *temporary* and *short-term* is relative. A sales project might have a life of two weeks, and a project to build a nuclear power plant might have a life of twenty years. But both are shorter than the life span of the organization; both are temporary.

■ *Project objectives are specific and measurable.* Project goals are stated in terms of specific performance objectives. Vague generalities that call for unspecified improvements won't provide the focus needed for a project.

You can measure the success or failure of a project by the degree to which the performance satisfies the objectives set out in its goal.

■ *Projects are constrained by time, cost, and delivering a satisfactory result.* A project exists to deliver a specific performance objective, and the quality of the performance must be satisfactory while staying within the time allowed and without going over the budget.

Usually, either the project start or finish date (or both) must meet some time requirement. The overall time constraint needs to be explicitly incorporated into the project goal statement. Individual tasks of the project might also be subject to time constraints.

Projects are subject to resource or cost constraints because there is always a limit to how much money you can spend to achieve the project objectives.

Projects frequently require resources that are already in demand elsewhere in the organization. The project manager must compete for resources with other projects and with the ongoing operations of the organization. Resources are usually the main source of cost for a project.

■ *Projects must be managed so that immediate goals are achieved without damaging the long-term viability of the organization.* A project is a relatively short chapter in the life of the organization. The project manager must not lose sight of the larger goals of the organization. If a project meets its immediate goals, but does damage to other projects or commitments of the organization, or to the community within which the organization exists, then the project is not really a success. You must include maintaining a healthy internal work environment as another constraint. If you undertake a project for a customer, you must include maintaining good long-term customer relations as a constraint.

Project management scholarly studies usually define a *project* as a collection of activities or tasks designed to achieve a specific but temporary goal of the organization, with specific performance requirements, and subject to time and cost constraints.

ON THE WEB

For an excellent paper on the full scope of project management, I recommend "A Guide to the Project Management Body of Knowledge," which you can download from the Web site of the Project Management Institute at **http://www.pmi.org**.

A successful project must meet deadlines, stay within budget, and meet its performance objectives according to specifications.

The manager of a project is responsible for planning the actions or tasks that will achieve the project objectives and for organizing the resources of the organization to carry out the plan. He or she must apply management principles to plan, organize, staff, control, and direct resources of the organization to successfully complete the project. That includes, of course, keeping all participants in the project informed about the project plan—one of the strongest features of Microsoft Project 98.

The staffing function for project management is often a question of negotiating resource commitments with internal line managers instead of recruiting new employees. The personnel often come from the existing work force, and the facilities and equipment often must be shared with the regular operations of the organization. Moreover, the project manager is not necessarily the supervisor for the resources that are used in a project—this function is usually the job of a line manager.

How Does Microsoft Project 98 Help with All This?

Microsoft Project 98 helps you achieve your project goal on time and on budget. Computer software can aid significantly in project management as a tool for recording, calculating, analyzing, and preparing presentations to help communicate the details of the project.

However, Microsoft Project cannot produce or even guarantee a successful project plan any more than Microsoft Word can produce or guarantee a successful computer book. Still, Microsoft Project can be invaluable in planning and managing your projects:

■ *Microsoft Project helps you develop a better plan.* Because the software requires you to specify precisely the tasks necessary for meeting the project goal, you must think carefully about the details of the project. The discipline imposed by entering these details helps you organize a better plan.

The screen views provide an organized presentation of the details of your plan, which can improve your ability to visualize, organize, and refine the plan.

- *Microsoft Project makes calculated projections easier and more reliable.* Based on the data you enter, the computer calculates a schedule that shows when each task should begin and end and when specific resources are scheduled to perform specific tasks. This schedule also shows the probable costs of the project.

- *Microsoft Project makes it easy to test various "what if" scenarios to search for the optimum project plan.* The computer lets you experiment with different elements of the plan to arrive at the best plan for your organization.

- *Microsoft Project helps you detect inconsistencies and problems in the plan.* The computer detects when resources are scheduled for more hours than they are available or when deadlines are impossible to meet given the constraints you've entered. The computer helps you find and resolve resource overallocations and problems with deadlines.

- *Microsoft Project helps you communicate the plan to others.* The software provides printed reports and Internet HTML displays that make it easier to sell the plan to upper-level management and get their approval. Similarly, it makes it easier to communicate the plan to supervisors and workers, and that simplifies getting their approval and cooperation.

- *Microsoft Project helps you track progress and detect potential difficulties.* After the project is under way, you replace the projected dates for the tasks in the schedule with actual dates as work on the tasks is begun and completed. The software revises the schedule to incorporate these actual dates, and it projects new completion dates and costs. This new projection provides you with valuable advance warning of potential delays or cost overruns, so you can take corrective measures if necessary.

If external circumstances change after the project is underway, for example, when new pay rates go into effect or your organization is subject to new regulations, the software makes it easier to adjust the plan and see the consequences.

It cannot be stressed too much, however, that project management software, like any software, is only as useful as the reliability and completeness of the data you supply. And that takes lots and lots of time, so plan on it—or hire someone to take care of it.

Some General, Commonsense Guidelines for Project Managers

These guidelines are offered to help promote your success with your project. Most of them are commonsense management techniques, but reviewing them from time to time is always a useful exercise:

- Remember that your success as a project manager depends largely on your ability to motivate people to cooperate in the project. No software program or well-designed plan can compensate for ineffective people skills. Computers might respond to logic, but people respond to human emotions.

- Establish your authority as project manager and your role as coordinator of project planning at the outset. If you are appointed, ask the officer making the appointment to distribute a statement that validates your authority. Don't post it outside your door unless you provide cork backing as protection against sharp-pointed projectiles.

- Make the planning stage a group effort as much as possible. You're sure to find that you can't think of everything, and a wider base of experience and expertise is immensely helpful. And you will find it much easier to secure approval of the plan and to get people committed to the plan if they help in its formulation.

- Set a clear project goal:

  - State the goal of the project precisely and simply in a manner that everyone associated with the project can understand. This includes your supervisors who approve the project, managers who work with the project, and those who actually do the work. Prepare a concise summary statement of the goal of the project. State your goal in realistic and attainable terms that can be measured. It will then be possible to measure success.

  - Secure agreement on the goal by all who must approve the project or who must provide supervision during the execution of the project.

  - State a definite time frame in the goal—it should be part of the commitment to the project. The goal "Install a new word processor throughout the company," for example, is ill-defined. "Select and install a new word processor throughout the company and train all personnel in its use by June 1" is more specific.

  - Define the performance requirements and specifications carefully.

  - Discover and record all fixed deadlines or time constraints.

  - Determine the budgetary limitations of the project.

  - State the performance or quality specifications of the project with great care. Write and then distribute these specifications, in a Statement of Work, to the creators of the specifications and to the supervisors and workers when they are assigned to tasks. Make sure no misunderstanding exists about what you expect. Misunderstood specifications are usually costly.

- Organize the tasks of the project into major phases or components and establish *milestones*, or interim goals, to mark the completion of each of these phases. Milestones serve as check points by which everyone can gauge how well the project is on target once the work begins. This is a *top-down* approach, and it provides organization for the project plan from the outset.

  For example, the conversion to a new word processing product might involve the following phases and milestones:

  - Determine the features required of the software.

  - Review available products.

- Select the product to be used.
- Software selected (milestone).
- Buy the software.
- Set up help desk.
- Install software.
- Software installed (milestone).
- Convert old documents if necessary.
- Train all users.
- Conversion complete (milestone).

■ List the tasks that must be completed to reach each milestone and estimate how long each task will take. If a task is too long (some say any more than two weeks) you will probably be better off breaking it down into more components.

■ Diagram the flow of activity to show the instances where tasks must be performed in a specific sequence.

■ Distribute the project plan to all who are responsible for supervising or doing the work. Secure their agreement that the assumptions of the plan are sound and that all involved are willing to do their part. Revise the plan as needed to secure agreement.

■ Distribute printed copies of the revised schedule with charts and tables to identify clearly the scope of the project and the responsibilities of all who must contribute to making the project a success.

■ Secure firm commitments to the work assignments outlined in the plan.

■ After work on the project is under way, monitor progress by tracking actual performance and results. This is the best way to discover problems early so you can take corrective actions before disaster strikes.

Tracking these performance details also helps document the history of the project so you can learn from the experience. It's especially helpful if you have problems meeting the goals, and it will be valuable to you if you have to explain why the project goals are not met.

If problems arise that jeopardize finishing the project on time or within budget, you can give superiors ample warning so they can adjust their expectations.

■ After the project is completed, acknowledge all participants who made the project a success.

A Checklist for Using Microsoft Project

Microsoft Project is so rich with options you can easily lose sight of the forest as you explore all the interesting new trees. The following sections give you an overview of planning a project with Microsoft Project.

Preliminaries

Before you start entering tasks in the computer, it's a good idea to define some basic parameters that govern how Microsoft Project treats your data. (These topics are covered in detail in Chapter 3, "Setting Up a New Project Document.")

1. Customize Microsoft Project's calendar of working time to define when the computer can schedule work on the project. This includes defining your organization's working days, non-working days, and regular working hours. And, while you're at it, be sure that you use the terms *day* and *week* to mean the same number of hours that Microsoft Project does.

TIP
When you enter a task that you estimated will take a day or a week, Project translates both terms into hours (actually "minutes," but hours will do for this explanation). If your "day" is not eight hours, or your "week" is not forty hours, you must define those terms for Project, or it will interpret your estimate incorrectly.

2. Enter some basic descriptions for the project: a project title, the name of the organization, the project manager, and the expected start or finish date. These descriptions will appear on reports.

3. Optionally, you can choose to prepare at the outset a list of the resources you will use in the project. This includes defining resource costs and recognizing working days and hours when a resource is not available. This can also be done later, but many users like to have the list ready when they start entering the tasks in the planning phase. That way they can assign resources as they create the task list without stopping to enter the details about the resource.

Planning

Planning is the phase in which you outline the project plan, refine it, and distribute it to all who are involved in the project. These topics are explored in detail in Chapters 5 through 14.

1. List the major phases of the project in outline form and then fill in the detailed tasks and milestones in the project. Estimate how long each task will take or how much work is involved. This is the topic of Chapter 5, "Creating a Task List."

2. If the start or finish date of a task is constrained to a fixed date, enter the date at this point. Also define the required sequencing of tasks, that is to say where tasks must be scheduled in a certain order. These topics are covered in Chapter 6, "Entering Scheduling Requirements."

3. Define the resources and assign them to tasks. Defining and assigning resources is covered in Chapter 8, "Defining Resources and Costs," and Chapter 9, "Understanding Resource Scheduling in Microsoft Project 98."

4. Assign all fixed costs to the tasks. Fixed costs are covered in Chapter 10, "Assigning Resources and Costs to Tasks."

5. Review the schedule that Microsoft Project has calculated so far, and correct all problems by taking the actions discussed in the following list:

- Identify and resolve scheduling problems where deadlines can't be met, or where resources are assigned to do more work than they have the time to do. These problems are discussed in Chapter 6, "Entering Scheduling Requirements," and Chapter 11, "Resolving Resource Allocation Problems."

- Identify costs that are over budget and find ways to lower the costs as described in Chapter 12, "Reviewing the Project Plan."

- If the time constraint for the overall project is not met by the schedule, you must find ways to revise the schedule to meet the requirements of the project goal. Auditing and refining the schedule are covered in Chapter 12, "Reviewing the Project Plan."

6. Distribute the project schedule for review by the managers who must approve the plan and by project supervisors and workers who must agree to do the work. Publishing the project schedule and assignments is covered in Chapters 13, "Printing Views and Reports," and Chapter 14, "Publishing Projects on the Web."

7. Revise the plan, if necessary, to accommodate suggestions or changes submitted in the review. See Chapter 12, "Reviewing the Project Plan."

8. Print and distribute the final schedule to all parties for final approval, and secure from each party a firm commitment to the plan.

Managing the Project

In this phase, you monitor progress on the project, recording actual experience and calculating a new schedule when actual dates fail to match the planned dates. These topics are covered in Chapter 15, "Tracking Work on the Project," and Chapter 16, "Analyzing Progress and Revising the Schedule."

1. Make a baseline (original) copy of the final schedule plan to use later for comparing actual start and finish dates with the planned dates.

2. Track actual start dates, finish dates, percentage of work completed, and costs incurred, and enter these details into the computer. Microsoft Project incorporates these changes in the schedule and calculates a revised schedule with revised cost figures.

3. Review the recalculated schedule for problems and, if possible, take corrective measures. Notify all participants about changes in the schedule that concern them.

4. After the project is completed, prepare final reports as documentation to show the actual work and costs and to compare those with the baseline copy of the plan you saved earlier.

Project Management Scheduling Techniques

The methods used by project management software to schedule dates and times for tasks (and the resources assigned to them) is ingenious. You will need to understand the general concepts if you are to use Microsoft Project effectively. However, you don't need to master the details of how calculations are made. Although the applications of these methods are reviewed as needed in upcoming chapters, gaining an overview can be useful before you get into the details of planning and coordinating a project.

You Must Provide the Raw Data

You must provide accurate task information for Microsoft Project to calculate a schedule for your project. This usually requires a lot of guess work, but without it, Project won't be as helpful to you. The less time you take in putting together reasonable task information, the less likely the computer projections will be reasonable.

- Enter a list of all the tasks that must be scheduled to complete the project. You must include the duration of each task (how long it should take to do the work). Include as *milestones* any decisive points in the project like the end of a major phase, or a point where new decision making is called for.

- You must also include any sequencing requirements (dependencies) that will govern when the task can be scheduled. A *sequencing requirement* is a requirement that the scheduled date for a task has to be tied to the scheduled date for some other task. When you build a house, for example, you schedule the carpenters to start erecting the walls after the date the foundation has been finished. You tie the date for starting the walls to the date when the foundation is scheduled to be finished.

- If a task must start or finish by a specific date, enter this requirement as a constraint on the scheduling of the task. For example, you might stipulate that a certain task can't start until the third fiscal quarter, due to cash flow problems. Or, you might have a contract that requires that a task be finished by a specific date. When calculating a schedule of dates for tasks, Microsoft Project normally schedules each task to begin as soon as possible, considering the task's position in the sequence of tasks. However, it will take note of your constraints and warn you if the schedule doesn't allow constraints to be met.

> **TIP** Do not enter start and finish constraints for tasks unless absolutely necessary. Especially *don't* use constraints to signify that resources won't be available until a certain date. Use Microsoft Project 98's new Available From resource field to define that limitation.

The Calendar Used for Scheduling

Microsoft Project uses its internal standard calendar to calculate a schedule for the tasks. The default standard calendar has no holidays and assumes that work can be scheduled from 8:00 a.m. to 5:00 p.m., Monday through Friday. You must customize the standard calendar to make it represent the work days and shifts of your organization. This standard calendar will be used to schedule all tasks that do not have resources assigned to them.

How Project Calculates the Schedule

Project starts calculating a schedule when you enter the first task. With each added detail, the schedule is updated. The primary method used in project management software for scheduling is called the Critical Path Method (CPM).

The CPM method calculates the overall duration of the project by chaining tasks together in their required sequences and then summing up the combined duration of all tasks in the chain.

Figure 1.1 illustrates a simple project that contains six tasks and a Project Finish milestone task. Tasks A, B, and C must be performed in sequence; tasks X, Y, and Z must also be performed in sequence. Both sequences can occur at the same time; however, both sequences must finish before the project is complete.

FIG. 1.1

The longest sequence of tasks (the critical path) determines the finish date for the project.

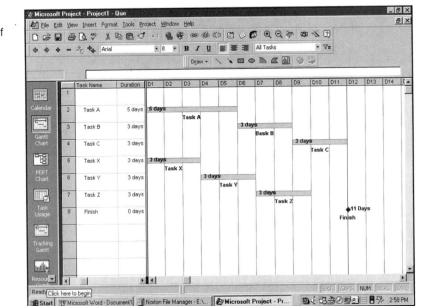

If parallel task sequences are in progress at the same time, the overall duration of the project is the duration of the longest of these task sequences. In Figure. 1.1, the sequence A-B-C takes 11 days, and the sequence X-Y-Z takes nine days. It takes 11 days to complete the project—the duration of the longest sequence.

You cannot complete the project on schedule unless the tasks on the longest sequence are finished on schedule. These tasks, known as *critical tasks*, are vital to keeping the overall project on schedule. A sequence of critical tasks is called a *critical path*. All tasks on the critical path must be finished on time as scheduled or the finish date for the project will slip.

In Figure. 1.1, tasks A, B, and C are critical tasks, and the sequence A-B-C is the critical path. The X, Y, and Z tasks are not critical to finishing the project on time. You could delay the completion of any one of these tasks for up to two days without causing a delay of the overall project. The X, Y, and Z tasks are said to have *slack*.

Critical tasks do not have slack. These tasks cannot be delayed if the project is to finish on schedule. So, having zero slack is one way to identify or define a critical task.

Why Should You Care About the Critical Path?

Identifying the critical tasks is an important time-saver in managing a project. Suppose you need to shorten the duration of the overall project (commonly known as *crashing* the schedule), and you're looking for tasks whose duration you can shorten to accomplish that. (For example, you might add more resources to a task in order to finish its work sooner, or you might reduce the scope of a task or the quality of the work so that it takes less time to complete.) You don't have to look at each and every task in the project to find potential time savings; you can safely limit your analysis to ways to shorten the critical tasks and not worry about shortening the non-critical tasks. That's because reducing the duration of non-critical tasks would have no effect on the finish date. This knowledge can save you a great deal of time in trying to find ways to shorten the project schedule.

How Resource Assignments Affect the Schedule

If you assign resources to tasks, the calculated schedule can change dramatically. Every resource has its own scheduling calendar, which shows those times when the resource is not available (such as vacations or attending conferences) or when the resource is available in addition to the standard times for the organization. The standard calendar is used to calculate schedules for tasks that have no resources assigned to them. When a resource is assigned, the task schedule will change to reflect the availability of the resource.

Changing the number of resources assigned to a task also affects its schedule. Some tasks have a *fixed duration*: no matter how many workers or resources you assign to the task, the duration remains unchanged. If you scheduled a task to deliver a small package to an outlying suburb, for example, you would assign a driver and a truck. You probably couldn't shorten the duration of the task by placing two drivers in the truck. In that case, the task would have a fixed duration. If, however, the task were to deliver a truckload of packages, a second driver could reduce the time it takes to load and unload the packages, and thus reduce the duration of the task. If changing the quantity of resources assigned to a task leads to a change in the duration of the task, the task's duration is said to be *resource driven*. The schedule for the task is driven or determined by the quantity of resources assigned to the task.

Microsoft Project assumes that tasks are resource driven—that is, that they are *not* fixed-duration tasks. If a task has a fixed duration, you must define the task explicitly as fixed duration. The program assumes that you can shorten the duration of a task if you increase the resources assigned to do the work.

From Here...

If you're experienced with Microsoft Project, see the following chapters:

- If you're new to Project, go on to Chapter 2, "Learning the Basics of Microsoft Project," for a review of the Microsoft Project user interface and then continue with the chapter order that follows.

- See Chapter 5, "Creating a Task List," and Chapter 6, "Entering Scheduling Requirements," for some of the new features—especially task splitting.

- Spend some time in Chapter 9, "Understanding Resource Scheduling in Microsoft Project 98," and Chapter 11, "Resolving Resource Allocation Problems," to learn about the many changes in the way Project calculates schedules for resource assignments.

Learning the Basics of Microsoft Project

In this chapter, you learn how to work in the Microsoft Office software environment using Microsoft Project. To get the most out of Project, you need to be familiar with all the screen elements you'll be working with. This chapter leads you into taking the first steps toward using Microsoft Project. ■

Start and exit Project

Take a look at starting Microsoft Project, using the Welcome! screen, and exiting Project using menu commands or keyboard shortcuts.

Getting acquainted

Learn to navigate through the screen components—views, menus, toolbars, the entry bar, and the status bar. Also learn about the new View Bar feature.

Using Help

Explore Microsoft Project's extensive online help, including accessing Project specific help through the World Wide Web.

Using Project views

Display different views of your project data. Learn to move around in the views and select tasks, resources, or individual task fields.

Starting and Exiting Microsoft Project

When you install Microsoft Project in Windows 95 or Windows NT 4.0, the Setup program places Microsoft Project on the Start menu, under Programs. Figure 2.1 shows the listing for Microsoft Project on the Start menu. To start Microsoft Project, choose Start, Programs, Microsoft Project.

FIG. 2.1
To start Microsoft Project, choose Start, Programs, Microsoft Project.

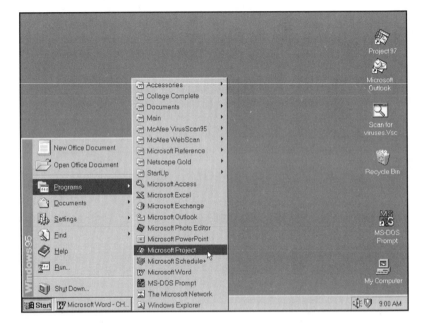

The program first displays a new project window in the background, with a blank document named Project1 and a Welcome! window in the foreground (see Figure 2.2). The following list describes the choices in the Welcome! dialog box:

FIG. 2.2
The Welcome! dialog box helps you choose how to get started.

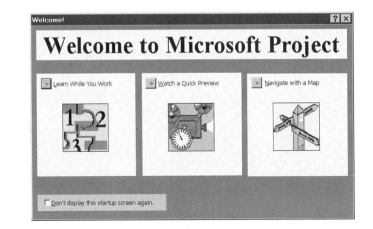

- Choose <u>L</u>earn While You Work for a tutorial that displays Cue Cards from the online Help system to guide you through setting up a new project document. This tutorial is divided into 12 basic lessons for creating a project and seven advanced lessons for managing a project.
- Choose <u>W</u>atch a Quick Preview for a demonstration and tutorial of the major features of project scheduling with Microsoft Project.
- Choose <u>N</u>avigate with a Map to view a graphical guide to the phases of project planning.

 In addition to the three main choices, you can also select the <u>D</u>on't Display this Startup Screen Again check box if you want to bypass the display of the Welcome! window the next time you start Microsoft Project. Use the close button in the upper-right corner of the Welcome! window to close the window without selecting any of the previous choices.

You can exit Microsoft Project by choosing <u>F</u>ile, E<u>x</u>it. Or you can click the application's close button in the upper-right corner of the window.

T I P   Use the Alt+F4 shortcut key combination to quickly close an application. You are prompted to save your latest changes before the application closes.

When you exit the application, all open project files close. If any changes have been made in a project file since you last saved it, a dialog box prompts you to save the changes before closing the file. Choose <u>Y</u>es to save the changes, choose <u>N</u>o to close without saving the changes, or choose Cancel if you want to return to work on the project.

N O T E   If the Planning Wizard asks you about saving a baseline when you save a file, you can safely choose the OK button without changing the default selection. The *baseline* is a copy of the way the schedule looks at this moment. The baseline copy does not change as you make changes in the project schedule. It's useful for comparing later versions of the schedule with the original intentions.

You can select the Don't Tell Me About this Again check box to avoid seeing the Planning Wizard baseline warning every time you close a file. ▨

▶ **See** "Setting the Baseline or Plan," **p. 474**

Exploring the Microsoft Project Window

 Once you move past the Welcome! screen, you see the Microsoft Project title bar at the top of the screen, along with the Microsoft Project menu, two toolbars, and an entry bar. On the left side of the screen are the active split bar and the View Bar, a new feature in Project 97. The View Bar has been added to Project to assist you in moving quickly between views (and help keep track of which view you currently have displayed). The status bar is visible at the bottom of the screen, and the data area in the center of the screen displays the project data (see Figure 2.3).

Part
I
Ch
2

FIG. 2.3
The Gantt Chart is the most commonly used view in Microsoft Project.

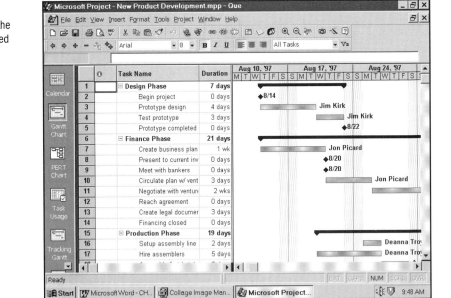

The display in the data area is a known as a *view*. The term *view* refers to the way the project data appears. The default view is the Gantt Chart, which is divided into two parts: a table on the left showing a list of task names, and a timescale on the right where a bar chart will show the beginning and ending of each task. Some views are *graphics images*, like the Gantt Chart, that present data in bar charts or network diagrams. For example, Figure 2.4 shows the PERT Chart view. This is the same project, but this view illustrates the sequencing of tasks in the project, similar to a flow chart.

Some views are *spreadsheets* that show data in columns and rows. The Resource Sheet view arranges information about the resources in a table (see Figure 2.5).

Some views are *forms* that show many details about one task or resource at a time. The Resource Form shows hourly rates and other details for Howard Thompson, one of the resources in this project, along with a list of all the tasks to which he is assigned (see Figure 2.6).

Still other views are combinations of these basic types. The Task Entry view shows the Gantt Chart at the top and the Task Form at the bottom to show details for the task that is selected in the Gantt Chart (see Figure 2.7).

FIG. 2.4

The PERT Chart is a graphic view that shows the sequencing of tasks in the project.

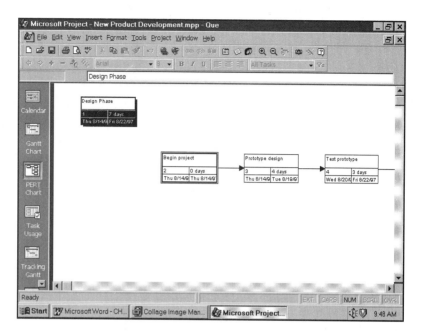

FIG. 2.5

Resource Sheet is a spreadsheet table displaying information about the project resources.

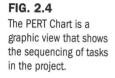

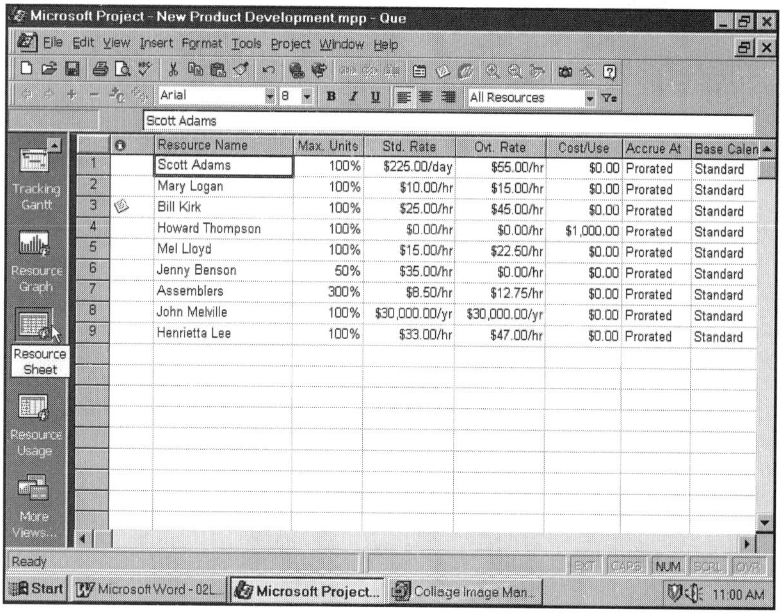

FIG. 2.6

The Resource Form view shows all the tasks assigned to one resource, among other things.

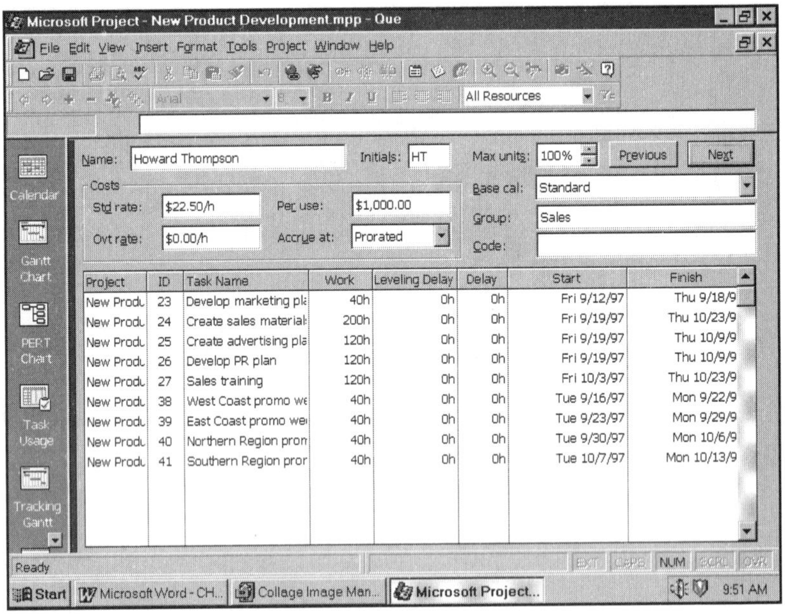

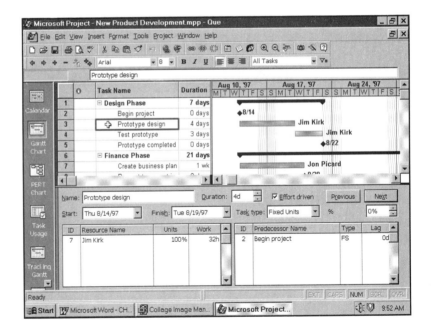

FIG. 2.7

The Task Entry view shows details for the selected task in the form at the bottom of the screen.

Each of these views draws on the same set of data, but presents it differently. Learning to make use of the different views is a key to the successful use of Microsoft Project. Later in this chapter, you will learn how to display other views in Project.

The Menu Bar

The Microsoft Project menu is very similar to the menus in the other Microsoft Office products (Word, Excel, PowerPoint, and Access). The menu commands are defined and described in detail in later chapters, as the functions they perform are discussed.

The Toolbars

Appearing below the menu bar are the toolbars that contain buttons you activate with the mouse to provide shortcut access to frequently used menu choices or special functions. The individual buttons on the toolbar are described as you encounter them in the following chapters. A brief description (called a *ScreenTip*) appears beneath a toolbar button if you rest the mouse pointer over the button for a second or two.

For more complete descriptions of the toolbar buttons, use the Microsoft Project Help menu. Choose Help, What's This?. By choosing this option, your mouse pointer now has a question mark attached to it. Simply click the tool you are interested in, and a mini help screen will provide you with additional information on that tool.

There are 12 toolbars provided in Microsoft Project 97. The two displayed initially are the Standard toolbar and the Formatting toolbar. You can add and remove toolbars to the display and create your own custom toolbars.

▶ **See** "Customizing Toolbars," **p. 876**

▶ **See** "Creating New Toolbars," **p. 880**

To show additional toolbars, or to hide one that is currently displayed, choose View, Toolbars. Toolbars that are checked are currently displayed (see Figure 2.8). Choose a checked toolbar to hide it; choose an unchecked toolbar to display it.

FIG. 2.8
Show or hide toolbars
through the View menu.

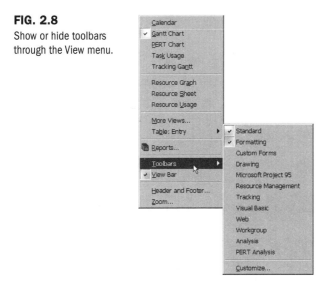

Part

I

Ch

2

T I P The shortcut menu is a quick way to show or hide toolbars. Position the mouse over any visible toolbar and right-click to display the shortcut menu (see Figure 2.9). Toolbars that are checked are currently displayed. Choose a checked toolbar to hide it; choose an unchecked toolbar to display it.

FIG. 2.9
You can use the shortcut menu to show or hide toolbars. Simply click the toolbar name to change its display status.

| ✓ Standard |
| ✓ Formatting |
| Custom Forms |
| Drawing |
| Microsoft Project 95 |
| Resource Management |
| Tracking |
| Visual Basic |
| Web |
| Workgroup |
| Analysis |
| PERT Analysis |
| Customize... |

The Entry Bar

The *entry bar* is on the line below the toolbars (see Figure 2.10). The entry bar performs several functions:

- The left end of the entry bar displays progress messages that let you know when Microsoft Project is engaged in calculating, opening and saving files, leveling resources, and so on.

- The center of the entry bar contains an entry area where data entry and editing takes place. During Entry and Editing modes, Cancel and Enter buttons also appear.

Use the entry area to enter data in a field or to edit data previously placed in a field. You use the entry area primarily when you change data in views that show a spreadsheet table or when you enter task data in the PERT Chart.

N O T E When the entry bar is active, many features of Microsoft Project are unavailable. Most menu commands, toolbar buttons, and shortcut keys are also unavailable. Make sure you close the entry bar by pressing Enter or by selecting the Confirm button on the entry bar (see Figure 2.10) after entering or editing data in a field. ▓

The View Bar

 The *View Bar* is a great new feature in this version of Microsoft Project. It helps you quickly identify which view you are looking at and provides you with quick access to the most commonly used views. There are scroll arrows on the View Bar to see additional views (see Figure 2.10). At the bottom of the list is the More Views option, which takes you to a dialog box listing of all the views in Microsoft Project.

To show or hide the View Bar, choose View, View Bar. Similar to the way views and toolbars are checked, choose the checked View Bar to hide it; choose the unchecked View Bar to display it.

Confirm button

Entry bar

FIG. 2.10
The entry bar is typically used to edit data in your project.

Cancel button

View Bar

Active split bar

Scroll arrow

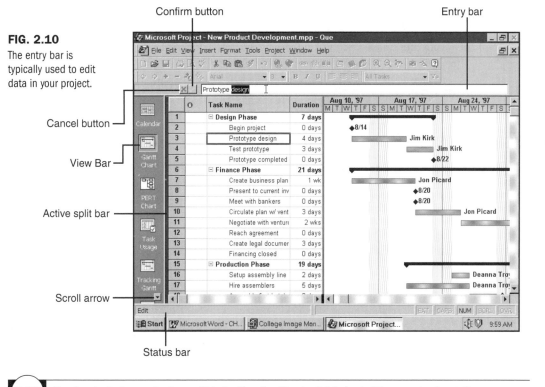

Status bar

TIP Use the shortcut menu to show or hide the View Bar. Simply click in front of the name to change its display status.

Whenever the View Bar is not being displayed, Project will still indicate which view you are in on the active split bar indicator. (See the section "The Active Split Bar" later in this chapter for more information.) As there are more than 25 views you can work with in Project, the View Bar and the active split bar will help you to quickly switch between the views and keep track of which view is being displayed. In order for a view to appear on the View Bar, the view has to be customized to display in the menu (which in turn displays it also in the View Bar). Chapter 22, "Customizing Views, Tables, and Filters," describes how to display views in the menu.

The Status Bar

The *status bar* is located at the bottom of the window. It shows the status of special keys and displays advisory messages (refer to Figure 2.10). At the left end of the status bar is the *mode indicator*. This indicator says Ready when Microsoft Project is waiting for you to begin an operation. The mode indicator says Enter when you initially enter data, and it says Edit when you edit a field where you have already entered data. It is also used to provide information for whatever action is currently taking place, including messages when you have a dialog box displayed, when you are opening or saving a file, and when you are previewing the document before printing.

The middle of the status bar displays warning messages when you need to recalculate and when you've created circular relationships while linking tasks. The far right end of the status bar indicates the status of the Extend (EXT), Add (ADD), Caps Lock (CAPS), Num Lock (NUM), Scroll Lock (SCRL), and Insert (OVR) keys. When you turn on one of these keys, the key name appears in the status bar. Choose Help, Contents and Index, and use the Index tab to look up status bar for more information on these keys.

Using the Online Learning Aids

Microsoft Project has an extensive online help facility, with many new special aids to help you learn how to use its features. The learning aids range in complexity from the immediate and brief ScreenTips to the analytical suggestions provided by the Planning Wizard and the step-by-step instructions contained in the new Getting Started tutorials.

Accessing Online Help

There are many sources of Help in Microsoft Project:

- The Help menu offers access to the online help topics as well as access to the new Office Assistant, a set of online tutorials featured in Getting Started, and Microsoft on the Web (if you are connected to the Internet).

- When the menu is unavailable, you can click the Office Assistant button on the Standard toolbar or press the F1 key to activate the Office Assistant.

- To access context-sensitive help, choose Help, What's This? or press Shift+F1. The mouse pointer changes into a question mark and an arrow. Choose a menu command or point to an area of the screen about which you want help and click the mouse button.

- Many dialog boxes feature a Help button in the title bar to explain parts of the dialog box. When you click this Help button, the mouse pointer becomes a question mark with an arrow. Click a feature of the dialog box to see an explanation of that feature.

- The Planning Wizard monitors your use of the program and offers tips of techniques that might be more efficient or warns you about potential problems you might create for yourself as a result of your current action. The Planning Wizard is automatically "turned on" in Microsoft Project. The section "Working with the Planning Wizard" later in this chapter provides more information on using this wizard.

- The Microsoft Project Help uses the new Office Assistant feature to provide a unique way to access Help topics. It's based on Microsoft's IntelliSense technology, which means it can interpret questions you type in your own, non-technical words and provide a list of Help topics that might be relevant to your question.

- If you have access to the Internet, Microsoft on the Web offers quick access to the Microsoft Web site. Free Software, New Product Information, and Frequently Asked Questions are among the topics available online from Microsoft.

Using the Office Assistant

 The Office Assistant, also known as Clippit, is one of the best ways to get help in Microsoft Project and is a significant improvement over the previous help feature known as the Answer Wizard.

The Assistant will help you find answers to your questions by interpreting questions you type in your own non-technical words and provide a list of Help topics that might be relevant to your question. Additionally, the Assistant works closely with the Planning Wizard to help explain problems and offer shortcuts on working more effectively with Microsoft Project.

Part

1

Ch

2

Accessing and Using the Office Assistant When you start Microsoft Project, the Office Assistant will be active (see Figure 2.11). Additionally, the Office Assistant may be accessed through the Help Menu or by using F1.

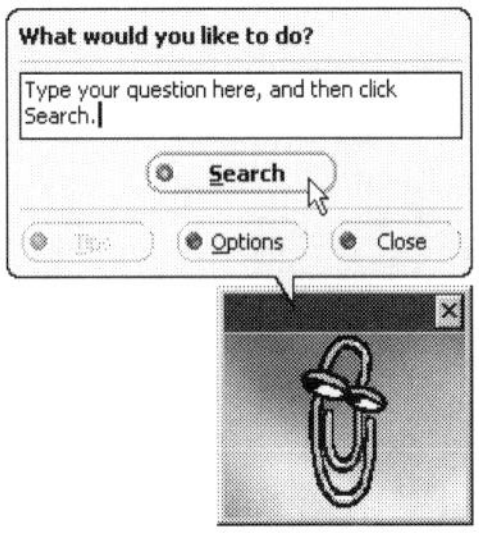

FIG. 2.11
The Office Assistant provides you with a quick way to ask questions while working with Microsoft Project.

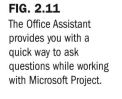

There are several ways to work with the Assistant:

- You can type a question in the What Would You Like To Do? box and click Search (see Figure 2.12). The Assistant will show several help topics that may answer your question.

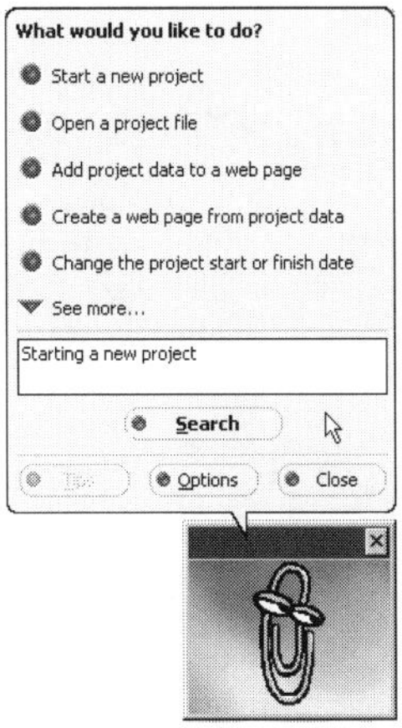

FIG. 2.12
The Office Assistant looks up references from questions you pose in your own words.

■ There is a Tips button to provide you with tips on using the Assistant.

■ The Options button lists the default settings for the Assistant.

■ Use the Close button, or press Esc, to close the Assistant's question box.

The Office Assistant is designed to move when it's in the way. If you want to hide the Office Assistant, choose the close button in the upper-left corner of the Assistant window (see Figure 2.13).

N O T E If the Office Assistant is open, then the Planning Wizard messages (suggestions and warnings) will be displayed by the Office Assistant. If you close the Office Assistant, then the Planning Wizard will use its own standard dialog boxes to display the messages. ■

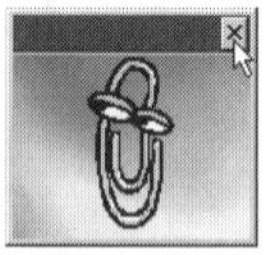

FIG. 2.13

Click the close button to temporarily hide the Office Assistant. The Office Assistant can be redisplayed quickly by pressing F1.

Changing the Office Assistant Options   The Assistant is shared by all the Microsoft Office programs. Changes you make to the Assistant options while working in Project affect the Assistant in all the Microsoft Office programs. The Office Assistant's Options dialog box (see Figure 2.14) indicates the current settings for the Assistant.

 You can choose other symbols to be your Office Assistant. To change the symbol, use the Gallery tab in the Office Assistant dialog box. Choose the Next button to see the other symbols. However, you may need your Microsoft Project CD to make the change.

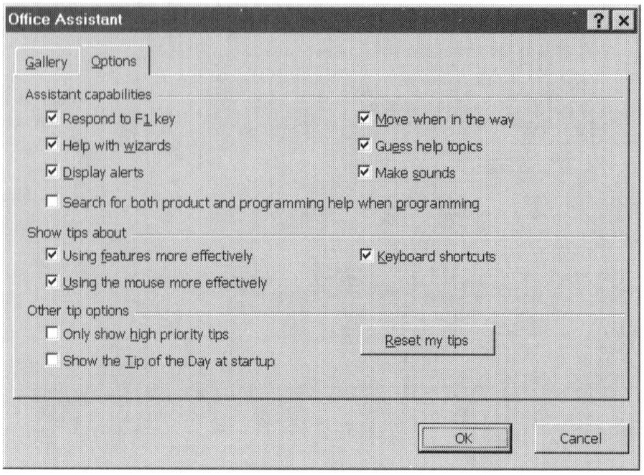

FIG. 2.14

You can set the options for the how the Office Assistant interacts with you.

Office Assistant	
Gallery **Options**	
Assistant capabilities	
☑ Respond to F1 key	☑ Move when in the way
☑ Help with wizards	☑ Guess help topics
☑ Display alerts	☑ Make sounds
☐ Search for both product and programming help when programming	
Show tips about	
☑ Using features more effectively	☑ Keyboard shortcuts
☑ Using the mouse more effectively	
Other tip options	
☐ Only show high priority tips	Reset my tips
☐ Show the Tip of the Day at startup	
	OK Cancel

T I P By default, the Assistant does not show tips about Keyboard Shortcuts. On the <u>O</u>ptions tab of the Office Assistant dialog box, you can activate this option.

Using Contents and Index

Through the Contents and Index options on the Help menu, you can browse or search the entire contents of Microsoft Project Help. The Help Topics: Microsoft Project dialog box has three avenues for getting help: a table of contents, an alphabetical index, and a text search capability (see Figure 2.15).

FIG. 2.15

The Help Topics dialog box provides multiple ways to search for help.

Part

Ch

2

Using the Contents Tab   The Contents tab displays a list of topics organized into categories, which represent different project scheduling processes you might want help with. Each topic has a book icon that changes to an open book when you double-click the topic and display the contents of the topic "book." You can drill down into topics until you find a category that seems promising (see Figure 2.16).

Many of the help screens offer numbered steps to accomplish specific tasks or interactive screens for you to click for additional information.

Using the Index Tab   All Help topics have short index references. Use the Index tab to locate key words in these index references (see Figure 2.17). Type a key word(s) in text box 1 to find it in the list of index entries. Each word is searched for independently in the alphabetized Index of Help topics. Select one of the matching index references displayed in list box 2, then choose the <u>D</u>isplay button to view the Help topic.

FIG. 2.16

Help topics are organized into procedural categories on the Contents tab.

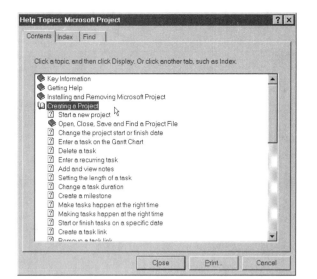

FIG. 2.17

Use the Index tab to search for key words.

TIP   You can also double-click the topic name to display it.

Using the Find Tab   Use the Find tab to search the body text of all Help topics to find matches for the letters or words you type in. The first time you use the Find tab, you will encounter the Find Setup Wizard (see Figure 2.18).

FIG. 2.18

You can choose how comprehensive the database of Help topic text words will be with the Find Setup Wizard.

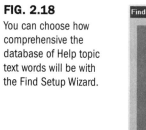

The first time you use the search facilities on the Find tab, Help builds a list or database of words that are contained in the Help files. Help asks you to choose how comprehensive the list should be by selecting one of three choices in the Find Setup Wizard dialog box (see refer to 2.18). The choices are:

- Choose the Minimize Database Size button to conserve disk space.

- Choose the Maximize Search Capabilities button to create the most comprehensive index of words with cross-referencing and other capabilities.

- Choose the Customize Search Capabilities button to choose which features will be included and which Help files will be included.

The wizard will guide you through the options when you choose the Next button. Once the list has been created, each time you select the Find tab from the Help Topics dialog box, you will see a new screen (see Figure 2.19).

Now that the word list has been generated, type in words or letters in the Find tab to search the body text of all Help topics (see Figure 2.19). As you type letters into text box 1, list box 2 displays a list of all words containing the letters you type. List box 3 displays a list of all Help topics that contain the letters you type in text box 1. By typing whole words, or by selecting whole words from the list in box 2, you can significantly narrow the search list displayed in list box 3.

You also can type more than one word into text box 1. Choose the Options button to display the Find Options dialog box and use the Search for Topics Containing option buttons to determine how to use multiple search strings (see Figure 2.20):

- The first button selects only Help topics that contain all the words you typed in any order.

- The second button selects all Help topics that contain at least one of the words you typed.

- The third button selects only those Help topics that contain all the words you typed in exact order.

FIG. 2.19

You can use the Find tab to search the actual text of Help topics for words or character strings.

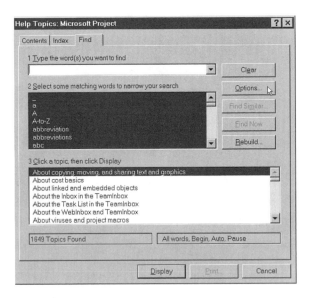

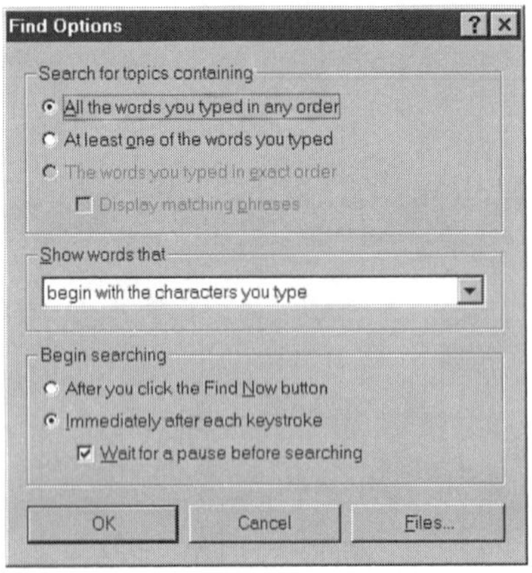

The Find Options dialog box is shown. It includes options for searching for topics containing, showing words that, and beginning searching.

FIG. 2.20

Use the Find Options dialog box to set preferences for the way Help conducts the word search.

Use the pull-down list in the Find Options dialog box to determine the display in list box 2 of the Find tab of words that match your typing. You can specify words that begin with, end with, contain, or match exactly the characters you type. You also can choose to display words having the same root as the word(s) you type.

The Find Options dialog box also offers control over when the search for matching words and topics begins. You can choose to have the search start only after you click the Find Now button on the Find tab. Or, you can choose to have the search begin immediately after each keystroke. The Help engine can also wait for a pause before searching.

Choose the Files button to choose which Microsoft application Help files you want examined in the search for matching words and topics.

Choose the OK button to save the settings on the Find Options dialog box or choose the Cancel button to close the dialog box without saving any changes in the settings.

Select a Help topic from list box 3 and choose the Display button to view the topic. You can also choose the Find Similar button to display a list of topics related to the one selected. Note that the Find Similar button is not available if you build the word list with the recommended setting (Minimize Database Size).

Choose the Rebuild button on the Find tab to generate the word list again with different options.

After reviewing the topic, choose the Help Topics button to return to the Find tab to select additional topics. Choose the close button of the topic window to leave Help and return to your document.

Getting Started

Microsoft has added three new help features for users new to Microsoft Project and project management. To access the new help options, choose Help, Getting Started. A submenu listing the three menu choices appears. These choices are: Quick Preview, Create Your Project, and Microsoft Project 101: Fundamentals.

Quick Preview   Choose Quick Preview from the Getting Started menu to access a brief tutorial that provides an overview of the capabilities of Microsoft Project (see Figure 2.21). This tutorial is an excellent way to introduce new Project users to Microsoft Project.

FIG. 2.21
First screen of the
Quick Preview tutorial.

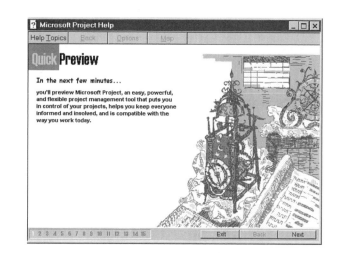

Create Your Project   Choose Create Your Project from the Getting Started menu to access a step-by-step tutorial to assist you in creating your first project (see Figure 2.22). This tutorial provides 12 lessons guiding you through the creation process. It also includes seven advanced lessons for managing your project.

FIG. 2.22

First screen of the Create New Project tutorial.

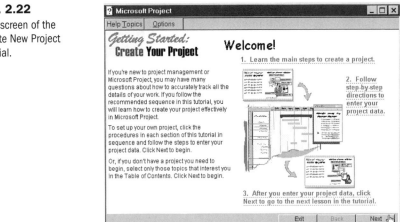

This tutorial provides 12 lessons guiding you through the creation process (see Figure 2.23). It also includes seven advanced lessons for managing your project (see Figure 2.24).

FIG. 2.23

The list of 12 lessons for creating your project.

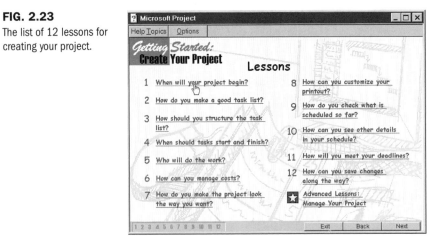

Microsoft Project 101: Fundamentals   Choose Microsoft Project 101: Fundamentals from the Getting Started menu. This feature is designed to assist new users in working with the software and designed to answer six specific questions (see Figure 2.25). The screens are interactive. When you click a caption, more information appears on the screen.

FIG. 2.24
The list of seven advanced lessons for managing your project.

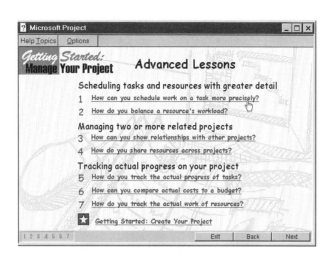

FIG. 2.25
Contents screen for Microsoft Project 101: Fundamentals.

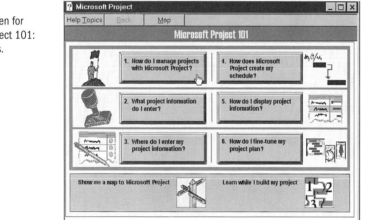

Microsoft on the Web

A dynamic new feature of Project 97 is the capability to access help on Project directly from Microsoft through the World Wide Web. If you have access to the Internet, a new means of finding answers to your questions is available. This assistance has been broken up into four distinct areas: Free Stuff, Product News, Frequently Asked Questions, and Online Support.

Choose Help, Microsoft on the Web to quickly access these key Microsoft Web site locations (see Figure 2.26).

FIG. 2.26
Microsoft on the Web provides quick access to Microsoft's Web site.

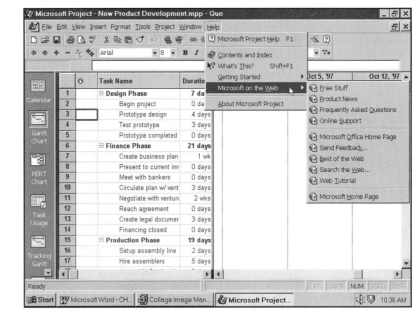

The first four topics mentioned are designed for Microsoft Project users specifically. Additionally, Microsoft has made it easy to access the Microsoft Office Web page, and has even provided a tutorial for those unfamiliar with using the Web. When you access one of the Microsoft on the Web help options, the system will even activate your Internet connection and your Web browser, if they are not currently active! Figures 2.27, 2.28, 2.29, and 2.30 show the initial screens for each of the Microsoft Project specific sites.

ON THE WEB

From this Web site, Microsoft provides tips, tricks, and how-tos on Microsoft Project. You can see a demonstration of the software and download sample template files and other free add-ins. There are a number of interesting Case Studies describing how companies used Microsoft Project to schedule and track various projects. WWW URL is **http://www.microsoft.com/project/work.htm**.

ON THE WEB

The Product News Web site provides a synopsis of all the late-breaking news. This includes any new tips and tricks, as well as the latest templates and other free add-ins. WWW URL is **http://www.microsoft.com/project/default.htm**.

FIG. 2.27
To access information about free trial copies of Microsoft Project or new template files, choose Help, Microsoft on the Web, Free Stuff.

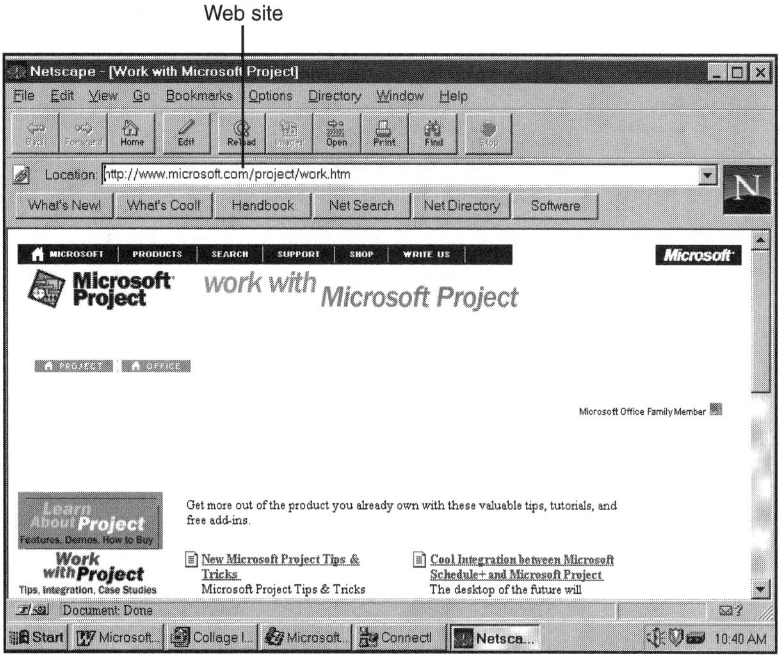

Web site

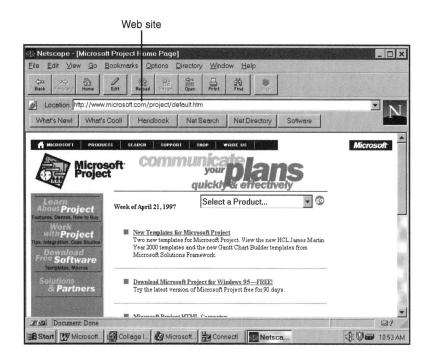

FIG. 2.28
To access information about Microsoft Project, choose Help, Microsoft on the Web, Product News.

Web site

FIG. 2.29
To see answers to the most commonly asked Project questions, choose Help, Microsoft on the Web, Frequently Asked Questions.

Web site

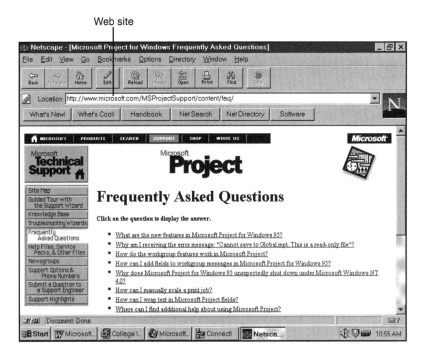

ON THE WEB

This Web site provides answers to the Frequently Asked Questions (FAQs). Additionally, you can use a wizard to troubleshoot a problem or ask for assistance with downloading files. Microsoft sponsors a newsgroup on Project—microsoft.public.project. Use any newsreader software to access this newsgroup. WWW URL is **http://www.microsoft.com/MSProjectSupport/content/faq/**.

ON THE WEB

The Online Support Web site lists a series of help topics for Project users and developers. These topics are typically more in-depth than those found under Frequently Asked Questions. New topics are easily found, because they are flagged with a "new" symbol next to the title. WWW URL is **http://www.microsoft.com/MSprojectsupport/**.

Working with the Planning Wizard

There are still more learning aids than those accessed with the Help menu. The Planning Wizard continuously monitors your work and suggests tips for easier ways to do things. It also intercepts actions that might cause problems and offers you solutions for avoiding the problems. For example, the message in Figure 2.31 appears when Planning Wizard detects that a task is being moved to a non-working day and suggests appropriate ways to complete the procedure.

Web site

FIG. 2.30

To connect to the technical support team for Microsoft Project, choose <u>H</u>elp, Microsoft on the <u>W</u>eb, Online Support.

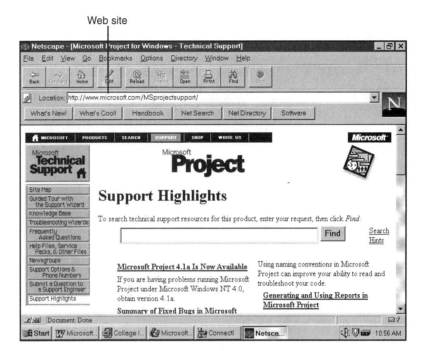

FIG. 2.31

The Planning Wizard monitors your work and offers suggestions to improve your use of Microsoft Project.

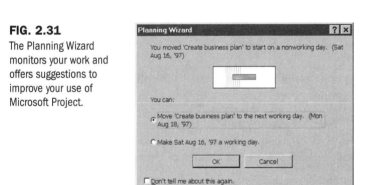

The Planning Wizard options are controlled on the General tab of the Options dialog box. To access the Options dialog box, choose <u>T</u>ools, <u>O</u>ptions.

There are other wizards active during specific activities to guide you through complex tasks. For example, the Gantt Chart Wizard helps you customize the graphics features of the Gantt Chart.

▶ **See** "Using the Gantt Chart Wizard," **p. 714**

Introducing the Gantt Chart View

The default view of a new project is the Gantt Chart view (shown in Figure 2.32). The Gantt Chart view is the most often used view for listing the project tasks.

FIG. 2.32
The Gantt Chart is the view most often in Microsoft Project because it shows both the outlined structure of the task list and the timescale for tasks.

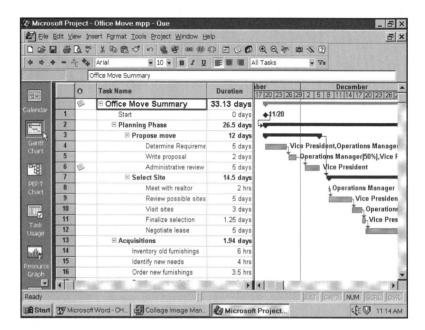

The Gantt Chart view is a graphical view that contains a spreadsheet table on the left side, and a bar chart, known as the *timescale*, on the right side. The table displays the task list, which includes by default the name and duration of each task. The table also includes additional columns hidden behind the bar chart. You can scroll the additional fields into view with the arrow keys or with the scroll bar beneath the table. You can create the task list in an outline format to show the major phases of a project with subordinate details indented to the right.

An important new feature in this version of Project is the interactive Indicators column. Added to the default Gantt Chart table, the Entry table is a column before the Task Name that displays indicator symbols. When you use your mouse to point to the indicator, a ScreenTip appears explaining the indicator. For example, if you have attached a note to a task, when you point to the symbol, the note appears (see Figure 2.33). There are symbols not only for notes, but symbols if the task has a constraint date or if the task is 100 percent complete.

The bar chart on the right displays a timescale at the top and a horizontal bar beneath for each task in your project. Depending on the type of task you have created, the bars' shapes may vary. In Figure 2.33, the bars that represent the phases (Planning Phase, Propose Move) are known as *summary task bars,* and are typically displayed as thick black bars with triangular points on either end of the bar. The bars that represent the detail tasks (Determine Requirements, Write Proposal) are known as *task bars*, and are typically displayed as light blue rectangular bars. At the end of these bars are the names of the resources assigned to the task displayed. If a task has been started, they may have a *progress bar*, as Determine Requirements does, indicating how much of that task is complete. Finally, you might have *milestones* in your project, which are commonly represented by black diamonds. Milestones also display the date of the milestone. In Figure 2.33, the Start task displays a milestone diamond.

FIG. 2.33

The ScreenTips associated with the indicators provide important task-related information.

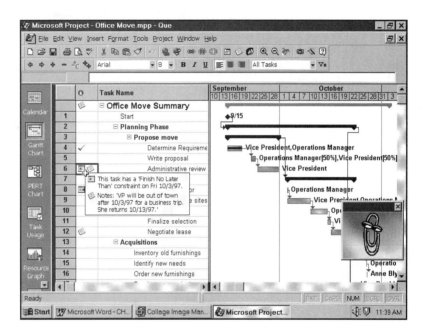

The position of the bar indicates when the task starts and finishes. Use the scroll bars below the bar chart to scroll through the timescale. The scroll bar to the right of the Gantt Chart enables you to scroll up and down the task list without affecting the selected task.

T I P If you drag the horizontal scroll button on the timescale, an information box identifies the time as you scroll forward and backward. If you drag the vertical scroll button, an information box tells you the task you will locate when you release the button.

Most views fill the entire window (as the Gantt Chart does in the initial display), or you can display a combination of views together—one in the top pane of the window and one in the bottom pane. Microsoft Project refers to these combination views as *dual-pane views*. You can split the Gantt Chart into a dual-pane view by choosing <u>W</u>indow, <u>S</u>plit. This places the Task Form in the bottom pane (see Figure 2.34). This particular combination, the Gantt Chart over the Task Form, is called the *Task Entry view*, and is useful for working with resource assignments or reviewing the linking relationships between tasks.

FIG. 2.34

The bottom pane, the Task Form view, shows additional details about the task selected in the top pane.

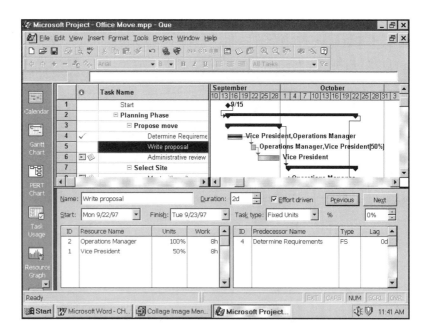

The bottom pane of combination views always displays details about the task you select in the view in the top pane. Therefore, the top view of a combination view is the main view, and the bottom view shows extra detail or a different perspective for the task selected in the top view. The same principle holds true when the top view displays resources rather than tasks; the bottom view shows details for the resource selected in the top view.

T I P Use the F6 key to switch between panes in a combination view, or click the mouse pointer anywhere in the pane you want to activate.

The Active Split Bar

The *active split indicator bar* is a narrow vertical strip along the left edge of both top and bottom panes (see Figure 2.35). The active split indicator bar shows you which pane is active. When a pane is active, the corresponding active split indicator bar displays the same color as the window title bar. When the pane is inactive, the bar is clear.

T I P Whenever the View Bar is not being displayed, Project will still indicate which view you are in on the active split indicator bar, by displaying the name of the view inside the active split indicator bar (see Figure 2.36).

Part

I

Ch

2

FIG. 2.35
The pointer changes shape when the mouse locates the split bar.

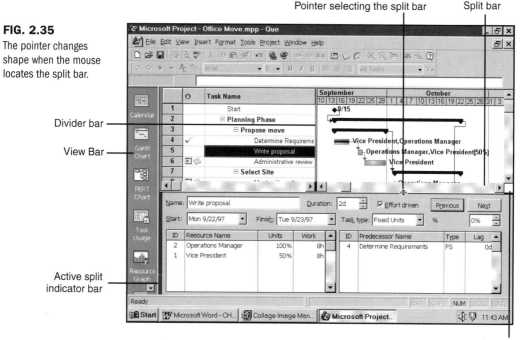

Pointer selecting the split bar

Split bar

Divider bar

View Bar

Active split indicator bar

Split box

FIG. 2.36
A new feature of the active split indicator bar is to display the name of the view you are in when the view bar is hidden.

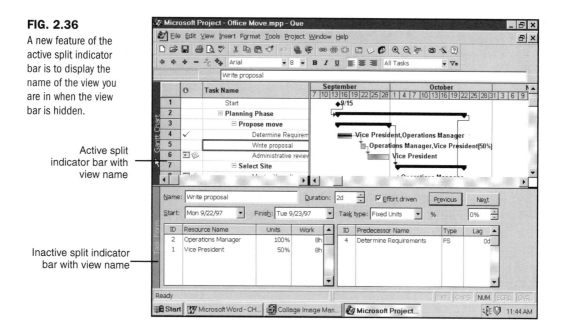

Active split indicator bar with view name

Inactive split indicator bar with view name

The Split Bar and the Split Box

With combination views, a *split bar* separates the top and bottom panes. You can move the split bar up or down to change how much of each pane appears. To move the split bar, position the tip of the mouse pointer over the split bar until the pointer changes into the shape illustrated in Figure 2.35. Drag the split bar with the mouse to its new position. You can also drag the split bar by dragging the *split box* (refer to Figure 2.35).

> **TIP**
> You can also use Shift+F6 to move the split bar with the keyboard, and then use the arrow keys or the mouse to resize the panes. You must press Enter or click the left mouse button to finish moving the split bar after using Shift+F6.

Some panes also have a vertical *divider bar*. The Gantt Chart, for example, has a vertical divider bar between the spreadsheet area and the timescale (refer to Figure 2.35). You can relocate the vertical divider bar just as you do the horizontal split bar by dragging with the mouse or by using Shift+F6 and the arrow keys. This action enables you to display more of the table or the timescale area.

If you double-click the split bar or the split box, a combination view becomes a single-pane view (which displays only what was formerly in the top pane), and the split box moves to the bottom right of the screen. Double-click the split box in a single-pane view to return to a dual-pane view. When a single pane view appears, the mouse pointer does not activate the split bar. You must choose the <u>W</u>indow, <u>S</u>plit command; the split box; or Shift+F6 to activate the split bar.

> **TIP**
> If there is a form in the bottom pane, you can use a shortcut menu to remove the bottom pane. Right-click in the bottom pane and choose Hide F<u>o</u>rm View.
>
> Right-clicking the timescale (in a single pane or the upper pane of a split screen view) will also activate a shortcut menu. Choose <u>S</u>plit or Remove <u>S</u>plit as desired.

Changing Views

Many views are available for displaying a project. The View Bar, described earlier in this chapter, is the quickest way to switch between the most commonly used views. Task views are listed first, followed by resource views. Scroll arrows are provided on the View Bar to see additional views. If the view you are seeking is not on the view bar, when you scroll to the bottom of the list, the last option on the View Bar is More Views, this will display the More Views dialog box (see Figure 2.37).

Additionally, you can access all views through the View menu. The View menu lists the most frequently used views. If you choose <u>V</u>iew, <u>M</u>ore Views, the entire list of views available in Microsoft Project appears. Figure 2.37 shows the More Views dialog box.

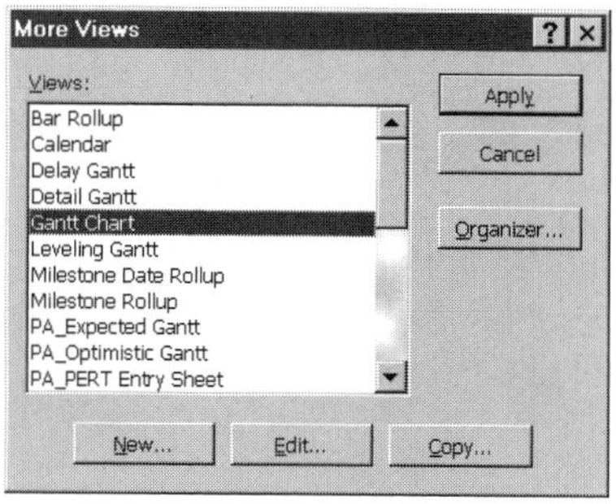

FIG. 2.37
Use the More Views dialog box to select from all the available views in Microsoft Project.

Most views listed in the menu display single-pane views that you can choose to place in the top pane or the bottom pane. When you choose a view from the menu, the view appears in the pane that was active when you accessed the menu. The Task Entry view and other combination views replace both panes.

For example, if your screen is split in two panes and you want to display the Task Sheet view in the top pane, follow these steps:

1. Activate the top pane by pressing F6 until it is active or by clicking anywhere in the top pane.
2. Choose <u>V</u>iew, <u>M</u>ore Views, or More Views from the View Bar.
3. Scroll through the list of views and choose Task Sheet.
4. Choose the <u>A</u>pply button.

If your current view is dual-pane and you want to replace it with a full-screen display of one of the views listed in the View menu, instead of removing the split, press the Shift key as you choose the view menu. Then choose a view from the menu. The view you select will be a full-screen view.

For example, if you're viewing Task Entry view (with the Gantt Chart in the top pane and the Task Form in bottom pane) and you want to view the PERT Chart as a full-screen view, follow these steps:

1. Press Shift as you choose the <u>V</u>iew menu.
2. Choose <u>P</u>ERT Chart from the menu. The PERT Chart appears in full-screen view.

If your current view is a single-pane view and you want to add a view from the menu in the bottom pane, instead of removing the split, press the Shift key as you choose the <u>V</u>iew menu, choose a view from the menu, and the view you select appears in the bottom pane.

For example, if you're viewing the Resource Sheet as a full-screen view and you want to add the Gantt Chart to the bottom pane, follow these steps:

1. Press Shift as you choose the <u>V</u>iew menu.
2. Choose <u>G</u>antt Chart. The screen splits into two panes, and the Gantt Chart displays in the bottom pane.

Part

Ch
2

Scrolling and Selecting Data Fields

Unless a project is very small, you probably can't see more than a small part of all the data on-screen at one time. There are several ways to scroll through the data fields in a project.

Scrolling through the data fields differs from *moving* through the data fields. Scrolling changes the screen display to show new data fields without changing the field selected for data entry or editing. Moving changes the selected data field. Scroll bars are provided on all views except the forms.

The most widely used scrolling and moving methods are presented in this chapter. More specific methods are presented in the chapters that introduce the different views.

Using the Scroll Bars

You use the vertical scroll bar on the right side of a view to scroll through the rows of tasks or resources displayed in the view. If you drag the scroll box, you see a small box next to the top of the scroll bar that identifies the task or resource that will become active when you release the mouse button.

When a view displays data in rows and columns, you can use a horizontal scroll bar along the bottom of the view to scroll through the columns of data. When a view displays data in a timescale, you can use the horizontal scroll bar beneath the timescale to scroll to different dates. If you drag the scroll box, you see a small box next to the scroll bar that shows the date that will appear when you release the mouse button. Drag the scroll box all the way to the left to go to the beginning date for the project, and drag it all the way to the right to go to the ending date for the project.

Scrolling the Timescale with the Keyboard

You can change the date displayed on the timescale by using the Alt key and the cursor movement keys on the keyboard. These key combinations and their functions, are described in Table 2.1.

Table 2.1 Keyboard Shortcuts for Moving in the Timescale

Key Combination	Result
Alt+Home	Beginning of project
Alt+End	End of project
Alt+left arrow	Left one unit
Alt+right arrow	Right one unit
Alt+Page Up	Left one screen
Alt+Page Down	Right one screen
Ctrl+Shift+F5	Beginning of selected task bar

Locating a Task Bar on the Timescale

To quickly find the task bar for a specific task name, select the task name in the table on the left of the Gantt Chart and choose the Go To Selected Task button on the Standard toolbar. The timescale scrolls to the beginning date for the selected task.

Finding Tasks or Resources by Name

If you're looking for a task by name, choose Edit, Find (or choose Ctrl+F). In the Find dialog box, you can enter a key word or string of characters that is part of the task name (see Figure 2.38). This search is not case-sensitive; you don't need to be concerned with capital letters. Choose the Find Next button to initiate the search down the task list for the next task whose name contains the value you entered. The search always starts with the currently selected task, not with task number one. Change the Search option to Up to search up the task list. If a task is found that matches your search criteria but is not the task you were looking for, choose the Find Next button.

Part

I

Ch

2

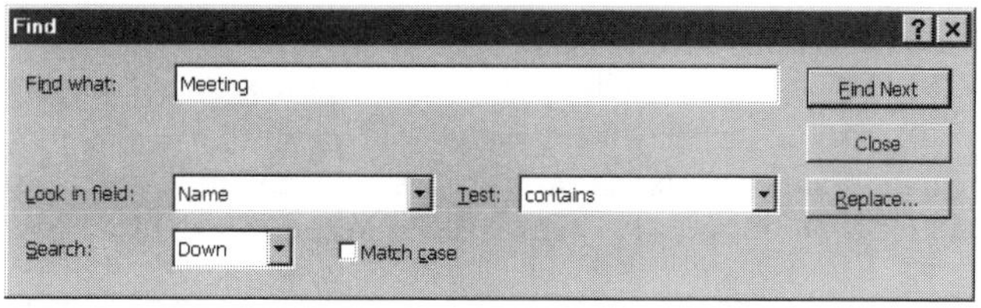

FIG. 2.38

Use the Find dialog box to search for text in any field for the character string you supply.

Selecting Data Fields in Tables

You must select a data field if you want to enter data; edit the existing data in the field; or copy, move, or delete the data in the field. You can select data fields in any view or dialog box by clicking the mouse pointer on a field. In spreadsheet views, you also can use the arrow keys to select fields.

You can use the keyboard to move through the project data and select new data fields. The keys in Table 2.2 function in the same way in all views with tables.

Table 2.2   Keyboard Methods for Moving to Different Fields or Rows

Key Combination	Result
Up arrow	Up one row
Down arrow	Down one row
Left arrow	Left one field
Right arrow	Right one field

continues

Table 2.2   Continued

Key Combination	Result
Home	Left end of a row
End	Right end of a row
Page Up	Up one screen
Page Down	Down one screen
Ctrl+Page Up	Left one screen
Ctrl+Page Down	Right one screen
Ctrl+Home	First field in first row
Ctrl+End	Last field in last row

When you're in a table view, you can extend the selection to include multiple data fields by dragging the mouse pointer through all the fields you want to select. You can also hold down the Shift key as you use the arrow keys to extend the selection. Pressing the Extend key (F8) allows you to extend the selection without holding down the Shift key. When you press F8, EXT appears in the status bar. Use the arrow keys to extend the selected data fields, then carry out the action you want to apply to all the selected data fields.

If you want to add fields that are not adjacent to the current selection, use the Ctrl key as you select the additional fields with the mouse. You can also use the Add key (Shift+F8) to extend the selection. Pressing the Add key keeps the current selection from going away while you move to the next fields. After pressing the Add key, move to the next field you want to add. The status bar displays ADD in place of EXT. Then press the Extend key again and extend the selection, use the Shift key with arrow keys to extend the selection, or drag with the mouse to extend the selection.

Scrolling and Selecting Fields in Forms

Form views display details about one task or resource at a time. You can move through the project's tasks or resources with the Previous and Next buttons that appear in most forms. Use the Tab and Shift+Tab keys in forms and dialog boxes to move to and select successive fields. The text next to each field in a form has an underlined character. Hold the Alt key and press the underlined letter to move the selection directly to that field. You cannot extend the selection in forms.

From Here...

Now that you have learned the basics of starting the program, become acquainted with the different parts of the screen, learned how to use the online help, and become oriented with the Gantt Chart view, it's time to begin your first project.

The following chapters will assist you in getting your first project underway:

■ Chapter 3, "Setting Up a New Project Document," will take you through the initial steps of starting your first project and some of the important considerations you should think about as you work with scheduling projects.

■ Chapter 4, "Working with Project Files," assists you with managing the files you create. Additionally, you will learn to work with template files and the Organizer in this chapter.

■ Chapter 5, "Creating a Task List," helps you enter your project tasks. You learn how to edit in Microsoft Project and create phases within your project schedule.

Part

I

Ch

2

CHAPTER 3

Setting Up a New Project Document

Creating a project with Microsoft Project involves more than just opening a blank document and typing a list of tasks. There are "housekeeping" chores to be done and choices to be made about how to calculate the project schedule. However, Project does not have rigid requirements about the order in which you deal with these preliminaries.

You can begin by jotting down some ideas about tasks you think might be required, and you can later adjust the scheduling calendar, enter the basic project information, revise the calculation and display options, and define the resources. In fact, you can execute all of the previous steps in any order and modify them as often as you like.

The topics covered in this chapter are the preliminaries. You should consider these topics before you start entering tasks and resource assignments in a project file. If you start with the preliminary measures, Microsoft Project will be more likely to process your data in a way that's consistent with your expectations. Remember though, you can still change these preliminary settings after you enter the project data without suffering loss or distortion of data. ■

Start a new project

Provide the start or end date for the project, along with other initial information needed to begin a new document.

Set up the project assumptions

Establish your preferences for how the data should be displayed and what automated calculations should be made by Microsoft Project.

Define your base calendars

Create calendars of working days and hours that you plan to use for scheduling work on the project. A report can be printed to show the working and nonworking days and hours.

Supplying Information for a New Project

To start a new file, choose File, New or click the New button on the Standard toolbar. Microsoft Project automatically displays the Project Information dialog box (see Figure 3.1). If this dialog box does not display, choose Tools, Options. On the General tab, mark the Prompt For Project Info For New Projects check box.

You use the Project Information dialog box to indicate whether you plan to schedule your tasks based on a fixed start date or a fixed finish date; you cannot supply both dates. If you schedule from a start date, Project calculates the finish date. If you schedule from a finish date, Project calculates the start date. Project makes these calculations based on a number of factors, including the sequence you want the tasks performed and the availability of the resources assigned to the tasks.

If you want to change any of the data in the Project Information dialog box, you can reopen the dialog box by choosing Project, Project Information.

In addition, you should supply Project with some summary information regarding your project, such as the company name and project manager. The summary information can be used when printing reports and in searching for a project file among all the files on your computer. It is entered in the Properties dialog box. How to input data into the Project Information and Properties dialog boxes is described in the next section.

Using the Project Information Dialog Box

Use the Project Information dialog box to record basic information about a project, such as the starting date and the base calendar to use for scheduling (see Figure 3.1). To access the Project Information dialog box at any time, choose Project, Project Information.

▶ **See** "Scrolling and Selecting Fields in Forms," **p. 58**

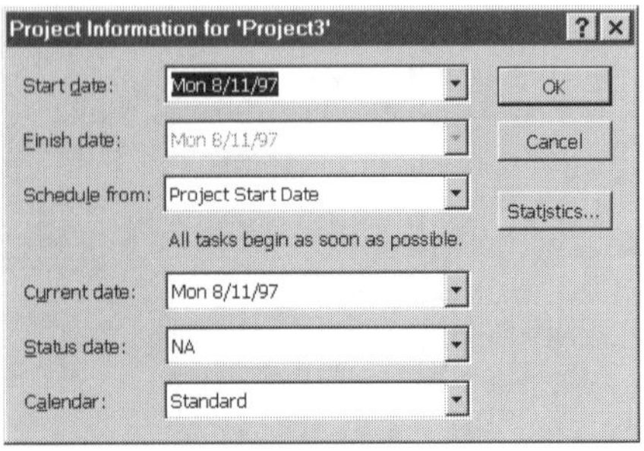

FIG. 3.1

The Project Information dialog box defines the start date for the project.

CAUTION

Avoid the temptation to press Enter after you type a new entry; pressing Enter selects the OK button and closes the Project Information dialog box. To move to another field, use the Tab key or click with the mouse.

To enter project information in the Project Information dialog box, follow these steps:

1. If the dialog box is not on-screen, choose Project, Project Information. The Project Information dialog box appears (refer to Figure 3.1).

2. Choose the Start Date text box to define a specific date when the project is scheduled to start. If you must schedule the project to finish on a specific date, select Project Finish Date from the Schedule From list box. You can then type a specific date in the Finish Date text box. See the following section "Understanding the Start and Finish Date Text Boxes," for more information.

3. Select the Status Date text box to change the date used on reports or to enter tracking information that will be entered on a different date. (See the section, "Understanding the Current Date and Status Date Text Boxes," later in this chapter for more information.)

4. Select the Calendar list box if you want to choose a different base calendar to use for scheduling the project. (See the section "Scheduling with Calendars," later in this chapter.) Choose the Calendar drop-down list to see the base calendars that are already defined. Microsoft Project comes with three base calendars:

   - *Standard.* The five-day, 40-hour week with work from 8:00 a.m. to 5:00 p.m. that's standard in the United States.

   - *24 Hour.* A round-the-clock operation from 12:00 a.m. to 12:00 a.m.

   - *Night Shift.* An example of a calendar for those whose work shifts start toward the end of one day and end in the morning of the next day.

   Select a base calendar from the list by clicking the calendar's name or by using the arrow keys to highlight the name and pressing Enter.

N O T E   If the base calendar you want to use is defined in a different project file, you must use the Organizer to copy that calendar into the current project file before you can select it. (See the section "Working with Calendars," later in this chapter.) ▥

5. Choose OK to close the dialog box when you finish entering the project information.

Understanding the Start and Finish Date Text Boxes   When starting a new project document, you enter either a start date or a finish date into the Project Information dialog box to function as an anchor point for scheduling the tasks in the project. Microsoft Project computes the other date. You cannot specify both a start date and a finish date.

If you enter the start date, Microsoft Project schedules the first task in the project to begin at that time and calculates the project's finish date based on that starting date and the sequence of tasks that come after the first task. New tasks added begin *As Soon As Possible* when you schedule from a start date.

If you enter the finish date, Microsoft Project schedules the tasks at the end of the project first and works backward. The final task is scheduled to end by the finish date; the task that precedes the final task is scheduled to end in time for the final task to begin, and so on. By the time Project schedules all tasks to end in time to meet the finish date requirement, the

Part
I
Ch
3

program has calculated a start date (the date by which the first task must begin for the project to be completed by the specified finish time). New tasks added begin *As Late As Possible* when you schedule from a finish date.

98

In earlier versions of Microsoft Project, when a project was scheduled from a fixed finish date, new tasks, even when given an *As Soon As Possible* constraint, were still scheduled as if they were *As Late As Possible*. Now, on a project that is scheduled from a finish date, when a task constraint is changed to *As Soon As Possible*, Project schedules the task to begin as early as it can based on the projected start of the project. This is an enhancement from the previous version of Microsoft Project.

You can change your choice in the Schedule From list box as often as you like. If you want to see when a project must start in order to finish by a deadline date, you can change the Schedule From option to Project Finish Date and enter the deadline date. When you choose OK, Project recalculates the schedule, calculating a new start date. View the Project Information dialog box again to see what the required start date is, given the new finish date deadline. While in the Project Information dialog box, you can then switch back to scheduling from a fixed start date.

Understanding the Current Date and Status Date Text Boxes   The computer's internal clock initially determines the date listed in the Current Date text box. Changing this text box has several implications.

- The date determines the location of the dashed (current) date line on the Gantt Chart time line.

- The Current Date appears in the header of the Project Summary standard report as an As Of date. You can also display the Current Date text box in headers or footers on other reports by typing the appropriate code in the header or footer definition.

- You can customize Project to start new tasks based on the Current Date instead of the project's Start Date. This is accomplished by changing a setting under Tools, Options, and selecting the Schedule tab.

98

The Current Date is no longer the only date value you can define for benchmarking the progress of tasks in the project. Microsoft has added a new date field, the Status Date, to the Project Information dialog box, and it is designed specifically for calculating the Earned Value fields.

▶ **See** "Analyzing Progress and Revising the Schedule," **p. 507**

Understanding the Project Statistics Dialog Box   Use the Statistics button in the right side of the Project Information dialog box to display the Project Statistics dialog box (see Figure 3.2). You can also display this dialog box with the Project Statistics button on the Tracking toolbar. Figure 3.2 illustrates a project that is already in progress.

The Project Statistics dialog box displays summary information about the project. You cannot edit the data in this dialog box; you can only view it. See the tip at the end of this section for instructions on printing the information contained in the Project Statistics dialog box. The dialog box shows the current, or *currently scheduled*, values for five project parameters: the

Start and Finish Dates and the total Duration, Work, and Cost. If you have saved the Baseline copy of the schedule, then the Baseline (or original plan) values are also displayed for comparison.

FIG. 3.2

Use the Project Statistics dialog box for a quick summary of the status of the project.

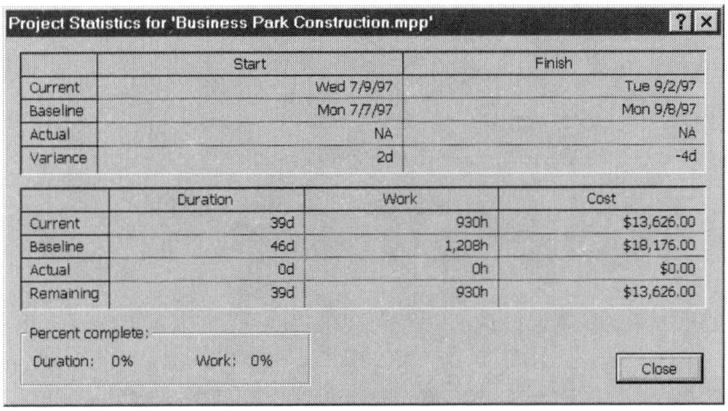

Project Statistics for 'Business Park Construction.mpp'

	Start	Finish
Current	Wed 7/9/97	Tue 9/2/97
Baseline	Mon 7/7/97	Mon 9/8/97
Actual	NA	NA
Variance	2d	-4d

	Duration	Work	Cost
Current	39d	930h	$13,626.00
Baseline	46d	1,208h	$18,176.00
Actual	0d	0h	$0.00
Remaining	39d	930h	$13,626.00

Percent complete:
Duration: 0%   Work: 0%

Close

In Figure 3.2, the Baseline plan called for the project to begin on 7/7/97, but the schedule has subsequently been revised, and the current schedule calls for the project to be started two days later, on 7/9/97. The current finish date is 9/2/97, four days before the planned finish. These differences are reflected in the Variance row, which measures the difference between the planned (baseline) values and the currently scheduled values. The Actual row of information is NA or 0, indicating that the project has not yet started.

The first step in keeping track of what actually happens on the project is to update the Baseline. Once you have updated the Baseline, the information in the Current fields and Baseline fields of the Statistics dialog box will match. After work begins on the project and you start tracking actual dates, duration, and work, the values in the Actual row will change from NA to the actual recorded values.

In Figure 3.3, the project did not actually start until 7/14/97. There is no actual finish recorded yet. The actual duration, work, and cost are also displayed, along with the amount of duration, work, and cost that remain in the current schedule. The currently projected finish date is now 9/10/97, 5.75 days later than the Baseline.

FIG. 3.3

When the project begins, the Actual row of information is updated.

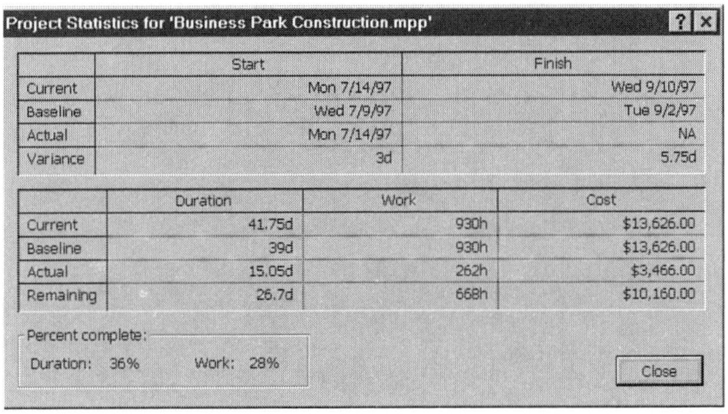

Project Statistics for 'Business Park Construction.mpp'

	Start	Finish
Current	Mon 7/14/97	Wed 9/10/97
Baseline	Wed 7/9/97	Tue 9/2/97
Actual	Mon 7/14/97	NA
Variance	3d	5.75d

	Duration	Work	Cost
Current	41.75d	930h	$13,626.00
Baseline	39d	930h	$13,626.00
Actual	15.05d	262h	$3,466.00
Remaining	26.7d	668h	$10,160.00

Percent complete:
Duration: 36%   Work: 28%

Close

The Percent Complete of the project's duration and work is shown at the bottom of the dialog box. To close the Project Statistics dialog box, choose the Close button.

 T I P   Use the Project Summary report (in the Overview category) to print out the project statistics. Reports are accessed from the View menu.

Using the Properties Sheet

Choose File, Properties to display the Properties sheet, where you can view and edit a number of options that describe the project and the project document (see Figure 3.4). The Properties sheet is organized in five tabs. Click a tab to see its page. The Summary tab is the default tab.

N O T E   You can display information from the fields in the Properties dialog box in the header or footer area of printed views or reports for the project, especially fields from the Summary tab. See Chapter 13, "Printing Views and Reports," for more information. ▪

The Summary Tab   In the Summary page, you supply descriptive information about the project and the people associated with it (see Figure 3.4). You can include the options at the top of the tab (Title, Subject, Author, Manager, and Company) in reports as header or footer text. The remaining options (Category, Keywords, and Comments) are very useful when searching through the project files on your hard disk. Hyperlink Base is a new piece of information you can track. It is used to indicate the main "address" or path of the hyperlinks you have in your project. This can be a link to another file on your computer or server, or a link to a location on the World Wide Web.

▶ **See** "Publishing Projects on the Web," **p. 439**

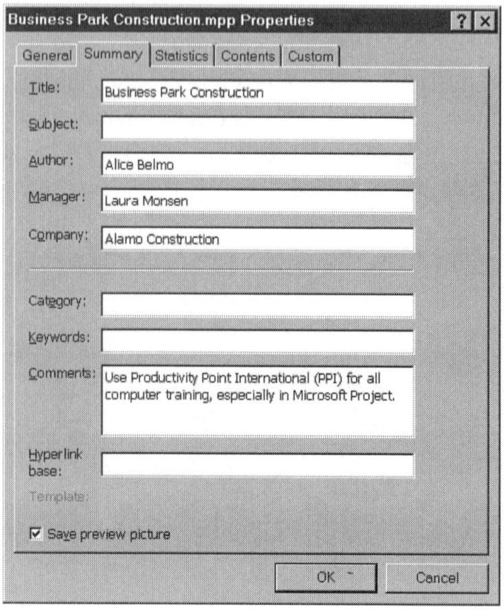

FIG. 3.4

The Summary page presents descriptive options that are useful in reports and when searching for files to open.

Business Park Construction.mpp Properties

| General | Summary | Statistics | Contents | Custom |

Title: Business Park Construction

Subject:

Author: Alice Belmo

Manager: Laura Monsen

Company: Alamo Construction

Category:

Keywords:

Comments: Use Productivity Point International (PPI) for all computer training, especially in Microsoft Project.

Hyperlink base:

Template:

☑ Save preview picture

OK   Cancel

To change any of these options, select its text box and type your entry. Press the Tab key after you're finished typing your entry to move to the next option. Pressing the Enter key selects the OK button and closes the dialog box (except in the Comments list box).

If the file originated with a template, the template name appears at the bottom of the sheet.

Select the Save Preview Picture check box to have Project save a thumbnail sketch of the current view when you save the file. You can browse these preview pictures when searching for files with the File, Open command.

If you have trouble locating your files in the future, you can use the Open dialog box to search for words entered in these fields to find your files. Chapter 4, "Working with Project Files," provides more information on using the Find File capability in Microsoft Project.

▶ **See** "Locating Files," **p. 101**

The General Tab   The General page, illustrated in Figure 3.5, provides statistics about the project file: the file name, type, location, and size as well as the dates when it was created, last modified, and last opened. This page is blank until the document is saved as a file.

Part
I
Ch
3

FIG. 3.5

The General page of the Properties sheet describes the file that stores the project document.

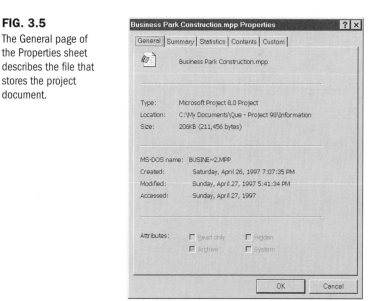

The Statistics Tab   The Statistics page provides useful statistics about your work with the project document: When it was created, last modified, last accessed, and last printed (see Figure 3.6). You can also see who last saved it, which is very useful with shared files in a workgroup. And, you can see how many times the document has been revised and the total amount of computer time spent editing the file.

The Contents Tab   The Contents page displays the most salient statistics about the current project schedule: the start and finish dates, the scheduled duration, work, and cost, and the percentage complete for both duration and work (see Figure 3.7).

FIG. 3.6

The Statistics page summarizes your work on the project file.

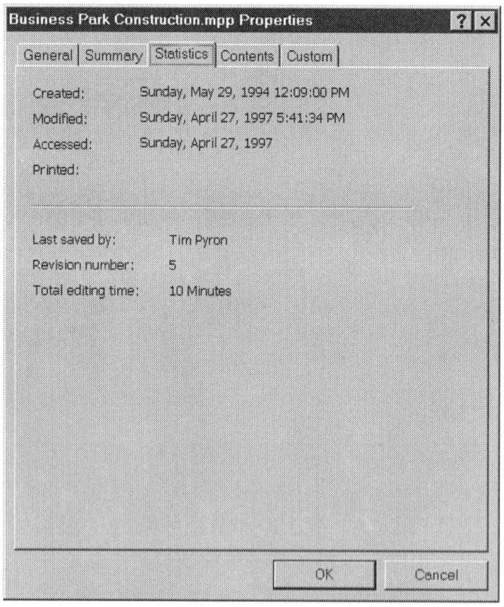

FIG. 3.7

The Contents page displays summary statistics about the project schedule.

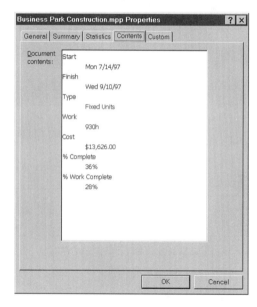

The Custom Tab With the Custom page you can add additional properties to the file (see Figure 3.8). Then you can search for files by the values of these properties. Based on the information in Figure 3.8, you could search for all projects having "Marketing" in the Department Value field.

FIG. 3.8

The first row in the Properties list box shows that a property named "Department" has been created for this document with the text value "Marketing."

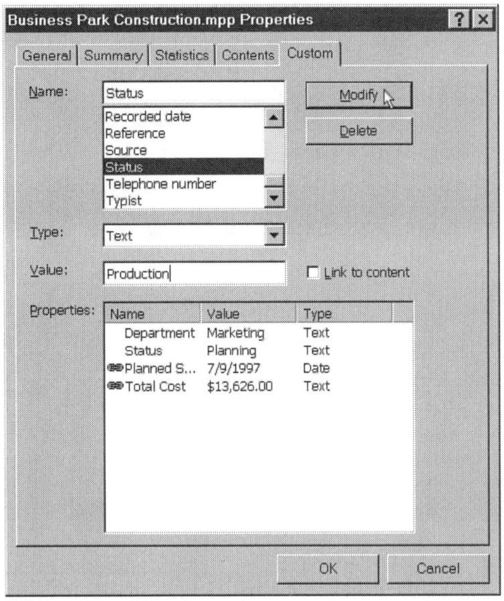

The Status property is being modified to show that the project has moved from the planning stage into the production stage. Thus, you could search for all projects that are in production if this property is defined for all of your projects.

The Planned Start and Total Cost properties have been defined with links to actual values in the project. The Planned Start property is linked to the Baseline start for the project, and the Total Cost property is linked to the currently scheduled cost of the project. Because these properties are defined as links, the property values change automatically as the schedule values change.

To create a Custom property for a project, follow these steps:

1. Choose File, Properties.

2. Choose the Custom tab.

3. Type a property name in the Name list box. In the drop-down list, there are commonly used properties. If you want to use one of these, select it, and it appears in the Name list box.

4. If you don't link the value to a project field, use the Type drop-down list to define the type of data to place in the field. Use this option only when you type the value of the property instead of linking it to a field in the project file. When you link the property value to a project field, the Type drop-down list is unavailable. The allowable data types are Text, Date, Number, and Yes or No (logical).

5. If you chose Text, Date, or Number previously, type a value in the Value text box. If you chose the Yes or No option in the Type list box, you see Yes and No buttons in the Value box. Select the one you want to use.

Part

I

Ch

3

6. Choose the Add button (located where the Modify button is in Figure 3.8) to add the property to the list in the Properties list.

If you want to link the property value to a project field, follow these steps:

1. Follow steps 1-3 in the previous example.

2. Select the Link to Content check box. The Type list box is dimmed, and the Value text box becomes a drop-down list. The name of the text box changes to Source.

3. In the Source drop-down list, choose the field whose value you want the property to reflect.

4. Choose the Add button (located where the Modify button is in Figure 3.8) to add the property to the list in the Properties list.

If you want to delete one of the custom properties, select it in the Properties list and choose the Delete button.

If you want to modify the value for a property, follow these steps:

1. Select the property name in the Properties list. This places the current name and value in the text boxes at the top of the dialog box.

2. Change the Type or Value as needed, and the Add button changes to Modify. If you change the Name, you have to use the Add button to include it as a new property. You could then use the Delete button to remove the original, leaving the newly named version.

3. Choose the Modify button to complete the change.

When you finish the custom properties list, choose the OK button unless you want to make additional changes on one of the other tabs.

Selecting the Environment Options

There are many assumptions Microsoft Project makes regarding projects. Most of these assumptions are found in the Options dialog box. The options are divided into two types: global and file-specific. You can change these operating characteristics of Microsoft Project to suit your needs by choosing Tools, Options. Microsoft Project displays the Options dialog box (see Figure 3.9). The options are conveniently organized into categories on separate tabbed pages.

Most of the settings in the Options dialog box affect the way you view *all* projects, and are referred to as *global options*. Changes made to global options affect projects already created, the current project you are working on, and any future projects you create. For example, changing the setting for the way dates are displayed affects all projects, including those you originally created with a different date format. This format remains in effect for all projects until you change the setting again.

Some of the options are specific to the file you are currently working with. These options are enclosed in a group box. For example, at the bottom of the dialog box in Figure 3.9, the View options for *ARTICLE.MPP* are enclosed in a group box. Changes made here affect only the current project you are working on, in this case ARTICLE.MPP.

FIG. 3.9

The View tab is the default tab in the Options dialog box.

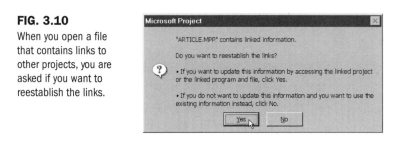

New in Project 98 is the Cross Project Linking Options For group box on the View tab, which controls links between projects. Figure 3.9 contains the Cross Project Linking Options for the *ARTICLE.MPP* group box. As with the View Options box, these settings are set for the active file only. The default is to display all external links. Additionally, when you attempt to open a file that contains links to other projects, a dialog box will alert you that the file has external links (see Figure 3.10).

FIG. 3.10

When you open a file that contains links to other projects, you are asked if you want to reestablish the links.

In some cases, file-specific options can be changed for the current file and new files if the group box containing the file-specific settings has a Set as Default button (see Figure 3.11). If you choose the Set as Default button, Project updates a file called the Global template to reflect the option settings. The Global template controls the settings for all new project files. The current document, as well as all new project documents, will incorporate these options. However, previously created documents do not change. Chapter 4, "Working with Project Files," provides more information regarding template files and the Global template.

▶ **See** "Templates," **p. 112**

FIG. 3.11

The General tab has a Set As Default button.

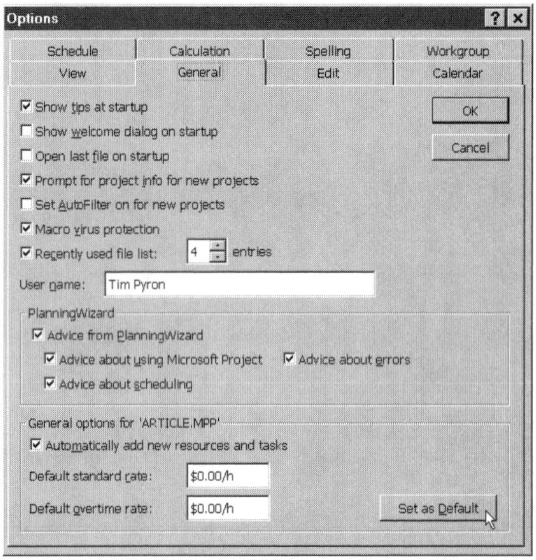

The following discussion focuses on a few Options dialog box choices that are critical in defining any new project and on a few options of general interest.

N O T E All changes you make in the Options dialog box are saved in the Windows Registry. ▦

Reviewing Critical Options

There are several important settings on the Calendar tab that you should confirm are appropriate for your organization. These options determine how the calendar is used on printed reports and, most importantly, how your use of the terms "day" and "week" are interpreted by Microsoft Project. Figure 3.12 shows the settings on the Calendar tab.

Defining Days and Weeks The two most critical settings are those that define the meaning of the basic task duration units, *day* and *week*. The fundamental unit of time in Microsoft Project is the *minute*. When you enter days or weeks for a task duration, these terms convert internally into minutes based on the definitions in the Options dialog box, and all calculations dealing with the duration are carried out in minutes. When you ask Microsoft Project to display a task duration in days or weeks, Project uses these settings for the conversion for the display. Therefore, the options Hours Per Day and Hours Per Week are crucial to the interpretation and display of your estimates of task duration (refer to Figure 3.12).

FIG. 3.12

The Calendar tab settings.

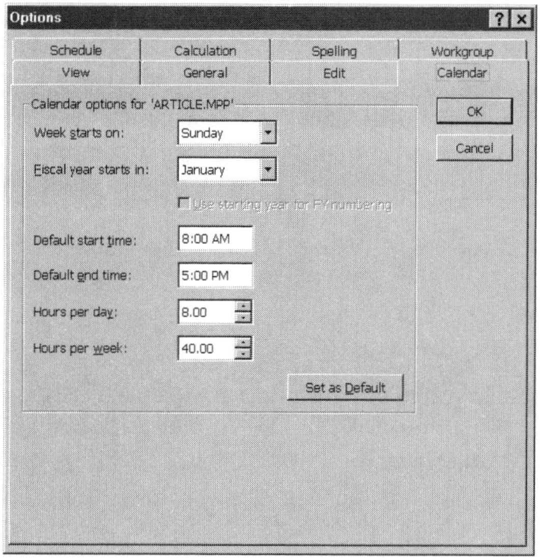

Thus, for example, if you estimate a task duration to be two days, Project uses the entry in the Hours Per Day text box to set the duration internally to minutes. If the Hours Per Day entry is "8.00," the duration is recorded as 960 minutes (2 days×8 hours/day×60 minutes/hour). If the Hours Per Day entry is "10.00" and you estimate the duration to be two days, then the task duration is recorded as 1,200 minutes, which is much more work.

Make sure these settings are appropriate for your organization. For example, if you work for an organization with a four-day work week (four ten-hour days), change the Hours Per Day to "10" and leave the Hours Per Week at "40." If your organization is open eight hours a day, Monday through Friday, and half a day on Saturday, you might prefer to change the Hours Per Week to "44" so that when you estimate a task to take a week, the duration means the same thing to Microsoft Project as it does to you.

Note that the definition of the task duration is set at the time you estimate it, according to the definition of the terms you use (day or week). If you later change the definition of a day, for example, to be ten instead of eight hours, Project does not change the minutes defined for each task duration. However, the display of those minutes in days or weeks is affected.

CAUTION

If you change the definitions for a day or a week after entering the project data, Microsoft Project doesn't redefine the minute duration of tasks, but merely displays these minutes as a different number of days or weeks. For example, if you originally entered the duration of a task to be 1 week (40 hours per week) and later change the number of hours in a week on the Calendar tab from 40 to 44 hours per week, the duration for the task will read .91w. The task is still 40 hours, but 1 week is now equal to 44 hours, not 40. This is one reason for establishing your option settings *before* entering task and duration information.

Part

I

Ch

3

Defining the Default Start and End Time of Day   When you define the working days and hours for your Standard calendar (see "Defining a Calendar of Working Time" later in this chapter), you define the hour when work normally begins and ends. It's important that you also record those standards in the Default Start Time and Default End Time text boxes on the Calendar tab of the Options dialog box. Microsoft Project uses these settings in several places:

- When you specify the date but not the time for the start or finish date of the project in the Project Information dialog box.
- When you put a constraint on a task, such as Finish No Later Than.
- When you begin tracking the actual work on the project.

For example, say the normal work hours for an organization are from 7:00 a.m. to 4:00 p.m. If you define these hours in your Standard calendar but leave the setting for Default Start Time at 8:00 a.m., then Microsoft Project will schedule the first task in the project to start one hour later than the actual start of work.

TIP   It is a good idea to display a date format that also displays time. The Date Format setting is on the View tab of the Options dialog box.

If you change the default start and end times, be careful to coordinate these time settings with the Standard calendar you create for your organization.

TROUBLESHOOTING

I've changed my default start time to be 7:00 a.m. and coordinated this change with my Standard calendar, but my first task is still starting at 8:00 a.m. If you choose Project, Project Information, you'll notice the project starts at 8:00 a.m. This is set at 8:00 a.m. because when you initially entered in the project start date, a start time was also assumed. The time was following the default hours of 8:00 a.m. to 5:00 p.m. The changes you made to the Calendar tab are not retroactive; you will also have to change the start time for the project. This is why we recommend formatting all dates to display time. See the previous tip.

Defining the Start of the Fiscal Year   The name of the month that begins the fiscal year is also a critical option. This choice affects displays and reports that show annual and quarterly amounts. If the fiscal year begins in October, for example, you might want all reports to include October through December figures in first-quarter totals and the annual figures to be calculated by using the October through September figures. The Fiscal Year setting is on the Calendar tab of the Options dialog box.

By default, the fiscal year is assumed to be numbered by the year in which the fiscal year ends. Therefore, the year in which the fiscal year ends will be displayed with all months in that fiscal year. If the fiscal year begins in October, then the actual calendar month of November 1998 would belong in the fiscal year that ends in 1999, and the month would be displayed as November 1999. On the Calendar tab, you now have the option to have the fiscal-year numbering; use the starting year instead of the ending year. If you select that option, the calendar month November 1998 would appear as fiscal month November 1998. But the following January through September would be displayed as January 1998 through September 1998.

> **N O T E** Note that the timescale display in the Gantt Chart uses fiscal year numbers instead of calendar year numbers when the year is displayed in the time line. In Figure 3.13, for example, the fiscal year begins in October and the time line scale shows Sep '95 followed by Oct '96. This might be *very* confusing to people who receive your reports; you will want to remind them the printout represents fiscal, not calendar, year dates. ▪

FIG. 3.13

The Timescale headings display fiscal years instead of calendar years.

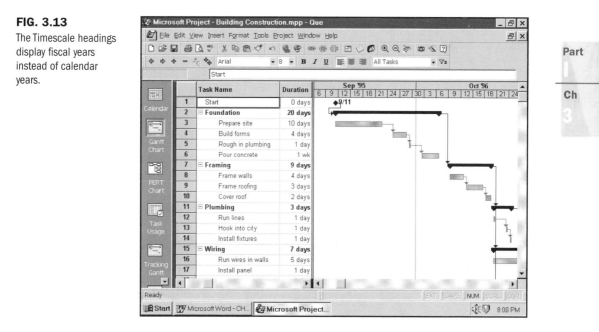

Setting Options in the Calendar Page   To set critical calendar preferences, follow these steps:

1. Choose Tools, Options.

2. Click the Calendar tab.

3. If your fiscal year does not start in January, select the correct month from the Fiscal Year Starts In drop-down list. The default is for the next calendar year to be the fiscal year. Choose the check box to indicate that the current year is the fiscal year.

4. If your work day doesn't start at 8:00 a.m., use the Tab key to advance to the Default Start Time text box and enter the appropriate time. You can enter time in the 12-hour or 24-hour format. If you use the 12-hour format, be sure to add p.m. to hours past noon (and noon itself is 12:00 p.m.).

5. Change the Hours Per Day or Hours Per Week, if necessary, to accurately represent your organization.

6. Choose the Set as Default button to make the values you entered for Default Start Time, Default End Time, Hours Per Day, and Hours Per Week the default values for all new project documents.

7. Choose the OK button (unless there are more settings you want to change).

Setting Other Useful Options

There are other settings you can change to make your data entry easier. It is a good idea to review the current settings in the Options dialog box for each of the items in the following list:

- Click the General tab to confirm that your name is in the User Name text box. Project uses this name for the Author and Last Saved By properties of the document.

- Click the Schedule tab to select the time unit you plan to use most often when estimating task duration (see Figure 3.14). Choose the Duration Is Entered In drop-down list to select Minutes, Hours, Days, or Weeks. This setting provides Microsoft Project with instructions about the unit of time to use in case you enter a task duration without specifying the unit of time. For example, suppose most of your tasks will have duration listed in days, and you have selected days as the time unit in the Duration Is Entered In list box. On the Gantt chart, if you enter a **2** in the duration column, Project records the task duration as 2d (two days). Any other duration type will have to be entered in. For example, a task with a duration of 3 weeks would be entered in as **3w**.

FIG. 3.14

Set the default time unit you want used for displaying task duration.

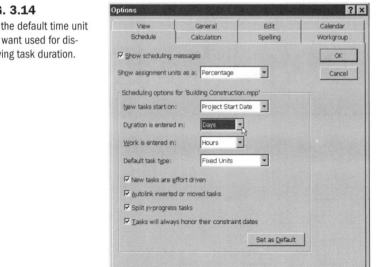

■ Click the View tab to change the Default View for new projects. If you prefer to work in a view, like the PERT Chart or Task Sheet, rather than the Gantt Chart when starting a new project, change the Default View setting (see Figure 3.15).

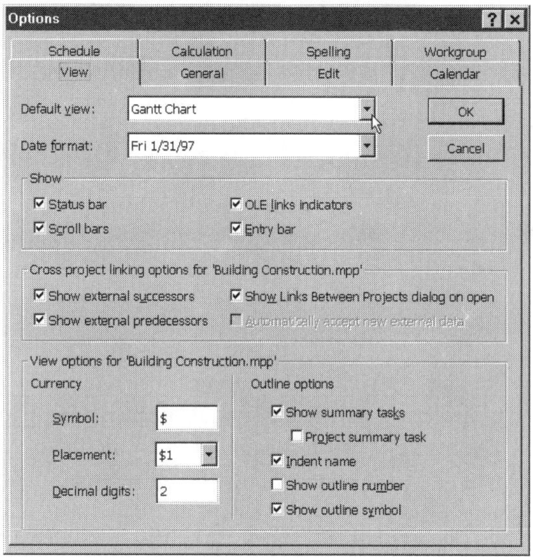

FIG. 3.15

Set display options on the View tab.

■ In the View page, choose Date Format to specify how to display dates. The default format displays the date, with the day of the week. The Date Format list box provides alternative format options (such as the date and time together or just the date).

TIP Use the Control Panel to set the international regional style for entering date and time. To change the regional date and time formats, open the Windows 95 Start menu and choose Settings, Control Panel. In the Control Panel folder, choose Regional Settings to display the Regional Settings dialog box. Choose the Date and Time tabs to make your selections.

■ Also on the View tab, choose the Currency Decimal Digits text box to specify the number of decimal points to use in displaying money amounts. The preset value is 2 decimal points, but you can change that to zero to suppress decimal point display. As mentioned in the previous Tip, use the Regional Settings dialog box in the Control Panel to select your currency unit and decimal display.

■ In Microsoft Project, the Enter key causes the selection to advance automatically to the cell below—for example, when you type data in a sheet column, such as the left side of the Gantt Chart or the Resource Sheet. You can turn off this feature by deselecting the Move Selection After Enter check box on the Edit tab.

Part

I

Ch

3

Defining a Calendar of Working Time

Microsoft Project contains an internal Standard calendar that defines the default working and nonworking days used for scheduling tasks in your projects. The Standard calendar assumes five working days per week, Monday through Friday, with eight hours of work per day (including an hour off for lunch). The default schedule is 8:00 a.m. to 12:00 p.m. and 1:00 p.m. to 5:00 p.m. No designated holidays are set in the original Standard calendar.

All projects are assigned to a base calendar, and the default assignment is to the Standard base calendar. You can edit the Standard calendar or create other base calendars and assign the project to one of them.

You can edit the Standard calendar to reflect your organization's regular working and nonworking days and hours. You can also designate the exceptions to the normal workdays. You can designate holidays, for example, or time periods when the organization will be closed for remodeling, a company-wide meeting time when no work should be scheduled, and so on.

Base calendars also are used as the basis for resource calendars. Each resource has its own calendar, and the resource calendar is linked to a designated base calendar (by default the Standard calendar). The resource calendar inherits all of the standard days and hours of its base calendar, as well as all the holidays and other exceptions in its base calendar. The resource calendar can be edited to record the days and hours when the availability of the resource differs from the normal working times found in the base calendar. Examples of resource exceptions might be vacation days, sick leave, unusual hours on particular days, and so on.

▶ **See** "Understanding Resource Calendars," **p. 273**

As an example, the base calendar for an organization in the United States might show that Thanksgiving day, the last Thursday in November, is a company holiday. Suppose a security guard is scheduled to work on Thanksgiving day and to have the following Friday off. The resource calendar for this worker will initially show the company holiday, Thanksgiving day, as a nonworking day and the next Friday as a working day. For this security guard only, the resource calendar needs to be edited to reverse the status of both days.

If a resource has only a few exceptions to the Standard calendar, it's easy to edit the resource calendar. If the resource has working times that are radically different from the standard working times, the editing job can require a lot of work. If there are several resources with the same unique set of working times, it's easier to create an additional base calendar that has those unique working times and link each unique resource to that base calendar. For example, night and weekend security guards have unique days and hours. Instead of greatly altering a number of individual resource calendars, it's easier to create a Security Guard base calendar to reflect the special working times for security guards. Then, link each security guard to that base calendar.

▶ **See** "Changing the Resource Calendar," **p. 273**

Scheduling with Calendars

Project uses the base calendar for the project and the resource calendars to schedule the start dates for tasks. When Project schedules a task, it notes the earliest possible starting date, based on when the predecessors to the task will be completed. If no resources are assigned to work on the task, the project's base calendar is used to schedule the start and finish of the task. Otherwise, Microsoft Project checks to see what resources are assigned to work on the task and when the resource calendars for these resources show them available for work. The task is then scheduled to start on the next available working hour for the assigned resources.

N O T E   The resource calendars take precedence over the project's base calendar. ▓

Editing the Standard Calendar

Changing the working days and hours on the Standard calendar affects the scheduled work time for all tasks that have no resources assigned to them and for all tasks whose resources are linked to the standard base calendar.

Changing Working and Nonworking Days   The original calendar shows all weekdays, Monday through Friday, as working days and all Saturdays and Sundays as nonworking days. You can change the status of any day to make the day working or nonworking, and you can specify the number of hours available for work on any day by defining the starting and ending times for work shifts on that day.

To edit the Standard calendar, choose Tools, Change Working Time. The Change Working Time dialog box appears (see Figure 3.16). The Change Working Time dialog box can display a calendar of working and nonworking times for any of the base calendars and resource calendars defined for the project.

Part

I

Ch

3

FIG. 3.16

Use the Change Working Time dialog box to define the days and hours when work can be scheduled by Microsoft Project.

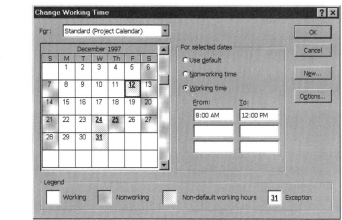

The dialog box contains a monthly calendar form, daily working times, and buttons to change the calendar. Additionally, Project 98 has now included a legend at the bottom of the dialog box that indicates how working and nonworking days will be displayed, along with days that have different hours from the default hours. Each date that is modified from the default will have the date underlined. If you modify a day of the week for the entire project, such as making the working time on every Monday from 1 p.m. to 5 p.m., the letter <u>M</u> in the Working Time calendar is underlined. Use the calendar scroll bar to change months and years. The calendar spans the period from January, 1984, to December, 2049.

To change the status of a single day or a consecutive period of days from working to nonworking or vice versa, click the day with the mouse. You can select consecutive days by clicking and dragging. You can select multiple days that are not consecutive by pressing the Ctrl key as you click the extra dates. On the right side of the dialog box, there are several buttons in the For Selected Dates area to change the working or nonworking status of a day.

In the For Selected Dates area of the dialog box, select the <u>N</u>onworking Time option button to make the selected day(s) nonworking. To make the selected day(s) working days, select the <u>W</u>orking Time option button.

TIP

To select days with the keyboard, use your arrow keys to move to the first day you want selected. Hold down the Shift key and use the arrow keys to select additional consecutive days.

You can also change the working status of any day of the week for all weeks throughout the year. If your organization works on Saturdays, for example, you will want to make all Saturdays working days.

To change the working status of a day for all weeks, select the day of the week by clicking the day letter at the top of the calendar (such as M for Monday). Select the <u>W</u>orking Time or <u>N</u>onworking Time option button in the For Selected Dates area of the dialog box.

Once the working status of a day of the week is set, that status becomes the *default* status for that day of the week. For example, suppose you have made every Friday a working day with the hours of 8:00 a.m. to 12:00 p.m. (noon). If you changed a particular Friday to either a full working day or a nonworking day and then want to change it back to the default hours for Fridays, use the <u>D</u>efault option button to reset the hours from 8 a.m. to 12 p.m. Selecting any specific date and using the <u>D</u>efault option button sets that date's working hours to the default for its day of the week.

Figure 3.16 shows the month of December 1997. The company is having a Holiday party on Friday, December 12. They don't anticipate any work on this project will be accomplished in the afternoon, and this day has been marked as a partial working day. Because the company gives all of its employees the afternoon of the 24th and all of the 25th of December to celebrate Christmas, these days are marked accordingly. Finally, to start the New Year off with a bang, all employees receive a half day off on December 31st. Partial working days are marked with slash marks; full nonworking days are marked in gray.

Changing the Standard Working Hours You can define the work periods for each day by supplying up to three work periods in the Working Time text boxes of the Change Working Time dialog box. Each work period has From text boxes and To text boxes. The default eight-hour work time periods are 8:00 a.m. to 12:00 p.m. and 1:00 p.m. to 5:00 p.m., equaling eight hours of work per day. Most of the time only the first four boxes are used. The remaining two boxes are typically filled in when the working times go across midnight. The section "Creating a New Calendar" later in this chapter provides a good example of when all six time boxes are used.

To change the working hours, follow these steps:

1. Select the From text box for the first time period you want to change.

T I P Use the Alt+F key to select the first From text box, then use the Tab key to advance to the other time boxes. Use Shift+Tab to return to previous boxes.

Part

Ch

3

2. Enter a time. For acceptable time formats, see the next section "Entering Time Formats."
3. Select the To text box and enter a time.
4. Repeat this process by clicking (or using the Tab key) each subsequent From and To text box to change the time in that box.

N O T E Project checks all time entries for consistency. Each successive time must be later in the day than the preceding time text box.

You cannot leave a work period blank and put data in a work period beneath it. Therefore, you must use the top From and To text boxes first; then you can fill the middle pair; only then can you fill the bottom pair.

Entering Time Formats You can use several formats for entering times in these text boxes. You can use either the 12-hour clock or the 24-hour clock to enter times. If you enter times based on the 12-hour clock, make sure that you use the a.m. and p.m. suffixes to ensure that the program understands your intent. If you enter a time without using an a.m. or p.m. suffix, the computer uses the first instance of the time following 8:00 a.m. (or whatever time you designate as the Default Start Time on the Calendar tab of the Options dialog box).

If you enter 3:30 without a suffix, for example, the computer assumes that you want to use 3:30 in the afternoon and attaches the p.m. suffix. If you want to set a work shift to start at 5:00 in the morning, enter 5 a.m. instead of 5:00 because the program interprets 5:00 to mean 5:00 p.m. (If the time you want to enter is on the hour, simply enter the hour number. For example, you can simply enter **10** for 10:00 a.m., and **5 p.m.** for 5:00 p.m.)

N O T E Noon is entered as 12:00 p.m., and midnight is entered as 12:00 a.m.

Deleting the Working Time Text Boxes   To remove a work period from the Working Time text boxes, you need to delete both the From time and the To time for that period. Follow these steps:

1. Select the From text box for the work period you want to remove.

2. Press the Delete key to clear the text box.

3. Move to the To text box. Select the time entry and press Delete to remove that time period.

T I P   Do not use the spacebar to remove an entry; you must highlight and delete each entry.

Resetting a Calendar   You can use the Use Default option button in the For Selected Dates area of the dialog box to cancel changes you made for calendar days. Selecting individual days and choosing Use Default returns those days to the working hours for those days of the week (the standard definition). Selecting the day of the week letters at the top of the calendar and choosing Use Default returns all days in the selected column to the standard 8-hour day, 8 a.m. to 5 p.m. Selecting all the weekday letters at the top of the calendar and choosing Use Default returns the entire calendar to the initial Standard calendar with no holidays and a 40-hour week.

Creating a New Calendar

Suppose you have a processing crew that works from 5:00 p.m. to 2:00 a.m., Monday through Friday. You can create a Processing Crew calendar to use as a base calendar for the resources in that group. The regular shift begins at 5:00 p.m. and continues to 2:00 a.m. the following day. An hour break is scheduled from 9:00 p.m. to 10:00 p.m.

N O T E   In the previous example, on Monday the crew starts at 5 p.m., breaks for dinner at 9 p.m., comes back to work at 10 p.m., and finishes that day at 12 a.m. (midnight). The work from midnight to 2 a.m. is entered on Tuesday. Tuesday through Friday the working times would show 12 a.m. to 2 a.m., then 5 p.m. to 9 p.m., and then 10 p.m. to 12 a.m. Saturday would reflect the last hour (12 a.m. to 2 a.m.) of Friday night's shift. Figure 3.20 later in this section illustrates this example. ▓

Create a new base calendar by following these steps:

1. Choose the New button on the right side of the Change Working Time dialog box to create a new base calendar. The Create New Base Calendar dialog box appears (see Figure 3.17).

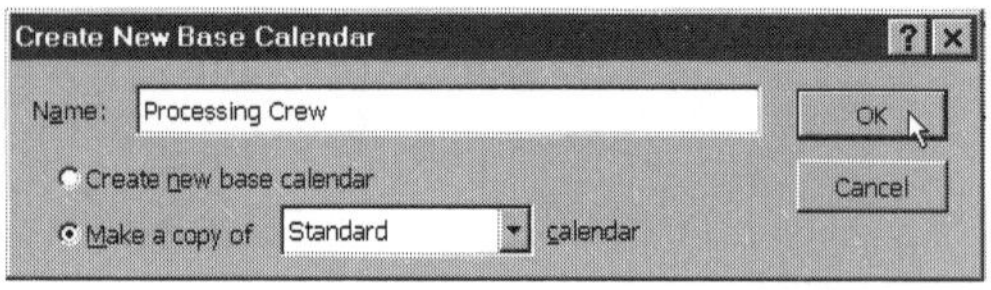

FIG. 3.17

You can start a new calendar from scratch, or you can use a copy of any existing base calendar.

2. Choose the N̲ame text box and type a distinctive name, such as **Processing Crew**, for the new calendar.

3. Click the Create N̲ew Base Calendar option button if you want to start with no holidays and the standard 40-hour week.

   Or choose the M̲ake A Copy Of Calendar option button to start with a copy of an existing base calendar and all its holidays and exceptions. Select an existing base calendar from the drop-down list. If you have already defined all regular company holidays on the Standard calendar, start with a copy of it so you don't have to enter those holidays again.

4. Choose OK to start defining the new calendar. If you made changes in another calendar that you haven't saved, you see the warning shown in Figure 3.18 before you can proceed to make changes in the new calendar. Choose the Y̲es button to save the changes you made in the other calendar.

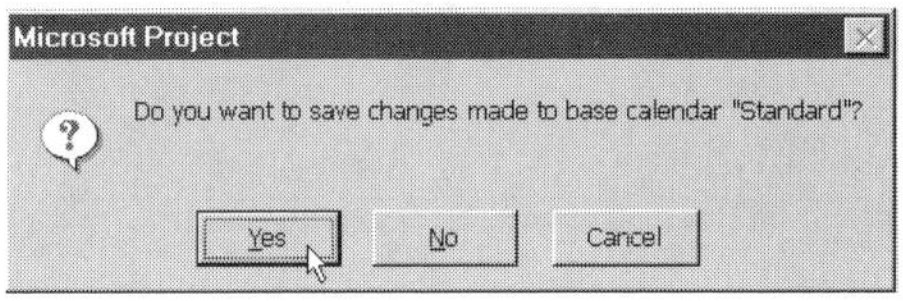

FIG. 3.18

You must save or discard earlier, unsaved changes in another calendar before you can start working on a new calendar.

The new calendar name now appears in the F̲or list box in the Change Working Time dialog box.

5. To change the hours for a weekday, such as Monday, select the letter at the top of the day column and enter the shift hours for that day in the F̲rom and T̲o text boxes (see Figure 3.19). The hours for Mondays are 5:00 p.m. to 9:00 p.m. and 10:00 p.m. to 12:00 a.m. The remainder of the shift is defined on the Working Time schedule for Tuesdays.

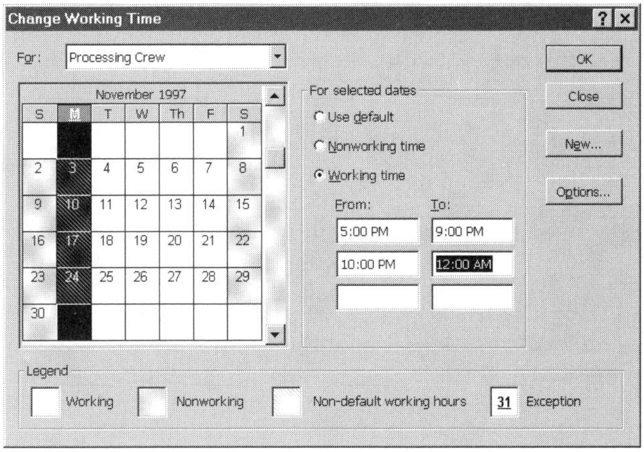

FIG. 3.19

Select the day letter at the top of a day column to change the hours for that day for every week.

6. To change the hours for several days that have identical hours, drag from the letter for the first day to the last day in the group and enter the common hours in the Working Time group. The Tuesday through Friday schedules require three shifts, as shown in Figure 3.20. The first shift is the continuation of the previous evening's shift. The second and third shifts show the periods for the beginning of the next evening's shift.

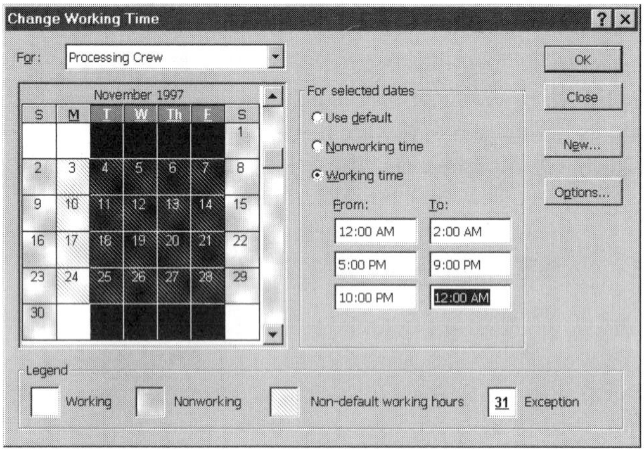

FIG. 3.20

You can select several days by highlighting the letters for the days at the top of the calendar display. Here, every Tuesday through Friday is selected so the working hours can be changed.

7. To set hours for a day that is currently a nonworking day, you first must make the day a working day. Then you can enter the hours in the Working Time text boxes. The Saturday hours in the Processing Crew calendar are just from midnight to 2:00 a.m. (see Figure 3.21). First, select the S at the top of the Saturday column and choose the Working button to make it a working day. Then you can enter the hours in the Working Time text boxes.

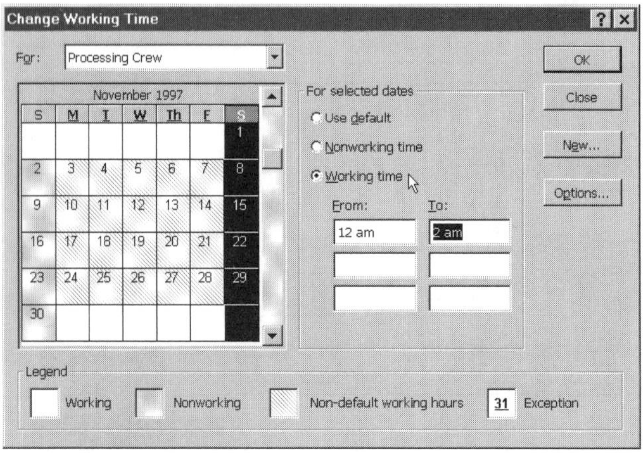

FIG. 3.21

You must first make a day a working day before you can define working times for it.

Saving or Canceling Your Changes

To finish editing base calendars and save the changes you made, choose the OK button on the right side of the Change Working Time dialog box. The Cancel button ignores all of the changes you have made.

Working with Calendars

All of the calendar information is saved along with the task and resource information in the project document. In earlier releases of Microsoft Project (Releases 3 and 1), the calendars were saved in a separate file named CALENDAR.MPC, and you had to copy the calendar file along with the project files to transfer a project document from one computer to another. Now you only have to copy the project file to transfer all information needed to process and display the project document.

If you create a base calendar in one project and want to use the same base calendar in future projects, you can use the Organizer to copy the calendar to the Global template (GLOBAL.MPT). The calendars in the GLOBAL.MPT file are automatically included in any new project file. You can also use the Organizer to copy a calendar to another existing project file, to delete a calendar from the active file, and to rename a calendar in the active file. The following section describes how to access the Organizer and how to use it.

N O T E The GLOBAL.MPT template is stored in the directory with the Microsoft Project program files, usually in C:\Program Files\Microsoft Office\Office. ▓

Part

I

Ch

3

Working with the Organizer

The Organizer is a feature that copies objects (such as calendars) from one project or template to another. You also use the Organizer to delete or rename a calendar. If you copy a calendar to the GLOBAL.MPT file (the template for all new projects), the calendar becomes part of all new project documents. For example, to customize the Standard calendar for all new projects, you must do the following:

1. Choose Tools, Change Working Times to edit the Standard calendar in an active project document to have the special working times, holidays, and hours that you want in the Standard calendar, as described in the previous section.

2. Use the Organizer to copy the customized Standard calendar to the GLOBAL.MPT file, replacing the existing Standard calendar in the GLOBAL.MPT file. The Standard calendar for all new projects will have your customized features. Specific steps to accomplish this are listed later.

You use the Organizer to manage not only calendars but also other customized elements (such as views, reports, macros, forms, tables, filters, toolbars, and menu bars). Therefore, you can activate the Organizer from several points in Microsoft Project—but not, unfortunately, from the Change Working Time dialog box where you define calendars.

In the previous version of Microsoft Project, accessing the Organizer was done in a roundabout manner. Because the Organizer is such a useful feature, you can now access the Organizer by choosing Tools, Organizer.

NOTE The Organizer can also be accessed through several other dialog boxes:

- View, More Views, Organizer
- View, Table, More Tables, Organizer
- Project, Filter For, More Filters, Organizer

The Organizer can no longer be accessed by choosing View, Toolbars. ▩

Copying Calendars to the Global Template

The following steps access the Organizer through the Tools menu. The active file, the file which contains the calendar, is referred to as the *source file*. The file in which you would like to place a copy of the calendar is referred to as the *target file*.

Follow these steps to copy a calendar to the GLOBAL.MPT template:

1. Choose Tools, Organizer to display the Organizer dialog box.
2. Choose the Calendars tab. Figure 3.22 show the Calendars tab from the Organizer. The calendars in the active file are listed on the right. The calendars in the GLOBAL.MPT file are listed on the left.

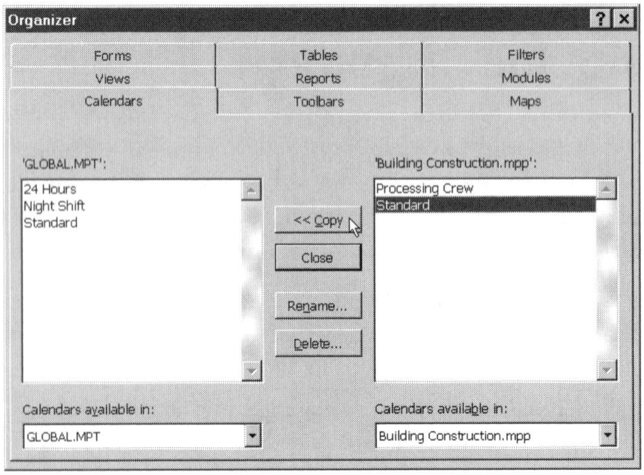

FIG. 3.22

The Organizer dialog box is used to make your customized calendars available to other projects you are working on.

3. Choose the calendar you want to copy from the list of calendars in your source file on the right side of the dialog box.
4. Choose the Copy button. If there is a calendar with the same name in the target file, such as the Standard calendar, Project will ask you for confirmation to override the former calendar (see Figure 3.23).

FIG. 3.23

You must confirm that you want to replace the Standard calendar in the GLOBAL.MPT with the Standard calendar from the source file.

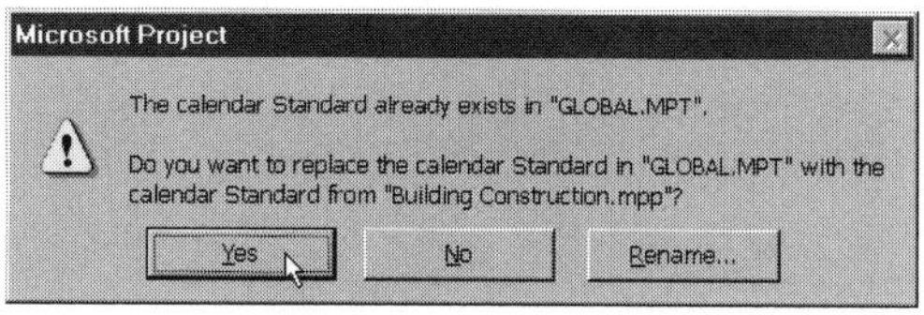

> **Microsoft Project**
>
> ⚠ The calendar Standard already exists in "GLOBAL.MPT".
>
> Do you want to replace the calendar Standard in "GLOBAL.MPT" with the calendar Standard from "Building Construction.mpp"?
>
> [Yes]   [No]   [Rename...]

5. Choose the Yes button to replace the calendar in the target file with the new calendar from your active file.

   Or you can use the Rename button to copy the calendar to the target file by using a new name that is not being used by another calendar.

6. Choose the Close button to exit the Organizer dialog box.

N O T E   You cannot edit the calendars in the GLOBAL.MPT template directly. To edit a calendar in the GLOBAL.MPT template, copy it to a project file with the Organizer. Edit the calendar in the project file, then use the Organizer to copy it back to the GLOBAL.MPT template. ▪

Copying a Calendar from One Project to Another

You can also use the Organizer to copy a calendar from one project document to another. For example, if you want to place a copy of the Processing Crew calendar from the Building Construction file into the Business Park Construction file, follow these steps:

1. Open the source and the target files.

2. Choose Tools, Organizer to display the Organizer dialog box.

3. Choose the Calendars tab. The calendars in the active file, Building Construction in Figure 3.24, are listed on the right. The calendars in the GLOBAL.MPT file are listed on the left. However, the source file does not always have to appear on the right; you can copy from right to left or left to right.

4. Use the Calendars Available In drop-down list box on the bottom-left side to choose the target file, in this case the Business Park Construction project (see Figure 3.24).

5. Choose the calendar you want to copy from the list of calendars in your source file.

6. Choose the Copy button. If there is a calendar with the same name in the target file, such as the Standard calendar, Project will ask you for confirmation to override the former calendar.

7. Choose the Yes button to replace the calendar in the target file with the new calendar from your active file.

   Or you can use the Rename button to copy the calendar to the target file by using a name that is not already being used by a calendar in the target file.

Part

I

Ch

3

8. Choose the Close button to exit the Organizer dialog box.

▶ **See** "Using the Organizer," **p. 114**

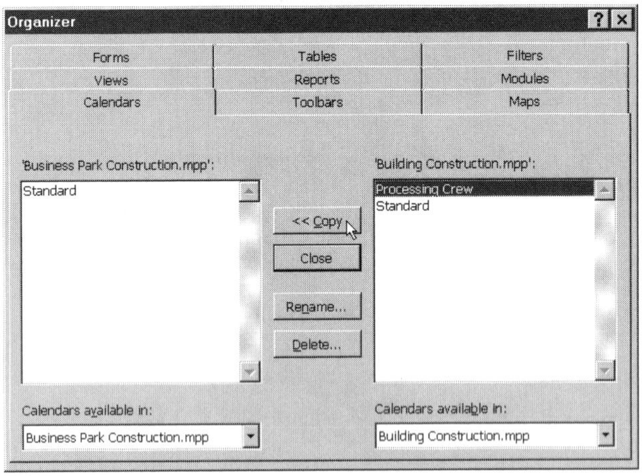

FIG. 3.24

Display both the target and the source files in the Organizer dialog box.

Using Calendars from Microsoft Project 3.0

Calendar Files, and any other Project 3.0 files, cannot be brought directly into Project 98. However, if your project files were saved in an .MPX format (either from Project 3.0, 4.0, or 4.1), you can open the project files in Project 98, and the calendar information will be included. The Organizer can then be used to copy the calendar(s) to the GLOBAL.MPT or to an .MPP file in Project 98.

Printing the Base Calendars

You can print a report to show the details of each of the base calendars in the active project file. Printing reports is covered in detail in Chapter 13, "Printing Views and Reports," and customizing the reports is covered in Chapter 24, "Customizing Reports." This section is a quick reference for printing the Working Days report, a report which provides information about the working and nonworking days in all of your base calendars.

To print the Working Days report, follow these steps:

1. Choose View, Reports. The Reports dialog box shown in Figure 3.25 appears.

2. Choose the Overview reports by double-clicking the Overview icon or by selecting the icon and choosing the Select button. The Overview Reports dialog box appears (see Figure 3.26).

3. Click the Working Days report. Choose the Select button to preview the report (see Figure 3.27).

FIG. 3.25

The Reports dialog box organizes reports into five standard categories plus a Custom option for customizing reports.

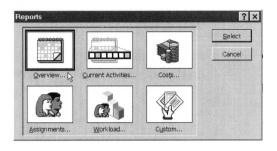

FIG. 3.26

The Working Days report prints all calendars for the active project.

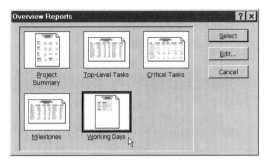

FIG. 3.27

The print preview screen shows you the layout of the report.

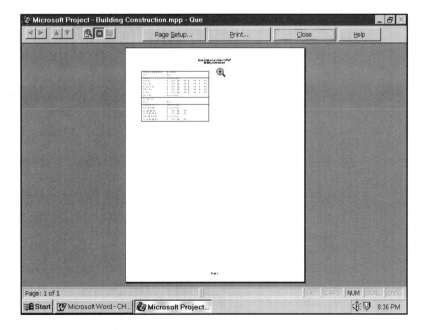

4. Choose the <u>P</u>rint button to access the Print dialog box and send the report to your printer. Choose the <u>C</u>lose button to return to the project workspace.

The report shows the standard working hours for each day of the week, followed by a list of the exceptions for individual days. Each base calendar prints on a separate page. Figure 3.28 is an illustration of the report for the Standard base calendar. Holidays are listed as exceptions below the standard days and hours.

FIG. 3.28

The Base Calendar report shows the standard working times plus the exceptions (such as holidays).

BASE CALENDAR:	Standard
Day	Hours
Sunday	Nonworking
Monday	8:00 AM - 12:00 PM, 1:00 PM - 5:00 PM
Tuesday	8:00 AM - 12:00 PM, 1:00 PM - 5:00 PM
Wednesday	8:00 AM - 12:00 PM, 1:00 PM - 5:00 PM
Thursday	8:00 AM - 12:00 PM, 1:00 PM - 5:00 PM
Friday	8:00 AM - 12:00 PM, 1:00 PM - 5:00 PM
Saturday	Nonworking
Exceptions:	
Date	Hours
Mon 7/4/94	Nonworking
Tue 7/4/95	Nonworking
Fri 12/12/97	8:00 AM - 12:00 PM
Wed 12/24/97	8:00 AM - 12:00 PM
Thu 12/25/97	Nonworking
Wed 12/31/97	8:00 AM - 12:00 PM

BASE CALENDAR:	Processing Crew
Day	Hours
Sunday	Nonworking
Monday	5:00 PM - 9:00 PM, 10:00 PM - 12:00 AM
Tuesday	12:00 AM - 2:00 AM, 5:00 PM - 9:00 PM, 10:00 PM - 12:00 AM
Wednesday	12:00 AM - 2:00 AM, 5:00 PM - 9:00 PM, 10:00 PM - 12:00 AM
Thursday	12:00 AM - 2:00 AM, 5:00 PM - 9:00 PM, 10:00 PM - 12:00 AM
Friday	12:00 AM - 2:00 AM, 5:00 PM - 9:00 PM, 10:00 PM - 12:00 AM
Saturday	12:00 AM - 2:00 AM
Exceptions:	
Date	Hours
Mon 7/4/94	Nonworking
Tue 7/4/95	Nonworking
Fri 12/12/97	8:00 AM - 12:00 PM
Wed 12/24/97	8:00 AM - 12:00 PM
Thu 12/25/97	Nonworking
Wed 12/31/97	8:00 AM - 12:00 PM

From Here...

In this chapter you learned how to start a new project file and many other things that need to be considered early on in the project, such as which options you want to change, and how to set up a project calendar. From here, you should look at these chapters:

- Chapter 4, "Working with Project Files," discusses saving your project and creating project templates, and gives you more detailed information on working with the Organizer.

- Chapter 5, "Creating a Task List," will step you through the process of entering in your tasks. This chapter also discusses outlining and printing your tasks, as well as some new editing features.

Working with Project Files

Understanding how to effectively work with your project files is important for project managers. In this chapter we will discuss manipulating your project files. ■

Locating and opening files

Learn how to find and open existing project files. The powerful Find File capability in Microsoft Project will assist you in locating files.

Saving your work

Learn to save your projects and protect your files with passwords. Save a group of files as a Workspace, allowing you to open up all your project files at once.

Exploring the uses of Project templates

Create and save Project templates for projects that repeat themselves. Use the templates provided by Microsoft.

Using the Organizer

The Organizer assists you in copying custom objects (like calendars, tables, and views) to other project files, including the GLOBAL.MPT template file.

Starting and Opening Project Files

Use the File menu to create a new file or open up an existing file. Each open project file resides in its own document window, and you can easily switch between your open projects. There can be up to 50 project files open at the same time in Microsoft Project.

Creating a New Project Document

Chapter 3 describes in detail how to set up a new project file. It involves more than choosing File, New, or using the New button on the Standard toolbar. When you create a blank project document, the new file inherits all the features of the Global project template (GLOBAL.MPT). All new documents, except those that are copies of templates, have generic document titles: Project1, Project2, and so on.

▶ **See** "Supplying Information for a New Project," **p. 62**

▶ **See** "Selecting the Environment Options," **p. 70**

N O T E   GLOBAL.MPT is a project template that is stored in the directory along with the program files (usually c:\Program Files\Microsoft Office\Office). Changes made to the GLOBAL.MPT template affect all new project files. The Organizer is used to make changes in the Global template. For more information on working with the Global template and Organizer, see "Using the Organizer" later in this chapter. ▪

When you save a new document, Project opens the File Save dialog box, which enables you to assign a file name to the document. See the section "Saving a File" later in this chapter.

Opening an Existing File

Use the File command to open a file or document. Choose File, Open, or choose the Open button on the toolbar, to display the File Open dialog box (see Figure 4.1). Use the Open dialog box to locate the file you want to work with. When the file name you want to open appears in the large list box in the center of the dialog box, select the name and choose the Open button. You can also double-click the file name to open it.

N O T E   In order to open multiple files at the same time, they must have been previously saved as a Workspace. This feature is discussed later in this section. ▪

N O T E   If the file you want to open contains links to other documents, you will see a warning message appear before the file opens. This message alerts you that the file you are about to open has external links and asks you if you want to reestablish (update) the links. ▪

T I P   When you activate the File menu, the pull-down menu displays a list of the four most recently saved project files below the list of commands. The most recently saved file is listed first. You can click one of these file names to open a recently used file without having to use the File Open dialog box.

You can expand the number of documents up to nine. Choose Tools, Options, and on the General tab, change the number of entries in the Recently Used File List spinner box.

FIG. 4.1
Use the File Open dialog box to locate a file you want to open, or manipulate the properties of an existing file.

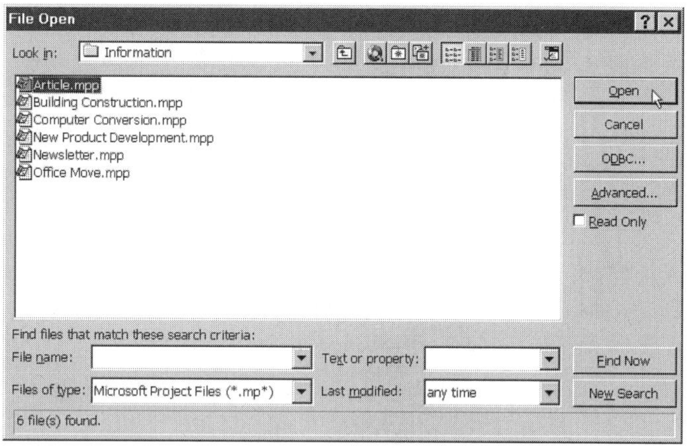

Using the File Open Dialog Box   The File Open dialog box is a powerful dialog box used by all Microsoft Office applications to locate and open files. It provides advanced search capabilities and is easy to use.

In addition to locating a file, many other file-related tasks can be accomplished from the File Open dialog box. You can open files, print files, copy files, move files to another folder, delete files, rename files, send files to communication and network destinations, and edit the properties of Microsoft Office application files.

Selecting a Different File Location to be Searched   By default, when you access the File Open dialog box, Windows looks in the My Documents folder. If the file you want to open is located in another folder, or on another drive, there are several ways to change the folder you are viewing. The toolbar in the File Open dialog box (see Figure 4.2) can assist you in changing the location of the files you are looking for.

Changing the Working Directory for Microsoft Project

The Open and Save As dialog boxes will initially open the My Documents folder in Windows 95 (or the Personal folder in Windows NT). Microsoft Project does not offer a way to change this default working directory. The Properties dialog box for the icon that starts Project has a Start In field, but this entry is intended to let you name a directory that contains an alternative GLOBAL.MPT file that you want to be used, not the directory where project files will be stored by default. The default working directory for Microsoft Project 98 is strictly governed by an entry in the Registry.

To change the working directory, you must use the REGEDIT applet. The Registry is a powerful, and dangerous, component of Windows 95. To change the default directory for storing files in Microsoft Project, follow these steps exactly:

continues

Part
I
Ch
4

continued

1. Exit Microsoft Project and all other applications. (You will need to restart Windows during this procedure.)

2. Click the Start button on the task bar.

3. Choose Run from the menu. This will display the Run dialog box.

4. In the Open text box type **regedit** and press the Enter key. This will open the Registry Editor.

5. In the Registry Editor window, click the plus sign next to the HKEY_CURRENT_USER folder.

6. Click the plus sign next to the Software folder.

7. Click the plus sign next to the Microsoft folder.

8. Click the plus sign next to the Windows folder.

9. Click the plus sign next to the CurrentVersion folder.

10. Click the plus sign next to the Explorer folder.

11. Click the User Shell Folders folder. This will display the names of the key values in the pane on the right.

12. In the Window pane on the right, double-click the Personal value in the Name column. This will display the Edit String dialog box.

13. In the Value Data text box, type the full path for the working directory that you want to use for storing and retrieving Project files. Then click OK.

    This directory does not have to exist at this point, but be sure that you create it before starting Microsoft Project again in step 16.

14. Close the Registry by choosing Registry, Exit.

15. Restart Windows.

16. Open Microsoft Project 98 and click the Open button on the toolbar. The new working directory should be opened automatically.

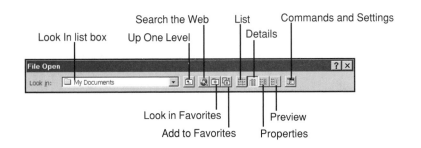

FIG. 4.2

The File Open dialog box toolbar provides many alternatives for changing the file location.

- Use the Look In list box to select a different folder or disk drive to view. Choose the list box arrow to display the tree structure of your desktop, including all drives and CD-ROMs on your computer and all network or modem connections to your desktop. Select the location you want to view and all folders in that location display. All files in that location also appear as long as they match the criteria defined at the bottom of the dialog box. Defining selection criteria is described in the section "Specifying Search Criteria for Finding Files" later in this chapter.

- Choose the Up One Level button to move up in the directory currently displayed in the Look In box.

- Choose the Search the Web button to open the search page of your Internet browser.

- Choose the Look in Favorites button to view a list of locations you have previously selected as favorite locations. These are locations you use frequently. The folders and file names in the Favorites list are *shortcut* icons that serve as cross-references to the locations of the real folders and files. See the section "Using the Selected File" later in this chapter for more information on working with the Favorites list.

Changing the File Names Display You can choose to display the list of file names in four different ways. The standard display, called the List display, lists just the names of files or folders.

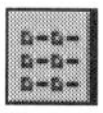

- Choose the List button to view a simple listing of the files or folders in the Look In box. Figure 4.1 illustrates the List display.

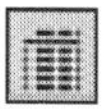

- Choose the Details button to display file names in a table format with columns for the name, size, type (as defined by the file name extension), and date last modified (see Figure 4.3). You can adjust the width of the columns by dragging the divider lines in the column headings.

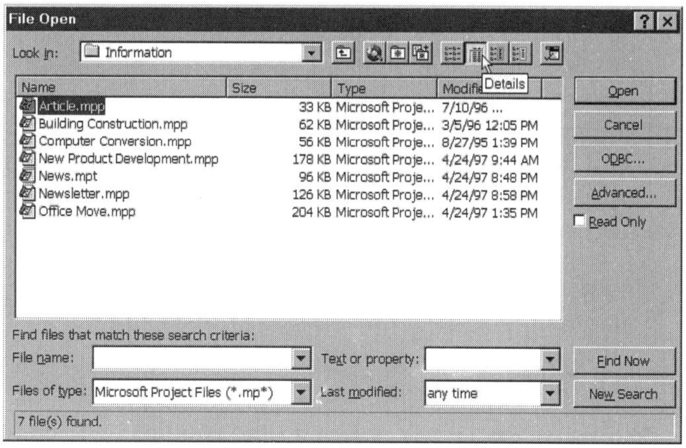

Part
I

Ch
4

FIG. 4.3
The Details button displays more information about the folders and files.

File Open				
Look In: Information				
Name	Size	Type	Modified	
Article.mpp		33 KB Microsoft Proje...	7/10/96 ...	Open
Building Construction.mpp		62 KB Microsoft Proje...	3/5/96 12:05 PM	Cancel
Computer Conversion.mpp		56 KB Microsoft Proje...	8/27/95 1:39 PM	ODBC...
New Product Development.mpp		178 KB Microsoft Proje...	4/24/97 9:44 AM	Advanced...
News.mpt		96 KB Microsoft Proje...	4/24/97 8:48 PM	Read Only
Newsletter.mpp		126 KB Microsoft Proje...	4/24/97 8:58 PM	
Office Move.mpp		204 KB Microsoft Proje...	4/24/97 1:35 PM	

Find files that match these search criteria:
File name: ___ Text or property: ___ Find Now
Files of type: Microsoft Project Files (*.mp*) Last modified: any time New Search
7 file(s) found.

Choose the Properties button to display file details such as Title, Author, Date Created, and Date Modified (see Figure 4.4). These are properties from the Summary and Statistics tabs of the Properties dialog box. Additional properties like Percent Complete, Cost, and Duration can be displayed if these items are added as custom properties. See "The Custom Tab" section later in this chapter for information on how to use custom properties in Project.

FIG. 4.4

Use the Properties button to display the Properties information for files.

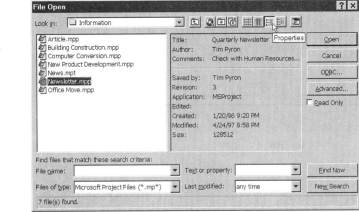

N O T E   You can scroll the list of properties to see additional information. Properties for other file types, like Excel and Word, can also be displayed.

   Choose the Preview button to display a thumbnail sketch of Microsoft Project files (see Figure 4.5). The Microsoft Project preview shows the view that was active when the project was saved.

N O T E   In order to preview files, a properties setting must be established and saved with the file prior to using the preview option. Choose File, Properties and on the Summary tab select Save Preview Picture. You must modify the properties for *each* file you want be able to preview.

Choose the Commands and Settings button to display a drop-down menu listing file commands and settings you can access from within the File Open dialog box (see Figure 4.6). From the drop-down menu choose the Search Subfolders command to display all files in all folders found in the selected location. Without this command, the display of files and folders is limited to those located directly in the location named in the Look In box.

Choosing this command automatically activates the Details display and the Group Files by Folder command so you see the organization of these folders in your computer. The list of file names includes all those found in the location named in the Look In box and in all subfolders under that location. On the left side of the File Open dialog box in Figure 4.6, the C drive is being viewed. All the Microsoft Project files on the C drive, along with the file structure they can be found in, is displayed.

If you deselect the Group Files by Folder command, only Microsoft Project file names appear in the list. Access the Commands and Settings button and deselect the Group Files by Folder command to display only the file names, not the complete file structure.

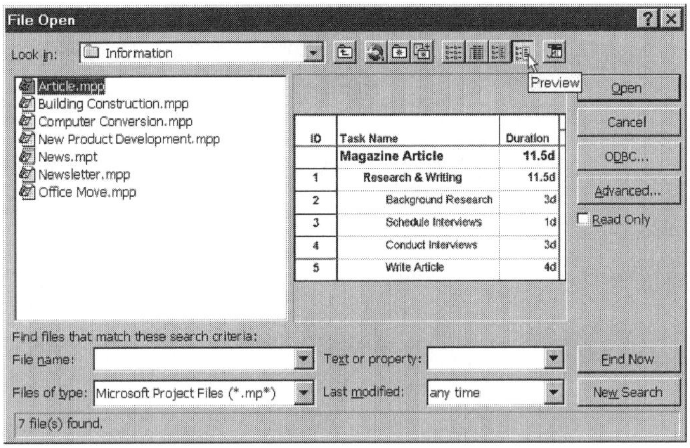

FIG. 4.5

View the contents of the file with the Preview button.

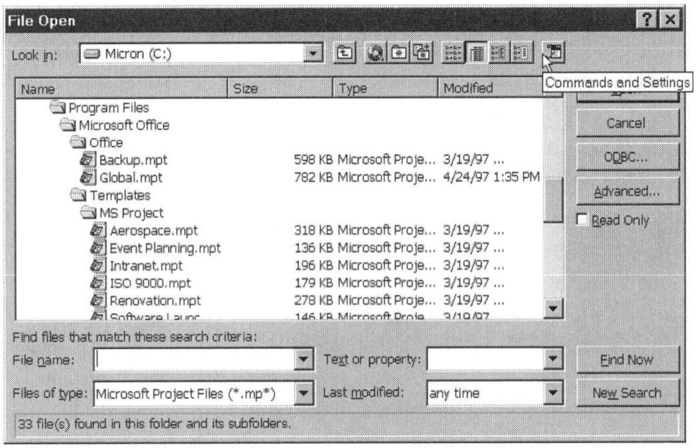

FIG. 4.6

You can view the contents of the selected location plus the contents of all subfolders in the selected location.

You can sort the list of file names or folders, regardless of which way you have displayed the list of file names. Follow these steps to sort the files:

1. Choose the Commands and Settings button to display a menu of options.

2. Choose the Sorting command to display the Sort By dialog box.

3. Choose the list arrow to display the sort options: Name, Size, Type, and Modified. Select the property category you want to use as a sort key. Choose Ascending or Descending as appropriate, and then choose OK.

Part

I

Ch

4

For the Size property, an ascending sort displays the smallest file size to the largest. A descending sort displays the largest file to the smallest. For the modified property, an ascending sort would display the most recently modified file first. A descending sort displays files that have not been modified recently at the top of the list.

 T I P To quickly sort files in the Details view, click the column heading once for an ascending sort, and a second time for a descending sort (see Figure 4.7).

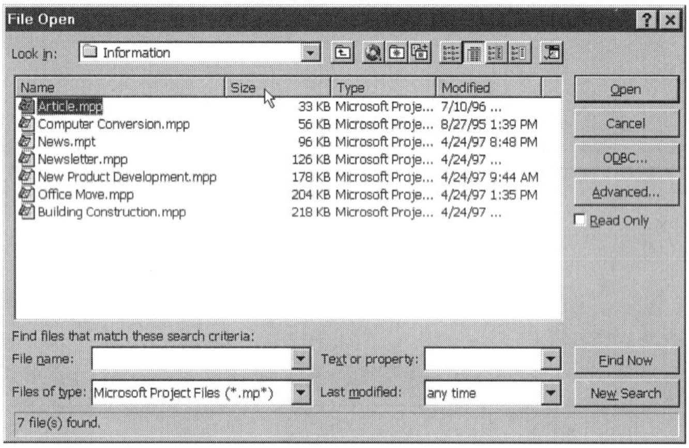

FIG. 4.7
Click the Size column heading in the Details view to sort the list of files from smallest to largest.

File Open				? X
Look in:	Information			
Name	Size	Type	Modified	
Article.mpp	33 KB	Microsoft Proje...	7/10/96 ...	Open
Computer Conversion.mpp	56 KB	Microsoft Proje...	8/27/95 1:39 PM	Cancel
News.mpt	96 KB	Microsoft Proje...	4/24/97 8:48 PM	
Newsletter.mpp	126 KB	Microsoft Proje...	4/24/97 ...	ODBC...
New Product Development.mpp	178 KB	Microsoft Proje...	4/24/97 9:44 AM	
Office Move.mpp	204 KB	Microsoft Proje...	4/24/97 1:35 PM	Advanced...
Building Construction.mpp	218 KB	Microsoft Proje...	4/24/97 ...	□ Read Only

Find files that match these search criteria:
File name: _____ Text or property: _____ Find Now
Files of type: Microsoft Project Files (*.mp*) Last modified: any time New Search
7 file(s) found.

Additional Options for Using the Selected File Although the most common use of the File Open dialog box is to retrieve a document for editing, you can also initiate a number of other file management actions after you select a file. Some of these options are available when you use the Commands and Settings button. Figure 4.8 shows the menu of choices available when you select the Commands and Settings button. Some file management actions are available only on the shortcut menu for the file. To access the shortcut menu (see Figure 4.9), right-click the file name.

FIG. 4.8
The file properties can be accessed from the Commands and Settings menu.

Open Read-Only
Open as Copy
Print
Properties
Sorting...
Search Subfolders
Group files by folder
Map Network Drive...
Add/Modify FTP Locations...
Saved Searches ▶

FIG. 4.9
A shortcut menu displays when you right-click the file name. Use this menu to manipulate your files.

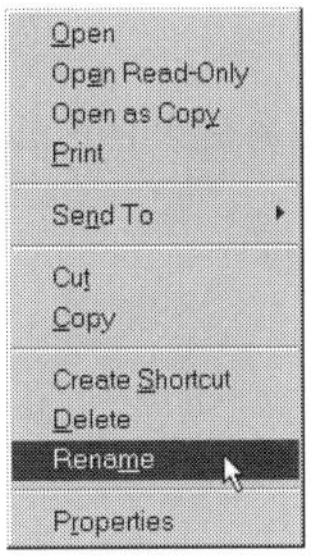

```
Open
Open Read-Only
Open as Copy
Print

Send To          ▶

Cut
Copy

Create Shortcut
Delete
Rename
Properties
```

- You can open the file by choosing the Open button, the Open command on the shortcut menu, or by double-clicking the file name.

- You may want to allow others to modify a file while you are viewing it, or to view a file without changing any of the values in the file. The Open Read Only command is available on both the shortcut menu and the Commands and Settings menu (refer to Figures 4.8 and 4.9). You can also use the Read Only option in the File Open dialog box, located on the right side of the dialog box under the Advanced button. Choose the file you want to open, then select the Read Only option and choose Open.

- You can delete a file by selecting it and pressing the Delete key, or by choosing Delete from the shortcut menu for the file. Choose the Yes button in the Confirm File Delete dialog box to complete the action.

- You can change the file's name by selecting the file name and pressing the function key F2, or by selecting Rename from the shortcut menu. Edit the name and then press Enter to complete the name change.

> **TIP** You can change the file's name by selecting the file name with two single clicks (clicking once, pausing, then clicking again). Remember, a double-click opens the file!

- You can send the file to the printer with the Print command on the shortcut menu. The view that was active when the file was saved will be the view that is printed.

- The shortcut menu also has a Send To command that lets you send a copy of the file to a floppy disk, to your fax modem, or to an e-mail post office address to send it to a co-worker.

- With the shortcut menu, you can copy or move the file to another location. Right-click the file name and choose Cut (to move the file) or Copy (to copy the file) from the shortcut menu. Choose another location in the Look In box and right-click the file name list area in that new location. Choose Paste from the shortcut menu that appears. The file is pasted in the new location.

  ▶ **See** "Supplying Information for a New Project," **p. 62**

- You can edit the file properties of Microsoft Office application files without actually opening the files. Right-click the file name and choose Properties from the shortcut menu. The Properties sheet for the file appears. Edit the fields on the various tabs as desired and then choose the OK button.

Part

Ch
4

To add a file or folder to the Favorites list, follow these steps:

1. Find the location of the folder or file and display the folder or file in the File Open list box.

2. Select the file or folder.

3. Choose the Add to Favorites button.

A shortcut to the item now appears when you choose the Look in Favorites button.

To remove an item from the Favorites list, simply select the item and press the Delete key; or right-click the item and choose <u>D</u>elete from the shortcut menu. Choose Yes to confirm that you want to send the item to the Recycle Bin. Because the item is a Windows shortcut, deleting it does not delete the folder or file that it represents. You are only deleting the reference to the folder or file.

> **CAUTION**
>
> Check to be sure that Favorites is displayed in the Look In box before deleting an icon. The icons in the Favorites folder are shortcuts, but the file icons in other folders usually are for the files themselves. A shortcut icon can be distinguished from other icons by the small arrow in the lower-left corner of the shortcut image.

Virus Protection

In this era of information exchange, files are frequently shared between people supporting a large project. When this happens, it is possible the file may pick up a computer virus. A *virus* is a computer program or macro that "infects" computer files by copying itself into your files and then when you open the infected files, the virus executes. Part of a virus' execution may be to spread the infection to other files or corrupting or deleting your files.

To safeguard against this, whenever a file that contains macros is opened in Microsoft Project, a warning is automatically displayed to alert you that the file contains one or more macros and reminds you that macros may contain viruses (see Figure 4.10).

FIG. 4.10
Virus alert message
for files that contain
macros.

You may choose to open the file with the macros enabled, open the file with macros disabled, or cancel the action of opening the file.

This warning message can be turned off if you do not want the system to display the warning each time you open files that contain macros. A control at the bottom of the dialog box allows you to disable this warning. The warning is also on the General tab of the Options dialog box (see Figure 4.11). Choose Tools, Options to display the dialog box. Choose Macro Virus Protection to activate or deactivate this warning.

FIG. 4.11

The General tab of the Options dialog box controls the display of the Macro Virus Protection warning message.

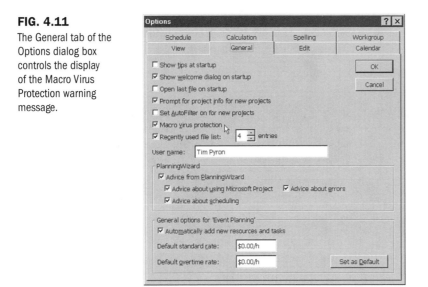

NOTE For additional information on macros, see Chapter 25, "Using Macros in Microsoft Project."

Locating Files

You can search for files by file name, location, and the date the files were created or last saved. Alternatively, files can be located by using the information you enter in the Properties dialog box for each file. You can also search for specific text that occurs in a project document. Specify search criteria as broadly or narrowly as you want. The more you narrow the search, the fewer number of files will be found.

The files found by using the search criteria are listed in the File Open dialog box. As described earlier in this chapter, with this list, you can browse through the directories you included in the search, sort the files in the list, and preview any file without opening it in Microsoft Project. Furthermore, you can view summary information about a file, specifically the file name, title, size, author, and date last saved, or you can view the properties information entered for a file. See the section "Additional Options for Using the Selected File" earlier in this chapter.

Part

I

Ch

4

If you know where the files you are looking for are located, you can indicate specific folders to search. This technique speeds up the process of finding the files because the program does not have to search the entire hard disk. For example, you might know that the files you want to find are in one of the subfolders of the \My Documents directory. In this case, you can limit the search to this subfolder. You also can specify a different drive for a search, such as a floppy drive or a shared network folder.

Specifying Search Criteria for Finding Files

Use the four criteria text boxes at the bottom of the File Open dialog box to select the file names to display. The default selection criterion is that all files must have a Microsoft Project extension (*.MP*). The criterion searches for files that have been last modified *any time*.

You can place search criteria or conditions in more than one of the fields, or in all of them. The more conditions you place on the search, the fewer the file names found and listed.

After you enter the search criteria, use the Find Now button to initiate the search. Use the New Search button to clear the criteria boxes and return them to the defaults.

Searching for Files of a Certain Type

As mentioned previously, the default file type must have a Project extension (*.MP*). The search pattern contains an initial asterisk to mean that the file name can be anything. The file extension must begin with the letters "MP" but the third character can be anything.

The file types that will be found by this pattern include all the extensions used by the latest release, Project 98, as well as those used in releases 3.0 , 4.0, and 4.1 (see Table 4.1).

Table 4.1   There Are Several Different Types of Files in Microsoft Project

Extension	Type of File
*.MPP	Microsoft Project project document
*.MPT	Microsoft Project template
*.MPW	Microsoft Project workspace
*.MPD	Microsoft Project database
*.MPX	Microsoft Project Exchange file for exchanging project data with older releases and with Microsoft Project on the Macintosh

N O T E   Microsoft Project 3.0 or earlier files (.MPP, .MPV, and .MPC) cannot be opened directly into Microsoft Project 98. Open and save these files in release 4.0 or 4.1, and then bring them into release 98 to convert them. Project 98 does not support files from release 3.0 or earlier. ▪

In this version of Microsoft Project, there has been a small change to the .MPX file format, and a new file type Microsoft Project Database (.MPD) has been added. The .MPX file format continues to be available for working with previous versions of Project. This format does not incorporate any of the new features of Project 98. The .MPD file format has been added to provide a more seamless transition between Microsoft Project and Microsoft Access, and provides a quicker way to export a project into Access.

▶ **See** "Exchanging Project Data with Other Applications," **p. 593**

To view a list of a particular file type, you can change the file type by changing the entry in the Files of Type list box. Choose the list arrow to show the file types that can be displayed in Project. Each file type mentioned in the list except the first (All Files *.*) can be imported into Microsoft Project to create new entries in a project document.

The other file types in the list include:

- Text files (*.TXT)
- Comma Separated Value files (*.CSV)
- Excel worksheet files (*.XLS)—Excel 5.0 and later releases only
- Access database files (*.MDB)

N O T E To open a Lotus 1-2-3 file, dBase or FoxPro database, see Chapter 19, "Exchanging Project Data with Other Applications." ▪

Part

I

Ch

4

Searching for Files by the Characters in Their File Names

You also can impose conditions on the file name itself by typing a criterion in the File Name text box. If you know the exact name, you can type it in. If you only know some of the characters in the name, you can use the traditional DOS wildcards (* and ?) to specify a pattern search to find the file name. The asterisk (*) is used for finding multiple characters, the question mark (?) finds a single character. For example, to find all file names containing the letters "plan" anywhere in the file name, type ***plan***. This would find files named: Planning, Game Plan, and Construction Plan. To find all budget files for the '90s (named BUDGET90, BUDGET91, BUDGET92, and so on) type **budget9?**. All file names matching the letters "budget9" exactly, plus one more unspecified character at the end of the name, will be selected.

Searching for Files that Contain Specific Text

Use the Text or Property text box to enter one or more words or character strings to be searched for in the body of the file or in its property fields.

A few rules exist for entering the text string to be used in searching files. You can use partial words or any combination of upper- and lowercase letters. If you search for "an," for example, you get a list of files that contain the words *annual* or *bank*, as well as any other files that have the letters "an" in them. To search for a phrase, such as "subdivision finished," enclose it in double quotation marks. You can use wild cards in the search, and you can combine words, as Table 4.2 shows:

Table 4.2 Examples of Searches Looking for Words or Phrases Which Occur in the Project File

To Search for	Type
A phrase (such as "bank loan")	" " (quotation marks enclose the phrase) Example: type **"bank loan"**.
One word *or* another word	, (comma) Example: type **subdivision,county** to find files containing either "subdivision" or "county."
One word *and* another word	& (ampersand or space) Example: type **subdivision & county** or **subdivision county** to find files containing both "subdivision" and "county."
Files not containing	˜ (tilde) Example: type **subdivision~county** to find files containing "subdivision" but not "county."

N O T E Your text search criteria are preserved for future use. Use the list arrow to see a list of previously used text search criteria and select one to use it again. ▪

Searching for Files by the Date Saved

Use the Last Modified field to search for files based on the date they were last saved. The default criteria is anytime; there is no constraint. Use the list arrow to display a date range to use in the search. You can search for the following times when a file was last saved: yesterday, today, last week, this week, last month, and this month. To use customized date criteria, choose the Advanced button on the right side of the File Open dialog box.

Using the Advanced Find Dialog Box

Use the Advanced button to display the Advanced Find dialog box for creating more complex search criteria (see Figure 4.12). Each of the criteria fields used in the File Open dialog box are represented as a criteria statement on a separate line in the list box at the top of this dialog box.

Use the Define More Criteria options to add more statements to the list of criteria. Enter a category in the Property list box by choosing the list arrow and then choosing a property type. Use the Condition list box to specify how to use the entry in the Value text box. The options displayed in the Condition list box depend on what Property category you choose.

As an example, Figure 4.13 shows a search for files that were last modified between 4/1/97 and 4/20/97. To perform this search, follow these steps:

FIG. 4.12

Use the Advanced Find dialog box to customize file search criteria.

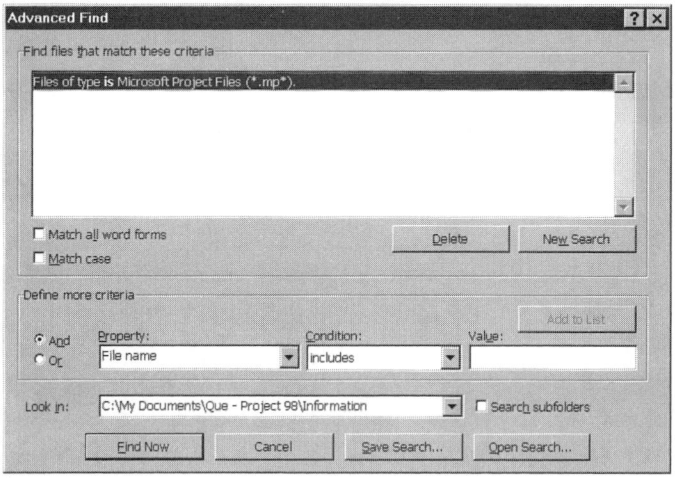

FIG. 4.13

Compose criteria statements with the fields in the Define More Criteria group.

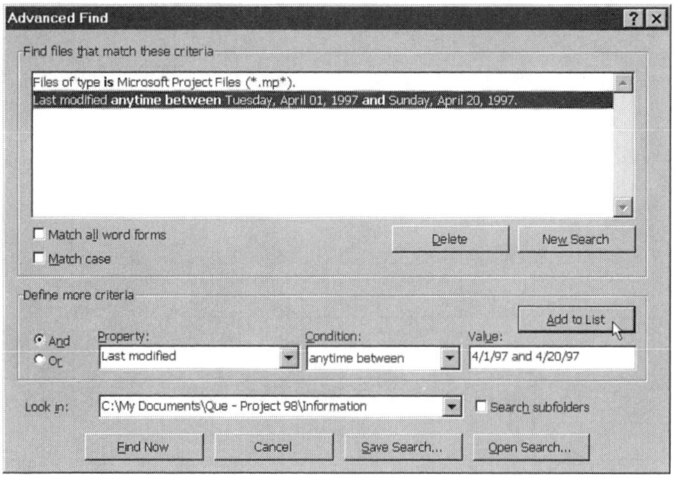

Part

I

Ch

4

1. Choose the And option button if the new criteria must be satisfied in addition to the existing criteria. Choose the Or option button if the new criteria can be used to include a file even if the other criteria are not met.

2. Select Last Modified from the Property list box.

3. Select Anytime Between from the Condition list box.

4. Type **4/1/97 and 4/20/97** (make sure you separate the dates with the word "**and**") in the Value text box.

5. Choose the Add to List button to add the criterion to the previous list.

You can edit criteria that have already been entered by double-clicking the criteria statement in the list. The criteria components are placed in the criteria boxes in the Define More Criteria group. Adjust the criteria definition and choose the Add to List button. Microsoft Project tells you if two conditions on the same property are not permitted, and lets you choose to replace the original criteria.

To remove a single criterion from the list, select it and choose the Delete button. To clear all criteria statements, choose the New Search button.

When your criteria involves searching for a specific word in the text of the file or its properties, select the Match All Word Forms check box to accept variations on the root word. For example, if you select this check box, a search for the word "write" would also accept "wrote" and "written."

If the upper- and lowercase spelling of a word must match exactly, select the Match Case check box.

You can use the Look In text box at the bottom of the dialog box to redefine the location for the search. Select the Search Subfolders check box to extend the search into subfolders that are found in the location you specify.

When you have set all the conditions, choose the Find Now button to initiate the search.

You can save the criteria set for future use by choosing the Save Search button. The Save Search dialog box appears (see Figure 4.14). Supply a name for the set of criteria in the Name for this Search text box and choose OK.

FIG. 4.14

Save customized searches for later use with the Save Search button.

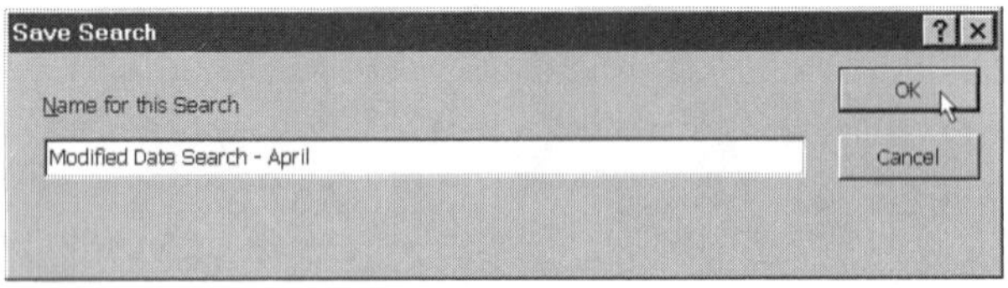

You can reuse a previously saved search by choosing the Open Search button. The Open Search dialog box appears with the list of saved searches in a list box (see Figure 4.15). Select the search you want to use and choose the Open button to load the criteria in the Advanced Find dialog box.

FIG. 4.15

Change the Advanced Find criteria to a previously saved set with the Open Search dialog box.

If you want to rename a saved search, select the old name in the Open Search dialog box and choose the <u>R</u>ename button. Type the new name in the Rename Search dialog box and choose the OK button.

Use the <u>D</u>elete button to delete a saved search. Complete the deletion by choosing <u>Y</u>es in the confirmation dialog box.

Using the ODBC File Open Option

ODBC, Open Database Connectivity, is an interface which allows developers to access data from both relational and non-relational databases. Project 98 can open and save entire projects in database formats. A database can be from any of three sources:

- *A Project 98 database.* The file extension is *.MPD.
- *An Access 97 database.* The file extension is *.MDB.
- *An ODBC source.* An ODBC source looks like a long file name, but it is really an alias for a data collection managed by another computer with drivers that translate between the ODBC source and Project. The actual file format could be Access, SQL, Oracle's database, or a few others that have ODBC drivers already defined.

The ODBC buttons on the File Open and Save dialog boxes just give you access to the sources that have been defined for your computer. The list of sources and drivers is managed by the ODBC applet in the Control Panel.

> **N O T E** It is more reliable when you open a project from a database format which was saved by Project in the first place. ▓

▶ **See** "Exchanging Project Data with Other Applications," **p. 593**

Part

I

Ch

4

Saving and Protecting Files

When you create a new file, or edit an existing one, you will want to save the project document. You can save files as project documents, HTML files, or Workspace files. Additionally, if you are working with a group of people who need access to your project file, you may want to protect the file from accidental changes.

Saving a File

The first time you save a file, the File Save dialog box appears, allowing you to specify how you want to save the file (see Figure 4.16). Choose <u>F</u>ile, <u>S</u>ave from the menu to save the file. Give the file a distinctive name (instead of Project1, Project2, and so on) and choose a different disk drive or directory in which to save the file if you need to.

> **N O T E** File names can be up to 255 characters, including spaces. Certain characters are not permitted, including: / ? \ : * , " < > | ▓

FIG. 4.16
Use the File Save dialog box to change any aspect of the way in which you save a file.

File Save
Save in: Information
Article.mpp
Building Construction.mpp
Computer Conversion.mpp
New Product Development.mpp
Newsletter.mpp
Office Move.mpp
Save
Cancel
ODBC...
Options...
File name: Project1.mpp
Save as type: Project (*.mpp)

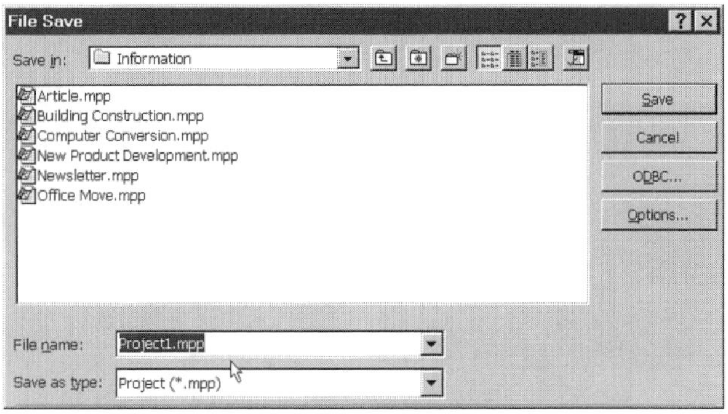

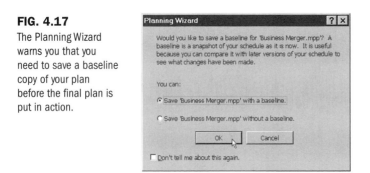

If you have entered tasks or resources into your file, when you save a document for the first time, you see a warning from the Planning Wizard that refers to saving a *baseline* (see Figure 4.17). Although it's very important that you save the baseline after you complete the project plan and before actual work on the project begins, it isn't necessary to save the baseline in the early stages of development. However, the Planning Wizard doesn't know when you add the final touches to your project plan, so it displays the warning from the outset. There's no harm in choosing OK and letting Microsoft Project add the baseline to your project. Just remember to set the final baseline before actual work begins on the project. See Chapter 15, "Tracking Work on the Project" for a description of the baseline and how to use it.

FIG. 4.17
The Planning Wizard warns you that you need to save a baseline copy of your plan before the final plan is put in action.

Planning Wizard
Would you like to save a baseline for 'Business Merger.mpp'? A baseline is a snapshot of your schedule as it is now. It is useful because you can compare it with later versions of your schedule to see what changes have been made.
You can:
Save 'Business Merger.mpp' with a baseline.
Save 'Business Merger.mpp' without a baseline.
OK
Cancel
Don't tell me about this again.

NOTE If you save a new project file, before any task or resource information is added, Microsoft Project will not prompt you to save a baseline. Only after some project data has been added will you see the Planning Wizard prompt about saving a baseline.

You must choose File, Save As if you later want to change any aspect of the way you saved a file. This includes changing the file's name, the location where it is saved, its password security, or the file format in which it is saved.

After you use the File Save dialog box once to establish how to save the file, you can choose File, Save or the Save button on the toolbar to save the file immediately—using its current save properties—without going through the Save As dialog box.

> **CAUTION**
>
> When working with programs (such as MS DOS or Windows 3.1) which only support file names of 8 characters or less, the file name used in Windows 95 or Windows NT 4.0 will be truncated. The first 6 characters of the file name will be followed by a tilde ˜, then by a number, usually a one (1). For example, the file name Office Move.MPP would be displayed as office~1.mpp.

Providing Security for Saved Files

In the File Save dialog box, you can choose the Options button to set the following security features (see Figure 4.18):

- You can make a backup copy of the previous version of a file every time you save the file.
- You can password-protect the file. A user cannot access the file without knowing a password.
- You can write protect the file so others can open and view the file under the original name—but cannot save any changes to using the original file name. Changes can be saved under a different name. This feature protects the data you placed in the file, yet allows others to view the data.
- You can save the file with a warning message saying that you prefer users open the file as a read-only file.

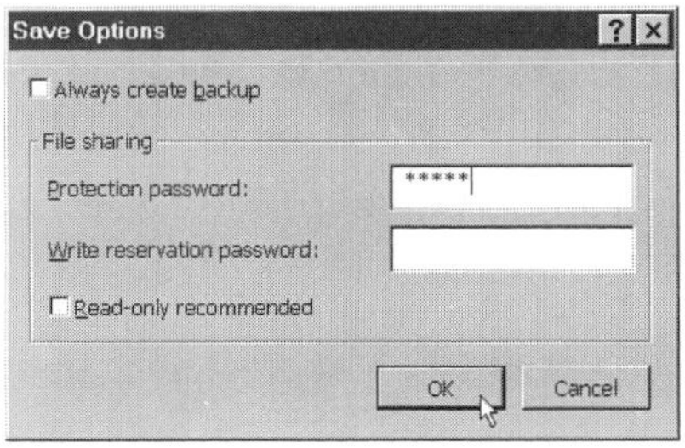

Part

I

Ch

4

FIG. 4.18
You can protect your file from being changed by others or even from being read by others.

Password-Protecting a File To protect a file, type up to 17 characters as a password in the Protection Password text box. You can enter any character, including spaces, numbers, and keyboard symbols. The password is case-sensitive: If you enter capitals anywhere in the password, you must use capitals for those same characters when you supply the password to open the file. As you type the password, each character is represented on-screen by an asterisk. When you choose OK, you are prompted to confirm the password by typing it again (see Figure 4.19). You are notified if you fail to type it exactly the same and will have to reenter the password and confirmation. Choose OK to close the warning and try again.

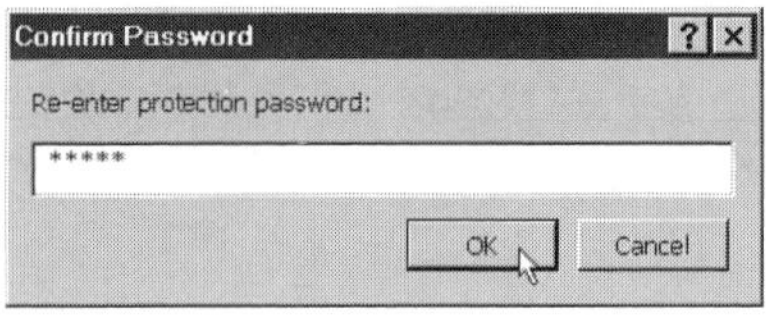

FIG. 4.19

You must type your password a second time to confirm it.

After you specify the security options, if any, choose OK to save the file. The password remains with the file each time you save the file.

When you attempt to open the file, you must enter the password exactly as typed when you saved the password (see Figure 4.20). If you do not enter the password correctly, including the upper- and lowercase of individual characters, you are warned and given another chance to type it correctly. There is no limit to the number of attempts you can make to type in the password.

CAUTION

While it is important to use passwords you can easily remember, it's also a good idea to write down your password and store it in a safe place. If you forget your password, there is absolutely no way to open the file. Not even the people at Microsoft can help you open the file with a lost password!

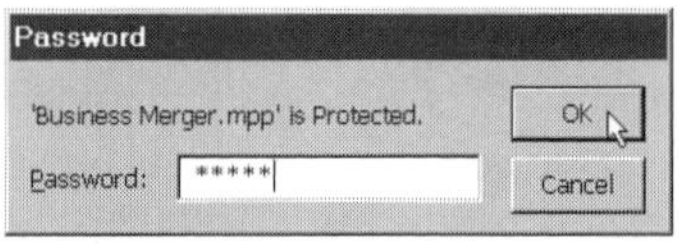

FIG. 4.20

You must match the spelling of the password exactly to gain access to the file.

To remove a password, choose File, Save As. In the Save As dialog box, choose the Options button. Delete all characters from the password field, and choose OK.

Saving a Read-Only File   You can also save a file with a Write Reservation Password by using the Options button in the File Save dialog box. This enables all users to open the file, but a warning appears stating that the file is write-reserved (see Figure 4.21). If the user supplies the correct password in the Password text box, the file opens and the user has the right to make changes and save the file under the same name. If the user doesn't supply the correct password (or forgets the password), the user can only open the file as read-only, and then save changes to the read-only file under a different name. Saving a file with a Write Reservation Password ensures that only users who have the password can replace the data in the file.

FIG. 4.21

Unless you know the password, you cannot open a write-reserved file and save changes to it. You can only open it as read-only.

Saving a File as Read-Only Recommended   If you select the Read-Only Recommended check box in the Save Options dialog box, users who try to open the file are warned that you want them to open the file as a read-only file (see Figure 4.22). Users can choose to accept the Read-Only default, or bypass the warning and open the file with read and write privileges. This option doesn't effectively prevent users from replacing the data in the file, but it does warn the users that the file is shared with others.

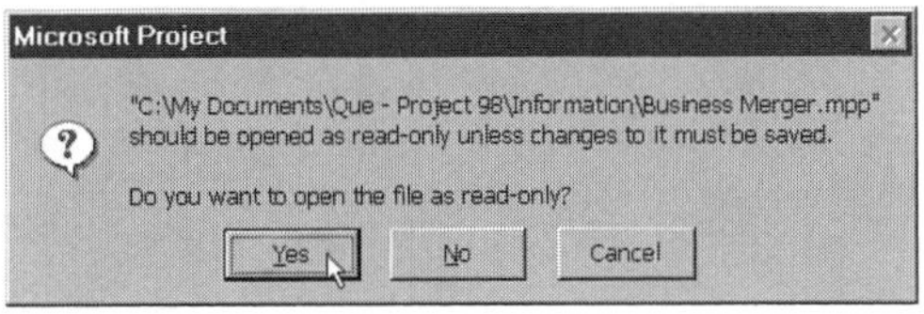

FIG. 4.22

Choose Yes to open a file that was saved as Read-Only Recommended unless you must make changes and save them in the original file name.

Using the Create Backup File Option   If you select the Always Create Backup check box each time you save the file, the original file is renamed by changing the extension from .MPP to .BAK. The revised version of the active file is then saved under the original name with the .MPP extension. This procedure retains a copy of the original version of the file on disk. For example, suppose you created a project file named MOVE.MPP in April. It is now July, and you open the file to make several changes. If the Always Create Backup is active when the revised file is saved, the April version is saved as MOVE.BAK, and the revised file is saved as MOVE.MPP. If you make additional changes to the file in September, the July version *replaces* the April version and is saved with the .BAK extension; the September version will now have the .MPP extension.

Part

I

Ch

4

Saving Files in HTML Format

Project files can be saved in the format (HTML) required by the World Wide Web. Your document can then be published on the Web. To save a file in HTML format, choose File, Save As HTML. For information on Web capabilities, see Chapter 14, "Publishing Projects on the Web."

Saving the Workspace

The File, Save Workspace command saves a small file that contains a list of the names of all the files currently open in memory. When you open a Workspace file, all the files contained in the related list of file names are opened. A Workspace file acts as a *pointer* to the files; it does not contain a *copy* of the files.

Suppose you're working on two files when you go to lunch. If you use the Save Workspace command before you save and close the individual files, you can restore all the files to the screen just by opening the one Workspace file.

The File Open dialog box does not allow you to select multiple files to open; each file has to be opened separately. Creating a Workspace file is the only way to open several project files at the same time, and is a great feature for people who are managing multiple project files.

When you choose File, Save Workspace, the program displays the Save Workspace As dialog box (see Figure 4.23). Workspace file names have the extension .MPW. Microsoft Project suggests a default Workspace file name of RESUME.MPW, but you can change the name in the File Name text box. Unless you choose another drive or directory, the Workspace file is saved in the current directory. Microsoft Project prompts you to save all open files that changed since the last save. You may also see the Planning Wizard warning about saving a baseline if tasks have been added that were not added to the baseline.

N O T E   Project files that are empty will not be added to the Workspace file. You will be prompted to make a decision about including documents in the Workspace file which have data entered in them, but that have not been saved. ■

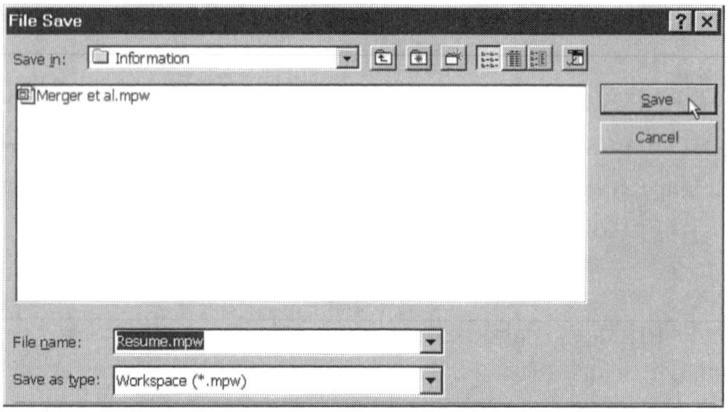

FIG. 4.23

Create and save a Workspace file when you want to be able to open all the Microsoft Project files that are currently open without having to open each individually.

File Save
Save in: Information
Merger et al.mpw
Save
Cancel
File name: Resume.mpw
Save as type: Workspace (*.mpw)

When you open a Workspace file, all active files will be closed before the Workspace file is opened. You will be prompted to save any active file in which changes have been made, but not yet saved. Choose File, Open to open a Workspace file and all the files contained in its list of file names.

Templates

A *template* is a project file that contains a typical or standard set of tasks or resources that is used as a starter for creating similar new project files. Microsoft Project provides six sample templates, but you can create your own templates for repeating or similar projects.

Opening Template Files

When you open a template, you are opening up a copy of the file, not the original template. You use this copy as a starting point for your new project.

To open a template file, choose File, Open or use the Open button on the Standard toolbar. Use the Look In list box to find the appropriate folder. You can also use the search criteria described in the "Locating Files" section earlier in this chapter to locate the template file you want to open. Once you have selected the template you want to open, choose Open, or double-click the file name.

With the exception of the GLOBAL.MPT, the copy of the template that appears will have the same name as the template. When you save the file, the File Save dialog box opens. The name of the template is the default project name. You can use this name or supply a different name.

The GLOBAL.MPT

When you create a new, blank project document, the new file inherits all the features of the Global project template, GLOBAL.MPT. All new projects have generic document titles: Project1, Project2, and so on. The GLOBAL.MPT is stored in the\Program Files\Microsoft Office\Office directory along with the Project program files.

Changes made to the GLOBAL.MPT affect all new project files. The Organizer is used to make changes in the Global template. See the "Using the Organizer" section later in this chapter for more information on modifying the GLOBAL.MPT.

Using the Microsoft Project Sample Templates

Microsoft Project provides several files as sample templates. Table 4.3 lists and describes the Project templates.

Table 4.3   MS Project Sample Template Files

Template Name	Description
Aerospace	This template provides a good illustration of a large multi-year project. Even if you don't have this type of project, the formatting used illustrates some dynamic ways to enhance the display of the project task names and task bars.
Event Planning	Planning a conference or other large event? Use this template to assist you. The three main phases in this project are: Pre-Planning, Event Preparation, and Event Wrap-Up.
Intranet	This template includes a task labeled "Notes about this Template." Use the Task Notes button on the Standard toolbar to view the entire note.
ISO 9000	A set of quality management and quality assurance standards. Tasks in this template include: Select a Project Leader, Initiate a Steering Committee, and Prepare Gap Analysis.
Renovation	This template offers some common steps when renovating a building, whether it be an office building or a private home. Phases include: Construction, Electrical, Plumbing, Telecommunication Installation, and Furnishings.
Software Launch	Marketing a new product? This template includes steps for Advertising, Public Relations, and Beta Testing.

Part

Ch

4

To access a sample template file, choose File, Open or use the Open button on the Standard toolbar. Use the Look In list box to get to the C drive. The sample templates are located in a special folder where all Microsoft application templates are stored. The path is:

C:\Program Files\Microsoft Office\Templates\MS Project

Once you have selected the template you want to open, choose Open, or double-click the file name. When you open one of Microsoft Project's templates, you are opening up a copy of the file, not the original template. Use this copy as a starting point for your own project.

Creating a New Template

Any of your existing project files can be saved as a template for similar or repeating projects.

T I P You can open the former project file, make your changes, and use the File, Save As command to save a copy of the new project with a different name. The advantage of creating a template is that when you save the file, because a template is a copy, you will automatically be prompted for the new file name, thus you will avoid accidentally saving the new file over the former project file.

To save an active file as a template, choose File, Save As. Enter the file name you want to use, and choose Template from the Save As Type list. The file name extension changes to .MPT automatically. When you open a template file, a copy of the file is displayed with the extension automatically changed to .MPP so you can save the working copy as a regular project file.

Modifying Template Files

If you would like to change a template file, there is no way to directly open the .MPT file. Instead, in order to make modifications to a template, you must open a copy of the template, make the desired changes, and save the file under the default name, with the .MPT extension. Choose Template from the Save As Type list to change the file type. The file name extension will change automatically.

Using the Organizer

When you have modified an existing object, like the Standard Base Calendar, or created a new customized view or report, the modified or custom object is only available to the project you are currently working with. The Organizer is a feature that copies objects from one project or template to another. It is most often used to copy modified or custom objects to other project files, or to the GLOBAL template. You also use the Organizer to delete an object which is no longer needed, or to rename an object. The Organizer is set up as a series of tabs, each tab focusing on a different type of object. Table 4.4 lists the types of objects the Organizer keeps track of.

Table 4.4 Objects in the Organizer

Type	Description
Views	Views are screen displays used to enter, organize, and examine your project information. There are views designed to look at primarily task information and views for examining resource oriented information. There are three types of views in Microsoft Project: charts or graphs, sheets, and forms. You can create custom views.
Reports	There are 25 predefined reports in Microsoft Project. You can create custom reports.
Modules	Modules are the location in which macros are stored. Microsoft Project uses Visual Basic to create macros. When you design your own macros, the macro is stored in a module.
Forms	Forms are a specific type of view which provide detailed information about a task or resource. As with views, you can design your own custom forms.
Tables	Tables are used with views like Gantt Chart, Task Sheet, and Resource Sheet. Tables are similar to spreadsheets in that the data is organized in rows and columns. You can create custom tables.
Filters	A filter is a tool used to highlight specific information in a view. There are two types of filters—task filters and resource filters. You can create custom filters.
Calendars	A list of the Base Calendars for a project appears under this tab. You can create custom Base Calendars.
Toolbars	There are 12 toolbars in Project 98. These toolbars can be customized, or you can create your own custom toolbars.
Maps	The Maps tab is used to track data exported to other programs. Export maps are a set of instructions that tracks exactly what types of data are to be exported, relating field to field or (when exporting to Excel) column to column.

Part

I

Ch

4

To make accessing the Organizer easier, Microsoft has added the Organizer to the Tools menu—choose Tools, Organizer.

N O T E The Organizer can also be accessed through several other dialog boxes by choosing:

- View, More Views, Organizer
- View, Table, More Tables, Organizer
- Project, Filter For, More Filters, Organizer

However, the Organizer can no longer be accessed by choosing View, Toolbars. ■

Using the Organizer to Modify the GLOBAL.MPT

In Project 98 you can now open the GLOBAL.MPT file directly, including earlier Global templates (from version 4.1 or 4.0) and transfer objects from your former Global into your Project 98 Global template. When you open the file, it displays the Organizer. If you upgrade Microsoft Project 98 over an older version of Microsoft Project (4.1 or 4.0), customized items in the old Global template will automatically be included in the new GLOBAL.MPT file.

TIP If you make a copy of your former GLOBAL.MPT file (4.0 or 4.1), naming it **GLOBAL41.MPT** for example, and then open this file in Project 98, you will be able to distinguish the two Global template files more easily in the Organizer. Otherwise, since the GLOBAL files in each version have the same name, it can be confusing which GLOBAL.MPT you are looking at.

Copying Objects with the Organizer

The steps that follow access the Organizer through the Tools menu. These steps are generic and can be used when copying any object managed by the Organizer. The active file, the file which contains the object, is referred to as the source file. The file in which you would like to place a copy is referred to as the target file.

Follow these steps to copy an object:

1. If you are copying an object to another file, rather than the GLOBAL.MPT, make sure that the target file is open.

2. Choose Tools, Organizer to display the Organizer dialog box.

3. Choose the tab which contains the object you want to copy. In Figure 4.24, the Tables tab is selected. The tables in the active file are listed on the right. The tables in the GLOBAL.MPT file are listed on the left.

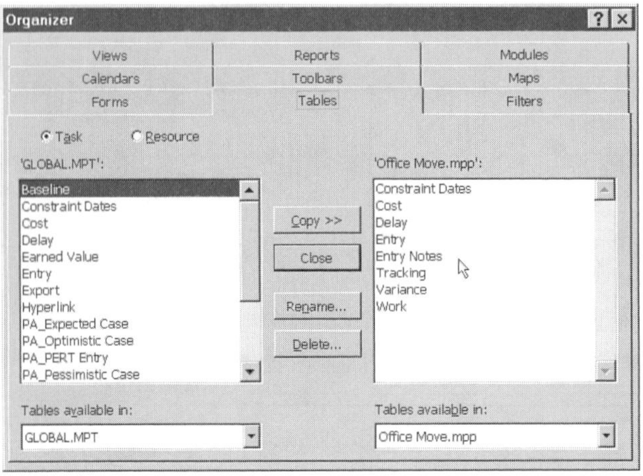

FIG. 4.24

The Organizer dialog box provides access to all the items which can be customized and shared in Project; the Tables tab is displayed in the figure.

If you are copying an object to a file other than the GLOBAL.MPT, use the Tables Available In drop-down list box on the bottom left side to choose the target file. On the right side of the dialog box in Figure 4.25, the Entry Notes table is highlighted in the source file (Office Move), and on the left side of the dialog box, the target file (Building Construction) is being selected.

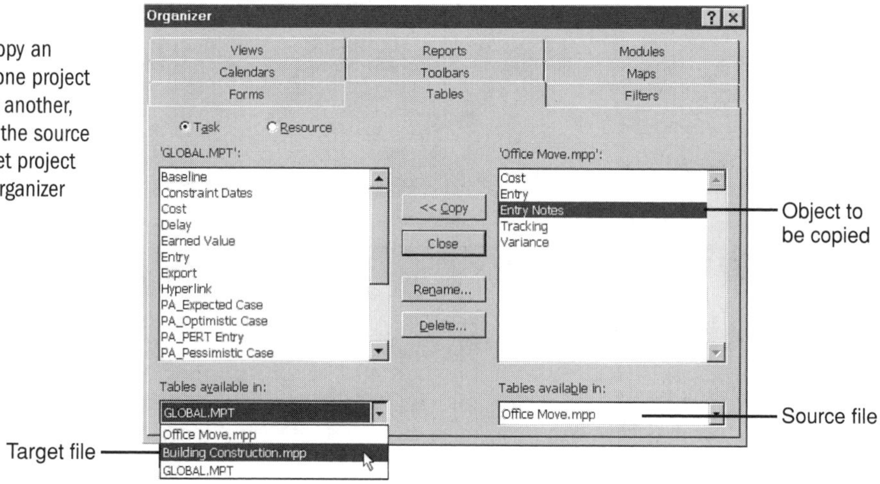

FIG. 4.25

In order to copy an object from one project document to another, display both the source and the target project files in the Organizer dialog box.

Object to be copied

Source file

Target file

4. Choose the table you want to copy from the list of tables in your source file on the right side of the dialog box.

5. Choose the Copy button. If there is a table with the same name in the target file, Project will ask you for confirmation to override the former table (see Figure 4.26).

FIG. 4.26

You must confirm that you want to replace the table by the same name in the target file.

6. Choose the Yes button to replace the table in the target file with the new table from your active file.

   Or, you can use the Rename button to copy the table to the target file by using a new name for the table, a name which is not already being used for another table.

7. Choose the Close button to close the Organizer dialog box.

Part

I

Ch

4

Renaming an Object with the Organizer

You must use the Organizer if you want to rename an object you created in a project document. To rename an object, follow these steps:

1. Open the Organizer and choose the tab for the object you want to rename. In Figure 4.27, the object is the Entry Notes table in the Office Move project.

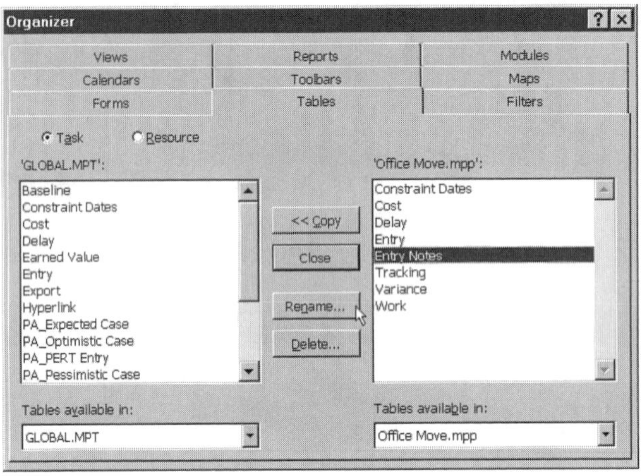

FIG. 4.27

Use the Organizer to rename an object.

2. Select the object to be renamed.

3. Choose the Rename button. The Rename dialog box appears (see Figure 4.28).

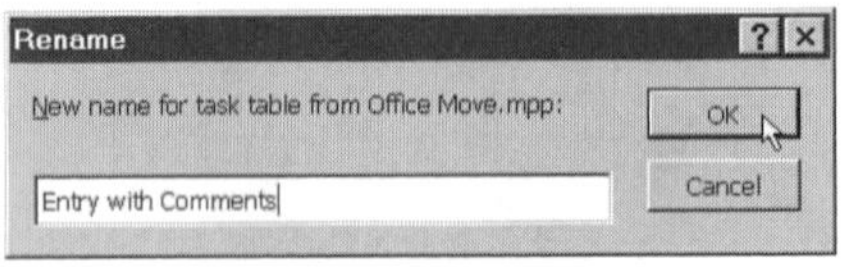

FIG. 4.28

Change the name of a project object in the Rename dialog box.

4. Type the new name for the object.

5. Choose the OK button to complete the name change.

6. Choose the Close button to close the Organizer.

Deleting an Object with the Organizer

Customized objects, like tables, that you create in a project document cannot be deleted with the same menu or dialog box that you used to create them. You must delete them with the Organizer. To delete an object, follow these steps:

1. Activate the Organizer by choosing Tools, Organizer.

2. Choose the tab for the object you want to delete. In Figure 4.29, the object is the Entry Notes table in the Office Move project.

FIG. 4.29

You must use the Organizer to delete customized objects from a project document.

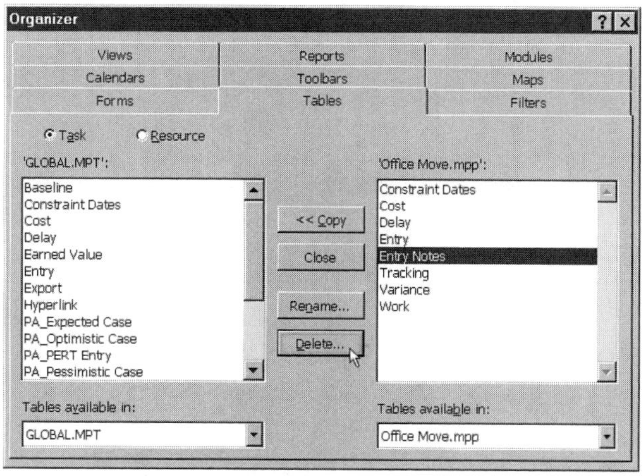

3. Select the object you want to delete.

4. Choose the Delete button. A confirmation dialog box appears (see Figure 4.30).

FIG. 4.30

You must confirm the deletion of any object.

5. Choose the Yes button to confirm the deletion.

6. Choose the Close button to close the Organizer.

Displaying and Closing Files

When you are working with more than one project file, you may want to alternate between your files, display them all at the same time, or close a file. Microsoft Project provides several alternatives for working with and closing your active files.

Using the Window Command

You can have up to 50 files open at the same time, each containing a separate project file. You can place one file at a time on-screen for viewing, or you can place all the files on-screen for simultaneous viewing by using the Window, Arrange All command.

The Microsoft Project Window menu lists up to nine open file windows at the bottom (see Figure 4.31). A check mark indicates the currently active file. You can choose the next file you want to activate by selecting a file from the list.

Part

I

Ch

4

FIG. 4.31

Activate document windows by choosing from the list in the Window menu.

If more than nine file windows are open in memory, the More Windows command appears at the bottom of the Window menu. Choose the More Windows command to access the Window Activate dialog box (see Figure 4.32). The Window Activate dialog box enables you to choose the window you want from a list. Select the file you want to activate, and choose the OK button.

FIG. 4.32

Use the Window Activate dialog box to scroll the entire list of open windows.

You also can use Ctrl+F6 to activate the next window. Pressing Ctrl+F6 again cycles through all the open windows until it returns you to the window you started with. Use Shift+Ctrl+F6 to cycle through the windows in the reverse direction. See Chapter 17, "Working with Multiple Projects," for more information on working with multiple files.

Closing Files

Use the File, Close command to remove an active document from memory. If you have made changes to the document since you last saved it, you are prompted to save the contents before closing. Choose from one of the three choices: Yes, No, or Cancel. Choose Yes to save the file and close the file. Choose No to close the file without saving your changes. Choose Cancel to leave the document open on the Workspace; the file is not saved or closed.

From Here...

In this chapter we discussed file manipulation: opening, locating, saving, protecting, displaying, and closing files. Additionally, you were introduced to project templates and the Organizer.

Now it's time to explore some other topics. The following chapters are recommended:

- Chapter 5, "Creating a Task List," will show you how to list a schedule of tasks in your project file, and create phases and milestones in your task list.
- Chapter 22, "Customizing Views, Tables, and Filters," and Chapter 27, "Customizing Toolbars, Menus, and Forms," describe how to customize project objects, tailoring Microsoft Project for your specific needs.

Part

I

Ch

4

Scheduling Tasks

5   Creating a Task List   125

6   Entering Scheduling Requirements   171

7   Working with the Major Task Views   215

Creating a Task List

Planning a project begins with the creation of a concise but comprehensive goal statement. If the goal of the project is not clearly in focus from the outset, the task list might need extensive revisions and could entail far more work in the long run. After the goal is agreed upon, the next major planning function is to draw up a list of activities or *tasks* that must be completed in order to achieve the project goal.

Using Microsoft Project to help create the task list can save a great deal of time and effort. At this stage of the process, the major contribution of the computer is as a word processing tool to help you enter, revise, and rearrange your ideas.

This chapter begins with the simple mechanics of creating and editing the task list. Alternative ways to enter, edit, and display the task list are described. The chapter ends with instructions for printing the project plan you develop using the procedures in this chapter.

The next chapter deals with defining the constraints (deadlines) and linking dependencies for your tasks. With that information, Project calculates a preliminary schedule with a project start and finish date, as well as start and finish dates for each task. Experienced users frequently enter tasks, outline and link them, and define constraints all at the same time. The steps are divided into separate chapters here because of the many options to be explained for each activity.

Approach the planning process

Methods for defining the task list are discussed. Depending on what information you have and how you think about your project, different methods work better for different people.

Enter and edit project tasks

Just as there are always several different ways to accomplish tasks in Windows, Project offers a variety of ways to capture information about your tasks.

Utilize task sheets and forms

Microsoft Project contains much information about your project; different views offer different perspectives and varying levels of detail that are needed during the life of the project.

Outline the task list

For projects longer or more complex than the simplest ones, an outline provides structure and flexibility for viewing information about your project.

Approaching the Planning Process

There are two basic approaches to creating a task list: the top-down approach and the bottom-up approach. The top-down approach starts by listing the major phases of the project. Then you fill in the details of each phase in an outline format. This method is probably the most common approach to project planning, and it provides an organizational structure that makes it easier to comprehend the scope of the project.

Outlining produces an organizational form that is almost identical to the organization-chart format, traditionally used by project managers, called the *Work Breakdown Structure*, or the WBS. (See Figure 5.1.) The Work Breakdown Structure identifies major components of a project and shows multiple levels of detail under each major component. Work Breakdown Structure (WBS) codes are traditionally used to number each task in such a way that the code identifies where the task fits into the hierarchical structure. These codes are identical to the outline numbers provided automatically by Microsoft Project and can be viewed either on the task list itself or on the Task Information Form (introduced later in this chapter).

FIG. 5.1

Work Breakdown Structure diagrams organize the project tasks into phases or functional groups that help visualize the scope of the project.

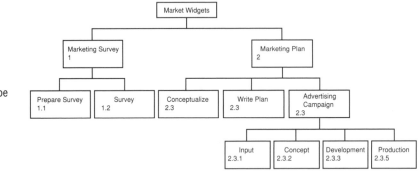

All the entries in an outlined project are *tasks*. All tasks that have subordinate detail tasks are called *summary tasks*. The subordinate tasks are called *subtasks*. The function of the summary task is to summarize the subtasks—whether they be actual things-to-do or other summary tasks.

If you use the bottom-up approach, you begin by listing all the task details. Although it is not required, many people prefer to have the list in somewhat chronological order. If your project is not too complex, this list might be adequate for understanding the scope of the project. For more complex projects, however, you will want to finish by organizing the task list into an outline.

Project simplifies both the top-down and the bottom-up approach. Follow the top-down approach by first entering the major phases as tasks and later insert indented subtasks under the major tasks. Project supports more levels of indentation for subtask detail than you will ever use (over 65,000!). With the bottom-up approach, you start by entering all the detail tasks and then insert summary items for groups of tasks that are indented underneath.

An outline is not necessary for a complete project plan. However, outlining has many advantages and can significantly enhance your project plan's flexibility and usefulness as a planning and reporting tool.

- Outlining encourages an orderly planning process, with less likelihood of leaving out crucial steps.

- You can display outlined projects with different levels of detail both on the screen and in printed reports. You can collapse the outline to major topics only, or to any level of detail, depending on the audience.

- The summary tasks in outlined projects automatically provide summary calculations for the subtasks under them, showing the aggregate duration, cost, and work involved for all the detail tasks taken as a whole.

Entering Tasks in the Gantt Chart

The initial view in Microsoft Project is the Gantt Chart view (see Figure 5.2). If the Gantt Chart view is not on-screen, click the icon for it in the View Bar or choose View, Gantt Chart.

▶ **See** "The View Bar," **p. 34**

FIG. 5.2

The Gantt Chart view of the Product project.

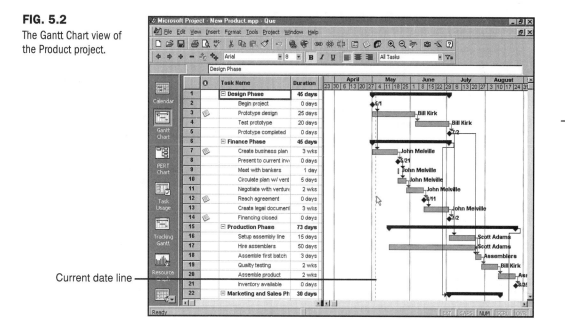

Current date line —

The Gantt Chart displays a list of tasks on the left side of the screen in a spreadsheet type format. On the right side of the screen is a timescale for representing task dates and durations in a horizontal bar-chart format. The task sheet portion of the Gantt Chart is ideal for creating and editing the task list. You can edit the list of tasks and easily rearrange their order. You can

Part

II

Ch

5

include up to 65,000 levels of outlining to organize the project into major phases or processes. Pop-up forms are easily accessible for any task to add or view more details than those provided in the table.

> **T I P** Microsoft Project also provides drag-and-drop features in the Gantt Chart for moving, copying, outlining, linking, and assigning resources.

As you add or edit tasks, the bar chart shows graphically the duration of each task and each task's temporal relationship to other tasks. The default Project bar chart shows the resources assigned to each task to the right of the task bar. Lines with arrows connect tasks to show the dependency links between them. The current date is displayed on the timescale as a vertical dashed line.

▶ **See** "Establishing Dependency Links," **p. 173**

▶ **See** "Formatting Gridlines," **p. 701**

> **N O T E** You also can use other views for creating the task list. Several of these views are discussed later in this chapter in the section "Using Other Views to Enter Tasks." ▪

You can enter a maximum of 1 million tasks in a single project, thus 1 million rows are available in the task table. If you want to visually separate groups of tasks, leave blank rows in the task list. The task IDs at the left of the table are record numbers in the database that Microsoft Project uses for referencing tasks instead of the task name, because duplicate task names are permitted. If you move a task to another location in the list, the task takes on the ID number of the new location.

The task sheet on the left side of the Gantt Chart contains more columns than just the ID, Indicator, Task Name, and Duration fields you initially see. The other columns (Start, Finish, Predecessors, and Resource Names) are hidden behind the timescale chart. You can view them by using the horizontal bar at the bottom of the task sheet. You can also use the mouse to move the vertical divider bar between the sheet columns and the timescale to display more columns or more of the timescale.

> **CAUTION**
>
> Don't enter start or finish dates in these columns. They are intended to be calculated dates based on dependencies that you create in the next chapter. If you enter dates here, a constraint is created which limits the ability of Project to recalculate dates of this task and others linked to it.

▶ **See** "Entering Tasks Constraints," **p. 205**

Creating Tasks in the Gantt Chart

Create a task by typing a name in the Task Name field in one of the rows of the task sheet portion of the Gantt Chart. As soon as you press Enter or move to another cell, Project supplies a default duration of one day for the new task, and displays a task bar starting at the current date under the timescale in the Gantt Chart to the right. Unless you define a different start or finish date in the Project Information dialog box, the start date of the project is initially set to the current date.

N O T E The start date of the project is controlled by a setting in the Options dialog box. On the Schedule tab is a drop-down list called New Tasks Start On. The two available options are Project Start Date (as identified in Project, Project Information) or current date (as specified by the computer's system clock).

To enter a task name, follow these steps:

1. Select a cell in the Task Name column.
2. Type the task name, using any combination of keyboard characters and spaces.

   Task names can contain up to 255 characters and do not have to be unique; you can use the same name for multiple tasks in the same project.
3. Complete the cell entry by pressing Enter, by clicking the green check mark in the entry bar, or by selecting another cell. You can cancel the cell entry before entering it by pressing the Esc key or by clicking the red "x" in the entry bar. The field reverts to its former contents.

If you press Enter to finish the cell entry, Microsoft Project moves the cell selection down to the next row. You can disable this feature by following these steps:

1. Choose Tools, Options. The Options dialog box appears.
2. Select the Edit tab.
3. Deselect the Move Selection After Enter check box.
4. Choose the OK button to close the Options dialog box.

If you disable the Move Selection After Enter option, you can still have the active cell selection move down automatically during data entry when you want by selecting the group of cells you plan to type in before you start typing:

- If you include more than one column in the selected group of cells, when you press Enter, the active cell moves from the bottom of one column to the top cell in the next column.
- Press the Tab key to move the active cell to the right instead of down, automatically advancing from the last column in a row to the beginning of the next row.
- Use the Shift key to reverse the direction of the move. Shift+Enter moves up and Shift+Tab moves left.

If you want several cells in a column to have the same entry (for example, many tasks with the same duration), place the entry in one cell and have Project fill the other cells with the same entry. To fill multiple cells with the same entry, follow these steps:

Part

II

Ch

5

1. Type the entry in one cell.

2. Press and hold the Ctrl key as you click other cells below and in the same column as the cell containing the entry. The cells do not have to be in adjacent rows.

3. Choose Edit, Fill and then the desired direction (Down, Right, Up, or Left) to fill the adjacent cells with the same entry that is in the selected cell. You can also right-click with the mouse pointer in the selected area and choose Fill Down.

Using the AutoCorrect Feature while Typing   Microsoft Project 98 includes an AutoCorrect feature that automatically corrects common typing errors as you type. These typing errors could be spelling, simple grammatical errors, or misplaced spaces. For example, if you type **comittee**, AutoCorrect replaces the word with the correctly spelled "committee" as soon as you press the space bar or place a punctuation mark. In addition, if you type **might of been**, AutoCorrect replaces the phrase with "might have been."

AutoCorrect also automatically capitalizes the names of the days of the week. If you mistakenly hold the Shift key too long and capitalize two letters at the beginning of a word (such as PRoject), AutoCorrect changes the second letter to lowercase.

▶ **See** "Checking for Spelling Errors," **p. 402**

If AutoCorrect changes a word you want left unchanged, you can simply change it back and AutoCorrect will leave it alone. If you never want a particular change to be made, you can add the word to the exceptions list in AutoCorrect. Of course, you can still run the spell checker to locate spelling mistakes.

You can turn off all or part of the AutoCorrect features, and you can add your own frequent misspellings to the list of corrections to be made automatically. You also can use AutoCorrect to replace abbreviations to save time as you type. For example, you can set AutoCorrect to replace "abc" with "ABC Manufacturing Co." To make changes in AutoCorrect, follow these steps:

1. Choose Tools, AutoCorrect. The AutoCorrect dialog box appears (see Figure 5.3).

FIG. 5.3

AutoCorrect can significantly speed up your typing because it corrects many of the most common typing mistakes.

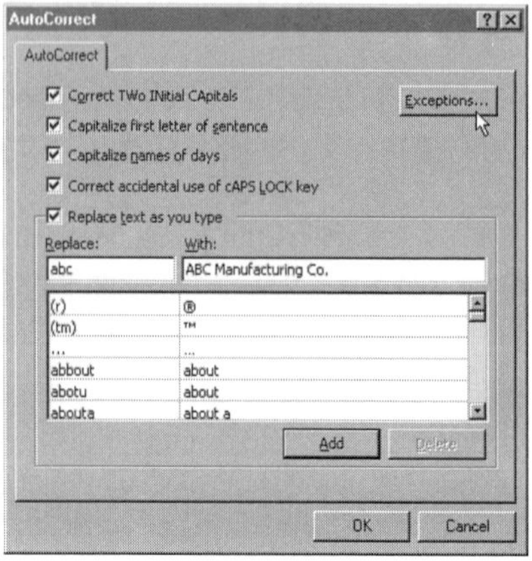

2. Deselect an option if you want to disable that AutoCorrect function. For example, deselect Replace Text as You Type if you don't want AutoCorrect to replace what you type with different spellings. (Select it again to turn it back on.)

3. In the Replace text box, type a word or character string you want to be replaced automatically each time you type it. For example, to replace "abc" with "ABC Manufacturing Co.," type **abc** in the Replace text box.

4. Press the tab key and type into the With text box the replacement word or phrase. For the "abc" example, type **ABC Manufacturing Co.**.

5. Choose the Add button to add your replacement text to the list at the bottom of the dialog box. Add as many replacement text items as you want by repeating steps 3 through 5.

6. Delete an AutoCorrect entry by selecting the entry in the list at the bottom of the dialog box and then choosing the Delete button.

7. When all additions and deletions are completed, choose the OK button to close the AutoCorrect dialog box.

If you want to change the replacement text supplied by AutoCorrect, follow these steps:

1. Choose Tools, AutoCorrect to open the AutoCorrect dialog box.

2. From the list at the bottom of the dialog box, click the item you want to change. This places it in the Replace and With text boxes, or, simply type the item in the Replace text box.

3. Enter or edit the text in the With box. The moment you add text to the With box, the Replace button becomes available (see Figure 5.4). In the figure, the abbreviation "Co." has been changed to "Company."

FIG. 5.4

You can modify the replacement text supplied by AutoCorrect.

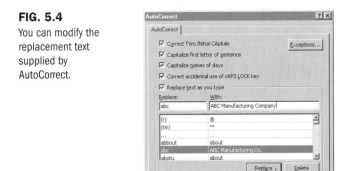

4. Choose the Replace button. A warning dialog box asks you to confirm the change (see Figure 5.5).

Part
II

Ch
5

FIG. 5.5

You must confirm any change to an AutoCorrect entry.

5. Choose Yes to confirm the change.

6. After you've entered all changes, choose OK to close the AutoCorrect dialog box.

If you want to change the way AutoCorrect makes changes to capitalization without turning the features off altogether, follow these steps:

1. Choose Tools, AutoCorrect to open the AutoCorrect dialog box.

2. Choose the Exceptions button.

3. Enter or edit the text in the Don't Capitalize After box on the First Letter tab or in the Don't Correct box on the INitial CAps tab.

4. Choose the OK button to close the AutoCorrect dialog box.

N O T E   The AutoCorrect list is shared among the various Microsoft products; therefore any entries added or changed are also reflected in any other Microsoft products that you use. Likewise, any changes made in the AutoCorrect list of other products will also be reflected in Project. ▪

Adjusting Column Widths in the Gantt Chart   If the task name is too long to see in the Task Name column, you can adjust the width of the column. To change the width of a column, follow these steps:

1. Move the mouse to the right edge of the column heading for the column you want to adjust. For example, to widen the Task Name field, move to the column divider line to the right of that heading (between the headings Task Name and Duration).

2. When the mouse pointer changes to a double-headed arrow, drag the column border to the right or left to suit your needs.

3. Release the mouse button.

You can also have Project calculate the widest entry in the column and adjust the column to that width. To adjust the column width to the longest entry, follow these steps:

1. Move the mouse pointer over the divider line to the right of the column heading for the column you want to adjust.

2. When the mouse pointer changes to a double-headed arrow, double-click the divider line, and the column adjusts automatically to the widest entry in the column.

T I P   If you don't place the mouse pointer directly on the divider line, double-clicking the mouse might open the Column Definition dialog box (shown in Figure 5.6). Select the Best Fit button to have Project adjust the column width to the widest entry or type a specific number of characters for the column width.

FIG. 5.6

Use the Column
Definition dialog box to
redefine properties of
the column.

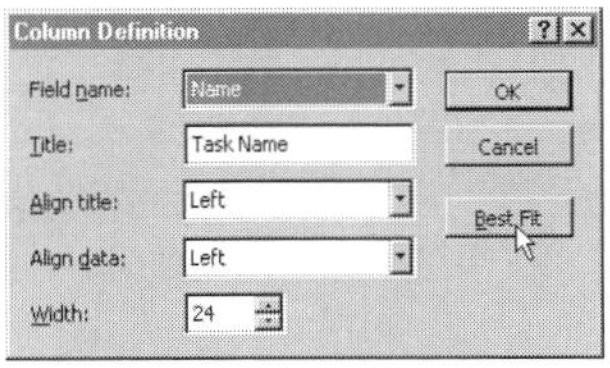

Adjusting the Height of Task Rows For long task names, you might want to use two or more
lines to display the task name. Project automatically word-wraps task names if extra lines are
available and the task name is longer than the column width can display. Figure 5.7 shows
word-wrapped task names.

FIG. 5.7

You can use more than
one row to display each
task in the Gantt Chart.
This allows long task
names to word-wrap.

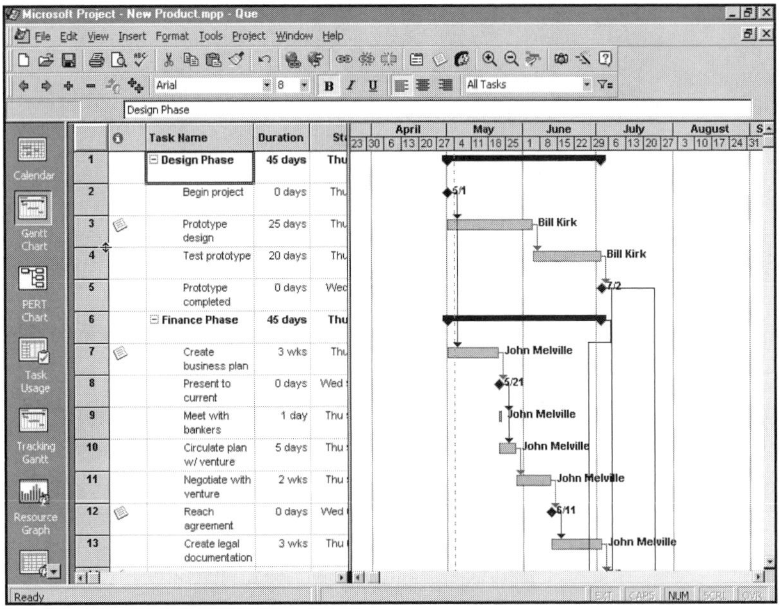

To adjust the number of lines displayed for each task name, follow these steps:

1. Position the mouse on the row divider line in the task ID column. The mouse pointer
changes to up and down arrows (notice the mouse pointer between task ID 3 and 4 in
Figure 5.7).

2. Drag the divider line up or down to change the height of the task rows. You cannot
change the height of just one task row; all row heights change together.

N O T E If you fail to position the pointer correctly you simply select multiple rows as you drag the
mouse pointer. The highlighted rows display in black. If this happens, click anywhere in the
task sheet and try again.

Part

II

Ch

5

Entering Task Durations

When you create a task name, Project assigns the task a default duration of one day. The display of one day may vary depending on the unit of time set for displaying duration and the default number of hours per work day. If the number of work hours per day is eight, the default duration will be displayed as 8h, 1d, or .2w.

> **T I P**   You can change the units in which the duration is expressed by choosing Tools, Options, and then from the Schedule tab choose the appropriate option from the Duration Is Entered In drop-down list.

▶ **See** "Selecting the Environment Options," **p. 70**

A horizontal bar for the task appears on the timescale side of the Gantt Chart. The bar starts at the current date unless you designated a different start date for the project. If the project start date is not the current date, the task bar might not be visible until you scroll to the date for the start of the project.

> **T I P**   Press Alt+Home to jump to the start date of the project on the timescale or Alt+End to jump to the end date of the project. Use the Go To Selected Task button on the Standard toolbar (or Ctrl+Shift+F5) to go to the beginning of the selected task.

You can enter estimates of task durations as you create the task names, or you can list all the task names first and come back to estimate the durations. This chapter follows the first course and discusses the duration field before finalizing the task list entries.

Understanding the Duration Field   The duration of a task is measured in time units: minutes, hours, days, or weeks. When entering duration units, you can use an abbreviation or the full word. For example, you can type **d**, **dy**, or **day**; **w**, **wk**, or **week**; and so on. When you enter a duration estimate in day or week units, Project internally converts these units to hours, based on the definitions for these terms as set in the Tools, Options dialog box. When you set a duration of 12 hours, you mean that it will be twelve hours of regularly scheduled work time from the time the task starts to the time it ends.

Suppose the base calendar for your project is the default Standard calendar with five eight-hour days of work per week. If you enter a 12-hour task that starts at 8:00 a.m., the task will be complete at 12 p.m. on the following workday. If work starts at 8:00 a.m. on a Friday, the task will end after 12 regular working hours—by noon the following Monday.

The task bar on the Gantt Chart starts at the scheduled start time and stretches to the scheduled finish time for a task. If the task duration spans an evening, weekend, holiday, or other non-working time period, the bar will cross over the intervening non-working time.

> **N O T E**   The task bar is normally solid from the start to the end of the task, appearing in front of any shading on the Gantt Chart for non-working time. Choosing Format, Timescale, you can display the non-working time shading in front of the task bar so the solid parts of the bar reflect only actual working time. ▪

▶ **See** "Changing the Display of Nonworking Time," **p. 707**

Defining Elapsed Duration   You can create a task to represent a *continuous* activity or process that continues around the clock. If a chemical process takes five hours, for example, that usually means five continuous hours. If the process starts at 3:00 p.m., it continues until 8:00 p.m. the same day. The Working Time calendar in Project assumes that work stops at 5:00 p.m. To schedule a task that should not be restricted by the working time calendar, enter the duration as *elapsed* time. To do this, insert the letter "e" before the time unit abbreviation. The duration estimate for the chemical process, for example, would be 5eh to represent five elapsed (continuous) hours.

> **CAUTION**
>
> Project automatically defines a task with an elapsed duration as a *fixed duration* task. This designation will only have an effect on your schedule if you assign resources to the task.

Figure 5.8 illustrates the differences between normal and elapsed duration. Task ID number 1 is a task with a normal five-day duration. Work begins on a Thursday but is interrupted by the weekend. Work is continued on the following Monday through Wednesday for a total of five work days. The task bar looks longer (seven calendar days) than the actual working days. Total work during the period is 40 hours (five 8-hour work days).

Task ID number 2 is a task with an elapsed duration of five days. Project schedules work on the task around the clock for five 24-hour time periods. Work continues through the weekend days and the holiday. Total work during the period is 120 hours (five 24-hour work days).

FIG. 5.8

Work on elapsed duration tasks proceeds through non-working times and continues for 24 hours per day.

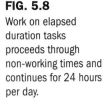

Part

II

Ch

5

Understanding Duration for Summary Tasks   Project calculates the duration for a summary task; you cannot modify this. The summary task start date is the earliest start date of any of its subtasks, and the summary task finish date is the latest finish date of any of its subtasks. The duration of the summary task is the amount of work time on the base calendar between that earliest start date and the latest finish date. A summary task whose first subtask starts at 8:00 a.m. one day and whose last subtask finishes at noon the next day would have a duration of 1.5 days (twelve working hours).

The duration for summary tasks is always displayed with the default setting for the Duration Is Entered In option on the Schedule tab of the Tools, Options dialog box. This is true even when the subtasks are expressed in other duration units. To change the duration units for summary tasks, you must change this setting. For further explanation, see the section "Outlining the Task List."

Estimating the Task Duration   When estimating durations, you should consider past experience with similar tasks, the experience and skill level of the resources you plan to use, and the number of resources you plan to use. When you assign the resources to the task, Project assumes the number of resource units you assign is the number you had in mind at the time you entered the duration.

▶ **See** "Understanding Resource-Driven and Fixed Duration Scheduling," **p. xxx** (Chapter 9)

Entering the Duration   The default duration for a new task is one day. If you want to enter a duration estimate of three days, you only have to enter **3** in the Duration column and the default duration unit d for day will be applied. You only need to supply a duration unit if the estimated duration is in a unit other than days.

To type a different duration estimate for a task, follow these steps:

1. In the Duration column of the Gantt Chart table, select the duration field for the task you want to change.

2. Type the duration, using the following abbreviations for the time units:

Abbreviation	Can Be Displayed As	Meaning
m or em	m, min, minute	Minutes or elapsed minutes
h or eh	h, hr, hour	Hours or elapsed hours
d or ed	d, dy, day	Days or elapsed days
w or ew	w, wk, week	Weeks or elapsed weeks

3. Complete the entry by pressing Enter or by selecting another field.

You can choose which label displays in the duration field using the Tools, Options dialog box. There is a drop-down list for each of the available time units on the Edit tab. These settings are for the current project file only. Choose the Set as Default button to have these settings apply to all newly created project files.

N O T E The duration labels in this version of Microsoft Project are smart. If the duration is greater than one, the label will change as appropriate. For example, 1 day, 2 days, 1 min, 2 mins, and so on. ▪

The default duration supplied when you enter a task name is always one day, but it can be displayed in minutes, hours, days, or weeks, depending on your selection in the Tools, Options dialog box. To change the default duration, follow these steps:

1. Choose Tools, Options to open the Options dialog box.
2. Choose the Schedule tab.
3. Change the Duration Is Entered In option.
4. Choose OK to close the Options dialog box.

If you defined Hours Per Day with something other than 8 hours on the Calendar tab of the Options dialog box, the default duration will not be an 8-hour day.

Using the PERT Analysis Toolbar to Estimate Durations   Quite often the task of estimating the duration for the tasks in your project is a project in itself. It's often reduced to guesswork. A popular technique is to use a weighted average of a combination of three estimates: a pessimistic one, an optimistic one, and the most likely one. Project now provides for the calculation of this weighted average for you and has a new toolbar to use.

Start by turning on the PERT Analysis toolbar. The easiest way to do this is to point to any place on a toolbar and right-click. Choose PERT Analysis from the shortcut menu that appears. You can also choose View, Toolbar, and then PERT Analysis (see Figure 5.9).

FIG. 5.9
The PERT Analysis
toolbar offers an easy
way to estimate
durations for tasks.

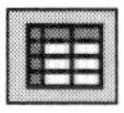

Part
II

Ch
5

With the PERT Analysis toolbar displayed, you have two choices of how to enter the three estimates. You can use the PERT Entry Sheet, a spreadsheet format with columns for optimistic, pessimistic, and expected durations (see Figure 5.10).

Instead of using a spreadsheet format, you may be more comfortable working with a form type format: the PERT Entry Form. This form displays one task at a time, with a field for each of the three duration estimates (see Figure 5.11). It doesn't matter which of these methods you use—either way the information is placed in the PERT Entry Sheet.

Figure 5.12 displays the dialog box that appears when you use the PERT Weights tool on the PERT Analysis toolbar. You can change the way each estimate is weighted in this dialog box. The default, shown in Figure 5.12, tends to give the most recognition to the value that you think is most likely. If situations make you feel overly optimistic or pessimistic, you may want to increase the number for those options. Notice that for reasons dictated by statistical theory, the total of the weights must add to 6.

FIG. 5.10

The PERT Entry Sheet provides one way to enter different duration estimates.

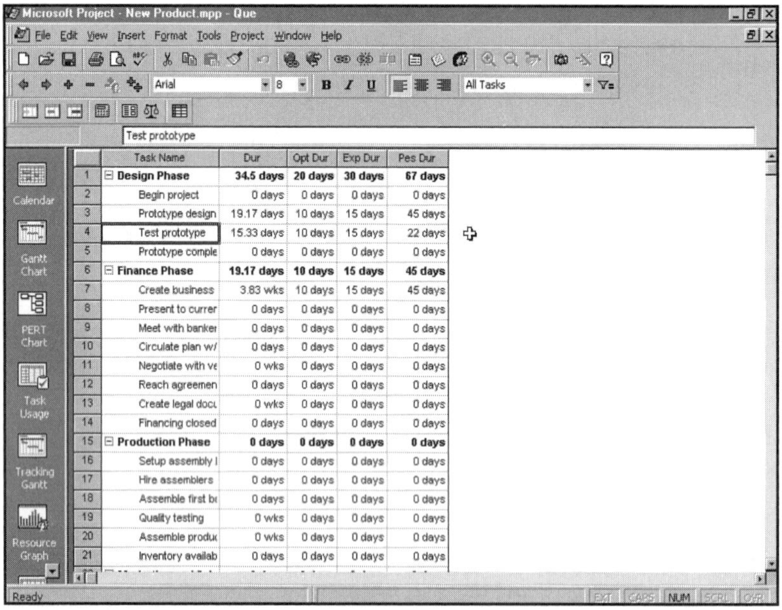

	Task Name	Dur	Opt Dur	Exp Dur	Pes Dur
1	**Design Phase**	**34.5 days**	**20 days**	**30 days**	**67 days**
2	Begin project	0 days	0 days	0 days	0 days
3	Prototype design	19.17 days	10 days	15 days	45 days
4	Test prototype	15.33 days	10 days	15 days	22 days
5	Prototype comple	0 days	0 days	0 days	0 days
6	**Finance Phase**	**19.17 days**	**10 days**	**15 days**	**45 days**
7	Create business	3.83 wks	10 days	15 days	45 days
8	Present to currer	0 days	0 days	0 days	0 days
9	Meet with banker	0 days	0 days	0 days	0 days
10	Circulate plan w/	0 days	0 days	0 days	0 days
11	Negotiate with ve	0 wks	0 days	0 days	0 days
12	Reach agreemen	0 days	0 days	0 days	0 days
13	Create legal docu	0 wks	0 days	0 days	0 days
14	Financing closed	0 days	0 days	0 days	0 days
15	**Production Phase**	**0 days**	**0 days**	**0 days**	**0 days**
16	Setup assembly l	0 days	0 days	0 days	0 days
17	Hire assemblers	0 days	0 days	0 days	0 days
18	Assemble first ba	0 days	0 days	0 days	0 days
19	Quality testing	0 wks	0 days	0 days	0 days
20	Assemble produc	0 wks	0 days	0 days	0 days
21	Inventory availab	0 days	0 days	0 days	0 days

FIG. 5.11

The PERT Entry Form.

FIG. 5.12

The Set PERT Weights dialog box enables you to adjust weights to be more pessimistic or more optimistic.

Once you have entered all the estimated durations, choose the Calculate PERT tool in the PERT Analysis toolbar. Project will calculate the duration. You can overwrite the calculated duration if you want, but it will be recalculated if you use the Calculate PERT tool again.

CAUTION

Save your file before using this feature! Any durations that have been manually entered will be set back to zero. If you want to keep Project from recalculating the duration estimates you don't want calculated, you have to fill in the three estimated fields with the same value you want returned by the calculation. If you accidentally set your durations to zero, close the file without saving and then open it again. Undo is not available for this feature.

The other tools on the PERT Analysis toolbar offer:

- The Optimistic Gantt chart shows a calculated set of optimistic durations. The statistical theory behind the PERT model says that you can be 95 percent certain that the actual durations will not be shorter than these optimistic calculations.

- A Gantt chart that uses your expected durations as a guide.

- The Pessimistic Gantt chart shows a set of pessimistic durations that you can be 95 percent certain are as bad as it will get.

Locating the Current Task Bar on the Gantt Chart

If you can't see the task bar for a task on the Gantt Chart, you can make Project scroll to the beginning date for the task by choosing the Go To Selected Task button on the Standard toolbar or by pressing Ctrl+Shift+F5. You can scroll instantly to the start date of the overall project by pressing Alt+Home. Scroll instantly to the finish date for the project by pressing Alt+End.

You can also use the Go To command to go directly to a specific task or a specific date on the timescale. Follow these steps:

1. Choose Edit, Go To (or press F5). The Go To dialog box appears (see Figure 5.13).

FIG. 5.13
Use the Go To dialog box to locate a specific date or a task by its ID number.

2. In the Date text box, enter the date to which you want to move or select the drop-down list to display a calendar from which you can select a date.

You can also enter **today** or **tomorrow** to jump directly to these dates. If you enter a three-letter weekday abbreviation, such as Tue., Wed., and so on, Project jumps directly past today's date to the next occurrence of that weekday.

3. To move to a specific task, type a task ID in the ID text box.

4. Choose OK.

Part
II

Ch

5

N O T E   If you supply a task ID number in the ID text box, Project scrolls to the row for the task ID
number and also scrolls the timescale to bring the beginning of the task bar into view. If
you specified a date, the timescale section of the Gantt Chart moves but the task list does not. ▪

Entering Milestones

The *milestone task* is a special type of task that represents a significant landmark, development, or turning point in the life of the project. You commonly use milestones to mark the completion of major phases or other major events in the project. A milestone is most easily defined by entering a task name and assigning it a duration of zero. Milestones typically do not represent the *doing* of work; they signal that the work has started or is completed. Milestones represent a point in time when something happens, whereas the ordinary tasks stretch out over time and represent continuing activity.

You might want to create milestone tasks at points you want to monitor closely in the project. In a project to construct a building, for example, one milestone might be the completion of all the tasks involved in laying the foundation. The milestone could be named Foundation Complete and have a duration of zero. If you enter **0** in the duration field for a task, Project makes the task a milestone.

N O T E   You can mark *any* task as a milestone, even if it has a non-zero duration. To change a task
to a milestone, or to remove its milestone designation, select the task and choose the
Information button on the Standard toolbar, or double-click the task. Choose the Advanced tab and
click the Mark Task as Milestone check box to change its milestone status. Choose OK to close the
dialog box. ▪

The Gantt Chart displays a milestone as a diamond shape, without a duration bar (see Figure 5.14). You can modify the symbol for a milestone and for all other task bars with the Format, Bar Styles command in the Gantt Chart view.

▶ **See** "Formatting the Gantt Chart," **p. 709**

Figure 5.14 illustrates a useful display of milestones. In this view, only milestone tasks are showing and the timescale has been adjusted to show the entire life of the project on one screen. This view focuses on the important dates in the project. To set up this view, follow these steps:

1. Open the project and choose the Gantt Chart from the View bar on the left side of the screen or from the View menu.

   ▶ **See** "Using the Standard Filters," **p. 686**

   | All Tasks ▾ |

2. To isolate just the milestones, choose Milestones from the filters drop-down list on the Formatting toolbar (see Figure 5.15).

Part

Ch

5

FIG. 5.14

Project represents milestones with the diamond shape on Gantt Charts.

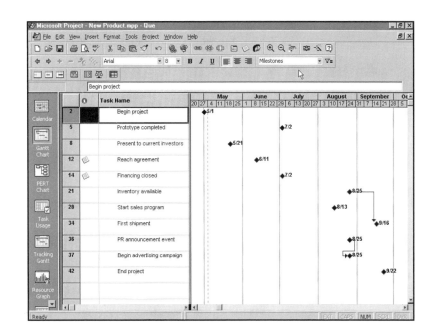

FIG. 5.15

Choose the Milestones filter to display only milestones.

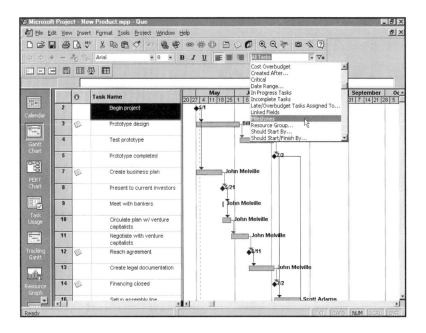

3. To compress the timescale to fit the entire project on one screen, choose View, Zoom. The Zoom dialog box appears (see Figure 5.16).

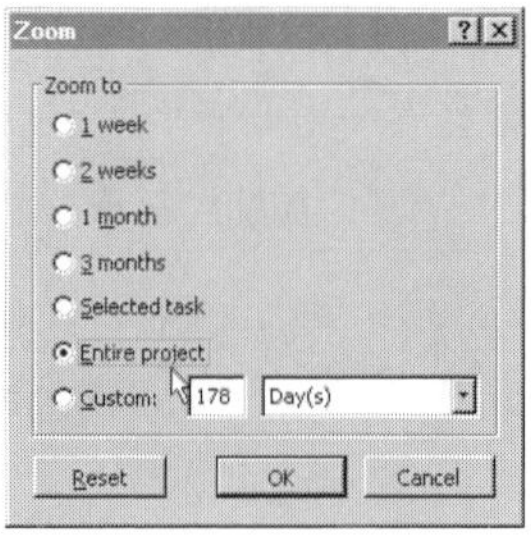

FIG. 5.16

Use the Zoom dialog box to compress the entire project to one screen.

Zoom ? X

Zoom to
○ 1 week
○ 2 weeks
○ 1 month
○ 3 months
○ Selected task
● Entire project
○ Custom: 178 Day(s)

Reset   OK   Cancel

4. Select the Entire Project option.

5. Choose OK to implement the change.

To return the display to the default timeline, choose View, Zoom again and choose the Reset button. Then choose OK to implement the change. To clear the filter, choose All Tasks from the filter drop-down list on the Formatting toolbar (or press F3).

 TIP You can also access the Zoom command by right clicking while pointing at the timescale heading.

Entering Recurring Tasks

Occasionally, you will need to add a task to your project that regularly repeats through the life of the project (such as recurring meetings, inspections, and so on). Project allows you to represent regularly recurring events as *recurring tasks*. A weekly project status meeting with a duration of three hours every Monday at 2:00 p.m. is a good example of a recurring task.

To insert a recurring task in your task list, follow these steps:

1. From any task view, select the Task Name field on the row where you want to insert the recurring task. You don't have to create a blank row for each recurring task, it is inserted automatically.

2. Choose Insert, Recurring Task. The Recurring Task Information dialog box appears (see Figure 5.17).

3. Type the task name in the Name text box and the duration of each occurrence of the task in the Duration text box.

4. From the This Occurs group, choose a general frequency: Daily, Weekly, Monthly, or Yearly. In Figure 5.17, the Weekly option has been selected.

5. Choose the specific frequency in the group to the right of This Occurs.

   This group varies depending on the general frequency you choose. If you choose Weekly, you can specify a frequency ranging from every week to every twelfth week in the Week On drop-down list. Next, select the day of the week you want to schedule the tasks on. The specific frequency choices for Daily, Monthly, and Yearly are discussed later in this section.

FIG. 5.17

Use the Recurring Task Information dialog box to add tasks that repeat regularly.

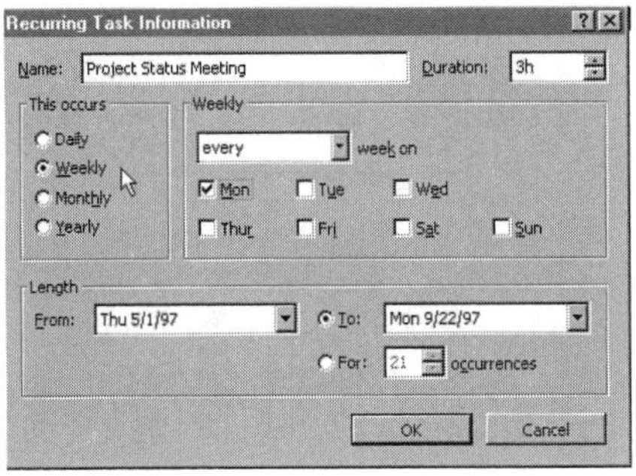

6. Next, define the length of the recurring task by defining the date range within which the tasks should be scheduled, or by specifying the number of times you want the task scheduled.

7. Choose OK or press Enter to complete the recurring task definition.

Once entered, the recurring task is placed in the task list as a specially formatted summary task (see Figure 5.18).

N O T E Initially, the From and To text boxes show the start and finish dates for the project and the For Occurrences text box shows the calculated number of occurrences that can be scheduled in that date range.

Specify a start date or time of day from the start date of the project in the From text box. For example, if you want the tasks to be scheduled at a specific time of day, enter the time as well as the date in the From text box. To select a date from a calendar, click the drop-down list next to either the From or To text box. If you want the first occurrence of the recurring task to start sometime after the project starts, change the From date. ■

N O T E If you are entering a whole hour, you need only type the number of the hour and either **am** or **pm** (refer to Figure 5.17). ■

N O T E Change the To text box if you want to specify when the last occurrence of the recurring task should be scheduled.

Alternatively, select the For Occurrences option and enter a number if you want to specify how many occurrences are to be scheduled. ■

CAUTION

If you enter a number larger than the calculated default, Project schedules the number you enter but the later occurrences will be beyond the original finish date of the project and it will extend the life of your project. You can tell if this has happened by looking up the project finish date in the Project Information dialog box (choose Project, Project Information) or any view that displays the finish date of the project, such as the Gantt Chart.

T I P An icon representing recurring tasks is displayed in the indicators column to the left of the task name. A tip showing the number of occurrences and the date range displays when the mouse rests on the icon for a moment.

The duration of the summary task is the number of working calendar days that lapse between the first occurrence and the end of the last occurrence of the recurring task. In Figure 5.18, the Duration column for the recurring task shows 125.38 days, but this doesn't mean that those who attend the meetings log a total of 125.38 days of meeting time. Rather, the last meeting ends 125.38 days after the first meeting begins.

In Figure 5.18, the task ID numbers between 5 and 30 do not appear. That's because the summary task for the recurring task has 26 subtasks (the individual meetings) that are hidden from view. Each of the subtasks is *rolled up* to the summary task bar; for example, the summary task bar displays markers for the subtasks and, in this special format, does not display a normal summary task bar.

FIG. 5.18

The summary task for recurring task displays on a single row of the Gantt Chart.

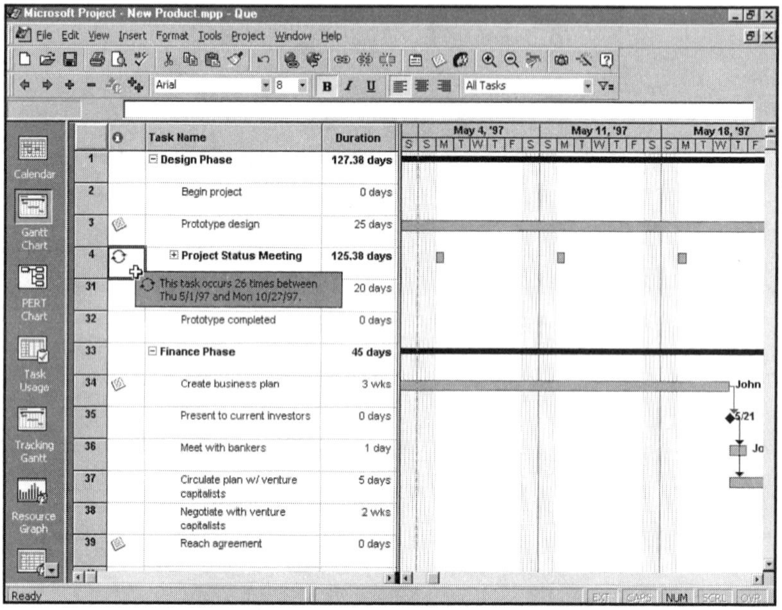

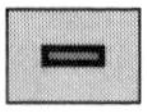

Figure 5.19 shows the project with the subtasks displayed. To display the subtasks, select the summary task name and choose the Show Subtasks button on the Formatting toolbar. To hide the subtasks, choose the Hide Subtasks button.

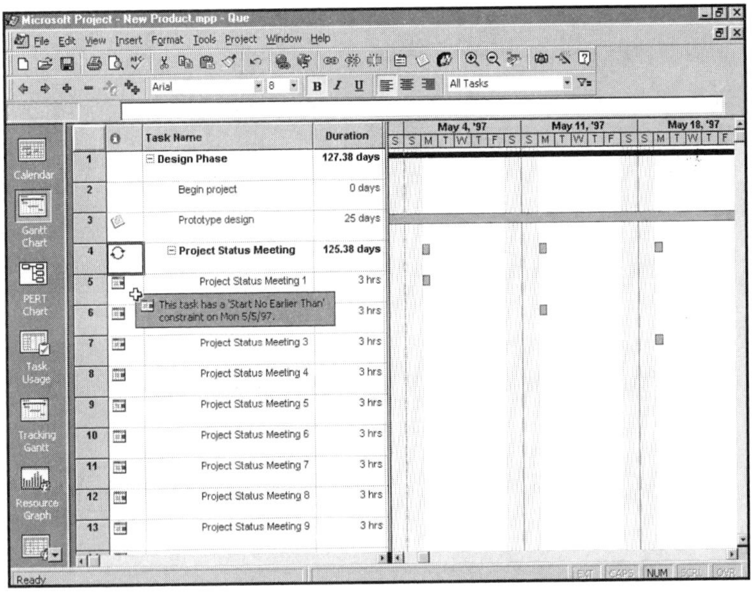

FIG. 5.19

You can display and hide the subtasks (recurring tasks) by clicking the outline symbol to the left of the summary task. If the outline symbol isn't showing, you can get the same result by double-clicking the task ID number.

CAUTION

Each of the subtasks in a recurring task is constrained to start-no-earlier-than its scheduled date. Constraints, even soft constraints like these, can create problems in a schedule if you make major changes in when the project is scheduled.

▶ **See** "Entering Tasks Constraints," **p. 205**

The previous steps describe how to create weekly recurring tasks. The processes for creating daily, monthly, and yearly recurring tasks are very similar. The steps below describe the differences in defining the specific frequencies of these tasks.

To create a series of daily recurring tasks, follow these steps:

1. As with the steps for the weekly tasks, choose the task row where you want to insert the recurring tasks and choose Insert, Recurring Task.

2. Select the Daily option to display the Daily specific frequency group (see Figure 5.20).

3. Choose a frequency interval ranging from every day to every 12th day from the Daily drop-down list box.

4. Select the Workday option to schedule tasks only on days defined as working days on the calendar.

   Or, select the Day option to schedule the tasks on non-working days as well as working days.

5. Choose OK to schedule the tasks.

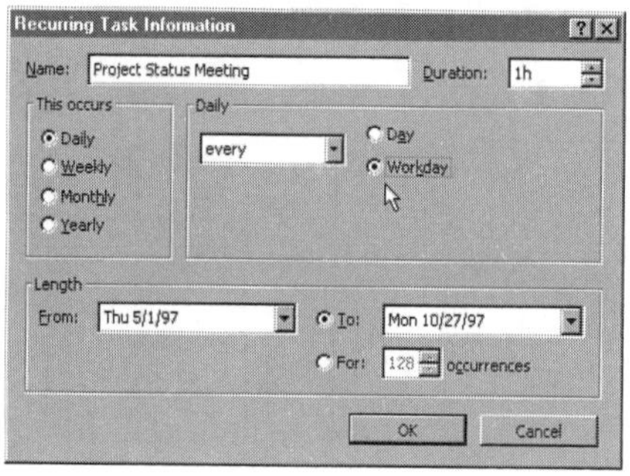

FIG. 5.20

You can schedule daily recurring tasks at intervals on regular working days as well as on non-working days.

To create a series of monthly recurring tasks, follow these steps:

1. As with the steps for the weekly tasks, choose the task row where you want to insert the recurring tasks and choose Insert, Recurring Task.

2. Select the Monthly option to display the Monthly specific frequency group (see Figure 5.21).

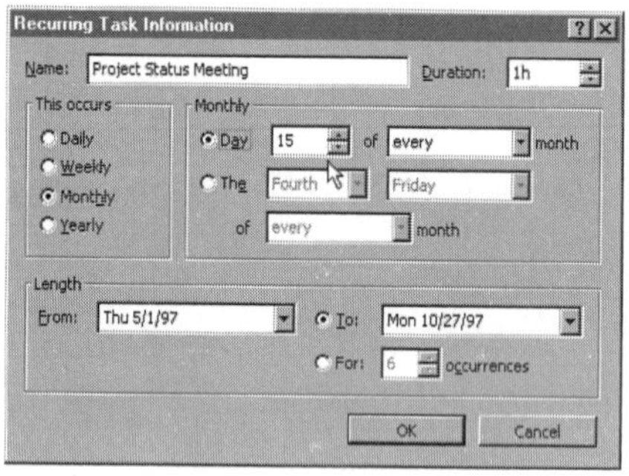

FIG. 5.21

You can specify a specific monthly date or a recurring weekday for monthly tasks.

3. Select the Day option if you want to pick a specific day of the month. In Figure 5.21, the meeting will be on the 15th of every month.

   You can also choose the nth day of the week of every month, every other month, and so on. For example, the 4th Friday of every month. Underneath the Day option you can select the list boxes to specify what day of the week and which month. For example, Figure 5.21 shows the Fourth Friday of every month displayed in the boxes. You can choose intervals from every month to every twelfth month.

4. Choose OK to schedule the tasks.

To create a series of yearly recurring tasks, follow these steps:

1. As with the previous steps, choose the task row where you want to insert the recurring tasks and choose Insert, Recurring Task.

2. Select the Yearly option to display the Yearly specific frequency group (see Figure 5.22).

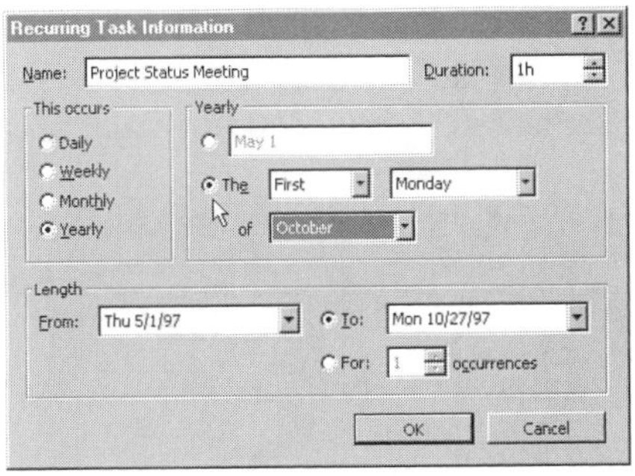

FIG. 5.22

You can specify a specific day of the year or a specific weekday in a specific month for yearly tasks.

3. Select the first option to type a specific date (without a year) in the text box. Select the second option to designate a date like the First Monday of October as illustrated in Figure 5.22.

4. Choose OK to schedule the tasks.

Sometimes, your definition of a weekly, monthly, or yearly recurring task might make Project place a task on a non-working day. If this occurs, Project warns you (see Figure 5.23). Choose the Yes button to let Project schedule the affected tasks at the earliest available working time. Choose the No button to skip those dates and leave those tasks out of the series of recurring tasks. Choose Cancel to stop the creation of the recurring task altogether.

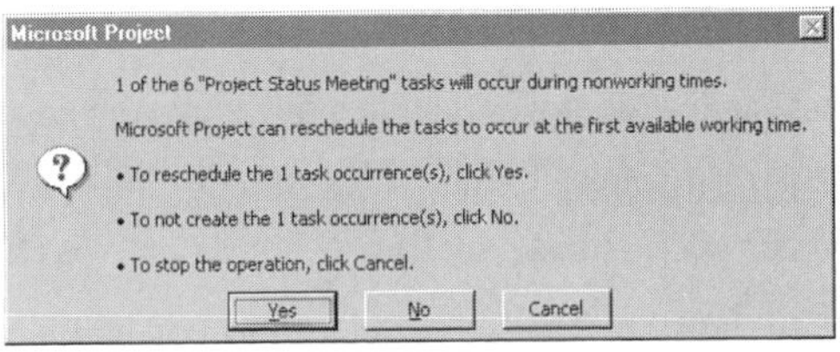

FIG. 5.23

Microsoft Project adjusts recurring tasks to the working calendar.

N O T E Recurring tasks are automatically created as Fixed Duration tasks. This has implications for assigning resources to tasks. See the section "Understanding Resource-Driven and Fixed Duration Scheduling" in Chapter 9 for details.

See the section titled "Editing the Task List" later in this chapter for information about editing a recurring task.

Using the Task Information Dialog Box

The Task Information dialog box appears when you choose the Task Information button on the Standard toolbar (see Figure 5.24). Because this dialog box is likely to be accessed frequently, there are a variety of ways to display it. You can also double-click a task name to display its Task Information dialog box. If you prefer the menu, choose Project, Task Information. Finally, fans of the keyboard will appreciate Shift+F2.

Five tabs organize the Task Information dialog box: General, Predecessors, Resources, Advanced, and Notes. These tabs contain additional details about the selected task; most of these additional fields are not immediately available on the Gantt Chart.

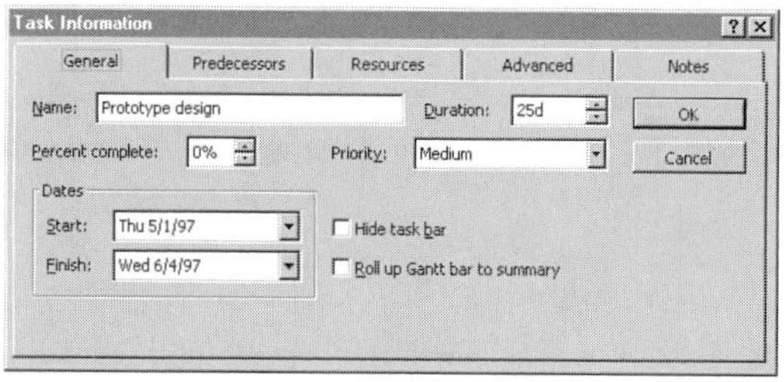

FIG. 5.24

Use the Task Information dialog box for quick access to commonly used task fields that are not available in the view you are currently using.

Task Information				? ×

General | Predecessors | Resources | Advanced | Notes

Name: Prototype design   Duration: 25d   OK

Percent complete: 0%   Priority: Medium   Cancel

Dates
Start: Thu 5/1/97   ☐ Hide task bar
Finish: Wed 6/4/97   ☐ Roll up Gantt bar to summary

Entering Data in the Task Information Dialog Box   To enter data in the Task Information dialog box, select the tab that contains the options you want to edit. To open a tab and view its page, click the tab. You can then move from option to option with the Tab and Shift+Tab keys. Move directly to an option by clicking it. You can also move directly to an option by pressing the Alt key plus the underlined letter in the field label. Press Alt+D, for example, to move directly to the Duration text box on the General tab.

You can mark a task as a milestone by selecting the Mark Task as Milestone check box on the Advanced tab. When you enter a duration of zero, a task is automatically marked as a milestone. You can mark any task as a milestone by selecting this check box, even if the task's duration is not zero. You can also remove the milestone status by deselecting this check box.

When you are finished, click the OK button or press the Enter key to enter the changes. To cancel all the changes you made, choose the Cancel button or press Esc.

Entering Task Note   Use the Notes tab of the Task Information dialog box to enter and display notes for each task (see Figure 5.25). These notes might be of use to you at this stage of planning the project. Include in your notes any assumptions that you are making for this task, or any other reminders that you need to document.

To enter notes about a task, select the task and choose the Task Notes button on the Standard toolbar. This button takes you directly to the Notes tab of the Task Information dialog box. Type a note in the Notes text box. Notes can contain over 3,000 characters. A special toolbar at the top of the Notes section (see Figure 5.25) provides formatting options for the notes. You can change the font and alignment for the notes, create a bulleted list, and even insert graphic images.

Project word-wraps in the Notes text box. If you want to force a new line or start a paragraph, press the Enter key. Use the following keys to move through the Notes text box:

Key	Effect
Home	Moves to the beginning of the current line
End	Moves to the end of the current line

Key	Effect
Ctrl+Home	Moves to the beginning of the note
Ctrl+End	Moves to the end of the note
Ctrl+left arrow	Moves one word to the left
Ctrl+right arrow	Moves one word to the right

FIG. 5.25

Use task notes as reminders and for explanations in reports.

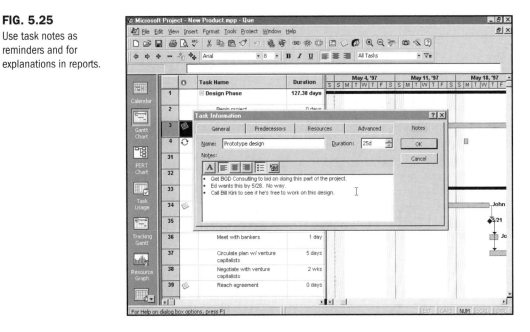

You can display notes in customized views, and you can print them in reports. Tasks with notes attached display a specific icon in the Indicator column to the right of the ID number in table views (refer to task 39 in Figure 5.25).

Using the Multiple Task Information Dialog Box   An important feature of the Task Information dialog box is its capability to make an identical change in several tasks at once. If you select multiple tasks before activating the form, the Multiple Task Information dialog box appears (see Figure 5.26). Any entry you make will be copied to all the tasks you selected. For example, to assign a duration estimate of two weeks to several tasks at once, select the tasks and then choose the Task Information button on the Standard toolbar. (The double-click method does not work when multiple tasks are selected.) Enter the duration on the General tab and choose OK to close the dialog box. Durations for all the selected tasks change to two weeks.

Using Other Views to Enter Tasks

Although the Gantt Chart is probably the most effective view in Microsoft Project for creating a task list, some people prefer other views. This section is a quick review of alternative views you

Part

Ch

5

might try out. Each has its strengths. You can access these alternate views either by clicking the appropriate icon in the View Bar or by choosing it from the <u>V</u>iew menu.

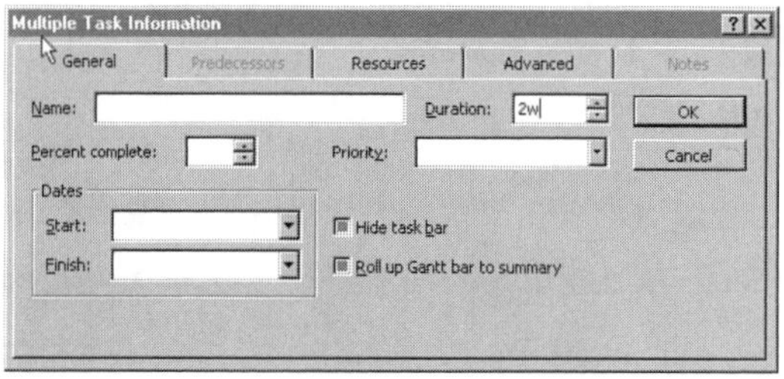

FIG. 5.26

Enter or change several tasks at once with the Multiple Task Information dialog box.

Using the PERT Chart

The PERT Chart (Program Evaluation and Review Technique) is a time-honored way to display the tasks in a project and is used by many, especially engineers, to enter and edit task lists (see Figure 5.27). The great advantage of the PERT Chart is that, when printed, it provides a road map of the sequencing of tasks in the project. However, it does not address time spans at all. That is the focus of the Gantt chart. Each task is represented on the PERT Chart by a box or a node, and a line is drawn from one task node to another to show that they are *linked* in a sequence chain. The disadvantage in using PERT charts to enter tasks is that you can't see very much of the project on one screen and some find it difficult to keep the overall structure in mind.

▶ **See** "Working with the PERT Chart View," **p. 225**

FIG. 5.27

The PERT Chart view of the Product project.

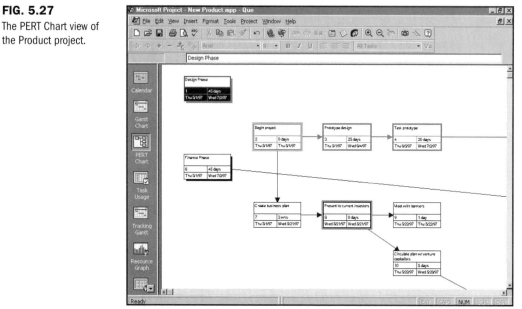

Using the Task Entry View

The Task Entry view is a combination view that displays the Task Form on the bottom pane, below the Gantt Chart. The Task Form in the bottom pane of the Task Entry view shows details for the task selected in the top pane (see Figure 5.28).

This view is not particularly useful if you are just typing task names and durations, but it's very efficient when you're assigning resources and linking tasks as you create the task list.

FIG. 5.28

The Task Entry view provides constant access to additional task fields for defining the task list.

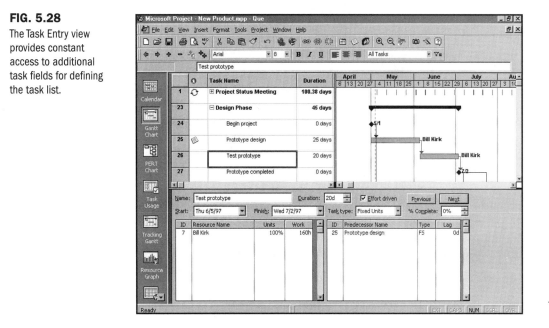

You can easily change the Gantt Chart view to the Task Entry view by merely splitting the screen to display the Task Form in the bottom pane. To display the Task Entry view, follow these steps:

1. If the Gantt Chart is not currently displayed, choose View, Gantt Chart.

2. Choose Window, Split.

N O T E The Task Form always appears in the bottom pane when you use the Split command with a task view. You can also just double-click the pane divider box in the bottom-right corner of the Gantt Chart. The Split command also appears on the shortcut menu that is displayed if you right-click over the graphics area of the Gantt Chart. ■

Only one of the two panes can be active at one time. The active pane is indicated by a narrow colored band on the left side of the view. You can either click anywhere on the inactive pane to activate it or use the F6 key to toggle back and forth between the two views.

Similar to the Task Information dialog box, the Task Form view has entry or editing fields for the task name and duration, plus other fields that don't appear on the standard task sheet portion of the Gantt Chart. The calculated start and finish dates that Project currently has scheduled for the task are shown on the form. There are also fields to identify how the task should be treated when resources are assigned. A Percent Complete field is useful when you begin tracking the actual work done on the task.

▷ **See** "Entering Task Constraints," **p. 205**

CAUTION

Do not enter dates in the Start and Finish date fields unless the task *must* start or finish on these dates. These fields are placed on the form mainly for viewing the scheduled dates for the task. If you enter a date in the Start field, Project assumes you want to constrain the task to start on or after that date (a Start No Earlier Than constraint). If you enter a date in the Finish field, Project assumes you want the task to be scheduled to finish no later than the date you enter. These constraints on tasks can create a lot of headaches for you later and should be avoided unless they are intended.

▷ **See** "Assigning a Name Resource," **p. 285**

Initially, the Task Form view displays entry tables for resource assignments and for predecessor relationships. The predecessor tasks are tasks whose scheduled dates must be considered when scheduling the current task. Use the Format, Details command to display other information at the bottom of the Task Form. For example, you can display the Notes text box, making it possible to add Notes to tasks without using the Task Information dialog box (see Figure 5.29).

To display the Notes text box at the bottom of the Task Form, follow these steps:

1. If the Task Form is not already active, select it by clicking anywhere on the Task Form (or by pressing F6).

2. Choose Format, Details, Notes. (You can also right-click on the form and choose Notes from the shortcut menu.)

TIP To return to the Resources and Predecessors details, choose Format, Details, Resources & Predecessors.

If you want to activate the Task Entry view from the menu often, you can add the Task Entry view to the View menu. To do this, follow these steps:

1. Choose View, More Views to open the More Views dialog box (see Figure 5.30).

2. Select Task Entry from the Views list.

3. Choose the Edit button to adjust the definition of the view. The View Definition dialog box appears (see Figure 5.31).

4. Select the Show in Menu check box.

5. Choose the OK button to close the View Definition dialog box.

6. Choose the Apply button on the More Views dialog box to display the view.

FIG. 5.29

You can keep the Notes text box on screen for constant access.

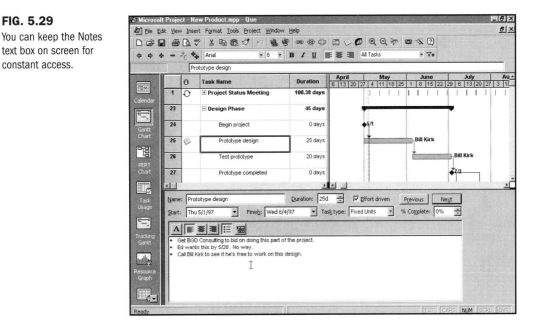

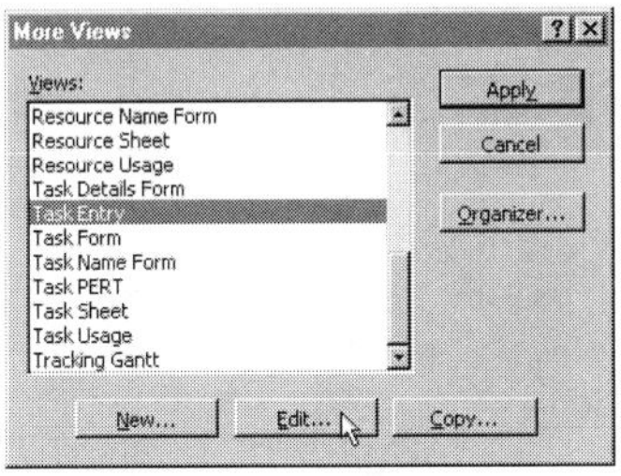

FIG. 5.30

The More Views dialog box lists all defined views.

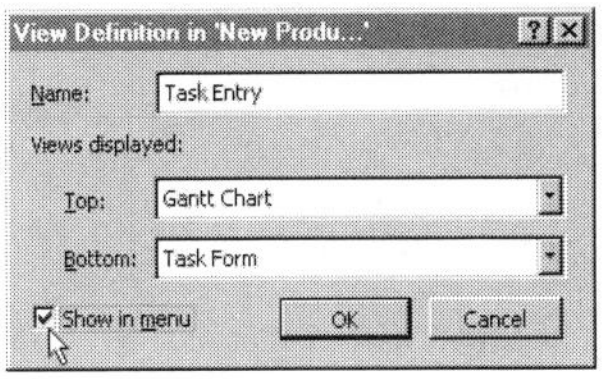

FIG. 5.31

Add a view to the View menu in the View Definition dialog box.

Using the Task Details View

You can view the Task Details view, shown in Figure 5.32, in the bottom pane to display more fields of data about the task than the Task Form view shows. However, the Task Details view compresses the area at the bottom of the form devoted to the optional detail tables and fields. To display the Task Details view, follow these steps:

1. Display the Gantt Chart at the top of the screen.
2. Choose <u>W</u>indow, <u>S</u>plit to split the screen.
3. To activate the bottom pane, click it or press F6.
4. Choose <u>V</u>iew, <u>M</u>ore Views. The More Views dialog box appears (refer to Figure 5.30).
5. Select Task Details Form from the <u>V</u>iews list.
6. Choose Appl<u>y</u> to display the form.

FIG. 5.32

The Task Details view shows even more fields than the Task Form.

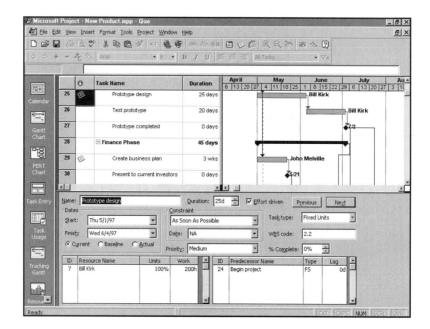

> **T I P** The Task Details view is useful when you are placing or editing a lot of task constraints.

Using the Task Sheet View

The Task Sheet view displays task information in a spreadsheet format, similar to the left side of the Gantt Chart without the timescale (see Figure 5.33). The Task Sheet view is a great tool for reviewing the major details of the task list, because you can see several columns for many tasks at the same time.

CAUTION

Be cautious in using the Start, Finish, Predecessors, and Resource Names fields until you have experience with Microsoft Project. Specifically, you will be tempted to enter dates for tasks, and if you do you will create many problems for yourself. However, experienced users of Project know that the Task Sheet view is very efficient when you have to enter details for a project already under way, with many tasks already completed, and therefore with the start and finish dates for many tasks already set.

▶ **See** "Viewing the Task Cost Table," **p. 483**
▶ **See** "Using the Tracking Table," **p. 497**

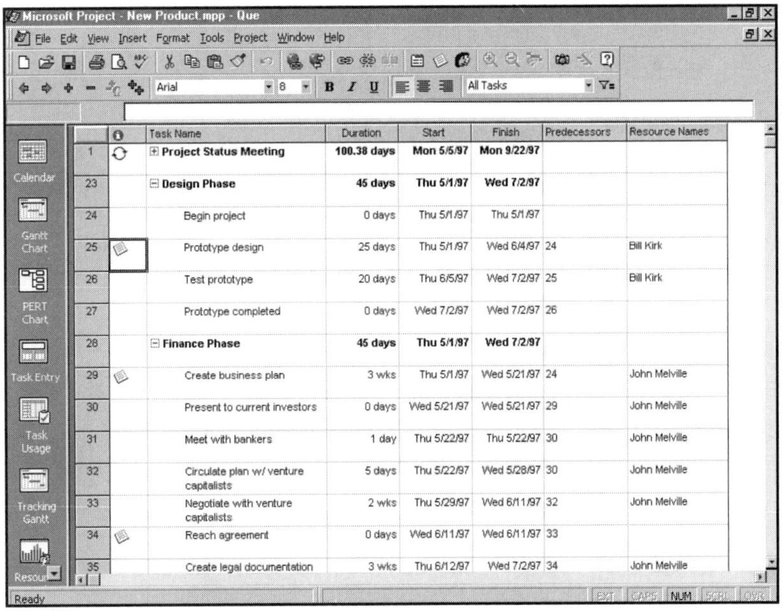

FIG. 5.33
The Task Sheet view of the Product project displays a lot of details.

To display the Task Sheet view as a full screen view, follow these steps:

1. If the screen is split in a dual-pane view, remove the split by choosing Window, Remove Split.
2. Choose View, More Views. The More Views dialog box appears.
3. Select Task Sheet from the Views list.
4. Choose Apply to display the view.

Creating Tasks with the Mouse

You can use the mouse to create task bars on the Gantt Chart and task nodes on the PERT Chart. You must then name the tasks, and you usually need to adjust the duration of tasks created this way. Although this feature is easy to use, it has its hazards, especially in the Gantt Chart. When you drag the mouse to create a task bar, the task is automatically assigned a soft constraint. If you drag from the start to the finish of the task, the task is constrained to start no earlier than the date you started the task bar on. If you drag from the finish to the start, the task is constrained to finish no earlier than the finish date you start on. These constraints can be very bothersome later as you edit the project, especially if you try to link subprojects to a master project. The best course is to rarely create tasks with the mouse.

▷ **See** "Understanding the Types of Constraints," **p. 203**

Editing the Task List

You can edit the list of task names and task durations in several views, as previously described. Changes made in one view are automatically reflected in all other views. The Gantt Chart or the Task Entry view (with the Task Form below the Gantt Chart), are probably the most useful views for editing and rearranging the task list.

Undoing Changes in the Task List

While you are revising the task list, you can undo nearly any change made in the task list with the Edit, Undo command. However, you can only undo the most recent change. Also, you can usually restore the last change just undone. When you use the Undo command a second time, if no other action was taken since the undo, Project treats the undo as a redo. When this is the case, the Undo command on the Edit menu is replaced by the Redo (u) command.

To undo or redo a change, follow these steps:

1. Choose Edit, Undo to reverse the most recent change in the project. You can also choose the Undo button on the Standard toolbar (or press Ctrl+Z).

2. Choose Edit, Redo (u) to reverse the undo you just executed, use the Undo button, or the shortcut key Ctrl+Z. These options all act as toggles.

Inserting, Clearing, and Deleting Tasks

As you revise a project, you often need to insert new tasks or remove tasks from the task list.

To insert a task between other tasks, follow these steps:

1. Select a cell in the row where you want the new task to appear. New rows are always inserted above the selected one. If you want to insert several tasks at the same location, extend the selection to include the number of rows that you want to add. All the details of the tasks included in the selection will shift down to make room for new blank rows.

2. Choose Insert, New Task (or press the Insert key).

Deleting an entire task is different from clearing the data from one or more fields for the task.

Follow these steps to delete one or more entire tasks:

1. Select at least one cell in each of the tasks to be deleted.
2. Choose Edit, Delete Task (or press Delete). The rows for the selected tasks are removed from the task list, and the remaining tasks close the gaps.

You can undo the deletion if you choose Edit, Undo before making another change.

The Edit, Clear command leaves the task row in place but clears the formatting or content from task fields. The command displays a cascading menu with the following choices:

- Choose All to clear the contents and formatting from the selected fields. If you had the task selected (by clicking the task ID), this option also clears the Notes from the selected task. Project leaves the row as a task and supplies a default duration immediately, even though the task is not named.
- Choose Formats to clear only the formatting of the selected fields. The content remains intact. (The Undo command is not available for clearing formats.)
- Choose Contents to clear the content of the selected field(s) only.
- Choose Notes to clear just the Notes field for the selected task.
- Choose Hyperlinks to clear any hyperlinks that have been attached to the task.
- Choose Entire Task to clear all cells and fields for the task and leave a blank row that is no longer a task.

  ▶ **See** "Publishing Projects on the Web," **p. 439**

It is also possible to clear only the active cell when you have selected many cells. To clear only the active cell of a selected group, follow these steps:

1. Select a group of cells by dragging the mouse or by using the Shift key with the arrow keys to extend the selection.
2. Press the Enter key or the Tab key (or their Shift combinations to move in reverse directions) to activate the cell you want to clear. It will display in white while all the remaining selected cells appear in black.
3. Press Ctrl+Backspace. This clears the active cell and activates the editing area of the entry bar so you can type a replacement entry.
4. (Optional) Type a replacement entry for the active cell.
5. Press Enter or Tab to activate another cell without losing the range selection.
6. Click anywhere or press any of the arrow keys to deselect the cells.

N O T E   Clear Contents is an option on the shortcut menu when you right-click tasks. ▓

Moving and Copying Tasks

You can use the Windows Clipboard if you want to copy or move cells or tasks to another location in the task list or to another project file. For both moving and copying, you must select only adjacent cells or tasks. The Cut command removes the selected tasks or cells from their location while the Copy command makes a copy of the selected tasks or cells, leaving them in their original location. The Paste command is used with both Cut and Copy to place the tasks or cells at the position of the insertion point.

> **CAUTION**
>
> Be careful when selecting the data cells for the Cut and Copy commands. If you want to cut or copy an entire task or group of tasks, you must select the task ID number. Use the mouse to select the ID number, which selects all cells in the task. If you select a limited number of cells in a task or group of tasks, only the data in these cells copies to the Clipboard.

T I P You can also press Shift+spacebar to select the entire row for a task.

To move a task or group of tasks, follow these steps:

1. Select the original task entries by clicking the ID number(s) for the tasks or by selecting all cells in a task row.

   Click the first task to be selected, press and hold the Shift key, and click the last task to be included. All tasks between those two points are included in the selection. You can also use the Shift key with the arrow keys to select adjacent task ID numbers.

2. Choose Edit, Cut Cell or Cut Task from the menu, or the Cut button on the Standard toolbar (or press Ctrl+X) to cut the original data from the task list to the Clipboard.

3. Select the task row where you want to relocate the data. Even if you are moving more than one task, select only the first row of the new location.

   If a task already resides on the row you selected, this task and all tasks below it automatically shift down to make room for the task or tasks you're moving.

4. Choose Edit, Paste from the menu or the Paste button on the Standard toolbar (or press Ctrl+V) to paste the Clipboard contents into the task list at the selected row. The Paste command inserts a new row or rows at the target selection point and copies the tasks in the Clipboard to the inserted rows.

To copy a task or group of tasks, take the following steps:

1. Select the original task entries using the techniques previously described.

2. Choose Edit, Copy Cell or Copy Task from the menu, or the Copy button on the Standard toolbar (or press Ctrl+C) to copy the selected data to the Clipboard.

3. Select the task row where you want the data duplicated. Even if you are copying more than one task, select only the first row at the new location.

   If a task already exists on the row you select, that task (and all tasks below it) shift down to make room for the new task or tasks you copy.

4. Choose Edit, Paste, the Paste button on the Standard toolbar, or press Ctrl+V to copy the Clipboard contents into the task list at the selected row. The Paste command inserts a new row or rows at the target selection point and copies the tasks in the Clipboard to the inserted rows.

TIP You can also access the Cut, Copy, and Paste commands by right-clicking the selected area.

After you copy data to the Clipboard, you can paste the data into many locations. The task data remains in the Clipboard until another copy or cut operation replaces the current Clipboard contents with new data.

If you select just the Task Name field for a task (rather than the entire task) before a cut or copy procedure, the Paste command doesn't insert a new row to create a new task at the target location. Instead, Paste copies the text from the Task Name cell to the existing target cell. If no task exists on the target row, the new entry creates a new task with a default duration.

CAUTION

Make sure you select the entire task or tasks, by selecting their ID numbers, *before* you begin a cut or copy operation if you intend to create new tasks at the paste site.

In addition to the cut-and-copy method for moving and copying tasks within the project, Project also includes a drag-and-drop feature to perform the same commands.

To *move* a task or group of tasks using the drag-and-drop feature, follow these steps:

1. Select the original task entries by clicking the ID number(s) for the tasks. You can also press Shift+spacebar to select all cells in a task row.
2. Move the mouse pointer over the ID number for any one of the tasks selected.
3. Hold down the mouse button and drag the mouse pointer directly below where you want to insert the selected tasks. A shadowed I-beam appears as you drag the pointer to its destination.
4. Release the mouse button and the selected task(s) move into the new position.

To *copy* a task or group of tasks using the drag-and-drop feature, follow these steps:

1. Select the original task entries by clicking the ID numbers for the tasks. You can also press Shift+spacebar and then Shift+down arrow to select entire tasks using the keyboard.

   Click and drag to select multiple task ID numbers that are next to each other.
2. Move the mouse pointer over the ID number for any one of the tasks selected.
3. Press and hold the Ctrl key and the mouse button, and drag the mouse pointer directly below where you want to copy the selected tasks. When you hold down both the Ctrl key

Part

II

Ch

5

and the mouse button, a small plus symbol appears next to the mouse pointer. This symbolizes a copy command using the drag-and-drop feature, rather than a move. A shadowed I-beam will follow as you drag the pointer to its destination.

4. Release the mouse button, and the selected task(s) copy to the new position.

Editing Recurring Tasks

If you select the summary task for a recurring task and choose the Information button, the Recurring Task Information dialog box appears as though you were beginning to create the recurring task. After you make your changes, choose the OK button. A Microsoft Project warning message warns that Project will change the frequency of the recurring task (see Figure 5.34). Choose OK if you do not mind losing the existing subtasks that will need to be deleted in order to change the frequency of the recurring task.

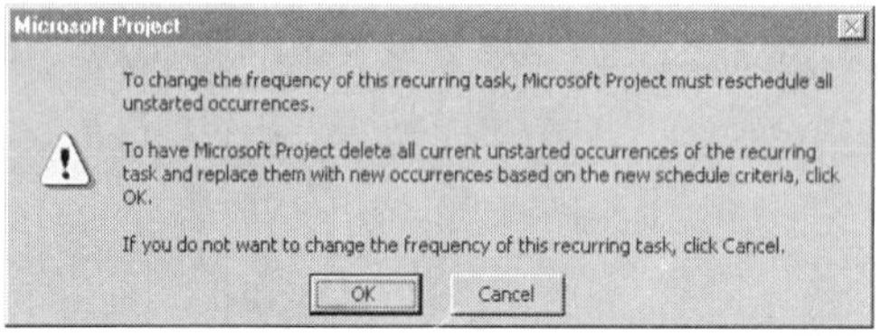

FIG. 5.34

Project must delete the existing tasks if you change the frequency of a recurring task.

Microsoft Project

To change the frequency of this recurring task, Microsoft Project must reschedule all unstarted occurrences.

To have Microsoft Project delete all current unstarted occurrences of the recurring task and replace them with new occurrences based on the new schedule criteria, click OK.

If you do not want to change the frequency of this recurring task, click Cancel.

[OK]   [Cancel]

Outlining the Task List

Outlining is Microsoft Project's method of organizing the details of a project into groups of activities that correspond to the major phases of a project. It is the equivalent of the traditional Work Breakdown Structure (WBS). The WBS is a diagram much like an organization chart. Each task is numbered, using the *legal* numbering system, and the number is called the *WBS number*. For example, the summary task would have a whole number like 1.0. The first level subtasks would be 1.1, 1.2, and so on. The second level would be 1.1.1, 1.1.2, and so on. The WBS number serves to identify the group containing the task in the overall structure of the project.

Like the Work Breakdown Structure, outlining organizes tasks into functional groups. Outlining usually is thought of in terms of its visual effect: you indent detail topics under major topics creating *subtasks*. See the expanded task list in Figure 5.35. The major topics, called summary tasks, control and summarize the subordinate detail topics. In project scheduling, the subordination of a task is called demoting the task, and the task you demote is a subtask. The task under which the task is subordinated automatically becomes a summary task that both controls and summarizes the subtasks. Unless you choose to display them differently, Project indents the display of subtasks beneath their summary tasks.

N O T E   What appears to be the first task in Figure 5.35 is actually a Project Summary task. When you use the multiple project feature, it is useful to be able to summarize an entire project with one task. See the section "Selecting the Display Options for Outlining" later in this chapter. ■

FIG. 5.35

Outlining helps you organize the details of the project.

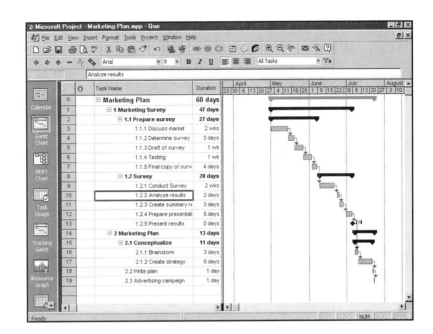

A summary task serves both to identify major groups of tasks and to summarize the duration, cost, and amount of work expended on its subtasks. When a task is transformed into a summary task, the task's start date is determined by the earliest start date of any of its subtasks, and the finish date is determined by the latest finish date of any of its subtasks. You cannot type a start date or finish date for a summary task. These dates can be calculated only from the related subordinates. The costs and amount of work associated with the subtasks are summarized in the cost and work fields of the summary task.

Part

II

Ch

5

CAUTION

If you demote a summary task, its subtasks are demoted even further. In fact, all actions you apply to a summary task also apply to its subtasks. If you delete, copy, move, promote, or demote a summary task, all of the subtasks, including subordinate summary tasks and their subtasks, are deleted, copied, moved, promoted, or demoted along with the summary task.

You can *promote* tasks already indented by shifting these tasks to the left. When you promote an indented task, the tasks immediately beneath the promoted task are affected in one of the following ways:

- If the tasks below are at the same level of indentation as the new promoted task, the tasks become subordinate to the new summary task.

- If the tasks below are subordinates of the promoted task, these tasks remain subordinates but shift to the left to follow the summary task.

■ If the tasks below are at a higher outline level (already further to the left than the promoted task), these tasks are unaffected by the promotion.

If you want to introduce a new task into the task list and make the new task a summary task, you must insert the task just above the task(s) you intend to make its subtasks. You can then demote the subtasks or, if the new summary task is inserted within an already indented list of tasks, you can promote the summary task rather than demoting its subordinates.

Indenting and Outdenting Tasks

There are several methods that you can use to indent (demote) or outdent (promote) a task or group of selected tasks. First, you must select the task or tasks you want to indent or outdent. Then do one of the following:

■ Choose Project, Outline, then choose Indent or Outdent.

■ Use the Indent or Outdent buttons on the Formatting toolbar to change the outline level of the selected tasks. The Indent button points to the right and the Outdent button points to the left.

■ Use the drag-and-drop technique: Place the mouse pointer over the first letters of the Task Name field until it becomes a double arrow pointing left and right. Drag the pointer to the left or right to change the Indent or Outdent level of the task. (You can only use drag and drop with one task at a time.)

■ Use the task shortcut menu to indent and outdent. Select the ID number for a task or group of adjacent tasks. Right-click the ID numbers and choose Indent or Outdent from the shortcut menu.

■ Use Alt+Shift+right arrow to indent a task or group of tasks. Use Alt+Shift+left arrow to outdent a task or group of tasks.

Collapsing and Expanding the Outline

A major advantage of outlining is that you can collapse the outline by hiding subtasks to view only the major components of the project (see Figure 5.36). Collapsing an outline merely suppresses the display of the subtasks, it does not delete the subtasks.

You can also collapse all but one part of the outline to show how the details of that part fit into the overall picture (see Figure 5.37).

To hide or show subtasks, follow these steps:

1. Select the summary task or tasks whose subtasks you want to hide.
2. Choose Project, Outline to display the Outlining submenu.
3. Choose Hide Subtasks to collapse that part of the outline or choose Show Subtasks to expand that part of the outline.

You can select the summary task and choose the Hide Subtasks button to hide its subtasks. You can also display subtasks with the Show Subtasks button. The Show Subtasks button has a single plus sign on its face.

FIG. 5.36

Look at the ID numbers to see which tasks are hidden.

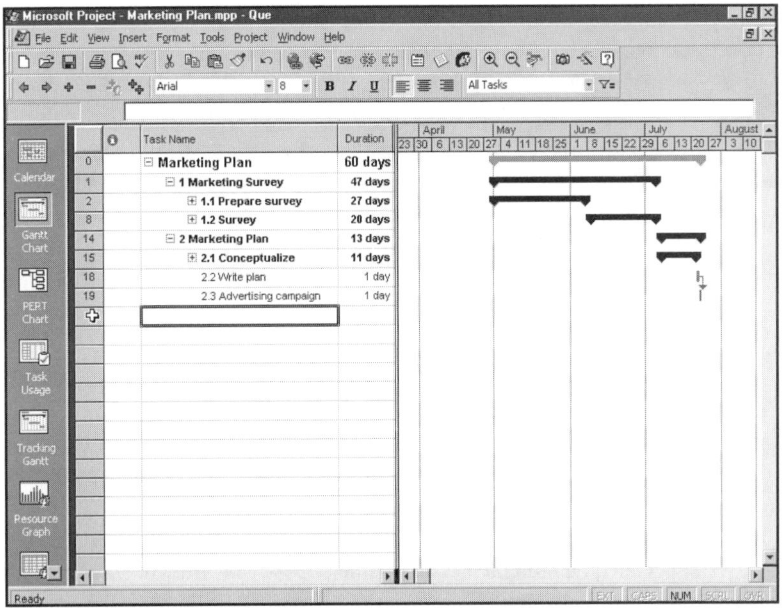

FIG. 5.37

Show the subtasks in one section of the plan but hide all other subtasks to highlight how those tasks fit into the overall project.

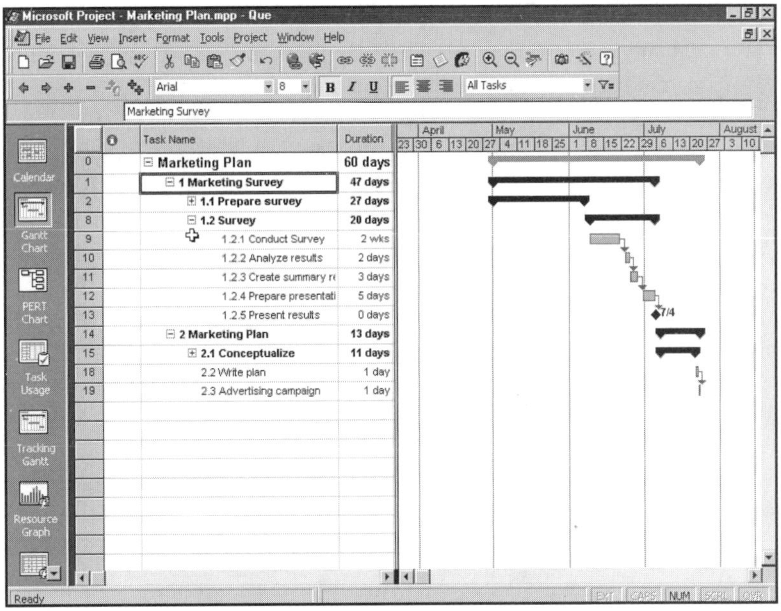

Part

II

Ch

5

TIP You can also simply click the outline symbol to the left of the summary task name to change the way its subtasks display. If the subtasks are displayed, clicking will hide them. If they are hidden, clicking will display them. You can also double-click the task ID—useful when the outline symbol is not visible.

If you have used the Hide Subtasks feature for parts of the project and would like to show all subtasks throughout the project, select any task and choose Project, Outline, Show All Subtasks. You can also choose the Show All Subtasks button on the Formatting toolbar.

T I P   A useful way to review the structure of a project is to click the Task Name column heading to select all tasks then choose the Hide Subtasks button. This collapses the outline to the first level tasks only. With the entire task list still selected, choose the Show Subtasks button, and all summary tasks expand to show one more level of subtasks. Choose the Show Subtasks button again, and another level of subtasks is revealed. When you're finished, choose the Show All Tasks button to be sure all tasks are displayed.

Editing Outlined Projects

When you delete, copy, cut, paste, promote, or demote a summary task, all its subtasks are included in the same operation. For example, if you delete a summary task, you also delete all its subtasks. If you demote a summary task, you further demote its subtasks. To use one of the operations listed above on a task that is a summary task, and to do so without affecting the subtasks, you must first promote the subtasks so they no longer are summarized by the task you want to change.

Selecting the Display Options for Outlining

Choose Tools, Options to change the formatting options for outlining. The outline options are on the View tab of the Options dialog box (see Figure 5.38).

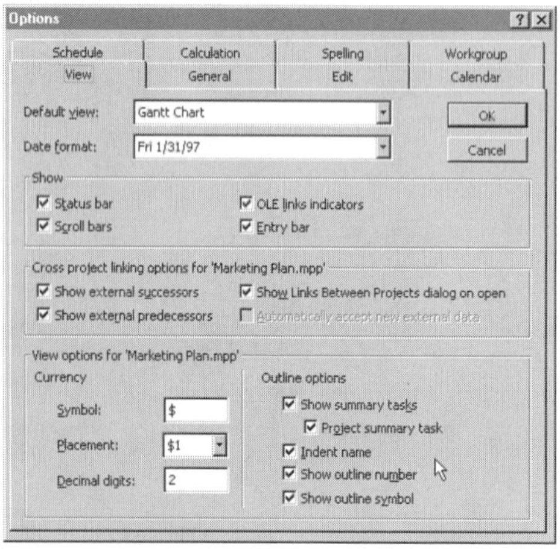

FIG. 5.38

The Options dialog box regulates the display of outlines.

There are five Outline Options from which you can choose:

- Deselect the Show Summary Tasks check box if you want to display only non-summary tasks. This leaves only the milestones and working tasks (the tasks that specify the actual activities in the project). This display is especially useful when you want to sort actual tasks by start date, duration, or alphabetically by task name. When you reselect the check box, summary tasks display again.

- When the Show Summary Tasks check box is selected, you can also select or deselect the Project Summary Task check box. This option creates a summary task for the entire project and displays it without an ID number at the top of the task list. The task in the first row of Figure 5.37 is a Project Summary task. Note that it has no ID number. Also note that all tasks are indented one level while the Project Summary task is displayed. The Task Name for the Project Summary task is taken from the project title you enter on the Summary page of the File Properties dialog box.

- Select the Indent Name check box if you want subtasks to be indented. Deselect this check box if you want subtasks left justified just like top level summary tasks. This is most useful when you're printing and you don't need to unnecessarily take up room with indented names.

- Select the Show Outline Number check box to display outline numbers to the left of each task name. The default is no outline numbers. The outline numbering scheme is the same scheme used in legal documents. The number for each task includes the position number for each of the summary tasks under which it is subordinated. The outline numbers shown in Figure 5.37 and previous figures are displayed by this option.

N O T E Outline numbers are ideally suited for use as Work Breakdown Structure (WBS) codes. Whether you choose to display outline numbers or not, the calculated outline numbers are placed in the WBS Code field for all tasks. You can view and edit this field in the Advanced page of the Task Information dialog box. If you want, you can replace the outline number with your own WBS codes. Note, however, that this does not change the display of outline numbers in the Gantt Chart. You can display the WBS Code field in reports and on screen by inserting a column.

- Select the Show Outline Symbol check box to display special symbols to the left of each task in a table view. The special outline symbols are a plus sign for summary tasks and a minus sign for all other tasks. These symbols are turned on by default.

  The outline symbols are useful when the outline is collapsed and you want to be reminded which tasks have subtasks that are not currently displayed.

To change an outline format option, follow these steps:

1. Activate a view in the top pane that shows a task list (either the Gantt Chart or the Task Sheet view).
2. Choose Tools, Options. Make sure the View tab of the Options dialog box is showing.
3. Select the options you want or deselect options.
4. Select OK when all options are set to your liking, or select Cancel to close the dialog box without making any changes.

Part
II

Ch
5

Printing the Project Task List

You can print the task list in a number of ways. You can print the Gantt Chart, the PERT Chart, or the Task Sheet view, all of which appear on paper much like they appear on-screen. You can also choose from among several standard, printable report forms. You cannot print the task forms.

▶ **See** "Printing Views and Reports" **p. 413**

▶ **See** "Formatting Views," **p. 695**

▶ **See** "Customizing Views, Tables, and Filters," **p. 741**

The following sections outline how to send a simple report to the printer.

Printing the Task Views

To print a view, follow these steps:

1. Display the view you want to print as a full-screen view or as the top pane of a split screen. It is always the top pane view that is sent to the printer.

 2. To preview how the report is going to look, choose File, Print Preview or select the Print Preview button on the standard toolbar (see Figure 5.39).

3. Select the Multipages button to get an overview of the full report. Figure 5.40 shows how the full Gantt chart spreads over multiple pages.

FIG. 5.39

Use Print Preview to review reports before they print.

Multipages button

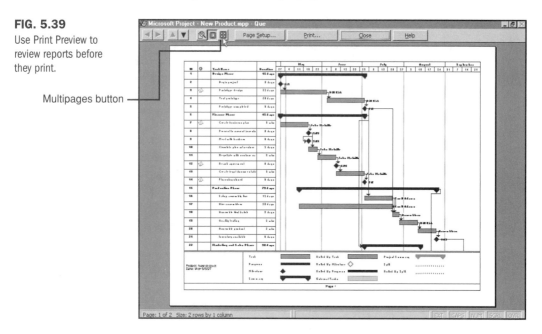

FIG. 5.40

The Multipages preview shows the layout of all pages in your printed view.

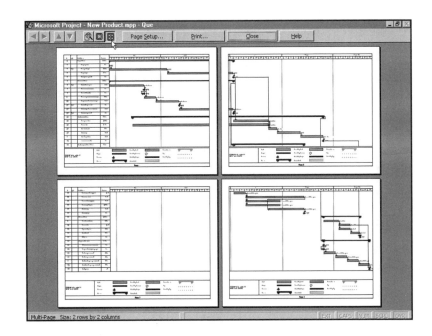

4. Place the pointer over any page of the report, and the pointer changes to a zoom pointer, an image of a magnifying glass that replaces the standard mouse pointer. Click to zoom in for a closer view of the page.

5. Use the triangle buttons in the upper-left corner of the screen (not the arrow keys) to scroll to different pages.

6. Choose the Page Setup button to change the page features of the report.

   ▶ **See** "Printing Views," **p. 416**

   ▶ **See** "Publishing Projects on the Web," **p. 439**

7. Choose the Print button to send the report to the printer. The Print dialog box appears as shown in Figure 5.41.

8. To start the print job, select the OK button.

Printing the Standard Task Reports

There are six report categories available for printing standardized and custom reports in Microsoft Project. Chapters 23, "Using the Standard Reports," and 24, "Customizing Reports," explain how to use and customize these reports. These reports are mentioned here in case you want to experiment with standard reports. At this stage, only the reports in the Overview category will make much sense. The reports in this category are as follows:

■ The Project Summary report is the printed version of the Project Statistics dialog box you see when you choose the Statistics button on the Project, Project Information dialog box.

Part

II

Ch

5

- The Top-Level Tasks report displays the task list but includes only those tasks in the first level of the outline.

- The Critical Tasks report lists the tasks that are critical—that must be finished on time if the project finish date is to be realized.

- The Milestones report lists all milestone tasks.

- The Working Days report summarizes the calendar information, showing the normal working days and hours plus all exceptions to those normal working times.

FIG. 5.41

Send the report to the printer by choosing the OK button on the Print dialog box.

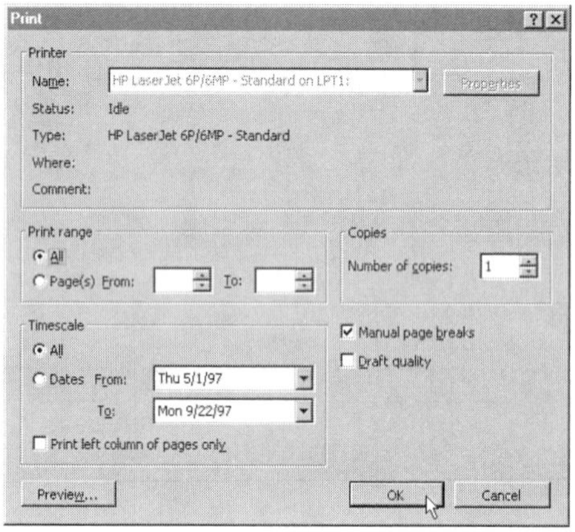

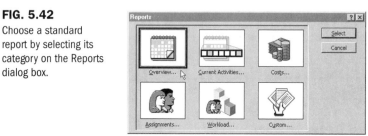

To print a standard report, follow these steps:

1. Choose View, Reports. The Reports dialog box appears (see Figure 5.42).

FIG. 5.42

Choose a standard report by selecting its category on the Reports dialog box.

2. Choose the report type you want to print from the six categories and choose the Select button.

3. Click the report you want to print and choose the Select button. This shows you the selected report in the Print Preview window.

4. Select the Print button in Print Preview to print the report.

From Here...

In this chapter, you learned how to create and edit the task list, as well as how to estimate and enter durations for the tasks. You viewed the various task forms used to enter additional task information. Finally, you learned how to outline the task list and the basic steps needed to print task reports.

Now that you know how to create the basic task list, you can investigate the scheduling tools available in Microsoft Project. These chapters will provide you with additional information you need to complete your project:

- Chapter 6, "Entering Scheduling Requirements," discusses the various task constraints available, as well as how to understand and create dependency links between the tasks.

- Chapter 8, "Defining Resources and Costs," discusses how to create a resource list to use when assigning resources to the tasks in your project plan.

- Chapter 10, "Assigning Resources and Costs to Tasks," discusses how to assign resources to the tasks in your project plan so that you can keep track of who is doing what, when.

- Chapter 12, "Reviewing the Project Plan," discusses the various tools and techniques available to check the schedule for correctness and to filter and sort the tasks and resources. It also reviews how to identify and shorten the critical path, one of the most useful tools provided by Microsoft Project.

Entering Scheduling Requirements

After you enter project tasks and estimate durations, you must focus on developing the schedule of start and finish dates. Up to this point, you've used Microsoft Project as a basic word processor or spreadsheet program—entering tasks and durations in a task view. In this chapter, you take a look at how to link these tasks to define the appropriate sequence of activity, thus giving Project specific information for calculating the schedule. You also examine how you record deadlines and constraints on the scheduling of tasks.

Scheduling: How it works

Understanding how Microsoft Project calculates the schedule, and the methods you can use to adjust the schedule.

Links

What is a link and why do I need it? Establish the links between tasks to define the appropriate sequence of events in your project. Insert delays or overlaps on your tasks. Remove links.

Reviewing links

With large, complex projects it is important to ensure the correct links have been created. Discover the best ways to review the links in your project.

Splitting tasks

A new feature of Project 98 is the ability to schedule interruptions in the work on the task.

Task constraints

Learn the best way to set deadlines for tasks, delay work on tasks until the last possible time frame, or set other external constraints. Explore the new soft constraint feature.

The project schedule depends on a number of factors:

■ The schedule either begins on a fixed project start date or is calculated to end on a fixed finish date. You determine which date by choosing Project, Project Information to open the Project Information dialog box.

▶ **See** "Using the Project Information Dialog Box," **p. 62**

■ Project schedules tasks only during the working times defined by the base calendar you select for scheduling the project, unless you assign a resource to a task. In this case, Project schedules work on the task during the working times on the calendar for that resource.

▶ **See** "Defining a Calendar of Working Time," **p. 78**

▶ **See** "Changing Working Times for Resources," **p. 273**

■ The schedule depends heavily on the durations estimated for the individual tasks. The longer the task duration for any given start date, the later the scheduled finish date for that task. Chapter 5, "Creating a Task List," covers estimating durations.

■ The schedule also depends on the requirements for the order or sequence in which to execute tasks. Typically, there are tasks whose start or finish dates must be scheduled in relation to the start or finish date of another task. This chapter is largely devoted to topics about linking tasks in an appropriate sequence.

■ The schedule can be affected by arbitrary limits or *constraints* that you impose on the start or finish of individual tasks. Imposing constraints are covered in the later part of this chapter.

■ The task schedule also depends on the availability of resources assigned to work on the tasks. Chapter 9, "Understanding Resource Scheduling in Microsoft Project 98," explains the effects on the schedule of resource availability.

■ The schedule will be altered if you schedule one or more interruptions in the work on a task by using the new Split Tasks feature. See the section "Task Splitting" later in this chapter.

■ The schedule will be affected if you delay a resource assignment to start after other resources have started, or if you contour the daily work assignment for a resource.

In practice, after you learn to use Microsoft Project, you probably will outline, link, and impose constraints on the task list as you enter the tasks. The process is divided into separate chapters in this book to focus on all the options and techniques possible for each activity. Chapter 5, "Creating a Task List," discusses entering and outlining your tasks. This chapter is devoted to linking tasks and added constraints. ■

Establishing Dependency Links

It's difficult to imagine a project in which no sequencing requirements exist for at least some of the tasks. Invariably, one or more tasks cannot be scheduled to start until one or more other tasks have finished. This relationship between tasks is known as a *dependency relationship*—the scheduled start or finish of one task must be set to coincide with, or *linked* to, the scheduled start or finish of another task.

There are several types of links you can use to show scheduling dependency, and Project provides a variety of tools and techniques for defining task links.

Understanding Dependency Links

When tasks are linked to show a dependency relationship, the dependent task is called the *successor* task and the task on which its schedule depends is called its *predecessor*.

Suppose, for example, you need to schedule the application of two coats of paint, a first coat and a final coat. When you have finished applying the first coat of paint, you can start applying the final coat. The date the Final Coat begins is dependent upon the date the First Coat is completed. The start date for the Final Coat (the dependent or successor task) should be linked to the finish date for the First Coat (the predecessor task). When you create a dependency relationship between tasks, the predecessor is listed first. In the painting example previously discussed, the dependency relationship is known as a Finish-to-Start link. It is one of the most common types of links. There are four different links available in Microsoft Project: Finish-to-Start, Finish-to-Finish, Start-to-Start, and Start-to-Finish. The section "Defining Types of Dependency Link Relationships" later in this chapter describes each of the four possible links in Microsoft Project.

Figure 6.1 illustrates two versions of this scenario that differ only in the duration of the predecessor. Project draws a small arrow from the predecessor task to the dependent task. The arrow is drawn from the finish of the predecessor to the start of the dependent task. The arrow always points to the task for which the dependency link is defined—the successor or dependent task.

FIG. 6.1
When you link a task, its schedule depends on the schedule for its predecessor.

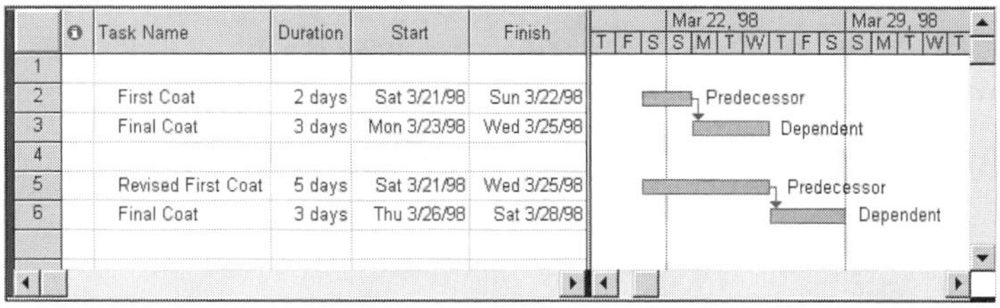

By establishing the link, you instruct Project to set the start date for Final Coat based on the scheduled finish date for First Coat. Any change that alters the calculated finish date for the predecessor causes Project to also reschedule the start date for the dependent successor task.

Part
II

Ch
6

The Revised First Coat in Figure 6.1 is longer by three days than the original First Coat task. Accordingly, the Final Coat task is delayed to start and finish later, reflecting the longer duration of its predecessor.

> **N O T E** To determine whether you need to link tasks together, ask yourself this question—if the first task gets delayed (or moved forward), do I want the second task to be delayed (or moved forward)? Changes in the scheduling of a predecessor task result in changes to the scheduling of the successor (or dependent) task. The successor task is dependent upon what happens to the predecessor task. The predecessor task always drives the scheduling of the successor task. ■

Allowing for Delays and Overlaps

You might need to allow for an artificial delay between tasks (known as a *lag*). You also might need to create an overlap, which is caused by starting a task before its predecessor is finished (known as a *lead*). A lead is a negative number entered into the lag field.

You can more realistically define dependency relationships by allowing for *lag time* when the start of the dependent (successor) task must be delayed beyond its predecessor's finish date. Looking back at the earlier example of applying two coats of paint, in the case where Final Coat is the successor to First Coat, you might want to allow for a two-day delay before applying the final coat to allow the first coat to dry completely. Figure 6.2 first group of tasks show the Final Coat following its predecessor immediately. The second group of tasks illustrates the same tasks with a lag that delays the Final Coat's start date. In both cases, the start of a third task, Clean Up, is dependent upon the finish of the Final Coat task.

FIG. 6.2

You can use lag time to delay the successor task. Lead time, however, allows tasks to overlap, thereby finishing earlier than would be possible otherwise.

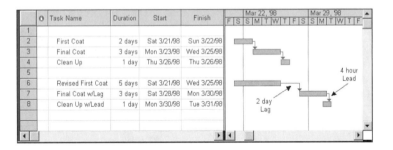

You might want to allow the dependent task to overlap or start before the predecessor task is finished. You can define *lead time* for a dependent task when the successor task could anticipate its predecessor. For example, a cleanup crew must clean up after the last coat of paint is applied. However, you might feel that you can start the Clean Up task before the last stroke of the final coat is applied. Accordingly, you can schedule the cleanup to start a couple of hours before the finish of the Final Coat task. Figure 6.2 shows a Clean Up task scheduled without any lead time. In the second pair of tasks, Figure 6.2 shows a Clean Up task scheduled with lead time and an overlap between the Final Coat and the Clean Up. The lead time allows the Clean Up task to finish earlier, which might allow the project to finish earlier.

TIP Identifying task relationships where overlap between tasks is possible is one of the best ways to shorten the overall time it takes to finish a project.

The section "Entering Lags and Leads," later in this chapter, has specific instructions for entering lag and lead time between tasks.

Using the Term *Successor*

The terms *predecessor* and *successor* imply that the successor task takes place after the predecessor task. Used in project scheduling however, the terms have a different meaning. Successor identifies a task that is dependent; it is dependent upon the predecessor task. A task that is dependent is called a successor task, and a task on which it depends is called its predecessor task. It can sometimes be confusing to use the term successor when the dependency does not describe tasks that take place one after the other in the usual sense of the words predecessor and successor. The successor might not always take place after its predecessor; it may take place at the same time or even before the predecessor task. To understand and use the types of dependency links, think of the successor task as the dependent task.

You might have need to schedule a dependent task to start as soon as its predecessor starts. For example, as part of building a house, we will have a subcontractor company tile the Jacuzzi area. While they are there, the subcontractor can also tile the laundry room. The predecessor task, tiling the Jacuzzi, and the dependent task, tiling the laundry room, can start at the same time. If the dependent task is a shorter task than its predecessor, then this successor will finish before its predecessor. Even more confusing is when the dependent (successor) task is completed *before* its so-called predecessor begins. Using the term *dependent* for *successor* as you decide how to link tasks is often very helpful.

Selecting the Dependent Task

Deciding which of two tasks is the dependent task and which is the predecessor is often self-evident. In many cases, the laws of physics decree the task sequence, and it is easy to decide which task is the predecessor and which the successor. Obviously, the Final Coat of paint always follows the First Coat of paint, so the First Coat is the predecessor and the Final Coat is the successor (dependent) task.

Sometimes the situation is more complicated, however. In manufacturing, for example, you must acquire the material inventory that you need for assembling the product before you can begin the assembly operation itself. However, you don't want to purchase a material inventory far in advance, for that requires that funds be tied up in idle inventory and storage costs. Instead, the purchase of material inventory is often scheduled to be completed just in time for the assembly operation to begin. If the schedule for the assembly operation is subject to extraneous factors that might change the start of the assembly task (like changes in orders placed by customers), Project will adjust the dates for purchasing materials to maintain the condition that materials be ready just in time for the start of assembly.

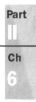
Part
II

Ch
6

The principle of just-in-time scheduling makes scheduling the Purchase Materials task dependent on the schedule for the Assemble Product task. The dependent task comes first chronologically; its scheduled finish date is dependent on the task that follows it. It is the scheduling dependency that the terms predecessor and successor are meant to define. Figure 6.3 is an illustration of the Purchase Materials task (dependent) occurring before the Assemble Product (predecessor) task.

FIG. 6.3

An example of just-in-time scheduling.

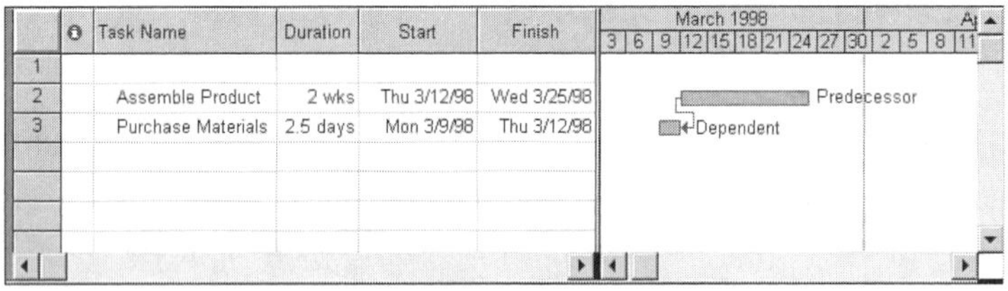

The decision as to which task should be the predecessor and which the dependent or successor task might hinge on which task you have more control over. If you have equal scheduling control over both tasks, make the task that must come first the predecessor and let the later task be the dependent successor. But, in cases where the schedule for one task is out of your control, you might want to arbitrarily make the more flexibly scheduled task the dependent task—regardless of which task actually must come first in time. For example, suppose one of your tasks is Receive Equipment. When you are relying on another organization to send the equipment, the actual sending (and subsequent receiving) of the equipment is out of your control.

A task that supports another task, which is a primary function of the organization, will frequently be scheduled as a dependent task with the primary function as its predecessor on the theory that the primary function should drive the scheduling of tasks that support it.

Defining Types of Dependency Link Relationships

There are four types of dependency relationships you can create, depending on whether you use the start dates or finish dates when linking tasks. The name for each dependency type includes a reference to either the start or finish date for the predecessor task, followed by a reference to either the start or finish date for the dependent task. Therefore, a *Finish-to-Start* relationship means the finish date of the predecessor task is used to schedule the start date of the dependent task. The predecessor is referenced first, then the dependent or successor task.

Project uses two-letter code abbreviations for the four dependency types, as shown in the following table. The first letter in the code refers to the predecessor and the second refers to the dependent task (the task being defined). Thus, the code for Finish-to-Start is FS. Table 6.1 shows the different dependency types and their corresponding codes.

Table 6.1 Linking Relationships Available in Microsoft Project

Dependency Type	Code
Finish-to-Start	FS
Start-to-Start	SS
Finish-to-Finish	FF
Start-to-Finish	SF

Using the Finish-to-Start (FS) Relationship   The finish date of the predecessor determines the start date for this task. For example, framing the walls of a new house should be scheduled to start after the foundation is finished (see Figure 6.4). The arrow is drawn from the finish of the predecessor task to the start of the dependent task. This is the most common dependency type and is the default relationship created by the Edit, Link Tasks command.

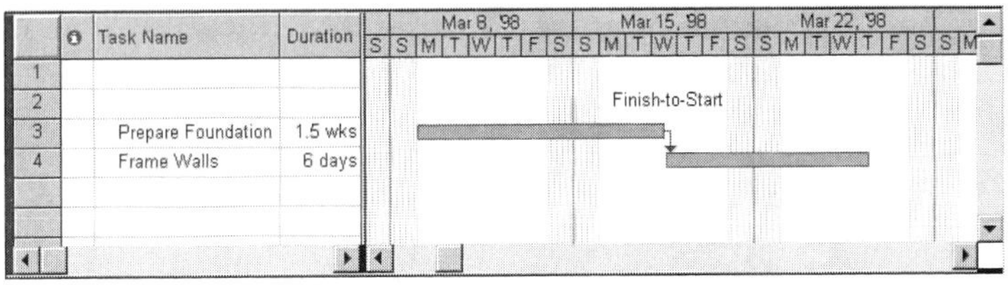

FIG. 6.4

The Finish-to-Start relationship is the most common linking relationship.

Using the Start-to-Start (SS) Relationship   The start date of the predecessor task determines the start date of this task. You are scheduling the two tasks to start at the same time with this link.

> **N O T E**   There is often a lag associated with Start-to-Start links. The start of the dependent task is delayed until the predecessor task is underway.

For example, suppose an organization leases new office space and moves to the new space when remodeling is completed. As part of the move from one office to another, there are several tasks that need to be accomplished—packing boxes, disconnecting desktop computers, disassembling furniture, and loading the boxes and furniture into the moving van. There are two ways you can approach this series of tasks. Because you can schedule the movers to start loading the vans almost immediately after the packing task starts, the start of the Load Vans task can be linked to the start of the Pack Boxes & Disassemble Furniture task, with a small amount of delay or lag time (see Figure 6.5). Pack Boxes & Disassemble Furniture is the predecessor task; Load Vans is the successor task. The arrow is drawn from the start of the predecessor to the start of the dependent task.

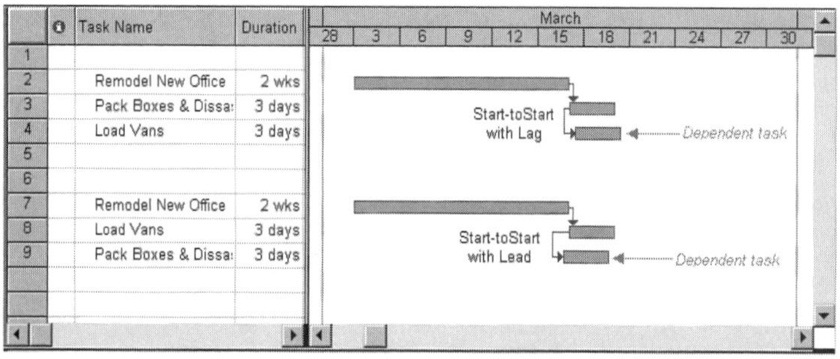

FIG. 6.5

You can link the start of the Load Vans task to the start of the Pack Boxes & Disassemble Furniture task, with a two-hour lag. Alternatively, you can link the Pack Boxes & Disassemble Furniture task to the Load Vans task with a two-hour lead.

In this example, you also could make Pack & Disassemble Furniture the dependent task, basing its start on the start of the Load Vans task, but with a small amount of lead time. The linking shown in the second set of task bars in Figure 6.5 illustrates this alternative. The start of the Pack & Disassemble Furniture task is linked to the start of the Load Vans task with a two-hour lead to assure that packing starts shortly before the loaders are ready to start. The choice as to which task is the predecessor is often arbitrary.

In the first example, if the packing is delayed, the loading is delayed—that is, the packing task drives when both tasks start. In the second example in Figure 6.5, if the loading van is delayed in arriving, we delay packing boxes and disassembling the furniture. The loading task drives when both tasks start.

Using the Finish-to-Finish (FF) Relationship   The finish date of the predecessor determines the scheduled finish date of this task. You schedule two tasks to finish at the same time. For example, in building or remodeling a kitchen, the acquisition of the kitchen appliances should be completed by the time the cabinet makers finish installing the kitchen cabinets, so the cabinet makers can install the appliances in (and around) the new cabinets (see Figure 6.6).

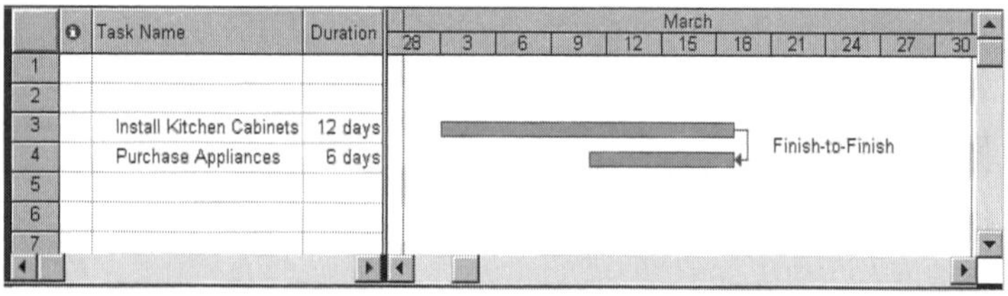

FIG. 6.6

The kitchen appliances should all be purchased by the time the kitchen cabinets are completed. This is a Finish-to-Finish relationship.

Using the Start-to-Finish (SF) Relationship   The start date of the predecessor task determines the scheduled finish date of this task. You might be scheduling a task to finish just in time to start a more important task which it supports. The following examples illustrate the Start-to-Finish relationship:

- When preparing for an important exam, most students schedule their studying to finish approximately when testing begins!

- When scheduling the delivery of merchandise to a new store, the Grand Opening date determines when the deliveries must be scheduled.

- Just-in-time scheduling in manufacturing is a policy that strives to finish acquiring raw materials just in time for the manufacturing process to begin. This policy saves money by not tying up cash in material inventories any longer than necessary.

Figure 6.7 illustrates a home building project that requires the framing materials to be purchased in time for framing the walls. In the first set of tasks, the Purchase Materials task is scheduled to finish just as the Frame Walls task begins. Purchase Materials is dependent on Frame Walls, making Frame Walls its predecessor. If the framing is delayed, the delivery will be delayed, too. The link is a Start-to-Finish link, and the arrow is drawn from the start of the predecessor to the finish of the dependent task.

FIG. 6.7
The Purchase Materials task must be completed in time for the Frame Walls task to begin, making its schedule dependent on the schedule for Frame Walls.

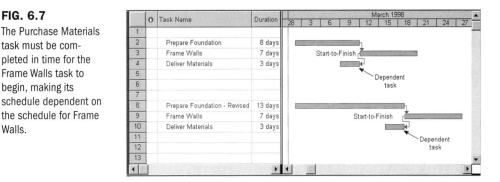

In the second set of tasks in Figure 6.7, the Prepare Foundation task has a longer duration, and that delays the scheduled start for Frame Walls. Automatically, Project delays the dependent Purchase Materials task just enough so it will still be finished just in time for the new start date of Frame Walls.

> **CAUTION**
> Remember—if changes occur in the scheduling of a predecessor task, this always results in changes to the scheduling of the successor (or dependent) task.

Entering Dependency Links

 You can define task dependencies in Project in several ways. If the dependency is a Finish-to-Start relationship (the most common), you can simply select the tasks you want to link and choose Edit, Link Tasks, or click the Link Tasks button on the toolbar.

Part
II

Ch
6

If the relationship is more complex, you need to use another method, or you need to edit the dependency link after it's been created.

Below is a brief listing of the different ways you can link tasks. Each of these methods is discussed in detail later in this chapter. Some can only be used in very restrictive circumstances, so read about all the methods before you try just one:

- If you are using a view with a task table and have already selected the tasks to be linked, you can use one of these options:
  - Menu command (Edit, Link Tasks)
  - Standard toolbar tool (Link Tasks)
- To create or edit a link to include lag time or lead time with a link, or to link tasks in an order other than the sequential ID order, select the dependent (successor) task and use one of these views:
  - Task Information dialog box (Predecessors tab)
  - Split screen (Task Form view)
  - Entry Table (Gantt Chart or Task Sheet views)
- To drag the mouse pointer from the predecessor to the successor task to create a link, use one of these views:
  - the timescale side of the Gantt Chart view
  - the PERT Chart view
  - the Calendar view

Creating Links Using the Menu or Toolbar

The simplest and easiest way to link tasks is to select the tasks and then choose Edit, Link Tasks, or click the Link Tasks button on the Standard toolbar (see Figure 6.8). You can also press Ctrl+F2 to create a link.

There is no limit to the number of tasks you can select for linking. You can link just one predecessor and one successor at a time, or you can link all the tasks in the project in the same operation. The order in which you add tasks to the selection makes a difference in defining the relationship. If tasks are selected by dragging to highlight contiguous tasks, tasks higher up on the task list (with lower ID numbers) are always predecessor to the selected task with the next higher ID number. If you select tasks that are not contiguous, the order does make a difference in linking the tasks. For example, if you select tasks 5, 2, and 12 in that order and then choose the Link Tasks button, task 5 is predecessor to task 2, and task 2 is predecessor to task 12.

TIP   To select a task, simply click the name of the task. You do not need to select the task ID number.

To select multiple, adjacent tasks in the task list, drag the mouse pointer to extend the selection to as many tasks as you want to link or use the Shift+down arrow or Shift+up arrow key combinations. For non-adjacent tasks, select the first task or tasks and add tasks to the selection by holding down the Ctrl key while clicking additional tasks or while dragging on additional groups of tasks.

FIG. 6.8

You can quickly link selected tasks with the Link Tasks button. This links the tasks in a Finish-to-Start relationship.

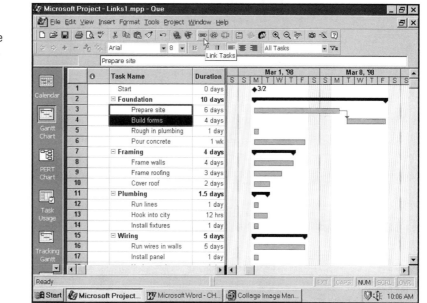

To link the selected tasks through the menu or toolbar, follow these steps:

1. Select the tasks you want to link.

2. Choose Edit, Link Tasks or click the Link Tasks button on the Standard toolbar. The tasks link automatically as Finish-to-Start links with no lag or lead.

This method is easy to use but it has its limitations. You can only define the simplest kind of dependency, Finish-to-Start. For a different type of relationship, you must use a different method or edit the link to change its type. Alternative methods are outlined in the next four sections in this chapter; techniques for defining more complex links are discussed in the next four sections.

Part
II

Ch
6

Creating Links Using the Task Information Dialog Box

You can also use the Predecessors tab of the Task Information dialog box to define task links (see Figure 6.9). Unlike the Edit, Link Tasks command, the Task Information dialog box allows you to choose the type of link and to enter lag or lead time.

▶ **See** "Entering Lags and Leads," **p. 191**

FIG. 6.9

Use the Task Information dialog box to define types of predecessor links and lag and lead time.

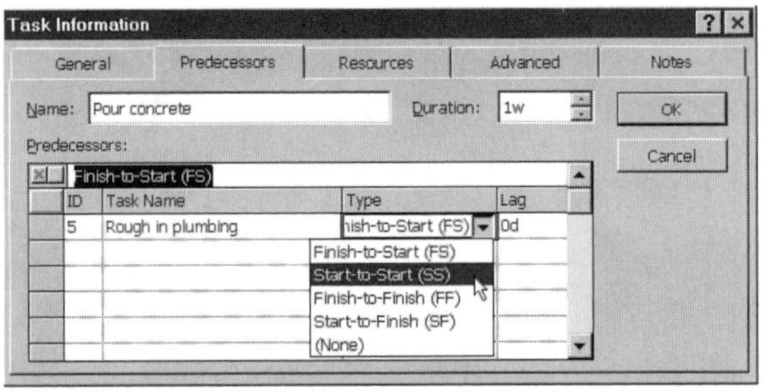

98

One improved feature of the Predecessors tab of the dialog box is the addition of drop-down list arrows (in place of list controls) in fields where a list of choices is available. This feature makes it easier to select the appropriate entry. The Task Name and Type fields have these new list arrows.

To create a dependency relationship using the Task Information dialog box, follow these steps:

1. Select the dependent (successor) task.

2. Open the Task Information dialog box by choosing Project, Task Information from the menu or click the Information button on the Standard toolbar.

TIP A quick way to access the Task Information dialog box is to double-click the task name.

3. Click the Predecessors tab to display that page.

   The Predecessors tab features a table in which you can define the predecessor task or tasks and the type of dependency relationship (refer to Figure 6.9).

4. Click in the Task Name field and a list arrow appears in the field. When you click the arrow, a list containing all tasks in your project is displayed. Choose the name of the task to be the predecessor task. Project will automatically supply the ID number and will supply the default Finish-to-Start link type with no lag, unless you choose otherwise.

   If you know the ID number, another method is to click the ID field in the Predecessors fields and enter the predecessor task ID. Project displays the text you type above the table in the entry bar. Press Enter to finish the cell entry or choose the green check button on the entry bar. Project automatically supplies the Task Name for that ID number and supplies the default Finish-to-Start link type with no lag.

5. To choose a dependency type other than the default Finish-to-Start, click in the Type field and a list arrow appears in the field. When you click the arrow, a list containing the four types of links is displayed. Choose the type of dependency relationship you want between these tasks, or choose (None) to remove the link to the predecessor task, and choose OK.

6. To enter in a lag time or lead time, click in the Lag field and type the amount of lag or lead time. Remember that positive numbers represent lag time and negative numbers

represent lead time. For more information on lag time and lead time, see the section "Entering Lags and Leads" later in this chapter.

7. If there are additional predecessors for this task, repeat steps 4-6 as needed for each predecessor.

8. Select OK or press Enter to complete the definition and close the dialog box.

Creating Links Using the Task Form View

With a task view like the Gantt Chart in the top pane, you can use the Task Form view in the bottom pane to define the predecessor and successor relationships. This is an easy way to define complex dependency relationships—relationships that contain leads or lags or that are not Finish-to-Start relationships.

When you display the Task Form view, the view usually displays entry fields for resource and predecessor information. There are other fields which can be displayed, including successor information, task notes, and resource work. The Format menu enables you to choose the entry fields that appear at the bottom of the Task Form. One of the choices available displays information pertaining to both predecessors and successors. This is frequently used when working with dependency links.

To place the predecessors entry fields on the Task Form view, follow these steps:

1. If the Task Form is not currently displayed, choose Window, Split to split the screen.

2. Activate the bottom pane by pressing F6 or by clicking anywhere in the bottom pane.

3. By default, the resource and predecessor fields appear in the lower pane. If these fields are not displayed, choose Format, Details, and then choose Resources & Predecessors or Predecessors & Successors.

> **T I P** You can also right-click the bottom pane and choose Resources & Predecessors or Predecessors & Successors (see Figure 6.10).

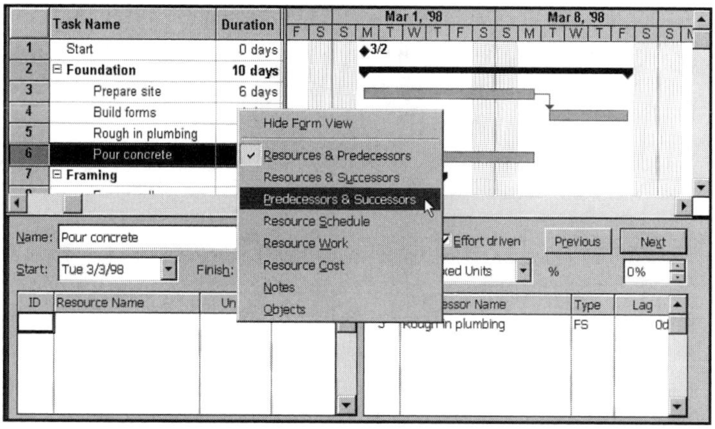

FIG. 6.10

The shortcut menu for the Task Form view offers several choices for the detailed information displayed in the bottom of the form.

One improved feature of the Task Form view is the incorporation of list controls in fields where a list of choices is available. This feature makes it easier to select the appropriate entry. The Predecessor Name and Type fields have these new list arrows.

After you display the predecessor fields, define a predecessor for the current task by following these steps:

1. Select the dependent task by clicking its task row in the top pane, or use the Previous and Next buttons in the lower pane to move to the desired task.

2. Select either the ID field or the Predecessor Name field in the predecessors area on the Task Form in the bottom pane.

3. If you selected the Predecessor Name field, a list arrow appears in the field. When you click the arrow, a list containing all tasks in your project is displayed. Choose the name of the task to be the predecessor. The Task Form view still shows the OK button because selecting the task name only completes the cell entry.

   If you selected the ID field, type the predecessor's ID number in the ID field and press Enter to complete the cell entry. Project automatically fills in the predecessor name when you choose the OK button to complete the linking definition.

   If you do not know the ID number of the predecessor, you can use the vertical scroll bar in the top pane to view the predecessor task. The ID field remains selected while you scroll the task list. Do not select the predecessor, just view its ID number. Type this number in the ID field. You can then press Enter or click the green check button on the entry bar to complete the cell entry.

4. Select the Type field if you want to define a link type other than Finish-to-Start. If you leave the Type field blank, Project supplies the default Finish-to-Start type when you choose the OK button. To choose a different type, either choose a two-letter code (FF, FS, SF, or SS) from the drop-down list or type in the two-letter code. Press Enter to complete the cell entry in the Type field.

5. Select the Lag field if you want to define a lag or lead. The default of 0d (zero days, meaning no lag or lead time) is supplied automatically when you choose the OK button if you leave this field blank. For more information on lag time and lead time, see the section "Entering Lags and Leads" later in this chapter.

6. You can add additional predecessors on other rows in the predecessors table by repeating steps 2 through 5.

7. Choose the OK button to execute the changes you entered in the Task Form. Figure 6.11 shows the completed field entries for a simple predecessor definition.

N O T E   When you edit a field in one of the tables at the bottom of a form, it activates the Entry bar at the top of the screen and the OK and Cancel buttons in the form. You must complete the editing by accepting or canceling the change. You can accept a change by pressing Enter, clicking the green check mark button in the Entry bar, or by choosing another field in the Task Form. However, until you choose the OK button, all changes you made to the Task Form are still temporary changes. Choose the OK button to complete the dependency definition or Cancel to reject the changes. If you choose

OK, the default predecessor Type and Lag will be provided if you have not completed those fields in the form. Once accepted or rejected, the OK button changes to read Previous; the Cancel button will read Next. This allows you to quickly move forward or backward in the list of tasks. ■

FIG. 6.11

You can use the predecessor fields on the Task Form to define a task's predecessor links.

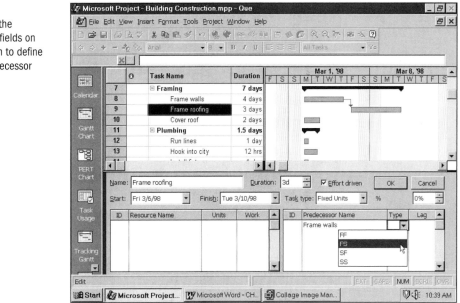

Creating Links Using the Entry Table

You can enter dependency relationships in the Predecessors field on the Entry Table. The Entry Table is the default table displayed on both the Task Sheet and Gantt Chart views. Using the Task Sheet, you accomplish this by selecting a task and defining the related predecessor relationship(s) in the Predecessors field. To see the Predecessors field on the Gantt Chart table, either move the vertical split bar or click the right arrow on the horizontal scroll bar at the bottom left side of the Gantt Chart. The Predecessors field is one of the additional fields that you can scroll into view. Figure 6.12 and Figure 6.13 show these two methods of viewing the Predecessors field.

You can enter the simplest relationship, the Finish-to-Start, by just entering the task ID number for the predecessor task in the Predecessors field. To enter one of the other relationships, you must enter the predecessor task ID number and the abbreviation for the type of link.

If there is a lag or lead, it is included as part of the cell entry. You enter leads and lags after the relationship type. Begin a lag with a plus sign and a lead with a minus sign. For example, to make task 4 a Start-to-Start predecessor task for task 5, with one day lead time, type **4SS-1d**. To make task 8 a Finish-to-Start predecessor for task 9 with four hours lead time, type **8FS-4h**. (See Figure 6.14 for an example of these two entries.)

Part

II

Ch

6

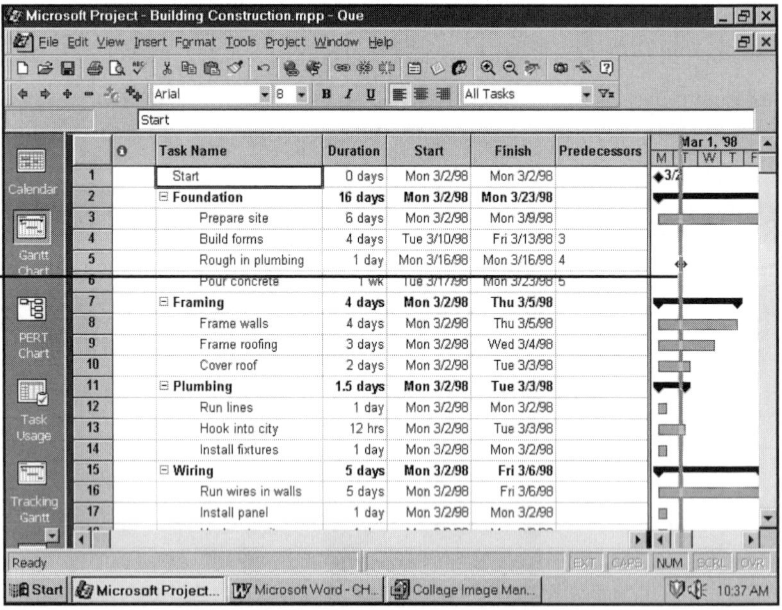

FIG. 6.12

Move the vertical split bar to see additional fields in the table portion of the Gantt Chart.

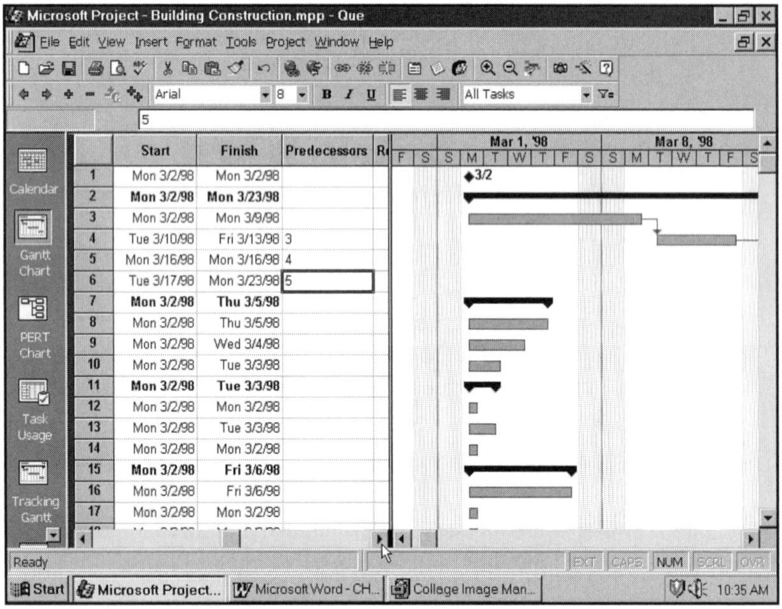

Vertical split bar ———

FIG. 6.13

Scrolling on the table side of the Gantt Chart view displays additional fields, including the Predecessors field.

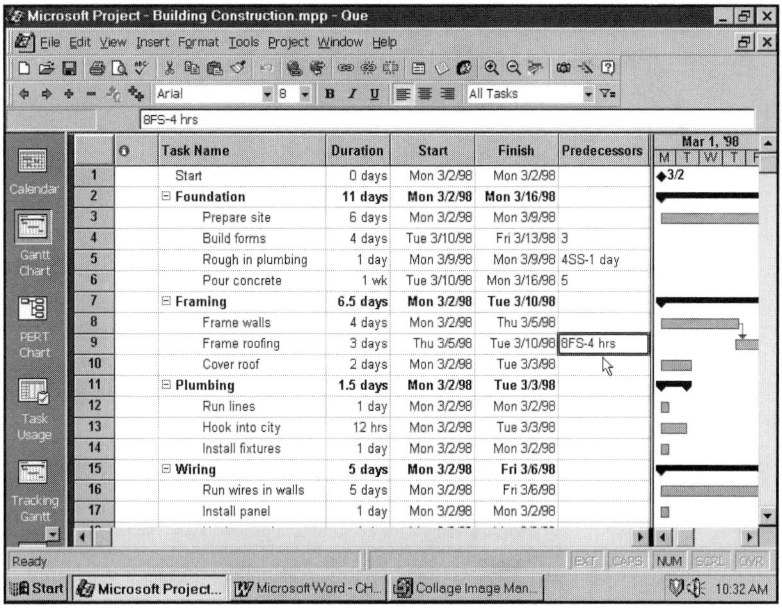

FIG. 6.14

Enter task links in the Predecessors field for the dependent task on the Entry Table.

If a task has more than one predecessor, separate the predecessor definitions by commas. Continuing the previous example, entering **8FS-4h,6FF+1h** indicates that task 6 is also a predecessor and the relationship is Finish-to-Finish with a 1-hour lag.

Using the tasks illustrated in Figure 6.14, to enter the predecessor relationship for the Wiring and Plumbing tasks, begin by selecting the Predecessors field in the row for Plumbing, the dependent (successor) task, and then enter the codes for the relationship you want to have between Wiring and Plumbing.

If you do not remember the ID number of the predecessor, you can use the vertical scroll bar to scroll in the task list to find the predecessor task. The Predecessors field in the Entry Table remains selected while you scroll the task list. Do not select the predecessor, just view its ID number. You can type this number, and it will be placed in the Predecessors field. If you need a link other than the default Finish-to-Start or want to add lag time or lead time, this should be typed in after the ID number. To complete your link, press Enter or click the green check button on the entry bar.

Creating Links Using the Mouse

You can use the mouse to link task bars on the timescale side of the Gantt Chart or in the PERT Chart or Calendar views. You can use the mouse to edit the linking relationship in the Gantt Chart or PERT Chart.

This technique for linking is most convenient when you can *see* both tasks you are trying to link on-screen at the same time. If both bars are not visible, you will probably do better with a

Part

II

Ch

6

different method of linking the tasks, such as the Task Form View method described earlier in this chapter.

CAUTION

Be careful! The mouse pointer is designed to perform a number of actions to tasks in these views. It is easy to accidentally move the task or mark the task as being partially complete. You must watch the shape of the mouse pointer carefully to make sure you're doing exactly what you intend to do. Make sure the mouse pointer is the shape of three chain links when you are over the successor task before releasing the mouse button. In the Gantt Chart, the mouse must be the four-arrow shape over the predecessor task, or it will not change into the chain-links shape, and you will not link the tasks. In both the PERT Chart and Calendar views, you must drag from the *center* of the predecessor task to the *center* of the successor task, or the mouse will not change into the chain-links shape, and you will not link the tasks.

T I P   It's easier if you start dragging *down* from the predecessor task and then onto the successor task.

Dragging the mouse pointer from one task bar to another task bar establishes a Finish-to-Start link between the tasks. The task you start on is the predecessor and the task you drag to is the dependent (successor) task. Make sure the mouse pointer has the four-arrow shape shown in Figure 6.15 before you press the button to start dragging the pointer.

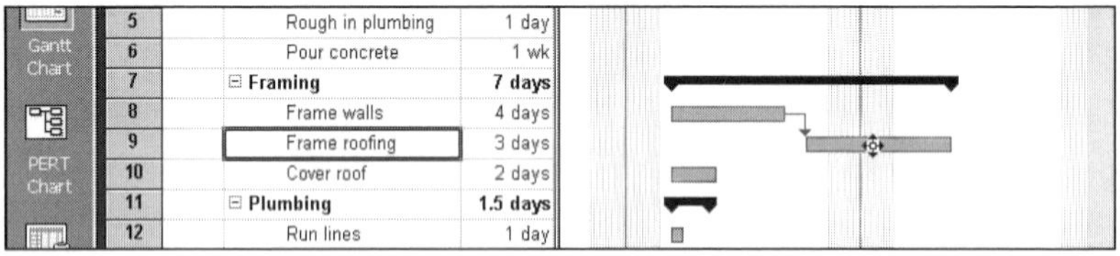

FIG. 6.15

Confirm that the starting mouse pointer is the four-headed arrow before dragging to link tasks.

To link tasks with the mouse, follow these steps:

1. Scroll the task list so the *predecessor* task is visible on-screen.

2. Position the mouse pointer over the middle of the predecessor task. It is not necessary to select the row for the task in the Gantt Chart table. In the Gantt Chart view, make sure the mouse pointer has the shape shown in Figure 6.15.

3. Click and drag toward the middle of the *dependent* (successor) task. The mouse pointer changes to the shape of three chain links (see Figure 6.16). In both the Gantt Chart and the Calendar, an information box identifies the predecessor task you started on and the dependent task bar you have positioned the mouse over.

   If the dependent task you are seeking is off the screen, move to the edge of the screen, and Project scrolls the task list or the timescale to bring the task bar into view.

   If you want to cancel the linking procedure, simply move the mouse over a blank area of the Gantt Chart or the Calendar and release the button. In the PERT Chart, you must return the mouse to the task you started with before releasing the mouse button, or you will create a new task with a link.

4. When the information box shows that you have selected the correct dependent task, release the mouse button to finalize the link.

FIG. 6.16

Drag from the predecessor task bar to the dependent (successor) task bar to establish a Finish-to-Start link.

Predecessor task

Successor task   Mouse pointer

The dependency type created by dragging is always a Finish-to-Start relationship. You can change the link type, add a lag or lead, or even delete the link with the mouse. To modify a link with the mouse, see the section in this chapter "Modifying, Reviewing, and Removing Dependency Links."

Working with the Automatic Linking Option

Microsoft Project has an option called *Autolink* that can help you manage the links in the task list when you move, delete, or insert tasks in a linked series of tasks. However, Autolink only works if the affected links are Finish-to-Start links. Autolink has these features:

- If you cut or delete a task from a chain of Finish-to-Start linked tasks, Autolink repairs the break in the chain by linking together the former predecessor and successor of the deleted task.

- If you insert a task in a chain of Finish-to-Start linked tasks, Autolink breaks the former link between the tasks. The new task is inserted between the existing tasks, and then the newly inserted task is linked to the task above and below it to keep the linked sequence intact.

- If you move a task, Autolink repairs the chain at the task's old site and inserts the new task into the chain at the new site.

In Figure 6.17, the first group of tasks shows a series of tasks before a task is inserted. The second group of tasks illustrates what happens if you insert the Inspect Foundation task with Autolink enabled. Autolink inserts the Inspect Foundation task between Foundation and Frame Walls, the new task automatically links to Foundation as its predecessor and to Frame Walls as its successor, and the former link between those tasks is removed. The third set of tasks shows what happens if you insert the Inspect Foundation task without Autolink enabled. The new task is scheduled to start at the beginning of the project and is not included in the linked chain of tasks.

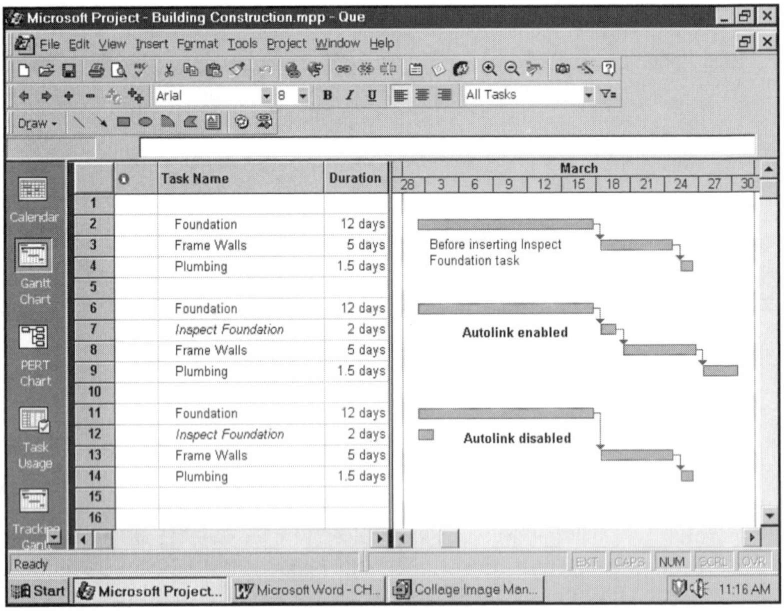

FIG. 6.17

Autolink retains the sequence of tasks when you insert or remove tasks from a linked chain of tasks.

N O T E   If you add or remove a task from the beginning or end of a linked chain, instead of the middle of the chain, Autolink does not include the new task in the chain. Thus, inserting a task at the beginning of a series of linked tasks or after the last task in a linked sequence does not cause Autolink to extend the chain to include the new task.

In order to include a task in a sequence, when the task has been added either to the beginning or ending of the sequence, you will have to link the tasks yourself. Use one of the traditional linking methods described earlier in this chapter. ■

By default, Autolink is enabled, but you can disable it by changing the status of the Autolink option. Follow these steps:

1. Choose Tools, Options. The Options dialog box appears.

2. Choose the Schedule tab.

3. Deselect the Autolink Inserted or Moved Tasks check box. This disables Autolink. To turn it back on, select the check box again.

4. To set the option status as a global default for all new projects, choose the Set as Default button. Otherwise, the change you make will only affect the active project document.

5. Choose the OK button to close the dialog box.

CAUTION

As convenient as Autolink can be when editing a task list, it can cause you problems by creating unintended task links. Be careful when this option is enabled, especially when inserting tasks. Check to see what links it creates and that they are as you want them. Unintended task links can become a vexing problem in a project schedule.

Modifying, Reviewing, and Removing Dependency Links

As you progress in auditing your project plan, it may become necessary to adjust the sequence of links you have established. You may want to modify the type of linking relationship between tasks, insert lag or lead time between tasks, or remove the link entirely. Additionally, before finalizing your schedule, you will certainly want to review the links to ensure the sequence is correct.

Entering Lags and Leads

As discussed earlier in this chapter, you might need to allow for a delay (lag) or an overlap (lead) between linked tasks. An earlier example discussed the need for a two-day delay between the first and final coats of paint to allow the first coat to dry completely before beginning the final coat. This is an example of a lag. If the clean up can begin before the last stroke of the final coat is applied, then the Final Coat and the Clean Up tasks can overlap. This is an example of a lead.

Lag and lead time are measured in time units, just like duration. Positive numbers represent lag time, and negative numbers represent lead time. You can enter lag or lead as a number followed by one of the time code letters you use for entering durations (minute, hour, day, or week). For example, use 2d to define a two-day lag and –4h to define a four-hour lead. If you type a number without a time unit (m, h, d, or w), Project appends the default unit. This default unit is controlled from a field on the Schedule tab of the Options dialog box. Choose Tools, Options to get to the Options dialog box. The default duration is Days in the Duration Is Entered In field.

You can also express lag or lead time as a percent of the predecessor's duration. Therefore, if a task can be started when its predecessor is within ten percent of being finished, you can enter a Finish-to-Start link with a ten-percent lead (entered as **–10%**). Project schedules the task to start so it overlaps the last ten percent of the predecessor task duration. Using percentage lags and leads allows the amount of lag or lead to vary with changes in the duration of the predecessor. Thus, the longer the duration of the predecessor, the more lag or lead would be scheduled.

There are several places you can enter a lag time or lead time. These include the Task Information dialog box, the Task Form view, the Entry Table, and on the timescale side of the Gantt Chart view.

Part
II

Ch
6

■ To activate the Task Information dialog box, double-click the task name. You can also choose the Information button on the Standard toolbar or choose Project, Task Information. On the Predecessors tab, click in the Lag field, type the amount of lag or lead time, and choose OK.

■ In the Gantt Chart view, split the screen to activate the Task Form view in the lower pane. Click once in the lower pane to active it. If necessary, choose Format, Details to display Resources & Predecessors. Choose the Lag field, type the amount of lag or lead time, and choose OK. Figure 6.18 shows a lag of 5 days being added between the Foundation phase (task 2) and the Framing phase (task 7) to give the foundation concrete a chance to dry and settle before framing the walls.

FIG. 6.18

Using the Task Form view is one of the most convenient methods. Here a lag of 5 days is being added between the summary tasks.

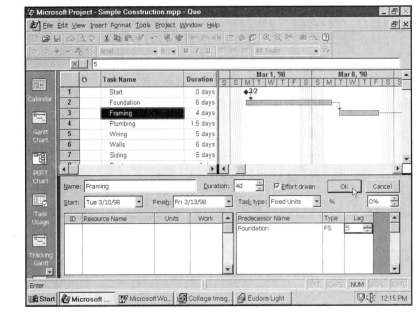

■ The Entry Table is the default table in the Gantt Chart and Task Sheet views. To enter in lag time or lead time, you must move to the Predecessors field. This field contains the task ID number of the predecessor task. For example, Figure 6.19 shows Schedule Interviews (task 3) has a predecessor of Background Research (task 2). The dependency relationship is Finish-to-Start, if no code is listed. Since we can begin scheduling the interviews as we are completing the research, the tasks can overlap by four hours. You would type in **FS-4h** after the task ID and press Enter. The predecessor field would then read **2FS-4h**. Even though the relationship is already Finish-to-Start, it is necessary when you enter a lag or lead to type in the relationship if one is not already there.

■ In the Gantt Chart or PERT Chart views, use the scroll bars to display the tasks so that you can see the linking line between the predecessor and dependent (successor) tasks. Position the tip of the mouse pointer on the line connecting the tasks where you want to add a lag or lead. Make certain the mouse pointer is a single white arrow pointing up and to the left. Double-click the linking line. The Task Dependency dialog box appears, as shown in Figure 6.20. Enter a lag or lead in the Lag text box, using positive entries for lags and negative entries for leads. Choose the OK button to complete the change.

FIG. 6.19
Entering lags and leads in the Entry Table.

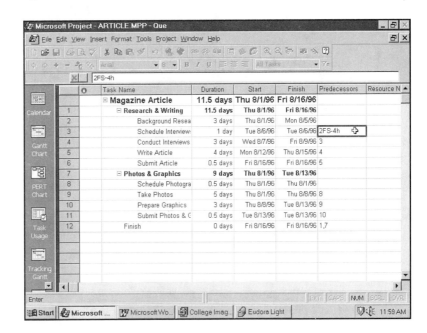

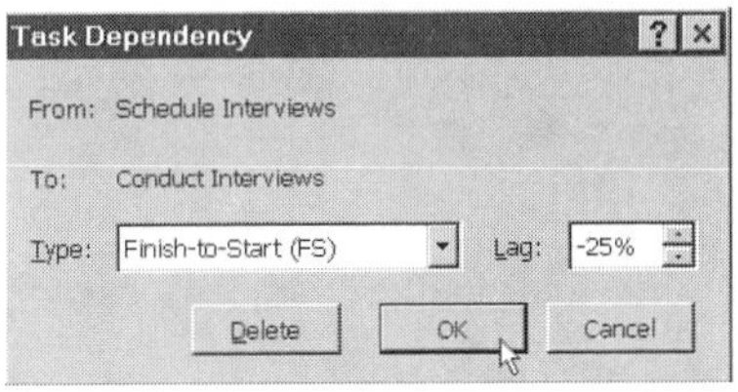

FIG. 6.20
Use the mouse to add a Lag or Lead in the timescale side of the Gantt Chart. The Task Dependency dialog box shows a 25% lead.

Removing Links

If you find a link between tasks is no longer necessary, or you prefer to create a link to another task, you will want to remove the current link. Just as there are several ways to create links, many of those methods are also used to remove links.

 Removing Links Using the Menu or Toolbar   You can easily unlink tasks using the menu or toolbar. Select the tasks you want to unlink and choose Edit, Unlink Tasks or click the Unlink Tasks button on the Standard toolbar. You can also press Shift+Ctrl+F2.

TIP If you select a single task and then choose Edit, Unlink Tasks or click the Unlink Tasks button, Project removes all predecessors for that task.

If you select multiple tasks and then choose Edit, Unlink Tasks or the Unlink Tasks button, Project removes all links between any pair of the selected tasks.

Select tasks for unlinking in the same manner you select tasks for linking. The unlinking operation works on all task relationships, not just the simple Finish-to-Start relationship.

To remove all links from the project, select all tasks by clicking a field name, such as a Task Name, in the spreadsheet table, and choose Edit, Unlink Tasks. You can also use the Unlink Tasks button.

Removing Links Using the Task Information Dialog Box   You can remove task links with the Task Information dialog box. To remove a link, follow these steps:

1. Select the dependent (successor) task.
2. Open the Task Information dialog box by double-clicking the task or choosing Project, Task Information.
3. Click the Predecessors tab to display the Predecessors page.
4. Select the row of the predecessor you want to remove.
5. Press the Delete key to delete the row listing, or change the Type to (None).
6. Repeat steps 4 and 5 for all predecessors you want to remove.
7. Choose the OK button to close the dialog box and the link, or links, will be removed.

Removing Links Using the Task Form View   To delete dependency definitions on the Task Form, follow these steps:

1. In the top pane, select the dependent task.
2. Select a field in the row for the predecessor in the bottom pane.
3. Press the Delete key to delete the row in the Predecessors table.
4. Complete the change by choosing the OK button.

Removing Links Using the Entry Table   To delete a task link on the Task Sheet, you can select both the predecessor and successor tasks and choose Edit, Unlink Tasks as previously described. You can also select the Predecessors field for the dependent task and use Ctrl+Delete to clear the cell entry.

> **CAUTION**
> When removing a link in the Table or Task Sheet, do *not* use the Delete key—this will delete the entire task!

Removing Links Using the Mouse   The dependency type created by dragging is always a Finish-to-Start relationship. You can change the link type, add a lag or lead, or even delete the link in the timescale with the mouse. To remove or modify a link with the mouse, follow these steps:

1. Position the tip of the mouse pointer on the line connecting the tasks whose link you want to delete or change.

> **CAUTION**
>
> Make certain the mouse pointer is a single white arrow pointing up and to the left.

2. Double-click the linking line. The Task Dependency dialog box appears (see Figure 6.21).

FIG. 6.21

Change or delete a dependency relationship with the Task Dependency dialog box.

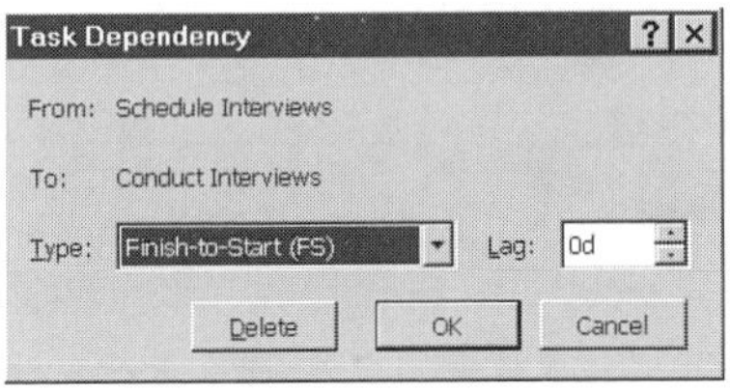

3. If you want to change the link, select the type of link you want to use from the Type list box.

4. To remove the link, choose the Delete button.

5. Choose the OK button to complete the deletion or change in the link definition.

Linking Outlined Task Lists

Linking in outlined task lists is more complicated than in non-outlined lists because more options are available. You can link the summary tasks to each other, you can link the subtasks in one summary group directly to the subtasks in other summary groups, or you can link summary tasks to subtasks of other summary groups.

Linking Summary Tasks   A summary task is implicitly linked to each of its subtasks. Unless the summary task has constraints on when it can start, its start date is derived from the earliest start of any of its subtasks. If the summary task is constrained, then its subtasks can start no sooner than the summary task. If the summary task is linked to another task, its predecessor and the type of dependency relationship dictate when the subtasks can begin.

Thus, there are implicit links already in place between a summary task and each of its subtasks. If you attempt to link a subtask to its summary task, Project displays a warning message indicating you cannot create the link.

Part

II

Ch

6

If you select all tasks and let Microsoft Project link the tasks in an outlined project, it links all tasks at the first outline level to each other, whether they are summary tasks or not. It then links the next level subtasks in any summary tasks, until all outline levels in all summary tasks are linked at their own level.

The advantage of linking summary tasks is that you can change the structure of the detail tasks in a summary group without worrying about the link between that group and any summary groups. If you add new detail tasks at the end of a summary group, for example, you don't have to worry about linking the new task to the first detail task in the next summary group to retain the overall sequence of tasks. In the first example of tasks in Figure 6.22, the last subtask in the Foundation phase (Pour Concrete) is linked to the first subtask in the Framing phase (Frame Walls). In the second example of tasks, the Foundation summary task is linked to the Framing summary task.

FIG. 6.22

The two approaches to linking between phases: linking the summary tasks or linking the subtasks.

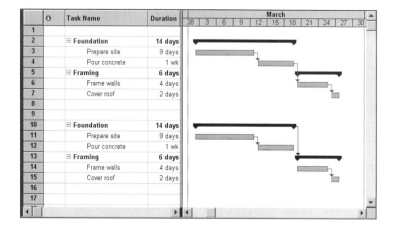

When new tasks are added to the Foundation phase, the links remain unchanged. If the new tasks have no impact on the Framing phase, keeping the link in the first example is appropriate. If the new tasks do have an impact on the Framing phase, linking the summary tasks together provides the most flexibility. No matter how many new tasks are added, the end of the Foundation phase will always dictate the start of the Framing phase, see Figure 6.23.

If automatic linking is enabled and you rearrange an outline, carefully review the links that result each time you move a task or group of tasks in the outline. You might have to edit the links to reflect exactly the relationship you want defined.

▶ **See** "Working with the Automatic Linking Option," **p. 189**

Leaving Summary Tasks Out of the Linking Chain   The other method of linking tasks in an outline is to ignore the summary tasks and link only the detail tasks. The predecessor for the first detail task in a summary group is a detail task in a previous summary group. This method of linking is harder to maintain. If you add tasks at the beginning or end of a group, you must maintain the proper link to other groups.

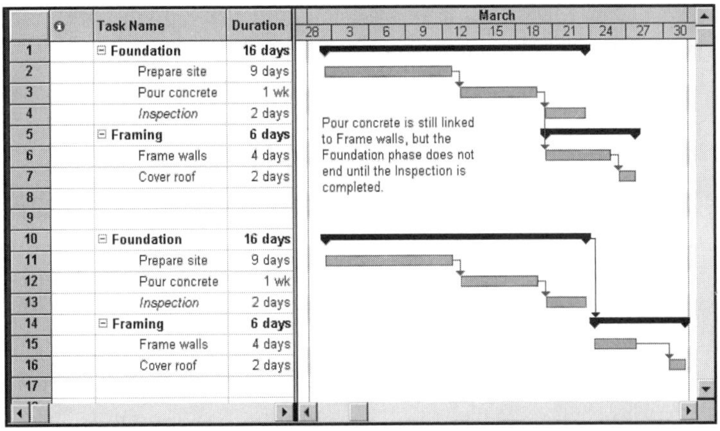

FIG. 6.23
When new tasks are added to the end of the Foundation phase, a different result will be produced, depending on the links you have originally created between the phases.

CAUTION

Make sure you establish no links to subtasks that require the subtask to start before the first subtask in the summary group. Using the illustration in Figure 6.24 as an example, if you link the first two tasks in the Production Phase (Setup Assembly Line and Hire Assemblers) in a Start-to-Start relationship with a lead time of five days, the linked task (Hire Assemblers) needs to start before its predecessor (Setup Assembly Line)—but that's before the Summary task (Production Phase) is scheduled to start. Project places the link but cannot change the schedule as required by the link. In other words, it ignores the lead time defined in the link and schedules both tasks to start at the same time, as shown in the start dates in Figure 6.24.

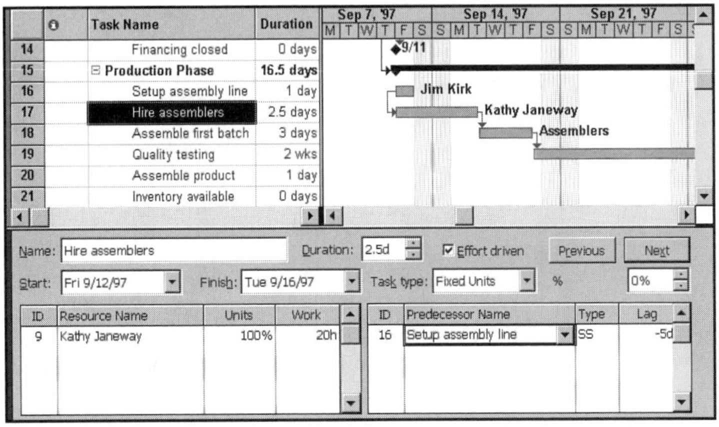

FIG. 6.24
Do not create links that have a subtask starting before the first subtask in the summary group.

Auditing the Task Links

The project schedule is heavily influenced by the linking relationships you establish among tasks. It is very easy to accidentally link tasks or break task links, and you should review the link relationships carefully before committing to the project schedule. Accidental links could easily skew the finish date of the project.

The Gantt Chart shows the task links as arrows connecting the task bars, with the arrow always pointing to the dependent (successor) task. There are additional views that are useful when reviewing the links defined in a project.

When you split the screen in the Gantt Chart view, the Task Form appears in the bottom half of the screen. Activate the lower half of the screen, and choose Format, Details to display predecessors and successors. For the task you have active, the predecessor and successor tasks are listed, along with any lag or lead associated with the link. Use the Previous and Next buttons in the bottom split to review the links.

The Task PERT view shows the predecessors and successors for just the selected task, and is useful for confirming that you defined the task relationships as intended (see Figure 6.25). You display the Task PERT view in the bottom pane while selecting tasks in another task view in the top pane, usually the Gantt Chart view. The selected task is represented by a box or node in the center of the Task PERT view, with predecessors on the left and successors on the right. The type of relationship and any lag or lead is shown next to the linked task nodes. For example, the Setup Assembly Line task has one predecessor—Prototype Complete in a Finish-to-Start relationship—and two successors—Hire Assemblers in a Finish-to-Finish relationship and Assemble First Batch in a Finish-to-Start relationship—with a four-hour lag.

FIG. 6.25
The Task PERT view offers a good review of the predecessor and successor links for a task.

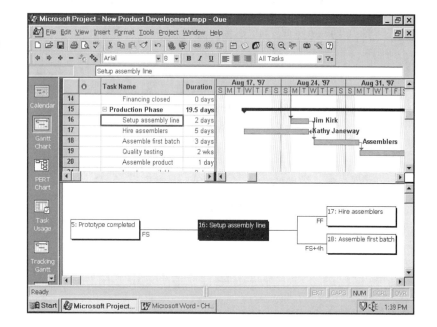

N O T E The Task PERT view is a display-only view; you can neither make changes nor can you print this view. ▩

To display the Task PERT below the Gantt Chart, follow these steps:

1. Display the Gantt Chart in the top pane by choosing <u>V</u>iew, <u>G</u>antt Chart.

2. Split the screen by choosing <u>W</u>indow, <u>S</u>plit. By default, the Task Form view appears in the lower pane.

3. Activate the bottom pane by clicking anywhere in the bottom pane or by pressing the F6 key.

4. Choose <u>V</u>iew, <u>M</u>ore Views, Task PERT.

5. Choose the <u>A</u>pply button to display the Task PERT view in the lower pane.

Select tasks in the top pane to see their predecessors and successors displayed graphically in the bottom pane.

T I P If you select multiple tasks in the top pane, you can use the horizontal scroll bar below the Task PERT to view the chart for each of the selected tasks. Pressing the Home key displays the view for the first of the selected tasks, and pressing the End key displays the view for the last of the selected tasks. Use these same techniques to select different tasks if you display the Task PERT as a full screen view.

Finally, another method of reviewing task links is in the PERT Chart view. The PERT Chart view concentrates on linking relationships by representing each task as a box with arrows from predecessor to successor tasks. Chapter 7, "Working with the Major Task Views," is devoted to using and understanding the major task views, including the PERT Chart.

Task Splitting

A new and powerful feature, *task splitting*, has been added to Microsoft Project 98. The assumption when you schedule a task is that the task will start, be worked on continuously, and finish. The reality is that certain tasks in your project may have a scheduled or unplanned interruption.

If you know there will be interruptions in a task, you can split the task when you create it. If the interruption happens after a task has started, you can split it and use the split to show when work will continue on the remaining portion.

Several examples of tasks that would be good candidates for task splitting are:

▩ Suppose someone is scheduled to work on a task, but there is a week-long business trip planned during the time she is scheduled to work on this task. The work on the task is going to stop during the week she is gone and will resume when she returns. You can incorporate the interruption in the planning stage of your project.

▓ Suppose the project has already begun. In a status meeting it is decided to redefine all of the project's remaining tasks. It may be necessary to interrupt any in-progress tasks to incorporate the revisions to the project. You can interrupt these ongoing tasks and then reschedule the remaining work.

There are certain properties of split tasks that you need to keep in mind:

A task can have an unlimited number of splits.

When you link to a task that is split, the link is to the task; you cannot create a link to a split portion of a task.

There are three views where you can create split tasks. The most accessible is the Gantt Chart. But you can also split tasks in the Task Usage view and, if resources are assigned to the task, in the Resource Usage view.

▶ **See** "Resolving Overallocations by Delaying Tasks," **p. 371**

To split a task in the Gantt Chart with the mouse, follow these steps:

1. Activate the Gantt Chart view.

2. Choose Edit, Split Task, click the Split Task button on the Standard toolbar, or right-click the task and select Split Task from the shortcut menu.

3. In the timescale side of the Gantt Chart, position the mouse pointer over the task bar you would like to split (see Figure 6.26). The Split Task information box allows you to indicate where you want the split to occur.

4. Click the task bar and the second segment of the split begins approximately 24 hours later. You can also click and drag the task bar to the desired new date and time.

T I P   Watch the start and finish dates in the Split Task information box carefully to determine when this segment of the split task resumes.

To remove the split, drag one of the split segments into another split segment. Whenever you drag a split, the Split Tasks information box appears.

To move a portion of the split task without moving the other, position the mouse pointer over the split task. The cursor will change to a four-headed arrow. Click and drag the task bar to the right or left to change the start date of this section of the task. Dragging the first section of a split task moves all sections of the task. Holding down the Shift key as you drag a later section of a split task also moves all sections of the task.

To change the duration of a split, follow these steps:

1. In the timescale side of the Gantt Chart, move the mouse pointer over the right side of any portion of the split task. The pointer will change to a right arrow with a line in front of it (see Figure 6.27).

FIG. 6.26

The Split Task information box accompanies the mouse pointer when you split a task.

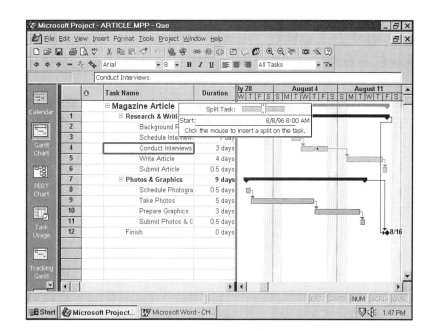

FIG. 6.27

Changing the duration of a split task.

Mouse pointer ——

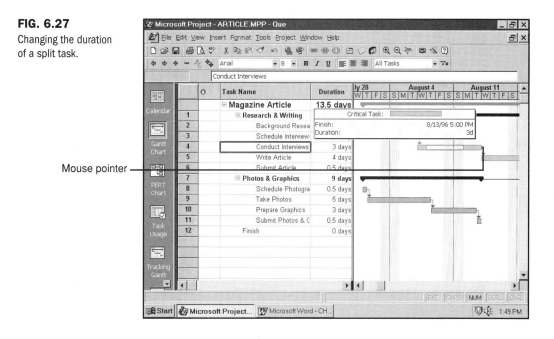

Part

II

Ch

6

2. To shorten the duration, drag the mouse to the left. To lengthen the duration, drag the mouse to the right. As you drag, the Split Tasks dialog box will indicate the new duration.

Working with Task Constraints

When you add a task to a project with a fixed start date, Microsoft Project schedules it by default to start as soon as possible. If the project is scheduled from a fixed finish date, the default is to schedule the task as late as possible. The program considers any sequencing requirements for the task's predecessors, and then schedules the task to begin as soon as possible after the predecessor tasks relationships are satisfied.

Some tasks, however, might be subject to deadlines from outside the project: deadlines imposed by customers, contractors, the government, or even internal company policies. Some situations are shown in the following examples:

- A manufacturing contract might call for delivery of the product no later than a stated date.
- A contract with a vendor might stipulate the earliest delivery date and delivery can be expected no earlier than that date.
- The financial task of preparing payroll reports is constrained by pay dates and tax reports.

In Microsoft Project 98, you now have the option to treat constraints as flexible *soft* constraints or as inflexible *hard* constraints. In previous versions of Project, a constraint was always a hard constraint, which meant that the constraint was honored even when it meant violating the conditions of its predecessor links. The default setting in Microsoft Project 98 is also to treat all constraints as hard constraints.

Figure 6.28 illustrates hard and soft constraints. Suppose that Frame Walls is a task with a Finish-to-Start link to its predecessor, the Pour Foundation task. Suppose further that the Frame Walls task has been given a constrained finish date and that the constraint deadline will just be met with the current schedule. If the predecessor task were to be delayed for any reason, the Frame Walls task would not finish until after its constraint deadline. With a hard constraint, Project ignores the predecessor relationship and schedules Frame Walls to finish by the constraint date, even though the schedule will show the Frame Walls task starting before the predecessor is completed. You will receive a strong warning from Project that the schedule is not accurate, and you will have to resolve the issue.

Treating constraints as hard constraints is still the default setting for Microsoft Project 98. However, you can also choose to have Microsoft Project 98 treat all of a project's constraints as soft constraints. With a soft constraint, the predecessor relationship is honored, and Project allows the constraint to be missed. A Constraint Violation icon appears in the indicator column to flag the task for your attention (see Figure 6.28). You still need to resolve the issue, but the schedule is more realistic now: You really do miss deadlines in the real world. You hardly ever start putting walls up before the foundation is in place.

FIG. 6.28
The impact of hard and soft constraints on a set of tasks.

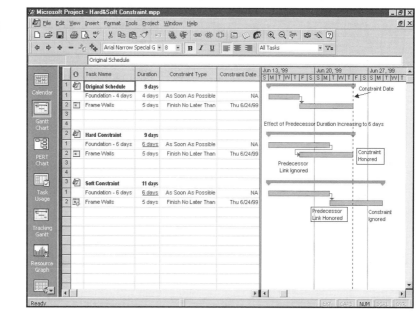

The section "Resolving Conflicts Caused by Constraints" later in this chapter discusses how to resolve constraint conflicts.

> **CAUTION**
> One of the most common mistakes a novice user of Microsoft Project can make is to accidentally impose constraints that make the schedule impossible to reconcile. You create task constraints any time you specify the scheduled start or finish dates for a task. For example, entering the dates in the Gantt Chart view or Task Information dialog box, or moving a task by dragging the task bar in the Gantt Chart or the Calendar view will add constraints to a task.

Part
II
Ch
6

Understanding the Types of Constraints

There are eight constraint types that describe the possible restrictions on the scheduling of a task, described in Table 6.2.

Table 6.2 The Constraint Options Available in Microsoft Project

Constraint Type	Abbreviation	Description
As Late As Possible	ALAP	Delays the task as long as possible, without holding up the finish of the project and without creating a conflict for any successor task that is constrained. There is no Constraint Date for this constraint.
As Soon As Possible	ASAP	Marks a task as not constrained, and does not have a Constraint Date.
Finish No Earlier Than	FNET	This task must not finish before the defined Constraint Date.
Finish No Later Than	FNLT	This task must complete on or before the defined Constraint Date.
Must Finish On	MFO	This task must finish exactly on the defined Constraint Date.
Must Start On	MSO	This task must start exactly on the defined Constraint Date.
Start No Earlier Than	SNET	This task cannot start until the defined Constraint Date or later.
Start No Later Than	SNLT	This task must start on or before the defined Constraint Date.

98

Whenever a task has a constraint other than As Soon As Possible or As Late As Possible, there will be an Indicator icon in the Indicators field in the table side of the Gantt Chart view. These icons appear like calendars, with either a blue or a red "dot" in the icon. The red dots indicate an *inflexible* constraint, and the blue dots indicate a *flexible* constraint.

When a project is scheduled from a fixed start date, the task schedule is pushed out from the project start date toward a project finish date. Adding or lengthening tasks makes it necessary to push the finish date out further. Any constraint that keeps tasks from being scheduled later can block this expansion toward later finish dates and create conflicts in the schedule. Such constraints are called *inflexible* constraints. For projects that have a fixed start date, the inflexible constraints are the Finish/Start No Later Than and the Must Finish/Start On constraints. The indicators for these tasks have a red dot when the project is scheduled from a fixed start date. The other constraints with dates (Finish/Start No Earlier Than) are considered *flexible* in a fixed start date project, and their indicators have a blue dot.

When a project is scheduled from a fixed finish date, the task schedule is calculated from the finish date and pushed back in time toward an earlier start date. Adding or lengthening tasks pushes the start date to earlier and earlier dates. Any constraint that keeps tasks from being scheduled earlier can block this expansion back to an earlier start time and create conflicts in the schedule. These inflexible constraints in a fixed finish date project are the Finish/Start No Earlier Than and the Must Finish/Start On constraints. The indicators for the inflexible constraints have a red dot. The other dated constraints (Finish/Start No Later Than) are considered flexible in a fixed finish date project and have blue dots in their indicators.

Table 6.3 summarizes the flexible/inflexible categories for the eight constraint types and the indicators you may see for them.

Table 6.3   Whether a Constraint Type Is Considered "Hard" or "Soft" Depends in Most Cases on the Context

Constraint Type Project	Abbreviation	Fixed Start Date Project	Fixed Finish Date
As Soon As Possible	ASAP	Flexible (no indicator)	Flexible (no indicator)
As Late As Possible	ALAP	Flexible (no indicator)	Flexible (no indicator)
Must Finish On	MFO	Inflexible (Red dot)	Inflexible (Red dot)
Must Start On	MSO	Inflexible (Red dot)	Inflexible (Red dot)
Finish No Earlier Than	FNET	Flexible (Blue dot)	Inflexible (Red dot)
Start No Earlier Than	SNET	Flexible (Blue dot)	Inflexible (Red dot)
Finish No Later Than	FNLT	Inflexible (Red dot)	Flexible (Blue dot)
Start No Later Than	SNLT	Inflexible (Red dot)	Flexible (Blue dot)

Entering Task Constraints

You can record task constraints in the Task Information dialog box. You can also display the Task Details Form view in the bottom pane if you want to view the constraint options continuously as you select different tasks.

To enter task constraints in the Task Information dialog box, follow these steps:

1. Select the task you want to constrain.
2. Choose Project, Task Information, or click the Information button on the Standard toolbar. The Task Information dialog box appears.

TIP You can also double-click the task name, or use the keyboard shortcut Shift+F2 to display the Task Information dialog box.

3. Choose the Advanced tab to display the Advanced page.
4. From the Constrain Task Type drop-down list, select the constraint type you want (see Figure 6.29).

Part

II

Ch

6

5. In the Constrain Task Date text box, enter the constraint date, if necessary. The As Soon As Possible and As Late As Possible constraints do not require a constraint date. All others require a date entry.

> **T I P**
> It is a good idea to add a note to the task indicating why the constraint was set. This will provide you with a reminder and, if you are sharing the project file with colleagues, will provide them with important information as well. To add a note to the task, simply click the Notes tab of the Task Information dialog box.

6. Select OK or press Enter to complete the entry.

FIG. 6.29

Choose the type of constraint from the Type entry list on the Advanced tab of the Task Information dialog box.

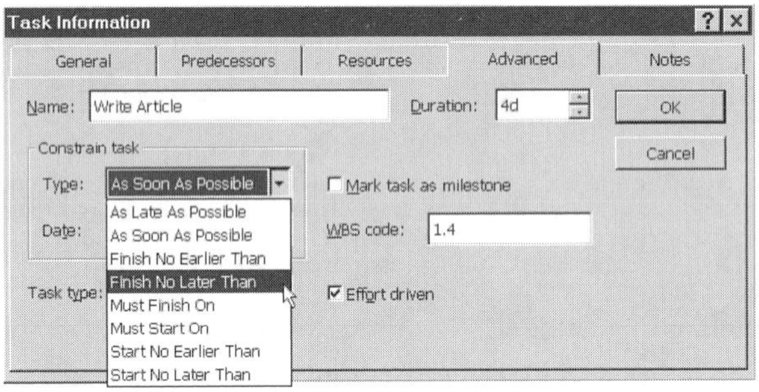

Constraints can interfere with Project's capability to freely adjust your schedule and can lead to scheduling conflicts. If you add a constraint to a task that is linked to other tasks, and those other tasks may be impacted by the constraint, the Planning Wizard warns you that your constraint could potentially create a problem either now or in the future (see Figure 6.30). The Planning Wizard dialog box offers three options:

- The default option is Cancel…. If the imposition of the constraint was accidental, accept this option and choose the OK button. The constraint will be canceled.

- The second option offers to continue after modifying the constraint to be less restrictive—a Start No Earlier Than or a Finish No Earlier Than constraint. These constraints offer less potential for disrupting the schedule, but they are not totally innocuous either.

- The third option lets you continue and add the constraint as entered.

Select one of the options and choose the OK button. Choosing the Cancel button is the same as choosing the first option.

See "Resolving Problems in the Schedule" later in this chapter for information about scheduling conflicts and how to deal with them.

To enter task constraints in the Task Details Form view, perform the following steps:

1. With a task view like the Gantt Chart in the top pane, split the screen and activate the lower pane.

2. Choose View, More Views. The More Views dialog box appears.

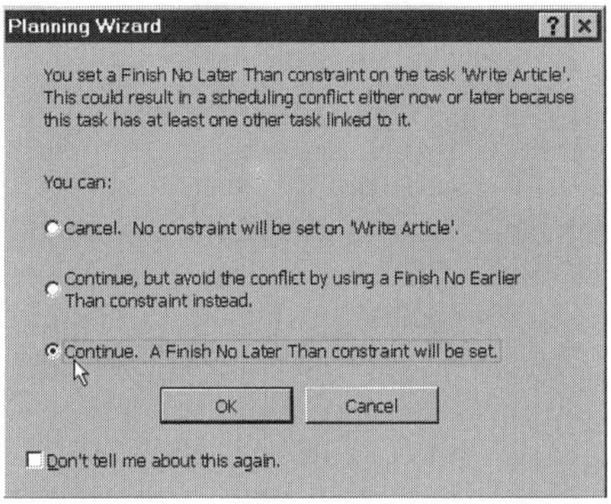

FIG. 6.30
The Planning Wizard alerts you when a constraint might cause a problem. This can save you from accidentally placing constraints you didn't intend.

3. Scroll toward the bottom of the list of views and select the Task Details Form view.

4. Choose the Apply button to display the form.

5. Select the Constraint field and click the drop-down list arrow or press Alt+down arrow to display the list of constraint options.

6. Select the appropriate constraint type.

7. Enter the constraint date, if required, in the Date field. As Soon As Possible and As Late As Possible do not require a constraint date.

8. Complete the entry by clicking OK or by pressing Enter.

You will want to verify which tasks have constraints—constraints you have intentionally set and ones that may have been created accidentally. You can use a standard filter to see those tasks which have constraints. This filter, Tasks With Fixed Dates, selects not only tasks that have Constraint Dates defined, but also tasks with Actual Dates defined. The Actual Date is the date when work actually began on the task and is an indicator that work has begun on the task. You can create your own filter for tasks with constraints by removing the Actual Date part of the filter definition.

▶ **See** "Creating Custom Filters with AutoFilter," **p. 763**

From the Formatting toolbar, choose the Filter drop-down list (which displays All Tasks by default). Scroll down and choose the Tasks with Fixed Dates filter.

▶ **See** "Using Filters," **p. 397**

Removing Task Constraints

To remove a task constraint, the constraint type needs to be changed to As Soon As Possible. Follow these steps:

1. Select the task.

2. In the Task Details Form view, select the Constraint field. Or in the Task Information dialog box, choose the Advanced tab and select the Constrain Task Type drop-down list.

Part

II

Ch

6

3. Select As Soon As Possible from the list. It is not necessary to remove the date in the date field; Microsoft Project will automatically do this for you.

4. Confirm the change by choosing OK or by pressing Enter.

If you want to return several tasks to an unconstrained status, select all the tasks you plan to change. Access the Task Information through the Information tool on the Standard toolbar, or by choosing Project, Task Information. Since more than one task is selected, the dialog box is titled Multiple Task Information. With multiple tasks, some options in the dialog box are not available. Choose the Advanced tab, and select As Soon As Possible from the Constrain Task Type drop-down list. When you select OK, the changes are made in all the selected tasks. To remove all constraints in the project, select a column heading in the task list table and choose the As Soon As Possible constraint in the Task Information dialog box.

Resolving Conflicts Caused by Constraints

Frequently, internal inconsistencies exist within the project plan—inconsistencies that reveal that the project plan simply cannot work. One of the most prominent of these inconsistencies is conflicting constraints placed on tasks which cause irreconcilable conflicts. You can identify and eliminate internal inconsistencies caused by task scheduling constraints with the help of the Planning Wizard and the Office Assistant.

In the example in Figure 6.31, we have set a Finish No Later Than constraint on task 6, Administrative Review. The Vice President will be out of town between 10/3/97 and 10/13/97 for a business trip, and she is the only one who can approve the Office Move Proposal. The constraint imposes a deadline of 10/2/97 on the Administrative Review task. The task duration is 5 days.

The Administrative Review (task 6) is scheduled to start on 9/24/97 and finish on 9/30/97, in ample time to meet its deadline of 10/2/97.

However, if the duration of Determine Requirements (task 4) is changed from 5 days to 10 days, this will cause a change in the scheduling of Write Proposal (task 5) which in turn causes a change in the scheduling of Administrative Review (task 6).

When you make a change to the schedule which conflicts with a constrained task, the Planning Wizard displays, as shown in Figure 6.32. The function of the Planning Wizard is to warn you about the potential scheduling conflict imposed by your action. The message in Figure 6.32 is created by changing the schedule of tasks performed prior to the Administrative Review. The Planning Wizard is alerting you that task 5 (Write Proposal) is linked to a task that cannot move. A successor task to task 5, in this case Administrative Review, is linked to task 5, which contains the constraint.

The choices presented in the message displayed in Figure 6.32 are to cancel and avoid the scheduling conflict or to continue and allow the scheduling conflict. Unless you have accidentally changed something which causes the conflict, you will most often choose to continue and allow the scheduling conflict.

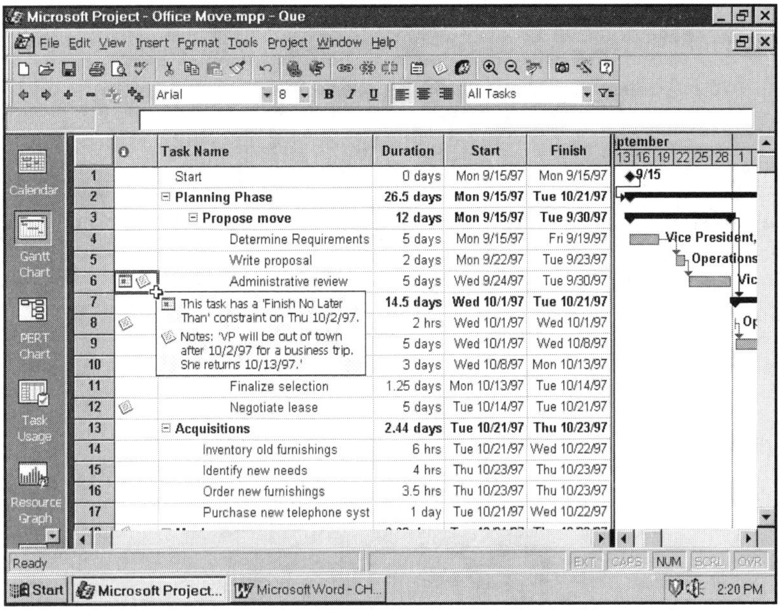

FIG. 6.31
A Finish No Later Than constraint imposes a deadline on a task.

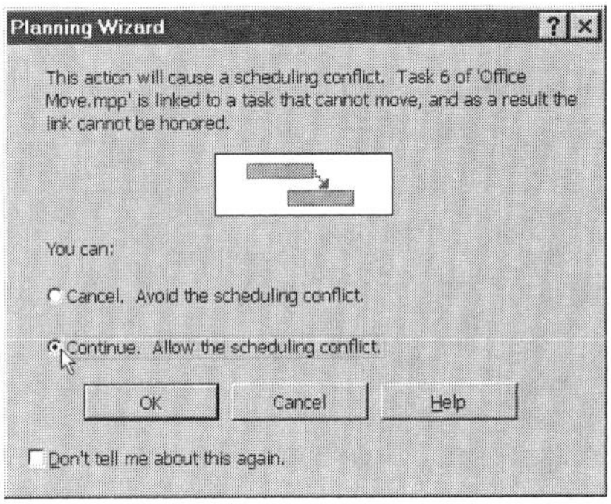

FIG. 6.32
A warning message appears when a task has a deadline that cannot move.

CAUTION

If you allow the scheduling conflict, it is important that you note the *task number* mentioned in the Planning Wizard dialog box. You will not be warned again of this conflict, or which task has the conflict.

Notice that you can discontinue the Planning Wizard by marking the Don't Tell Me About This Again check box. This check box refers not only to this particular conflict but also to all scheduling conflicts. It is recommended that you leave the Planning Wizard active to assist you in working with Microsoft Project. Use the options in the General tab of the Options dialog box to turn the Planning Wizard to the on or off position.

Figure 6.33 shows the result of an unresolved scheduling conflict. Notice the start and finish dates for the tasks. The deadline for the Administrative Review is still 10/2/97. However, we won't finish determining the requirements, let alone write the proposal, before the Administrative Review is scheduled to start.

FIG. 6.33

The linking lines that wrap from the finish of task 5 to the start of task 6 are another indication that task 6 has a constrained date.

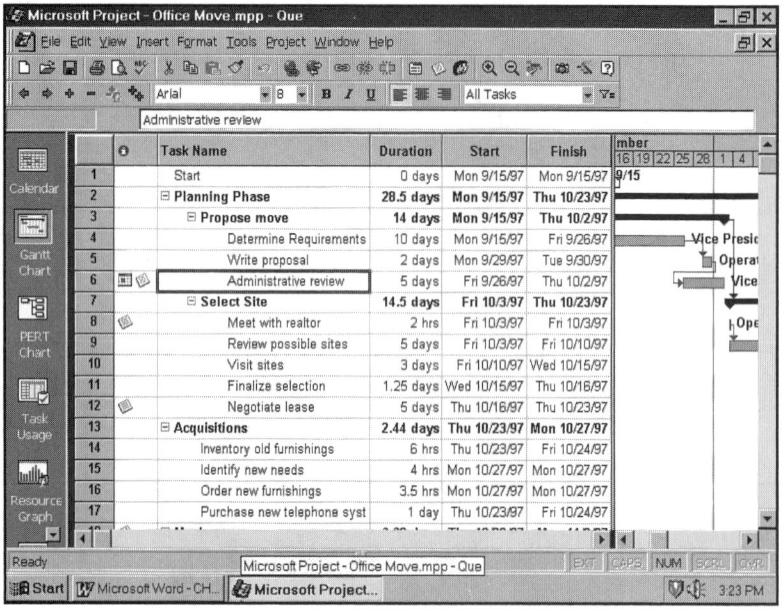

If you do not resolve the conflict, Project will not warn you again.

The cause of this scheduling problem almost always is a constraint. The problem also can be caused by a successor task that already had an actual start date recorded. In either case, the constraint keeps the successor start date from being rescheduled, or the existence of an actual start date keeps the start date from being rescheduled.

The task named in the message has one or more successors that have fixed dates—dates that can't be rescheduled to accommodate changes in the schedule. These dates are fixed either because of constraints on the dates or because the actual event has already happened—and you can't reschedule history.

TIP A constraint or an actual date may be accidentally added to a task by dragging the bars on the Gantt Chart with the mouse.

There are four fundamental solutions to a constraint date scheduling problem:

■ Reassess the need for the constraint and the conditions that make the successor task dates fixed.

- If you must have fixed date constraints, you may want to re-evaluate the dependency relationships. You may be better off removing the link.

- Change the conditions governing the finish date for the predecessor—the task named in the Planning Wizard message (or earlier tasks in the schedule which impact the predecessor)—so that you can schedule the task to finish by the date it is constrained.

- Change the scheduling option—making it a soft constraint versus a hard constraint. This is a new feature in Project 98. This does not, however, resolve the conflict in your assumptions, the assumptions that led you to link the tasks and to place the constraint. It just avoids the Wizard messages and schedules the tasks more realistically. (See the section "Working with Task Constraints" earlier in this chapter for more information on soft and hard constraints.)

You need to choose the course of action that makes the most sense in your project. Frequently, a careful review of the tasks, the constraints, and the task relationships reveals that new definitions are called for—conditions may have changed since the original definitions were entered, and the definitions are now more restrictive than they need be.

Your job is to identify the nature of the problem and change the constraints or the relationship definition. If you can't change the tasks, then you need to find ways to make it possible to finish the task or soften the scheduling of the task.

Display the Task Information dialog box for the task by clicking the Information button on the Standard toolbar. Choose the Advanced tab and examine the constraint type; if it's not As Soon As Possible, examine the constraint date.

T I P   Check to see if there is a note associated with the task which might explain why the constraint was set. This might provide you with some guidance as to how you can resolve the conflict.

Changing the date to a later date, if possible, may resolve the conflict. Changing the constraint type back to the unconstrained As Soon As Possible certainly removes the conflict (at least as far as this task is concerned).

- If the task isn't constrained, you need to examine whether there has been an Actual date imposed on this task. Choose Tools, Tracking, Update Tasks. You can also click the Update Tasks button on the Tracking toolbar. Look to see if an Actual Start date has been inadvertently entered. If no actual date was entered, the Actual Start drop-down list box displays the value NA (see Figure 6.34).

- If the task has already started and a date has been entered, then consider redefining the task relationship.
  - If an Actual Start date was entered by accident, select the current entry (use Alt+S or click and drag across the current entry) and press the Delete key or type **NA** to return the field to an unrecorded status.
  - Examine the task relationship. You can remove the predecessor task to break the relationship. You can also redefine the relationship to allow for lead time to check whether the successor has started before the predecessor is scheduled to finish.

Part

II

Ch

6

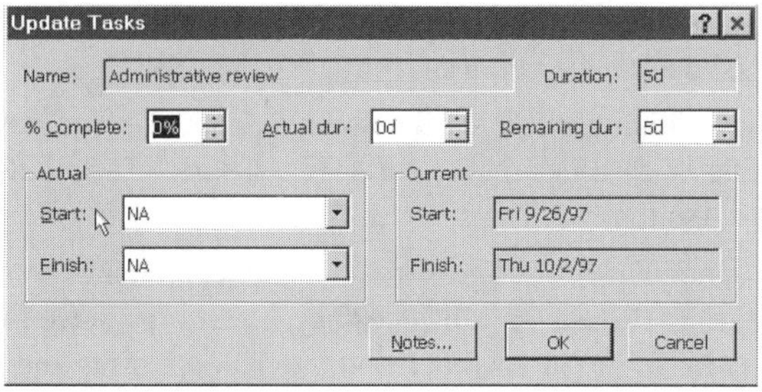

FIG. 6.34

Use the Update Tasks dialog box to check whether Actual dates have been entered for the task.

- If none of the successor tasks have Actual Start dates or constraints, then the task in the Late date message must have a summary task that links to a task with fixed dates or to another summary task with fixed dates in one of the subordinate tasks. You need to examine the successor to the summary task. If the successor is another summary task, you must examine all the subordinate tasks for the constraint.

- If none of the previously suggested changes is feasible, you can review the conditions that cause the scheduled date of the task in the message to be later than the late date and attempt to find a way to move the scheduled finish date forward in time to match the late date.

  ▶ **See** "Shortening the Critical Path," **p. 405**

- A new alternative has been added to resolving this scheduling conflict. In previous versions of Microsoft Project, you did not have the choice of ignoring the constraint. When a task had a fixed date, the schedule for all subsequent tasks was based on this fixed date. With this version, you can choose to "soften" the constraint. Choose Tools, Options and select the Schedule tab. Turn off the new option Tasks Will Always Honor Their Constraint Dates. When turned off, the dates the task can be scheduled for, based on the dates of its predecessor, will be displayed in the Start and Finish date fields. Figure 6.35 shows an example of these tasks with a hard constraint on Administrative review. Note the message in the indicator field. Figure 6.36 shows an example of the new, soft constraint capability. The constraint indicator has added a red exclamation symbol to provide you with an alert. The message about the constraint also changes.

Using the Adjust Dates Macro

The Adjust Dates macro helps you reschedule the start (or finish) of a project with constrained tasks when you want the constraints to change by the same number of days that you changed the start (or finish) of the project to. This macro is especially helpful when using a project template that has milestones, which are given constraint dates relative to the start of the project. For example, suppose you have designed a project template that has three major phases which are constrained to be completed two, four, and five months from the start date of the project. If you need to delay the start of this project for six months, you could use the Adjust Dates macro to enter the new start date and adjust the constraints. The macro calculates the number of days by which you change the start date and adjusts all constraints by that same number of days.

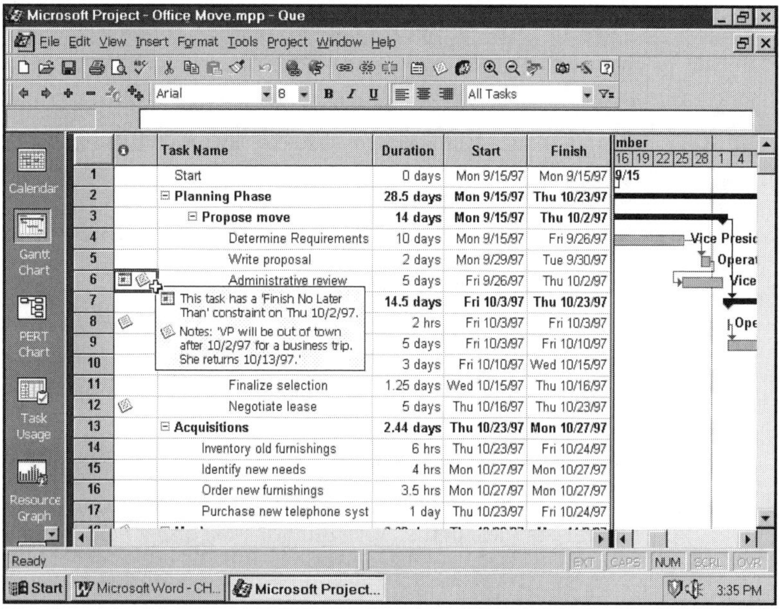

FIG. 6.35

The constraint indicator when a constraint is marked to always honor their constraint dates—a hard constraint.

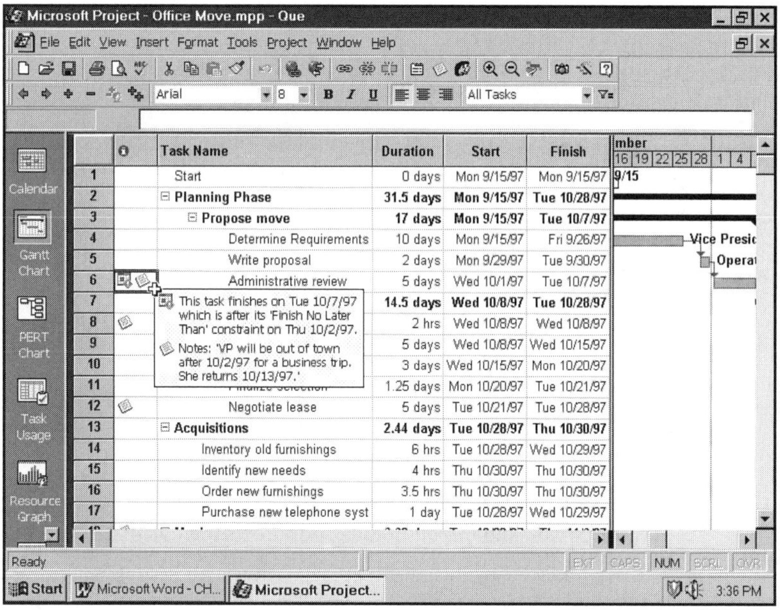

FIG. 6.36

The new constraint indicator when a constraint has been softened.

Part

II

Ch

6

To use the Adjust Dates macro, follow these steps:

1. Open the project document whose dates you want to adjust. Don't adjust the project start or finish date yet; let the macro do that for you.

2. Choose Tools, Macro, Macros… to display the Macros dialog box.

T I P   To quickly get to the Macros dialog box, use the keyboard shortcut Alt+F8.

---

3. Select the AdjustDates macro from the list of macros.

4. Choose the Run button. An input box will display (Figure 6.37) with a request for the new start date. If this project is scheduled from a fixed finish date, the input box would request a new finish date. Choose Project, Project Information to view the Schedule From field on the Project Information dialog box.

5. Enter the start date (or finish date) in the input box.

6. Choose the OK button. Microsoft Project will enter the new date in the Start Date (or Finish Date) field of the Project Information dialog box and adjust all task constraint dates by the same number of days.

   ▷ **See** "Running the Macro," **p. 842**

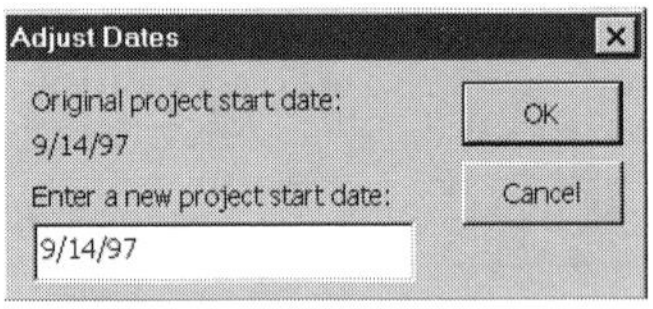

FIG. 6.37

The Adjust Dates macro first asks you to enter the new start date (or finish date) for the project and then adjusts all constraints for you.

Adjust Dates	☒
Original project start date:	OK
9/14/97	
Enter a new project start date:	Cancel
9/14/97	

From Here...

You now understand how Microsoft Project calculates the schedule dates. We have taken a look at how to link these tasks using the four dependency relationship, along with lag time and lead time to define the appropriate sequence of activities for your project. You also examined how you set deadlines and constraints for tasks and to adjust those constraints if necessary. The next step is to define the resources that will work on the tasks.

▪ Chapter 8, "Defining Resources and Costs," will introduce to you entering resource information and understanding how costs are calculated.

▪ Chapter 12, "Reviewing the Project Plan," will help you identify tasks that have constraints by using the Tasks with Fixed Dates filter.

Working with the Major Task Views

In addition to the Gantt Chart view, there are two other task views which are useful for working with a project. The Calendar view and the PERT Chart view provide alternative representations of your project tasks.

The Gantt Chart view can be significantly enhanced through graphics and text objects, which are used to draw attention to or explain particular events within the project. ∎

Explore the uses of Calendar view

Shown in the familiar Sunday through Saturday monthly calendar format, use this view to build or modify projects. Display and print a list of tasks for individual resources.

Work with the PERT Chart view

See your projects displayed in a large scale flow chart. Use this unique view to create or edit projects.

Enhance the Gantt Chart view

Add textual comments, arrows, and other graphics objects directly to the Gantt Chart timescale to annotate events within your project.

Working with the Calendar View

You will often find it useful to display your project on the familiar calendar background. After creating a project file using the other views provided by Microsoft Project, it can be very helpful to distribute reports showing all tasks or selected tasks in the calendar format. Although it isn't the best view for designing and creating lengthy or complex projects, you can use the Calendar view to create simple, short duration projects.

Understanding the Calendar View

Display the Calendar view by clicking the Calendar button on the view bar or by choosing View, Calendar. The standard Calendar view appears (see Figure 7.1). The Calendar view cannot be displayed in the bottom pane of a split screen view.

FIG. 7.1

Present your project in Calendar view; most people are familiar with this format and can easily decipher your data.

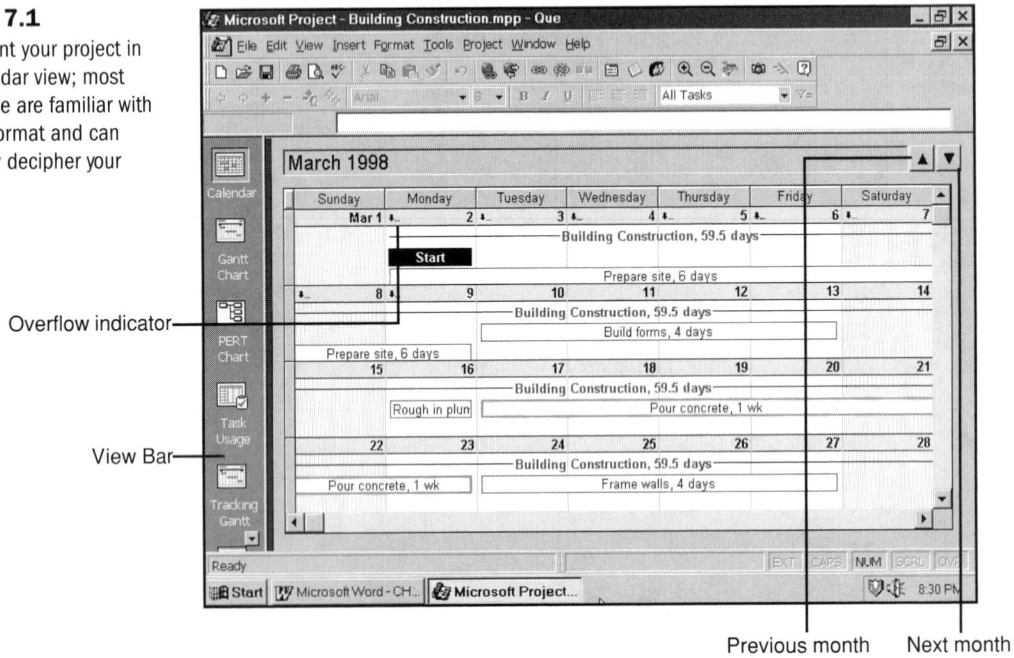

Overflow indicator

View Bar

Previous month   Next month

The Calendar view features a month and year title, and shows one or more weeks of dates with task bars stretching from their start dates to their finish dates. The default display shows four weeks at a time and includes bars or lines for all tasks except Summary tasks. You can include Summary tasks and you can change many other features of the display by customizing the Calendar view. Milestone tasks are represented by black task bars with white text. In Figure 7.2, the Start milestone task is displayed.

In some cases, there isn't enough room in the calendar to display all the tasks whose schedules fall on a particular date. When this happens, you see an overflow indicator in the left-hand corner of the date box (refer to Figure 7.1). The overflow indicator is a black arrow with an ellipsis that indicates there is more available.

You can see all the tasks scheduled for a given date by displaying the Tasks Occurring On dialog box for that date (see Figure 7.2). To display the Tasks Occurring On dialog box for a specific date, double-click the gray band at the top of the date box, or follow these steps:

1. Position the mouse pointer over any portion of the gray band at the top of the date box. (The day number appears at the right of this gray band in the default calendar layout.)

2. Right-click to display the shortcut menu for dates.

3. Choose Task List from the shortcut menu. The Tasks Occurring On dialog box appears for the specific date you pointed to.

4. Double-click a task to see the Task Information dialog box for that task. Click the OK button to close the Task Information dialog box.

5. After reviewing the list of tasks, choose the Close button to close the dialog box.

FIG. 7.2

All tasks that occur on a specific date are shown in a list. Double-click any of the tasks to see details for that task.

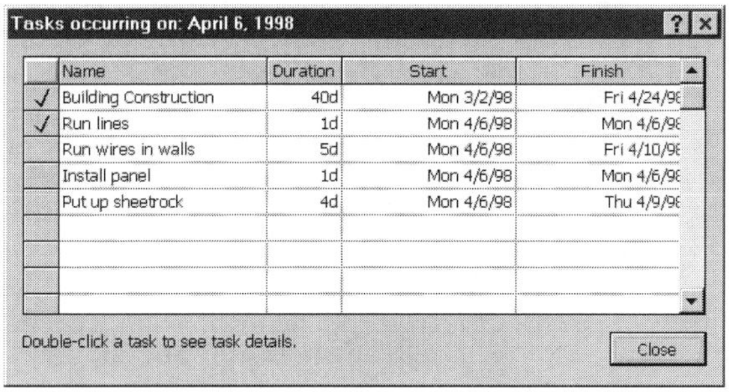

Tasks occurring on: April 6, 1998

	Name	Duration	Start	Finish
√	Building Construction	40d	Mon 3/2/98	Fri 4/24/98
√	Run lines	1d	Mon 4/6/98	Mon 4/6/98
	Run wires in walls	5d	Mon 4/6/98	Fri 4/10/98
	Install panel	1d	Mon 4/6/98	Mon 4/6/98
	Put up sheetrock	4d	Mon 4/6/98	Thu 4/9/98

Double-click a task to see task details.   Close

The Tasks Occurring On dialog box lists all tasks whose schedule dates encompass the date you selected. Those tasks whose bars appear in the calendar have a check mark to the left of the listing. To increase the number of tasks that appear on the calendar, you can use the Zoom command (see "Using Zoom" later in this chapter) or you must make changes in the calendar format.

The Calendar view, like other views, has a number of shortcut menus available. One way to approach learning about this view is to just start right-clicking different spots on the view. There are navigation options like Go To and Zoom on shortcut menus. Additional shortcut menus offer access to the Task Information dialog box, a list of tasks occurring on specific dates, and formatting options for virtually every element of the calendar.

Moving Around in Calendar View

As with other views, your effective use of the Calendar view depends on your ability to move around and find the information you want to focus on. It's helpful to know how to change the display of the calendar to show only selected information.

Part

II

Ch

7

Scrolling the Calendar   Use the scroll bars to move forward and backward in time on the calendar. When you drag the scroll box on the vertical scroll bar, a date indicator pop-up box helps you locate a specific date (see Figure 7.3). The beginning and end points on the scroll bar are approximately the start and end dates of the project.

FIG. 7.3

Drag the scroll box to move quickly to a specific date.

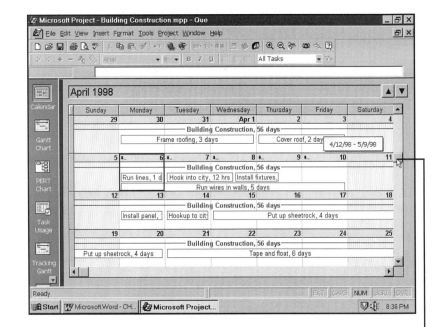

Scroll button ─┘

Press Alt+Home and Alt+End to jump to the beginning and ending dates of the project, respectively. You also can use the Page Up and Page Down keys to scroll through the display showing successive weeks in the life of the project.

Scroll through the months of the year with the up and down arrow buttons to the right of the month and year title. As you scroll through the months, the beginning of each successive month appears in the first row of the calendar, no matter how many weeks you displayed in the view. The Alt+up arrow and Alt+down arrow keys also scroll by months through the project calendar.

Locating a Specific Task or Date   You can quickly move to a specific date anywhere in the calendar, including dates outside the date range of the project. You also can locate a specific task by specifying its task ID or by searching for tasks by name.

Use the Go To command to move directly to a specific task ID or date. You can access the Go To command by right-clicking the month and year title (or by right-clicking anywhere but directly on a task bar) and choosing Go To from the shortcut menu that appears. You can also choose Edit, Go To. The Go To dialog box appears (see Figure 7.4).

FIG. 7.4

Use the Go To dialog box to quickly locate a specific date or task ID.

▶ **See** "Formatting the Calendar," **p. 716**

CAUTION

By default, the summary task bars do not display in the Calendar view. The Go To command (and the Find command described later in this section) cannot select tasks that don't display task bars in the Calendar view. Therefore, you can't go to a summary task. You change the Calendar to display summary task bars through the Format, Bar Styles command.

When a given date has more tasks than can be shown in the Calendar view display, it shows the first few tasks and indicates there are more by an arrow next to the date. If you enter an ID for a task whose task bar is not visible on that date, Project selects the task, and its beginning date scrolls into view—but you can't see the task or a selection marker to indicate which date is the beginning date. However, because the task is selected, you can choose the Information button on the toolbar to view its Task Information dialog box. The task start date is on the General tab. Close the Task Information dialog box by choosing the Cancel button. Double-click the start date for the task to see the other tasks scheduled on that date.

You can use the Find command to locate tasks by their field values, usually by the value in the Name field. As with the Go To command, if the task you find is not currently displayed in the calendar, you cannot see it.

T I P

You must select a task bar in the Calendar view before you can use the Find command.

To find a task by searching for one or more characters in its name, follow these steps:

1. Select any task. If you want to search from the beginning of the task list, press Alt+Home to scroll to the beginning of the project and then select the first task bar displayed.
2. Choose Edit, Find (or press Ctrl+F). The Find dialog box appears (see Figure 7.5).
3. In the Find What text box, type the characters you want to search for. You can enter whole words or phrases, or just parts of words. In Figure 7.5, the word **Inspection** is being located.

Part
II

Ch
7

FIG. 7.5

Search for a task by name or any other field value with the Find command.

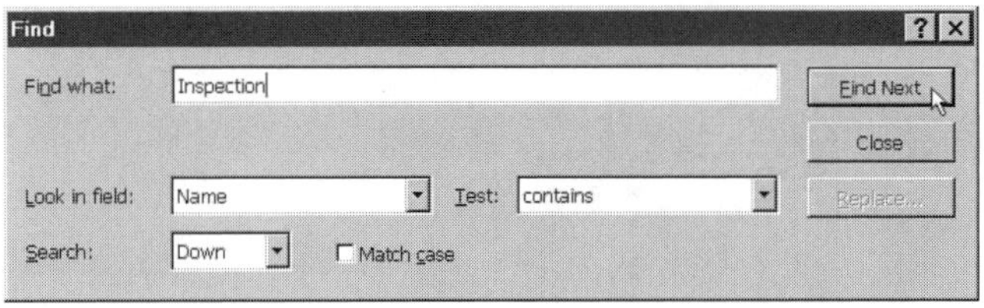

Find	? X
Find what:	Inspection	Find Next
		Close
Look in field:	Name ▼	Test:	contains ▼	Replace...
Search:	Down ▼	☐ Match case

4. By default, the Name field is searched. However, you can select any task field. Select the Look In Field and use the drop-down list box to choose the task field you want to search. Figure 7.5 has the Name field selected.

5. The Test box provides the criteria for the search. The default is Contains. Other options include: Equals, Is Greater Than, Is Greater Than or Equal to, and so forth.

6. Choose the direction to be searched from the Search drop-down list box. The choices are Down or Up from the selected task.

7. You can further tailor the search by making it case-sensitive. Marking the Match Case option requires the results to match the text typed in the Find What text box.

T I P If you've closed the dialog box, to use your last Find criteria again press Shift+F4 to search further toward the end of the task list, or press Ctrl+Shift+F4 to search further toward the beginning of the task list.

N O T E If the bar for the task is not visible, try using the Zoom In button to see more task bars for each day or use the Task Information button to see details for the task. Both of these features are described in the following sections. ▪

Using Zoom You might want to look at your calendar from different perspectives, backing away at times to see the big picture (although this has practical size limitations) or zooming in on the details for a specific week. To change the perspective, choose View, Zoom, or use the Zoom In and Zoom Out buttons on the Standard toolbar. Each click on one of these buttons displays one, two, four, or six weeks in ascending or descending order depending on the button you use.

The calendar in Figure 7.6, for example, is zoomed in to a two-week view to get a good understanding of the tasks going on during that time.

T I P You often have more options when accessing the dialog box for a feature than you do when using the toolbar button.

Choose View, Zoom to display the Zoom dialog box (see Figure 7.7). You can also right-click an empty spot on the calendar, and choose Zoom from the shortcut menu that appears. You have many options in the Zoom dialog box. You can zoom to a Custom level, specified in weeks, or you can determine a From date and a To date.

Zoom In button   Zoom Out button

FIG. 7.6
Click the Zoom In
button to display fewer
weeks and more tasks
per day.

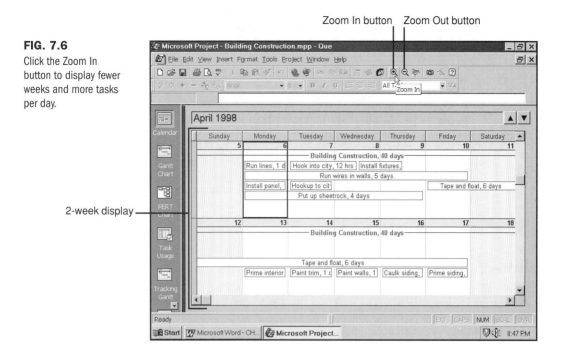

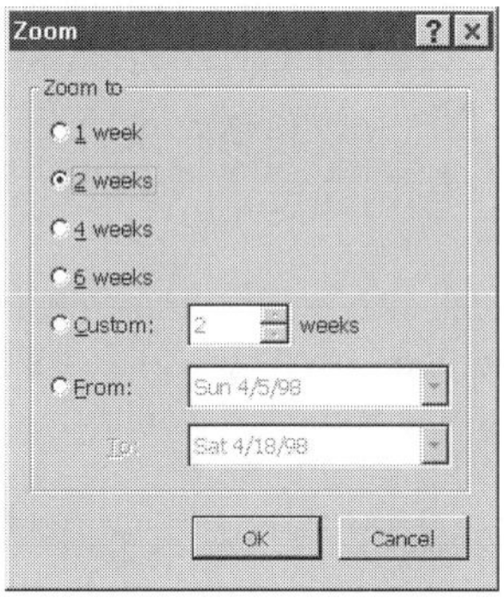

2-week display —

FIG. 7.7
Use the Zoom dialog
box to customize the
number of weeks to
display in the Calendar.

Using the Zoom command on the Calendar view has no effect on the printed Calendar view; it only affects the screen display. See Chapter 13, "Printing Views and Reports," for more information about using the Page Setup dialog box to control the printing of calendars.

Using Filters to Clarify the Calendar View   When a project has many overlapping tasks, the Calendar view can quickly become very cluttered. As previously discussed, you can zoom in to see more detail, but you can also use *filters* to narrow the list of tasks that display at one time. A filter limits the display of tasks to just those that match the criteria defined in the filter. For example, you can have Project display only the critical tasks in the project by applying the Critical filter. You might also choose to display tasks that a specific resource is working on by applying the Using Resource filter.

To apply a filter to a Calendar View, do one of the following:

All Tasks ▼

■ Choose the Filter button on the Formatting toolbar. Select from the available filters on the drop-down list.

■ Choose Tools, Filtered For and choose from the predefined filters.

■ If you want to highlight a particular category of tasks, choose Tools, Filtered For, More Filters. Select the filter you want to apply and then choose the Highlight button.

When you focus on the deadline and, therefore, the critical path, use the Critical filter. When you want to give each resource a list of its assigned tasks, choose the Using Resource filter. When the project is underway and you want a record of what has been accomplished so far, use the Completed Tasks filter. Filters are discussed in detail in Chapter 12, "Reviewing the Project Plan."

▶ **See** "Using Filters," **p. 397**

Editing a Project in Calendar View

As mentioned in the section "Working with the Calendar View" at the beginning of this chapter, it isn't recommended to use the Calendar view to create a complex project. This view really is more useful for reviewing and printing tasks and the time frames in which they occur. This section includes techniques for looking up and modifying task information. It could be helpful, for example, to be able to add and modify task notes when reviewing the calendar.

Viewing Task Details in Calendar View   The display of individual task information is minimized in the Calendar view. You can view and edit details about a task by selecting the task and opening the Task Information dialog box. Alternatively, you can use the Calendar as the top part of a dual-pane view, then select a task in the calendar and view its task details in the lower pane.

You can open the Task Information dialog box, shown in Figure 7.8, for a task in Calendar view in several ways. You can use any of the methods listed here for tasks that display task bars. If the task bar is not displayed, you must use one of the last two methods.

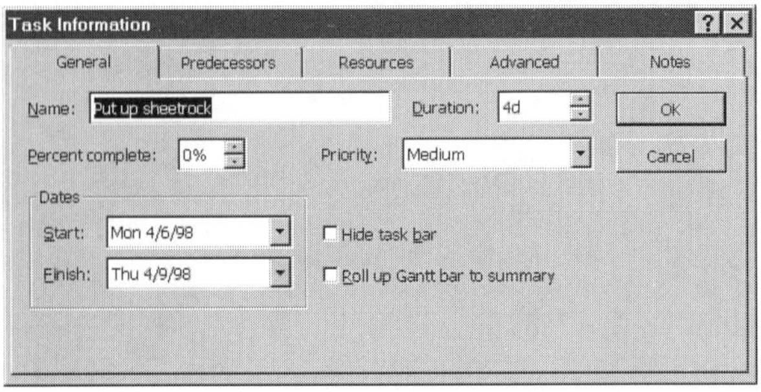

FIG. 7.8

The Task Information dialog box offers easy access to most of the data fields for a task.

To display the Task Information dialog box for tasks that display task bars, use one of these methods:

■ Double-click the task bar to both select the task and display the Task Information dialog box.

■ Right-click the task bar. This selects the task and displays the shortcut menu (see Figure 7.9). Choose Task Information to see the General tab of the Task Information dialog box, or choose Task Notes to go directly to the Notes tab of the Task Information dialog box.

FIG. 7.9

The shortcut menu for a task is helpful for displaying task information.

If the task bar is not displayed, you must first select the task using the Go To command or the Find command as described in the earlier section "Locating a Specific Task or Date." After you select the task, you can use one of the following methods to display the Task Information dialog box:

■ Choose Project, Task Information. (Choose Project, Task Notes if you want to go directly to the Notes tab of the Task Information dialog box.)

■ Choose the Information button on the Standard toolbar to view the General tab of the Task Information dialog box. (Choose the Task Note button if you want to go directly to the Notes tab.)

Another way to view task details is to combine the Calendar view with another view in the bottom pane. For example, if you put the Task Form view in the bottom pane, it displays task information for a task selected in Calendar view. You can choose Format, Details, Notes to see the notes for the selected task. If you display the Task PERT view in the bottom pane, it illustrates task dependencies for the task selected in Calendar view.

You can split the view window into two panes using one of the following methods:

■ Choose Window, Split.

■ Right-click anywhere in the calendar (except a task) to open the shortcut menu and choose Split.

When you choose the Split command, Project puts Task Form view in the bottom pane by default. You can replace Task Form view with any view you want (except the PERT Chart, which cannot be displayed in a bottom pane).

Inserting Tasks in Calendar View   You can create tasks in Calendar view by choosing Insert, New Task or by dragging the mouse to create a new task bar in the calendar. Although it's easy to create tasks in the Calendar view, you might not want to use the Calendar view in this manner for two reasons:

■ With the Gantt Chart view, as well as others, you can insert a new task in the middle of the project and near other tasks to which the new task is related. The task is given an ID number where it was inserted. When creating a task in Calendar view, however, it is

Part
II
Ch
7

always given the next highest ID number in the project, regardless of where the task was inserted. If you view the new task in Gantt Chart view (or any view with a table), the task is at the bottom of the list—even if its dates fall in the middle of the project or you link it to tasks in the middle of the task list.

- The task you create in Calendar view is often automatically given a date constraint. You would want to remove the constraint as soon as you create a task in the Calendar view. To remove the constraint, set the constraint type to As Soon as Possible in the Advanced Tab of the Task Information dialog box.

CAUTION

Adding tasks to a project in Calendar view can result in task constraints that, unless removed, needlessly produce scheduling conflicts.

Whether tasks created in the Calendar view are constrained depends on what you have selected when you create the new task: a task or a date.

- If you select a task and you insert the new task with the menu or the Insert key, the new task will not be constrained (its constraint type will be As Soon As Possible).
- If you select a date when you create the new task, or if you create the task by dragging with the mouse (which automatically selects the date where you start dragging), the new task will be constrained.

If the task is constrained when you create it, the constraint type depends on whether you schedule your project from a fixed Start Date or a fixed Finish Date. If you create the task by dragging with the mouse, the constraint type also depends on the direction you drag the mouse: from start to finish or from finish to start. Remember to check the Constraint Type of any task you create in the Calendar view (following the steps that are outlined below) and change it appropriately.

To insert a task using the menu, follow these steps:

1. Select the date for the start of the task if you want the start date constrained, or select any task if you do not want the task to be constrained.

2. Choose Insert, New Task. You also can simply press the Insert key that is the shortcut key for the Insert Task command. Project inserts a new, untitled task in the project with a default duration of one day. Because the task has no name yet, its task bar only displays its duration. If there is no room to display the bar for the new task, it seems to disappear. Regardless, the new task is selected.

3. Choose Project, Task Information (or choose the Information button on the Standard toolbar) to open the Task Information dialog box.

4. Provide a name and any other information for the task. For example, you probably need to enter the Duration. You might also want to choose the Notes tab and type comments about the task.

5. Because most tasks created in Calendar view are automatically given a date constraint, choose the Advanced tab and change the entry in the Constrain Task Type field as appropriate.

6. Choose OK to close the dialog box.

To insert a task with the mouse, follow these steps:

1. Scroll the Calendar until you see the start date (or finish date) for the task.

2. Drag the mouse from the start date to the finish date for the task (or from the finish date to the start date).

3. Click the Information button to display the Task Information dialog box and supply the task name (and any other information you want to specify).

4. Choose the Advanced tab and correct the Constrain Task Type as appropriate.

5. Choose OK to close the dialog box.

Deleting Tasks in Calendar View   To delete a task, simply select it and choose Edit, Delete Task or press the Delete key. If the task bar is not displayed, you must use the Go To command or the Find command to select it. (See the section "Locating a Specific Task or Date" earlier in this chapter.) If you accidentally delete a task, use the Undo feature to get it back. Just click the Undo button; choose Edit, Undo; or press Ctrl+Z.

T I P   You must do this right away though, because Undo can only undo your last action.

Creating Links Between Tasks in Calendar View   There are several ways to create task dependency links in Calendar view. One method is to select the tasks you want to link (use the Ctrl key to add tasks to the selection). Then choose the Link button on the Standard toolbar.

You can also use the mouse. Simply click the center of the bar for the predecessor task and hold the mouse button until the mouse pointer turns into chain links. Drag down to the intended successor task. The mouse pointer changes to a link and, after you start dragging, a pop-up box indicates the creation of a Finish-to-Start relationship between the two tasks.

To change to a different kind of relationship or to add lag or lead time, you must display the Task Information dialog box for the dependent (successor) task and choose the Predecessors tab.

Working with the PERT Chart View

Part

II

Ch

7

The PERT Chart is a graphic display of tasks in a project, in which each task is represented by a small box or *node*. Lines connect the nodes to show task dependencies. The PERT Chart is most useful for an overall view of how the process or flow of task details fit together. You can also use the PERT Chart as the original entry view.

While in the PERT Chart view, you cannot filter the task list, and you cannot use the Clipboard to copy or move entire tasks. You can, however, use the Clipboard to cut, copy, and paste individual field entries.

Understanding the PERT Chart View

The PERT Chart is named for the *Program Evaluation and Review Technique (PERT)*, a project management methodology introduced by the Special Projects Office of the U.S. Navy in 1958. The PERT Chart has evolved into several species of network diagrams. The popular version used in Microsoft Project reveals information about the individual task, as well as information about the task's place in the flow of activity.

Figure 7.10 shows the standard PERT Chart view of the PRODUCT project. In this figure, Design Phase is the currently selected task. The default format for nodes displays five fields for the task: the name, ID, duration, start, and finish. You can select other fields to display.

FIG. 7.10

The PERT Chart view focuses on the links between tasks; use it as a road map for the flow of work in the project.

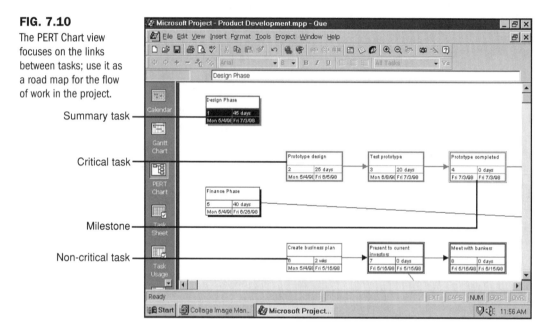

Each node represents a task, which is connected to predecessors and successors by lines. In the diagram, dependent (successor) tasks are always placed to the right of or beneath predecessors. Different border styles or colors distinguish summary tasks, critical tasks, and milestones. Summary tasks are above and to the left of subordinate tasks.

Table 7.1 describes a few of the node borders displayed in Figure 7.10.

Table 7.1   Each Type of Task Has a Unique Node Border

Type of Tasks	Node Borders
Summary tasks	Thin border with shadow box
Milestones	Double borders

Type of Tasks	Node Borders
Critical tasks	Red heavy borders
Non-critical tasks	Black heavy borders

To view the PERT Chart, follow these steps:

1. If you want the PERT Chart to be half-screen display, select the top pane.

2. Click the PERT Chart button in the view bar or choose View, PERT Chart.

N O T E You cannot display the PERT Chart in the bottom pane in a split screen.

Zooming the PERT Chart View

The PERT Chart in Figure 7.10 displays each node enlarged enough to read the field data easily. If you want to get an overview of the links among more tasks, you can zoom the view to show more tasks. Figure 7.11 shows the same task selected, Test Prototype, as in Figure 7.10. In the zoomed view, you get a better feel for how that task fits into the overall project.

FIG. 7.11
Normally, the PERT Chart displays dashed lines to show where page breaks occur when you print the view.

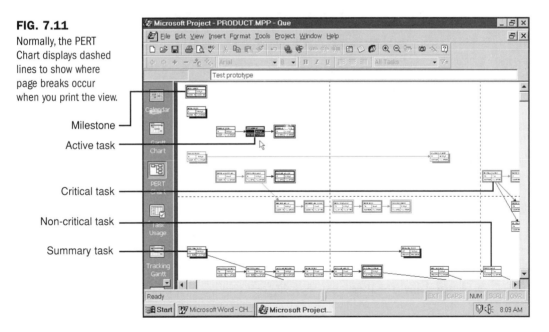

You can zoom out to view more tasks using the Zoom Out button on the Standard toolbar. Zoom in to see the task details using the Zoom In button. The Zoom In and Zoom Out buttons increment and decrement the zoom percentage by 25 percent each time you click the button. The supported zoom range is from 25 percent to a maximum of 400 percent. The normal magnification is set to 100 percent.

You have more options for zooming when you choose View, Zoom. The Zoom dialog box appears (see Figure 7.12). To change the zoom percentage, select one of the percentage buttons or fill in the Custom text box with a value between 25 percent and 400 percent. Select the Entire Project button to select the percentage between 25 percent and 400 percent, which just fits the entire project in the window. If the entire project cannot be displayed in one screen at 25 percent, the Zoom command displays a warning (see Figure 7.13). Choose OK to close the alert.

FIG. 7.12

The Zoom dialog box gives you precise control over the scope of the view.

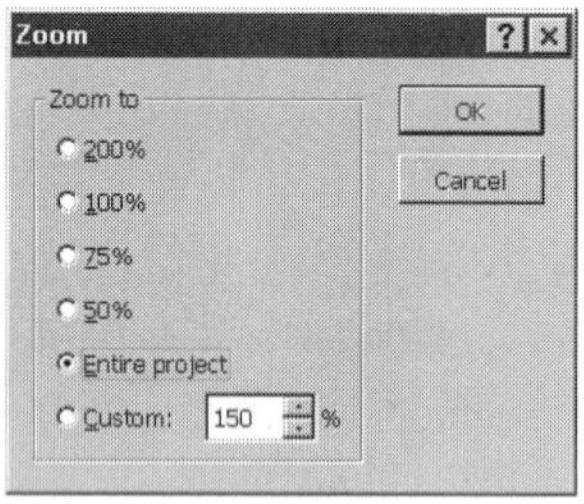

> **N O T E**   Using the Zoom command affects only the screen view in the PERT Chart. It does not affect how much of the chart is printed. ▪

FIG. 7.13

The warning appears if the entire project cannot be displayed on one screen.

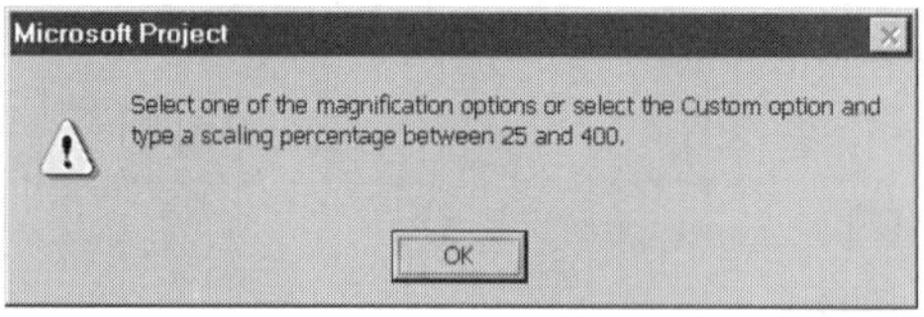

Scrolling and Selecting in the PERT Chart

You can use the horizontal and vertical scroll bars or the movement keys (the arrow keys, Page Up, Page Down, Home, and End) to scan through the PERT chart. However, the rules for each method are quite different.

Scrolling does not change the currently selected node. After you scroll, you probably cannot see the selected node, although the name remains in the Entry bar.

To put the selected node back in the center of the screen, press the Edit key (F2) as though you plan to change the selected node. To cancel the editing, press the Esc key. To select one of the visible nodes after scrolling, just click the node.

You can also use the selection keys to move around the PERT Chart, selecting different nodes as you go. The rules that the selection keys follow in selecting the next node are not apparent. The following list defines the rules of the selection keys:

▪ *Right arrow key.* Selects nodes to the right until there are no more nodes directly to the right. It then selects the next node down and to the right and continues to the right.

- *Down arrow key*. Selects nodes directly below until there are no more nodes. It then selects the next node that is down and to the right and continues down.
- *Left arrow key*. Selects nodes to the left until no more nodes lie directly to the left. It then selects the next node up and to the left and continues to the left.
- *Up arrow key*. Selects nodes directly above until there are no more nodes. It then selects the next node above and to the left and continues up.

The rest of the selection keys simulate repeated use of the arrow keys. The newly selected task name appears in the Entry bar. If the selected task is not visible after the move, press the Edit key (F2) and press Esc to place the selected task in the center of the screen. Here's what the other selection keys do:

- *Page Down*. Simulates repeated down arrow for one screen.
- *End*. Simulates repeated down arrow until it reaches the bottom row of the PERT Chart.
- *Page Up*. Simulates repeated up arrow for one screen.
- *Home*. Simulates repeated up arrow until it reaches the top row of the PERT Chart.
- *Ctrl+Page Down*. Simulates repeated right arrow for one screen.
- *Ctrl+Page Up*. Simulates repeated left arrow for one screen.
- *Ctrl+End*. Simulates repeated right arrow until it reaches the last column of the PERT Chart.
- *Ctrl+Home*. Simulates repeated left arrow until it reaches the first column of the PERT Chart.

TIP To move to the beginning of the PERT Chart, press Ctrl+Home and then Home.

You also can use the Go To command and select task ID number one, assuming you didn't leave a blank row at the top of the task list.

To go to the start of the project, follow these steps:

1. Choose Edit, Go To (or press F5).
2. Type the ID number for the first task in the project (usually number 1).
3. Choose the OK button.

Editing a Project in the PERT Chart

You can use the PERT Chart view to change task data, add and delete tasks, and create and modify task links.

Changing Task Data in the PERT Chart   To change the field data displayed in a node, follow these steps:

1. Select the task to edit by clicking the mouse pointer on the node or by using the selection keys.
2. Select the field to edit using the Tab and Shift+Tab keys or by clicking the field.

3. In the Entry bar, type the new data or edit the existing data.

4. Complete the change by pressing Enter, by selecting the Enter box in the Entry bar, or by selecting a different field or node.

If you want to change data in fields that don't appear in the node (such as constraints, fixed duration, and so on), you must use the Task Information dialog box. To use the Task Information dialog box, follow these steps:

1. Select the node you want to edit.

2. Choose Project, Task Information to display the Task Information dialog box.

T I P   You can also double-click the center of the node to display the Task Information dialog box. You may also choose the Task Information button on the standard toolbar. Double-clicking the border of a node takes you to a formatting dialog box.

3. Select the tab in the Task Information dialog box where you want to make your changes.

4. Choose the OK button.

Adding Tasks in PERT Chart View   You can add tasks directly to the project in the PERT Chart view. You must select the insertion position carefully, however, if you want to control the ID number of the new task. Project inserts a task you add in PERT Chart view just after the currently selected task. So, to insert a task just after a specific task, first select the task you want the new task to follow.

To add a new task, follow these steps:

1. If possible, select the task you want the new task to follow. This step makes sure the new task node will be placed to the right of the selected task and has an ID number that follows that of the selected task.

2. Choose Insert, New Task (or press the Insert key) to insert a blank node to the right of the selected task.

   The ID number for the new task is one greater than the selected task, and all existing tasks with ID numbers higher than the selected task increase by one. The new task appears directly to the right of the selected task. If there is already a task in that position, the new task hides it. In Figure 7.14, task #3 (Prototype Design) was selected before the new task was inserted. The new task is numbered #4 (notice it does not have a task name) and completely hides the task that was formerly #4 and is now #5 (Test Prototype).

FIG. 7.14

Insert new tasks in PERT Chart view by selecting the task that is to precede it and pressing the Insert key.

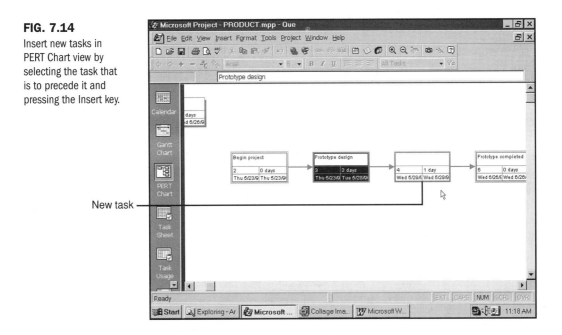

New task ──

3. Type the name for the new task. Tab to the Duration field and estimate the duration. Do not enter the start or finish date unless you want the task constrained to one of those dates.

You can also create a new task node by dragging the mouse pointer to form a rectangle in an empty area of the PERT Chart (see Figure 7.15). The ID number of the new task is still one greater than the currently selected task. In Figure 7.15, task #4 is selected; so, the new task will be #5.

N O T E Automatic linking of tasks is not enabled while you add, delete, or move tasks in PERT Chart view. ▓

Deleting Tasks in PERT Chart View You can delete tasks while in PERT Chart view. However, you cannot delete summary tasks in the PERT Chart view. Also, Autolink is not operative in PERT Chart view. If you delete a task in the middle of a linked chain of tasks, you must manually rejoin its predecessor and successor to preserve the chain.

To delete a task, select the task and choose Edit, Delete Task (or press Delete).

Part

II

Ch

7

FIG. 7.15

Drag the mouse to create a rectangle in the position you want the new task to occupy.

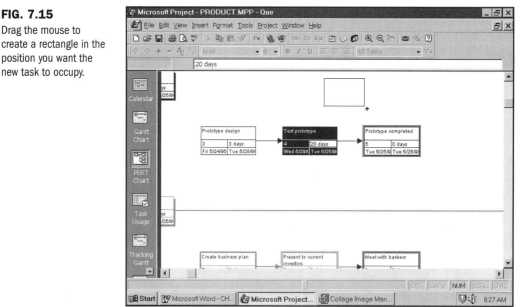

In previous versions of Project, you could not undo a deleted task in the PERT Chart view. With Project 98, you can undo your deletions, but only your last action.

Linking Tasks in PERT Chart View   You can create task links in PERT Chart view by dragging the mouse from the *middle* of the predecessor task to the middle of the successor task (see Figure 7.16). Make sure you start in the middle of task node. Dragging the border of a task node merely repositions the node. The task relationship is Finish-to-Start with no lead or lag. If you want to change the relationship, enter lead or lag time. If you want to delete the task link, you must activate the Task Dependency dialog box, then double-click the line that links the two tasks. The Task Dependency dialog box appears, allowing you to redefine the task relationship.

To redefine a task relationship in PERT Chart view, follow these steps:

1. Double-click the line between the tasks to display the Task Dependency dialog box. In Figure 7.17, the link between Test Prototype and Prototype Completed is being edited. The Task Dependency dialog box shows the predecessor and successor task names in the From and To fields.

T I P   Make sure the very tip of the mouse pointer is on the line that links the tasks when you double-click.

FIG. 7.16

Drag from the center of one node to another to link the nodes.

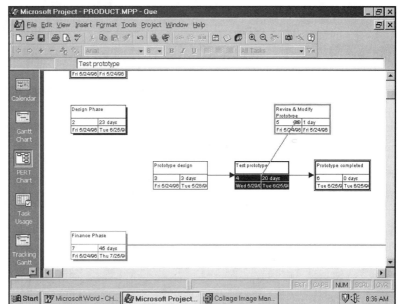

FIG. 7.17

The Task Dependency dialog box can be used to edit or remove task links.

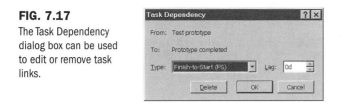

2. Change the relationship in the Type list box.

3. Enter a lead or lag in the Lag text box, if needed.

4. Choose the Delete button if you want to remove the link altogether.

5. Choose OK to complete the change.

Moving Task Nodes in PERT Chart View You can change the layout of the PERT Chart by moving individual task nodes or groups of nodes to new positions in the PERT Chart view. If you move a group of nodes simultaneously, the nodes retain position relative to each other as you move them. The linking lines also follow task nodes to the new locations.

TIP If you want to see more task nodes on a printout of the PERT Chart view, you do not have to move the nodes. Instead, you can change the Page Setup options to scale the printout. See Chapter 13, "Printing Views and Reports," for information using the scaling option.

Part

II

Ch

7

To move a task node with the keyboard, select the task and then hold down the Ctrl key as you press the arrow keys to move the node. To move the task node with the mouse, follow these steps:

1.   Move the mouse pointer to the border of the task node you want to move.

2.   Hold down the mouse button. Initially, this selects the node for moving as indicated by a gray border surrounding the node.

3.   Drag the node to the new location (see Figure 7.18). The node remains selected for moving even after you release the mouse button.

FIG. 7.18

You can reposition nodes with the mouse.

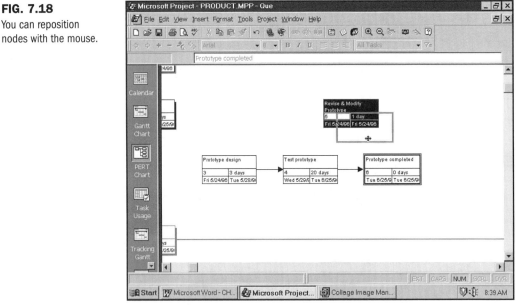

> **T I P** You might find it useful to zoom out so you can see an overview as you redesign the layout of the PERT Chart.

To move a group of task nodes together, follow these steps:

1.   Select the border of the first node of the group you want to move.

2.   Select other nodes to be moved at the same time by pressing the Ctrl key as you click their borders.

3.   When you've selected all nodes, drag the border of one of the selected nodes and drop them in the new location. All selected nodes move to the new.

You can also select nodes to be moved as a group by drawing a selection box around them. This is sometimes called *lassoing* the items to be selected. To select multiple nodes with a selection box, follow these steps:

1. Imagine a rectangle that encloses only the nodes you want to select.

2. Move the mouse pointer to one of the corners of this imaginary rectangle.

3. Hold down the mouse button and drag the mouse pointer diagonally to the opposite corner of the imaginary rectangle, creating the rectangle as shown in Figure 7.19. Release the mouse button. All task nodes that fall even partly in the area of the rectangle are selected for moving. In Figure 7.19, tasks 2 through 6 are inside the selection box.

FIG. 7.19

You can use a selection box to select multiple task nodes.

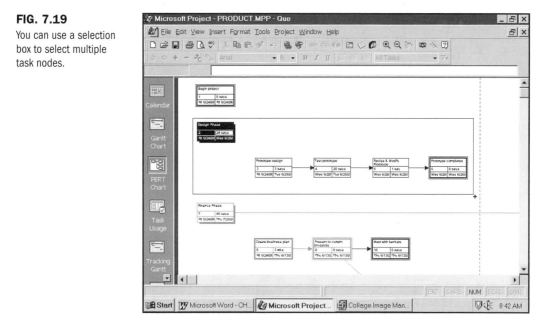

4. Drag the border of one member of the selected group, and the entire group moves to the new location.

N O T E Press the Shift key as you select the border of a task, and Project selects that task plus all its dependent (successor) tasks. You can quickly select all of a summary task's subtasks by holding down the Shift key as you click the border of the summary task. Drag the border of any task in the selected group to move the entire selected group. ▨

When you rearrange the PERT Chart, you want to see the page break lines so you don't place a task node on a page break. If you place a node on a page break line, part of the node prints on one page, and the remainder prints on another page. The following section explains how to display and use page break lines.

Customizing the PERT Chart with the Layout Dialog Box

You can customize the layout of the PERT view with the choices in the Layout dialog box (see Figure 7.20). The following choices are available:

■ By default, the dependency lines are drawn diagonally from predecessor to successor tasks. With the Links options, you can choose to draw orthogonal lines so that only right angles are used to display the dependency lines.

■ Select the Show Arrows check box to show (or deselect to remove) the arrow tips from the successor end of the dependency lines. Removing the tips will leave lines with no explicit direction.

■ Deselect the Show Page Breaks check box if you want to hide the dotted page break lines. Select the check box when you want to use the page break lines.

■ Select the Adjust for Page Breaks check box if you want Project to automatically adjust task nodes to avoid page break lines when you execute the Layout Now command (see the following section). This way, no task node can be split by a page break. If a node must be adjusted to avoid a page break, Project moves the node to the right or down until it fits entirely on the next page.

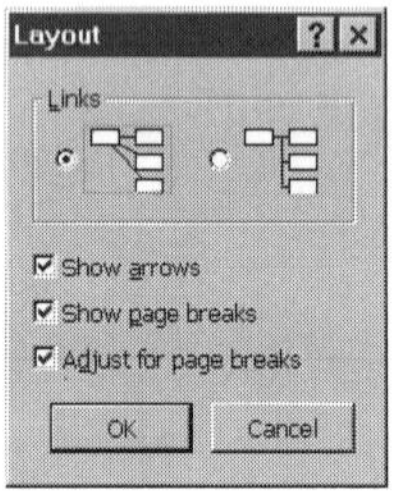

FIG. 7.20
The PERT Chart Layout dialog box controls PERT Chart display features.

To change one or more of the Layout dialog box options, follow these steps:

1. Choose Format, Layout (or right-click an empty space in the PERT Chart and choose Layout) to display the Layout dialog box.

2. Select the desired Links style.

3. Select or deselect the check boxes to Show Arrows, Show Page Breaks, or Adjust for Page Breaks. A check mark in the check box indicates that the feature is turned on.

4. Select the OK button to activate your choices. The Links, Show Page Breaks, and Show Arrows options implement immediately. The Adjust for Page Breaks option doesn't implement until the next time you choose Format, Layout Now.

CAUTION

The Layout Now command forces Project to redraw the PERT Chart. This causes all changes you made by moving task nodes to be lost. To have Project redraw the PERT Chart, choose Format, Layout Now. Unless there is a specific reason, it is best not to manually move task nodes. Manually moving the nodes makes it difficult to maintain as the task list changes.

In addition to the positioning and layout of the PERT Chart described in this chapter, Project allows you to control the data displayed in the nodes, the number of data fields displayed, text styles for different categories of task, the size of the task nodes, and the borders around the task nodes. See Chapter 21, "Formatting Views," for an in-depth explanation of these formatting options.

Adding Graphics and Text to Gantt Charts

Microsoft Project provides a set of drawing tools to help you enhance the appearance of your Gantt Charts. The drawing tools produce graphics objects that can be moved, resized, placed in front of, along side of, or behind the task bars.

Included among the drawing tools is a Text Box tool that lets you place free text anywhere in the Gantt Chart display. This chapter shows you how to create and modify graphics and text on the Gantt Chart. Note that graphic objects you have placed on the Gantt Chart are not displayed when the Gantt Chart is in the bottom pane of a combination view.

Introducing the Drawing Toolbar

Text and graphic objects are created on the Gantt Chart with the Drawing toolbar. When the toolbar is displayed, you can create objects by selecting an object button and creating an example of the object on the Gantt Chart area. After they are created, you can modify the objects to create the effect you desire. Figure 7.21 shows an example of a text message overlaid on the Gantt Chart, with an arrow directing your attention to the circled tasks the message describes.

FIG. 7.21

Text and graphics elements can be used to annotate a Gantt Chart or to emphasize one of its aspects.

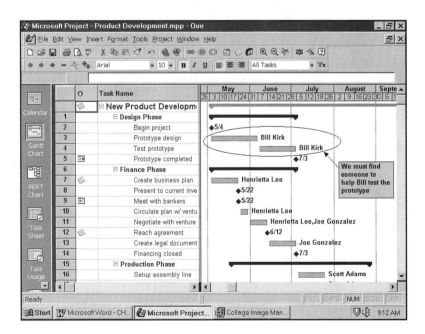

To display the Drawing toolbar, choose Insert, Drawing. The Drawing toolbar is displayed underneath the Formatting toolbar.

 ▶ **See** "The Toolbars," **p. 33**

 ▶ **See** "Introducing the Gantt Chart View," **p. 50**

Descriptions of the Drawing Buttons

Like many of the toolbars in Project 98, this toolbar has been updated. The first button is a drop-down menu providing options for arranging and editing the objects you draw.

The next seven buttons on the toolbar create objects on the Gantt Chart graphic area. These buttons create lines, arrows, rectangles, ovals, arcs, polygons, and text boxes. The remaining two buttons provide access to various editing possibilities.

The first button on the toolbar is a drop-down list. The Draw button provides you with options for arranging and editing the objects you draw. It includes options to:

  ▪ *Bring to Front*. Bring a selected object to the forefront, placing it before all other objects that originally overlaid it.

  ▪ *Send to Back*. Send an object to the back, placing it behind all other objects in the same area.

  ▪ *Bring Forward*. Move an object in front of other objects, one at a time, toward the viewer. Objects in front hide objects that are behind them.

  ▪ *Send Backward*. Move an object behind other objects, one at a time, away from the viewer.

  ▪ *Edit Points*. Change the shape of a polygon.

When you choose one of the seven drawing buttons, the mouse pointer becomes a set of crosshairs. Position the pointer where you want to begin drawing an object and drag it to create the object. After it has been created, the object has small black resizing handles at each corner and along each side. The handles are used to change the dimensions of the object.

Figure 7.22 shows samples of the figures that you can draw. The buttons that draw the objects are described in the following sections. Table 7.2 shows each of the seven drawing buttons and describes their uses.

TIP With some objects, the Shift key can be used to create a perfectly symmetrical object, for example, a perfect square, a perfect circle, or a perfect arc. To draw a square or circle, select the appropriate drawing button, and then hold down the Shift key as you begin to drag the mouse to create the object.

FIG. 7.22
You can draw a variety of geometric figures, lines, and arrows, in addition to placing text among the other figures.

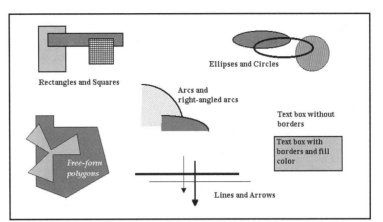

Table 7.2 Drawing Buttons on the Drawing Toolbar

Button	Name	Click and drag to...	Shift+Click and drag to...
D-2	Line	lines without arrowheads	(n/a)
D-3	Arrow	lines with arrowheads	(n/a)
D-4	Rectangle	rectangles	perfect squares
D-5	Oval	elliptical figures	perfect circles
D-6	Arc	elliptical arcs	symmetrical arcs from circles
D-7	Polygon	a many-sided figure of any configuration	(n/a)
D-8	Text Box	a rectangle box for typing text	a perfect square for typing text

The last two buttons on the toolbar are the Cycle Fill Color button and the Attach to Task button. The Cycle Fill Color button allows you to change the fill color of the selected object, cycling through the palette of color choices each time you click the button. With the Attach to Task button, you open the Format Drawing dialog box to change how an object is anchored to the Gantt Chart or modify the attributes of the object.

TIP Double-click the Polygon button to have the computer draw the final line that connects the last point to the starting point, producing a closed figure.

Part
II

Ch
7

Working with Drawing Objects in the Gantt Chart View

Once you have drawn objects in the Gantt Chart view, you may want to modify the object. You can attach an object to a specific task or date so that when you zoom out, the object stays with the task or date it is attached to. You can hide, move, resize, copy, or delete objects you have drawn. The color of the border surrounding the object and the inside the object can be changed to enhance its visual appearance.

However, before you can make any of these changes, you must first select the object you want to modify.

Selecting Objects   In the Gantt Chart view displayed, you can select task fields in the table area; you can select a task bar (when you use the mouse to modify the task); or you can select objects that you have placed in the graphics area.

You can use the mouse to select objects in the graphics area if you watch the mouse pointer carefully. Move the tip of the mouse pointer to an object's line or border. When a small cross appears below and to the right of the pointer arrow, click to select the object. When the object is selected, small black resizing handles appear around it. Only one object can be selected at a time.

> **N O T E**   For solid figures (rectangles, ellipses, arcs, or polygons with a fill pattern), you can point to the interior of an object to select it. This might be easier than pointing to the border. ▣

You also can use the keyboard to select objects. The F6 function key toggles back and forth between selecting the task table and a graphic object. (If a combination view is displayed, the bottom view is also selected in turn by the F6 key.)

> **T I P**   If you have created multiple drawing objects, when one of them is selected, you can use the Tab key to cycle the selection to the other drawing objects one at a time. Shift+Tab can be used to cycle backwards through the drawn objects.

Attaching Objects to a Task Bar or a Date   When you create an object, it is automatically attached to a date on the timescale where you created it on the Gantt Chart, with a vertical offset to show how far down from the timescale it should be displayed. The object stays with that date as you scroll the timescale or as you zoom the timescale.

> **CAUTION**
> Be aware that if you zoom out in the Gantt Chart, your objects may be placed on top of each other due to the compressed timescale.

If an object is attached to a date in the timescale, when you move the object, it remains attached to the timescale but at the new date and vertical position where you move it. You can see the attachment by examining the Size & Position tab of the Format Drawing dialog box for the object (see Figure 7.23).

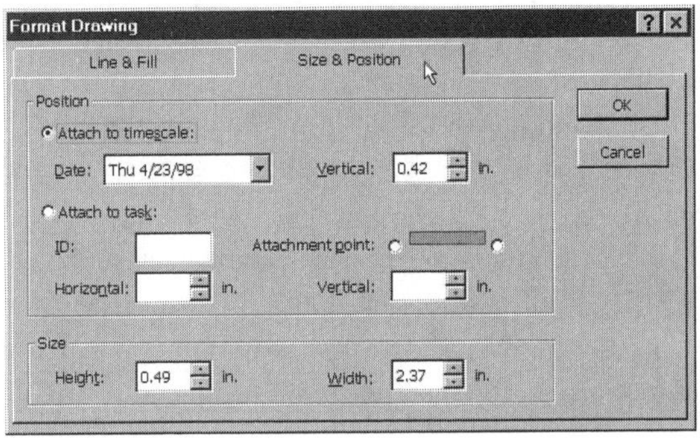

FIG. 7.23
Use the Format Drawing dialog box to attach an object to a task or to the timescale.

To view the Format Drawing dialog box, you can simply double-click the object. Be sure to double-click the border of text boxes, because double-clicking the center of the box opens the text area for editing.

There are several other ways to view the Format Drawing dialog box. You can select the object and use the Attach to Task button on the Drawing toolbar. If you prefer to use the menu bar, choose Format, Drawing and choose Properties from the submenu. Or, to use the shortcut menu (see Figure 7.24), position the mouse pointer over the object so that the pointer displays the small cross to its right. Click the secondary mouse button to see the shortcut menu and select Properties. Selecting Properties will bring up the Format Drawing dialog box shown in Figure 7.23.

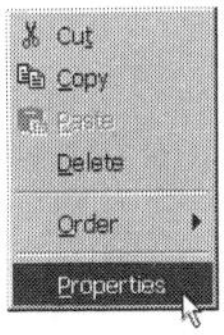

FIG. 7.24
The drawing objects shortcut menu is a quick way to work with drawn objects.

To attach an object to a task, follow these steps:

1. Note the ID number of the task to which you want to attach the object. You need to enter the ID number on the dialog box but there is no way to browse or search for the ID number when the dialog box is active.
2. Activate the Format Drawing dialog box and choose the Size & Position tab.
3. Choose the Attach to Task option button.
4. Enter the task number in the ID text box. If you do not remember the ID number, you will have to close the dialog box, find the number, and then come back to the dialog box.

Part
II
Ch
7

5. Attach the object to the beginning or the end of the task bar by choosing the Attachment Point at the beginning or the end of the sample task bar.

6. The Horizontal and Vertical fields show the offset from the attachment point where the object's top-left corner will be placed. Positive offset values are to the right horizontally and down vertically. Negative offset values are to the left horizontally and up vertically. Enter zero in both these text boxes unless you are absolutely certain that you know the values that will look best. The zero values ensure that the drawing object is displayed next to the task bar when you finish this procedure, and you do not have to search the Gantt Chart to find it. You then can use the mouse to reposition the drawing as desired.

   Once the object is attached to the task, you can move it with the mouse, and the horizontal and vertical offset values are recorded automatically. The object remains attached to the task as you move the task (unless you come back to the Size & Position tab and attach it to the Timescale).

7. Choose OK to return to the workspace.

If you later decide to unlink the object from the task in order to fix it at a particular date, return to the Size & Position tab and choose the Attach to Timescale button. Then move the task with the mouse to the preferred position.

Hiding Objects on the Gantt Chart The objects you place on the Gantt Chart remain visible and print with the Gantt Chart unless you elect to hide them. You can hide them for one printing, for example, and then display them again later.

To hide the drawing objects:

1. Choose Format, Layout. The Layout dialog box is displayed (see Figure 7.25).

2. Clear the Show Drawings check box at the bottom.

3. Choose OK to implement the change.

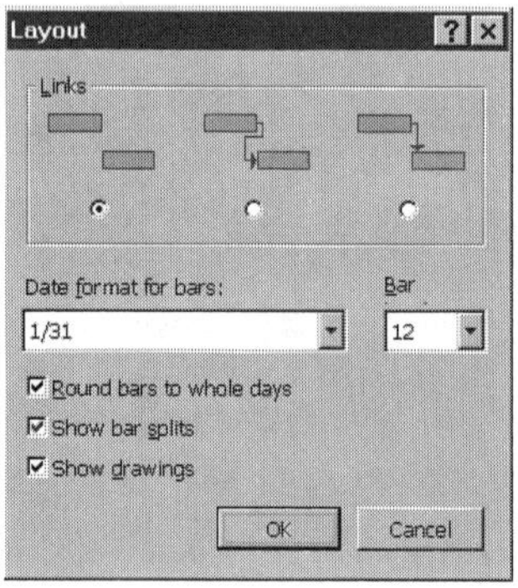

FIG. 7.25

Graphic objects are hidden from view if you clear the Show Drawings check box on the Layout dialog box.

Moving Objects You can move an object by moving the mouse pointer over the object, away from the selection handles. Watch for the small cross to appear to the right of the pointer arrow. Then drag the object to a new position.

CAUTION

It is very easy to accidentally move a task bar or create a new task bar when your intention is to move or resize an object. If the mouse pointer does not have the cross beside it, you will not be moving the object. Do not click the mouse until the cross appears.

Resizing Objects Although you can size an object with the Height and Width fields at the bottom of the Size & Position tab in the Format Drawing dialog box (see Figure 7.23), it is much easier to use the mouse to achieve the same end.

When a two-dimensional object is selected, its selection handles are evident in a rectangular array around the object. Line and arrow objects display selection handles at each end of the object. You can change the size of the object by moving the mouse pointer over one of the selection handles until the pointer changes into a pair of opposing arrows. Drag the handle to the position you desire (see Figure 7.26).

FIG. 7.26

Use the selection handles to resize an object.

The corner handles resize both sides that meet at the corner. The handles along the top and bottom midpoints resize vertically, and the handles along the sides resize horizontally.

T I P Use the Shift key with one of the corner handles to resize the object proportionally along both horizontal and vertical dimensions.

The selection handles of a polygon disappear when you click the Edit Points option on the Draw drop-down list on the Drawing toolbar (see Figure 7.27). Instead, you see reshaping handles at the connecting nodes of its line segments. Use these handles to reposition the connecting nodes and thus change the shape of the drawing. To move a connecting node, position the mouse pointer directly over the handle (it turns into a large plus sign). When you are finished reshaping the figure, click the Edit Points tool again to display the selection handles again.

FIG. 7.27

The Edit Points option on the Drawing toolbar allows you to edit the points on a polygon.

> **CAUTION**
>
> It is just as easy to accidentally move a task bar or create a new task bar when trying to resize an object as it is when moving an object. If the mouse pointer has not become opposing arrows, you will not be resizing the object, and you should refrain from clicking the mouse.

If you want to increase or decrease the size of a polygon without changing its shape, you can make proportional changes to its Size fields on the Format Drawing dialog box. For example, to double the size of a polygon, follow these steps:

1. Select the polygon.
2. Activate the Format Drawing dialog box by double-clicking the polygon or by using the secondary mouse button over the polygon to activate the shortcut menu and selecting Properties.
3. Choose the Size & Position tab.
4. Double the values entered in the Height and Width fields.
5. Choose OK to close the dialog box.

Copying Objects   You can make a copy of an object to display in another area of the Gantt Chart or in another document. Follow these steps to copy an object with the mouse:

1. Select the original object.
2. Use the Ctrl key as you drag away from the original object. You will be dragging a copy of the original.
3. Continue dragging the copy until it is in its new position. The copy appears in outlined form until you release the mouse button.
4. Release the mouse button when the copy is in position.

You also can use the Clipboard to copy an object; this method must be used if you are copying the object to another file:

1. Select the original object.
2. Choose Edit, Copy.
3. If you want to place the copy in the same project document, choose Edit, Paste. A copy of the object appears at the top-left corner of the visible part of the Gantt Chart graphic area. If you want to place the copy in another document, you must activate that document and then choose Edit, Paste to place the copy in the new document.
4. Drag the copy of the object into its desired position.

Changing the Line and Fill Style of an Object   You can change the thickness and color of lines and object borders. You can also choose the background pattern and color that fills the interior of the figure. Both the line and fill are selected on the Line & Fill tab of the Format Drawing dialog box (see Figure 7.28).

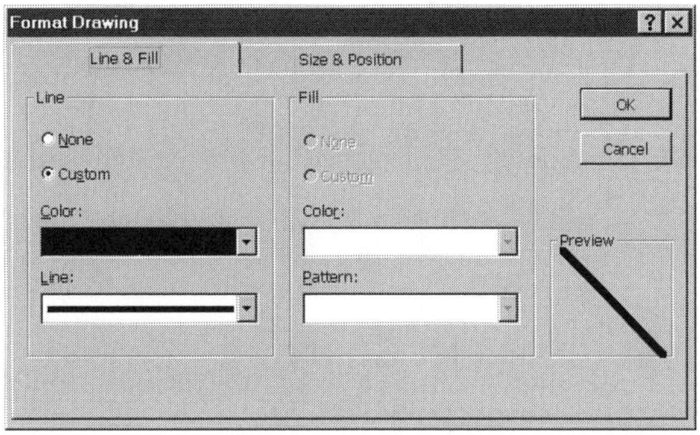

FIG. 7.28

You can customize the attributes of border lines and the interior fill of objects.

To change an object's border line and fill attributes, follow these steps:

1. Select the object and display the Format Drawing dialog box by double-clicking the object. Alternatively, you can choose Format, Drawing, and choose Properties to display the dialog box.

2. Choose the Line & Fill tab.

3. If you want the line or border to be invisible, choose the None button in the Line section. If you select a line color or line style, the Custom button is activated automatically.

4. If you want to select the color for a line, choose a sample color band from the entry list below the Color label.

5. If you want to select the thickness of a line, choose a sample line from the entry list below the Line label.

6. If you want the background of the object to be transparent so that you can see task bars or other objects behind this object, choose the None button in the Fill section of this tab. If you choose a Color or a Pattern, the Custom button is activated automatically.

7. The default fill pattern is solid; the default color is white. If you want to display a different color in the interior of the object, simply select a different color from the entry list below the Color label. The color of an object can also be changed by selecting the object and using the Cycle Fill Color button on the Drawing toolbar.

8. Whatever is black in the pattern is displayed in the color you select. Whatever is white in the pattern remains white. If you leave the default white color selected and select a pattern, you will have a white pattern color on a white background. Select a color for the pattern to see the pattern on the object.

9. Choose a pattern by selecting a sample from the entry list below the Pattern label. The first pattern in the entry list appears white. It is a "clear" pattern, equivalent to choosing the None button in the Fill section. The second pattern in the entry list is solid black. Choose the solid band for a solid background in the color you chose from the Color field. The remaining patterns are displayed against a white background, with the pattern appearing in the foreground in the color you choose from the Color field.

Part

II

Ch

7

10. Use the Preview box at the lower-right corner of the tab to assess the choices you have made. Change the choices until the Preview box looks the way you want the object to look.

11. Choose OK to implement the changes. Choose Cancel to leave the object unchanged.

Deleting Objects   You can delete objects by simply selecting them and then pressing the Delete key on your keyboard.

Placing Free Text on the Gantt Chart

Use the Text Box drawing button to place free text on the Gantt Chart. After you place the text box on the screen, you enter the text into the box. You can change the line and fill attributes and position of the text box as described in the preceding sections. You can also edit the text and choose the fonts for the text display.

Creating a Text Box   To display a text message in the Gantt Chart, you need to bring into view the area where the message is to appear and then follow these steps:

1. Choose the Text Box button on the Drawing toolbar.

2. Drag the mouse in the Gantt Chart to create a box at the approximate location and of the approximate dimension you need. You can adjust the box to fit the text later. An insertion point cursor blinks in the text box.

3. Type the text you want to appear in the box. The text automatically word-wraps within the current size of the text box. It also word-wraps automatically when you resize the text box later. Press Enter to start new lines in the text box.

4. When you are finished entering text, click outside the text box.

Editing the Text in a Text Box   Periodically, it may become necessary to modify the text in a text box. Follow these steps to edit the text:

1. Select the text box. The mouse pointer changes into an I-beam within the text box.

2. Select the place in the text that you want to edit by clicking the I-beam at that point (see Figure 7.29).

3. Click outside the text box when you are finished editing.

TIP   If you want to move a text box, you must select its border with the mouse. Unlike the other objects, selecting the interior of this object does not allow you to move it. Instead, you are allowed to edit the text.

FIG. 7.29

You can use normal editing techniques in a text box.

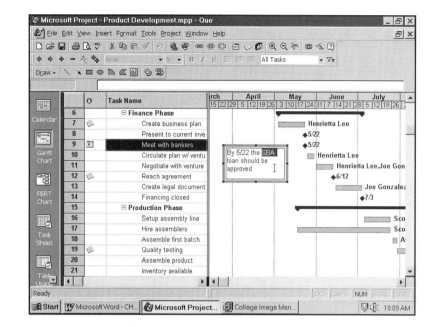

Changing the Text Font   The only method for changing the font or font attributes is through the menu; the formatting options on the Formatting toolbar are deactivated when the object is selected. You can choose the font or font attributes for the text in a text box by selecting the text box and choosing Format, Font. Choose the font type, color, style, or size desired.

Your selections are applied to all text within the text box. You cannot apply different fonts or font attributes to individual words or phrases within the text box. Text within a text box is left-aligned. It cannot be centered or right-aligned.

Changing the Properties of the Text Box   When you create a text box, it is automatically given a lined border and a white background fill. If you want the text to float freely without lines so that the Gantt Chart shows through, you must choose the None button in both sections of the Line & Fill tab on the Format Drawing dialog box.

To clear the lines and fill for a text box:

1. Select the text box.
2. Double-click the text box border to display the Format Drawing dialog box.
3. Choose the None button in the Line section and the None button in the Fill section.
4. Choose OK to effect the change.

Part

II

Ch

7

TROUBLESHOOTING

My drawing won't stay with the task bar I want it associated with. Just choose Format, Drawing, Properties to attach the drawing to the task.

The task bars are hidden by the drawing and I can't see them. You need to select the drawing and use the shortcut menu to move the drawing back.

If an object seems to disappear after you attach it to a task bar, open the Format Drawing dialog box again and change the Horizontal and Vertical offset values to zero. Then the object appears right next to the task bar, and you can reposition it with the mouse.

From Here...

Now that you have learned about working with some of the major task views, you may find the following chapters worthwhile:

- Chapter 8, "Defining Resources and Costs," will introduce you to the Resource Sheet view, one of the major resource views used in Microsoft Project.

- In Chapter 20, "Using the Standard Views, Tables, and Filters," you will explore some of the other task and resource views available in Microsoft Project.

- Should you need to customize a view, Chapter 22, "Customizing Views, Tables, and Filters," will guide you through the steps to modify the existing views, or create your own views.

Assigning Resources and Costs

8   Defining Resources and Costs   251

9   Understanding Resource Scheduling in Microsoft
Project 98   283

10   Assigning Resources and Costs to Tasks   307

11   Resolving Resource Allocation Problems   345

Defining Resources and Costs

This chapter focuses on resources: understanding what resources are, how to create a resource pool, and how costs are calculated in Microsoft Project. We will examine the association between tasks and the resources and costs assigned to tasks. You will learn how to define resources and their costs and how to define costs that are not associated with a particular resource. With this foundation you will then be ready to assign resources to tasks, modify those assignments, and resolve conflicts that arise with overallocated resources. ■

Understanding resources and costs

What are Resources? How can costs be added to tasks and the project? We will examine the association between tasks and the resources and costs assigned to tasks. You will learn how to define resources and their costs and how to define fixed costs not associated with a particular resource.

Defining your resources and their availability to work on your project

Learn to enter resource information in Resource views and create calendars for resources that Microsoft Project can use for scheduling resources and, thereby, for scheduling the tasks that these resources are assigned to work on.

Sort, filter, and print the resource list

Produce more meaningful and informative reports by learning to sort and filter your resource information.

Understanding How Project Uses Resources and Costs

You don't have to assign resources and costs to plan a project with Microsoft Project. You can enter the tasks and let Project schedule the project based on the project calendar, the duration of the tasks, the task constraints, and the dependency relationships you define for the list of tasks. When you don't assign resources to a task, Project uses the base calendar you assigned to the project in the Project Information dialog box and schedules the tasks during the working hours defined in that calendar. You can also assign costs, known as *fixed costs*, to individual tasks without defining resources. If you fail to define and assign resources to tasks, however, you miss an advantage of using Microsoft Project: the program's capability to schedule tasks when the necessary resources are available and its capability to advise you that you have overallocated a resource's time.

If you do assign resources in a project, Project schedules work on a task according to the availability of the resources assigned to work on the task, and uses several factors to determine when resources are available. One factor is the resource calendar, described in the "Understanding Resource Calendars" section of this chapter. Another factor is the dates the resource is available to work on the project, described in the "Using the Resource Information Dialog Box" section of this chapter. This is a new feature with this release of Microsoft Project which allows you to specify a range of dates a particular resource is available to work on the project.

When you assign resources, Project calculates the amount of work or effort associated with the assignment in hours and calculates the cost of that work. The cost is based on a standard cost rate per unit of work time, and you define the standard rate when you define the resource.

> **CAUTION**
>
> Microsoft Project calculates cost figures for your project plan that you can include when estimating the cost of the project. If you track actual work on the project in Microsoft Project, it generates "actual" cost figures. In all cases, however, these calculations are no better than the data you provide the program. And you must *not* expect Microsoft Project to serve as a cost accounting system; it was not designed for that purpose.

You can define a comprehensive list of resources at the outset, including resource cost rates and availability information, and then later assign these resources to the respective tasks, or you can define the resources as you make the assignments. When you assign new resource names to a task, Project will add these names to the roster of resources. If you create resources on the fly, you must remember to go back later and enter the resource cost rates and availability information.

TIP   The Automatically Add New Resources option (available on the General tab of the Options dialog box) determines how Project treats undefined resources you assign to tasks. See the section "Setting the Automatically Add New Resources Option" later in this chapter for more information about this option.

Understanding Resources and Costs

Resources in your project include the people, facilities, equipment, and supplies that contribute to the work on a task. You can also use resource assignments to designate the people who have responsibilities for tasks, and to record the outside contractors or vendors who contribute to the project.

Costs can include the cost of the resources you assign to tasks, and expenses not related directly to resources, such as overhead and fixed costs.

Defining Resources

The term *resource* primarily is applied to people and assets that must be assigned to perform or facilitate work that is required to complete a task. Resources can include workers, supervisors, management, plant and equipment, facilities, and critical supplies or material deemed necessary to complete a task. You also might choose to assign as resources people who don't do actual work on the task or whose work you do not need to measure (such as outside contractors or vendors), but whose name you want associated with the task. The list of resources available for work on a project is known as the *resource pool*.

Some resource names you add to the resource pool represent a single individual or asset. You can use a person's name, for example, as a resource name, or you can name a single piece of equipment as a resource. You can also define a resource that represents a *group* of resources with similar skills or job descriptions that are considered to be interchangeable units in the project. For example, you might define a group of three assemblers as an Assemblers resource, or a group of five electricians as the Electricians resource. Group resources are called "resource sets" in Microsoft Project.

> **CAUTION**
>
> Individuals in a group resource will have cost rates that are common to the group and will be scheduled by a single resource calendar that is common to the group. You cannot assign unique cost rates to individual members of a resource group, and you cannot recognize individual vacation days or other nonworking times for members of the group.

> ▶ **See** "Understanding Resource-Driven and Fixed Duration Scheduling," **p. 283**
> ▶ **See** "Assigning Resources and Costs to Tasks," **p. 307**

Defining Costs

There are two types of costs in Project, resource costs and fixed costs, and together they add up to Total Cost. *Resource costs* are those costs which derive from the resources assigned to the task. *Fixed costs* are costs that you associate with the task but are not attributable to a named resource. Additionally, when a resource is defined or a fixed cost is entered, you must specify when the costs will be recognized (accrued) in reporting costs.

Resource Costs   When you assign a resource to a task, Project calculates a cost value for the task by multiplying the number of units of work for the resource (in minutes, hours, days, or weeks) times the cost rate for the resource. The result is a cost per unit of time. If you assign multiple resource names to a task, the sum of all the individual resource costs is recorded as the resource cost of the task. Table 8.1 provides some examples of how task costs are calculated. Resource rates can be entered in by minute, hour, day, week, or year.

Table 8.1   Sample Cost Calculations

Work	Resource Rate	Calculated Cost	Notes
10 hours	$5 per hour	$50	
10 hours	$100 per day	$125	Project converts the daily rate of $100 into an hourly rate of $12.50 ($100 divided by the hours per workday—here assumed to be 8). This hourly rate is then multiplied by the number of work hours to calculate the cost.
10 hours	$35,000 per year	$168.27	Project converts the annual rate of $35,000 into an hourly rate of $16.826923 ($35,000 divided by 52 weeks per year divided by 40 hours per week). This hourly rate is then multiplied by the number of work hours to calculate the cost.

The resource cost calculations described so far are designed for resources like labor, equipment, or facilities where the resource cost is based on the amount of work the resource does on the task. If the task takes more work than anticipated, the resource cost will increase. On the other hand, some resources like materials have a one-time cost for each unit used in the task, and this resource cost is not affected by the duration or work on the task. The *Cost Per Use* field is designed to capture these costs.

As an example, a magazine planning a photo essay would assign a photographer, models, cameras, crew, and rolls of film to tasks in the project. The rolls of film could be listed in the resource pool with only a Cost Per Use (no standard rate). The cost of film for each task would depend only on the number of rolls used by the photographer on a shooting assignment.

In another example, the construction task of pouring a foundation involves materials like concrete, among other things. Concrete costs would be based on the number of truckloads of mixed concrete delivered multiplied by the Per Use cost for each truckload. For this example, the cost of a truckload of delivered concrete would be entered in the Per Use field, and the number of truckloads needed would be entered in the Units field. The duration of the task would have no direct correlation with the materials cost.

The Per Use value is charged for each unit of a resource assigned to a task, and is charged to all tasks the resource is assigned to.

Fixed Costs   Fixed costs are costs that are independent of the number of resources needed to complete a task. The legal fees associated with a contract or the construction permit fees could be treated as Fixed Costs. A vendor's fixed fee for doing the work of a task could be entered as a Fixed Cost for, although there may be resources involved in the task, those resources that are under the vendor's control and do not need to be tracked by the project manager.

▶ **See** "Defining Fixed and Total Cost," **p. 262**

Cost Accrual   When you define a resource or enter a fixed cost, you also must specify when the costs associated with that resource or fixed cost will be recognized in financial reports. As Actual Work is recorded, Microsoft Project calculates Actual Cost based on the accrual method that you select for each resource.

TIP This distinction is important only when preparing interim cost reports while the project is in progress. Once the project is completed, all costs are recognized by each of the accrual options.

- Normally, costs are prorated over the duration of the task, so as work is done on the task, a proportional amount of the cost is considered as already incurred. If, for example, you were to print a cost report at a time in the project when an Assembly task was marked as 60% complete, Project would include 60% of the scheduled resource cost as Actual Cost (cost already incurred) for the Assembly task.

- You can also stipulate that all the costs be considered incurred as soon as the task is begun. In the preceding example, the report would include 100% of the scheduled cost as Actual Cost at the time of the 60% completed report.

- A third option is to count costs as incurred only after all work on the task is completed. In the example above, Project would show Actual Cost as zero in the interim report at the 60% completion date, and 100% after the task has finished.

Understanding the Resource Fields

The resource fields are accessible on several views. The Resource Sheet is the most efficient view for creating a resource list (see Figure 8.1). You can also use the Resource Form to change resource information, but it isn't a good view for creating the resource pool (see Figure 8.2).

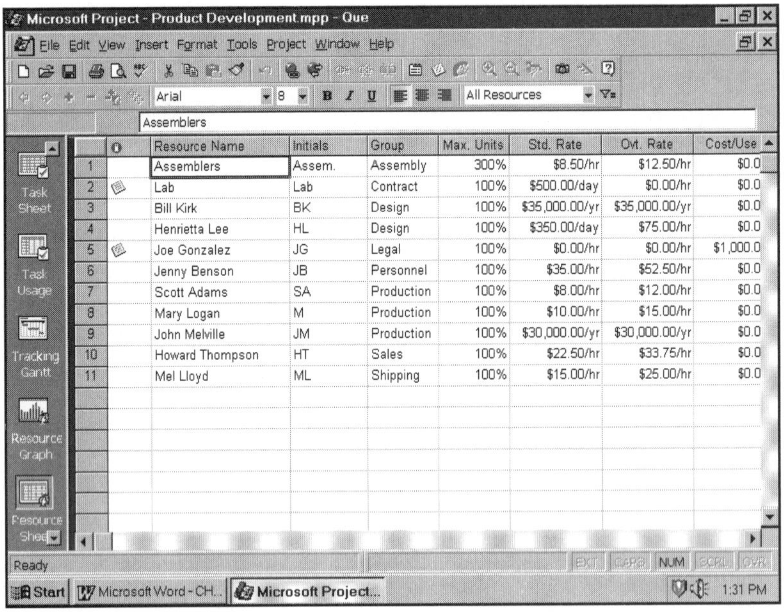

FIG. 8.1

The Resource Sheet is the primary data entry view for defining resources. You can see many resources at once.

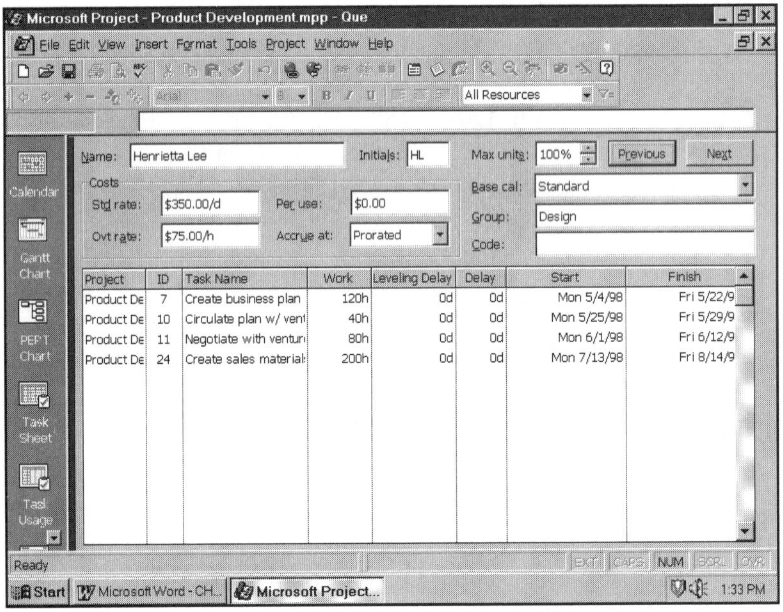

FIG. 8.2

You can also use the Resource Form to modify resource definitions. Choose View, More Views to access this form.

However, Microsoft Project 98 introduces a number of new resource fields that are not—or cannot be—included on the Resource Sheet or the Resource Form. The new fields include multitiered rate schedules for resources, dated rate increases for resources, availability dates for resources, and more. Almost all of these fields are included on the Resource Information dialog box (see Figure 8.3), and you must use this dialog box to record these new features of a resource definition. The Resource Information dialog box also now includes the resource calendar for editing.

▶ **See** "Using the Resource Information Dialog Box," **p. 270**

N O T E The Resource Information dialog box does not appear automatically. Use the information tool on the Standard toolbar or choose Project, Resource Information to display this dialog box. ▪

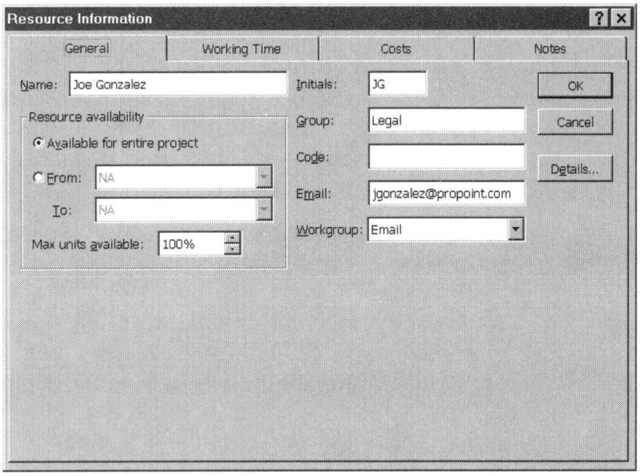

FIG. 8.3

Use the Resource Information dialog box to create new resource definitions or modify existing ones.

When you define a resource, you must provide a resource name. You might fill in data for the remaining options as described in Table 8.2, or you can leave the options with the default or blank values.

Table 8.2   Resource Fields in the Resource Sheet View

Option	Purpose
ID	When you add a resource to the resource pool, Project assigns the next available resource ID number to the resource. As with tasks, resources are identified by their ID number. You cannot assign the ID number; Project assigns the ID number. This field does not appear in the Resource Information dialog box.

continues

Table 8.2   Continued

Option	Purpose
Indicators	Resource notes and warnings regarding resource overallocations will be represented by symbols in the Indicator field in the Resource Sheet. In Figure 8.1 there are note indicators displayed next to The Lab and Joe Gonzalez. Indicator is a new field in Project 98.
Name	Always identify the resource with a name. The name can contain any characters except the comma and the square brackets ([]). Resource names can be up to 255 characters long, and they don't have to be unique (because resources are identified by their ID numbers). However, if you assign a resource name to multiple tasks, Project uses the first resource with that name in the resource list. The resource name can be a specific resource name like Anita Salinas or a group of resources like Electricians.
Initials	To save space, you can use the initials for the resource on Gantt Charts and PERT Charts rather than the full name. You can also use initials when assigning resources in the Task Form view to save the time of typing the full resource name.
Group	This provides a place to enter an identifying code word or number you can use for sorting and filtering resources. You can identify all management personnel, for example, by entering **Management**; all equipment resources by entering **Equipment**; and all vendors and contractors by entering **Vendors**. With these entries, you then can use the Group Resource filter to view the data for only one of the group categories, such as Management. If you want, you can enter in several "groups" that the resource belongs to by separating the groups with spaces or commas. When applying a filter to locate one of the words in the group however, wild cards will be necessary. See Chapter 20, "Using the Standard Views, Tables, and Filters," for more information on using filters. You can enter anything in this field—any combination of letters, numbers, spaces, or other characters, up to 255 characters in length. Don't confuse this field with the concept of resource groups, which are multiple, interchangeable units of a resource that are identified with one ID and name. The Group text box provides a means for organizing resource names into meaningful groupings.
Max Units	Here you can define the maximum number of units a resource is available for assignment at any one time in the project. The units can be defined as a percentage or decimal; the default is percentage. You can change the format for the Max Unit field on the Schedule tab of the Options dialog box. Choose Tools, Options, and select the Schedule tab. Choose the Show Assignment Units As A list box, and select either Percentage or Decimal.

Option	Purpose
	The default percentage is 100%, but you can enter a value between 0% and 1,000,000%. For a single unit resource, 100% means this resource is available to work full time on this project. If the resource is working on other projects, a smaller percentage of his or her time would be available to devote to this project. If you are grouping your resources, you would enter in a percent greater than 100%. If you have two full-time writers and one part-time writer, for example, enter **250%**.
	The default decimal value is one, but you can enter any value between zero and 10,000. For a single unit resource, enter **1** if the resource is available full time. Enter a fraction if the resource can only work part time on tasks in this project. For example, enter **.5** if the resource is to work no more than half of each day on any task in this project.
	For groups of resources, you enter in the number of units available. If you have three trucks available to use for this project, enter **3**. You can also enter fractional values. If you have two full-time writers and one part-time writer, for example, enter **2.5**.
	Project uses this field to calculate when a resource is overallocated. Because you can assign resources to multiple tasks (and to multiple projects), it's possible to assign the same resource to tasks that are scheduled at the same or overlapping times. If the sum of the assignments of a resource to all tasks at a given moment exceeds the entry in the Max Units text box, Project calculates that the resource is overallocated, and displays a symbol in the Indicator field to flag the resource for you.
Standard Rate	The standard rate is the cost per unit of time to charge for the use of the resource. Type the standard rate as a number, followed by a *forward* slash, and one of the following time unit abbreviations: m (minute), h (hour), d (day), w (week), or y (year). You can use the year as a time unit when defining annual rates for resources. If you type just a number (without a time unit) Project assumes it's an hourly rate. For example, type **600/w** for $600 per week, **35000/y** for $35,000 per year, and **15.5** for $15.50 per hour.
	When you assign the resource to a task, the standard rate is converted to an hourly rate and is applied to the number of hours of work it takes to complete the task. For annual rates, the hourly rate is calculated by assuming 52 weeks, and the number of hours per week is derived from the entry in the Options dialog box for default hours per week. For the standard workweek of 40 hours, the annual rate is divided by 2,080 to get an hourly rate.

continues

Table 8.2 Continued

Option	Purpose
Overtime Rate	Use the overtime rate when you add overtime hours to the work schedule. If the rate for overtime work is the same as the regular rate, you must enter this amount again in the Overtime Rate text box, or overtime hours will be charged at the zero default rate.
	You can use the Overtime Rate field in two ways. If you want Project to estimate the cash outlays on a project, the overtime rate must match actual payments for overtime work. With salaried employees, for example, leave a zero if they are not paid for their overtime hours.
	You can also use the overtime rate to reflect the opportunity cost of using a resource in overtime. For example, say a salaried employee is assigned to do all the work on a task in overtime. If the overtime rate is zero, the task will add nothing to the cost of the project. With this approach, an hour spent in overtime on a task might not cost any additional amount in payroll, but that time could have been used on other tasks or other projects, and the cost of using it on the assigned task should be measured. By this logic, the overtime rate should never be zero; it should be the same as the standard rate if no premium is paid to the employee for working overtime, or it should reflect the actual overtime rate.
Cost Per Use	The Cost Per Use is a charge added once for each unit of the resource assigned to any task, regardless of the duration of the task. It is mainly used for material resources. Suppose the Cost Per Use charge is $100 and one unit of the resource is assigned to Task A. The Cost Per Use charge for Task A is $100. If two units of the same resource are also assigned to Task B, the per use charge for Task B would be $200.
	The cost of the task derived from the cost of resources (the resource cost) is the sum of the standard rate charges, the overtime charges, and the Cost Per Use charges. (**Note:** To see the remaining fields in the Resource Sheet view, scroll to the right.)
Accrue at	You can choose one of three options: Start, End, and Prorated. The accrual method determines how Project calculates actual costs accrued when a task has started but not finished.
	The default accrual method is Prorated, which means that if 20% of the work on the task is completed, the cost will be estimated to be 20% of the scheduled or estimated cost.
	If you choose Start, then when you enter an actual start date for the task, Project calculates the entire cost of the task as actual cost, beginning on the start date. Any report generated after the actual start is recorded will show the entire cost of the task as already incurred.

Option	Purpose
	If you choose End, Project defers recognition of the actual cost until you enter a finish date or until the task is 100 percent complete.
	The Accrue At option is relevant only in interim reports when the project has started, but not finished. If a task is 20 percent completed when you print a cost report, the Prorated option would show 20 percent of projected costs as Actual Costs (already incurred); the Start option would show all of the costs as Actual Costs; and the End option would show zero Actual Costs.
Base Calendar	This identifies the base calendar for this resource. Choose a base calendar from the drop-down list. The calendar for the resource inherits all the working days and working hours from the calendar on which it is based. There are three base calendars built into Project: 24 hours, Night Shift, and Standard. The default base calendar is Standard. Chapter 3 "Setting Up a New Project Document" discusses base calendars.
Code	You can enter any kind of information and can use any combination of up to 255 symbols and characters. The most common use of the Code text box is to place accounting codes so you can group task cost information by accounting codes for exporting to other applications.

There are a number of new fields which only appear in the Resource Information dialog box. These fields are described in Table 8.3.

Table 8.3   New Resource Fields in the Resource Information Dialog Box

Option	Purpose
Resource Availability	If the resource will not be available for the entire duration of the project, you can specify the dates the resource will be available. Project will let you assign resources outside the range of available dates, but an overallocation will be noted.
Email	You can specify an e-mail address for the resource. A MAPI-compliant, 32-bit e-mail system is required in order to send messages, such as task assignments, from within Microsoft Project. Chapter 18, "Using Microsoft Project in Workgroups," can provide you with more information on this capability.
Workgroup	A workgroup can be set up in Project to allow for communication between project participants. Communication can be made via e-mail, the World Wide Web, or both. Messages can be sent to project participants, and those recipients can send replies. See Chapter 18, "Using Microsoft Project in Workgroups," for more information.

continued

Table 8.3 Continued

Option	Purpose
Details	In the Resource Information dialog box, you have an additional option. The Details button is used to identify any particulars of the e-mail address that the mail program may require to send the e-mail, including the type of e-mail system being used (for example, SMTP, cc:MAIL, and so on).
Time Stamped Cost Rates	You can now allow for the inflation factor in defining resource cost rates. You can assign one cost rate for a specified period of time and another rate for a different period of time. For example, suppose the cost of renting computer equipment is $50 per day through 1/14/98, then the rate goes up to $65 per day. The first Effective Date entry indicates the beginning of the project. Dates when the rate changes are entered in subsequent rows. When your computer date/time clock reflects 1/15/98, the new rates will automatically be applied. The most common use of this new feature will be for increased personnel costs. You can enter up to 25 timed rate changes.
Cost Rate Tables	The Cost Rate Tables provide up to five different rates you can define if the rate charged for the resource varies depending on the type of work performed. For example, Table A could contain fees for verbal consultations, and Table B could contain fees for hands-on labor. As with the rates in the Resource Sheet, you can enter in a standard rate, overtime rate, and per use cost, and can indicate when the rates should accrue. The rates in Table A are the default rates that will be used. You can select other rates in the Assignment Information dialog box. (See "Assigning Resources and Costs to Tasks" in Chapter 10.)

Defining Fixed and Total Cost

The Fixed Cost field is displayed on the Cost table, which you can apply to the Gantt Chart and to the Task Sheet. Figure 8.4 shows the Task Sheet with the Cost table in the top pane and the itemized resource costs in the bottom pane. The Fixed Cost field adds $1,000 to the itemized resource costs in the Total Cost field.

To display the Task Sheet view as shown in Figure 8.4, follow these steps:

1. Choose View, More Views. In the More Views dialog box, choose Task Sheet from the view list and choose Apply.

2. To apply the Cost table, choose View, Table, Cost.

3. To display the Task Form in the bottom pane, choose Window, Split.

4. To display the itemized resource costs in the Task Form, choose Format, Details (or right-click the Task Form to display the shortcut menu), and then choose Resource Cost.

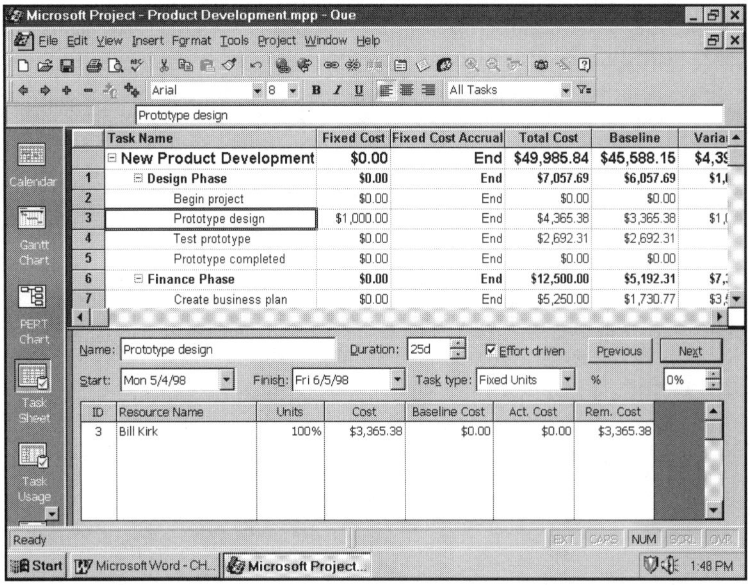

FIG. 8.4

The Total Cost field includes resource costs and fixed costs.

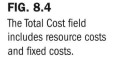

Like the variable costs associated with a resource, you can indicate when the fixed cost will accrue. The choices are exactly the same: Start, Prorated, and End. The default is End. This is a new feature in Project 98.

The Total Cost field sums the resource costs and the fixed costs. If resources are not assigned to a task, you can enter cost directly into the Total Cost field or in the Fixed Cost field. If resource costs do exist, any entry you make in the Total Cost field is ignored. To see how this process works, enter a cost amount in the Fixed Cost field. The amount you enter is added to the resource costs to calculate the Total Cost.

N O T E For clarity, the Cost field is labeled Total Cost on the Cost table, but the field name is Cost. ▓

Defining the Resource Pool

As mentioned earlier, the list of resources available for work on a project is known as the resource pool. Microsoft Project will calculate resource costs based on your definitions of each resource in the resource pool.

You usually define the resource pool in each project. You can also stipulate that a project will use the resource pool already defined in another project.

▶ **See** "Sharing Resources among Projects," **p. 558**

Part

III

Ch

8

TIP Many users create a project template that contains no tasks but defines the organization's standard resources and costs. When a new project file is desired, the project is created from this template file of resources. See the section, "Creating a Resource Template," later in this chapter for the steps on creating a resource template file.

There are several ways you can create and add to a pool of resources. You can create the resource pool before you define the tasks. Use the Resource Sheet or Resource Form to create or add resources to the pool. Resources can also be added to the pool automatically when you assign a new (undefined) resource to a task. You can use any task view that has a field for resource assignments to assign and define resources. See the section "Setting the Automatically Add New Resources Option" later in this chapter. Understanding how this option works before you assign resources to tasks is important.

Using the Resource Sheet

Use the Resource Sheet view to enter many resources at one time. Refer to the section, "Understanding the Resource Fields," earlier in this chapter for descriptions of these fields.

To display the Resource Sheet, choose View, Resource Sheet or select the Resource Sheet from the View Bar. The Resource Sheet view appears (see Figure 8.5). To enter the field information, see the section "Filling in the Resource Fields" later in this chapter.

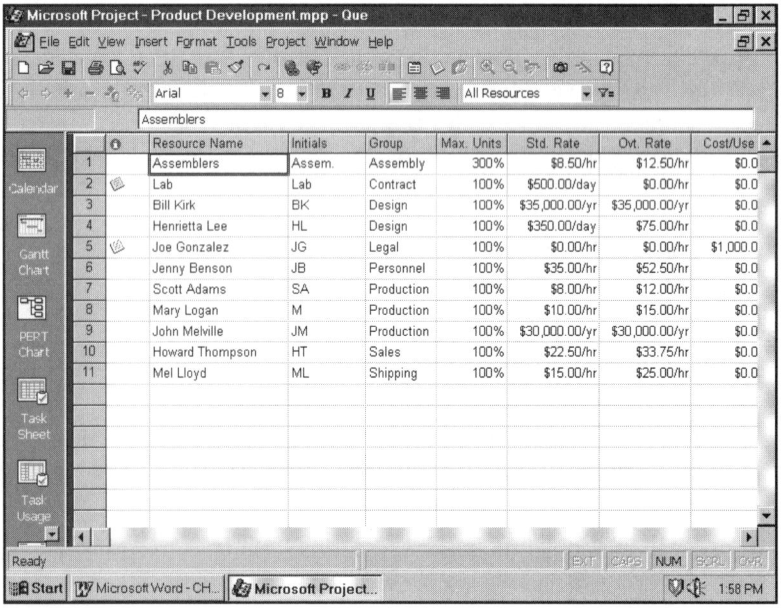
Microsoft Project - Product Development.mpp - Que
File Edit View Insert Format Tools Project Window Help
Arial
8
All Resources
Assemblers
Calendar
Gantt Chart
PERT Chart
Task Sheet
Task Usage
Resource Name | Initials | Group | Max. Units | Std. Rate | Ovt. Rate | Cost/Use
1 Assemblers | Assem. | Assembly | 300% | $8.50/hr | $12.50/hr | $0.0
2 Lab | Lab | Contract | 100% | $500.00/day | $0.00/hr | $0.0
3 Bill Kirk | BK | Design | 100% | $35,000.00/yr | $35,000.00/yr | $0.0
4 Henrietta Lee | HL | Design | 100% | $350.00/day | $75.00/hr | $0.0
5 Joe Gonzalez | JG | Legal | 100% | $0.00/hr | $0.00/hr | $1,000.0
6 Jenny Benson | JB | Personnel | 100% | $35.00/hr | $52.50/hr | $0.0
7 Scott Adams | SA | Production | 100% | $8.00/hr | $12.00/hr | $0.0
8 Mary Logan | M | Production | 100% | $10.00/hr | $15.00/hr | $0.0
9 John Melville | JM | Production | 100% | $30,000.00/yr | $30,000.00/yr | $0.0
10 Howard Thompson | HT | Sales | 100% | $22.50/hr | $33.75/hr | $0.0
11 Mel Lloyd | ML | Shipping | 100% | $15.00/hr | $25.00/hr | $0.0
Ready
NUM
Start
Microsoft Word - CH...
Microsoft Project...
1:58 PM

FIG. 8.5
The Resource Sheet view is used to enter information about the pool of resources which will be required on your project.

You can add notes while entering the resource pool on the Resource Sheet (see Figure 8.6). Simply split the screen with the Resource Sheet in the top pane, and the Resource Form will appear in the bottom pane. Then display the Notes field in the Resource Form. Add resources in the top pane and add comments in the Notes field in the bottom pane.

FIG. 8.6
Display the Notes field in the bottom split and the Resource Sheet in the top split for the most efficient creation of a resource pool.

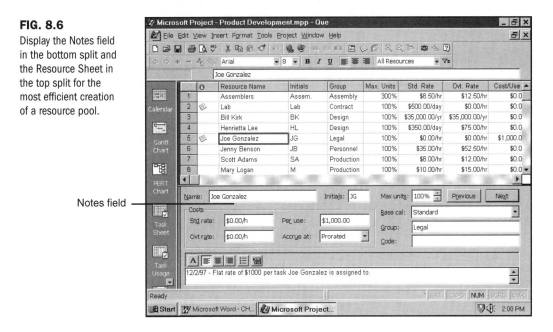

Notes field

To create the combination view displayed in Figure 8.6, follow these steps:

1. Display the Resource Sheet as a full screen view. If the current view is a full screen view, choose View, Resource Sheet. If the current view is a split screen view, hold down the Shift key as you choose View, Resource Sheet.

2. Split the screen by choosing Window, Split. The Resource Form appears in the bottom pane.

3. Click the bottom pane to activate it (or press F6).

4. Choose Format, Details, Notes (or right-click the Resource Form and choose Notes from the shortcut menu).

Using the Resource Form

The Resource Sheet view displays the resource data in a spreadsheet arrangement. You can also enter the resource pool by filling in the fields on the Resource Form. To create a new resource on the form, you must have a blank form. If there are already resources in the pool, choose the Next button to move through the existing resources until you get a blank form.

TIP One advantage of using the Resource Form for entering resources is that you can display the Notes field at the bottom and add notes about each resource (see Figure 8.7).

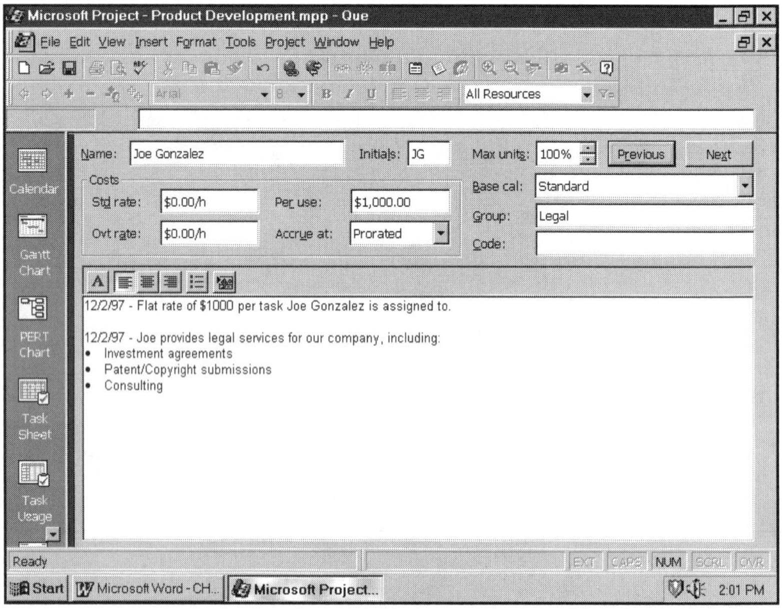

FIG. 8.7

You can add resources in the Resource Form when it is displayed full screen.

To display the Resource Form, follow these steps:

1. If the current view is a split screen view, remove the split by choosing Window, Remove Split. You can also select the top pane; the Resource Form must be in the top pane if you want to use it to create new resources.

TIP Holding down the Shift key while selecting the View menu automatically will remove the split screen when you choose another view.

2. Choose View, More Views.

3. From the More Views dialog box, choose Resource Form and choose Apply.

You can attach notes to resources if you display the Notes field at the bottom of the form. To display the Notes field on the Resource Form, follow these steps:

1. Click the Resource Form view to activate it.

2. Choose Format, Details, Notes.

N O T E You can also right-click the Resource Form and choose Notes from the shortcut menu that appears. ▪

If some resources are already in the pool, you must choose the Next button until a blank form for adding a new resource appears. Fill in the fields, as described later in the section "Filling in the Resource Fields." To save the new resource, choose the OK button.

Setting the Automatically Add New Resources Option

The setting of the Automatically Add New Resources option determines how Project reacts when you assign a resource to a task, and the resource is not currently in your pool of resources. This type of resource is often referred to as an *undefined resource*. Choose Tools, Options and select the General tab to access the Automatically Add New Resources option.

Whenever you assign a resource name to a task, Project checks the resource pool for the name you enter. If the name is not yet defined, Project will add the resource to the list. By default Project automatically adds any new resource to the resource pool, without confirming the addition with you or allowing you to enter in other pertinent resource information, like cost rates and base calendar. When the resource is added, the default settings for the fields in the resource sheet are filled into the Resource Sheet.

> **CAUTION**
>
> You are not reminded that the resource was added or that the resource information was not defined. You must remember to go back and fill in the resource information later.

The default setting for the Automatically Add New Resources option can be the cause of miscalculations in your costs if you neglect to go back and fill in the data for the new resource. It can also be the cause of duplicate resource names. For example, suppose you have created a pool of resources which includes: Peter, Maria, and Ivan. As you are assigning resources to tasks, you type in **Pete** instead of Peter. A new resource (Pete) has been added to your list of resources; you now have Peter, Maria, Ivan, and Pete. The default settings for the fields in the Resource Sheet are the only resource information entered for Pete. Unless you changed the default standard and overtime rates in the Options dialog box, the default rates for Pete are zero, which causes your cost information to be inaccurate.

If the Automatically Add New Resources option is disabled, Project will prompt you to decide if you want the resource added to the resource pool (see Figure 8.8). Project asks you to confirm each new resource before adding it to the resource pool. If you confirm that you want to add the resource, the resource is added. However, you will still have to define the information for the resource.

FIG. 8.8

The prompt which displays when you are assigning a new resource to a task and the Automatically Add New Resources option is deselected.

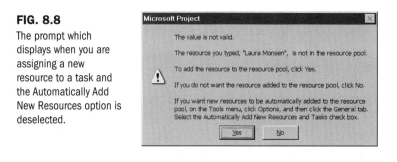

▶ **See** "Assigning Resources and Costs to Tasks," **p. 307**

The Resource Information dialog box is the quickest, and most complete way to define a resource when you are in a task view, like the Gantt Chart view. To open the dialog box, double-click the resource name or select the resource name, then choose the Information button on the Standard toolbar. See the section "Using the Resource Information Dialog Box" later in this chapter for detailed instructions on adding or modifying information in this dialog box.

To set the Automatically Add New Resources option for automatic addition of resources, follow these steps:

1. Choose Tools, Options. The Options dialog box appears.

2. Choose the General tab (see Figure 8.9).

3. Select the Automatically Add New Resources check box (near the bottom section of the dialog box) if you want Project to add resource names to the resource pool without asking you for confirmation.

   Or

   Deselect the Automatically Add New Resources check box if you want Project to add resources only after you confirm that you want them added.

4. Choose the OK button to close the dialog box.

> **TIP** Generally, you should disable the Automatically Add New Resources option. If it is enabled, Project automatically adds to the resource pool the resource names you assign to tasks—even if they're mistyped. When the option is disabled, Project warns you that the resource doesn't exist and asks if you want to add the new name to the resource pool.

Filling in the Resource Fields

Use the Resource Sheet or Resource Form to fill in the resource fields. The resource fields were described in detail in the section "Understanding the Resource Fields" earlier in this chapter and while brief examples of typical entries are provided with the steps below, refer to this previous section for more information on using these fields. To fill in the fields in the Resource Information dialog box, see the next section in this chapter "Using the Resource Information Dialog Box."

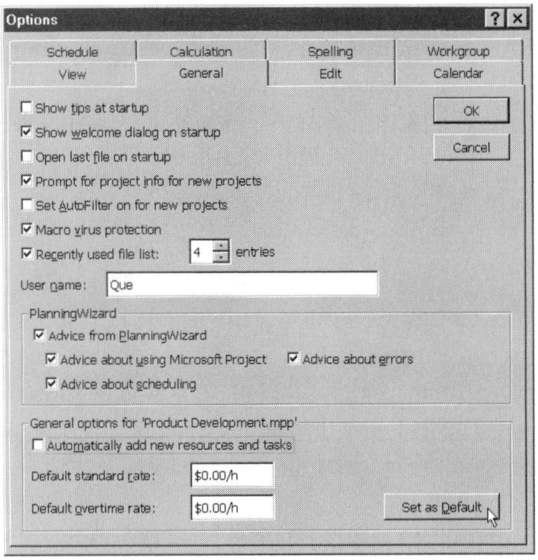

FIG. 8.9

Choose whether to automatically add resources to the resource pool in the Options dialog box.

To fill in the resource fields follow these steps:

1. Enter a name of up to 255 characters. Although you can use either upper- or lowercase letters, remember that reports print the names exactly as entered. You cannot use a comma or square brackets ([]) in resource names.

2. The default initial is the first letter of the resource name. If you want to display initials on the Gantt Charts, Calendar, or PERT Chart or use initials as a shortcut for assigning resources in the Task Form, enter unique initials for each resource. Project doesn't reject duplicate initials, but if you use duplicates, it can certainly result in confusion.

3. Enter a Group identifier for the resource, and you can sort or filter resources according to the identifiers you enter in this field. (You can enter any kind of information in this field—not just a group name, but any combination of letters, numbers, spaces, or other characters up to 255 characters in length.)

4. Enter the maximum percentage of the time the resource is available to work on one task or a combination of tasks simultaneously. The default value is 100%, but you can enter a value between 0% and 1,000,000%. For a single unit resource, 100% means this resource is available to work full time on this project. If the resource is working on other projects, a smaller percentage of his or her time would be available to devote to this project. If you are grouping your resources, you would enter in a percent greater than 100%. If you have two full-time workers and one part-time worker, for example, the Maximum Units field should have a value of 250%. This field can also display units in decimal numbers like 20 or 5.5.

5. Enter the standard rate for charging cost to tasks on which the resource works. Type the standard rate as a number, type a forward slash, and then type one of the following time unit letters: m (minute), h (hour), d (day), w (week), or y (year).

If you enter a number but do not include a time unit, Project uses the number as an hourly rate. For example, type **600/w** for $600 per week, **35000/y** for $35,000 per year, and **15.5** for $15.50 per hour.

6. Enter the overtime rate. The overtime rate calculates resource costs when overtime hours are entered in the work schedule. If the rate for overtime work is the same as the regular rate, you must enter this amount again, or overtime hours are charged at the zero default rate.

7. Enter the Per/Use cost. This is the cost associated with each unit of the resource and will be applied to each task the resource is assigned to. For example, if photographic film is a resource, which costs $5.25 per roll, the Per/Use cost is $5.25. If three rolls of film are assigned to task 7, the resource cost calculated will be 3 × $5.25 = $15.75. If four more rolls are used with task 11, a cost of $21.00 will be added to task 11.

8. Select the accrual method for calculating actual costs. From the Accrue At drop-down list, select Start, End, or Prorated.

9. Enter the base calendar to use for scheduling the resource. By default, the resource calendar for this resource inherits all the standard working days and hours of the base calendar and all the exceptions, both nonworking days and extra working days. Assign a different base calendar to the resource by choosing one from the Base Calendar drop-down list.

10. Enter a Code for the resource if you want to sort or filter resources according to the entries in this field. You can use any combination of up to 255 characters. The most common use of the Code field is to place accounting codes so cost information for the task can be grouped by accounting codes for exporting to other applications.

Using the Resource Information Dialog Box

 The Resource Information dialog box has been significantly altered in Project 98 to provide comprehensive information about your resources. It now displays all the information you need regarding a particular resource. In addition to the fields found on the Resource Sheet, there is information about the resources availability, the resource calendar, variable costs rates, and notes.

 To access the Resource Information dialog box from a resource view, like the Resource Sheet or Resource Form, you can select the resource name and click the Information icon on the Standard toolbar to display the Resource Information dialog box. With some resource views (like Resource Sheet and Resource Usage) you can also double-click the resource name to produce the Resource Information dialog box.

N O T E The Resource Information dialog box can also be accessed from certain task views, like the Task Form view. The Task Form is the default view displayed in the lower pane when you split the window while displaying the Gantt Chart view. Select the Resource Name field before attempting to access the Resource Information dialog box. ▪

Figure 8.10 shows the General tab of Resource Information dialog box. From this tab, you can indicate the resources availability, maximum units, group, and even the resource's e-mail address.

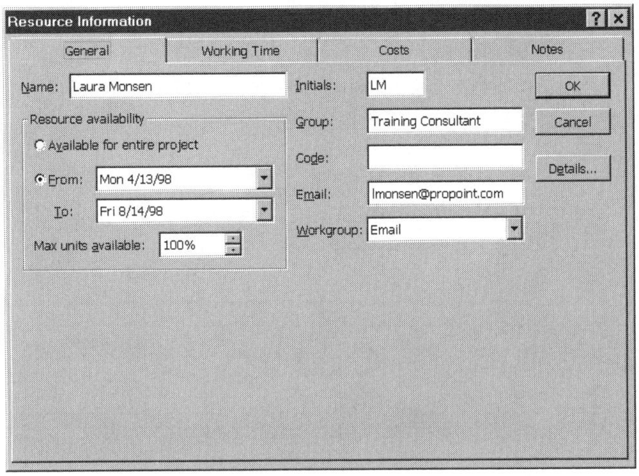

FIG. 8.10

The General tab displays when you activate the Resource Information dialog box.

Some of the fields on the General tab are the same as those in the Resource Sheet and Resource Form. Several fields are new, however, and are described in the section "Understanding the Resource Fields" earlier in this chapter.

Figure 8.11 shows the Working Time tab of Resource Information dialog box. The fields on this tab are a duplicate of the fields when you choose Tools, Change Working Time. The section "Changing Working Times for Resources" later in this chapter discusses each of these fields in detail.

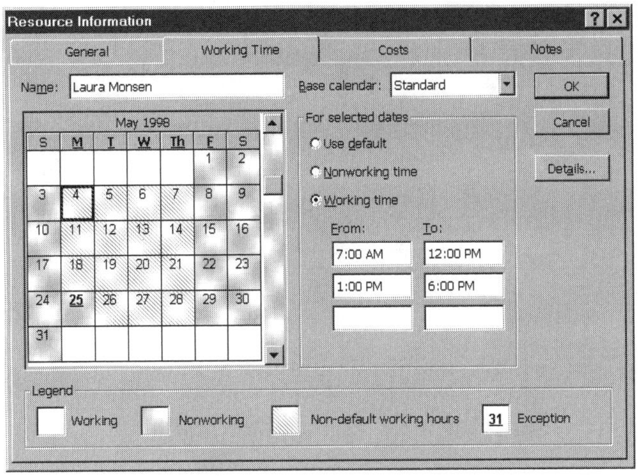

FIG. 8.11

The Working Time tab on the Resource Information dialog box displays the resource calendar information.

Figure 8.12 shows the Costs tab of Resource Information dialog box. These fields provide you with the ability to assign variable resource rates, a new feature in Project 98.

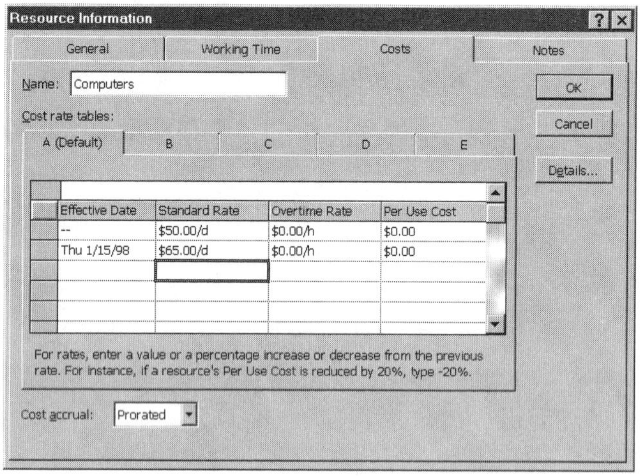

FIG. 8.12

The Costs tab on the Resource Information dialog box displays five cost rate tables.

While a few of the fields on the Costs tab are the same as those in the Resource Sheet and Resource Form, there are many new features provided here. See the section "Understanding the Resource Fields" earlier in this chapter for a description of how these fields are used.

Figure 8.13 shows the Notes tab of the Resource Information dialog box. While the capability to add notes to a resource has been available in Project for some time, the capability has been expanded to include: font formatting, text alignment, bulleted text, and inserting a bitmap object, sound and video clips, a Word document, or an Excel spreadsheet.

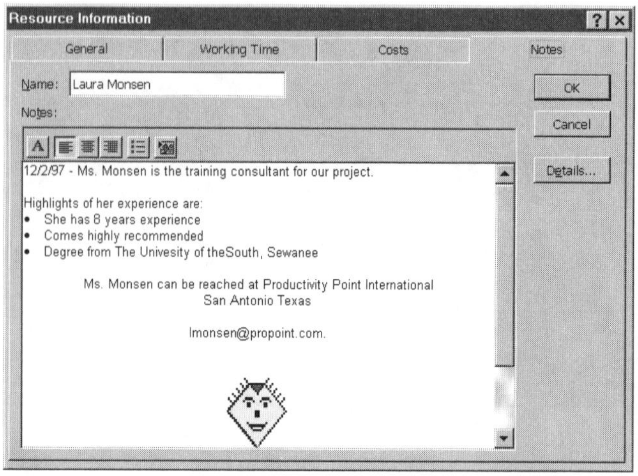

FIG. 8.13

The Notes tab provides quick access to enter or view notes about the selected resource.

Changing Working Times for Resources

Use the resource calendar to record details about the daily working availability of individual resources. Each resource calendar is tied to one base calendar, and the resource calendar inherits all the information contained in the base calendar: the standard working hours and days and the exceptions to these standard working times (holidays, extra workdays, and so on). You then adjust the resource calendar for each resource to show exceptions to the base calendar's working times, holidays, and so on for the resource. The default base calendar for resources is the Standard calendar.

▶ **See** "Defining a Calendar of Working Time," **p. 78**

Understanding Resource Calendars

You edit resource calendars to indicate the exceptions to the base calendar that apply to each resource. For example, if the resource represents an individual, you would enter vacation days, personal/sick days, and any other days the resource will not be available to work on the project—like going on an out-of-town business trip. You can edit resource calendars by choosing Tools, Change Working Times or by accessing the calendar on the Working Time tab of the Resource Information dialog box.

If several resources have similar exceptions to the base calendar used in the project, creating an additional base calendar to be used by these resources is worthwhile. Therefore, if a group of nightshift workers will be assigned to work on a project, and they all have the same basic schedule of nightwork hours, creating a base calendar for nightshift work and then using that base calendar for all workers with those hours saves you time. With this method, you only define the hours once, instead of customizing each nightshift worker's resource calendar.

N O T E If you create several base calendars for use by resources, remember to make company-wide changes in working days and hours to all base calendars. If your company decides to make December 24 a holiday, for example, you need to edit each base calendar used by resources to apply the holiday to all resources. ▨

Changing the Resource Calendar

After you add a resource to the resource pool, you can edit the resource's calendar to change its working times. There are two ways to access the resource's calendar: through the Change Working Time dialog box and through the Resource Information dialog box.

To access the resource calendar from the Resource Information dialog box, follow these steps:

1. From any resource view, select the name of the resource. Choose Project, Resource Information. (Double-clicking the resource name only works in some resource views.)

2. Choose the Working Time tab in the Resource Information dialog box. The same information which appears in the Change Working Time dialog box is displayed (see Figure 8.14).

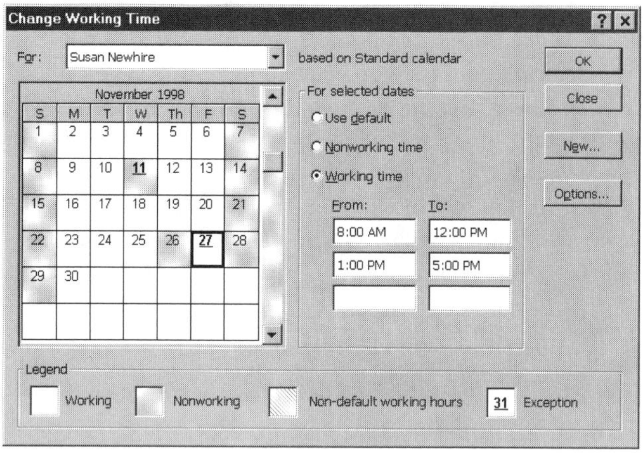

FIG. 8.14

The Working Time tab from the Resource Information dialog box.

To access the resource calendar from the Change Working Time dialog box, follow these steps:

1. Select the top pane. You cannot access the calendars from the bottom pane.

2. Choose Tools, Change Working Time. The Change Working Time dialog box appears (see Figure 8.15).

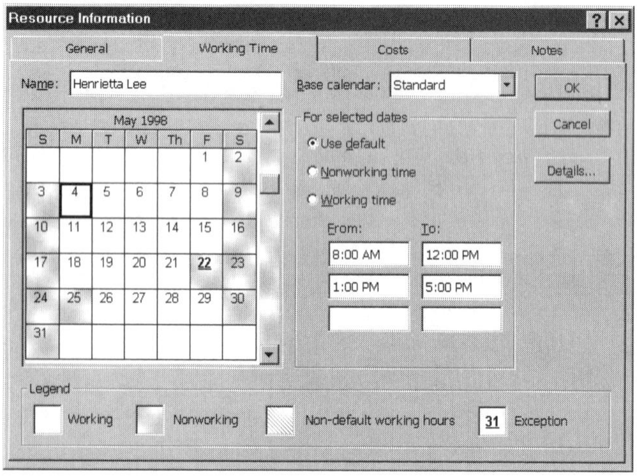

FIG. 8.15

The Change Working Time dialog box, as accessed from the Tools menu.

Regardless of which method you use to access the Working Time options, use the following steps to modify the resource calendar:

1. If you accessed the Working Time options by double-clicking the resource name, the calendar for that resource is automatically displayed in the Resource Information dialog box. If you accessed the Working Time options by displaying the Change Working Time

dialog box, you may need to select the correct resource calendar. Note in Figure 8.15, there is a For drop-down list at the top of the dialog box to select the correct calendar. If the resource you want to edit is not the currently displayed calendar, select the resource you want to edit from the For drop-down list. The name of the base calendar that is used for the resource appears to the right of the resource name you select.

2. Edit the calendar and hours, using the techniques described in Chapter 3, in the section "Defining a Calendar of Working Time," for editing the base calendar.

   Use the Working Time and Nonworking Time option buttons to mark days that differ from the base calendar. If November 26 and 27 are holidays on the base calendar, these dates are shaded as nonworking days on the resource calendar. If a worker has agreed to work on the 27th, select that day and then select the Working Time option button. This shows that the worker will work this day, regardless of what the base calendar shows. The 27th will appear underlined to indicate this is an exception to the base calendar. Similarly, select the Nonworking Time option button to mark vacation or sick days when the resource cannot work, regardless of what the base calendar shows. These resource-specific nonworking days will appear grayed out with an underline, noting the exception to the base calendar. Any exceptions to the base calendar are indicated by the date appearing with an underline.

   Select the Use Default option button when you want to undo an exception on the resource calendar. If a day is marked nonworking on the resource calendar, but you need the day to be a Working day (reverting to the base calendar's original setting), set the day with the Use Default option button. If you reset the day as a Working day, the worker is expected to work on this day, even if the base calendar date subsequently was changed to a nonworking day. The Use Default option button enables the base calendar to determine the status of the day.

   The days marked as nonworking days on the base calendar are shaded gray on the resource calendar, just as they are on the base calendar. Exceptional days, however, are additionally marked by an underline. For example, in Figure 8.15, November 11 appears shaded in gray with an underline because Susan Newhire is not available to work on the project that day; a nonworking day is indicated. Days marked as nonworking on the base calendar that are working days for the resource have no shading, but are underlined to indicate the exception to the base calendar. For example, in Figure 8.15, November 27 appears underlined because Susan Newhire is taking it as a working day to make up for her day off on November 11.

3. Choose the OK button to record the changes in the resource calendar, or choose the Close button to abandon the changes.

You can make whole months nonworking days by dragging the mouse from the first square on the calendar to the last square. This procedure selects all the month's days, and you then can choose the Nonworking Time option button. Advancing to the next month with the scroll bar leaves all days selected, allowing you to easily mark long periods of time as nonworking by selecting the Nonworking Time option button on each month in the period.

You can make the same weekday a nonworking day throughout all months and years of the calendar by selecting the weekday letter above the calendar and choosing the Nonworking Time option button. Reverse the procedure by selecting the weekday and choosing the Use Default option button.

A legend indicates how working and nonworking days will be displayed, along with days that have different hours from the default hours. Each date that is modified from the default will have the date underlined. If you modify a day of the week for the entire project, such as making the working time on every Monday from 1 p.m. to 5 p.m., the letter M in the Working Time calendar is underlined. This legend is a new feature with Project 98. Use the calendar scroll bar to change months and years. The calendar spans the period from January 1984, to December 2049.

Sorting Resources

You can sort the resource list for special purposes. For example, you might want an alphabetical listing of resources (see Figure 8.16). Or, if you apply the Cost table to the Resource Sheet, you can sort the resources by the Total Cost with the most costly resource assignments listed first (see Figure 8.17).

If you sort the list by Resource Name, Project looks at the entire field entry. It does not distinguish between multiple words in the field, like first names and last names. The sort is performed based on the first characters that appear in the field.

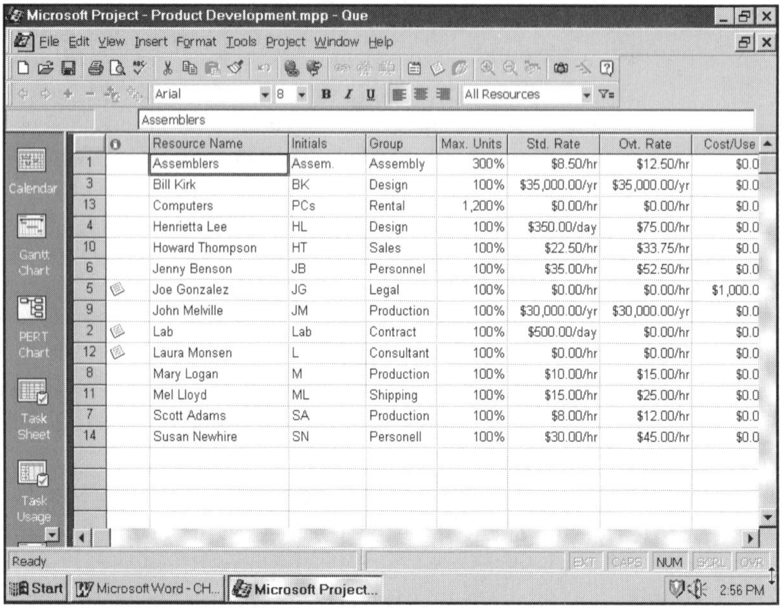

FIG. 8.16
You can sort the resource pool alphabetically for special reports.

		O	Resource Name	Initials	Group	Max. Units	Std. Rate	Ovt. Rate	Cost/Use
	1		Assemblers	Assem.	Assembly	300%	$8.50/hr	$12.50/hr	$0.0
	3		Bill Kirk	BK	Design	100%	$35,000.00/yr	$35,000.00/yr	$0.0
	13		Computers	PCs	Rental	1,200%	$0.00/hr	$0.00/hr	$0.0
	4		Henrietta Lee	HL	Design	100%	$350.00/day	$75.00/hr	$0.0
	10		Howard Thompson	HT	Sales	100%	$22.50/hr	$33.75/hr	$0.0
	6		Jenny Benson	JB	Personnel	100%	$35.00/hr	$52.50/hr	$0.0
	5		Joe Gonzalez	JG	Legal	100%	$0.00/hr	$0.00/hr	$1,000.0
	9		John Melville	JM	Production	100%	$30,000.00/yr	$30,000.00/yr	$0.0
	2		Lab	Lab	Contract	100%	$500.00/day	$0.00/hr	$0.0
	12		Laura Monsen	L	Consultant	100%	$0.00/hr	$0.00/hr	$0.0
	8		Mary Logan	M	Production	100%	$10.00/hr	$15.00/hr	$0.0
	11		Mel Lloyd	ML	Shipping	100%	$15.00/hr	$25.00/hr	$0.0
	7		Scott Adams	SA	Production	100%	$8.00/hr	$12.00/hr	$0.0
	14		Susan Newhire	SN	Personell	100%	$30.00/hr	$45.00/hr	$0.0

FIG. 8.17

Sorting the resource list by Total Cost identifies those resources that add the most cost to the project.

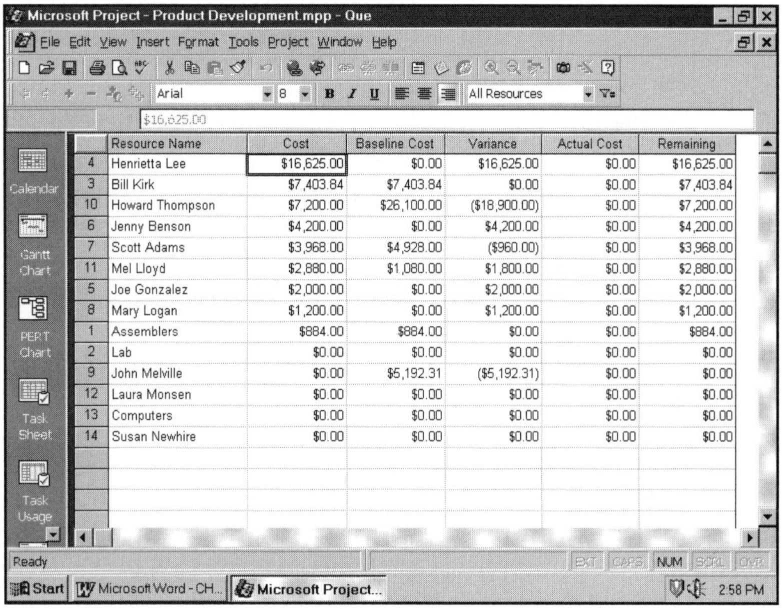

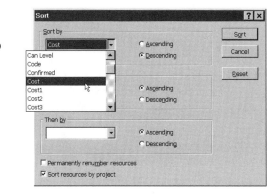

To produce a view with the resource list that shows the Cost fields sorted by cost in decreasing order, perform the following steps:

1. Display the Resource Sheet by choosing View, Resource Sheet.

2. Display the Cost table by choosing View, Table, Cost.

3. 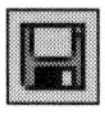 It is a good idea to save the document just before a sort operation in case you want to restore the original order of the rows. Choose File, Save or choose the Save button on the Standard toolbar.

4. Choose Project, Sort, Sort By. The Sort dialog box appears (see Figure 8.18).

FIG. 8.18

The Sort dialog box allows you to sort on up to three fields.

5. In the Sort dialog box, select Cost from the Sort By drop-down list shown in Figure 8.18. (You can type the letter **C** to quickly move to the first field name that begins with that letter, then scroll to locate the exact field.)

6. Select the Descending button to the right of the Sort By list box.

7. Make sure the Permanently Renumber Resources check box (at the bottom of the Sort dialog box) is deselected, unless you want current sort choices to permanently sort the resource list.

8. Choose the Sort button to execute the sort.

> **T I P** When you are ready to return the list to the ID order, you can either press F3 or choose All Resources from the Filter menu.

Strategically sorting your lists can greatly enhance the list's usefulness as a report. For example, after examining the list in Figure 8.17, management might look for cheaper resources on the list who could substitute for Henrietta Lee to possibly reduce the cost of the project. Since Bill Kirk is in the same group as Henrietta (see Figure 8.16), he would be a prime candidate to substitute for Henrietta to help lower the project costs. Alternatively, there may be someone from another group who is also a less expensive resource that could be substituted for Henrietta.

Filtering Resources

Microsoft Project includes several filters for selectively restricting the listing of resources or for highlighting resources that match specific filter criteria. A common use of filters for resources, for example, is the Overallocated Resources filter. This filter displays only resources scheduled to work on more than one task at the same time (the resources whose time is overallocated). Figure 8.19 shows the Resource Sheet in the top pane with the Overallocated Resources filter applied. Only Bill Kirk and Henrietta Lee are overallocated resources. The bottom pane shows the Resource Form, with the tasks assigned to the selected resource. The Filter list box on the Formatting toolbar shows that the resource list is currently filtered for Overallocated Resources.

To display this view, follow these steps:

1. Display the Resource Sheet as a full screen view. If there is already a full screen view displayed, choose View, Resource Sheet. If the current display is a split screen, hold down the Shift key as you choose View, Resource Sheet.

2. Filter the resource names by choosing Project, Filtered, Overallocated Resources. You can also choose the Filter drop-down list box from the Formatting toolbar to see the standard filters available for the resources (see Figure 8.20).

3. Choose Window, Split. Project displays the Resource Form in the bottom pane. The task details appear for the resource selected in the top pane.

FIG. 8.19
The Overallocated Resource filter allows you to focus on those resources which are overallocated.

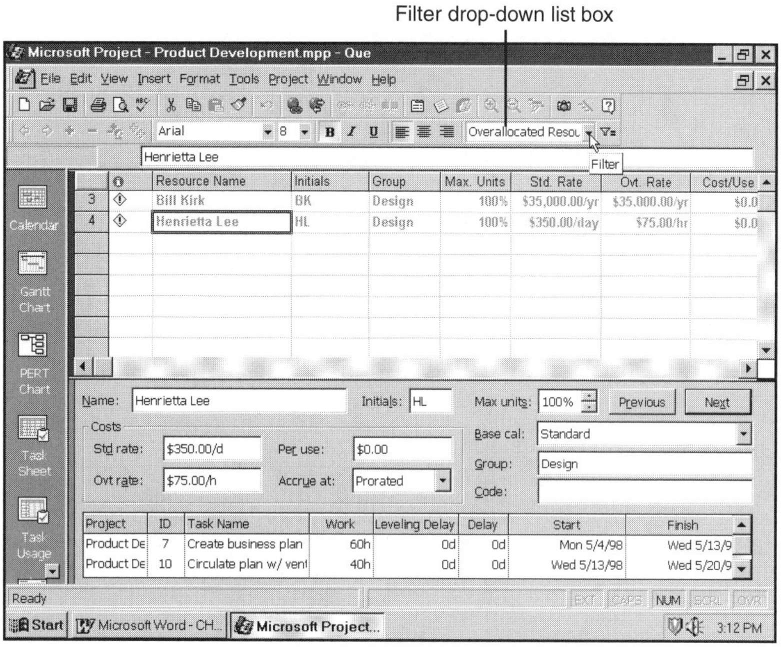

FIG. 8.20
The Filter drop-down list box on the Formatting toolbar provides a shortcut to the complete list of filters.

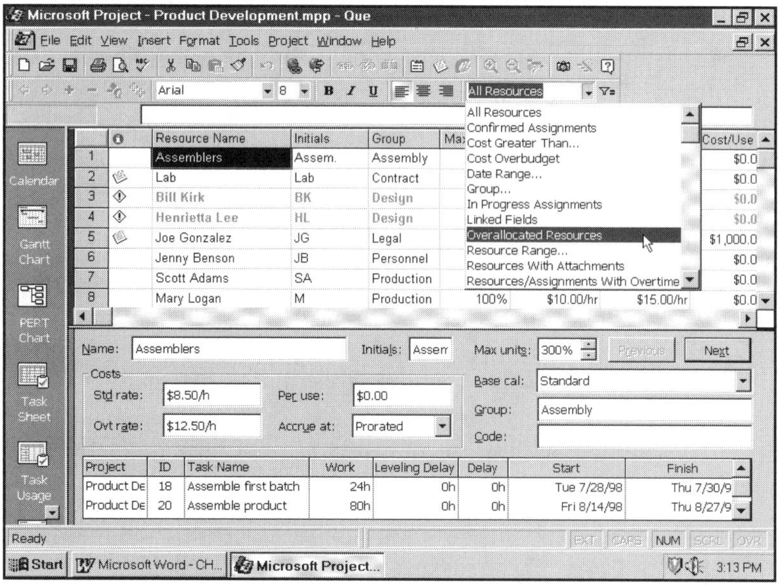

The view shown in Figure 8.20 is a good device for reviewing the tasks that contribute the most to the workload of individual overallocated resources.

Creating a Resource Template

If you plan to use the same set resources in many different projects, you'll save time by defining these resources and their associated costs in a template document, which you can use when you start a new project that uses those resources. When you open the template file, a new project is opened based on the template file data. You can now add your tasks for the new project, without having to define the project resources and costs.

If you need to include standard tasks in these projects, include a task list in the template to avoid having to type them for each new project. The list of tasks will also keep you from accidentally leaving out one of the standard tasks.

To save a project file containing resources as a template, follow these steps:

1. Enter the resource information and related costs in an empty project file.
2. Choose File, Save As.
3. Type the project file name in the File Name text box.
4. In the Save as Type list box, choose Template. When you save a project file as a template file type, Project appends the .MPT file extension.
5. Choose the correct location for saving the file in the Save In list box.
6. Click Save or press Enter to save the project file.

To create a new project file that is a copy of the template, follow these steps:

1. Choose File, Open or choose the Open button on the Standard toolbar to display the File Open dialog box.
2. Choose the location where the template is stored in the Look In list box.
3. The default selection in the Files of Type list box includes template files, so the templates will already be displayed. However, if you want to list templates only, select Templates (*.MPT) from the Files of Type list box.
4. Select the template file name from the File list box.
5. Choose Open or press Enter to open a new project file based on the template you selected.

The new file will have the same name as the template, but its file extension will automatically be changed to the .MPP extension of regular project documents. When you save the document, Project prompts you to supply a new name in the File Save dialog box. You should give the file a new name in order to distinguish it from other copies of the template.

Printing the Resource List

You can print the Resource Sheet view with the File, Print command. Printing the Resource Sheet view gives you a listing of the resources used in the project along with their associated costs.

To print a view, follow these steps:

1. Display the view either in the top pane or as full screen. You cannot print a view displayed in the bottom pane.

2. Select filters or perform the sorting you want in the printed report.

3. To preview how the report is going to look, choose File, Print Preview (or choose the Print Preview button).

4. To get an overview of the full report, click the Multiple Pages button (see Figure 8.21). Use the arrow buttons to scroll to different pages.

Click the One Page button, or any page in the multiple-page preview, to display single pages at a time. Click any part of a page in the single-page preview to enlarge that section of the page (see Figure 8.22).

FIG. 8.21

The Multiple Pages button displays all the pages in the printout so you can see the overall layout.

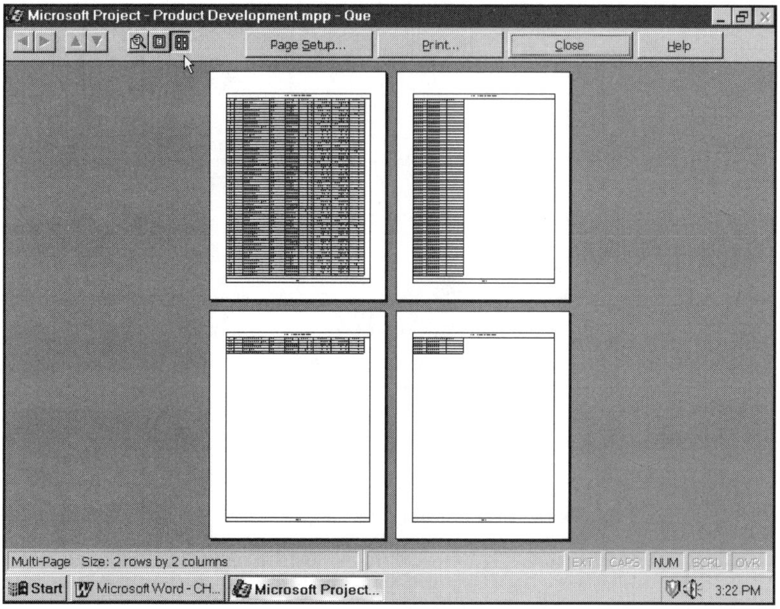

5. Choose the Page Setup button to change the page features of the report. The Page Setup dialog box appears.

▶ **See** "Changing the Page Setup," **p. 420**

6. Choose the Print button to send the report to the printer. The Print dialog box appears.

7. Choose the OK button to start printing.

▶ **See** "Using the Print Commands," **p. 414**

FIG. 8.22

You can read the details of a preview page by clicking that section.

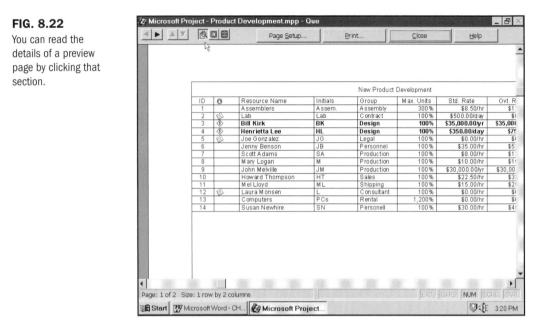

From Here...

This chapter is designed to acquaint you with resources, how to create a resource pool, and how costs are calculated in Project. With this foundation you are now ready to assign resources to tasks, modify those assignments, and resolve conflicts that arise with overallocated resources.

Check out the following list of chapters to learn more about how Project 98 works with resources:

- Chapter 9, "Understanding Resource Scheduling in Microsoft Project 98," explores an impressive new feature in Project which allows you to specify exactly when a resource performs the work on a task. Additionally, the ability to take a task and show that work will stop for a period of time, and resume later, is explored.

- Chapter 10, "Assigning Resources and Costs to Tasks," will discuss: assigning resources, full time or part time, to tasks; how work is calculated by Project; and deciding if the duration of a task should be fixed or resource driven.

- Chapter 11, "Resolving Resource Allocation Problems," introduces you to a number of methods to correct overallocations that invariabl arise in project scheduling.

Understanding Resource Scheduling in Microsoft Project 98

This chapter gives you the background and understanding you need to use resource scheduling successfully. There are numerous calculations that Microsoft Project performs in the background as you edit the data for resource assignments, and many of them are not obvious if you're not trained in project management software. It can be very frustrating to make a change that you assume will have only a small effect on one resource's schedule, and then find that Project has amplified that small change into a chain reaction that affects many other resources and costs. This chapter will help you understand how Project proceeds with its calculations and will help you understand and predict the consequences of your data entries.

You have already seen, in Chapter 8, the data fields that you use in Microsoft Project 98 to define resources and costs. This chapter shows you how some of those fields help explain the way Project schedules work when you assign a resource to a task.

How assigning resources affects the project schedule

The moment you assign resources to a task, it is possible for your schedule to change.

How changes in resource assignments affect the schedule

Task duration is tied to resource units and work in the internal workings of Project.

How to choose the task type

Learn how to use the new task types.

How to delay and split tasks or individual assignments

You can work your schedule around interruptions by delaying or splitting a task or a single assignment for the task.

Understand the new, smarter calculation of task duration

Project 98 has a new method of calculating task duration when multiple resources work different schedules.

Use resource contouring to provide flexible scheduling

Resource assignments can be scheduled to work with varying amounts of effort during the assignment.

The resource fields that will be used in this chapter are:

- The resource name
- The maximum number of resource units that are available for work on tasks in the project
- The date range when the resource is available to the project
- The working hours and nonworking hours on the resource calendar

With the topics in this chapter under your belt, you will be better able to focus on the many views, tools, and features of Project that you will see in the next chapter as you go through step-by-step instructions for actually entering the details of resource assignments. ▦

Reviewing the Essential Components of Resource Assignments

After a resource has been added to the project, you can assign the resource to work on individual project tasks. You can also assign work to resource names that have not yet been defined in the resource pool, and Project will add the new resource names to the pool for you.

As you saw in Chapter 8, you should require that Project alert you before a new name is added to the resource pool, because it is possible that you accidentally mistyped an existing resource name. If you don't have the chance to intervene, Project will create a new variation of the same resource in the pool, with a slightly different spelling. Furthermore, the workload of the correctly spelled resource will be misrepresented because it will not include the assignments that were given to its typographically challenged cousins.

▶ **See** "Setting the Automatically Add New Resources Option," **p. 267**

When a resource is assigned to work on a task, Microsoft Project will initially schedule work for the resource in specific time periods based on a number of data field values.

- Normally, Project will schedule the resource work to start at the time that the task is scheduled to start, and will schedule the work to continue uninterrupted and at a steady rate until the work assigned to the resource is completed.
- Project will only schedule work during the dates and times that are defined as working time on the resource's calendar. Therefore, Project will not schedule work for a resource during weekends, vacations, or other times which have been marked as nonworking on the resource calendar.
- If you define the assignment units as less than 100%, less than full-time activity for the resource, then Project will schedule less work each period than the resource calendar defines as available working time. For example, if you assign the resource to spend only 25% of its time on the task, then Project will schedule work equal to 25% of the available working time in any calendar period.
- Conversely, if you have defined the resource to have multiple units available for assignment (for example, a team of carpenters, a staff of nurses, a fleet of delivery trucks, or the *corps de ballet*), then you can assign multiple units of the resource to a task. Project

will schedule an amount of work that is a multiple of the available time on the resource calendar. For example, if you assign three nurses to an eight-hour shift, Project will schedule twenty-four hours of work during the period.

Microsoft Project 98 allows you to override its initial schedule calculations in order to adjust the assignments to suit specific requirements or the needs of your resources.

Part

III

Ch

9

- You can introduce a delay in the start of the work scheduled for one resource, leaving other resources to start the task as originally scheduled. The delay is measured from the start of the task (when the other resources start). For example, if a resource performs a specialized function on the task that is not needed until the task is almost finished, then the work schedule for that resource can be delayed until the end of the task.

- You can interrupt the flow of assigned work by splitting the assignment, setting periods of no work for this resource in the middle of the schedule while other resources continue to work. For example, you can pull a resource off of a long task temporarily to work on something more pressing by splitting the assignment on the long task to allow for the interruption.

- You can override the even distribution of the work that Project normally schedules by manually adjusting the amount of work assigned in each period, thus creating periods of high and low activity on the task for the resource. For example, if you know that a resource will only be needed part-time on a task during the second week on the task, but full-time otherwise, you can edit the assignment for the resource during that week to be fewer hours per day than Project assigned.

- You can instruct Project to apply one of its predefined assignment contours that vary the amount of effort scheduled during the assignment. For example, the front-loaded contour schedules the resource to put its full effort into the early periods of the assignment but to taper off to part-time involvement as the task nears completion.

Before tackling the more advanced topics of customizing a resource assignment, you must first understand the basic assignment fields.

Understanding the Resource Assignment Fields

When you assign a resource to a task, you must at least name the resource. You can optionally also specify the number of full-time resource units to dedicate to the task or the amount of work that the assignment entails. The fields in which you enter this information are described in the following list and can be seen in the Task Form illustrated in Figure 9.1.

Assigning a Resource Name

You must identify the resource by its resource ID number or by its name. When you assign resources in the Task Form, you can also identify the resource with its initials.

Assigning the Units

The Units field defines the number of full-time resource units to be assigned to the task. If you don't enter a value for Units, Project will supply the default value, 100%. The value "100%" means the equivalent of the full-time effort of one unit of the resource.

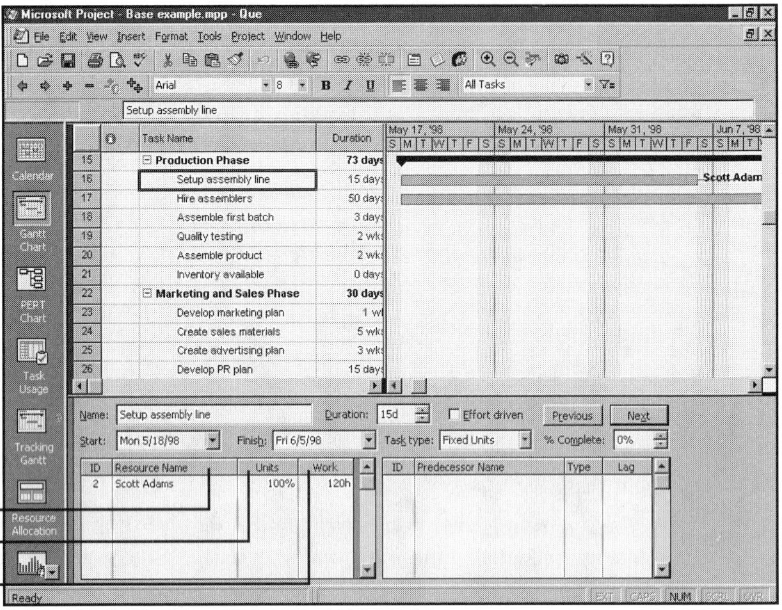

FIG. 9.1

A Task Form displays all three key assignment fields in the Resource details area.

Resource Name field
Assigned Units field
Assigned Work field

T I P The display format for Units defaults to a percentage in Microsoft Project 98. To view Units in decimals instead of percents, choose Tools, Options, select the Schedule tab, and in the Show Assignment Units As A field, select the Decimal setting.

If you are assigning one unit of the resource to work part time on the task, enter a percentage that is less than 100%. For example, if you want the resource to spend only 25% of its time on the task, enter **25%** in the Units field.

If multiple resource units are to work on the task full time, enter the Units as a multiple of 100%. For example, if you want to assign the full-time services of three forklifts to move inventory in a warehouse, enter **300%** in the Units field. If you want to assign the three forklifts half-time to the task, enter **150%** in the Units field.

You can also assign a resource to a task with 0% units. In that case, Project will not calculate a work schedule for the resource. Project will calculate the work as zero, and consequently will calculate the cost of the work as zero, also. For instance, you would assign zero units when you assign a contractor to a task and the contractor agrees to complete the task for a fixed fee. The work is the responsibility of the contractor. All you need to record is the fee, which you would enter in the Fixed Cost field.

▶ **See** "Assigning Fixed Costs and Fixed Contract Fees," **p. 337**

CAUTION

If you use the default display (Percentage) for the assignment Units field and type a units value that includes a decimal point, be sure to include a percent sign after the number, or Project will interpret your entry in Decimal format instead of percentage format. If your entry does not include a decimal point, Project will interpret it as percentage format.

For example, if you type **12.5%**, Project treats that entry as **12.5%**, and if you type **12**, Project treats that as 12%; but if you type **12.5**, Project treats it as 12.5 units and displays 1,250%. If you include a decimal, you must also include the percent sign for the entry to be treated as a percent.

N O T E You can enter fractions of a percent in the Units assignment, but they will display as rounded whole percent numbers. So if you want to specify that a worker spends one hour per eight-hour day on a task (one-eighth or 12.5% of a day), you will see 13% displayed after you enter **12.5%**. Project will actually use fractional percents in its calculations (down to tenths of a percent)—it just doesn't display them. ▣

Assigning the Work

Work, which is also called effort, measures the effort expended by the resources during the assignment. Work is always measured in hours in Microsoft Project, and it can be entered by the user or, if not, will be automatically calculated by Project.

If a resource works full-time on a task that lasts a week (forty hours), the resource will do forty hours of work. But, if the resource is only assigned half-time to the task, then it will only do twenty hours of work. If two resource units work full-time all week, there will be eighty hours of work.

Other things equal:

> The longer the duration of the task, the more work will be scheduled.

> The more resources assigned, the more work will be scheduled.

The amount of work scheduled is tied to the duration of the task and the number of units assigned to the task. The next section defines this relationship more precisely.

Understanding the Work Formula

The formula for calculating work is

$$\textbf{Duration} \quad \times \quad \textbf{Units} \quad = \quad \textbf{Work}$$

or, in symbols:

$$\textbf{D} \quad \times \quad \textbf{U} \quad = \quad \textbf{W}$$

In words, multiply the task duration by the assigned units to calculate work.

Simple algebra can be used to reformulate this equation to calculate values for Duration when Work and Units are given:

Duration = Work/Units

or, in symbols:

D = W/U

Also, when Duration and Work are given, Project can calculate Units with this variation of the formula:

Units = Work/Duration

or, in symbols:

U = W/D

Although duration can be displayed in minutes, hours, days, or weeks, Project converts duration to hours when calculating work. Thus, if a one-day task has 100% units assigned to it (one, full-time unit of the resource), the work would be calculated as:

D × U = W

8hrs × 100% = 8hrs

Applying the Work Formula in New Assignments

When you first assign a resource to a task, the duration will already be defined (that happened when you created the task).

■ If you just enter the resource name, but don't provide either the Units value or the Work value of the assignment, Project will assume the Units value is 100% and will calculate the Work from the Duration and Units.

■ If you enter the Units value, Project will use that value with the Duration to calculate the Work. For example, if you assign a resource to a four-day task (32 hours, assuming you define a day as eight hours) and enter **50%** in the Units field, Project will calculate the Work as follows:

D × U = W

32hrs × 50% = 16hrs

■ If you enter the Work value, but do not supply the Units, then Project assumes you want the default Units (100%) and will calculate a new value for the Duration based on the specified Work and the assumed value of 100% for Units. For example, if you assign a resource to a two-day task (16 hours) and enter 32 hours for the Work value but nothing for the Units, Project will calculate a new Duration using this variation of the Work formula:

$$D \quad = \quad W/U$$

$$D \quad = \quad 32h/100\% \quad = \quad 32 \text{ hours} \quad \text{(or 4 days)}$$

- Now, you may wonder why Project chose to recalculate the Duration instead of calculating a value for the Units. The reason is that Project does not calculate new values for Units except in rare circumstances (where you leave it no alternative). It will help you predict what Project will recalculate when you make changes by remembering this set of "biases" that are programmed into Microsoft Project.

N O T E Project is programmed with a bias to calculate changes in Duration before changing Work, and to calculate changes in Work before changing Units.

- If you enter both the Units and the Work, then Project will recalculate the task Duration using the values you entered. (There is one exception to this rule, which will be explained later.) For example, if you assign Units the value 200% and Work the value 32 hours, Project will calculate a new task Duration using this variation of the Work formula:

$$D \quad = \quad W/U$$

$$D \quad = \quad 32h/200\% \quad = \quad 16 \text{ hours} \quad \text{(or 2 days)}$$

If you use the Task Form to assign resources, you can prepare a list of resources to assign to the task and then execute all assignments at once. In this event, Project calculates each of the assignments independently as outlined previously and then calculates the task duration to be equal to the longest duration needed by any one of the resources to complete its work. (See the section "Understanding the Driver Resource Concept" later in this chapter.)

Applying the Work Formula to Changes in Existing Assignments

These arithmetic examples have assumed that Project is free to recalculate any of the three variables in the work formula. If you were to change one of the values in an existing assignment, Project would accept the new value you enter and would have to calculate a change in one of the other values to maintain the equation. Actually, Project is programmed with a default bias to leave changes in assigned units and work up to you (when you enter changes in those values) and to adjust duration when possible. If Project cannot change duration in a calculation (either because you have entered a new duration value or have told Project that duration is to be kept fixed), its bias dictates that it chooses to change work before it changes units.

- In general, if you were to change the entry in either the Units or the Work field for an existing assignment, Project would adjust the Duration (because it's programmed to adjust duration before adjusting either of the other two fields).

- If you were to change the entry in the Duration field, Project would choose to change Work before changing Units.

Choosing the Task Type

Suppose that you add a task to the project whose duration must remain fixed, and that you don't want Project to change it. Or, suppose that you want to edit an assignment to a task, and just for this particular change, you don't want Project to change the duration as it normally would. As you will see in this section, you can select a *task type* to instruct Project to leave any one of the three variables Duration, Work, or Units unchanged in its calculations.

By selecting a task type, you choose how you want Project to calculate changes in the task assignment schedule as it keeps the resource work formula in balance. You can assign a task type as a permanent attribute of the task, but you can also change the task type temporarily to control how Project will treat a particular change in one of the Duration, Units, or Work fields.

For example, suppose that you want to create a task with a duration you want to remain fixed, and in addition, you want to define the total work that must be done to complete the task, but need Project to tell you how many resource units are needed to do that amount of work within the fixed duration. In this example, you would need to tell Project that the task has a fixed duration and that when you enter the work required, you want Project to calculate the necessary units.

Each of the task types listed defines one of the variables, duration, work, or units, as fixed in calculations:

- *Fixed Duration*. Some tasks have a defined duration that should not be changed. Perhaps the duration is set by a client, by government, or another organization, and you must work within that time frame. If a task's duration should not be changed, then select the task type *Fixed Duration*. Then if you need to change the Work value in the equation, Project will adjust the Units value, or if you change the Units assigned, Project will adjust the Work value. Of course, *you* can change the Duration value, but Project avoids recalculating it if you define the task as the Fixed Duration type. If you change Duration yourself for a Fixed Duration task, then Project will recalculate Work.

- *Fixed Units*. For some tasks, you may feel that you want to be the sole decision maker about how many units of each resource are assigned to the task. For those tasks, you should select the task type *Fixed Units* so Project will know that if the Work value is changed, it should recalculate Duration, not Units, and if Duration is changed, it must adjust Work. Of course, *you* can change the Units value, but want to reserve that prerogative. Fixed Units is the default task type in Project. If you change the Units yourself, Project will recalculate Duration.

- *Fixed Work*. For some tasks, you may want to stipulate that the total Work is fixed. As an example, you might contract to provide a fixed amount of work for a client. If the amount of Work is not to change should Duration or Units change, then define the task as a Fixed Work task, and Project will not adjust Work to keep the equation in balance. If you change assigned Work for a Fixed Work task, Project will recalculate Duration.

You can define a task's type in the Task Information dialog box, in the Task Entry or Task Details views, or by adding a column for the field Type to any task table. Figure 9.2 shows the

Task Type field on the Task Information dialog box. Figure 9.3 shows the field on the Task Entry view.

FIG. 9.2

The Task Type can be set in the Advanced folder tab in the Task Information dialog box.

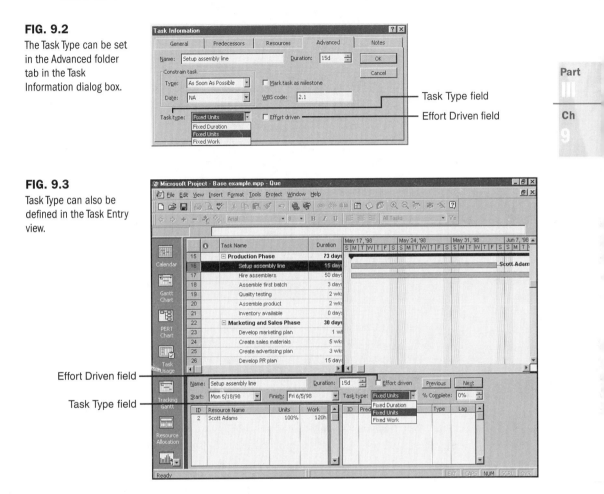

FIG. 9.3

Task Type can also be defined in the Task Entry view.

The default task type for Project is *Fixed Units*, which means that Project normally leaves it up to you to change the units assigned and will recalculate Duration if you change Work, or will recalculate Work if you change Duration. You can change the default task type for a project with the Tools, Options menu. In the Options dialog box, select the Schedule tab and select the type you want as the default in the Default Task Type field. (See Figure 9.4.)

When Project processes your resource assignments, it must maintain the Work equation (Work = Duration × Units), but the task type governs how Project chooses to keep the equation in balance. Project will respond in the following ways when you create a new assignment for a task:

FIG. 9.4
You can change the default task type in the Options dialog box.

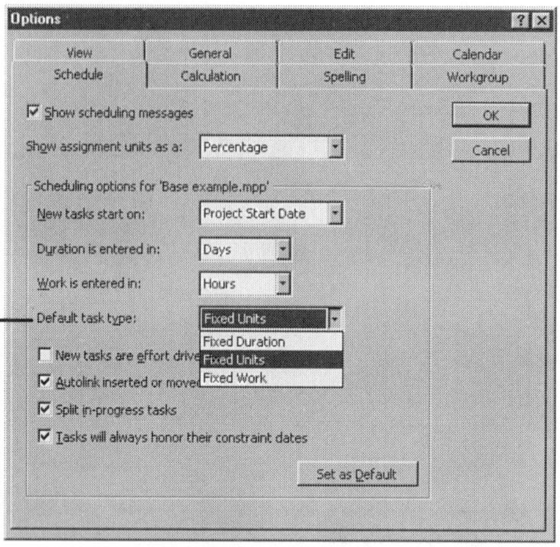

Default task type ———

- If you entered a value in Units, and left the Work field blank, Project will calculate the unknown Work (because both Units and Duration have been given values). This will be true no matter what the task type is.

- If you entered a value in Work and left the Units blank, Project's calculation will depend on the task type, because Project is programmed to leave changes in Units up to the user if at all possible.

  - As long as the task is not a fixed duration task (if it's fixed units or fixed work), then Project will adjust the Duration. It assumes that the Units will be the default (100%) and calculates the Duration that is necessary for the resource to complete the amount of work you assigned.

  - However, if the task is a fixed duration task, then Project cannot change the Duration entry and will calculate the Units needed to complete the Work you entered and place that value in the Units field.

- If you entered values in both Units and Work, Project again bases its calculations on the task type.

  - As long as the task is not a fixed duration task (for example, it's of the type fixed work or fixed units), Project adjusts the Duration to accommodate the Work and Units you entered.

  - If the task is a fixed duration task, Project keeps the Work amount you entered and calculates a new Units value that can do the specified work in the given (fixed) Duration.

N O T E The previous example is an exception to the rule that Project avoids calculating Units if it can choose to recalculate Work. When the task type is fixed duration and you change both the work and units for an assignment, Project keeps your work entry and recalculates the units within the fixed duration.

Understanding Effort Driven Tasks

Closely related to task type, is the choice you have as to whether a task is *Effort Driven* or not. This choice only affects scheduling when you change the list of named resources already assigned to a task (in other words, when you change the number of resource names assigned to the task). The Effort Driven status has no effect on the calculations when you first assign resources to a task, even if you use the Task Form and create a list of resource names before clicking the OK button to process the assignments.

If a task is Effort Driven, that means the total work (effort) on the task is to remain the same after a change in the number of resource names assigned. Consequently, if you add a resource to an Effort Driven task, the workload remains the same but there are more resources to share the fixed work. Each resource will be assigned less work, though the total work remains the same, and the task Duration will be reduced.

If a task is not Effort Driven, that means the workload on the task will change when the number of named resources changes. If you add a resource to this task, Project will leave all previously assigned resources doing the same amount of work as before, will leave Duration unchanged, and will add the work of the new resource to the total work for the task.

You can change the Effort Driven status for a task on the Task Information dialog box (refer to Figure 9.2) or on the Task Form (refer to Figure 9.3).

The default status for new tasks in Project is Effort Driven, but you can change the default in the Options dialog box, right next to where you change the default Task Type (see Figure 9.5). Choose Tools, Options from the menu and select the Schedule tab on the Options dialog box. Deselect the New Tasks Are Effort Driven check box to change the default setting.

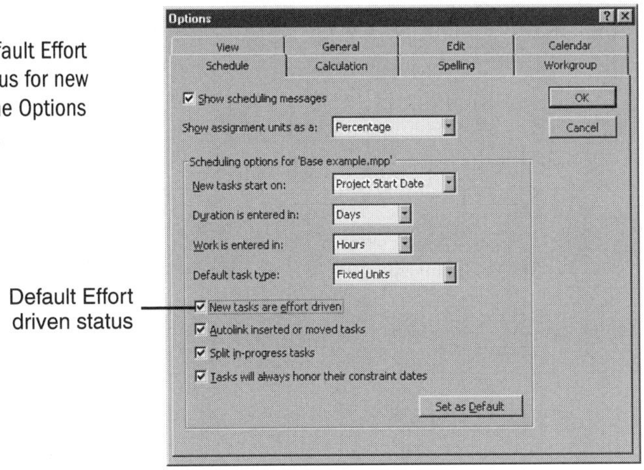

Part

III

Ch

9

FIG. 9.5
Set the default Effort Driven status for new tasks on the Options dialog box.

Default Effort driven status

If your original resource assignment to a task includes multiple resources, Project performs these same calculations for each of the resources independently. It doesn't matter if the tasks are Effort Driven or not. Subsequent changes to the list of resources assigned to the task, however, are subject to the Effort Driven status of the task.

If, after the initial assignment of resources to a task, you add more resources or remove some of the resources, then Project must consider the Effort Driven status of the task in its calculations. If Effort Driven is on, as it is by default, Project redistributes the total work for the task across the revised resource list, weighting the work for each resource by its fraction of the total number of units assigned.

For example, suppose that Mary and Scott are assigned to an Effort Driven task as in the following table:

Resource	Units	Work	% Total Units
Mary	50%	20 hours	33%
Scott	100%	40 hours	67%
Total	150%	60 hours	100%

Then Pat is assigned to the task at 50% units. The total work is assumed by Project to remain unchanged (since this is an Effort Driven task) and total units assigned has increased from 150% to 200%. The following table is designed to help you see how Project calculates the new work assignments.

Resource	Units	Work	% Total Units
Mary	50%	15 hours	25%
Scott	100%	30 hours	50%
Pat	50%	15 hours	25%
Total	200%	60 hours	100%

Because Scott contributes 50% of the units after Pat is assigned to the task, Scott will be assigned 50% of the work, or 30 hours. Mary and Pat are each assigned 25% of the total work, or 15 hours each.

If Effort Driven is off, Project assumes that the work of a newly assigned resource is to be added to the existing work of all other named resources. The assignments of the existing resources are not changed. Similarly, if you remove a named resource from the task, Project reduces the total work for the task by that resource's work assignment and does not recalculate other resource assignments.

You can change the Effort Driven field for a task temporarily if you need to. For example, suppose that you created a task for 20 hours of work moving stock in a warehouse and assigned warehouse workers to the task but forgot to assign the forklifts they would be using. If the task is Effort Driven and you add forklifts to the list of resources, Project will reduce the current duration of the task and reassign work from the warehouse workers to the forklifts. However, you simply want to add the forklifts without changing the duration because you entered the 20 hours of work, originally assuming the workers would have the forklifts to work with. Before adding the forklifts, turn off the Effort Driven field. Then add the forklifts with Effort Driven off. Then you can turn Effort Driven back on for future calculations.

Understanding Duration with Multiple Resources Assigned

Part

III

Ch

9

When there are multiple resources assigned to a task, they may not all have the same work schedule. Some resources may not be available during all of the task duration. Individual schedules for some resources can be modified to delay an assignment or to split the assignment with a period of inactivity.

Duration, in the simplest cases, is just the number of work days between the start and finish of a task. But this definition assumes that work goes on continuously during that time. Duration is now defined by Microsoft Project as the number of time periods during which any resource is working on a task.

For example, suppose Bill Kirk and Mary Logan each have 20 days of work to do on a task, the task Duration will be 20 days if they do their work during the same time periods. But suppose that Bill is on vacation for 5 days when Mary starts working on the task and works 5 days longer than she does to finish his portion of the assignment. Bill's start and finish dates will not match Mary's. The earlier start of the two, and the later finish of the two, become the Start and Finish dates for the entire task. However, the Duration will be the number of time periods during which any one of them worked on the task. The duration of the task in this example will be 25 days—5 days when Mary worked alone while Scott was on vacation, 15 days when they were both working on the task, and 5 days when Scott worked alone after Mary finished

Understanding the Driver Resource Concept

The *driver resource* refers to the fact that in some cases one or more resources are fully occupied with work throughout a task's duration (the driver resources) and other resources have less work to do during the same period (non-driver resources).

For example, if you create a task with a duration of one day and then assign Mary, Pat, and Scott to the task with the work amounts given in the following table, Project will calculate the task duration to accommodate the longest time needed by any one of the resources. In this case, both Mary and Pat need 5 days to complete their assignments, so the task duration will be changed by Project to 5 days. Scott will work only the first 2 days on the task.

Resource	Work	Units	Duration	Driver Resource
Mary	40 hours	100%	5 days	Yes
Scott	16 hours	100%	2 days	No
Pat	20 hours	50%	5 days	Yes

In a case like this example, Mary and Pat are said to be *driver resources* because their assignments drive the task duration. If you change the assigned work or units for Mary and Pat, it will likely have an effect on the duration of the task. However, you could make changes in Scott's assignment, within limits, without affecting the duration of the task.

- You could increase the work assigned to Scott from 16 hours up to 40 hours without needing to increase the task's duration.

- You could also change Scott's Units from 100% down to as low as 40% before it would impact his ability to complete his assignment in the current duration.

- Similarly, you could reduce the task duration from 5 days down to 2 days without affecting Scott's ability to do the work currently assigned to him (16 hours at 100% effort).

If you change either the assigned units or the assigned work for a resource that is not a *driver resource* (a resource like Scott that doesn't need the entire task duration to complete its assigned work), and the duration required by that resource after the change is still less than the task duration, then Project will not need to change the task duration.

If there are multiple resources assigned to a task when you change the Duration field entry, only the *driver resources* (those that must work for the full task duration to complete their work) will be affected. However, if you shorten the task duration so much that non-driver resources cannot complete their work, then they would be affected, also.

To summarize these points:

- When you change the duration for a task, only the assignments for driver resources (those who need the full duration to complete their assignments) will be affected. Project will apply the work formula to calculate changes in the assignments. Non-driver resources will not be affected as long as the change in duration still leaves them the time they need to complete their assignments.

- When you change the assigned units or work for driver resources, task duration will be affected, and Project will recalculate the assignment values for all driver resources, but not those for non-driver resources.

- When you change the assigned units or work for a non-driver resource without making it a driver resource, Project does not recalculate the assignment for that resource or for any other resources assigned to that task..

Modifying Resource Assignments

We have seen that you can define a resource assignment by specifying the task duration, assignment units, and assigned work for the assignment. We have seen that your choice of the task type or Effort Driven status of the task also impacts resource assignments. In this section, we will examine other options you have for fine-tuning resource assignments. Your choices include:

- Assigning overtime work on a task

- Applying one of the predefined work contours to an assignment.

- Manually adjusting a resource contour on a task

- Splitting a resource's schedule on a task to accommodate time when she is needed elsewhere
- Splitting an entire task and rescheduling the remaining work
- Adding delay to a resource's arrival on a task

Contouring Resource Usage

P98

The only resource work pattern allowed in earlier versions of Microsoft Project was the so-called *Flat pattern*. The Flat pattern schedules all of a resource's work to begin and end as early as possible on a task. There is no allowance for an initial buildup of effort, or tapering of effort at the end of a task, or any other variation in the amount of effort allocated by the resource at different time periods. Varied scheduling patterns are now available in Microsoft Project 98. The default resource schedule in Microsoft Project is still the Flat pattern, but you can have Project change an assignment by applying one of its predefined *work contours*.

To change the scheduling pattern, use the Task Usage view (see Figure 9.6) or the Resource Usage view (see Figure 9.7). These views display tasks and resource assignment information. Double-click an assigned resource name in the Task Usage view, or the task name in the Resource Usage view, to bring up the Assignment Information dialog box (see Figure 9.8).

Part
II

Ch
9

FIG. 9.6
Task Usage View

Task ——
Contour indicator ——
Resource assignment ——
Assignment details ——

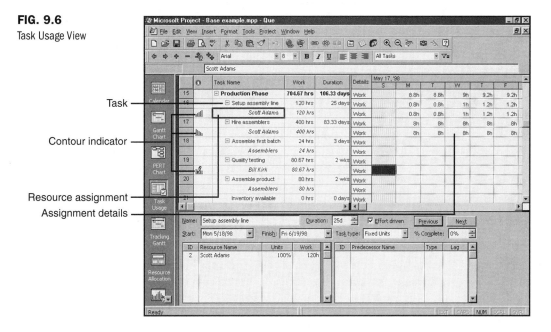

TIP Shift+F2 is a quick access to Information dialog boxes. Depending on what is selected when the keys are pressed, it will bring up the Task Information, the Resource Information, or the Assignment Information dialog box.

FIG. 9.7
Resource Usage view

Resource ———

Task assignment ———

Assignment details ———

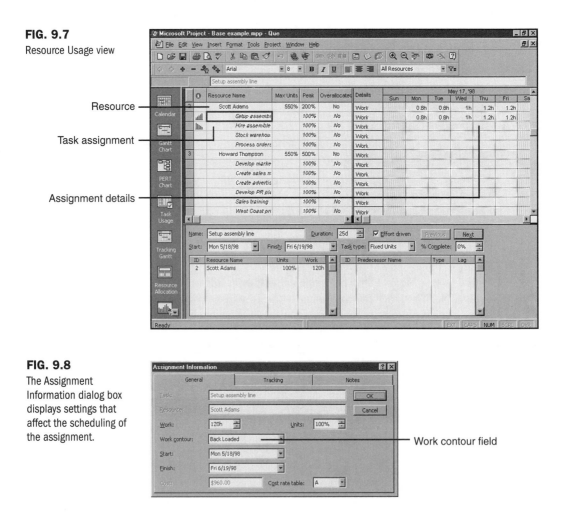

FIG. 9.8
The Assignment
Information dialog box
displays settings that
affect the scheduling of
the assignment.

Work contour field

If the pattern has been changed from a Flat assignment, an icon will appear in the Indicator column for that resource on the Task Usage view (refer to Figure 9.6), or for that task on the Resource Usage view (refer to Figure 9.7). In either of those views, you may also manually change the assigned hours over the course of a task, regardless of the underlying scheduling pattern you used. In other words, any resource assignment pattern can be manually adjusted. If you make manual changes, the icon in the Indicator column shows a pencil imposed on the Scheduling Pattern icon (refer Figure 9.6).

Microsoft Project 98 provides seven predefined work contour patterns that you can apply to a resource assignment. These are in addition to the default assignment pattern, called *flat*, that is used when Project initially calculates an assignment. The contour patterns are listed as follows and illustrated in Figure 9.9.

Part

III

Ch

9

- *Flat.* This is the pattern used in the initial assignment calculation by Project—all work is assigned as soon as the task starts and continues until the assignment is completed. There is no icon for this pattern.

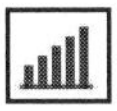

- *Back Loaded.* Heaviest daily load is at the *end* of the task.

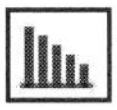

- *Front Loaded.* Heaviest daily load is at the *beginning* of the task.

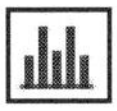

- *Double Peak.* Resource's efforts come and go throughout the task.

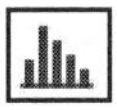

- *Early Peak.* Heaviest daily load is *near* the beginning of the task.

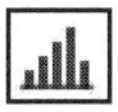

- *Late Peak.* Heaviest daily load is *near* the end of the task.

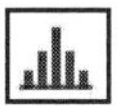

- *Bell.* Heaviest daily load is in the middle of the task.

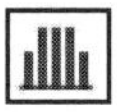

- *Turtle.* Similar to early peak, with a slightly heavier load at the beginning of the task.

FIG. 9.9
Work contours redistribute assigned work over a longer duration.

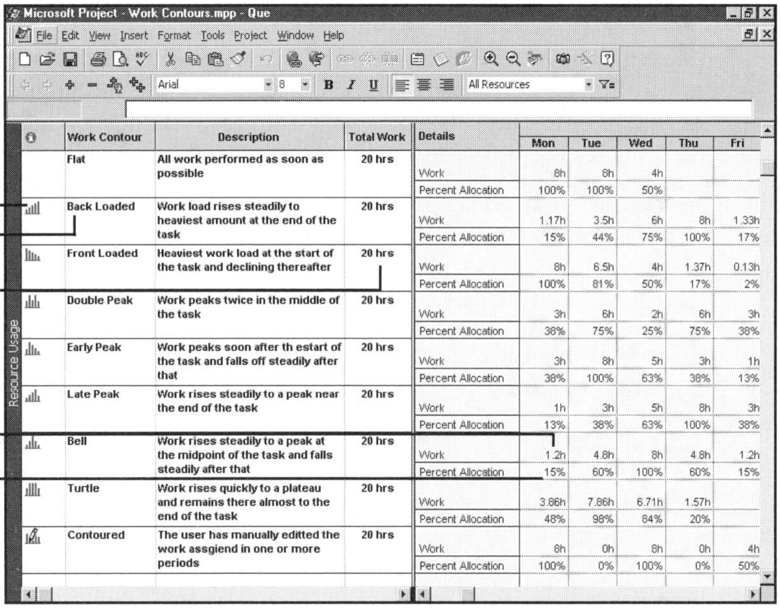

Contour indicators
Contour types

Total work

Work assigned per day
Unit assignment per day

Figure 9.9 illustrates the contour types in an actual calculation by Microsoft Project. The first row, labeled Flat, shows how an initial assignment of 20 hours of work was scheduled for a resource that has a unit assignment of 100% to the task (for example, the resource will devote 100% of its time to the task).

In the timescale on the right, you can see the Work and Percent Allocation for each day. The resource is assigned 100% to the task, and for the first two days, 100% of its time is allocated to the task, with 8 hours of work each day. On Wednesday, the assignment is completed after 4 hours of work. The Percent Allocation row shows only 50% of the resource's time being allocated to this task for that day.

Each of the other rows show how Project would schedule the work if one of the other contours were applied. The Total Work remains 20 hours in all cases, as seen in the Total Work column. The Work assignment for each day varies depending on the contour pattern, as does the Percent Allocation.

Each of the contours reduces the unit assignment during selected days in the assignment; the choice of which days determines the pattern that is the source of the different contour names. Because less work is scheduled in some days, the total assignment will necessarily take longer to complete. Note that the duration of the task is extended when the contours are applied. Instead of completing the task on Wednesday, work must continue until Friday.

The last row in Figure 9.9 is labeled Contoured and represents a case where the user has manually created a unique "contour," in this case by scheduling the work for Monday, Wednesday, and Friday only (scheduling no work on Tuesday and Thursday).

Using Overtime to Shorten a Task

You can reduce the duration for a task by allowing some of a resource's work to be scheduled as overtime work. The total work to be done on the assignment remains the same, but the amount of work scheduled during regular working time hours is reduced. Also, the overtime rate for the resource will be charged for the overtime work.

For example, suppose that Bill Kirk has been assigned full-time (100% units) to write a report that is scheduled to take 60 hours of work to complete, for a duration of 7.5 days to complete the report. This example is illustrated as the task "Report" (task number 1) in the Task Usage view at the top of Figure 9.10. Bill is scheduled to start on a Monday and finish at midday on Wednesday, one week later. The Cost of the task is $1,200 (based on Bill's standard rate of $20/hour). The assignment details on the right show the daily work and cost extending for seven days and part of the eighth day, Wednesday of the second week.

But Bill's manager now must have the report in no more than five days, so he authorizes 20 hours of overtime work for Bill on this task. Bill will still spend 60 hours on the report, but 20 hours will be overtime hours and only 40 hours will be scheduled in the regular working time made available by his resource calendar. This change is represented by task 2 in Figure 9.10, Report (w/Overtime). (Normally, you would modify the original task to add overtime, but using two tasks in the illustration allows you to compare the two versions of the task.) The task duration with overtime is only 5 days, and there is no work scheduled after the first week; however, the Cost of the task has risen from $1,200 to $1,400. This is because Bill is paid $10 more for overtime hours ($30/hour), and 20 hours of overtime add $200 to the total cost.

FIG. 9.10

Scheduling overtime work shortens task duration but may lead to increased cost.

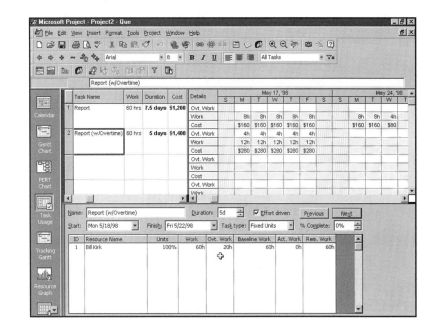

The assignment details on the right show 4 hours of overtime work for each of the five days in the task schedule. The Work details show 12 hours per day (regular hours plus the overtime hours). The Cost details show $280 per day, which is regular cost of $160 (8 hours a day at the regular rate, $20/hour), plus overtime cost of $120 (4 hours a day at the overtime rate, $30/hour).

Overtime work can be entered on a Task or Resource Form that has been formatted to show resource work. Figure 9.10 shows the Task Form in the lower pane with Resource Work details displayed. The Overtime Work field contains 20h, and the Work field (which is total work) shows 60h.

If you have applied a work contour pattern, Microsoft Project automatically allocates the overtime work in the same contour pattern. So a front-loaded resource will also have his or her overtime work scheduled more heavily at the beginning of the task. Previous versions of Microsoft Project scheduled all overtime work at the end of a task, which distorted the true day-by-day work pattern for the resource.

N O T E Overtime work that is scheduled by Microsoft Project cannot be adjusted manually. However, when you are tracking progress on the task, you can enter the amount of actual overtime work in each time period to show exactly how the work was performed. ■

Splitting a Task Assignment

Task splitting has been enhanced in this version of Microsoft Project. Work assignments on split tasks now truly reflect the time during which the work is interrupted, when the work is scheduled to resume, and how the remaining work has been rescheduled. There are two basic methods for splitting a work assignment:

- You can split the task, and Project will automatically split each resource assignment for the task, with zero work scheduled during the period of the split.

- You can split an individual resource assignment by inserting one or more periods of zero work in the middle of the assignment.

If you introduce a split in an individual resource assignment, Project does not show a split in the task unless it is the only resource assignment for the task or unless you introduce the same split in all assigned resources.

Figure 9.11 shows three tasks to which Bill Kirk is assigned. The view has a Gantt Chart in the top pane and the Task Usage view in the bottom pane. The work detail in the bottom pane for his assignment to the Plan Conference task shows a split highlighted in the assignment—three days with zero work scheduled. The task bar in the top pane shows that the task is split, also. The split was created by inserting three days of no work in his schedule, and the task split was a consequence of the assignment split.

FIG. 9.11

Introduce a split in a task assignment when the resource needs to work on another task temporarily.

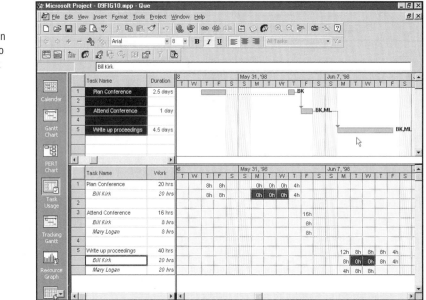

Bill Kirk also has a two-day split in his assignment to the Write Up Proceedings task. But the task bar in the top pane of Figure 9.11 is not split because Mary Logan, who is also assigned to the task, continues to work on those days while Bill is diverted to another task.

Scheduling a Late Start for an Assignment

Sometimes, one of the resources assigned to a task is expected to perform a function that is not needed at the beginning of the task, but only after some work on the task has been completed. For example, a group charged with proposing a new product might need to run their preliminary ideas for a proposal by technical experts for feedback on the feasibility of the ideas. If an expert is too expensive to engage in the preliminary debates, the expert's assignment to the task can be delayed to start only after the task has been underway for an appropriate amount of time.

You would also need to delay an assignment if one of the resources assigned to a task is needed more urgently elsewhere in the project at the time that the task is scheduled to start.

You can delay the start of an assignment by entering a value in any one of several places in Microsoft Project:

■ The assignment Delay field is displayed in the Resource Schedule details of both the Task Form and the Resource Form. In Figure 9.12, the Task Form is displayed in the bottom pane. Mary Logan's assignment has **1d** entered in the Delay field. As a consequence, although the Start date for the task is Monday, 6/8/98, the Start date for her assignment is Tuesday, 6/9/98.

If you enter a value in the Delay field, Project automatically calculates the delayed dates for the Start and Finish date fields.

N O T E The default entry in the Delay field is 0d which means no delay. The Delay field is never blank. You can remove a delay by entering zero in the Delay field; you cannot erase an entry and try to leave the field blank. ■

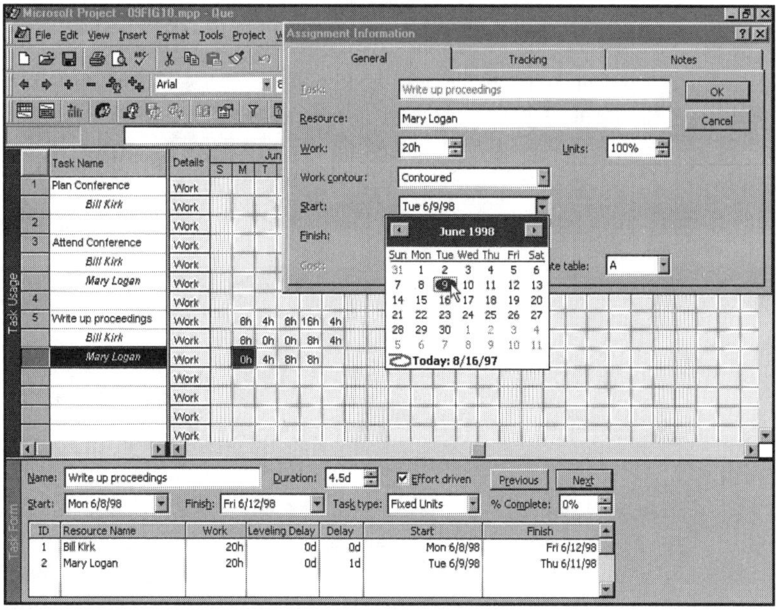

FIG. 9.12
Create a delay in an assignment to recognize the fact that the resource is not necessary at the start of the task.

▓ You could also enter a delayed start date in the Start field to the right of the Delay field. Project would automatically calculate the value for the Delay field.

N O T E   If you enter a date in the Finish field to the right of the Delay field, Project does not calculate a delay—instead it recalculates the amount of work that will be completed between the (unchanged) Start of the assignment and the new Finish you entered. ▓

▓ You can enter a delayed start date in the Assignment Information dialog box. The Assignment Information dialog box in Figure 9.12 was displayed by double-clicking the assignment row at the bottom of the Task Form. The Start field is on the General tab. Click the calendar control to the right of the field and select a start date.

The Delay field does not appear on the Assignment Information dialog box, but its value is recalculated if you enter a new date in the Start field.

▓ You can also create a delay for an assignment by editing the work details in the timescale of the Task Usage view or the Resource Usage view. Figure 9.12 shows the Task Usage view in the top pane, with Mary Logan's assignment selected. The timescale shows 0h highlighted on the Monday for her assignment. The delay could have been created by inserting this day of zero work in the timescale. Project would then have automatically calculated the value displayed in the Delay, Start, and Finish fields in the Task Form in the bottom pane and in the Assignment Information dialog box.

This discussion about delaying assignments has been presented in terms of projects which are scheduled from a fixed start date. In those projects, Microsoft Project schedules tasks and assignments as soon as possible, calculates the start date for both tasks and assignments first, and then calculates their finish dates. A delay in an assignment is tantamount to a late start, and it offsets that assignment schedule from other resource assignment schedules on the same task.

If your project is scheduled from a fixed finish date, Microsoft Project first schedules the last tasks in each chain of linked tasks to end on the fixed finish date. Task and assignment finish dates are calculated first and then their start dates are calculated. Project then works backward along the chain of linked tasks, scheduling later tasks before earlier tasks until the start of the project is reached and a project start date is calculated.

You cannot introduce delays (late starts) for assignments in fixed finish date projects, because that would delay the project finish date—which is fixed by definition. You can, however, modify assignments to show that some resource assignments are offset from others by introducing an early finish for an assignment.

An early finish for an assignment in a fixed finish date project is entered in the same Delay field we used previously, but it is entered as a negative number. Alternatively, you can enter an early finish date in the assignment's Finish field, and Project will calculate the (negative) Delay value for you and a new date for the Start field.

As a corollary to the note, if you were to enter a different date in the assignment Start field, Project would not adjust the Delay value but would calculate a new amount of work for the assignment based on the (unchanged) finish date and the start date you entered.

N O T E You can enter negative amounts in the assignment Delay field only if the project is scheduled from a fixed finish date. You can enter positive amounts only if the project is scheduled from a fixed start date.

From Here...

The new Microsoft Project scheduling engine adds resource contouring options and new task types. Enhanced views and dialog boxes are available to access these options. The following chapters will provide more information for working with these new features.

- Chapter 10, "Assigning Resources and Costs to Tasks," will show you the mechanics of assigning resources and costs to tasks.

- Chapter 11, "Resolving Resource Allocation Problems," will give you the techniques you need to adjust resource assignments to avoid overallocations.

Assigning Resources and Costs to Tasks

You will usually assign resources to tasks because you want Microsoft Project to help you schedule and monitor the work the resource will do on the task. You can also use resource assignments to associate a cost with the task, like the contract fee of a vendor who will deliver the completed task without requiring you to schedule and monitor the work. Finally, you can use a resource assignment to associate a name with the task just for reporting purposes. This chapter will show you how to use Microsoft Project's views and tools to assign resources and to modify resource assignments. To benefit the most from this chapter, you should understand the contents of Chapter 8, "Defining Resources and Costs," and Chapter 9, " Understanding Resource Scheduling in Microsoft Project 98." There are intricate relationships among task and resource fields that are covered in those chapters.

Choose the right task type

You can control how Project responds to changes in resource assignments by defining the task type.

Enter resource assignments

Use different views, tools, and dialog boxes to record the pertinent facts about a resource assignment.

Select a Cost Rate table

You can choose one of five different cost rates for each task assignment.

Fine-tune assignments with delays, interruptions, and custom work patterns

You can now record exactly when the resource will do the work on an assignment.

Schedule overtime

Use overtime to get more done in a shorter time period.

Understand how changes in the assignments will affect the schedule

Project responds in varying, but predictable ways, to different changes in the resource assignments.

Print reports to show assigned tasks and resources

Reports can outline who is working on what task when.

When first assigning resources to tasks, there are a number of data fields you can use to give Microsoft Project the information it needs to calculate schedules and costs as you intend:

- You can choose the task type to control how Project will calculate changes in the schedule when you change assignments to the task.

- You *must* provide the resource name when you assign it to a task.

- You can define the units assigned or let Project assign the default number of units.

- You can define the amount of work the resource will perform or let Project calculate that from the task duration and number of units.

- You can let Project use the default cost rates for the resource or select a special Cost Rate table you have defined if the task is to be charged different rates than normally charged for this resource.

- To speed up progress on the task, you can assign the resource overtime work, or modify the resource calendar to provide additional available hours on specific days.

- You can accept the default work pattern for the assignment, which is an even amount of work each day until the task is complete, or you can modify the work *contour* to schedule more work at different times in the assignment. You can also delay the start of the assignment beyond the start of the task and split the assignment to work around interruptions in the resource availability.

As you can see, Project provides you the opportunity to fine-tune resource assignments so that schedule and cost calculations can be very precise. You can also get by with just the minimum amount of definition if you don't need all that sophistication.

This chapter will show you how to enter all the information listed previously. You will also see how to use the quick tools that record the minimum amount of information needed to get the job done. There are a number of different views and tools you can use to assign resources, and you will see how to use all of them. Each offers its own advantages. ■

Selecting the Appropriate Task Type

Unless you assign resources to tasks, you do not have to be concerned with selecting the task type. The task types were defined and explained in detail in Chapter 9. Only a summary of the distinctions among the task types will be given here. Similarly, the data fields that define a resource were covered in detail in Chapter 8 and will not be explained again in detail here.

▶ **See** "Choosing the Task Type," **p. 291**

▶ **See** "Understanding the Resource Assignment Fields," **p. 285**

By selecting a task type, you choose how you want Project to calculate changes in the task schedule when any one of the three variables in the resource Work formula is changed. The Work formula, you will recall, is

Work = Duration * Units

or

$$W = D \times U$$

where

- Work is the amount of work the resource will do
- Duration is the task duration
- Units is the number of units of the assigned resource

When one of these values is changed, either one or both of the other values *must* change to keep the equation valid. Project automatically recalculates the values in the equation any time one of the values changes.

In choosing a task type, you let Project know which value it should *not* change—which value it should leave *fixed*. You must choose one of the three task types:

- Choose *Fixed Units*, which is the default for Project, if you want Project to avoid recalculating Units when either Work or Duration change. Project will then recalculate Work if Duration changes and will recalculate Duration if Work changes. If you change the Units yourself, Project will recalculate Duration, not Work.

- Choose *Fixed Duration* if you want Project to leave this task's Duration unchanged if either Work or Units is changed for a resource. Work and Units will be linked, then, in that changing one will change the other for this task. If you change Duration yourself for a Fixed Duration task, then Project will recalculate Work.

- Choose *Fixed Work* if you want Project to leave assigned Work unchanged when either Duration or Units change. Changing Duration will lead to a change in Units and vice versa. If you change assigned Work for a Fixed Work task, Project will recalculate Duration.

The default type for new tasks in Microsoft Project is *Fixed Units*, which means that Project normally lets you change the units assigned and will recalculate Duration if you change Work and will recalculate Work if you change Duration.

NOTE This is also the default in earlier versions of Microsoft Project. However, in earlier versions you can only choose to make a task Fixed or to leave it Not Fixed. Fixed is the same as Fixed Duration in Project 98, and Not Fixed is the same as Fixed Units in Project 98. There is no Fixed Work type in earlier versions.

You can make any one of the three task types the default for new tasks by following these steps:

- Choose Tools, Options to display the Options dialog box.
- Select the Schedule tab.
- In the Default Task Type field, use the drop-down list to select the type you want to be the default.

Part
III

Ch
10

To verify or change the Task Type setting, follow these steps:

1. Select the task.
2. Click the Task Information tool to display the Task Information dialog box.
3. Select the Advanced tab.
4. Set the Task Type by choosing the list arrow and selecting Fixed Duration, Fixed Units, or Fixed Work (see Figure 10.1).
5. Choose OK.

FIG. 10.1

Use the Task Information dialog box to access additional fields of information about each task.

You can also select the task type on the Task Form, which is the view displayed in the bottom pane when you split a full-screen task view. To change the task type settings using the Task Form, follow these steps:

1. If not already displayed, choose a task view like the Gantt Chart, the Task Sheet, or the Task Usage view.
2. Split the view by choosing Window, Split. The bottom pane will display the Task Form view (see Figure 10.2).
3. Activate the bottom pane. If resource details are not visible, choose Format, Details and select one of the options that includes resources, like Resources & Predecessors.
4. Use the Task Type list box to choose a new task type.

Closely allied to the choice of a task type is the choice of whether or not a task is *Effort Driven* or not. The default for new tasks in Microsoft Project is Effort Driven, but you can choose to cancel that setting. This choice only has importance when you change the number of resource names assigned to a task. It does not have any effect if you change the number of units where there is only one assigned resource.

If the task is Effort Driven, then when you add new resource names to the assignment list, Project will divide the pre-existing work up among all the resources, and that will result in less work for the pre-existing resources and a shorter duration for the task. Conversely, if you re-move a named resource from a task, Project will assign its work to the remaining resources. and the task duration will increase.

If a task is not Effort Driven, then Project will not change the workloads of existing resources when you add a new resource and task duration will not change. Total work for the task will increase due to the addition of a new resource.

FIG. 10.2
The Task Type field can also be accessed on the Task Form.

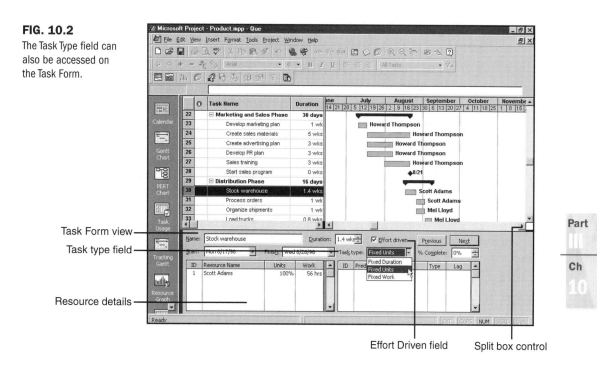

Task Form view
Task type field
Resource details

Effort Driven field   Split box control

The default status for new tasks in Project is Effort Driven, but you can change that on the Options dialog box, right next to where you change the default Task Type. Choose Tools, Options and select the Schedule tab on the Options dialog box. Deselect the New Tasks Are Effort Driven check box to change the default setting.

To verify or change the Effort Driven setting for a task, follow these steps:

1. Select the task.

2. Click the Task Information tool to display the Task Information dialog box.

3. Select the Advanced tab.

4. Select the Effort Driven check box to change its status (refer to Figure 10.1). If the check box is filled, the task is Effort Driven; if empty, the task is not Effort Driven.

5. Choose OK.

The Effort Driven field also appears on the Task Form.

Assigning Resources to Tasks

There are a variety of methods and techniques you can use to make the assignments of resources to existing tasks. These include:

- The Assign Resources dialog box, where drag and drop is available.
- The Task Information dialog box, where a pick list of resource names is available.

Part
III

Ch
10

- The Task Entry view, which displays the Gantt Chart in the top pane, and Task Form, which included resource assignment fields in the bottom pane.

- The Task Usage view, which replaces the Gantt Chart task bars in the timescale with a grid of cells that show details about the assignment during each period in the timescale. You can edit the cells to change work assignments in individual time periods.

- Any task sheet which displays the Resource Names column.

The Assign Resources dialog box and the Task Information dialog box offer pop-up accessibility from any task view, but they accept and display a limited amount of data. The Task Entry and Task Usage views are not pop-up objects, but they display a great deal of information at a glance and in combination with each other. The pop-up dialog boxes offer the widest set of choices for controlling the details of resource and cost assignments. We will keep the Task Form with its resource details in the background as we demonstrate the pop-up dialog boxes so you can see more of the details.

Using the Assign Resources Dialog Box

The Assign Resources dialog box is a versatile tool for adding resource assignments to tasks. In addition, you can use the dialog box to remove resources from selected tasks and replace resources for selected tasks. You can use the Resource Assignment dialog box to assign resources to one or more selected tasks (see Figure 10.3). You display the Resource Assignment dialog box by selecting Tools, Resources, Assign Resources. You can also click the Assign Resources tool.

Figure 10.3 shows the Assign Resources dialog box over the Task Entry view in the background. The selected task is Preliminary Design. You can see the assigned resources in the Assign Resources dialog box with check marks next to their names to indicate that they are assigned to the selected task. You can also see more detail about the assignments in the Resources area of the Task Details Form in the bottom pane.

Adding Resources   To add a resource assignment to a selected task or group of tasks, follow these steps:

1. Select the task or tasks to which you want the resource assigned.

2. Display the Assign Resources dialog box by choosing Tools, Resources, Assign Resources or by clicking the Assign Resources tool on the Standard toolbar.

3. Select the resource name from the Name list, or type in the name for a new resource.

4. Select the Units field and type the resource units to assign to the task. The default for the Units field is 100%. As a result, Project supplies a value of 100% effort for the resource unless you specify a different value for the Units field. Remember that a smaller percentage means that a resource devotes only the designated fractional part of each day to the task. If you enter **0** as the units value, neither work nor resource cost is calculated for the resource for this task. The Fixed Cost field described later in this section will be used to record costs for the tasks that do not depend on the amount of work a resource performs.

FIG. 10.3

Use the Assign Resources dialog box to assign resources to selected task(s).

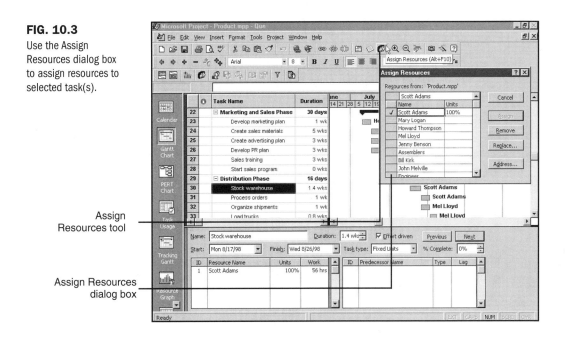

Assign Resources tool

Assign Resources dialog box

The units should be no greater than the maximum units available for this resource. If you do not know the maximum units available, double-click the resource name to see the Resource Information dialog box (see Figure 10.4).

FIG. 10.4

The Resource Information dialog box shows additional information about resources.

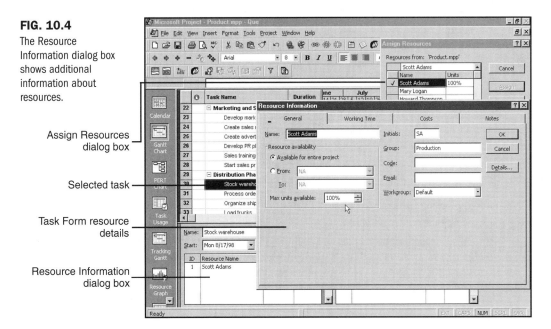

Assign Resources dialog box

Selected task

Task Form resource details

Resource Information dialog box

Part

III

Ch

10

5. Click the <u>A</u>ssign button or press Enter to assign the resource and unit information to the selected tasks.

6. If you are adding more resources to the same tasks, select the next resource name to be assigned, type the number of units in the Units field, and select <u>A</u>ssign to assign this resource to the selected tasks.

7. After the resource list is completed, select the Close button to close the Assign Resources dialog box.

N O T E When you click the <u>A</u>ssign button on the Resource Assignment dialog box, a check mark appears to the left of the resource assigned, as shown in Figure 10.3. This check mark will only appear when the task is selected in the view. ▦

Scheduling Resources for a Specific Amount of Work   The Assign Resources dialog box can also be used to calculate the number of resource units needed to complete a specified amount of work within the task's current duration. Normally you enter a simple percentage in the Units column of the Assign Resources dialog box. If you enter a work amount in the Units column (a number followed by a time unit instead of a number and a percentage), then Project calculates the number of units of that resource needed to do that much work within the current duration for the task.

N O T E This procedure will not work if the task is Effort Driven and this is the first assignment to the task. ▦

To assign resources using a work amount, follow these steps:

1. Select the task or tasks to which you want the resource assigned.

2. Display the Assign Resources dialog box.

3. Select the resource name from the Name list.

4. Select the Units field and type the work amount followed by the unit it's measured in (h, hr, d, dy, w, wk, and so on).

5. Click the <u>A</u>ssign button or press Enter to assign the resource and unit information to the selected tasks. Project automatically converts the work value to a percentage.

6. After the resource list is completed, select the Close button to close the Assign Resources dialog box.

Adding Resources Using Drag and Drop   With the Assign Resources dialog box, you can assign resources to a task by using the drag-and-drop method as well. An advantage to using the drag-and-drop assignment feature is that you do not have to preselect the task for which a resource should be assigned. This provides a quick and efficient way of assigning different resources to one task at a time. However, Project gives you no choice but to use a unit value of 100% for the resource assignment you create with this technique. Of course, you can change the units assignment later, but that will lead to other automatic calculations which may not be intended.

CAUTION

Do not use drag-and-drop assignments unless you want the unit assignment to be 100%.

To assign resources to a task by using the drag-and-drop feature, perform the following steps:

1. Display the Assign Resources dialog box by clicking the Assign Resources tool.
2. Select the resource by clicking in the Name field.
3. Position the mouse pointer in the gray rectangle just to the left of the resource name. The Assign Resources graphic appears below the mouse pointer (see Figure 10.5).

FIG. 10.5
When you point to the gray button beside a selected resource, the mouse pointer appears as a selection arrow carrying a resource.

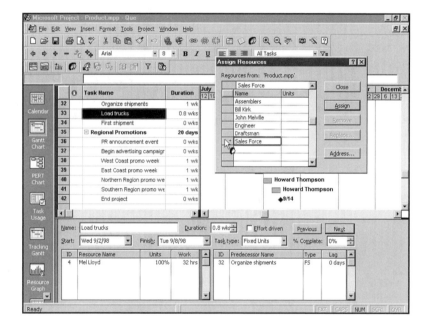

4. Hold down the mouse button (a plus sign appears next to the pointer graphic) and drag the mouse pointer to the task for which the resource should be assigned.
5. When the task is highlighted, release the mouse button to assign the resource.

TIP To assign multiple resources to a task using the drag-and-drop feature, hold down the Ctrl key while selecting the resource names in the Assign Resources dialog box. When you drag the mouse pointer to the task, all selected resources are assigned at once.

Removing Resource Assignments from One or More Tasks   To remove a resource assignment from one or more selected tasks, perform the following steps:

1. Select the task or tasks in the view that have resource assignments you want to remove. In Figure 10.6 the task is West Coast promo week.

2. Display the Assign Resources dialog box by clicking the Assign Resources tool.

3. Select the resource or resources you want to remove from assignments by clicking the check mark or the resource name. The Draftsman, who is mistakenly assigned, is selected in Figure 10.6.

N O T E   Resources assigned to the selected task are identified by check marks to the left of the resource name. If a check mark is gray instead of black, then your task selection in the view includes some tasks that have that resource assigned to them and some that do not. ■

4. Choose the Remove button. The resource (or resources) that are selected in the Assign Resources dialog box are removed from any assignments they may have with the task or tasks that are selected in the view.

FIG. 10.6

Delete unwanted assignments with the Remove button on the Assign Resources dialog box.

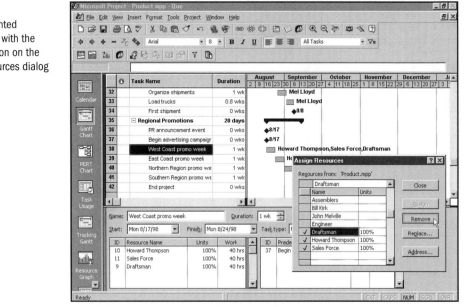

T I P   To remove a group of resources from the selected tasks, hold down the Ctrl key while you select the resources.

Changing Resource Names and Unit Assignments   Use the Assign Resources dialog box to change the resource name or unit assignment for tasks. Each resource name and unit assignment must be replaced individually. Different techniques are used to replace resources depending on whether you want to replace a resource with another resource or whether you want to change the amount of work units assigned to a resource. For example, to change a full-time assignment for Scott Adams to part-time, replace the unit assignment of 100%, with the new unit assignment of 50% (to represent part-time); then either press Enter, click the check mark on the edit box of the dialog box, or choose Replace. To replace Scott Adams with another resource such as Bill Kirk, you would select Scott Adams and then choose Replace. Then in the Replace Resource dialog box, select Bill Kirk.

To replace an assigned resource with another resource name, perform the following steps:

1. Select the task. You can select multiple tasks by using the Ctrl key if you want to make an identical assignment change in all of them.

2. Display the Assign Resources dialog box by clicking the Assign Resources tool.

3. Select the Resource Name to be replaced.

4. Click the Replace button (see Figure 10.7). Project will display the Replace Resource dialog box over the Assign Resources dialog box.

5. Select the new resource name.

6. Select the Units field for the selected resource and enter the value if you want it to be something other than 100%.

7. Choose OK or press Enter.

FIG. 10.7

A second dialog box, Replace Resource, provides a list of replacement resources to choose from.

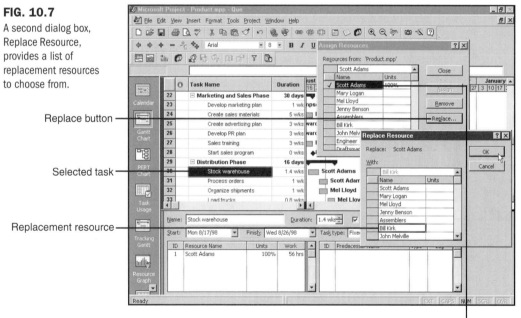

Replace button

Selected task

Replacement resource

Currently assigned resource

N O T E The Replace Resource dialog box lists all resources on the project. Microsoft Project does not filter the list for availability during the dates for the task or suitability to the task. Therefore, many of the names in the list may not be available or appropriate to the task assignment.

To replace the number of units in a resource assignment, follow these steps:

1. Select the task in the view. You can select multiple tasks if you plan to make an identical assignment change in all of them.

2. Display the Assign Resources dialog box by clicking the Assign Resources tool.

3. Select the Units field for the resource whose assignment is to be changed.

4. Type the new unit assignment for the resource.

5. Choose Close or press Enter.

N O T E   Changing the number of resource units assigned to a task causes Microsoft Project to recalculate the task duration (unless the task is a Fixed Duration task). ▓

To replace the amount of work assigned to a resource, follow these steps:

1. Select the task in the view. You can select multiple tasks if you plan to make an identical assignment change in all of them.

2. Display the Assign Resources dialog box by clicking the Assign Resources tool.

3. In the Assign Resources dialog box, select the Units field for the resource whose assignment is to be changed.

4. Type the new amount of work for the assignment. Remember to add the time units for the work amount (h, hr, d, day, and so on).

5. Choose Close or press Enter. Project will recalculate the number of resource units needed to complete the new amount of work.

N O T E   Although you cannot enter work amounts in the Assign Resources dialog box for Effort Driven tasks when making the initial assignment, you can do so for subsequent assignments or changes in the assignment. ▓

TROUBLESHOOTING

I assigned a resource to a task and the duration allowed for the task changed. This impacted the rest of the project. How can I control this? You can change the task to a Fixed Duration task so that the duration will not change regardless of how many or how few resources are assigned to the task.

Assigning Resources with the Task Information Dialog Box

You can use the Task Information dialog box to assign resources to a single task or to multiple tasks in the project. The procedures for assigning tasks by using this form are quite different from those used in the Assign Resources dialog box.

You can use the Task Information dialog box to add, change, and delete the resource assignment information for the selected task. Follow these steps:

1. Select the task for which you want to assign or change a resource.

2. Display the Task Information dialog box by choosing Project, Task Information. You can also click the Task Information tool on the toolbar. The fields in the dialog box show the current data for the task (see Figure 10.8).

TIP You can also access the Task Information dialog box by selecting the task, clicking the secondary mouse button, and choosing Task Information from the pop-up shortcut menu. Still another method is to use the shortcut key Shift+F2.

3. Select the Resources folder tab to assign or view the resource information for the selected task.

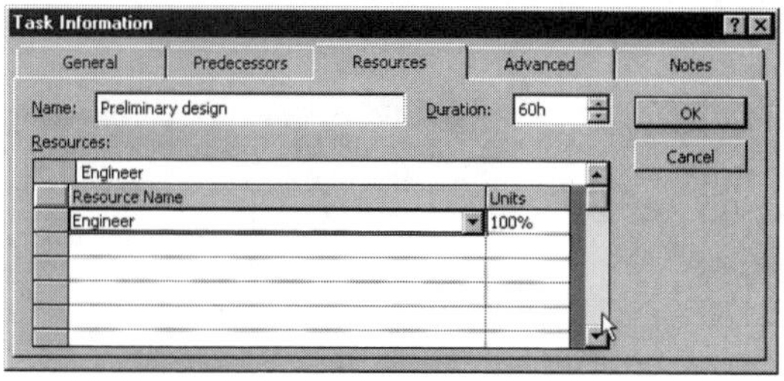

FIG. 10.8

The Task Information dialog box contains a Resources tab which can be used to assign or edit resources.

4. In the Resource Name box, edit an existing entry or choose a blank row to add a new resource. To add or change the resource, select a resource from the drop-down list in the field.

5. Type the unit assignment for the resource in the Units field. The default for the Units field is 100%. As a result, Project supplies a value of 100% effort to the resource unless you specify a different value for the Units field.

6. To add additional resources to the selected task, click the next Resource Name field and repeat the preceding steps.

7. After you complete all resource assignments for the task, choose OK.

If you use the Ctrl key to select more than one task before opening the Task Information dialog box, Project displays the Multiple Task Information dialog box so that any resource you select will automatically be assigned to all selected tasks (see Figure 10.9).

The resource assignment entries you make in the Multiple Task Information dialog box are added to existing resource assignments for the selected tasks.

NOTE You cannot change existing resource assignments for multiple tasks by using the Multiple Task Information dialog box. ▨

Part
III

Ch
10

FIG. 10.9
Select multiple tasks to make changes to all at one time.

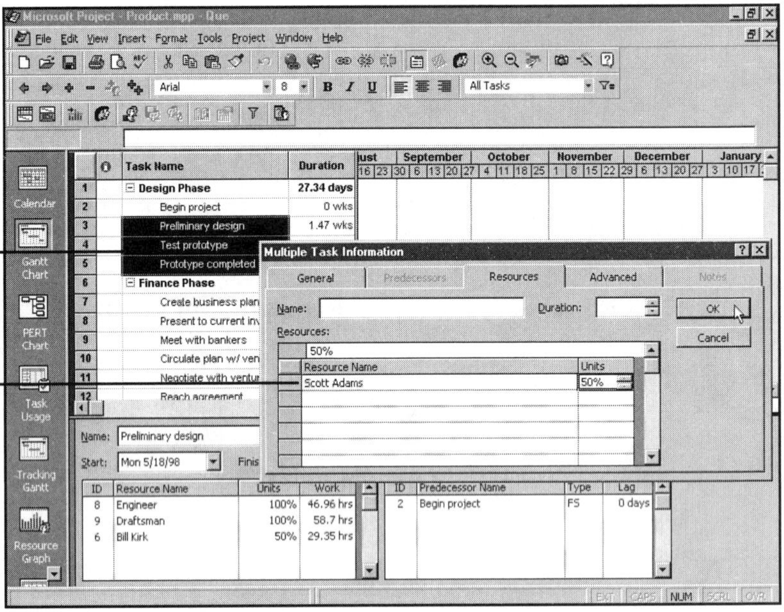

Multiple tasks selected —

Resource to be assigned to multiple tasks —

Assigning Resources with the Task and Task Details Forms

Both the Task Form and the Task Details Form can display resource assignment details in a table at the bottom of the form. The most commonly displayed details are resource ID, Name, Units, and Work for each assigned resource. This table is a convenient place for assigning resources because it allows you to enter either resource Units, Work, or both for each resource assignment.

You will generally want to use these forms in the bottom pane of a task view such as the Gantt Chart, the Task Sheet, the PERT Chart, or the Task Usage view. With a combination view like this, you can see how a task relates to other tasks in the top pane along with a lot of detail about the task in the bottom pane. To display such a combination view, follow these steps:

1. Use the menu or the View Bar to select the view you want in the top pane. For example, choose View, Gantt Chart or View, PERT Chart. Or, you can click the icon for the view you want to display on the View Bar.

2. Split the view by choosing Window, Split. You can also double-click the split box control below the vertical scroll bar.

   When you split a task view, the Task Form is automatically displayed in the lower pane. If you want the Task Details Form in the bottom pane, activate the bottom pane and choose View, More Views. In the More Views dialog box, select Task Details Form in the Views list and click Apply to display it.

3. Activate the bottom pane with the F6 key (or by clicking anywhere in the bottom pane) so that you can choose the details displayed at the bottom of the form.

4. Choose F_ormat, _Details to display the Details menu. You can also display the Details shortcut menu by right-clicking anywhere in the Task Form.

5. From the Details menu, choose R_esources & Predecessors, Resources & S_uccessors, or Resource W_ork (see Figure 10.10).

The assignment details in these three choices include the Units field along with Name and Work. The Resource S_chedule details do not include Units, so you can't manage assignment units in that display.

FIG. 10.10

The Details menu for the Task Form shows the current display with a check mark and lets you select a new display.

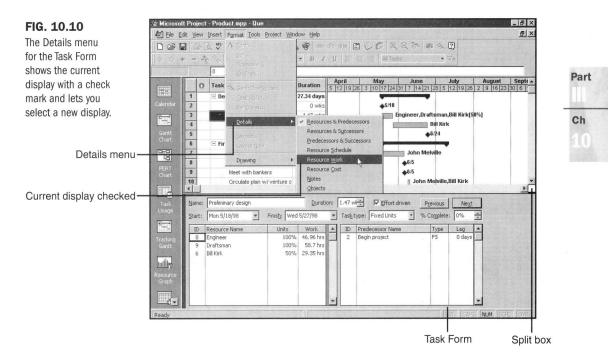

Details menu

Current display checked

Task Form   Split box

The procedures for assigning resources with both forms are the same. To assign resources using the Task Form, follow these steps:

1. Select the task in the top pane.

N O T E   If the bottom pane is active, you can change the task selection in the top pane with the Previous and Next buttons in the lower pane. If the task you want to select is near to the currently selected task, this will be faster than activating the top pane, selecting the task, then activating the bottom pane again.

2. Select the Resource Name field.

3. Identify the resource by typing the resource name, typing the resource initials, or by selecting the resource name from the drop-down list available in the Resource Name field.

4. If you leave the Units field blank, Project will assign the default (100%). If you want to specify the units for the assignment, select the Units field and enter the units you want to assign.

5. If you leave the Work field blank, Project will calculate the work based on the task duration and the assigned units. If you want to specify the amount of work for the assignment, select the Work field and type in the work amount. Work must be entered with a number plus the unit of measure (h, hr, hour, d, day, wk, and so on).

6. If you are assigning multiple resources, you can enter these resources in the next rows of the Resource Name column.

7. After all resource assignments are made for the task, choose the OK button.

When you click OK, Project will calculate the values for those fields you did not fill in, in accordance with the principles discussed in Chapter 9, " Understanding Resource Scheduling in Microsoft Project 98."

When you assign a resource to a task, Project schedules the work to start when the task starts. Sometimes, however, one or more of the resources assigned to a task perform a specialized function that doesn't take place until other work on the task is partly completed.

For example, if you assign a marketing manager, an engineer, and a draftsman to draw up a preliminary design for a product, the draftsman's work on the task doesn't really start until some design details have already been proposed. To accurately schedule the draftsman's work, Project needs to delay the start of the draftsman's scheduled work to some time after the task starts.

Microsoft Project has a Delay field for resource assignments which you can use to force a delay in the scheduled work for a resource beyond the start of the task. If you want to enter a value in the Delay field, then you need to display the Resource Schedule details in the Task Form or Task Details Form where the field is available for editing (see Figure 10.11).

N O T E You can also get to the Delay field by replacing the Task Form with the Resource Form and displaying the Schedule details (which is just like the Resource Schedule details on the Task Form).

You can also enter delays on the Task Usage and Resource Usage views. The Task Usage view will be discussed in the next section. The Resource Usage view is explored in great detail in Chapter 11, "Resolving Resource Allocation Problems." ▨

Figure 10.11 shows the Task Form with the Resource Schedule details displayed. The Preliminary Design task is selected, and the three assigned resources are listed in the assignment details. The draftsman is only scheduled to work 12 hours, much less than the 50 hours for each of the other resources.

You can also see in Figure 10.11 that Project has scheduled all three resources to start at the start of the task, which is Monday, May 18, 1998. In reality, the Draftsman is expected to execute his assignment in the last 12 hours of the task, after the other two resources have completed 38 hours of their assignments.

FIG. 10.11

The Resource Schedule details let you control when work is assigned.

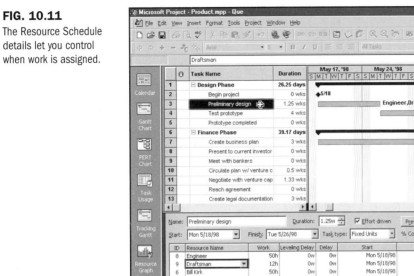

Assignment Delay field | Assignment dates | Resource Schedule details

Figure 10.12 shows a delay of 38 hours entered for the Draftsman's assignment. Note that the Start and Finish dates for the assignment have been changed and that all three resources finish their assignments on the same date (which is also the finish of the task).

To enter a delay in an assignment, you can follow these steps:

1. Display the Task Form or Task Details Form in the bottom pane of a task view, as described in the numbered steps at the beginning of this section.

2. Activate the form in the bottom pane and display the Schedule details by choosing Format, Details, Resource Schedule.

3. Select the task for the assignment in the top pane.

4. Select the row for the resource name you want to delay in the bottom pane, and move to the Delay field.

5. Enter a delay value, using a number followed by the measurement units for the delay (minutes, hours, days, or weeks). Alternatively, you can enter a delayed start date for the assignment in the Start field.

6. Click the OK button to complete the entry.

As pointed out in step 5, you can enter a later start date in the Start field, and Project will calculate the delay and a new Finish date value, just as when you enter a value in the Delay field.

Part

III

Ch

10

FIG. 10.12
Delaying the start of the Draftsman's assignment by 38 hours places his work at the end of the task.

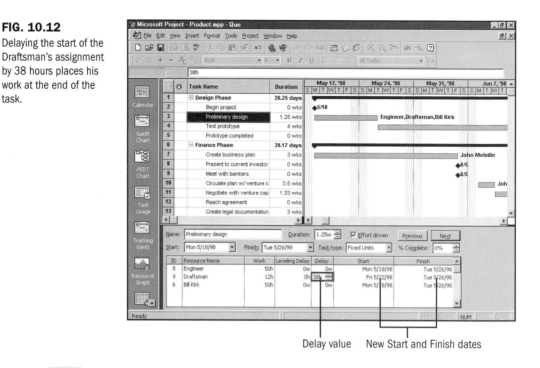

Delay value   New Start and Finish dates

N O T E   This discussion is based on a project with a fixed start date. If your project has a fixed finish date, then the delay field accepts negative numbers only (assignments are started earlier than the task). You could enter an earlier date in the Finish date field, and Project would calculate the negative delay for you.

If you enter a new date in the Finish date column, and the project has a fixed start date, Project doesn't calculate a Delay that would cause the assignment to finish on that date. Instead it recalculates the Work value of the assignment. Similarly, if your project has a fixed finish date, and you enter a new date in the Start date column, Project recalculates the Work value of the assignment instead of a delay. ▪

To remove a delay for an assignment, enter a zero value in the Delay field and click the OK button. Project will schedule the assignment at the start of the task.

Assigning Resources with the Task Usage View

The Task Usage view is a new view introduced in Microsoft Project 98. You can do everything we have covered so far in this chapter in the Task Usage view, and in addition, you can do things we can't do in the views already covered. You can use the Assign Resources dialog box to assign resources to tasks in the Task Usage view, or you can display the Task Form in the bottom pane to assign resources.

The attractiveness of the Task Usage view lies in its features that let you fine-tune assignments after they are created. For example, you can:

- Modify assignments by splitting scheduled work around interruptions where the resource is busy on other tasks.

- Change the flat, even distribution of work during an assignment to a *contoured* distribution that has more work scheduled at some times during the assignment than at others.

- Use the resource Cost Rate Tables to assign different standard rates to different tasks.

Figure 10.13 shows the Task Usage view in the top pane and the Task Form in the bottom pane. The Task Usage view is similar to the Resource Usage view which is described in great detail in Chapter 11, "Resolving Resource Allocation Problems." You can apply all the features described for the Resource Usage view to the Task Usage view.

FIG. 10.13

The Task Usage view offers time-phased detail about individual task assignments for viewing and editing.

Selected task ———

Assigned resources ———

Time-phased work Details ———

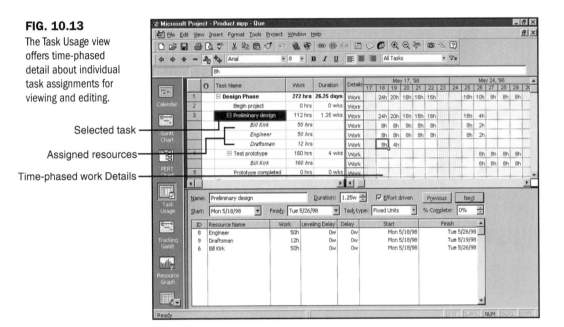

To display the Task Usage view, you can simply click the icon for the view on the View Bar, or you can follow these steps:

1. Choose View, More Views.

2. From the Views list in the More Views dialog box, select Task Usage.

3. Click the Apply button to display the view.

The table area of the Task Usage view displays all the tasks in the project. Indented under each task are rows for each resource that is assigned to that task. The Work field for the task is the sum of the Work field values for the assigned resources.

The right side of the view is a timescale grid of cells that show assignment details by time period. In Figure 10.13, the Work details are displayed in the grid. This is the default assignment detail, but you can display other details if desired. The value in the Work field for each resource in the table is the sum of the values displayed in the cells on the row for that resource in the timescale.

You can edit the entries in the cells to change the work assigned for specific time periods. For example, you could change the work amounts for the Draftsman on the 18th and 19th to zero and enter those hours in the cells for the 25th and 26th at the finish of the task.

▶ **See** "Task Usage," **p. 670**

Modifying Work Schedules with the Task Usage View   As mentioned previously, you can delay and split task assignments and customize the amount of work scheduled for each time period with the Task Usage view.

To change the amount of work scheduled for any given time period in the Task Usage View, simply select the cell, type in a new value, and either press Enter or select another cell. When you type in a value, Project will assume the unit is hours unless you provide a different measurement unit.

As soon as you complete a cell entry, Project will immediately recalculate:

- The Work field entry for the resource in the table.
- The Summary work for time period in the task row in the timescale.
- The Total work for the task in the table.
- The Duration for the task.

For example, to revisit the previous example where we needed to delay the Draftsman's assignment, we can edit the cells in the Task Usage view directly to achieve that goal. We would:

1. Enter zeros in the cells for May 18–19.
2. Enter **8h** in the cell for May 25. We could also just enter **8** since the default unit is hours.
3. Enter **4h** in the cell for May 26.

Figure 10.14 shows the result of changing the cell entries to delay the start of the Draftsman's assignment.

The Edited Contour icon now appears in the Indicator column to signal that the work on this assignment has been edited.

Perhaps the easiest way to shift the assigned work to later periods, as we are doing with the delay, is to insert blank cells where the assignment starts, pushing each work amount to the right until the date for the assignment is reached.

To insert blank cells in the grid, select the first of the cells to be moved to the right and choose Insert, Cells to shift that cell to the right. Or better yet, you can simply press the Insert key to insert a blank cell.

FIG. 10.14

The time-phased distribution of work can be edited directly in the Task Usage view.

Revised task totals for each period

Contour indicator

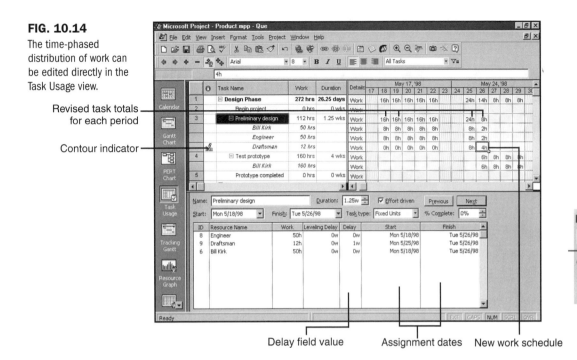

Delay field value   Assignment dates   New work schedule

If you select a string of cells before you choose Insert, the Insert, Cells command will insert as many blank cells as you have selected. Figure 10.15 shows the Draftsman's scheduled days selected, along with the remaining days in the week. When you choose Insert, Cells, all the selected cells will be pushed to the right (past the selection), and blank cells will be inserted in their place.

You can also delete cells and shift all cells on the right of the deleted cell to the left. To delete a cell or a block of cells, select the cell or cells and then choose Edit, Delete Cells; or simply press the Delete key to delete the selected cells.

By manually editing cells and inserting or deleting cells, you can adjust the work pattern for a resource assigned to the task.

Using the Assignment Information Dialog Box

The Assignment Information dialog box can be displayed by selecting an assignment row in either the Task Usage or the Resource view and then choosing Project, Assignment Information. You can also display the dialog box by clicking the Assignment Information tool on the Standard toolbar, or by double-clicking the assignment row.

Figure 10.16 shows the Assignment Information dialog box for the Draftsman's assignment. As you can see, the dialog box provides several fields that we have already worked with on forms and tables, including the assigned Work, the assigned Units, and the Start and Finish dates for

Part

III

Ch

10

the assignment. You can also change the name of the assigned <u>R</u>esource here, but there is no list to select from, and you must know how to spell the name correctly.

FIG. 10.15

You can insert a block of cells in one step.

Selected cells —

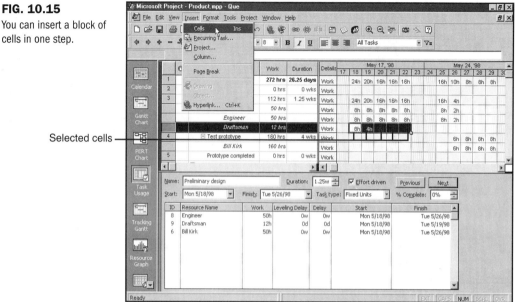

FIG. 10.16

The Assignment Information dialog box is the most accessible method of changing the new assignment fields in Microsoft Project 98.

Notes tab —

Work contour selection —

Cost of this assignment —

Cost Rate Table selection —

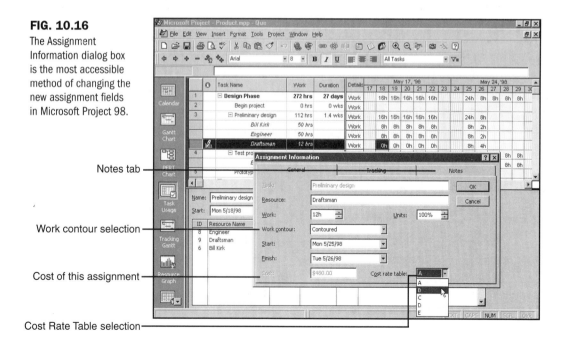

There are four new assignment fields on the Assignment Information dialog box:

- The Work Contour field lets you choose from a set of predefined work contours. A *contour* is a planned pattern of scheduled work spread over the duration of an assignment. For example, the Bell contour schedules a few hours per day at the beginning and end of an assignment, but increases the assigned hours toward the middle of the assignment.

  The default contour is *flat*, which means that the resource is scheduled from the start of the task to work as much as possible each day until the assignment is complete. Thus, the work load will tend to be the same every day until the assignment is finished. If you have edited the assignment, you can return it to the standard schedule by choosing the Flat contour.

  The only other way to access and select the predefined contours is to display the Contour field as a column in the Usage table.

- The Cost Rate Table field lets you select one of the five different Cost Rate tables that you can define for a resource as the standard and overtime rates for this assignment. The default assignment is table A. The Cost Rate Table field can also be displayed as a column in the Usage table. (The Usage table is the table displayed on the Task Usage and Resource Usage views.)

- The Cost field is a display-only field that shows you the scheduled cost of the assignment.

- On the Notes tab, the Notes field lets you record notes about an assignment. For instance, you could make a note here about why you delayed the assignment.

Selecting a Predefined Contour By default, the work that Project schedules for an assignment is evenly distributed across the time periods of the assignment. However, you can edit the assignments in individual time periods to customize the schedule. You can also choose one of eight predefined contour patterns for Project to apply to an individual assignment. Figure 10.17 shows the eight predefined contours, the indicators that identify them, and a sample work distribution over a ten-period assignment. The last row, labeled Contoured, is included to show the indicator for manually edited assignments.

Thus, if a resource schedule needs to show lots of hours up front with a tapering off toward the end, you can assign the Front Loaded contour to the assignment, and Project would change the work in the individual periods to reflect that pattern.

To select a contour for an assignment, follow these steps:

1. Select the assignment in the Task Usage view or the Resource Usage view.
2. Display the Assignment Information dialog box by choosing Project, Assignment Information, by clicking the Assignment Information tool, or by double-clicking the assignment row.
3. On the General tab, use the list arrow in the Work Contour field to select one of the predefined contours.
4. Click OK to have Project calculate the new assignment pattern.

Microsoft Project - Contours.mpp - Que
File Edit View Insert Format Tools Project Window Help
Calendar
Gantt Chart
PERT Chart
Task Usage
Tracking Gantt
Resource Graph
Resource Sheet
Work Contour
Description
1 2 3 4 5 6 7 8 9 10
Flat
Even distribution across the assignment
8h 8h 8h 8h 8h 8h 8h 8h 8h 8h
Back Loaded
Starts low and peaks toward the finish
0.8h 1.2h 2h 4h 4h 6h 6h 8h 8h 8h
Front Loaded
Peaks at the start and starts tapering off
8h 8h 8h 6h 6h 4h 4h 2h 1.2h 0.8h
Double Peak
Peaks twice during the assignment
2h 4h 8h 4h 2h 2h 4h 8h 4h 2h
Early Peak
Rises to an early peak and then tapers off
2h 4h 8h 8h 6h 4h 4h 2h 1.2h 0.8h
Late Peak
Rises to a late peak and then tapers off
0.8h 1.2h 2h 4h 4h 6h 8h 8h 4h 2h
Bell
Has a Bell shaped curve, peaking in the middle
0.8h 1.6h 3.2h 6.4h 8h 8h 6.4h 3.2h 1.6h 0.8h
Turtle
Rises to a plateau in the middle then tapers off
2h 4h 6h 8h 8h 8h 8h 6h 4h 2h
Contoured
Has been manually edited (random peaks)
8h 2h 6h 1h 0h 7h 1h 10h 0h 8h
Ready
NUM

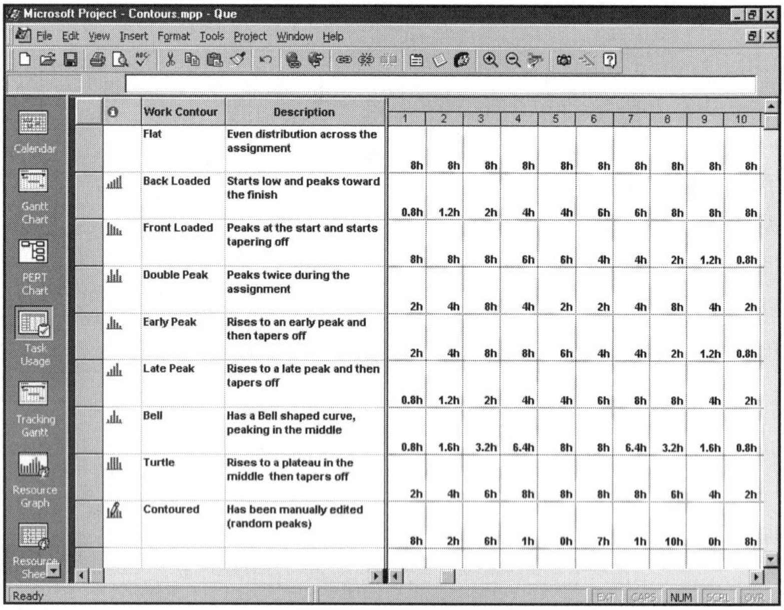

FIG. 10.17
The predefined assignment contours feature work patterns that rise, peak, and taper at different stages.

When you assign a contour Project will keep the total work of the assignment constant (see the Caution below for an exception), but the duration of the assignment may change.

CAUTION

If you assign a contour to a Fixed Duration task, the task duration cannot change, and the contour assigned may not allow all the work to be completed within that duration.

If you want to restore the assignment contour to the default pattern, or if you have edited the assignment and want to restore the original assignment, choose the predefined contour named Flat.

P98

Selecting a Cost Rate Table for an Assignment One of the important new features in Microsoft Project 98 is the ability to define a graduated scale of standard and overtime cost rates for a resource so that work on some assignments can be charged more than work on other assignments. For example, a computer consulting company might assign a systems programmer to some highly technical tasks at exorbitant rates, but to other more mundane tasks at lower, merely outrageous rates.

The only convenient way to select the Cost Rate table for an assignment is through the Assignment Information dialog box, and the only way to display the Assignment Information dialog box is with either the Task Usage or Resource Usage views. Figure 10.16 shows the Cost Rate Table list opened for selection. Choose one of the lettered tables and click OK to assign the standard rate and overtime rate on that table to the assignment.

N O T E The Cost Rate tables can be edited only in the Resource Information dialog box. Display a view with fields for resources and either double-click a resource name or click the Information tool on the standard toolbar to display the Resource Information dialog box. Click the Costs tab to display the five Cost Rate Tables, A through E. ▨

Assigning Resources on a Task Table

You can also use a task table to assign resources to a task or group of tasks selected on a task view. However, entering the resource assignment data on a task table is not quite as easy as entering it on the other views described.

On a task table, the Resource Name field is a text entry field (see Figure 10.18). The text entry must follow the pattern as on Task 4, Test Prototype, below. You must enter the resource assignment by using the following notation pattern:

```
ResourceName1[Units],ResourceName2[Units], ...
```

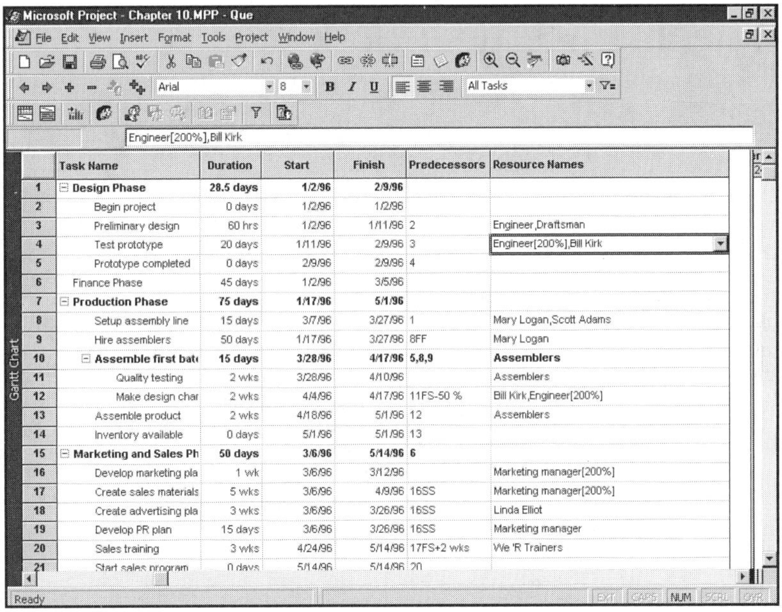

FIG. 10.18
Use the Resource Names field to assign resources.

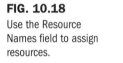

When entering data using this format, note that the Units value follows immediately after the resource name, without an intervening space and is placed in square brackets. Unit values of 100% do not need to be included. Notice, too, that multiple resource assignments are separated by commas.

To assign resources to tasks in the Task Sheet view, perform the following steps:

1. View the Gantt Chart.

2. Choose View, Table and apply any table which includes a Resource Name column, such as the Entry table.

3. Select the Resource Names column of the task table for the task to which you want to assign resources.

4. Enter the resource name. You can select the name from the drop-down resource list, which appears in the cell when the Resource Names column is active.

5. If the number of units is other than 100%, follow the name immediately with the percent of effort, including the % sign, enclosed in square brackets, by typing in the Edit bar.

6. If you want to assign more resources to the same task, use the list separator (a comma in North America) to separate each resource and repeat steps 4 and 5 until all resources are complete.

TIP To change the list separator, open the Control Panel, use Regional Settings (in Windows 95) or International (in Windows NT 3.51) and select the Number tab.

7. Press Enter or select any other cell to complete the resource assignment.

Assigning Overtime Work

Overtime means that a resource works at a time outside the normal working schedule. This definition explains how Microsoft Project sees overtime. To Microsoft Project, if part of the work on a task is done in overtime, that much of the task work is not scheduled during the regular working times on the resource calendar.

Understanding How Microsoft Project Schedules and Charges for Overtime

When you instruct Project to schedule a certain amount of time in overtime hours, the program makes a note to reduce the number of regular hours that are needed to complete the assignment. Note that when you enter overtime work hours, you do not designate the exact days and hours when the overtime work takes place—you just tell Project that a certain number of hours on the task are overtime hours. Project uses this instruction to reduce the number of regular calendar hours scheduled for the task and notes that the overtime rate is used for costing purposes for those overtime hours.

The cost of the overtime hours is calculated by using the overtime rate that you define on the Resource Sheet or Resource Information dialog box (see Figure 10.19).

As you can see, if you use overtime, providing Project with the needed information for assessing the cost of overtime hours is vitally important. If you don't enter an overtime rate when defining the resource (leaving the field with the default zero value), overtime work is charged at the rate of zero. Tasks that use overtime work for which no overtime costs are recorded appear to use fewer of the limited resources than what actually is used. The overtime hours of all resources (even salaried professionals) should be charged as a cost to reflect the opportunity cost of having done one task instead of others.

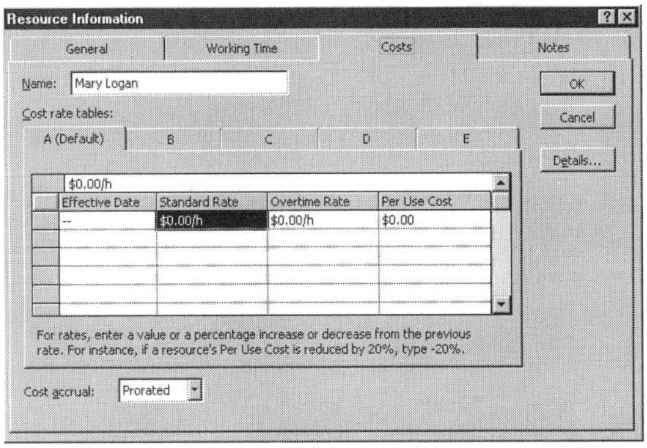

FIG. 10.19

The Cost Rate tables for a resource can be entered on the Resource Information form.

Another way of scheduling extra time is to change the resource calendar and increase the hours when a resource is available. You edit the resource calendar and make these days and hours working times rather than non-working times. Be aware, however, that Microsoft Project charges no overtime rate for work done during the regular calendar hours. If you do not pay premium overtime rates, then editing the calendar is satisfactory. Indeed, editing the calendar gives you the ability of stating explicitly when the extra work time takes place. If you pay premium overtime rates, however, you should enter overtime hours in the Overtime field so that costing will be done at the overtime rate.

Microsoft Project 98 has an improved way of scheduling with overtime. This is the procedure it follows:

- Your entry in the Overtime Work field is subtracted from the assignment's total work, and the difference is called *Regular Work*.

- The new, reduced Regular Work is scheduled during the hours available on the resource calendar. If you have selected a work contour for the assignment, the new work schedule is apportioned over time in the same pattern as the contour.

- The Overtime Work is then scheduled with the same contour over the same period of time as the Regular Work.

N O T E In earlier versions of Microsoft Project, the entire amount of overtime was scheduled at the end of the assignment. ▓

Although you can display the scheduled overtime work detail in the Task Usage and Resource Usage views, you cannot edit the overtime assignment. When tracking actual work performed, however, you *can* edit the overtime work detail to place actual overtime in the time period when it was actually performed.

Entering Overtime Work

Scheduled overtime can be viewed in the Task and Resource Usage views, but you cannot enter overtime in those views. The Overtime field appears on three forms for you to edit, and in each case, you must use the Format Details command to apply the Resource Work table at the bottom of the form. You can enter overtime in the following places:

- On the Task Form, with the Resource Work entry table displayed at the bottom of the form

- On the Task Details Form, with the Resource Work entry table displayed at the bottom of the form

- On the Resource Form, with the Work entry table displayed at the bottom of the form

TIP If you want to clear an overtime entry, you must enter a **0**. You cannot leave the field empty. This field must have a value.

You can see the total overtime worked by a resource for all tasks by viewing the Resource Usage view or the Resource Sheet and applying the Work table to either one.

NOTE If you assign all the work to be done in overtime, Project reduces the duration of the task to zero and automatically flags the task as a milestone. You can remove the milestone flag by opening the Task Information dialog box and clearing the Mark Task as Milestone check box on the Advanced tab. The milestone symbol will no longer appear in the Gantt Chart for the task, although its duration will still be zero.

Using the Task Form to Enter Overtime

You can use any of the task-oriented views (Calendar, Gantt Chart, PERT Chart, Task Usage, Tracking Gantt, and Task Sheet) in the top pane to display and select the task for which you want to record overtime. The Task Form in the bottom pane can then be used to enter the amount of overtime. Whether you use the Task Form in the bottom pane or display the Task Form to cover the entire window, the procedures for recording overtime are the same.

To enter overtime in a combination view, perform the following steps:

1. Choose a task-oriented view from the View menu for the top pane.

2. Select the task for which you want to schedule overtime.

3. Display a combination view by choosing Window, Split.

4. Press F6 to activate the Task Form in the bottom pane. If you prefer the Task Details Form in the bottom pane, choose View, More Views and select the Task Details Form to view in the bottom pane.

5. In the bottom pane, choose Format, Details and select Resource Work, or right-click the Form and select Resource Work from the shortcut menu to display the Resource Work fields in the entry table (see Figure 10.20).

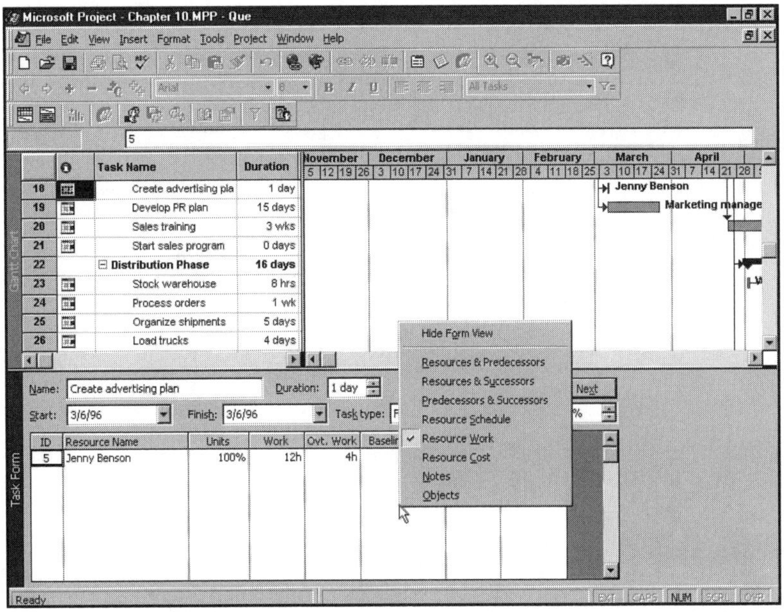

FIG. 10.20

You can enter overtime hours, and reduce task duration, in a combination view.

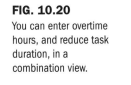

6. Select the Ovt. Work field and enter the amount of work that you are scheduling in overtime. Enter a number followed by a time unit abbreviation (h, hr, hour for hours., and so on), and then press Enter or click the Enter box on the Edit bar. Do not reduce the entry in the Work field. That field's entry must show the *total* amount of work to be done, including both the regular work and the overtime work.

7. Choose OK to complete the overtime assignment.

In Figure 10.21, the resource designated for overtime is Jenny Benson, whose work load for this task is 12 hours. Her 12 hours of work take 1.5 days calendar days. After recording the overtime of four hours for Jenny Benson, the task duration is reduced to one day. Usually, overtime is scheduled for just this reason, to reduce the overall time taken to complete a task.

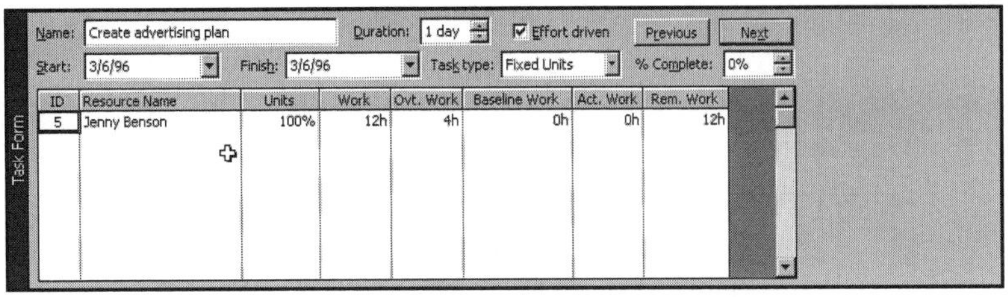

FIG. 10.21

The task duration is reduced to one day by allowing four hours of overtime.

Using the Resource Form to Enter Overtime

If you apply the Work fields entry table, you can use the Resource Form to enter overtime hours. You can also use this form to enter the default overtime rate for the resource. This is the overtime rate that appears on the Cost Rate table labeled "A" in the Resource Information dialog box for the resource.

To enter overtime in the Resource Form, perform the following steps:

1. Choose a task-oriented view from the top of the View menu.

2. Select the task for which you want to schedule overtime.

3. Display a combination view by choosing Window, Split.

4. Press F6 to activate the Task Form in the bottom pane.

5. Choose View, More Views and select Resource Form to place it in the bottom frame.

6. To place the Work fields in the entry table at the bottom of the form, choose Format, Details, Work, or select Work from the shortcut menu (see Figure 10.22).

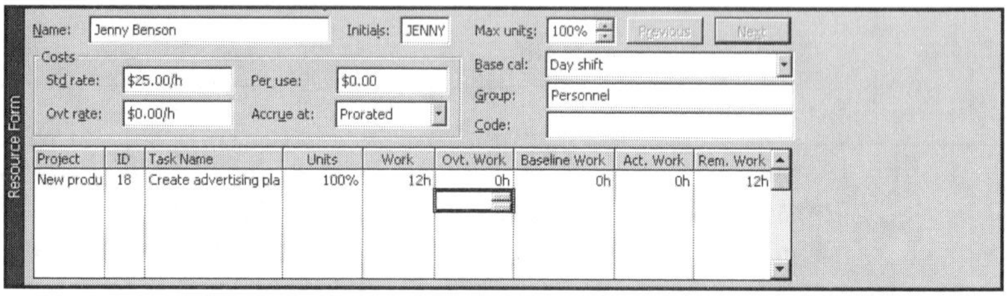

FIG. 10.22

You can use the Resource Form to enter overtime hours.

7. Because the Resource Form shows details for only one resource at a time, you might need to use the Next or Previous buttons to select the resource for which overtime is to be entered.

TIP

You also can use Find to select the resource. Press Ctrl+F, or choose Edit, Find to display the Find dialog box. Type all or part of the resource name and choose Find Next to move forward to this resource. Or set the Search option to Up in order to search backward in the project.

8. The Work table shows a row for each task to which the resource is assigned. If the task to which you want to assign overtime is not visible, use the scroll bar on the right of the form to bring the task into view.

9. Select the Ovt. Work field for the task.

10. Enter the amount of overtime work using a number and a time unit abbreviation (h, hr, and so on), and press Enter or click the Enter box on the Edit bar.

11. Edit the Ovt. Rate value at the top of the form, if necessary. The rate entered in this field will be stored as the overtime value in the default Cost Rate Table A.

12. Choose OK to complete the overtime assignment.

Viewing Scheduled Overtime

After allowable overtime hours are entered, Project schedules them across the new duration of the task for each resource. In previous versions of Project, overtime was assumed to take place at the end of the task, which distorted schedules and cost reports. Project now schedules the overtime parallel with the resource's effort on the task. Assume Mary Logan has a 40-hour task, with the default Flat resource contour, and will do her work Monday through Friday. The Task Usage view with details formatted to show resource work and overtime displays the values (see Figure 10.23).

FIG. 10.23
The Task Usage view is for displaying overtime, not entering data.

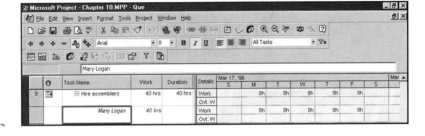

Let's say, for example, that suddenly Mary Logan's manager needs the task to be completed no later than sometime on Thursday, so he authorizes 10 hours of overtime for the task. First, Project reduces the duration of the task by the 10 hours of overtime, making the new duration 3.75 days. Then Project divides the 10 overtime hours over the new duration of 3.75 days, resulting in 2.67 overtime hours per full 8 hour day. Lastly, Project adds the 2.67 hours to the original 8 hours each day of the task, so her total work per day is now 10.67 per 8 hour day and 8 hours total on the .75 fourth day. Project follows these steps to calculate overtime schedules for resource contours other than Flat, as well. The new values display in the Task Usage view (see Figure 10.24).

FIG. 10.24
Project allocates overtime according the resource schedule contour.

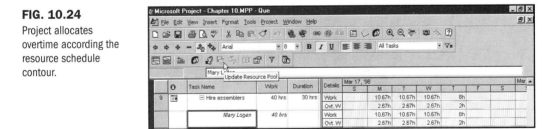

Assigning Fixed Costs and Fixed Contract Fees

For some tasks, you need to assign costs that aren't linked to the task duration or the resource assignment. These costs, known as *fixed costs*, are entered on the Gantt Chart or the Task Sheet with the Cost table for tasks applied.

You also use fixed costs when the work on a task is done by a contractor or vendor at a fixed fee. You do not want Project to track the work estimate for this kind of task because the amount of work is important to the contractor or vendor but not to you. Your cost isn't affected if the work takes more time or money than estimated. For these tasks, make the task a Fixed Duration task and assign the contractor or vendor as a resource to the task. Enter a zero in the Units field. The work amount is calculated as zero. Therefore, resource cost values from this resource are also zero. Then enter the contract cost in the Fixed Cost field of the task Cost Table.

Figure 10.25 shows an application of the procedure for recording contractors and fixed costs. You want to transfer performance of the Quality Testing task to a vendor named Quality Testing Labs. The vendor agrees to a delivery price of $1,000 and agrees to complete the testing within the two-week time frame originally scheduled for the task's duration. Bill Kirk's work load is reduced manually from 80 hours of testing work to ten hours of coordinating and overseeing the testing process.

FIG. 10.25

A vendor and a fixed bid can be added to a task.

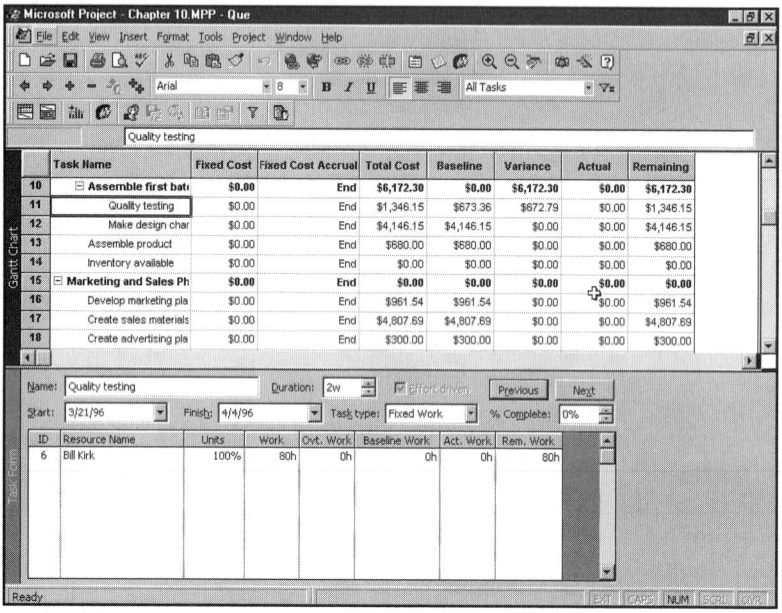

To enter the cost of a fixed contract fee for a task, follow these steps:

1. Choose a task-oriented view from the top of the View menu.

2. Select the task to assign to a contractor or vendor.

3. Apply the Cost table by choosing View, Table, Cost.

4. Display a combination view by choosing Window, Split.

5. Select Fixed Duration as the Task type on the Task Form and deselect Effort Driven. Choose OK to set these changes.

6. Assign the contractor as a resource in the Resource Name field in the bottom pane.

7. Enter the resource units as zero (**0**).

8. To complete the resource assignment, choose OK.

9. Activate the top pane; press F6.

10. Select the Fixed Cost field for the task.

11. Enter the Fixed Cost amount and press Enter, or select the Entry box in the Edit bar.

The Fixed Cost is added to the resource costs in the Total Cost column.

N O T E   You can enter the fixed cost without assigning the contractor or vendor as a resource. Assigning the resource name just gives you a reference for determining who is responsible for doing the work.

Also note that if no resources are associated with this task, you can enter the fixed cost amount in the Total Cost field. Project copies the amount to the Fixed Cost field. ■

The task is first made into a Fixed Duration task because the work is handled outside the company's resources. The vendor name is added to the resource listing, but the units are set to 0. At the same time, you can reduce Bill Kirk's work load to ten hours.

This illustration assumes the contractor has already been entered in the resource sheet or resource pool, along with the contractor's standard, overtime and per use rates. The vendor quoted a fixed price for this job, but also has quoted the hourly rates and a setup fee charged for most jobs. Note that the setup charge and standard rates do not affect the cost of this task because the unit assignment is 0. Finally, the $1,000 fixed fee is entered in the Fixed Cost field of the Cost table (see Figure 10.26).

FIG. 10.26

The task duration has been fixed and the cost for the vendor has been added to the Cost table.

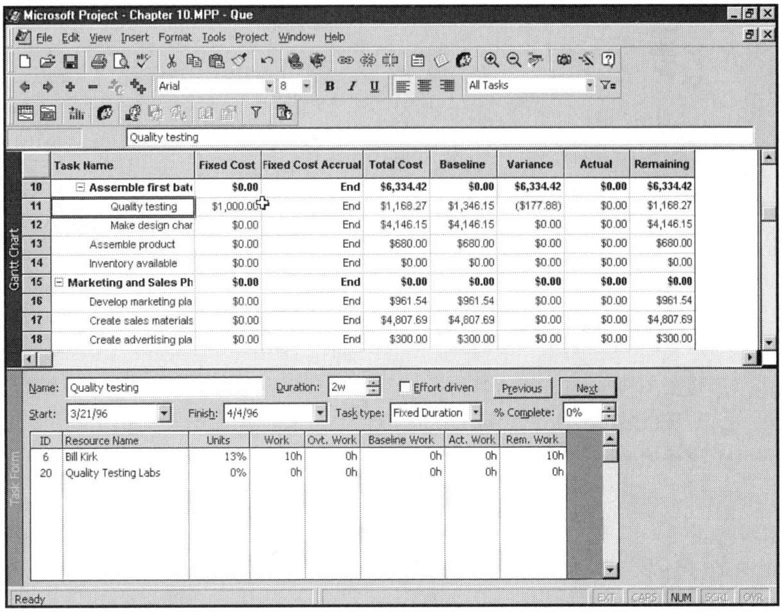

If the manager of this project has already captured an original project plan, the Baseline column of the Cost table shows the original estimate for this task. The new cost of the task may be more if the contractor expense more than offsets the savings from reducing Bill's effort. A positive value in the Variance column indicates the scheduled cost for the task now exceeds the original estimate.

Using Alternate Views of Resources and Resource Assignments

So far, this chapter has concentrated on how to enter and assign project resources and costs to individual tasks or groups of tasks. Several views have been used for data entry, including the Resource Form and the Resource Sheet. Several tables and format displays have been introduced, including the Cost and Work tables for sheet views of tasks and resources, and the Cost and Work details fields on the Task Form.

Besides these tools, several resource views are available that provide interesting insights into the resource work loads in your project. The Task Usage, Resource Usage, Resource Allocation, and Resource Graph views are especially helpful and are briefly described in the following sections.

Understanding the Enhanced Usage Views

The Task and Resource Usage views have a timescale similar to the Gantt Chart, but the right side—the details side—shows number values instead of bars. The Task Usage view lists all tasks and their assigned resources; the Resource Usage view provides a list of all resources. For each resource, a list also is provided, showing all tasks to which they have been assigned. By default, the Usage detail rows show the scheduled number of hours each resource is assigned to a task (see Figure 10.27). To display the either usage view, choose from the View menu.

The Resource Usage view shows the amount of time each resource is scheduled to work on the selected task, as well as on other tasks in the project. It also displays the dates for which each resource's time is scheduled. If the resource name appears in the color red, the resource is overallocated at some time period during the project.

 N O T E   You can increase the time span covered in each unit of the timescale with the timescale Zoom Out tool. If the time unit is currently days, selecting the Zoom Out tool twice displays the total amount of work by week for the resources. Press the timescale Zoom In tool twice to return to the daily timescale. In a combination view, the top pane must be active to use the timescale Zoom tools on the toolbar. ▩

T I P   If pound signs fill the field in the grid, the column of the grid is too narrow to display the information. Double-click the timescale to display the format Timescale dialog box and increase the Enlarge percentage in the lower-left corner.

FIG. 10.27

The Resource Usage view identifies the number of hours each resource is obligated each time period.

Usage detail area

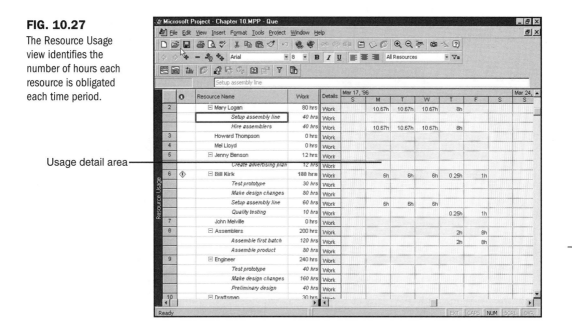

Rows for other values can be added to the usage detail area. These values include Cost, Actual Work, and Cumulative Work. For more information about adding and removing detail rows, turn to Chapter 21, "Formatting Views."

Understanding the Resource Allocation View

The Resource Allocation view is a valuable tool for dealing with overallocated resources. The Resource Allocation view also is useful for reviewing the work assignments by resource. The Resource Allocation view puts the Resource Usage view in the top pane and displays all resources. A Gantt Chart appears in the lower pane (see Figure 10.28), which only shows the tasks assigned to the resource selected in the top pane. The Gantt Chart used here is known as the Leveling Gantt because it adds a field and formatted task bar for the Leveling Delay field. The Leveling Delay field shows how much a task has been delayed due to resource leveling.

▶ **See** "Resolving Resource Allocation Problems," **p. 345**

To display the Resource Allocation view, follow these steps:

1. Choose <u>V</u>iew, <u>M</u>ore Views, select the Resource Allocation view, and choose Apply.

2. Another method is to select the Resource Allocation View tool on the Resource Management toolbar.

The top pane lists all the resources in the resource pool and shows the timescale, with the scheduled hours of work during each time unit. Select a resource name, and the lower pane shows a list of all tasks on which the selected resource is assigned to work, with a task bar in the timescale to show when the task is scheduled for work. Figure 10.28 shows the Resource

Part III

Ch 10

Allocation view focusing on all of Bill Kirk's tasks in this project. The usage of this view is described in greater detail in Chapter 11, "Resolving Resource Allocation Problems."

FIG. 10.28

Use the Resource Allocation view to identify overallocation of resources.

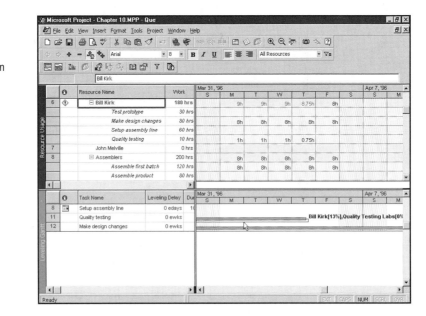

TIP To see the task bar for a particular task, select the task in the bottom pane and choose the Go To Selected Task tool on the Standard toolbar.

To review the assigned work schedule for the resource over the life of the project, scroll the timescale. Use Alt+Page Down to move the timescale forward and Alt+Page Up to move the scale back through time, or drag the horizontal scroll box.

Understanding the Resource Graph View

The Resource Graph view not only shows information about the allocation of the resource per time period, but also shows the maximum available units of the resource in the same time frame. You can see the Resource Graph most effectively by placing the graph in the bottom pane, beneath the Resource Usage view (see Figure 10.29).

When you display the Resource Usage view in the upper pane, the schedule of work per re-source is displayed. To add to or change the rows of information you need, choose Format, Details and turn the field displays to the on or off position. Please refer to Chapter 21, "Formatting Views," for additional Resource Graph formatting options.

To view the Resource Graph view in the bottom pane, follow these steps:

1. Choose View, More Views.

2. Select the Resource Allocation view and choose Apply.

3. Press F6 to activate the bottom pane.

4. Choose View, Resource Graph.

FIG. 10.29

The Resource Graph view gives an overall picture of resource allocation.

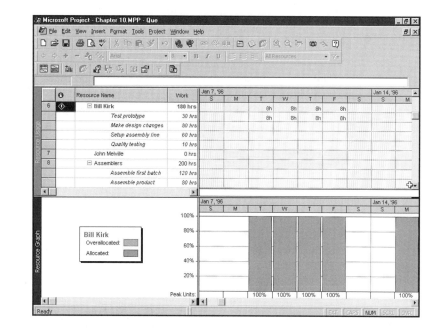

The left half of the Resource Graph view shows the graph legend and resource name. To the right is the timeline that graphically shows the number of units allocated for a resource. The blue bar shows the amount of units allocated. The red bar shows the overallocated units. To display a graph of other values, such as peak units, make sure the graph is the active pane, then choose Format, Details. To display allocation for a different resource, select the resource name in the top pane.

Printing Resource Work and Cost Reports

Several report formats are available to help you monitor and evaluate the scheduled tasks for the resources and resource costs for the project (see Figure 10.30). Reports are covered in more detail in Chapter 23, "Using the Standard Reports."

FIG. 10.30

The Reports dialog box displays available report categories.

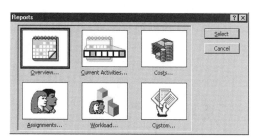

Part III

Ch 10

Reports that reflect resource information are included in the following report categories:

- *Costs* reports provide budget information for the resources as well as for tasks. Special reports are designed to display specific information. One reports only those resources currently over budget, while another displays tasks over budget, and a third monitors the weekly cash flow of the project.

- *Assignments* reports are designed to identify each resource and the tasks to which the resource is assigned. One report design lists only the resources, a second report design adds a timescale for each task, whereas yet a third identifies only overallocated resources. The fourth report format creates a weekly To-Do list for each resource.

- *Workload* reports include a Resource Usage report, which resembles the Resource Usage view. It lists the resources and tasks assigned to each resource along with their work assignment over a time period.

To choose one of these report formats, follow these steps:

1. Choose View, Reports.

2. Choose the report category containing the desired report format.

3. Select the report design.

When you select a report, the report automatically is displayed in the Print Preview window. From this screen, you can zoom the report to see the data close up, choose Page Setup to format the report layout, or choose Print to send the report to the printer.

From Here...

This chapter has presented methods for making resource assignments and discussed assignment consequences. The project plan now needs a careful review to ensure that it meets scheduling, loading, and budgeting goals. The following chapters focus on the techniques for analyzing and modifying the plan.

- Chapter 11, "Resolving Resource Allocation Problems," will give you some techniques for adjusting resource requirements to achieve optimal loading.

- Chapter 12, "Reviewing the Project Plan," will discuss a variety of techniques for investigating other aspects of the project schedule.

- Chapter 20, "Using the Standard Views, Tables, and Filters," and Chapter 23, "Using the Standard Reports," give additional information on resource views and reports for printed output.

Resolving Resource Allocation Problems

When resources are assigned more work than they can complete in a given time period, the project schedule is unrealistic and the actual work on the project will not be exactly as planned. Either some tasks—maybe even the project itself—will not finish on time or not all the tasks will be completed. You need to identify these over-allocations and modify the project plan to eliminate them. This chapter will show you how to recognize resource allocation problems and how to correct them.

Previous chapters have shown you how to define and schedule tasks and how to define and assign resources. You found that creating task dependencies and constraints can make it impossible to meet constraints if the dependencies are honored. When this situation occurs, your project plan is not really workable and has to be adjusted.

Similarly, after you assign resources to tasks, you frequently find that the task schedule has a resource assigned to more than one task at the same time. If the conflicting assignments require more work than the resource can possibly do in the scheduled time period, then the resource is said to be *overallocated*.

What causes resources to be overallocated

Project does not normally consider the other demands on a resource's time when scheduling the resource, so overallocations are likely to happen.

Identify resources that are overallocated

Find out if resources are overallocated, when they are overallocated, and what assignments contribute to the problem.

Review strategies for resolving resource overallocations

Examine the alternatives you should consider for correcting resource overallocations.

Use Microsoft Project 98's special features to analyze and correct allocation problems yourself

The best solutions usually require you to analyze individual cases and make adjustments. Project has a number of tools to help you.

Use Project's Leveling command for a quick but simplistic solution

Project's Leveling command resolves the issue by simply delaying some of the assignments until overallocations are eliminated.

The following sections will show you how to recognize the overallocation problem and find solutions for it. Microsoft Project 98 offers an impressive arsenal of new (and old) tools to help you deal with resource allocation problems.

- Project 98 highlights all overallocated resource names and displays an overallocated indicator next to those that need your attention.

- Recognizing that many *short-term* overallocations are in reality easily resolved by the people doing the actual work, Project 98 lets you define what time period will be considered short-term and reserves the overallocation indicator for the longer-term problems only.

- The new Task Usage view and the revised Resource Usage view allow you to edit the actual time periods when individual resource assignments are scheduled.

- When you call on Project 98 to calculate a solution to the overallocation problem—which is a process called *leveling*—the results are far more sophisticated than in earlier versions. In earlier versions, leveling delays entire tasks, and all resources assigned to those tasks, until the overallocation is resolved. Now, Project 98 can:

  - Limit its changes to the individual resource that is overallocated instead of changing the entire task and all other resources assigned to the task.

  - Split a task at the point where the overallocation occurs and reschedule just the remaining work to a later date to help resolve a resource conflict.

  - Split the rescheduled work assignments for a resource to work around fixed commitments that cannot be changed.

  - Enable you to exempt an individual resource's assignments from being changed by the leveling process, much as you have always been able to exempt an individual task.

  - Enable you to use the Leveling Gantt, a new view that shows task bars for both before and after the leveling operation to let you easily see the effects of leveling on individual tasks.

- Whereas earlier versions of Microsoft Project can only level projects that are scheduled from a Fixed Start Date, Project 98 can also level projects with a Fixed Finish Date.

With these new features, you can resolve resource allocation problems with more real-world relevance than ever before. ■

Understanding How Resource Overallocations Occur

A resource is overallocated when assigned to work more hours during a given time period than the resource has available for work on the project. The number of hours that the resource has available for the project during any time period is determined by two values that you control:

- The *units* of full-time effort that the resource has available to the project, as defined in the Max Units field on the Resource Sheet or the Resource Information dialog box.

> The *working hours* defined for the resource for the time period in the resource calendar on the Resource Information dialog box.

Multiplying the *units* available for the resource by the calendar working hours in a given time period determines the hours of work the resource has available during that time period. Table 11.1 shows several examples of the availability calculation. A single employee resource typically has eight hours available per day and has maximum units available to the project of 100% (one full-time unit). Case A shows that this employee can be assigned up to eight hours of work a day. But, if the employee works only half-time, then the units available is only 50%, and Case B shows that you are limited to assigning up to four hours a day to that resource. Case C shows that the same limitation would result if the employee works full-time but has only four hours of working time on the calendar for the day.

Table 11.1 Determining the Work Hours Available for a Resource in a Time Period

Case	A	B	C
Maximum Resource Units Available	100%	50%	100%
Calendar Working Hours for the Period	8 hrs	4 hrs	8 hrs
Maximum Work Hours Available for the Period	8 hrs	4 hrs	4 hrs

Overallocations generally occur for only two reasons:

> A resource will be overallocated if you assign more units of the resource to a single task than the maximum units available for that resource. For example, if you assign a part-time employee (50% units available) to work full-time (100%) on a task, you would automatically overallocate that resource. You would also automatically overallocate a group or team resource that has five units available (500%) if you assigned six units (600%) of the resource to a task.

> A resource will also be overallocated if you assign the resource to multiple tasks that happen to be scheduled at the same time period and that in combination have more units assigned than the maximum units available. This second case is the most common cause of overallocated resources.

When scheduling tasks for you, Microsoft Project can easily create an overallocated resource by scheduling multiple task assignments at the same time. Before resource assignments are made, Project schedules tasks to start as soon as possible based on:

> The first possible date, as determined by the start of the project and any predecessors for the task

> The earliest date that will leave constraints or deadlines satisfied

> The next available working time on the project base calendar

Part
III

Ch
11

N O T E This explanation and most others in this chapter (except where specifically noted) are worded in terms of projects that are scheduled from a *Fixed Start Date*. Microsoft Project automatically schedules tasks in such projects *As Soon As Possible* in order to achieve the shortest overall duration for the project. If a project is scheduled from a *Fixed Finish Date*, then tasks are automatically scheduled *As Late As Possible* in order to achieve the shortest overall duration for the project. ▪

When you assign a resource to work on the task, Project substitutes the resource calendar for the project base calendar, and schedules the task assignment on the first available date on the resource calendar. However, Project does not normally look to see if the resource is already assigned to other tasks during the times it selects for the new assignment. Because Project ignores existing assignments when scheduling new assignments, it is easily possible for a resource to be overallocated.

T I P The *default* behavior for Project is to ignore other assignments. However, you can change the default and have Project check for other assignments each time it schedules a resource and, if necessary, delay the new assignment until the resource is free to work on it. Before you decide to change this default, however, you should read the rest of this chapter, especially the section "Understanding the Pitfalls of Automatic Leveling."

Identifying Resource Overallocations

Microsoft Project 98 lets you know which resources are overallocated by displaying those resource records in red in any view that displays a resource table. For example, in both the Resource Sheet and the Resource Usage views, overallocated resources will appear in red. In the Resource Sheet in Figure 11.1, three resource rows appear in red: Mel Lloyd, Scott Adams, and Howard Thompson.

Actually, Microsoft Project defines a resource as overallocated if at any moment in time the sum of the units assigned for the resource is greater than the maximum units of the resource available. There is a resource field named Overallocated that contains Yes for resources that are Overallocated and No for those that are not.

The maximum units available is defined on the Resource Sheet or on the Resource Information dialog box in the Max Units available field. Project also maintains a resource field named Peak Units that contains the largest number of assigned units at any minute in the project. If Peak Units is greater than the Max Units available field, then the Overallocated field will be automatically set to Yes, and the resource name will appear in red in a table view.

Figure 11.1 shows the Resource Sheet with both the Peak Units and Overallocated fields displayed to the right of the Max Units field. Each of the first three resources is flagged as overallocated because the Peak Units value exceeds the Max Units value. If the Overallocated field was not displayed, you would still know these resources were overallocated because of the red highlight used for the overallocated resources.

In previous versions of Microsoft Project, as soon as any overallocation is detected, you are warned by a message in the status bar that you have a "leveling" problem. The message text is Level <resource > where *resource* is a resource that is overallocated. You must then go in search of the resource names displayed in red, try to find where in the schedule the problem occurs, and determine what to do about it.

FIG. 11.1

Resource views containing tables show the names of overallocated resources in red.

Overallocated resources in red

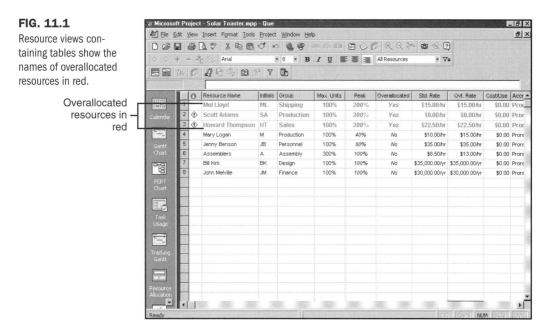

N O T E The terms *level* and *leveling* derive from the need to make changes in the schedule so that the excessive peaks in a resource workload are "leveled out" by redistributing the work to other time periods.

However, not all overallocations really need the project manager's attention. Sometimes the overallocation is a mere technicality. For example, suppose a regular full-time employee is only scheduled to work on two tasks on a given day, and each task will only take an hour to complete. That's only 2 hours of work for the day and is hardly an overallocation for an eight-hour day. But suppose that both tasks have been scheduled by Project to begin first thing in the morning. Then Project would flag the resource as overallocated, because it is scheduled to do two hours of work in one hour. In reality, the resource could easily finish both tasks in the day by delaying one until the other is finished. The project manager may prefer not to be bothered by warnings like this when the overallocation is small enough to be handled by the resource on a day-by-day basis.

To help you focus only on those overallocation cases that you think really warrant your attention, Microsoft Project 98 has introduced a leveling sensitivity setting that is based on the amount of work and the resource's work availability for the time frame. In the example just given, there is a need to do something if we consider only the one-hour time period when the

Part
III

Ch
11

tasks are scheduled (or any minute within that hour). But if we consider the whole eight-hour day, there really is no need for concern. Now you can select a sensitivity time frame for Project to use when evaluating overallocations. Your choices are:

- Minute by minute (minute by minute is the only setting available in prior versions of Project)
- Hour by hour
- Day by day
- Week by week
- Month by month

If you were to select either the minute or hour leveling time frame in the example we have been using, Project would still alert you that the resource needs leveling. However, with a day-by-day or longer timeframe setting, Project would not display the warning about the need for leveling.

The leveling warning itself is no longer a text message in the status bar. Now Project displays a leveling indicator in the Indicator field for any resource with an overallocation judged excessive by the current leveling sensitivity setting. All resources with any overallocation still appear in red on resource tables, but if you don't see the leveling indicator, the overallocation is acceptable within the leveling sensitivity setting.

In Figure 11.1 the resource names Mel Lloyd, Scott Adams, and Howard Thompson appear in red to indicate that there is at least one time period where their workloads exceed their availabilities. Both Scott and Howard have the leveling indicator, and the project manager needs to look at the overallocations for those resources. Figure 11.2 shows the same resources in the Resource Usage view. Instead of emphasizing the resource definition fields, the Resource Usage view emphasizes a timescale with the scheduled activity for each resource broken down into discrete time periods. In this example, the Peak Units and the Work fields are displayed for each day in the timescale.

If you rest the mouse pointer over an indicator, Project displays the meaning of the indicator. In Figure 11.2 you can see the ScreenTip where the mouse is resting over the indicator next to Howard Thompson. The ScreenTip explains that `This resource should be leveled based on a Week by Week setting`.

TIP

You can pause the mouse pointer over a leveling indicator to see a ScreenTip that identifies the leveling sensitivity time frame. This is quicker than opening the Leveling dialog box where the leveling sensitivity is defined.

Mel Lloyd is overallocated because his Max Units is 100%, but he is assigned for 200% units on Tuesday. He does not have a leveling indicator because the leveling sensitivity setting is Week by Week, and Mel has less than 40 hours of work to complete in the week. Although Mel is overallocated, his assignment does not need leveling because he can do the work he has been assigned.

FIG. 11.2

The leveling indicator appears in the Indicator column in resource views with a table, like the Resource Usage view shown here.

Leveling indicator

Indicator ScreenTip

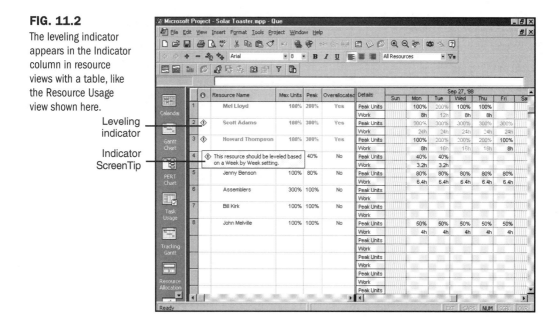

Both Scott Adams and Howard Thompson have far more than 40 hours of work assigned during the week; therefore, on a Week by Week basis, they need leveling.

Viewing Resource Overallocations

To identify all the overallocated resources by name, you need to use one of the three resource views that display a table: the Resource Sheet, the Resource Usage view, or the Resource Allocation view. Figure 11.1 shows the Resource Sheet, and Figure 11.2 shows the Resource Usage view. The Resource Allocation view includes the Resource Usage view and will be discussed more in later sections of this chapter. If a resource is overallocated during any period in the life of the project, the resource name will be highlighted in red in any of these views.

To display the Resource Sheet or the Resource Usage view, choose the View menu, and then either Resource Sheet or Resource Usage. To display the Resource Allocation view, you must use the More Views command.

1. Choose the View menu.
2. Select the More Views command. This will display the More Views dialog box.
3. In the Views list of the More Views dialog box, select Resource Allocation.
4. Click the Apply button to display the selected view.

Filtering Overallocated Resources

If your resource list is extensive, you can filter the resource list to display only those resources with an overallocation. This will display all overallocated resources, not just those with the leveling indicator. In Figure 11.3, the Resource Sheet is filtered for overallocated resources; in this case, only three resource names appear.

Part

III

Ch

11

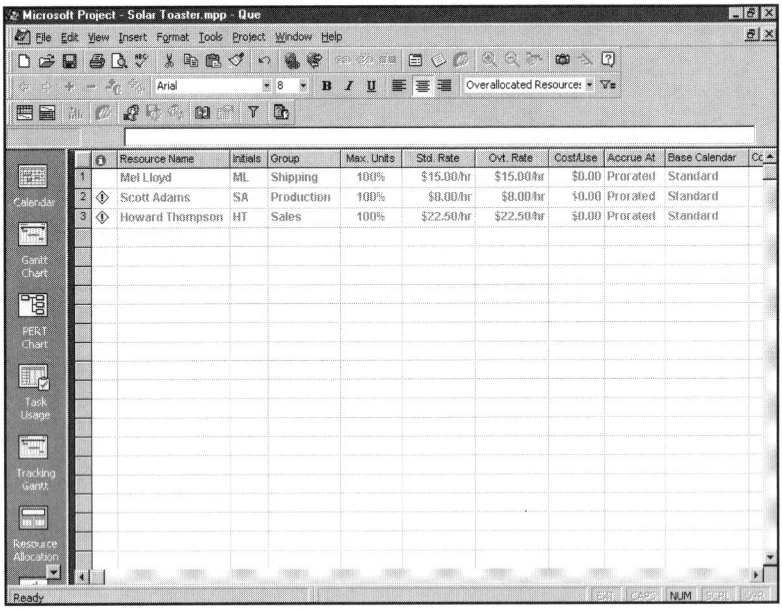

FIG. 11.3

Applying the Over-allocated Resources filter reduces the display to just those resources that have overallocation problems.

To apply the Overallocated filter, select the top pane view if you are in a combination view, and choose Project, Filtered For, Overallocated Resources. Filters affect only the top pane, because the bottom pane is already filtered to show details for the selection in the top pane.

If you were to correct the overallocation problem for one of the resources displayed by the filter, the resource would remain in the display until the filter is applied again. This is because Project filters are not automatically recalculated. You can apply the filter again with the menu, or you can press Ctrl+F3, the key combination that recalculates the current filter.

To remove the filter, choose Project, Filtered For, All Resources, or simply press the F3 function key.

Working with the Resource Usage View

You must use a resource view with a timescale if you want to see assignment data for each time period or to see exactly when a resource overallocation occurs. The Resource Usage view is a standard view that has been enhanced in Microsoft Project 98 to show a great deal more resource assignment information than in earlier versions of Project. In addition to listing all the resources, and highlighting those that are overallocated, you can display rows indented under each resource for all of the resource's task assignments (see Figure 11.4). Furthermore, you can display multiple assignment field values for each of the assignments, and some of the fields can be edited right in the cells of the timescale grid. In Figure 11.4 both the Peak Units and the Work values are displayed for each assignment and summarized for each resource. The cells in the timescale grid break down the assignment values into discrete time periods. Since you can choose the time unit displayed in the timescale, you can zoom in to view the assignment details minute by minute or zoom out to see summaries for months, quarters, or years.

FIG. 11.4

The Resource Usage view allows you to list all assignments under each resource.

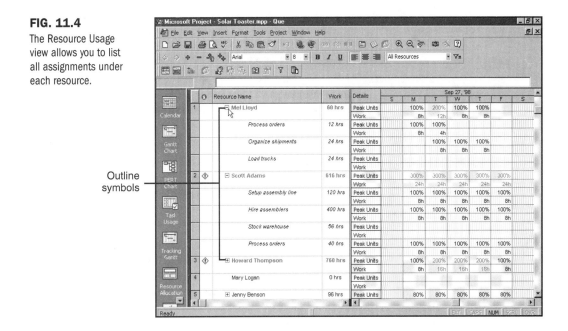

Outline symbols

To display the Resource Usage view, choose <u>V</u>iew, Resource <u>U</u>sage, or choose the Resource Usage icon from the View bar. If you are currently viewing a combination view and want to see the view as a full screen view, press the Shift key as you select the <u>V</u>iew menu or the Resource Usage icon on the View bar.

The Resource Usage view in Figure 11.4 shows the individual assignments for Mel Lloyd and Scott Adams. The individual assignments for Howard Thompson are hidden from view, but they are summarized on the rows for Howard Thompson. You can click the outline symbol that appears to the left of a resource name to hide or display the assignments for that resource. If there are undisplayed assignments, the outline symbol will be a plus sign (see Howard Thompson and Jenny Benson in Figure 11.4). If the assignments are displayed, the outline symbol will be a minus sign (see both Mel Lloyd and Scott Adams in Figure 11.4). If a resource has no assignments, there will not be an outline symbol next to the name (see Mary Logan in Figure 11.4).

You can also use the Hide Assignments tool on the Formatting toolbar to hide or display the assignments for one or more resources that you have selected. To hide or display all assignments, select one of the column headings, like Resource Name, to select all resources, then click the Hide Assignments tool.

For each assignment row in the Resource Usage view, the cells in the timescale show values for assignment fields for the time period spanned by each cell. The cells in the rows for the resource names sum the values in the assignment rows beneath them. If a resource is overallocated during any time period, the resource name will be highlighted in red. Furthermore, the display of the summary data will be highlighted in red in those time periods where an overallocation exists. This allows you to see the exact time periods when overallocations occur.

N O T E If there is an overallocation at any time during the period spanned by a cell, Project 98 will highlight that period's values in red no matter which assignment field values you may choose to display and no matter how far you may zoom out to compress the timescale.

In older versions of Project, the display is highlighted in red only if the value for the field being displayed is greater than the availability for that field for that time period. Thus you would always see Peak Units highlighted when there was an overallocation, but Work values might not be highlighted if the assigned work was not excessive for the time period covered by the cell. In essence, the display in older versions corresponds to the leveling sensitivity concept adopted in Project 98.

The benefit of this change is that you can always locate time periods when overallocations occur in Project 98, but it is sometimes not apparent in earlier versions. If the wrong field values are being displayed, or the time unit is large, you may not see any red highlight in older versions to help you locate the time period for overallocations. ▪

Using the Go To Next Overallocation Tool If you are in a timescale view and have displayed the Resource Management toolbar, you can use the Go To Next Overallocation tool to find the next time period in which a resource has an overallocation. The timescale automatically scrolls to the beginning of the next time period that has an overallocation period detected by the tool. Click the Go To Next Overallocation tool again to find the next overallocation. It will stop on the next task involved in the current overallocation or move on to another date.

If you want to search through the entire project, you must first scroll the timescale to the beginning date of the project. To move the timescale to the beginning of the project, you must first click any cell in the timescale area, then press Alt+Home to move to the beginning date of the project.

If you use the Go To Next Overallocation tool in a view with a resource list, such as the Resource Usage view, the search for overallocated time periods is limited to those tasks to which the selected resource is assigned. If you select a resource name, the Go To Next Overallocation tool will find the next time period during which that resource is overallocated.

If you want to search through the entire project for overallocated resources, select all resources first by clicking one of the column headings in the resource view, and move to the beginning date of the project with the Alt+Home key combination. When you use the Go To Next Overallocation tool, the first time period with an overallocation will be identified, and the first assignment that is associated with an overallocation during this time period will be selected in the resource list.

If you use the Go To Next Overallocation tool in a view with a task list, such as the Gantt Chart or the Task Sheet, the task list will scroll to the first task associated with an overallocation and select that task. Successive use of the Go To Next Overallocation tool selects other tasks assigned to overallocated resources during the same time period. When all tasks for that time period have been identified, the Go To Next Overallocation tool will identify the next time period with an overallocated resource and select the first task for that time period.

Changing the Usage Fields Displayed   The Resource Usage view allows you to display rows for assignments and to choose different field values to display in the timescale grid. Each field value you choose to display will have its own row in the display. If you display assignment rows and four field values, then there will be four rows for each assignment under each resource. The default value displayed in this view is the Work field, the total hours of assigned work per unit of time.

To change the details displayed in the timescale, complete the following steps:

1. Display the Resource Usage view and click anywhere in the timescale grid to activate that part of the view.

2. Choose F_ormat from the menu bar to display, among others, both the Detail S_tyles command and the _Details command. You can also right-click in the timescale grid to display the shortcut menu with both these options. The Detail S_tyles command allows you to choose which field details will appear on the short list displayed by the _Details command. We will describe the Detail S_tyles command first, then use the _Details command to actually display the field value rows.

3. Choose the Detail S_tyles command. The Detail Styles dialog box will open (see Figure 11.5). It has two tab pages: Usage Details and Usage Properties.

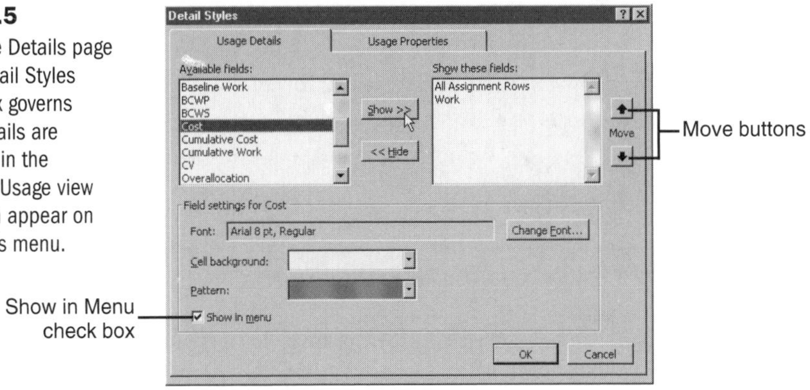

FIG. 11.5

The Usage Details page of the Detail Styles dialog box governs which details are displayed in the Resource Usage view and which appear on the Details menu.

Show in Menu check box

Move buttons

4. On the Usage Details page, select a field to display or add to the Details menu from the list in the A_vailable Fields list box. The list in the Sh_ow These Fields scroll box tells which fields are currently displayed. The first entry in the Sh_ow These Fields list in Figure 11.5 is All Assignment Rows, which is really not a field but is used to turn on and off the display of the assignment rows under each resource name.

5. Select the Show in M_enu check box to add the selected field to the D_etails menu. Note that this does not display the field; it just adds it to the D_etails menu.

6. Click the Show button to add the field to the Show These Fields scroll box and to the current display in the timescale. Click the Hide button to move the item you have selected in the Show These Fields scroll box back to the Available Fields scroll box.

7. You can change the order of the displayed fields with the Move arrows. Select a field name and move it up or down with the arrows.

8. To change the display characteristics of an assignment field row, click the field in one of the boxes at the top of the page and click the Change Font button to select a different font format. Select the Cell Background drop-down box to change the color of the row of cells and the Pattern drop-down box to change the fill pattern for the cells in that row.

9. Choose the Usage Properties tab for additional controls (see Figure 11.6).

FIG. 11.6

The Usage Properties page of the Detail Styles dialog box governs how the details are displayed.

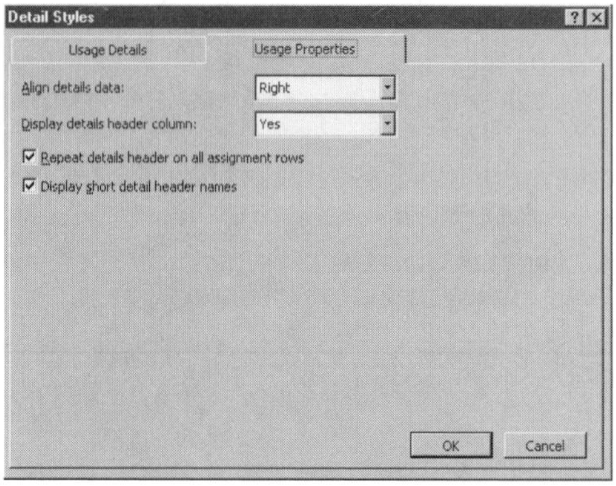

10. Change the cell value's alignment with the list arrow in the Align Details Data list box.

11. Select Yes or No in the Display Details Header Column list box to display row headers for each assignment field row. Without these headers, you cannot tell what the value display represents.

N O T E In combination views, the row headers will *not* display if both panes contain a timescale and only one of the panes contains a Usage view (Resource Usage or Task Usage).

12. Select the Repeat Details Header on All Assignment Rows check box to display the headers on every row in the display, for resource and assignment rows alike. Leave the check box empty if you want the row headers to appear next to the resource name itself and to not be repeated for each assignment row.

13. Select the Display Short Detail Header Names check box to use shorter names for the detail headers. Leave the check box empty to use the long names.

14. When all settings are completed, choose OK to return to the Usage view. The fields displayed in the Show These Fields scroll box on the Detail Styles page will be displayed, and the properties you selected will be in place.

If you right-click anywhere in the timescale grid, the shortcut menu will appear, giving you the option to view the Detail Styles dialog box again (see Figure 11.7) or to change the display status of the fields you placed on the Details menu. Fields with check marks are currently displayed. Click a field to add a check mark or to remove one that is already there.

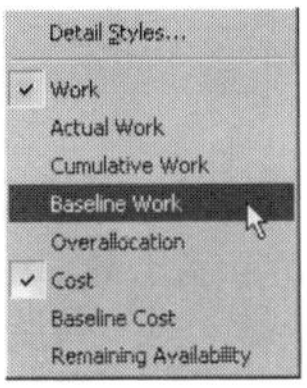

FIG. 11.7
The Details shortcut menu displays check marks for the fields that are currently displayed and lets you change the display by clicking a field name.

Detail Styles...
✓ Work
Actual Work
Cumulative Work
Baseline Work
Overallocation
✓ Cost
Baseline Cost
Remaining Availability

Strategies for Eliminating Resource Overallocations: an Overview

Part III
Ch 11

The existence of overallocated resources in your project plan means that the resources will not be able to complete all of their assignments in the scheduled time period. Some of the assigned work will not be completed within that time period—either the work will not be done or it will have to be done at a later time. If the work is never done, then the full scope of the project delivery will not be realized. If the work is done later, then the project finish date may well be delayed, and you won't meet your final deadline.

You can resolve the overallocation by looking for ways to do either or both of the following:

- You can increase the availability of the resource during the time period in question.
- You can reduce the total work assigned to the resource in that time period.

The following sections present an overview of strategies you might use for achieving each of these objectives. Later sections will show you how to use Microsoft Project to implement each of these possible solutions.

Increasing the Availability of the Overallocated Resource

If you want to try to increase the availability of an overallocated resource, remember that the availability during any time period depends on the settings in both the Resource Availability section of the Resource Information dialog box and the Resource Calendar (the Working Time section).

- The Resource Information dialog box lets you indicate if the resource is Available for the Entire Project or only From and To specific dates. If you have indicated a limited time of availability and a task assignment falls outside that time period, Project will permit the assignment but will show it as an overallocation (because the availability in the assignment period is zero). You may be able to change the availability period for the resource to encompass the overallocated assignment.

■ You can increase the entry in the Max Units Available field if you are able to increase the units of the resource that will be available. This entry is typically 100% (or 1) for individual resources and a larger number than that for group or team resources. If an individual resource has less than 100%, you can see if the resource can work full-time. If a group resource is overallocated, you can increase the number of Units available by adding more workers to the group.

T I P Although part-time workers can be given a Max Units Available setting less than 100% to show that they are part-time, it is generally best to enter the units as 100% and modify their available working hours on the calendar to reflect exactly *when* they are available each day. In that way, they are available 100% during those hours when they are scheduled to work. If the part-time resource uses flexible working hours, however, and works at different times as needed, you could give that resource a regular 8-hour calendar setting and enter 50% in the Max Units field.

If additional workers have to be hired to increase the number of units, you must consider the substantial added costs of searching, hiring, increased payroll, fringe benefits, and all the other factors associated with permanent employment. This solution is generally not feasible unless there is a demonstrated need for a permanent increase in the employment roster. If additional workers can be added as temporary employees, then the added cost is probably less than a permanent hire, but still must be figured into the decision. If the group resource already is made up of non-employees, for example contract workers or workers supplied by a vendor for an out-sourced task, then requesting additional units to work during the peak demand time is not necessarily an added cost to the project. If those workers were going to be paid for completing this task over a longer duration, you can just as easily employ more workers for a shorter time period to meet the demand.

■ If the overallocation is not substantial, you can see if the resource is willing to work more hours during the period of overallocation. One way to show this in Project is to schedule overtime hours for the overallocated resource. Overtime hours are charged to the task at the overtime rate defined for the resource and, therefore, potentially increase the cost of the task since Project substitutes these hours for hours during the regular calendar hours.

■ Alternatively, you can increase the working time temporarily by changing the working hours on the resource calendar during the overallocation time period. Use this alternative instead of assigning overtime when the resource is not paid a premium wage rate for working overtime. You can control exactly when the additional hours are available with this solution, but you cannot specify when overtime hours will be worked in the schedule.

T I P As in earlier releases of Project, you cannot schedule overtime hours for specific dates or time periods. You assign the resource to work overtime on a specific task, and Project schedules the overtime work. In Microsoft Project 98 the schedule spreads the overtime evenly over the duration of the task, whereas in earlier releases all the overtime was scheduled on the last day of the task. When tracking actual work in Microsoft Project 98 you can, however, record the actual overtime work in the time period when the work was done.

Reducing the Workload for the Overallocated Resource

To reduce the workload for a resource in an overallocated period, you can:

- Reduce the total work defined for one or more task assignments during the period
- Reduce the number of tasks assigned to the resource during the period
- Shift the work load for one or more assignments to other periods by changing the contour of the assignment to shift work to later time periods for those tasks

If you reduce the total work defined for a task, that can help ease the overallocation for the resources assigned to the task. This reduction might result from lowering the performance requirements for completing the task, removing unnecessary work or "frills" from the task definition, or reassessing the work estimate for completing the task. But you must consider the effect of this "downscaling" of the project on the scope and goal expectations of the project.

You can reduce the number of tasks assigned to the resource during the overallocated period in several ways:

- You can cancel one or more tasks. This option may reduce the scope of the project's delivered outcome. But, to the extent that the task list included unnecessary elements or "frills," you have some latitude in removing tasks without seriously affecting the project scope.
- You can substitute other resources for the overallocated resource in the assignments for the task. This is frequently the most satisfactory solution for resolving resource overallocations. However, this solution requires more investigative work for the planner.

You can keep the resource assigned to all the tasks if you can postpone or delay the assigned work for some of the tasks to a later period when the resource has more availability for the work. Delaying any of the assigned work in the project schedule naturally extends the duration for the task and may compromise finishing the project on time.

To delay some or all of the work on an assignment, you can try one of the following solutions:

- The traditional delaying technique, called *leveling*, shifts the schedule for one or more tasks to a later date in order to free the overallocated resource to work on higher priority tasks. This may not be a viable option when deadlines are important because delaying tasks may extend the project finish date. If critical tasks are delayed, the project finish date will by definition be delayed. Microsoft Project 98 has made leveling far more sophisticated and flexible.

- You can also delay the start of just one resource's assignment to a task. Other resources may continue to work as scheduled, but this resource will do its part later in the project. Microsoft Project 98 can delay just the overallocated resource's assignment to a task to relieve the overallocation.
- If the resource has already started working on a task, you can split the task to stop work temporarily, thus freeing the resource for other tasks during the overallocation period. Splitting the task will stop work for all resources assigned to the split task.

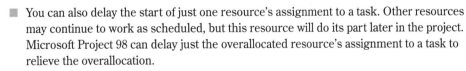

- You can change the assignment contour to shift more of the work to later time periods. The default assignment contour is "flat," which means that work is evenly distributed throughout the duration of the task. You can choose one of several other predefined contours that set higher work loads at later points in a task's schedule. You can also edit the resource's work assignment on each task yourself to reduce the workload during the overallocated time period.

Eliminating Resource Overallocations Yourself

The previous section provided an overview of the possible ways to resolve resource overallocations. This section shows you how to use Microsoft Project's views to analyze the facts and use your own judgment to implement the strategy you think best fits the situation. The last section shows how Microsoft Project's Leveling command can eliminate overallocations using the sole strategy of delaying assignments.

Increasing the Availability of the Overallocated Resource

The first set of strategies revolve around increasing the availability of the resource that is overallocated. After negotiating with the resource, you can use the tools in this section to implement the changes.

The best place to change the availability of a resource is in the Resource Information dialog box because more of the fields that govern availability are accessible there. To display the dialog box, you must be in a view that contains resource data fields, and you must be able to display a record for the resource you want to change. Use either the Resource Sheet, the Resource Usage view alone, or the top pane of a combination view to see all resources listed. The Resource Allocation view places the Resource Usage view in the top pane. After selecting a resource name, click the Resource Information tool to display the Resource Information dialog box.

> **N O T E**   Although resource names seem to appear in the Task Usage view, the records are really *assignment* records, not *resource* records, and the Information tool on the toolbar will display the Assignment Information dialog box instead of the Resource Information dialog box. ■

You can also get to the Resource Information dialog box from a view in the bottom pane of a combination view if the view in the bottom pane contains resource fields. However, you must first select a record in the top pane that is associated with the resource name you want to change. Then the resource name will appear in the bottom pane, and you will be able to select the resource and display the Resource Information dialog box.

> **T I P**   You can access the Resource Information dialog box by double-clicking the resource name in most views where the resource name is displayed. The views where this doesn't work are the Resource Form and Resource Name Form.

Increasing the Resource Availability Settings   To change the dates when a resource is available (assuming that it is not available for the entire project) or to add to the maximum number of available units of a resource, follow these steps:

1. Select the resource name in a view on-screen, as discussed in the introduction to this section.

2. Click the Resource Information tool to display the Resource Information dialog box and choose the General tab page (see Figure 11.8).

FIG. 11.8

Increase the Max Units available in the Resource Information dialog box.

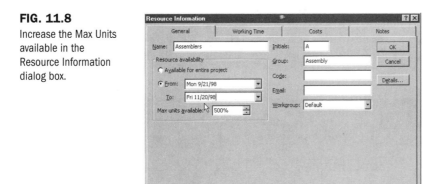

Part

III

Ch

11

3. To change the units available select the Max Units Available field and enter the new value.

4. To increase the range of dates when the resource is available (when Available for Entire Project is *not* selected) move the From date to an earlier date or the To date to a later date. If the resource is only available after a fixed From date (when, for example, that is the date the resource is hired or purchased) and is available from then on, be sure the To date has the letters "NA" to indicate that a fixed end date is not applicable.

5. Choose OK to complete the entry.

Scheduling Overtime for the Resource   You also can schedule overtime hours for the resource to supplement the regular calendar working hours. If you enter overtime hours, Microsoft Project subtracts this number of hours from the total amount of work that was to have been scheduled during the normal working hours defined on the resource calendar. The total work will still be the same, so do not change the total amount of work hours for the task when adding overtime hours. Simply enter the quantity of hours that will be worked overtime. Of course, overtime hours are frequently paid for at premium hourly rates. Using overtime to solve overallocation problems may be a costly method of solving the problem, but not usually as costly as hiring new resources.

In Microsoft Project 98 overtime hours are scheduled over the same duration as the regular (non-overtime) work. When you enter overtime hours for an assignment, Project subtracts those hours from the total work assignment, schedules the remaining regular work hours, and then spreads the overtime hours over the same time period. If the work assignment is contoured, the overtime hours distribution will reflect the same contour.

You can enter overtime on the Task Form or on the Resource Form. In either case, you need to display the Work details to see overtime. If you use the Task Form, you see only one task listed at a time. If you use the Resource Form, all tasks on which the resource is assigned to work are displayed in the Work fields listing, and you can assign overtime to multiple tasks from the same screen.

Figure 11.9 displays the Resource Usage view in the top pane and the Resource Form in the bottom pane with Work details selected. The timephase section of the Resource Usage view has been formatted to display details for Work, Overtime Work, and Regular (non-overtime) Work. In the figure the overtime hours are already calculated for Scott Adams's work on the Process Orders task.

FIG. 11.9

This figure illustrates entering overtime work to solve an over-allocation problem.

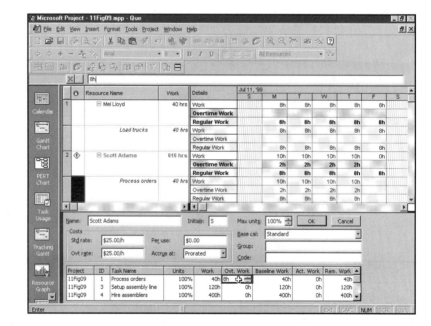

The data from the figure is summarized in Table 11.2. Before adding the overtime, the 40-hour task was scheduled for eight hours a day for five days. When eight hours of overtime were scheduled, the regular work became only 32 hours, and Project scheduled that during the first four days of the week. Then, the overtime was spread out over the same period. Note that total work for each time period includes both regular and overtime hours, so total work has not changed.

Table 11.2   The Effect of Adding Eight Hours of Overtime to the Process Orders Assignment

Details	Before Overtime					After Overtime				
	M	T	W	T	F	M	T	W	T	F
Work	8h	8h	8h	8h	8h	**10h**	**10h**	**10h**	**10h**	0h
Overtime Work	0h	0h	0h	0h	0h	**2h**	**2h**	**2h**	**2h**	0h
Regular Work	8h	8h	8h	8h	8h	**8h**	**8h**	**8h**	**8h**	0h

To enter overtime hours for a task using the Resource Form, follow these steps:

1. Select the pane in which to place the Resource Form. In this example, the bottom pane is used. With the Resource Usage view in the top pane you can just double-click the split box to display the Resource Form (this always works when a resource view is in the top pane).

2. Make the Resource Form the active pane.

3. Choose Format, Details, Work. Or right-click the Resource Form and choose Work from the shortcut menu.

   The Resource Work fields are displayed at the bottom of the form (see Figure 11.9).

4. If the Resource Form was placed in the bottom pane, as it is in this example, you can select the resource in the top pane or use the Next and Previous buttons on the Resource Form until you find the resource. If the Resource Form is in the top pane, use the Next and Previous buttons to select the resource name. Figure 11.9 shows Scott Adams selected in the top pane.

5. Select the task for which you want overtime hours scheduled. In this example, the task selected was Process Orders.

6. In the Overtime Work field, type the amount of overtime work. You must use a number, followed by a time unit. If you don't specify a time unit, Microsoft Project assumes that the time unit is hours. In Figure 11.9, for example, **8h** is entered in the bottom pane for Scott Adams on the Process Orders task.

7. Choose OK to complete the entry.

N O T E   If the resource is paid for overtime work, be sure that the resource doesn't have a zero overtime rate in the cost fields of the Resource Form. Some users mistakenly leave the overtime rate zero if no premium pay exists for overtime hours—if overtime is paid at the same rate as regular hours. If you leave the overtime rate set to zero, however, overtime hours are charged at a zero rate. ▨

Note that Project has spread the overtime evenly among the days of the assignment. You cannot change the assignment per period to specify exactly when the overtime hours are worked.

Part
III

Ch
11

You can specify in Project only which task has the overtime hours applied. You will settle the actual hours with the resources themselves as a separate matter. When you enter the Actual Overtime work, however, you can place it in the time periods when it took place.

Extending the Available Hours on the Resource Calendar If resources work extra hours and the overtime rate is the same as the regular rate, you then can adjust the calendar for the resource to show the extra hours. All regular working hours on the calendar are charged at the standard rate for the resource.

If only certain resources work the added hours, make the change on the individual resource calendars. If the added hours are worked by all resources, you can make the change on the base calendar (and on all base calendars used for resources in the project).

To extend the normal working hours for the resource, follow these steps:

1. Display the Resource Information dialog box for the resource and choose the Working Time tab. Alternatively, you can choose Tools, Change Working Time from the menu and use the For drop-down list to select the resource whose hours you want to extend.

2. Select the date or dates on which you want the extra hours worked.

3. Enter the extra time in the Hours text boxes.

4. Click OK to close the dialog box and execute the changed hours.

Figure 11.10 shows Scott Adams's resource calendar modified to extend his hours during the week of July 11, 1999 by adding two hours a day, starting at 6 p.m.

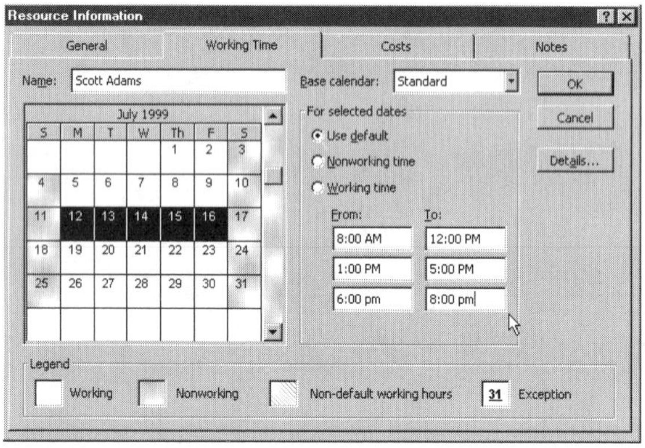

FIG. 11.10
You can increase the working hours on the calendar to extend a resource's availability.

◆ **TROUBLESHOOTING**

When I try to select Tools, Change Working Time, the Change Working Time command is grayed out. If Change Working Time is grayed out (unavailable) make sure the upper pane of a combination view is active. As an alternative you can click any Resource field that is visible, in either the top or bottom pane, and click the Resource Information tool on the Standard toolbar to view the Resource Information dialog box.

TIP To select nonadjacent days on a calendar, use the Ctrl key when clicking the days.

Reducing the Workload of the Overallocated Resource

Coming from the other side, instead of increasing the availability of the resource that is overallocated, we can look for ways to reduce the demands on the resource during the overallocated period. We can cancel non-essential tasks, reassign tasks to other resources, or delay one or more assignments until the resource has time to work on them. We will first look at the Resource Allocation view, which is an efficient view to use for all these strategies.

 Using the Resource Allocation View to Substitute Resources   The Resource Allocation view provides a good starting point for tackling the problem of reducing the demand for an over-allocated resource. This view has its own tool on the Resource Management toolbar, offering easy access, or you can access it by choosing View, More Views and choosing Resource Allocation from the Views list. Once it is selected, click the Apply button to display the view.

 This composite view shows the names and task assignments of all resources in the top pane, highlights overallocated resources in red, and displays the leveling indicator for those tasks that need attention. The bottom pane displays the Leveling Gantt, a new view in Microsoft Project 98, which shows the tasks to which the selected resource name is assigned during any period on the timescale. The Leveling Gantt has a specially formatted Gantt Chart that will be especially helpful when we discuss leveling resource assignments.

You can use the Go To Next Overallocation tool in either pane to pinpoint overallocated re-source assignments. In the top pane, the Go To Next Overallocation tool identifies *resources* that are overallocated. In the lower pane, the Go To Next Overallocation tool identifies *tasks* that are associated with an overallocation of the resource you selected in the top pane.

You can use this view to remove a task assignment from an overallocated resource if you do not yet know which other resource will replace the overallocated resource. You can also use this view to redefine the task duration if that is your choice for reducing the demand for the over-allocated resource. The next section will cover using this view to reassign a task to another resource.

If you want to remove an assignment from a resource without finding another resource to take its place, you can simply select the assignment and choose Edit, Delete Assignment (or press the Delete key). The assignment will disappear from under the resource and will reappear in the Unassigned category at the top of the Resource Usage view. You can move the assignment to another resource later. You can also select the row for the assignment and drag the assign-ment to the Unassigned group.

If you want to redefine the duration for a task, select the overallocated resource in the top pane; then select the task in the bottom pane. Either double-click the task or use the Task Informa-tion tool to display the Task Information dialog box.

Part

III

Ch

11

Substituting Underused Resources for Overallocated Resources   Probably the most conventional method of dealing with the problem of overallocated resources is to find substitute resources to take some of the load off the overallocated resources. To use this approach in a cost-effective manner, you need to consider a number of things, including the following:

- *The list of overallocated resources and their current work loads per time period.* This tells you when the overallocations occur. These resources are identified in the Resource Usage view, the top pane of the Resource Allocation view.

- *The tasks that each overallocated resource is currently assigned to work on during the periods of overallocation.* This identifies the tasks for which you should seek substitutes. These tasks are also identified in the Resource Usage view.

- *The total work commitment for each of the tasks for which resources may be substituted.* This helps you decide which of two tasks to give to a substitute and which to keep for the overallocated resource. You can give the task that involves the most total work to the cheaper resource to keep costs low. The Work field is displayed by default in the Resource Usage view.

- *The availability of other resources during the overallocated time periods.* This helps you find resources that may be used as substitutes. Though not displayed by default in the Resource Usage view, the Remaining Availability is one of the Details you can choose to display in the timescale grid. Because the bottom pane of the Resource Allocation view has a timescale, the detail labels will not be displayed. But you can assign a distinctive format to any of the details to help identify those values easily. In the example that follows (see Figure 11.12), the Remaining Availability has been formatted in **bold underlining** to distinguish it from the Work field.

- *The standard rate cost for using each of the resources.* This tells you the cost of substituting other resources for those currently assigned to the tasks. Though not in the default display of the table in the Resource Usage view, the Standard Rate field can be added as a column in the table. In Figure 11.12, it is added to the right of the Work field.

- *The skill level of other resources available to do the work and the time it may take them to learn the tasks that need to be done.* Comparing skill levels of resource substitutes can be used to reassess how long the assignment will take and how many units of the substitute resource should be assigned. This is not a standard field in Microsoft Project, but you can customize one of the resource text fields to hold this data and then display it in the table on the Resource Usage view for reference when reassigning tasks.

It is certainly not required that you add the information suggested in the previous list (standard rate, remaining availability, and skill rating), but the additional information promotes more cost-effective assignments.

Since the default table for the Resource Usage view is the Usage table, you can add the Standard Rate field to that table. The following steps show the quickest method of adding this column:

▶ **See** "Customizing Views, Tables, and Filters," **p. 741**

1. Click the column heading for the Work column. In this example, we will insert a column to the left for the Standard Rate field.

2. Choose Insert, Column to display the Column Definition dialog box (see Figure 11.11).

3. Type an **s** in the Field Name field to jump to the field names in the list that start with an "S," and Standard Rate will appear since it is the first "S" field in the list. Click Standard Rate or press Enter.

4. Select the Title text box and type a shorter name. Std.Rate is used in this example.

5. Click the OK button to finish defining the new column.

6. If necessary, adjust column widths and the vertical divider bar so you can see both the Std.Rate and Work columns.

Displaying details in the Resource Usage timescale is described earlier in this chapter in the section "Working with the Resource Usage View." See that section for instructions on displaying and formatting the Remaining Availability field in the timescale. The resulting view will be similar to the one in Figure 11.12.

Part

III

Ch

11

StdRate field

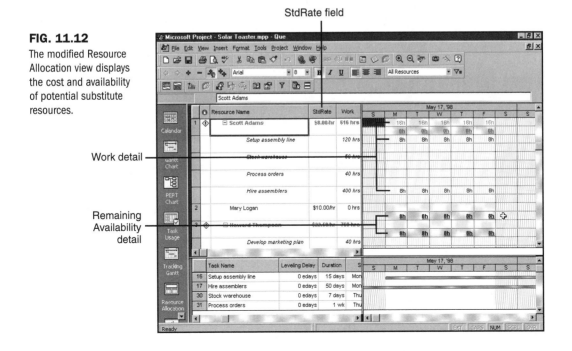

FIG. 11.12

The modified Resource Allocation view displays the cost and availability of potential substitute resources.

Work detail

Remaining Availability detail

To substitute another resource for one of the assignments of an overallocated resource, first select the overallocated resource in the top pane. Use the Go To Next Overallocation tool to find the next time period when the resource is overallocated.

Decide which task will be reassigned to another resource and select that task in the lower pane. In Figure 11.12, the two tasks in conflict are Setup Assembly Line and Hire Assemblers. Both Mary Logan and Howard Thompson show available time, at least during the period shown in this figure. You should use the Zoom Out tool to see if Mary or Howard is available for the whole duration of one of the tasks in question. In fact it appears that both Mary and Howard are free for the duration of the Setup Assembly Line task.

Mary's Standard Rate is less than Howard's is, so it is more cost-effective to substitute Mary for Scott.

After a task and resource combination is selected, you can use the Resource Assignment dialog box to replace one resource with another:

1. Select the task for the substitution in the lower pane. In this example the task will be Setup Assembly Line (see Figure 11.13).

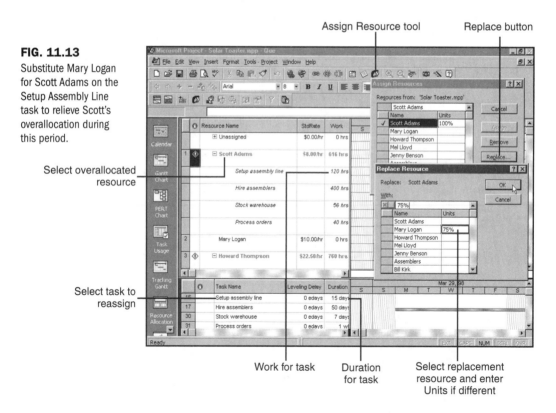

FIG. 11.13

Substitute Mary Logan for Scott Adams on the Setup Assembly Line task to relieve Scott's overallocation during this period.

2. Click the Resource Assignment tool to display the Resource Assignment dialog box. (You can also use Alt+F8 to open this dialog box.)

3. First, select the resource you want to replace (Scott Adams) and click the Replace button. Notice the slight difference in the dialog box (refer to Figure 11.13). The words Replace and With have been added at the top.

4. Select the name of the resource that you want to assign as a substitute.

5. Change the Units assigned if there is a difference in skill levels. Mary Logan is presumed to be more efficient than Scott Adams in this example, and she can do the same task with 75-percent effort compared to Scott's 100-percent effort. Consequently, the Units is set to 75% for the new assignment.

6. Choose OK to complete the substitution.

NOTE Be careful when working in the Assign Resources dialog box. It will appear that your substitution was not made because the dialog box is still open, and the resource you were making substitutions for is still listed. Notice, however, that the list of tasks in the Gantt Chart is different now than it was earlier. The task whose resource was replaced is no longer in the list. If you choose Mary Logan's name in the Resource Usage view, you will see that she has a new task. The Resource Assignment dialog box will actually stay open until you specifically close it. ■

Figure 11.14 shows the schedule after substituting Mary Logan for Scott Adams. Scott's workload is reduced, and he is no longer overallocated in this period. Mary's workload is increased, but due to the 75-percent effort assigned, she is not working full-time on the task. The task's duration has not changed, but the total work on the task has fallen from 120 hours to 90 hours due to the fact that Mary can complete the same task with 75 percent of the effort.

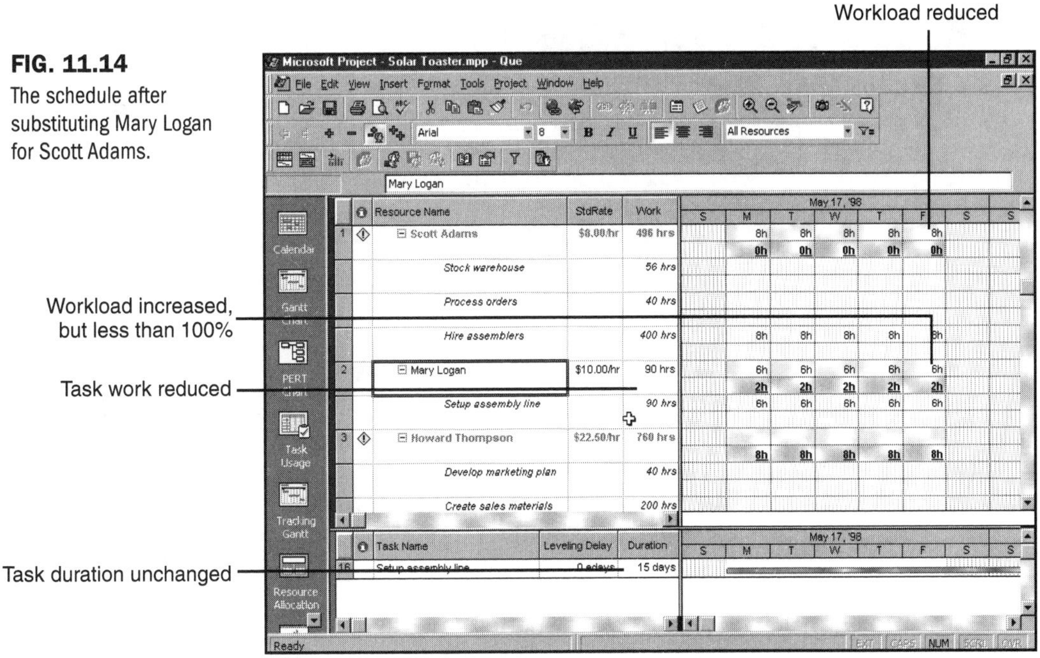

FIG. 11.14
The schedule after substituting Mary Logan for Scott Adams.

Workload reduced

Workload increased, but less than 100%

Task work reduced

Task duration unchanged

Once the new assignment has been added to the replacement resource, you can modify the assignment with the Assignment Information dialog box. Select the assignment row in the top pane and click the Assignment Information tool.

If Mary Logan were to work full-time on the new task assignment, she could finish the task sooner and thereby reduce the task duration. In Figure 11.15 the Assignment Information dialog box is used to change her Units to reflect 100%. For this illustration, the Assignment Information dialog box shows both how the change was made and the effect it had on values in the schedule. After the change, the task work is still 90 hours, but the duration has fallen from 15 days to 11.25 days.

FIG. 11.15

Make changes in individual assignments with the Assignment Information dialog box.

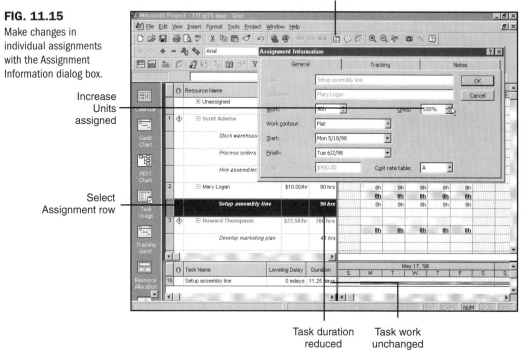

This example has attempted to show that using the data, views, and tools of Microsoft Project 98 to find and resolve resource overallocations gives you the opportunity to *optimize* the solution to the problem, where optimizing means that you examine many factors and make choices that solve the problem in a cost-effective, efficient manner. Substituting resource assignments is generally the most effect approach to resolving resource overallocations. The drawback is the time it takes to analyze the situation and reach a decision.

Resolving Overallocations by Delaying Assignments

If resource overallocation is the result of scheduling multiple tasks at the same time, you can delay one or more task assignments to level or spread out the demands on the resource over a longer period of time, and thereby reduce the demand in currently overallocated periods. You can delay assignments yourself by examining the schedule and selecting the assignments to delay, or you can have Microsoft Project choose the assignments to delay—either on your command or automatically as task assignments are added to the schedule. This section shows you how to level assignments yourself, on a case-by-case basis. Using Project's Leveling command is reserved for a later section.

If you choose to delay assignments yourself, there are several ways you can go about it—most of which are new with this release of Microsoft Project.

- You can use the Delay field of the task database to enter a delay in the start date for a task, thus delaying all assignments to that task.

- If work on a task is scheduled to have started already when the overallocation begins, you can split the task at that point and resume the task when the overallocated resource is available again. Of course, other resources assigned to the task will have their assignments split also.

- You can use the Assignment Delay field to delay the start of the assignment for just the resource that is overallocated, leaving other resources' assignments for the task unchanged.

- Instead of splitting the task, and all assignments, you can split just the assignment of the overallocated resource, leaving other resource assignments unchanged.

- Instead of delaying *all* the work on the overallocated resource's assignment, you can merely *reduce* the hours assigned during the period of overallocation and increase the hours at a later period. This is called *contouring* the assignment and can be done by manually editing the assigned work in each period or by choosing one of the predefined contour patterns to apply to the assignment.

Delaying the Task Use the Resource Allocationview when leveling resource work loads manually. With the Resource Usage view in the top pane to help you select the overallocated resources, the bottom pane displays the Leveling Gantt with the Leveling Delay field in the table next to the task name. The Delay field is usually zero, but if you enter an amount of time in the field, then Project delays the start of the task, and therefore all assignments to the task, by the amount of that delay value. You can enter delay amounts directly in the field in this view.

Delay amounts are shown in elapsed time. Elapsed time ignores the distinction between working time and nonworking time on calendars. Using elapsed time makes it easier for you to estimate the amount of time you should enter in this field. You can count the time units in the timescale of the Gantt Chart and enter that number without having to check to see if any of those units fall on nonworking days.

Part
III
Ch
11

The Delay table also includes the Successors field to give you information about what tasks are directly affected if you delay the selected task. You must scroll the columns in the table to see the Successors field. The task bars display the names of assigned resources to the right of the bar (see Figure 11.16). The Leveling Gantt shows the amount of any *free slack* (the amount of time between the end of a task and the start of a successor task) as a thin bar extending beyond the bottom edge of the task bar. You can delay a task by as much as the free slack, without affecting the scheduling of other tasks. Of course, if you delay tasks beyond the free slack, then successor tasks are also delayed; if you delay a task beyond the total slack, the whole project is delayed.

N O T E　*Free slack* is the amount of time that a task can be delayed without delaying successor tasks. *Total slack* is the amount of time that a task can be delayed without delaying the project. ▪

FIG. 11.16

The Leveling Gantt shows resource names to the right of task bars and includes a thin bar for free slack to the right of the bar.

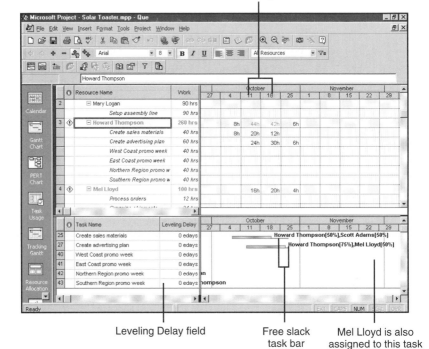

As shown in Figure 11.16, Howard Thompson is an overallocated resource in the weeks of October 11 and 18. Selecting his name in the top pane causes the tasks to which he is assigned to appear in the bottom pane. After using Alt+Home (to move to the beginning of the project), click the Go To Next Overallocation tool to locate the first time period during which Howard Thompson is overallocated. The first overallocation occurs the week of October 11 when tasks

25 and 27 overlap. By zooming out to compress the timescale, you get a more comprehensive picture of the situation. You can see that there are other resources assigned to these tasks as well.

One way to eliminate this overallocation is to delay the start of the Create Advertising Plan task. In Figure 11.17 the Leveling Delay has been set to 9 edays (9 elapsed days). As a result, the tasks no longer overlap, and Howard Thompson has no overallocation during this period. The Leveling Gantt displays this bar preceding the task bar to show the amount of the delay. Since the entire task was delayed, the assignment for the other assigned resource was delayed also. This could create an overallocation for that resource.

FIG. 11.17

The Leveling Gantt shows the amount of the delay as a thin bar to the left of the main task bar.

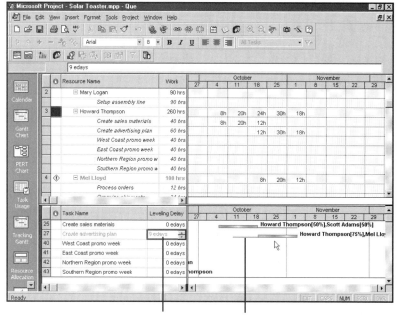

Delay value   Delay bar

Part

III

Ch

11

You can use Undo (Ctrl+Z) immediately after entering a delay amount to restore the previous values to the delay field entries. You also can remove a delay by entering a zero in the delay field. Note that you can't delete a value and then leave the entry blank. If there are many delay values to be cleared, you may want to use the Clear Leveling menu command. To use the menu to return the delay values to zero for a single task or group of tasks, follow these steps:

1. Select the tasks for which you want to reset the delay to zero. Click and drag to select adjacent tasks. Press Ctrl while clicking to select nonadjacent tasks.

2. Choose Tools, Resource Leveling.

3. From the Resource Leveling dialog box, click Clear Leveling. The Clear Leveling dialog box appears (see Figure 11.18).

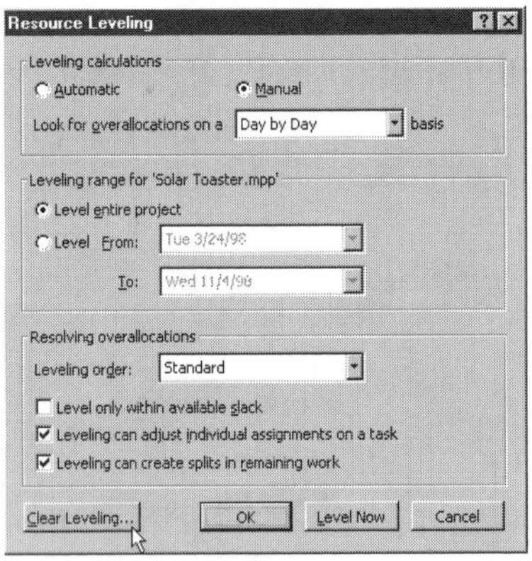

FIG. 11.18

The Clear Leveling dialog box resets the values in the Delay field to zero for all tasks or for selected tasks.

4. Choose the Selected Tasks option to change the values for only the tasks that you selected. If you want to remove all delay values for all tasks, use the Entire Project option.

5. Choose OK. All tasks with nonzero delay values are reset to zero delay.

Splitting a Task

In the preceding example, all work on the task was delayed to clear the overallocation. If one of the conflicting task assignments has already started, you can split the ongoing task and let it start again when the resource is free to continue working. In Figure 11.19 the Create Sales Materials task was split until after the Create Advertising Campaign task was completed. Notice the contour indicator in the Indicator column for the Create Sales Materials assignment in the top pane. There would be a similar indicator for the other resources assigned to the split task. And also notice that Howard Thompson no longer is overallocated during this period. However, other resources affected by this change may now be overallocated.

To split a task in the Leveling Gantt Chart, follow these steps:

1. Activate the pane with a task view, in this case the Leveling Gantt in the lower pane.

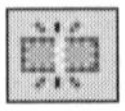

2. Click the Split Task tool to activate the Split Task information box. The information box will reflect the task over which the mouse pointer is located as you move around the screen and will indicate the time at which the split will occur if you were to click at that moment. Do not click anywhere now until you are in position to click the task bar you want to split.

3. Click the task bar you want to split at the point where you want the split to occur.

4. Drag the split part of the task you want to reschedule to a new start date.

TIP You will find it easier to be precise with the split and with dragging the part of the task to its new start date if you zoom in to the time unit most appropriate for selecting the split. When dragging part of the task to a new date, if the destination date is off the screen, drag the pointer just beyond the edge of the screen slowly and the timescale will scroll until you reach the destination.

FIG. 11.19
When two tasks contend for the same resource, you can split one task around the other.

Contour indicator

Split bar

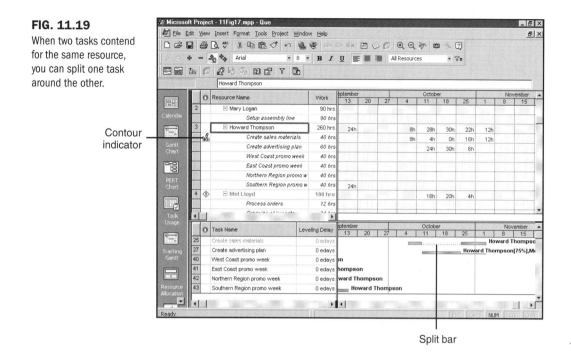

To remove a split in a task, simply use the mouse to drag part of the task toward the part you want to remain stationary. When they touch, Project will remove the split and rejoin the tasks.

Delaying Individual Assignments

When tasks have multiple resources assigned to them, it is better to resolve overallocations for just one of the resources by changing the assignment for just that resource, leaving the other resources unchanged. This section will show you how to delay individual assignments for tasks.

Returning to the previous example, instead of delaying the Create Advertising Plan task as we did in Figure 11.17, we will delay Howard Thompson's assignment to that task. But, we must first find out when his assignment on the other task ends, then delay his assignment to start the next day. To see the dates for an assignment, select the assignment and click the Resource Information tool. The Assignment Information dialog box (see Figure 11.20) lets you view or edit the Start and Finish of an assignment. In this case, the task finishes on 10/20/98. We will set the start date for the other assignment to the following day, 10/21/98.

To delay the start of an assignment, follow these steps:

1. Select the assignment in the Resource Usage or Task Usage view.

2. Click the Assignment Information tool or choose Project, Assignment Information. You can also double-click the assignment row. The Assignment Information dialog box will appear (see Figure 11.21).

3. Enter the delayed start date in the <u>S</u>tart field or click the date control and select the date from the calendar.

4. Click OK to complete the entry.

FIG. 11.20

Use the Assignment Information dialog box to view information about an assignment.

Select assignment

View finish date

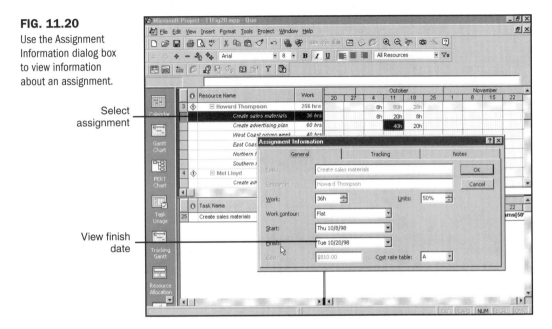

FIG. 11.21

Use the Assignment Information dialog box to change the start or finish dates for individual assignments.

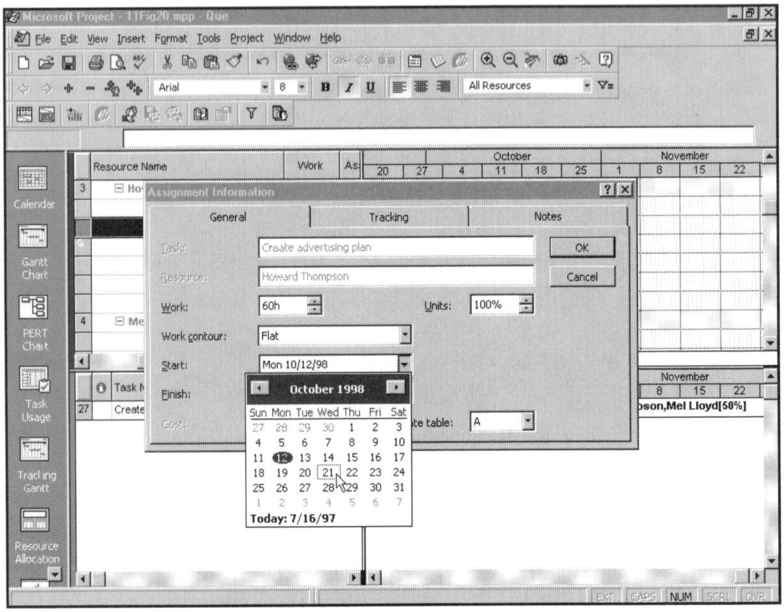

Figure 11.22 shows the effect of delaying Howard Thompson's assignment. The original cell for the start of his assignment now has "0h" in it, and Howard Thompson is no longer overallocated. You can also see that Mel Lloyd's assignment information for the same task at the bottom of the grid has not changed. Mel still starts the week of the 11th.

FIG. 11.22

The time-phased data in the Resource Usage view shows the delay of the assignment for one resource without a delay for the other resource.

"0h" inserted for Howard Thompson

Mel Lloyd still starts on the same date

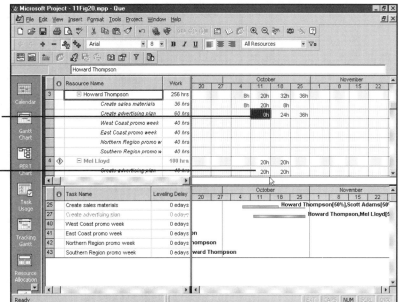

Removing assignment delays is not as straightforward as removing task delays. When you delay an assignment with the Start field of the Assignment Information dialog box, Project translates the difference in the previous start date and the one you enter into an *assignment delay* and stores that value in the Assignment Delay field.

The Assignment Delay field is not on any standard table, and the Clear Leveling command does not reset assignment delays to zero. Perhaps the easiest method to use if you want to remove the delay is to display the Assignment Delay field in the Resource Usage or Task Usage view.

You can insert a column for the Assignment Delay by clicking the column heading for the Work field and then choosing Insert, Column. For the Field Name, choose Assignment Delay (see Figure 11.23). Click the Best Fit button to widen the column for the title and close the dialog box.

You may need to adjust the vertical divider bar so you can see all of the new column. Note that the task you delayed has a non-zero value in it (see Figure 11.24). To remove the delay, type a zero or use the spin control to select zero. Do not press the Delete key, for that will delete the assignment. As you can see, having this field available is an alternative to entering assignment delays in the Assignment Information dialog box.

Part

III

Ch

11

FIG. 11.23
Use the Column
Definition dialog box to
define a new column in
a table.

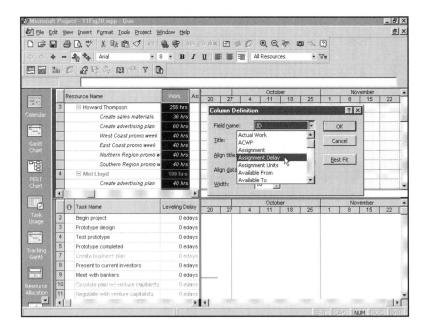

CAUTION

Do *not* press the Delete key to clear a field in an assignment row. Like task tables and resource tables, the Delete key removes the row that has the selection.

N O T E The Assignment Delay field only accepts zero or positive numbers for projects that are scheduled from a fixed start date. It only accepts zero or negative numbers for projects that are scheduled from a fixed finish date. ▓

T I P If you have many assignment delays to remove, it would be worth your while to design a filter to display only those tasks where the Assignment Delay field is not equal to zero. Using Not Equal to Zero instead of Greater Than Zero will allow the filter to serve both projects with positive delay values (scheduled from a fixed start date) and projects with negative delay values (those scheduled from a fixed finish date).

▶ **See** "Creating Custom Filters," **p. 754**

Splitting Individual Assignments

In Figure 11.19 we split the Create Sales Materials task to resolve an overallocation problem. Now we will split the assignment to that task for the resource that is overallocated, thus leaving other assigned resources on their existing schedule. To split an assignment you must view either the Resource Usage view or the Task Usage view and edit the time-phased data in the cells to insert a gap with no work into the existing assignment.

FIG. 11.24

You can use the Assignment Delay field in a table to enter and remove assignment delays.

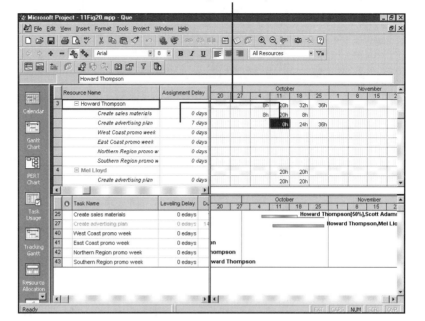

Assignment delay

In Figure 11.25 the Zoom In tool has been used to view individual days. The cell is selected where the split in the Create Sales Materials task will occur. You can create the split by choosing Insert, Cell from the menu or by pressing the Insert key. The contents of that cell will be shifted to the right, and all cells to the right of the insertion point will be shifted also.

> **CAUTION**
>
> If you type a zero into an assignment cell, you will create a split in the assignment, but the work scheduled for that day will be lost.

In Figure 11.26, you can see that the Insert key has been pressed three times, shifting work after the split further out into the future. The task bar in the Gantt Chart does not show a split because other resources are continuing to work during the split period for this assignment. The total work for the assignment has not changed. Notice the contour indicator on the assignment row, indicating that the time-phase values for the assignment have been edited.

TIP To select a series of assignment cells, hold down the Shift key as you use the arrow key to extend the selection, or after selecting the first cell, hold down the Shift key as you click the last cell to select. You can then press the Insert key to shift work assignments past the last selected cell.

Cell selected to start split

FIG. 11.25

Select the cell where the split in the assignment will be and press the Insert key.

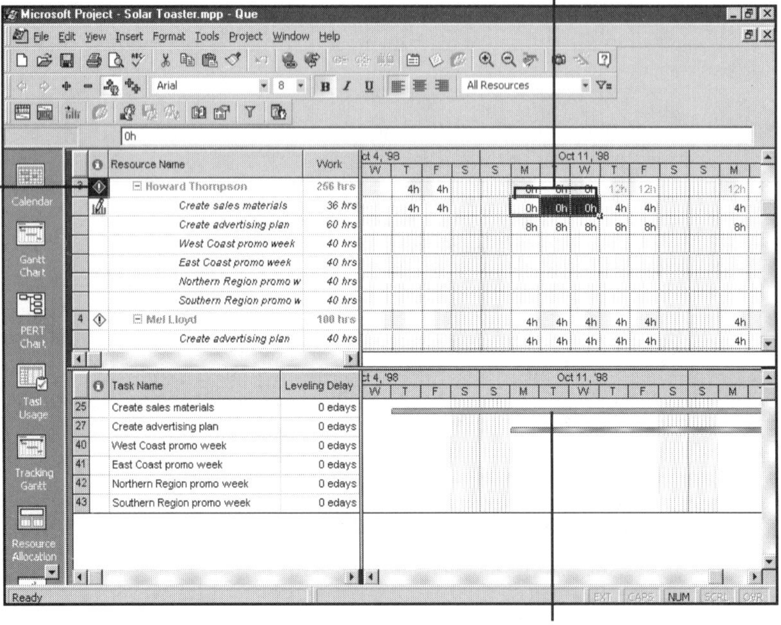

Create sales materials begins

Create advertising plan begins

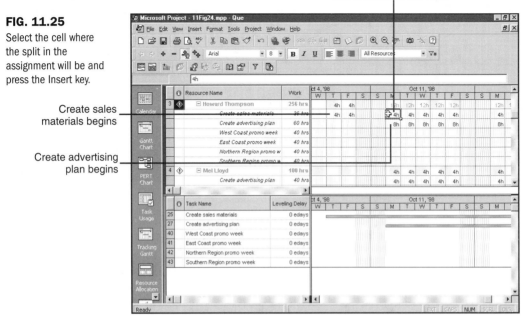

Split in the assignment

FIG. 11.26

The split appears as cells with zero work in the assignment row.

Contour indicator

Task Gantt shows no split

To remove the splits in an assignment, select the cell or cells you want to remove and press the Delete key. Unfortunately there is no easy way to identify those assignments that have been edited, other than the existence of the contour indicator on those assignment rows.

Project Can Level Overallocated Assignments for You

Instead of delaying, or *leveling* individual tasks and assignments on your own, you can also have Project calculate task delays to remove resource overallocations. If the project is scheduled from a fixed Start Date, Project adds *positive* delays to tasks to remove overallocations. If the project is scheduled from a fixed Finish Date, Microsoft Project 98 adds *negative* delays to tasks to remove overallocations. A negative delay causes a task to start *earlier*, and the effect of leveling on a fixed Finish Date project is to schedule the Start date for the project sooner. Earlier versions of Microsoft Project do not level projects with fixed finish dates.

T I P Do not attempt to use the Leveling command until after you enter all the tasks and all the information about each task and resource. If you do use leveling prior to entering all information, you will need to repeat the leveling operation after adding more tasks or redefining resources and resource assignments to accurately reflect the changes.

Configuring the Settings in the Resource Leveling Dialog Box

There are a number of settings you should confirm or change before using Project's Leveling command. Choose Tools, Resource Leveling to open the Resource Leveling dialog box with all the choices for leveling functions provided by Microsoft Project (see Figure 11.27). There are several new settings in this dialog box that affect how Microsoft Project performs its leveling command. The leveling indicator that displays on resource tables depends on your selection in the Look for Overallocations On A list box. As you change this selection, the red highlight for overallocated resources will not be affected, but the leveling indicator appears less often if you select larger time units. Thus, if you increase the time basis from Day by Day to Week by Week, some leveling indicators may disappear.

Table 11.3 outlines the choices in the Resource Leveling dialog box and provides a brief description of each choice.

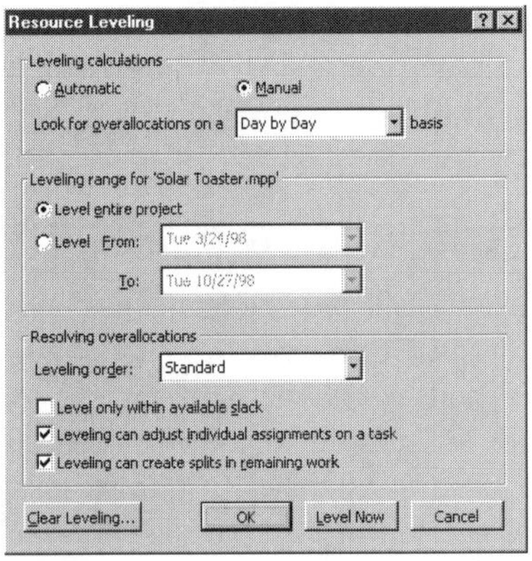

FIG. 11.27

The Resource Leveling dialog box has many new settings that determine how Project calculates the schedule when it does leveling calculations for you.

Table 11.3   The Leveling Options

Option	Description
Automatic	Instructs Project to level tasks the moment one or more overallocated resources is detected. Automatic leveling takes place as you enter the tasks into the project.
Manual	Leveling is executed only when you choose Tools, Resource Leveling, Level Now. Manual is the default status for leveling.
Look For Overallocations On A x Basis	This setting determines the timescale sensitivity of leveling calculations. The choices in this drop-down list box are: Minute by Minute, Hour by Hour, Day by Day, Week by Week, and Month by Month.
Level Entire Project	With this option, Project searches for overallocations that need leveling from the beginning to the end of the project. This is the only option in earlier versions of Project. This choice does not keep you from choosing to level just selected resources or all resources.
Level From, To	With Microsoft Project 98, you can limit the date range that Project scans for overallocations to be corrected. Overallocations outside this date range are allowed to remain.

Option	Description
Leveling Order	This option provides three choices for establishing how Project decides which of several tasks to delay when the tasks cause a resource overallocation conflict. The choices are ID Only, Standard, and Priority, Standard. A description of these choices follows this table.
Level Only Within Available Slack	If this box is selected, tasks are delayed only within the amount of total slack, and the finish date of the project is not delayed. With this constraint, the leveling operation may not resolve the overallocation problem. If you clear this box, and no task constraints exist to serve as impediments, Project can resolve the resource overallocation through leveling, though usually with a delay in the finish date of the project.
Leveling Can Adjust Individual Assignments on a Task	With this new feature, Microsoft Project 98 can delay only the work assignments of the resources that are overallocated on a task. Other resources are not affected. The task duration is increased because the work effort is more spread out.
Leveling Can Create Splits in Remaining Work	If a resource assignment is delayed, Project can split the remaining work into pieces that can fit into available time slots for the resource, thus working around later task assignments that have constraints.

The Leveling Order drop-down list box has three possible values, as described in the following list:

- *ID Only.* If the ID number is the only basis for selecting which of several tasks will be delayed, then tasks with higher ID numbers are always delayed before tasks with lower ID numbers. If the task list is created in chronological order—with earlier tasks listed at the top of the list and with one sequence of tasks leading to the finish date—the ID Only scheme essentially delays tasks with the later start dates. Delaying the tasks with later start dates minimizes the number of successor tasks affected by imposing delays.

- *Standard.* The Standard order, which is the default leveling order for Microsoft Project, uses five factors to determine which of several tasks is to be leveled first. One of those factors is the Priority rating which you can assign to tasks. In the Standard order, your Priority rating has relatively less weight than most of the other factors.

Part
III

Ch
11

■ *Priority, Standard.* The same factors considered in the Standard order are used for the Priority, Standard order. Primary weight is given to the Priority assignment of each task (a factor which you can control).

In deciding which of two tasks is delayed and which is left untouched, both the Standard and Priority, Standard orders use the same set of five factors, the difference lying only in the greater weight assigned to the tasks' Priority value in the Priority, Standard order. The factors, listed in descending order of importance, are:

1. *Predecessor.* Tasks that do not have dependencies are picked before those that have dependencies.

2. *Amount of total slack.* Tasks with more total slack are chosen before those with less slack.

3. *Start date.* Tasks that start later are delayed before those that start earlier.

4. *Priority value.* You can raise or lower each task's priority value in the selection of those to delay. The lower priority tasks are chosen for delay before the higher priority tasks.

5. *Constraints.* Tasks with constraints are less likely to be delayed than those without constraints.

 You can enter Priority assignments in the Task Information dialog box, which you can open by clicking the Task Information tool.

There are two other fields that influence how Project treats tasks and resources when it is calculating the leveling delays. Both influence how likely it is that the task or resource assignment will be delayed. With these fields, you can instruct Project not to level a task or to level it only after all other options are exhausted.

■ *Can Level.* This resource field contains a Yes or No value. If the value is the default Yes, then Project can delay assignments for that resource, if it needs to, in its leveling calculation. If the value is No, Project will not delay the resource's assignment. The field does not appear on any prepared views or information forms. You can add the field to any task table and enter No for those tasks you want to keep from being delayed.

■ *Priority.* This task field lets you assign priority values to tasks. Those with the lower priority values are selected before those with high priority values when Project selects tasks to be delayed.

To assign a Priority value to a task, complete the following steps:

1. Select the task in a view that displays one or more task fields. You can select multiple tasks if you want to set them all to the same priority value with one step.

2. Click the Task Information tool on the Standard toolbar to display the Task Information dialog box (see Figure 11.28) or the Multiple Task form if more than one task has been selected.

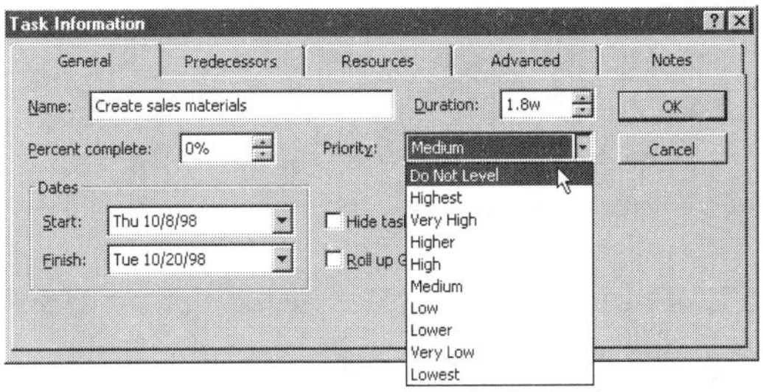

FIG. 11.28

Setting priorities for a task controls how likely it is to be delayed in leveling.

3. Select the General tab and click the list arrow in the Priority list box to display the priority choices. The first choice, Do Not Level, will assure that the task is never delayed in a leveling calculation. Choices further down the list make the task more and more vulnerable to being delayed if necessary.

4. Choose the priority level.

5. Click OK.

Using the Level Now Command

After establishing your choices in the Resource Leveling dialog box, you can instruct Project to level the project with the Level Now command. If you select this command from a task view, the leveling occurs immediately, without prompts. If you select the command from a resource view, you see the Level Now dialog box (see Figure 11.29).

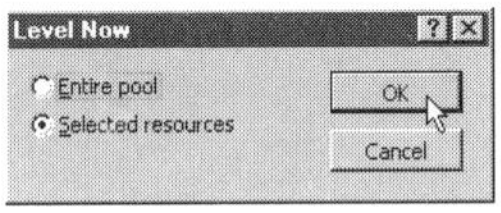

FIG. 11.29

You can level assignments for all over-allocated resources or for just those you have selected.

If you choose Selected Resources, only the overallocations for the resources in the selection are reviewed for leveling operations. If you select Entire Pool, all resources and all tasks are reviewed.

When you choose OK, Project tries to resolve the resource overallocations by leveling—within the bounds you specify in the Resource Leveling dialog box. For the first overallocation problem it encounters, Project identifies the tasks causing the overallocation and notes tasks that *cannot* be delayed. These include tasks that have hard constraints, tasks that have Do Not Level priority assignments, and tasks that are already started. If more than one task exists that you can delay, Project uses the set of five rules previously discussed to select one or more of the tasks to delay.

In Figure 11.30, you see the result of the leveling operation for the resource Howard Thompson. Only one delayed task is seen in this time frame (Create Advertising Plan). Note the new task bars in the Gantt Chart. When the Level Now command is executed, Project saves the current start and finish dates of all tasks into new fields called Preleveled Start and Preleveled Finish. The Leveling Gantt displays these dates as *preleveled* bars above the newly delayed *scheduled* bars for tasks so that you can easily see the effects of leveling. Notice in Figure 11.30 that the lower bar for Create Advertising Plan is shifted to the right (reflecting the Leveling Delay) of the preleveled bar just above it.

FIG. 11.30

After the Level Now command has changed the schedule, the Leveling Gantt displays preleveled task bars for comparing the original schedule with the delayed schedule.

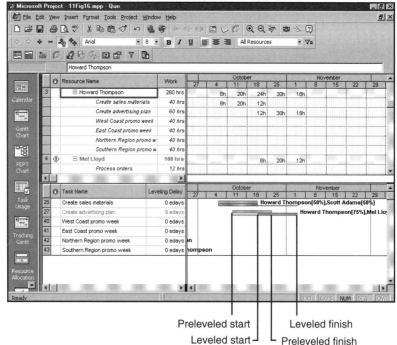

Preleveled start Leveled finish

Leveled start Preleveled finish

If one or more dates where overallocations occur can't be resolved, you see a message similar to the message in Figure 11.31.

FIG. 11.31

Sometimes Project can't resolve all the overallocation problems.

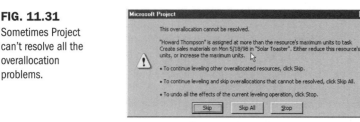

To respond to the Unresolved Overallocations message, do one of the following:

■ Choose Skip to have Microsoft Project skip this resource and continue looking for other overallocations.

■ Choose Skip All to have Project skip this resource and all others that cannot be resolved without alerting you to those that cannot be resolved.

■ Choose Stop to stop the leveling process and erase all the delays that have been entered so far.

Clearing the Effects of Leveling

You can use the Clear Leveling command on the Resource Leveling dialog box to remove all leveling delays or just those from selected tasks. To use this command, you must be in a task view. Choose Tools, Resource Leveling, Clear Leveling. The Clear Leveling dialog box will display (see Figure 11.32). Select Entire Project or Selected Tasks and click OK. All Leveling Delay fields will be reset to zero for the project or the selected tasks.

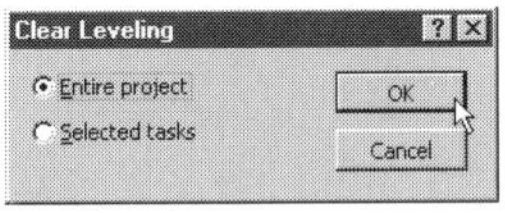

FIG. 11.32
You can quickly remove all leveling delays from the entire project or from selected tasks with the Clear Leveling command.

Understanding the Pitfalls of Automatic Leveling

The first option on the Resource Leveling dialog box is Automatic Leveling. If you select this option, then Microsoft Project will watch for resource overallocations *as* you assign resources and as the project schedule changes. The moment Project detects an overallocation, it will quietly attempt to resolve it by delaying tasks in the background as you go on building the schedule. This seems like a powerful and useful option, but it has very clear drawbacks.

Most importantly, you are a far better judge of the best choices for your schedule. You can't provide Microsoft Project with all the information you bring to the decision-making process as you make scheduling choices. If you use Automatic Leveling, you will not be aware of the leveling decisions going on in the background. Had you seen a leveling indicator, you might well have had an alternative that doesn't require delaying tasks and, most often, the project finish. It's not uncommon to wind up with a bloated schedule that has lots of unproductive time because of all the leveling delays.

You also should note that Project doesn't optimize the leveling strategy. The program doesn't examine all possible combinations of task delays in order to choose the best solution in terms of lowest cost, earliest project finish date, or any other consideration.

From Here...

In this chapter you have seen how to deal with the ever present problem of overallocated resources. You saw how to identify overallocations and how to use a variety of strategies to resolve overallocation problems. You also saw to use the Level Now command to let Project take care of overallocations with the single solution of delaying task assignments until the problems are all gone.

■ See Chapter 15, "Tracking Work on the Project," for information about entering the actual work and costs for the project.

■ See Chapter 16, "Analyzing Progress and Revising the Schedule," for help with understanding what's going on after work on the project and tracking has begun.

■ See Chapter 17, "Working with Multiple Projects," for information about resource pools and combining projects

■ See Chapter 18, "Using Microsoft Project in Workgroups," for suggestions about communicating with resources and other members of the project team.

IV

Reviewing and Publishing the Project

12   Reviewing the Project Plan   391

13   Printing Views and Reports   413

14   Publishing Projects on the Web   439

CHAPTER 12

Reviewing the Project Plan

At this point, the tasks are defined, the resources involved in the project have their respective tasks assigned, and costs have been calculated. You may want to step back from all the details and look at the overall project. You need to evaluate how successfully the project plan meets the objectives of the project, as stated in the project goal. Microsoft Project offers many tools to make this evaluation easy.

Often, the first draft of a project plan includes costs that exceed budget limits, or the scheduled finish date of the project is later than acceptable. There may also be inconsistencies in the plan. For example, deadlines for individual tasks may not be met. This chapter shows you how to get an overview of your project, identify and shorten the critical path, and identify and reduce costs for the project. ■

View your project to get the overall picture

Learn the many display options that allow you to focus on a careful review of the project plan.

Use filters

Using filters allows you to focus on the tasks and resources that need special attention.

Sort task and resource lists

You can control the sort order in a variety of ways to provide a better order when reviewing tasks and resources.

Identify the critical path and reduce its duration

Part of the review process often includes attempts to reduce the duration of the project to meet deadlines. First you must identify the critical path, then you can test out different strategies for reducing its duration.

Identify associated project costs and review strategies for reducing costs

If the calculated project budget exceeds expectations, Project offers ways to test strategies for reducing costs.

Looking at the Big Picture

You probably feel overwhelmed by the multitude of details in a large project. From time to time, you may need to step back and look at the overall project to keep a global perspective. You can review the Project Statistics sheet to note specifics about the scheduled start and finish dates and the planned costs. You can collapse the timescale when viewing the Gantt Chart to get a macro-time perspective. You can filter the summary tasks and milestones, or collapse the outline to view and compare the schedules and costs of the major phases of the project.

After you define the tasks, durations and constraints, dependency relationships, and resource assignments, Microsoft Project calculates the scheduled start and finish date for each task and also the scheduled finish date for the project. You can use the Project Statistics dialog box shown in Figure 12.1 to view the scheduled start and finish dates for the project. All the data in the Project Statistics dialog box is calculated—you cannot edit any of the fields on the form.

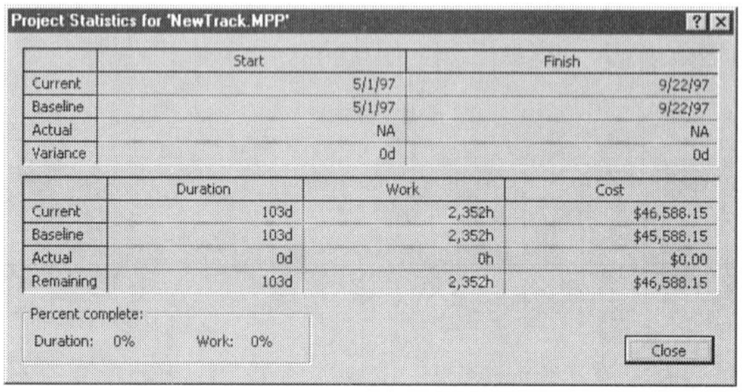

FIG. 12.1

Examine the Project Statistics dialog box for a quick summary of the project's start and finish dates.

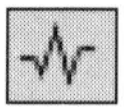

To display the Project Statistics dialog box, choose the Project Statistics button on the Tracking toolbar (or right-click anywhere on a displayed toolbar and choose Tracking from the shortcut menu), or choose Project, Project Information to display the Project Information dialog box; then choose the Statistics button.

At a glance, you see the Current Start and Finish dates, the Duration for the project, and the planned amount of Work and Cost. After you set the baseline copy of the schedule, you see the Baseline Start and Finish dates. After you start work on the project and enter tracking information, you also see the Actual Start of the project, the Variance for the Start and Finish dates, and the Actual and Remaining Duration, Work, and Cost.

If the project is scheduled from the Start date, use the Project Statistics dialog box to identify the currently calculated Finish date; if the project is scheduled from the Finish date, use the Project Statistics dialog box to view the currently calculated Start date. If the calculated date is inconsistent with the project goal statement, you need to find ways to shorten the life of the project.

The scheduled cost figure in the Project Statistics dialog box tells you at a glance the sum of all resource costs and fixed costs that you previously defined for the project. If this figure is too high to be consistent with the goals of the project, you need to search for ways to reduce costs without sacrificing the time objectives of the project goal.

Compressing the Timescale

You usually can gain an overview of the flow of activity in the project by viewing the Gantt Chart with the timescale compressed. In Figure 12.2, for example, the project is displayed with the timescale compressed to show months in the major scale and weeks in the minor scale units of time. (For clarity, resource names have been removed from the task bars.)

FIG. 12.2

Compress the timescale to get an overall view of the time dimension of the project.

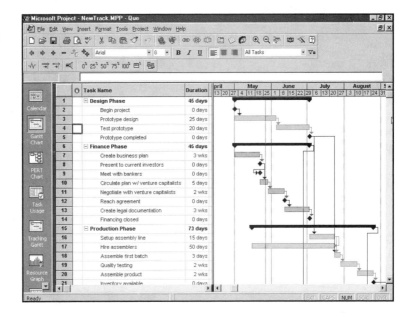

 To compress the timescale with the toolbar, click the Zoom Out button on the Standard toolbar to automatically select larger time units represented in each unit of the timescale. The display of weeks in Figure 12.2 is the result of clicking the Zoom Out button twice. Use the Zoom In button on the Standard toolbar to subdivide time into smaller units of time.

▶ **See** "Formatting Views," **p. 695**

To make more explicit changes than these tools provide, choose Format, Timescale. To make references easier to follow in the discussion, for example, the illustrations in this chapter label the days on the timescale with the day number rather than with the weekday letter. See the instructions in Chapter 22, "Customizing Views, Tables, and Filters," to make this change in your project.

It is also useful to Zoom the screen to view the whole project at once. You can do this by choosing View, Zoom, Entire project. To return the screen to the default timescale of months and weeks, choose View, Zoom and select the Reset button.

T I P You can also double-click any part of the timescale headings in the Gantt Chart to access the Timescale dialog box.

Collapsing the Task List Outline

The compressed time display may be more meaningful if you also collapse the outline or filter the task list to view only the summary tasks or the milestones. In Figure 12.3, the task list is collapsed to show only the first-level summary tasks (all subtasks are hidden). This view provides an overview of the start and finish dates of the major phases of the project. You can collapse the outline to any level of detail by first collapsing the task list to the first-level tasks, and then expanding the list to show the next level of subtasks.

FIG. 12.3

Hide the subtasks in an outlined project to focus on the major phases of the project.

		Task Name	Duration
	1	⊞ Design Phase	45 days
	6	⊞ Finance Phase	45 days
	15	⊞ Production Phase	73 days
	22	⊞ Marketing and Sales Phase	30 days
	29	⊞ Distribution Phase	16 days
	35	⊞ Regional Promotions	20 days

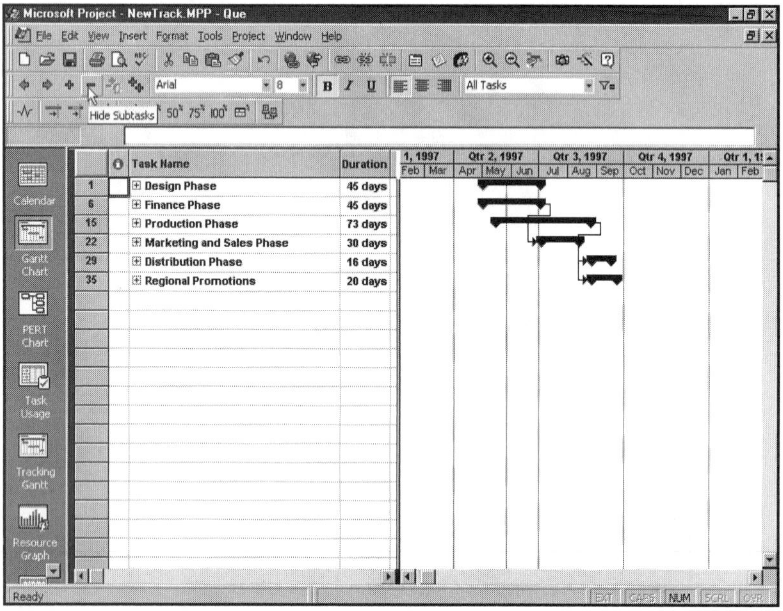

To collapse the outline to the first level, follow these steps:

1. Activate a pane that displays a task list table (the Gantt Chart, for example).

2. Select all tasks by clicking the Task Name heading at the top of the task column). All tasks are highlighted.

3. Click the Hide Subtasks button to hide all subtasks. You also can choose Project, Outline, Hide Subtasks to hide all subtasks.

Click the Show Subtasks button to open up successive levels in the outline. For example, if your project had five levels in the outline and you wanted to display tasks down to the third level, click the Show Subtasks button twice. To remove the highlight on all tasks, select any cell in the task list.

Similarly, you may find it constructive to view just the milestones in order to focus on the completion dates of the important sections of the project. The next section shows you how to filter the display to show just certain tasks or resources.

Filtering the Task or Resource List

When you filter the task list, you impose conditions that must be met to display a task. All the tasks that meet the conditions are allowed to filter through to be displayed and are known as *filtered tasks*. All those tasks that fail to meet the conditions are not displayed. You can apply a filter, for example, to display only the milestones (as shown in Figure 12.4), only the critical tasks, or only the summary tasks. You also can use filters to just highlight the tasks selected by the filter, leaving the rest of the tasks displayed but not highlighted (see Figure 12.5). Filters also can be used in resource views to display specific resources.

FIG. 12.4

A filtered task list that shows only milestones lets you focus solely on important completion dates.

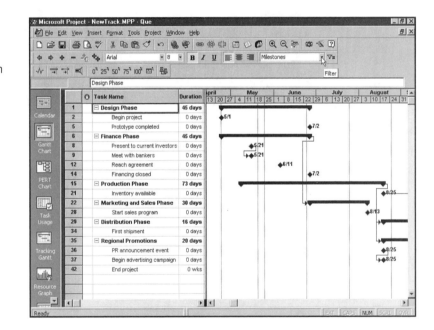

NOTE The summary tasks for filtered tasks will display based on a setting in the Filter Definition dialog box. If you don't want to display summary tasks when filtering, edit the filter by choosing Project, Filtered For:, More filters. Select the filter and then click the Edit button. Clear the Show Related Summary Row check box. ■

Microsoft Project has many predefined task filters, and you can add custom filters to the list. Some are interactive filters: When you select the filter, a dialog box with the name of the filter in the title bar appears from which you specify values to use in selecting the filtered tasks. The Date Range filter, for example, prompts you for two dates, and then displays all tasks whose

Part
IV

Ch
12

schedules include dates that fall within those two filter dates. The Using Resource filter prompts for a resource name and then only displays the tasks assigned to that resource.

FIG. 12.5
Having filtered tasks appear highlighted makes them stand out in the display.

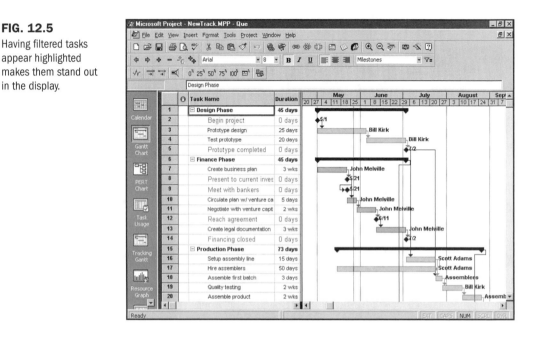

You may find the following list of task filters useful for reviewing the project after the tasks are all entered:

Filter	Description
Critical	Filters only critical tasks
Date Range	Filters only those tasks scheduled for work between the two dates that you enter when prompted
Milestones	Filters only milestone tasks
Summary Tasks	Filters only summary tasks
Tasks With Fixed Dates	On the More Filters list; filters all tasks that have any date constraint other than As Soon As Possible

N O T E   The Summary Task filter is not usually a good substitute for collapsing the outline, as described in the preceding section. The Summary Task filter shows only summary tasks, but all levels in the outline are displayed. Furthermore, if any first-level task in the outline is not a summary task, the task is not included in the list of tasks filtered by the Summary Task filter. If you want to focus only on the tasks up to a certain level in the outline, collapsing the entire outline to that level of tasks is the preferred method.

Using Filters

To filter the task list or the resource list, choose Project, Filtered For and choose the filter that you want to apply. If you choose an interactive filter, respond to the prompts by typing the requested information, and then choose OK. For example, to view only the milestone tasks for the project, choose Project, Filtered For:, and choose Milestones from the list of filters. Note that the currently applied filter appears in the Filter combo box on the Formatting toolbar.

> **T I P** You also can use filters to merely highlight the tasks that meet the filter criteria without hiding the other tasks. If you want to apply one of the filters on the initial filters menu as a highlight filter, hold down the Shift key as you select the Filtered For: menu option. You can then select the filter that you want to apply, and it will be implemented as a highlight filter. This technique works whether you are opening the menu from the keyboard or using the mouse. You must hold down the Shift key until you have selected the Filtered For: menu option. After that, you can release the Shift key.

> **T I P** If you edit the tasks or resources while a filter is applied, you may change that element of a task or resource that is tested by the filter. You must then reapply the filter to make the filtered display accurate. The quick key, Ctrl+F3, updates the display to accurately reflect the filter criteria.

You also can display a highlight filter by following these steps:

1. Choose Project, Filtered For:.
2. Choose More Filters.
3. Select the filter you want to use in the More Filters dialog box.
4. Choose the Highlight button.

When you finish using the filter, you can remove it by pressing F3, or by choosing Project, Filtered For, and selecting the All Tasks filter.

One of the most useful filters is the filter for Tasks With Fixed Dates. This filter is used to identify all the tasks that have constrained dates. Novice users of Microsoft Project often inadvertently place constraints on tasks, and then they don't understand why Project doesn't recalculate start and finish dates as expected. Use the Tasks With Fixed Dates filter to display tasks that have constraints. You can then review the tasks and be certain that the constraints are in fact necessary.

To apply the filter for constrained tasks, follow these steps:

1. Choose Project, Filtered For:.
2. Choose More Filters from the cascading menu. The More Filters dialog box is displayed (see Figure 12.6).

Part
IV

Ch
12

FIG. 12.6

There are additional useful filters listed in the More Filters dialog box.

3. Select the Tasks With Fixed Dates filter.
4. Choose the Apply button to activate the filter.

To clear a filter, you have several options. You can use the Filter button on the Standard toolbar. When you open the drop-down list from the Filter button on the Standard toolbar, choose All Tasks at the top of the list. A quick alternative is to use the F3 shortcut key.

▶ **See** "Exploring the Standard Filters," **p. 685**

Viewing the Costs

The Gantt Chart focuses on the time relationships among the tasks. If you want to focus on the costs of the major phases of the project or on the amount of work scheduled for each major phase, view the Task Sheet with the Summary table. Figure 12.7 shows the Duration, summary Cost, and Work hours, of all the tasks in the PRODUCT project. Figure 12.8 shows the same information, but with the Summary Task filter applied.

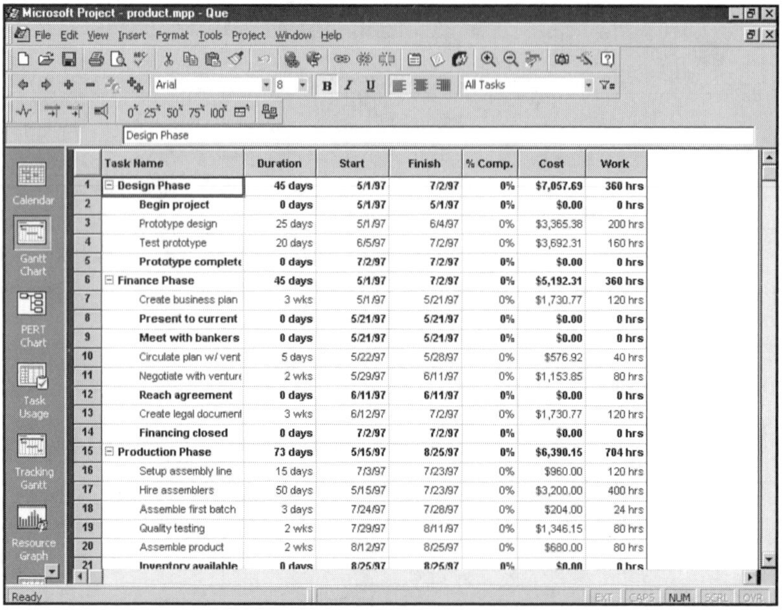

FIG. 12.7

The Summary table shows Duration, Cost, and Work details for the project.

		Task Name	Duration	Start	Finish	% Comp.	Cost	Work
	1	⊟ Design Phase	45 days	5/1/97	7/2/97	0%	$7,057.69	360 hrs
	2	Begin project	0 days	5/1/97	5/1/97	0%	$0.00	0 hrs
	3	Prototype design	25 days	5/1/97	6/4/97	0%	$3,365.38	200 hrs
	4	Test prototype	20 days	6/5/97	7/2/97	0%	$3,692.31	160 hrs
	5	Prototype complete	0 days	7/2/97	7/2/97	0%	$0.00	0 hrs
	6	⊟ Finance Phase	45 days	5/1/97	7/2/97	0%	$5,192.31	360 hrs
	7	Create business plan	3 wks	5/1/97	5/21/97	0%	$1,730.77	120 hrs
	8	Present to current	0 days	5/21/97	5/21/97	0%	$0.00	0 hrs
	9	Meet with bankers	0 days	5/21/97	5/21/97	0%	$0.00	0 hrs
	10	Circulate plan w/ vent	5 days	5/22/97	5/28/97	0%	$576.92	40 hrs
	11	Negotiate with venture	2 wks	5/29/97	6/11/97	0%	$1,153.85	80 hrs
	12	Reach agreement	0 days	6/11/97	6/11/97	0%	$0.00	0 hrs
	13	Create legal document	3 wks	6/12/97	7/2/97	0%	$1,730.77	120 hrs
	14	Financing closed	0 days	7/2/97	7/2/97	0%	$0.00	0 hrs
	15	⊟ Production Phase	73 days	5/15/97	8/25/97	0%	$6,390.15	704 hrs
	16	Setup assembly line	15 days	7/3/97	7/23/97	0%	$960.00	120 hrs
	17	Hire assemblers	50 days	5/15/97	7/23/97	0%	$3,200.00	400 hrs
	18	Assemble first batch	3 days	7/24/97	7/28/97	0%	$204.00	24 hrs
	19	Quality testing	2 wks	7/29/97	8/11/97	0%	$1,346.15	80 hrs
	20	Assemble product	2 wks	8/12/97	8/25/97	0%	$680.00	80 hrs
	21	Inventory available	0 days	8/25/97	8/25/97	0%	$0.00	0 hrs

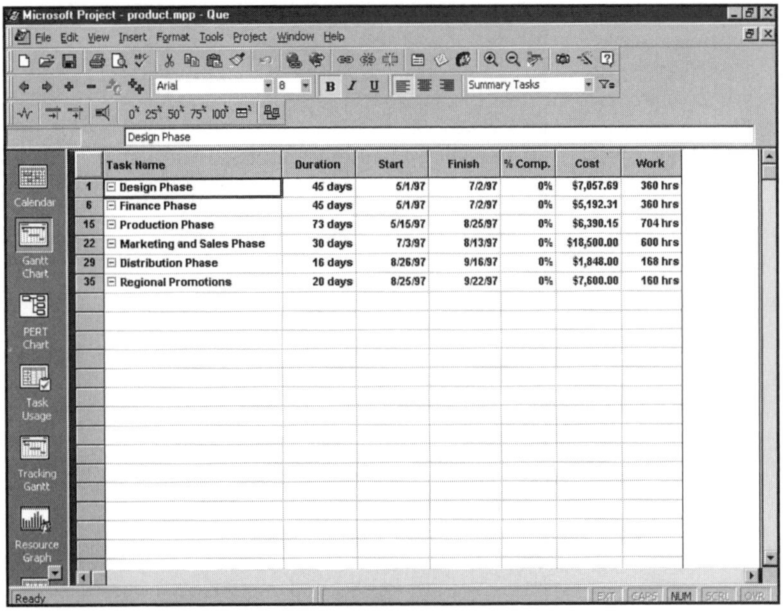

FIG. 12.8

Collapsing table shows Duration, Cost, and Work details for the project.

To view the Summary table for the Task Sheet, follow these steps:

1. View the Task Sheet by choosing View, More Views, select the Task Sheet from the resulting More Views dialog box, and then click the Apply button.

2. Choose View, Table, and choose Summary from the drop-down list of tables.

The Summary Table view of the project affords an opportunity to see the project from a larger perspective and to see which tasks or phases entail the most work, cost, and duration.

Sorting the Task and Resource Lists

You can sort the task list or the resource pool to view the rows in a different order. Although the tasks or resources are displayed in a different order after sorting, the ID numbers do not change, and the schedule is unaffected (see Figure 12.9). When you finish using the sorted order, you can return the task list to the original order. However, you also have the option of instructing Microsoft Project to permanently renumber the task IDs according to the current sort order. This section gives details on how to accomplish these options.

When you sort an outlined project, you can retain or ignore the outline structure. If you retain the outline structure, all tasks at the first outline level are sorted (carrying their subtasks with them); within each summary task, all subtasks at the next outline level are sorted (carrying their subtasks with them), and so forth. If you choose not to keep the outline structure, subtask groups are broken up and dispersed throughout the task list, independent of their summary task. If you do not keep the outline structure, you will probably want to suppress the display of summary tasks and the indentation of subtasks, as shown in Figure 12.9. See the following numbered steps for instructions on suppressing summary tasks and indentation.

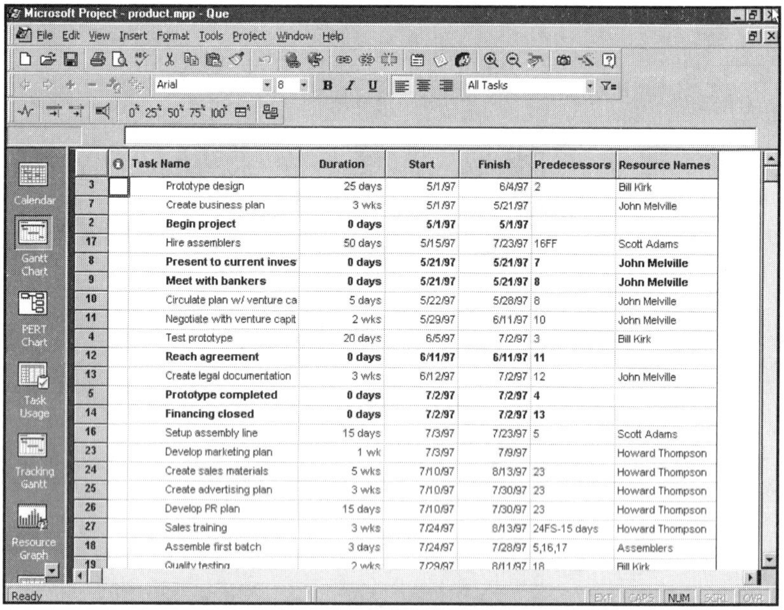

FIG. 12.9
The list of working tasks is sorted here in chronological order by start date. Summary tasks have been omitted from the list.

		Task Name	Duration	Start	Finish	Predecessors	Resource Names
3		Prototype design	25 days	5/1/97	6/4/97	2	Bill Kirk
7		Create business plan	3 wks	5/1/97	5/21/97		John Melville
2		**Begin project**	0 days	5/1/97	5/1/97		
17		Hire assemblers	50 days	5/15/97	7/23/97	16FF	Scott Adams
8		**Present to current inves**	0 days	5/21/97	5/21/97	7	**John Melville**
9		**Meet with bankers**	0 days	5/21/97	5/21/97	8	**John Melville**
10		Circulate plan w/ venture ca	5 days	5/22/97	5/28/97	8	John Melville
11		Negotiate with venture capit	2 wks	5/29/97	6/11/97	10	John Melville
4		Test prototype	20 days	6/5/97	7/2/97	3	Bill Kirk
12		**Reach agreement**	0 days	6/11/97	6/11/97	11	
13		Create legal documentation	3 wks	6/12/97	7/2/97	12	John Melville
5		**Prototype completed**	0 days	7/2/97	7/2/97	4	
14		**Financing closed**	0 days	7/2/97	7/2/97	13	
16		Setup assembly line	15 days	7/3/97	7/23/97	5	Scott Adams
23		Develop marketing plan	1 wk	7/3/97	7/9/97		Howard Thompson
24		Create sales materials	5 wks	7/10/97	8/13/97	23	Howard Thompson
25		Create advertising plan	3 wks	7/10/97	7/30/97	23	Howard Thompson
26		Develop PR plan	15 days	7/10/97	7/30/97	23	Howard Thompson
27		Sales training	3 wks	7/24/97	8/13/97	24FS-15 days	Howard Thompson
18		Assemble first batch	3 days	7/24/97	7/28/97	5,16,17	Assemblers
19		Quality testing	2 wks	7/29/97	8/11/97	18	Bill Kirk

N O T E If you choose to ignore the outline structure during sorting, you cannot permanently renumber the tasks to match the new sort order—that would restructure the outline. ■

Normally, the task and resource lists are sorted according to the numbers in the ID field, and the default sort order is ascending order. When you choose Project, Sort, Sort By, you are asked to identify the field to use for sorting and the direction of the sort—whether to sort in ascending (normal) order or in descending (reverse) order. For example, you could sort the resource list by the group they are in, and for duplicates within a group, sort by the Standard Rate paid to the resources, with the highest pay rates listed first. The sort fields in this instance are Group, Ascending and Standard Rate, Descending (see Figure 12.10).

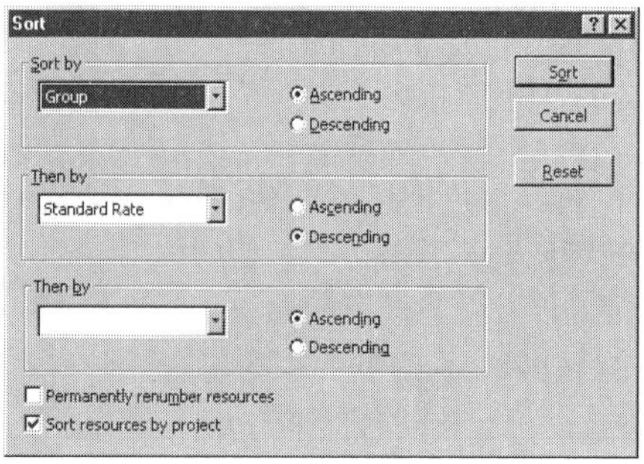

FIG. 12.10
Here the resource sheet is first sorted in ascending order by group and then in descending order by the standard pay rate.

You can use up to three sort fields, which enable you to apply a second and third sort order for groups of tasks or resources that have the same entry in the first sort field. If, for example, you sort tasks by Duration and many tasks have similar estimated durations, you may use the second sort field to sort all the tasks with the same duration by name. If several tasks have the same duration and the same name, you can use a third sort field to arrange the tasks within this similar group according to their scheduled start dates. The process is the same as when you sort a mailing list by state, and within states by city, and within cities by name.

N O T E If the tasks are filtered when you sort or if some tasks are hidden because the outline is collapsed, the suppressed tasks still are not displayed after sorting. ▪

To sort tasks or resources by more than one field, follow these steps:

1. Choose Project, Sort. Some of the most commonly used fields for sorting appear in a short list. If the field you want to sort on is listed, and you want to sort in normal order, and you want to sort by that field only, choose the field from the list. If the field you want is not listed, or you want to sort in descending order, or you want to use more than one sort key, choose the Sort By command. The Sort dialog box appears (see Figure 12.11).

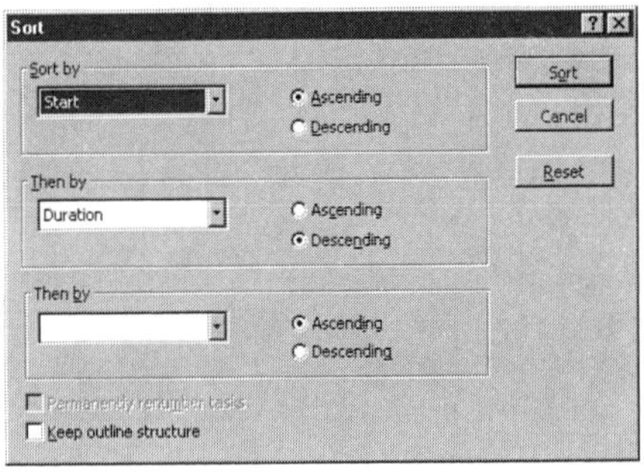

FIG. 12.11

Use the Sort dialog box to tailor the way the task or resource list is sorted.

Part

IV

Ch

12

CAUTION

If the Permanently Renumber Tasks (or Resources) option (at the bottom of the Sort dialog box) was selected the last time the Sort command was used, it will be used when you sort by selecting from the short list of sort fields.

2. Choose the Sort By area to identify the name of the field that you want to serve as the primary sort key. Choose the entry list arrow to view the field names or type the first letter of the field name to activate the entry list. Scroll to and choose the field you want to use.

3. Choose Ascending or Descending order for the first key. A descending sort is good for dates (most recent first) and costs (higher figures first).

4. Choose the Then By area and choose another field from the field list. This field will be used for sorting the duplicates that occurred in the first field that was sorted.

5. Choose Ascending or Descending order for the second field.

6. Repeat steps 4 and 5 for the second Then By area if necessary.

7. Clear the Keep Outline Structure check box to sort tasks independently of their summary task groups if desired. (This also makes it impossible to permanently renumber the tasks.) If you mark the check box, first level tasks in the outline are sorted, then second level tasks in the outline are sorted within their summary tasks, and so on.

8. Choose the Sort button to initiate the sort.

If you want to hide the display of summary tasks and remove the indentation from the display of subtasks, follow these steps:

1. Choose Tools, Options.

2. Choose the View tab on the Options dialog box.

3. Clear the check boxes for Show Summary Tasks and for Indent Name.

4. Choose OK to close the Options dialog box.

After you edit a sorted list, you may want to sort the modified list again to take into account the values that have changed, because they may affect the sort order. To sort the list again using the current sort keys, press Ctrl+Shift+F3, or you can activate the Sort dialog box again. The sort keys are still defined as you last set them, and you can simply select the Sort button again.

To reset the list to normal (ID number) order, press Shift+F3, or access the Sort dialog box and choose the Reset button and then the Sort button.

To permanently renumber a list, follow these steps:

1. Choose the sort keys as in the preceding steps. If you are renumbering a task list, double-check that the Keep Outline Structure check box is active. You cannot renumber tasks unless Keep Outline Structure is turned on.

2. Choose the Permanently Renumber Tasks check box for tasks or the Permanently Renumber Resources check box for resources.

> **CAUTION**
>
> You can undo the renumbering, provided you act immediately. Choose Edit, Undo Sort. If you don't undo the sort immediately, you can always close the file without saving and then open it again. This is why it is suggested that you always save before sorting.

Checking for Spelling Errors

Microsoft Project has a spelling checker that you can use to verify spelling in one or all fields for names, notes, and special text for both tasks and resources.

Using the Spelling Command

 To activate the spelling checker, click the Spelling button on the Standard toolbar or choose Tools, Spelling. When Project cannot find a word in the dictionary, the Spelling dialog box appears (see Figure 12.12).

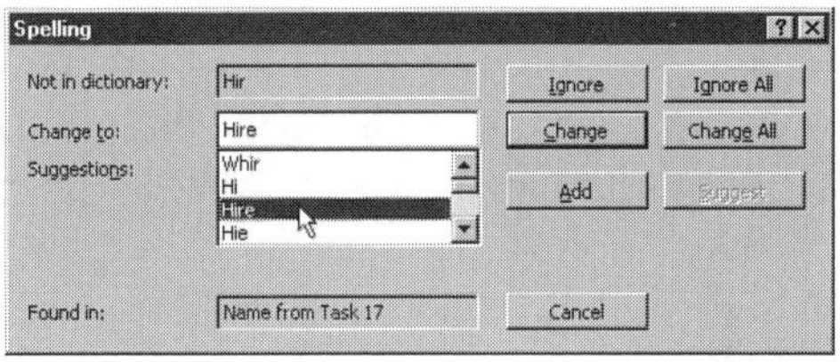

FIG. 12.12
Use the Spelling dialog box to decide how to treat words that are not in the dictionary.

The text boxes in the Spelling dialog box show you the problem word and where the word is found and offer options for responding to the problem. These text boxes are defined in the following list:

Field	Definition
Not in Dictionary	Display-only field that shows the problem word.
Change To	Text entry field in which you type a replacement for the word. If Always Suggest is enabled on the Spelling tab of the Options dialog box, a suggested replacement from the Suggestions list is placed in the field automatically.
Suggestions	Optional list of possible replacements culled from the dictionary (and from your custom dictionary).
Found In	Display-only field that shows the field and task or resource where the problem word is found.

The following list defines the action buttons found in the Spelling dialog box:

Button	Use
Ignore	Select Ignore to ignore the problem word in this instance.
Ignore All	Select Ignore All to ignore the word here and anywhere else it appears.
Change	Select Change to have the entry in the Change To field replace this instance of the problem word.
Change All	Select Change All to have the entry in the Change To field replace this and all other occurrences of the problem word.
Add	Select Add to add the problem word to your custom dictionary. The spelling checker ignores this occurrence and all future occurrences with the same spelling.

Part

IV

Ch

12

Cancel (Close)	Select Cancel to quit the spelling checker before any words are changed. If any words have changed, the Cancel button changes to a Close button. Select Close to quit the spelling checker immediately. Words that you changed remain changed.
Suggest	Select the Suggest button to display a list of suggested alternatives for the problem word when the Suggestions list is not already displayed. This button is only available when the Always Suggest option is not selected in the Spelling tab of the Options dialog box (see the following section) or when you type into the Change To field.

Setting the Spelling Options

The Spelling tab of the Options dialog box provides you with an opportunity to determine some characteristics of the spell check operation. The Spelling tab, shown in Figure 12.13, provides the following options:

FIG. 12.13

Use the Spelling tab in the Options dialog box to regulate how spell checking works.

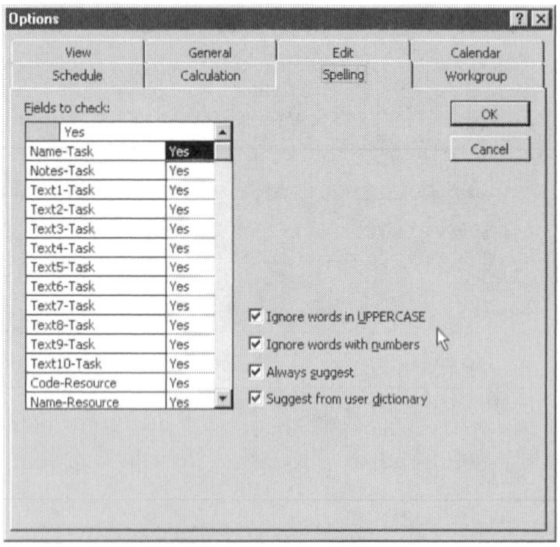

Option	Description
Fields to Check	Contains a selection list of text fields in the task and resource databases. All fields are initially marked Yes to be included in the spell checking operation. Change any field settings to No if you don't want the field checked.
Ignore Words in UPPERCASE	Causes UPPERCASE words to be ignored. If you always enter task names in upper case, this would be a good option to turn off.
Ignore Words with Numbers	Causes words that contain numbers to be ignored.

Always <u>S</u>uggest	Activates the Suggestio<u>n</u>s list each time the spelling checker is used.
Suggest from User <u>D</u>ictionary	Besides the standard dictionary, checks problem words against the custom dictionary.

To change the spelling options, follow these steps:

1. Choose <u>T</u>ools, <u>O</u>ptions.

2. Choose the Spelling tab in the Options dialog box and change the necessary options.

3. Choose OK to implement the choices.

N O T E   The user's custom dictionary is stored in the folder Program Files\Microsoft Office\Office and is named CUSTOM.DIC. You can edit the custom dictionary with a text editor. Make sure, however, that the entries are in alphabetical order before you save the edited file. ■

Shortening the Critical Path

The preceding sections looked at the project plan from a variety of perspectives: changing the timescale, zooming in or out for more or less detail, filtering the list to only see certain tasks, and rearranging the task list in a different order. This section turns its attention to making some changes that might have been identified as a result of the earlier work and reducing the overall duration of the project to schedule the finish date sooner (or the start date later for a project that is scheduled from the finish date). The popular phrase for this process is *crashing the schedule*.

Part
IV

Ch
12

To reduce the duration of the project, you must reduce the duration of the tasks or overlap the tasks so that the combined duration of all the tasks is not as great. Reducing the duration of individual tasks may be no more complicated than reassessing the estimated duration and entering a more optimistic figure. Often, however, more effort is required. You may need to increase the quantity or quality of the resources assigned to the task. You may be able to schedule overtime to shorten the duration of a task. By changing the relationships among tasks, you may be able to realign the task dates to allow for more overlapping of tasks. You may define lead time for some Finish-to-Start relationships, or you may be able to redefine a Finish-to-Start relationship to be a Start-to-Start or Finish-to-Finish. If tasks that were originally scheduled end-to-end are allowed to overlap in time, you probably can shorten the project schedule by redefining the task relationships.

Of course, working on shortening noncritical tasks or scheduling these tasks to overlap, would waste time. You should focus your attention only on critical tasks, because only critical tasks count when trying to crash the schedule. Keep in mind that changes you make in the schedule may change the status of a noncritical task to critical. But at all times you need to focus on the critical tasks, because these are the ones that determine the duration of the project. Only delays to critical tasks impact the end date of the project; delays to noncritical tasks do not.

Identifying the Critical Path

 You can use any task view to identify the critical tasks. The basic Task Entry view on the More Views menu is popular because this view displays, in either the top or bottom panes, many fields relevant to crashing the schedule. (This view is also accessible using the Task Entry View button on the Resource Management toolbar. Turn on the Resource Management toolbar by right-clicking any portion of a displayed toolbar.) You also can use the PERT Chart to identify the critical tasks. However, it's not as easy to get to all the fields you may want to change as you revise the project.

You can identify the critical tasks most dramatically by filtering the task list in the Gantt Chart view or the Task Sheet view to show only the critical tasks. However, as you redefine the project, some tasks may change from noncritical to critical. The filter does not automatically recalculate, although you can use Ctrl+F3 to quickly reapply the current filter. You also can highlight the critical tasks by choosing a highlight filter, and then all tasks are in view at all times, and the critical tasks are highlighted. The same problem exists, however, in that the highlight filter is not recalculated as you change the project. The most satisfactory results are derived from formatting the text of critical task names to appear in a highlighted color, because the format choice is constantly updated as the status of a task changes.

To filter the critical tasks, follow these steps:

1. Select the top pane if a combination view is in place.
2. Display a task list view by choosing Gantt Chart from the View menu or Task Sheet from the View, More Views menu.
3. Choose Project, Filtered For:, and then Critical from the drop-down menu.

To highlight the critical tasks, hold down the Shift key as you perform these same steps. Instead of hiding the tasks that are not critical, Microsoft Project highlights the names of critical tasks in blue. Otherwise the steps are the same as listed previously.

▶ **See** "Formatting Text Displays for Categories of Tasks and Resources," **p. 697**

To format the display of critical tasks to show a highlight color at all times, follow these steps:

1. Display a task list view in the top pane as shown in the preceding steps.
2. Choose Format, Text Styles. The Text Styles dialog box appears (see Figure 12.14).
3. Select Critical Tasks from the Item to Change list.
4. Choose the formatting feature to use as a highlight. Select Bold from the Font Style text box, for example, to bold critical tasks, or choose the Color drop-down list and select a color to use as a highlight.
5. After you make all the desired selections, click OK.

Another popular combination view for crashing the schedule places the Task Details Form in the top pane and the Task Name Form in the bottom pane (see Figure 12.15). Next, format the top pane to display Predecessors & Successors fields and the Resource Work fields in the bottom pane. You can filter the top pane to display only Critical tasks (but note that you need to recalculate the filter fairly often). Use the P<u>r</u>evious and Ne<u>x</u>t buttons in the top pane to change the tasks as you review the task definitions. You can change task definitions, relationship definitions, and resource assignments (including overtime) all on the same screen. You will not have the benefit, however, of the graphical displays that help you keep the project organized in your head.

FIG. 12.14
Use the Text Styles dialog box to change the format of critical tasks.

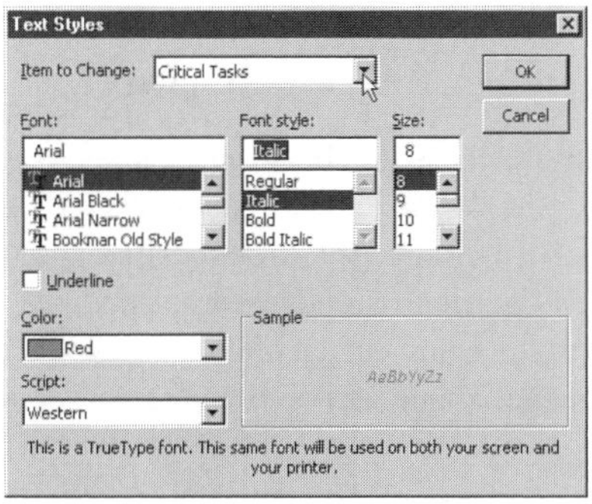

FIG. 12.15
Use two task forms to access task and resource information.

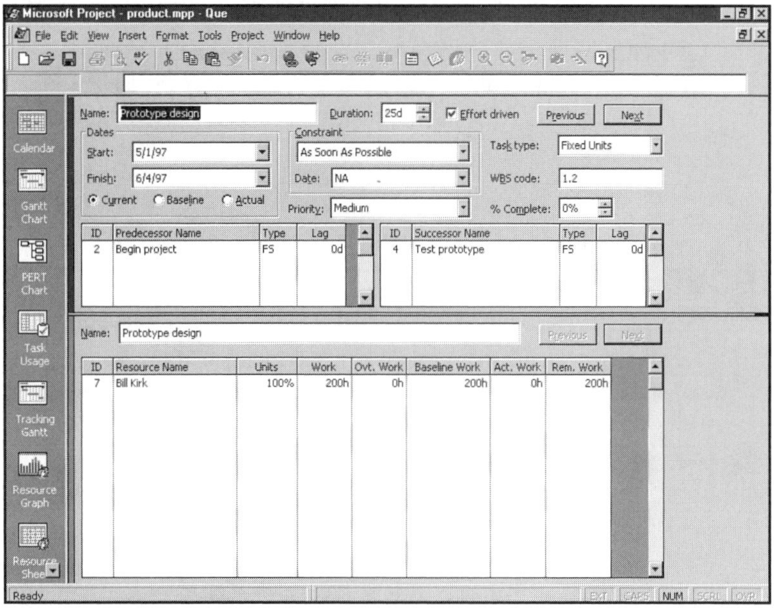

Part
IV

Ch

12

Strategies for Crashing the Schedule

No matter which view you use, move through the project from one critical task to the next, looking for the opportunities from the following list:

■ Review with an intent to reduce task durations that are unnecessarily long. Assigning more resources or more skilled resources may be one way to do this.

▪ Examine the predecessor and successor relationships and try to identify the relationships that you can change from Finish-to-Start to one of the overlapping relationships (Start-to-Start, Finish-to-Finish, or Finish-to-Start with lead time). This strategy usually is one of the most fruitful because many users hastily define all relationships as Finish-to-Start when more lenient definitions can be applied. Ask the question: Does the predecessor to this task really have to be 100 percent complete or would almost finished be good enough?

▪ Schedule overtime to reduce the number of regular work hours that a task may take.

You may find it easier to concentrate on each of these strategies if you go through the project task list once for each of the areas identified in the preceding list. Remembering what you are looking for is sometimes easier if you look for the same thing as you examine task after task. Make one complete pass through the project, looking for duration estimates that you can trim. Next, make another pass through the complete list of critical tasks, looking for changes in task relationships. Finally, do the same for changing resource assignments and scheduling overtime.

After you make changes, remember that some formerly noncritical tasks now may be critical and that these tasks should be reviewed along the same lines for possible duration reductions.

A useful combination view at this point is the Gantt Chart or Task Sheet in the top pane and the Task PERT in the bottom pane. You can move from one task to another easily in the top pane and view the task relationships for the selected task in the bottom pane.

▶ **See** "The Task PERT Chart," **p. 669**

▶ **See** "Creating a Combination View," **p. 746**

Reducing Costs

If the project costs are above expectations, you can examine the project schedule for possible cost savings. Because the variable costs all derive from resource assignments, you may want to focus on ways to reduce the cost of the resources assigned to individual tasks.

Reviewing the Cost Schedule

You can view the task list with the cost and total amount of work for each task if you view the Task Sheet and apply the Summary table. If you want to focus on only tasks with costs in excess of some determined amount, you can create a filter to display only these tasks. If you display the Task Form in the bottom pane and choose the Resource Work fields from the Format menu to appear at the bottom of the form, you can see the resource assignments, including overtime work, in detail.

You also may use the Resource Substitution view, discussed in the section titled "Creating a New View for Resource Substitution" in Chapter 11, to identify less expensive resource substitutes to assign to tasks.

To display the Summary table in the top pane and the Resource Work table in the bottom pane, follow these steps:

1. Select the top pane if currently displaying a combination view.
2. Choose View, More Views.
3. From the More Views dialog box, choose Task Sheet.
4. Click the Apply button.
5. Choose View, Table, Summary.
6. Select the bottom pane. If you are not currently displaying a combination view, choose Window, Split first.
7. The Task Form appears because it is the default when you split a window underneath a Task Sheet or Gantt Chart.
8. Choose Format, Details, Resource Work to display the work fields.

▶ **See** "Creating Custom Filters," **p. 754**

Strategies for Reducing Costs

Less expensive resources that perform the same quality of work in the same amount of time obviously will lower your costs. You also can reduce costs if you can substitute more expensive but more efficient resources. You can justify the extra cost if the number of hours of work that complete the task is more than reduced proportionally. For example, if the standard rate of the new resource is 20 percent higher than the old resource, but you can reduce the work hours by 25 percent, this substitution would result in a cost savings. Let's suppose you have an 8-hour task when a $10/hr resource is assigned to it. This task would cost $80. What if a $12/hr resource could accomplish the same task in 6 hours? The task would only cost $72.

You also may be able to assign tools or equipment to the task and thereby increase the efficiency of the labor so that reduced hours of work result in reduced total labor costs. If the reduction in labor time and costs is enough to match the cost of the tools or equipment, the added capital expense results in a cost savings overall.

Printing Summary Reports

Several overview reports are available for printing at this point in your project. You can run these reports by choosing View, Reports. A dialog box appears that displays an icon for each category of reports (see Figure 12.16). Double-click the icon for the category desired and another dialog box appears with the reports included in that category. Figure 12.17 displays the reports in the Overview category. Click a report, and it is displayed in print preview format.

FIG. 12.16

The Reports dialog box offers a variety of report categories.

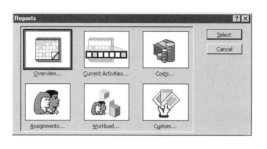

FIG. 12.17

The reports provided in the Overview category are useful when auditing the task schedule.

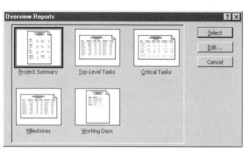

Each report is described in detail in Chapter 23, "Using the Standard Reports." Customizing reports is covered in Chapter 24, "Customizing Reports." A brief discussion is included here of the reports that are most useful at this stage of project development.

The Overview Report category offers several reports that are helpful in documenting this stage in project design:

- The Project Summary offers a one-page snapshot view of the project, including start and finish dates, total duration of the project, total hours of work, and dollar costs. It shows the same information that is displayed in the Project Statistics dialog box. It also includes the Comments you enter on the Summary tab of the File Properties dialog box.

- The Top-Level Tasks report displays the summary duration, cost, and work information for the top level summary tasks.

- The Critical Tasks report identifies all critical tasks of the project, noting their dependencies and any lag or lead times. It is here that you can start to pinpoint inconsistencies behind the logic of the project plan.

- The Milestones report highlights the major landmarks of the project. This report is useful in communications with members of the project team and other interested parties.

- The Working Days report documents the calendars defined in your project. It lists the normal working days and hours and any exceptions for all defined base calendars and resource calendars.

The Cost Reports category of reports also includes two reports that are helpful when completing the design phase of the project.

- The Cash Flow report is instrumental in providing information needed in funding the project—planning to have the correct amount of money at the correct time.

- The Budget report may also be helpful at this point, listing each task and its fixed and variable costs. If the project is over budget, it is easy to pinpoint the most expensive tasks with this report.

When you finish the initial design of the project, use these tools to step back from the details and look at the big picture. Does it make sense? Is the project going to finish on time? Are costs within budget? If not, then you have the tools to decide where changes are necessary.

From Here...

Before you can call the project plan complete, a careful review is in order. This chapter introduces a variety of ways to modify the display of the project plan to explain it to others, to identify potential problems, and to improve its efficiency.

The following chapters provide more information depending on the direction you seek:

- Chapter 13, "Printing Views and Reports," shows you how to transfer your project plan onto paper.

- Chapter 14, "Publishing Projects on the Web," shows you how to transfer your project plan to others via the Internet.

- Chapter 15, "Tracking Work on the Project," provides the steps necessary to keep track of activities on the project as they occur as well as the reasons for doing so.

Part
IV

Ch
12

CHAPTER 13

Printing Views and Reports

One of the main functions of project management software is to print reports that communicate a project plan to others in a clear and informative format.

There are two ways to print your project data: Frequently, you just print the view of the data that appears on-screen. The printed version is nearly identical to the display format on-screen. A few views cannot be printed, however, including combination views (a split screen with one view in the upper pane and another in the lower pane), the Task PERT Chart, and the forms (such as the Task Form, the Resource Form, and the Tracking Form). Also, Microsoft Project provides 25 predesigned reports for printing. The report formats include a monthly calendar with tasks shown on the scheduled dates, comprehensive lists of tasks and resources, and a summary page that resembles the Project Statistics dialog box.

Get ready to print

Adjust the timescale, sort the data, and set manual page breaks before you begin printing.

Setting the options

Learn how to set margins and orientation. Create and customize headers, footers, and legends.

Preview before you print

Get a glimpse of what the printout will look like before you print. Preview any adjustments you've made to the Page Setup options. Control the page or date range that is printed.

Selecting the Print button sends a copy of the current view to the printer immediately; you do not have a chance to exercise control over the way the report looks. Use the commands in this chapter to make changes to the page setup before using the Print button. Choosing the Print Preview button enables you to see what the printed copy will look like and also gives you access to the Page Setup and Print commands. You should almost always start a print job with the Print Preview button instead of the Print button. ■

Using the Print Commands

As in all Windows applications, the printer commands are located on the File menu (see Figure 13.1). The Page Setup command defines headers, footers, page orientation, and so on, for printed views. You can also use Page Setup to select the printer and to change any printer-specific options available for your printer. The Print Preview and Print commands are used to print views. There are 25 predesigned reports in Microsoft Project that are accessed by choosing View, Reports. The Page Setup and Print buttons displayed when viewing a report work the same way the Print commands on the File menu do.

FIG. 13.1

Use the Print commands on the File menu before or after a project is created to establish your print settings.

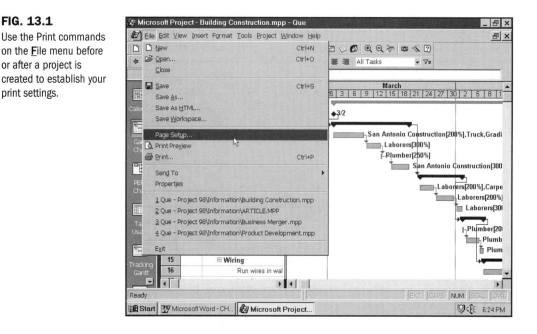

Changing the Printer Setup

Make sure that you select the correct printer before you start a print job. You can select the default printer for any Windows application by selecting the Start button on the taskbar and choosing Settings, Printers.

The default printer is selected when you start to print in Microsoft Project. If you want to use a printer other than the default printer, you can select the printer or the desired printer options by choosing File, Page Setup, and choosing the Printer button; the Print Setup dialog box appears (see Figure 13.2).

FIG. 13.2

From the Print Setup dialog box, choose the printer you want to use.

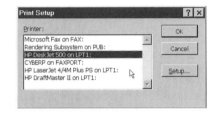

The list of installed printers appears in the Printer list box. If you only want to change the printer you are printing to, select the printer you want and choose OK. If you want to change the way the printer is set up, choose the printer for which you want to change the setup, and then choose Setup.

Some of the options available may be selecting legal size paper rather than the standard letter size, selecting a paper feeder source, or changing the resolution of graphics objects. You also can change the orientation of the report on the paper from portrait (upright) to landscape (sideways). An information box appears the first time you choose the Setup button to advise you that the portrait or landscape orientation setting is managed in the Page Setup dialog box for individual views and reports.

If the information box appears, choose OK to go on to the Properties dialog box, which displays the options for the printer. Figure 13.3 shows the options for a Hewlett-Packard DeskJet; your printer may have different options. Select the options you want and choose OK when finished, and then choose OK in the Print Setup dialog box. Until you change the printer or the options, Microsoft Project continues to use this printer definition as the default.

You can also use File, Print to change the printer setup. Use the Printer Name list box in the Print dialog box to select a different printer (see Figure 13.4) and the Properties button to change the paper size, orientation, graphics resolution, and print quality (see Figure 13.3).

Part
IV

Ch
13

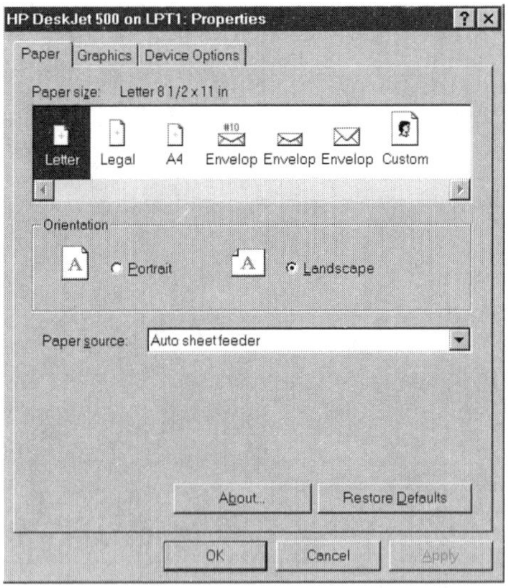

FIG. 13.3

A sample Properties dialog box, used to select orientation, resolution, and print quality for your output.

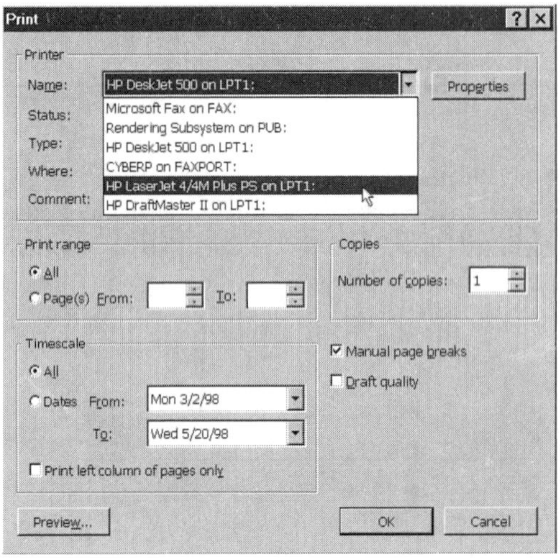

FIG. 13.4

Choose the desired printer from the Print dialog box.

Printing Views

Most of the time you will be printing views, such as the Gantt Chart view or the Resource Sheet view. This section provides a few pointers about preparing the screen view for printing. Chapters 7, 20, and 21 contain detailed instructions for refining the display with special formatting and graphics features. This chapter focuses on the use of the Print commands after the screen presentation is established.

▶ **See** "Introducing the Drawing Toolbar," **p. 237**
▶ **See** "Using and Creating Tables," **p. 748**
▶ **See** "Using the Format Options in the Standard Views," **p. 696**

Preparing the View for Printing

The first step is to set up the screen to display the project data just as you want the information to appear on the printed report. You choose from the View menu, possibly from the Tools menu, and (most likely) from the Format menu to get the combination of data and display features that presents your data in the best way.

Choosing the View Fundamentals   You first must choose the appropriate view to print. You can view tasks or resources in either a worksheet table layout or a graphic layout. In views that contain timescales, the timescale displayed is printed. For instance, in the Gantt Chart view, the timescale can be displayed in minutes, hours, weeks, months, quarters, or years. Zoom in or out to adjust the timescale. If you filter the tasks or resources, only the data displayed is printed.

Moreover, if you have split the screen into panes you must choose the pane from which the view is printed. If the top pane is active, all tasks or all resources are printed unless you filter the data. If the bottom pane is active, only the tasks or resources associated with the selection in the top pane are printed. You may decide to print from the bottom pane, for example, if you want to isolate all the resources assigned to a selected task, or you may want to print a list of all the tasks to which a selected resource is assigned.

To display a view, select the View menu and choose the desired view from the list. If the screen is split into panes, the selected pane will have a colored bar on the far left side of the screen next to the pane. The default color is dark blue. To select a different pane, click the desired pane or use the F6 key to toggle between the upper and lower panes.

If the view contains spreadsheet-like columns of data, you may need to choose View, Table to select the most appropriate set of data columns. The various tables were introduced in previous chapters as tools to use in the process of building and managing a project. Chapter 16 addresses ways to use the different tables, and Chapter 20 describes how you can create customized tables. To simply change the table currently displayed, choose View, Table, and choose the table you want to use.

NOTE   In views that show a table to the left of a timescale, check the columns of the table that are visible on-screen. Unless you choose the Print All Sheet Columns option on the View tab of the Page Setup dialog box, the rightmost column that is completely visible is the last column of the table that appears on the printed report. For example, in the initial Gantt Chart view (where the ID, Task Name, and Duration are the only columns visible), the printed report doesn't show the other columns in the table unless you scroll to display more columns or choose to display all columns on the View tab of the Page Setup dialog box.

TROUBLESHOOTING

I've changed the display in the Gantt Chart view to view only the task ID by moving the partition to the far left. Yet both the ID and the Indicator columns continue to be printed. By default, the ID and Indicator columns are both printed on the Gantt Chart even if you change the screen display to show only the ID column. First make sure that only the ID column is being displayed on the screen, and then edit the table that is currently being used in the view by choosing View, Table, More Tables. Choose the Edit button to display the Table Definition dialog box. You need to uncheck the Lock First Column check box. When this box is not checked, only the first column, ID, will print.

Finally, if you want the printed view to focus on just part of the project, you may want to choose a filter to display only a subset of the tasks or resources. Most of the filters are useful tools in building and managing a project. Chapter 12, "Reviewing the Project Plan," describes the general use of filters, including how to use the new AutoFilter capability. In Chapter 20, "Using the Standard Views, Table, and Filters," you learn about the built-in filters and their uses. Chapter 22, "Customizing Views, Tables, and Filters," describes how to customize filters. To apply a predefined filter, choose Tools, Filtered For, and choose the appropriate filter.

> **TIP**
>
> A quick way to apply a filter is to use the Filter drop-down list box on the Formatting toolbar.

Sorting the Display   After displaying the data you want to print, you may want to rearrange the order of the tasks or resources. To sort the table lists, follow these steps:

1. Choose Project, Sort. A drop-down list appears with several sort choices. Choose the Sort By option. The Sort dialog box appears.

> **CAUTION**
>
> Most of the time you will sort tasks or resources temporarily to display or print project information differently from how it appears in the view. Make sure the Permanently Renumber Tasks check box is deselected if you are only temporarily sorting the data.

2. Choose the Sort By list box, and select the column on which to sort the records.
3. Choose Ascending or Descending for the order of the sort. If you anticipate duplicates to occur in the first column you are sorting on, use the two Then By list boxes to create second and third level sorts, if necessary.
4. Choose the Sort button to execute the sort.
   ▶ **See** "Sorting the Task and Resource Lists," **p. 399**

Figure 13.5 shows the Sort dialog box where all the tasks will be sorted by Cost in descending order, from highest to lowest. One of the choices at the bottom of the dialog box is Keep Outline Structure. This would result in a sort where the detail tasks remain with their summary tasks and are only sorted within the "phase" they are in.

FIG. 13.5

The Sort dialog box provides three levels of sorting.

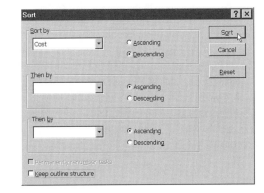

If you print the report, it shows the data in the order displayed on-screen. If at some point you want to return to the default sort order, choose the Reset button in the Sort dialog box.

Enhancing the Display of the Text Data   You can format text data to emphasize or highlight selected categories of tasks or resources. For example, you may want to display summary tasks in bold, milestones in italics, or overallocated resources (in a resource view) as underlined. The display of the gridlines and the column and row separator lines can be customized. In views with a timescale, you can customize the time units and labels used to represent the time units. In graphics views, special graphical features from a *palette* may be selected. All these customizing features are covered in detail in Chapter 22. Use these display enhancements selectively to improve the presentation quality of your printed reports.

Setting and Clearing Page Breaks   You can force a page break when printing task and resource lists so that a new page starts at a specific task or resource—even if the automatic page break doesn't occur until further down the list. Page breaks are tied to the task or resource you select when you set the page break. Even if you sort the list or hide a task by collapsing the outline, a new page starts at the task or resource where the page break was set.

Page breaks also affect the printing of the built-in reports. The final dialog box you see just before printing offers an option to use or ignore the page breaks you set manually. This feature prevents you from having to remove all page breaks for one special printout and later having to replace the breaks. You can remove one page break or all page breaks with relative ease.

To set a page break, select the row just below the intended page break. This row becomes the first row on a new page. Choose Insert, Page Break. A dashed line appears above the selected row to indicate the presence of a manually inserted page break.

Part

IV

Ch

13

To remove a page break, reselect the row just below the page break. Choose Insert, Remove Page Break. (Notice that when a page break row is selected, the menu choice changes to Remove Page Break.) The selected page break is removed.

To remove all page breaks, select all the rows in the active view by clicking the first column heading on the far left side of the view. Typically, this is an empty gray rectangle above the task or resource ID number. Choose Insert, Remove All Page Breaks. (The wording of the Page Breaks command changes to Remove All Page Breaks.)

N O T E   You cannot set the page breaks on the PERT Chart, but you can move the task nodes to either side of the automatic page breaks. You also can instruct Microsoft Project not to allow a task node to fall on a page break. To display page breaks in the PERT Chart view, choose Format, Layout. The Show Page Breaks check box controls whether lines are drawn on-screen to indicate where the page breaks occur in printing. Select the Show Page Breaks option to display page breaks. With the page breaks displayed, you can see where you need to move task nodes relative to the page breaks. ▪

To keep Microsoft Project from placing PERT Chart task nodes on a page break, make sure the Adjust for Page Breaks option is chosen on the Layout dialog box.

T I P   This setting doesn't take effect until you choose Layout Now to redraw the PERT Chart.

▶ **See** "Moving Task Nodes in the PERT Chart View," **p. 233**

 In PERT Charts, page breaks are automatically displayed, but you may have to zoom out to see them. Choose View, Zoom, or choose the Zoom Out button to see the page breaks in the PERT Chart. You cannot set the page breaks on the PERT Chart, but you can move the task nodes to either side of the automatic page breaks. Choose Format, Layout, and check the Show Page Breaks and the Adjust for Page Breaks options. With the page breaks displayed, you can see where you need to move task nodes relative to the page breaks.

▶ **See** "Formatting the PERT Chart" **p. 719**

TROUBLESHOOTING

Project is ignoring the manual page breaks I have set. Check the Print dialog box and make sure that there is an X in the Manual Page Breaks check box.

Changing the Page Setup

You can change features about the appearance of the pages in any view with the Page Setup command. For example, the margins, orientation, headers and footers, and legend for graphic views can be modified. A separate page setup configuration is available for each of the views and reports. This means that changing the header and footer you design for Gantt Charts does not change the header and footer you design for Task Sheets.

To change the page settings for the active view, choose File, Page Setup or choose the Page Setup button in Print Preview. (If the active view cannot be printed, the File, Page Setup command is not available.) The Page Setup dialog box is displayed for the active view.

Figure 13.6 shows the Page tab of the Page Setup dialog box for Gantt Charts. Notice the name of the active view appears in the title bar.

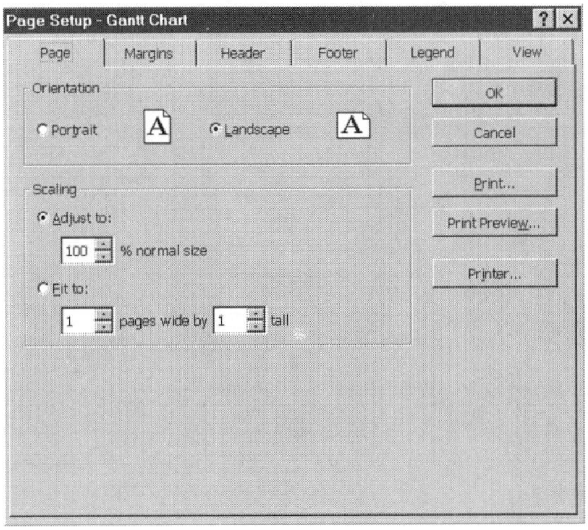

FIG. 13.6

Use the Page tab in the Page Setup dialog box to set the page orientation for printing.

Make the changes described in the following sections and then choose OK.

▶ **See** "Organizing Views in Project Files," **p. 764**

Using the Page Setup Dialog Box   The current settings on the Page Setup dialog box for any view are saved with the project file. They are not used when you print the view with other project files. If you want to use the settings from another project file, use the Organizer feature of Microsoft Project.

As with other dialog boxes, the Page Setup dialog box has multiple tabs. Each tab at the top accesses a different collection of settings. To see the settings for a particular topic, choose the appropriate tab.

Selecting the Orientation   The Page tab (refer to Figure 13.6) contains options used to set the page orientation to Portrait (upright) or Landscape (sideways). This setting overrides the default orientation set in the Print Setup dialog box. If you intend to add the printout to another document or if you have a number of tasks and a short timescale, the Portrait orientation would be best. If on the other hand you have a longer timescale, the Landscape orientation would display more of the timescale per printed page.

Scaling the Printout   In previous versions of Microsoft Project, scaling the printout was only available if you had a PostScript printer. Now scaling options are available for all printers, not just PostScript printers. These options allow you to enlarge or reduce the printouts either by a specified percentage or by a given number of pages.

Part
IV

Ch
13

Scaling can be used to reduce or enlarge your printout. In Figure 13.7, the final task is being printed on the bottom two pages. You can adjust the printout to compress the pages so the last task is included in the other pages. Select the Fit To option in the scaling area of the Page tab (refer to Figure 13.6). In this case, you would set the printout to fit to two pages wide by one page tall.

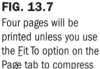

FIG. 13.7
Four pages will be printed unless you use the Fit To option on the Page tab to compress the printout.

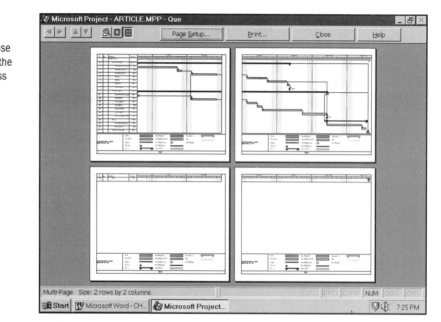

Specifying the Margins   Choose the Margins tab in the Page Setup dialog box to set the margins as appropriate (see Figure 13.8). The default margin is half an inch (.5) for the top, bottom, left, and right margins. Microsoft Project prints with a quarter inch (.25) margin, even if you reduce the margin to zero (0). If a header or footer is added or if borders are displayed on every page, the margin automatically expands to fit the text, though no change is displayed in the setup dialog box.

Placing Borders   Also on the Margins tab of the Page Setup dialog box are options for placing borders on the printed view. You can use borders to surround the page and separate the body of the report from the header, footer, and legend. By default, borders are printed with every page. For multiple-page PERT Charts that you want to tape together, this capability makes cutting and pasting easier if you place borders around the outer pages only.

To enclose each page in a lined border, choose Every Page in the Borders Around section on the Margins tab of the dialog box. To place borders on the outside pages only, choose Outer Pages (for PERT Charts only). To suppress all borders, choose None.

FIG. 13.8

The Margins page is used to change the width of the margins of your printout.

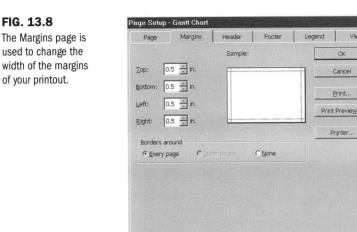

Descriptions of the Header and Footer Buttons   On the Header and Footer tabs of the Page Setup dialog box are seven buttons that can be used to format, insert system codes, or insert pictures into the header or footer (see Figure 13.9). Most views have a default footer indicating the printed page number.

The buttons shown in Figure 13.9 are described in the following list:

- *Font.* Displays the Font dialog box. Options for formatting font, font style, size, and color are available. Text you type in, system codes inserted, or any of the project information items added from the list box may be formatted using the Text Styles button. You must first highlight the text or code to be formatted before choosing the Font button.

- *Page Number.* Inserts the code &[Page] for the current page number. Only the page number is printed. If you want the header or footer to display Page 2 where 2 represents the number of the page, you must type the word **Page** followed by the code. The header or footer would show Page &[Page].

- *Total Page Count.* Inserts a code &[Pages] for the total number of pages. Only the number representing the total number of pages is printed. If you want the header or footer to display Page 2 of 10 where 2 represents the current page and 10 the total number of pages, you must type the word **Page** followed by the Page Number code, and then type the word **of** followed by the Total Page Count code. The header or footer would show Page &[Page] of &[Pages].

- *Current System Date.* Inserts a code &[Date] in the header or footer that is based on the date in your computer system. This is used when you want to indicate the date your view or report was printed.

- *Current System Time.* Inserts a code &[Time] in the header or footer that is based on the time in your computer system. This is used when you want to indicate the time your view or report was printed.

FIG. 13.9

The Header tab of the Page Setup dialog box enables you to customize your headers.

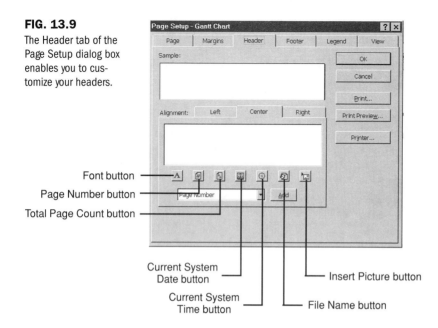

Font button

Page Number button

Total Page Count button

Current System Date button

Current System Time button

Insert Picture button

File Name button

N O T E It is very useful to print the date and time on your view and reports, especially if you are producing several revisions in a single day or over several days. ▪

- *File Name.* Inserts a code &[File] in the header or footer that reflects the name of the project file. The file extension (.MPP) is not displayed with the file name.

- *Insert Picture.* Inserts any type of picture file including: WMF, PCS, CGM, TIF, BMP, and GIF. This is particularly useful for inserting your company logo.

Entering Headers and Footers You can enter up to five lines of header text and three lines of footer text to repeat on each page of the printed document. You can type literal text in the header and footer, or you can place codes that are replaced with system variables (date, time, file name, or page number) or with field values from the project file (project name, company name, project file name, start date for the project, and so on).

Unless you use alignment codes to specify otherwise, the header and footer appear centered between the margins, as indicated by the center alignment tab. In either the Header or Footer tab of the Page Setup dialog box, the Sample text box at the top of the tab shows what your header or footer will look like. The default footer is the word Page followed by a system code for the current page number. To enter a header or footer, follow these steps:

1. Select either the Header or Footer tab of the Page Setup dialog box.
2. Choose the desired Alignment tab (Left, Center, or Right).
3. Use the box below the Alignment tabs to type the appropriate text you want to appear on the header or footer.

Or, choose one of the buttons to insert a system code—for example, page number, total page count, date, time, or file name.

Or, select the pull-down box below the buttons to insert information from the project—for example, project name, project manager, project start date, or the name of a filter applied to the view. Scroll in the list, as there are many options to choose from. If you use one of the items in the pull-down box, click the Add button to insert the information into the header or footer.

4. If you want to format any of the text or codes in the header or footer, highlight the text or code and use the Font button. See Figure 13.10 for a sample header.

TIP There are also keyboard shortcuts for applying formats. Select the text or code and use Ctrl+B to apply bold formatting. Ctrl+I italicizes, and Ctrl+U underlines the selection.

FIG. 13.10
A header contains the Project Title, Company, and Project Manager displayed in the upper-left corner of each printed page. The text has been formatted using the Text Style button.

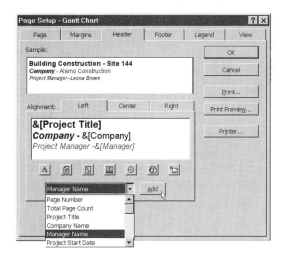

Using Legends   If the view you are printing has graphic elements (as do the PERT Chart, the Gantt Chart, and the Resource Graph), you can place a legend in the printout to explain the graphic elements used. Choose the Legend tab to display choices for configuring the display of the legend (see Figure 13.11).

You can enter up to three lines of legend text in each of the three alignment areas to repeat on each page of the printed document. Just as with the Header and Footer tab, seven buttons on the Legend tab of the Page Setup dialog box can be used to format, insert system codes, or insert pictures into the legend. Additionally, a drop-down list box enables you to insert information specific to the project.

The default legend displays the project title and date the view or report was printed in the Left alignment tab.

FIG. 13.11

The Legend tab of the Page Setup dialog box provides you with options for customizing the legend in your printout.

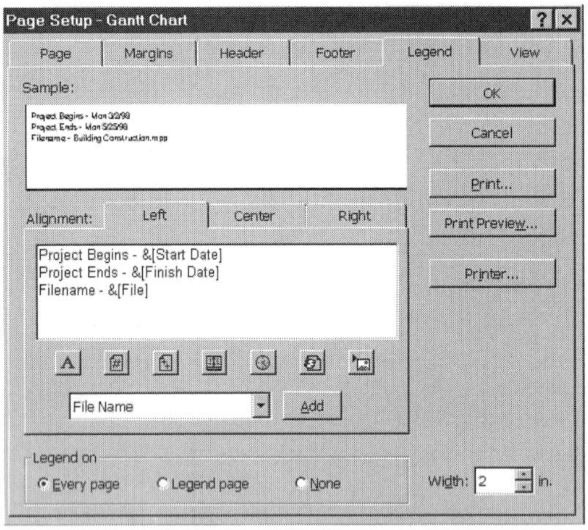

The text area can occupy up to half the legend area. You regulate the width of the legend text area by typing a number from 0 to 5 in the Width box; the number represents how many inches of the legend area are devoted to the text. Typing a **0** means all the legend area is devoted to the graphical legends. Typing a **5** means 5 inches of the area is reserved for text.

The formatting of the legend text is regulated with the Font button on the Legend tab, in the same manner as header and footer text is.

The last option on the Legend tab enables you to select where to display the legend. You can choose from the following commands:

- *Every Page*. Prints the legend at the bottom of each page.
- *Legend Page*. Prints the legend once on an extra page at the end of the report.
- *None*. Suppresses the display of a legend entirely.

Figure 13.11 shows the Legend tab for a legend to be placed at the bottom of all pages. The legend text is used to display the start and finish dates for the project and the project file name. The text area occupies two inches of the legend area width. (Skip to Figure 13.19 for a sample legend that has a picture and the start date in the legend text area.)

Formatting Header, Footer, and Legend Text The Font button is available for changing the text formatting of header, footer, and/or legend text. This button appears as a capital A (refer to Figure 13.9) and is just to the left of the code buttons for inserting file and system variables, as discussed in the section on headers, footers, and legends. First select the Alignment tab that has the text you want to format. Project gives you the option of formatting all the text on that tab the same, or you can apply a different format to each line of text.

It is necessary to select the text before you choose the Font button. Project 98 enables you to format part or all of the line. This is a new feature in Project. Choose the Font button to display the Font dialog box (see Figure 13.12), which you use to apply formatting to the text in the header, footer, and legend.

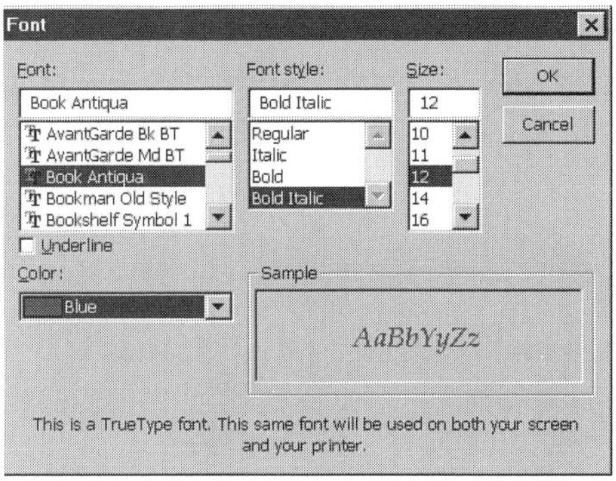

FIG. 13.12

The Font dialog box enables you to format all of the text or apply a different format to each line of text.

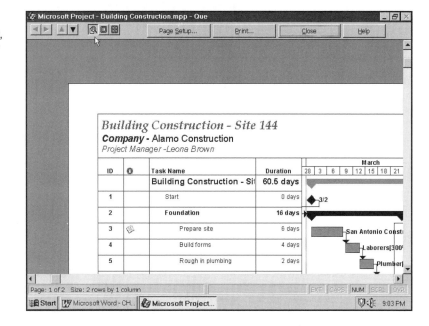

You can choose a font by selecting the entry list arrow to the right of the Font box. Choose the print attributes you want (bold, italic, or a combination) by selecting from the Font Style list box. Turn on underline by checking the Underline check box. After you choose the font and the font styles, choose the font point size (if multiple sizes are available) by selecting from the Size list box. If you are using a color printer or plotter, you also can choose the Color of the text. After all items are formatted, choose OK to return to the Page Setup dialog box.

Figure 13.12 shows the Font as Book Antiqua, with a font style of Bold Italic. The size is 12-point with a blue color. Figure 13.13 shows these settings as applied to the top line of a header.

FIG. 13.13

A preview of the header, zoomed in. Each line or part of a line can be formatted differently.

Part

IV

Ch

13

After you configure all page setup options, choose OK to close the Page Setup dialog box. Alternatively, you may choose to view your changes with the Print Preview button or to print directly with the Print button.

TROUBLESHOOTING

I've selected a font, but the font size I want is not listed in the Size list box. If the point size you want doesn't appear to be available, highlight the current font size and type the size in the box directly below the Size heading for a custom font size.

Selecting Special Options for Views Choose the View tab in the Page Setup dialog box, shown in Figure 13.14, to see options specific to the view being printed. These settings are for all views except the Calendar view. Some options on the View tab do not apply to all views and are displayed in dimmed mode (are inactive) for these views.

FIG. 13.14

The View tab of the Page Setup dialog box, for all views except the Calendar view.

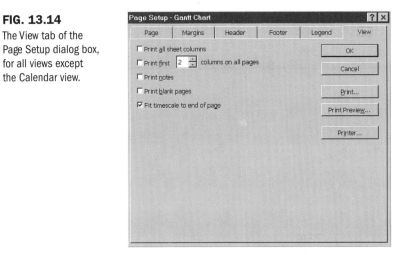

The View tab displays some of the most valuable print settings. When printing the Calendar view, the options on the View tab will be different than those listed here:

- For views with sheets like the Gantt Chart, Delay Gantt, Detail Gantt, Task Sheet, and Resource Sheet, click the Print All Sheet Columns check box to print all columns of the sheet, regardless of whether they are completely visible on the screen.

- Select the check box for Print First x Columns on All Pages to override the default of only printing the ID numbers, indicators, and task names on the first column of pages (refer to Figure 13.14). This option enables you to print a specified number of columns on all pages.

■ Select the Print <u>N</u>otes check box to print notes that have been entered for Tasks or Resources.

■ Uncheck the Print <u>B</u>lank Pages option to suppress the printing of blank pages. The default is for all pages to print.

■ Leave the check box for Fit Timescale to End of Page checked to ensure that a timescale unit (a week, for example) does not break across pages.

The following options are available for the Calendar view on the View tab of the Page Setup dialog box (see Figure 13.15):

■ Select <u>M</u>onths Per Page and choose either <u>1</u> or <u>2</u> months on a page.

■ Marking the Only Show <u>D</u>ays in Month check box will display a blank box indicating a day from another month, like a placeholder. However, the calendar will not display the dates or tasks in boxes for days in other months. For example, if September is the current month and the 1st of September begins on a Tuesday, then the dates and tasks for Sunday and Monday of that week (August 30th and 31st respectively) do not display on the printout.

If you mark the <u>O</u>nly Show Weeks in Month check box, only those weeks from the month are displayed. Weeks from other months are not printed. If the Calendar view is displaying six weeks—all five weeks in September and a week in October—only those weeks in September will print. The printout will not reflect the sixth week (in October).

■ Select Wee<u>k</u>s Per Page and type the number of weeks in the entry box. This is very useful if you have many tasks and want to print one or two weeks on a page. If you have more than eight weeks per page, the information becomes unreadable.

FIG. 13.15

The View tab of the Page Setup dialog box, for the Calendar view.

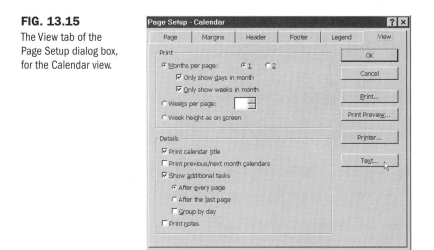

■ Use the Week Height as on <u>S</u>creen option if you want the printed calendar to match the week height on the screen display of Calendar view.

- The calendar title is printed at the top of each page when the Print Calendar Title check box is marked. You can change the format of the title by choosing Format, Timescale.

- Select the Print Previous/Next Month Calendars option to have miniature calendars of the previous and next months appear in the upper-left and upper-right corners of the printed calendar. Only the dates are printed for the miniatures; no project information is displayed.

- The Show Additional Tasks option is used when more tasks exist than can be displayed on the calendar. You have the choice of printing these overflow tasks After Every Page or After the Last Page. The default for displaying additional tasks is After Every Page.

  The Group by Day check box displays the overflow page with each day listed. If a task occurs across several days, it will be listed beneath every date the task is being worked on. By default this check box is not selected, and the additional tasks are listed once, based on the day the task starts.

- Check the Print Notes option to print the notes for the tasks. The notes are printed on a separate page after the calendar or overflow page. The task ID and name appear with the note.

- The Text button enables you to format the font type, font style, size, and color for all printed text; monthly titles; previous/next month miniature calendars; or overflow tasks (see Figure 13.16).

FIG. 13.16
For Calendar view, you have the option to format the way certain text appears when printed.

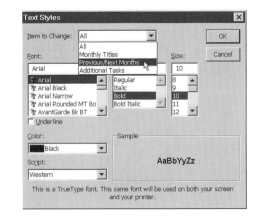

Using Print Preview

You can choose File, Print Preview to preview on-screen the look of the printed document. You also can choose the Print Preview button in the Page Setup dialog box or the Print Preview button from the toolbar. Figure 13.17 shows the Print Preview screen for the settings illustrated to this point in this chapter.

The initial preview screen shows the entire first page of the view being printed. If multiple pages exist, you can use the buttons at the top left of the preview screen to scroll left, right, up, and down one page at a time (see Table 13.1). You can zoom in on the details of a page by choosing the Zoom button or by using the mouse pointer, which changes to a magnifying glass when positioned over a page. Simply click the part of the page you want to see in greater detail. The magnifying glass only appears while the pointer is over the page (otherwise, the pointer is an arrow).

FIG. 13.17
Always preview before you print.

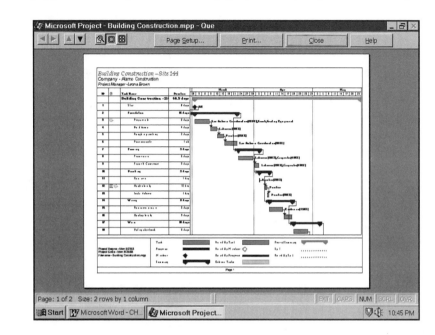

Table 13.1 The Print Preview Buttons

Button	Effect	Keyboard Shortcut
◀	Move left one page	Alt+left arrow
▶	Move right one page	Alt+right arrow
▲	Move up one page	Alt+up arrow
▼	Move down one page	Alt+down arrow
🔍	Zoom in on one page	Alt+1 (one) (Click area of page to zoom into)
▤	View one full page	Alt+2 (Click specific page to view)
▦	View multiple pages	Alt+3 (Click area outside of page)

Part
IV

Ch
13

Use Alt+Z to switch between the Zoom, One Page, and Multiple Page views. Alt+1, 2, and 3 only use the numbers above the alphanumeric keys, not those on the number pad.

N O T E   If the Print Blank Pages option on the View tab of the Page Setup dialog box is not checked, blank pages are displayed with a gray shaded background and are not printed. ■

Figure 13.18 shows the zoomed-in view of the title area of page 1 of this preview, and Figure 13.19 shows the zoomed-in legend text area in the bottom-left corner of the page. Figure 13.20 illustrates the multiple page preview of the same report. Note that the status line in Figure 13.20 indicates there are 12 pages and that the size of the printout will be three rows by four columns. Pages are numbered down the columns, starting from the left. Therefore, page 3 of the report is the bottom page in the left column on-screen.

FIG. 13.18

A preview of a Gantt Chart, zoomed in to show the title area.

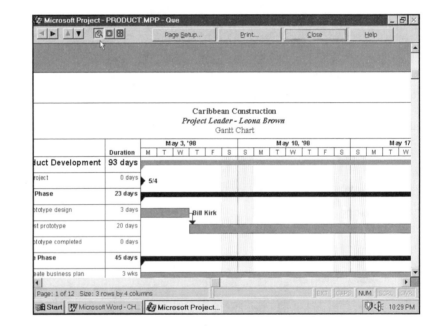

You can open the Page Setup dialog box from the Print Preview screen by choosing the Page Setup button at the top of the preview screen. If you have a question about one of the available options, choose the Help button for context-sensitive online help. When you are ready to print, choose the Print button (see the following section). To make modifications, or if you decide against printing at this time, choose the Close button to return to the project view.

T I P   Ctrl+P is a shortcut key combination that you can use instead of choosing File, Print.

FIG. 13.19
A preview of a Gantt
Chart, zoomed in to see
the legend area.

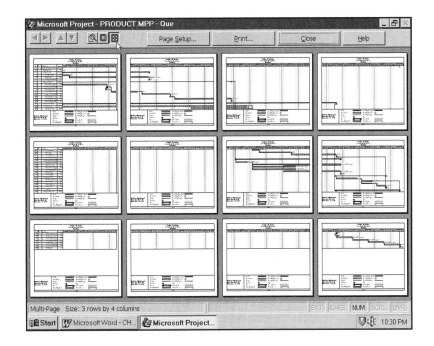

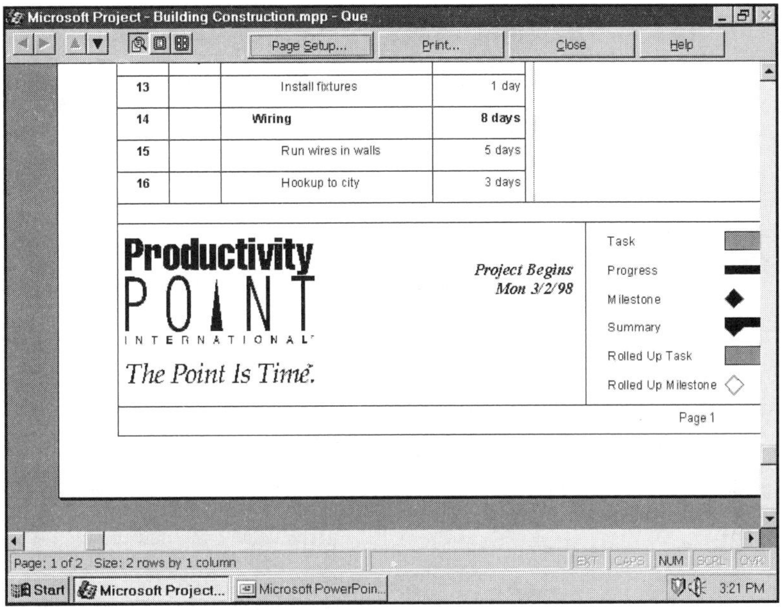

FIG. 13.20
The multi-page view of
a Gantt Chart, in the
preview screen.

Once you have established the print options, these settings become a permanent part of the
project file. You may change the settings at any time.

Using the Print Command

When the view is refined on-screen and the page setup and printer options are selected, the final step in printing is to choose File, Print. The Print dialog box appears and presents you with choices for printing the current screen view. You also can choose the Print button from the Print Preview screen or the Print button from the toolbar.

> **CAUTION**
>
> The Print button on the toolbar sends the view to the printer directly, without first presenting the dialog box where you choose your print options.

When you choose File, Print or select the Print button in the preview screen, the Print dialog box appears (see Figure 13.21).

FIG. 13.21

Choose what to print, the quality of the printout, and the number of copies from the Print dialog box.

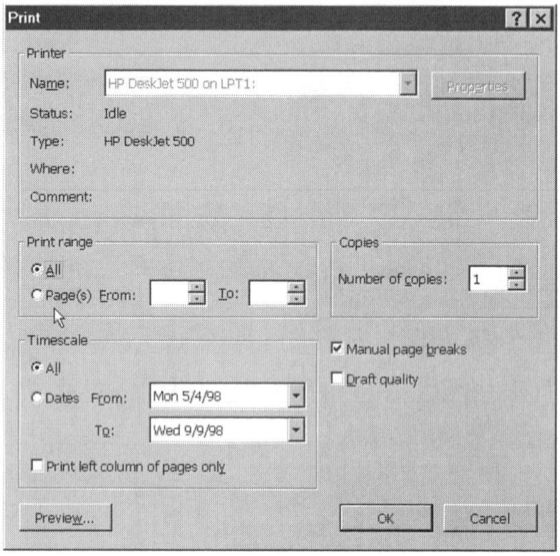

Some options on the Print dialog box do not apply to all views and may be displayed in dimmed mode (meaning they are inactive) when printing from these views.

Selecting the Pages to Print   In the Preview screen, you can see the number of pages that will print. When you display the Print dialog box, the default is to print all pages, as indicated in the All option of the Print Range area. If you only want to print some of the pages, enter the starting page number in the Page(s) From box and the ending page number in the To box. To reprint just page 5 of a view, for example, type **5** in both the Page(s) From and To fields. On views that include a timescale, the default is to print from the start date of the project through the finish date. You can limit the printed output to a specific time span. See the upcoming section, "Printing Views with a Timescale," for details.

If you embedded manual page breaks in a task list or a resource list, these page breaks are not used in printing unless the Manual Page Breaks check box is marked. Unmark the check box if you want to ignore the manual page breaks.

> **N O T E** Printing with manual page breaks is inappropriate if you previously sorted the list for a particular report, because the manual page breaks make no sense in the sorted order. See earlier sections in this chapter—"Sorting the Display" and "Setting and Clearing Page Breaks"—for more information. ◼

Selecting the Quality and Number of Copies   Mark the Draft Quality check box to speed up printing, or leave the box unmarked to use final-quality printing.

For multiple copies of a view, enter a number in the Number of Copies box. You must collate the multiple copies by hand because Microsoft Project instructs the printer to print all copies of the first page, and then all copies of the second page, and so on.

Printing Views with a Timescale   For views that contain timescales, you can print the full date range of the project, from the start date to the finish date of the project, which is the default setting. Alternatively, you can print the timescale data for a limited range of dates. Choose the All option button to print the entire project, or choose the Dates From option button to specify a limited range of dates. Enter the starting date in the Dates From box and the ending date in the To box.

Reminder—the screen display dictates whether the information is printed showing weeks, months, quarters, or years. Choose View, Zoom or choose the Zoom In/Zoom Out buttons on the Standard toolbar to change the timescale on the screen.

TROUBLESHOOTING

When I print my Gantt Chart view, the timescale begins flush to the task names columns. It also chops off my resource names on the last few tasks of the printout because they extend beyond the finish date. How do I avoid this? By default, the start and end dates of the project are displayed in the Timescale section of the Print dialog box. This causes the printout to display the beginning of the Gantt Chart bars flush against the task names on the left side of the printed view. It also has the printout stop when the last task is completed, regardless of whether or not the resource names printed to the right of the last few task bars can be seen.

You want to display a gap between the table side of the Gantt Chart and the beginning of the task bars and leave a few extra days at the end of the printed project view. You can accomplish this by changing the Dates From entry to a date slightly earlier (two or three days) than the beginning of the project. This starts the Gantt Chart timescale at that date, which pushes all task bars slightly to the right for better display on paper. If you can't see the resource names on the last few tasks, extend the Dates To entry slightly (two or three days). Use the Preview button to see how this will look before you begin printing your pages.

Choose the Print Left Column of Pages Only check box to print only the pages on the far left side in Print Preview, Multi-Page Layout. If you refer to Figure 13.20, for example, the three pages that contain the task descriptions are the left column of pages.

 Sending the View to the Printer Before you print the document, you should preview it, especially if you have made changes in the Print dialog box. You can choose the Preview button in the Print dialog box or the Print Preview button in the Page Setup dialog box to review the effects of the choices you made. If you are not currently viewing the Print or Page Setup dialog boxes, you may also access Print Preview by using the Print Preview button on the Standard toolbar. If you selected a limited number of pages to print, the Print Preview screen still shows the entire report. Nevertheless, when you are actually printing, only the selected pages are printed.

To start the print job, in the Print dialog box choose OK. Or you can use the Print button on the Standard toolbar.

Printing Standard Reports

Project has designed reports for you to use; you can customize these reports, or create your own reports. The 25 predesigned reports have been divided into five standard categories of reports and are available by choosing View, Reports. Choose this command to display the Reports dialog box shown in Figure 13.22.

FIG. 13.22
Select one of the categories on the Reports dialog box to choose from several impressive built-in reports.

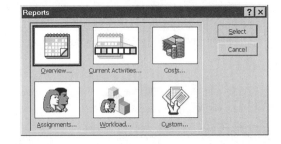

Double-click the category of reports that you want to view, or click a category and choose Select. A subsequent dialog box lists the individual reports available for each category. Table 13.2 lists those individual reports.

Table 13.2 The Standard, Predefined Reports

Category	Report Name
Overview	Project Summary
	Top-Level Tasks
	Critical Tasks
	Milestones
	Working Days

Category	Report Name
Current Activities	Unstarted Tasks
	Tasks Starting Soon
	Tasks In Progress
	Completed Tasks
	Should Have Started Tasks
	Slipping Tasks
Costs	Cash Flow
	Budget
	Overbudget Tasks
	Overbudget Resources
	Earned Value
Assignments	Who Does What
	Who Does What When
	To-do List
	Overallocated Resources
Workload	Task Usage
	Resource Usage

The Custom category accesses a dialog box with numerous preformatted reports, many of which were in the categories previously discussed.

Once a report has been selected, you are taken into the Print Preview screen. From there, you can access the Page Setup and Print dialog boxes. To print a report, simply choose the Print button in the preview screen.

The Page Setup dialog box, the Print Preview screen, and the Print dialog box options are used the same way for reports as for the views, as discussed in earlier sections of this chapter. Due to the nature of the reports, some of the Page Setup and Print options may not be available. See the earlier section "Changing the Page Setup" and "Using the Print Command" for more information on these options.

▶ **See** "Using the Standard Reports," **p. 767**

▶ **See** "Customizing Reports," **p. 793**

From Here...

Now that you have learned how to preview views and reports, change the page setup options, and print the views or reports, there are many other capabilities within Project to customize the views or reports before you print.

The following chapters will assist you in customizing Microsoft Project:

▪ Chapter 21, "Formatting Views," shows you how to customize the look of the text and timescale bars, which includes working with sorting, fonts, color, and using the Gantt Chart Wizard.

Part
IV
Ch
13

■ Chapter 22, "Customizing Views, Tables, and Filters," assists you in tailoring these items for your specific needs. You learn how to customize the existing views, tables, and filters, as well as create your own from scratch.

■ Chapter 23, "Using the Standard Reports," explores the 25 predesigned reports in Microsoft Project. Most importantly, you learn why you might use a particular report.

■ Chapter 24, "Customizing Reports," helps you change the existing reports to make them more useful to you and design your own reports from scratch.

CHAPTER 14

Publishing Projects on the Web

Microsoft Project 98 offers many new Internet features, including saving your project to an HTML document and creating hyperlinks to other Web pages on the Internet or corporate intranet. In this chapter, we examine in depth all of the new Internet features of Microsoft Project 98. ■

Overview of Project 98's Internet features

Learn about saving a project as an HTML document for your Internet Web site or corporate intranet.

Navigating with hyperlinks

Discover Microsoft's Internet Explorer, Uniform Resource Locators (URLs), sending e-mail from a Web page, and navigating to Internet and intranet documents.

Exporting Project data to Web pages

Save your project as an HTML document, use maps to choose which Project fields to save to your Web page, and even include graphics in your Web document.

Adding, modifying, and deleting a hyperlink in your project

Learn to create hyperlinks to the Microsoft Project home page, link to a Word document on an intranet, or set up a hyperlink to a project resource's Internet home page.

Publishing your Web document

Master the steps for sending Web pages to a Web server or Internet server so that they can be viewed through a browser.

Overview of Project 98's Internet Features

Project 98 has many new features that integrate it with the Internet. Consistent with Word, PowerPoint, Excel, and Access, Microsoft Project includes a Save as HTML feature which lets you save your project as an HTML document that can be published to your Internet Web site or corporate intranet (see Figure 14.1).

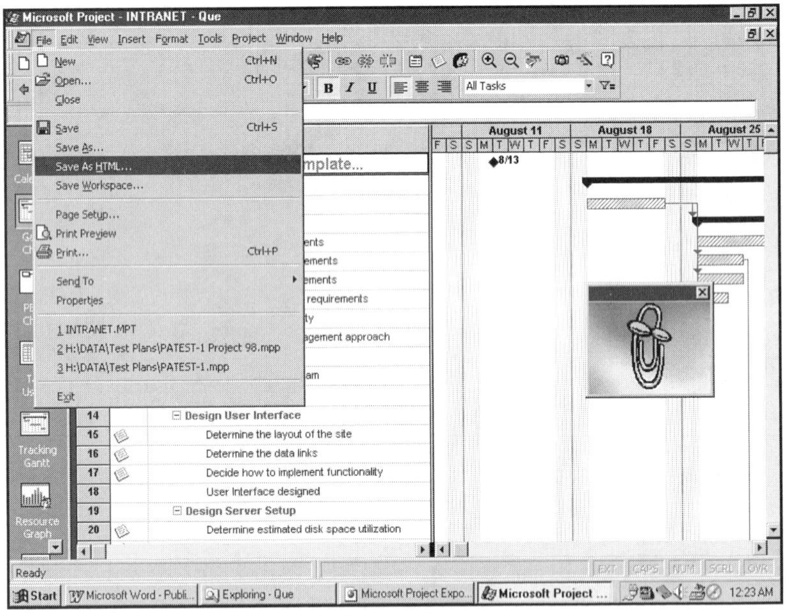

FIG. 14.1

Select Microsoft Project 98's Save as HTML menu item to save your project as a Web document.

In addition, Project 98's other new Web features include:

- The ability to save your Project information as an HTML document.

- The ability to create an Import/Export map which allows you to select the specific task, resource, and resource assignment fields to be included in your HTML document.

- The ability to set up templates for your Microsoft Project Web pages to include graphics for your company logo, custom backgrounds and colors, and fonts which you specify.

- Several new Web-related task and resource fields which store information as hyperlinks, which can be used to navigate to Web sites on the Internet or to documents stored on your Web server.

- The ability to communicate project information via your corporate intranet using the new Web browser-enabled workgroup features of Project 98. (For more information on this topic, see Chapter 18, "Using Microsoft Project in Workgroups.")

- The ability to save your project as a Microsoft Project Database (MPD) file, which can be used to generate Web pages which contain dynamic content from your project plan.

A Microsoft Project template which includes all the tasks for designing, rolling out, and supporting a corporate intranet.

The remainder of this chapter describes in detail each of these topics, including many real-world examples of how you can integrate Microsoft Project 98 with the Internet.

Navigating with Hyperlinks

The purpose of this section is to introduce you to some basic Internet concepts and terminology that provide the foundation for moving forward with how Microsoft Project 98 integrates with the Web.

Applications that are used to view documents on the Internet are called *Web browsers*. The two most popular Web browsers are Netscape Navigator and Microsoft Internet Explorer. The latest version of Microsoft's Web browser, Internet Explorer, is included for free on the Project 98 CD. A browser lets you navigate to a specific Internet site by referencing its Web address, also known as its *URL* (*Uniform Resource Locator*). For example, the URL for Microsoft's home page is **http://www.microsoft.com/**. By typing this URL in the address field of Internet Explorer (see Figure 14.2), the browser will navigate you directly to this site.

FIG. 14.2
View Microsoft's home page through Internet Explorer 3.0.

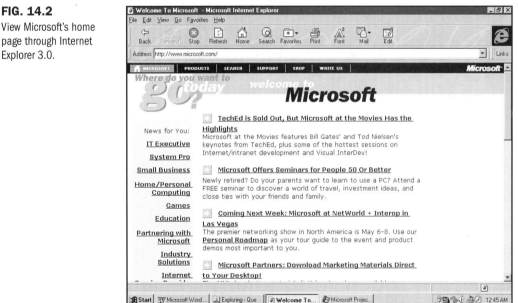

Hyperlinks provide the ability to quickly and easily jump from one document to a related document by simply clicking on a graphic or underlined text. For example, Windows Online Help frequently uses hyperlinks to jump from one topic to another within the help file.

The Internet has expanded the concept of hyperlinking in that a Web page on the Internet can navigate someone to another Web page stored on a server anywhere in the world.

A Web page (or Web document) is formatted using *Hypertext Markup Language*, or *HTML*. The HTML code contains all of the text, formatting, font and color information, and references to graphics that determine how a document will display in a Web browser. In addition, the HTML code may include hyperlinks which can navigate someone to another location on the Web.

N O T E Until recently, the only way to create documents for a Web site was to become an expert in writing HTML code (or hire someone to do it for you). Fortunately, Microsoft Project (as well as the other Office 97 applications) will *automatically* generate the HTML code for you by selecting the Save as HTML option. Once the HTML document is created, it can be opened directly into Internet Explorer (or any other Web browser) so you can immediately see how your documents will look when they are published on the Web. ▦

Later in this chapter, in the section "Modifying Project's Standard HTML Template," you will learn how to enhance the overall appearance of your Web pages by modifying the HTML code created from Project 98 to include specific font references and background graphics.

Exporting Project Data to Web Pages

In this section, you will step through several examples of saving your project as an HTML document. After you complete each example, you'll open the resulting HTML file in Internet Explorer so you can immediately see what it would look like if it were published on the Web.

For each of the following examples, the INTRANET.MPT template that comes with Project 98 (typically located in the Microsoft Office\Templates\Microsoft Project directory on your computer) is used, but you can use one of your Project files if you prefer.

Saving Your Project as an HTML Document

To save your project as an HTML document, follow these steps:

1. Open your Project file, and select File, Save as HTML. This will open the File Save dialog box (see Figure 14.3).

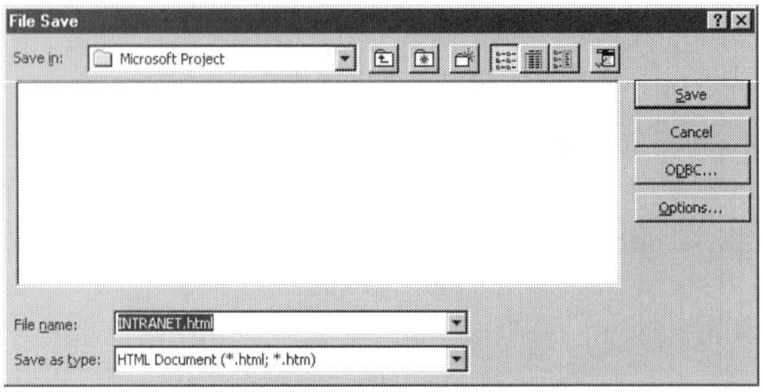

FIG. 14.3
The Microsoft Project
File Save dialog box
allows you to save your
project as an HTML
document.

2. Navigate to the directory where you want to save the document, and type the name of the HTML document in the File Name field. The document will automatically be assigned the .HTM extension.

3. Click the Save button, and the Export Format dialog box will open (see Figure 14.4).

FIG. 14.4

Microsoft Project 98's Export Format dialog box allows you to select an import/export map on which to base your HTML document.

4. Click the New Map button, and the Define Import/Export Map dialog box opens (see Figure 14.5).

FIG. 14.5

The Define Import/ Export Map dialog box allows you to define the type of project data (tasks, resources, and assignments) you want to export to your HTML document.

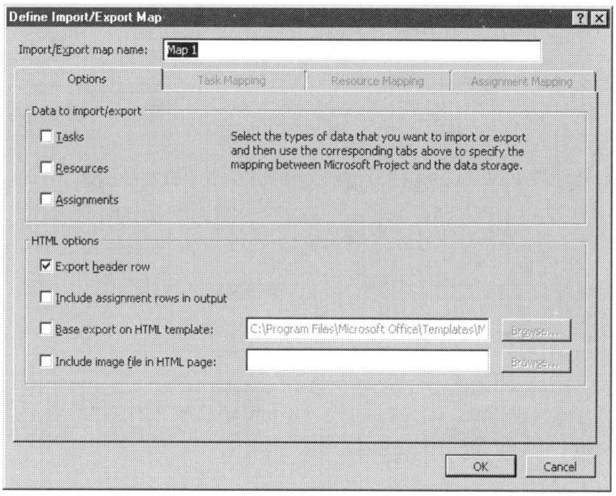

N O T E   An Import/Export map is a new feature of Project 98 which allows you to define the type of information to be included in your HTML document. You can create an Import/Export map which exports task data, resource data, resource assignment data, or any combination of the three. Once you select which *type* of data to export, you will then select the specific fields you want to export to your HTML document. ▓

5. In the Import/Export Map Name text box at the top of the dialog box, type a descriptive name for the Import/Export map. For example, if this map will contain task schedule information, you would type **Task Schedule Map** in this field.

6. In the Data to Import/Export section, select one or more check boxes for the type of data you want to export (refer to Figure 14.5).

N O T E   For each type of project data you select in the Define Import/Export Map dialog box (Tasks, Resources, or Assignments), the corresponding tab on the dialog box will be enabled (Task Mapping, Resource Mapping, or Assignment Mapping). When you select the Task Mapping, Resource Mapping, or Assignment Mapping tab of the dialog box, you will be presented with a screen that gives you the ability to select the specific fields to be exported for that type of project data. ▨

7. Select the tab corresponding to the type of data you are exporting (for example, Task Mapping), and the Import/Export dialog box will display the mapping options for that type of data (see Figure 14.6).

FIG. 14.6

This figure shows Microsoft Project 98's Define Import/Export Map dialog box displaying Task Mapping options. This dialog box is used to select the specific task, resource, or resource assignment fields to be exported to your HTML document.

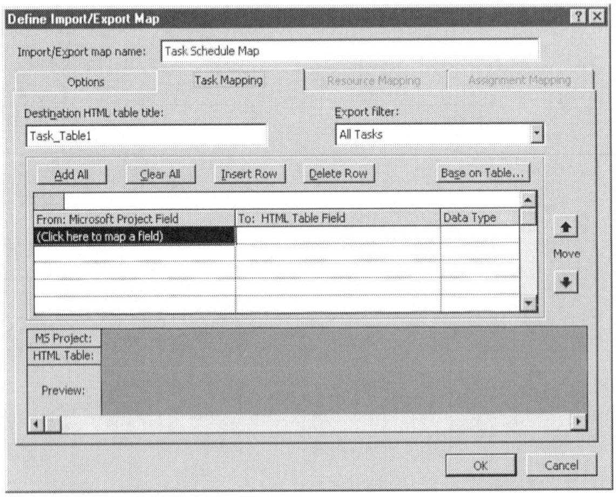

N O T E   Each type of data you export (Tasks, Resources, and Assignments) will be displayed in a separate table in the HTML document. ▨

8. In the Destination HTML Table Title field, type a descriptive name for the table, which will be generated in the HTML file for this data type. For example, if you are defining task fields to be exported for a corporate intranet project, you could type the name **Corporate Intranet Project Tasks**. This descriptive name will be displayed above the corresponding table in the HTML file (see Figure 14.7).

FIG. 14.7

The Destination HTML Table Title text box shows the title "Corporate Intranet Project Tasks." This title will display above the task table in your HTML document.

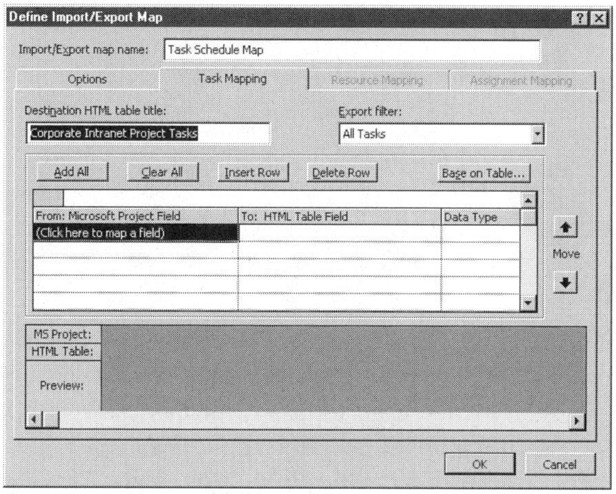

9. From the Export Filter drop-down list, select the filter to be used for the tasks or resources you are exporting to an HTML file. If you want to export all of the tasks or resources from your project, select the corresponding filter (All Tasks or All Resources).

N O T E The Export filter only applies to Task Mapping and Resource Mapping, since filters do not exist for assignments in Microsoft Project. ▪

TIP If you have not yet created the task or resource filter to be used with this Import/Export map, you can click the OK button to close the dialog box, create the filter, and select Save as HTML once again to continue where you left off.

10. The next step in setting up your Import/Export map is to define which fields you want to export to your HTML document. For example, to create a task schedule table, you would most likely select the ID, Name, Start, Finish, and Duration fields to be exported to the HTML document.

TIP If you have an existing Microsoft Project table that contains the same fields you want to export to your HTML document, click the Base on Table button and select the existing table on which you want to base your HTML table (see Figure 14.8).

11. In the From: Microsoft Project Field column, click the (Click Here to Map a Field) cell. From the drop-down list, select the first field you want to include in your table.

TIP A quick way to select the field you want from the drop-down list is to type the first letter of the field name once you have clicked the list. This will navigate you directly to the fields which start with that letter, rather than having to scroll down the entire list. This technique will work on any drop-down list in a Windows application.

Part
IV

Ch
14

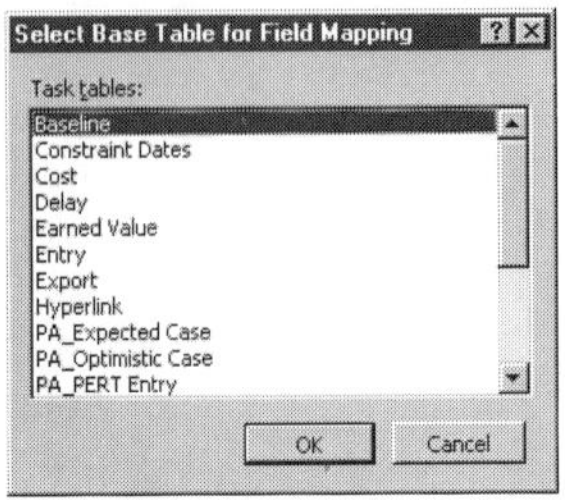

FIG. 14.8

The Select Base Table for Field Mapping dialog box allows you to select an existing Microsoft Project table on which to base your HTML table.

12. If you would like to display a header for this field other than the Microsoft Project field name in your HTML document, click the To: HTML File Field column, and type the new name you would like to use. For example, you may want to display "Task ID" as the column header instead of "ID" in your HTML document.

13. Repeat steps 11 and 12 for each field you want to export to your HTML document (see Figure 14.9).

Also, you can change the order of the fields in your table by clicking the Move Up and Move Down arrows on the right of the dialog box.

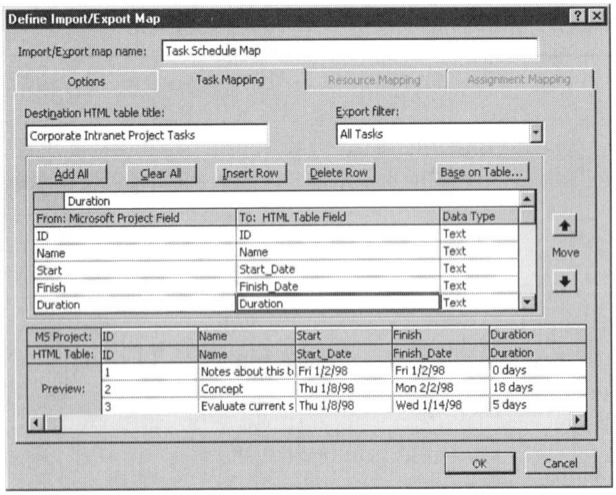

FIG. 14.9

This figure shows the Define Import/Export Map dialog box with several task-related fields selected.

N O T E As you build your table, you can use the Insert Row and Delete Row buttons to add or delete fields to your table. Or, you can use the Add All button to add every field for the corresponding data type to the table. Although this sounds intriguing, it is unlikely you will want to create a huge table in your HTML document containing *every* field available in Microsoft Project for that data type! ▪

14. Once you have selected the fields you want to export for this data type, repeat steps 7 through 13 for each of the other data types you are exporting.

15. Click the OK button to close the Define Import/Export Map dialog box, and click the Save button to save your project as an HTML document.

N O T E The Import/Export map is *automatically* saved in your GLOBAL.MPT file, and will be available for all of your other future projects. ◼

Viewing Your Project as an HTML Document

Now, you get to view the HTML file that was created in your Web browser. Start up your Web browser. For this example, we will be using Internet Explorer, but Netscape has a similar option.

1. Select File, Open, and the Open dialog box will open. Click the Browse button to navigate to your HTML file, and click Open.

2. From the Open dialog box, click the OK button (see Figure 14.10), and your Web browser will display the HTML document you created in Microsoft Project (see Figure 14.11).

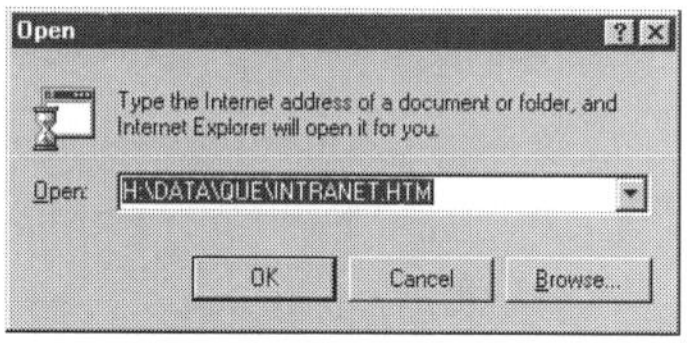

FIG. 14.10

The Microsoft Internet Explorer Open dialog box allows you to open a Web document by referring to its Internet address or file name.

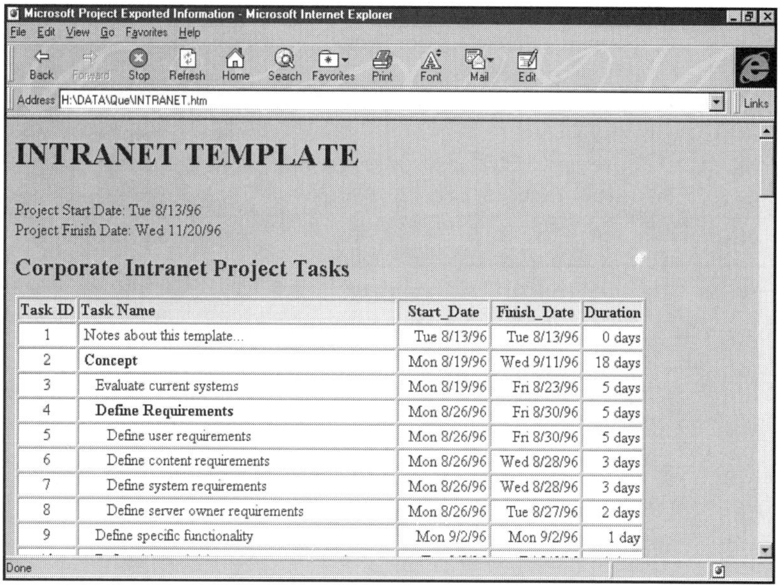

FIG. 14.11

This figure shows Microsoft Internet Explorer displaying the HTML document created from your project.

Part

IV

Ch

14

Defining Import/Export Map HTML Options

Now that you have created your first HTML document from Microsoft Project, let's examine some of the other available options you can choose when exporting your Project.

1. Open a plan in Microsoft Project, and select File, Save as HTML.

2. From the File Save dialog box, navigate to the directory where you want to save the document.

3. Type the name of the HTML document in the File Name field.

4. Click the Save button, and the Export Format dialog box will open (see Figure 14.12).

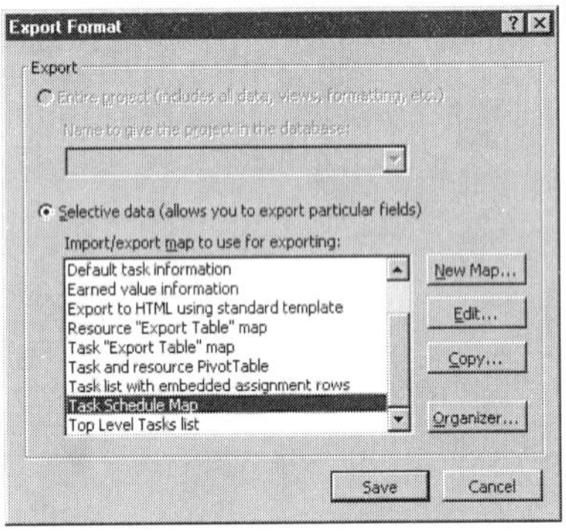

FIG. 14.12

The Export Format dialog box allows you to select the Import/Export map on which you want to base your HTML document.

5. From the Import/Export Map to Use for Exporting list box, select the Task Schedule Map used in the previous example and click the Edit button. The Define Import/Export Map dialog box will display.

N O T E   If you prefer to keep your original map intact, you can click the Copy button to make an exact copy of your first map.

6. The Export Header Row option on the Define Import/Export Map dialog box will export the HTML file field names to the first row of the table in your HTML document (see Figure 14.13). If you do not check this option, the first row of the table will contain the actual data (see Figure 14.14).

7. If you want to include the resources assigned to each task directly below the task row in your HTML document, check the Include Assignment Rows in Output option in the Define Import/Export Map dialog box. Figure 14.15 shows the results of selecting this option as displayed in Internet Explorer 3.0.

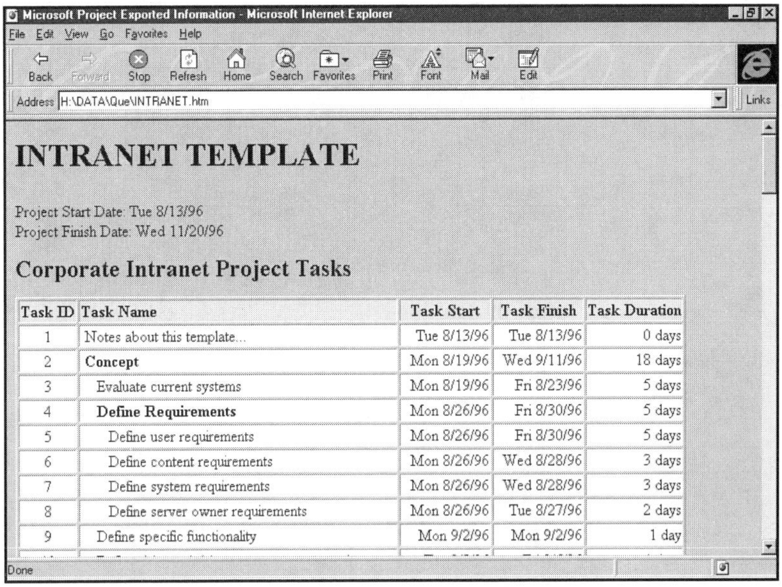

FIG. 14.13

This figure shows the HTML document displayed with the task field names in the first row of the table (for example, Task ID, Task Name, and so on) since the Export Header Row option was checked in the Define Import/Export Map dialog box.

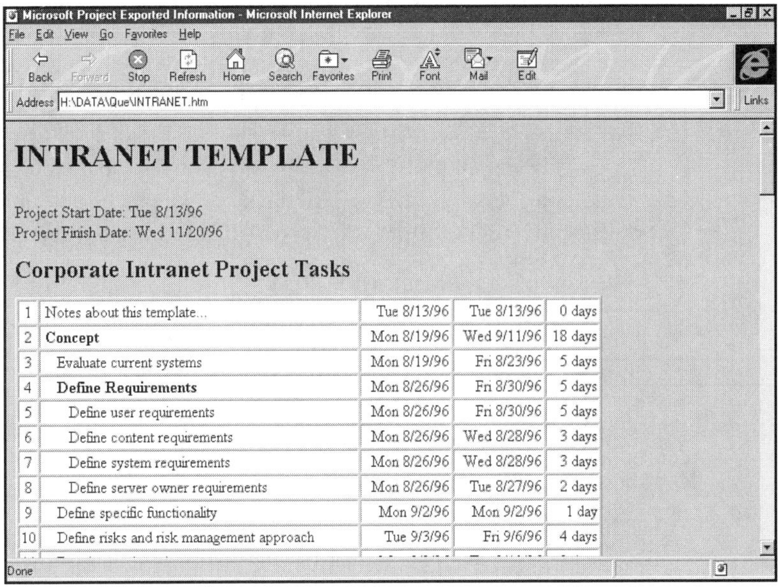

FIG. 14.14

This figure shows the HTML document displayed without the task field names in the first row of the table since the Export Header Row option was not checked in the Define Import/Export Map dialog box.

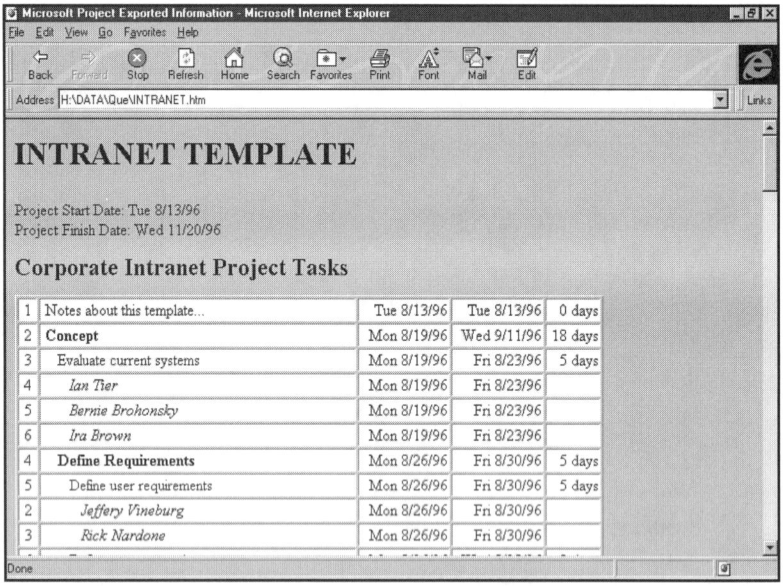

FIG. 14.15
The task table in your HTML document displayed with resource assignments below each task.

8. Microsoft Project comes with a default template named Standard Export.Html on which all of your HTML documents are based when you use the Save as HTML feature. In addition, Project also includes several other HTML templates on which you can base your HTML document. These templates contain formatting and other information that determines how your document will display in your Web browser.

   The Base Export on HTML Template option in the Define Import/Export Map dialog box allows you to select the HTML template on which you want to base your HTML document. To select a template for your HTML document, check the Base Export on HTML Template option. Then, click the Browse button to select the template you want to use for your HTML document. These templates are typically stored in the Program Files\Microsoft Office\Templates\Microsoft Project Web directory on your computer.

9. Once you have selected the appropriate options in the Define Import/Export dialog box, click OK, and the Export Format dialog box will display. Click the Save button, and your project will be saved as an HTML document.

The next section discusses how you can modify the Standard Export table to improve the layout and format of a Microsoft Project Web page.

Modifying Project's Standard HTML Template

In this section, you will explore some of the ways you can change the Standard Export HTML template that comes with Microsoft Project 98. You can actually modify the HTML code that is contained within the template to change several characteristics of the template's appearance, including:

- The background color of the HTML document
- Defining a background graphic for the template
- Adding graphic images, such as a company logo, to your Web page
- Changing the text which appears in the title bar of your browser when displaying your Web page
- Defining the font type, color, size, and justification of the HTML header
- Adding hyperlinks to other Web pages on the Internet or your corporate intranet
- Adding the ability to send an e-mail directly from your Web page

In each of the following examples, you will walk through the process of modifying the Standard Export.Html template that comes with Project 98. The Standard Export.Html template is a text document that can be edited in any text editor such as Notepad, or if you prefer, a word processor such as Microsoft Word.

As we proceed through each example below, we will continue to add modifications to the Standard Export template to create a highly customized, professional-looking Web page.

Changing the Background Color of Your Web Page

In the first example, we will change the background color of the template from the standard Windows gray to a light blue. Use the following steps to edit the Standard Export HTML template:

1. From your text editor, open the Standard Export.Html file, typically located in the Program Files\Microsoft Office\Templates\Microsoft Project Web directory (see Listing 14.1).

Listing 14.1   HTML Code from the Standard Export.html File

```
<HTML>
<HEAD>
<TITLE>Microsoft Project Exported Information</TITLE>
<META HTTP-EQUIV="Content-Type" CONTENT="text/html; charset=ISO-8859-1">
</HEAD>

<BODY>
<H1><!--MSProjectTemplate_ProjectTitle--></H1>
<P>
<!--MSProjectTemplate_Image-->
<P>
Project Start Date:<!--MSProjectTemplate_StartDate-->
<BR>Project Finish Date:<!--MSProjectTemplate_FinishDate-->
<P>
<H2><!--MSProjectTemplate_TaskTableTitle--></H2>
<!--MSProjectTemplate_TaskTable-->
<P>
<H2><!--MSProjectTemplate_ResourceTableTitle--></H2>
<!--MSProjectTemplate_ResourceTable-->
```

Part
IV

Ch
14

continues

Listing 14.1   Continued

```
<P>
<H2><!--MSProjectTemplate_AssignmentTableTitle--></H2>
<!--MSProjectTemplate_AssignmentTable-->
<P>

<!--- Footer --->
</TABLE>
<HR>
<CENTER>
<TABLE WIDTH=500 BORDER=0>
<TD ALIGN=CENTER>
<A HREF="HTTP://WWW.MICROSOFT.COM/MSPROJECT"><B>Microsoft Project Home
Page</B></A></TD>
<TD ALIGN=CENTER>
<A HREF="HTTP://WWW.MICROSOFT.COM"><B>Microsoft Home Page</B></A></TD>
</TABLE>
<!--- End Footer --->

</BODY>
```

2. From your text editor, save this file with the name Export Project with Custom Options.Html, or you may save the file using any name you want.

3. Six lines down from the top of the code, you will see the text <BODY>. Change the text inside the brackets <> to <BODY BGCOLOR="#CCFFFF">.

N O T E   The BGCOLOR= parameter tells your Web browser the background color to use when displaying your HTML document. If you leave out the BGCOLOR= parameter, your browser will typically display the Web document with a gray background. The #CCFFFF used in the previous example is the hexadecimal representation of the light blue color for the background of the Web page.

TIP   A great way to figure out the hexadecimal value for your desired background color is to create a new document using Microsoft Word, and save it as an HTML file. Then, select Format, Background, and Word will display a dialog box which will allow you to graphically select a background color for your document (see Figure 14.16). Once you have selected the background color, select View, HTML Source. Microsoft Word will display the source for the HTML document (see Listing 14.2).

TIP   From the line <BODY LINK="#0000ff" VLINK="#800080" BGCOLOR="#ffff00">, copy the hexadecimal value of the color and set the BGCOLOR in your Microsoft Project template equal to the same value.

FIG. 14.16

This figure shows how you can select a background color in Microsoft Word to help figure out the hexadecimal value of the background color for your HTML document.

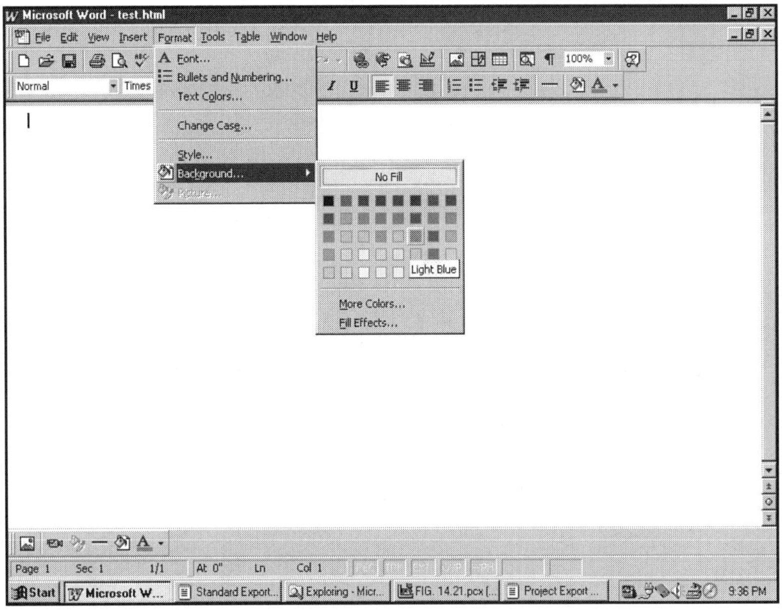

Listing 14.2 HTML Source from a Microsoft Word HTML Document

```
<HTML><HEAD><META HTTP-EQUIV="Content-Type" CONTENT="text/html; charset=windows-
1252"><META NAME="Generator" CONTENT="Microsoft Word 97"><META NAME="Template"
CONTENT="C:\PROGRAM FILES\MICROSOFT OFFICE\OFFICE\html.dot">
</HEAD>
<BODY LINK="#0000ff" VLINK="#800080" BGCOLOR="#ffff00">

<FONT SIZE=2><P> </P></FONT></BODY>
</HTML>
```

4. Once you have selected a background color for your HTML document, save and close the file in your text editor.

5. Open the project you want to save as an HTML file in Microsoft Project, and select File, Save as HTML.

6. From the File Save dialog box, navigate to the directory where you want to save the document.

7. Type the name of the HTML document in the File Name field.

8. Click the Save button, and the Export Format dialog box will open.

9. From the Import/Export Map to Use for Exporting list box, select the Task Schedule Map used in the previous example and click the Edit button.

10. Select the Base Export on HTML Template check box, and click the Browse button to select the template you created in step 2.

11. Click the OK button to close the Define Import/Export Map dialog box, and from the Export Format dialog box, click Save.

12. Now, open the HTML document in your Web browser to see the result of changing the background color. Start up your Web browser, and open the HTML document you created in this example. Notice how the Web page now displays with the custom background color you selected.

Defining a Background Graphic for the Template

In this example, we will modify the template we created in the previous example to add a background graphic to the HTML template. A background graphic is often used instead of a background color to give your Web page a rich, textured look. The Microsoft Office CD includes several GIF files that can be used as a background graphic for your Web page. These graphic files are typically installed in the Program Files\Microsoft Office\Web Page Templates\Styles directory.

To add a background graphic to your Project template, do the following:

1. Copy the file you want to use for your background graphic into the same directory where you will save your HTML document. In this example, we will use the file Brick Wall.gif as the background graphic.

2. From a text editor such as Notepad, open your customized Microsoft Project HTML template created in the previous example (or any other Project HTML template you want to modify).

3. About six lines down from the top of the code, locate the text <BODY... (the exact text after the word BODY will vary depending on any other changes you may have already made to the template).

4. Change the text inside the brackets (<>) to <BODY BACKGROUND="*xxxxxx.gif*">, where *xxxxxx.gif* represents the name of the background graphic file you want to display on your Web page. In this example, set the text inside the brackets to <BODY BACKGROUND="Brick Wall.gif">.

5. Save the template, and close the file in your text editor.

6. Open the project you want to save as an HTML file in Microsoft Project, and select File, Save as HTML.

7. From the File Save dialog box, navigate to the directory where you want to save the document.

8. Type the name of the HTML document in the File Name field.

9. Click the Save button, and the Export Format dialog box will open.

10. From the Import/Export Map to Use for Exporting list box, select the Task Schedule Map used in the previous example and click the Edit button.

11. Select the Base Export on HTML Template check box, and click the Browse button to select your customized Project HTML template.

12. Click the OK button to close the Define Import/Export Map dialog box, and from the Export Format dialog box, click Save.

13. Now, open the HTML document in your Web browser to see the result of changing the background graphic. Start up your Web browser, and open the HTML document you created in this example (see Figure 14.17). Notice how the Web page now displays with the custom background graphic you selected.

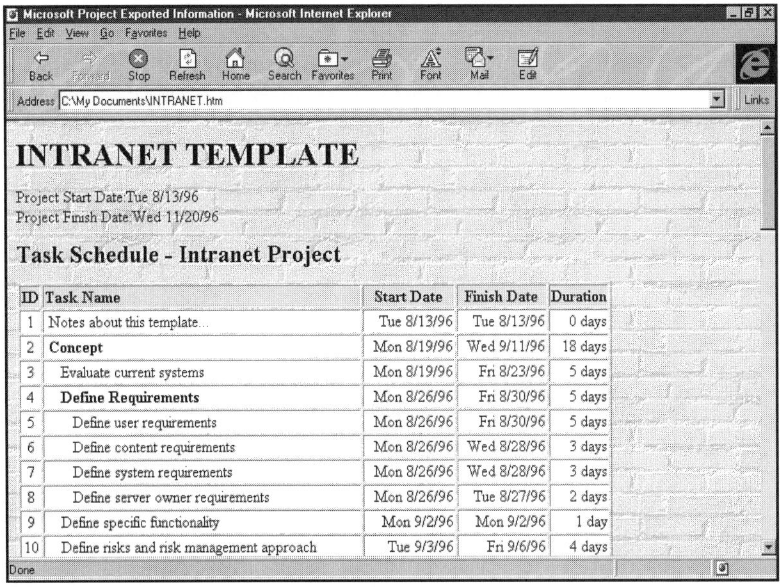

FIG. 14.17
This figure shows the HTML document displayed with a custom background graphic.

Microsoft Project Exported Information - Microsoft Internet Explorer

File Edit View Go Favorites Help

Back Forward Stop Refresh Home Search Favorites Print Font Mail Edit

Address C:\My Documents\INTRANET.htm

INTRANET TEMPLATE

Project Start Date Tue 8/13/96
Project Finish Date Wed 11/20/96

Task Schedule - Intranet Project

ID	Task Name	Start Date	Finish Date	Duration
1	Notes about this template...	Tue 8/13/96	Tue 8/13/96	0 days
2	Concept	Mon 8/19/96	Wed 9/11/96	18 days
3	Evaluate current systems	Mon 8/19/96	Fri 8/23/96	5 days
4	Define Requirements	Mon 8/26/96	Fri 8/30/96	5 days
5	Define user requirements	Mon 8/26/96	Fri 8/30/96	5 days
6	Define content requirements	Mon 8/26/96	Wed 8/28/96	3 days
7	Define system requirements	Mon 8/26/96	Wed 8/28/96	3 days
8	Define server owner requirements	Mon 8/26/96	Tue 8/27/96	2 days
9	Define specific functionality	Mon 9/2/96	Mon 9/2/96	1 day
10	Define risks and risk management approach	Tue 9/3/96	Fri 9/6/96	4 days

Done

Displaying a Graphic Image on Your Project Template

Microsoft Project allows you to easily include a graphic image in your template without having to make any modifications to the HTML source code. You may want to include your company logo or other graphic to enhance the appearance of your Web page.

To add a graphic to your Project HTML template, do the following:

1. Open the project you want to save as an HTML file in Microsoft Project, and select File, Save as HTML.

2. From the File Save dialog box, navigate to the directory where you want to save the document.

3. Type the name of the HTML document in the File Name field.

4. Click the Save button, and the Export Format dialog box will open.

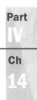

Part

IV

Ch

14

5. From the Import/Export <u>M</u>ap to Use for Exporting list box, select the map you want to use for this export, and click the <u>E</u>dit button (or you may create a new map, if you prefer).

6. Select the <u>B</u>ase Export on HTML Template check box, and click the Browse button to select the Project HTML template you want to use for this export.

7. Select the <u>I</u>nclude Image File in HTML Page check box, and click the Browse button to select the graphic you want to use in your template.

8. Click the OK button to close the Define Import/Export Map dialog box, and from the Export Format dialog box, click Save.

9. Open the HTML document in your Web browser to see the result of adding the new graphic. Start up your Web browser, and open the HTML document you created in this example (see Figure 14.18). Notice how the Web page now displays with the graphic you selected.

FIG. 14.18

This figure shows the HTML document displayed with a graphic image.

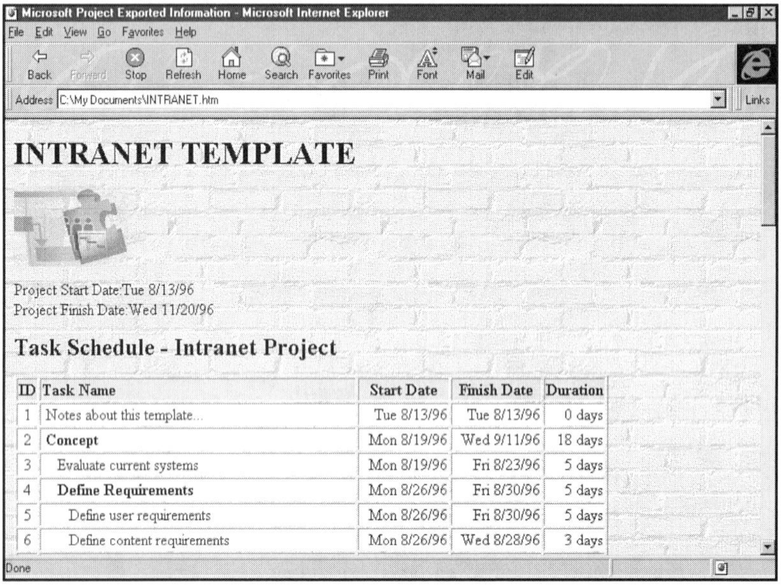

Changing the Title Bar Text

Another way you can customize your Microsoft Project Web page is to change the text that will display in the title bar of the Web browser when your page is opened. By default, the Standard Export.Html template that comes with Microsoft Project displays the text Microsoft Project Exported Information in the title bar of the browser.

To change your HTML template to display your company name or the name of your project in the title bar text of your Web browser, do the following:

1. From a text editor such as Notepad, open your customized Microsoft Project HTML template created in the previous example (or any other Project HTML template you want to modify).

2. About three lines down from the top of the code, locate the text `<TITLE>Microsoft Project Exported Information</TITLE>`.

3. Replace the text `Microsoft Project Exported Information` with the text you want to display in the title bar of the Web browser. For example, you could change the title bar text to display `ABC Corporation Intranet Project`. Be careful not to change the `<TITLE>` and `</TITLE>` tags that surround the title bar text.

4. Save the template, and close the file in your text editor.

5. Open the project you want to save as an HTML file in Microsoft Project, and select File, Save as HTML.

6. From the File Save dialog box, navigate to the directory where you want to save the document.

7. Type the name of the HTML document in the File Name field.

8. Click the Save button, and the Export Format dialog box will open.

9. From the Import/Export Map to Use for Exporting list box, select the map you want to use for this export, and click the Edit button (or you may create a new map, if you prefer).

10. Select the Base Export on HTML Template check box, and click the Browse button to select the Project HTML template you want to use for this export.

11. Click the OK button to close the Define Import/Export Map dialog box, and from the Export Format dialog box, click Save.

12. Now, open the HTML document in your Web browser to see the result of changing the title bar text. Start up your Web browser, and open the HTML document you created in this example (see Figure 14.19). Notice how the Web page now displays the text `ABC Corporation Intranet Project` in the title bar of the window.

Formatting Text in Your Project HTML Template

In this next example, we will modify the formatting of the header text that displays at the top of the Standard Export.Html template. Specifically, we will define the font, size, color, and justification of the header text. These same techniques can be used in other places in your template as well.

The Standard Export.Html template will automatically include the project title at the top of the HTML document.

Part

IV

Ch

14

Custom title bar text

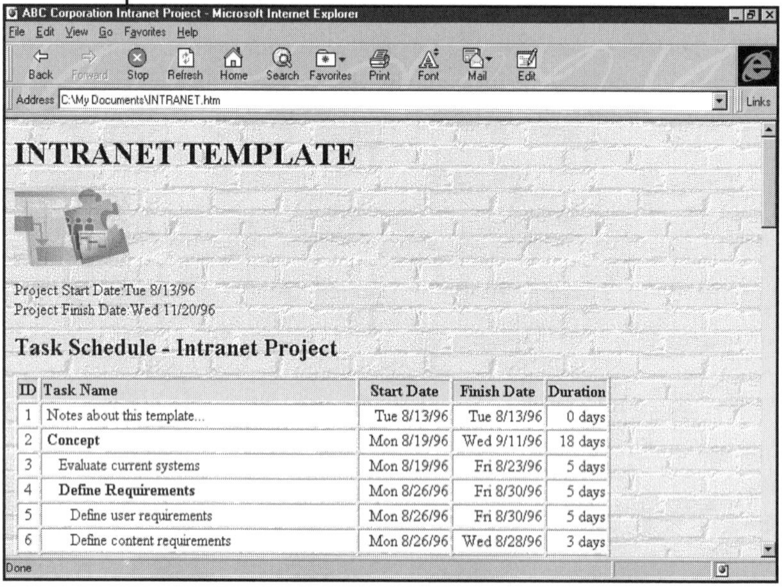

FIG. 14.19

This figure displays the HTML document with custom title bar text "ABC Corporation Intranet Project."

N O T E You can easily change the project title in Microsoft Project by selecting File, Properties, and typing the new project title in the Title field on the Summary tab. If you do not select the project title yourself, Microsoft Project will automatically use the name of the file as the project title. ∎

To format the header text in your HTML template, do the following:

1. From a text editor such as Notepad, open your customized Microsoft Project HTML template created in the previous example (or any other Project HTML template you want to modify).

2. About seven lines down from the top of the code, locate the text `<H1><!--MSProjectTemplate_ProjectTitle--></H1`. When you save your project as an HTML document, Microsoft Project will insert your project's title directly after the comment `<!--MSProjectTemplate_ProjectTitle-->`.

3. Modify the line with the following HTML code in Listing 14.3.

Listing 14.3   HTML Code from Customized Project HTML Template

```
<H1><CENTER><FONT FACE="Arial" COLOR="#0033FF">
<!--MSProjectTemplate_ProjectTitle--></FONT></CENTER></H1>
```

N O T E You can choose any Windows font next to the FACE= parameter, but you should try to avoid non-standard fonts that a user may not have installed on their computer. Also, you can select any color for the text that you want (the one in the previous example is blue) by specifying the hexadecimal code for the color. To determine the hexadecimal code for the color, follow the tip given in step 3 in the section "Changing the Background Color of Your Web Page" earlier in this chapter. The <CENTER> tag that appears in the previous code will center all text and graphics which follow it, up until the </CENTER> tag.

4. Save the template, and close the file in your text editor.

5. Open the project you want to save as an HTML file in Microsoft Project, and select File, Save as HTML.

6. From the File Save dialog box, navigate to the directory where you want to save the document.

7. Type the name of the HTML document in the File Name field.

8. Click the Save button, and the Export Format dialog box will open.

9. From the Import/Export Map to Use for Exporting list box, select the map you want to use for this export, and click the Edit button (or you may create a new map, if you prefer).

10. Select the Base Export on HTML Template check box, and click the Browse button to select the Project HTML template you want to use for this export.

11. Click the OK button to close the Define Import/Export Map dialog box, and from the Export Format dialog box, click Save.

12. Now, open the HTML document in your Web browser to see the result of formatting the header text. Start up your Web browser, and open the HTML document you created in this example (see Figure 14.20). Notice how the header text displays the title of your project with center justification and a blue Arial font!

FIG. 14.20

This figure shows the HTML document with the customized header text "ABC Corporation Intranet Project."

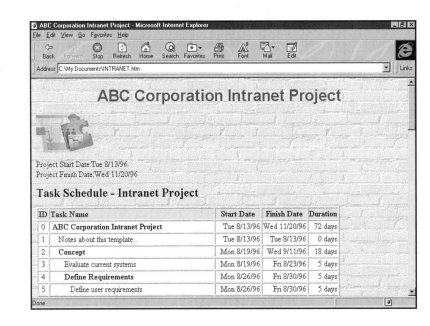

Part
IV

Ch
14

Adding Hyperlinks to Your Project HTML Template

Another useful customization you can make to a Project HTML template is to include hyperlinks to other Web pages. For example, you can include a link that will navigate visitors to your company's home page on the Internet or Microsoft's Internet Explorer home page, or even allow a visitor to download a demo file that describes your company's products or services.

Another type of hyperlink you can add provides visitors to your site the ability to send an e-mail to the Webmaster of your Web site or president of the company. This type of hyperlink is referred to as a *mail link*.

To add hyperlinks to your Microsoft Project HTML template, do the following:

1. From a text editor such as Notepad, open your customized Microsoft Project HTML template (or any other Project HTML template you want to modify).

2. Toward the bottom of the HTML code in Listing 14.4, locate the section that begins with the comment `<!--- End Footer --->`.

Listing 14.4   HTML Code from Customized Project HTML Template

```
<!--- Footer --->
</TABLE>
<HR>
<CENTER>
<TABLE WIDTH=500 BORDER=0>
<TD ALIGN=CENTER>
<A HREF="HTTP://WWW.MICROSOFT.COM/MSPROJECT"><B>Microsoft Project Home
Page</B></A></TD>
<TD ALIGN=CENTER>
<A HREF="HTTP://WWW.MICROSOFT.COM"><B>Microsoft Home Page</B></A></TD>
</TABLE>
<!--- End Footer --->

</BODY>
```

N O T E   The Standard Export.Html template that comes with Microsoft Project 98 includes hyperlinks to the Microsoft Project home page, as well as the Microsoft Corporation home page. Let's examine the syntax of a hyperlink so we can add two additional links to your template:

`<A HREF="xxxxxxxx">yyyyyyyy</A>`

The *xxxxxxxx* represents the address of the site you want to navigate to, and *yyyyyyyy* represents the displayed text that the visitor will click to navigate to the site.

3. Add an additional hyperlink to the Project HTML template that will navigate to ABC Corporation's home page on the Internet. Directly *below* the link to the Microsoft home page and *above* the `</TABLE>` tag toward the bottom of the Project HTML template, add the following:

```
<TD ALIGN=CENTER>
<A HREF="http://www.abc-corporation.com"><B>ABC Corporation
Home Page</B></A></TD>
```

The HTML code should now appear as shown below (see Listing 14.5).

Listing 14.5   HTML Code with a Hyperlink to ABC Corporation's Home Page

```
<TD ALIGN=CENTER>
<A HREF="HTTP://WWW.MICROSOFT.COM"><B>Microsoft Home Page</B></A></TD>
<TD ALIGN=CENTER>
<A HREF="http://www.abc-corporation.com">
<B>ABC Corporation Home Page</B></A></TD>
</TABLE>
<!--- End Footer --->
</BODY>
```

Consider adding one more hyperlink to the template. It is very common to provide visitors to your home page with the ability to send an e-mail to someone in your organization, such as the Webmaster of your Web site or a technical support engineer. When a visitor to your home page clicks this hyperlink, it will automatically start up his or her e-mail application and create a new e-mail message addressed to this individual.

An e-mail hyperlink (also referred to as a *mail link*) uses the structure <A HREF="mailto:xxxxxxxx">yyyyyyyy</A>, where xxxxxxxx represents the e-mail address you want to send mail to, and yyyyyyyy represents the displayed text that the visitor will click to start his or her e-mail application with the new e-mail message.

To create a mail link that will send an e-mail to the Webmaster of ABC Corporation when the visitor clicks it, do the following:

1. Directly below the link to the ABC Corporation Home Page and above the </TABLE> tag toward the bottom of the Project HTML template, add the following:

   ```
   <TD ALIGN=CENTER>
   <A HREF="mailto:webmaster@abc-corporation.com"><B>Click
   here to send email to the ABC Corporation
   Webmaster</B></A></TD>
   ```

   The HTML code should now appear as shown in Listing 14.6.

Listing 14.6   HTML Code with an E-mail Hyperlink

```
<TD ALIGN=CENTER>
<A HREF="http://www.abc-corporation.com">
<B>ABC Corporation Home Page</B></A></TD>
<TD ALIGN=CENTER>
<A HREF="mailto:webmaster@abc-corporation.com">
<B>Click here to send email to the
 ABC Corporation Webmaster</B></A></TD>
</TABLE>
<!--- End Footer --->
</BODY>
```

2. Save the template, and close the file in your text editor.

3. Open the project you want to save as an HTML file in Microsoft Project, and select File, Save as HTML.

4. From the File Save dialog box, navigate to the directory where you want to save the document.

5. Type the name of the HTML document in the File Name field.

6. Click the Save button, and the Export Format dialog box will open.

7. From the Import/Export Map to Use for Exporting list box, select the map you want to use for this export, and click the Edit button (or you may create a new map, if you prefer).

8. Select the Base Export on HTML Template check box, and click the Browse button to select the Project HTML template you want to use for this export.

9. Click the OK button to close the Define Import/Export Map dialog box, and from the Export Format dialog box, click Save.

10. Now, open the HTML document in your Web browser to see the result of adding the new hyperlinks. Start up your Web browser, and open the HTML document you created in this example (see Figure 14.21). Scroll down to the bottom of the Web page, and you will see the two new hyperlinks you added to your Project HTML template.

FIG. 14.21

This figure shows the HTML document with hyperlinks to ABC Corporation's home page and a mail link to the Webmaster of ABC Corporation.

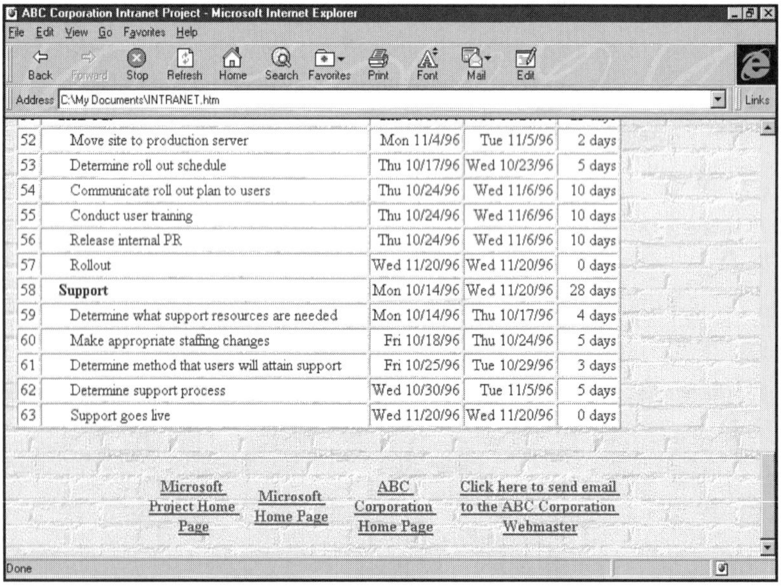

Adding, Modifying, and Deleting Hyperlinks in Your Project

In addition to being able to publish your project as an HTML document, Microsoft Project 98 now includes several new Internet-related task and resource fields. In this section, you will take a look at each of these fields to see how they are used by Microsoft Project 98. In addition, we will take a look at some practical examples of how hyperlinks can help you work more effectively when managing a project.

Adding a Hyperlink to a Task or Resource   To add a hyperlink to a task or resource in your project plan, do the following:

1. Select the task or resource to which you want to add a hyperlink, and click the Insert Hyperlink button on the Standard toolbar (or if you prefer, select Insert, Hyperlink from the menu). The Insert Hyperlink dialog box opens (see Figure 14.22).

FIG. 14.22

Microsoft Project's Insert Hyperlink dialog box gives you the ability to add a hyperlink to a task or resource in your project.

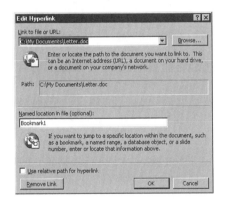

N O T E   If necessary, Microsoft Project will prompt you to save your project before creating a hyperlink. ▇

2. In the Link to File or URL field, type the file path of the document you want to link to or the URL of the Web site you want to navigate to from this task or resource. You can also click the Browse button to select a file from your hard drive or network.

3. In the Named Location in File field, you have the option to refer to a specific section of a document to navigate to. For example, you can specify a bookmark in a Word document, a cell or named range in an Excel file, a specific slide number in a PowerPoint presentation, or a table in a Access database (see Figure 14.23).

Part

IV

Ch

14

FIG. 14.23

The Edit Hyperlink dialog box allows you to modify an existing hyperlink in your project.

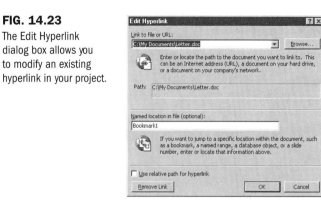

4. If you select the Use Relative Path for Hyperlink check box, the location for the file you are pointing to will be referenced in relation to the location of the Microsoft Project file. For example, you may set up a hyperlink to a document that is stored in the same directory as your Project file, but sometimes that directory may be local, and other times you may be opening the file from a network. If you check this option, the hyperlink will look for the file in the same location as your Project file. If you do not check this option, the hyperlink will always try to locate the document from its absolute location (independent of the location of the project file).

5. Click the OK button, and the hyperlink will be created.

Editing a Hyperlink for a Task or Resource   To edit a hyperlink to a task or resource in your project plan, do the following:

1. Select the task or resource for which you want to edit a hyperlink, and click the Insert Hyperlink button on the Standard toolbar (or if you prefer, select Insert, Hyperlink from the menu). The Insert Hyperlink dialog box opens.

2. Enter the hyperlink information as described in the previous section, "Adding a Hyperlink to a Task or Resource."

3. Click the OK button, and the hyperlink will be modified with your new information.

Deleting a Hyperlink for a Task or Resource   To delete a hyperlink to a task or resource in your project plan, do the following:

1. Select the task or resource for which you want to delete a hyperlink, and click the Insert Hyperlink button on the Standard toolbar (or if you prefer, select Insert, Hyperlink from the menu). The Insert Hyperlink dialog box opens.

2. Click the Remove Link button, and the hyperlink will be deleted from your task or resource.

Navigating to a Hyperlink   Once you have set up a hyperlink in your project, you can very easily navigate to the associated document or Web site by simply clicking the Hyperlink field from the task or resource in your project.

An easy way to display the hyperlink fields in your project is to display the Hyperlink table (available from both a task view and a resource view).

To navigate to a hyperlink from a task or resource, do the following:

1. From either a task view or a resource view in Project, select View, Table, Hyperlink. The Hyperlink table will open (see Figure 14.24).

FIG. 14.24

This figure shows a hyperlink from a task to the Microsoft Project home page on the Web.

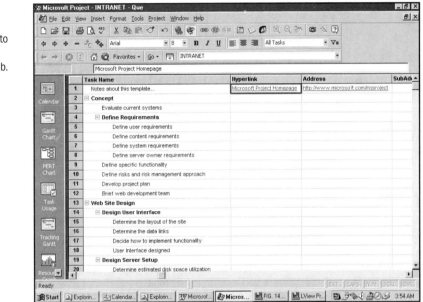

N O T E   Initially when you create a hyperlink for a task or resource, both the Hyperlink field and Address field contain the same information. It may be helpful to replace the information in the Hyperlink field with descriptive information for the location. For example, if you were setting up a link to the Microsoft Project Web site, you could type **Microsoft Project Home Page** in the Hyperlink field. Then, when you click the hyperlink, you will still be navigated to the location specified in the Address field.

Managing a Project with Hyperlinks   Hyperlinks can be very useful in helping you manage a project by allowing you to associate specific references to information stored on the Internet or your corporate intranet to a task or resource in your plan. For example, you may have developed a PowerPoint presentation which is always delivered when you kick off a new project in

Part

IV

Ch

14

your organization. By creating a hyperlink from this task in your plan, you can easily navigate a user directly to this presentation (or even a specific slide within the presentation) at the click of a mouse.

Another example of how a hyperlink can be effective is the capability to associate detailed reference information for a task to help a person successfully perform the task in your project. A hyperlink could navigate a person to a Word document which details the step-by-step instructions on how to complete a task in your plan, or even to a Web site which is always being updated with the latest information on a particular topic.

Creating Web Pages from MPD Files

Although Microsoft Project has provided the ability to save a project to a database file since version 4.0, Project 98's Save as MPD option has been enhanced to the point that now literally every Project object can be saved to an Access database file.

Saving your project as an MPD offers many benefits. Because it is a true relational database file, you have the ability to write custom queries and reports that let you tap into your Project data in ways not possible in native Microsoft Project by itself.

But probably the most exciting aspect to being able to store your project plan as an Access database is that you can utilize the new Internet features of Microsoft Access to create static or dynamic Web content from your Microsoft Project data.

Microsoft Access includes a very robust wizard that lets you create HTML pages from any Access object. For example, you can create an Access report to generate HTML pages of your Project data, you can publish data from any Access table of query, and you can even generate a Web page from an Access form to collect Project data from project team members on a Web server.

Updating Your Project Web Pages

With Microsoft Access 97, it is possible to create a dynamic Web page whose content is generated by connecting to an Access database and executing a query on the database. The advantage of a dynamic Web page is that that it is not necessary to re-create HTML pages with fresh content, because the page is automatically generated with the latest information whenever someone accesses it.

Since a Microsoft Project MPD file is an Access database, you can create dynamic Web pages that query the MPD file to refresh the content of the Web page. Furthermore, you can create a dynamic Web page to update the Project MPD file with the latest information from Project team members.

N O T E For more information on how to set up a dynamic Web page from an Access database, refer to Chapter 18, "Creating Dynamic Web Pages," in Que's *Special Edition Using Microsoft Access 97*. ■

Publishing Your Web Documents

Once you have created your "Web assets" (for example, HTML documents, graphic files, and so on), the next step is to publish those assets on the Internet or corporate intranet.

If your Web documents will be viewed from a corporate intranet, all you need to do is copy the files to the required location on a server (as specified by your intranet administrator). If your files will be viewed from an Internet Web site, you will need to upload the files to the Web server of your Internet Service Provider. As your Project HTML documents change over the course of a project, it will be necessary to copy the latest files to the server to refresh the content.

An easy way to publish your Web assets is to use the Web Publishing Wizard, which ships as part of the Office 97 CD. The Web Publishing Wizard will literally walk you through the entire process of publishing your files to your server.

To publish your Project Web pages using the Web Publishing Wizard, do the following:

1. Start up the Web Publishing Wizard by selecting Start, Programs, Accessories, Internet Tools, Web Publishing Wizard. The Web Publishing Wizard dialog box opens (see Figure 14.25). Click the Next button to start this wizard.

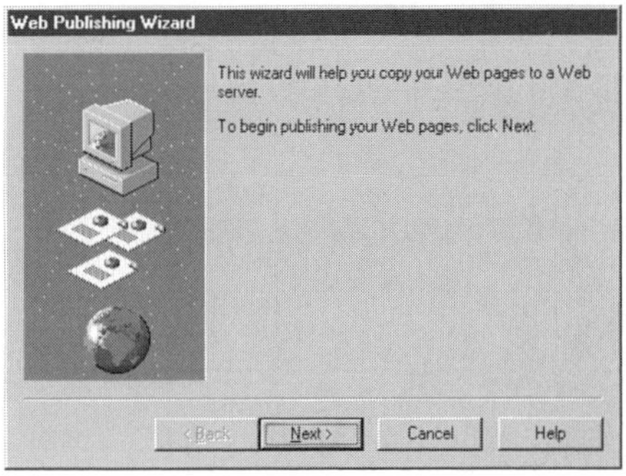

FIG. 14.25
The Microsoft Web Publishing Wizard will lead you through the process of publishing your HTML documents on the Internet or corporate intranet.

2. From the next screen of the Wizard, select the Web document you want to publish (see Figure 14.26). Or, if you will be publishing several files, select the directory where the files are stored and click Next.

3. Select the name of the Web server that you will be publishing to from the drop-down list (see Figure 14.27), or click the New button to add a new server to the list of available destinations (see Figure 14.28) and click the Next button.

4. Depending on the Web server you have selected in step 3, the Web Publishing Wizard will lead you through the specific steps required to transfer files to that Web server.

5. Once your files have been transferred, use your Web browser to make sure you are able to access and view your files from the server.

Part
IV
Ch
14

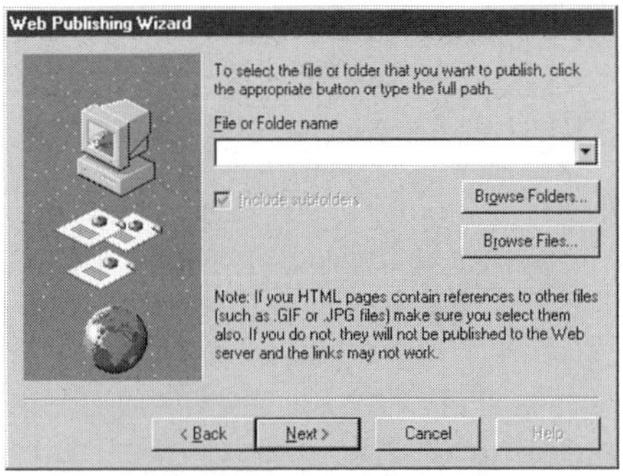

FIG. 14.26

This screen from the Web Publishing Wizard allows you to select the files or folders you want to publish.

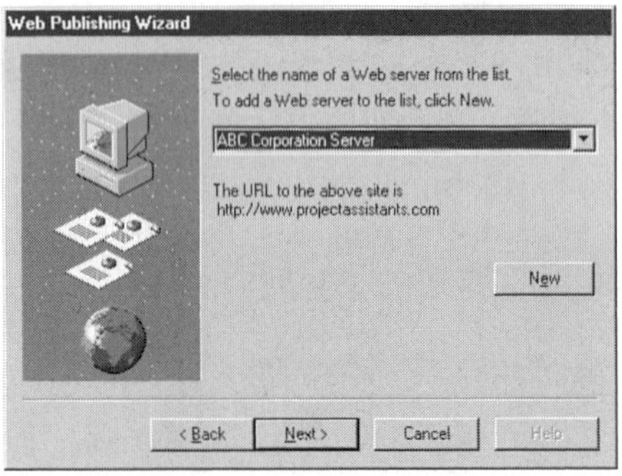

FIG. 14.27

This screen from the Web Publishing Wizard allows you to select the Web server to which to publish your Web documents.

FIG. 14.28

This screen from the Web Publishing Wizard allows you to select your Internet Service Provider.

From Here...

Microsoft Project 98, with its Web-enabled features, gives you an entirely new method for communicating important information about your project. By saving your project as an HTML file, it is possible for others to view your critical Project data directly from a Web browser—even without having Microsoft Project installed on their computer. In addition, by using

Project's HTML template features, you can customize the look of your Web documents by including such enhancements as graphics and hyperlinks to your HTML documents. See the following chapter for more information:

- Chapter 18, "Using Microsoft Project in Workgroups," provides information about Project 98's Workgroup features that have been enhanced to allow you to communicate project status and to request updates from other team members via your Web browser.

Part

IV

Ch

14

Tracking and Analyzing Progress

15   Tracking Work on the Project   473

16   Analyzing Progress and Revising the Schedule   507

CHAPTER 15

Tracking Work on the Project

Previous chapters showed you how to create a plan for a project. In Chapter 3, "Setting Up a New Project Document," you established the background information for the project, which included naming the project, setting the date objectives, and establishing the calendar. In Chapters 5, "Creating a Task List," and 6, "Entering Scheduling Requirements," you entered all the tasks and defined their characteristics in terms of durations, constraints, and task relationships. In Chapters 8, "Defining Resources and Costs," 9, "The New Microsoft Project Scheduling Engine," and 10, "Resource Contouring," you added resources to the project file and assigned resources to the tasks. You refined the schedule in Chapters 11, "Resolving Resource Allocation Problems," and 12, "Reviewing the Project Plan," to remove inconsistencies, and you tweaked the schedule, called *crashing the schedule,* to bring it in line with the dates and costs specified in the project goal statement. You now have a finalized plan that meets the project objectives in a workable way. After the plan is finalized, you are ready to begin the work and execute the project.

If you fail to take advantage of the forecasting powers of Microsoft Project, you miss some of the greatest benefits Project can provide. ■

Save a copy of the finalized plan or baseline for future reference

Saving a baseline allows you to capture what your original plan predicted. Once you start entering actual data, you can compare it to the original plan.

Track actual events on your project

Recording facts about what actually happened on a task-by-task level is a worthwhile endeavor, especially if your projects are similar.

Examine the revised schedule to identify potential problems

If you have a baseline and you've entered information about what is actually happening on your project tasks, Microsoft Project provides a variety of views to compare the two. If you can identify problems early enough in the process, you can make adjustments in the plan to keep the problems from getting bigger.

Modify the plan to adjust for events that are throwing your project off track

If everything happens exactly as you planned, you have no need to re-schedule subsequent tasks. If the actual finish dates for tasks differ from the planned dates, however, Microsoft Project can use the real dates to reschedule the remaining tasks in the project.

Setting the Baseline or Plan

After you finalize the planning of the project, set aside a copy of the finalized project schedule for future reference. Actually, the *final plan* is final only because the plan shows the final product of the initial planning effort. The copy that you make of the finalized plan is the baseline that you use to compare actual performance with planned performance. As work progresses on the project, you might have to modify the plan to respond to changing circumstances or as a result of new information. Resource availability can change, duration estimates can change, and so on. You also begin to record the actual start and finish dates for tasks. If actual dates match the planned dates exactly, you have performed a miracle. In all probability, some tasks will finish late, and other tasks will finish early. As you enter these actual dates, Microsoft Project reschedules successor tasks to reflect the changed circumstances.

Figure 15.1 illustrates the evolution of the schedule. The *planning stage* culminates in a finalized plan, the copy of which is known as the *baseline*. As the *execution stage* gets underway, changes and revisions in the plan often are necessary. As these changes are added to the computer version of the plan, Microsoft Project recalculates the schedule to incorporate the revisions. As work on the project progresses, the actual dates and durations of tasks are entered into the computer version of the plan, and Microsoft Project replaces the calculated start and finish dates with the actual dates and recalculates the remaining schedule. Therefore, as the project goes forward, the current schedule is revised by the addition of changes and actual data. You can print reports that show the variances or differences between the planned dates and the actual dates, the planned amount of work and the actual amount of work, the planned cost and the actual cost.

FIG. 15.1
This figure shows the evolution of the project plan schedule.

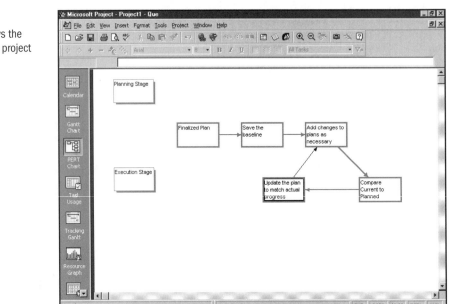

The baseline is like an architect's final drawings for a building project. After construction gets underway, plan changes are penciled in, and some features are whited out. If changes are significant, new plans are drawn. By setting aside a clean copy of the original plans at the start of construction, you can compare the original intentions with the final result.

In managing your project, you can set aside copies of the printouts from the original plan for comparison purposes. You might find, however, that having an electronic set of the planned dates, planned work, and planned cost is more useful. This allows the computer to print comparisons or variances to show how work is progressing, how well the plans are being realized, and how likely you are to meet the project goals.

Capturing the Baseline

Microsoft Project provides two ways to capture the baseline. The first is with a Planning Wizard. The first time you save a file, the Planning Wizard asks if you want to save the file with a baseline (see Figure 15.2). If you select the option to save the baseline and click OK, Project will save a second set of start and finish dates for each task, duplicating the currently calculated start and finish dates. This second copy of dates is called the *baseline*. As you enter actual information about each task, when it started and finished and how long it actually took to complete, Project will recalculate the start and finish dates of all successor tasks. Because of this continual recalculation, you need those baseline dates in order to compare reality with what you had planned.

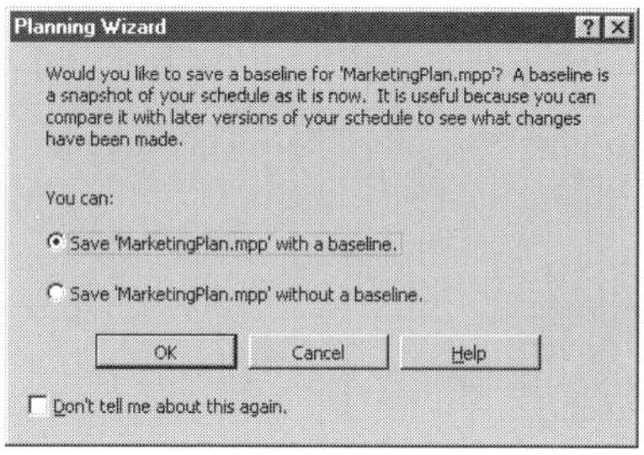

FIG. 15.2

The Planning Wizard stands ready to save baseline information when you first save a project file.

▶ **See** "Saving a File," **p. 107**

When you close a file without saving first, you are normally prompted for whether you want to save your changes. When you indicate Yes, if there is at least one task that does not have baseline information, the Planning Wizard again prompts to save baseline information as well as the changes made to the file. As shown in Figure 15.3, you have several options at this point.

As with other Planning Wizards, you may elect not to be reminded of this in the future. If you mark the Don't Tell Me About This Again check box and later want to turn the feature back on, use the General tab in the Options dialog box. The Advice About Scheduling option is unchecked. Recheck the box to once again have the Planning Wizard prompt you for updating the baseline.

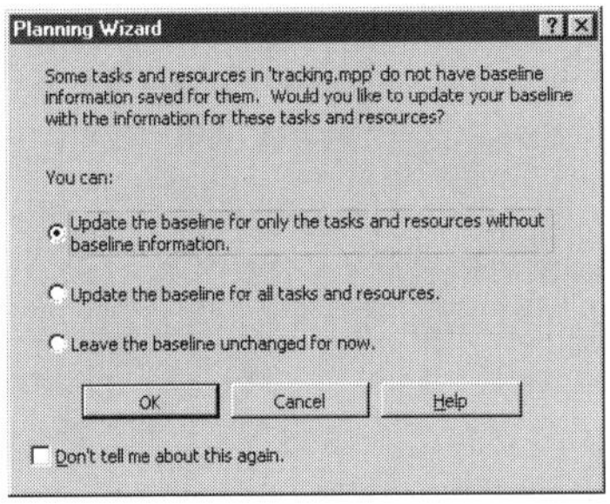

FIG. 15.3

Each time you save the file, the Planning Wizard watches for changes and updates all tasks or just new tasks with baseline information.

The second method of saving the baseline is by choosing Tools, Tracking, Save Baseline. This command copies the currently calculated start and finish dates, duration, work, and cost data into a set of fields, respectively known as Baseline Start, Baseline Finish, Baseline Duration, Baseline Work, and Baseline Cost. You can execute the Save Baseline command from any Task view, but not from the Resource views.

The Save Baseline command offers an option of copying data for the entire project or for selected tasks. Use the selected task option when you want to correct mistakes for selected tasks or add data for tasks that you added to the plan after the baseline was captured. Use the entire project option when you create the baseline for the first time or when you want to update the baseline for all tasks.

To save the baseline plan, take the following steps:

1. Activate any Task view, such as the Gantt Chart or the Task Sheet.

2. Choose Tools, Tracking, and then Save Baseline. The default settings for the Save Baseline dialog box appear in Figure 15.4.

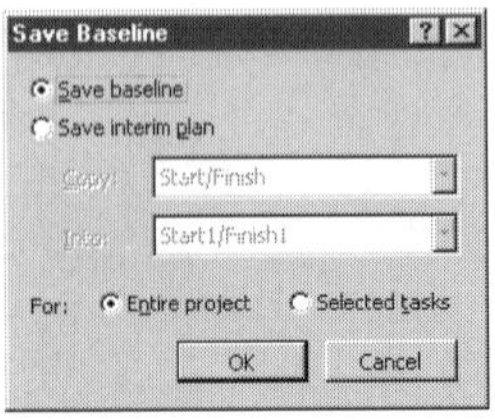

FIG. 15.4

The Save Baseline dialog box allows you to specifically save the baseline information.

3. Choose OK to save the baseline. You will see no evidence that the field data was copied until you look at views that display baseline data fields. The following section explains how to view and verify the baseline data.

Viewing the Baseline

The fields that are changed with the Save Baseline command are the Baseline Duration, Baseline Start, Baseline Finish, Baseline Work, and Baseline Cost. These fields are displayed in the Baseline table (see Figure 15.5).

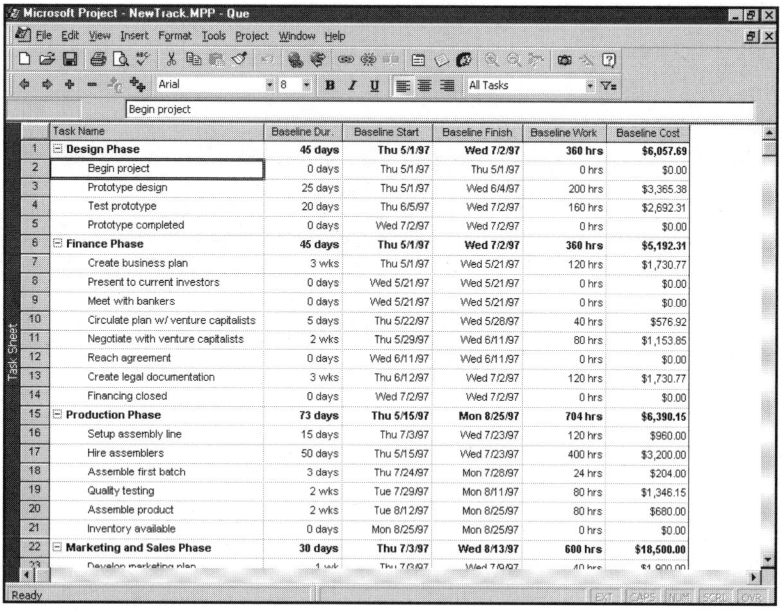

	Task Name	Baseline Dur.	Baseline Start	Baseline Finish	Baseline Work	Baseline Cost
1	**Design Phase**	**45 days**	**Thu 5/1/97**	**Wed 7/2/97**	**360 hrs**	**$6,057.69**
2	Begin project	0 days	Thu 5/1/97	Thu 5/1/97	0 hrs	$0.00
3	Prototype design	25 days	Thu 5/1/97	Wed 6/4/97	200 hrs	$3,365.38
4	Test prototype	20 days	Thu 6/5/97	Wed 7/2/97	160 hrs	$2,692.31
5	Prototype completed	0 days	Wed 7/2/97	Wed 7/2/97	0 hrs	$0.00
6	**Finance Phase**	**45 days**	**Thu 5/1/97**	**Wed 7/2/97**	**360 hrs**	**$5,192.31**
7	Create business plan	3 wks	Thu 5/1/97	Wed 5/21/97	120 hrs	$1,730.77
8	Present to current investors	0 days	Wed 5/21/97	Wed 5/21/97	0 hrs	$0.00
9	Meet with bankers	0 days	Wed 5/21/97	Wed 5/21/97	0 hrs	$0.00
10	Circulate plan w/ venture capitalists	5 days	Thu 5/22/97	Wed 5/28/97	40 hrs	$576.92
11	Negotiate with venture capitalists	2 wks	Thu 5/29/97	Wed 6/11/97	80 hrs	$1,153.85
12	Reach agreement	0 days	Wed 6/11/97	Wed 6/11/97	0 hrs	$0.00
13	Create legal documentation	3 wks	Thu 6/12/97	Wed 7/2/97	120 hrs	$1,730.77
14	Financing closed	0 days	Wed 7/2/97	Wed 7/2/97	0 hrs	$0.00
15	**Production Phase**	**73 days**	**Thu 5/15/97**	**Mon 8/25/97**	**704 hrs**	**$6,390.15**
16	Setup assembly line	15 days	Thu 7/3/97	Wed 7/23/97	120 hrs	$960.00
17	Hire assemblers	50 days	Thu 5/15/97	Wed 7/23/97	400 hrs	$3,200.00
18	Assemble first batch	3 days	Thu 7/24/97	Mon 7/28/97	24 hrs	$204.00
19	Quality testing	2 wks	Tue 7/29/97	Mon 8/11/97	80 hrs	$1,346.15
20	Assemble product	2 wks	Tue 8/12/97	Mon 8/25/97	80 hrs	$680.00
21	Inventory available	0 days	Mon 8/25/97	Mon 8/25/97	0 hrs	$0.00
22	**Marketing and Sales Phase**	**30 days**	**Thu 7/3/97**	**Wed 8/13/97**	**600 hrs**	**$18,500.00**
23	Develop marketing plan	1 wk	Thu 7/3/97	Wed 7/9/97	40 hrs	$1,000.00

FIG. 15.5 The Baseline table applied to the Task Sheet view displays baseline information.

To view the baseline fields in a Task view, take the following steps:

1. Be sure that you are in either the Task Sheet view or the Gantt Chart view. If you are in a combination view and you want to see all tasks, you must be in the top pane.
2. Choose View, Table, and then More Tables to see the full list of standard tables.
3. From the More Tables list, select the Baseline table.
4. Choose the Apply button to display the table.

Correcting the Baseline

If you want to correct the entries for any task, or if you need to add tasks to the baseline because they were not in the plan as originally conceived, select the tasks to be added or corrected to the baseline plan and choose Tools, Tracking, Save Baseline. This time, however, select the Selected Tasks option button in the Save Baseline dialog box rather than the Entire Project option button.

You also can make changes directly to the Baseline table. Be careful when you use this option, however, because Microsoft Project doesn't check entries for consistency. Typographical and calculation errors are not corrected by Project. If you change the baseline duration, for example, Project doesn't change the baseline finish date. For most changes, the best route is to use the Save Baseline command to be sure that all the data entries are consistent.

You can also view the baseline dates in the Task Details form as shown in Figure 15.6. This view is useful when you want to see more information about each task and focus on one task at a time. In this case, form views are better than sheet views that show limited information about each task but many tasks at once. As in the sheet view, use caution when changing baseline data. Microsoft Project doesn't automatically make any recalculations with changes that you make to baseline information.

FIG. 15.6

Verifying baseline dates on the Task Details form.

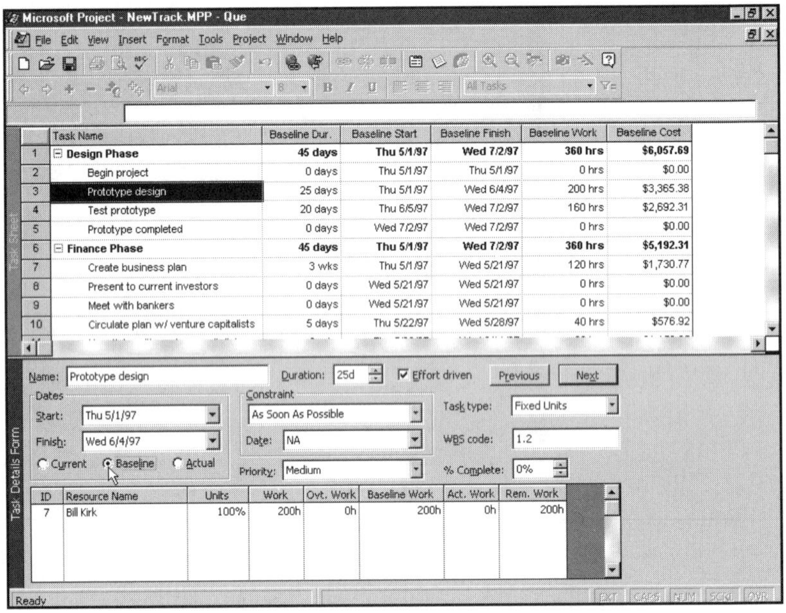

If you need to verify the baseline work or cost for individual resource assignments on the Task Details form, choose Format, Details to view the Resource Work or Resource Cost fields. To see the Baseline Work or Cost fields from the perspective of a resource rather than a task, use the Resource Form (as shown in Figure 15.7) with the Format, Details, set to Work or Cost. Again, Microsoft Project does not automatically recalculate related fields when you make a manual entry in Baseline Work. Add the resource as you normally would, and then update the baseline by choosing Tools, Tracking, Save Baseline for selected tasks. All related fields will be automatically recalculated.

The new Task Usage and Resource Usage views also have the capability of showing baseline information. As a matter of fact, these views offer more flexibility in what can be displayed and edited than the Task Sheet, Task Form, or Resource Form. Figure 15.8 shows the Task Usage view with the baseline dates turned on, as well as the calculated start and finish dates. The Task Sheet portion of the Task Usage view has the Baseline table applied.

FIG. 15.7

The Resource Form with details set to Work or Cost shows baseline information from the resource's perspective.

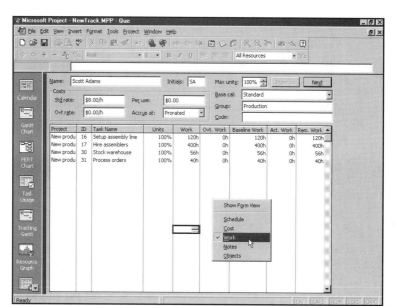

Saving Interim Schedules

At key points during the project, either during the planning stages before the baseline plan is saved or after work is under way on the project, you may want to make a record of the current (calculated) dates for tasks at this point in the evolution of the project plan. A good reason to do this is when the entire project is put on hold for a period of time. When you resume work on the project, you want to have a new set of baseline dates against which to compare your progress. Otherwise, it would appear that you were always behind schedule, if only because of the delay.

Ten sets of baseline date fields are available for each task, which represent ten sets of Start and Finish dates, aside from the date fields saved in the baseline. Because each date set is numbered, you will see fields named Start1 through Start10 and Finish1 through Finish10 for each task. By using the Save Baseline command, you can capture interim date schedules by copying the Current Start and Finish dates in one or more of these sets of date fields. Note that only the date fields are copied for each task—the work and cost values are not copied.

To save interim project dates, take the following steps:

1. Choose a Task view.

2. Choose Tools, Tracking, Save Baseline.

3. Choose the Save Interim Plan option button. The Copy and Into date fields are then available.

4. Select the Entire Project option button (although you also can choose to copy only selected tasks).

5. Both sets of date fields have a list of ten sets of Start/Finish date fields. Do not use the Baseline Start/Finish fields because performing this process wipes out the original baseline dates. Choose an appropriate set of dates from each entry list.

6. Choose OK to copy the date values.

You can use the copies of the dates in reports or display them in customized views. You can also control the titles that are visible in the selected task view.

▶ **See** "Creating New Views," **p. 742**

▶ **See** "Adding and Changing the Columns in the Table," **p. 749**

In long projects, the project plan may change so dramatically over time that a new baseline is considered worthwhile. Although you can keep as many as ten sets of date values for comparison purposes, you can maintain only one set of baseline duration, work, and cost figures. If a new baseline is needed, and you want to preserve the work and cost estimates of the old baseline, you need to find a creative solution to the problem of saving data for which no automatic-saving provision exists. Several options are available to achieve this task. One option is to save a copy of the project file under a different name, and then open the originally named file again and continue setting a new baseline. Another option is to export the baseline field data to a spreadsheet or database for storage until you need to use the data.

If you only want to preserve the dates of the original baseline and are not concerned about the work and cost estimates, you can copy the dates to one of the ten sets of interim dates.

To copy the baseline dates to an interim set of dates, follow the preceding steps for saving interim dates, except that you should choose Copy, Baseline Start/Finish when you reach step 4.

No standard views or reports are available that display the interim date fields. You can however, create, views and reports; or modify any view or report that displays the baseline dates and substitute the interim dates for the Baseline date fields.

▶ **See** "Creating New Views," **p. 742**

▶ **See** "Using and Creating Tables," **p. 748**

▶ **See** "Creating Reports," **p. 797**

▶ **See** "Customizing Task Type Reports," **p. 805**

Comparing the Baseline with the Current Schedule

Because comparing what you planned to what is actually happening is such a useful project management task, there are several views and reports that allow you to see baseline data next to the currently calculated plan. You can use the new Task Usage view which allows you to turn on the display of Baseline Work. You can use the Task Sheet view with three different sets of tables. You can also use the Tracking Gantt for a more graphical view. The Gantt Chart Wizard has five different predefined options for formatting the baseline information. Many of the reports in the Current Activities and Costs categories compare actual progress to baseline information.

Using the Task Usage View to See Baseline Information   The new Task Usage view allows you to turn on the display of baseline data. By default, the timescale portion of the view displays planned hours of work for each task, spread across the days when the work is planned to occur. If you right-click the timescale portion of the view, you can also turn on the display of Baseline Work as well (as shown in Figure 15.8).

FIG. 15.8

The Task Usage view with Baseline Work displayed allows you to compare very precisely when work was supposed to occur with when it actually occurs.

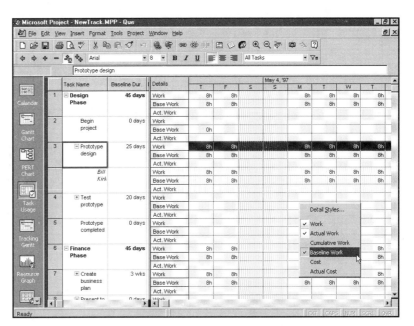

▶ **See** "Exploring the Standard Views," **p. 660**

Using Tables to View Baseline Data   The baseline data is displayed beside the currently calculated data in three separate task tables—the Variance table, the Cost table, and the Work table. You can display each table in the Task Sheet or in one of the Gantt Chart views. You can use all three tables to print progress reports.

In each table, the currently calculated field values are displayed along with the baseline field values. Variances are calculated to show the difference between the current and the baseline data.

The current values represent predicted or anticipated values until actual tracking data is entered. Actual data always replaces the currently calculated data, so that the schedule always contains the most accurate information available. Therefore, after tracking begins, the current fields show anticipated values for tasks that have not yet begun and actual values for tasks that already have actual data recorded.

T I P To quickly choose different tables, right-click the button at the top of the task IDs, just to the left of the Task Name column.

Viewing the Task Variance Table The Baseline Start and Baseline Finish date fields are displayed in the task Variance table (see Figure 15.9). The Variance table focuses on dates only. The start and finish dates are calculated dates until actual dates are entered. Therefore, the Start Variance and Finish Variance columns show anticipated variances based on the actual information entered for predecessor tasks. Once actual information has been entered for tasks, these variances are real. Incidentally, it is impossible to tell from the Variance table alone whether the current start and finish dates are actual dates or just the currently planned dates.

FIG. 15.9

The Variance table applied to the Task Sheet concentrates on date differences in the schedule.

	Task Name	Start	Finish	Baseline Start	Baseline Finish	Start Var.	Finish Var.
1	⊟ **Design Phase**	5/1/97	7/3/97	5/1/97	7/2/97	0 days	1 day
2	Begin project	5/1/97	5/1/97	5/1/97	5/1/97	0 days	0 days
3	Prototype design	5/2/97	6/5/97	5/1/97	6/4/97	1 day	1 day
4	Test prototype	6/6/97	7/3/97	6/5/97	7/2/97	1 day	1 day
5	Prototype comple	7/3/97	7/3/97	7/2/97	7/2/97	1 day	1 day
6	⊟ **Finance Phase**	5/1/97	7/7/97	5/1/97	7/2/97	0 days	2.25 days
7	Create business	5/1/97	5/21/97	5/1/97	5/21/97	0 days	0 days
8	Present to currer	5/21/97	5/21/97	5/21/97	5/21/97	0 days	0 days
9	Meet with banker	5/21/97	5/21/97	5/21/97	5/21/97	0 days	0 days
10	Circulate plan w/	5/22/97	6/2/97	5/22/97	5/28/97	0 days	2.25 days
11	Negotiate with ve	6/2/97	6/16/97	5/29/97	6/11/97	2.25 days	2.25 days
12	Reach agreemen	6/16/97	6/16/97	6/11/97	6/11/97	2.25 days	2.25 days
13	Create legal docu	6/16/97	7/7/97	6/12/97	7/2/97	2.25 days	2.25 days
14	Financing closed	7/7/97	7/7/97	7/2/97	7/2/97	2.25 days	2.25 days
15	⊟ **Production Phase**	5/16/97	8/26/97	5/15/97	8/25/97	1 day	1 day
16	Setup assembly l	7/4/97	7/24/97	7/3/97	7/23/97	1 day	1 day
17	Hire assemblers	5/16/97	7/24/97	5/15/97	7/23/97	1 day	1 day
18	Assemble first br	7/25/97	7/29/97	7/24/97	7/28/97	1 day	1 day
19	Quality testing	7/30/97	8/12/97	7/29/97	8/11/97	1 day	1 day
20	Assemble produc	8/13/97	8/26/97	8/12/97	8/25/97	1 day	1 day
21	Inventory availab	8/26/97	8/26/97	8/25/97	8/25/97	1 day	1 day

In Figure 15.9, the scheduled start for task 3 was changed to one day later than originally planned. Now, the start is a day later than the baseline start, and the variance fields show a resulting variance of one day. Note that the delay in task 3 also delays task 4, task 3's successor; the variance also shows up for task 4. The variance for task 3 is real, while the variance for task 4 is predicted. If the duration for task 3 could be reduced enough so that the task still finishes by its calculated finish date, the variance of task 4 would go back to zero, or back on schedule. The tasks in the Finance Phase group are unaffected because these tasks are not successors to the group that includes task 4. The Production Phase however, is a successor and is also delayed.

To display the task Variance table, choose View, More Views, Task Sheet, and then Apply to display the Task Sheet in the top pane. Then choose View, Table, Variance to display the Variance table.

Viewing the Task Cost Table The Baseline cost field appears in the task Cost table (see Figure 15.10). The Total Cost values in the Cost table equal the actual values if tracking data was already entered for the tasks, and variances are either anticipated or actual, depending on whether actual data was entered.

- For tasks that have not yet begun, the values in the Actual column are zero and the values in the Total column are the currently calculated data. The Remaining cost equals the Total Cost.
- For completed tasks, the Total and Actual data is the same, and the Remaining cost is zero.
- For tasks still in progress, the Actual cost plus the Remaining cost equals the Total Cost.

An unexpected Fixed Cost of $1,000 was entered for task 4, as shown in Figure 15.10, and as a result the Total Cost field becomes $1,000 greater than the Baseline Cost, and the Variance field shows the $1,000 disparity. Microsoft Project creates values in the Actual field when tracking data is entered.

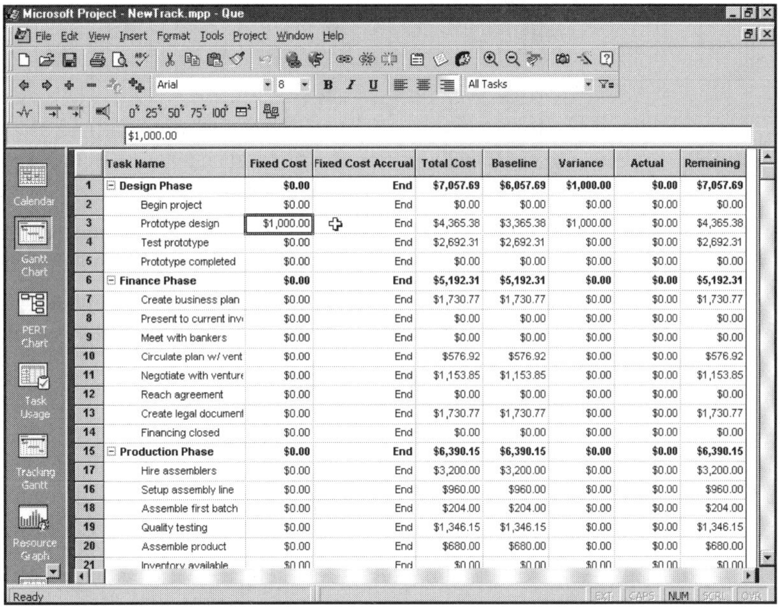

	Task Name	Fixed Cost	Fixed Cost Accrual	Total Cost	Baseline	Variance	Actual	Remaining
1	Design Phase	$0.00	End	$7,057.69	$6,057.69	$1,000.00	$0.00	$7,057.69
2	Begin project	$0.00	End	$0.00	$0.00	$0.00	$0.00	$0.00
3	Prototype design	$1,000.00	End	$4,365.38	$3,365.38	$1,000.00	$0.00	$4,365.38
4	Test prototype	$0.00	End	$2,692.31	$2,692.31	$0.00	$0.00	$2,692.31
5	Prototype completed	$0.00	End	$0.00	$0.00	$0.00	$0.00	$0.00
6	Finance Phase	$0.00	End	$5,192.31	$5,192.31	$0.00	$0.00	$5,192.31
7	Create business plan	$0.00	End	$1,730.77	$1,730.77	$0.00	$0.00	$1,730.77
8	Present to current inv	$0.00	End	$0.00	$0.00	$0.00	$0.00	$0.00
9	Meet with bankers	$0.00	End	$0.00	$0.00	$0.00	$0.00	$0.00
10	Circulate plan w/ vent	$0.00	End	$576.92	$576.92	$0.00	$0.00	$576.92
11	Negotiate with venture	$0.00	End	$1,153.85	$1,153.85	$0.00	$0.00	$1,153.85
12	Reach agreement	$0.00	End	$0.00	$0.00	$0.00	$0.00	$0.00
13	Create legal document	$0.00	End	$1,730.77	$1,730.77	$0.00	$0.00	$1,730.77
14	Financing closed	$0.00	End	$0.00	$0.00	$0.00	$0.00	$0.00
15	Production Phase	$0.00	End	$6,390.15	$6,390.15	$0.00	$0.00	$6,390.15
17	Hire assemblers	$0.00	End	$3,200.00	$3,200.00	$0.00	$0.00	$3,200.00
16	Setup assembly line	$0.00	End	$960.00	$960.00	$0.00	$0.00	$960.00
18	Assemble first batch	$0.00	End	$204.00	$204.00	$0.00	$0.00	$204.00
19	Quality testing	$0.00	End	$1,346.15	$1,346.15	$0.00	$0.00	$1,346.15
20	Assemble product	$0.00	End	$680.00	$680.00	$0.00	$0.00	$680.00
21	Inventory available	$0.00	End	$0.00	$0.00	$0.00	$0.00	$0.00

FIG. 15.10 The Cost table applied to the Task Sheet focuses on differences in costs over what was planned.

To display the task Cost table, display the Task Sheet in the top pane. Then display the Cost table by choosing View, Table, Cost.

Viewing the Task Work Table The Baseline Work field is displayed in the task Work table (see Figure 15.11). The values in the Work column equal the actual work amounts if tracking data was already entered for the tasks, and variances are either anticipated or actual, depending on whether actual data was entered.

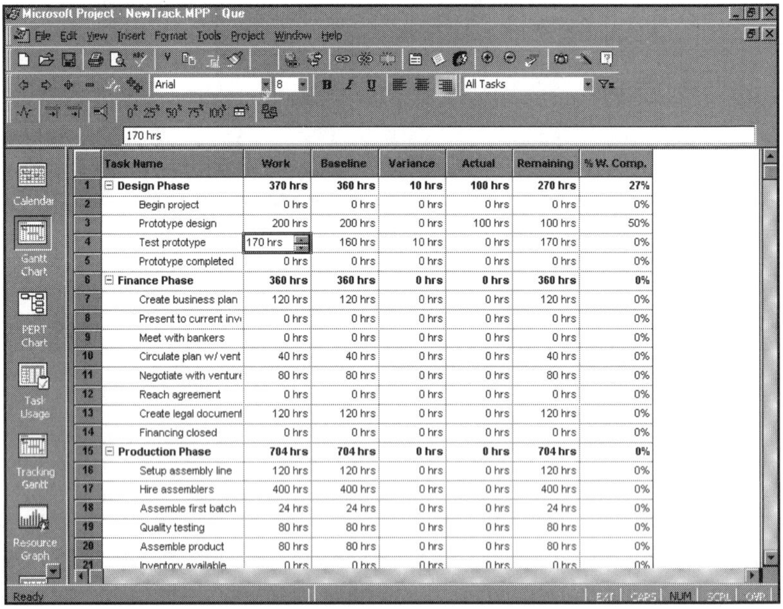

	Task Name	Work	Baseline	Variance	Actual	Remaining	% W. Comp.
1	Design Phase	370 hrs	360 hrs	10 hrs	100 hrs	270 hrs	27%
2	Begin project	0 hrs	0 hrs	0 hrs	0 hrs	0 hrs	0%
3	Prototype design	200 hrs	200 hrs	0 hrs	100 hrs	100 hrs	50%
4	Test prototype	170 hrs	160 hrs	10 hrs	0 hrs	170 hrs	0%
5	Prototype completed	0 hrs	0 hrs	0 hrs	0 hrs	0 hrs	0%
6	Finance Phase	360 hrs	360 hrs	0 hrs	0 hrs	360 hrs	0%
7	Create business plan	120 hrs	120 hrs	0 hrs	0 hrs	120 hrs	0%
8	Present to current inv	0 hrs	0 hrs	0 hrs	0 hrs	0 hrs	0%
9	Meet with bankers	0 hrs	0 hrs	0 hrs	0 hrs	0 hrs	0%
10	Circulate plan w/ vent	40 hrs	40 hrs	0 hrs	0 hrs	40 hrs	0%
11	Negotiate with venture	80 hrs	80 hrs	0 hrs	0 hrs	80 hrs	0%
12	Reach agreement	0 hrs	0 hrs	0 hrs	0 hrs	0 hrs	0%
13	Create legal document	120 hrs	120 hrs	0 hrs	0 hrs	120 hrs	0%
14	Financing closed	0 hrs	0 hrs	0 hrs	0 hrs	0 hrs	0%
15	Production Phase	704 hrs	704 hrs	0 hrs	0 hrs	704 hrs	0%
16	Setup assembly line	120 hrs	120 hrs	0 hrs	0 hrs	120 hrs	0%
17	Hire assemblers	400 hrs	400 hrs	0 hrs	0 hrs	400 hrs	0%
18	Assemble first batch	24 hrs	24 hrs	0 hrs	0 hrs	24 hrs	0%
19	Quality testing	80 hrs	80 hrs	0 hrs	0 hrs	80 hrs	0%
20	Assemble product	80 hrs	80 hrs	0 hrs	0 hrs	80 hrs	0%
21	Inventory available	0 hrs	0 hrs	0 hrs	0 hrs	0 hrs	0%

FIG. 15.11
The Work table applied to the Task Sheet displays differences in number of hours worked over what was planned.

- For tasks that have not yet begun, the Actual work amount is zero, and the Work amount is the current Baseline amount. The Remaining work equals the value in the Work column because all the work remains to be done.
- For completed tasks, the Work and Actual work amounts are the same, and the Remaining work is zero. The %W. Comp. (percent of work completed) field is 100 percent.
- For tasks still in progress, the Actual work plus the Remaining work equals the Work. The percent of work completed (%W. Comp.) reflects the completed portion.

The Work field was increased for task 4 from 160 hours to 170 hours in Figure 15.11, and because Work is now greater than Baseline work, the Variance field shows the 10 hour difference. The Actual field is updated during tracking of the project.

To display the task Work table, display the Task Sheet in the top pane. Then display the Work table by choosing View, Table, Work.

Viewing the Tracking Gantt Chart An extremely informative graphic view of baseline values compared to the current schedule is called a *Tracking Gantt* (see Figure 15.12). It is accessible from the View menu or from the View Bar. The Tracking Gantt view shows two task bars for each task. The upper bar represents the baseline start and finish dates for the same task while the lower bar represents the currently calculated start and finish dates for the task.

FIG. 15.12

The Tracking Gantt displays two sets of bars for each task, one that you planned and one that reflects reality.

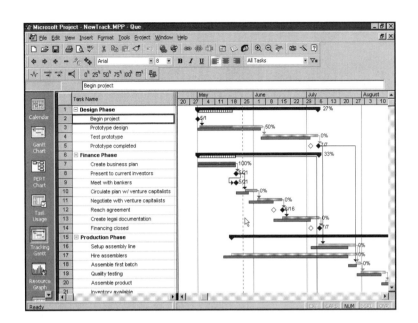

You can also use the Gantt Chart Wizard to display baseline information. In step 2 of the Gantt Chart Wizard, select the Baseline option. Instead of Baseline option, you can also choose from one of four baseline formats under the Other option (see Figure 15.13). The baseline formats created by the Gantt Chart Wizard also display two bars for each task, one with baseline information and one with calculated dates. The only difference is the colors and position of each bar.

 **See** "Using Gantt Chart Bars to Analyze Progress," **p. 526**

FIG. 15.13

The Gantt Chart Wizard will display baseline information for you.

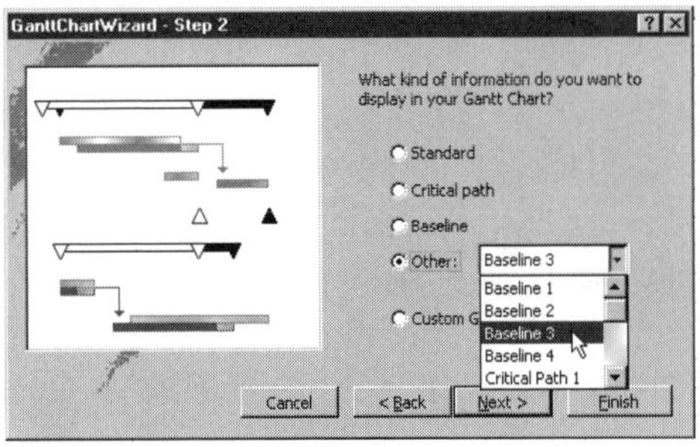

As long as the project proceeds according to the plan, the dates on the two bars will match. When the dates of any task deviate from the baseline, however, you can see the discrepancy immediately. In Figure 15.12, for example, the delayed start for task 3 is reflected in the shift to the right from the start of the lower bar. The added work that was imposed on task 4 is reflected in the even further shift to the right of the scheduled finish date. Note that any successor tasks would also be similarly affected.

Notice also in Figure 15.12 the mouse pointer is pointing at the current date line. This line has been reformatted to display more prominently. It helps identify where you currently are in the project. Any tasks straddling the today line should be in progress. All bars that are mostly on the left side of the line should be almost done. Any bars approaching the line from the right are due to be starting soon. This information alone can be very useful to a project manager.

▶ **See** "Formatting Gridlines," **p. 701**

N O T E   A new feature in this version is Progress Lines, described in detail later in this chapter. One option for the Progress Line is to show progress as compared to the baseline. See the next chapter, "Analyzing Progress and Revising the Schedule," for details on working with Progress Lines. ▢

Printing the Views That Show Baseline Comparisons

Each of these views that display comparisons between baseline values and values in the current schedule can be printed without extensive adjustments. The default print settings are adequate for simple reports.

To print any of these views, display them on-screen and choose File, Print. For a list of reports that display current activities compared against baseline values, choose View, Reports, and then choose the Current Activities and Costs report categories on the Reports dialog box.

▶ **See** "Printing Views," **p. 416**
▶ **See** "Printing Standard Reports," **p. 436**

Tracking Actual Performance and Costs

After the project gets underway, you may find that some tasks start or finish early or late, or that completing a task takes longer or costs more than expected. As you respond to these unexpected changes in the project, you may need to adjust estimated durations for later tasks—based on the experience of the earlier tasks—and you may want to change task relationships. If the cumulative effects of the changes threaten the cost and finish date as set forth in the project goal, you may need to crash the schedule again and find ways to reduce costs.

If you record the actual dates, durations, and work for tasks as events unfold, Microsoft Project uses this data to reschedule tasks affected by the changes. You can see right away the implications for the rest of the project when the actual work doesn't go according to plan. With this knowledge beforehand, you can take corrective measures to minimize unwanted consequences. By entering actual performance data in the computer on a timely basis, you can predict problems and do something about them early in the project. You also can use the project schedule to try *what-if* tests to measure the effects of alternative compensating actions.

The frequency with which you update the project is determined by the criticality of the project. A project plan is like a financial plan or budget in that the plan is a blueprint for reaching a goal.

If accounting data is not recorded in a timely fashion, then management does not have the accounting reports that may warn of possible problems in meeting budgeted profits. Similarly, if the project data is not recorded regularly, the project manager doesn't have reports that may warn of problems with the project. Therefore, the project may not be completed on time and within budget.

Updating the project schedule can be a time-consuming task and, probably for this reason, is often neglected by project managers. A lot depends on how much detail you intend to track. The level of detail you intend to track is determined by how much information you need back and how much time you can spend on tracking. You may choose to track dates and durations carefully but not spend the time needed to track individual resource work and cost. You must base this decision on the usefulness of the data, as opposed to the cost of gathering and entering the information. If you take this route, Microsoft Project still can help warn you about tasks that slip (are not on schedule) and can help you keep the project on course. The cost data, however, will be less accurate because cost is primarily calculated from the work expended by individual resources.

There are a wide variety of views, tables, and forms that you can use to enter actual data. The ones you choose depend to a large degree on what kind of information you are entering and how much information you need to see as a result of the actual information. It also depends on whether you prefer working with sheet views, forms, or graphic views. As with the entering of the original project data, information you enter in one view is automatically reflected in all other relevant views.

In addition to the views that display baseline information, there are several views that display progress on a task, for example, work that has occurred during the completion of the task. The Gantt Chart displays a progress bar in the middle of the task bar for tasks that have already begun. The progress bar appears differently depending on whether you are showing baseline bars. If you are displaying baseline bars (as discussed in the previous section) the progress bar is overlaid on the lower bar and is a solid dark bar of the same color as the lower bar (see task 3 in Figure 15.12). If you are not displaying baseline bars (as in a standard Gantt Chart), the progress bar is a narrower black bar inside the task bar that represents the percentage complete. Figure 15.14 shows the project with progress already noted for tasks 3 and 7.

The PERT Chart also can display a record of progress, but only in a general way (see Figure 15.15). If a task is completed, the task node (the rectangular box representing the task) shows crossing diagonal lines (as though the node was crossed out). If the task is in progress but not complete, you see a single diagonal line drawn through the node. No diagonal lines appear in tasks that are not yet started.

▷ **See** "Using the Box Styles Options," **p. 720**

The sections that follow describe the views that you can use to enter and review actual progress data.

FIG. 15.14

The progress bars indicate tasks that have already started.

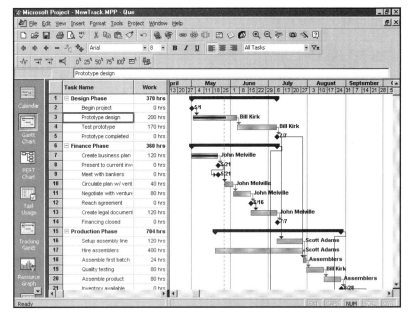

FIG. 15.15

Progress marks on the PERT Chart nodes indicate tasks that have started or are complete.

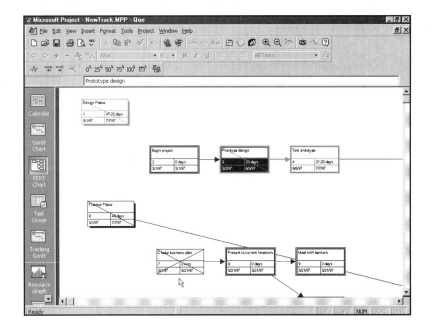

Establishing a Procedure for Updating Tasks

The updating procedure is a simple process if work on tasks proceeds according to the schedule. Updating becomes progressively more time-consuming when dates, work amounts, durations, and costs differ from the schedule. A well-established procedure for gathering actual performance data and regularly updating the computer files is needed to keep the project file current, as shown in the following steps:

1. First, gather information about the progress on each task. You should gather information on both what was actually done and new estimations about tasks yet to do. You need to know if duration estimates were revised or if the estimated amount of work for a resource on a task was revised. You may want to print a progress report form that you distribute to all personnel who work on the project. You also may want to require these personnel to submit regular updates. This data can provide the basis for the actual data that you enter as you track progress.

TIP The Tracking table applied to the Task Sheet, filtered by the Using Resource filter, is a useful tool here. Give each resource a printed copy to keep track of their work on the project.

▶ **See** "Using Microsoft Project in Workgroups," **p. 565**

2. Next, revise the *scheduled* description of tasks to match the actual events or revised estimates before you record that actual work was begun or completed. If the progress reports indicate that the actual duration, amount of work, or cost for a task doesn't match the predicted values as outlined in the schedule, change the description of the task in the schedule to match the actual events. If the progress reports suggest that you should make changes in the planned schedule for unfinished tasks, enter adjustments to the scheduled duration, work, and costs before you enter actual dates and percentages completed. If the workers on a task, for example, took 30 hours to complete the task rather than the scheduled 20 hours, you can more easily revise the scheduled duration before recording the actual work date. If you also want to track total work and costs effectively, make these entries for each resource in the Work fields at the bottom of the Task or Resource Form before you enter actual dates and duration as completed.

3. Having revised the schedule to make task descriptions fit the reality of actual performance, you then can use one or more of the views, forms, and tools described in the following section to record actual dates when work began and, if completed, when work was finished. If work is not completed, you can optionally record the estimated Percentage Complete. When you enter the dates and Percentage Complete for tasks, Microsoft Project can calculate the interim and completed work and cost figures. If necessary, you can enter your own figures for work and cost after tasks are completed.

Understanding the Fields Used in Updating

You can enter one or more of the following tracking fields for tasks. Many of these fields are calculated by Microsoft Project when an entry is made in one of the others in the list.

- Actual Start date
- Actual Finish date
- Percentage Complete (percentage of the task's Duration)

- Actual Duration (to date)
- Remaining Duration
- Revised Scheduled Duration
- Actual Work
- Percentage of Work Completed
- Remaining Work
- Actual Fixed Cost
- Actual Cost
- Remaining Cost

No one view displays all these fields—with the possible exception of the Export table. Some of these fields lead to automatic recalculation of other fields. Some fields are calculations only, and your entries are ignored. The Work and Cost fields are special cases; if you are tracking work and cost carefully, you do not enter actual in-progress work or costs for the task, but rather you enter the in-progress work for the resources assigned to the task. The work that you enter for the resources is the source of the cost calculations.

You can save time if you understand how these fields are interrelated. You then can select the fields to update and select the view or form that provides the fields you want to use. The tracking fields are described in the following sections, with emphasis on the impact made by entering a change in one of the fields. You become more successful in tracking projects if you understand these relationships.

Actual Start Date　　Prior to having an Actual Date entered, the Actual Start field's value is "NA." When you record actual dates, Microsoft Project changes the current calculated Start and Finish dates to show the actual dates. Therefore, as the project progresses, your entries of actual dates replace the calculated (predicted) entries for task dates, and the schedule contains more and more reality, as compared to prediction.

You can enter the Actual Start date on all the tracking views and forms either directly or indirectly through setting some other field value. For example, if you set a Percentage Complete other than zero, the calculated Start date is set for the Actual start date. If you set the Percentage Complete to 100, the Actual Start and Actual Finish are set to whatever the calculated dates were.

Actual Finish Date　　This field displays NA until the task finish date is entered or calculated. You can enter the Actual Finish date on all the tracking views and forms, either directly or indirectly, by having the finish date calculated. If you enter a date in the Actual Finish date field, Microsoft Project performs the following procedures:

- Moves the Actual Finish date to the current Finish date.
- Sets the Percentage Complete (of the Duration) to 100 percent.
- Sets the Actual Start date to equal the current Start date, if no Actual Start date is entered.

▓ Calculates the Actual Duration field, and changes the Duration, if necessary, to match the Actual Duration.

▓ Sets the Remaining Duration field to zero.

▓ Calculates the Actual Work and Actual Cost fields, based on the Actual Duration. If the Actual Duration differs from the original Duration, Work and Cost are adjusted proportionally.

▓ Changes the task display to non-critical if it was critical (its completion can no longer endanger the finish date of the project).

If you want to enter actual work and cost information that differs from the calculated work and cost, make the changes in the calculated data for the individual resources on each task before setting the actual completion date of the task. See the section, "Recording Actual Work and Costs," later in this chapter.

Percent Complete   After a task is started, you can track the progress of the task by entering the percentage completed on a regular basis. You also can track progress by entering either the actual duration to date for the task or the remaining duration. See the "Actual Duration" and "Remaining Duration" sections later in this chapter. The relationship among these three variables (Percentage Complete, Actual Duration, and Remaining Duration) are defined by these equations:

Percentage Complete = Actual Duration/Duration

Remaining Duration = Duration–Actual Duration

When you record a finish date for a task, Microsoft Project displays 100% in the Percentage Complete field for the task. If you want to track interim progress on a task, you can enter partially completed percentage numbers.

You can enter this field on almost all updating views and forms.

When the Percentage Complete field is changed, Microsoft Project performs the following procedures:

▓ Sets the Actual Start date to equal the current Start date, unless an Actual Start date was already entered. If the task did not start on schedule, first update the Start date with the Actual Start date, and then enter the Percentage Complete.

▓ Sets the Actual Finish date to match the current Finish date if 100% is the percentage value that is entered. If the Actual Finish date is not the same as the calculated date, type the Actual Finish date rather than entering 100%.

▓ Sets the Actual Duration field to equal the Percentage Complete figure times the scheduled duration. Therefore, if a task is marked 60 percent complete when the scheduled Duration was 10 hours, the Actual Duration field is calculated and set to 6 hours.

▓ Sets the Remaining Duration field to equal the scheduled Duration minus the Actual Duration. Using the preceding example, the Remaining Duration field is calculated as 10 minus 6 and set to 4.

■ Sets the Actual Work and Actual Cost fields to match the Percentage Complete times the scheduled Work and Cost amounts, but only if the check box for Updating Task Status Updates Resource Status is marked. You can find this check box on the Calculation tab of the Options dialog box.

In Microsoft Project 98, you can now enter the Percentage Complete field for a summary task. This has the effect of marking each of the subtasks with the same value entered for the summary task. Obviously, this is a fast way to enter actual information for tasks that are all the same in terms of progress.

> **N O T E**   The Updating Task Status Updates Resource Status option on the Calculation tab of the Options dialog box instructs Microsoft Project as to whether it should translate actual duration into actual work and actual work into actual costs. If the option is set to Yes, Microsoft Project calculates the Actual Work and Actual Cost for each task by adding up the actual work and cost for each resource assigned to the task as work on the task progresses. Therefore, you will see prorated cost figures appear as you indicate progress on the task (if the Accrue At field for the resources has been set to Prorated). See the section, "Recording Actual Work and Costs," later in this chapter. ■

Actual Duration   This field is available only on the Tracking table and the Update Tasks dialog box. You can access the Update Tasks dialog box by choosing Tools, Tracking, Update Tasks. When you enter a value in this field that is less than or equal to the scheduled Duration, Microsoft Project assumes work on the task is progressing according to plan. Accordingly, the program automatically sets the Actual Start date as scheduled (unless it has been set previously) and calculates the Percentage Complete and the Remaining Duration field by comparing the Actual Duration with the originally entered or calculated Duration.

If you enter an Actual Duration that is greater than the original Duration, Microsoft Project assumes that the task is finished and took longer than scheduled. The current Duration is changed to match the new, longer duration, and then the Percentage Complete and Remaining Duration fields are set to 100% and 0, respectively, to indicate that the task is complete.

If the Updating Task Status Updates Resource Status option is on, the work and cost figures for resources also are updated based on the task information entered.

Remaining Duration   If you enter a value in the Remaining Duration field, Microsoft Project assumes that work has begun as scheduled, and that all but this amount of the scheduled Duration has been completed. The program calculates and sets the Actual Duration and the Percentage Complete based on the new value and the original Duration. If not already set, Microsoft Project sets the Actual Start date as whatever was scheduled. If the option Updating Task Status Updates Resource Status is on, and resources were assigned to the tasks, work and costs are updated for the resources and summed for the task.

If you enter **0** in the Remaining Duration field, it is the same as entering **100%** in the Percentage Complete field. The Actual Finish date will be updated as originally scheduled.

If you enter a figure in the Remaining Duration field that is larger than the existing figure, Microsoft Project assumes that you are simply entering a new estimation of the total duration and not tracking actual progress. If no entry has been made to show that the task has started, this new Remaining Duration value is simply used to increase the scheduled duration of the task. If the task has already been marked as started, the new Remaining Duration entry is used to extend the scheduled Duration. The new scheduled Duration will be equal to the Actual Duration already shown, plus this new estimate of the amount of time left to complete the task. Percentage Complete is recalculated to show the Actual Duration figure as a percent of the new, longer total Duration; and the work and cost figures are recalculated proportionally.

For example, suppose that a task with an estimated Duration of 10 days has already had 3 days of Actual Duration recorded. The Remaining Duration field shows 7 days, and 30% displays in the Percentage Complete field. If the entry in the Remaining Duration field is changed to 9 days, Microsoft Project takes that to mean that 9 more days (after the 3 days already recorded) are necessary to complete the task instead of just 7. The total Duration is changed automatically to 12 days, and the Percentage Complete is reduced to 25 percent (3 days of 12 total days).

The Scheduled Duration   Revised estimates of the scheduled (originally planned) Duration can be entered in any of the locations discussed in previous chapters for defining a task.

If you change the scheduled Duration after a task has already started and Actual Duration is greater than zero, the already recorded Actual Duration is left unchanged, and the Percentage Complete and Remaining Duration fields are adjusted to reflect the new estimate of total Duration.

Recording Actual Work and Costs   Work and cost values are calculated by Microsoft Project for individual resources and summed for the tasks to which the resources are assigned. If a task has no resources assigned, you must manually enter the work and cost values when the task is completed. You can enter the work and cost values for individual resources while work is in progress, but you cannot override the summed work and cost values for the tasks until the tasks are marked as completed.

In this version of Microsoft Project, you can now edit the Actual Work field on a summary task. In previous versions it was only a calculated field. As you enter work for the summary task, the subtasks are allocated their portion of the work depending on how the tasks are linked. If the subtasks are not linked, as you enter work hours for the summary task, the hours are split equally between the subtasks until any of the subtasks reach their total originally calculated hours of work. Thereafter, the work hours are split between the remaining subtasks that are not yet complete. If the tasks are linked, the hours of work entered for the summary task are allocated to the first task in the link. If that task has two successors, once the first task is complete, additional hours are split between the two successors. For example, you can see in Figure 15.16 that 9 hours of work have been added to the summary task. The first 8 were allocated to subtask 1 because it was first to be performed. Both subtasks 2 and 3 are successors, and the remaining hour has been split between them.

FIG. 15.16

Entering work for summary tasks makes it easier to enter actual work data.

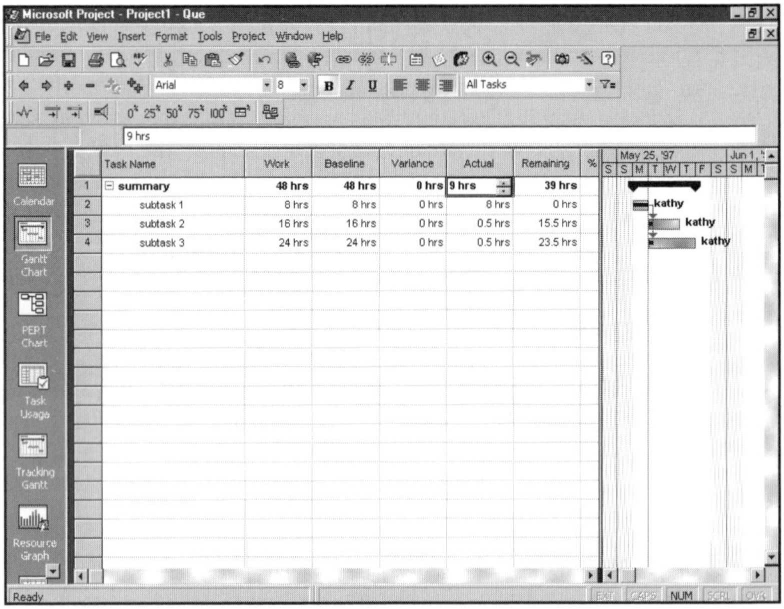

You cannot increase the work beyond the total calculated work for the subtasks, however. Figure 15.17 displays the error message if you try to increase the work beyond the calculated work for the subtasks. If the work for the summary task was greater than that originally calculated, you would have to enter the actual work for each of the subtasks and have the summary task's work calculated.

FIG. 15.17

This figure shows that you can't enter total work for a summary task that exceeds what was originally calculated.

To successfully update work and cost amounts, you have to understand the following points:

■ If no resources are assigned to a task or if resources are assigned and the Updating Task Status Updates Resource Status check box on the Calculation tab of the Options dialog box *is not* marked, you can enter actual work and cost amounts directly into the Actual Work and Actual Cost fields for the task, just as you can enter actual dates and duration.

■ If resources are assigned and the Updating Task Status Updates Resource Status check box *is* marked, Microsoft Project translates each resource assignment's actual duration into actual work and actual work into actual costs. If you enter actual work for a resource while this setting is marked, Microsoft Project translates this into Percentage Complete for the task.

- If resources are assigned and the check box for Actual Costs are always calculated by Microsoft Project is turned on, you cannot enter actual cost values into the task tracking fields while the task is in progress (before it is marked completed). The values are being calculated from the actual work data for each resource, and all entries you make are replaced immediately by the calculated value. After the task is marked as completed, however, you may override the calculated work and cost figures with your own entries.

To track work and costs while the task is in progress, you can enter the actual work and cost amounts for the resources or for the task itself. If you enter work for the task, Project assumes that the work was split between resources assigned to the task. If the resources worked a different number of hours on the task, it is better to enter the hours worked for the resources. Project will sum the hours for the task.

The Task and Resource Usage views are the best for entering this level of detail. The Task Usage view is best when you are looking at work from the perspective of the task. The Resource Usage view is best when you working from the perspective of the work performed on many tasks by a resource. These views allow you to enter work details on a timescale basis. For example, tasks that span more than one day can have hours of work performed across the days when the task was being worked on.

If you are not interested in that level of detail and want to enter the total hours worked on a task, without regard to when they were performed, use the Task Details Form, or Resource Form, to enter actual work and cost values for each resource. The work and cost fields are available at the bottom of these forms by selecting the appropriate format choice from the menu when the form is displayed. If the check box for Updating Task Status Updates Resource Status is checked, the Percentage Complete field is calculated accordingly.

Using the Facilities Provided for Updating Tasks

Several views, menu commands, tools, and custom forms are available for updating tasks. This section starts with the facilities that provide the greatest detail and the greatest range of options. The shortcut tools and commands are covered at the end of the section. Before using shortcuts, you should understand the details of the operation and the results of using the shortcut tools.

The facilities that can be used for tracking actual performance are described in the following list:

- The Task and Resource Usage views both allow for the entering of actual data at either the task level or the resource level. You can either enter the hours worked into the timescaled grid or double-click a resource assigned to the task and use the Tracking tab in the Assignment Information dialog box.

- The Task Sheet, with the Tracking, Variance, Work, or Cost tables applied, provides access to all the fields described in the preceding section "Understanding the Fields Used in Updating." The Tracking table focuses only on the tracking or actual fields. The other tables show scheduled, baseline, actual, remaining, and variance values.

■ The Task Form provides the Duration and Percentage Complete tracking fields. The Task Details Form provides the actual dates fields. Both forms provide entry fields for resource work and resource costs by choosing the appropriate option from the F̲ormat, D̲etails menu command.

■ The Resource Form with the details set to Work provides a column for Actual Work, and with details set to Cost provides a column for Actual Cost.

■ The T̲ools, Trac̲king menu command has two commands in addition to S̲ave Baseline: Update T̲asks and Update P̲roject. Update Tasks allows you to enter very specific actual information when the task is not proceeding according to plan. Update Project provides a date-sensitive facility for updating the actual dates, duration, and percent complete for tasks that have scheduled dates that fall before a designated *as of* date.

■ The Tracking toolbar (see Figure 15.18) has a series of buttons that can make tracking progress easier, including a button to access the Update Tasks dialog box.

FIG. 15.18

The Tracking toolbar enables easy access to updating actual information.

Project Statistics
Update as Scheduled
Reschedule Work
Add Progress Line
0% Complete
25% Complete
50% Complete
75% Complete
100% Complete
Update Tasks
Workgroup Toolbar

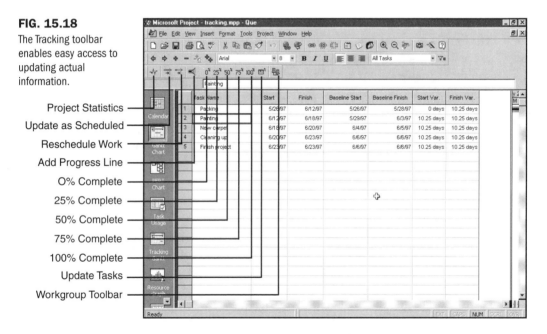

Using the Usage Views   The Usage views provide the greatest level of detail on a per re-source, per task, day-by-day basis. When resources use timesheets to keep track of their work, these are the best views to capture that information. If you are tracking exact hours of work and subsequent costs, these are probably the best views to use.

By default the Task Usage view displays a timescaled work value for each task with a break-down by resource assigned to the task. You can add a row for each assignment and task that displays an editable region for actual work (see Figure 15.19). Right-click anywhere in the timescale portion and choose Actual Work from the shortcut menu. You can also choose

Format, Details from the menu and choose Actual Work from the cascading menu. As you enter actual hours for resources, the task work hours are totaled from the assigned resources. If you enter actual hours for the task, they are distributed to the resources assigned in a smart way. If all resources are working on the task for the whole duration of the task, the hours are split evenly between the resources. If a delay has been placed on when a resource begins work on the task, that resource is not given any actual hours until the delay has been covered.

FIG. 15.19

The Task Usage view with an Actual Work row displayed allows for detailed tracking of work.

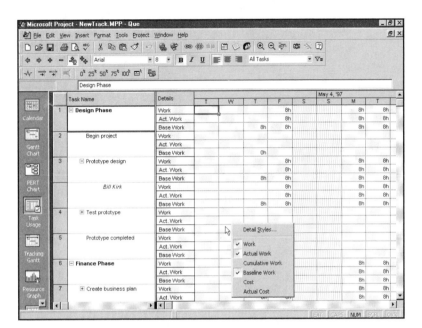

The Resource Usage view (as shown in Figure 15.20) works much the same way but from the perspective of the resource. This is a better view to use when a resource hands in a timesheet with hours performed for various tasks.

Using the Tracking Table   The Task Sheet views can display a Tracking table that provides columns for tracking the percentage complete, actual dates, and so on. To view the Tracking table, choose View, Task Sheet. Again open the View menu, but this time choose Table and then choose Tracking (see Figure 15.21).

The Tracking Table has fields for entering progress on tasks. Note that the Actual date fields in the Tracking table display NA when no actual date is yet recorded. This table also displays the Percentage Complete, Actual Duration, Remaining Duration, Actual Cost, and Actual Work fields. You see the values in these fields calculated immediately after you enter any of the fields that signal work has been done on the task. The calculated entries are the same proportion of their scheduled values as the value displayed in the Percentage Complete field. For example, if you enter a Percentage Complete of 60% on a 10 day task, it will calculate an Actual Duration of 6 days and a Remaining Duration of 4 days.

FIG. 15.20

The Resource Usage view allows you to enter detailed work hours from a resource's timesheet.

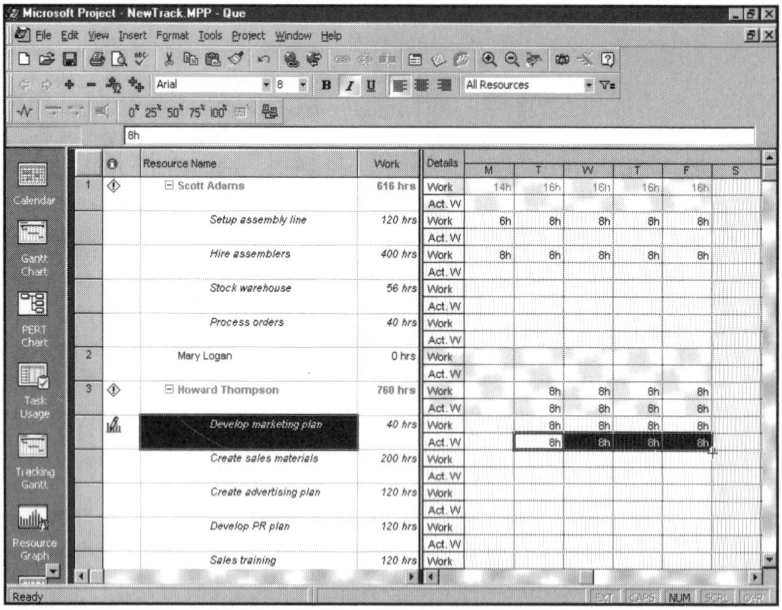

FIG. 15.21

The Tracking table provides a spreadsheet format for collecting data on tasks that are in progress.

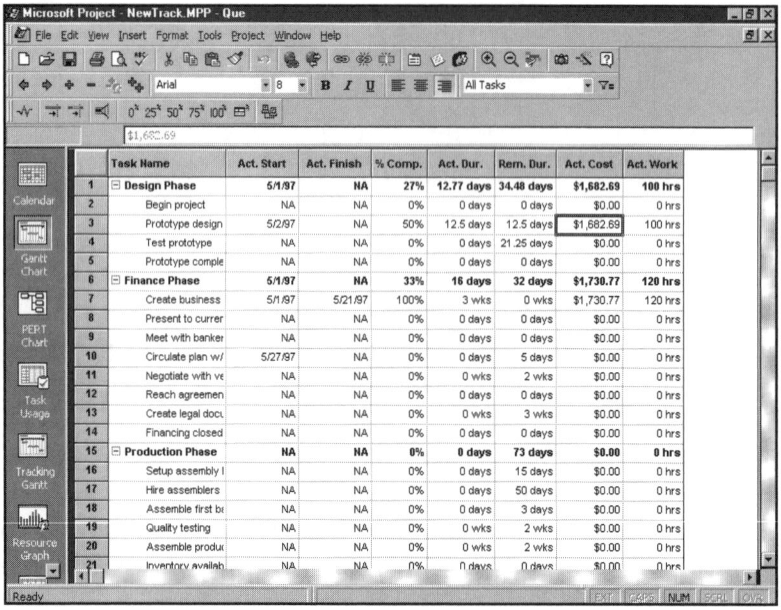

There is a new option on the Calculation tab of the Options dialog box: Actual Costs Are Always Calculated by Microsoft Project. If resources are assigned to tasks and this check box is marked, you cannot change the entries in actual cost. Notice the entry bar in Figure 15.21. The value for total cost is dimmed and therefore not available for change. If you clear the check mark, you will be able to enter your own cost figures but Project will not calculate any. Be careful about turning the option back on again after manually entering any cost figures. They will be overwritten as shown in the warning box displayed in Figure 15.22.

FIG. 15.22

Manually entered cost figures will be overwritten if you turn on the Actual Costs Are Always Calculated by Microsoft Project option.

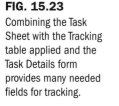

Microsoft Project

Any actual costs that have been manually entered will be removed so that Microsoft Project can calculate all actual cost values.

To continue, click OK.

To keep any manually entered actual cost values, click Cancel.

[OK]   [Cancel]

Using the Task Form for Tracking   The Task Form and the Task Details form both provide fields for entering tracking information, although the Task Details form offers much more flexibility, partly because you can enter actual dates. You must first activate the actual fields by choosing the Actual option button. Figure 15.23 shows the Tracking table applied to the Task Sheet in the top pane and the Task Details form in the bottom pane.

FIG. 15.23

Combining the Task Sheet with the Tracking table applied and the Task Details form provides many needed fields for tracking.

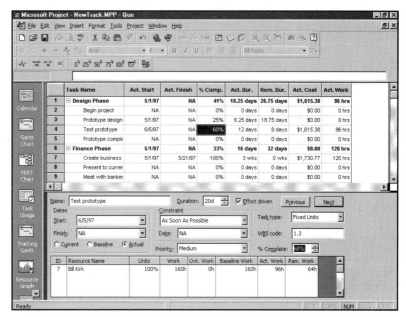

In Figure 15.23 task number 4 was updated to show that the task is 60 percent complete, which means that the duration is 60 percent complete. As a result, in the Tracking table you can see that Microsoft Project calculated that the actual duration is 12 days (60 percent of 20 days), the remaining duration is 8 days, and the Start date has been placed in the Actual Start column. Notice that the Actual Work field shows that 96 hours of work has been done (60 percent of the

160 hours assigned to Bill Kirk), and the Actual Cost is set to $1,615.38, which is based on the standard rate for Bill Kirk and the actual work value. With the Task Details Form set to display work, you can enter total hours of work performed by each resource, but not on a timescaled basis as in the Usage views. With the Usage views (either Task Usage or Resource Usage), you can track actual hours of work on a day-by-day basis.

▶ **See** "Reviewing the Format Options for the Form Views," **p. 727**

Project uses the work data to calculate the resource costs for each task. If actual costs differ from the scheduled cost for the values entered in the Actual Work fields, you need to have a way to enter actual costs. To do this, display the Resource Cost fields at the bottom of the Task Details Form and record actual costs by resource for each task. This method will only work if the option Actual Costs always calculated by Microsoft Project is not turned on in the Options dialog box (see Figure 15.24).

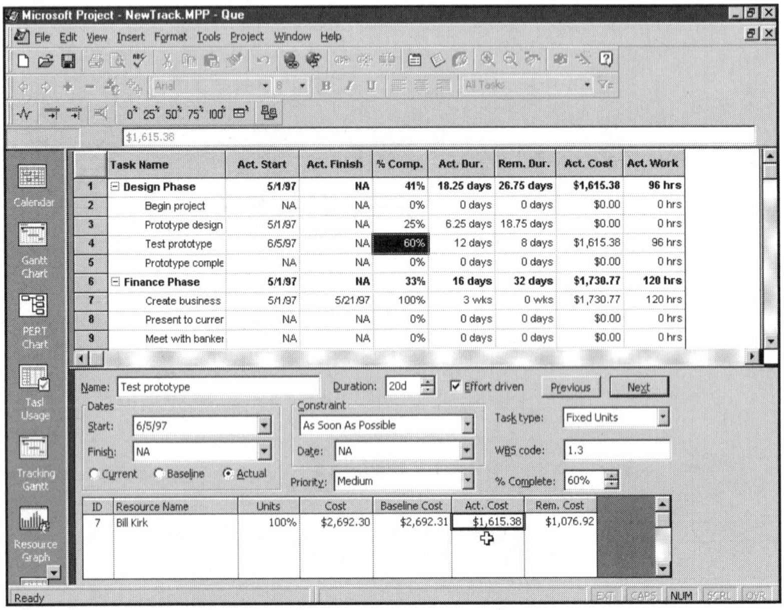

FIG. 15.24

This figure shows the Resource Cost fields on the Task Details Form.

   Using the Update Tasks Dialog Box   Access the Update Tasks dialog box by using either the Tools, Tracking, Update Tasks menu command or the Update Tasks button on the Tracking toolbar (refer to Figure 15.18 for a look at these buttons). Use this dialog box to enter all the tracking fields discussed in this section except the actual work and cost (see Figure 15.25). For example, if you enter 100% complete, Project sets the Actual Start and Actual Finish to what they were scheduled to be. If you set an Actual Duration of 6 days on a 10 day task, Project calculates Percentage Complete to be 60%, and a Remaining Duration of 4. On the other hand, if you enter a Percentage Complete of 60%, then Project calculates the Actual Duration to be 6 and a Remaining Duration of 4.

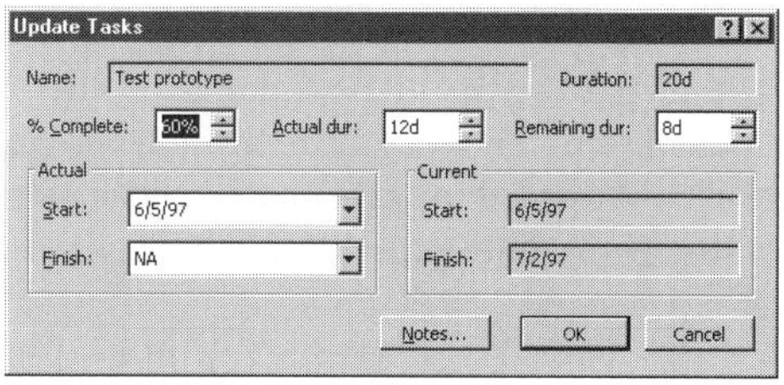

FIG. 15.25
Use the Update Tasks dialog box for individual or groups of tasks to provide actual information for tasks that are not proceeding according to plan.

If you select several tasks before accessing the Update Tasks dialog box, the dialog box appears blank. Any change you enter here is added to all the selected tasks. You could record, for example, all tasks completed yesterday by selecting the tasks and typing yesterday's date in the Actual Finish date field.

Using the Percent Complete Buttons If one or more tasks have started and finished on schedule, you can select the tasks and use the various percent complete buttons to copy the scheduled start and finished dates to the actual dates and to enter the appropriate percentage in the Percentage Complete field (refer to Figure 15.16 for a look at the percent complete buttons).

You also can use the following methods to mark a task as completed; these buttons, however, are the fastest way to show tasks that are on schedule either as completed or in varying stages of completion.

Using the Update Project Command Choosing Tools, Tracking, Update Project is a convenient way to update a group of tasks scheduled to start or finish by a certain date. Either enter or select a date in the Update Work As Complete Through text box. Only the tasks with scheduled activity before the update date are affected by this command. When you choose this command, the dialog box displayed in Figure 15.26 opens.

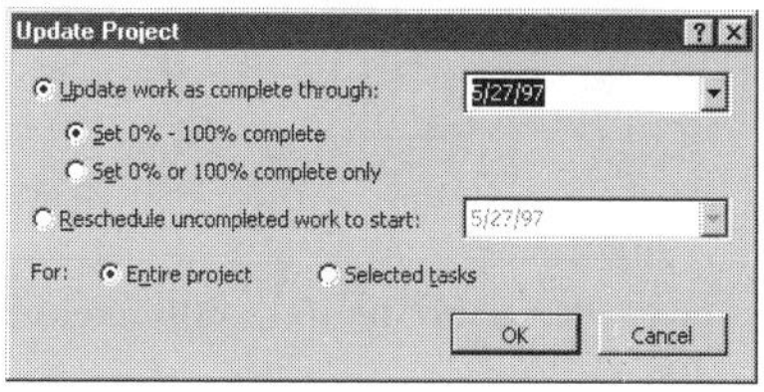

FIG. 15.26
The Update Project dialog box allows you to schedule tasks.

The Update Project dialog box offers choices for updating tasks that are on schedule and tasks that are slipping. The updating options you can choose in this dialog box are as follows:

- *Set 0% - 100% Complete.* Sets the actual dates as originally scheduled and also calculates the Percentage Complete. The Percentage Complete is calculated as the percentage of the duration that was scheduled for completion by the update date.

- *Set 0% or 100% Complete Only.* Leaves the percent complete field at zero until the Actual Finish date is updated, at which time the percentage is set to 100 percent. This option is useful for cases where the Percentage Complete is to be either 0 percent or 100 percent.

▨ *Reschedule Uncompleted Work to Start.* Reschedules slipping tasks to start on the update date as entered in the top-right corner of the dialog box. If the task already has some amount of actual duration recorded for it, the remaining duration is split off from the part already completed and rescheduled to begin on the update date. If a task has not yet started but should have, Project moves the start of the task to start on the update date.

N O T E   The Split In-Progress Tasks check box must be marked (the default) on the Schedule tab of the Options dialog box before you can use the Reschedule Uncompleted Work to Start option.

To mark this option, complete the following steps:

1. Choose Tools, Options and then choose the Schedule tab.
2. Make sure that the Split In-Progress Tasks check box is marked.
3. Choose OK. ▨

To use the Update Project command, take the following steps:

1. Select the task or tasks that you want to update, if only selected tasks are to be updated. If you want to include all tasks that start before the update date, it doesn't matter whether you have tasks selected or not.
2. Choose Tools, Tracking, Update Project. The Update Project dialog box opens (refer to Figure 15.26).
3. Choose the Entire Project or Selected Tasks option button, depending on whether you want all tasks considered for updating or only tasks that you selected.
4. Choose the operation that you want performed. Select one of the options as described in the previous list.
5. Change the date field to the date you want to use as a cut-off date—all uncompleted tasks *before* the update date are processed by the command. By default the update date is the status date, as set in the Project Information dialog box. Access this dialog box by choosing Project, Project Information.
6. Choose OK to execute the update.

Figure 15.27 shows the results of using this button. Note that all task bars that lie to the left of the status date (June 3) show progress bars right up to the update line.

CAUTION

The use of the Update as Scheduled button assumes the status date, as specified in the Project Information dialog box (choose Project, Project Information). If you want to update as of some other date, make sure to enter it before using this button.

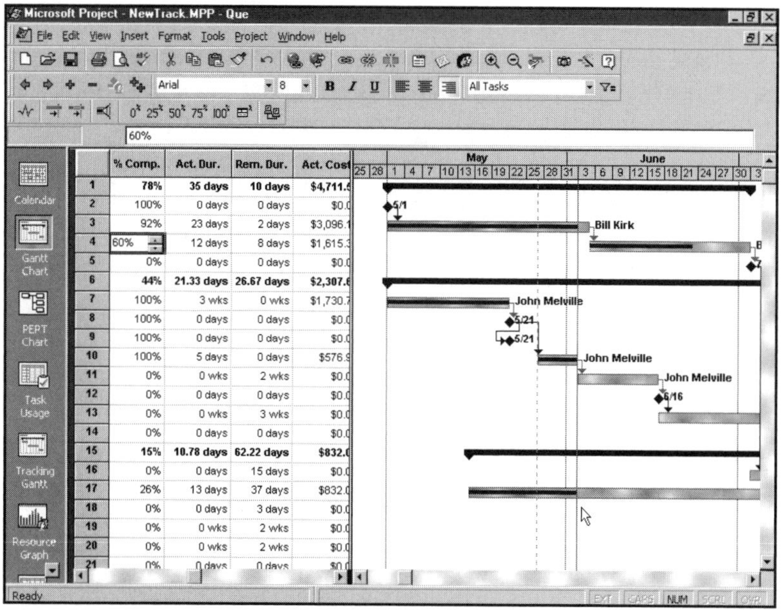

FIG. 15.27

All tasks have been automatically updated as of an "update" date.

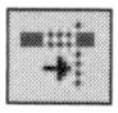

Using the Reschedule Work Button on the Tracking Toolbar The Reschedule Uncompleted Work to Start option in the Update Project dialog box is useful when the scheduled start date falls before the status date and the task has not yet started; the task is rescheduled to start on the status date. If the task has started but the actual duration is less than expected by the current date, the remaining duration of the task is split off and scheduled to start on the current date. The two fields controlled by this button are Stop and Resume. In earlier versions, these fields were calculated fields but can now be edited.

Using the Mouse in the Gantt Chart You can use the mouse in the Gantt Chart to drag the progress bar from the start date of a task to the percentage completed point on the task bar. To enter Percentage Complete with the mouse, complete the following steps:

1. View the Gantt Chart in the top pane by choosing View, Gantt Chart.

2. Move the mouse pointer to the beginning of the task bar for a task you want to update. The pointer changes to a percent sign (%).

3. Click and drag the mouse to the right to increase the Percentage Complete. As you move the mouse, an information box appears to the left of the task bar to indicate the date the task is complete through a certain date, which is specified as you drag the mouse. When the correct date is reached, release the mouse button. Drag the mouse all the way to the finish date to indicate 100 percent complete.

The percentage of work complete changes to the value that you set with the mouse, and the actual start date is set to the date on which the task was scheduled to start.

You can extend the duration of a task by dragging the scheduled end date to the right. Move the mouse pointer to the right end of the task bar until the pointer changes to a right-pointing arrow. As you drag the pointer to the right, an information box appears to let you know the duration that will be set when you release the mouse button.

After you record an actual start date for a task, you can use the mouse to change the date. Move the mouse pointer to the left end of the task bar until it turns into a left-pointing arrow. Then click and drag to the right as the information box indicates an actual start date. Release the mouse button when the start date indicated is what you want.

Be careful when using the mouse to update tasks on the Gantt Chart. If the mouse is in the middle of the task bar, the pointer turns into a double-arrow symbol, and if you drag the mouse, you set a task constraint of Start No Earlier Than. These constraints are insidious because you probably will not be aware that you have set a constraint.

▶ **See** "Resolving Conflicts Caused by Constraints," **p. 208**

If you accidentally start any of these mouse actions in the Gantt Chart and want to escape, you can drag the mouse down from the task bar before releasing the button to prevent any changes. Depending on where you pointed when any of these actions were initiated, the mouse pointer may change to a chain link. If this happens, make sure that you drag to an open space sufficiently away from other task bars so as not to inadvertently create a task link.

TIP   Don't forget about Undo if you inadvertently make a change to a task with the mouse.

The tracking facilities presented so far are used for the more difficult cases, which actually may be the more common cases. When tasks start on time and finish within the scheduled duration, quicker ways exist to record the actual data. You also can update many tasks at the same time (refer to the section, "Using the Update Tasks Dialog Box," earlier in this chapter).

TROUBLESHOOTING

I've already saved the baseline and begun work on the project; then I get a new set of tasks assigned. What do I do? Add the new tasks and make sure to link them to the rest of the project as necessary. Then select the tasks and choose Tools, Tracking, Save Baseline. Make sure to mark the option button for selected tasks.

The project's baseline has already been saved and initial phases of the project have begun. Then the project is delayed. How can I reset the baseline without losing the one I have already? Choose Tools, Tracking, Save Baseline as before, but make sure to mark the Interim Plan option button, and then choose one of the alternate sets of dates—for example, Start1, Start2, Start3, and so on.

I get tracking information from people out in the field. How can I provide them with a tool that allows them to capture the information I need? Print out the project using the Task Sheet with the Tracking table applied. The Task Sheet has several blank columns where information can be entered as soon as it is available. If the project is long, filter the project for a specific date range. The Using Resource filter would also be helpful to only print the tasks that a particular resource is responsible for.

As I track my project I want to manually track the actual time worked on a project rather than have the software do it, but when I indicate that a task has started, the work and cost fields are filled in and I can't change them. Unmark the Updating Task Status Updates Resource Status option on the Calculation tab of the Options dialog box. When you deselect this option, the work and cost fields are not calculated automatically; you can enter information of your own. Or, simply wait until the task is 100% complete and then enter your data.

From Here...

This chapter has covered in great detail how to keep track of your progress on a project using the extensive tracking features of Microsoft Project. You have seen how to compare actual experience with the original plan so that you can tell how you're doing.

At this point you probably want to print out progress reports for management and staff. You may want to refer to the following chapters:

- Chapter 13, "Printing Views and Reports," discusses the mechanics of printing your views and reports and the options you have to make changes in the manner in which they are printed.

- Chapter 14, "Publishing Projects on the Web," describes how to work with projects that involve people available through the Internet.

- Chapter 17, "Using and Creating Views," demonstrates how to modify existing views or create views of your own using custom tables and filters, as well as combining different views in new combination views.

- Chapter 18, "Using Microsoft Project in Workgroups," explains the techniques offered by Microsoft Project to assist in tracking a project that involves many people on a network.

CHAPTER 16

Analyzing Progress and Revising the Schedule

In this chapter, we'll initially take a look at the tools that Project provides to help us analyze our project schedules, work estimates, and budget at both the task and resource level of detail. We'll then complete the treatment of this subject by seeing how to use the tools that Project provides to help us revise and adjust our project plan to keep our plans reflective of reality. ■

Why are variances important?

An overview of why it is important for project managers to analyze variances and revise the schedule.

Reviewing summary progress information

Learn how to review high-level variance information for the overall project plan.

Analyzing task variances

Discover how to analyze variances at the task detail level.

Analyzing resource variances

Find out how to analyze variances at the resource detail level.

Analyzing trends in your plan

Learn how to determine if things are getting better or worse by capturing and reviewing week-to-week trends.

Plan revision

Discover how to know when to make adjustments in the project schedule.

Analyzing Variances and Revising the Schedule

As you may recall, the initial project definition stage culminates in the development of what is commonly referred to as the project business plan, proposal, or statement of Work. In this all-important first deliverable you'll typically find the project budget, schedule, and scope, in addition to goals, objectives, approach, and project completion criteria. In order to ensure successful completion, it is important to maintain project control through sound project management practices. Project control is typically attained through tracking, analysis, revision, scope management, and communication.

As we execute our project plans, we find it necessary to track and analyze actual progress to ensure that our goal of on-time, on-budget completion remains achievable. If tasks are being completed late or in excess of their original work estimates, we have to spot these trouble signs sooner rather than later to be sure that we proactively revise our project plan to adjust to the day-to-day realities of the project. If progress is not as expected, we have to start thinking about revising our plans to extend the scheduled finish date, adjust resource assignments, or reduce scope.

We can begin the process of analysis by regularly looking for tasks that are not progressing as originally planned. You'll typically start to analyze progress after you have captured tracking progress by entering **%Complete** or keying the Actual Work, Remaining Work, Actual Start, and Actual Finish. Once you have captured this information you're ready to analyze plan variances—that is, tasks where progress is out of sync with the baseline (original estimates).

Analyzing Progress

The easiest way to hone in on unfavorable variances is to apply a set of tables, filters, views, or reports to quickly locate these variances. Let's take a look at the different techniques we can use to catch trouble early.

Predicting the future is risky, even for a skilled project manager. The foundation of project control is to know which of your predications are proving to be inaccurate. Analyzing progress and revising the schedule is an important process that occurs after the plan is initially baselined and throughout the execution of your project. Once you have spotted trouble in your project (unfavorable variances), the next step is to figure out how you will revise your work plan to complete the schedule within the available time and budget.

There are two primary ways to make sure your plan remains dynamic and up-to-date: rescheduling unstarted or late tasks, and rescheduling remaining work on in-progress tasks. These rescheduling processes help you avoid stagnant work plans, a common problem for late, overbudget projects. In the last sections of this chapter (see "Revising the Schedule to Complete on Time and on Budget"), we'll review how to use Project to achieve a realistic, revised schedule.

Definitions

Before we perform our first work plan analyses, let's take a look at how Project calculates and stores information that will help to analyze the plan.

Project automatically calculates the difference between current progress and original estimates and places the result into fields called variances.

You may find it easier to remember these fields as follows: think of work as Current Estimated work and baseline work as Original Estimated work. The work variance then is the difference between your Current Estimated work and your Original Estimated work. The same holds true for the other four variance fields listed later.

Note that any time the Current Estimated values are higher than the Original Estimated (baseline) values, the resulting variance will be a positive number. This means that any variance that is greater than zero is exceeding your original estimates and is considered unfavorable. A list of how Project calculates variances follows:

> Work Variance = (Work – Baseline Work)
>
> Cost Variance = (Cost – Baseline Cost)
>
> Finish Variance = (Finish – Baseline Finish)
>
> Start Variance = (Start – Baseline Start)
>
> Duration Variance = (Duration – Baseline Duration)

In addition, Project automatically calculates two types of percent complete: %Complete and %Work Complete. It is important to understand the differences between these two fields because they give you two different flavors of project progress:

- *%Complete*, the percentage of completion based upon the tasks' actual duration divided by estimated duration times 100. If you key directly into the %Complete field, Project calculates the Actual and Remaining Duration for the task, and sets the %Work Complete.

  Microsoft Project 98 no longer calculates your Actual Work and Remaining Work automatically, based upon the %Complete. In previous versions of Microsoft Project, the Updating Task Status Updates Resource option was selected by default, as an option. This default was a problem if you did not want Project to calculate your Actual Work and Remaining Work. The new default for Project 98 (unselected) ensures that Project will not change your Actual Work and Remaining Work, unless you specifically change this default option. If you want Project 98 to automatically calculate your Actual Work and Remaining Work, you need to select the Updating Task Status Updates Resource option. To select this option, choose Options from the Tools menu, click the Calculation tab, and check the option. Note that this option was on the Schedule tab in previous versions of Project.

> **CAUTION**
>
> If you set this option, Project may change your Actual Work and Remaining Work, even if you have keyed values in these fields.

■ *%Work Complete*, the percentage of completion based upon the tasks' actual work divided by total estimated work duration times 100. If you key directly into the %Work Complete field, project calculates the Actual and Remaining Duration for the task, and sets the %Complete.

Reviewing Summary Progress Information

There are two easy ways to analyze how your entire project is performing against your original plan. The first method is to display the Project Summary Task, combined with work, variance, or tracking table. To display the Project Summary Task, choose Tools, Options, then click the View tab. Note the Project Summary Task option in the lower right-hand corner of the screen under Outline Options. Check this option and Project automatically displays a summary task for the entire plan.

Analyzing the Work Variances for the Entire Project Once you've displayed the project summary task, try applying the Work table. Choose View, Table, Work.

Figure 16.1 shows that for the Software System Implementation project, the total Work Variance is –997.0 hours (favorable).

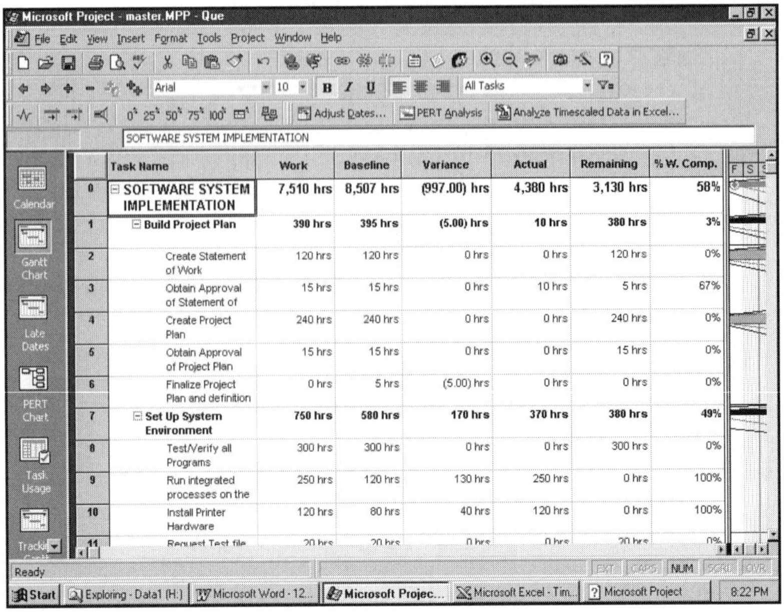

FIG. 16.1

This summary project task shows the Work table applied.

		Task Name	Work	Baseline	Variance	Actual	Remaining	% W. Comp.
	0	⊟ SOFTWARE SYSTEM IMPLEMENTATION	7,510 hrs	8,507 hrs	(997.00) hrs	4,380 hrs	3,130 hrs	58%
	1	⊟ Build Project Plan	390 hrs	395 hrs	(5.00) hrs	10 hrs	380 hrs	3%
	2	Create Statement of Work	120 hrs	120 hrs	0 hrs	0 hrs	120 hrs	0%
	3	Obtain Approval of Statement of	15 hrs	15 hrs	0 hrs	10 hrs	5 hrs	67%
	4	Create Project Plan	240 hrs	240 hrs	0 hrs	0 hrs	240 hrs	0%
	5	Obtain Approval of Project Plan	15 hrs	15 hrs	0 hrs	0 hrs	15 hrs	0%
	6	Finalize Project Plan and definition	0 hrs	5 hrs	(5.00) hrs	0 hrs	0 hrs	0%
	7	⊟ Set Up System Environment	750 hrs	580 hrs	170 hrs	370 hrs	380 hrs	49%
	8	Test/Verify all Programs	300 hrs	300 hrs	0 hrs	0 hrs	300 hrs	0%
	9	Run integrated processes on the	250 hrs	120 hrs	130 hrs	250 hrs	0 hrs	100%
	10	Install Printer Hardware	120 hrs	80 hrs	40 hrs	120 hrs	0 hrs	100%
	11	Request Test file	20 hrs	20 hrs	0 hrs	0 hrs	20 hrs	0%

Analyzing the Date Variances for the Entire Project   Now try applying the Variance table. Choose View, Table, Variance.

Figure 16.2 shows the date variance fields for the Software System Implementation project. You can see that even though the project is tracking ahead of plan on work estimates, the project has a Start Variance of positive 11 days (unfavorable). This means the project started later than expected.

Part

V

Ch

16

FIG. 16.2

This summary project task shows the Variance table applied.

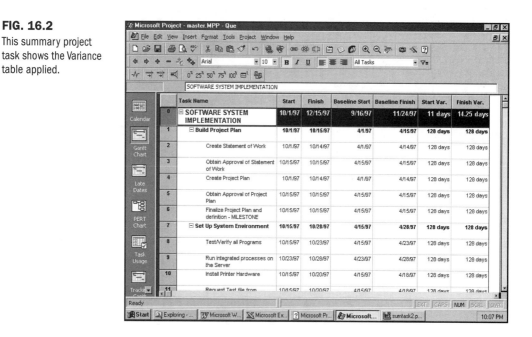

It can be tempting to focus too heavily on analyzing work variances. If you analyze your work variances and your work estimates are accurate, you might assume that you will meet your objective of on-time delivery. It's possible to be completing tasks according to the original (baseline) work estimates, but miss your objective of on-time delivery due to these tasks starting or finishing late.

As we can see in the current example, the work Variance is favorable (refer to Figure 16.1), but if we look at the Finish Variance, the entire project is forecasted to complete 14.25 days later than originally estimated (refer to Figure 16.2).

TROUBLESHOOTING

Are date variances affecting my critical path? During the tracking process, you should key in Actual Start and Actual Finish dates for each task. When you key an Actual Finish date that is later than originally estimated, your project's overall Finish Date can be pushed to a later date. When this happens, it means that slipping tasks have extended the critical path for the project.

Analyzing Cost Variances for the Entire Project   To analyze your overall project costs, try applying the Cost table. Choose View, Table, Cost.

Figure 16.3 shows the Cost Variance field for the Software System Implementation project. The project summary task shows a total Cost Variance of –$25,950.00 (favorable). The original estimated Cost (baseline) was $86,250, but based on current progress, the project is expected to be completed under budget at a Total Cost of $60,300.

FIG. 16.3

The summary project task shows the Cost table applied.

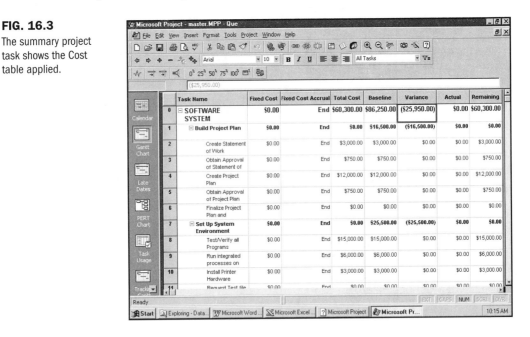

Displaying Project Statistics   Another quick way to see your project's progress in a single view is to display the Project Statistics dialog box. You can show this view from the Tracking toolbar by clicking the Project Statistics tool button. When you click this tool button, you'll see the entire project summarized as shown in Figure 16.4. Note that this dialog box summarizes project start and finish dates, duration, work, and cost for the project. You can also display this view by choosing Project, Project Information. In the Project Information dialog box, click the Statistics button.

The Project Summary Report   Project also provides a convenient report, called Project Summary, that shows a summary analysis of the entire project. Choose View, Reports. On the Reports dialog box, click Overview, then Select. Choose the report called Project Summary, then click Select. You'll be presented with the report as shown in Figure 16.5. Note that this report provides a summary of your overall project dates, duration, work, costs, and summary task status.

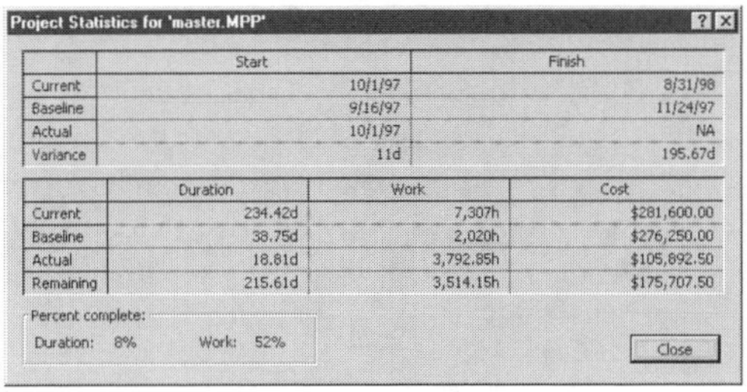

FIG. 16.4

Here is the Project Statistics dialog box.

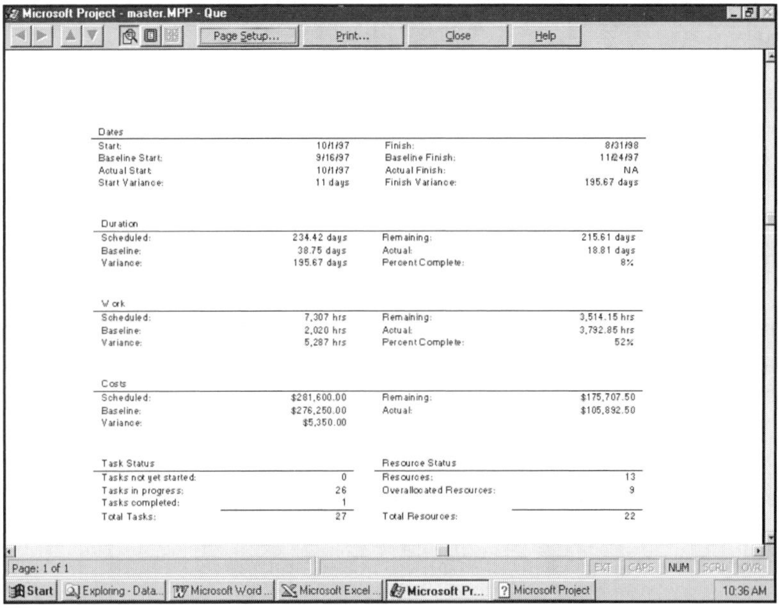

FIG. 16.5

This is the Project Summary report.

TROUBLESHOOTING

I've looked at the project summary task and want to start analyzing the next level of detail in my project plan. Is there an easy way to focus on analyzing the next highest level of detail in my plan? Now that we've seen how to analyze the overall project, let's go to the next level of detailed analysis: analyzing the highest level summary tasks in your project. These high-level summary tasks are often called *phases*. Instead of focusing only on the project summary task, we can apply the Cost, Work, or Variance tables combined with the filter called Top Level Tasks. The Top Level Tasks filter chooses all tasks with an outline level of 1, that is, any tasks that were not indented.

continues

continued

To find the Top Level Tasks filter, you'll have to go to the More Filters dialog box. Choose Project, Filtered For, More Filters. Scroll down the More Filters dialog box until you see the Top Level Tasks filter. Select the filter, then choose Apply. Figure 16.6 shows the More Filters dialog box with Top Level Tasks selected. Try applying the Cost, Work, or Variance tables combined with this filter to analyze how the phases in your project are progressing.

FIG. 16.6

This figure shows the Top Level Tasks filter being selected.

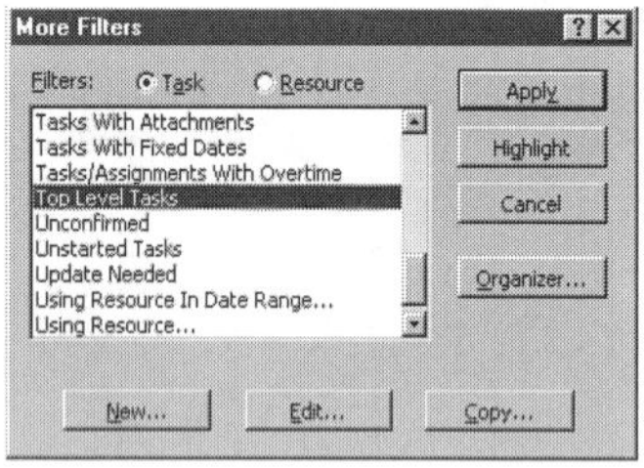

Reviewing Progress Information at the Task Level

It's a good idea to plan to analyze variances in your work plan at least as often as you track progress. If you apply actual and remaining work on a weekly basis, plan to analyze variances on a weekly basis. It doesn't do much good to key in actuals every week, and then not see what these numbers are telling you. Subtle increases of work and costs over your original baseline can add up quickly. The sooner you spot trouble and revise your plan, the more likely you are to achieve your project's objectives of on-time, on-budget completion.

Project provides a number of views, filters, and reports to assist you in spotting trouble at the task level of detail. Let's take a look at how we can analyze variances that are occurring on individual tasks in your plan.

Finding Task Work Variances   You may recall that work variances are created whenever your current work estimates are different than your baseline work. A negative work variance is favorable and a positive work variance is unfavorable. The fastest way to see the work variances for each task in your plan is to apply the Work table. From the View menu, choose Table, Work. Figure 16.7 shows the Work table. Note that the Variance column displays the work variances for each task in your plan.

To focus on trouble spots, you'll want to look at tasks with unfavorable variances. Project provides a filter, called Work Overbudget, for this purpose. Figure 16.8 shows the contents of this filter. Note that the tasks will be selected if work is in excess of baseline work, the task was baselined, and the task is not finished (remaining work not equal to zero). See Figure 16.9.

You can combine the Work table and Work Overbudget filter into a new single view. This new view can be applied any time you want to spot tasks quickly that are forecasted to exceed their original work estimate. Figure 16.10 shows the new Work Variance view. This same configuration can be used to build an Underestimated Tasks report. To build this view or report, refer to Chapter 22, "Customizing Views, Tables, and Filters," and Chapter 24, "Customizing Reports."

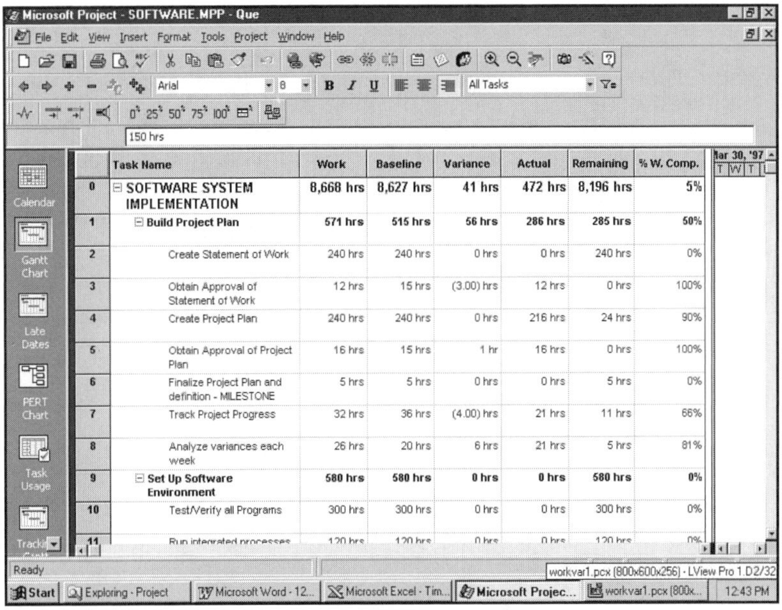

FIG. 16.7
Gantt Chart with Work table applied.

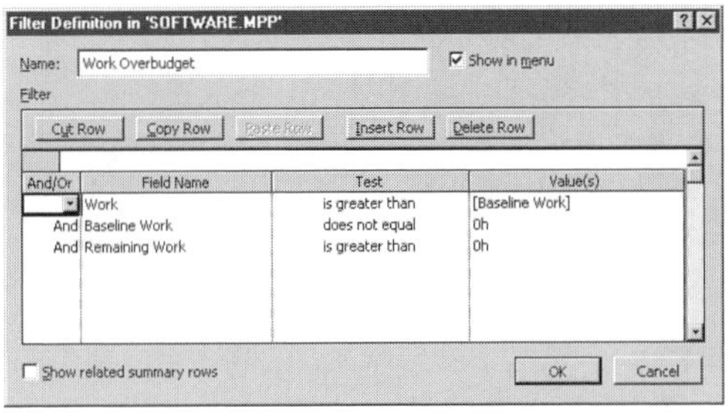

FIG. 16.8
The contents of the Work Overbudget filter shows the logic used to select tasks that have exceeded their baseline estimates.

◆ **TROUBLESHOOTING**

I keyed in actual and remaining work then looked at my work variances and they're all large numbers, even though my work estimates seem to be fairly accurate. Why am I seeing such large work variances? Variances are meaningless unless your work plan has been baselined. If you haven't baselined your plan, all of your work variances will be equal to your work. If you see this happening, you need to baseline your plan. If you've already keyed in actuals, rebaselining your plan may cause your baseline to be different than what you originally intended, especially if some of your work or date estimates are proving to be inaccurate.

To be able to recover from a problem like this, you'll need a backup of your plan that reflects the condition of your plan before you keyed in your first actuals. Open your backup copy of the plan, baseline the plan, then reapply the actuals.

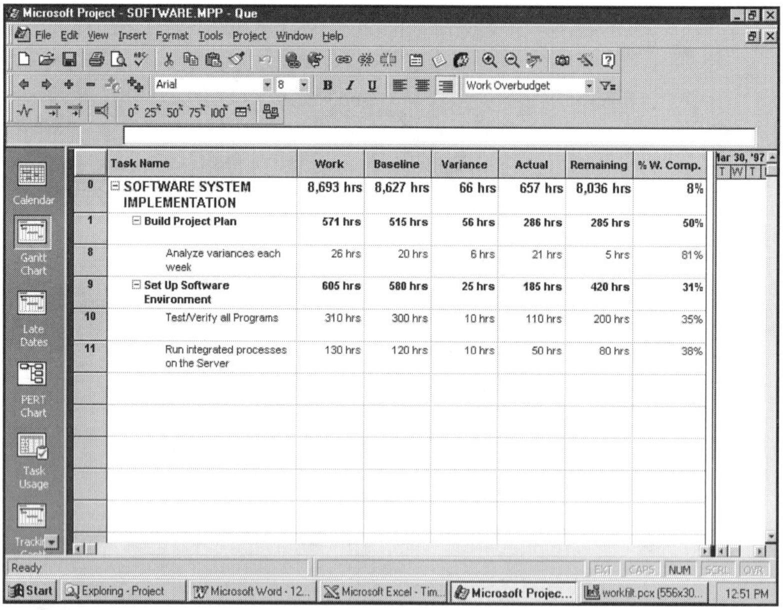

FIG. 16.9

The results of applying the Work Overbudget filter, showing those tasks that have exceeded their original (baseline) estimate.

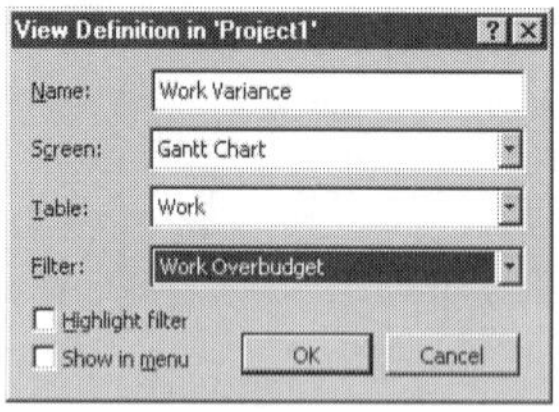

FIG. 16.10

The newly created Work Variance view which combines the Work Table with the Work Overbudget filter.

Finding Task Start and Finish Date Variances   Date variances are created whenever your current start and finish estimates are later than the baseline dates. This can happen in a variety of ways:

- A predecessor task is delayed or completed early, forcing a successor task to be re-scheduled.

- You set a new start or finish date for a task since it could not be completed as originally scheduled.

- You set an actual start or finish date that's different than the baseline date.

- Actual work is higher or lower than originally planned, causing the task's duration and dates to change.

To see all date variances for your project, display the Variance table. Choose View, Table, Variance. Figure 16.11 shows the work plan with the Variance table displayed. Note that you can see the start and finish date, baseline start and finish dates, and date variances.

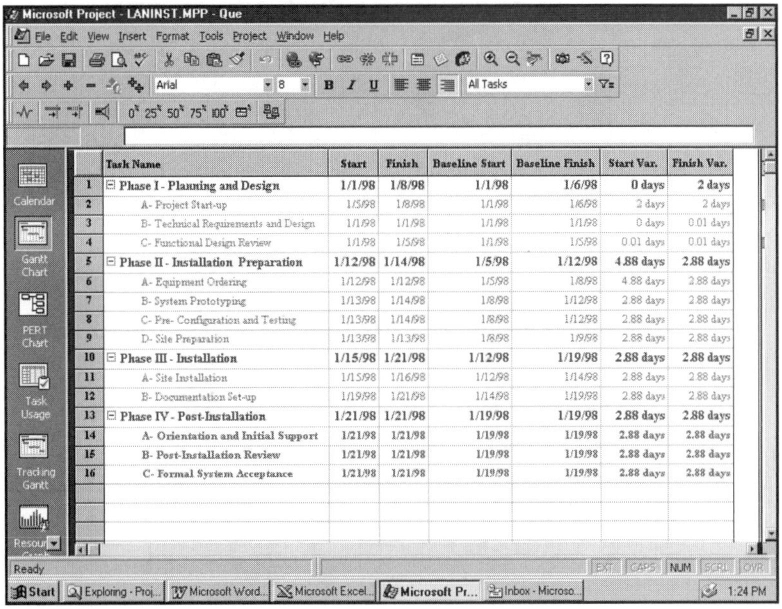

	Task Name	Start	Finish	Baseline Start	Baseline Finish	Start Var.	Finish Var.
1	Phase I - Planning and Design	1/1/98	1/8/98	1/1/98	1/6/98	0 days	2 days
2	A- Project Start-up	1/5/98	1/8/98	1/1/98	1/6/98	2 days	2 days
3	B- Technical Requirements and Design	1/1/98	1/1/98	1/1/98	1/1/98	0 days	0.01 days
4	C- Functional Design Review	1/1/98	1/5/98	1/1/98	1/5/98	0.01 days	0.01 days
5	Phase II - Installation Preparation	1/12/98	1/14/98	1/5/98	1/12/98	4.88 days	2.88 days
6	A- Equipment Ordering	1/12/98	1/12/98	1/5/98	1/8/98	4.88 days	2.88 days
7	B- System Prototyping	1/13/98	1/14/98	1/8/98	1/12/98	2.88 days	2.88 days
8	C- Pre- Configuration and Testing	1/13/98	1/14/98	1/8/98	1/12/98	2.88 days	2.88 days
9	D- Site Preparation	1/13/98	1/13/98	1/8/98	1/9/98	2.88 days	2.88 days
10	Phase III - Installation	1/15/98	1/21/98	1/12/98	1/19/98	2.88 days	2.88 days
11	A- Site Installation	1/15/98	1/16/98	1/12/98	1/14/98	2.88 days	2.88 days
12	B- Documentation Set-up	1/19/98	1/21/98	1/14/98	1/19/98	2.88 days	2.88 days
13	Phase IV - Post-Installation	1/21/98	1/21/98	1/19/98	1/19/98	2.88 days	2.88 days
14	A- Orientation and Initial Support	1/21/98	1/21/98	1/19/98	1/19/98	2.88 days	2.88 days
15	B- Post-Installation Review	1/21/98	1/21/98	1/19/98	1/19/98	2.88 days	2.88 days
16	C- Formal System Acceptance	1/21/98	1/21/98	1/19/98	1/19/98	2.88 days	2.88 days

FIG. 16.11
The Variance table shows the current estimated start and finish dates, the original (baseline) start and finish dates, and any variances from the baseline start and finish dates.

Next, you may want to focus on tasks that are forecasted to finish later than originally estimated. To do this, you'll look for tasks with finish variances greater than zero that have not yet finished. Project provides the Slipping Tasks filter for this purpose. Figure 16.12 shows the contents of the Slipping Tasks filter. This filter shows you tasks that are not yet finished, that have a baseline, and have a current estimated finish date later than the baseline finish date. This filter can be used to find tasks that you can still do something about. They're forecasted to finish late, but they're not finished yet.

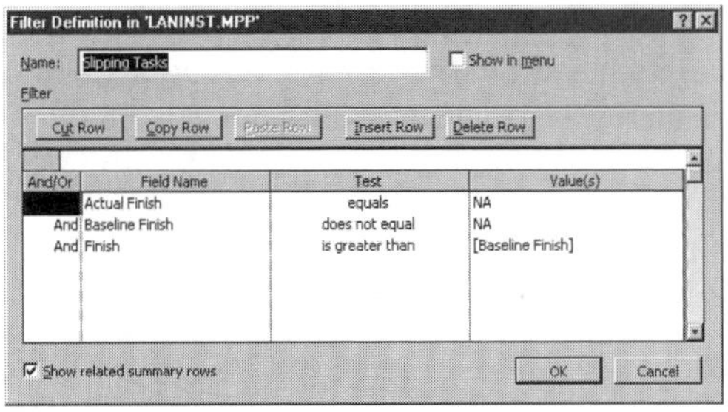

FIG. 16.12
The Slipping Tasks filter shows tasks that are currently planned to complete later than originally planned.

Project supplies another filter that looks for similar problems with tasks forecasted to finish late, called the Slipped/Late Progress filter. Figure 16.13 shows the contents of the Slipped/Late Progress filter. Note that the filter looks for tasks that have a baseline finish date (the task was baselined) and either the finish date is greater that the baseline finish date, or the BCWS is greater than the BCWP. (For more information on the BCWS and BCWP fields, see the list of definition fields used on the Earned Value Table and Report, later in this chapter.)

FIG. 16.13

The Slipped/Late Progress Filter shows tasks that have a baseline finish date and either the finish date is greater that the baseline finish date, or the BCWS is greater than the BCWP.

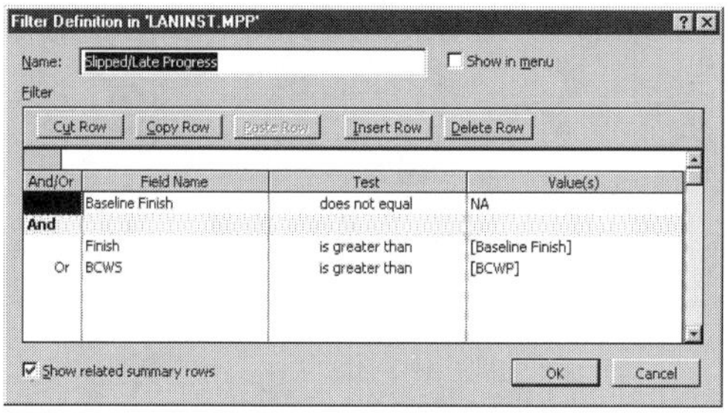

You may want to view all tasks that have unfavorable start and finish dates. You can quickly build a filter for this purpose. Figure 16.14 shows an example of this new custom filter. Display this filter with the Variance table and you'll quickly isolate all the tasks in your plan that have unfavorable date variances.

FIG. 16.14

Use a custom filter to view tasks with unfavorable date variances.

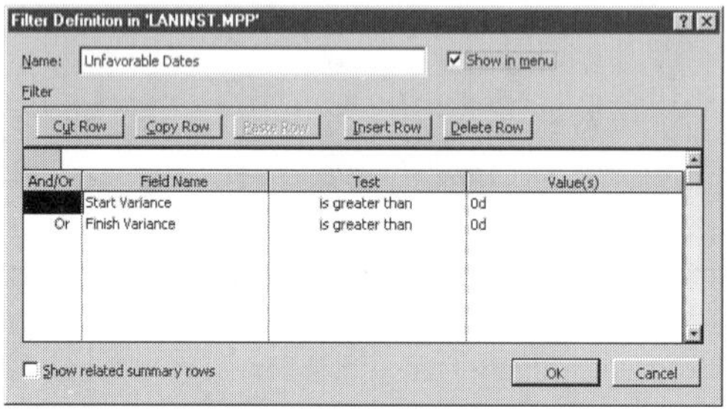

To isolate unfavorable variances for only the Start Variance field, you can quickly apply an AutoFilter. First apply the Variance table. To run an AutoFilter on the start variance field, click the AutoFilter button.

Click the AutoFilter drop-down list on the Start Variance column heading and choose Custom from the drop-down list. Set the test to Is Greater Than and set the value to 0d. When you're done the Custom AutoFilter will be built, as shown in Figure 16.15.

The same concept can be applied to the Finish Variances for your project.

FIG. 16.15

The Custom AutoFilter is showing unfavorable start variances.

◆

TROUBLESHOOTING

I've started and finished a number of tasks late, but am not seeing unfavorable variances. What's causing this to happen? You may not see date variances for a large number of the tasks in your project. Don't forget that whenever a task %Complete is greater than zero, Project automatically copies the estimated task Start date to the Actual Start date. If you don't explicitly key an Actual Start date, Project will assume it started on the estimated Start date. Also, when a task %Complete is 100 percent, Project automatically copies the estimated task Finish date to the Actual Finish date. Again, if you don't explicitly tell Project when the task actually finished, Project will assume it finished on the estimated Finish date.

Part

V

Ch

16

Finding Task Cost Variances   Cost variances are created whenever your current cost estimates are higher than your baseline cost estimates. Tasks can start and finish on time and complete within their original estimates, but still have cost variances. For example, if you estimated that the programming would be completed with a VBA programmer at $50 per hour but you're forced to reassign the task to a programmer whose rate is $60 per hour, your costs will be over budget if the hours remain constant. Hopefully, the programmer with the higher rate can complete the task in fewer hours, but this will not always be the case.

To spot problems with unfavorable costs, you can apply the Cost Overbudget filter. Figure 16.16 shows the contents of the Cost Overbudget filter. As you can see, this filter looks for tasks that were baselined, where the current estimated cost is greater than the baseline cost (or original estimate).

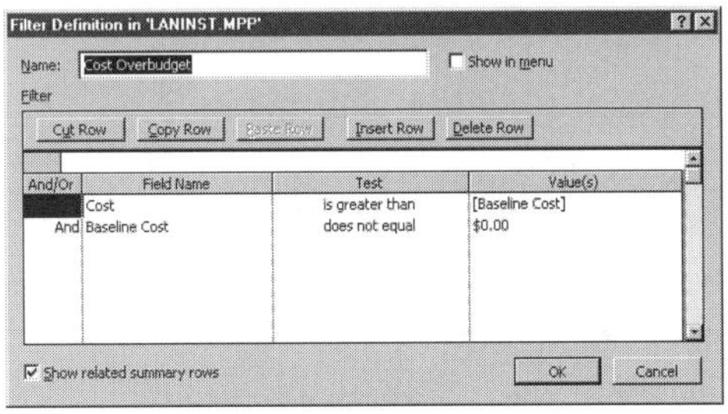

FIG. 16.16

The Cost Overbudget filter is useful for quickly finding tasks that were baselined, and the current estimated cost is greater than the originally estimated cost.

And/Or	Field Name	Test	Value(s)
	Cost	is greater than	[Baseline Cost]
And	Baseline Cost	does not equal	$0.00

You can combine the Cost table and Cost Overbudget filter into a new view. This new view can be applied any time you want to spot tasks quickly that are forecasted to exceed their original cost estimate. Figure 16.17 shows the new Cost Variance view. This is the same configuration used for the Overbudget Tasks report. To build this view, refer to Chapter 22, "Customizing Views, Tables, and Filters."

Analyzing Variances at the Resource Assignment Level   Project now allows you to view specific resource assignments that are late or overbudget for a specific resource. To view late or overbudget assignments you apply the Late/Overbudget Tasks Assigned To filter. From the Project menu, select Filtered For, More filters. From the More Filters dialog box, choose

Late/Overbudget Tasks Assigned To. Because this filter is interactive, you will be prompted to enter the name of the resource you want to analyze. Figure 16.18 shows the contents of the Late/Overbudget Tasks Assigned To filter.

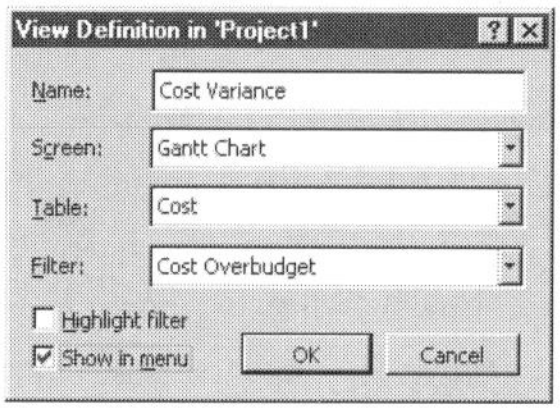

FIG. 16.17

Custom Cost Overbudget view combines the Cost table and Cost Overbudet filter. This view can help you quickly spot tasks that are exceeding their original budget.

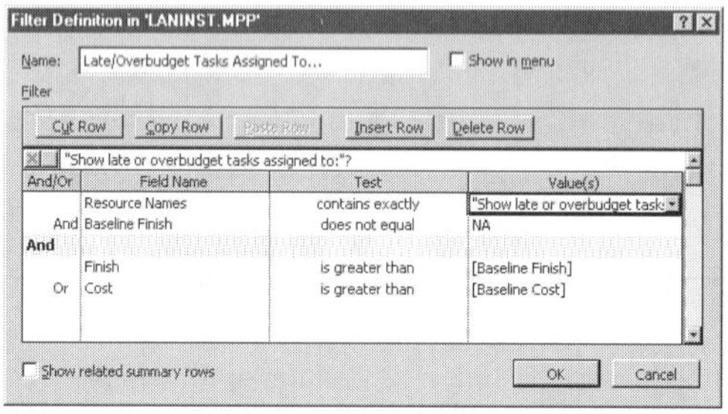

FIG. 16.18

The Late/Overbudget Tasks Assigned To filter provides detailed variance information about specific resources assigned to specific tasks. This level of detailed analysis was not possible in previous versions of Project.

You can compare baseline work to work at the resource assignment level of detail in your plan. Use the following steps:

1. Display the Task Usage View by clicking the Task Usage icon.
2. In the Task Usage grid, click your right mouse button. Choose Baseline Work.
3. You are now able to review the current work estimate against the baseline work estimate at the detailed resource assignment level of detail.

Figure 16.19 shows the Task Usage view with work and baseline work displayed.

You can perform this same analysis from the Resource Usage view. The information presented is basically the same, except that the information is presented by task within resource, instead of resource within task.

TROUBLESHOOTING

What should I do if my variances are favorable? Managing a project that is ahead of schedule is an enjoyable, though sometimes rare position to be in. It's very tempting to tell everyone when you find yourself in this enviable position. Before you do, consider what sometimes happens if you report that you're ahead of schedule:

- Scope: Because you have extra time on your hands, your project scope may be increased.

- Budget: Because you don't need all the money you originally asked for, your budget may be cut to be in line with current projections.

- Schedule: Because you're ahead of schedule, your project finish date can be adjusted to complete earlier than originally planned.

- Resources: Because you're completing tasks early, in fewer hours than originally predicted, some of your resources can be diverted to other efforts.

Carefully consider the right time to report favorable variances. It's a good idea to wait, if you can, until you're fairly certain that these trends will continue.

FIG. 16.19

Task Usage view with work compared to baseline work. This view provides the ability to quickly compare current progress with baseline estimates at the resource assignment level of detail.

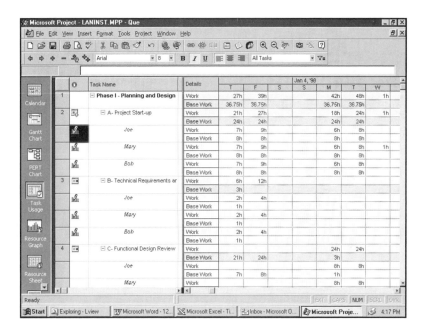

Now that we've learned how to locate which tasks require additional attention to get back on schedule, we need to revise our schedule to achieve on-time, on-budget completion. But before we do that, let's take a look at how we can isolate variances for resources.

Reviewing Progress Information at the Resource Level

You can also analyze variances for resources. The concept is very similar to many of the analyses that you performed on tasks in the previous section. By analyzing resources, you may find a pattern in the tasks that have variances. You might be able to determine that the reasons for variances are resource-related:

- Resources arrived late onto the project.

- Tasks were assigned to resources with the wrong skills to perform the task.

- Tasks for one resource were consistently underestimated.
- Resources have not been able to apply the percentage of time to the project that was originally anticipated.
- Tasks that are slipping seem to be assigned to the same resource or combination of resources.
- The original cost of a resource was under- or overestimated.
- Customer or user resources are not applying the appropriate effort to the project.

To find these kinds of patterns, you can view variances for resources. Rather than repeat the previous steps that we performed on tasks for work, date, and cost variances, Table 16.1 shows the variances you can select.

Table 16.1 Suggested Variance Analyses from Resource Sheet

Table	Filter*	Custom Filter Criteria	Shows You
Cost	Cost Overbudget	—	Resources whose current estimated cost is higher than originally estimated baseline cost.
Entry	Slipping Assignments	—	Resource assignments that are forecasted to finish later than originally estimated.
Entry	Should Start/Finish By…	—	Resource assignments that should have started or finished by a date that you specify. (This is an interactive filter.)
Entry	Should Start By…	—	Resource assignments that should have started by a date that you specify. (This is an interactive filter.)
Work	Work Overbudget*	Work is greater than [Baseline Work]	Resources whose current estimated work is higher than originally estimated baseline work.

Filters with an asterisk can be built. Refer to Chapter 22, "Customizing Views, Tables, and Filters." These filters can also be set in AutoFilter mode.

Graphically Analyzing Tasks in Your Plan: Adding Progress Lines   Project 98 provides a new feature that enhances the visual display of your project's progress line on the Gantt Chart. The progress line is a line drawn as of the date you specify. The progress line is drawn vertically down the Gantt Chart and connects the actual duration of each task to the vertical date you have specified. There are two basic ways to display a progress line:

- Using the Add Progress Line tool button on the Tracking toolbar.
- Choosing <u>T</u>ools, Trac<u>k</u>ing.

Using the Add Progress Line tool button   When you click the Add Progress Line tool button, the mouse pointer changes shape to look like a progress line and the Progress Line ToolTip box pops up as you move your cursor over the Gantt Chart area. Note that the ToolTip displays the date it will use to display the progress line. Figure 16.20 shows the ToolTip box that will pop up.

When you move your pointer to the desired date, click your primary mouse button and the progress line will display, connecting each task's actual duration at the progress date you specify. Figure 16.21 shows the resulting progress line. Note that the progress line is drawn using 10/20/97, since this is the date that was displayed in the ToolTip pop-up box when you clicked the Gantt Chart.

Displaying Progress Lines From the Tools Menu   Project provides many additional options for displaying progress lines from the Tools menu. From the <u>T</u>ools menu, choose Trac<u>k</u>ing, Progress <u>L</u>ines. You are then presented with the Progress Lines dialog box (see Figure 16.22).

The most common way to show a progress line is at the current Status Date. You may remember from Chapter 15, "Tracking Work on the Project," that the Status Date is a date you select that signifies the date you consider to be current for your project. The Status Date will not change unless you change it. (See Project Information on the Project menu to view or modify how your project's Status Date is currently set.)

To display a progress line at the Status Date, check the first box titled Always Display Current Progress Line, then check the option At Project Status Date. Note that the progress line displays in red on the Gantt Chart. You can also choose to display the current progress line At Current Date. This option will use the Current Date setting to display the progress line. The Current Date can be changed, but by default is set to the date on your system clock.

Let's explore some of the other progress line settings. Note the option boxes at the bottom right of Figure 16.22. You can Display Progress Lines in Relation To one of two options: Actual Plan, or Baseline Plan. The default setting, Actual Plan, shows the progress line based on the Actual Duration of the task. If you choose the Baseline Plan option, the progress line connects the Baseline Start date for any task with 0% Complete or the Actual Duration for tasks with progress.

FIG. 16.20

The Progress Lines ToolTip box will display to show you the date on which the progress line will be placed.

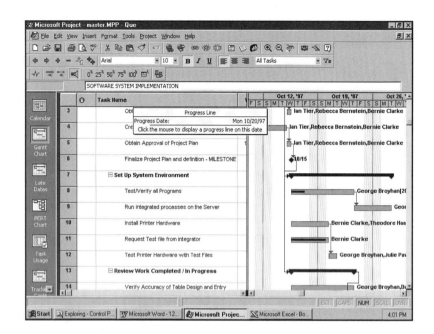

FIG. 16.21

The Progress Line will display, connecting the current progress line within each Gantt Bar.

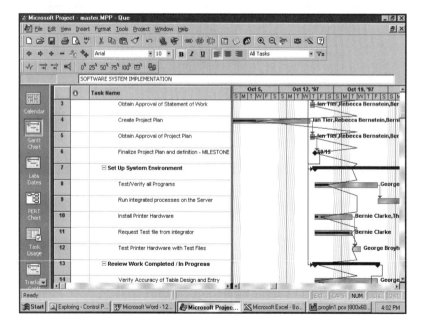

N O T E   The progress line does not stretch and connect Gantt lines with future dates. It always shows progress up to, but not past, the Project Status Date. ▪

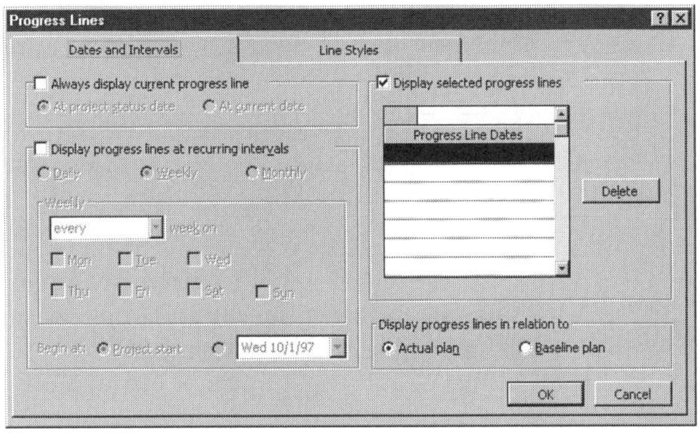

FIG. 16.22

The Progress Lines dialog box provides numerous options for controlling formatting of the Progress Line. These options provide the ability to override the defaults used when using the Progress Lines tool button.

Displaying Progress Lines at Regular Intervals   Figure 16.22 also shows an option called Display Progress Lines at Recurring Intervals. This option allows you to display multiple recurring progress lines on the Gantt Chart. This option can be used for "what if" type scenarios. For example, if you choose the Monthly option, you'll see what the progress lines will look like with each passing month on your project. You may recognize these recurring options if you've ever used a recurring task.

Choosing Daily allows you to select either every day of the week or only the working days. Note that the edit drop-down list provides many more options than every day (every other, every 3rd, and so on). If you choose Weekly, the options automatically change to the days of the week you want to use and again offers a drop-down list with options for every other, every 3rd, and so on. If you choose the Monthly option, the options now change to options for the day of the month on which you want to show the progress line. Table 16.2 shows these intervals and their options.

N O T E   You can use both the Always Display Current Progress Line and Display Progress Lines at Recurring Intervals options. If you choose both options, the current progress line will display in red, by default.

Table 16.2   Options for Progress Lines at Recurring Intervals

Interval	Options
Daily	Every Day
	Every Work Day
	Drop-down allows every day through every 12th day
Weekly	You can choose any day of the week (Mon through Sun)
	You are not limited to only one day of the week. You can choose one day, through all seven days of the week.
	Drop-down list allows every week through every 12th week.

continues

Table 16.2   Continued

Interval	Options
Monthly	You can choose day 1 through 31 of every month. Drop-down list allows every month through every 12th month.
	or
	You can choose the first or last day (or workday or nonworking day or any day of the week). Drop-down allows every month through every 12th month.

TROUBLESHOOTING

What if I want to show progress lines at irregular intervals not offered in the Table 16.2? For example, during the first two months of the project I want to see progress lines every other week, then for the remaining four months I want to see progress lines only once a month. If you select the Display Selected Progress Lines, you can type the dates directly into the list of progress line dates. You can also use Date Picker control to graphically select dates from the drop-down list on each line of the grid.

Note that you can also delete dates by clicking the date you want to delete, then clicking the Delete button.

TIP Once you show a progress line, you may want to change the options you originally selected. One easy way to do this is to double-click anywhere on the progress line. Project then automatically displays the Progress Lines dialog box.

Changing the Look of Progress Lines   The Line Styles tab on the Progress Lines dialog box provides numerous options for displaying progress lines. These display options give you a high degree of control over the types, colors, shapes, and date interval of the progress line. Figure 16.23 shows the Progress Lines dialog box with the Line Styles tab selected.

Any time you set the baseline for a task, or the entire project, you will reset the variance fields to zero (or NA for dates). If your project is already under way, you may not want to lose your variances when you reset the baseline. Project provides the intermediate baseline fields to allow you to store intermediate variances to avoid wiping out your variances.

On the other hand, you may find that resetting variances to zero is just what you want. Maybe your original estimates were incorrect, but you were just given permission to re-estimate the unfinished tasks in your plan. You can apply a filter for Uncompleted Tasks, select those uncompleted tasks, and set the baseline For Selected Tasks.

Using Gantt Chart Bars to Analyze Progress   You can analyze your project progress by simply looking at the standard Gantt Chart. To analyze the standard Gantt Chart, you look for tasks with a progress bar that is to the left of the current date line. Figure 16.24 shows a project plan with the current date set to 1/7/98. Note the progress line for tasks 3 and 4 are left of the current date, indicating that they're behind schedule. Task 2 is right on schedule and task 6 is ahead of schedule.

FIG. 16.23

The Progress Lines dialog box allows you to format the look of the progress line.

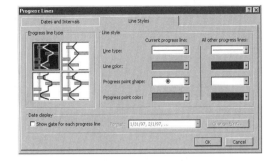

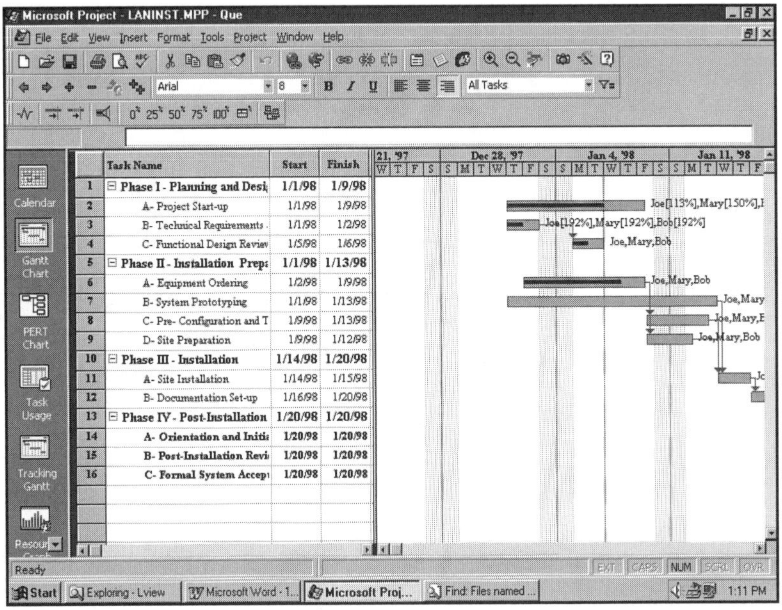

Part

V

Ch

16

FIG. 16.24

Progress lines show tasks ahead of and behind schedule.

Besides the standard Gantt Chart view, Project also supplies a different view called the Leveling Gantt, which can be used to see slack and slippage. Figure 16.25 shows the Leveling Gantt chart. Note that tasks that are slipping have a line to the left of the progress bar and the number of days of slippage is also displayed. For example, task 6 has slipped 4.88 days.

 You can also use the Gantt Chart Wizard to build customized Gantt Chart views. One useful configuration compares baseline to plan. To build this customized Gantt Chart, click the Gantt Chart Wizard tool button on the Standard toolbar. When you run the wizard, choose Baseline for Step 2.

FIG. 16.25

The Leveling Gantt shows the amount of slippage for each task by displaying a thin line to the left of the Gantt bar.

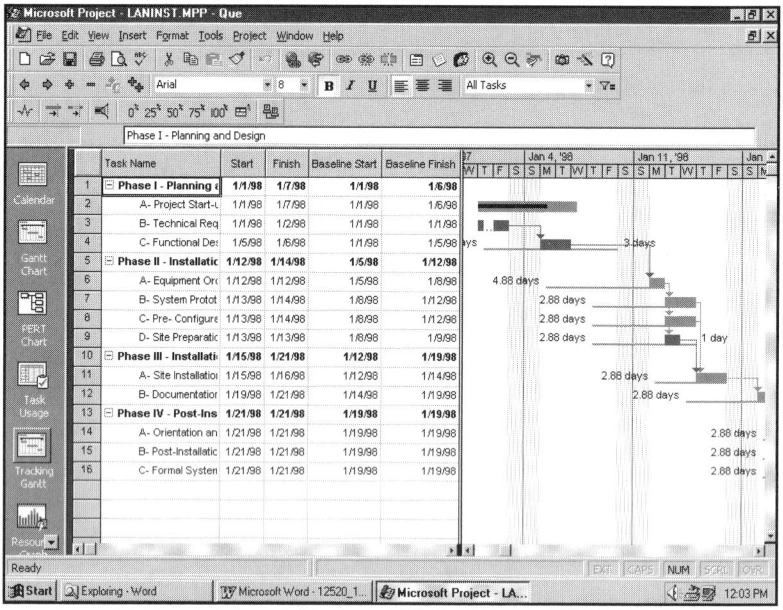

Figure 16.26 shows the resulting Gantt Chart. Note that task 2 has started as planned, is not yet finished, but is forecasted to complete a little late. The remaining tasks (from task 4 on) are not yet started but are planned to start later than the baseline start date.

FIG. 16.26

Gantt Chart with Baseline task bars. This customized Gantt chart shows the baseline start and finish as well as the current estimated task start and finish dates. This Gantt chart makes it easy to graphically analyze your plan.

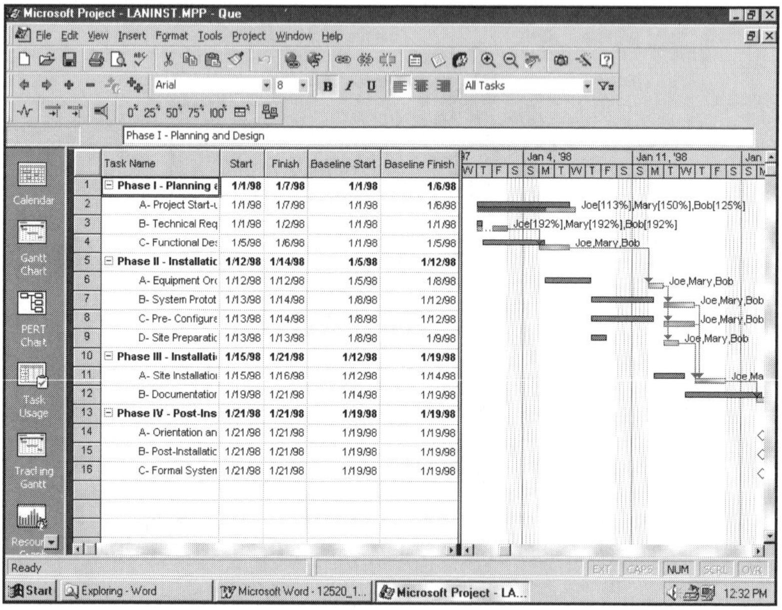

The Earned Value Fields and Report   One of the best ways to analyze variances in your plan is to compare how much of your budget you should have spent compared to how much you've actually spent. This concept is sometimes referred to as Estimated Burn Rate versus Actual Burn Rate. Project supplies a number of fields that are automatically calculated called Earned Value. Let's take a look at what fields are available and how they're used.

The earned value fields now carry a much greater level of precision due to Project's ability to consider time-phased data. The time-phased earned value fields give Project new abilities to provide enhanced information about data that is spread over some period of time. For example, Project now considers each resource's Base Calendar when making earned value calculations for time-scaled data.

98

Part

V

Ch

16

For example, the BCWS (budgeted cost of work scheduled) field contains the cumulative time-phased baseline costs up to the status date or today's date. This time-phased field shows cumulative BCWS as distributed over time, up to the status date or today's date.

The following is a list of definition fields used on the Earned Value Table and Report.

- *BCWS (Budgeted Cost of Work Scheduled)*. The planned (or scheduled) earned value of the task. Project first determines the planned completion percentage based on today's date and the task's baseline start and finish dates.

  BCWS = Planned Completion Percentage×Planned Cost

  The BCWS field shows how much of the budget should have been spent on a task or resource by now (depending on which sheet view you apply).

N O T E   The planned completion percentage is an internally calculated field that cannot be displayed. Project calculates this field by figuring out what the percent complete should be for a task by taking the difference between the planned start date for the task and the project status date. ▪

T I P   You can calculate the planned completion percentage for a task by using some algebra on the BCWS calculation:

Planned Completion Percentage = BCWS÷Planned Cost

Example Calculation of Planned Completion Percentage: The baseline cost for an assignment is $100, and is evenly distributed over its duration. The baseline start for the assignment is September 1 and the baseline finish is September 30. If today's date is September 15, then the BCWS for the assignment is $50. By dividing the planned cost of $100 into the BCWS of $50, you can calculate a Planned Completion Percentage of 50 percent.

- *BCWP (Budgeted cost of work performed)*. This field is often referred to as the earned value of the work that has been performed on the task.

  BCWP = Percent Complete×Baseline Cost

  Example, if the baseline cost for a task is $100 and the task is now 75 percent complete, the BCWP is $75.

> **TIP** Because you can calculate planned completion percentage and Project stores the task's actual percent complete, try comparing these two numbers. If a task's planned completion percentage is 75 percent and the percent complete is 50, you are running 25 percent behind the planned burn rate for that task.

- *ACWP (Actual cost of work performed)*. This field represents the cost of actual work plus any fixed costs for the task, up to the project status date. The calculation of the ACWP depends on each resource's Accrue At settings in the Resource Information dialog box (or Resource Sheet). The resource's cost accrual method is used in conjunction with the actual work recorded for each resource, any fixed costs for the task, and the status date or today's date.

  Actual Cost = (Actual Work times Standard Rate) + (Actual Overtime Work×Overtime Rate) + Resource Per Use Costs + Fixed Cost

- *SV (Schedule Variance)*. The difference between the current schedule and the baseline schedule. If the schedule variance is negative, the project is ahead of schedule; if the schedule variance is positive, the project is behind schedule.

  Current Schedule – Baseline Schedule

- *CV (Earned Value Cost Variance)*. The difference between the baseline costs and the scheduled costs (current estimate). If the cost variance is negative, the cost is currently under the budgeted (or baseline) amount; if the cost variance is positive, the task is over budget.

  Earned Value Cost Variance = Cost – Baseline Cost

- *EAC (Estimate at Completion)*. This field is simply an alternate column heading for the Cost field.

- BAC *(Budgeted at Completion)*. This field is simply an alternate column heading for the Baseline Cost field.

- *VAC (Variance at Completion)*. This field is simply an alternate column heading for the Cost Variance field.

Analyzing Time-Scaled Data in Excel

 Project has a new macro that allows you to export the timescaled data from Project for analysis in Microsoft Excel. To initiate this function, display the Analysis toolbar and click the Analyze Time-Scaled Data in Excel tool button.

Once you click this tool button, Project starts a macro that presents the options to you in a wizard format with Steps 1 through 5 as follows:

1. The first screen lets you pick whether you want to export all tasks in the project or only the currently selected tasks. If no tasks are currently selected, the second choice is deactivated.

2. Select the fields to be exported. On the left side of the screen (available fields), all of the fields stored at the resource assignment level are offered for export to Excel. You click

the field you want to add and click the Add button. The field selected is then displayed on the right side of the screen (fields to export). If you decide you don't want a field you've already selected, you select it on the right side of the screen and click Remove.

3. The next step provides you the ability to set the date range and units you would like to use for the export. The default date range is the project start and finish dates. The default unit is Days.

4. Next, you are offered the opportunity to automatically graph the time-scaled data in Excel. Choose Yes or No.

5. The final step offers one large button labeled Export Data. Click the button and the export process begins.

Part

V

Ch

16

N O T E You can select Finish at any one of the previous steps and accept the defaults without going through all five steps. ■

Once you select Finish or Export Data, the macro will automatically export the data to Excel and display the information. This function requires Excel version 5.0 or higher.

Figure 16.27 shows the sample graph that is drawn in Excel. Note the Excel sheet name tabs at the bottom of the Excel workbook, which are labeled Timescaled Data Graph and Timescaled Data. If you click the Timescaled Data tab you will then see the data sheet with the numbers that were used to draw the data graph.

FIG. 16.27

Sample graph of timescaled data in Excel, which visually represents the amount of total work for each day of the project.

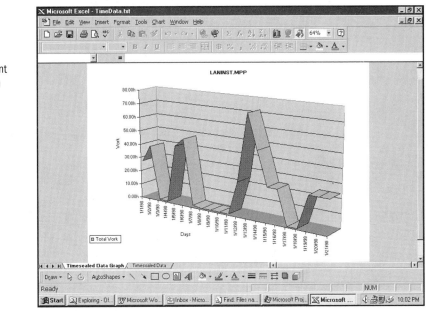

N O T E Project 98 now provides the ability to display S-curves, which show cumulative costs or hours over time. As the name implies, the term S-curve is derived from the fact the

continues

continued

cumulative cost and work quantities tend to start slowly, rapidly increase, then wind down at the end of a project. To see S-curves for your project, you can select from fields such as BCWS, cumulative % complete, cumulative cost, or cumulative work fields in step 2 of 5 in the Analyze Timescaled Data Wizard. In step 4 of 5, you will then be asked, "Do you want to graph the time-scaled data in Excel?" Choose Yes, Please, and the S-curves will then be plotted in Microsoft Excel.

Figure 16.28 shows a sample data sheet. If you scroll to the bottom of the data sheet, you'll see totals for each time period column in the sheet, based on the units you selected in Step 3 of the wizard.

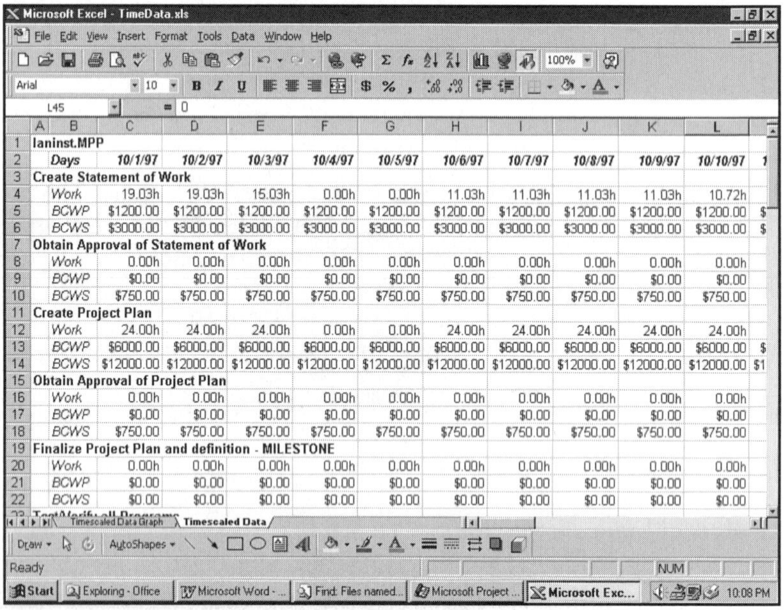

	A / B	C	D	E	F	G	H	I	J	K	L
1	**laninst.MPP**										
2	*Days*	*10/1/97*	*10/2/97*	*10/3/97*	*10/4/97*	*10/5/97*	*10/6/97*	*10/7/97*	*10/8/97*	*10/9/97*	*10/10/97*
3	**Create Statement of Work**										
4	*Work*	19.03h	19.03h	15.03h	0.00h	0.00h	11.03h	11.03h	11.03h	11.03h	10.72h
5	*BCWP*	$1200.00	$1200.00	$1200.00	$1200.00	$1200.00	$1200.00	$1200.00	$1200.00	$1200.00	$1200.00
6	*BCWS*	$3000.00	$3000.00	$3000.00	$3000.00	$3000.00	$3000.00	$3000.00	$3000.00	$3000.00	$3000.00
7	**Obtain Approval of Statement of Work**										
8	*Work*	0.00h	0.00h	0.00h	0.00h	0.00h	0.00h	0.00h	0.00h	0.00h	0.00h
9	*BCWP*	$0.00	$0.00	$0.00	$0.00	$0.00	$0.00	$0.00	$0.00	$0.00	$0.00
10	*BCWS*	$750.00	$750.00	$750.00	$750.00	$750.00	$750.00	$750.00	$750.00	$750.00	$750.00
11	**Create Project Plan**										
12	*Work*	24.00h	24.00h	24.00h	0.00h	0.00h	24.00h	24.00h	24.00h	24.00h	24.00h
13	*BCWP*	$6000.00	$6000.00	$6000.00	$6000.00	$6000.00	$6000.00	$6000.00	$6000.00	$6000.00	$6000.00
14	*BCWS*	$12000.00	$12000.00	$12000.00	$12000.00	$12000.00	$12000.00	$12000.00	$12000.00	$12000.00	$12000.00
15	**Obtain Approval of Project Plan**										
16	*Work*	0.00h	0.00h	0.00h	0.00h	0.00h	0.00h	0.00h	0.00h	0.00h	0.00h
17	*BCWP*	$0.00	$0.00	$0.00	$0.00	$0.00	$0.00	$0.00	$0.00	$0.00	$0.00
18	*BCWS*	$750.00	$750.00	$750.00	$750.00	$750.00	$750.00	$750.00	$750.00	$750.00	$750.00
19	**Finalize Project Plan and definition - MILESTONE**										
20	*Work*	0.00h	0.00h	0.00h	0.00h	0.00h	0.00h	0.00h	0.00h	0.00h	0.00h
21	*BCWP*	$0.00	$0.00	$0.00	$0.00	$0.00	$0.00	$0.00	$0.00	$0.00	$0.00
22	*BCWS*	$0.00	$0.00	$0.00	$0.00	$0.00	$0.00	$0.00	$0.00	$0.00	$0.00

FIG. 16.28
This figure shows a sample data sheet for timescaled data in Excel.

For more information on manipulating the information in Excel, please refer to Que's book *Special Edition Using Microsoft Excel* or your Microsoft Excel User's Guide.

Capturing and Reviewing Week-to-Week Trends

The information that has been covered so far in this chapter deals with analyzing variances as a snapshot in time. These snapshots only tell part of the story. The full story involves watching what your project variances are doing over time. A project that has a total work variance of 100 hours this week may appear to be in trouble, but what if the total work variance was 500 hours last week? Despite the current 100-hour work variance, it looks like the situation has improved significantly over last week.

If you want to watch variance trends over time, you can keep track of these changes in Excel. By filling in a simple spreadsheet in Excel with the week-ending dates of your analyses, the total baseline work, total work, and work variances, you can calculate the percent variances and graph them using the Chart Wizard in Excel.

Figure 16.29 shows an example of weekly trends plotted in Excel. For more information on using graphs to plot Project data in Excel, please refer to Que's book *Special Edition Using Microsoft Excel* or your Microsoft Excel User's Guide.

FIG. 16.29

This figure shows weekly variance trends plotted in Excel.

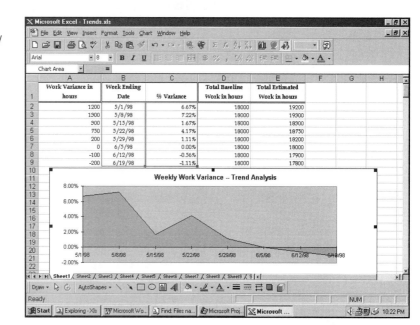

Updating the Schedule

As your project progresses you'll find that it becomes necessary to update your project's schedule. These next two sections review the different techniques you'll employ to keep your schedule in sync with what's really happening on your project. This part of the chapter covers techniques for updating your schedule, while the final section covers techniques for modifying the results of your updated schedule to ensure that you deliver within your original project objectives, schedule, and budget.

Rescheduling Remaining Work

Whenever you key in actual and remaining work, Project assumes that the remaining work will continue as originally scheduled. Unfortunately, tasks get interrupted and it is sometimes necessary to reschedule the remaining work for a task to a date that is later than originally planned. Project provides an easy way to reschedule remaining work.

N O T E   Before you try to reschedule remaining work for a task, be sure your project options are set to allow this activity.

continues

continued

Choose Tools, Options. The Schedule tab on the Options dialog box has an option called Split In-Progress Tasks. This option must be checked to be able to use the reschedule remaining work functions. Figure 16.30 shows the Split In-Progress Tasks option.

FIG. 16.30

Use the Options dialog box for splitting in-progress tasks.

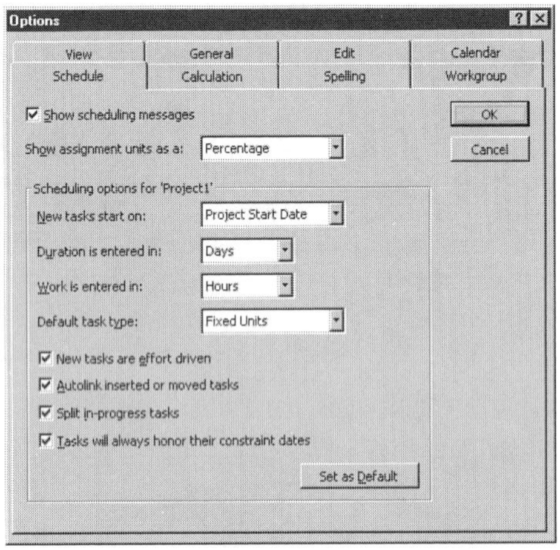

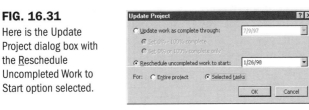

You can reschedule remaining work in one of two ways: from the Tracking toolbar, or from the Tools menu.

- *Rescheduling remaining work from the Tracking toolbar.* The Reschedule Work tool button on the Tracking toolbar automatically reschedules all remaining work for the selected tasks to start on the current date.

- *Rescheduling remaining work from the Update Project dialog box.* If you don't want remaining work to be rescheduled on the current date, you can use the Update Project function on the Tools, Tracking menu. Figure 16.31 shows the Update Project dialog box with the Reschedule Uncompleted Work to Start option selected. Note that you can set the date that you want the remaining work to start.

FIG. 16.31

Here is the Update Project dialog box with the Reschedule Uncompleted Work to Start option selected.

For tasks that are partially complete, Project automatically splits the task between the completed work and the remaining work. Figure 16.32 shows that Task 4, Functional Design Review, was set to start on 1/2/98. The eight hours of actual work was complete by 1/5/98, and the remaining work was rescheduled to 1/13/98.

Note that the Gantt bar is broken to show the gap between the actual work of eight hours and remaining work of eight hours for this task.

FIG. 16.32

Note that the Gantt bar for Split Tasks shows a dotted line representing the amount of time when no work is scheduled for the task.

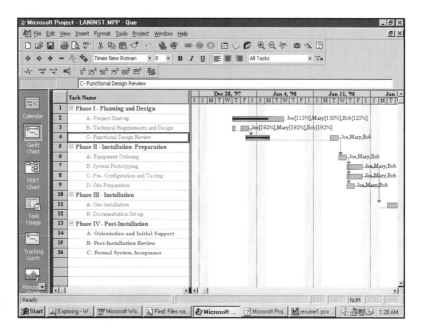

CAUTION

Rescheduling the remaining work may change task constraints. For a task with a Must Finish On constraint, rescheduling the remaining work task causes the task finish date to go beyond the constraint date and Project changes the constraint type to As Soon As Possible.

N O T E When you reschedule remaining work for a task, Project sets the Stop date to the date when the last actual work was applied and the Resume date is set to the date you specified on the Update Project dialog box. Figure 16.33 shows the Stop and Resume fields for the Task 4 from the previous example. Note that the last actual work was applied on 1/5/98 and the task's remaining work is scheduled to resume on 1/13/98. ■

Rescheduling remaining work is conceptually the same as setting a second Start date for a task. The Resume date is the date when the remaining work will start. A task with rescheduled remaining work looks the same as a split task on the Gantt Chart.

Rescheduling Tasks That Haven't Started

Besides rescheduling the remaining work for a task, you may sometimes be forced to reschedule an entire task. Any task that was scheduled to start before today's date that has not yet started should be rescheduled. To identify these tasks, try applying the Should Start By filter. Figure 16.34 shows the selection criteria for this filter. Note that this filter allows you to specify a date by which tasks should have started. The tasks in your plan are compared to the date you key. Any task that has not started (Actual Start = NA) by the date you keyed is returned by this filter.

This filter basically shows you unstarted tasks that are scheduled to start on a date that has already passed. This is a sign of a plan that is not reflective of reality. You should change the start dates of these tasks to a new date when you think they can be performed.

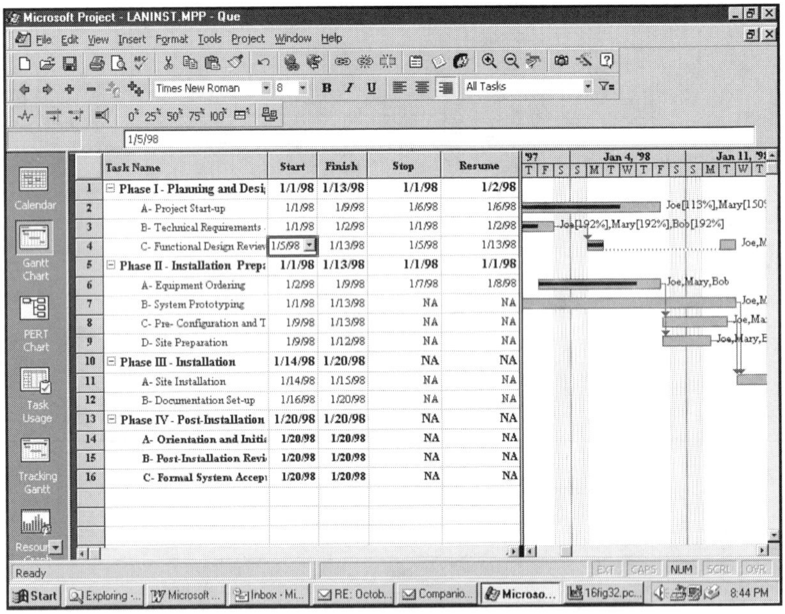

FIG. 16.33
Here, a split task shows Stop and Resume dates.

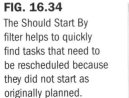

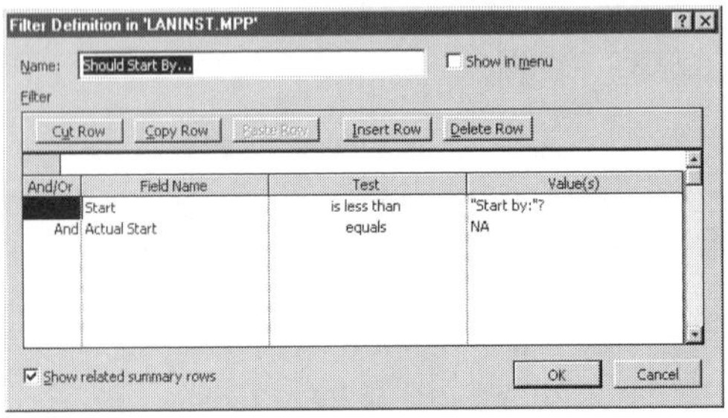

FIG. 16.34
The Should Start By filter helps to quickly find tasks that need to be rescheduled because they did not start as originally planned.

Revising the Schedule to Complete on Time and on Budget

Once you have determined that your plan is encountering unfavorable variances you have to do something about it. If the project is in trouble it's important to remember one thing—use the plan to manage the project; don't deviate from the plan, change it! Depending on the type of problem you are having, there are different strategies you'll need to employ to get your plan back on track. The bottom line is that something needs to change if you still plan to deliver on time and on budget with high quality and all expectations met.

Project provides many tools to help you revise your schedule, but first you have to know what will work for you, on this project, in your particular situation. Remember that when it comes to revising a project plan there are limited options: scope, schedule, and resources (people, machines, and money). Some projects that fail to recognize the need to adjust one of these factors end up cutting something that should not be touched—quality.

Before you even begin to modify the plan in Project, chances are that there are users, customers, sponsors, and managers that you'll need to talk to before you can reflect your strategy in Project. Whatever you decide, you are likely to be forced to make trade-offs. If you use a cheaper resource to stay within budget, the work estimates may increase due to lack of experience of the cheaper resource. If you reduce scope, you are probably sacrificing some of your objectives to stay within schedule and budget. If you overlap tasks, you increase the risk of failing. The harsh reality is that if there were serious oversights when the plan was developed, the chances of completing your plan according to all of its original expectations will take quite a bit of creativity on your part.

Let's take a look at what these options mean in Project:

Cutting Scope. When you cut scope, you're reducing function, taking something out of your project objectives, delivering less than originally committed. Reducing function in Project can be deployed in limited ways:

- Deleting tasks
- Reducing work

Reducing Schedule. If your targeted project finish date is in jeopardy, reducing schedule means you first have to find out which tasks are extending the schedule, then figure out some way to make those tasks finish sooner. In Project, you can reduce schedule by:

- Adding more resources to your project, so that some tasks can be completed sooner.
- Breaking links between tasks and allowing them to occur simultaneously, usually a risky proposition (and not always possible).
- Overlapping dependent tasks by introducing lead (the opposite of lag).
- Reducing duration by increasing a resource's percent commitment to tasks, including overtime.
- Replacing inexperienced resources with more experienced resources to your plan. You may be able to reduce work estimates, thereby completing tasks in less time.
- Using resources more efficiently; underallocated resources are a problem, too.

Adding Resources. Adding resources is sometimes an effective way to recover a schedule that is falling behind, but usually comes at a price—the budget. Adding resources is easy in Project (view Resource Sheet, Insert Resource). Finding the right resource at the right time for the right price can be pretty challenging.

If you do add resources, there are some things you'll need to do:

- Reassign work to the new resource.
- Reschedule late tasks to complete sooner, with the help of your new resource.
- Modify work estimates so that they are realistic for the new resource.
- Rebaseline, if setting your variances back to zero is what you desire.

Let's see how we can deploy some of the strategies that are listed previously. Many of them are easy to do in Project. The hard part is likely to depend on your ability to convince your project team and sponsors that your strategies for adjusting the plan are acceptable to all involved.

 TIP Before you adjust your project plan, it's a good idea to take frequent backups of your Project's .MPP file. You may decide that the changes you are making to your schedule are not working out. Rebuilding the plan without a good backup can be pretty painful if you're not careful.

Reducing Scope

Negotiating a reduction in scope for your project can be one of the more difficult tasks you'll face as a project manager. Once you define your initial project objectives, removing functions from your deliverables is often technically complicated, requiring advice from many different members of the team. It's hard to decide what you can take out and still have everything function smoothly. Add to this dilemma a group of sponsors who have had high expectations and you'll find yourself in a pretty tough situation. Assuming you're able to overcome these hurdles, here are some ways to reduce the scope of your project.

Project provides an easy way to delete tasks: Highlight the tasks you want to delete and press the delete key or choose Edit, Delete Task.

There are two easy ways to modify work by task: By displaying the Task Form in the bottom pane of a split Gantt Chart, or by modifying work by keying directly in the grid of the Task Usage view. If, on the other hand, you want to reduce work by resource, your best bet is to make your modifications in the Resource Form in the bottom pane of a split Resource Sheet, or by modifying work by keying directly in the grid of the Resource Usage view.

Reducing Schedule

Schedule reductions can be accomplished in a variety of ways, but the decision to do so needs to be made with great caution. Many elements of risk are introduced to your project plan when you agree to reduce work, overlap tasks, add resources, and maintain scope. Reducing the schedule may lower your confidence in completing on time while increasing your risk of delivering quality. Despite these concerns, we are sometimes forced to revise the plan and bring it in early. Here are some ways to reduce the schedule:

- *Overlapping dependent tasks.* If two tasks are linked, Project sets the default relationship to Finish-to-Start and the Lag to 0d. You can overlap tasks by setting the lag to a negative number. A negative lag is usually referred to as "lead." If you introduce lead for tasks on the critical path, the project finish date will be made earlier.

- *Increasing a resource's percent commitment to a task.* For tasks with fixed work, increasing the resources units on a task will reduce the task's duration. To display a unit as a percent, refer to the Schedule tab on the Options dialog box. Project shows resource units as a percentage, by default.

- *If a resource is already 100 percent committed to a task*, consider using the Overtime Work field to reduce duration. The overtime field can be viewed for each resource assigned to a task on the Task Form with details Work displayed.

- *Look for underallocated resources.* The Resource Usage view is often used to look for resource overallocations. This view can also be used to look for underallocated resources. Keep your resources assigned up to their maximum availability to ensure that your schedule is as efficient as possible.

T I P When you reduce schedule, Project will not automatically remove unneeded occurrences of a recurring task. Don't forget to get rid of unneeded tasks, such as weekly status meetings, by modifying the number of occurrences on your recurring tasks (on the Task Information dialog box), or by deleting individual occurrences.

- *Adding more experienced resources to your task.* If you decide to replace a resource with a different, more experienced resource, you can use the Resource Assignment dialog box. In this case, the trade-off is higher cost versus lower work estimates:

  1. Select the task for which you want to replace a resource.
  2. Click the Resource Assignment tool button. On the Resource Assignment dialog box click the resource you want to replace and click the Replace button. Figure 16.35 shows the Resource Assignment dialog mode in Replace mode.
  3. Now select the new resource who'll be replacing the original resource.

T I P After you have revised your plan, it may be appropriate to rebaseline, if setting your variances back to zero is what you want.

When you're done revising your schedule, chances are that your resources may have become overloaded. Load-leveling is the final step to ensuring that a revised schedule remains realistic.

From Here...

Analyzing progress and revising the schedule are key project management activities that form the foundation of project control. To manage a project without performing these activities is to roll the dice on your chances of completing on time and within budget. Your ability to meet your project's objectives relies on your ability to spot trouble early through analysis, and make necessary course corrections through schedule revision With the multiple demands placed on a project manager during the execution stage of a project, only the most disciplined will find the time to perform these fundamental control activities.

FIG. 16.35

The Assign Resources dialog box in Replace mode.

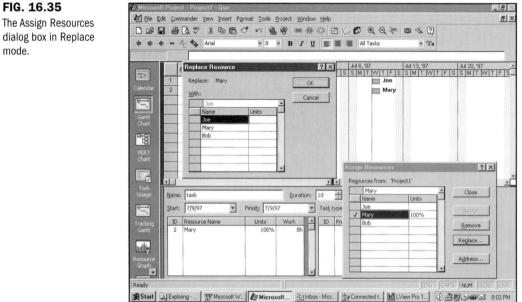

If you've taken the time to gather tracking data (actual work, remaining work, percent complete, actual start, and actual finish), the time will have been well invested when you follow through by analyzing and revising your schedule. Your ability to predict the future will be all too apparent when you analyze your work estimates, start and finish dates, and costs.

- For more information on modifying the tracking data that generate variances, see Chapter 15, "Tracking Work on the Project."

- For more information on using Excel to analyze your Project data, see Chapter 19, "Exchanging Project Data with Other Applications."

- For more information on standard views and reports you can use to analyze variances, see Chapter 20, "Using the Standard Views, Tables, and Filters," and Chapter 23, "Using the Standard Reports."

- For more information on building customized Project objects for analyzing variances, see Chapter 22, "Customizing Views, Tables, and Filters," and Chapter 24, "Customizing Reports."

Coordinating Projects and Sharing Data

17 Working with Multiple Projects   543

18 Using Microsoft Project in Workgroups   565

19 Exchanging Project Data with Other Applications   593

CHAPTER 17

Working with Multiple Projects

There are several instances where working with one project file does not allow you to accomplish your objectives. Working in a Windows environment typically offers the capability to work with more than one file at a time, and this is certainly true with Microsoft Project. With this in mind, consider the following situations where it would be beneficial to work with more than one file at a time: A task in one project may depend on a task in another project. For example, the start date for one task may need to be linked to the start or finish date for a task in another project. Several projects, managed by different people, may be placed under the supervision of a manager who provides coordination of dates and resources between the various projects. A project may be so large that it is easier to organize and manage by breaking it into several smaller, more manageable units. These separate files can then be linked back together enabling you to see the whole project. This benefit is similar to those gained by outlining a project, but on a larger scale. Several projects may use the same group of resources and need to be coordinated so that the right resources are available to each project at the right time. A project may be too large to fit into the computer's memory at one time. Breaking it into smaller projects can overcome the memory limitations. ■

Move between open projects

Learn to move back and forth quickly between open projects.

View or print several projects together

Viewing and printing multiple projects are made easy.

Share a common pool of resources among multiple projects

See what resources are doing across all projects at once, not just one at a time.

Insert one project file into another

See the impact of a project that is a part of another project by inserting one project file into another.

Cross link project tasks

When otherwise independent projects have interdependent tasks, you can cross link them.

Using the Window Commands

In keeping with the standard Windows convention, you can have more than one project file open at a time. In fact, in this version of Microsoft Project, you can have 50 files in separate windows open at once. If you are using inserted projects, you can have up to 1,000 in any one file. When there are multiple files open at once, the Window command is used to control and move between the various open windows. You can also use the Ctrl+F6 shortcut key combination to move between active project windows. As shown in Figure 17.1, a list of open project files appears at the bottom of the Window menu. A check mark appears in front of the name of the active window. When more than nine files are open at once, there will be an additional More Windows option at the bottom of the Window menu. When chosen, More Windows displays all project files that are open. Choose the project file that you want to make active. Other files are not closed; they are simply moved to the background.

> **N O T E** This list of files is different than the one displayed at the bottom of the File menu, which is simply a list of the last four files that were opened, but which are not necessarily open now.

FIG. 17.1

The Window menu includes a list at the bottom that you can use to locate other open project files.

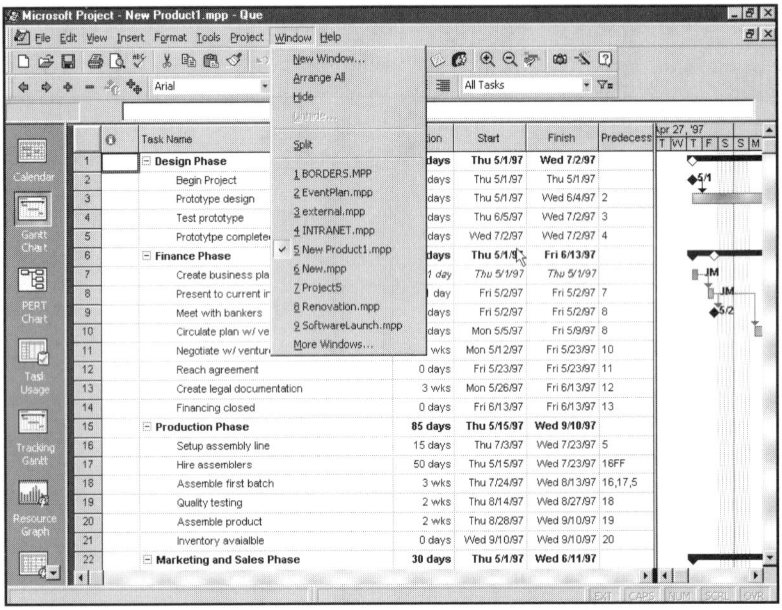

The Window, Split command, discussed previously, is used when dividing the screen for a combination view. Combination views can be very helpful during many different stages of a project's life.

> **See** "Introducing the Gantt Chart View," **p. 50**
> **See** "The Task Entry," **p. 678**

▶ **See** "Resource Allocation," **p. 679**

▶ **See** "Creating a Combination View," **p. 746**

Viewing All the File Windows at the Same Time

The <u>W</u>indow, <u>A</u>rrange All command is useful when you want to view more than one project file in its own distinct window at the same time. Open the projects that you want to see on-screen at once and then choose this command. Depending on how many project files are open at once, each window will be sized and moved (tiled) so that each file can be seen on-screen simultaneously. As you can see in Figure 17.2, the name of each file will be displayed in its title bar, with the active window having the brighter color title bar as well as the active pane indicator (the colored narrow bar at the left side of the active pane). The title bar of the inactive files will be gray (assuming the default Windows colors). This is obviously only practical when a small number of project files are open at once or when some of the project files are hidden (see the next section).

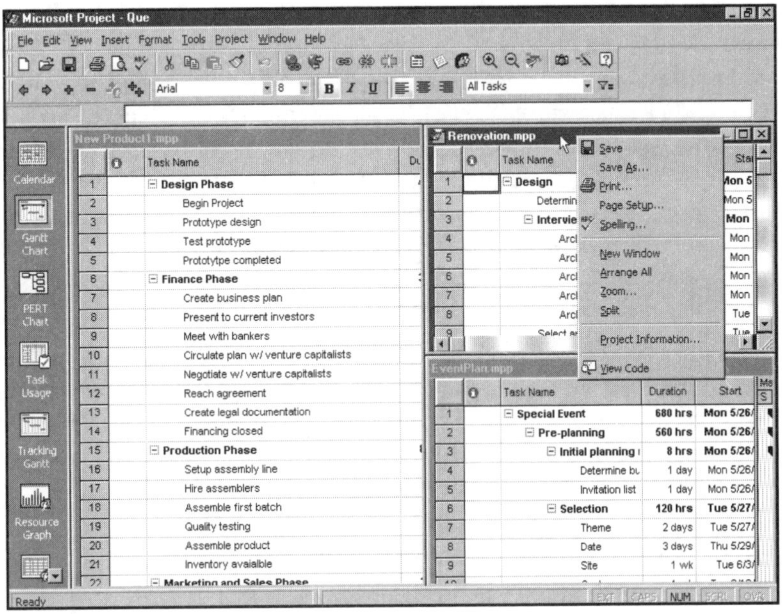

FIG. 17.2

Several windows displayed at once can be very convenient when coordinating several project files.

Part

VI

Ch

17

TIP Whichever window is active when you choose the <u>W</u>indow, <u>A</u>rrange All command will appear at the top left corner of the screen and will remain active.

TIP When a project file is not maximized, there is a handy shortcut menu that appears when you right-click the title bar of the file. Useful commands on this shortcut menu include: Save, Print, Spelling, Project Information, and most of the Window commands.

When you maximize any one window, all other windows will become maximized as well. You won't be able to see them because the active file is covering the full screen, but when you move to any other file, it will already be maximized.

Hiding and Unhiding Open Windows

If there are any project files that are open that you don't want included in the Arrange All display, instead of closing them, you need only temporarily hide them using the Hide command. To redisplay the hidden window, choose the Window menu again. If any files have been hidden, an Unhide command is now on the menu. If you choose the Unhide command, the Unhide dialog box opens and displays a list of files that have been hidden. Choose the file you want to unhide and choose OK. If you exit Project with windows hidden, you will be prompted to save them if necessary.

Combining Tasks from Different Files into One Window

The Window, New Window command deserves special attention, especially in light of significant advances made in this new version. Combined with the Insert, Project command, you can merge multiple project files into one window to edit, view, print, or even link their tasks in one view. Each task retains its native ID number, so you will see more than one task with ID number 1. You can modify the display to add a column that identifies the file that each task came from. You can sort the task list as if it were one file; you can filter the merged list in the same way you use filters in one file. You can apply any table or view to see the merged view, except the PERT Chart. You can print views or reports from the merged window as though it were a single project file. You can even insert and delete tasks.

There are two basic approaches to combining projects together into one window. One is with the Window, New Window command. This approach assumes that all the files to be combined are already open. The second is with the Insert, Project command which enables you to access files that are not currently open.

Using the Window, New Window Command

To combine the tasks from multiple projects that are currently open into the same view, follow these steps:

1. Choose Window, New Window to display the New Window dialog box (see Figure 17.3).
2. From the Projects list, select all the file names you want to include in the new window. Use the Ctrl key to add non-adjacent file names to the selection.
3. Choose the View list box located at the bottom of the dialog box and change the view if you want. You can change the view later, after the new window is displayed.
4. Click OK to display the new window.

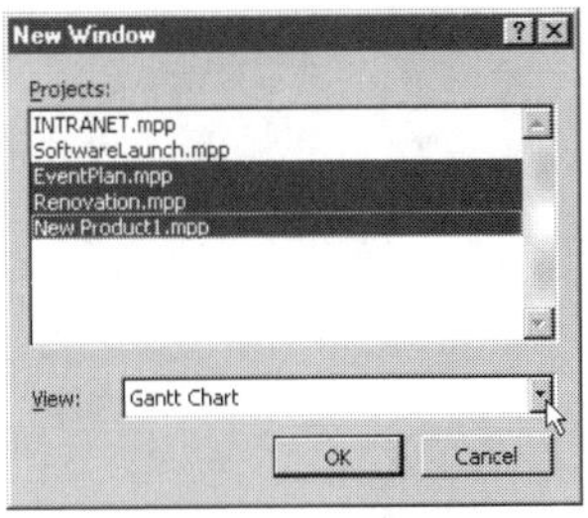

FIG. 17.3

In the New Window dialog box, choose the projects that you want to combine into one window.

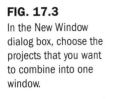

The merged window has the title Project#, where # is a consecutively assigned number for each time that you create a new project file. When you open the Window menu, you see that the Project# choice is now a separate entry on the open projects list, while the individual project files have been left open. You can save the merged window for further use with the regular File, Save command.

As you can see in Figure 17.4, when any of the task sheet views are active (including any of the Gantt Charts), the Indicators column will display an icon for an inserted project. Point at the icon to display a message with the name of the source file. An inserted project is simply a copy of all the tasks from another file inserted into this new window.

At the beginning of each file's tasks there will be a Project summary task added. The task ID for this Project summary task indicates the order in which the selected files were merged. You can use the Outline symbol in front of the Project summary task name to hide the details of the task, just like working with the tasks in an outline. On the timescale side of the Gantt Chart, there will be a gray bar that appears much like a summary task bar.

TIP When using the Show All Subtasks button in the formatting toolbar, only the subtasks in the selected inserted project will display. You need to select each inserted project or select all by clicking the Task Name column heading before using the Show All Subtasks button.

N O T E You might also use the Window, New Window command when you want to see two window views of the same project. This, in essence, allows you to see more than the standard combination view. Using this method, you could see either two separate combination views, two full screen views at once, or one combination view and one full screen, all of the same project. To do this, choose Window, New Window, but select only one project file. The title bar of the new window has the project name followed by a colon and a number, indicating the second instance of this project file. You can use either the Window command or Ctrl+F6 to move between them. Any changes that you make and save to one instance of the project file will be saved in the other window as well. There is only one file open here: it's simply displayed in two separate windows, much like the combination views you have already seen.

Part
VI

Ch
17

FIG. 17.4

There are several ways to get information about an inserted project.

Icon indicating inserted project

Click this outline symbol to hide or show the details of the inserted project

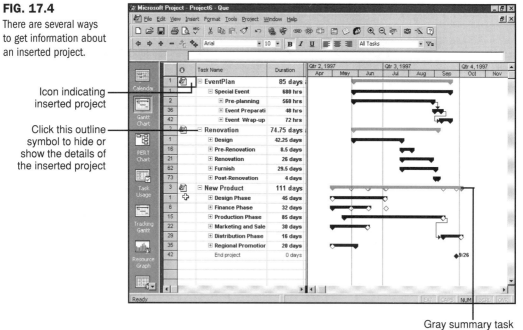

Gray summary task identifies task bar identifies inserted project

Combining Projects into One File

If a project that you want to combine with another is not already open, you will need to use the Insert, Project command. To insert an entire project into another, follow these steps:

1. Select the task below where you want the new inserted project to be placed.

2. Choose Insert, Project to access the Insert Project dialog box (see Figure 17.5).

FIG. 17.5

Use the Insert Project dialog box to identify the file to be inserted into another.

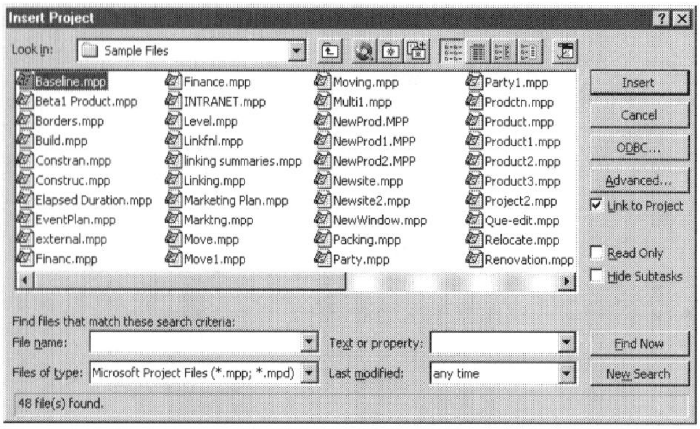

3. Select the file to be inserted.

4. Select the Read Only check box to open this copy as one that is read-only. You will not be able to make changes to the source copy.

5. Select the Hide Subtasks check box to initially hide the subtasks of the inserted project and display only a Project summary task.

6. Select OK when you are finished. The tasks of the inserted project will now be available in the original file as if they had been entered there.

> **N O T E** The ODBC button in the Insert Project dialog box allows you to insert a file that is stored in a database. This topic is covered in detail in Chapter 19, "Exchanging Project Data with Other Applications." ▪

Working with Inserted Projects

You can see information about the inserted project by choosing the Advanced tab in the Task Information dialog box. Access the dialog box using the Task Information button in the Standard toolbar, double-click the task, or right-click any portion of the inserted project task and choose Task Information from the shortcut menu. Then choose the Advanced tab. When you access the Task Information dialog box for a task that represents an inserted project, the title of the dialog box changes to Inserted Project Information. Notice in Figure 17.6 that the title bar indicates that this is an inserted project.

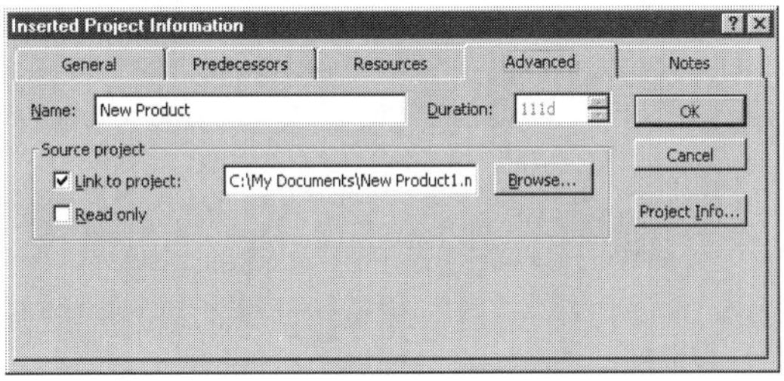

Part

VI

Ch

17

FIG. 17.6

The Task Information dialog box for an inserted project displays information about the link back to the source file and offers access to project information for that file.

You can choose whether to maintain a link with the individual source files. The Link to Project check box determines whether or not changes made in this file should be linked back to the original file. If checked, any content-related changes that you make to the new file will also be made in the original source file. By default, there is a link between the inserted project and the original file that it came from. Regardless of your choice, any changes made to the *formatting* in the new window will not be reflected in the source files. The obvious advantage here is that you can make formatting changes in the new window for the purpose of printing reports for different audiences without having those changes reflected back in the original working file.

By default, files are opened as read-write, but you can change that to read-only. Select the Read Only check box if there is a link maintained and you prefer to protect the original source files. If the inserted file is set to read-only, the icon in the Indicators column of the Gantt Chart will show an exclamation mark, and the message will indicate that it is read-only.

Use the <u>B</u>rowse button to change the link to another file or to restore the link when the file has been moved or renamed. (See upcoming sections on moving, deleting, and renaming inserted projects for detailed information.)

You can access the Project Information dialog box for the source file by using the Project <u>I</u>nfo button in the Inserted Project Information dialog box.

N O T E The reference to the location of the original source file is stored in the Subproject field for the inserted project task. If the Read Only check box is active, a Yes is stored in the Subproject Read Only field. You will only see these fields if you add them on your own to a table. ▦

▶ **See** "Printing Views," **p. 416**

▶ **See** "Using the Format Options in the Standard Views," **p. 696**

N O T E It's important to note that when you combine project files by choosing <u>W</u>indow, <u>N</u>ew Window or Insert, <u>P</u>roject, these project files are only displayed together in one window, but so far are not linked to each other. ▦

Initially, all the tasks are grouped by the file from which they came. For the most part, you can sort or filter the list in the normal way. When sorting, you must choose <u>P</u>roject, <u>S</u>ort, <u>S</u>ort By in order to gain access to the check box that keeps the outline structure. You will most likely want to be able to sort by start date, for example, and allow the tasks to move out of their original project order. The predefined sort options on the Sort menu are set to retain the outline structure. When you allow the sort to not retain the outline structure, the outlining tools in the Formatting toolbar are not available. The task list in Figure 17.7 includes three inserted projects whose tasks have been sorted in start date order. You can still see which project each task comes from using the Project column. Both the Summary tasks and the Project summary tasks have been temporarily hidden.

N O T E When filtering and sorting, you might want to turn off the display of the Project summary task and regular summary task. This is controlled by the Outline options on the View tab of the <u>O</u>ptions dialog box.

If you turn off the display of the Project Summary task, you might want to see the project name next to each task. You can add a column to the table to display the Project field. Right-click a column heading and choose Insert <u>C</u>olumn from the shortcut menu. Then choose Project for the Field Name. ▦

▶ **See** "Using and Creating Tables," **p. 748**

N O T E If you used the previous version of Microsoft Project, this ability to combine files would have required the use of the Consolidation command. This command is no longer available; its features have been consolidated with the <u>I</u>nsert, <u>P</u>roject and <u>W</u>indow, <u>N</u>ew Window commands. ▦

FIG. 17.7
Sorting a file with inserted projects can make it easier to see when tasks from several projects are scheduled.

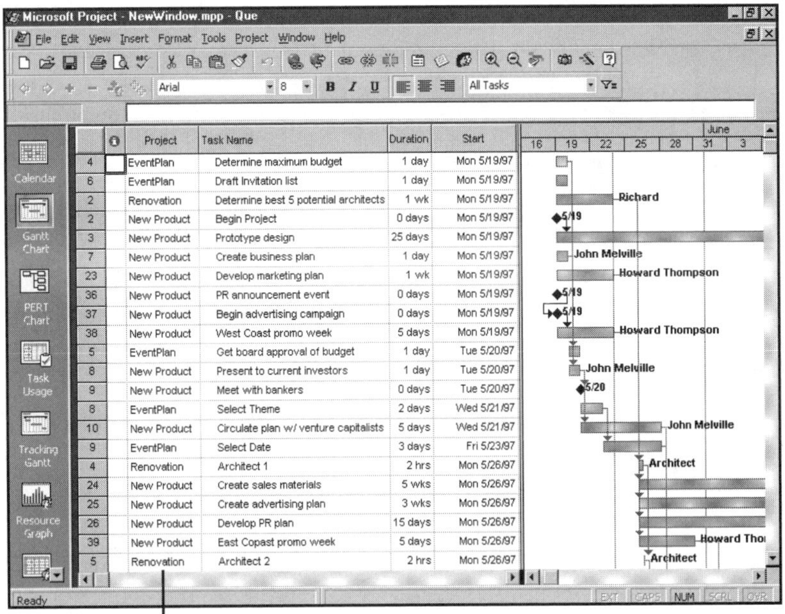

The Project column identifies the
Project file where each task is from

TROUBLESHOOTING

When I use the Window, New Window command, I can't tell which task is from which file, especially if I have sorted the tasks by their start date. Modify the table that you are using to also display the project file name, which is most likely just before the ID number for the task. This way, you can see the file name and the task ID together to distinguish between files. Right-click a column heading, choose Insert Column and then choose Project for the Field Name.

You can create inserted projects at any level of an outline, as well as inserting a project into a project that is itself inserted into another. Microsoft Project checks to be sure that no circular references exist within the levels.

Breaking a Large Project Apart Using Inserted Projects

You can create inserted projects by moving tasks from a large project into new project files, and then defining the new files as inserted projects. Some preparation is involved in making the move as easy and successful as possible.

If you move one or more tasks which are linked to tasks that will remain behind, you will lose the links and have to redefine them later. It is easier to copy the tasks that are going to become a new project file rather than cut them, save the copied tasks as a new file, insert the new project file, change the links, and then delete the original copied tasks.

To move tasks to a new project file, follow these steps:

1. Select the task IDs of the tasks that you plan to move. This ensures that all fields will be selected and that all relevant data will be copied. If the tasks to be moved include a Summary and all the subtasks indented underneath it, you need only select the summary task.

2. Choose Edit, Copy Task (or press Ctrl+C) to copy the task data to the Clipboard.

3. Choose File, New to create a new project file. If the Prompt for Project Info for New Projects check box is checked on the General tab of the Tools, Options dialog box, the Project Information dialog box will open.

   ▶ **See** "Creating a New Project Document," **p. 92**

4. With the Name field of the first task selected in the new file, choose Edit, Paste (or press Ctrl+V). The task data is copied.

5. Choose File, Save to save the new file. Fill in the dialog box to save the file and click OK.

6. Return to the original file by choosing the file name from the list at the bottom of the Window menu. Alternatively, press Ctrl+F6 until the project document reappears.

7. Select the task in the row below where the inserted task will be placed and create the inserted project as described in the section "Working with Inserted Projects."

Maintaining Inserted Projects

You can change the name of the inserted project by changing the name in the Source Project field on the Advanced tab of the Task Information dialog box. You can use the Browse button to locate the file instead of typing it in. If the new file name exists, it will be used as the source project file instead of the one just replaced. If the file name is simply deleted, the link between the two projects is severed, and the inserted project task becomes a default 1-day duration task.

Be careful about moving or renaming projects that are used as inserted projects. When you open a project that contains an inserted project, if Microsoft Project can't find the file, it displays a message as shown in the title bar in Figure 17.8. To maintain the link, you would need to locate the file before proceeding. Project will allow you to cancel the dialog box but the link with the inserted project will be broken. The tasks for the inserted project will still be in the project file but there will no longer be a link between the two. Notice the indicator in Figure 17.9.

If a file is simply renamed, the warning message does not display, but the link will still not be maintained. If you point to the indicator for the inserted project, you will see that the file name was not updated with the new file name. If you make changes in either file, the changes will not be automatically reflected in the other linked file.

FIG. 17.8

You need to re-identify an inserted project when the original is moved or deleted.

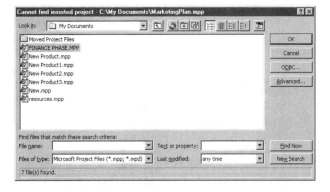

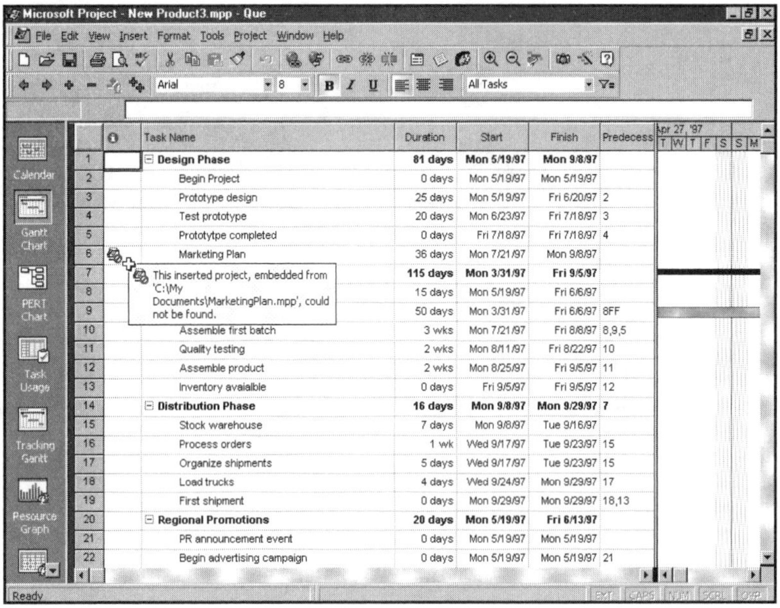

FIG. 17.9

The Task Indicator helps you identify that an inserted project cannot be found.

Identifying Tasks That Are Inserted Projects

In addition to the indicator for inserted projects in the Indicators column, you can use the Subproject File field, where the name of the inserted project is stored. You can design a table to display that field and thereby identify the tasks. Figure 17.10 shows the Subproject File field substituted for the Resources field.

TIP   You can't create a filter directly for inserted projects because the Subproject field for regular tasks is blank, and there is no test for blank fields. As shown in Figure 17.10, you can use one of the 20 available Flag fields which can only be set to Yes or No. As you create inserted projects, set the flag to Yes. Then design a filter that looks for Yes on the Flag field that you used. This would be a worthwhile exercise if you have many inserted projects and would like to have a printed report documenting them.

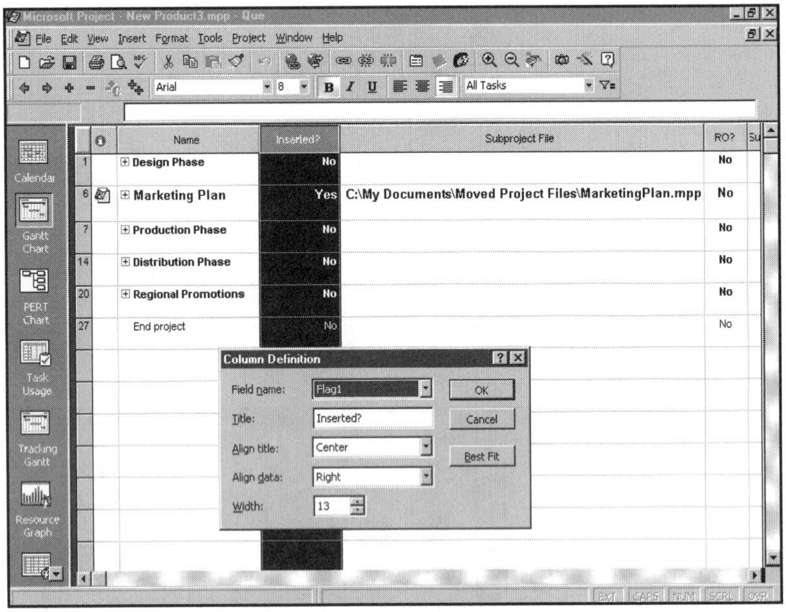

FIG. 17.10
Create a table with a subproject field to see which tasks are inserted projects.

▶ **See** "Using and Creating Tables," **p. 748**
▶ **See** "Creating Custom Filters," **p. 754**

Deleting Inserted Projects

You delete an inserted project in much the same way you delete a summary task. Simply select it and then press the Delete key on the keyboard, or right-click the task ID and choose Delete Task from the shortcut menu. You will be warned about deleting more than one task with the warning message shown in Figure 17.11. When the Office Assistant is being used, the warnings will appear in the Office Assistant's question box rather than the standard Windows dialog box.

Creating Links Between Tasks in Separate Projects

There are two basic types of links that you can create between projects. One is when all of the tasks of one project taken together are the predecessor or successor to a group of tasks in another project. For example, in the New Product project file, the design phase is probably handled by a completely separate department also using Microsoft Project. Many other tasks in the New Product project can't proceed until the design phase is complete. You could insert the entire project for the design phase and link it as you would link any other task.

A second kind of link occurs when a specific task in another project, not the project start or finish, needs to be linked to a specific task in the current project file. For example, in the design phase, there is a task called *Prototype Complete*. Although the design phase as a whole may not be complete, once the Prototype is complete, some sales and marketing tasks could begin.

FIG. 17.11
Deleting an inserted project deletes all of the tasks that were part of that project.

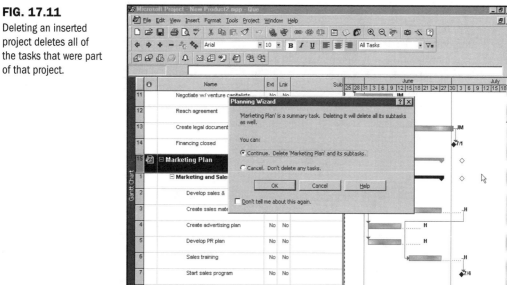

Whichever situation you have, the method for creating the links is the same. It's as simple as entering the file name and task ID of the task to be linked in the Predecessor or Successor ID in any of the views that allow the entering of the predecessor or successor information. If you have inserted a whole project into another, you have easy access to the task to be linked. You can even use the Link Tasks button in the Standard toolbar. If you are linking to another task in a project that has not been inserted, you will need to enter the full path of the project file. The format should be as follows:

drive:\directory\sudirectory\taskID

▶ **See** "Publishing Projects on the Web," **p. 439**

For example, c:\my documents\design phase.mpp\3 would create a link to task ID#3 in the design phase file.

N O T E On networked computers, in Windows 95 or Windows NT, it's not necessary to use a drive name; a network share can be used instead. \\networkshare\directory\subdirectory\ taskID is the format. Files can even be stored on FTP sites and then inserted through the Insert Project dialog box by pulling up the predefined FTP site under the drop-down list box for the Look In field. ▪

These cross links between files can use any of the standard task relationships (FS, SS, FF, and SF) as well as support lag and lead time.

▶ **See** "Establishing Dependency Links," **p. 173**

When the link is established, the name of the task being linked to will appear in the task list in gray text. The duration, start, and finish will also display in gray. No other information will be immediately available. If the task that is linked to has a duration, the task bar will appear in gray as well. If the task being linked to is a milestone, it will not appear any different from a regular milestone. If you double-click the linked task, it will open the project plan that contains the linked task. In the source project for the linked task, the task that was linked to from the destination project plan also appears in gray, and you can double-click it to return to the original project plan. If you access the Task Information dialog box for either of the two grayed tasks, you will be able to view information about the task but you will not be able to change it.

CAUTION

Project will allow you to enter a note about a grayed task but it will not be linked back to the original task.

TIP

When you create a link to a task in another Project file, the External Task field is set to Yes. This means that you can create a filter for all tasks that have an external link. This filter, combined with a table including the predecessors and successors columns, would provide a view of all external links and their source. Combine this tip with the tip about using the Flag1 field to identify inserted projects to get a printout of all external sources of data.

For example, in the New Product file, suppose that the FINANCE PHASE is in a separate file that for some reason you don't want inserted. You can't set up the assembly line until both the Prototype is completed as well as Financing Closed. In the New Product file, you would create a predecessor task to Set Up Assembly Line as shown in Figure 17.12.

FIG. 17.12

A predecessor or successor that refers to a task in another project creates a cross-linked task.

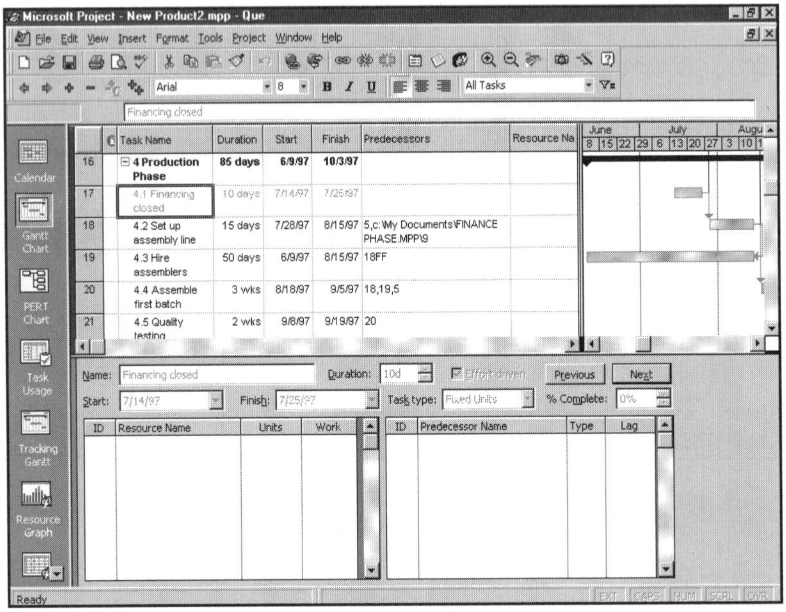

Notice the gray text of the task Financing Closed. This task is only part of the New Product plan to the extent that it is a predecessor to Set Up Assembly Line. If you double-click the Financing Closed task, the FINANCE PHASE project file is opened as shown in Figure 17.13. Notice the gray text of the Set Up Assembly Line task. This task is only part of the FINANCE PHASE plan to the extent that it is a successor to Financing Closed. If you double-click the Set Up Assembly Line task, you will be returned to the NEW PRODUCT file.

FIG. 17.13

Grayed task names indicate cross-linked tasks and allow easy movement back and forth between files.

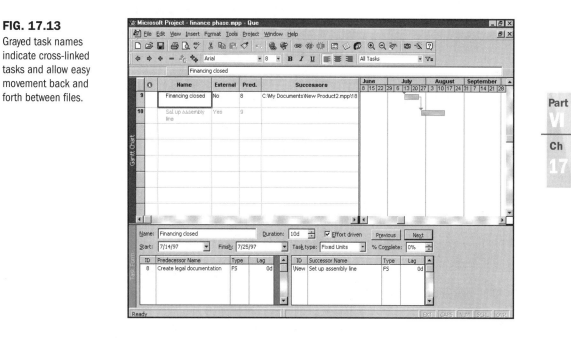

Part
VI

Ch
17

From here on out, any changes in the Finance Phase project plan that cause the Financing Closed task to change will have an impact on the New Product project plan. Otherwise, the two project plans function independently of each other.

When you open a file that has cross-linked predecessors, a Links between Projects dialog box will automatically appear, advising of any changes that have taken place to the external tasks. You can access this dialog box at any time by choosing Tools, Links Between Projects. Use this dialog box not only to refresh any changes made to the external files, but also to reestablish file locations or delete links. The Differences column shows what kind of changes have taken place. Notice in Figure 17.14 the full path is shown for the selected task in the title bar of the dialog box.

If you create links that would cause a circular relationship between tasks—one task acting as a predecessor and a successor of another—the dialog box in Figure 17.15 will open. You will need to explore the relationships between the linked tasks, locate the erroneous link, and remove it.

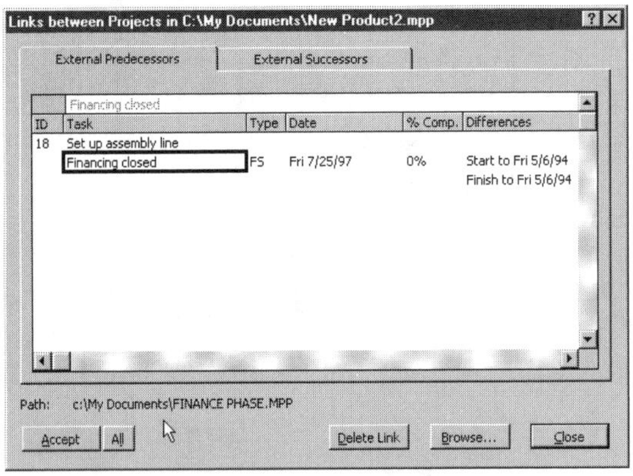

FIG. 17.14

The Links between Projects dialog box identifies changes made in cross-linked tasks.

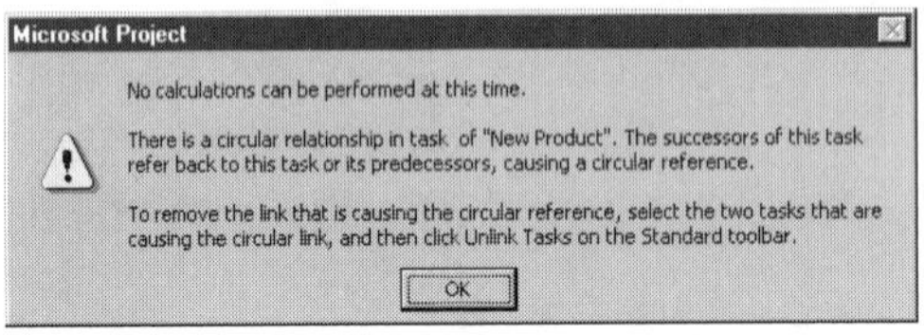

FIG. 17.15

Project displays an error message if any cross-linked tasks create a circular relationship.

Sharing Resources Among Projects

It is not unusual to have several projects that use the same set of resources. When this is the case, it's cumbersome to manage the same resources in several different project files. You can't easily see what each resource is doing for all projects. You may want to have Microsoft Project store the resource information in one file and only the assignment information in the project files. You do this by entering all resources in one project file (which may very well not even have any tasks) and by instructing the other project files to use the resources defined in the file with the resources.

If projects share the same list of resources, you can open all the projects at the same time and view the allocation of resources across the projects. Microsoft Project warns you when a resource is overallocated because of conflicting assignments in different projects, and you can use the leveling command to resolve the resource overallocation by delaying tasks in different projects.

▶ **See** "Resolving Resource Allocation Problems," **p. 345**

Creating the Resource Pool

Any file can be the one that contains the resource pool definitions. If your resources typically work on many different kinds of projects, you can create a project file that has no tasks defined in it but that defines all your resources. If your resources typically work on many projects of the same basic type, you might benefit from creating a template that contains the basic tasks as well as the setting to use the resources in another file.

▶ **See** "Templates," **p. 112**

Using the Resource Pool

By choosing Tools, Resources, Share Resources, you can define any project file to use the resources of another project file. If both files have resources defined in them at the time the link is established, the resource pool will be enlarged to include all resources defined in both files. If the same resource is defined in both files and there is a difference in the definition between the two files, you must tell Microsoft Project which file takes precedence in settling definition conflicts. The Share Resources dialog box provides a check box for this purpose.

You can look at the Resource Sheet in either file to see the complete list of resources, and you can change the resource definitions in either file. When you close the files, each includes a copy of the entire resource pool. In this way, you can open the project file that uses the resource pool independently of the file that actually contains the resources, if needed, to modify and manage that project file.

To enable a project file to use the resources of another file, follow these steps:

1. Open both project files: the one containing the resource pool and the one that is to share that pool. Make sure that the active project is the one that is to use the other project's resources.

2. Choose Tools, Resources, Share Resources to display the Share Resources dialog box (see Figure 17.16). Choose the Use Resources option button and use the From drop-down box for a list of currently open files from which you can choose.

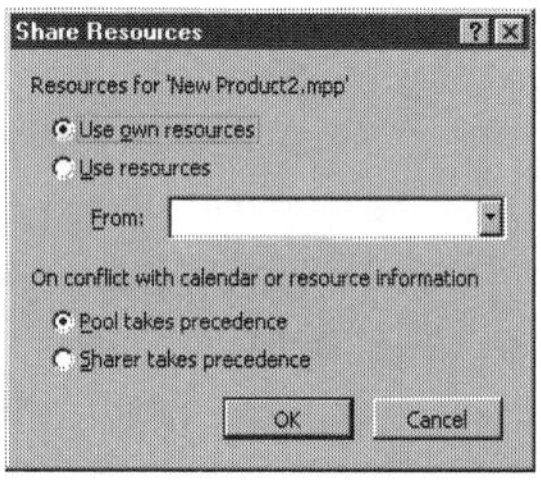

FIG. 17.16

Use the Share Resources dialog box to use a resource pool from another project file.

3. Select the Pool Takes Precedence option button if you want conflicting definitions to be settled by the entry in the file that contains the resource pool. Select the Sharer Takes Precedence option button if you want resource definition conflicts to be settled by the entry in the file that uses the resource pool.

4. Click OK to complete the link.

If the file containing the resources is not open when you open a file that uses its resources, an Open Resource Pool Information dialog box opens (see Figure 17.17). You can choose to have Project open the resource pool, as well as all other project files that use the resources. However, you can work on the file even if you do not have the resource pool project open, because a copy of the pool is saved with each file that uses the common resource pool.

Part
VI

Ch
17

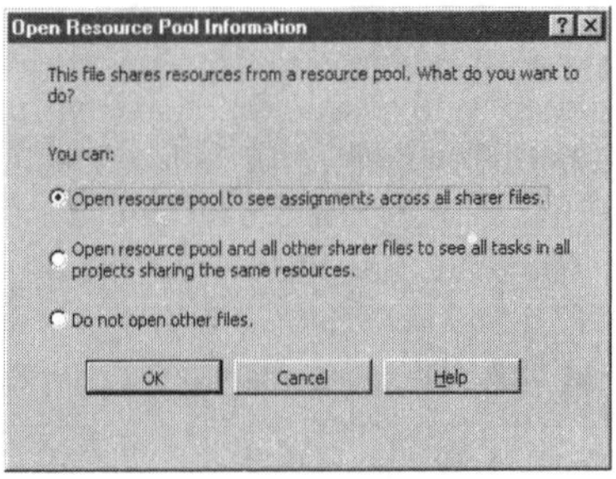

FIG. 17.17

Microsoft Project offers to open the file containing the resources.

After a project is defined to use another project's resource pool, changes you make to the resource pool while both files are open are recorded directly into the shared pool and are shared by both files immediately. If you work with the dependent file alone, however, and you make changes in the copy of the resource pool, the changes may not be saved back to the resource pool. If you merely add new resources with different names, the resources are added to the resource pool when both files are open together the next time.

If you change the definition of the resource (for example, the pay rate, maximum units, or working days on the resource calendar), the changes may be lost when both files are loaded in memory together the next time. If you marked the Pool Takes Precedence option button in the Resource Sharing dialog box, the changes are lost; if you left the check box unmarked, the changes are recorded in the resource pool. If you enter a resource definition change in the sharing file when only this file is opened, and you want to have the change copied to the resource pool, mark the option button before opening the file with the resource pool.

CAUTION

Be very careful about choosing the Pool Takes Precedence option button when resolving differences between resources with the same name. The calendar and resource information in the file that is sharing resources of another project will have its resource information changed permanently, even after returning to using its own resources.

Saving Multiple Files in a Workspace

If you want to open all the files that share the same resource pool at the same time, you can save the workspace in addition to saving the individual files. To save the workspace, follow these steps:

1. Choose File, Save Workspace.

2. If any files have unsaved changes, you are prompted to save the individual files. In the File Save dialog box, choose the Yes button.

3. The Save Workspace As dialog box displays. Select the directory for the workspace if you want to store it somewhere other than the default directory (see Figure 17.18). The

name of the workspace file will initially be resume.mpw (so that you can resume later with the same files), but you can change it by typing in a new name in the File Name text box.

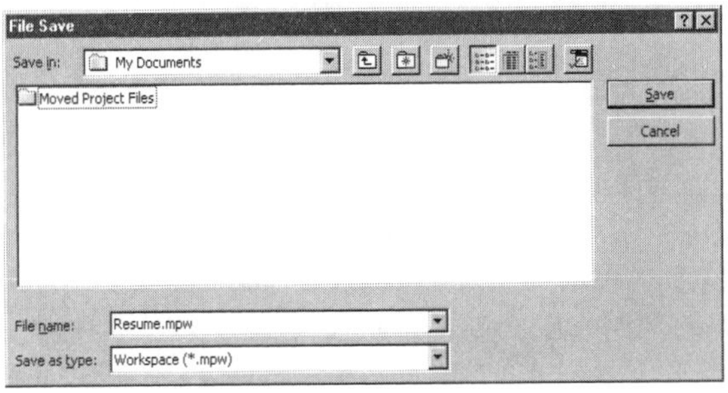

FIG. 17.18

Saving a workspace saves time by loading multiple files that are used together.

4. Click the Save button to complete the operation.

To open all the files, choose File, Open. Select the workspace file and click OK.

N O T E   Workspace files are automatically saved with the extension .MPW. ▪

Discontinuing Resource Sharing

You can discontinue the sharing of resources at any time. Simply open the file that uses another file's resources, open the Resource Sharing dialog box (choose Tools, Resources, Share Resources), and choose the Use Own Resources option button. The resources in the resource pool are no longer available to the file. However, any resources that were assigned to tasks in the file are copied into the file's resource list and are saved with the file. Likewise, any resource in the file that was sharing the resource pool of another project is copied into the pool and remains there, even after sharing is discontinued.

To discontinue a project file's dependence on another file's resource pool, perform the following steps:

1. Open both the file that contains the resource pool and the file that is to become independent (and use its own resources).
2. Make the file that is to use its own resources the active file window.
3. Choose Tools, Resources, Share Resources.
4. Choose the Use Own Resources option button in the Share Resources dialog box.
5. Click OK to execute the new definition.

The message in Figure 17.19 confirms the removal of the connection between the two files.

FIG. 17.19

Microsoft Project confirms that you want to remove the connection between a project file and a resource pool.

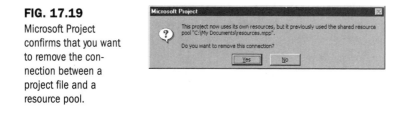

N O T E   If you were to have the file that contained the resources active when you chose the Tools, Resources, Share Resources command, you would see a different dialog box (see Figure 17.20). In this dialog box, you would see a list of files that are linked to yours, including the one that is sharing resources. After selecting it, you could then choose the Break Link button and then click OK. ■

Identifying Resource Pool Links

The resource-sharing connection is recorded in the file that contains the resource pool and in the file that uses the resource pool. However, the existence of the link is stored in different places in the two files.

To verify that a project file uses the resources of another project file, you must view the Share Resources dialog box. Choose Tools, Resources, Share Resources to see the dialog box. The Use Own Resources option button will be selected if it is an independent file, or if the project uses resources from another file, the name of that file appears in the From drop-down box.

To determine whether a project file's resources are used by other project files, you also use the Tools, Resources, Share Resources command. When the active file is one whose resources are being used by another project, you will see a different dialog box when using this command.

To view the resource-sharing links between the file that owns the resource pool and other files, follow these steps:

1. Choose Tools, Resources, Share Resources. A different Share Resources dialog box appears (see Figure 17.20).

FIG. 17.20

The Share Resources dialog box for the file with the resources displays all the files that are sharing those resources.

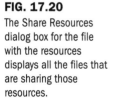

2. You may choose to open one or all of the project files that shares resources with the file containing the resources by selecting the file from the Sharing Links list and then choosing either the Open button or the Open All button.

3. You can choose the Break Link button to break the link that currently exists between these project files. This is essentially the same as choosing the Use Own Resources option button in the project file that was using the file containing the resources.

4. The precedence option buttons at the bottom of this dialog box exert the same control as described previously in the "Using the Resource Pool" section.

5. Click OK to save changes.

> **TIP** When you first begin to experiment with inserted projects, cross project links, and sharing resource pools, it would be worth your while to create a table that includes the following columns: External, Linked Fields, Predecessors, Successors, Sub Project File, Sub Project File Read Only, and Notes. As you begin working with the files, you can see exactly what is happening and where Project is storing the information. Change the column titles to an abbreviation so that you can make the columns narrow in order to see more on-screen without scrolling.

Part
VI

Ch
17

From Here...

This chapter has dealt with the important issues associated with working with more than one project file at a time. You learned about moving from one window to another, displaying multiple project files in one window, linking tasks between projects, and inserting one project file into another. You also learned how to use a separate file for the storage of resource information and linking that file to the project files that need to use those resources.

The following chapters will explore issues of working with more than one application or more than one user:

- Chapter 14, "Publishing Projects on the Web."
- Chapter 18, "Using Microsoft Project in Workgroups."
- Chapter 19, "Exchanging Project Data with Other Applications."

Using Microsoft Project in Workgroups

Projects are usually group endeavors. You can use Microsoft Project to schedule your own personal projects or agenda, but more likely you will use it to plan and track projects that involve many planners and many resources who do the work of the project. Previous versions of Project allowed project leaders to communicate with their resources by e-mail, using MAPI (Messaging Application Programming Interface)-compliant applications (Microsoft Mail or Microsoft Exchange) and VMI-compliant applications such as Lotus Notes.

Microsoft Project 98 enhances workgroup communications with intranet and Internet functionality, in addition to e-mail communications via any 32-bit MAPI-compliant mail application such as Microsoft Mail, Microsoft Exchange, and Outlook. (At the time of this writing, the next version of Lotus Notes was announced to be MAPI-compliant.) The new Internet features enable project managers to communicate with their resources over a corporate intranet or the World Wide Web, making it possible to manage a project with resources located almost anywhere in the world.

Additionally, Internet-style hyperlinks can be used to link to components of other Office 97 applications, making it easier than ever to include Word documents, Excel charts, or other objects in projects.

Setting up a workgroup

Learn how to set up an e-mail, intranet, or Internet workgroup for a project, with a workgroup manager and resources.

Sending task assignments to resources

As a workgroup manager, find out how to send task assignments to resources in the project workgroup using TeamAssign or the WebInbox.

Accepting or declining tasks

As a workgroup member, learn how to accept or decline tasks sent by the workgroup manager.

Updating tasks to the workgroup manager

As a resource in a workgroup, discover how to use TeamUpdate to update work on tasks to the workgroup manager.

Sending messages to other workgroup members

As a workgroup manager, learn how to send Team Status messages to workgroup members. As a resource or workgroup manager, learn how to send Schedule Notes and documents to other members of the workgroup.

This chapter describes workgroup communications using Outlook and Microsoft Mail, as well as communicating via a corporate intranet or the World Wide Web. Because the basic techniques for assigning and updating tasks are similar, detailed information is given for standard e-mail communications, with sections on the special requirements of intranet/Internet communications. For more details on the new intranet/Internet features, see Chapter 14, "Publishing Projects on the Web." ■

Exploring Project's Workgroup Features

The examples in this chapter assume that you have created a software development project called SortWare and assigned resources to it. The project has two levels representing the major phases and subphases of a software development project. The tasks are linked as needed to indicate which tasks must be completed before others are started, and each task is assigned to one or more resources. For information on creating a project see Chapter 3, "Setting Up a New Project Document."

Helen is the project manager for the SortWare project. She needs to communicate with her superior, Mike, and with resources, named Al and Susan, that she has assigned to tasks in the project. The sample project is shown in Figure 18.1.

FIG. 18.1

This figure illustrates the SortWare sample project.

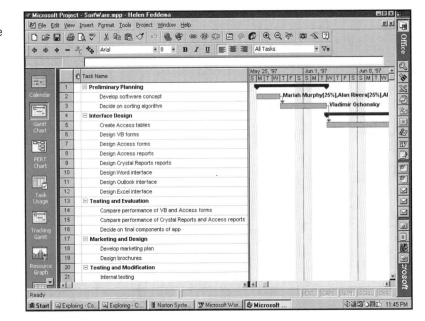

All resources have Windows 95 installed and the members of the workgroup use Microsoft Outlook or Microsoft Exchange for mail and tasks, running on Microsoft Mail or Exchange Server services. Some, but not all, of the features described here would also work with other electronic-mail platforms.

Deciding on E-Mail, Intranet, or Internet Workgroup Communications

With Project 98, you have the option of communicating with workgroup members by e-mail alone, or via an intranet or the World Wide Web. An e-mail workgroup is the basic type of workgroup. Intranet and Internet workgroups add some extra functionality to the basic e-mail communications to enable communications with workgroup members outside of a local network without requiring them to phone in to an Exchange server via Dial-Up Networking.

If all the members of a workgroup can communicate by e-mail (either on a LAN or using Dial-Up Networking), then you can set up an e-mail workgroup. If the workgroup members need to communicate on a corporate intranet or the World Wide Web, you will need to set up Internet-enabled communications.

Communicating with a Workgroup by E-Mail

All members of an e-mail workgroup need to have access to a MAPI-compliant, 32-bit, e-mail system (such as Microsoft Outlook, Microsoft Exchange, or Microsoft Mail). Additionally, each member of the workgroup must have a unique e-mail address.

A workgroup needs a workgroup manager and resources to work on the tasks. The workgroup manager is the person who creates and maintains the project schedule, sends out assignments, and updates the project with the responses from resources. The resources work on the tasks composing the project.

The workgroup manager must have Microsoft Project installed. Workgroup members don't need to have Project, but if they don't have Project they need to run the WGsetup.exe utility from the Microsoft Project CD to enable correct processing of workgroup messages they receive.

Communicating with a Workgroup on an Intranet

The workgroup manager and members need to have access to a common Web server, the one running the corporate intranet. When the workgroup manager sets up Microsoft Project to use Web communications, the TeamInbox is installed on the Web server. This lets the workgroup manager send tasks and messages to workgroup members as an alternative to the regular TeamAssign and TeamUpdate commands and the Outlook Inbox. Just like a standard e-mail workgroup, each member of the intranet workgroup must have a unique e-mail address.

 Setting Up a Web Server for Your Intranet   If you are running Windows NT 4.0, you already have an activated Web server, Internet Information Services (IIS). If you are running Windows 95, you need to install a Web server. Project 98 includes the Personal Web Server (PWS) on its CD. If you want to set up an intranet using PWS, install it from the CD, then follow these steps:

1. Open the Control Panel.
2. Double-click the Personal Web Server icon.
3. Click the Administration tab, then the Administration button.

4. Click the WWW Administration hyperlink.

5. Click the Directories tab.

6. For your PWS home directory (default: C:\Webshare\wwwroot), click Edit in the Action column.

7. Select the Execute check box in the Access section.

8. Click OK.

To verify that the PWS is working properly, go to another computer on the same network, open the Internet Explorer (without connecting to the Internet), and type the following address (substituting your computer's name for *computername*):

http://*computername*/default.htm

You should see the default PWS home page, as shown in Figure 18.2 (or your modified home page, if you have customized it).

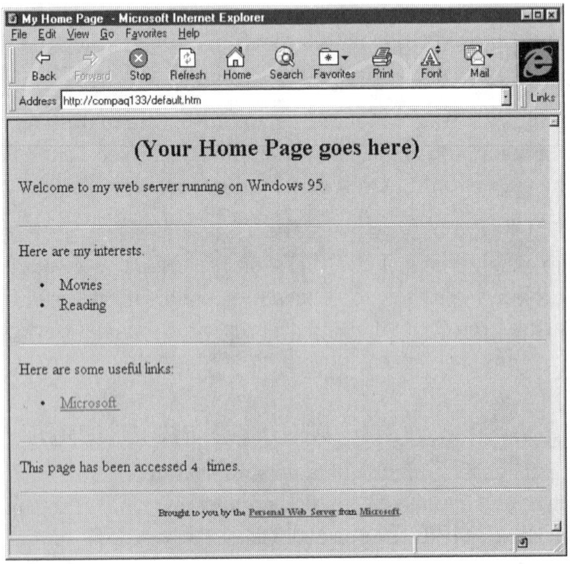

FIG. 18.2

Here is the default Personal Web Server home page, as viewed from another computer on the network.

If you get an error message when trying to view the PWS home page, you may find one or more of the following troubleshooting tips helpful:

- Open the PWS and click the Startup tab. The Web Server State should say that the Web Server is running. If not, click the Start button, as shown in Figure 18.3.

- Verify that the PWS is running, then click the Services tab and check whether the HTTP service is started. If it is stopped, highlight it and click the Start button, as shown in Figure 18.4.

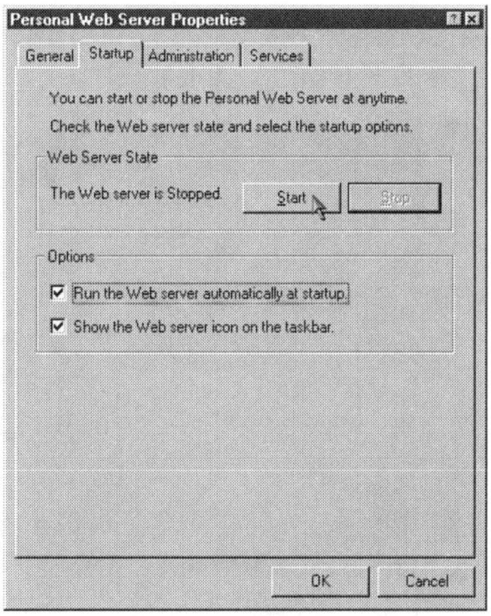

FIG. 18.3

Check the Personal Web Server Properties sheet to see if PWS is running.

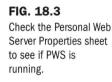

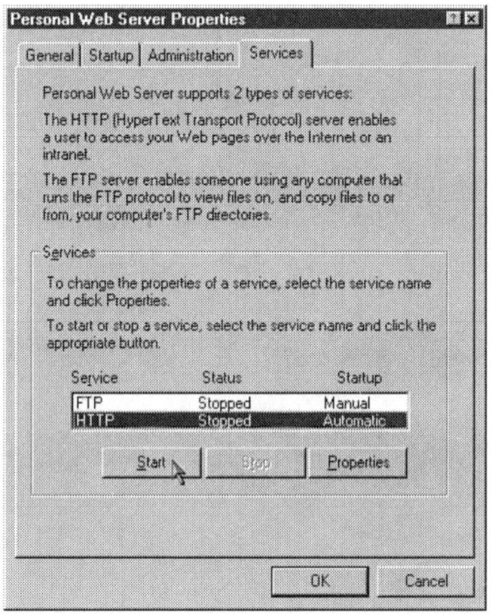

FIG. 18.4

Check that the HTTP service is running in the Personal Web Server.

- If the PWS is running and HTTP started, and you still can't access the PWS home page, check that you have the correct computer name by double-clicking the Network icon in the Control Panel and clicking the Identification tab, as shown in Figure 18.5.

- To verify that the PWS server computer can be accessed from other computers on the network, click the Start button on another computer, then select Find, Computer, and type in the computer name you verified in the preceding step. The computer should be found.

N O T E The Personal Web Server requires that you have the TCP/IP protocol installed for your LAN adapter, and have valid IP addresses for all computers on the network. Refer to Windows 95 Help for information on adding and configuring the TCP/IP protocol, if needed. ■

FIG. 18.5

Check your computer's name in the Network properties sheet.

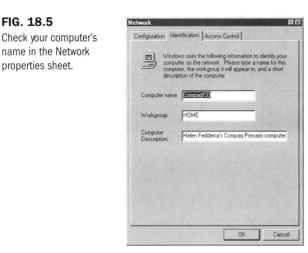

Next, you need to share the Web server folder so workgroup members can have access to it. Use the following steps to share the Web server folder:

1. Open the Windows Explorer and highlight the Web server folder (default: C:\Webshare).

2. Right-click the Webshare folder and select Sharing from the menu.

3. On the Sharing tab of the Webshare Properties dialog box, select the Shared As option and accept the default share name of Webshare, as shown in Figure 18.6.

FIG. 18.6

Set the share options for the Webshare folder.

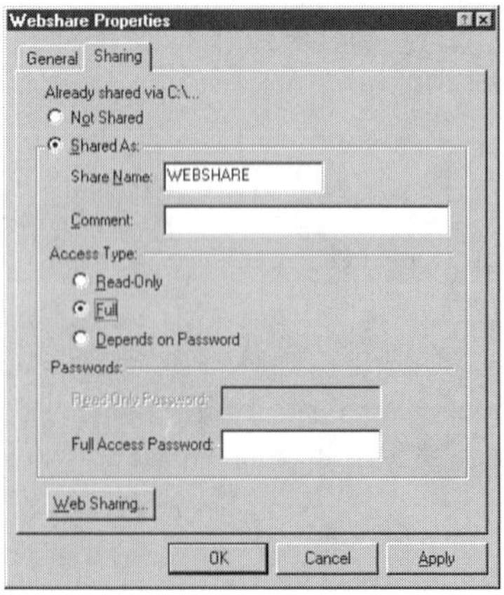

4. Select the Full option under Access Type.

5. If desired, enter a password for full access.

6. Click the Web Sharing button, and check the Share Folder for HTTP, Read Only, and Execute Scripts check boxes, as shown in Figure 18.7.

FIG. 18.7
Set options for sharing
the Webshare folder.

7. Click OK twice to close the dialog boxes.
8. The Webshare folder should now display with a hand under it, as shown in Figure 18.8.

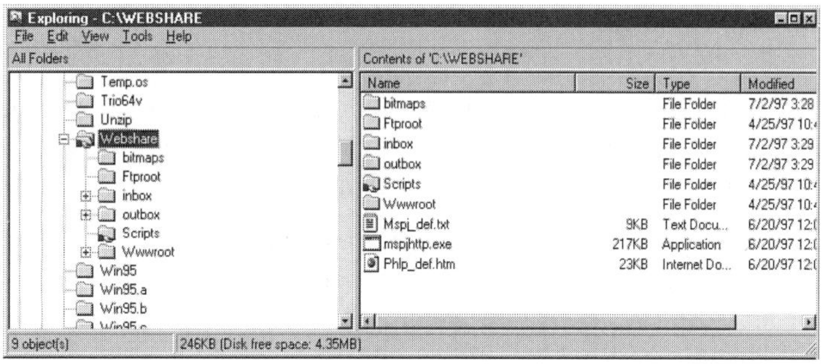

FIG. 18.8
The Webshare folder is
shown with a hand icon
indicating that it is
shared.

Using the WebInbox and TeamInbox on an Intranet To enable workgroup communications on an intranet, choose Tools, Options, then click the Workgroup tab. The default selection for the Default Workgroup Messaging for Resources drop-down list is Email, so you need to change it to either Web or Email and Web. Next, for the Web Server URL enter the URL the resource uses to connect to the Personal Web server. Use the syntax http://*computername*/ *sharename*—for example, **http://compaq133/Webshare**.

Next, for the Web Server Root enter the path to the folder where you installed the Personal Web Server, in this case **C:\Webshare**.

Finally, if desired, check the Notify when New Web Messages Arrive and the Send Hyperlink in E-Mail Note check boxes. Figure 18.9 shows the completed Workgroup tab in the Options dialog box.

When you click OK to apply your settings, you will get a confirming dialog box. Click the Yes button to copy the needed files to the share folder.

Each project can have its own workgroup settings. To ensure that your preferred workgroup settings are the default for new projects, click the Set as Default button.

To confirm that Web connectivity is working, check the Workgroup toolbar in Project; the WebInbox tool should be enabled.

FIG. 18.9
Fill in the intranet settings on the Workgroup tab of the Options dialog box.

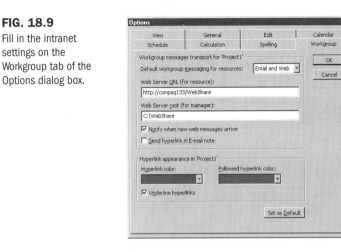

Once Web communications have been enabled, when the workgroup manager sends tasks or messages to workgroup members on an intranet, the messages are stored in the TeamInbox on the intranet Web server, under the root folder (default: C:\Webshare).

Resources open the TeamInbox with a Web browser such as Microsoft Internet Explorer or Netscape Navigator, just as they would open any other Web site using the URL syntax http://*computername/sharename/*mspjhttp.exe (for example, **http://compaq133/Webshare/mspjhttp.exe**).

The first TeamInbox screen has a logon for security purposes, as shown in Figure 18.10.

FIG. 18.10
This figure illustrates logging on to the TeamInbox.

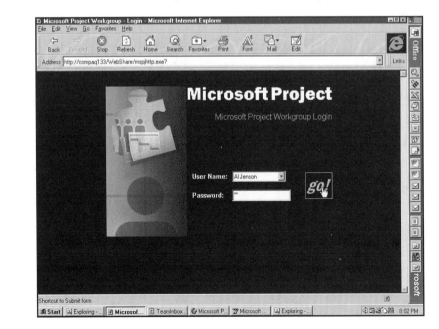

Once you have logged on to the TeamInbox Web page, you will see the actual WebInbox screen, listing messages from your workgroup manager, as shown in Figure 18.11.

FIG. 18.11

A resource's TeamInbox shows a new message from the workgroup manager.

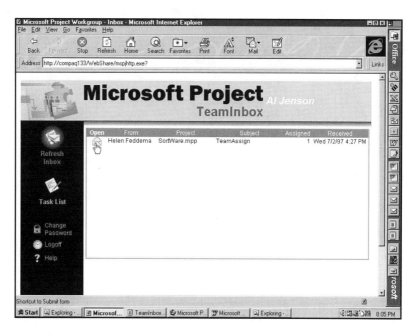

When the resource opens the message, a reply form is generated where the resource can enter comments to send back to the manager, as shown in Figure 18.12.

FIG. 18.12

Respond to a task assignment in the TeamInbox.

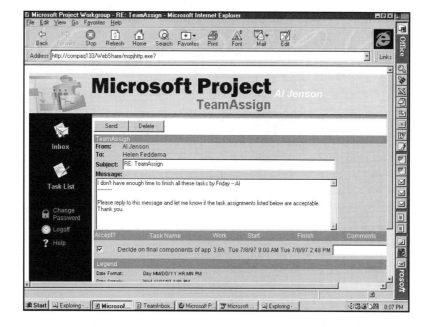

When a resource replies to a message in the TeamInbox, TeamInbox alerts Microsoft Project, which then alerts the workgroup manager. Next, the workgroup manager can view responses from resources in the WebInbox within Microsoft Project (see Figure 18.13) and update the schedule right inside Project.

FIG. 18.13

The workgroup manager's WebInbox contains responses from a resource.

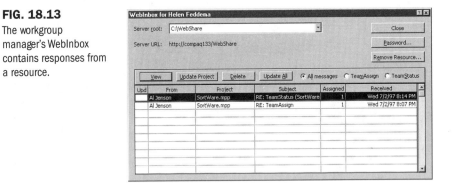

Clicking the Task List icon on the Web page opens a list of the assigned tasks, as shown in Figure 18.14.

FIG. 18.14

Here is a resource's task list in the TeamInbox Web page.

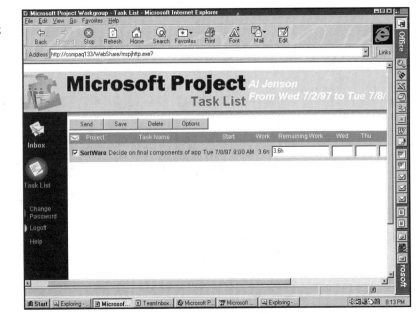

Scrolling across the page reveals a timesheet-like interface where you can enter hours worked on a task to update the project.

N O T E When you enter work done on a task in the TeamInbox, the hours worked are not automatically deducted from the hours remaining; you have to update that hours remaining number separately. ▪

Workgroup members who use TeamInbox don't need to use Microsoft Project to access it. There is no need to run the WGsetup.exe program, as in the case of e-mail workgroups.

Communicating with a Workgroup on the Internet

 The workgroup manager and members need to have access to a common Web server. When the workgroup manager sets up Microsoft Project to use Web communications, the TeamInbox is installed on the Web server. This lets the workgroup manager send tasks and messages to workgroup members via the TeamInbox as an alternative to the regular TeamAssign and TeamUpdate commands and the Outlook Inbox.

Just like a standard e-mail workgroup, each member of the intranet workgroup must have a unique e-mail address.

 When the workgroup manager sends tasks or messages to workgroup members via the Internet, the messages are stored in the TeamInbox on the shared Web server. Resources open the TeamInbox using a Web browser such as Microsoft Internet Explorer or Netscape Navigator, just as they would open any other Web site, except that the TeamInbox screen has a logon for security purposes. The TeamInbox screens for the Internet are similar to those for the intranet TeamInbox illustrated in the previous section, "Using the WebInbox and TeamInbox on an Intranet."

Once you have logged on to the TeamInbox Web page, you will see messages from your workgroup manager, which you can open in a familiar e-mail message interface. When you reply to a message in the TeamInbox, TeamInbox alerts Microsoft Project, which then alerts the workgroup manager. Next, the workgroup manager can view responses from resources in the WebInbox from within Microsoft Project, and can conveniently update the schedule from inside Project.

Workgroup members who use TeamInbox don't need to use Microsoft Project to access it. There is no need to run the WGsetup.exe program, as in the case of e-mail workgroups.

Part
VI

Ch
18

Circulating the Project Schedule for Review

Routing your project plan to key managers and technical experts for comments and approval is critical to the success of any project. You need to be sure that the plan is workable and that you have the support that is needed to complete the project. The Send command in Microsoft Project will create an electronic-mail message for you, with your project file attached. You can address the message as you send it, or you can attach a routing slip that can be used over and over to communicate with the same group or to send the message sequentially to each person on the list. To circulate a project schedule, do the following:

1. Open the File menu.

2. Select the Send To command.

3. Select the Mail Recipient command from the next menu.

Using the Send Command

The Microsoft Project Send command is similar to the Send command in the other applications in the Microsoft Office group. The Send command opens a new mail message form where you can compose and address a message, and the currently active document is automatically attached to the message. Each addressee will get a copy of the project file in Microsoft Project. You can, if you want, remove the attached project file and send the message without it.

The steps that follow assume that you have not previously attached a routing slip to this project and that you must address the message before you can send it. See the next section ("Using a Routing Slip") for information about creating and using routing slips.

To address and send a copy of a project file through electronic mail, follow these steps:

1. Open the project file and activate its window.

2. Choose File, Send To, Mail Recipient, or choose the Send To Mail Recipient button on the Workgroup toolbar.

   For more information about displaying the Workgroup toolbar, see Chapter 2, "Learning the Basics of Microsoft Project."

3. The Outlook Choose Profile dialog box appears if you are not already logged in to the mail system. Select the appropriate profile and choose OK to continue.

4. If you connect to an Exchange server to do e-mail communications and you have set up Outlook to offer you a choice of connecting to a network or working offline when you log on, you will next get the Microsoft Exchange Server dialog box where you can choose to Connect or Work Offline (see Figure 18.15).

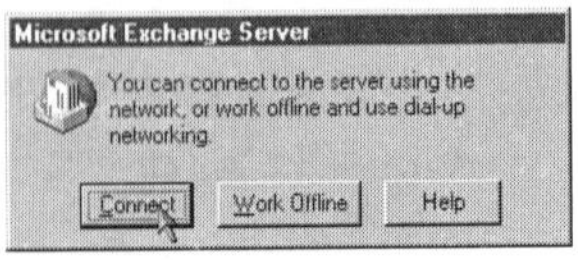

FIG. 18.15

This is the Microsoft Exchange Server dialog box you may get when logging on to Outlook.

5. When the Outlook mail message form appears, there will be an icon in the message area representing the attached project file (see Figure 18.16). You will need to address the message and add appropriate text (if desired) in the message area.

6. Click the To button to open the Select Names dialog box in Figure 18.17. There you can select the names of the recipients for your message (in the To field) and the names of those you want to copy the message to (in the Cc field). You can also type in the names manually; if you type multiple names in either list, you must separate the names with semicolons.

FIG. 18.16
Here is the Outlook mail message form with the project file name in its title bar and a Project icon representing the attached Project file.

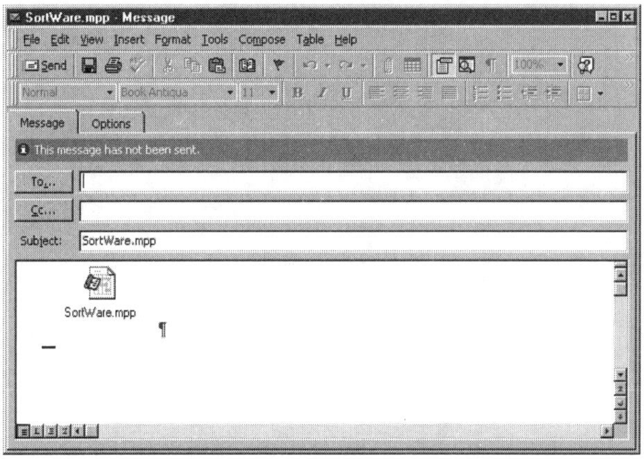

FIG. 18.17
The Outlook Select Names dialog box allows you to select recipients for a mail message.

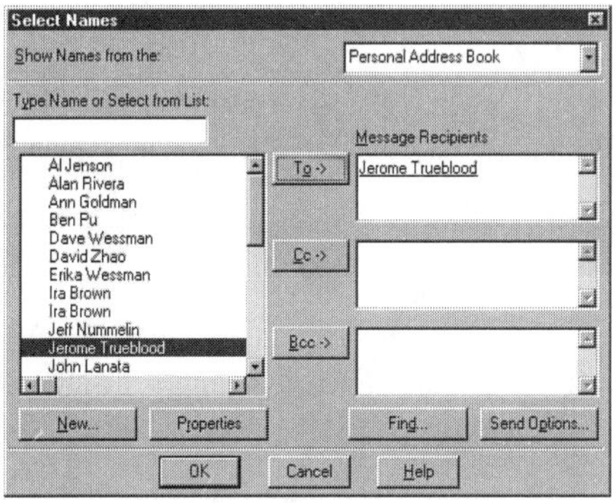

Part
VI

Ch
18

7. If you create a new mail message in the Outlook Outbox and choose the A_ddress button, the Address Book dialog box appears (see Figure 18.18), and you can select mail recipients from it just as with the Select Names dialog box described previously.

CAUTION

When you send a file directly from Project, you may not see the same selection of address books as when you compose a mail message directly in Outlook. To make sure your address book includes the recipients you need for sending Project files, copy the addresses from their native address books to your Personal Address Book, which is always visible when sending files from Project.

TIP

After entering the recipients, select _Tools, Check Names, or press Alt+K to verify the accuracy of the address list you type. Names that are found in the mail directory will be underlined. Those that are not found will be selected for you to correct. Using commas instead of semicolons to separate names will cause the name check to fail.

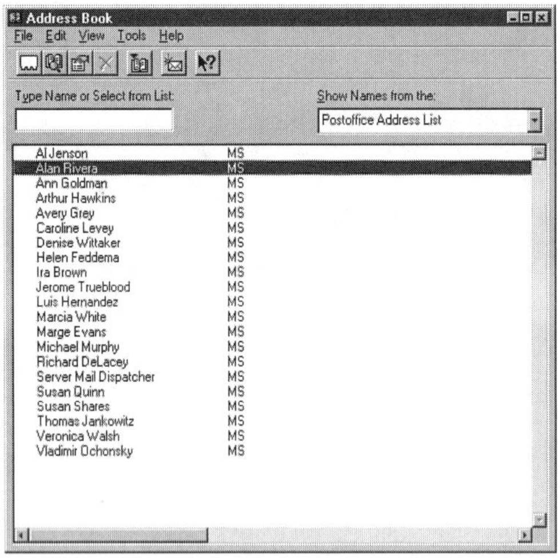

FIG. 18.18

The Address Book dialog box for selecting mail recipients from an Outlook address book has the Postoffice Address List selected.

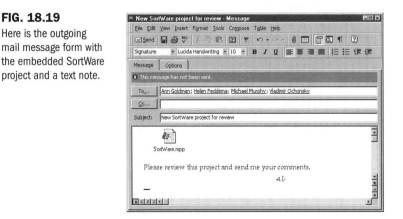

T I P You can start typing the name you want to use, and when enough letters have been typed to identify the name, it will appear selected in the list. Then you can press Enter to place the name in the To list, or press Alt+C to place the name in the Cc list.

---

8. Type the text of your message in the message area at the bottom of the mail form, either before or after the icon for the attached file (see Figure 18.19). If you don't need to send the Project file, you can select and delete the icon for the attached file, making your message text only.

FIG. 18.19

Here is the outgoing mail message form with the embedded SortWare project and a text note.

9. When the addresses and message are complete, choose the Send button to transmit the message with the accompanying copy of the project file.

When the addressees receive the message, they can double-click the file icon in the message area to open Microsoft Project with the project file displayed.

Using a Routing Slip

If you will be corresponding regularly with the same group about the project, you will want to prepare a routing slip to attach to the project file. The routing slip can be used repeatedly to circulate the same file from one recipient to another, accumulating suggested changes in the project file. You also will be notified automatically as each recipient forwards the message and file on to the next person on the routing slip list. These status notes will keep you informed of the progress of the message.

You can reuse the routing slip to send later messages and new versions of the project. You also can change the names on the list and change the message text. You can choose to have the project and message sent to all names on the address list simultaneously, or one after another in the order they are listed. If you route the message to one recipient after another, you can choose to have tracking notices sent to you each time the message is forwarded to the next name on the list.

To attach a routing slip to a project file, follow these steps:

1. Open the project file and activate its window.

2. Choose File, Send To, Routing Recipient, or choose the Send to Routing Recipient button on the Workgroup toolbar. The Routing Slip dialog box appears (see Figure 18.20). You can use the Cancel button to close the dialog box without changing anything.

FIG. 18.20

Create a permanent address list and an accompanying message with the Add Slip command.

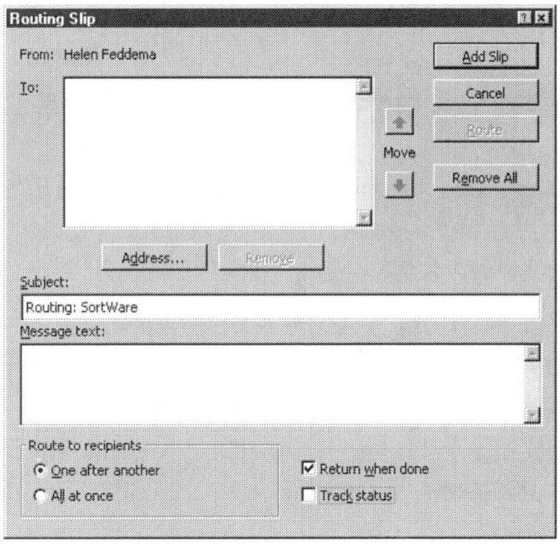

3. Add to the address list and remove names from the list with the Address and Remove buttons. You can remove all names from the list (and clear the message area) by choosing the Remove All button).

If you are routing the message to recipients one after another, you can move names up or down in the list to alter the routing order. Move a name by selecting the name and then clicking one of the arrows above or below the Move label. Al Jenson is currently first on the list to receive the message. Al Jenson is selected and the down arrow can be used to move him down the list. In Figure 18.21, Al Jenson has been moved to the bottom of the list and will be the last to receive the message, enabling him to review all comments and changes.

FIG. 18.21

This figure shows the routing slip with Al Jenson moved to the last position using the Move button.

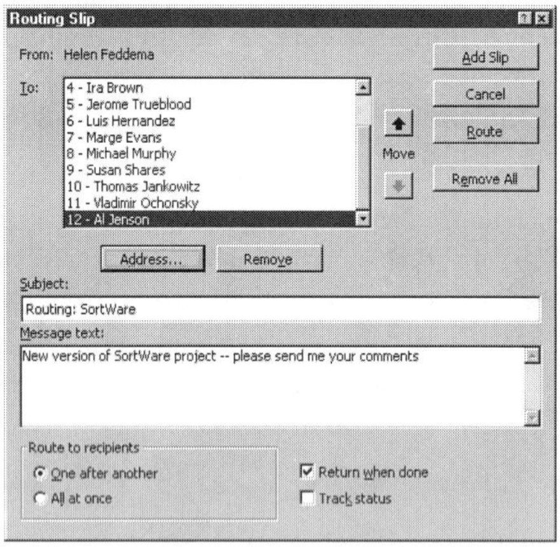

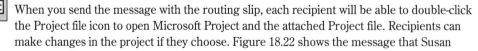

4. Type a subject heading into the Subject text box.

5. Type the message you want delivered with the file in the Message Text box.

6. In the Route to Recipients area, choose how you want the message routed. Choose One After Another to let one copy of the message make the circuit of all recipients, accumulating responses and changes in the project file as it moves down the list in the order you have entered the names. Choose All at Once to send a separate copy of the message and file to each recipient.

7. If you route the message one after another, you can choose to receive tracking notices as each recipient passes the message on to the next name on the list. Fill the Track Status check box to receive progress messages.

8. Fill the check box for Return When Done if you want the project file, including modifications by the people on the routing list, to be returned to you after all others on the routing slip have seen it.

9. If you are ready to send the message immediately, choose the Route button. If you want to attach the routing slip to the project but are not ready to send the message just yet, choose the Add Slip button.

Once a routing slip has been attached to a Project file, the labels of two buttons on the Workgroup toolbar change: The Send to Mail Recipient button label changes to Next Routing Recipient, and the Send to Routing Recipient button's label changes to Other Routing Recipient. After the file has been sent to all recipients, the labels of these buttons change back to Send to Mail Recipient and Sent to Routing Recipient.

When you send the message with the routing slip, each recipient will be able to double-click the Project file icon to open Microsoft Project and the attached Project file. Recipients can make changes in the project if they choose. Figure 18.22 shows the message that Susan receives. The message about the routing slip and how to continue the routing is supplied automatically by Microsoft Project and the mail application.

FIG. 18.22
The mail message contains the routed project file, with instructions to use the Send To, Next Routing Recipient command to continue the routing.

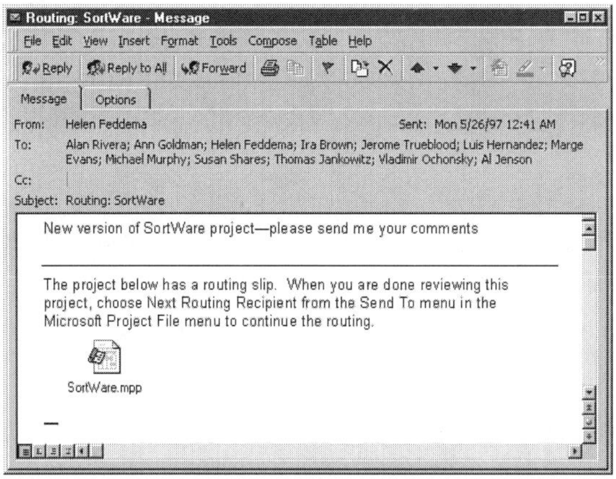

To forward the message and file on to the next name on the routing slip (or back to the originator when the route is complete), the recipient must open the project and use the Send To, Next Routing Recipient command. The Routing Slip dialog box will appear (see Figure 18.23). You can choose to continue the routing (Michael Murphy is the next name on the list), or you can choose to send the project to an address you supply.

Part
VI

Ch

18

FIG. 18.23
The Routing Slip dialog box has the next recipient's name automatically filled in.

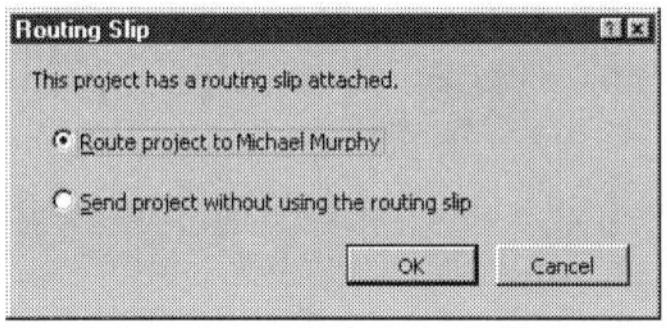

To review and forward a project you have received as a recipient on a routing slip, follow these steps:

1. Open the mail message that contains the routed project file.

2. Double-click the icon for the Microsoft Project file.

3. Review the project, making changes and adding notes to tasks or resources as you think appropriate.

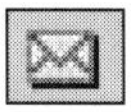

4. Choose File, Send To, Next Routing Recipient (or click the Next Routing Recipient button on the toolbar) to forward the message and the edited file to the next name on the routing slip. The Routing Slip dialog box appears (refer to Figure 18.23).

5. Choose the option button next to Route Project to *nextname*, and choose the OK button to send the message.

6. Close the project file and save the changes.

When routing–slip recipients forward the message to the next name on the list, a status message is automatically sent to the originator of the routing slip if the Track Status check box is filled on the routing slip.

When the last recipient of the routed message sends the file on, the file is returned to the author of the routing slip. Figure 18.24 shows the message that indicates the routing is completed.

FIG. 18.24
Here is the message sent to the originator of the routing after all messages have been routed.

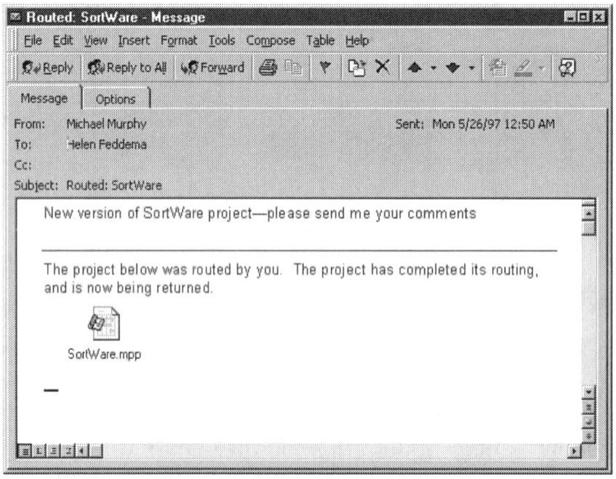

Sending Task Requests with TeamAssign

Microsoft Project 98 has a new utility called TeamAssign for assigning tasks to resources. The workgroup manager uses TeamAssign to assign tasks to resources by e-mail. For intranet- and Internet-enabled workgroups, the WebInbox is used for communications (see the "Communicating with a Workgroup on an Intranet" and "Communicating with a Workgroup on the Internet" sections earlier in this chapter for details). Resources can then respond to the workgroup manager to accept or reject the task assignments, to send the resources revision notices, and to ask them to supply tracking information.

All of these messages are composed automatically, and the information supplied by the resource can be inserted into the project as updates, without the workgroup manager having to key the responses in. Microsoft Project 98 enhances the automatic tracking capability of earlier versions by adding the functionality needed to assign and track tasks over an intranet or the Internet.

Composing the TeamAssign Form

The workgroup manager can create and send a TeamAssign message by following these steps:

1. Select the tasks you want to assign to resources.

2. Choose the TeamAssign button, or choose Tools, Workgroup, TeamAssign. The TeamAssign dialog box appears (see Figure 18.25).

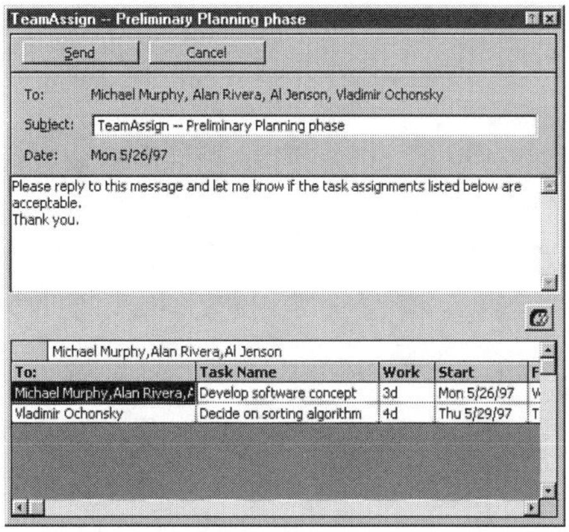

FIG. 18.25

This figure shows assigning tasks to resources using the TeamAssign form.

3. Add to or change the Su**b**ject if you want.

4. Add to the message text if you prefer.

5. You also can add to the task assignments with the Resource Assignment button above and to the right of the task list at the bottom of the dialog box.

6. When the dialog box is complete, choose the **S**end button to transmit the request to the resources.

7. A confirmation message appears, reminding you that all resources must have Windows Messaging installed in order to receive task assignments.

8. You will briefly see a series of Send Message dialog boxes, each saying that a task is being sent to *ResourceName*, Task *x* of *y* tasks.

After sending the tasks, an icon appears in the Indicator column of the project, with a ToolTip telling you that the resources assigned to a task have not all responded to the task assignment.

Responding to TeamAssign Requests

When the resource receives the request, it will look like Figure 18.26. After choosing the **R**eply button, the resource can add to the message text, answer Yes or No to the Accept? column at the bottom of the dialog box, and enter comments in the column to the right of the Finish date.

To respond to the task request, follow these steps:

1. View the mail message, which will be titled TeamAssign.

2. Choose the **R**eply button to enter your response. A message with the subject "RE: TeamAssign" will appear (see Figure 18.27).

3. Add to the **M**essage text as necessary.

4. If you must decline a task request, change the Yes in the Accept? column to No.

5. Enter an explanation in the Comments column to the right of the Finish date column.

6. Choose the **S**end button to send your reply.

Part
VI

Ch
18

FIG. 18.26

The TeamAssign dialog box can be used to accept or decline resource assignments.

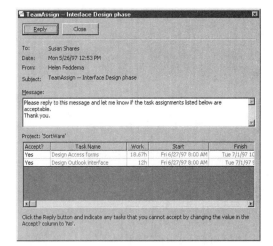

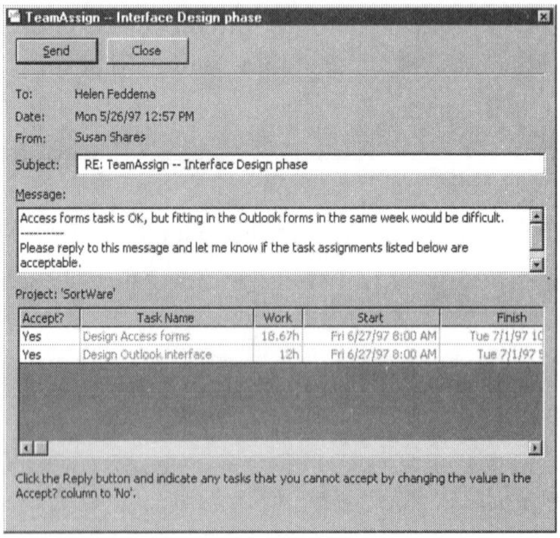

FIG. 18.27

The TeamAssign response form allows you to provide explanations and comments about your acceptance or rejection of task assignments.

Project automatically generates Outlook tasks from team assignments. Figure 18.28 shows some tasks in the Outlook task list. Note that they were created under a category (also created by Project) with the same name as the project.

Workgroup Manager Feedback to Resources

When the project manager receives the reply to the Task Request message, he or she can continue the dialog by adding to the Message text and sending a Reply, or the response can be accepted and incorporated into the project with the Update Project button.

To add the acceptances (or rejections) by resources to the project, follow these steps:

1. View the response from the resource (see Figure 18.29).

FIG. 18.28

This figure shows tasks created by Project in the Outlook task list.

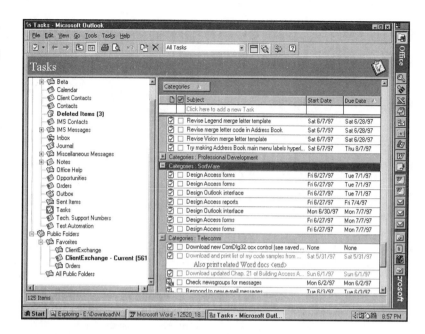

FIG. 18.29

The response from the resource about task assignments can become part of a continuing dialog, or it can be used to update the project.

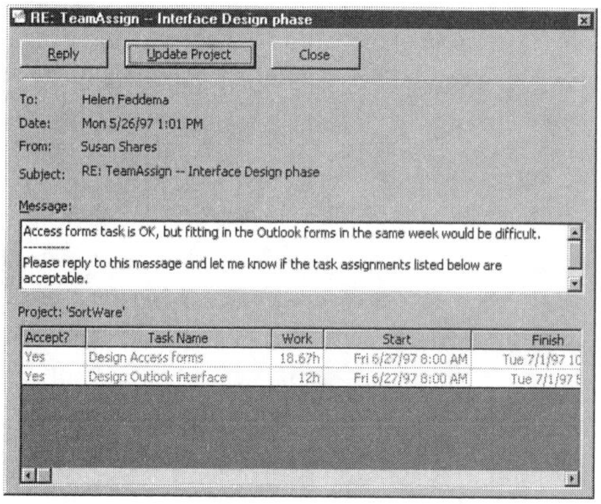

Part

VI

Ch

18

2. Choose the Update Project button to add the acceptance value and the Comments from the resource to the project file. If the resource accepts the assignment, the task assignment Confirmed field will have the value Yes. When all resources assigned to the task have confirmed the assignment, the Confirmed field for the task will have the value Yes. If the resource typed text into the Comments field, the comment will be added to the task Note field with attribution to the resource.

Requesting and Submitting Status Reports with TeamStatus

 As a workgroup manager, once the project is underway, you need to be informed about progress on individual tasks, and to revise the schedule to incorporate this information. Only in this way can Microsoft Project help you anticipate the consequences of variances from the planned schedule.

In the past, the project manager has been overwhelmed with the time and effort required to keep the project schedule current by recording actual events. Now, Microsoft Project and Outlook have combined forces to relieve much of that burden. Although you must still get task status information from resources, the response from the resource can now be automatically incorporated into the schedule as actual updates.

As a workgroup manager, you now can use the new TeamAssign command to easily send e-mail messages to targeted resources requesting progress updates on their tasks. The request message lists the tasks the resource is assigned to work on, and provides fields for recording when work actually started, the amount of work that is completed, the amount of work that remains, and comments about the status of the task. The resource merely has to fill in the electronic-mail message, which resembles a timesheet, and send the reply back to the project manager.

At any time during the progress of a project, the workgroup manager can send TeamStatus messages to resources working on the project, and automatically incorporate their responses into the project schedule.

> **CAUTION**
>
> If you are a workgroup manager using e-mail to update your schedule, be careful not to update resource usage based on percent complete for each task, as this will wipe out the information entered by the resource in the status request message and incorporated into your schedule.

To send a TeamStatus message to all resources assigned to a task or group of tasks, follow these steps:

1. Select the tasks for which you want feedback from resources.
2. Click the TeamStatus button, or choose Tools, Workgroup, TeamStatus.
3. Select either the All Tasks or Selected Task option button from the small dialog box.
4. The TeamStatus form opens, as shown in Figure 18.30.
5. Type the Subject of the status request.
6. Type a message in the message box, if desired.
7. Click the Send button to send the message.

FIG. 18.30

The TeamStatus form is where the workgroup manager requests status updates from project resources.

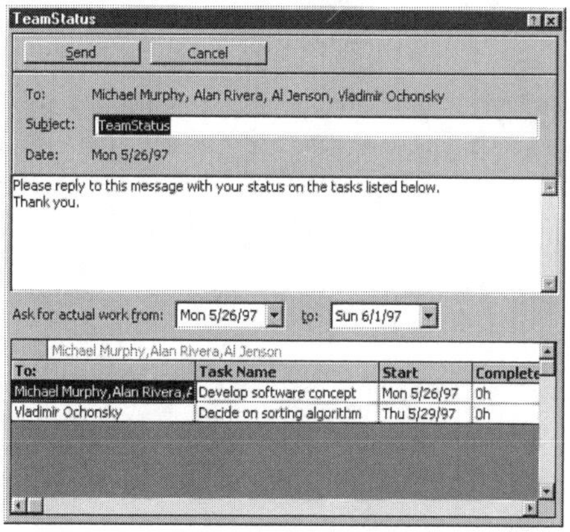

As a workgroup manager, when you receive responses to TeamStatus request messages, you can incorporate the responses into the project schedule automatically by clicking the Update Project button in the response message.

Sending Task Updates with TeamUpdate

As a workgroup manager, when you revise the project in response to actual work or changes in the plan, resources need to be notified of changes in the schedule for their tasks. The start or finish dates may have changed, or the resource may no longer be assigned to the task. Microsoft Project keeps track of which resources need to be notified because their task assignments have been modified. The resource needs to enter their actual hours of work to update the project. Use the TeamUpdate command to transmit these changes to the affected resources, or to the workgroup manager.

For a workgroup manager to send task updates to resources, follow these steps:

1. Select the tasks for which you want to send updates. If you want to include all tasks, select the column heading for one of the task fields.
2. Choose the TeamUpdate button on the Workgroup toolbar, or choose Tools, Workgroup, TeamUpdate. The Task Updates dialog box appears.
3. Add to the message text if you want.
4. Choose the Send button to transmit the updates.

Setting Task Reminders

Use the Set Reminder command to place alarms on tasks in Outlook. You can choose to have the reminder alarm set to the start or finish dates for the selected tasks, and you can choose how long in advance of the event the alarm will sound.

CAUTION

If the tasks are subsequently rescheduled, the alarm is not adjusted in Outlook. Although you can use the Set Reminder command again to capture the new scheduled date, you must manually remove the old alarms in Outlook.

To set alarms in Outlook to give a warning before a task's start or finish date, follow these steps:

1. Select the tasks you want to set alarms for.

2. Choose the Set Reminder button on the Workgroup toolbar, or choose Tools, Workgroup, Set Reminder. The Set Reminder dialog box appears, as shown in Figure 18.31.

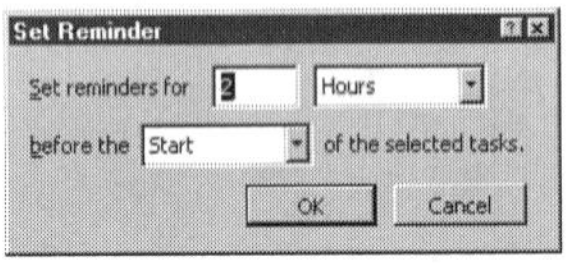

FIG. 18.31

You can set reminders for the start or finish of tasks.

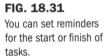

3. In the Set Reminders For field, type a number of units and select the unit to be used from the entry list to the right.

4. In the Before The field, select Start or Finish to indicate where the reminders should be placed.

5. Choose the OK button to set the reminders.

Sending Schedule Notes

The Send command described in the section "Using the Send Command" earlier in this chapter sends the entire project file to the recipients of the message. If you would like to send a message about a limited selection of tasks, or if you want to send a special copy of the project file without losing your routing slip, you can use the Send Schedule Note command by choosing Tools, Workgroup, Send Schedule Note.

The Send Schedule Note dialog box appears (see Figure 18.32) to offer you choices about creating the message. Fill the check boxes at the top to have the message addressed automatically to the Project Manager, the assigned Resources for the tasks that are included, or the Contacts that have been named for the tasks. Choose the Entire Project button to select those recipients for all tasks in the project, not just those currently selected. Choose the Selected Tasks option button to choose the resources and contacts for only the selected tasks.

N O T E The Contact field is designed explicitly for use with workgroup messaging. You can type the name (which is the e-mail address) of any person on your mailing list in the Contact field for those tasks you want that person to be posted on. Then, when you send messages, the Contact person can be included automatically for each of those tasks.

The Contact field does not appear on standard forms or views. You can add the field to a table in order to assign Contact names to tasks. ▒

▶ **See** "Exploring the Standard Tables," **p. 679**

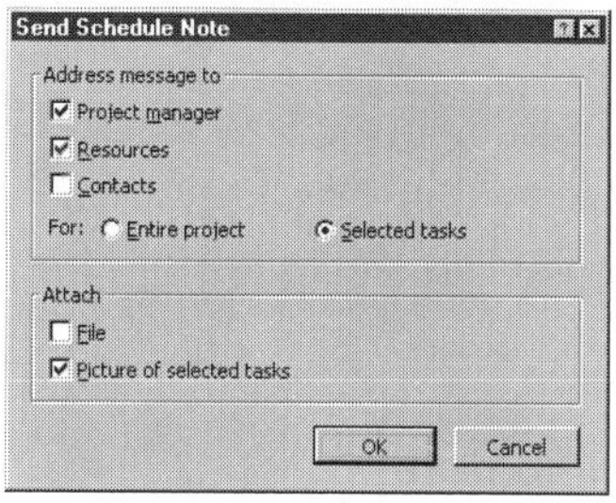

FIG. 18.32

Use the Send Schedule Note dialog box to prepare special notes for special categories of workgroup members.

You can attach the entire project File to the message. You also can choose the Picture of Selected Tasks button to attach a graphic of the way the active view displays the tasks that are selected.

To send a schedule note, follow these steps:

1. If you plan to attach a picture of selected tasks, apply the appropriate view and select the tasks.

2. Choose Tools, Workgroup, Send Schedule Note. The Send Schedule Note dialog box is displayed (refer to Figure 18.32).

3. If you want names of people who are defined in the project file to receive copies of the message, fill the check boxes for the appropriate categories to be selected: Project Manager, Resources, or Contacts.

4. If you fill one or more of the category check boxes, choose whether names are to be selected for those categories from the Entire Project or only from the Selected Tasks.

5. If you want to attach the project file, fill the File check box.

6. If you want to attach a picture of the selected tasks as displayed in the active view, fill the Picture of Selected Tasks check box.

7. Choose OK to continue assembling the message. An Outlook Mail Message dialog box will appear (see Figure 18.33). The dialog box is initially titled to match the project file, but the title will change to match the subject of the message.

8. You are free to add or remove names from the To list of direct recipients and the Cc list of copied recipients. Use the Address Book button to help select mail addresses.

9. Type the message Subject. The Subject will replace the dialog box title as soon as you leave the field.

10. Type the message text before or after the attachment icons (if there are any).

11. Choose the Send button to send the message.

Part
VI

Ch
18

FIG. 18.33

Finalize the message from the Send button in the mail message dialog box.

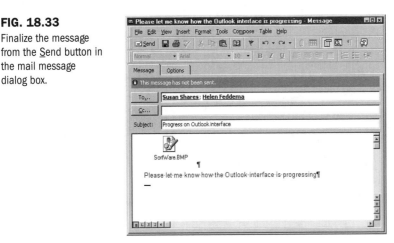

TROUBLESHOOTING

I attempted to send mail and the message was returned to me by the System Administrator with the message `No transport provider was available for delivery to this recipient.` This means that the Outlook profile you are using doesn't contain the appropriate service for the message. For example, if you are sending a message to resources on a LAN, you would need either the Microsoft Mail or Exchange Server service in your profile. If the profile you are using contains only the Internet Mail and Microsoft Network services, the message can't be sent to these recipients. To fix this problem, select Exit and Log Off from the Outlook File menu, log on again to the correct profile, then open the returned message in the Inbox and resend it.

I need to select recipients from a Postoffice address book, and this address book is not available for selection from the Select Names dialog box invoked from Project. You can compose the message in Outlook instead; the Address Book dialog box in Outlook has all available address books. For convenient access to all recipients from Project, when you have the Postoffice Address Book open in Outlook, right-click the recipient's name and select Add to Personal Address Book from the menu to copy the recipient to your Personal Address Book (see Figure 18.34).

From Here...

This chapter has introduced the new e-mail and Internet workgroup features of Microsoft Project 98. These features are among the most exciting improvements in project management found in Microsoft Project. You have learned to share project data with members of your workgroup on an e-mail network, an intranet, or the World Wide Web. You also have learned how to use Outlook, Exchange, or Microsoft Mail to notify resources about their task assignments and changes in the schedule for those assignments. Finally, you have learned how to use electronic mail to track progress on the project.

- For guidelines on distributing printed reports, see Chapter 13, "Printing Views and Reports."

- For information about combining workgroup projects, see the section on consolidating projects in Chapter 17, "Working with Multiple Projects."

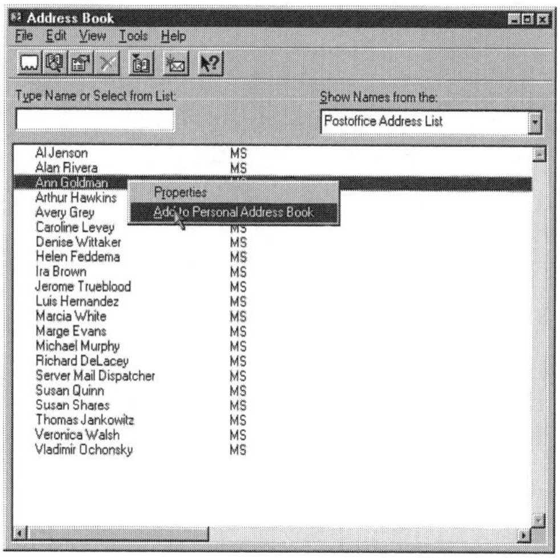

FIG. 18.34

This figure illustrates copying a recipient from the Postoffice Address Book to the Personal Address Book.

Exchanging Project Data with Other Applications

There are many reasons why you might find it useful to be able to copy all or part of a Microsoft Project 98 document to another software application. One common reason is the desire to prepare reports in other applications. Other purposes include using another application for additional analysis or processing of Project data, and archiving an organization's history of projects. Similarly, it is often useful to copy data from other applications into Microsoft Project, especially to avoid re-typing large amounts of data. The following scenarios illustrate the need for a data-exchange capability:

- **Save projects in the new Microsoft Project Database format**

  Use the Microsoft Project Database format for projects that can be opened by Project as well as by products that support the Access format.

- **Import and export data**

  Prepare and use data exchange maps that let you copy field data between Project and applications that don't recognize the Microsoft Project format.

- **Link field values between Project and other applications**

  Paste linked data values between Project and other applications.

- **Copy and paste limited sets of data between applications**

  Exchange static copies of data between Project and other applications.

- **Share data "objects" with other applications**

  Embed data formatted in the style of another application (like an Excel graph) within a Microsoft Project view, and embed Project formatted data (like a Gantt Chart) in other applications.

■ You might want to copy some of your Project information to a PowerPoint presentation or to a report you want to put together in Word or Excel (or other similar office software applications).

■ You might have a list of tasks or resource names in Word or Excel that you want to use in a Project document. It is faster and more accurate to import the data than to key it in again in Project.

■ You might want to process some of your Project data using the special facilities or calculating power of Microsoft Excel.

■ There might be others in your organization who want to query aspects of the project but who don't know how to use Project. If the project is saved in a database, you can work on it in Project, and they can use Access-aware applications to view the Project data details.

■ You may want to keep an archive of all projects for a department or organization, which can be used to review the history for a resource or to calculate performance statistics over a longer time period.

■ You might need to make the project available to someone who still has an older version of Microsoft Project, or to someone who uses another project management application.

■ You might want to build a link between a task start or finish date in Project and a date that is stored in another application. If the date in the other application changes, Project will automatically change the date for the task. Or, reversing the direction of the link, you might want changes in critical dates in the Project schedule to be automatically reflected in presentations or reports in another application.

■ You may prefer to distribute new schedule notices or other reports on a corporate intranet or on the Internet, via Web pages.

This chapter will help you choose the best method for exchanging data between a Microsoft Project 98 data file and other software applications. As illustrated by the previous examples, you can transfer all the Project data or only a part of it. It can be a static copy (which is not automatically updated) or a linked copy (which *is* automatically updated).

For small amounts of data, you may well just use the copy and paste facilities of the Windows Clipboard. For larger transfers, it will be easier to export and import data files. If you need to exchange Project data that is not stored in data fields (such as the calendar of working times, or the display format of a particular Gantt Chart), then you must use the file-transfer mechanism. ■

File Formats Supported by Microsoft Project 98

You can import and export entire projects or selected sets of project data using the File, Open and File, Save As menu commands. These commands allow you to read and write the project data in formats other than Project's native MPP format. After an overview of the file formats supported by Microsoft Project 98, we will examine in detail exporting and importing with each of the formats.

▶ **See** "Working with Project Files," **p. 91**

Microsoft Project now supports three *native* formats that store all Project data, including views, filters, and field data. Additional formats are supported for exchanging data with other applications that don't read the Project native formats. Table 19.1 summarizes the list of file formats that you can use with Microsoft Project 98. In general, if the format can handle the entire set of Project data, Microsoft Project will create copies of all of its tables and fields in the new format. If only part of the Project data is to be exchanged, then you will need to use an import/export map to match Project fields with the fields in the other format.

N O T E The file extensions referred to in Table 19.1 and the text will only be visible in Project's File Open and File Save As dialog boxes if Windows 95 is displaying file extensions. To display file extensions, choose Start (on the Windows 95 taskbar), Programs, Windows Explorer. On the Exploring - Main Menu choose View, Options. On the View tab clear the check box for Hide MS-DOS File Extensions for File Types That Are Registered. Click the Apply button and then the OK button. ■

Table 19.1   File Formats Supported by Microsoft Project 98

File Format	Extension	Import/Export Map	Description
Native Formats			
Project	MPP	Not needed	This is the traditional format for Project document files. It saves the complete set of Project data.
Template	MPT	Not needed	Templates save standard or *boilerplate* information that you use frequently in your Project documents. When opened, the template produces a new Project document.
Project Database	MPD	Not needed	This format is based on the Microsoft Access 97 (version 8.0) file format, although it uses a proprietary extension. The entire project data set is saved in this format, including field data, views, calendars, and formatting. The files can be queried, opened, modified, and saved either in Microsoft Project or Microsoft Access.

continues

Part
VI

Ch
19

Table 19.1   Continued

File Format	Extension	Import/Export Map	Description
Other Formats			
MPX 4.0	MPX	Not needed	The MPX format was used in past versions of Microsoft Project to exchange data between versions of Project or with other project management software. The MPX 4.0 format is retained in Microsoft Project 98 for backward-compatibility so that you can save your Project 98 documents in a format that can be opened by users with Microsoft Project 4.0 or Microsoft Project 4.1. You can save most of the field data in this format, but not the entire project because there are many new fields in Microsoft Project 98 and new capabilities, for example, split tasks and resource contours.
Microsoft Access 8.0 Database	MDB	Optional	This is the Microsoft Access 8.0 database format. You can save all or part of the project data in this format, and any application that recognizes this format can open the file or query it for reports.
ODBC	varies	Optional	ODBC databases are data storage sources that can be accessed by a wide variety of applications, both commercial software products and custom applications developed within the organization. You can store entire projects or selected project data in ODBC data stores.

File Format	Extension	Import/Export Map	Description
Other Formats			
Microsoft Excel Workbook	XLS	Required	Project can export to the Microsoft Excel 5.0/7.0 format. You can export field data in this format but not project elements like calendars and views. The resulting file can be opened directly in Microsoft Excel 97 as a workbook or in any application that supports the Excel 5.0/7.0 format. Although you can read Excel 8.0 data into Microsoft Project 98, you cannot save data in the Excel 8.0 format from Project 98.
Microsoft Excel PivotTable	XLS	Required	This is the format used in Excel for its PivotTable. You only export field data to a PivotTable, not all of the Project data. You cannot import from an Excel PivotTable into Microsoft Project.
Hypertext Markup Language	HTM	Required	This is the HTML format used by browser programs on the World Wide Web and intranets. You can export field data, but not an entire project, to the HTML format; and you cannot import from HTML files into Microsoft Project.
ASCII Text	TXT	Required	This is a generic text format that is widely used for data transfers between applications and platforms. Field data is tab-delimited. You can only transfer field data for a single Microsoft Project table in this format.

Part

VI

Ch

19

continues

Table 19.1 Continued

File Format	Extension	Import/Export Map	Description
Other Formats			
Comma Separated Value	CSV	Required	This is another generic text format widely used for transferring data between applications and platforms. Originally, field values were separated by commas, but now the format uses the default system list separator. You can only transfer field data for a single Microsoft Project table in this format.

N O T E The Project Workspace format, with the extension MPW, also appears in the list of file types in both the File Open and File Save As dialog boxes. However, this is not really a data file format. It merely saves the *workspace settings* (not any field data) for all the open files on the workspace so that you can open all those same files in the same window configuration by simply opening the Workspace file.

The sections that follow will examine all these file formats except the standard Project document (MPP) and Project template (MPT) types. These were covered earlier in this book, most explicitly in Chapter 4, "Working with Project Files."

Most of these "non-native" formats require that you use an export/import map to define which field values in Project are to be associated with data locations in the other format. The creation and use of a map will be presented in detail with the first file format that requires it (see the section "Creating Import/Export Maps for Access and ODBC Sources").

Exporting Project 98 Data to Older Releases of Microsoft Project

In the past, the most comprehensive exchange of data between Microsoft Project and other products was through the MPX (Microsoft Project Exchange) format. This was a standardized protocol for exchanging project data between project management software applications. This MPX file is an ASCII text file that stores not only task and resource field information, but also resource assignments, work and cost data, calendars, and other project information. Microsoft Project can open or save one of these files as simply as it can open or save a regular Microsoft Project data file.

However, MPX has been replaced by the Microsoft Project Database format as the preferred vehicle for exchanging all project data. The MPX format has not been updated in Microsoft Project 98. That is to say, it does not incorporate the new features found in Microsoft Project 98. The MPX format is included only for backward-compatibility, so you can save a Project 98 document in a format that can be opened in Microsoft Project 4.0 or 4.1. Because those Project formats did not allow for the new fields in Microsoft Project 98, like the time-scaled resource assignments, the data saved in the MPX format is not the complete data found in the Microsoft Project 98 document. The new Microsoft Project Database format is now the standard medium for transporting all project data to other applications.

To save a project file in the MPX format, use these steps:

1. Choose File, Save As.
2. Modify the target directory and file name in the Save In and File Name text box if necessary.
3. Display the entry list for the Save as Type text box and select MPX 4.0.
4. Choose Save to execute the command.

   ▶ **See** "Saving a File," **p. 107**

To open a file in Microsoft Project 98 that was saved in the MPX format, choose File, Open. After selecting the search directory in the Look In text box, the list of files you can open will include any MPX files in that directory along with the rest of the Project files. Select the MPX file name and choose the Open button.

Saving the Entire Project in a Database

Part VI

Ch 19

We will examine first the options you have for saving the entire Project data set in other formats. All aspects of the Project document are saved, including all the field data, calendars, views, filters, and format settings. When you create a file in one of these formats, Microsoft Project creates tables and fields in the new format that mirror its own tables and fields. There is no need for you to worry about an import/export map to assist in the process.

Using the Microsoft Project Database Format

The Microsoft Project Database format saves the entire project to a Microsoft Access database format with the extension MPD. This format has replaced the MPX format as the standard interchange format for project data. You can store multiple projects in the same MPD file. You can open individual projects from the MPD file in Microsoft Project, or in Microsoft Access, or any application that supports the Microsoft Access format. You can query the MPD file with any application that can query an Access database.

N O T E For technical information about the Microsoft Project Database and Access formats, see the documentation that is included with Microsoft Project 98 in the file DATABASE.WRI that is copied to your disk when Project is installed. The complete path to the document, starting with the root directory of the disk drive on which you installed Microsoft Project, is **\Program Files\Microsoft Office\Office\ Database.wri**. ▨

Saving a Project in a Microsoft Project Database   When you save a project in the Microsoft Project Database format, you have the choice of appending the project to an existing MPD file or creating a new MPD file. When you open an MPD file that contains multiple projects, you are asked to select the project you want to retrieve.

You cannot save just selected parts of a project in a Microsoft Project Database—the entire project is saved, including all field data for tasks, resources, and assignments, plus all other information such as views, formats, calendars, and so on.

N O T E Although not required, it's a good idea to supply the project document with a Title in the File, Properties dialog box before starting to save a project to a database, especially when saving it to a database that already contains multiple projects. The database file itself will have a name, and each of the projects within the database has a name. Having the document title defined will help you keep track of the names you will be asked to supply when saving to a database. ▨

To save a Project file as a new Microsoft Project Database, use these steps:

1. Choose File, Save As to display the File Save dialog box.
2. Select the location for the new database file in the Save In box.
3. Pull down the list of file types in the Save as Type list box and select Project Database (*.MPD). If there are any MPD files in the location you have selected, they will appear in the file list at this point. The extension on the default file name will change to .MPD also.

   In Figure 19.1, the project document had been named LANS98.MPP originally, but the name is changed to LANS98.MPD when the MPD file type is selected. Also, an existing Project database named Product Development appears in the file list.

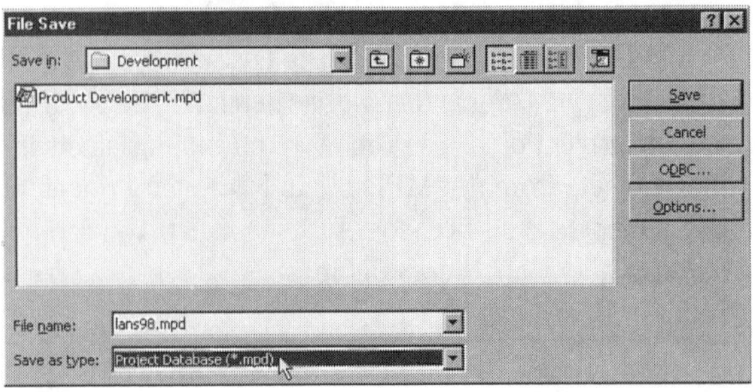

FIG. 19.1

Selecting Project Database as the file type changes both the list of files in the location and the extension on the default file name.

4. Supply the name for the database in the File Name text box. The default database name is the same name that was attached to the project file. To give the database a distinct name, you must type in the new name.

In Figure 19.2 a new database named System Support will be created for the LAN project and other future System Support projects.

N O T E When choosing the name for a new Project database, bear in mind that you may decide to store many project documents in the database. Unless you know that you will only store one project in the database, choose a general name that will help you identify the current project you are saving and all others that you will likely store in the same database file. ▪

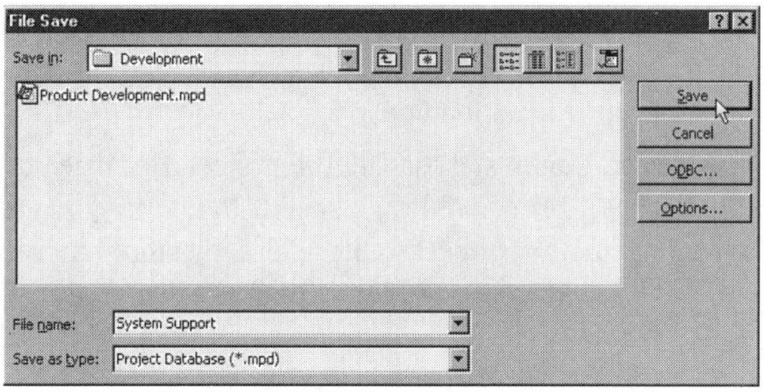

FIG. 19.2

Changing the database name to something more general than the current project's name allows other projects to be saved in the database.

5. Choose the Save button to start saving the data. The Export Format dialog box will appear (see Figure 19.3). Entire Project is the only available option when saving a Microsoft Project Database. The options for Selective Data are not applicable, so that option's choices are dimmed.

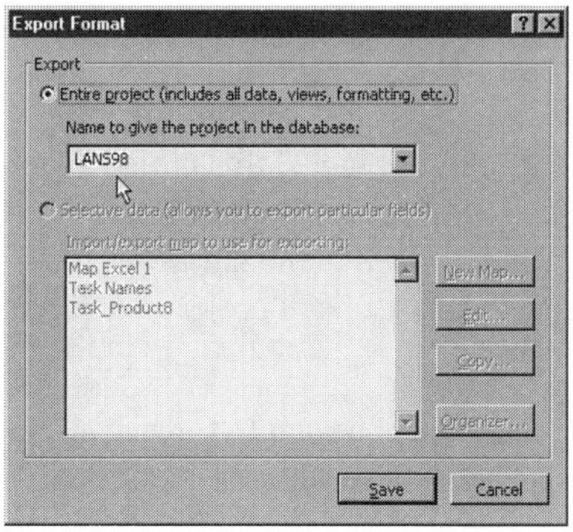

FIG. 19.3

Provide the name to identify this project in the database in the Export Format dialog box.

Part

VI

Ch

19

6. Select the text box labeled Name to Give the Project in the Database if you want to change the name of the project and type in a new name.

If the Project document already has a file name, it will appear in the text box. If the file has not been saved previously, the project title will appear as a default name for the project. The project title is maintained in the File Properties dialog box, on the Summary tab. (See Chapter 3, "Setting Up a New Project Document.")

7. Choose <u>S</u>ave to begin creating the database. A Saving progress bar will appear on the left of the status bar to let you know the file is being saved.

To save your project in an already existing database requires a few additional steps:

1. Choose <u>F</u>ile, Save <u>A</u>s to display the File Save dialog box.

2. Use the Save <u>I</u>n box to select the location where the database file is stored.

3. Pull down the list of file types in the Save as <u>T</u>ype list box and select Project Database (*.MPD). This will display the Microsoft Project Database files in that location.

4. Choose the database name in the list. Note that the original project name in the File <u>N</u>ame text box disappears and the database name replaces it. You will restore the project's unique name in a moment.

5. Choose the <u>S</u>ave button to start saving the project. Because you are adding a project to an existing database, Microsoft Project needs to know if you are replacing that database or just appending another project to those already stored there. A dialog box appears to let you choose the next step (see Figure 19.4).

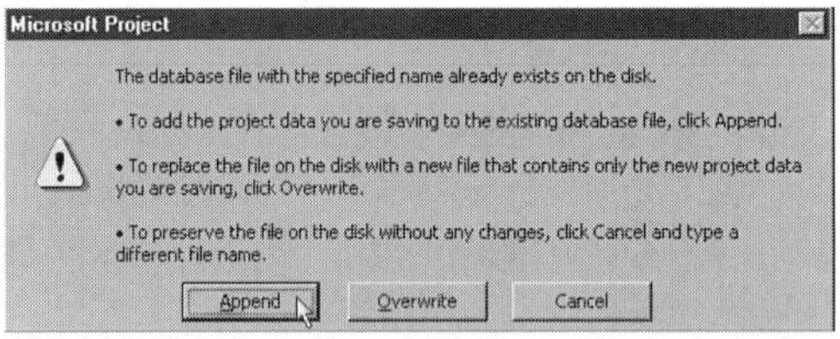

FIG. 19.4

When adding a project to a Project Database, you can append the project to those already in the database, or you can replace the existing projects in the database with the new project you are saving.

Microsoft Project

The database file with the specified name already exists on the disk.

- To add the project data you are saving to the existing database file, click Append.
- To replace the file on the disk with a new file that contains only the new project data you are saving, click Overwrite.
- To preserve the file on the disk without any changes, click Cancel and type a different file name.

[Append]   [Overwrite]   [Cancel]

6. Choose the <u>A</u>ppend button if you want to add this project to those already in the database. You must also choose the <u>A</u>ppend button if you want the project you are saving to replace another project already saved in the database. You will have to give the new project the same name in the database as the project that it replaces.

Or

Choose the <u>O</u>verwrite button only if you want to remove all existing projects from the database and save the new project in that file.

Or

Choose the Cancel button if you want to back out of the process and leave the database file unchanged. If you choose <u>A</u>ppend or <u>O</u>verwrite, the Export Format dialog box will appear as in the previous example.

7. Use the list arrow in the Name list box to review the names of other projects stored in the database file (see Figure 19.5). If you are replacing a project, choose that project's name from the list. Otherwise, you can keep the default name of the new project or change the name by typing in the Name list box.

FIG. 19.5
Review the list of projects stored in the database in the Name list box.

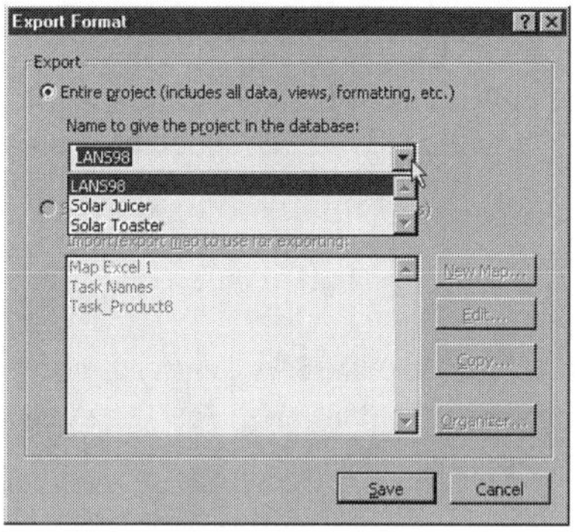

8. Choose Save to begin saving the project in the database.

Opening Projects from a Microsoft Project Database   Open a project that was saved in a Microsoft Project Database with the File, Open command.

1. Choose File, Open.

2. Select the location of the database file you want to open in the Look In box. The Microsoft Project Database files in that location will be displayed along with other project files stored there.

3. Choose the database name from the list and choose the Open button. The Import Format dialog box will appear (see Figure 19.6).

FIG. 19.6
Select the project name to be opened from a Microsoft Project Database file.

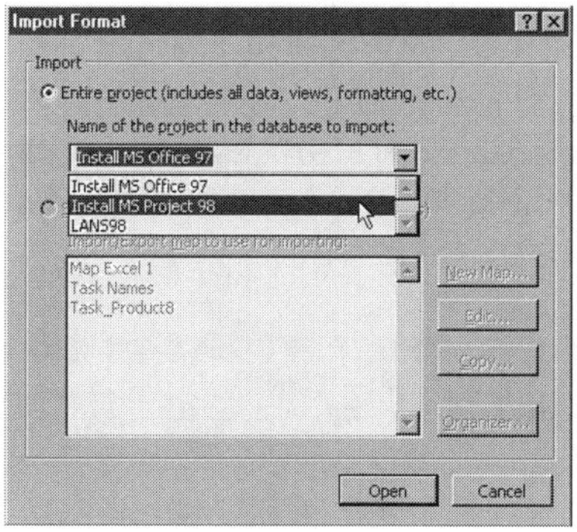

4. Use the list arrow to display the names of the projects stored in the database and choose the project you want to open from the list.

5. Choose the Open button to begin loading the project from the database.

Part
VI

Ch
19

If project data has been changed by another application in the MPD file, then when it is imported into Project 98 the program will attempt to determine which field was changed and will make appropriate adjustments to other data that may rely on the changed field. If the new data is inconsistent with the Project scheduling engine or with other fields, Project will generate an error log noting the inconsistency.

After opening and working with a project stored in an MPD file, you can save your work as you would with any other file: simply choose File, Save from the menu or choose the Save button on the Standard toolbar. The project will be saved in the database it came from, replacing the older version of the project.

> **CAUTION**
>
> If you choose the File, Save As command instead of the Save command, Project will change the extension of the project file to MPP and, unless you correct it, the project would be saved in a new standard project document instead of back in the database it came from.

Saving Projects in Microsoft Access Format

You can also save the entire project in a standard Microsoft Access 8.0 database. The Microsoft Project Database is also stored in the native Microsoft Access 8.0 format. More applications recognize the Access MDB extension, however. A further distinction is that you must save all of the project data in the Microsoft Project Database format, whereas you can choose to save all or only selected parts of the project in the Microsoft Access format.

The steps for saving an entire project in the Access format are virtually the same as those used to save a Microsoft Project Database.

To save all of an open project document in a Microsoft Access 8.0 database, use these steps:

1. Choose File, Save As to display the File Save dialog box.

2. Select the location for the new database file in the Save In box.

3. Pull down the list of file types in the Save as Type list box and select Microsoft Access 8.0 Database (*.MDB). If there are any MDB files in the location you have selected, they will appear in the file list at this point. The extension on the default file name will change to .MDB also (see Figure 19.7).

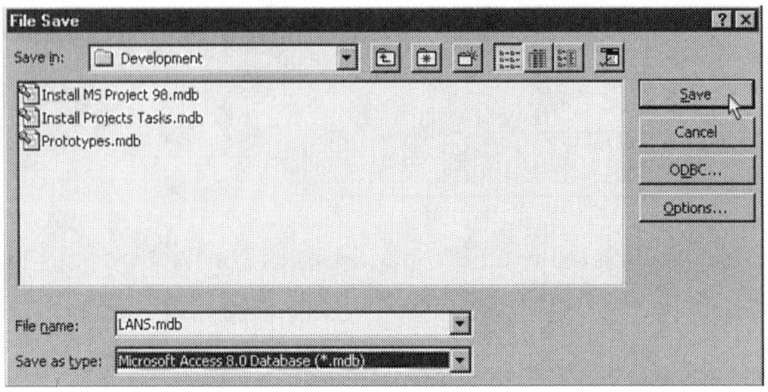

FIG. 19.7

Save a project in an Access 8.0 database the same way you save one in a Project 98 database.

4. To create a new database, supply the name for the database in the File Name text box. The default database name is the same name that was attached to the project file. To give the database a distinct name, you must type in the new name. Remember that if other projects are to be stored in this database, an inclusive name might be better than the current project's name. To add the project to an existing database, select the database name from the file list.

5. Choose the Save button to start saving the data.

6. If you are adding to an existing database file, the dialog box in Figure 19.4 prompts you to choose what will happen to the existing database.

   Choose Append to add this project to the others contained in the database, or to replace one of the existing projects in the database with the data in this project.

   Or

   Choose Overwrite to replace the database file, and all the projects contained in it, with a new database that contains only the project you are saving.

   Or

   Choose Cancel to stop saving the project.

7. When the Export Format dialog box appears, be sure that the default option Entire Project is selected.

8. Supply the name given to this project by typing it into the Name text box. You can accept the default name, type in a new name, or use the name of one of the existing projects in the database (if you want to replace that project's data with the data in the project you are saving).

9. Click the arrow in the list box to see the names of other projects stored in this database. Click one of those names if you want to replace that project.

10. Choose Save to begin saving the project in the database.

You open a project that was saved in a Microsoft Access database with the File, Open command.

1. Choose the File, Open command from the menu.

2. Select the location of the database file you want to open in the Look In box.

3. Pull down the list of file types in the Files of Type list box and select Microsoft Access Databases (*.MDB).

4. Choose the database name from the file list and choose the Open button. The Import Format dialog box will appear (see Figure 19.8).

CAUTION

If the database does not contain any complete project files (in other words it only contains parts of one or more projects), the option Entire Project will be dimmed. You can import data from the database, but you must create a map to access it (see the section "Creating and Using an Import Map" later in this chapter).

Part
VI

Ch
19

FIG. 19.8

Choose one of the complete projects stored in an Access database to open it as a project document.

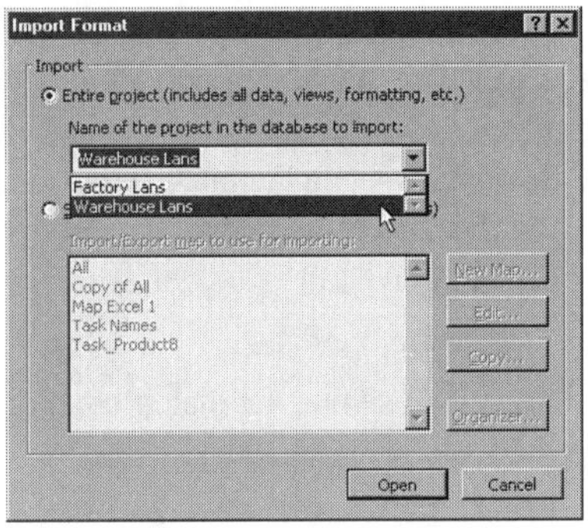

5. Use the list arrow to display the names of the projects stored in the database and choose the project you want to open from the list.

6. Choose the Open button to begin loading the project from the database.

After opening and working with a project stored in an Access database, you can save your work as you would with any other file by choosing File, Save or selecting the Save button on the Standard toolbar. The project will be saved in the database it came from, replacing the older version of the project.

Saving Projects in a Microsoft ODBC Data Source

You can store and retrieve project data with ODBC (Open Database Connectivity) data sources, such as Microsoft SQL Server, as well as other programs that provide ODBC drivers to access their data files. ODBC database sources are ideal for customized applications that draw data and reports from many different organization-wide databases. ODBC is not a file format, it is a set of protocols, drivers, and instructions for storing the way to access and work with different data sources.

N O T E Microsoft Project 98 and Microsoft Access 97 require 32-bit ODBC drivers to connect to client/server RDBMS's (Relational Database Management Systems). You must obtain 32-bit updates for all ODBC drivers. ▓

Saving a Project in an ODBC Database You can save a project in an ODBC database almost as easily as in any other format. There are a few additional steps involved in identifying the ODBC data source. The data source definition is not a database itself, but a reference to a database. You can create some databases on the fly in which to store your project. Others have to be created by server administrators. See your database administrator if you need help with the data sources available to you.

To save an entire project in an ODBC database, follow these steps:

1. Choose File, Save As.

2. Choose the ODBC button on the right side of the File Save dialog box. This will display the Select Data Source dialog box (see Figure 19.9).

FIG. 19.9

The ODBC Select Data Source dialog box lets you create a new data source definition or use an existing one.

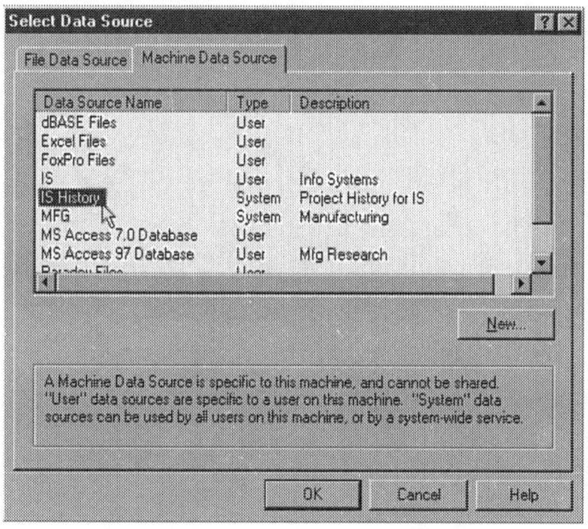

3. Choose either the File Data Source tab or the Machine Data Source tab to show the list of data sources (databases) already defined on your system. If you want to create a new data source, choose the New button and follow the instructions for defining a new data source.

4. If required by the data source you selected, enter your logon ID and password and then click OK. The Export Format dialog box is displayed.

5. Be sure the option Entire Project is selected.

6. Provide the name you want to use for this project in the database.

7. Choose the Save button.

Importing a Complete Project from an ODBC Source   You must be careful when importing a project from an ODBC source that was not originally created in Microsoft Project. The source database must have been carefully structured to parallel the database structure used by Microsoft Project. To open a project from an ODBC database:

1. Choose File, Open.

2. In the File Open dialog box choose the ODBC button.

3. Select the tab (File Data Source or Machine Data Source) that lists the data source you want to open.

4. Choose the data source and then click OK.

5. In the Import Format dialog box select the option Entire Project.

6. Click the arrow in the list box to display the projects saved in the source.

7. Choose the project you want to open.

8. Click the Open button to open the project data.

Part

VI

Ch

19

Exchanging Selected Parts of a Project with Other Formats

For some file formats you are only allowed to store selected field values from a Project file. This is true for the Microsoft Excel format, the HTML format for Web browsers, and the text formats. In other instances, you simply may not want to store all of the Project information. For example, a colleague might ask you to supply an Access database that records just the task names, scheduled work, and actual work for your project as a source to help that person estimate task work in a similar project.

When you save an entire project, Microsoft Project automatically creates a standard set of tables in the new database format with the standard Microsoft Project field names.

If you choose to save only parts of the project in one of the export formats, you must use an export format map to define which fields you want to export from Project and what you want to call the table or tables in which they will be stored. If you plan to change the values in the other format and then import the data back into Project, you must use that same map or a similar map to tell Project where the imported data goes in the Project data structure.

Working with Import/Export Maps

All import/export maps are similar in design: they specify tables and fields in another file source that will be matched with tables and fields in Microsoft Project. A map allows you to define up to three tables in the non-Project format to match data in Project. The non-Project format tables are listed here:

- A task table for values that match Project's task fields
- A resource table for values that match Project's resource fields
- An assignment table for values that match Project's assignment fields

For each table you define, you specify the field name in Project and the corresponding field name (or other location) in the export or import format. Option buttons make it very easy to add all Project fields to the table, or to add the same set of fields that appear in one of the defined tables in Microsoft Project.

For export maps, you can choose to export only a subset of the tasks or resources in the project by applying one of the Project's *filters*.

For import maps, you can choose how the imported data will fit into the open Project file. Your options are as follows:

- You can place the imported records into a new Project document. Project will create a new MPP document file with the field values you have selected. This file is a standard Project MPP file and saving it does not update the source data.

- You can have the imported records appended to the tasks, resources, or assignments already in the open Project. Project will add new tasks, resources, or assignments below the existing tasks, resources, or assignments.

- You can have the values in the imported records merged into the existing Project records. This means that Project will attempt to match the records coming in with those already in the open document. Where there is a match, the field values coming in will replace the existing field values. In order for Project to match the records coming in with those in the current file, you will have to define one field as a "key" field to be used for matching records. For example, you could import resource names and standard rates in order to update the pay rates in the resource table. In this case, you would probably use the resource names as the key field to match records.

The maps are not file format specific; that is, if you design a map to export data to Access, you can also use the same map to export data to an Access database, to a text file, or to an Excel spreadsheet. However, the different file formats often convert non-text fields into different field types and different values. For example, the same export map will save 8 hours of work to an Excel spreadsheet as text (as 8 hrs) and to an Access database as the number 480,000 (1,000 times the number of minutes).

N O T E   When you choose to save Project data in a nonproject format, Project will modify the options that are shown on the import/export map to match the format you chose. For example, if you choose to Save As an HTML format, and then choose an import/export map that was originally designed for exporting to an Excel spreadsheet, the spreadsheet options will be replaced by HTML options.

You must be very careful when using import maps that were designed for a different data source. A map designed for one database or spreadsheet source may specify tables or fields that are not used in another data source. Always check the structure of the map before applying it to import.

Import/export maps are saved in the GLOBAL.MPT file, not in the Project file that is open when you create them. You must use the Organizer to delete a map. However, you can rename a map without having to go to the Organizer. When you edit a map, you have the option to change its name.

▶ **See** "Deleting an Object with the Organizer," **p. 118**

Part
VI

Ch
19

Reviewing the Predefined Import/Export Maps

Microsoft Project 98 includes eleven predefined import/export maps for general purpose use. Some are like predefined Project reports, views, or tables, while others are intended for a specific file format. The predefined maps are listed and described in Table 19.2.

Table 19.2 The Predefined Import/Export Maps

Map	Description
"Who Does What" Report	This maps resource names and their task assignments (including Start and Finish dates and total hours of Work).
Compare to Baseline	This maps schedule, baseline, and variance values for tasks (including the Duration, Start and Finish dates, Work and Cost).
Cost Data by Task	This maps tasks with their costs (scheduled, baseline, and variance). It includes Fixed Cost, Total Cost, Baseline Cost, Actual Cost, Variance, and Remaining Cost.
Default Task Information	This maps the task Entry Table fields (ID, Name, Duration, Start and Finish Dates, Predecessors, and Resource Names).
Earned Value Information	This maps the earned value fields for tasks. It includes these fields: ID, task Name, BCWS, BCWP, ACWP, SV, CV, Baseline Cost, and Cost Variance.
Export to HTML using Standard Template	This maps task, resource, and assignment fields into three separate tables. The task table includes the ID, Name, Duration, Start and Finish Dates, Resource Names, and % Complete fields. The resource table includes the ID, Name, Group, Max Units, and Peak Units fields. The assignment table includes the Task and Resource Names, Work, Start and Finish Dates, and % Work Complete fields. See the "Exporting Project Data to the Internet or an Intranet" section later in this chapter for more details about the HTML format.
Resource "Export Table" Map	This maps all the fields in the predefined resource Export Table, which is a comprehensive set of 25 resource fields that covers definition of the resource as well as scheduled, baseline, and tracking work and cost values for all assignments for each resource.
Task "Export Table" Map	This maps all the fields in the predefined task Export Table, which includes nearly five times as many fields as the resource Export Table.

Map	Description
Task and Resource PivotTable	This maps two tables: a task table and a resource table. If used to create an Excel PivotTable, each table will also have an accompanying PivotTable. The task table includes task Names, resource Names assigned to the task and their Groups, Duration, Start and Finish dates, and task Cost. The resource table includes the resource Group and Name along with the total Work and Cost of assignments. See "Exporting to an Excel PivotTable" later in this chapter for more details about the PivotTable format.
Task List with Embedded Assignment Rows	This maps a task table along with all the resource assignments to each task and includes the Work, Duration, Start and Finish Dates, and % Work Complete for each assignment.
Top Level Tasks List	This maps a task table that is filtered for top level tasks (tasks at the first outline level). The fields include the task ID, Name, Duration, Start and Finish dates, % Complete, Cost, and Work.

The sections that follow explain how these maps are put together and how they are to be used.

Creating Import/Export Maps for Access and ODBC Sources

Creating an import/export map is fairly straightforward, once you understand the mechanism. Project does most of the work, at least if you stick to general cases. To illustrate, we will first create an export map to send selected cost data for tasks, resources, and assignments to an Access database. Then we will modify the same map to import a more limited set of data from the Access database. The same map could be used for an ODBC database as well.

Creating and Using an Export Map   Export maps are easier to create than import maps for the simple reason that the Project field names are the source of the data, and you can create field names in the target format that are similar to the Project field names. With import maps, the field names in the source may not be as easy to relate to the set field names in Microsoft Project.

To create a map for exporting Project data to an Access 8.0 database, use these steps:

1. Open the Project file you want to export.
2. Choose File, Save As.
3. Select the directory in the Save In list box.
4. In the Save as Type list box, select the Microsoft Access 8.0 Database (*.MDB) file type.

Part

VI

Ch

19

5. If you are adding to an existing database, select it from the file list. If you are creating a new database, type its name in the File Name text box.

   Don't add partial project data sets to a database that already contains complete projects. The table names will get confusing.

6. Select the Save button. The Export Format dialog box will be displayed (see Figure 19.10).

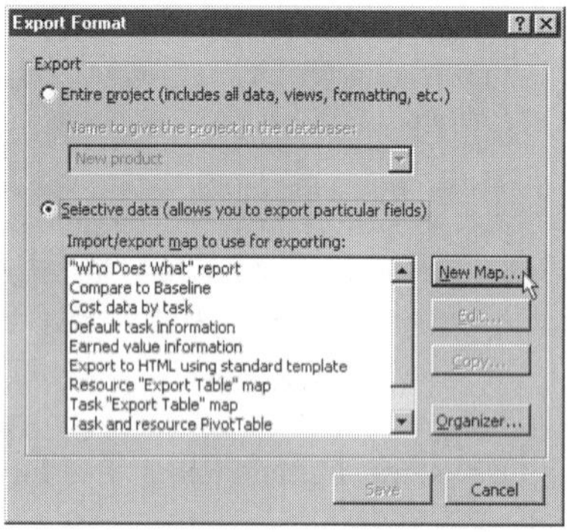

FIG. 19.10

Use the Export and Import Format dialog boxes to manage the maps that determine how data is exchanged with other formats.

7. In the Export Format dialog box, select the Selective Data option button. The map list and buttons for managing maps will become available.

   You can select an existing map to use, create a New Map, Edit an existing map, Copy a map as a starting point for a map to edit, or open the Organizer to copy maps from other Project files and other templates to this list.

8. Choose the New Map button to advance to the Define Import/Export Map dialog box (see Figure 19.11).

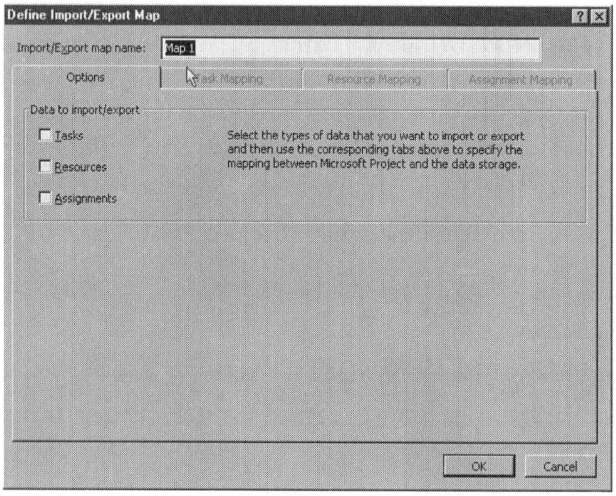

FIG. 19.11

Use the Options tab of the Define Import/ Export Map dialog box to assign a name to the map and to choose what type of tables will be created.

9. On the Options tab, type a name for the map that will help you remember the map's focus in the Import/Export Map Name text box. Also, select one or more of the check boxes for the types of data you want to store in the new format. When you check a table check box, the tab for that table type becomes available.

In Figure 19.12, the map name will be Cost Data and all three table types are checked.

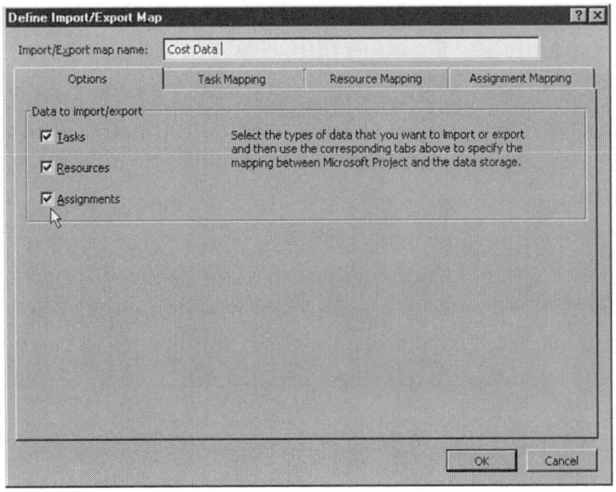

FIG. 19.12

This map will be called Cost Data and will include fields from the task, resource, and assignment tables in Microsoft Project.

10. Select the tab for the table type(s) you checked on the Options tab. We will start with the Task Mapping tab.

11. Supply a descriptive name for the table on this tab in the field labeled Destination Database Table Name.

12. If you want to limit the tasks that will be exported, use the list of filters in the Export Filter field (see Figure 19.13) to select a task filter. Any of the currently defined filters can be chosen. You cannot design a new filter at this point. Filters must be defined ahead of time.

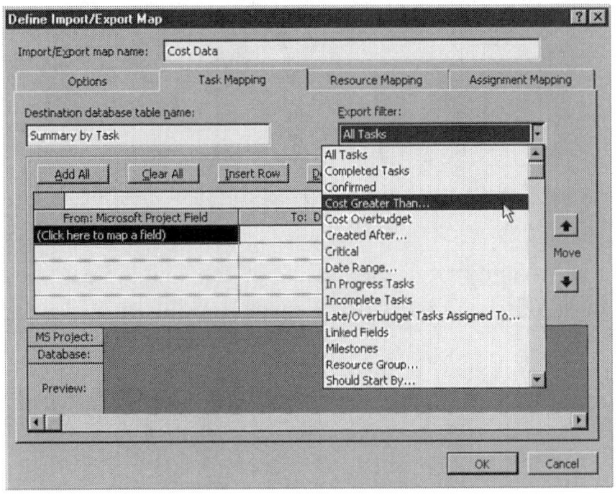

FIG. 19.13

To control which tasks will be exported, you must already have defined an appropriate task filter.

Part
VI

Ch
19

13. Now you must define the task fields that will be exported in the mapping table. You must list each of the Project fields that are to be exported in the column labeled From: Microsoft Project Field. You must create a name for the database field that will hold that data in the column labeled To: Database Field. The data type will be filled in automatically from the Project field types.

Click the list arrow in the first cell in the left-hand column—the cell that displays the prompt (Click Here to Map a Field). The complete list of Microsoft Project task fields will be displayed (see Figure 19.14).

14. Select the field to be exported from the list of Project fields and press Enter to complete the selection. A default field name is inserted in the second column (for the exported database) and the field data type will be inserted in the third column.

You can change the export field name to suit your tastes. Be sure, however, that you don't violate any field-naming rules of the format you are creating. For example, for an Access database field names can't have leading spaces or include periods, exclamation marks, or square brackets. You can, however, replace the underscore separator in the field names suggested by Project. Below the mapping table, you will see a sample of the fields you have added and the data they contain.

FIG. 19.14

Select a Project field name to be exported from the list.

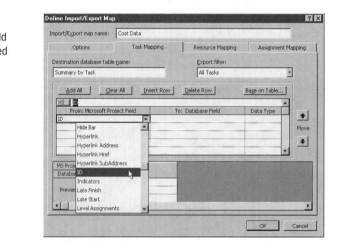

15. Continue this process for each field you want to export.

16. There are several buttons that can speed the process of managing the field mapping table:

   - To move a field row in the list, select the row to be moved and use the Move arrows on the right side of the mapping table to move the row up or down in the list.

   - To insert all of the task fields in Microsoft Project, select the Add All button.

   - To clear the mapping table, select the Clear All button.

- To insert a blank row for a new field in the middle of the list, select the place where the row should be inserted and click the Insert Row button.

- To remove a field row, select the row to be removed and click the Delete Row button.

- To populate the mapping table with the same fields that are contained in one of the task tables in Microsoft Project, select the Base on Table button. The Select Base Table for Field Mapping dialog box will appear (see Figure 19.15) with a list of all the currently defined task tables. Select the table you want to use and click OK. The \field list will be cleared from the mapping table, and the fields that are defined in the table you selected will be inserted in the mapping table.

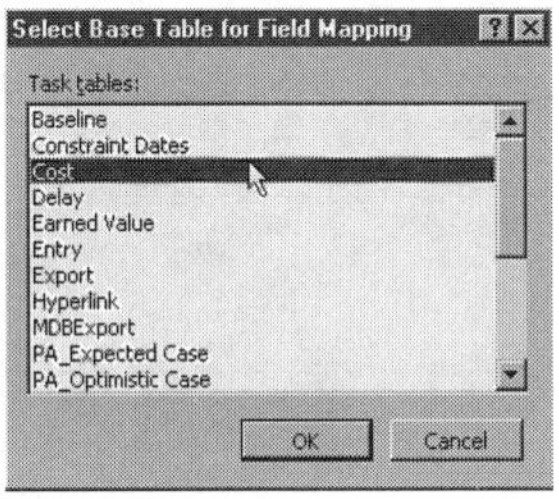

FIG. 19.15

You can fill the mapping table with the fields defined in a Project table by using the Base on Table button.

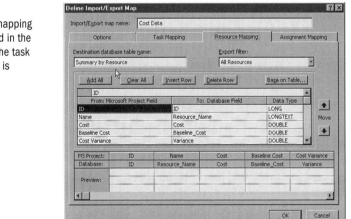

17. When the task mapping table is completed, move on to the next table you have elected to include in the database export. In the example, the Resource Mapping tab is selected (see Figure 19.16). The table name will be Summary by Resource and the fields were filled in by selecting the Cost table from the list displayed by the Base on Table button.

    Note that you can also apply a resource filter to select a subset of the resource records to be included in the export table.

FIG. 19.16

The resource mapping table is defined in the same way as the task mapping table is defined.

Part
VI

Ch
19

18. Finally, if you are including assignment fields, choose the Assignment Mapping tab and repeat the process (see Figure 19.17).

    The assignment records are the details that are combined for the task and resource cost summaries. Because there is no table in Microsoft Project for assignments (they only appear in the Task Usage and Resource Usage views and on certain forms), you cannot choose a table as a template for the fields to be included. Also, there are no filters for assignments. Both these options are dimmed on the Assignment Mapping tab.

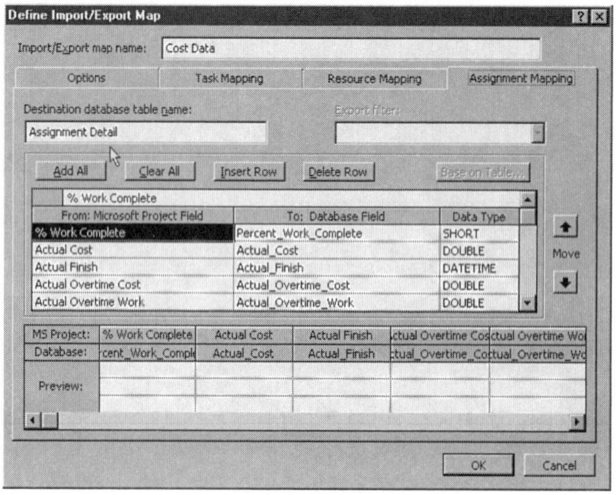

FIG. 19.17

The assignment mapping table has fewer options than the task and resource mapping tables.

19. When all the tabs are filled in, click OK to save the export map. You will be returned to the Export Format dialog box, and your new map will appear in the list of maps.

20. Choose the Save button to export the selected data to the database name you entered in the Save As dialog box at the beginning of these steps.

Creating and Using an Import Map   When you want to import data into Microsoft Project from another source, you must find a workable import map or create one of your own. If the data was originally exported from Microsoft Project, then use the same map for the import that you used for the export. Or, if you want to make slight changes, it is easy to copy the export map and edit the copy to produce the new import map.

The options for an import map are slightly different from those found on the export map:

- The source tables are already defined (whereas you defined the target tables in the export map). For example, there may be many tables in the source database that have task information in them. You must choose the table containing the task data you need. Similarly, you must identify the source tables that are appropriate for supplying resource or assignment fields.

    If you created the source by exporting fields from Project, then it will be much easier because the field names will be recognizable. But, if the source table was created from a source other than Project, the field names will have to be translated.

▪ You cannot import only a portion of the records using any of the Project filters. If you want only part of the records from the source, you will have to filter the source first to produce a new database and then import the resulting tables into Project. Alternatively, you could import all the data into Project and then delete the unwanted records.

▪ When importing, you can choose whether the imported data will be stored in a new project file. You can also choose whether the data will be appended to or merged into an existing project file.

To illustrate importing from another file format, we will import from the database that was created earlier in explaining the export process. Follow these steps:

1. If you intend to add the imported data to an existing Project document, then you must open that project before starting the import process. Otherwise, it doesn't matter which project documents are open when you import, because Project will create a new document.

2. Choose File, Open or click the Open toolbar button.

3. Select the location of the data source in the Look In list box.

   If you are importing from an ODBC data source, choose the ODBC button instead and select the data source in that dialog box.

4. In the Files of Type list box, select the format of the data source.

5. Choose the data source file from the file list and click the Open button.

6. In the Import Format dialog box choose the Selective Data option (in many cases it will be your only choice).

7. Find the map that you plan to use for importing.

   Or, start a New Map (following the same techniques outlined for creating an export map).

   If there is an existing map that is similar to the map you need, then copy it and edit the copy.

8. You should always edit the map you plan to use to be sure that it defines the desired import process. Figure 19.18 illustrates the errors you will see in the mapping tables if you choose the wrong map. If the map names source fields that don't exist in the file you have started to open, the field name entries will have OUT OF CONTEXT: prefix.

9. Look at each tab to verify the settings. You should pull down the list of names in the Source Database Table Name field to verify that the appropriate table has been chosen for each tab.

   Figure 19.19 shows the import map that is derived from the export map we created earlier, with the Task Mapping tab selected. The Source Database Table Name list is pulled down to show all the tables in the source database.

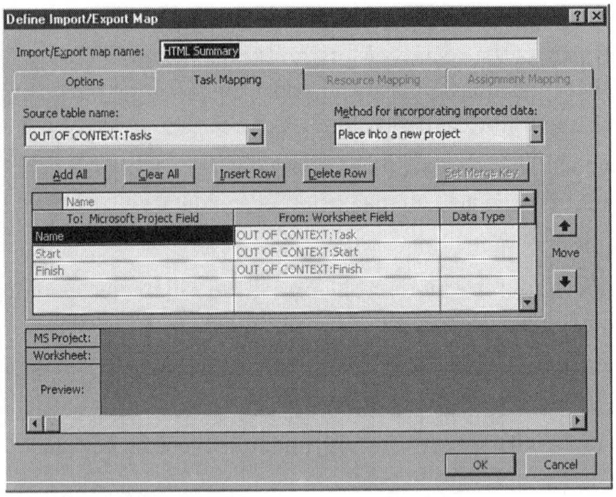

FIG. 19.18

If you have chosen the wrong predefined map for an import file, it will be apparent if you examine its tabs.

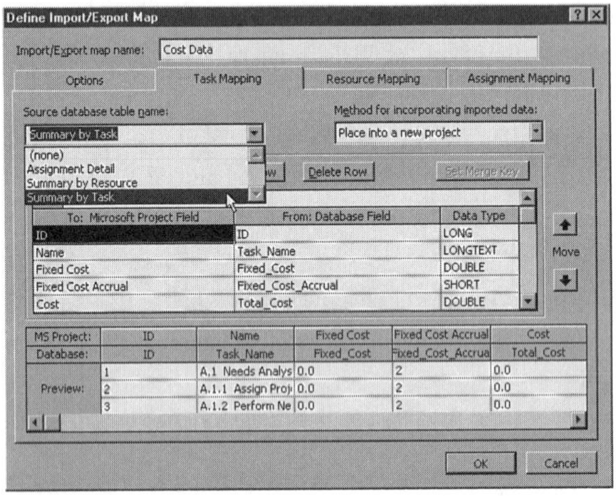

FIG. 19.19

The import map for a map you defined as an export map will be slightly different from the original export map.

10. Examine the option labeled Method for Incorporating Imported Data (see Figure 19.20).

   • Choose Place Into a New Project to start a new Project document with the imported data.

   • Choose Append to End of Current Project to add these records (task records in this case) beneath the task records already in the project.

   • Choose Merge (By Key) Into Current Project to have Microsoft Project match incoming records with existing records and update the fields with the imported values.

11. If you choose to merge the imported data, the Set Merge Key button becomes active. Select a field that will have the same values in both the existing Project file and the imported table.

For example, the task ID field would match tasks as long as the task list has not been edited since the exported data was created. Better yet, the Unique ID field doesn't change once a task is created and is a more reliable key field.

Once the key field is selected, click the Set Merge Key button. The field name will change to MERGE KEY: field name (for example, MERGE KEY: ID in Figure 19.21). If you need to change the MERGE KEY field, simply select the new key field and click the Set Merge Key button again.

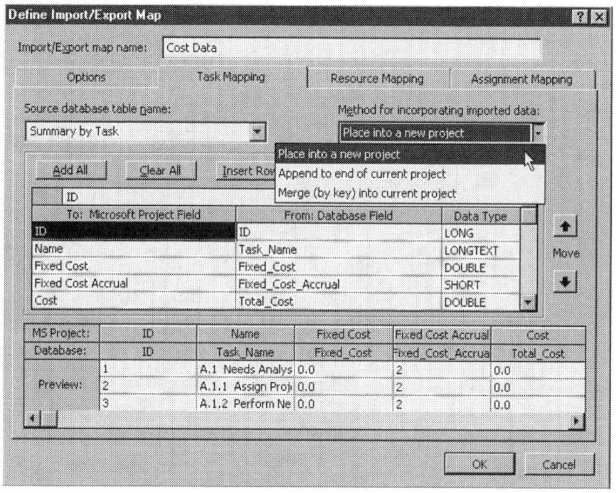

FIG. 19.20

You can start a new project file with the imported data, or you can incorporate the imported data into an existing project file.

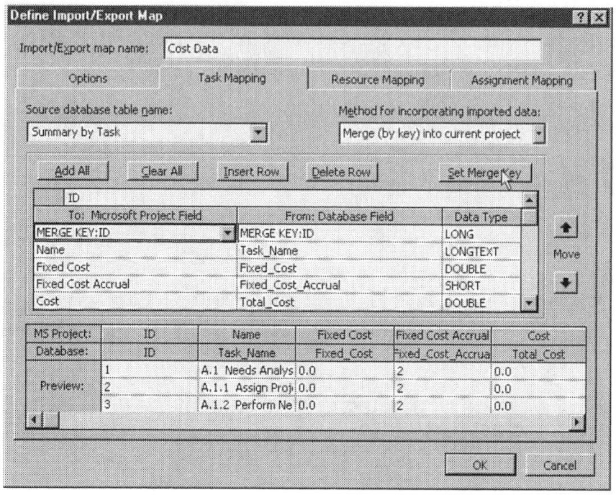

FIG. 19.21

One field must be selected as the Merge Key field to identify matching records when imported data is to be merged with existing data.

12. Once all the tabs have been set correctly, choose the OK button to save the import map.

13. Choose the Open button on the Import Format dialog box to begin the import.

TROUBLESHOOTING

I imported data into Microsoft Project but I can't see the data in Project. Make sure you have used an appropriate import map. If the field names in the map don't exist or are mismatched with Project fields, you may not have imported any data. Also, make sure you are using the appropriate view or table. If you imported resource data and are using a Task view, you would not see the data. Likewise, if the Project table in the current view does not include the fields you imported, you will not see the imported data.

Working with Microsoft Excel Formats

You can export field data to Microsoft Excel 97 workbooks as spreadsheet data or as PivotTable data. You can import field data from Excel 97 and Excel 5.0/7.0 workbooks (excluding PivotTables).

There are a few options on the import/export map for the Excel format:

- You can choose whether or not to export field names as the first row of the spreadsheet. If you choose not to export field names, the worksheet column numbers will be used for the worksheet field names.

- You can instruct Project to include assignment rows like those displayed on the Task Usage and Resource Usage views. However, the assignment rows will not be automatically outlined and indented in the Excel workbook as they are in Project.

  Of course, you can use Excel's Outlining command to group assignments under the task or resource, and this will make it possible to hide and display the assignment rows at will (as in Project). But, you will have to do this by hand and when the assignment rows are displayed, they still will not be indented.

TIP

Remember to change Excel's default grouping direction. Choose Data, Group and Outline, Settings and clear the Summary Rows Below Detail check box.

Exporting Project Data to an Excel Worksheet You can use an import/export map you created for other formats to export Project data to Excel. You may want to create a copy and save it with a name that indicates it's for Excel. In the following example, the map for exporting to Excel is based on the Cost Data map developed previously for exporting to Access.

To export Project data to an Excel workbook, use these steps:

1. Open the Project document that you want to export.
2. Choose File, Save As to display the File Save dialog box.
3. Select the location for the new file in the Save In list box.
4. Change the Save as Type selection to Microsoft Excel Workbook (*.XLS).
5. Supply the name for the file in the File Name text box.

6. Choose the Save button. Project will display the Export Format dialog box.

7. Select or create a map to use for exporting the data. Be sure you open the map for editing if it was created earlier. There are options for Excel that don't appear on maps when used for Access, for example. Figure 19.22 shows the Cost Data map open for editing.

FIG. 19.22

You can include assignment rows with task and resource data.

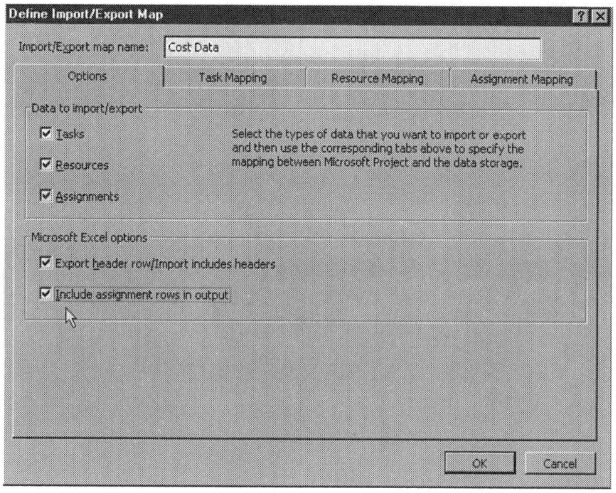

8. On the Options tab, in the Microsoft Excel Options group, fill the check box labeled Export Header Row/Import Includes Headers. If filled, the first row on each sheet in the workbook will display field names as column headers. If this check box is empty, there will be no labels at the top of the columns in the workbook.

9. If you want tasks and resources to show assignment details (as in the Task Usage and Resource Usage views), fill the check box labeled Include Assignment Rows in Output.

TIP Assignment rows will be indistinguishable from Task or Resource rows in the Excel worksheet. You can add the task field named Assignment to the map (or the resource field named Assignment) to identify assignment records. The Assignment field displays Yes for assignment records and No for task or resource records.

CAUTION

If you export the rows for the assignment details in a task mapping, the assignment rows will appear to be just additional tasks in the workbook that is created. If you imported that workbook back into Project, the resource assignments would indeed be listed as tasks—even if you included the task Assignment field in the exported data. Similarly, exported assignment details in a resource mapping results in the assignments being treated as additional resources; and they cannot be imported back into Project satisfactorily. Assignment records cannot be imported into Project unless you are importing a full project with the Microsoft Project Database format or the Microsoft Access format.

Part VI

Ch 19

10. Click OK to save the revised map.
11. Choose the Save button on the Export Format dialog box to initiate the export.

When the exported data is opened in Excel, there is a worksheet for each of the tables that was defined in the export map in Project (see Figure 19.23). As specified in the export map, the field names appear in the first row of the worksheet and the assignments for each resource are listed under the row for the resource.

FIG. 19.23
The Excel file shows the Project data that was exported. The assignments for Scott Adams are selected on the Summary by Resource worksheet.

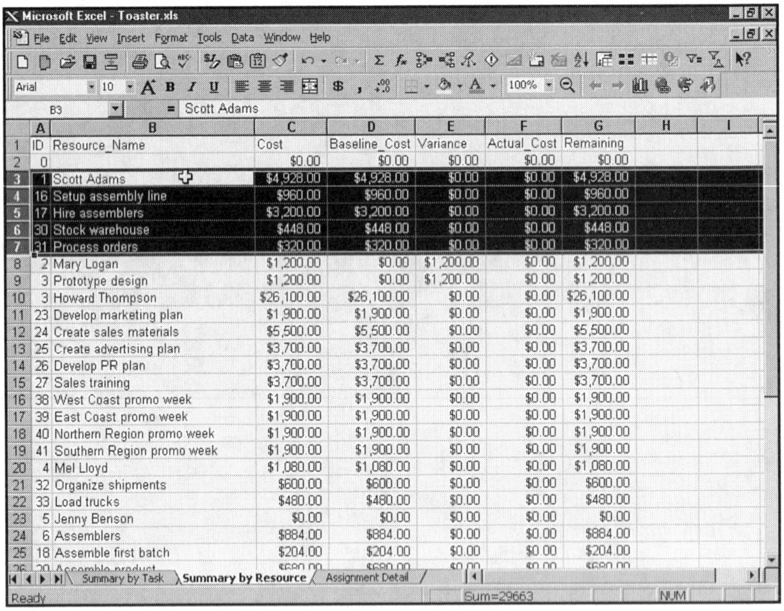

	A	B	C	D	E	F	G
1	ID	Resource_Name	Cost	Baseline_Cost	Variance	Actual_Cost	Remaining
2	0		$0.00	$0.00	$0.00	$0.00	$0.00
3	1	Scott Adams	$4,928.00	$4,928.00	$0.00	$0.00	$4,928.00
4	16	Setup assembly line	$960.00	$960.00	$0.00	$0.00	$960.00
5	17	Hire assemblers	$3,200.00	$3,200.00	$0.00	$0.00	$3,200.00
6	30	Stock warehouse	$448.00	$448.00	$0.00	$0.00	$448.00
7	31	Process orders	$320.00	$320.00	$0.00	$0.00	$320.00
8	2	Mary Logan	$1,200.00	$0.00	$1,200.00	$0.00	$1,200.00
9	3	Prototype design	$1,200.00	$0.00	$1,200.00	$0.00	$1,200.00
10	3	Howard Thompson	$26,100.00	$26,100.00	$0.00	$0.00	$26,100.00
11	23	Develop marketing plan	$1,900.00	$1,900.00	$0.00	$0.00	$1,900.00
12	24	Create sales materials	$5,500.00	$5,500.00	$0.00	$0.00	$5,500.00
13	25	Create advertising plan	$3,700.00	$3,700.00	$0.00	$0.00	$3,700.00
14	26	Develop PR plan	$3,700.00	$3,700.00	$0.00	$0.00	$3,700.00
15	27	Sales training	$3,700.00	$3,700.00	$0.00	$0.00	$3,700.00
16	38	West Coast promo week	$1,900.00	$1,900.00	$0.00	$0.00	$1,900.00
17	39	East Coast promo week	$1,900.00	$1,900.00	$0.00	$0.00	$1,900.00
18	40	Northern Region promo week	$1,900.00	$1,900.00	$0.00	$0.00	$1,900.00
19	41	Southern Region promo week	$1,900.00	$1,900.00	$0.00	$0.00	$1,900.00
20	4	Mel Lloyd	$1,080.00	$1,080.00	$0.00	$0.00	$1,080.00
21	32	Organize shipments	$600.00	$600.00	$0.00	$0.00	$600.00
22	33	Load trucks	$480.00	$480.00	$0.00	$0.00	$480.00
23	5	Jenny Benson	$0.00	$0.00	$0.00	$0.00	$0.00
24	6	Assemblers	$884.00	$884.00	$0.00	$0.00	$884.00
25	18	Assemble first batch	$204.00	$204.00	$0.00	$0.00	$204.00
26	20	Assemble product	$680.00	$680.00	$0.00	$0.00	$680.00

Exporting to an Excel PivotTable One of the most convenient export options for analyzing the data in your project is the ability to export data directly into an Excel PivotTable. PivotTables quickly summarize data in cross-tab calculations, and they offer truly impressive flexibility for easily changing which calculations will be presented and in what level of detail.

For example, we will export task and resource assignment records to an Excel PivotTable. Each record will contain the name of a task (and the name of its summary task—the phase of the project), the name of a resource assigned to the task, and the scheduled cost of the assignment. The resulting PivotTable (see Figure 19.24) easily displays this data in a compact table that neatly summarizes the following items:

- The total cost for any phase of the project along with the distribution of that cost among contributing resources in dollar amounts and in percentage terms.
- The distribution for each resource of work and cost among the phases of the project

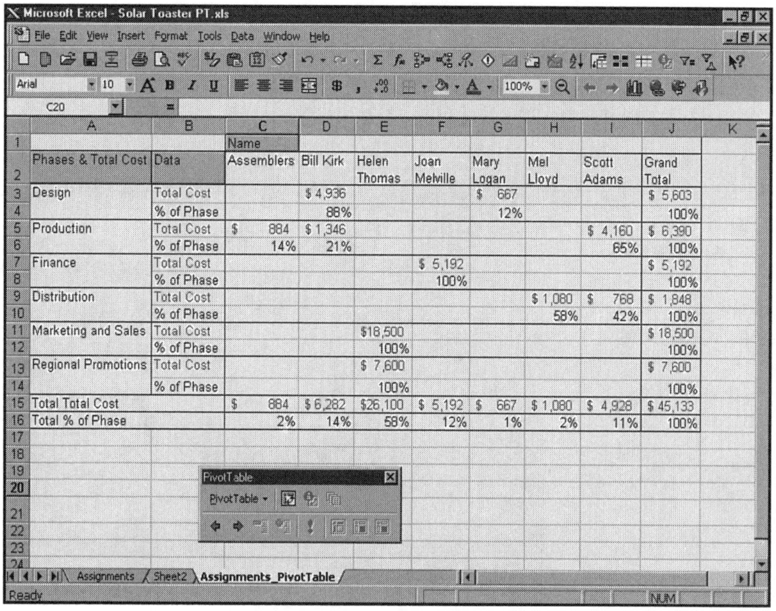

FIG. 19.24

Reading across the PivotTable, you see which resources worked on each phase and the percentage of distribution of costs among resources for that phase. Reading down, you see which phases on which a given resource worked.

The row headings of the PivotTable are the task's summary task name values. The column headings are the resource names. The table data (the numbers in the body of the table) are calculated by Excel by summing the cost amount from all assignment records that have the same combination of summary task name and resource name. This is called *cross-tabbing* the data.

Creating a PivotTable such as this involves exporting the data and then fine-tuning the PivotTable in Excel to produce the results you want.

To export Project data to an Excel PivotTable, follow these steps:

1. Open the Project file from which you want to export data.

2. Choose File, Save As.

3. Select the location for the new Excel file in the Save In list box, and provide a name for the file in the File Name text box.

4. Choose the file type Microsoft Excel Pivot Table (.XLS) in the Save as Type list box. Note that this Project menu choice spells Pivot Table as two words, while Excel spells PivotTable as one word. The Excel spelling is used in this presentation.

5. Choose the Save button.

6. In the Export Format dialog box, choose New Map to display the Define Import/Export Map dialog box.

7. Provide a name for the map in the Import/Export Map Name text box.

8. Select one or more of the data category check boxes in the Data to Import/Export group: Tasks, Resource, and Assignments.

You can only use one category for each PivotTable. If you export fields from all three categories, you will produce three separate, unrelated PivotTables in the same Excel file. In Figure 19.25 the Assignment fields will be exported to create a Cost PivotTable similar to the one illustrated in Figure 19.24.

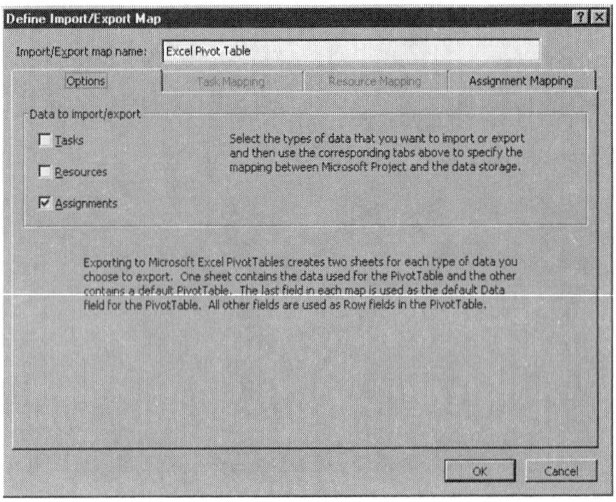

FIG. 19.25

You can include tasks, resources, and assignments when exporting to a PivotTable, but each category will be a separate PivotTable in the resulting Excel workbook.

9. Click the tab for the first data category you have selected.

10. Provide a name for the worksheet in the Destination Worksheet Name text box (see Figure 19.26).

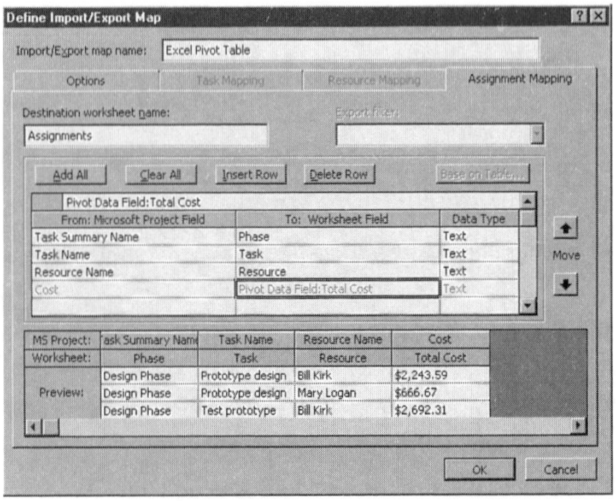

FIG. 19.26

The last field in the mapping table will appear in red with the prefix "Pivot Data Field" to remind you that this field will be the calculated body of the PivotTable.

11. Enter the names of the Project fields you want to export in the From: Microsoft Project Field column. When you enter a Project field name, Project will supply the field name for the worksheet in the To Worksheet Field column.

The last field entered in the mapping table will be the field that Excel uses for the table data (the calculated numbers in the body of the PivotTable). To remind you of this, Project displays the last field row in red, and adds the prefix Pivot Data Field: before the export field name. If you edit the export field name, Project will replace the prefix as long as it is the last field name row.

N O T E Even though a map may be designed for exporting to a PivotTable, if you start the Save As command by choosing any format other than Microsoft Excel PivotTable, then the map will not display the last field in red and will generate a regular spreadsheet instead of a PivotTable. ▨

T I P If you plan to group the data in the PivotTable by major categories with minor category details listed under them, put the major category fields above the minor category fields in the field mapping. In this example, Task Summary Names will be called Phase and will summarize the task details under each summary group.

Always make the field you want to be used for calculations the last field in the field mapping list. In this example, Cost will be called Total Cost and is the last field listed.

12. When the field map is completed, repeat the process for any other data category tab you have chosen to use in the export.

13. Choose OK to save the import/export map.

14. Choose the Save button on the Export Format dialog box to begin saving the exported data into Excel.

Now, you can open Excel and look at the PivotTable. Be prepared to see something that you will probably think is a mistake. Just a little tinkering will fix it up in a hurry.

You will see two worksheet tabs for each data category you exported (see Figure 19.27). The first sheet contains the raw data you exported in a table. The second sheet contains the default PivotTable. You will need to fine tune the PivotTable in almost all cases. Not only will you need to format things like column widths and the display of numbers; you will also need to adjust the layout of the PivotTable. Specifically, there are no column categories, and we want the Resource names to appear as column headings. Fortunately, Excel makes this *very* easy.

1. First, click the PivotTable Wizard on the PivotTable toolbar that floats over the worksheet. This will activate the PivotTable Wizard dialog box (see Figure 19.28), which you can use to redefine the layout of the PivotTable.

Notice that all the fields you exported are represented by small bars on the right side of the dialog box; all but the last of these has been copied into the Row section of the layout model. The Total Cost field is in the Data section. We need to move the Resource bar from the Row section into the Column section. Then the Resources will be listed across the column headings of the table.

Part
VI

Ch
19

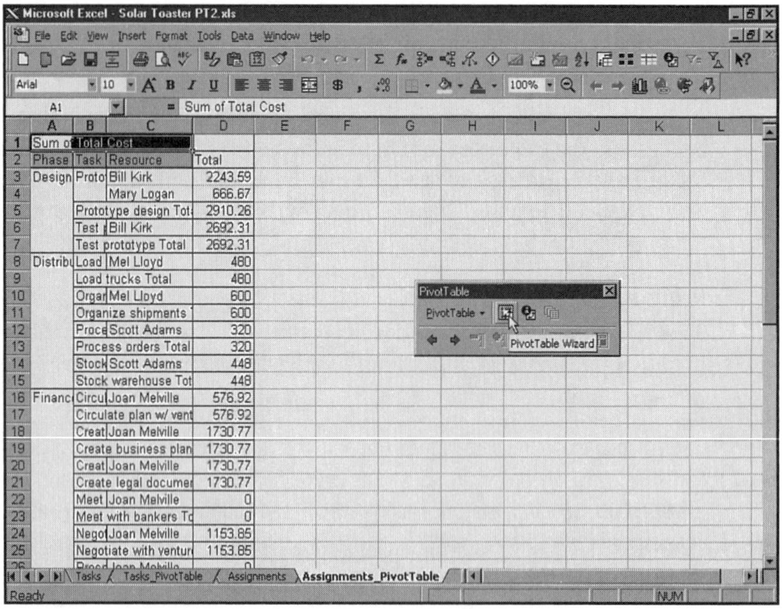

FIG. 19.27

The default PivotTable usually looks like a mess. But just a little touching up produces impressive results.

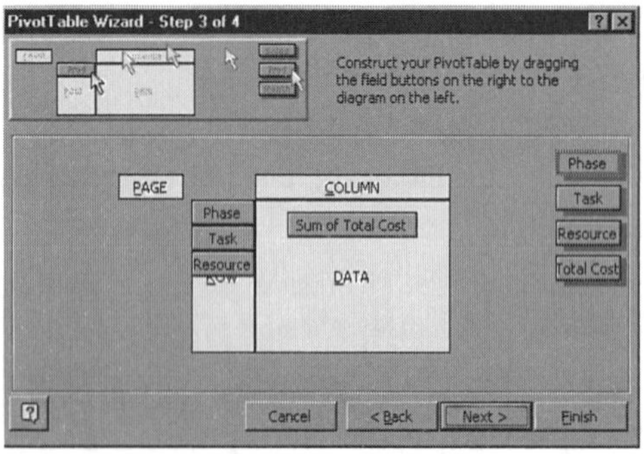

FIG. 19.28

All the fields you exported are in the Row section of the PivotTable layout, except for the last field in your list (Total Cost in this case) which is placed in the Data section as a summary calculation.

2. Use the mouse to drag the Resource bar from the Row section to the Column section (see Figure 19.29). Although there are many options you can use in the PivotTable Wizard, we can't begin to cover them in this book. Get Que's *Special Edition Using Microsoft Excel 97, Bestseller Edition* for very helpful and thorough coverage of PivotTable options.

3. Click the Finish button to return to the PivotTable worksheet (see Figure 19.30). The Resource names are now column headings and the Cost amounts in the body of the table are summarized by task and resource name combinations.

   I have widened the first two columns so you can read the Phase and Task text. The only other change we will make in this example, out of the many that could be made, is to hide all the task details and show just the summary costs for the project phases.

FIG. 19.29

You simply drag a field bar into the section of the PivotTable where you want that field's data to be displayed. If you drag it into the Data section, the field's data will be used for the calculation in the table. If you drag it into the Column section, the field's data will appear as column headings in the PivotTable.

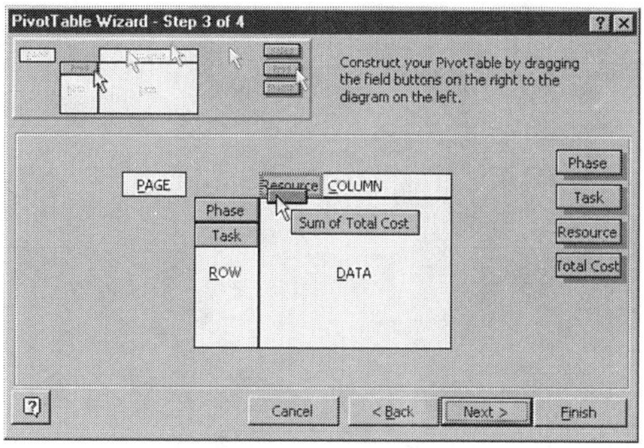

FIG. 19.30

Now the resource names are column headings and the amounts are costs summarized by resource and task.

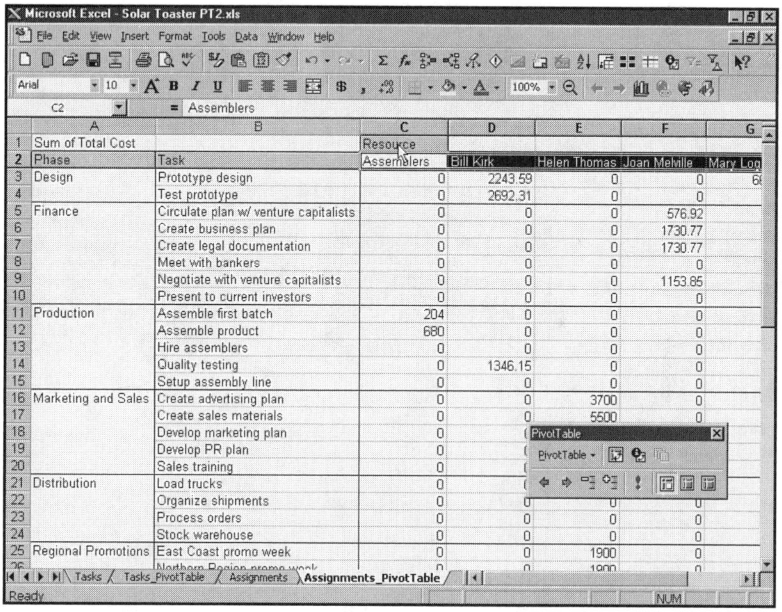

	A	B	C	D	E	F	G
1	Sum of Total Cost		Resource				
2	Phase	Task	Assemblers	Bill Kirk	Helen Thomas	Joan Melville	Mary Log
3	Design	Prototype design	0	2243.59	0	0	66
4		Test prototype	0	2692.31	0	0	
5	Finance	Circulate plan w/ venture capitalists	0	0	0	576.92	
6		Create business plan	0	0	0	1730.77	
7		Create legal documentation	0	0	0	1730.77	
8		Meet with bankers	0	0	0	0	
9		Negotiate with venture capitalists	0	0	0	1153.85	
10		Present to current investors	0	0	0	0	
11	Production	Assemble first batch	204	0	0	0	
12		Assemble product	680	0	0	0	
13		Hire assemblers	0	0	0	0	
14		Quality testing	0	1346.15	0	0	
15		Setup assembly line	0	0	0	0	
16	Marketing and Sales	Create advertising plan	0	0	3700	0	
17		Create sales materials	0	0	5500	0	
18		Develop marketing plan	0			0	
19		Develop PR plan	0			0	
20		Sales training	0			0	
21	Distribution	Load trucks	0		0	0	
22		Organize shipments	0	0	0	0	
23		Process orders	0	0	0	0	
24		Stock warehouse	0	0	0	0	
25	Regional Promotions	East Coast promo week	0	0	1900	0	
		Northern Region promo week	0	0	1000	0	

4. To hide the task detail, click the Phase column heading to select the Phase field and click the Hide Detail button on the PivotTable toolbar (see Figure 19.31).

The PivotTable in Figure 19.32 shows the Task rows hidden. You could display the detail again by selecting the Phase column and clicking the Show Detail button on the PivotTable toolbar. This figure also shows a few minor formatting changes (zero values are suppressed, decimals are removed, and so forth) just to improve the display. Your final step would be to enhance the PivotTable by adding other PivotTable features, or by using Excel's formatting features to create the look that you want to print.

Part
VI

Ch
19

FIG. 19.31

If there are multiple row fields, click one on the left and use the Hide Detail button to hide the fields to its right. Use the Show Detail button to display the hidden rows.

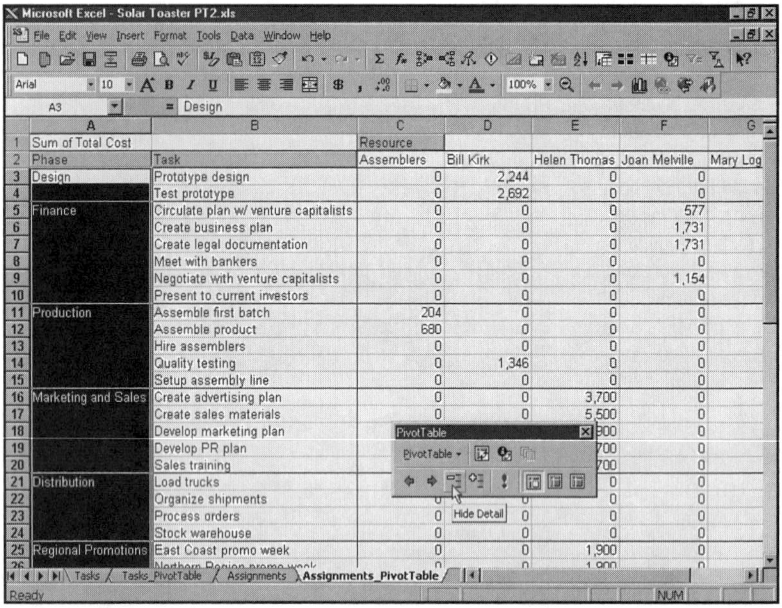

FIG. 19.32

With task details suppressed, and a few other formatting changes, the PivotTable is presentable. With a relatively small effort, you can export Project data to Excel PivotTables for a powerful reporting tool.

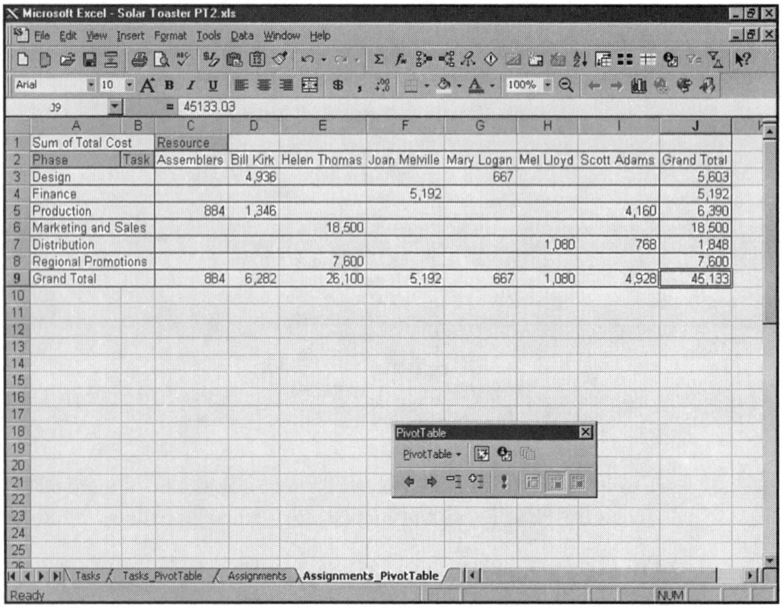

TIP When there are many zero values in the PivotTable, your audience will be able to better focus on the numbers if you suppress the display of zero values. To suppress zeros, use Excel's Tools menu, select Options, use the View tab, and clear the check box next to the Zero Values option.

Importing Project Data from the Excel Format Importing data from original sources outside Microsoft Project into a Project document has to be done with extreme care. You will have to be sure that the data is mapped to the correct Project fields and that the data type is appropriate for those fields.

> **CAUTION**
>
> As explained earlier, if the Excel workbook was created by exporting tasks or resources from Microsoft Project, and if the option to include rows for resource assignments was selected, then some of the rows in the workbook will be tasks (or resources) and others will be assignment details. Do not attempt to import data from a workbook like this. Identify and remove the assignment details before attempting to import the data back into Project.

The simple example that follows shows how to add a list of new employees to the resource roster in a Project file. The list is stored in Sheet 1 of an Excel worksheet. The names are to be added to the Resource data in the Solar Toaster project file where a new product development is being planned. The column headings are not exact matches for Project field names, and there are text entries in the overtime rate field where Project expects to find only numbers. Table 19.3 shows the data from the worksheet.

Table 19.3 New Employees to Be Added to Project

Employee	Hourly	Overtime
John Marshall	15.00	22.50
Mary Weaver	45.00	67.50
Allen Rickert	35.00	N/A
Molly Andrews	25.00	37.50
Alice Benson	10.00	15.00
Willis Kirk	30.00	45.00
Melville White	20.00	N/A
Ardo Muni	18.00	27.00
Lisa Mularky	20.00	30.00

To import the data from Excel into the Project file, use these steps:

1. Open the Project file into which you want to import the data, unless you plan to have Project create a new document file for the imported data. Figure 19.33 shows the Project Resource Sheet before the import.

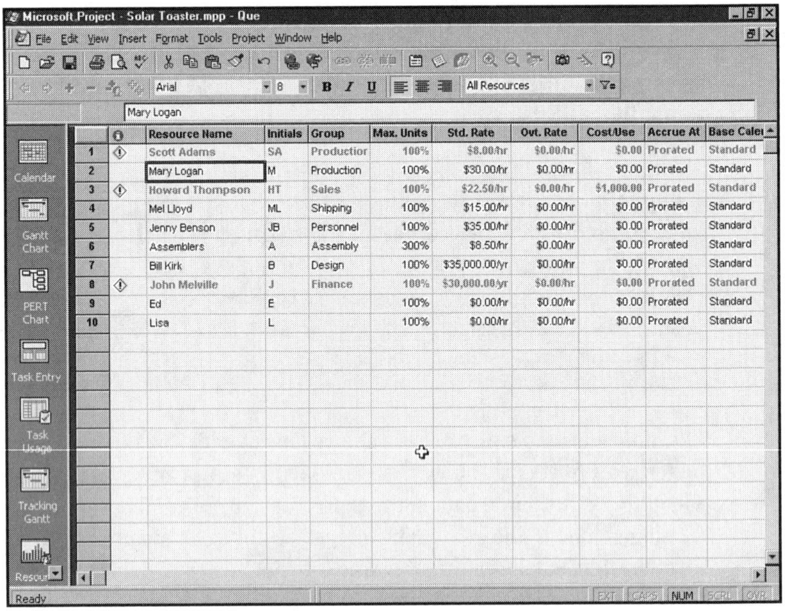

FIG. 19.33

The current resource roster in the Solar Toaster Project file contains 10 names.

2. Although not necessary, choose a view in Project that will show the data when it is imported. This is especially helpful if you're not sure what Project field names to use for some of the imported data. For example, in the Resource Sheet the employee's name should go in the column labeled Resource Name, but the actual name of that field is just Name. Similarly, the real field name for the Std. Rate and Ovt. Rate columns are Standard Rate and Overtime Rate. You must know these field names when you map the imported data.

TIP If you don't know the Project field names you need to use, display a table in Project that includes the field and then look at the definition for the field. To see the field definition, double-click the column heading for the field to display the Column Definition dialog box. Figure 19.34 shows the column definition for the column labeled Resource Name. Resource Name is the Title for the column, but the Field Name is the Name. Choose Cancel to close the dialog box without changing the column definition.

3. Choose File, Open to display the File Open dialog box.
4. Use the Look In list box to select the location in which the Excel workbook is saved.
5. Change the Files of Type selection to Microsoft Excel Workbooks.
6. Select the Excel file from the file list and choose the Open button.
7. Choose the New Map button in the Import Format dialog box to display the Define Import/Export Map dialog box.

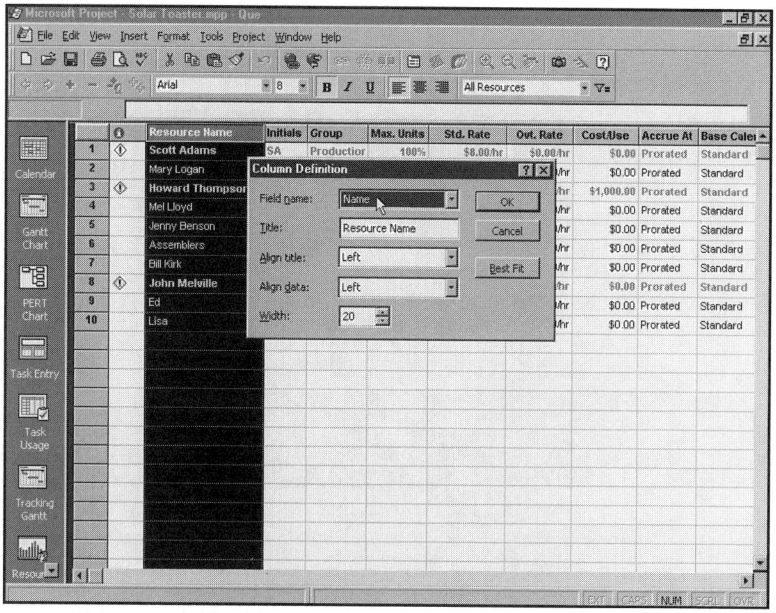

FIG. 19.34

The column definition for the Resource Name column shows that the name of the field is Name. Be sure to click Cancel to avoid changing the column definition.

8. On the Options tab select the check boxes for the type of data you are importing. In this example, we are importing only Resource data.

   Also, be sure there is a check mark in the box labeled Export Header Row/Import Includes Headers (see Figure 19.35). Note that the option to import assignment detail rows is not available. Project has no way of knowing which rows are tasks (or resources) and which are assignment details.

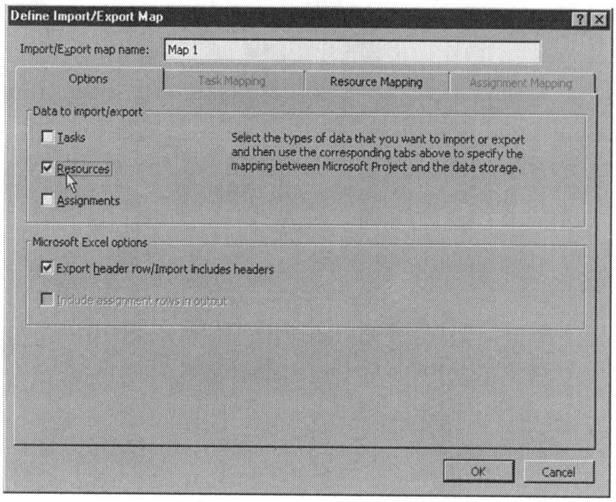

FIG. 19.35

You will need the headers to be imported to help you match the imported data with Project fields.

Part

VI

Ch

19

9. Choose the tab for the data types you are importing. In this example, the Resource Mapping tab is selected (see Figure 19.36).

FIG. 19.36

You must select which sheet in the workbook contains the data you want to import.

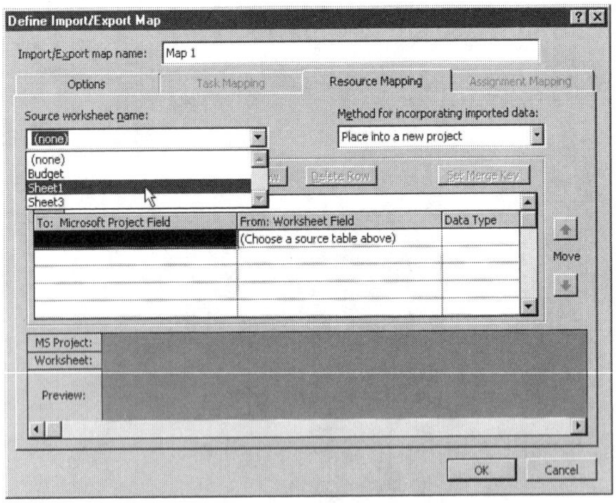

10. Use the list arrow in the Source Worksheet Name list box and select the worksheet you want to use. In this case, we will use Sheet 1.

When the source worksheet is selected, Project fills the From column in the center of the mapping table with the column headings from the worksheet, and attempts to find a matching field name from Project in the left-hand column. You can see in Figure 19.37 that Project was not able to find a close match for the first two fields, and found an incorrect match for the third field.

FIG. 19.37

Project is not able to match the worksheet column headings with Project field names unless the worksheet contains exact matches for Project's field names.

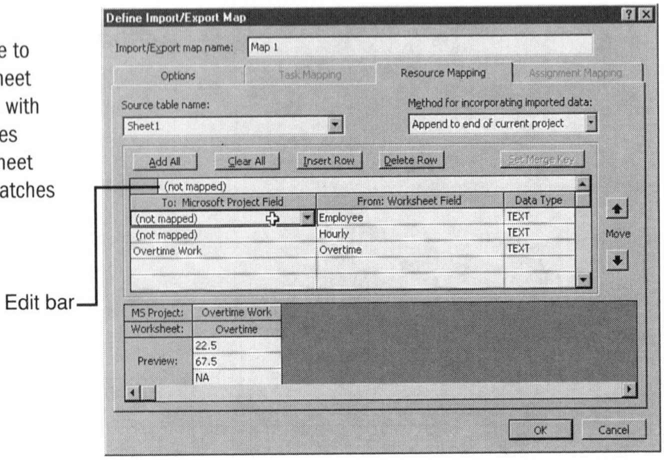

11. Supply the correct field names in the first column of the mapping table. You can type the field name into the Edit bar just above the table, or you can use the in-place arrow control to display the list of all Project field names and select the correct one from the list.

12. Select the appropriate method for importing the data in the list box labeled Method for Incorporating Imported Data. In this example, the imported data will be appended to the bottom of the existing resource sheet.

13. Choose OK to save the import map.

14. Choose the Open button in the Import Format dialog box to begin the import.

15. If there is a problem with the data types being imported into any field, you will see a warning message like that displayed in Figure 19.38.

- Choose Yes to continue importing and to continue seeing error messages. You should generally choose this option unless you know what the problems are and what corrective action you will need to take in the Project document as a result.

- Choose No to continue importing without seeing further error messages.

- Choose Cancel to stop importing.

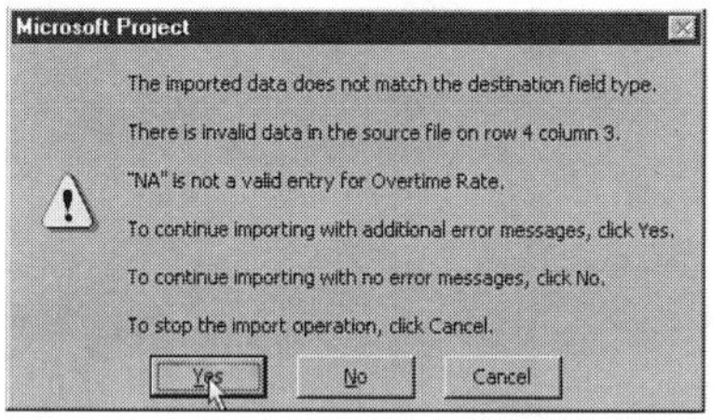

FIG. 19.38

If there is a data mismatch during importing, Project will warn you and let you choose how to proceed.

Part VI

Ch 19

CAUTION

The mismatched data will not be imported into Project, and the affected field in Project will display a default value. You will need to find these holes in the data and manually supply the correct information.

It's a good idea to jot down the source references in the warning message (see Figure 19.38). If you are importing a lot of data at once, the references will help you locate the problem in the source file so you can determine where you need to look in the Project file to fill in the missing information.

16. Review any data type mismatches and correct the entries in the Project file.

In the example here, the problems resulted from the NA text entries in the Overtime Rate column. The imported resource names were added below the existing names in the roster (see Figure 19.39) and Project set the Overtime Rate values for the problem values to zero.

FIG. 19.39
The imported names
are appended to the
bottom of the resource
roster.

			Resource Name	Initials	Group	Max. Units	Std. Rate	Ovt. Rate	Cost/Use	Accrue At	Base Calen
	1	◇	Scott Adams	SA	Production	100%	$8.00/hr	$0.00/hr	$0.00	Prorated	Standard
	2		Mary Logan	M	Production	100%	$30.00/hr	$0.00/hr	$0.00	Prorated	Standard
	3	◇	Howard Thompson	HT	Sales	100%	$22.50/hr	$0.00/hr	$1,000.00	Prorated	Standard
	4		Mel Lloyd	ML	Shipping	100%	$15.00/hr	$0.00/hr	$0.00	Prorated	Standard
	5		Jenny Benson	JB	Personnel	100%	$35.00/hr	$0.00/hr	$0.00	Prorated	Standard
	6		Assemblers	A	Assembly	300%	$8.50/hr	$0.00/hr	$0.00	Prorated	Standard
	7		Bill Kirk	B	Design	100%	$35,000.00/yr	$0.00/hr	$0.00	Prorated	Standard
	8	◇	John Melville	J	Finance	100%	$30,000.00/yr	$0.00/hr	$0.00	Prorated	Standard
	9		Ed	E		100%	$0.00/hr	$0.00/hr	$0.00	Prorated	Standard
	10		Lisa	L		100%	$0.00/hr	$0.00/hr	$0.00	Prorated	Standard
	11		John Marshall	J		100%	$15.00/hr	$22.50/hr	$0.00	Prorated	Standard
	12		Mary Weaver			100%	$45.00/hr	$67.50/hr	$0.00	Prorated	Standard
	13		Allen Rickert			100%	$35.00/hr	$0.00/hr	$0.00	Prorated	Standard
	14		Molly Andrews			100%	$25.00/hr	$37.50/hr	$0.00	Prorated	Standard
	15		Alice Benson			100%	$10.00/hr	$15.00/hr	$0.00	Prorated	Standard
	16		Willis Kirk			100%	$30.00/hr	$45.00/hr	$0.00	Prorated	Standard
	17		Melville White			100%	$20.00/hr	$0.00/hr	$0.00	Prorated	Standard
	18		Ardo Muni			100%	$18.00/hr	$27.00/hr	$0.00	Prorated	Standard
	19		Lisa Mularky			105%	$20.00/hr	$30.00/hr	$0.00	Prorated	Standard

CAUTION

When importing task Start or Finish dates, Project treats the imported dates as though you had typed them instead of letting Project calculate them. In other words, the tasks are assigned the soft constraint Start No Earlier Than (for fixed start date projects) or Finish No Later Than (for fixed finish date projects). You can reset these task restraints to As Soon As Possible or As Late As Possible once the tasks are imported into Project.

Exporting Project Data to the Internet or an Intranet

You can create pages for your intranet or the Internet by exporting Project data to the HTM format. The HTML (Hypertext Markup Language) is currently the standard format for Internet browsers. You can save Project data to the HTML format, but you cannot import Project data from the HTML format.

If you want to include graphic images of views like the Gantt Chart or the PERT Chart, you must first create the graphic file (GIF format) and then include the GIF file in the HTML format.

In this example, we will save a summary of the phases in the project to publish on the intranet. The HTML file will include a picture of the Gantt Chart. First, you must save the graphic image. Then, you can export the data to an HTML format file.

 To create a "browser-ready" graphic image of a view in Microsoft Project, you must display the view on the screen just as you want it to appear in the graphic image. Then you use the Copy Picture button on the Standard toolbar to create the graphic file. If you want to include only selected rows from a view with a table, you must select the rows before you select the Copy Picture button.

To save a graphic image of a view, follow these steps:

1. Prepare the view you want to capture. Apply any filters or special formatting you want to use. For this example, a new table was applied to the Gantt Chart that omits the ID and Indicator columns.

2. If only part of the rows in a table view are to be included, select those rows now.

 3. Click the Copy Picture button. The Copy Picture dialog box is displayed (see Figure 19.40).

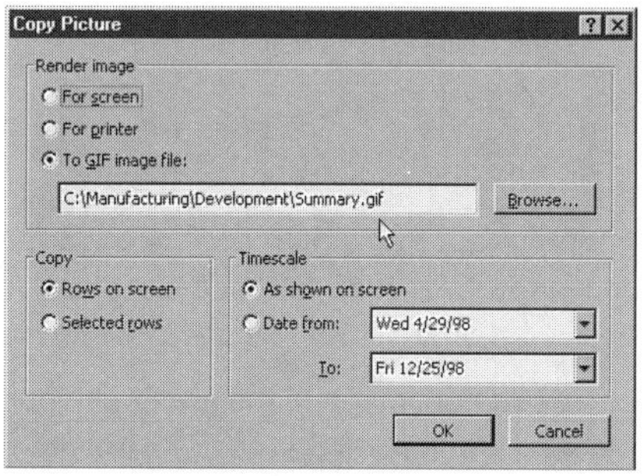

FIG. 19.40

The Copy Picture command now includes GIF images for Internet browser views.

4. In the Render Image group, select To GIF Image File.

5. Supply the path and file name for the GIF file in the text box. You should generally save the picture file in the same directory you plan to save the HTML format file that displays it.

6. In the Copy group, select Rows On Screen if you want the picture to include all the rows displayed on the current screen. This will not include all rows in the project unless they are on the screen when the picture is taken.

   Choose Selected Rows if you want the picture to include only the rows you have selected.

7. In the Timescale group, select As Shown On Screen if you want the picture to include exactly the date range displayed on the current screen.

   Select Date From and fill in the Date From and To boxes if you want to specify the date range to include.

8. Click OK to save the picture file.

Part

VI

Ch

19

Once the graphic image is ready, you can save the HTML format file. To create the HTML file for part of the project data, use these steps:

1. Open the project you want to export if it is not already open.

2. Choose File, Save As HTML to display the File Save dialog box.

   This new command is a shortcut for choosing File, Save As, and then selecting HTML document (*.HTM) in the Save as Type list box.

3. Select the location in which you want to save the Web page file in the Save In list box.

4. Supply the name you want to use for the export file in the File Name text box.

5. Choose the Save button. The Export Format dialog box will be displayed.

6. Choose the New Map button.

7. The Delete Import/Export Map dialog box has four special HTML options (see Figure 19.41).

   - If you want the column headings you choose to be exported, fill the check box labeled Export Header Row.

   - If you want assignment details to be included with tasks or resources, fill the check box labeled Include Assignment Rows in Output.

   - If you want to use an HTML template for the layout of the page, fill the check box labeled Base Export on HTML Template and select the template file in the text box to the right.

   - If you want to select a graphic image to include in the page, fill the Include Image File in HTML Page check box and provide the path and file name for the image file in the text box to the right.

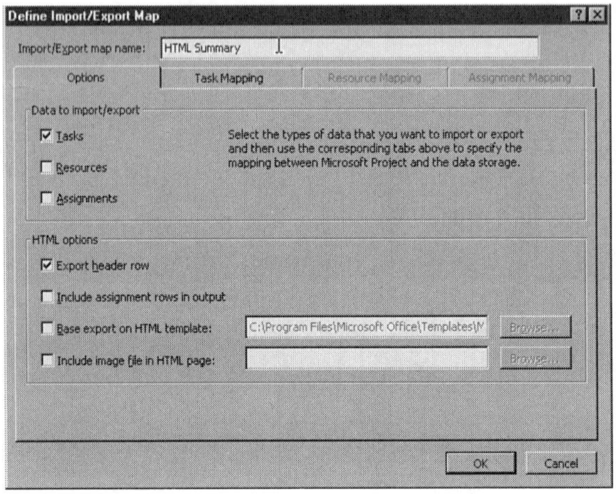

FIG. 19.41

The Define Import/ Export Map dialog box has special options for the HTML format.

8. Select the Tasks, Resources, or Assignments check boxes as appropriate and fill out the tabs for each data group you selected. In this example, only the Task Mapping tab needs to be filled in (see Figure 19.42).

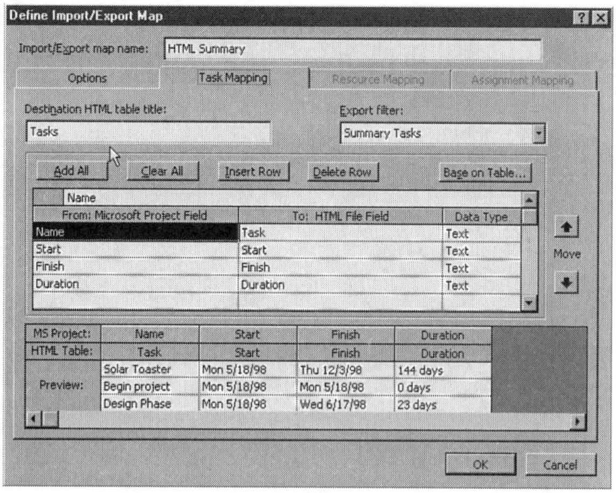

FIG. 19.42

This export table will include only Summary tasks (because of the filter) and a limited set of fields.

9. As with other exporting operations, save the map by choosing the OK button and save the export data by choosing the Save button.

10. Use your browser to view the page you created (see Figure 19.43). From the browser menu choose File, Open and select the browser page you just saved. Or, you can use the Explorer to find the file and double-click it to open it. The association for the HTM extension should already be defined and the file will be opened in your browser.

TROUBLESHOOTING

I included an image file in my HTML export, but it's not displayed when I view the HTML file with my browser. If you move the HTML file to a new location, be sure to move all the image files also or they will not display when you view the page in the new location.

Working with Text File Formats

Project supports two ASCII text formats: tab-delimited and CSV (comma-separated value). The import/export maps for both these formats are almost the same as the import/export maps for Excel. However, you can import or export with all three of Project's data field tables at once in Excel (Tasks, Resources, and Assignments); but you can only import or export one Project table at a time with the text formats.

Part
VI

Ch
19

FIG. 19.43

The basic browser page shows the fields you exported in a table format.

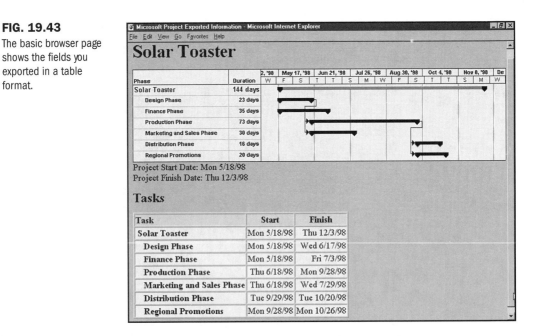

Exporting Project Data in the Text Formats Suppose you want to export a list of project milestones to a text file. You would follow these steps:

1. Open the project file you want to export from.

2. Choose File, Save As.

3. Select the directory for the new text file in the Save In list box.

4. Select the file format in the Save as Type list box. For a tab-delimited file select Text (Tab delimited, *.TXT). This format places tab characters between each field of data in a record (with quote marks surrounding field values that contain commas), and separates the records with a paragraph mark (carriage return and line feed).

   For a comma-delimited file select CSV (Comma delimited, *.CSV). This format places commas between each field of data in a record (with quote marks surrounding field values that themselves contain commas), and separates the records with a paragraph mark (carriage return and line feed).

5. In the Export Format dialog box choose New Map if you do not have a map for this purpose.

6. The Define Import/Export Map dialog box has radio buttons instead of check boxes for selecting the data (Task, Resource, or Assignment) to export or import. The Milestones map in Figure 19.44 shows the Tasks data selected. The Task Mapping tab was used to define the fields to exchange. Otherwise, the text map is used just like an Excel map.

FIG. 19.44

The Define Import/
Export Map dialog box
allows you to work with
only one table at a time.

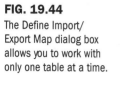

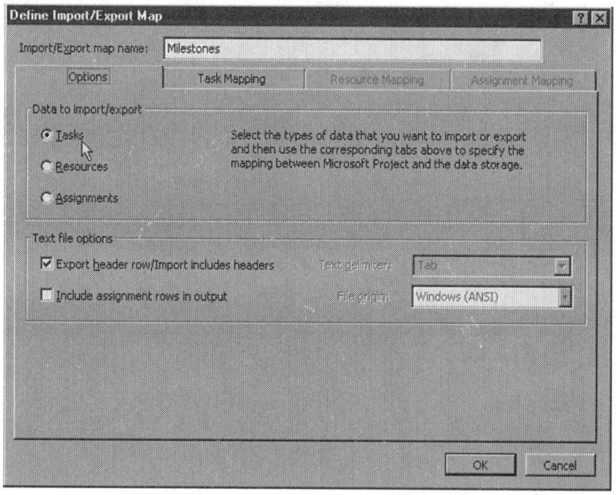

7. When the map is complete, choose OK to save the map.

8. Choose the Save button on the Export Format dialog box to create the file.

Importing Project Data from the Text Formats Importing from a text file is similar to importing from an Excel workbook, except that you can only import one type of data at a time—Tasks, Resources, or Assignments. (See the previous section "Importing Project Data from the Excel Format.") The same problems in matching field names are likely to occur with text files that are found with Excel formats when the import source file was not originally exported from Project.

Copying Selected Data Between Applications

If you do not need to transfer all the information in a file (for example, you need just one or a few values from the source document), you can use the Windows Clipboard to copy and paste the data from one document (the source) to the other (the destination). You can choose to simply paste a copy of the values, or you can paste a permanent link that displays the current value from the source document but also can be updated on demand to display new values if the source document is changed (see Figure 19.45).

When pasting Clipboard data into a Project document, it is very important that you select the correct field(s) to receive the data (see Figure 19.46). With importing files, the import/export map defines where the field data is pasted. But with the copy/paste procedure, it all depends on where you click the mouse when you use the paste command.

If you are pasting a single value, it's easy to select a recipient field that is appropriate for the value you are copying. If you are copying a block of two or more values, however, you will have to have a Table view in Project that has the appropriate columns next to each other to receive the block of copied values.

Part
VI

Ch
19

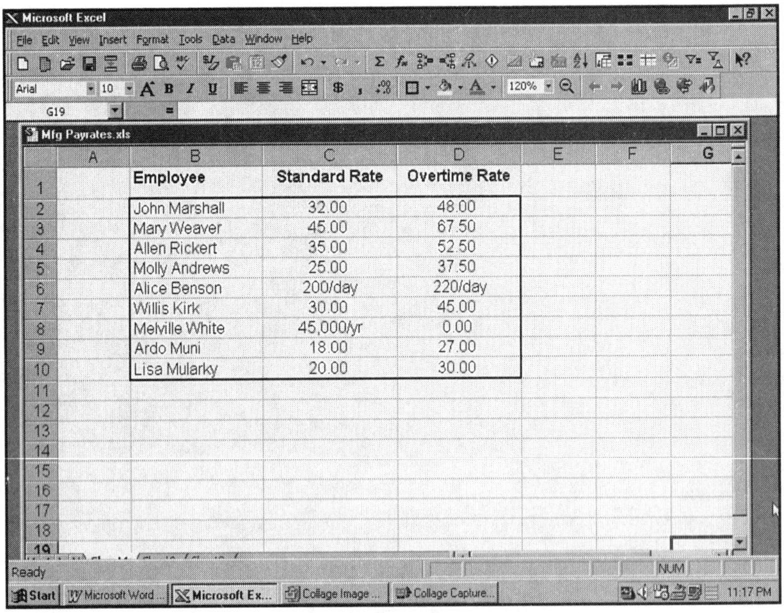

FIG. 19.45

If you paste the resource names and cost rates in this table to the Project Resource Sheet...

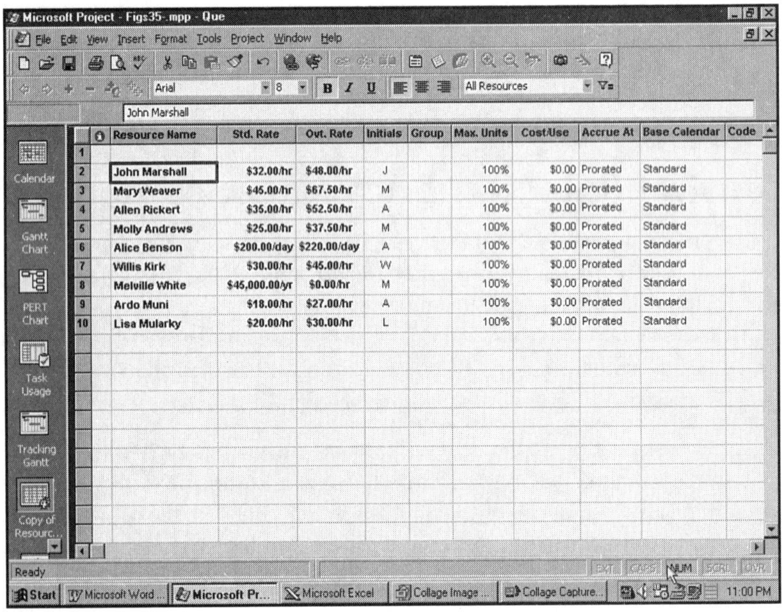

FIG. 19.46

...in Project the Standard Rate and Overtime Rate columns must be moved next to the Resource Name column, or the cost values would be pasted in the wrong columns.

Frequently, this will mean that you must define a special table in Project to display the data field columns in the same order as the data that you are copying. When you paste the data into Project, the special table must be displayed in the Current view.

Furthermore, you must be sure that the cell you select before executing the Paste command is the cell that should receive the upper-left cell of the pasted block. The cell containing John Marshall was selected before pasting.

Copying Data from Other Applications

To copy data to Microsoft Project from another application, follow these steps:

1. Select the source data. You may select a single value or several values. If you select several values, be sure that the order of the values matches the order of the values in the Microsoft Project table that will serve as the destination.

 2. Place the data in the Clipboard by choosing Edit, Copy or by pressing Ctrl+C.

3. Move to Microsoft Project and select a view with a table containing columns in the same order as the data you are copying.

T I P Do not close the other application if more data is to be moved. Use Alt+Tab to switch between Project and the other open application.

4. Select the task or resource row and the first field in the table that is to receive the data. If you select blank rows, Microsoft Project creates new tasks or resources with the data you copy. If you select rows that already contain data, Project replaces the existing data with the newly copied data.

N O T E If you overwrite an existing resource, you are simply changing field values for that resource. Any tasks assigned to that resource are still assigned to it—even though the resource name may have been changed.

 5. Choose Edit, Paste (or press Ctrl+V).

Paste places a static copy of the current value from the source document in the field that you selected. Microsoft Project cannot update this value if the value in the source document is changed (unless you execute another copy and paste).

If you selected a field that does not support the data type you are importing, you will see a Pasting Error message like the one illustrated in Figure 19.47. Choose one of the option buttons:

FIG. 19.47
The Pasting Error message gives you clues about the type of data mismatch that has occurred.

Part
VI

Ch
19

- If you want to continue pasting and continue receiving error messages, choose <u>Y</u>es. The mismatched value will be pasted into the cell and Project will attempt to make sense of it.

- If you want to continue pasting but without having to deal with any more error messages, choose <u>N</u>o.

- If you want to stop the pasting operation, choose Cancel. Note that you were pasting a block of values and several have already been pasted. They will remain in the Project document but no more will be added.

> **CAUTION**
>
> Note that pasting dates into the Start or Finish fields for tasks creates Start No Earlier Than Constraints for those tasks. You can adjust the constraint definition on the Advanced tab of the Task Information dialog box.

▶ **See** "Resolving Conflicts Caused by Constraints," **p. 208**

Copying Microsoft Project Data into Other Applications

To copy data from Microsoft Project to another application, follow these steps:

1. Place a view on-screen with a table that displays the data you want to copy to the other application.
2. Select the source data. You can select a single value, several adjacent values, or whole task rows or resource rows.

3. Place the data in the Clipboard by choosing <u>E</u>dit, <u>C</u>opy or by pressing Ctrl+C.
4. Move to the other application and select where you want to place the data.
5. Choose <u>E</u>dit, <u>P</u>aste.

Paste places a static copy of the current value from the project file. This value is not updated if the value in the project is changed.

Linking Selected Data Between Applications

The copy operations described in the preceding section produce static copies; once the copy of the data has been pasted it doesn't change as the original data changes. You can also paste a value from another application that is a *linked reference* to the data location in the source document. The linked reference can be updated to reflect changes in the value stored in the source document.

Use <u>E</u>dit, <u>C</u>opy in the source document and use the equivalent of the Paste <u>L</u>ink command in the target document to create the dynamic link.

Linking Microsoft Project Data Fields to Other Sources

To link Microsoft Project field values to values stored in other sources:

1. Select the source data, for example, a cell or range of cells in an Excel worksheet. You can select a single value or several values. If you select several values, be sure that the order of the values matches the order of the values in the table that you view when you paste the values into Microsoft Project.

2. Place the data in the Clipboard by choosing <u>E</u>dit, <u>C</u>opy or by pressing Ctrl+C.

3. Move to Microsoft Project and select a Sheet view and a table with the columns arranged to match the order of the data that you are copying.

4. Select the task or resource row in the table to receive the data. If you select blank rows, Microsoft Project creates new tasks or resources with the data that you are copying into the file. If you select rows in which data already exists, Microsoft Project replaces the existing data with the data being copied.

5. Choose <u>E</u>dit, Paste <u>S</u>pecial. The Paste Special dialog box appears (see Figure 19.48).

FIG. 19.48

The Paste Special dialog box lets you specify the format for the data that will be pasted into the receiving file.

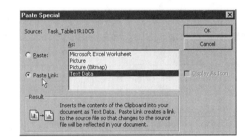

6. Choose the Paste <u>L</u>ink option button.

TIP Choose the Paste <u>L</u>ink option button before you select the format of the pasted data in the <u>A</u>s box. Changing the link option changes the selections in the <u>A</u>s box.

7. In the <u>A</u>s box, choose Text Data as the type of link if you want the data to become text in a table. Project attempts to convert text data into number data in a number field or a date in a date field.

   If you are in a Gantt Chart, however, there are more options for the format in which the data is pasted (as shown by the graphics options in Figure 19.48). Choose the Worksheet or Picture option if you want the data to be a picture *object* in a graphic area. (See the section "Pasting Objects into Microsoft Project" later in this chapter.) In the Gantt Chart view, for example, both those options would create a graphic object in the bar chart area of the view.

8. Choose OK to establish the link. Project will display a small triangle in the lower-right corner of each cell that is linked to a source for its data. You can see the link indicators in the Standard Rate and Overtime Rate values in Figure 19.49. The cost rate table is linked to an Excel worksheet where the cost rates are maintained.

FIG. 19.49

Linked cells in a Table view display a link indicator, a small triangle in the lower-right corner of the cell.

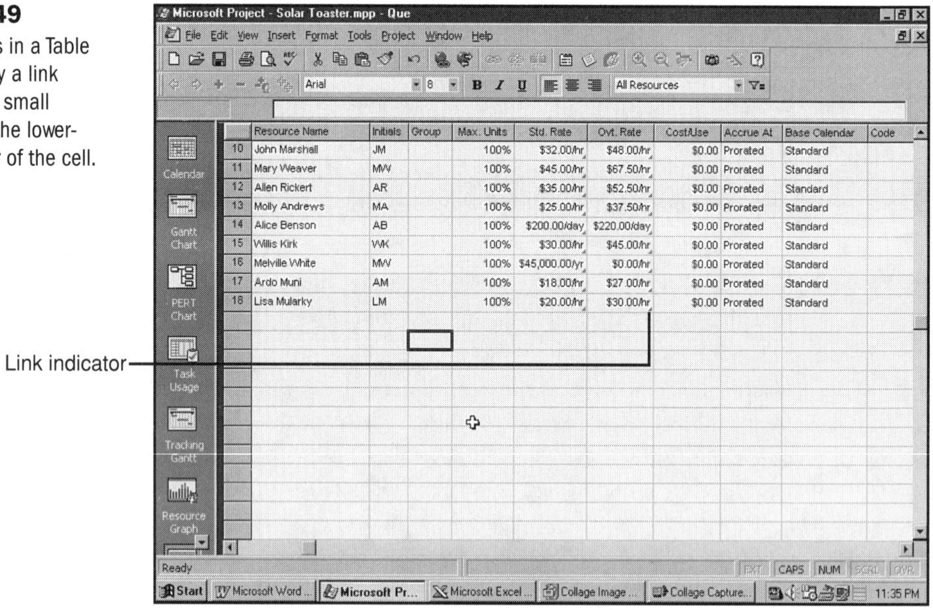

Link indicator—

TIP

Double-clicking a cell that is linked to an external source actually opens the external source so that you may view or edit it. If you want to see the Information dialog box for the task, resource, or assignment that contains the linked cell, click a cell in that row that is not linked. You can also right-click the cell and select the Information option from the shortcut menu, or use the Information button in the Standard toolbar.

If you attempt to paste a link with mismatched data, you will receive an OLE error message that the operation cannot be completed (see Figure 19.50). Unlike the regular Paste command, if there is a data mismatch while pasting a block of values, Project halts the operation and removes all values pasted in during that operation. These values are removed because a block of cells is considered one link. If one cell contains a mismatch, the entire paste link must be ignored.

FIG. 19.50

Unlike pasting static values, if you paste a linked value that is a data mismatch, Project will reject the paste operation and will not attempt to interpret the mismatched data.

> **Microsoft Project**
>
> The OLE paste operation cannot be completed.
>
> OK

Refreshing Linked Data in Microsoft Project

While the source document and Microsoft Project are both in memory, the linked data in Microsoft Project is instantly refreshed each time the project file is recalculated.

When you save the project file that contains linked values, Project saves the current values of the linked fields along with the reference to the source for the value. That way, when you open a file with linked values, Project can display the most recent values.

When you open a Project document that contains links to other files, Project attempts to update the linked values. If the source files for the links are already open in memory, then Project refreshes the linked values automatically. If the source files are not already open in memory, then Project will inform you that the file contains linked information and asks you if you want to refresh the links before displaying the project document (see Figure 19.51). If you select Yes, Project will quickly look into the source files and retrieve the current (saved) values of the link sources. If you select No, Project will open the document and display the last saved values for the linked cells. You can update the links yourself later.

FIG. 19.51

When opening a project document with links to other files, you can have Project refresh the links or use the saved values.

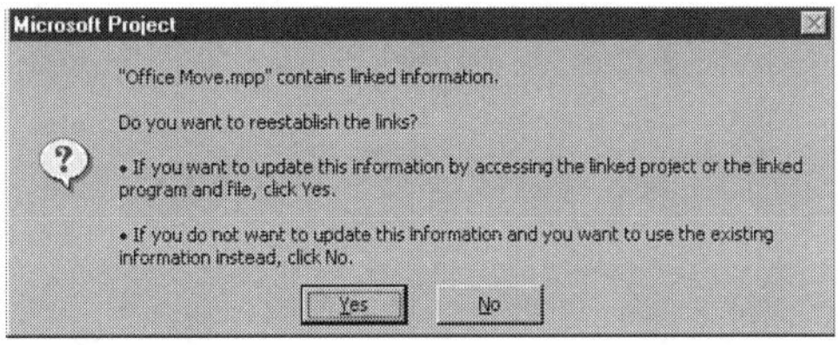

You can update the linked values in a Project document at any time with the Edit, Links command. The source application does not need to be opened for the linked values to be refreshed. The Links dialog box lists all the external links in the current document (see Figure 19.52).

FIG. 19.52

All external sources of linked data are identified in the Links dialog box.

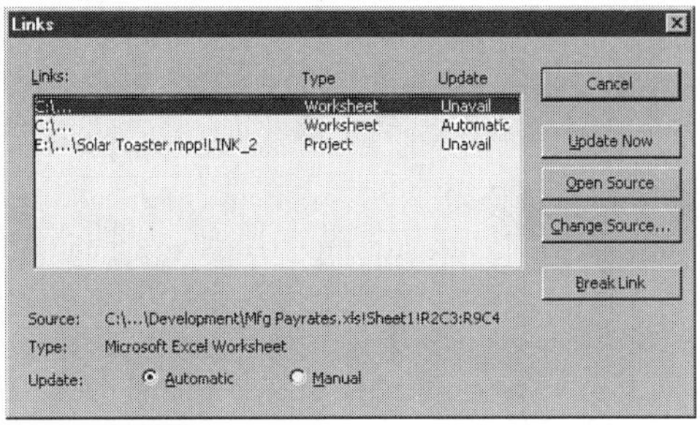

The list of links displays the path to the source, the document type of the source file, and the update status of the link. These three items are displayed in greater detail at the bottom of the dialog box for the selected link.

Part

VI

Ch

19

TIP   If there is no path or document name listed, then the link needs to be updated (see the following paragraph) to refresh that information.

Thus, for the first link in Figure 19.52, the detail shows the truncated path to the file (because it's too long for the display), the file name (Mfg Payrates), and the location of the linked data within the file (the range R2C3:R9C4 or C2:D9 in standard A1 notation). The Type is identified as a Microsoft Excel Worksheet. The Update status is Automatic, which means that the value has been updated at least once since this file was opened. If the Update status is Manual, then the source has not been made available and you have to manually update the links with this dialog box.

N O T E   Notice in this example that there is just one link reference in the Links dialog box for the whole range of cells that was pasted in the link operation. If you need to maintain each of the cells as separate links, you should copy and paste each of the cells individually. ▮

To update the data links to external sources, follow these steps:

1. Choose Edit, Links from the menu to display the Links dialog box (refer to Figure 19.52).

TIP   If the Links option is dimmed, then the document has no linked values.

2. Select all links that you want to refresh. To select all links, click the first link and hold down the Shift key as you click the last link. To add nonadjacent links to the selection, hold down the Ctrl key while making the additional selections.

3. Choose the Update Now button to refresh all the data links you have selected. The source for each link that you select is searched for the current values.

   If you want to open the application document named in the link reference, choose the Open Source button. You can open only one link source at a time. If you want to remove the link(s), choose the Break Link button. The current value will remain in the link location, but the reference to an external source will be gone.

If you want to change the source of the linked data, you can do so in the Change Source dialog box. Choose one of the links in the Links box and choose the Change Source button. The Change Source dialog box appears (see Figure 19.53), in which you can choose another file to link to. Although you can browse through the files for the file name of the new source, you must know the location within the new source file to complete the change. For that reason, it is usually better to paste new links over the old instead of using this dialog box.

Deleting Links to Other Sources

If you attempt to type over a field value that is a link to another file, you are warned that the link will be lost (see Figure 19.54) and you are offered the opportunity to proceed or to cancel the data entry. If you choose Yes (to proceed with the change), the DDE link reference is lost.

Fortunately, you can undo the change with the Edit, Undo command. Choose No to abandon the editing change and preserve the link.

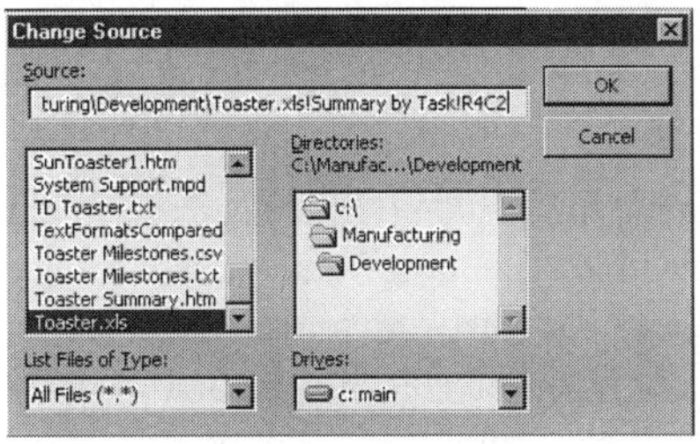

FIG. 19.53

The Change Source dialog box can be used to redefine the link source—but only if you know the address of the specific location within the file.

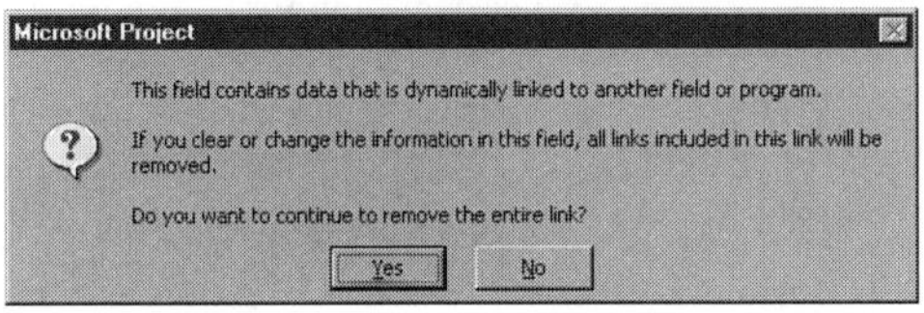

FIG. 19.54

If you edit or clear a cell that contains a linked value, you will lose the link.

To delete the data and its link to an external source, you can select the field whose link you want to remove and choose Edit, Clear. Then select the Contents option. You are then asked to confirm the deletion. Choose Yes to complete the deletion.

> **CAUTION**
>
> If you delete a link that is part of a linked range of fields, the link to all of them is removed, not just the one cell or field. The Edit, Undo command will restore the links.

TIP You can also use the shortcut Ctrl+Del in place of the Clear command.

If you want to paste links to Microsoft Project data into other applications, you simply reverse the steps outlined in this section, copying the source data in Project and pasting the links into another application.

Identifying Tasks or Resources with Links Attached

You can filter the task or resource list to determine which tasks or resources use linked data from other sources. For either a Task view or a Resource view, choose Project, Filtered For. Choose More Filters to display the More Filters dialog box, and choose the Linked Fields filter. Choose the Apply button to display only the tasks or resources that have one or more linked fields. Choose the Highlight button to highlight those tasks or resources that have linked values in one or more fields.

Part
VI

Ch
19

Working with Objects

The preceding sections focused on sharing data values as text between applications. For example, a group of cell entries in an Excel workbook can provide the task names and durations in a Microsoft Project document. Or, if you paste Excel data as text into a Project Gantt Chart view, each cell is placed in a separate field in the table, as in Figure 19.49.

An *object*, on the other hand, is a picture of data (usually a group of data or a special format for data) that exists in another application. The most frequent use of objects is to show graphic data (for example, Excel charts, MS Paint artwork, or special displays like the PERT Chart or the Gantt Chart from Microsoft Project) in an application that doesn't normally generate similar graphics images. It is common to refer to the application that generates an object as the *server* application and the application that has the object pasted in it as the *client* application. These terms will be used in the following discussion where they help clarify.

If you paste Excel data as a picture object in Microsoft Project, a mini-spreadsheet would be displayed in the graphics area of the Gantt Chart, complete with gridlines. If you paste a copy of an Excel chart, it will also appear in the graphics area (see Figure 19.55). You can position and resize the picture within Microsoft Project.

FIG. 19.55

In this illustration the Project data is paste-linked into an Excel spreadsheet, the Excel data is used to generate an Excel chart, and the chart is paste-linked back to Project as an object in the Gantt Chart.

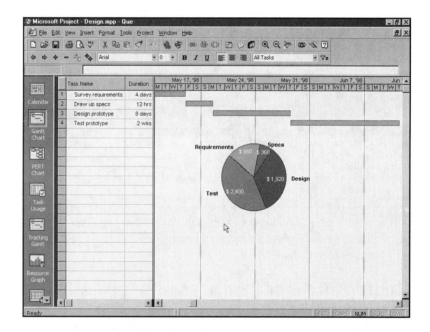

If task rows from a Gantt Chart in Microsoft Project are pasted into a Microsoft Word document as text, each row of task information becomes a row of ordinary text in the document. If they are pasted in Word as an object, they will be displayed as a graphic figure. In Figure 19.56 the same Project task rows are pasted first as text and then as a picture object. The task fields appear as an ordinary tab-separated list in Word. The picture of the tasks includes the Gantt Chart table cells along with the task bars and the timescale above the task bars.

FIG. 19.56
A Microsoft Word document can show a Microsoft Project image within its page of text.

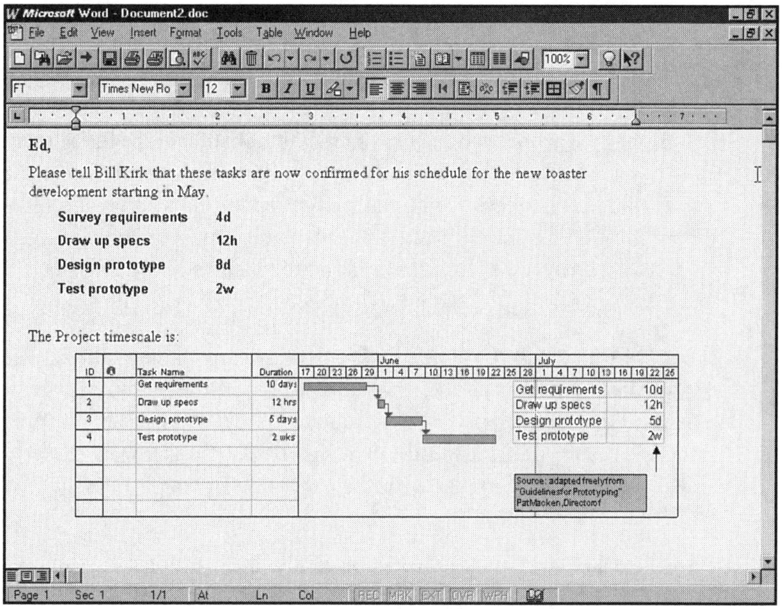

Objects can be pasted regardless of whether they are linked or not. If they are not linked, the pasted image cannot be updated to show changes in the source document. You must copy and paste the image again.

Pasting Objects into Another Application

To paste linked or unlinked picture objects from one application into another, copy the data to the Clipboard in the server (the source) document and paste the object from the Clipboard into the client (the destination) document. The only difference is that when you paste an object, you choose the picture or object format rather than the text data format.

Pasting Objects into Microsoft Project   You can paste graphic objects into three locations in Microsoft Project:

- In the graphics area of the Gantt Chart
- In the Notes box of the Task, Resource, or Assignment Information forms
- In the special Objects field in the Task Form or the Resource Form (see the following paragraphs)

Pasting Objects into the Gantt Chart   The Gantt Chart is the premier view in Microsoft Project. It can be enhanced by pasting Project drawings (see Chapter 7, "Working with the Major Task Views") or objects from other applications into the timescale area. To paste an object into the Gantt Chart, use these steps:

Part
VI

Ch
19

1. Activate the source (the server application), select the object, and copy it to the Clipboard with the Edit, Copy command.

2. Activate Project (the client application) and view the Gantt Chart.

3. Choose Edit, Paste Special.

4. In the Paste Special dialog box, choose the Paste button or the Paste Link button as appropriate.

5. In the As box, you may have an option that includes the server application's name, and you always have the Picture option. Both choices produce picture images that look similar. The option with the server application's name shows more of the special formatting that the server application is capable of displaying. The Picture option is less responsive to special formats and to changes in the formats.

6. Choose OK to paste the image.

Pasting Objects in the Notes Field   You can attach notes to all three of Project's main record types: tasks, resources, and assignments. To see the notes, you must use a view that displays fields of the record type you want to attach the note to. Then you must select a field for the specific record (task, resource, or assignment) that you want to attach the note to. Then display the Information form for the record. Assignment Information forms are new in Microsoft Project 98.

To paste an object into the Notes field of an Information form, follow these steps:

1. Copy the object to the Windows Clipboard from another application.

2. Switch to Microsoft Project, activate an appropriate view, and select the record whose note you want to paste into.

    - To paste in a task note, activate one of the many views that display fields for tasks and select the task you want to use.

    - To paste in a resource note, activate one of the many views that display fields for resources and select the resource you want to use.

    - To paste in an assignment note, you must activate either the Task Usage view or the Resource Usage view and select the assignment record you want to use.

3. Choose Project, Task (or Resource or Assignment) Notes from the menu or choose the Notes button on the Standard toolbar. The Notes tab on the Task/Resource/Assignment Information form will be displayed (see Figure 19.57).

4. Click in the Notes box and use the Windows paste key combination, Ctrl+V, to paste the object in the note. (Neither the menu nor the toolbar buttons are available in the dialog box.)

5. If you want to resize the object, click in the middle of the object to display the sizing handles around the object. Use the mouse to drag the sizing handles to the direction you want.

6. Choose OK to save the note.

▶ **See** "Working with Drawing Objects in the Gantt Chart View," **p. 240**

FIG. 19.57
The Information Notes field can now have rich text formatting, including graphic images.

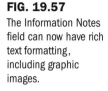

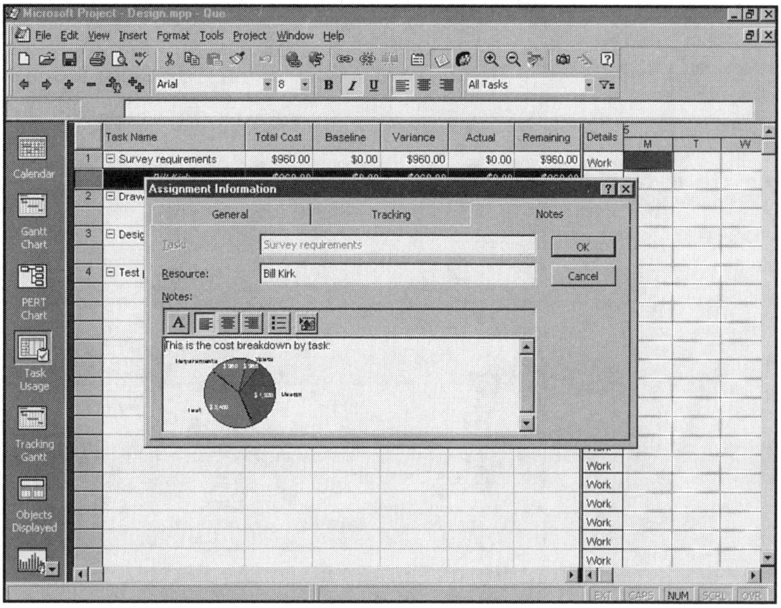

Pasting Objects in the Task or Resource Objects Box   The objects pasted into the Task Objects box or the Resource Objects box can be viewed only in the Task Form or Resource Form (or in their abbreviated versions: the Task Name Form and the Resource Name Form). You can also include the objects that are pasted in the Objects box in custom reports (see Chapter 24, "Customizing Reports").

There is also an Objects *field* for both tasks and resources that displays the number of objects that have been pasted into the Objects box for each task or resource. If you display the Objects field in a table, it shows the number of objects attached to the task or resource. You can filter this field for values greater than zero to identify those tasks and resources that have objects attached.

To paste an object into an Object field, follow these steps:

1. Paste the object into the Windows Clipboard from the source (server) application.

2. In Project, display the Task Form, Task Name Form, the Resource Form, or the Resource Name Form, depending on the type of record you want to paste the object into. In Figure 19.58, the Resource Name Form is displayed in the lower pane below the Resource Usage view. A Word document that contains both text and a chart is pasted in the Objects box.

   The table in the Resource Usage view has been modified to display the Objects field. It shows that there are two objects attached to this resource. You would use the scroll bar next to the Objects box to see the next object.

Part

VI

Ch

19

FIG. 19.58

The Object field displays graphic or other objects that are attached to an individual task or resource. However, the objects can only be viewed in the Task or Resource Forms, or on custom reports.

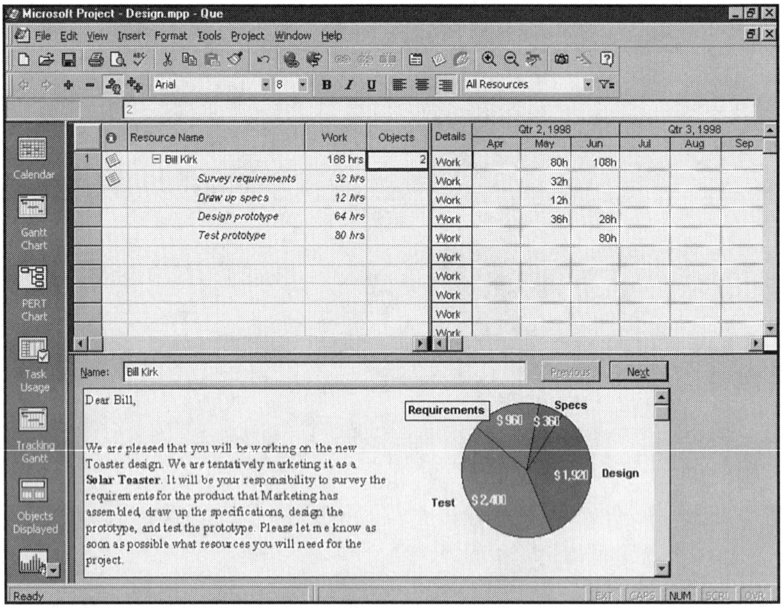

3. Make the form active, right-click the mouse to display the Details menu, and choose Objects to display the Objects box. You can also use the Format menu, and choose Details, Objects.

4. Click in the Object field at the bottom of the form to select it.

5. Choose Edit, Paste Special from the menu to display the Paste Special dialog box (refer to Figure 19.48).

6. Choose Paste or Paste Link.

7. Choose the Picture option in the As list box of formats.

8. Choose OK to save the picture.

You can paste multiple objects to the Objects box. The scroll bar to the right scrolls through the objects.

TIP The Objects box scroll bar does not scroll through a single object, even if it is too large for the area it is displayed in. If you can't see the entire object, increase the size of the form. You cannot resize the objects that are pasted in the Objects box.

If you want to delete an object in the Objects box, scroll to display that object and press the Delete key. The object will be deleted from the project document.

Pasting Project Objects into Other Applications   Microsoft Project has a number of distinctive graphical views that can be very effective when pasted into other applications. The graphics views include:

- Any of the various Gantt Chart views
- The PERT Chart view
- The Calendar view
- The Task Usage and Resource Usage views
- The Resource Chart view

When copying a Microsoft Project object to the Clipboard, you have the choice of using the Edit, Copy command or the Copy Picture button on the Standard toolbar. You should generally use the Copy Picture button because you have more control over the way the object is prepared for its target.

The Copy Picture dialog box (see Figure 19.59) offers choices that vary depending on the view you are copying. For all views you have choices about the format in which the picture is rendered:

- Choose For Screen if you are pasting the picture into another application just to be viewed on-screen.

- Choose For Printer if you are pasting the picture into an application for printing. The format of the picture will be determined by the printer you have selected in Project at the time you save the picture. If you change printers before you print, you should save the picture again.

- Choose To GIF Image File if you plan to use the picture in a Web site display. The image will be saved in a GIF format file (a Graphics Interchange Format compressed bitmap) that the most widely used browsers can display with various controls. You must enter the path and file name for the file that is to be created. A Browse button is available if you want to search the directory structure, or to search for a file name to replace.

Part
VI

Ch
19

FIG. 19.59
Use the Copy Picture dialog box to tailor what the image includes and how it is rendered.

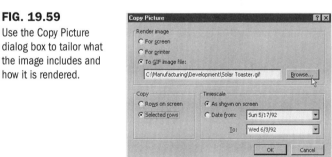

If the view you are copying includes a table display, you will have the choice of including:

- The Rows On Screen (just those visible when you take the picture)
- The Selected Rows (those in which you have selected one or more fields)

  If the rows you select are not adjacent, the picture will leave out rows in between, and your selected rows will appear to be adjacent in the picture.

If the view contains a timescale, you will have the choice of:

- Using the dates As Sh<u>o</u>wn on Screen, which means that you can arrange the timescale on the screen that you want, and then capture just that range of dates in picture.
- Or, using a range of dates that you specify in the Date <u>F</u>rom and <u>T</u>o boxes.

To copy a Microsoft Project object to the Clipboard, use these steps:

1. Select the task or resource data to be included. You can select the entire task or resource rows in a table, or just several adjacent fields. You can also select non-adjacent fields.
2. Choose the Copy Picture button to display the Copy Picture dialog box (refer to Figure 19.59).
3. Choose either For <u>S</u>creen, For <u>P</u>rinter, or To <u>G</u>IF Image File. If you chose To <u>G</u>IF Image File, supply the path and file name for the GIF file in the text box.
4. If you are in a table display, choose Ro<u>w</u>s on Screen or Selected <u>R</u>ows.
5. If there is a timescale in the display, select either As Sh<u>o</u>wn on Screen or Date <u>F</u>rom and <u>T</u>o.
6. Choose OK to save the picture. Or, choose the Cancel button to quit without saving the picture.
7. Switch to the client application and choose the equivalent of the Paste or Paste Link command, depending on whether you want a linked relationship.

As with linked field data, you can find out which tasks or resources have objects attached to their Objects boxes by using a filter. However, you must define this filter because there is no standard filter to identify attached objects. The Objects field for each task and resource contains the number of objects attached to that task or resource. You can design a filter to test for values greater than zero in this field to identify the tasks or resources.

▶ **See** "Creating Custom Filters," **p. 754**

Embedding Objects

In the preceding examples, an object was created in the source (server) application and then was copied and pasted into the target (client) application. The purpose for this is usually to avoid retyping data values, or to take advantage of the special formatting features of the server application. But in all cases, the source data for the pasted object was another application.

It's also possible, with OLE2 compliant applications, to create data within Microsoft Project and then temporarily "borrow" the formatting capabilities of another application to produce effects that are not native to Microsoft Project. Both the data and the special formatting functionality are said to be *embedded* in Microsoft Project. In this case, the functionality of the server application is made available on call to Microsoft Project.

For example, Figure 19.60 shows a Gantt Chart with a text watermark formatted by Microsoft WordArt 2.0. The image was created from within Microsoft Project by calling on WordArt to insert a formatted object. You could also call on Microsoft Excel to chart some project data and display it in the Gantt Chart area. These are called *embedded* objects. The data resides solely within the client application, but the functions to process the data are borrowed from another application. This powerful process is made possible by Microsoft OLE and OLE2.

FIG. 19.60

Embedded objects are not based on any external data, although they are formatted by calling on other applications. WordArt was used here to provide a watermark for the Gantt Chart display.

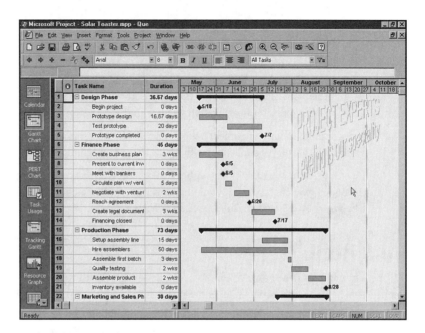

The logo for Project Experts is displayed as an embedded object on the Gantt Chart. To embed an object in Microsoft Project, follow these steps:

1. While in Microsoft Project, choose Insert, Object. The Insert Object dialog box appears, as shown in Figure 19.61.

FIG. 19.61

The Insert Object dialog box lets you choose a server application to create an embedded object in your Microsoft Project data.

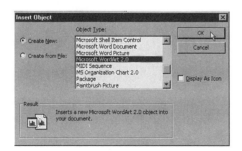

2. Select the Create New button to generate a new object, or select the Create from File option button and select the file from the file names dialog box that will be displayed in that case.

3. If you choose the Create New option button, choose the server application in the Object Type box.

4. Choose OK to open the server application on top of Microsoft Project.

5. Prepare the object in the server application. You may have to copy and paste the Microsoft Project data into the server application to begin processing. However, the data only remains in the server application as long as the server application is being used by Project to create this object.

6. When the object is ready to be put back in Microsoft Project, exit the application to return to Project. For some applications, you will have a menu choice to return to the client application (Project in this case). For others, like WordArt 2.0, you can simply click outside the server application window in the Project window to return.

If you want to modify the object using its server application, you can simply double-click the object and the server application will open. Make your changes, and exit back to Project.

If you want to format the object within Project, for example, you might want to move or resize the object, you can use the techniques described in the section "Working with Objects" in Chapter 7, "Working with the Major Task Views."

From Here...

This chapter has shown you how to exchange Microsoft Project data with other file formats, some of which can contain all of the project data and some of which can only contain small sets of project data. For related information, refer to the following chapters in the book.

- See Chapter 14, "Publishing Projects on the Web," for more information about using the HTML export feature.

- See Chapter 16, "Analyzing Progress and Revising the Schedule," for hints about reviewing projects that you have imported.

- See Chapter 17, "Working with Multiple Projects," to see how to consolidate projects.

Working with Views and Reports

20   Using the Standard Views, Tables, and Filters   659

21   Formatting Views   695

22   Customizing Views, Tables, and Filters   741

23   Using the Standard Reports   767

24   Customizing Reports   793

CHAPTER 20

Using the Standard Views, Tables, and Filters

In previous sections of this book, many of the available views, tables, and filters have been used to illustrate their usefulness during various stages of a project's life. Some are most useful during the planning stages of project design, while others are not practical until the project is being tracked. The purpose of this chapter is to provide a detailed description of each view, table, and filter, along with comments about when and where each should fit into the project. ■

■ **Differentiate between the types of views**

Different types of views provide different perspectives on your project. Sheets, graphs, and forms allow for different work styles.

■ **Determine the best view to use during different stages of the project**

The information that is needed varies widely during the different phases of a project. Recognizing not only what information is necessary, but also which view provides it is an important skill to develop.

■ **Apply appropriate tables of data to display the most useful fields**

With over 60 different fields of data stored in every task, you have to know how to narrow the field to focus on the right information.

■ **Apply the filters necessary to see only the tasks or resources that meet certain criteria**

This last major building block of Project allows you to focus on categories of tasks, hiding ones that don't match specified criteria. In projects with many tasks, you need to be able to identify certain kinds of tasks automatically.

Exploring the Standard Views

Views can be categorized in two different ways. The first logical breakdown of views is whether they display tasks or resources. All views focus on one or the other, but not both. The next method of categorizing views is by their format. There are basically three different formats for views: sheets, forms, and graphs. The following list summarizes the predefined views using these two category breakdowns. Graph views are listed first, then sheets, then forms. The Task views are listed in the column on the left, while the Resource views are listed on the right. The views marked with an asterisk must be accessed by choosing View, More Views.

View Type	Task Views	Resource Views
Graphical views	Calendar Gantt Chart (Bar Rollup*, Detail Gantt*, Leveling Gantt*, Milestone Date Rollup*, Milestone Rollup*, PA_Expected Gantt*, PA_Optimistic Gantt*, PA_Pessimistic Gantt*, Tracking Gantt) PERT Chart Task PERT*	Resource Graph
Sheet views	Task Sheet* Task Usage PA_PERT Entry Sheet	Resource Sheet Resource Usage
Form views	Task Form* Task Details Form* Task Name Form*	Resource Form* Resource Name Form*
Combination views	Task Entry*	Resource Allocation*

The views listed with the Gantt Chart are fundamentally the same as the Gantt Chart, except that they have a different table applied, and the bars are formatted differently. See the section "Exploring the Standard Tables" later in this chapter for a discussion of these different tables.

The combination views are actually two standard views displayed on the same screen. They provide a unique combination of information that will be summarized at the end of the chapter.

The following sections will describe each of the views, with all the task views listed first and then the resource views.

The Calendar

In the popular Calendar view (see Figure 20.1), tasks are displayed in a familiar calendar format. Each task is displayed as a bar that spans the days and weeks during which the task is scheduled to occur. For many people, it is easier to visualize a project when it is displayed in this familiar format.

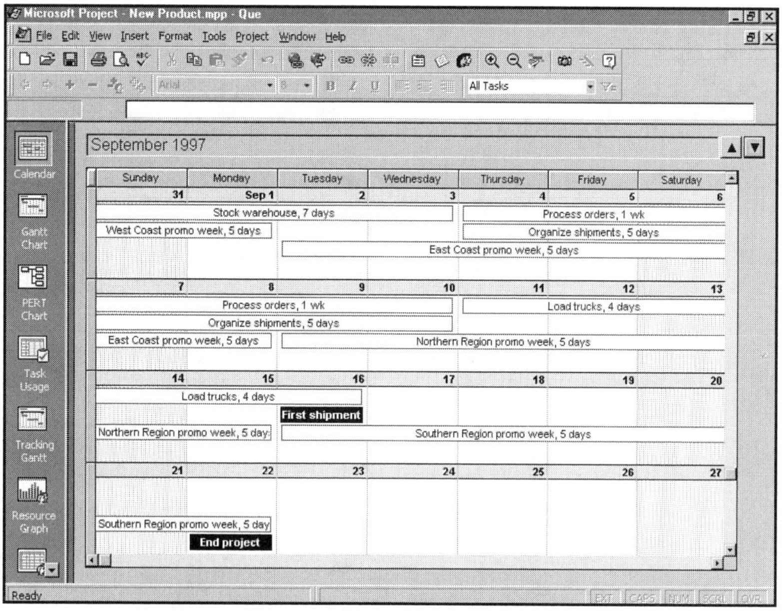

FIG. 20.1

The Calendar view displays tasks in a familiar format as you view, edit, or print your project.

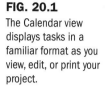

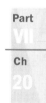

While it is possible to create a project using the calendar, it is not generally advisable to do so. Creating tasks on the calendar causes constraints to be applied to the tasks. This view can be very useful, however, for reviewing the project plan, for editing a project after the initial design has taken place, and for printing.

▶ **See** "Inserting Tasks in the Calendar View," **p. 223**

▶ **See** "Resolving Conflicts Caused by Constraints," **p. 208**

Quite often, the calendar displays too many tasks at once, and it becomes difficult to see what you want. Many filters can be applied to hone in on particular categories of tasks; for example, tasks that are in progress, top-level tasks, or tasks using a particular resource. This last filter is very helpful when you want to give each resource a list of respective tasks. Filters in general are discussed at the end of this chapter. See Chapter 7, "Working with the Major Task Views," for more information about using filters specifically with the Calendar view.

The Gantt Chart

The Gantt Chart, one of the most popular project management views, is actually a Task Sheet on the left side and a bar chart on the right (see Figure 20.2). The chart is a list of tasks displayed as bars overlaying a timescale. The length of the bars is determined by the duration of the tasks. The placement of the bars on the timescale is determined by the start and finish dates of the tasks. Dependency lines are drawn to show the predecessor and successor relationships between tasks.

Part
VI

Ch
20

FIG. 20.2

The Gantt Chart draws bars on a timescale to show when tasks occur.

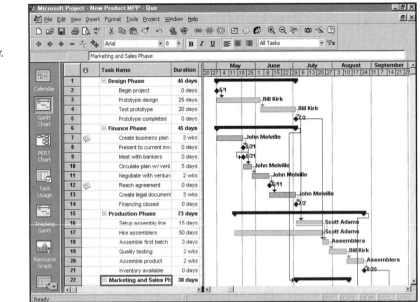

The Gantt Chart is useful during many stages of the project. During the initial planning stages of a project, you can enter tasks, make determinations about dependency relationships, and even assign resources. After the initial planning phase, you will probably need to crash the schedule, which basically means that you reduce the amount of time taken to complete the whole project. The Gantt Chart immediately displays the effect of your efforts. After the project is underway, the Gantt Chart offers practical displays of tasks that are in progress, behind, or ahead of schedule.

The options for formatting the Gantt Chart are so numerous that there is even a special automated tool, the Gantt Chart Wizard, that walks you through the process.

▶ **See** "Using the Gantt Chart Wizard," **p. 714**

▶ **See** "Strategies for Crashing the Schedule," **p. 407**

The Rollup Views

Several of the views based on the Gantt Chart view are grouped together because they are all rollup views. The technique of using rollups was discussed in greater detail in Chapter 12, "Reviewing the Project Plan." This section will describe the various predefined rollup views that are available, what information they provide, and how they are different from each other.

If you use outlining in your project task list, you can choose to display specified task names and dates on the summary task bar. This is useful when the outline level for that task is collapsed and you still want to see where that task falls along the summary task. A problem associated with rollups occurs when task names are long or the timescale is zoomed out to view a long time period. The text tends to overlap.

Each of the rollup views use the Rollup table to add a column in the Task Sheet called Text Above. This field offers a drop-down list with Yes and No as the options. When Yes is selected, the task name appears above the summary task bar, rather than below (which is the default). Figure 20.3 displays the advantages of using a collapsed outline with rollups. In this figure, the outline is collapsed, and milestones are set to rollup to the Gantt Chart. Some of the milestones have the Text Above field set to Yes to stagger their titles.

> **CAUTION**
>
> On any of the rollup views, no tasks will automatically rollup. You must specifically mark a task as rolled up on the General tab of the Task Information dialog box.

FIG. 20.3

Rollups can increase the level of detail available in a collapsed outline.

Task names rolled up to the summary task

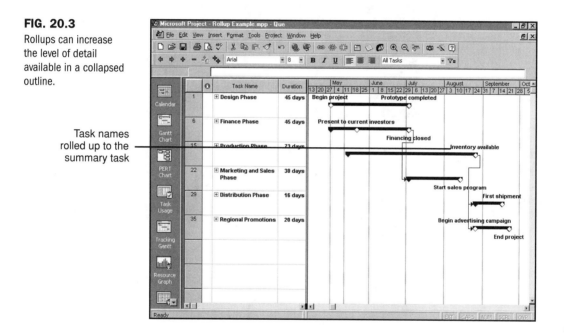

Bar Rollup   If you rollup a task (rather than a milestone), the summary task bar appears more like a task than a summary. This is useful when you want to highlight certain tasks when task details are not displayed. As shown in Figure 20.4, the rollup of the Quality Testing task emphasizes its importance.

Milestone Date Rollup   The Milestone Date Rollup view is very similar to the Bar Rollup view. The difference is that the milestone dates rollup as well as their names. As shown in Figure 20.5, the names of the milestones appear above the summary task bar (you don't have to change the Text Above field) and the date appears below. Triangles only appear on the end of the summary task bar if you rollup a milestone to it.

FIG. 20.4
The Bar Rollup view allows you to emphasize specific task details in a collapsed outline.

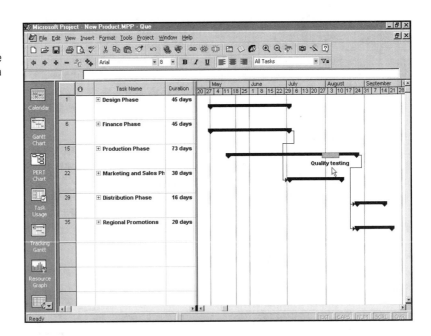

FIG. 20.5
The Milestone Date Rollup view automatically puts names above the summary task bar and dates below.

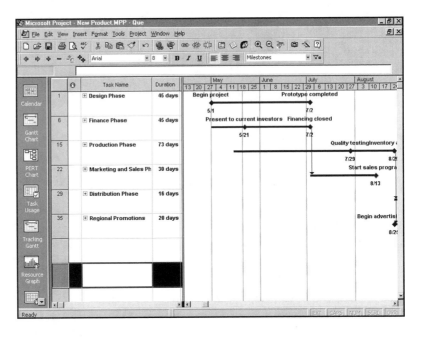

CAUTION

Because all of the rolled up task names appear above the summary task bar, there is an increased likelihood that the task names will overlap. You may need to increase the span of the timescale, shorten the task names, or be more selective about which tasks are rolled up.

Milestone Rollup   The Milestone Rollup view is similar to the previous two rollup views. As displayed in Figure 20.6, when tasks are marked as Rolled Up, the task name is rolled up, but not the date. A field in the Task Sheet allows you to choose to have the text of the name appear above the summary task bar. If tasks are rolled up (rather than just milestones), only a triangle shows for it on the summary task bar, rather than a bar, as in the Bar Rollup view.

FIG. 20.6

The Milestone Rollup view allows you to selectively place some rolled up task names above the summary task bar and some below.

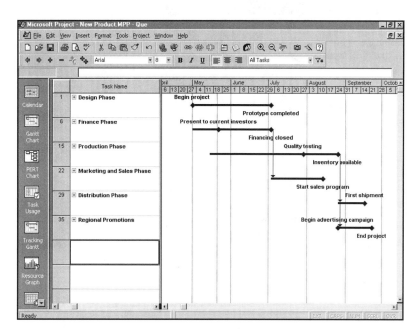

The Leveling Gantt

Following the same general format as the Gantt Chart, the Leveling Gantt has been specifically formatted for use while resource overallocation problems are being resolved, either through manual leveling or leveling performed by Microsoft Project.

The left side of the Leveling Gantt uses a special table that includes the leveling delay field. This is where Project or you enter a delay in a task because the resource is too busy with other tasks. Several bars have been added for each task (see Figure 20.7). Extending to the left of each task is a very narrow delay bar, which is drawn from the earliest date a task can

Part
VII

Ch
20

start (early start) to its scheduled start. This bar shows graphically the delay that has either been manually entered or calculated by Project during automatic leveling. Extending to the right of each task bar is another very narrow bar that depicts free slack (the amount of time that a task can be delayed without delaying any other tasks). This bar is drawn from the scheduled finish date to the amount of free slack. Using this bar, you can see how much a task can be delayed without causing a delay in the project. Assuming the default settings, a blue colored bar shows the task as currently scheduled, while a green colored bar shows the task before it was leveled. A dotted line shows where the task has been split as a result of leveling.

▶ **See** "Resolving Overallocations by Delaying Assignments," **p. 371**

▶ **See** "Splitting a Task," **p. 374**

FIG. 20.7
The Leveling Gantt allows for the input of and shows the effects of delaying tasks.

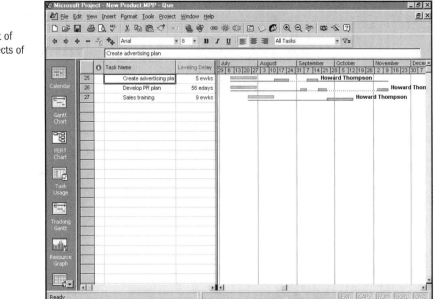

The Detail Gantt

Based on the same general format as the Gantt Chart, the Detail Gantt is very similar to the Leveling Gantt in that it shows where delays have been created as a result of leveling, whether performed by Project or by you. The leveling table displays the leveling delay field. On the timescale portion of the Gantt Chart, additional bars are drawn to display how much a task can be delayed without causing the project to slip, how much a task has already been delayed, and where tasks have been split.

For example, in Figure 20.8 you can see that task #25 has been delayed for five weeks and could still be delayed eight more weeks without causing the project deadline to be missed. Work on that same task was also performed at two different times (it was split) in order to accommodate other more pressing tasks assigned to the resource.

The difference between the Detail Gantt and the Leveling Gantt is that the Detail Gantt does not show how the task was scheduled before it was delayed.

FIG. 20.8

The Detail Gantt offers another view to keep track of tasks that have been delayed or that could be delayed to resolve resource overallocations.

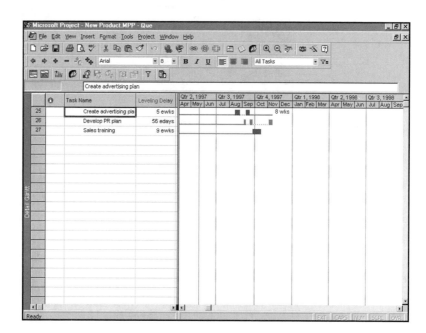

The Tracking Gantt

The Tracking Gantt is also based on the basic Gantt Chart and displays an additional gray bar below the regular task bar with the baseline information. The standard progress bars have been modified slightly; instead of a narrow black bar extending across the task bar, there are two bars of equal height for each task. The lower bar is gray and depicts baseline information. The top colored bar displays progress with a solid color and similar color shading for the remaining work to be done for the task (see Figure 20.9). Text for the percent complete is included on the right side of all task bars.

▶ **See** "The Tracking Gantt Chart," **p. 667**

Part
VII

Ch
20

CAUTION

The baseline bars will not display if the baseline has not been saved.

FIG. 20.9

The Tracking Gantt gives a snapshot of how the project is progressing.

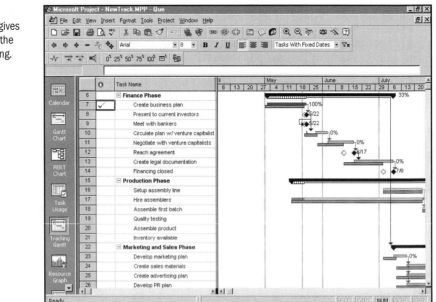

PERT Analysis Gantt Charts

Another group of views that are based on the Gantt Chart are the views used by the PERT Analysis method of estimating durations. They include PA_Expected Gantt, PA_Optimistic Gantt, and PA_Pessimistic Gantt. The only difference between them is the table that is applied, and therefore the columns that are displayed. These columns are described in more detail in the section "Exploring the Standard Tables," which appears later in this chapter. There is also a PA_PERT Entry Sheet that is the Task Sheet portion of the Gantt Chart with the columns for each estimate type. This view is primarily for entering the different estimates.

The easiest way to access these views is through the PERT Analysis toolbar, but you can also access them by choosing View, More Views. Basically, the PERT Analysis is a method for estimating durations using a weighted average of worst, best, and most likely cases. After Project performs the calculations to determine a duration, you can easily flip back and forth between a Gantt Chart that shows all optimistic estimates, all pessimistic estimates, and all most likely estimates. It could be a useful approach when you want to see the impact of all of those estimates, rather than just one task at a time.

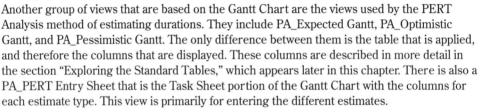

▶ **See** "Using PERT Analysis Toolbar to Estimate Durations," **p. 137**

The PERT Chart

The PERT Chart is another graphical view of a project, which focuses on the dependency relationships between tasks. There is no reference to time at all, as there is in the Gantt Chart. As shown in Figure 20.10, the PERT Chart resembles a flow chart with boxes (nodes) for each task. Lines are drawn to illustrate predecessors and successors. The display in Figure 20.10 was created using the Zoom Out tool in the Standard toolbar. Notice the mouse pointer that is close to the entry bar. When you click a task node, the name of the task is displayed there. When you double-click a task node, the Task Information dialog box for that task is displayed.

This view is primarily intended for use during the initial design phase of a project. It is here that you can ensure that the plan is logical.

▶ **See** "Establishing Dependency Links," **p. 173**

▶ **See** "Working with the PERT Chart View," **p. 225**

FIG. 20.10

The PERT Chart helps define the logic of predecessors and successors for the project plan.

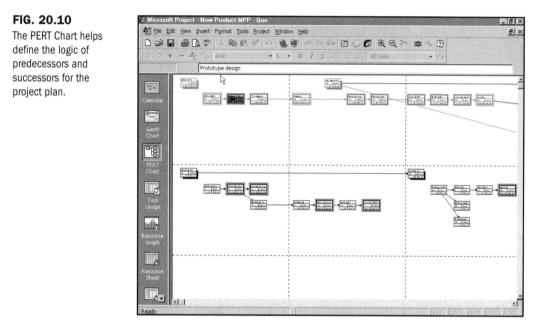

The Task PERT Chart

As the name implies, the Task PERT is a special kind of PERT Chart. As shown previously in Figure 20.7, the Task PERT is typically displayed at the bottom of a task list (Task Sheet or Gantt Chart). It only shows the *immediate* predecessors and successors for the task selected in the top pane. This is a very useful view when examining the task dependencies of the project, particularly when making sure that every task is linked and that the links all make sense. For example, the dependencies for task 18 are much more clear in the Task PERT view at the bottom of Figure 20.11 than in the Gantt Chart at the top. The type of relationship is also displayed. For example, each of the tasks related to task 18 in Figure 20.11 has a finish-start (FS) relationship.

▶ **See** "Understanding Dependency Links," **p. 173**

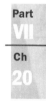

Part

VII

Ch

20

TIP When working with combination views, it might be useful to turn off the View Bar. Point to a blank spot on the View Bar, press the right mouse button, and choose View Bar. When this is done (as shown in Figure 20.11), the view name shows at the left edge of the view.

FIG. 20.11
Use the Task PERT to ensure that every task has at least one predecessor and successor and that all relationship links make sense.

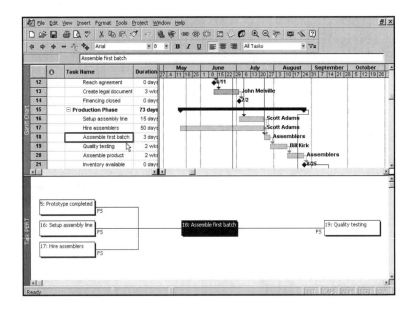

The Task Sheet

The Task Sheet view is a spreadsheet format of information. Tasks are displayed in rows with fields of information about those tasks displayed in columns. The fields (columns) that are displayed are determined by the table that has been applied. (See the section "Exploring the Standard Tables" later in this chapter for more details about tables.) Located on the View, More Views menu, the Task Sheet can be used during many different phases of the project, and is preferred by people who like working in a spreadsheet format rather than with a form or with a graphical view. Figure 20.12 displays the Task Sheet with the Entry table applied.

▶ **See** "Resolving Problems Caused by Constraints," **p. 208**

> **CAUTION**
>
> Don't change the start or finish dates in the Task Sheet when you see them. These are dates calculated by Project, and you may inadvertently create a constraint.

Task Usage

The new Task Usage view displays on a timescale the hours of work that are to be performed. As shown in Figure 20.13, task 23 is a one-week task assigned to Howard Thompson. In the timescale grid on the right side of the view, the task begins on Thursday with eight hours of work and continues through the following Wednesday, skipping the weekend. This view is primarily intended for resource contouring, which is discussed in detail in Chapter 10, "Assigning Resources and Costs to Tasks."

FIG. 20.12

The Task Sheet with the Entry table applied makes viewing a lot of detail information on one screen possible.

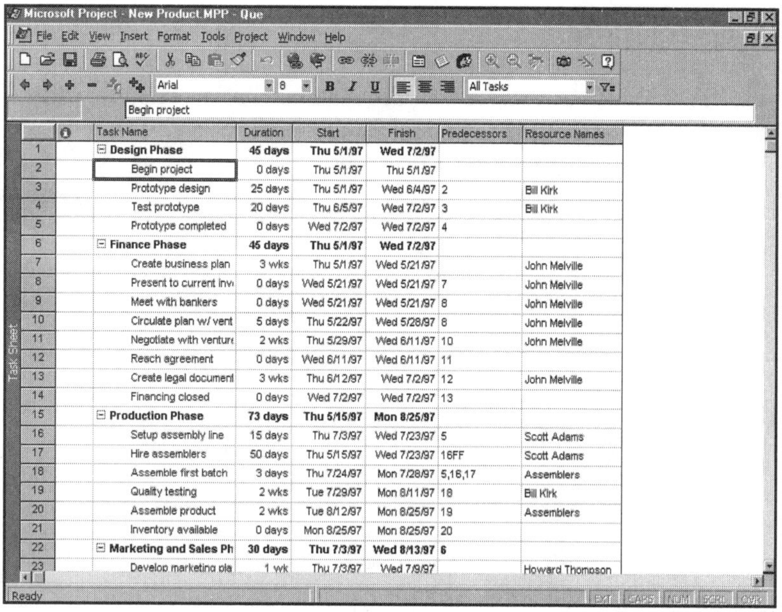

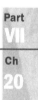

FIG. 20.13

The Task Usage view displays exactly when work is scheduled to occur.

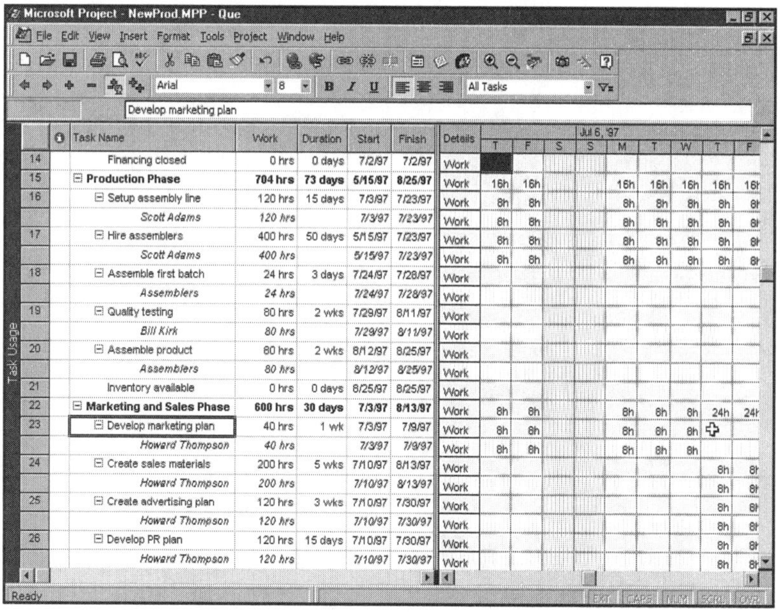

Part

VII

Ch

20

The Task Form

In contrast with the Task Sheet, the Task Form presents basic information about only one task in a form format (see Figure 20.14). It is possible, therefore, to see more information about one task at a time than in a sheet view. Accessed by choosing View, More Views, the Task Form is often used in the bottom pane to display more detailed information about the selected task in the top pane. If displayed in a single pane view, as in Figure 20.14, you can move from one task to another using the Previous and Next buttons.

The bottom portion of the form view can be set to display a variety of options, including notes. These options can be found by choosing Format, Details or by right-clicking anywhere in the form itself. It is also possible to create custom forms if the predefined ones do not meet your needs.

▶ **See** "Using the Task Form for Tracking," **p. 499**

▶ **See** "Formatting the Task and Resource Forms," **p. 727**

▶ **See** "Using Custom Forms," **p. 899**

FIG. 20.14

The Task Form allows you to focus on one task at a time.

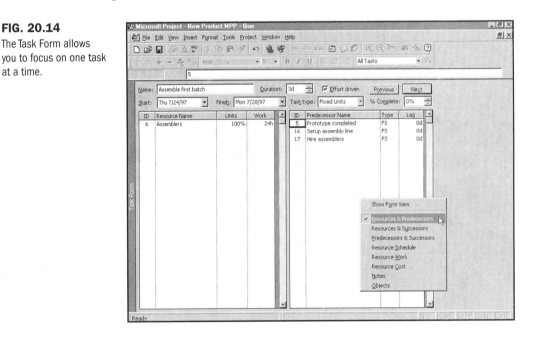

The Task Details Form

The Task Details Form shown in Figure 20.15 is similar in format to the Task Form but shows more detail. Notice in particular the options for Current, Baseline, and Actual Dates. You could use this form for tracking the progress of tasks already underway. Constraints are also displayed on this form, making them more apparent than they were in the Task Form. As with the Task Form, open the Task Details Form by choosing View, More Views. Also as with the Task

Form, the bottom portion of this form can display a variety of fields when you choose Format, Details from the main menu or right-click the form and choose an option from the shortcut menu.

FIG. 20.15
The Task Details Form is useful during scheduling and tracking.

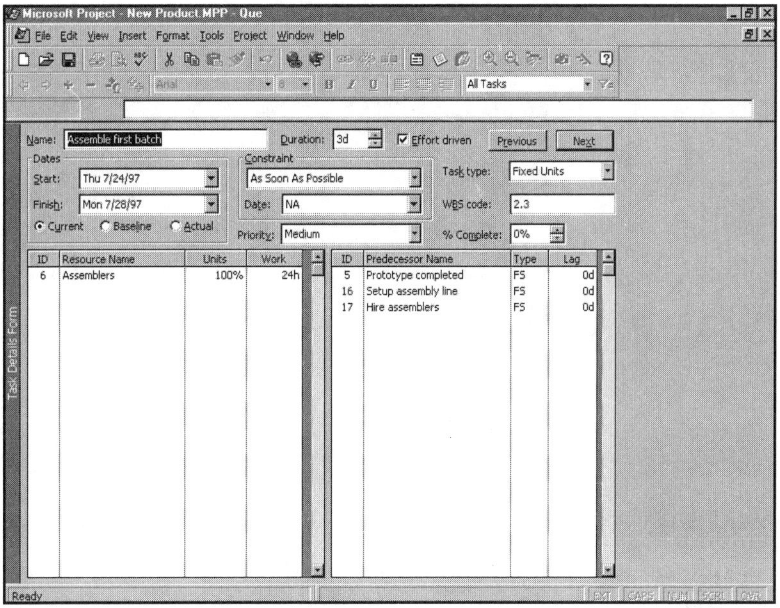

The Task Name Form

The Task Name Form shown at the bottom of Figure 20.16 is, as its name implies, a simplified form which displays only its task name in the top portion of the form. The bottom portion of the form has the same formatting options as the Task Form and the Task Details Form. It is accessed by choosing View, More Views. The Task Name Form is an effective form to use when you want a form in the bottom pane of a combination view and don't want to waste screen space with redundant information.

The Resource Graph

The Resource Graph is a graphical view displaying resource allocation over time (see the top pane in Figure 20.17). Found on the main View menu and on the View Bar, it can be a single pane view, or it can be used as part of a combination view, in either the top pane or the bottom pane. Used in conjunction with the Go To Next Overallocation button on the Resource Management toolbar, it can be very useful in determining when resources are overallocated, and by how much. For example, you can see in Figure 20.17 that beginning in the week of July 6, Howard Thompson has way too much to do.

▶ **See** "Understanding the Resource Graph View," **p. 342**

Part
VII

Ch
20

FIG. 20.16

The simple Task Name Form doesn't distract the user with too much detail.

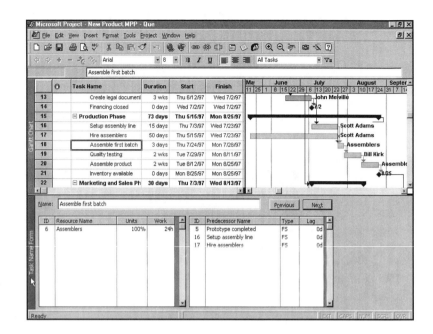

FIG. 20.17

The Resource Graph illustrates resource overallocations graphically on a timescale.

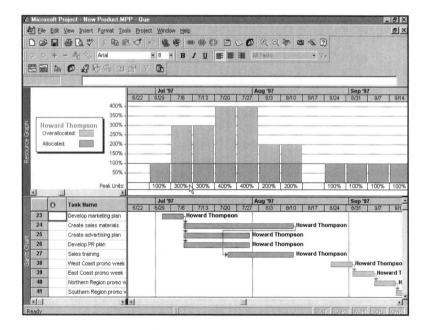

TIP A very handy combination view is a view with the Resource Graph in the top pane and the Gantt Chart in the bottom pane (refer to Figure 20.17). With this combination view, once you have identified an overallocated resource and determined the time frame during which the overallocation occurs (the top pane), you can see which tasks the resource has been assigned to (the bottom pane).

Resource Usage

The Resource Usage view, accessed through the main View menu, is a sheet view that lists resources on the left and their allocation to tasks on a timescale on the right (see Figure 20.18). This view displays information similar to the Resource Graph information, but in a different format, showing actual numbers rather than graphical representations of those numbers. Resources are listed on the left with the tasks assigned to them indented underneath. A symbol similar to the outline symbol in the task list allows you to hide or show the tasks assigned to the various resources. For example, in Figure 20.18, tasks for Scott Adams have been hidden; the plus symbol to the left of his name indicates that there is information not currently displayed. A diamond-shaped icon with an exclamation point displays in the Indicators column for the resources that need to be leveled. When you point to the icon, a message that identifies the type of leveling setting that is required (day by day, week by week, and so on) appears.

FIG. 20.18

Use the Resource Usage view when resolving overallocation problems.

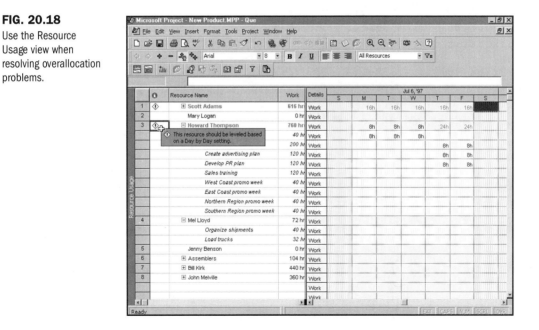

The allocation information on the right side can be set to display hours of work, hours of overallocated work, cost, available time, and so on.

Part

VII

Ch

20

This view is primarily used when resolving overallocation problems. Much like the Resource Graph, it is useful when displayed in a combination view, particularly with the Gantt Chart in the bottom pane to display the tasks assigned to each resource.

▶ **See** "Understanding the Resource Allocation View," **p. 341**

▶ **See** "Working with the Resource Usage View," **p. 352**

The Resource Sheet

The Resource Sheet shown in Figure 20.19 is a list of resource information displayed in a familiar spreadsheet format. Accessed by choosing View, More Views or using the View Bar, it can be used to enter and edit data about resources. Each resource is in a row with fields of resource data in columns. The Indicators column displays an icon for overallocated resources. The fields that are displayed depend on the table that has been applied. (See the section "Exploring the Standard Tables" later in this chapter for more details.) This view is most often used for creating the initial resource pool.

▶ **See** "Defining the Resource Pool," **p. 263**

▶ **See** "Using the Resource Sheet," **p. 264**

▶ **See** "Copying Data from Other Applications," **p. 641**

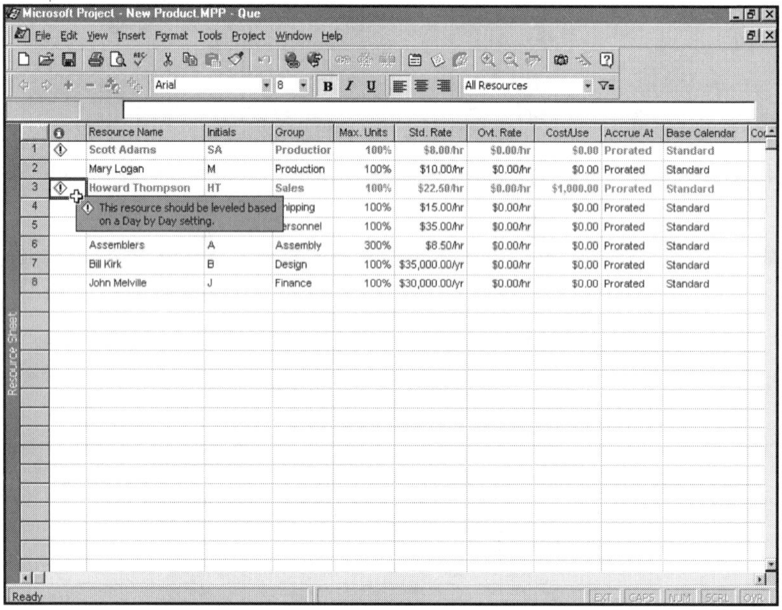

FIG. 20.19

The Resource Sheet provides a spreadsheet format for entering and editing basic resource data.

The Resource Form

Displaying much the same information as the Resource Sheet, the Resource Form only shows one resource at a time, allowing you to focus on one at a time (see Figure 20.20). The information in the top portion of the Resource Form is the same as in the Resource Sheet. The bottom portion can be set to display a schedule of tasks to which the resource is assigned—the hours of work that are currently assigned (including overtime), costs associated with this resource, notes, and so on. You can find these choices by choosing Format, Details.

FIG. 20.20

Use the Resource Form to display both basic and detailed information about any resource.

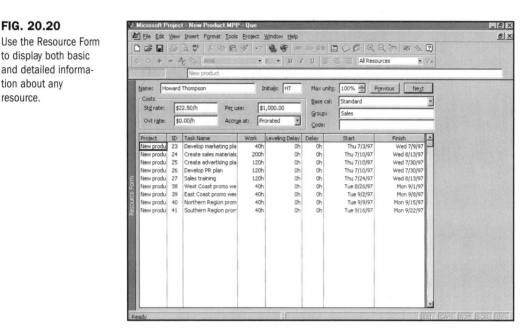

The Resource Form can be accessed by choosing View, More Views for display in a single or combination view. The top portion of the Resource Form can also be accessed by double-clicking a resource name in any view that displays it (see Figure 20.21). The form will appear this time as a dialog box for easy viewing and editing.

▶ **See** "Using the Resource Form," **p. 265**

Part
VII

Ch
20

The Resource Name Form

Similar to the Task Name Form, the Resource Name Form is a simple form that only displays the Resource Name in the top portion (see Figure 20.22). The bottom portion can be formatted to display a variety of fields about resources. To access this form, choose Format, Details.

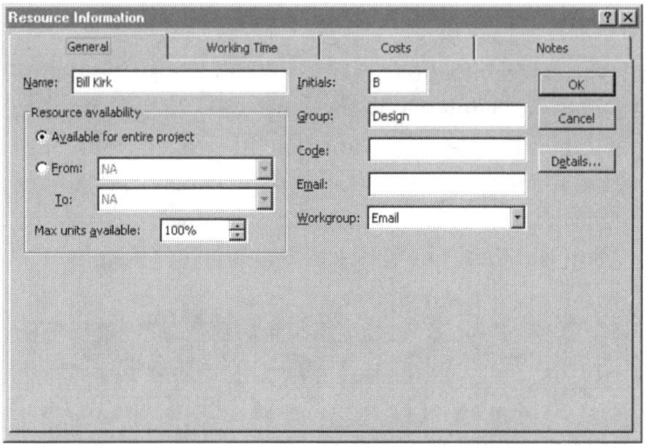

FIG. 20.21

The top part of the Resource Form can be displayed by double-clicking any resource in any view.

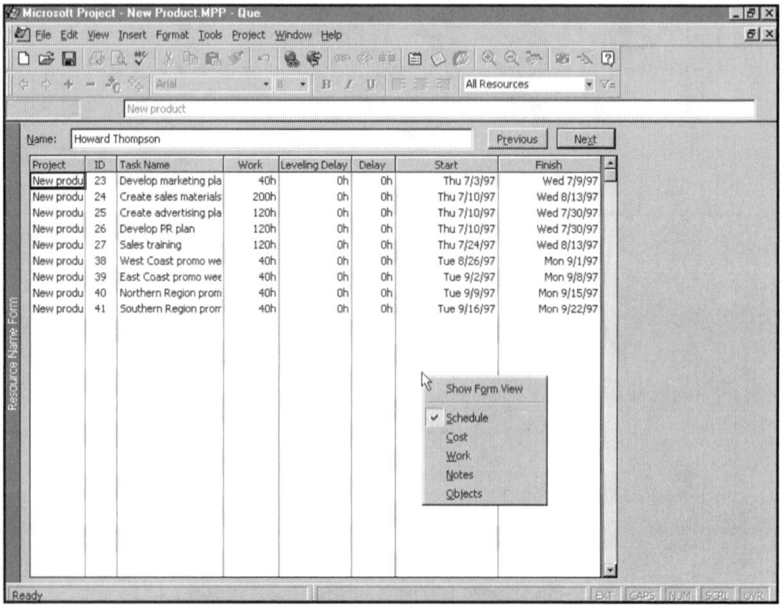

FIG. 20.22

The Resource Name form doesn't distract the user with too much detail.

The Task Entry

The Task Entry view is actually a combination of two views already described—the Gantt Chart in the top pane and the Task Form in the bottom pane (see Figure 20.23). It is a useful view because you can see several different types of information at one time: tasks on a timescale at the top and detailed information about the selected task at the bottom. This view can be accessed in three ways: by choosing View, More Views; by clicking the Task Entry button on the Resource Management toolbar; or by merely splitting the window by choosing Window, Split when a Gantt Chart view is active. The Task Form is the default view that displays automatically when the window is split.

FIG. 20.23

The Task Entry view offers several different perspectives on your project.

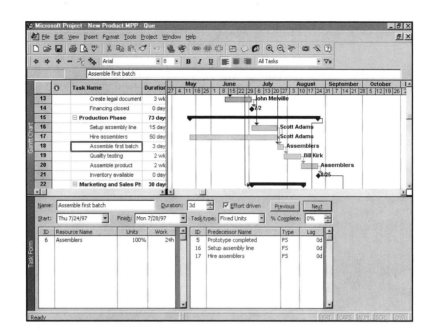

Resource Allocation

The Resource Allocation view is another predefined combination view that uses views that have already been described: the Resource Usage view at the top and the Leveling Gantt at the bottom (see Figure 20.24). As its name implies, this view was designed for resolving resource overallocations. In the top view, you determine which resources are overallocated, during what period of time, and to what degree. Then in the Gantt Chart at the bottom, you can determine which tasks are assigned to that resource. With this information, you can make decisions about how to handle the overallocation. For example, in Figure 20.24 the top pane identifies the week of July 6 as a problem for Howard Thompson. The bottom pane identifies the tasks that Howard has been assigned. Each of these tasks requires his full attention. With this information, you can make a wise decision about how to handle the problem.

▶ **See** "Identifying Resource Overallocations," **p. 348**

This view can be accessed in two ways: by choosing <u>V</u>iew, <u>M</u>ore Views or by clicking the Resource Allocation View button on the Resource Management toolbar.

Exploring the Standard Tables

In the sheet views, the fields (columns) that are displayed are controlled by tables. You can choose different tables by choosing <u>V</u>iew, <u>T</u>able, <u>M</u>ore Tables. If you are in a table view, the list of task tables is displayed. If you are in a resource view, a list of resource tables is displayed.

Part
VII

Ch
20

When you access the More Tables dialog box, you can view either the task or resource list of tables by choosing the appropriate option button in the top-left corner of the dialog box. The most commonly used tables are listed on the Ta<u>b</u>le menu, but all tables are listed in the More Tables dialog box. You can only apply tables, however, for the appropriate view format—that is, you can only apply a task table when you are in a task view.

FIG. 20.24

Use the Resource Allocation view to see when and by how much a resource is overallocated, as well as what tasks the resource is assigned during that time period.

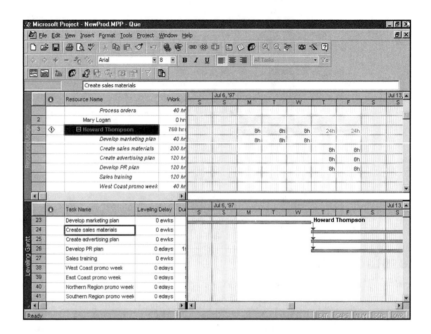

The following list displays all of the predefined tables, with the task tables on the left and the resource tables on the right. Tables marked with an asterisk must be accessed by choosing <u>V</u>iew, Ta<u>b</u>le, <u>M</u>ore Tables.

Task Tables	Resource Tables
Cost	Cost
Entry	Entry
Hyperlink	Hyperlink
Schedule	Summary
Summary	Usage
Tracking	Work
Usage	Earned Value*
Variance	Export*
Work	
Baseline*	

Constraint Dates*

Delay*

Earned Value*

Export*

PA_Expected Case*

PA_Optimistic Case*

PA_PERT Entry*

PA_Pessimistic Case*

Rollup Table*

You can customize and even create your own tables. The purpose of this section is to describe each of the predefined tables that are included with Microsoft Project. The fields that are included in each table will be listed but not described in detail.

▶ **See** "Using and Creating Tables," **p. 748**

The Task Tables

By choosing <u>V</u>iew, Ta<u>b</u>le, the most frequently used tables available for tasks appear directly. There are a number of other tables that can only be accessed by choosing <u>V</u>iew, Ta<u>b</u>le, <u>M</u>ore Tables. You can also edit, copy, and even create new tables in this dialog box. You must be in a task view before any of these tables are available.

The Cost Table   The Cost table is a task table that displays cost information about tasks. The fields that are displayed include: ID, Name, Fixed Cost, Fixed Cost Accrual, Cost, Baseline Cost, Cost Variance, Actual Cost, and Remaining Cost. This table is most useful when you are tracking a project and need to see how costs are varying from what you had originally planned.

The Entry Table   The Entry table is a task table that is the default table used for the Gantt Chart. It is particularly helpful during the data entry stage when you create your project. The fields that are displayed include: ID, Indicators, Name, Duration, Start, Finish, Predecessors, and Resource Names.

The Hyperlink Table   The Hyperlink table is a task table that allows you to create a hyperlink to a file on your own computer, a network in your organization, an intranet in your organization, or the World Wide Web. The fields that are displayed include: ID, Indicators, Name, Hyperlink, Hyperlink Address, and Hyperlink SubAddress.

▶ **See** "Navigating with Hyperlinks," **p. 441**

The Schedule Table   As its name implies, the Schedule table displays scheduling information about tasks. Fields that are included are ID, Name, Start, Finish, Late Start, Late Finish, Free Slack, and Total Slack. With this information, you can pinpoint tasks that can be adjusted when you are trying to reduce the overall duration of the project (crash the schedule). You know that you can delay noncritical tasks, but by how much? By providing the calculated values of free slack and total slack, you can tell how much a task can be delayed.

The Summary Table   The Summary table provides basic task information. Fields displayed include: ID, Name, Duration, Start, Finish, Percent Complete, Cost, and Work. This view can be useful to management when printed as a summary of all the tasks that are part of the project.

The Tracking Table   The Tracking table provides a place to view or enter actual information on tasks as the project progresses. Fields that are displayed include: ID, Name, Actual Start, Actual Finish, Percent Complete, Actual Duration, Remaining Duration, Actual Cost, and Actual Work. Print the Task Sheet with this table applied and give it to personnel who do not work in an office with a computer. The printout serves as their tracking tool. Notes taken on the printout can then be entered back into the file.

The Usage Table   The Usage table is used by the new Task Usage view and provides information about the hours of work expended for each task. The fields that are displayed include: ID, Indicators, Name, Work, Duration, Start, and Finish.

The Variance Table   The Variance table is another task table that summarizes the difference between what was planned and what has actually happened in the project. Fields that are displayed include: ID, Name, Start, Finish, Baseline Start, Baseline Finish, Start Variance, and Finish Variance. For example, with the calculated variance fields it's possible to identify resources that start their tasks late but finish on time, or resources that start on time but finish late. These are two different kinds of resource problems and should be handled differently.

The Work Table   The Work table displays total hours of work required and performed for tasks. Fields that are displayed include: ID, Name, Work, Baseline Work, Work Variance, Actual Work, Remaining Work, and Percent Work Complete. This is information useful when you need to identify tasks that require more time than originally expected, and which of these tasks are in trouble because they took so long to complete. These tasks may need additional resources or different resources.

The Baseline Table   The Baseline table displays information about what you planned during the design phase of the project. As you enter actual information, Project continues calculating start and finish dates for the tasks that follow. Baseline dates are created at the time the baseline is set. Those dates will not be recalculated, but instead provide the comparison to what you planned. Fields that are displayed include: ID, Name, Baseline Duration, Baseline Start, Baseline Finish, Baseline Work, and Baseline Cost.

▶ **See** "Setting the Baseline or Plan," **p. 474**

The Constraint Dates Table   Available only through the More Tables command, this task table is an invaluable tool for locating tasks that have had constraints applied, whether they were applied intentionally or not. Fields that are displayed include: ID, Task Name, Duration, Constraint Type, and Constraint Date.

▶ **See** "Resolving Problems Caused by Constraints," **p. 208**

The Delay Table   The Delay table is used by the Detail and Leveling Gantt views, but you can use it directly if you want. It is helpful when you are trying to resolve overallocation problems. If you are using the Resource Leveling command, you can use this table to see where delays have been imposed on a task. If you are leveling resources on your own, this table offers a place to enter the delay information. This table is basically the entry table with the Leveling Delay field added. Fields that are displayed include: ID, Indicators, Name, Leveling Delay, Duration, Start, Finish, Successors, and Resource Names.

▶ **See** "Resolve Overallocations by Delaying Assignments," **p. 371**

The Earned Value Table   The Earned Value table is used to compare actual progress against expected progress (based on work completed by resources). It can also be used to predict whether a task will come in under budget (based on costs incurred thus far). All of the fields are calculated and include: ID, Name, Budgeted Cost of Work Scheduled (BCWS), Budgeted Cost of Work Performed (BCWP), Actual Cost of Work Performed (ACWP), Schedule Variance (SV), Cost Variance (CV), Estimate at Completion (FAC), Budgeted at Completion (BAC), and Cost Variance. This table is probably not for the casual user.

The Export Table   This task table was designed with exporting to another application in mind. Most of the task fields, including many that are calculated, are displayed: ID, Unique ID, Name, Duration, Type, Outline Level, Baseline Duration, Predecessors, Start, Finish, Early Start, Early Finish, Late Start, Late Finish, Free Slack, Total Slack, Leveling Delay, Percent Complete, Actual Start, Actual Finish, Baseline Start, Baseline Finish, Constraint Type, Constraint Date, Stop, Resume, Created, Work, Baseline Work, Actual Work, Cost, Fixed Cost, Baseline Cost, Actual Cost, Remaining Cost, WBS, Priority, Milestone, Summary, Rollup, Subproject File and numerous customizable fields, Text 1-Text 10, Cost 1-Cost 3, Duration 1-Duration 3, Flag 1-Flag 10, Marked, and Number 1-Number 5.

▶ **See** "Exchanging Project Data with Other Applications," **p. 593**

The Resource Tables

When a Task Sheet is part of a view, the task tables described previously focus on task information. When a resource sheet view is displayed, the columns are also controlled by tables. Only the resource tables are available when you are in a resource view. The most commonly used tables are available directly by choosing View, Table. All resource tables are available when you choose View, Table, More Tables.

The Cost Table   There is also a Cost table for resources. Instead of calculating costs on a task-by-task basis, the Cost table for resources provides cost data by resource. Fields that are displayed include: ID, Resource Name, Cost, Baseline Cost, Cost Variance, Actual Cost, and Remaining Cost. This table can be helpful in determining which resources are the most and least expensive and which ones are over budget and under budget. When applied to the Resource Usage view, this table allows you to see the cost information for the resource during the whole project, as down on a task-by-task basis.

The Resource Entry Table   Very similar to the Entry table for tasks, the Entry table for resources displays information about resources that are usually gathered when the resource pool is being created. It is the default table used by the Resource Sheet. Fields that are displayed include: ID, Indicators, Resource Name, Initials, Group, Maximum Units, Standard Rate, Overtime Rate, Cost Per Use, Accrue At, Baseline Calendar, and Code.

▶ **See** "Defining the Resource Pool," **p. 263**

The Hyperlink Table   The Hyperlink table for resources is very similar to the Hyperlink table for tasks. It is used for storing hyperlink references to a file on your computer, a network, an organization's intranet, or even the World Wide Web. The fields that are displayed include: ID, Indicators, Resource Name, Hyperlink, Hyperlink Address, and Hyperlink SubAddress.

The Summary Table   Similar to the Summary table for tasks, the Summary table for resources provides a synopsis of information about each resource in the pool. Fields that are displayed include: ID, Resource Name, Group, Max Units, Peak, Standard Rate, Overtime Rate, Cost, and Work. As with the Summary table for tasks, a useful printout for management would be the Resource Sheet with the Summary table applied.

The Usage Table   The Usage table provides information about the quantity of resources that are being used. Fields that are displayed include: ID, Indicators, Resource Name, and Work. With this table, it is easy to see which resources are being overutilized and which are being underutilized.

The Work Table   This resource table provides work information about each resource. Fields that are displayed include: ID, Resource Name, Percent Work Complete, Work (total hours assigned), Overtime Work, Baseline Work (planned), Work Variance, Actual Work, and Remaining Work. From this table, you can tell a number of things about each resource. You can tell how much progress the resources have made on their assigned tasks and how much work they have left to do. You can also tell how long they work on tasks compared to how much time was allocated for the task, as well as how much of the work has been overtime (in some cases incurring overtime costs).

The Earned Value Table   Using traditional project management calculations, this resource table is useful for comparing the budgeted work and costs with the actual cost of the work. All of the values in this table are calculated. It is used for analysis only, not for entering or editing data. The fields that are displayed include: ID, Name, Budgeted Cost of Work Scheduled (BCWS), Budgeted Cost of Work Performed (BCWP), Actual Cost of Work Performed (ACWP), Schedule Variance (SV), Cost Variance (CV), Estimate at Completion (EAC), Budgeted at Completion (BAC), and Variance at Completion (VAC). This table is probably not for the casual user.

The Export Table   Like the Export table for tasks, the Export table for resources provides a vehicle for resource information to be exported to other applications. Fields that are displayed include: ID, Unique ID, Resource Name, Initials, Max Units, Standard Rate, Overtime Rate, Cost Per Use, Accrue At, Cost, Baseline Cost, Actual Cost, Work, Baseline Work, Actual Work, Overtime Work, Group, Code, Text 1-Text 5, and Email Address.

▶ **See** "Exchanging Project Data with Other Applications," **p. 593**

Exploring the Standard Filters

As discussed, tables are a central building block of Microsoft Project. They determine which fields are displayed for tasks or resources. Filters are another major building block that determine which tasks or resources are displayed, depending on criteria that you provide.

All the views except the PERT Chart and the Task PERT can have filters applied. All the standard views have been assigned the all-inclusive filter (All Tasks or All Resources).

▶ **See** "Selecting the Filter for the View," **p. 745**

N O T E Any view in the bottom pane of a combination view will not have any filters available. The bottom pane is already being filtered by virtue of being the bottom pane, which is always controlled by what is selected in the top pane. ▪

A filter helps you identify and display only the tasks or resources (depending on the view) that match one or more criteria. All other tasks or resources are temporarily hidden. If a filter is applied as a highlight filter, all tasks or resources are displayed, but those selected by the filter are displayed with highlight formatting features such as a different color, bold, italic, underline, and so on, as defined by choosing Format, Text Styles. Any filter can be applied as a highlight filter or a display-only filter.

▶ **See** "Formatting Text Displays for Categories of Tasks and Resources," **p. 697**

You define the criteria for a filter by specifying one or more field values that must be matched for a task or resource to be selected by the filter. For example, Microsoft Project maintains a field named Milestone for tasks, and automatically places the value Yes in the field if you define a task as a milestone; tasks that you don't mark as a milestone are given the value No in that field. The Milestone filter stipulates that the Milestone field must equal the value Yes.

In addition to these simple filters, there are special filters known as interactive filters that ask the user to supply the value or values to be searched for in the field. The Date Range filter, available by choosing Project, Filtered For, for example, asks the user to enter two dates and then displays all tasks that have a Scheduled Start or Finish date within this range of dates.

N O T E Any of the filters on the Project, Filtered For menu command that contain an ellipsis are interactive filters. ▪

T I P You can also apply an existing filter by using the Filter list box on the Formatting toolbar.

Another type of filter, the calculated filter, determines what item to display by comparing the values in two fields in the database. For example, the Cost Overbudget filter compares the value in the Cost field (which is the total scheduled cost for a task) with the value in the Baseline Cost field for that same task. If the scheduled cost is greater than the planned cost, the filter selects the task.

Part VII
Ch 20

Some filters use more than one test for selecting the items to display. For example, the In Progress Tasks filter selects all the tasks that have an Actual Start date recorded (the Actual Start field no longer displays NA) but do not have an Actual Finish date recorded (the Actual Finish field still displays NA). In this case, both conditions must be met for a task to be selected: The Actual Start must not have NA, and the Actual Finish must still have NA. This kind of criterion is usually called an *and* condition or criterion. For a task to be selected, both this condition *and* that condition must be satisfied.

| All Tasks ▾ |

Another example of a filter that applies more than one test is the Tasks With Fixed Dates filter, which is accessed by either choosing Project, Filtered For, More Filters or by selecting it from the Filter list box on the Formatting toolbar. This filter locates all the tasks that either have constrained dates (the Constraint Type setting is not As Soon As Possible) or that already have an actual start date recorded (the Actual Start field no longer shows NA). This filter is useful for resolving scheduling problems caused by fixed dates. In this case, Project selects all the tasks that have a constraint imposed on them *or* that have already started and cannot be rescheduled. This type of criterion is called an *or* condition or criterion. For a task to be selected, either one *or* the other of the conditions must be satisfied.

▶ **See** "Resolving Conflicts Caused by Constraints," **p. 208**

Using the Standard Filters

Not every view can be filtered, and there are other limitations to using filters. The following points summarize these limitations:

■ You can only apply task filters to task views and only resource filters to resource views.

■ You cannot apply a filter to a bottom pane view. The reason is that the bottom pane view is already filtered: It displays only the tasks or resources that are associated with the item or items selected in the top pane.

■ The PERT Chart and Task PERT cannot be filtered, but the standard filters are available for all other views.

■ You cannot apply a highlight filter to a form. Using a filter as a highlight makes sense only for the views that display lists, because the purpose of a highlight is to make selected items stand out from the rest. Thus, only the views that contain a table can accept a highlight filter.

■ Each filter considers the entire set of tasks or resources for selections. Using the Filter drop-down list on the Standard toolbar or the standard filters on the Project, Filtered For menu, you cannot use successive filters to progressively narrow the set of selected tasks or resources. For example, if you filter the task list to show Milestones, and then you apply the Critical filter, you will see all critical tasks related, not just critical milestones. You must either create a filter, edit an existing one, or use the AutoFilter option in order to use more than one criterion at a time.

▶ **See** "Creating Custom Filters," **p. 754**

TIP   You can create successive filters using the AutoFilter feature covered in an upcoming section.

Any view that can accept a filter can have one defined as part of the view: When the view is selected, the filter is automatically applied. All the standard views initially have the All Tasks or All Resources filters designated as part of the view definition.

▶ **See** "Selecting the Filter for the View," **p. 745**

Describing the Standard Filters

`All Tasks ▼` The standard filters supplied with Microsoft Project provide standard selection criteria useful in many situations that you will encounter. You may never need to create your own filters. Tables 20.1 and 20.2 describe the standard task filters and resource filters, respectively. An asterisk marks a filter not found on the standard Project, Filtered For menu command, but which is found instead on the More Filters menu. All filters are listed in the Filter list box on the Formatting toolbar as well.

Table 20.1   The Standard Task Filters

Filter Name	Purpose
All Tasks	Displays all tasks.
Completed Tasks	Displays tasks that are marked as 100% complete.
Confirmed*	Displays tasks for which the requested resources have agreed to take on the assignment.
Cost Greater Than...*	Displays a prompt asking for the cost to be used in a test for tasks that are greater than that cost.
Cost Overbudget*	Displays all tasks that have a scheduled cost greater than the baseline cost if the baseline cost is greater than 0.
Created After...*	Displays a prompt asking for a date to be used in a test for tasks that were created after that date.
Critical	Displays all critical tasks.
Date Range...	Displays a prompt asking for a range of dates to be used in a test for tasks that either start or finish within that range of dates.
In Progress Tasks*	Displays all tasks that have started but have not finished.
Incomplete Tasks	Displays all tasks that have a percent complete not equal to 100%.
Late/Overbudget Tasks Assigned To...*	Displays a prompt asking for a resource name to be used in a test for tasks assigned to that resource where the task's finish date is later than the baseline finish or the cost is greater than the baseline.

Part

VII

Ch

20

continues

Table 20.1 Continued

Filter Name	Purpose
Linked Fields*	Displays all tasks that are linked to another application.
Milestones	Displays all milestones.
Resource Group...*	Displays all tasks assigned to the specified resource group.
Should Start By...*	Displays all tasks that should have started but have not started by a date supplied by the user.
Should Start/Finish By...*	Prompts for a range of dates which are used to display tasks that should have started by the beginning date or should have finished by the end date.
Slipped/Late Progress*	Displays tasks where the finish date is later than the baseline or the Budgeted Cost of Work Scheduled is greater than the Budgeted Cost of Work Performed.
Slipping Tasks*	Displays all tasks not finished and whose scheduled finish date is later than the planned finish date.
Summary Tasks	Displays all tasks that have subordinate tasks defined below them.
Task Range...	Displays all tasks that have ID numbers within a range specified by the user.
Tasks With Attachments*	Shows tasks that have objects attached, such as a graph or a note in the Notes field.
Tasks With Fixed Dates*	Displays all tasks that have a constraint other than As Soon As Possible or that have already started.
Tasks/Assignments With Overtime*	Displays all tasks where overtime work has been assigned.
Top Level Tasks*	Displays all highest level summary tasks.
Unconfirmed*	Displays all tasks for which the requested resources have not yet committed to the task.
Unstarted Tasks*	Displays all tasks which have not yet started. For example, the Actual Start field is still set to NA.
Update Needed*	Displays all tasks that have incurred changes, such as revised start and finish dates or resource reassignments, and needs to be sent for update or confirmation.
Using Resource in Date Range...*	Displays all tasks that use the resource named by the user during the range of dates also supplied by the user.

Filter Name	Purpose
Using Resource...	Displays all tasks that use the resource named by the user.
Work Overbudget*	Displays all tasks where the actual hours of work performed are greater than what was planned (the baseline work).

Table 20.2 The Standard Resource Filters

Filter Name	Purpose
All Resources	Displays all resources. This is the default filter.
Confirmed Assignments*	Displays resources who have confirmed their task assignments.
Cost Greater Than...*	Displays resources where the cost is greater than the amount specified by the user.
Cost Overbudget	Displays all resources that have a cost that is greater than the baseline cost.
Date Range...*	Displays resources who have tasks that are occurring during a range of dates specified by the user.
Group...	Displays all resources that belong to the group specified by the user (which have the same entry in the Group field).
In Progress Assignments*	Displays resources who have tasks that are being worked on. For example, the tasks have an actual start date but no actual finish.
Linked Fields*	Displays all resources with fields that are linked to another application.
Overallocated Resources	Displays all resources that are overallocated. For example, resources that have too many hours of work assigned to them during some time period of the project.
Resource Range...	Displays all resources that have ID numbers within the range specified by the user.
Resources With Attachments*	Displays resources that have objects attached or a note in the Notes field.
Resources/Assignments With Overtime*	Displays resources where some of the work assigned to them is incurred as overtime.

Part

VII

Ch

20

continues

Table 20.2   Continued

Filter Name	Purpose
Should Start By...*	Displays resources assigned to tasks that have not started where the calculated start falls after a date specified by the user.
Should Start/Finish By...*	Displays resources assigned to tasks that have not started where the start or finish of the task falls between a date range specified by the user.
Slipped/Late Progress*	Displays resources with tasks assigned where the finish date is later than the baseline or the Budgeted Cost of Work Scheduled is greater than the Budgeted Cost of Work Performed.
Slipping Assignments*	Displays resources with tasks assigned that are not finished and whose scheduled finish date is later than the planned finish date.
Unconfirmed Assignments*	Displays resources with tasks assigned for which a commitment has not yet been made.
Unstarted Assignments*	Displays all resources assigned to tasks which have not yet started but that have been confirmed. For example, the Actual Start field is still set to NA.
Work Complete*	Displays resources assigned to tasks that are 100% complete.
Work Incomplete*	Displays resources assigned to tasks that have started but are not 100% complete.
Work Overbudget	Displays all resources with scheduled work that is greater than the baseline work.

Applying a Filter to the Current View

All Tasks ▼   To apply a filter to a view, you can choose Project, Filtered For or use the Filter list box on the Formatting toolbar. If the filter that you want is on the Project, Filtered For menu, select the filter name, and it will be applied immediately. If the filter is not on the Project, Filtered For menu, first choose More Filters, and then choose the filter name from the complete list of filters in the More Filters entry list (see Figure 20.25). Choose the Apply button to apply the filter so that only filtered tasks or resources that satisfy the filter appear. If you want to apply the filter as a highlight filter (so that filtered items are highlighted and all other items remain displayed), choose the Highlight button instead of the Apply button.

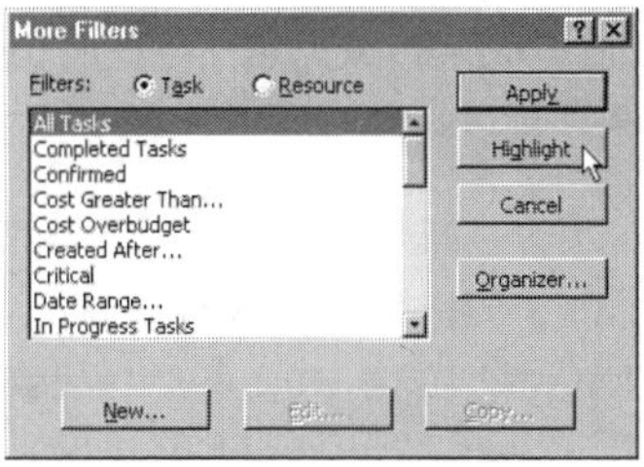

FIG. 20.25

The More Filters dialog box lists all filters that are available for both tasks and resources.

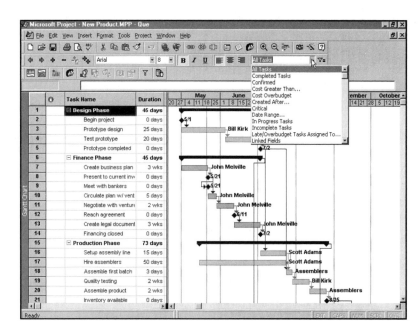

T I P You can also apply filters as highlight filters by holding down the Shift key as you choose Project, Filtered For and select the filter name.

You can also apply a filter to the current view by selecting the filter name from the Filter list box on the Formatting toolbar (see Figure 20.26). When you select the filter name from the list, the filter is applied immediately. You cannot apply the filter as a highlight filter when using the Filter list box.

FIG. 20.26

The Filter list box on the Formatting toolbar provides access to all filters.

Part
VII

Ch

20

CAUTION

When you apply a filter, all tasks or resources that satisfy the criteria at that moment are selected by the filter. If you change a value in a field, you might change how this value satisfies the filter criteria. The task or resource will continue to be displayed or highlighted, however, because the filter criteria are evaluated only at the moment the filter is applied. You may need to apply the filter again if you make significant changes in the project.

TIP
The filter does not automatically reflect changes to task or resources that would cause it to be included or not included in the filter. You can reapply the filter by pressing Ctrl+F3. You can set a filter back to the default All Tasks or All Resources by pressing F3.

After you apply an interactive filter, a dialog box appears in which you must supply the values to be used for testing the tasks or resources. For example, Figure 20.27 shows the Using Resource filter dialog box. This filter will select all tasks assigned to the resource that you choose from the entry list.

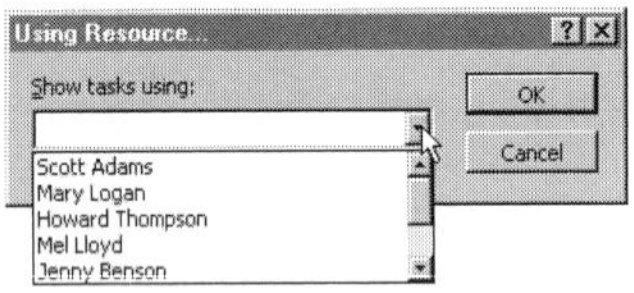

FIG. 20.27
The Using Resource filter dialog box allows you to choose from a list of available resources.

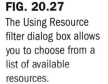

Using the AutoFilter

A new feature with this version of Microsoft Project is the AutoFilter. It is very similar to the AutoFilter feature in Microsoft Excel. To turn on the AutoFilter feature, you can choose the AutoFilter tool on the Formatting toolbar or from the menu, choose Project, Filtered For, AutoFilter.

When enabled, the AutoFilter places a drop-down menu with AutoFilter values at the top of each table column (see Figure 20.28). To filter that column, choose an option from the drop-down menu. The column heading will turn blue to indicate that the column is filtered. You can apply a filter in this way to more than one column to perform successive filters. For example, in Figure 20.28 filters have been used to display only tasks assigned to John Melville that are starting this month.

The duration field has AutoFilter options for ranges less than 1 week, more than 1 week, and so on. Date fields have options for ranges as well—for example, this week, this month, next month, and so on (see Figure 20.28).

Each of the drop-down menus also has a custom option which allows you to create and save a filter with more than one condition, using either an *and* or an *or* condition (see Figure 20.29).

▶ **See** "Creating Custom Filters," **p. 754**

TIP
The keystrokes that reapply the filter (Ctrl+F3) and set a filter back to the default All Tasks or All Resources (F3) also work with the AutoFilter.

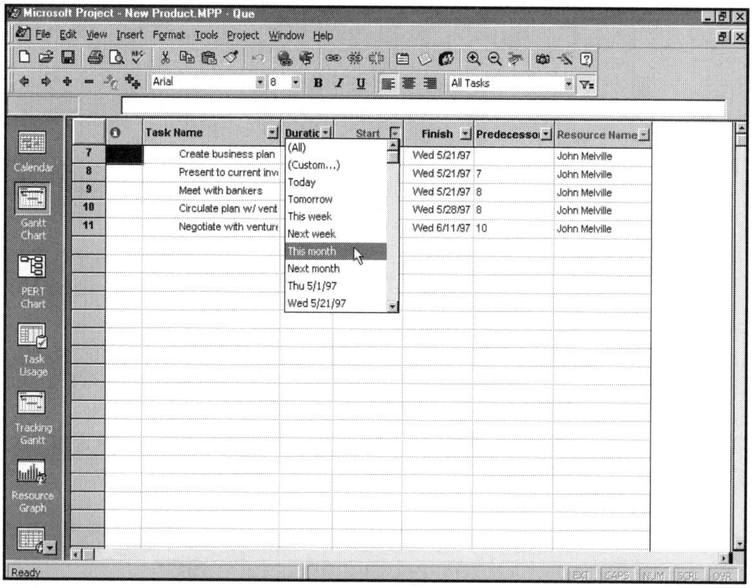

FIG. 20.28

Use the AutoFilter to easily narrow down a list of tasks or resources.

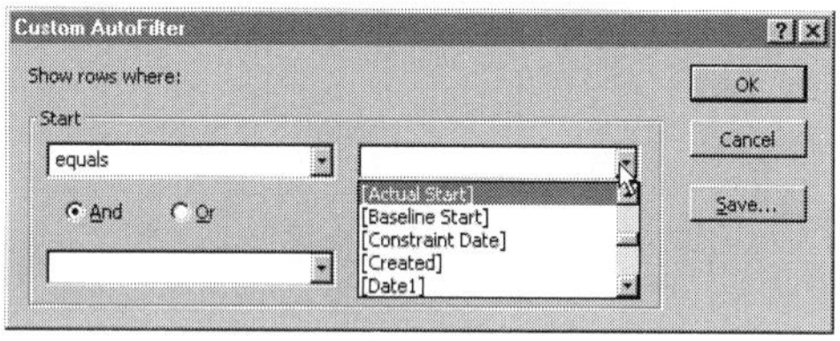

FIG. 20.29

Create multiple condition fields that can be saved with the Custom AutoFilter option.

From Here...

This chapter has described the views, tables, and filters that come with Microsoft Project and the situations in which they would be useful. The following chapters describe how to make changes to these essential building blocks. You can change the information that displays, or you can change the way it displays.

- Chapter 21, "Formatting Views," will show you how to change the default formats for virtually any component of any view.

- Chapter 22, "Customizing Views, Tables and Filters," will show you how to edit the existing definitions for each of these building blocks as well as create new ones of your own.

- Chapter 23, "Using the Standard Reports," will describe the various predefined reports that come with Microsoft Project.

- Chapter 24, "Customizing Reports," will show you how to modify the predefined reports and create new ones of your own.

Part

VI

Ch

20

CHAPTER 21

Formatting Views

Being able to customize the standard views and reports, along with creating new ones is a major strength of Microsoft Project. In the previous chapter you saw how to use the basic building blocks of tables and filters to create new views. This chapter shows you how to enhance the appearance and serviceability of the standard views.

A number of menu commands provide options for changing the appearance and content of the major views. Most of these options are on the Format menu, but you will also find choices on the View and Project menus.

Views are basically broken down into three category types: sheets, forms, and graphical views. Views of the same type share similar customizing options. Sheet and graphical views all contain gridlines; therefore, you can use the Format, Gridlines command to change the appearance of the gridlines in all of these views. Many graphical views also contain a timescale, so use the Format, Timescale command in all these views. Use the Format, Text Styles command to change the font, size, and color of text in all views. ■

Zoom in and out to change the perspective on the project

Get a different timeframe perspective on the project at different phases of the project.

Modify the timescale display to change perspectives

Instead of using Zoom, you can be more precise and specific about how the timescale should be displayed.

Choose the font, size, and color of text

Project allows you to customize on an individual task-by-task basis or by categories of tasks.

Change the display of graphical objects on views

In the graphical views, you can customize nearly everything, graph type, color, shapes, colors, shading, and so on.

Change the type of values that are calculated

Learn how many different kinds of values can be calculated and graphed based on the information needs of the project manager.

Sort tasks and resources in an order that you specify

Instead of viewing data in a default sort order and manually looking for information in categories, it makes more sense to sort in alternate orders.

Using the Format Options in the Standard Views

Unlike tables and filters (described in the previous chapter), the options on the Format menu do not create named objects, but only change the look of the current view. Suppose you change the timescale on the Gantt Chart to show months instead of days. Until you change the timescale again, you will see this format for the timescale each time you use the Gantt Chart. However, if you switch to another view that also has a timescale (the Resource Usage view, for example), you will find that the timescale in that view does not incorporate the changes in the Gantt Chart timescale, but instead reflects the way the Resource Usage view was last displayed. These changes are saved with the project file only. If you change to another project file, you won't see changes you made in other files. You can borrow settings from another file or a template called GLOBAL.MPT that stores all of your default settings using the Organizer.

▶ **See** "Organizing Views in Project Files," **p. 764**

Sorting the Tasks or Resources in a View

Sorting is especially relevant for views that display tasks or resources in a table or list layout, but you also can sort the order in which tasks or resources appear in the form views as you scroll with the Next and Previous buttons. You can't sort the displayed items in the PERT Chart and Task PERT views, however.

The Sort command, on the Project menu, enables you to sort by a number of pre-defined fields, as well as a combination of up to three columns or fields that you specify. The pre-defined fields for sorting vary from one view to another. For example, in a resource view, pre-defined sort fields include By Cost, By Name, or By ID. The pre-defined fields in a task view include By Start Date, By Finish Date, By Priority, By Cost, and By ID. In addition, for both task and resource views, you can choose the Sort By option to specify other fields, a combination of fields, and the order of the sort.

For example, for resources, you might want to sort first by the group in which they are located. Then sort within each group by the standard rate the resources are paid—but in descending order, so that the highest paid are listed first within each group. If some of the people in the same group are paid the same standard rate, you also can alphabetize these people by name in ascending (normal) order.

To sort the entries in a view, choose Project, Sort. A cascading menu appears with the pre-defined sort fields (see Figure 21.1). If you choose from one of these, the tasks or resources will be sorted immediately but only by that one field and in ascending order. If you select the Sort By option, the Sort dialog box appears offering more choices (see Figure 21.2).

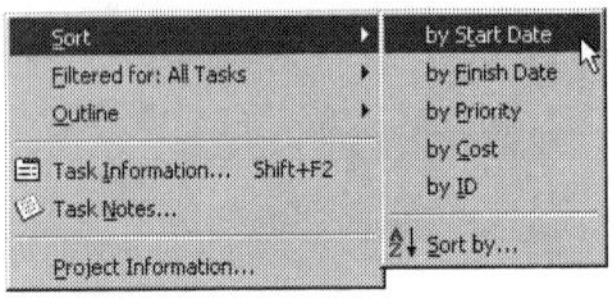

FIG. 21.1

The cascading sort list offers easy access for sorting tasks or resources.

FIG. 21.2
The Sort dialog box offers more extensive options for sorting.

Selecting the Sort Keys   Use the drop-down list arrow in the Sort By area to select the major sort field. Select the Ascending or Descending button to specify the sort order. If you want to further sort the list within the groups that are placed together by the first sort field, choose the two Then By fields, similarly indicating the sort order for each of these fields. In Figure 21.2, the Resource Sheet is being sorted by Group name first, in ascending (normal) order. Within each group, the resources are being sorted by their Standard Rate of pay in descending (highest paying) order. Notice that the second Then By field is selected so that the resources earning the same standard rate will be further sorted in ascending order by resource name.

Selecting the Sort Operation   After you define the fields to sort by, you need to indicate whether you want the tasks or resources to be permanently renumbered. Although the option to undo a sort is available, it is a good idea to save your project file before sorting in case the Undo function is not available. For task views, you can also choose to keep all tasks under their summary tasks, but to sort subordinate tasks within their summary task, mark the Keep Outline Structure check box. To sort all tasks without regard for their position within an outline, clear this box.

▶ **See** "Outlining the Task List," **p. 160**

For resource views, there is also a check box for sorting the resources by the projects to which they are assigned. This is useful when you are using the same pool of resources for more than one project.

▶ **See** "Sharing Resources Among Projects," **p. 558**

To sort the list immediately, choose the Sort button. To return the sort keys to the standard sort—by ID numbers only—choose the Reset button. Note that Reset will not display the original order of the list if Permanently Renumber Tasks was selected.

Choosing the Cancel button cancels all changes you made to the Sort dialog box and returns you to the workspace.

▶ **See** "Sorting the Task and Resource Lists," **p. 399**

Part
VII

Ch
21

Formatting Text Displays for Categories of Tasks and Resources

Most of the views enable you to choose special formatting options for displaying text. You can differentiate categories of tasks or resources by the font, type size, style, or color of text used to display the data. For example, you can format critical tasks to be displayed in red, or summary tasks to appear in bold. In table views, you can format the column headings. In timescale views, you can format the unit labels in the timescale. Text formatting also defines the appearance that highlight filters will use to display items selected by the filter.

▷ **See** "Filtering the Task or Resource List," **p. 395**

▷ **See** "Using the Standard Filters," **p. 686**

To change the display of text for *categories* of tasks or resources in a view, choose Format, Text Styles. The Text Styles dialog box appears (see Figure 21.3). If the Text Styles command doesn't appear in the Format menu, you can't change the text display in this view. To change the text display for selected tasks or resources that don't fall into any particular category, see the section "Formatting Selected Text," later in this chapter.

FIG. 21.3
Use the Text Styles dialog box to change text style for categories of tasks or resources.

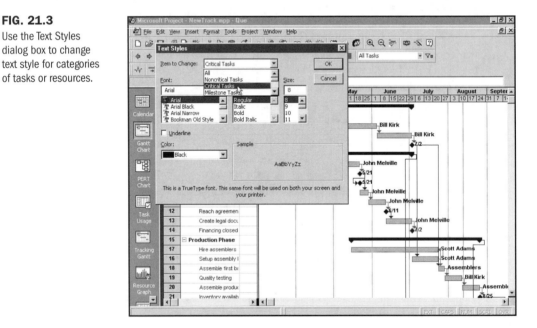

Selecting the Item to Change   From the Item to Change drop-down list, choose the item you want. Some items in the list take precedence over others when a task or resource falls into two or more categories. Here are the task items, listed in order of precedence (with the highest priority at the top):

▓ Highlighted Tasks (by a filter)

▓ Marked Tasks

▓ Summary Tasks

▓ Milestone Tasks

▓ Critical Tasks

Therefore, if a Milestone task also is a Summary task, the display is governed by the text format for Summary tasks rather than for Milestone tasks. If the same task is selected by a highlight filter, the task shows the Highlight display rather than either the Summary or the Milestone display.

Highlighted tasks are those selected by a highlight filter. Use Format Text Styles (as described in this section) to determine how highlighted tasks or resources will be displayed. Use the Project, Filtered For command with the Highlight option to display tasks or resources with the highlight format.

▶ **See** "Using the Standard Filters," **p. 686**

TIP You can choose to highlight tasks selected by the filter rather than hide other tasks by pressing the Shift key while choosing Project, Filtered For.

Marked tasks have the logical value Yes in the Marked field of the task database. Use the Marked field to manually select tasks without defining a filter (or when there is no logical test that can be expressed for the filter). You can define any task table or custom form to display the Marked field for editing purposes. When you mark tasks, you can filter or use a special text format for them.

▶ **See** "Entering Milestones," **p. 140**

▶ **See** "Outlining the Task List," **p. 160**

▶ **See** "Identifying the Critical Path," **p. 406**

Milestone tasks have the logical value Yes in the Milestone field. The Milestone field is set to Yes when you enter a duration of zero for a task, but you can also designate any task as a Milestone task by checking the Mark Task as Milestone check box on the Advanced tab of the Task Information dialog box. Access the Task Information dialog box by double-clicking the task name or by choosing the Task Information tool on the standard toolbar. You can also place the Milestone field in a table for editing purposes.

▶ **See** "Using and Creating Tables," **p. 748**

The All item in the Item to Change drop-down list on the Text Styles dialog box lets you easily make the same change in all items at once. If you make a change in the format options for the All item, this change is made for every other item in the selection list. You may use the All item initially, for example, to set an overall font type or size, leaving all other options clear. This procedure sets the same font type and size in all categories. You can then override the font and size on individual categories. If you later choose the All item again, however, and make a change in the font or point size, all categories change again.

The items listed after All are specific to tasks or resources, depending on which view is currently displayed. After those items are features of the active view. When the Gantt Chart is the active view, for example, the first items listed deal with tasks: critical, noncritical, milestones, and so on. After that, the item list includes Row & Column Titles (for the table part of the view), Major Timescale and Minor Timescale (for the unit measures at the top of the timescale), and Bar Text (for displaying field values next to the bars in the bar chart in the timescale).

Part

VII

Ch

21

Changing the Font   Use the Font scroll bar in the Text Styles dialog box to move through the list of font choices for the selected item. The fonts listed are the ones that have been installed in Windows 95 for the selected printer. After selecting the font, you may choose the size (in points) for the selected font from the Size list. You can use the scroll bar to move through the list. You must choose the font before selecting a size because not all sizes are available for all fonts.

Changing the Text Style   Select from the Font Style list to add bold, italic, or a combination of the two to the text. Choose Regular to clear a previous choice. Mark the Underline check box to turn on underlining.

Use the Color drop-down list to choose the color for the selected item's text. If you don't use a color printer, all the colors print as black (but with different shading on grayscale printers). The clear color option causes an item's text to be transparent in the display, although the row for the item still appears on-screen and on paper. The use of color on-screen is still useful, even if you use a black-and-white printer.

If all items in the Item to Change drop-down list have the same setting for one of the format features, this setting appears selected when the All item is selected. If all items use the same font, for example, you see the font name displayed when the All item is selected. If one or more items use a different font, however, the font name remains blank when you select the All item. The Underline check box will be marked if all items apply to that feature, not marked if no items use the option, or dimmed if at least one, but not all, item uses the feature.

Formatting Selected Text

There are two additional choices for formatting text: using the Format, Font command and using the Formatting toolbar. The choices available using Format, Font are the same as in the Text Styles dialog box, except that you don't have a choice for Item to Change. Changes that you make in this dialog box will be made to any tasks that are selected, not to categories of tasks or resources.

The Formatting toolbar offers drop-down lists for changing the font and point size, as well as buttons for bold, italic, and underline. Additionally, there are three buttons for the alignment of selected text: left, center, and right.

You can copy formatting options you've created for a single task or resource using the Format Painter button on the Standard toolbar. To use this button, select the task or resource with the format you wish to copy. Click the Format Painter button. The mouse pointer changes to a cross with a paintbrush attached. Select the tasks or resources to which you want to copy the format. Formatting changes created using this button are the same as if you used the Formatting toolbar or the Format, Font command.

Use caution when using this button, however, because Undo is not available. If you change your mind about the format, you have to use the Formatting toolbar options or the Format, Font command to reset the changes you made.

CAUTION

The difference between using the Format Text Styles dialog box and using Format, Font (or the Formatting toolbar) is significant. When using the latter two options you are making changes to *selected* text only, not to *categories* of tasks or resources. When additional tasks or resources belonging to a certain category are added, the formatting applied using the Format, Font command or the Formatting toolbar are not taken into account. Any text display changes are made only to selected tasks or resources.

Formatting Gridlines

Views that contain tables have gridlines between the rows and columns of the table and between the column and row titles. Views that have a timescale can have horizontal and vertical lines to separate the major and the minor timescale units. The Gantt Chart also can have gridlines between the bars in the bar chart. A very useful gridline is Current Date which appears on any timescale view.

To change the display of gridlines, choose Format, Gridlines. The Gridlines dialog box appears. Figure 21.4 shows the Gantt Chart Gridlines dialog box.

T I P You can also access the Gridlines dialog box by pointing to any blank area of the Gantt chart and right-clicking. The Gridlines option also may be found on the shortcut menu.

FIG. 21.4

Change the way lines appear using the Gridlines dialog box.

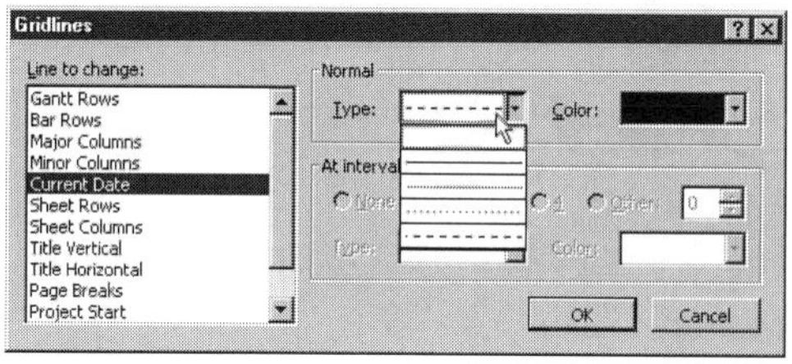

From the Line to Change list, choose the kind of line you want to change. The settings in the Normal box are applied to every line of the type that you choose unless a selection in the At Interval box also is active (in which case a different line and color appears at regular intervals). Only a few line categories can be given a distinguishing interval line type and color. Sheet Rows and Sheet Columns in table views, for example, can have intervals, and in the Gantt Chart and the Resource Usage views, rows and columns can have interval colors and line types.

Use the Type drop-down list in the Normal box to choose one of the five options (no line, solid, dotted, small dashes, and large dashes). Use the Color drop-down list arrow in the Normal box to choose a color. Select the At Interval line type and color if you want a distinguishing line (if available). Activate the At Interval Type and Color fields by choosing an interval. Choose 2, 3, or 4; or choose Other and type the interval number.

Part

VII

Ch

21

For timescale views, you can define the style of the Current Date line. For table views, you can define the style of page break lines as seen on-screen (page break lines do not print). After you complete the procedure, click OK to accept the changes or click Cancel to return to your previous settings.

Using the Outline Options

Views that list tasks (the Gantt Chart and the Task Sheet) can display the tasks in ways that show information about their places in the outline structure. You can hide or display summary tasks, or indent subordinate tasks to show their level in the outline; outline numbers can be displayed next to each task; and summary tasks can be displayed either with or without a special symbol to show that these tasks have subordinate tasks.

▶ **See** "Outlining the Task List," **p. 160**

To change the display of the outlined tasks, choose Tools Options, and click the View tab. The Outline display default options are shown in Figure 21.5. Figure 21.6 shows the effects of each of these choices when they are marked.

FIG. 21.5

Options for displaying outlines on the View tab of the Options dialog box.

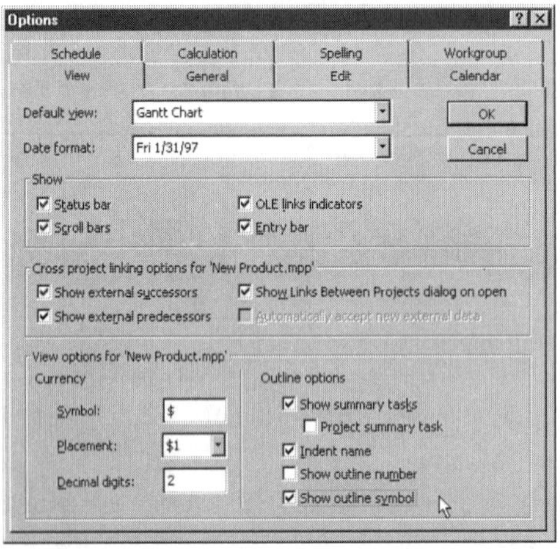

NOTE Make sure you're in a view that can display outlines (Gantt Chart or Task Sheet) before accessing the Options dialog box; otherwise, the Outline Options section won't be available. ▨

■ If Show Summary Tasks is marked, you see the summary tasks included in the list of tasks. If the check box is not marked, the summary tasks do not appear in the list. If subtasks are currently hidden, summary tasks will also be hidden. Notice also that the outlining commands on the Formatting toolbar are no longer available when summary tasks are not shown. If you clear the check box, you should clear the Indent Name check box also, so all the subordinate tasks align at the left margin. This is useful when you are linking tasks and you don't want to include the summary task in the link. It is also useful when applying a filter and then performing some action on all of the tasks meeting the criteria of the filter. For example, this is useful when you want to mark all milestones to be rolled up to the summary task.

▶ **See** "Using the Multiple Task Information Dialog Box," **p. 147**

▶ **See** "Establishing Dependency Links," **p. 173**

▶ **See** "The Rollup Views," **p. 662**

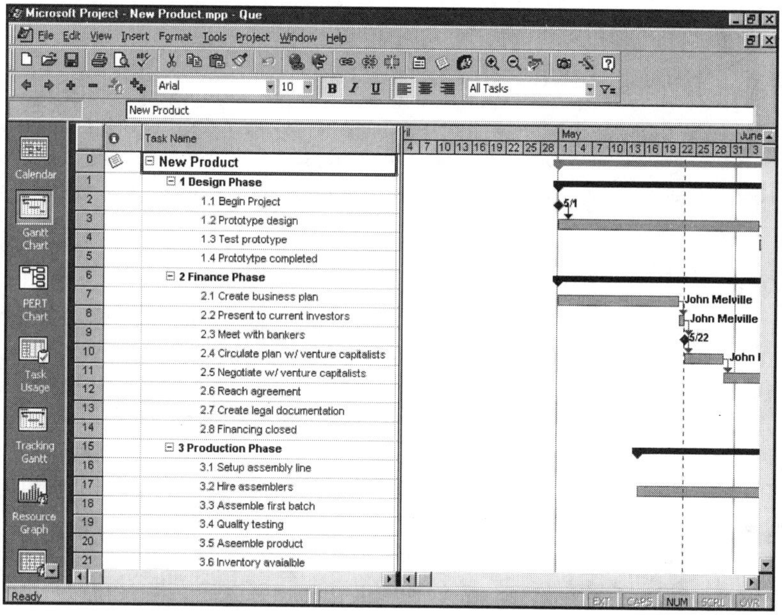

FIG. 21.6

An outline with Project Summary Task, Indent Name, Show Outline Number, and Show Outline Symbol selected.

If Project Summary Task is marked, you will have an additional summary task at the beginning of the task list that summarizes the entire project. This is useful when consolidating projects. (This topic was covered in Chapter 17, "Working with Multiple Projects.")

If the Indent Name box is marked, the tasks are indented to show their subordinate status. If the box is not marked, all tasks are aligned at the left margin.

If the Show Outline Number check box is marked, the task names are preceded by an outline number that identifies each task's place in the outline. The outline numbering is in the so-called legal style, with each task number including the related summary task numbers. This is the same number you see in the Task Information dialog box under the Advanced tab marked WBS (Work Breakdown Structure) code. If this box is not marked, you will not see the outline numbers.

If the Show Outline Symbol check box is marked, summary tasks are preceded by a plus (+) or a minus sign (–) depending on whether the subtasks for that summary task are hidden or shown. A plus sign indicates that the summary task has subtasks that are not currently being displayed, while the minus sign indicates that all tasks under the summary task are showing. If the Show Outline Symbol check box is not marked, no outline symbols are displayed.

TIP   When printing reports that include outlined tasks, you can save space by turning off the Indent Name option. If you do this, turn on the Show Outline Number option so that you can see where your outline is located.

TROUBLESHOOTING

I'm working on a project that has an outline, but my outline symbols on the formatting toolbar are grayed out. Why can't I use them? The Show Summary Tasks option has been turned off in the Tools, Options dialog box. The outlining tools will display again if you select Show Summary Tasks.

Formatting Timescales

Views that display a timescale offer you the option of choosing the time units and the date formats for the timescale display. The timescale normally uses two levels of time units for clarity in interpreting the timescale. These levels are known as the *major units scale* and the *minor units scale*, either of which can be suppressed.

TIP   You can also use the View, Zoom command to zoom in on a variety of predefined time periods, including the entire project.

To change the timescale, choose Format, Timescale. The Timescale dialog box appears (see Figure 21.7).

TIP   You can also access the Timescale dialog box by double-clicking anywhere the timescale units are displayed or by right-clicking the timescale headings and choosing Timescale from the shortcut menu.

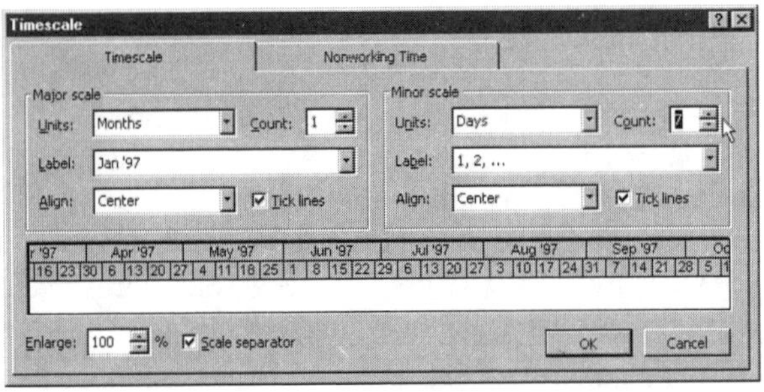

FIG. 21.7
You can be very specific about how the time frame is displayed with the numerous options in the Timescale dialog box.

The Timescale dialog box provides areas for defining both the Major Scale and the Minor Scale. Below these areas is a sample display area that instantly shows you what the timescale will look like as you select different options.

Changing the Major Scale   You define the major and minor scales separately. The only requirement is that the units selected for the major scale be at least as large as the units selected for the minor scale. To change the Major Scale units, use the Units drop-down list to choose one of the options provided: Years, Half Years, Quarters, Months, Thirds of Months, Weeks, Days, Hours, and Minutes.

N O T E   To change the month that begins the fiscal year (so that Quarter 1 covers the months used by your organization in its reports), you must change the Fiscal Year Starts In option on the Calendar tab of the Options dialog box. (Choose Tools, Options to open this dialog box.) Using the drop-down list, change from the default, January, to the month you want to use. If you choose a month other than January, there is also a check box to indicate that you want to use the starting month for FY (fiscal year) numbering. Similarly, if you want the week to begin on a day other than Sunday (the default), you must change the Week Starts On item in the same location. ▪

To include more than one time period within each major unit, choose the Count text box and enter a number other than 1. To have the major scale show fortnights (two weeks), for example, select Weeks as the Units and 2 for the Count. For the same effect, you also could select Days as the Unit and 14 for the Count. You can establish whatever kind of timescale you want to display for your project.

N O T E   If the major scale tick lines that separate the units of the major scale don't change in the sample area immediately after you change the count, you may need to select the Tick Lines check box twice to refresh the tick line display. ▪

To choose the label to display in each major scale time unit, use the Label drop-down list. The list of options is extensive and depends on the units selected for the display. You can use three basic types of labels for any of the time units:

- The specific time period named, such as the year, quarter number, month name or number, and day number. Many choices are available, including abbreviations, full or partial specifications, numbers, and words. Figure 21.8 shows a partial list of options available for the Weeks unit.

- The number of the time period in the life of the project, starting from the beginning of the project or counting down from the end of the project. These units are designated with either (From Start) or (From End) as part of the label definition. If the unit is Week 1 (From Start), for example, the time periods are labeled Week 1, Week 2, and so on, if you are counting from the beginning of the project. If you are counting down from the end of the project, the time periods are labeled Week 40, Week 39, and so on. This labeling scheme is useful in the early planning stages of a lengthy project, before specific start and finish dates are established or when a project file is used as a template.

▶ **See** "Templates," **p. 112**

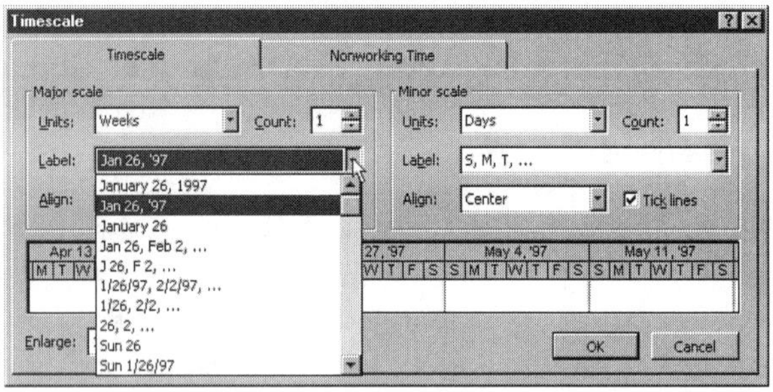

FIG. 21.8

The Major Scale Units Label options is shown for the Weeks unit.

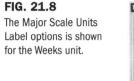

■ No label. If minor scale labeling is sufficient, you can suppress any labeling of the major scale unit. You can't, however, avoid having a major timescale unit.

T I P   When working with a project that spans more than a single calendar year, be sure to include the year number in the label.

You can center, left-align, or right-align the time units labels. Use the Align drop-down list arrow to choose an alignment specification, or just type the specification.

You must mark the Tick Lines check box to display tick lines separating the major time units. You use the Count text box to determine how the tick lines are spaced.

Changing the Minor Scale   The Minor Scale options are virtually the same as the Major Scale options, with the following exceptions:

■ You can't have a minor scale unit that is larger than the major scale unit. Specifically, the time span of the minor scale unit, including its count factor, can't be longer than the timescale of the major scale unit. You won't be notified of this until you choose OK, but you can see that there is a problem in the sample box at the bottom of the dialog box because it is blank.

■ You can choose not to have a minor scale at all by choosing None in the Units drop-down list. This display is useful when you want to show the big picture of a project without displaying too much distracting detail.

Otherwise, selecting the minor scale is identical to selecting the major scale.

Completing the Timescale Definition   Notice the two options at the bottom of the Timescale tab in this dialog box; Enlarge and Scale Separator. You use these options to adjust the overall look of the timescale. To change the width of the minor timescale units, choose the Enlarge box and enter an adjustment percentage. For example, if the values in the Resource Usage view are too large to fit within the cells of the minor timescale units, type **120%** or **150%** to enlarge the minor scale unit space. Likewise, if you are happy with your timescale settings but you just want to shrink the whole thing down so more fits on the screen or on paper, choose a number smaller than 100 percent. You can remove the horizontal line that separates the major scale labels from the minor scale labels. Just clear the S̲cale Separator check box.

After you enter all the changes, choose OK to put the new timescale format in place. The timescale changes affect only the display of the view that was active when you changed the timescale. Each timescale view has its own timescale format. For example, changes you make to the Gantt Chart timescale will not have any impact on the timescale in the Resource Usage view.

TROUBLESHOOTING

I have set up the major and minor scale on my timescale exactly the way I like it, but it's a little too small. Is there anything I can do without changing the setup? Yes, simply change the 100 percent in the E̲nlarge text box to a larger number. You may have to play with the number until you get the size right. Likewise, if your timescale is a little too big, change the E̲nlarge number to 85 or 90 percent or whatever number gets the look you're after.

CAUTION

If you have customized your timescale settings, specifically the labels, when you use the Zoom In and Zoom Out buttons in the Standard toolbar, you will lose your customized settings.

Changing the Display of Nonworking Time   Use the Nonworking Time tab in the Timescale dialog box to make changes to the way Nonworking Time is displayed on the Gantt Chart. You can choose Fo̲rmat, Ti̲mescale and then click the Nonworking Time tab to bring it to the front. Alternatively, you can point at a blank spot on the timescale (not at a bar or a heading), press the right mouse button, and then choose Nonworking Time from the shortcut menu. Or, you can double-click the shaded working time. The choices on this tab are shown in Figure 21.9.

CAUTION

Don't confuse the shortcut menu for the body of the Gantt Chart with the shortcut menu for the timescale. The shortcut menu for the timescale provides a Change Working Time option which accesses the Calendar and lets you redefine what should be considered nonworking time. The shortcut menu for the body of the Gantt Chart provides a Nonworking time option, which simply changes the way nonworking time is displayed.

Choose the calendar for which you want to change the nonworking time. Use the drop-down list if you want to select an individual's resource calendar. Otherwise the Standard (Project

Part
VII

Ch
21

Calendar) will be used. The options in the Draw section determine the way the bars are drawn when spanning nonworking time (evenings and weekends, for example). Nonworking time is shaded with a color and pattern of your choice. Whether this time is displayed depends on the Timescale format. For example, if your major timescale unit is set to Months, and the minor timescale unit is set to Weeks, you won't be able to see nonworking time.

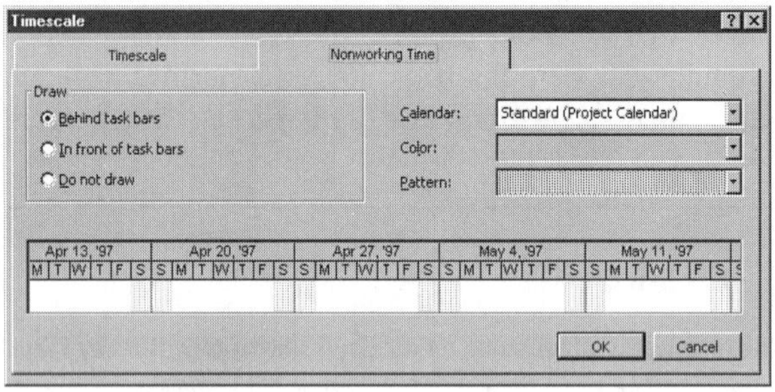

FIG. 21.9

Changing the display of Nonworking Time on the Gantt Chart.

The options for shading include Behind Task Bars (the default), In Front of Task Bars (leaving a gap in the bars), or Do Not Draw. This last option effectively eliminates the shaded display of nonworking time altogether. Nonworking time is still displayed, but the display is no different from working time. Task bars that span nonworking time will simply be longer than you might expect from their duration value.

Choosing to display nonworking time in front of the task bars more clearly indicates that the tasks are not being worked on—over weekends, for example. The bars are longer not because their duration is longer, but because they span nonworking time.

Using Page Breaks

Page breaks force the start of a new page when you print the view but have no effect on the screen display (other than an optional dashed line to indicate where the page break falls within the data). You can format the appearance of the page break line with the Format, Gridlines command.

▶ **See** "Setting and Clearing Page Breaks," **p. 419**

To force a page break in the views that permit it, select any cell in the row below the intended page break. This row will become the first row on the new page. Then choose Insert, Page Break.

To remove a page break, select the row below the page break and choose Insert, Remove Page Break.

To remove all page breaks from the view, select all tasks by clicking the Task or Resource Name column heading before choosing the Insert, Remove All Page Breaks.

The page breaks that you have entered manually are honored by the Print command *only* if the Manual Page Breaks check box in the Print dialog box is marked. To print the report without using the manually inserted page breaks, clear this check box.

Formatting the Gantt Chart

The Gantt Chart is one of the most important presentations in project management reporting; therefore, many format choices have been made available for this presentation. You can either format it yourself or use the Gantt Chart Wizard.

Reviewing the Format Options for the Gantt Chart

The Format menu for Gantt Charts includes the following options: Font, Bar, Timescale, Gridlines, Gantt Chart Wizard, Text Styles, Bar Styles, and Layout. The options for Font, Timescale, Gridlines, and Text Styles were described in previous sections of this chapter. Refer to the appropriate sections for instructions on using these features. The following sections show you several ways to change the look of the bar chart in the timescale section of the Gantt Chart view.

Using the Bar Styles Options

One way to change the display of the bar chart section of the Gantt Chart view is to choose Format, Bar Styles. The Bar Styles dialog box appears (see Figure 21.10).

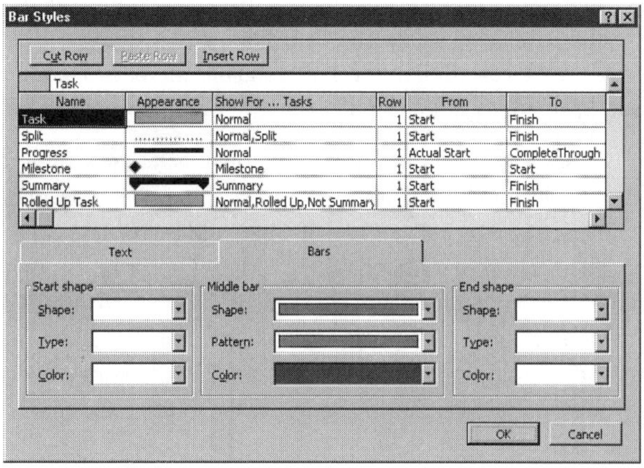

FIG. 21.10
Use the Bar Styles dialog box to change the display of categories of task bars in the Gantt Chart.

> **TIP**
> You can also open the Bar Styles dialog box by right-clicking a blank spot on the timescale portion of the Gantt Chart and choosing Bar Styles from the shortcut menu, or by double-clicking anywhere in the Gantt Chart background except at a specific bar.

The top half of the Bar Styles dialog box contains a definition table with rows for each of the bars and symbols that appear in the Gantt Chart. The bottom half of the dialog box contains two tabs. The Bars tab has drop-down lists for specifying the formatted look of the bars and symbols. You can specify the way a bar will look at the start, end, and in between. The Text tab has text boxes where text fields can be added in various locations around the bars. The second column in the table at the top of the dialog box displays a sample of the formatted look that you composed.

To insert a new bar within the table, select the row you plan to define the bar in and select the Insert Row button at the top of the dialog box.

To delete a bar from the definition, select the row that defines the bar and choose the Cut Row button. You can paste this definition into a new location; just select the new location and choose the Paste Row button. A blank row is inserted, and a copy of the row that you cut is placed in the new row.

To copy a row (for example, to create a bar that closely resembles a bar already defined), cut the row to be copied (use the Cut Row button) and immediately paste it back to the same location (use the Paste Row button). Next, move to the location for the copy and paste the row again.

Supplying the Bar Name Use the first column of the definition table to enter a name for the bar. The bar name can be anything you choose and has no significance, except that the name appears in the legend next to the bar symbol when the Gantt Chart is printed.

Defining the Bar Appearance The second column shows what the bar or symbol looks like when the Palette definition is applied. Change the look of the sample with the Start Shape, Middle Bar, and End Shape sections on the Bars tab at the bottom of the dialog box.

You can define the Shape, Type, and Color of the start shape at the left edge of the bar. Use the Shape drop-down list to scroll the list for the shape you want. Use the first option, which is blank, if you don't want a symbol to mark the start of the bar. Use the Type drop-down list to choose Dashed, Framed, or Solid. Finally, use the Color drop-down list to choose a color.

In the Middle Bar section, use the Shape drop-down list to view the options for the size and height of the bar itself. The list includes no bar at all, a full bar, a top half of a bar, a small bar in the center of the bar space, a bottom half of a bar, and heavy lines at the top, middle, and bottom of the bar space. These bar shapes can overlap. The Progress bar (the solid black center of the task bar when the *percentage complete* is greater than zero) for example, is formed by displaying the thin center bar for the progress amount, and the full bar for the duration of the task. When you have multiple bars drawn for one task, the bars closer to the top of the dialog box are displayed first. Bars further down in the list in the dialog box are laid on top of the bars higher up in the list.

Use the Color drop-down list to choose the color of the bar. Use the Pattern drop-down list to choose the fill pattern or shading for the bar. The bar can be clear, have an outline only, be solid, or have any one of nine fill patterns.

To select the shape for the end of the bar, follow the same procedure as for selecting the shape for the start of the bar. Use the Shape drop-down list to choose the shape, and the Type drop-down list to choose the type. Use the Color drop-down list to choose the color.

The Appearance column in the table at the top of the dialog box displays the effect of the choices. You must go through these steps for each bar or symbol that you place on the Gantt Chart. Before choosing any options at the bottom of this dialog box, make sure that the intended task is selected at the top.

Selecting the Tasks That Display the Bar   Select the third column (Show For...Tasks) in the definition table at the top of the Bar Styles dialog box to define the category(ies) of tasks for which the bar is displayed. When you click in this column, a drop-down list will appear. Choose a bar category from the drop-down list or type the category. If you want to use two or more task categories, separate the task categories' names with commas (or the list separator character specified in Window's Control Panel, Regional Settings).

The drop-down list contains a large number of task types. All tasks fall into one of the first three categories: Milestone, Summary task, or Normal (any task that is not a Milestone or a Summary task). You can use these three kinds of tasks in combination with the other types in the list to more narrowly define specific types of tasks—for example, Normal, Critical and Normal, Noncritical instead of just Normal (which includes both Critical and Noncritical). If a task falls into more than one category, it shows the formatting features of both categories. If one formatting feature overwrites another, the feature that is lowest in the definition table will be applied last and will remain visible in the display.

To select all tasks *except* the type named, you can place the word *Not* before the type name. Examples are Not Summary, Not Milestone, and Not Rolled Up.

The Rolled Up type refers to a special field for subordinate tasks that instructs Microsoft Project to show a symbol for the Finish Date of the task on the Summary task bar. You designate tasks as Rolled Up tasks using the Task Information button on the Standard toolbar. This opens the Task Information dialog box. The General tab has a check box for Roll up Gantt Bar to Summary. Figure 21.11 illustrates the use of rollup symbols. Notice the mouse pointer is at a triangle that represents a subtask that has been hidden but rolled up to the summary task.

FIG. 21.11

Using rolled up dates to make Summary Tasks more descriptive.

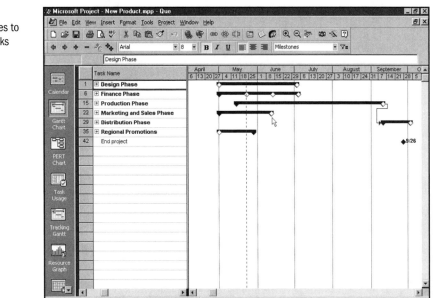

Part

VII

Ch

21

Each of the milestone tasks has been defined as a Rollup task, which means the <u>R</u>oll up Gantt Bar to Summary check box on the Task Information dialog box is selected. The mouse pointer is at one of the rollup symbols, a small diamond shape.

▶ **See** "The Rollup Views," **p. 662**

Selecting the Row for the Bar   You can place up to four rows of bars on the Gantt Chart for each task, or you can use the extra rows for displaying text. Notice in the dialog box in Figure 21.10 that the Progress bar is placed in Row 1 along with the Task bar. Because the shapes of the bars differ, the effect is to superimpose one over the other.

> **CAUTION**
>
> The order in which you list superimposed bars in the definition table is important. The bars in the Gantt Chart are drawn in the order listed in the definition table. If the Progress bar in this example were defined above the Normal bars, the Progress bar would be drawn before the Normal bars, and the larger Normal bars would hide the Progress bar.

Defining the Length of the Bar   The length and placement of every bar or symbol on the Gantt Chart is determined by entries in the From and To columns of the definition table at the top of the Bar Styles dialog box. You can use date fields or one of several measures of time (Percent Complete, Total Slack, Free Slack, and Negative Slack, Actual Start, Late Start, and so on). Choose an entry from the drop-down list.

> **CAUTION**
>
> Choosing from the drop-down list for From and To requires a strong knowledge of what each of these dates represent. If you are not familiar with these, it may be easier to use the Gantt Chart Wizard.

Placing Text in the Bar Chart   On the Text tab of the Bar Styles dialog box is a column for designating a position next to the bar where data from one or more fields can be displayed. You can display field data at the left, right, top, and bottom of the bar, as well as inside the bar. You can't type literal text in these columns; you can only designate fields that contain text to display the values in the selected fields. Thirty user-defined Text fields (Text1, Text2, through Text30) are available, in which you can type text that you want to display in the bar chart. For easy access when you want to enter text in these fields, either insert a column in an existing table or edit the table definition to include your custom fields.

TROUBLESHOOTING

I want to add text to the task bars but there's not enough room. Add the text to a different row. You don't have to have a bar on the row; you can use it for text only.

▶ **See** "Using and Creating Tables," **p. 748**

> **T I P** Figure 21.12 shows the text columns and the selection that produces a display of Resource Initials next to the task to which they are assigned rather than a full Resource Name which often takes up too much room.

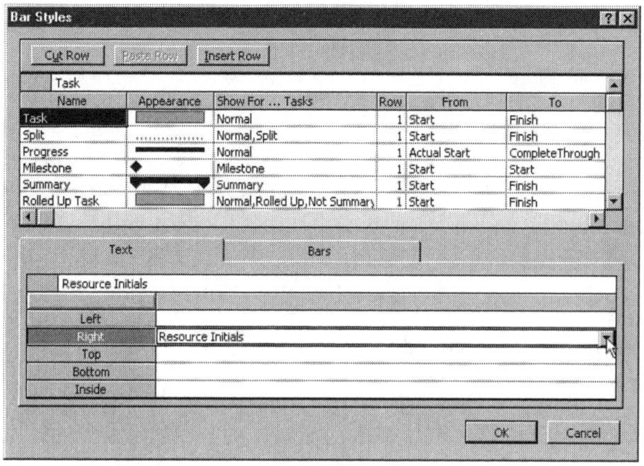

FIG. 21.12

Use the Text tab of the Bar Styles dialog box to place text from fields around the bars of the Gantt Chart.

To select a field to be displayed beside a bar, select the row for the desired position on the bar, and select the name from the drop-down list. Select OK to accept your changes or select Cancel to close the dialog box without implementing them.

> **N O T E** If you want to change the format of specific bars that don't fall into one of the categories available, choose Format, Bar. This command has the same options as the Bar Styles dialog box, but it will only apply changes to the *selected* tasks. ■

TROUBLESHOOTING

I would rather have information around the task bars than in columns on the left. Add the text around the bars as previously discussed. Then create and apply a table that only has one column in it, the task ID. You have to print at least one column but the information in the other columns can be placed around the task bars.

Changing the Layout of the Gantt Chart   The Layout option on the Format menu accesses the Layout dialog box (shown in Figure 21.13), which offers a number of additional choices for the way bars are displayed on the Gantt Chart. Although the primary focus of the Gantt Chart is a list of tasks occurring on a timeline, it's often helpful to see the dependency relationships between tasks. In the Links section of this dialog box, you can choose whether to have lines drawn to designate the dependency linkages between tasks, and if so you can choose between two styles of lines.

FIG. 21.13

Use the Layout dialog box to further define the appearance of task bars on the Gantt Chart.

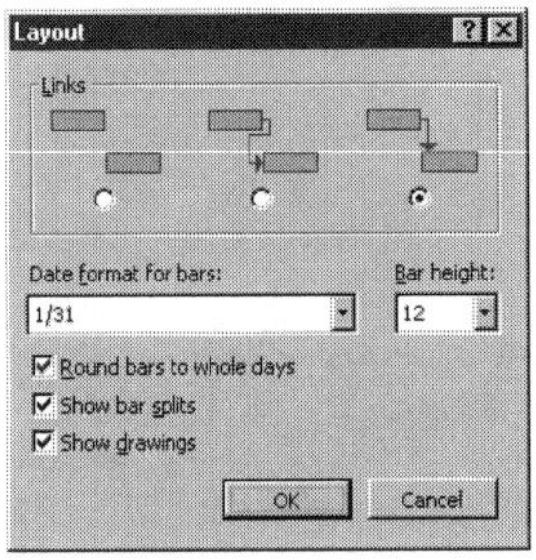

When dates are displayed as text around the bars, use the Date Format for Bars drop-down list to choose from a list of available formats. This won't change the default format for dates displayed elsewhere in the project. The first option on this list is Default, which returns you to the same format as specified on the View tab of the Tools, Options dialog box.

Use the Bar Height drop-down list to choose a size for the bars. Sizes vary from 6 to 24 points with a default of 12.

The Round Bars to Whole Days option determines how tasks with a duration less than the time period by the minor timescale are displayed. For example, if a task with a duration of five hours is displayed in a Gantt Chart with a minor timescale of days, and this box is cleared, then the bar will display a length of exactly five hours. If the Round Bars to Whole Days check box is marked, the bar will extend to a full day. Only the display of the task is modified, the actual duration and calculated start and finish dates remain the same.

The Show Bar Splits check box instructs Project to display tasks that have been split. If this box is not checked, the task bar will simply extend the duration of the task from start to finish, including the split. If this box is checked, it will be very clear where work stopped and then resumed on the task.

The Show Drawings check box enables you to place graphics in the Gantt Chart.

▶ **See** "Adding Graphics and Text to Gantt Charts," **p. 237**

Choose OK to accept your changes or select Cancel to close the dialog box without implementing them.

Using the Gantt Chart Wizard

Microsoft Project includes a feature that makes formatting the bars on the Gantt Chart extremely easy. This automated feature walks you through the various formatting options, asking questions about how you would like to have the bars displayed. The options are basically the same as those already covered, but the wizard takes you through the process step by step. To access the Gantt Chart Wizard, you can choose Format, Gantt Chart Wizard, use the Gantt Chart Wizard button on the Standard toolbar, or choose Gantt Chart Wizard from the Gantt Chart shortcut menu (accessed by right-clicking on any blank area of the Gantt chart).

You are initially presented with an introductory dialog box with a series of buttons at the bottom. Choose the Next button to see your first set of choices (see Figure 21.14). Notice that the title bar includes the step at which you are currently working. There are actually 14 separate steps, but you will only see every step if you choose the Custom Gantt Chart. As you make your choices, you are taken to the next appropriate step, depending on your choice. Simply choose the desired option, and then choose the Next button to move to the next step. You can click Back, Cancel, or Finish at any time. If you are unsure of the meaning of a particular option, click the help button in the top-right corner (it appears as a question mark) and then click the option about which you have a question.

FIG. 21.14

The Gantt Chart Wizard walks you through the formatting options for the Gantt Chart.

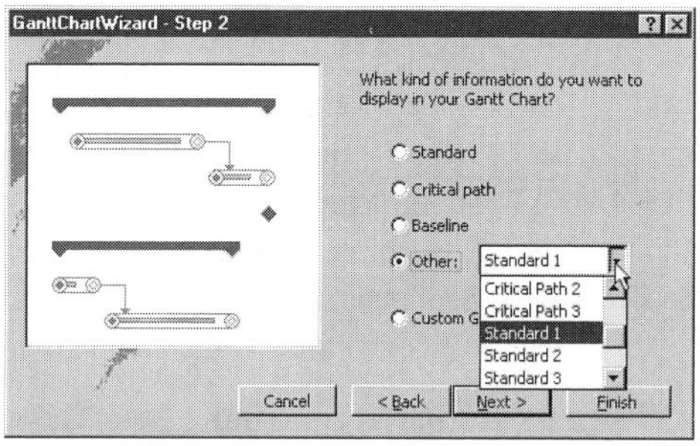

The first question you must answer involves selecting the way that tasks are displayed. Your choice here acts as a starting point for setting up the format of the bars on the Gantt Chart.

- Standard uses the same bars that are used in the default Gantt Chart.

- Critical Path is a helpful view to use when trying to reduce the total duration of the project (referred to as "crashing the schedule" in project management circles) or identifying those tasks that must be completed on time in order to meet the project deadline.

  ▶ **See** "Shortening the Critical Path," **p. 405**

- Baseline is an appropriate choice when tracking a project already underway.

- Other offers a list of 13 pre-defined formats you can use as is or modify as desired (refer to Figure 21.14).

- Custom Gantt Chart offers the most extensive choices and walks through all the choices for formatting one step at a time. These options include choices for the colors, patterns, and shapes of Critical, Normal, Summary, and Milestone tasks. You also have an option for adding bars for baseline information or slack. You can also choose to place text next to bars.

After you make your initial choice, you are prompted for the kind of text to display in and around the bars. Here again, you have a custom choice which allows for distinct definitions for the text formats of Normal, Summary, and Milestone tasks. The final question involves whether or not the link lines should be drawn to display dependency relationships between the task bars.

Once you have made all your changes, the Gantt Chart Wizard does the rest. All you have to do is choose the Format It button and then choose the Exit Wizard button from the final dialog

Part

VI

Ch

21

box that appears. You still have the option of making further changes using the techniques covered in previous sections.

Formatting the Calendar

You can modify the display of the Calendar View in many ways to meet your specific needs. As with other views, you can use the Zoom command on the View menu, or you can use the Zoom In and Zoom Out buttons on the Standard toolbar to cycle through preset options for zooming. This is convenient if you have many tasks occurring at the same time.

A number of mouse methods are available for changing the height and width of the squares where the dates are displayed. Point to any vertical line in the calendar, and the mouse pointer changes to a double-headed arrow. Drag left or right to narrow or widen the column. Likewise, if you point to a horizontal line, the mouse pointer again changes to a double-headed arrow indicating that you can drag up or down to make the date box taller or shorter. This is particularly useful when you have more tasks on a given day than can be displayed at once.

The options that are available on the Format menu for the Calendar view include Timescale, Gridlines, Text Styles, Bar Styles, Layout, and Layout Now. The Text Styles and Gridlines options are the same as discussed in previous sections. The options for Timescale, Bar Styles, and Layout are unique to the Calendar view and are discussed in detail here.

Formatting the Timescale for the Calendar

The Timescale dialog box has three tabs that offer choices for headings and titles, for additional data elements that can appear in the date boxes, and for applying shading on certain days.

The Week Headings tab is shown in Figure 21.15. Here you have numerous choices of labels for the month, the days of the week, and for each week. This figure shows a label for each week that counts down to the end of the project. Additionally, you can choose a five- or seven-day week, and you can choose to show the previous and next month, much like printed calendars.

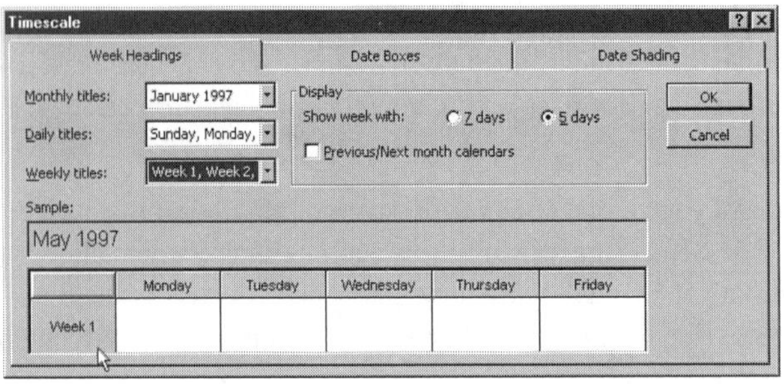

FIG. 21.15
Customize the calendar display with the Week Headings tab on the Timescale dialog box.

The Date Boxes tab, shown in Figure 21.16, allows you to place additional data elements in the top or bottom row of each individual date box. There are many choices here. The default setting includes an overflow indicator and the date in the top row. The overflow indicator appears when all tasks scheduled to occur on a given day can't be displayed with the date box. When printing, overflow tasks appear on a separate page. A pattern and color can also be chosen for emphasis.

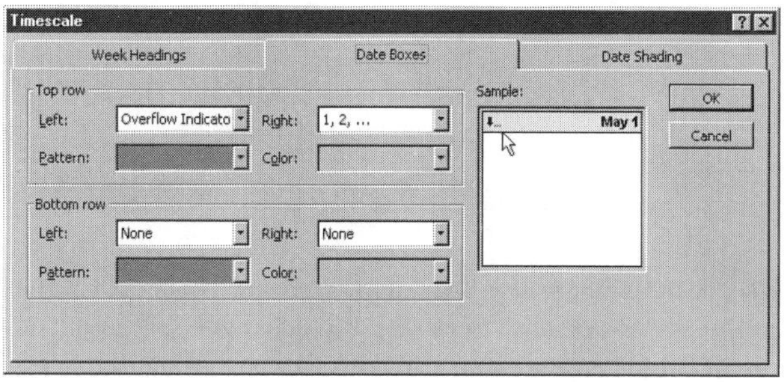

FIG. 21.16

Customize each date box with additional information in the Date Boxes tab of the Timescale dialog box.

Finally, on the Date Shading tab (see Figure 21.17) you can shade a variety of categories of working or nonworking dates for the base calendar or individual resource calendars as specified in the Show Working Time For drop-down list. First choose the type of date that you want to shade in the Exception Type list. Then choose a pattern and color from the drop-down lists at the bottom of the dialog box. A sample is displayed on the right as you make your choices. When you're finished making changes, click OK. You are returned to the Calendar view to see the effect of your formatting changes.

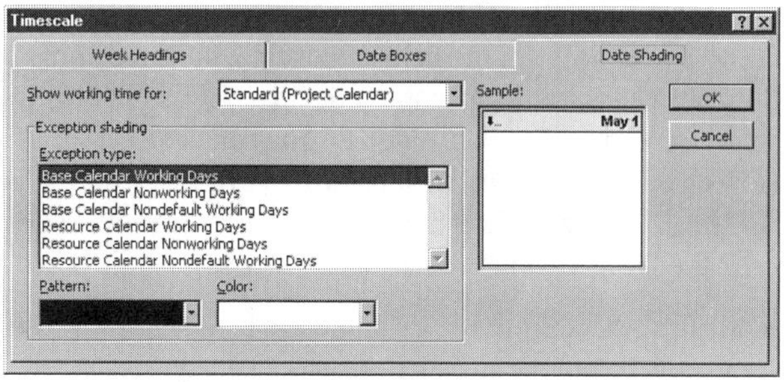

FIG. 21.17

Indicate working and nonworking days on the calendar with options in the Date Shading tab of the Timescale dialog box.

Selecting Calendar Bar Styles Options

As with the Gantt Chart, you have control over how the bars in the calendar appear, including text that can be displayed as part of the bars. Access the Bar Styles dialog box by choosing Format, Bar Styles, or use the shortcut menu (right-click any spot other than a specific bar in the calendar portion of the view, not the headings). Select the Bar Styles option, and the Bar Styles dialog box appears (see Figure 21.18).

FIG. 21.18

The Bar Styles dialog box offers choices for changing the display of task bars in the Calendar view.

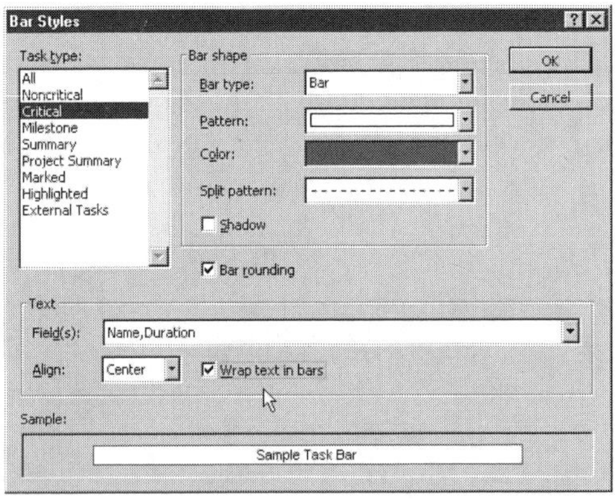

First, select the type of bar you want to modify in the Task Type list box. Then use the drop-down lists in the Bar Shape area to modify the Bar Type, Pattern, and Color for the bar. You have a variety of choices for pattern and color. As for the bar type, you can have a bar or a simple line extending across the days of the task's duration. There are also choices of different displays for tasks that have split. If you choose a bar for the bar type, you can also apply a shadow for emphasis.

The Bar Rounding check box, deals with tasks whose durations are not a whole day (for example, durations of a half day or a day and a half). If the check box is left marked, the bar on the calendar will be rounded to a full day.

In the Text area, you can choose any number of fields to be displayed in the bar either by typing in their names (separated by commas) or by choosing them from the Fields drop-down list. If you want to have more than one field listed on the bar and you are choosing from the drop-down list, make sure to deselect the field name and type in a comma before selecting another field from the list. Otherwise, if you choose another field while the first field is still selected, the first field is replaced rather than added to. You can deselect a field name either by pressing the right arrow or by clicking with the mouse at the right end of the field name. Alignment options for the text of these fields can be centered, left, or right. When text is long, it may be useful to check the Wrap Text in Bars check box.

For all categories of tasks except All, a sample will be displayed at the bottom of the dialog box to show you the effect of your choices. If All is the task type selected, and some, not all, of the task types have a check box option turned on, the check box will be displayed with a gray shading. When all of the task types have the check box turned on, there will be a check mark in the check box. When none of the task types have the check box turned on, the check box will be empty.

Choose the OK button when finished. You are returned to the calendar to see the effects of your changes.

> **CAUTION**
>
> Depending on your choices in the Bar Styles dialog box, you may see a message from the Planning Wizard that indicates that some of the calendar bars will have different heights. There are instructions for how to position those bars.

Setting the Layout Options for the Calendar View

The Layout dialog box (shown in Figure 21.19) can be accessed either by choosing Format, Layout or using the calendar shortcut menu. The options presented here determine the order of tasks displayed in each date box. The default is Use Current Sort Order. The alternative to this is Attempt to Fit as Many Tasks as Possible without regard for sorting. The check box for Show Bar Splits determines whether a task that has been split displays any differently than a regular task. By default when a task is split, a dotted outline will be drawn during that portion of the task when work was not underway. The check box for Automatic Layout specifies that the settings in this dialog box will be initiated automatically as tasks are edited, added, or deleted. When Automatic Layout is not selected, you must choose Layout Now from either the Format menu or from the calendar shortcut menu to apply the changes.

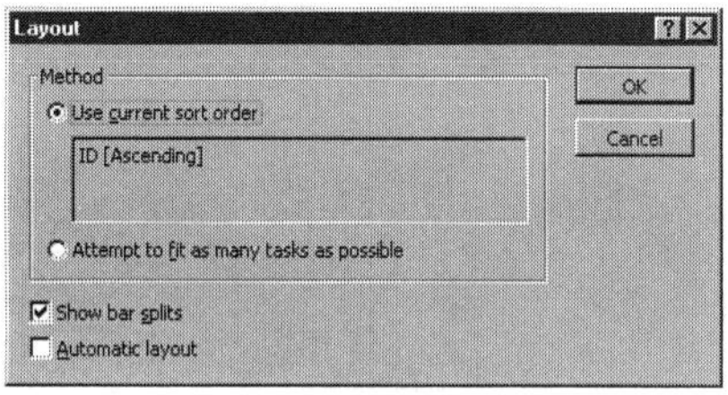

FIG. 21.19
The Layout dialog box allows you to determine how and when tasks are sorted within each date box.

Formatting the PERT Chart

You can customize the PERT Chart by rearranging the layout of the task nodes and by changing the size of the nodes, the borders around the nodes, and the fields displayed within each node. You can also change your perspective by zooming in or out to see more or less of the entire project.

Reviewing the Format Options for the PERT Chart

The Format menu for the PERT Chart view contains the options Text Styles, Box Styles, Layout, and Layout Now. You can also use the Zoom option on the View menu or the Zoom In and Zoom Out buttons on the Standard toolbar.

The use of the Format menu to change the display of text was covered earlier in this chapter. The Zoom, Layout, and Layout Now commands were covered in previous chapters but are summarized here for completeness. The Box Styles commands are covered in detail in the following sections.

Part

VII

Ch

21

Using the Box Styles Options

You can customize the boxes that surround the nodes to display eight border styles and colors. Figure 21.20 shows the seven options and identifies the standard border assignments.

FIG. 21.20

This figure displays the
Borders options for
PERT Chart nodes.

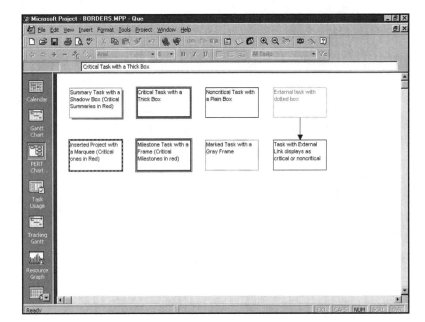

You can assign each box one of 15 colors—16 if you count transparent as a color. If you have a color printer or plotter, the use of color can be an effective tool. If you have a black-and-white printer, you can't distinguish one color from another.

The border styles and colors are assigned by kinds of tasks. Table 21.1 lists the variety of tasks used for border assignments and shows the default border and color assigned to each kind of task. The default color for all critical tasks is red, and the default color for all non-critical tasks is black.

Table 21.1   Border Styles and Colors for PERT Charts

Task Type	Critical	Noncritical
Normal	Thick Box, Red	Plain Box, Black
Milestone	Frame, Red	Frame, Black
Summary	Shadow Box, Red	Shadow Box, Black
Inserted Project	Marquee, Red	Marquee, Black
Marked	Gray Frame, Red	Gray Frame, Black
External	Gray Dotted Box	Gray Dotted Box

To assign border styles and colors to tasks in the PERT Chart, follow these steps:

1. Choose Format, Box Styles or double-click the border of one of the nodes on the screen. The Box Styles dialog box appears with the Borders tab selected (see Figure 21.21).

FIG. 21.21
First choose the type of task to change, and then choose a style and color for the box.

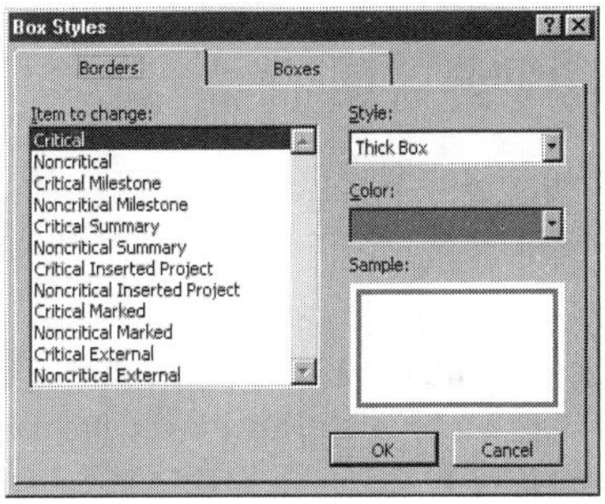

2. Change the borders for different categories of tasks using the Borders tab on the Box Styles dialog box. Choose a task type from the Item to Change list.

3. Use the Style drop-down list to choose a style. The sample display under the Colors drop-down list shows the style you have selected.

4. Use the Color drop-down list to choose one of the available colors.

5. After you make all the border selections, choose OK to accept the changes and close the dialog box.

Using the Boxes Tab in the Border Styles Dialog Box

You can regulate what is displayed within each node, as well as the size of the node, with the Boxes tab. This tab enables you to perform the following procedures:

- Change the fields that appear in each of the five positions.
- Reduce the number of field positions displayed.
- Increase or decrease the size of the task node.
- Change the format for the dates displayed in PERT nodes without having to change the format for dates in other displays.
- Suppress the gridlines that separate the display of the field data.
- Turn the markings on or off that show tasks in progress and tasks completed.

To display the Box Styles dialog box for the PERT Chart, access the PERT Chart view by choosing View, PERT Chart or click the PERT Chart in the View Bar. Then choose Format, Box Styles, or double-click the background of the PERT Chart screen. Figure 21.22 shows the Box Styles dialog box for the PERT Chart. Note that the layout of the dialog box mirrors a node.

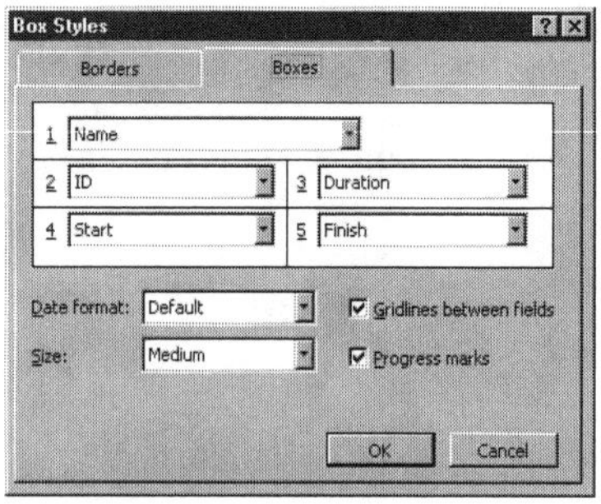

FIG. 21.22

Change the way a PERT Chart node is displayed in the Boxes tab of the Box Styles dialog box.

Changing the Fields Displayed   By default, the PERT nodes display five fields of data: Task Name, ID number, Duration, Start Date, and Finish Date. You can change the field displayed in any node by choosing the field position (1, 2, 3, 4, or 5) and then using the drop-down list next to the field to choose a field name.

If you want the position in the node to remain blank, you can select the blank at the top of the drop-down list. If both positions 4 and 5 are left blank, these positions on the task node are removed, and the task node shrinks in size accordingly. Likewise, if both positions 2 and 3 are left blank, the task node shrinks even further. By leaving tasks 2 through 5 blank, you can create small task nodes that show only the task name. You then can print PERT Charts that show less detail but display more nodes per page. Figure 21.23 shows a sample PERT Chart with only the task name showing in each node. The size of the node in the figure has also been reduced.

FIG. 21.23

The PERT Chart here shows only the task name.

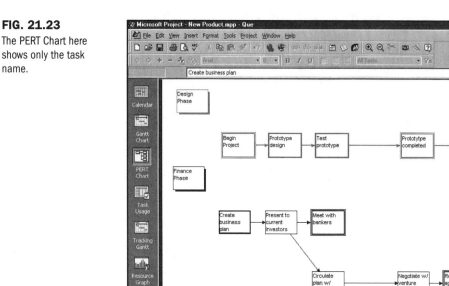

Changing the Node Size Select the Size text drop-down list at the bottom of the Box Styles dialog box to change the size of the node display. You can select Smallest (ID only), Small, Medium, or Large from the drop-down list. The shortcut menu for the PERT Chart (right-click a blank spot) has an option for Hide and Show Fields which acts as a toggle. When fields are hidden, nodes are displayed only with the ID field (as shown in Figure 21.24). This causes the nodes to be smaller; subsequently, more of them fit on the screen.

Changing the Date Format You can change the format for displaying dates in the PERT Chart without changing the default date formats used in other views. Select the Date Format drop-down list and choose the format that suits you best. Use the Default option if you want the same date format you have chosen on the View tab of the Tools, Options dialog box. Shorter date formats will fit better in the smaller space available for PERT Chart nodes.

Displaying Gridlines To display gridlines that separate the field positions in the task node, mark the Gridlines Between Fields check box. Clear this check box to suppress gridlines.

Selecting Progress Marks If you select the Progress Marks check box, the nodes for completed tasks are displayed with two diagonal lines drawn over the nodes to indicate completion. The nodes for tasks that are in progress, but not completed, have a single diagonal line displayed across them. Clear the Progress Marks check box to suppress this display. Figure 21.24 illustrates the use of progress marks. Task 7 is complete; task 8 has started but hasn't finished. The Summary task, task 6, is also in progress.

FIG. 21.24
PERT Chart progress marks are used to show the progress of work on tasks.

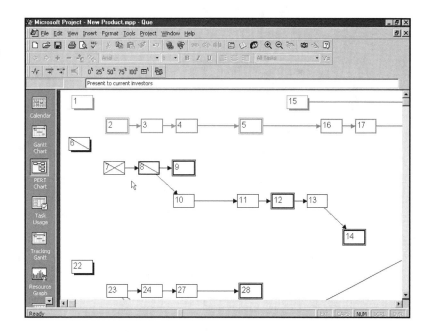

After you have completed the Box Styles dialog box, choose OK to implement the new box and border styles.

Part
VII

Ch
21

Using the Zoom Command

When viewing the PERT Chart, it's often helpful to change the perspective, either pulling back to see the big picture or moving in closer for a more detailed view. This feature is especially useful when you manually move the nodes around to redesign the chart. You can choose View, Zoom, use the shortcut menu, or click either the Zoom In or Zoom Out button on the Standard toolbar. You can zoom from 25 to 400%.

When you use the Zoom In and Zoom Out buttons, you are moved through the various preset zoom levels. When you use either the shortcut menu or the View menu, the Zoom dialog box appears. Choose any of the preset zoom values or enter a value of your own choice in the Custom text box. Figure 21.25 shows the same PERT Chart that was illustrated in Figure 21.24, but it's zoomed out to the maximum extent. You can print the PERT Chart in any of the Zoom levels.

FIG. 21.25

The PERT Chart zoomed to a different perspective.

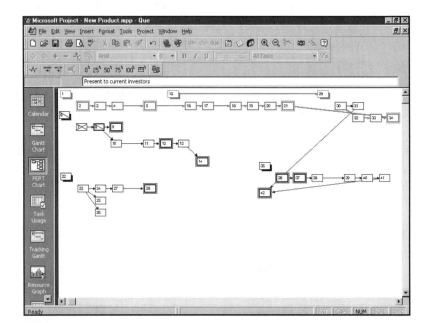

Selecting Layout Options

The Layout Now command on the PERT Chart Format menu redraws the PERT Chart according to the following standard rules of node placement:

- Successor tasks are placed to the right of or below their predecessor tasks.

- Summary tasks are placed above and to the left of their subordinate tasks.

- Linked task nodes are connected with straight lines (diagonal lines if necessary), and an arrow is placed at the successor task's end of the line to indicate the direction of the relationship.

■ Where page breaks would fall when printing is not taken into consideration. This could result in a node being split between two pages.

To some extent, you can modify these rules by choosing Format, Layout when the PERT Chart is the active view.

The Layout dialog box, shown in Figure 21.26, provides several options for changing the way the PERT Chart is drawn by the Layout Now command. To open the dialog box, choose Format, Layout. To close the Layout dialog box, choose OK to implement your changes or Cancel to ignore them.

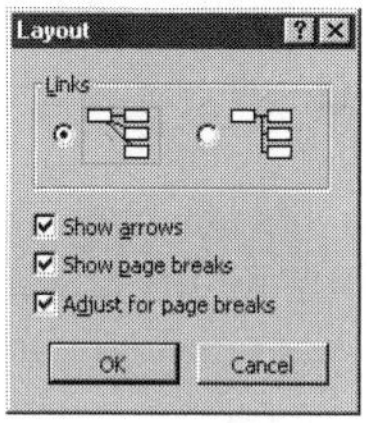

FIG. 21.26

Change the way lines are drawn and how page breaks are handled using the PERT Chart Layout dialog box.

Changing the Type of the Linking Lines

The linking lines that indicate dependency relationships are usually drawn straight from the predecessor to the successor. If the linked tasks aren't on the same row or column of the chart, the linking line is drawn diagonally over the shortest distance between the linked nodes. A PERT Chart can become a messy picture if many diagonal lines intersect nodes and other lines. You can choose to have the dependency lines drawn as right-angled (orthogonal) lines only. To select the orthogonal lines, first choose Format, Layout. When the Layout dialog box appears, select the orthogonal diagram in the Links area.

You may often need to move nodes manually in the chart to clarify the relationships if you use the orthogonal Links option.

Figure 21.27 shows orthogonal lines. The line leading into task 33 implies that task 21 is a predecessor to task 33. Task 21, however, is the predecessor to task 34, and the line is just passing through task 33 on the way to task 34.

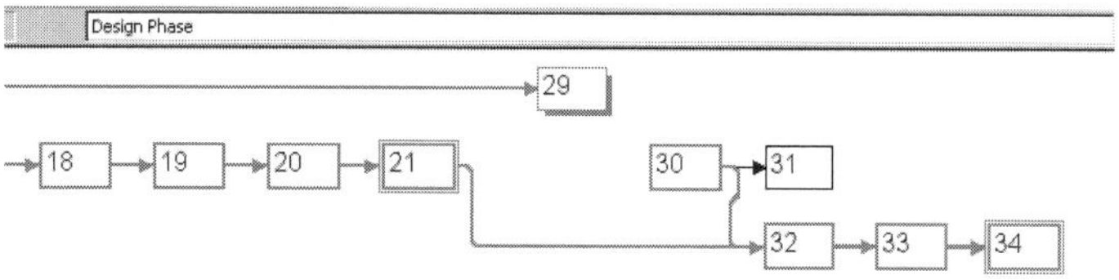

FIG. 21.27

A PERT Chart with orthogonal linking lines.

Figure 21.28 shows the same PERT Chart after manually adjusting the placement of the nodes to clarify the relationships between tasks 21 and 34. You can drag the border of a node to move it. You can also select the node and use the arrow keys.

FIG. 21.28

The same PERT Chart, with task nodes moved for clarity.

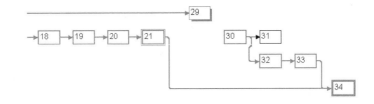

Showing Arrows, and Displaying and Adjusting for Page Breaks   Clear the Show Arrows check box on the PERT Chart Layout dialog box to remove the arrows from the successor end of the dependency linking lines. Mark the check box again to restore the display of the arrows.

To see where page breaks will fall, mark the Show Page Breaks check box. This helps you identify problem areas before printing. Figure 21.29, for example, shows the page break lines falling across several of the task nodes. If you print in this manner, getting a clean *paste together* of the split nodes becomes difficult. You can manually move the task nodes away from the page break lines. You also can mark the Adjust for Page Breaks check box to instruct Microsoft Project to avoid placing nodes on page breaks, and then redraw the PERT Chart with the Format, Layout Now command.

FIG. 21.29

The PERT Chart with page breaks displayed highlights where nodes fall on a page break.

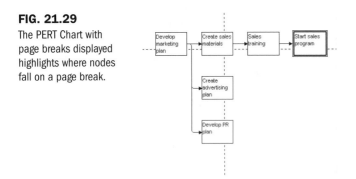

If this check box is marked and Layout Now is executed, task nodes are moved to the right or down to avoid having nodes fall across the page breaks. Figure 21.30 shows the same PERT Chart shown in Figure 21.29, but after Layout Now has redrawn the chart with the Adjust for Page Breaks check box marked. If you clear this check box, page breaks are ignored when Layout Now is used.

FIG. 21.30

The same PERT Chart as the previous figure but automatically adjusted for page breaks.

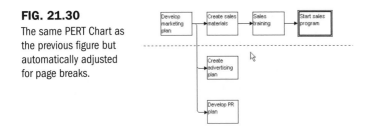

Redrawing the PERT Chart with the Layout Now Command

To redraw the PERT Chart, choose Format, Layout Now. The layout options specified in the Layout dialog box govern the way nodes and lines are placed in the chart. You can also right-click a blank spot in the PERT Chart and choose Layout Now from the shortcut menu.

Formatting the Task and Resource Forms

Like the other forms, the Task and Resource Forms can't be printed, and the formatting choices are limited. If the form is active in the top pane, you can view all resources with the form. Use the Next and Previous buttons to change the task or resource displayed in the form. If the form is active in the bottom pane, you can display only tasks or resources that are associated with the items selected in the top pane.

To display the Task or Resource Form, select the pane in which you want the form to appear, and then choose View, More Views, and then select Task or Resource Form from the More Views dialog box.

Reviewing the Format Options for the Form Views

The Resource and Task Forms have a limited number of format options. The Project menu for both the Resource and Task Form view provides a Sort option, and the Format menu provides a Details option that offers various entry field tables that you can place at the bottom of the form.

The Sort option changes the order in which resources or tasks appear when you use the Next and Previous buttons.

To sort the resource or task list for display while using the Form view for either, choose Project, Sort. Follow the same procedure for using the Sort dialog box (for all views), as described earlier in this chapter, "Sorting the Tasks or Resources in a View."

Using the Entry Field Options

To select a different set of entry fields for the Task or Resource Form, you can choose other options by choosing Format, Details. These options are available for form views only and are described in this section.

 TIP You can also see a list of alternative formats for forms by right-clicking anywhere in the form and choosing from the shortcut menu.

The Resource Form and the Task Form have several detail options that are the same. In the Resource Form, the various tasks assigned to that resource are listed. Changing the details changes the display of the information about the tasks assigned. The Task Form displays information about the resources assigned to the tasks. Therefore, changing the details in the Task Form changes the way the resource information is displayed.

Part
VII

Ch
21

In the Task Form, to display fields for when work is scheduled as well as entry fields for imposing a delay either on the task itself or when the resource begins work on the task, choose Format, Details, Schedule. Notice the columns named Leveling Delay and Delay (see Figure 21.31). You can use the Delay field to delay the start of work on a task by the resource. The Leveling Delay field is a delay for the task itself and is the same field that appears on the Delay Table on the Detail and Leveling Gantt Charts. The Delay field is a delay for the resource only. If the resource is the only one assigned to work on a task, the effect of a resource delay has the same effect on the schedule as the effect of a task delay: both choices delay the start of the task. However, suppose several resources are assigned to a task and one of the resources needs to spend only the last several hours on the task (during the finishing stage, for example). The assignment of this resource to the task can be accompanied by a delay in when the resource begins work on the task, but does not result in a delay for the task.

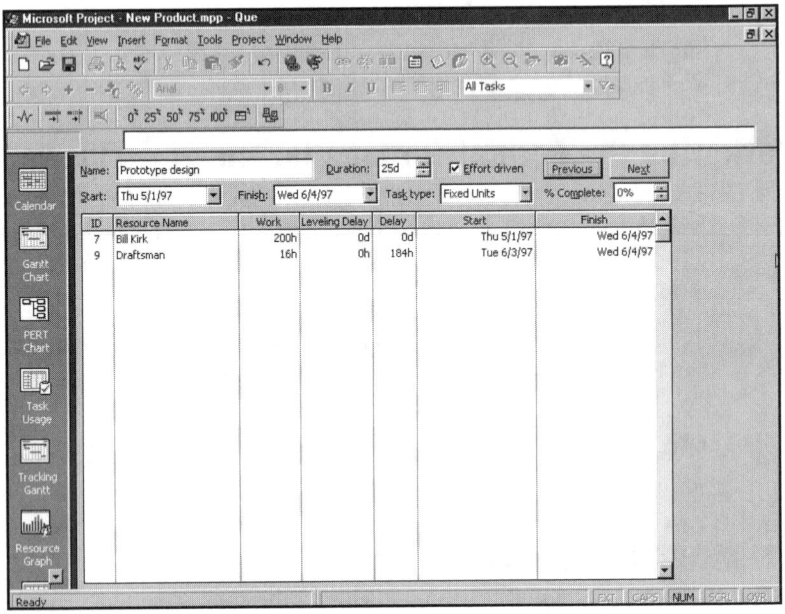

FIG. 21.31

Choose Format, Details, Schedule to display Schedule fields on the Task Form.

To display the cost fields for the resource for each task (on the Task Form) or the cost of each task to which the resource is assigned (on the Resource Form), choose Format, Details, Cost. Figure 21.32 shows the cost of each resource assigned to the Prototype Design task.

To display the fields for work on different tasks, choose Format, Details, Work. Use this version of the form to record the actual work and overtime spent on tasks by the resource.

Choose Format, Details, Notes to display the Notes field for the task or resource (see Figure 21.33).

FIG. 21.32

The costs for each resource by task are displayed on the Task Form.

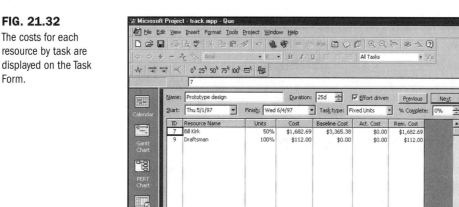

FIG. 21.33

The Notes field is shown here on the Task Form.

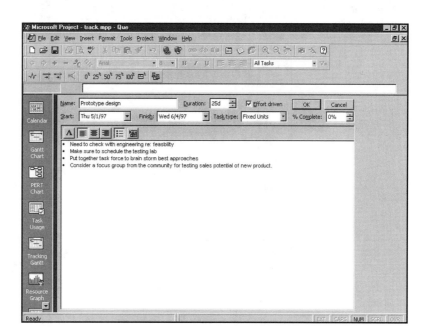

TIP You can also attach a note to any selected task or resource by using the Task Notes button on the Standard toolbar, or right-click any part of a task (the name, the ID, or the bar) and choose Notes from the shortcut menu.

Choose F<u>o</u>rmat, <u>D</u>etails, <u>O</u>bjects to display objects that were attached to the task or resource.

▶ **See** "Adding Graphics and Text to Gantt Charts," **p. 237**

Choosing F<u>o</u>rmat, <u>D</u>etails shows several additional choices for display in the Task Form. The standard display shows the <u>R</u>esources and Predecessors entry fields for the selected task. You also can choose to display Resources and S<u>u</u>ccessors, or <u>P</u>redecessors and Successors.

Formatting the Resource Graph

The Resource Gr<u>a</u>ph shows values derived from the task assignments of one or more resources; these values are graphed along a timescale. To display the Resource Graph, choose <u>V</u>iew, Resource Graph or click the Resource Graph icon in the View Bar. Figure 21.34 shows a histogram, or bar chart (in the lower pane), for the allocated and overallocated task assignments for Howard Thompson during the weeks of May 4 and 11. The value measured in this example is the Peak Units, or largest number units of work assigned during each time period (in this case, each day).

▶ **See** "The Resource Graph," **p. 673**

FIG. 21.34

The Resource Graph showing peak units displayed below the Resource Usage view.

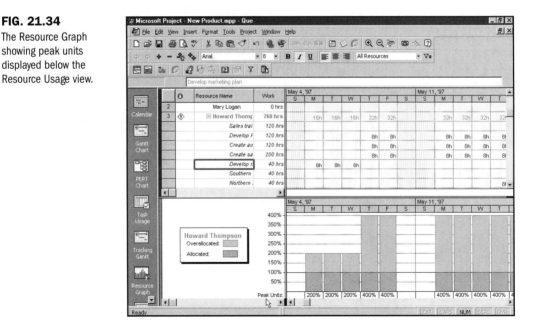

You can use the graph to show the following measurements for a resource time period:

▪ Peak Units

▪ Amount of work assigned

- Cost of the assignments
- Overallocation of the resource
- Percent Allocation
- Cumulative work or cost
- Availability of the resource

The graph can show these measurements for one resource, for a group of resources, or for the resource and the group together. The values can be for selected tasks or for all tasks during each time period.

If the Resource Graph is displayed in the bottom pane below a task view, the displayed values are for one resource only. You can show values for this resource's assignment to one task (the selected task) or to all tasks during each period measured on the timescale. Figure 21.34 shows the assignment bars for Howard Thompson for all tasks during each day. This figure provides a quick glimpse of the overassignment in terms of numbers of tasks assigned.

When the Resource Graph is in the top pane, or in the bottom pane but below a resource view, the values displayed are for all tasks and may be for one resource, for a group of resources, or for that one resource compared to the group of resources. If group data is displayed, the group is defined by the filter currently in use. If the All Resources filter (the default filter) is in use, for example, the data summarizes all resources for all tasks. Figure 21.35 shows the total costs associated with Howard Thompson's task assignments, relative to the total costs of all resource assignments in the project.

FIG. 21.35

The Resource Graph for costs associated with Howard Thompson compared to the costs of all other resources.

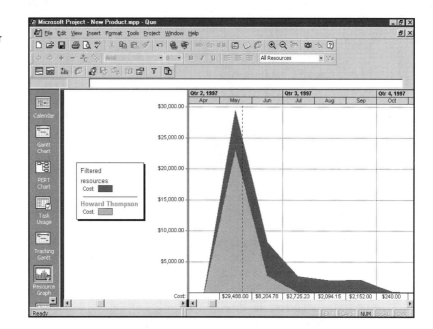

Table 21.2 summarizes the values displayed for different placement locations for the Resource Graph.

Table 21.2   Values Shown in the Resource Graph

Location of Graph	Group Value	One Resource Value
Top pane or bottom pane below a resource view	Value is for all tasks for all filtered resources	Value is for all tasks for the selected resource
Bottom pane below a task view	Value is for one resource but for all tasks	Value is for one resource but for only the tasks selected in the top pane

Reviewing the Format Options for the Resource Graph

As with other views, the Zoom command on the View menu is available for the Resource Graph and works (as discussed previously in this chapter) to modify the timeframes that are displayed. Likewise, the Zoom In and Zoom Out tools on the Standard toolbar can be used in this view.

The Format menu for the Resource Graph contains dialog box options—described previously in this chapter—for formatting the timescale, gridlines, and text styles. The Bar Styles dialog box, however, also offers features unique to the Resource Graph. These features are discussed in the following section.

The Format menu also provides a Details option. The choices on this list of calculated values control what information is displayed in the timescale portion of the Resource Graph. Because the Bar Styles dialog box changes are based on these values, the Details options are described first.

Selecting the Values To Display

The Format, Details menu displays a list of choices of what values will be calculated and graphed in the Resource Graph.

N O T E   When work is chosen, the unit (hours, minutes, or days) is determined by the Work Is Entered In option on the Schedule tab of the Tools, Options dialog box. The display of costs is determined by the Currency Symbol, Currency Placement, and Currency Decimal Digits choices on the View tab in the same dialog box. ▪

Displaying Peak Units   Peak Units measures the largest number of units of a resource assigned at any moment during each time period on the graph. If the number of assigned units exceeds the available number, the excess is shown as an overallocation. An availability line shows the number of units available.

Note that Peak Units are measured in *units assigned*, not work assigned. As such, Peak Units may mislead you when it shows an overallocation. Suppose a person is assigned full-time to two tasks during the same day. The peak units is 2, and because only one unit of a person is usually available per time period, the peak of 2 is an overallocation and is displayed as such. If each of the two tasks is a one-hour task, however, the person should have no problem completing both tasks during the day.

The Peak Units measurement is very useful, however, with multiple-unit resources in which the number of maximum units available is more than one. In these cases, the overallocation warning is more likely to be accurate.

Displaying Work   The Work choice on the Format, Details menu is measured in hours and is the number of units of each resource assigned to each task multiplied by the duration in hours of the tasks per time period displayed. For example, two programmers are assigned to work on a task that is estimated to take one eight-hour day. Project would calculate this task to have 16 hours of Work.

The amount of work available to be done by the resource is determined by the number of units of the resource and by the resource calendar during the time unit. If the total work for the time period exceeds the available amount of resource hours, the excess is shown as an over-allocation.

Displaying Cumulative Work   Another choice on the Format, Details menu is Cumulative Work. This is a measurement of the total work for the resource since the beginning of the project. This running total includes the work during the time period shown.

Displaying Overallocation   The Overallocation value shows the overallocation of work for the resource for the time period. The Overallocation option shows just the amount of the over-allocation, not any work hours that occurred during the normal work day. See the section, "Displaying Work," earlier in this chapter for the way Work is measured.

Displaying Percent Allocation   The Percent Allocation value is a measurement of the allo-cated work versus the available work. The Percent Allocation shows the amount of work as a percentage of the amount available. See the previous section, "Displaying Work," for the way in which Work is measured.

Displaying Availability   The Availability value is a measurement of the unallocated work for the resource during the time period. The Availability option shows the unused or unallocated work time that is still available. This is a useful option when you want to see who has some available time to work on tasks, or to see if you are available when new tasks are assigned to you. (See the previous section "Displaying Work.")

Displaying Cost   The Cost value is the scheduled cost of the resource work during the time period. If the resource cost is to be prorated (as defined in the Cost Accrual field on the Costs tab of the Resource Form), the costs will appear in the time period when the work is done. If there is a Per Use Cost associated with a prorated resource, that cost is shown at the start of the task. If the resource cost is to accrue at the start or end of the task, the entire cost will appear in the graph at the start or end of the task.

Displaying Cumulative Cost   The Cumulative Cost display adds each period's cost to the preceding period's cumulative cost to show a running total of costs. You can use this measurement to show total cost over the life of the project if you use only the group graph and include all resources in the group (see the Bar Styles dialog box instructions in the next section).

Using the Bar Styles Dialog Box

The Bar Styles dialog box allows you to specify what type of graph you would like to display (bar, area, step, line, and so on), as well as how it should look. It also allows you to specify whether you want to see groups or just selected resource information. When the Resource Graph is displayed, choose Format, Bar Styles to open the Bar Styles dialog box. A different Bar Styles dialog box appears for each of the value measurements just described. However, all of these dialog boxes have the same layout and are used the same way. Figure 21.36 shows the Bar Styles dialog box for the Work value. As with all the Resource Graph Bar Styles dialog boxes, this dialog box has four main sections plus three options at the bottom of the box.

N O T E   The different areas of this dialog box that are available will depend on the Details option that is set by choosing Format, Details.

FIG. 21.36
The Resource Graph Bar Styles dialog box for Work values.

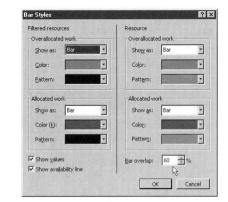

You use the two top sections to specify the display of overallocated amounts (if applicable), and the two bottom sections to specify the display of the allocated value up to the maximum available. The sections on the left side of the dialog box are for specifying the display of group data, and the sections on the right side are for specifying the display of one selected resource. Be aware that some of the values on the Details menu can display only two of the sections.

After the dialog box is closed, you may see multiple sets of double bars, and in some cases, each bar has an upper and a lower segment. The upper segment is the overallocation measurement. The lower segment is the allocation up to the overallocation level. Where you see pairs of bars, the left bar is the group measurement (again, note the similarity in the dialog box), and the right bar is the selected resource measurement. Recall that the resource group is defined by the filter that is applied when the Resource Graph is in the top pane or as a single pane. In this case, the group represents all resources because no filter has been applied.

Therefore, where you see a pair of bars in the graph (see Figure 21.37), the bar on the right (slightly in front) is the bar for the resource (Howard Thompson in this case), and the left bar (slightly behind) is the bar for the group (all resources in this case). Note that a horizontal line extends across the graph at this level. This line is the availability line for the resource.

FIG. 21.37

The Resource Graph demonstrates Howard Thompson's over-allocation compared to that of the entire resource pool.

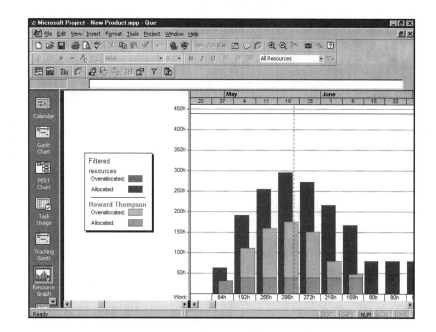

At the bottom of the graph, the work values are displayed in the time periods where the resource is allocated.

All these features are defined by the dialog box. (The graph in Figure 21.37 is defined by the settings in the dialog box in Figure 21.36.) The check boxes at the bottom are marked to show the values and to show the availability line. The bars overlap by 60 percent to show that they are paired.

The shading patterns are determined by the selections in the four sections of the dialog box. For each section, you choose three features that determine how the value is represented. Use the Show As drop-down list to choose the general form of the representation. The Bar is the usual choice, but you also can use lines and areas. The choice Don't Show suppresses all representation of the value. Choose Color (k) to select the color of the image, and choose Pattern for the pattern that fills the bar or area. (Notice that the underlined letters for these options are different in each section.)

You manage what is displayed by choosing to display or not to display in each of the four sections of the dialog box. If you want to display only the values for the selected resource, with no representation of the group values, choose Don't Show from the Show As drop-down list for both sections on the left. If you want to show only the totals for all resources, choose Don't Show for both sections on the right. When you choose Overallocation on the Format Details menu, the Bar Styles dialog box has both of the bottom sections dimmed to show that the sections are unneeded. When you finish making changes, choose OK to implement them or choose Cancel to ignore them.

To prepare the resource graph as shown in Figure 21.35, follow these steps:

1. Choose Format, Details, Cost.

2. Choose Format, Bar Styles.

3. In the Bar Styles dialog box in the Filtered Resources area, change the Show As option for the Resource cost (top left) to area.

4. Set the Show As option for the selected Resource cost (top right) to area. Choose a different color as well.

5. Click OK to close the dialog box.

6. Zoom the timescale to a major scale of quarters and a minor scale of months. You can use the Zoom out button on the standard toolbar or the Format, Timescale menu option to do this.

Formatting the Resource Usage View

The Resource Usage view shows the same data displayed in the Resource Graph, except that the values appear as number entries in a grid under the timescale. Figure 21.38 shows the Resource Usage view above the Resource Graph to demonstrate the similarity of the data presented. In both views, the value displayed is Work. The Format menu for the Resource Usage view includes text styles, formatting fonts, gridline formatting, and timescale formatting. As with the other views, sorting is also available on the Project menu, and page breaks can be inserted using the Insert menu. These are all topics covered previously in this chapter under their own headings. See those sections for information about using these format options.

Choosing the Details

The choices available by choosing Format, Details are the same value choices that were described under the Resource Graph: Work, Actual Work, Cumulative Work, Overallocation, Cost, and Remaining Availability. Select the value to display in the timescale grid by selecting one of these options.

If the Resource Usage view is placed in the bottom pane under a task view, the resources that are displayed will be resources assigned to the task that you selected in the top pane. The values displayed next to the resource name, are the total values for all tasks during the time periods shown. A breakdown of other tasks assigned to that resource are displayed under the resource name.

Figure 21.39 shows the Resource Usage view below the Gantt Chart. The values in the usage timescale table (in the same row as his name) show Work assigned to Howard Thompson for all tasks during each time period. Underneath his name and spread out across the timescale grid is a breakdown of the tasks that generated the totals. The values show that the resource is overallocated for a normal 40-hour work week, 8-hour work day.

FIG. 21.38
The Resource Usage view is shown in the top pane with the Resource Graph in the bottom pane, both showing Work as the value displayed.

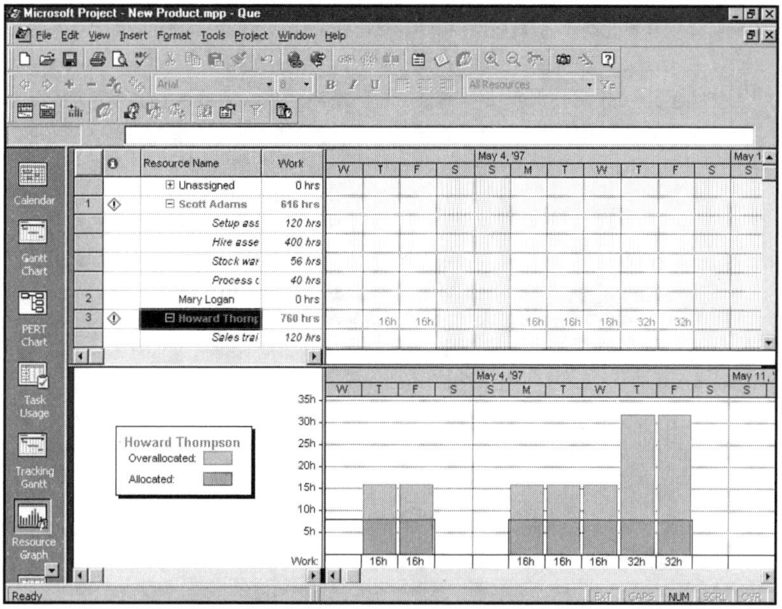

FIG. 21.39
The Resource Usage view is displayed below the Gantt Chart, with hours of Work displayed for the resource.

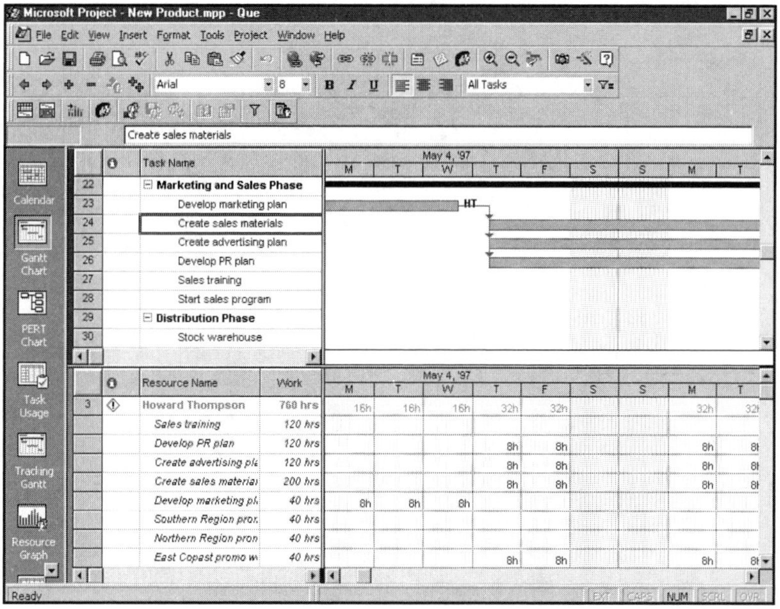

Part
VII

Ch
21

Formatting the Detail Styles

A new option with this version of Microsoft Project is the option for formatting how the details are displayed and how many of them are displayed at once. When the Resource Usage view is active, the Format menu contains an option for Detail Styles. Choosing this menu displays the dialog box displayed in Figure 21.40. Here, you can choose from a wide variety of fields, each with its own font, background color, and pattern. From the Available Fields list on the left, simply select a field to be displayed and use the Show button. To remove a field from being displayed, select it from the Show These Fields list on the right and use the Hide button. To rearrange the order in which the fields will be displayed, use the Move Up and Move Down buttons on the right side of the dialog box. The Usage Properties tab contains options for how the detail data should be aligned, and whether to display headings for the various columns and rows. Figure 21.41 displays the additional rows of information for each task assigned to Howard Thompson. Not only are these additional rows useful for reviewing, you can enter data into this view. This would be a handy place to enter actual information when you are tracking progress on your project.

▶ **See** "Using the Facilities Provided for Updating Tasks," **p. 495**

FIG. 21.40

The Detail Styles dialog box offers many choices for how much detail to display in the timescale grid of the Resource Usage view.

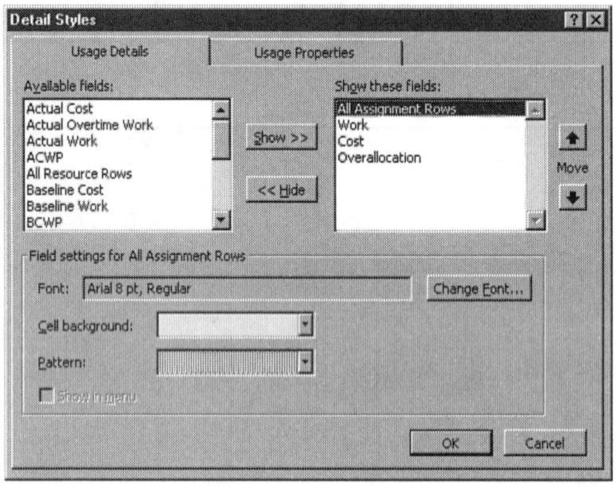

Formatting the Task Usage View

The options for formatting the new Task Usage view are identical to the Resource Usage view. The main difference between the views is the focus. While the Resource Usage view is looking at the information from the perspective of the resource, the Task Usage view looks at each task, providing totals for various details and then a breakdown by each resource that is assigned to work on the task. As shown in Figure 21.42, the task Prototype Design has two resources assigned, each has its own hours and costs, with a total for the task.

Formatting the Sheet Views

The Task and Resource Sheets both display a table of field values for the list of tasks or resources. The Format menu for both the Sheet views only includes options for changing Fonts,

Gridlines, and Text Styles. Also, as before, the Project menu has a Sort option, and the Insert menu offers a choice for inserting page breaks. These features were discussed previously in this chapter under their own headings. The columns that are displayed depend on the table applied to the sheet.

▶ **See** "Using and Creating Tables," **p. 748**

FIG. 21.41
Hours of work, costs for those hours of work, and overallocated hours can provide useful information when making decisions about your project.

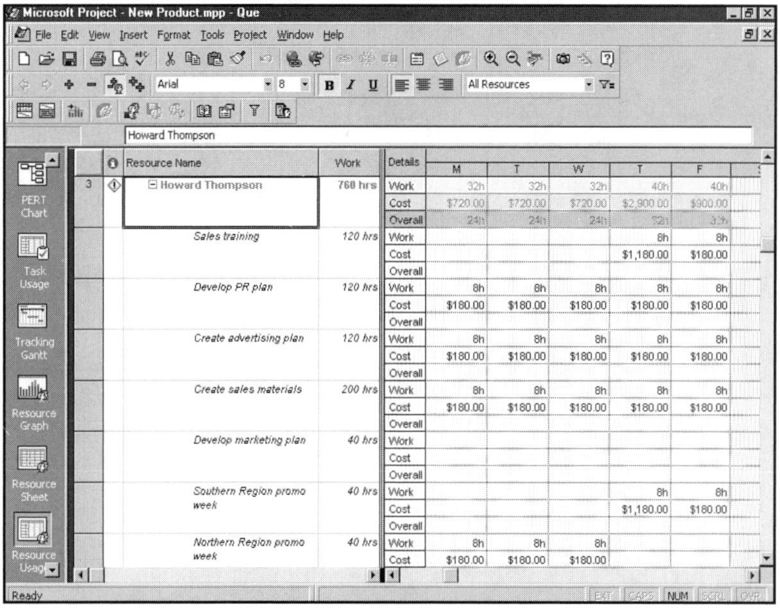

FIG. 21.42
Adding extra rows to the Task Usage view can make it a useful tracking tool.

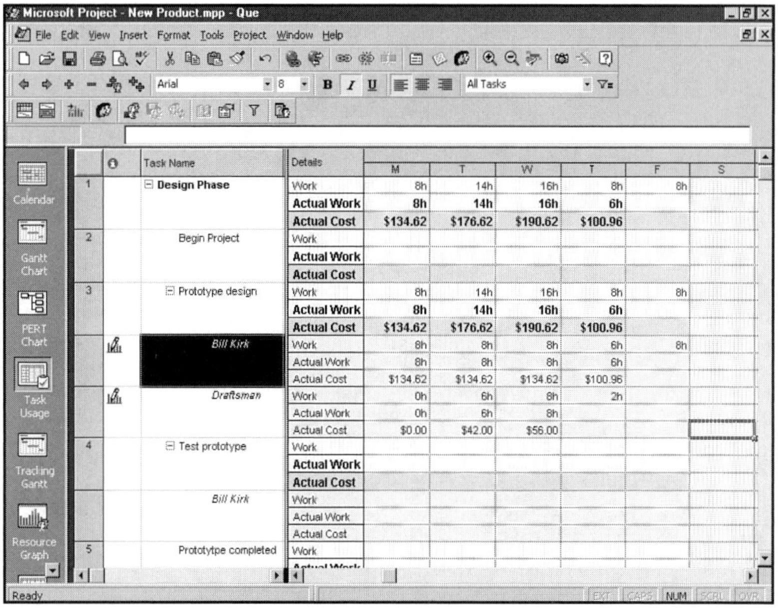

From Here...

This chapter described most of the standard customizing features for the many views in Microsoft Project. In addition to these standard features for customizing views, you can add text and graphics of your own creation. There are also numerous options for customizing reports. When you find yourself using these same features repeatedly, you may want to automate them with macros. To learn more about these subjects, refer to the following chapters:

- Chapter 7, "Working with the Major Task Views."
- Chapter 24, "Customizing Reports."
- Chapter 25, "Using Macros in Microsoft Project."

CHAPTER 22

Customizing Views, Tables, and Filters

One of the major strengths of Microsoft Project is the variety of tools that are available for customizing the standard views and reports and for creating new views and reports to serve specific needs. This chapter shows you how to use the basic building blocks in Microsoft Project to create, customize, and store new views.

Create new views for the project

When you are creating a new view, normally you would work from the bottom up by creating a new table or a new filter first. This chapter works from the top down by first discussing views, and then looking at tables and filters.

Customize and create new tables of data

Tables are named objects; their settings can be saved for future use. If you change the fields displayed in a table, for example, all views that use that table will display the new fields.

Use filters to control which tasks are displayed

Filters are also named objects; for example, if you change the criteria specifications of a filter, all views (and reports) that use that filter will display the results of the changed criteria.

Organize and manage the new view definitions in project files, and make them part of the global template

Instead of recreating the same views, tables, and filters in every project file, you can share your customizations with other specific files or with all new files that are created.

Creating New Views

You can change the views that are available on the <u>V</u>iew menu or in the More Views dialog box by editing the standard views or creating new views. When creating a new view, you can save time by copying an existing view and making changes in the copy (leaving the original view undisturbed). If none of the standard views are satisfactory, you can create a new view from scratch.

Creating a new view by editing an existing one uses the same techniques as creating a view from scratch. After you are familiar with the basics, copying, and editing views will be easy.

To start, choose <u>V</u>iew, <u>M</u>ore Views. The More Views dialog box appears (see Figure 22.1).

FIG. 22.1

You can create new views or edit existing ones in the More Views dialog box.

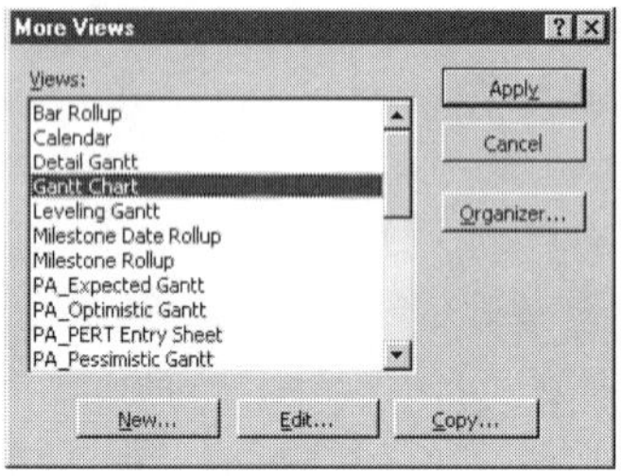

This dialog box has been used previously to change from one view to another. This chapter discusses the three buttons at the bottom of the dialog box: <u>N</u>ew, <u>E</u>dit, and <u>C</u>opy. The <u>N</u>ew button is used when you want to create a new view from scratch. The <u>E</u>dit button is used when you want to make changes to an existing view, overwriting the original. The <u>C</u>opy button is used when you want to make changes to an existing view but you don't want to overwrite the original. The steps are the same whether you choose New, Edit, or Copy. For this example, choose <u>N</u>ew. The Define New View dialog box appears as shown in Figure 22.2.

TIP   If you want to preserve the standard tables in their original form, use the <u>C</u>opy command rather than the <u>E</u>dit command and edit the copy of the table. You then will have both the original and the revised copies to use.

◆ TROUBLESHOOTING

I've already modified a standard view by editing it and now I want to get back the original. Use the Organizer to copy the view that you modified back into your project. Make sure to rename the view that you modified to a new name so that your original isn't overwritten.

FIG. 22.2

Create a new view in the Define New View dialog box.

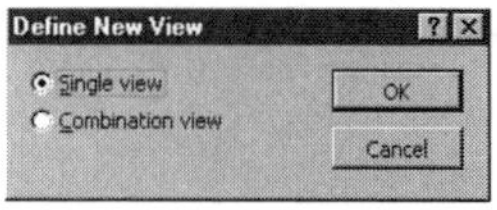

The purpose of the Define New View dialog box is to give you a place to indicate whether the new view will be a single pane view or a combination view. A combination view is simply a display of two views: one in the top pane and one in the bottom pane (see Figure 22.3). Two commonly used combination views include the Task Entry view (the Gantt Chart and the Task Form) and the Resource Allocation view (Resource Usage and the Gantt Chart). Indeed, when two views are often used in combination to perform standard tasks, it is advantageous to save the view combination for easy access. The new view can even be displayed in the menu if used often enough. See the upcoming section "Creating a Combination View" for step-by-step instructions.

FIG. 22.3

Use the View Definition dialog box to set up a new combination view.

Before you can create a combination view you must have created or determined which single pane views you want. To create a new single pane view, choose the New button from the More Views dialog box. When the Define New View dialog box appears choose Single View. The View Definition dialog box appears (see Figure 22.4).

FIG. 22.4

The first step in creating a new view starts with the View Definition dialog box for a single pane view.

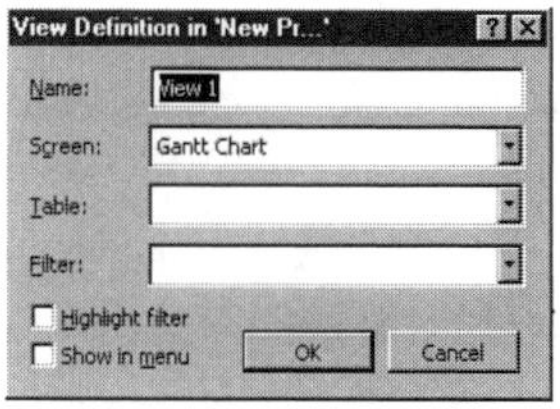

The View Definition dialog box has text boxes and check boxes for defining the following options:

- The Name of the new view.
- The basic Screen or general view format used.
- The Table used (if the chosen screen uses a table).
- The Filter that should be used, and whether it is a highlight filter or a limited display filter.
- Whether the new view appears in the main View menu.

N O T E   If an existing view is copied, the screen option cannot be changed.

TROUBLESHOOTING

I want to change the screen used for a view and I can't. Instead of copying an existing view you
must create a brand new view. You may first want to edit the view that you were copying to see the
settings that were used. Then create a new view.

Entering the Name of the View

You should enter a name that readily identifies the features you are incorporating into the view.
If the view is to appear on the View menu, you must mark the Show in Menu check box at the
bottom of the dialog box. You can designate a letter to use to choose the view from the View
menu using the keyboard rather than the mouse. Type an ampersand (**&**) before the chosen
letter when you type the view name. When the view is displayed in the menu, this letter is
underlined to indicate that this character is used to select the table. For example, if you enter
&Dependencies in the Name text box, the Checking Task Dependencies view will appear on
the menu as Checking Task Dependencies; you can type the letter **D** to select the view from
the menu.

N O T E   Try to make sure that you designate a letter not already used by another view. If you choose
a letter already being used by another menu command, you may have to press the letter
twice to select the view.

Selecting the Screen

Microsoft Project provides a number of basic screens, used alone or in combination, to produce
the standard views listed on the View menu and on the More Views dialog box. All views must
use one of these basic, prefabricated screens.

You cannot change the screen assigned to one of the pre-defined views listed in the View
menu. You can, however, create custom forms that resemble the basic screens.

▶ **See** "Using Custom Forms," **p. 900**

Here are the basic screens:

Calendar	Resource Usage
Gantt Chart	Task Details Form
PERT Chart	Task Form
Resource Form	Task Name Form
Resource Sheet	Task PERT
Resource Graph	Task Sheet
Resource Name Form	Task Usage

You can modify some of these screens extensively to customize a view; other screens, however, can be changed only in limited ways. You can create your own table to apply to the views that contain tables. You can define a filter that will be permanently attached to the view for all but the PERT Chart views. Format choices can be customized in varying degrees for each of the views, and the format settings can be saved as part of the view. See Chapter 21, "Formatting Views," for a refresher on formatting.

To define the screen on a new view, first select the Screen drop-down list from the View Definition dialog box, and then choose a screen from the list that appears.

Selecting the Table for the View

If the screen that you choose displays a table of field columns, you must define the table to use in the view. To define the table, select the Table drop-down list from the View Definition dialog box, and then choose a table name. The entry list contains all tables that are included in the More Tables menu for the screen type (task or resource) that you have chosen. If you wanted to include a customized table, it must exist before you can include it in a view. See "Using and Creating Tables" later in this chapter.

Selecting the Filter for the View

All views (except the PERT Chart and Task PERT view) have a filter attached. For all the standard views, the filter that is originally attached is the All Tasks or All Resources filter. Select the Filter drop-down list to select one of the defined filters. In Figure 22.5, the Tasks With Fixed Dates filter is defined as a highlight filter for the view, which means that all tasks will be *displayed*, but tasks with fixed dates will be *highlighted*.

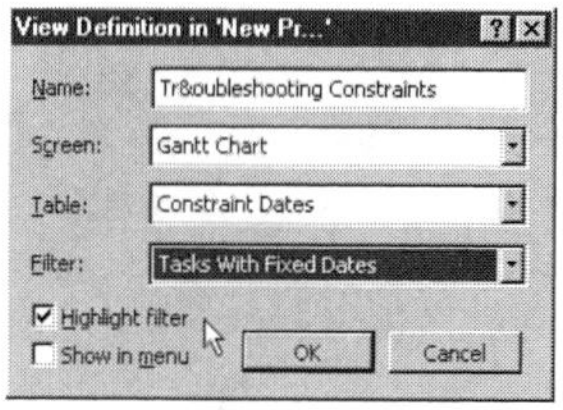

FIG. 22.5

This figure illustrates completing the View Definition dialog box.

A highlight filter shows all tasks or resources, but those selected by the filter are displayed with the highlight formatting features bold, italic, underline, and so on, as defined with the Format, Text Styles command for highlighted items.

If you want to filter by something other than the variables that are included with the standard filters, you must define the filter first before you can use it in a view.

▶ **See** "Formatting Text Displays for Categories of Tasks and Resources," **p. 697**

Displaying the View Name in the Menu

To display the view name in the View menu and on the View Bar, mark the Show in Menu check box. All views always appear in the More Views list.

Saving the View Definition

When you have finished using the View Definition dialog box, select the OK button to save your definition. You are returned to the More Views dialog box, where you can take one of the following actions:

- Select the Apply button to place the view on-screen immediately.
- Select the Close button to leave the current view on-screen, but save the view you have just defined.
- Select the New, Copy, or Edit buttons to continue working with the list of views.
- Select the Organizer button to save the newly defined view along with all other views to the global file. See the upcoming section, "Organizing Views in Project Files," for more details.

Creating a Combination View

If the view is a combination view (a view that defines other views to be placed in the top and bottom panes), the views for each pane must be defined before you can define the combination view. To define a combination view, access the More Views dialog box by choosing More Views from the View menu. Select the New button to display the Define New View dialog box (refer to Figure 22.2). Then select the Combination View button. The View Definition dialog box that appears is designed for defining a combination view (refer to Figure 22.3).

In the Name field enter a name for the view. Include an ampersand (&) in front of a letter to designate the selection letter for the view when the name appears on the menu. From the Top drop-down list, choose the view to place in the top pane. All single pane views that have been defined are available for selection. From the Bottom entry list, choose the view to place in the bottom pane. All single pane views (except PERT Charts, which cannot appear in the bottom pane) are available for selection. Mark the Show in Menu check box if you want the view to appear on the View menu and on the View Bar. Clear this check box if you want the view to appear in the More Views dialog box only.

To complete the view definition, click the OK button. Select the Apply button in the More Views dialog box to display the view immediately, or select the Close button to save the view but leave the screen unchanged. Figure 22.6 displays the new combination view that was defined in Figure 22.3.

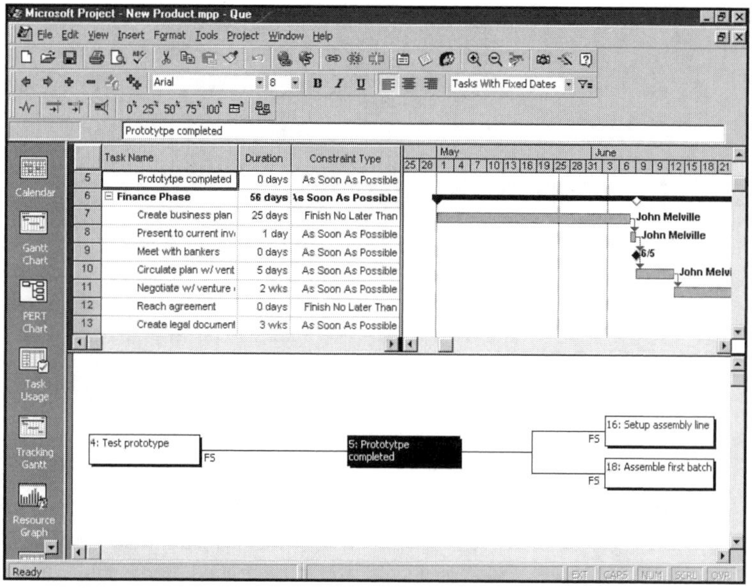

FIG. 22.6

A newly created combination view allows you to focus on specialized tasks.

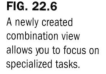

If you define a combination view that uses other customized views you have defined, and if these views use customized tables and filters you have defined, you must plan the order in which the customized components are developed. In other words, you must work from the bottom up. The following sequence is for the most complex case. In this example, you define a combination view that uses new views you have defined; these views use tables and filters you have defined which contain specific formatting changes you want to use.

1. Define all new tables that you plan to use. It doesn't matter whether their names appear on the View, Table menu, because you probably won't use them individually; they will be used automatically by the new view that you are creating.

2. Define any new filters that you plan to use. These filters do not have to appear on the Project, Filtered For menu; appearing on the More Filters menu is sufficient.

3. Define the single pane views that you want to include in your combination view using the basic screens that are appropriate. Assign to these views the tables and filters that you want the views to use.

4. Format each of the views with the special formatting options that you want to use.

   ▶ **See** "Formatting Views" **p. 695**

5. Define the combination view by naming the new customized views to be placed in the top and bottom panes. If you want to have this view directly available from the View menu, mark the Show in Menu check box. The definitions you have created are saved with the project file.

N O T E   If you later decide that you want to use this view in another project file you can copy it to a single project file or to GLOBAL.MPT—a template that makes views, tables, and filters available to all project files. See the section, "Organizing Views in Project Files," later in this chapter.

Using and Creating Tables

This section shows you how to use the View, Table command to change the appearance and content of the column data in the sheet views. Tables are the building blocks of Microsoft Project that control which fields are displayed in sheet views. This includes Gantt Charts because the left side of a Gantt Chart is actually a task sheet. Through the manipulation of tables, you can determine the data displayed in each column, the width of the column, the alignment of the data within the column, the title that appears at the top of the column, and the alignment of the column title. With the Table Definition dialog box, you can add new columns, delete columns, rearrange the order of columns, and make other changes in the definition of the table.

To change the display of a table, select View, Table and choose More Tables. The More Tables dialog box appears on-screen, with the currently displayed table highlighted (see Figure 22.7). You use this dialog box to perform the following procedures:

■ Display a table that is not included on the main Table menu (there are several task and resource tables that are only available from this dialog box).

■ Create new or delete existing tables.

■ Change the features of any of the tables in the list box.

FIG. 22.7
The More Tables dialog box offers choices for customizing tables.

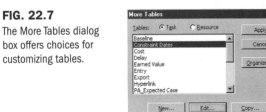

The names of either task tables or resource tables appear in the list box, depending on the view that was active when you chose the More Tables command. To switch between task tables and resource tables, choose between the Task or Resource option buttons at the top of the dialog box.

To apply a table to the current view, choose the desired table from the list and choose the Apply button. Note, however, that if the current view is a task view, you cannot display a resource table on this view.

To edit an existing table, choose the table from the list box and choose the Edit button. If you want to create a new table that is similar to an existing table, choose the original table from the list and choose the Copy button. To create a new table from scratch, choose the New button.

Whenever you choose the New, Copy, or Edit button, the Table Definition dialog box appears. If you choose New, the fields in the dialog box will be empty. If you choose either Edit or Copy, the fields will contain the values for the table you selected from the list box in the More Tables dialog box. Figure 22.8 illustrates a dialog box for a copy of the Entry table. The explanations that follow also apply when you are editing or creating new tables.

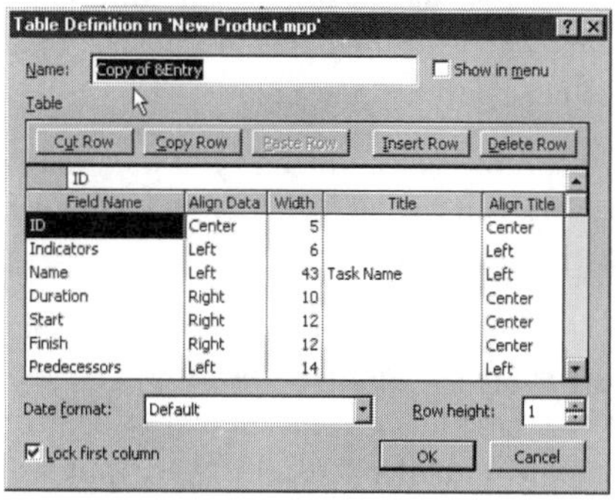

Part

VII

Ch

22

FIG. 22.8

The Table Definition dialog box is illustrated with a copy of the Entry table.

Entering a Table Name

When you create a new table or edit a copy of another table, you will want to supply a new name for the table. If the table name is to appear on the Table menu, use an ampersand (&) before any character in the name to indicate that this character is used to select the table.

Adding and Changing the Columns in the Table

If you are starting with a new table, simply access the drop-down list at the right side of the field name column, as shown in Figure 22.9. Choose a field by scrolling through the list and choosing the one you want.

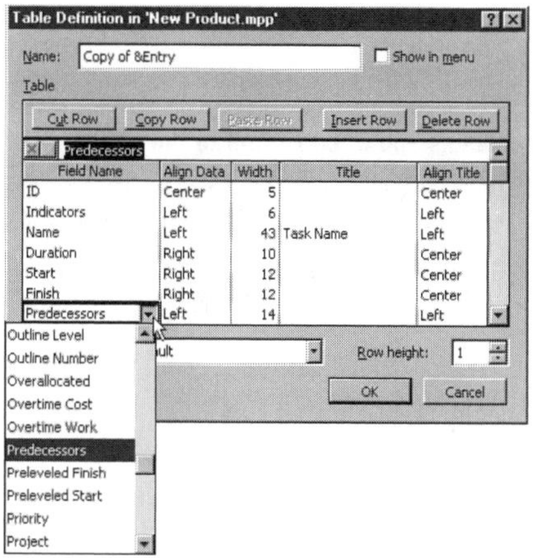

FIG. 22.9

Use the long list of field names in the Table Definition dialog box to choose the columns to display in a table.

If you want to add additional fields, move the cursor down to the next blank row, using the scroll bar on the right side of the dialog box if necessary. To insert a field between the existing fields, select the row below where you want to place the new field, and use the Insert Row button to insert a blank row. Select from the field drop-down list as described previously.

To remove a field from the table, select any item (that is, Field Name, Width, and so on) in the row that contains the field to be deleted and use the Delete Row button. To replace a field with a new field, select the Field Name entry for the old field and select the new field from the drop-down list. This replaces the old field with the new field.

To rearrange the columns in your table, select the one you want to move and use the Cut Row button. Select the row below where you want the cut row to be moved and use the Paste Row button. There is no need to insert a blank row first.

When you use the drop-down list to choose a name from the Field Name list, the default Alignment and Width for the field are supplied automatically. However, you can change the alignment to Left, Center, or Right by typing this specification or by selecting the alignment from the drop-down list. Type a different Width for the field if you want a width other than the default. Use the Title column to supply a column name if you want one that is different from the field name. Leave the Title column blank if you want to use the field name as the title.

Completing the Definition of the Table

At the top of the dialog box, the check box labeled Show in Menu must be marked if you want the table to appear on the View Table menu (rather than just on the More Tables dialog box). The View Table menu displays as many as 20 table names.

Mark the check box labeled Lock First Column if you want the first column of the table to remain on-screen at all times. As you scroll to the right in the table, if this box is checked, the first column will not scroll out of view. However, it is not editable when it is locked. In the standard sheet views, the first column is the task or resource ID.

TROUBLESHOOTING

I'm working in a table with many columns and when I scroll to the right side of the table the task names disappear. Is there any way to lock them in place? Yes, edit the table and move the task name field to the very first column. Make sure the Lock First Column check box is selected. The only problem with this arrangement is that you can't move your cursor into the column for editing. Edit your table in this way after your task names have been finalized or edit the table again and unlock the column.

Use the Date Format area to specify the format for date fields in the table. If you leave the Default entry in place, the date format selected through the Tools, Options command is used. Select the drop-down list to display the other date formats that you can elect to use rather than the default format. The change in date format will not change your default or the date format used in other views.

The normal row height in a sheet view is 1, which means that one row of text is displayed for each task or resource *row* in the table. If the row height is greater than 1, long text entries in any column of the table automatically wrap if the width of the column is insufficient to display them on one line. Choose Row Height and enter the number of text lines to be displayed for each task. Note that all rows are the same height and additional lines take up space even if they are blank. Figure 22.10 shows the definition for a new table named Bid, which displays tasks with ID, Indicators, Name, Duration, Start, and Text1 with a Title set to the word "Comments." Note that the titles for several of the fields have been changed, the Date Format has been changed, and the Row Height has been changed to 3 to facilitate displaying the long text entries that may be found in the Text1 field.

> **TIP**
> When you use a name in the Title field for one of the custom fields (Text1-30), it is actually an "alias" that can be used to reference that same custom field in other tables that you work with.

Figure 22.11 shows the Bid table (as defined in Figure 22.10) when applied to the Task Sheet view.

FIG. 22.10

This figure illustrates the table definition for the Bid table.

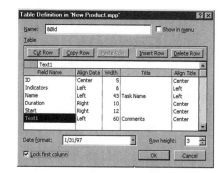

> **TIP**
> A very useful yet simple table is one with only one field, the task ID. Use this table in conjunction with a Gantt chart that has the task names placed next to the task bars for a completely graphical view. It's much easier to read the task names when they are close to the task bars, and columns of text take up a lot of valuable space.

Changing Table Features from the View Screen

Most of the features that you define in the Table Definition dialog box can be changed from the view screen without having to go through the View, Table command. For example, you can access the Column Definition dialog box to insert, delete, and edit the definitions of columns directly in the table, without using the More Tables menu.

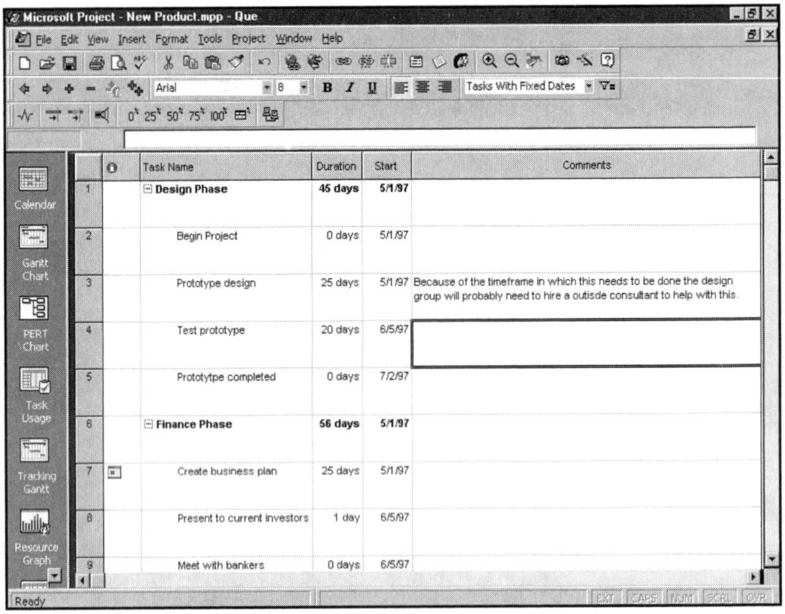

FIG. 22.11

This figure illustrates the Bid table applied to the Task Sheet view.

To change the definition of a column from the view screen, double-click the title of the column. The Column Definition dialog box appears, as shown in Figure 22.12, with the current column settings displayed in the selection fields. To redefine a column, change the selections in any of the following entry fields:

- ▨ Choose Field <u>N</u>ame to view the list of field names, and select a field from the list.

- ▨ Choose <u>T</u>itle if you want to type a different text title to appear at the head of the column. When you change the title for a custom field (Text 1-30), you can use the same title to reference the field in other tables.

- ▨ Choose <u>A</u>lign Title to change the alignment for the column title and Align <u>D</u>ata to change the alignment for the column data.

- ▨ Choose <u>W</u>idth if you want to set the width of the column manually. Enter the width in number of characters. You also can use the <u>B</u>est Fit button to set the width to the widest entry in the column.

FIG. 22.12

This figure shows the Column Definition dialog box.

Complete the new definition of the column by choosing either OK or Best Fit. Choose OK if you want to apply the new column definition, including the Width setting. Choose Best Fit, however, if you want Microsoft Project to calculate the width needed to fully display both the title and the longest data value that initially goes into the column. The Best Fit button closes the dialog box and applies the new definition, but with the calculated column width.

To insert a new column, follow these steps:

1. Select the entire column currently located where the new column is to be placed. Select a column by selecting the column title.

2. Choose Insert, Column, or press the Insert (Ins) key. The Column Definition dialog box is displayed with values for the ID field supplied in the definition fields. Select the values for the new column, as previously described.

> **T I P** You can also point at the column title for the column to the right of where the new column will be inserted and right-click. Insert Column is one of the options on the column shortcut menu.

The new column is inserted in front of the column that was selected.

To remove a column from the table, first select the column (by selecting the column title). Then choose Hide Column from the Edit menu or press the Delete key. You can adjust the column width directly on the view screen by using the mouse. Follow these steps:

1. Move the mouse pointer into the row at the top of the table where the column titles are displayed, and position the pointer on the right gridline of the column you want to adjust.

2. Drag the gridline to the right or left to adjust the column width.

3. Double-click the gridline to have Microsoft Project calculate and adjust the column width to the best fit for the data in the column. The width is set to the necessary space for a full display of the widest entry found in any row of the column.

Any column width that you set using the mouse is automatically recorded in the Table Definition dialog box.

> **T I P** If you drag the right side of the column far enough to the left you can make the column seem to disappear. It merely has a column width of zero. To display the column again, simply edit the table definition in the Table Definition dialog box and specify a width greater than zero.

You can also change the row height with the mouse. Point to the bottom gridline in the first column (usually the ID column). When the mouse pointer changes to a double-headed arrow, drag up or down. This action adjusts the number of lines to be allocated for all rows in the table.

If you want your table to appear when you select a view, you must define the view to include the table name. To display the Task Sheet view shown in Figure 22.11, open the View menu, choose More Views, and select Task Sheet. Then open the View menu, choose the Table command, and select the Bid table. (If you didn't include the Bid table on the menu, you will need to choose More Tables and then Bid.) If you choose Task Sheet again, the screen would revert to the table defined for that view—the Entry table. See "Creating New Views," earlier in this chapter, for instructions on defining a view that always displays a custom table.

Creating Custom Filters

Before reading this section, be sure to read the section "Using the Standard Filters" in Chapter 20, "Using the Standard Views, Tables, and Filters." This section covers creating your own customized filters, including ones which prompt the user for input, calculate values, and allow multiple criteria to be entered. At the end of this section, the custom AutoFilter feature is discussed.

A good way to begin creating your own filters is to examine the definitions of the standard filters. To look at a filter definition, perform these steps:

1. Choose Project, Filtered For and select More Filters from the list.

2. Select a filter from the list.

3. Choose the Edit button.

The Filter Definition dialog box appears. Figure 22.13 shows the Filter Definition box for the In Progress Tasks filter.

FIG. 22.13

This figure shows the Filter Definition dialog box for the In Progress Tasks filter.

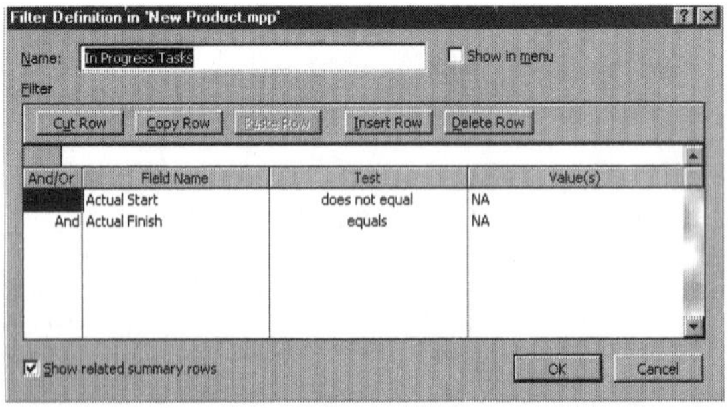

The In Progress Tasks filter applies two tests. The first test examines the Actual Start field to be sure that the value is *not equal* to NA (that is, the task has been started), and the second test examines the Actual Finish field to see whether the value is NA (the task has not finished). The logical operator And has been entered in the And/Or field, meaning that both the first *and* the second conditions must be met for a task to be selected.

Figure 22.14 illustrates the interactive Date Range filter. In this filter, the Finish field is tested to see whether the Finish date value falls after the entered value and whether the Start date falls before the entered value. However, the filter is designed to prompt the user to supply the dates at the time the filter is applied. Note that the *prompt* in the Values column is written within double quotation marks, and the *pause* for the user to enter a response is defined with the question mark. Prompts appear with a question mark immediately following the prompt.

For multiple prompts, use a comma (or the list separator specified in the Options dialog box) to separate the values.

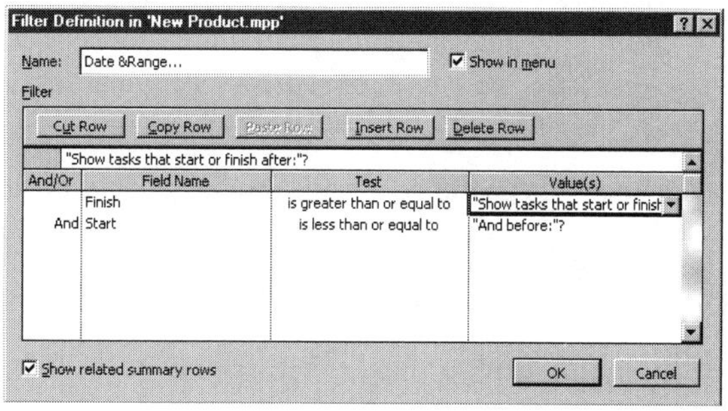

FIG. 22.14

The Filter Definition dialog box for the Date Range filter illustrates the prompts used to get criteria from the user at the time the filter is run.

To define a filter, choose More Filters from the Project, Filtered For menu. If you want to create a new filter unlike any filter already defined, choose the New button. Otherwise, select an existing filter name from the Filters entry list if you want to edit or copy an existing filter. In all three cases, New, Edit or Copy, the Filter Definition dialog box is displayed. The following sections show you how to develop an over budget filter that displays all tasks with a budgeted cost in excess of $1,000.

Naming the Filter

Provide a name for the filter by typing in a name in the Name field of the dialog box. If the filter name is to appear in the Filtered For menu, use an ampersand (&) before the letter that will be underlined (this letter is used to choose the filter from the menu). The check box labeled Show in Menu at the top of the dialog box must be selected for the filter name to appear in the menu.

In the example of the over budget filter, enter the name as **O&ver Budget by 1000** (with v as the selection letter), and mark the Show in Menu box so that the filter is placed on the Filtered For menu (see Figure 22.15).

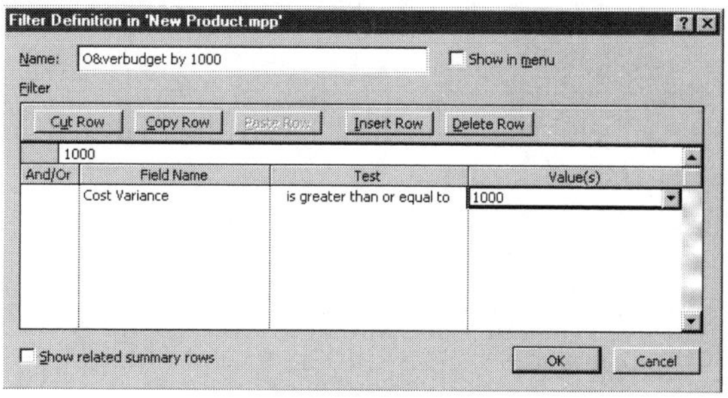

FIG. 22.15

This figure illustrates the finished Overbudget by 1,000 filter.

Defining the Filter Criteria

To define the criteria, you will be using the Filter area. For each test to be imposed on the database, you must fill in a row of this area. Each row must identify a Field Name, the nature of the Test to be conducted in the field, and the Value(s) to be looked for in the field. If multiple tests are to be imposed as part of the filter, the And/Or column must indicate the relationship of the criterion rows.

Selecting the Field Name Type the field name or use the drop-down list to select a field name from the drop-down list. In the example in Figure 22.15, the field name is Cost Variance.

Selecting the Test Select the cell in the Test column and use the drop-down list to view the tests you can select. Select the appropriate test or type the test phrase. In the example, the test is to be *greater than or equal to*.

Table 22.1 describes the use of each of the items in the Test entry list.

Table 22.1 The Filter Test Options

Test	Meaning and Example	Field Name	Value(s)
Equals	Field values must match value(s) exactly Critical	Critical Tasks	Yes
Does not equal	Field value must differ from Value(s) entry Task has started	Actual Start	NA
Is greater than	Field value must be greater than Value(s) entry Task started after 8/1/97	Actual Start	NA
Is greater than or equal to	Field value must be greater than or equal to Value(s) entry Budgeted cost $1000 or over	Planned Cost	1000
Is less than	Field value must be less than Value(s) entry Duration less than 1 day	Duration	1d
Is less than or equal to	Field value must be less than or equal to Value(s) entry Task finishes before 9/1/97	Actual Finish	9/1/97

Test	Meaning and Example	Field Name	Value(s)
Is within	Field value must lie on or between the range of Value(s) entry Duration is between 5 and 10 days	Duration	5d,10d
Is not within	Field value must lie outside the range of Value(s) entries Tasks that are not in the middle of production	% complete	25%,75%
Contains	Field value must contain the string in Value(s) Resource assignment includes Mary Logan, among others	Name (Resource)	Mary Logan
Does not contain	Field value must not contain the string in Value(s) Resource assignments include everyone except Mary Logan	Name (Resource)	Mary Logan
Contains exactly	Field value must contain the exact string in Value(s) Resource assignment includes only Mary Logan	Name (Resource)	Mary Logan

Entering the Value(s)   To enter the value to test for, select the cell in the Value(s) column. Type a value for the test or place an interactive prompt for interactive filters, or use another field name for calculated filters. The drop-down list for this column is used for calculated filters and contains the names of the fields, with each field name automatically enclosed in square brackets as required by the calculated filters. In Figure 22.15, the value is $1,000.

Completing the Filter Definition   Use the Insert Row button to insert a blank row before the criterion rows you have selected. Use the Delete Row button to remove a criterion row from the definition.

If the filter is to appear in the Filtered For menu, be sure that the Show in Menu check box is selected. Mark the Show Related Summary Rows check box if you want the summary task for any task selected by the filter also displayed.

Choose the OK button to complete the definition and return to the More Filters dialog box. Choose the Apply or Highlight button to apply the filter immediately, or choose Close to save the filter definition but not apply the filter at this time.

Using More Filter Criterion Tests

This section illustrates various types of filter criteria. These samples should help you design almost any kind of filter.

Testing for Logical Values   Many of the fields in the databases contain only the logical values Yes or No. For example, the Milestone field contains Yes for Milestone tasks, and No for all other tasks. The standard filter for Milestone tasks looks for the value Yes in the appropriate field (see Figure 22.16).

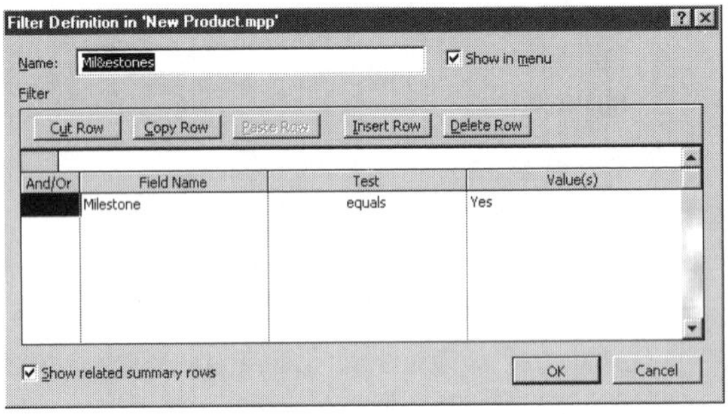

FIG. 22.16

The Milestone task filter searches for the value Yes.

Using the Within and Not Within Tests   Use the Is Within test to look for values that lie within and include the upper and lower values in the Values column. Use the Is Not Within test to identify values that fall outside a range of values. The range of values being used in the test is entered in the Value(s) column, with a comma separating the lower and upper values. In Figure 22.17, the Finish field is searched to find tasks that finish on 8/10/97 or by 8/15/97.

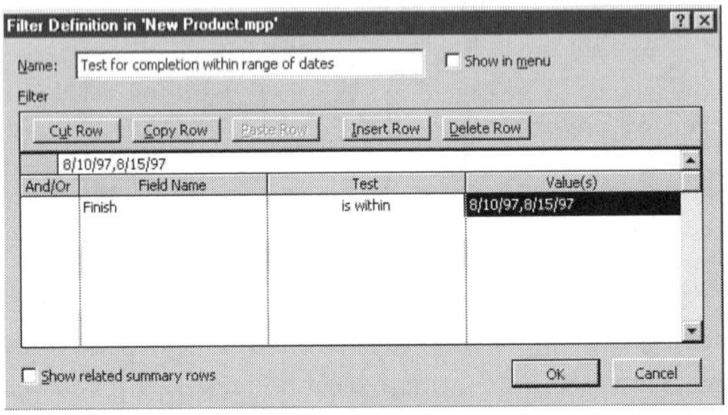

FIG. 22.17

This figure shows a filter that uses the Is Within test.

Using the Contains Test   Some text fields (most notably, Resource Names, Predecessors, and Successors) may contain lists of entries separated by commas. The Resource Names field contains the list of all the resources assigned to a task, and the Predecessors field contains a list of all the predecessors to the task. These are really text fields. The Contains test examines the text to see whether a string of characters that you enter in the Value(s) column is contained within the field contents. The Contains test is useful when you want to locate all of the tasks whose name includes a specified string of characters. Figure 22.18 shows a filter criterion that looks for the tasks whose name not only includes the word "sales" but other words as well, either before or after sales.

FIG. 22.18

This figure illustrates the Contains test.

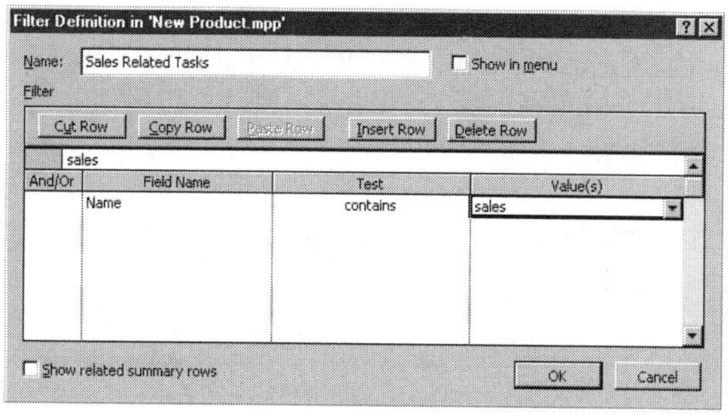

Using Wild Cards in a Value(s) String

Text field entries can be searched with wildcard characters in the search string. You must use only the Equals or Not Equals test for strings that include wild cards. The wildcard characters in Microsoft Project are similar to wildcard characters used in DOS: the asterisk (*) and the question mark (?).

A wild card can match any character that falls in the same place as the wild card in the search comparisons. Therefore, the test string ab?d is matched by any character in the third position as long as the *a*, *b*, and *d* are in the right places. The asterisk represents any number of missing characters or no characters, whereas the question mark represents just one character. Note the following examples:

Test String with Wild Card	Possible Matches
f?d	f*a*d, f*b*d, f*c*d, f*d*d, f*e*d, f2d
f??d	f*in*d, f*or*d, f*oo*d, f23d
f*d	fd, f*a*d, f*ee*d, f*ormatte*d
f*	f, f1, f123, find this text
12-?06	12-*A*06, 12-*1*06, 12-*X*06
12-*06	12-*A*06, 12-06, 12-*abc0*06

The filter in Figure 22.19 is defined to search the WBS field for entries that end in .1. This could conceivably produce a list of first steps under each summary task. For example, you might use this to assign a supervisor to the first step in any new summary task to get the work started.

Using Interactive Filters

An *interactive filter* increases the versatility of a filter that must search for different values in a field from one time to the next. For example, the filter in Figure 22.20 is designed to locate tasks in which the word "sales" is included. To search for a different word, you must redefine the filter. You can, however, replace the specification of the word "sales" with instructions to ask the user for the word to be located. Then the filter can be used to locate the tasks for any resource. This is similar to the Find feature, but is more useful because as a filter it not only can find the tasks with the specified word but also can hide all tasks that don't include the word or merely highlight the tasks that do include the word. Also, because it can be included on the menu and is automatically included on the filter drop-down list in the Formatting toolbar, it can be designed for use by people who aren't necessarily familiar with the software but can still use it to review project details.

FIG. 22.19

This figure illustrates a filter that finds WBS entries ending in .1 which will locate all first steps.

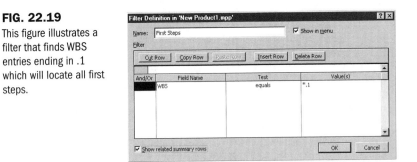

Interactive filters are created by typing a message and a question mark in the Value(s) column of the filter definition. When the filter is applied, the message is displayed (in a dialog box) as a prompt for the user, and the question mark causes Microsoft Project to wait for the user to fill a blank that follows the message in the dialog box. For example, the message "What words are you looking for in task names?" is a suitable prompt. The entry in the Value(s) column of the filter definition would look like the entry in Figure 22.20.

FIG. 22.20

This figure illustrates an interactive filter to locate tasks with specified words.

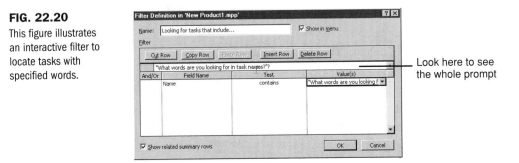

Look here to see the whole prompt

Another example would be a useful modification to the filter illustrated in Figure 22.17 which looks for Finish dates that fall within the range 8/10/97 and 8/15/97. You can replace both of these specific dates with prompts, as shown in Figure 22.21. If you are using an Is Within test with dates, you can prompt for both of them. Simply place a comma in between the two prompts. The resulting dialog box with prompts for this filter is shown in Figure 22.22.

FIG. 22.21

This figure illustrates an interactive filter with multiple prompts which allows more flexibility.

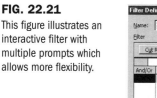

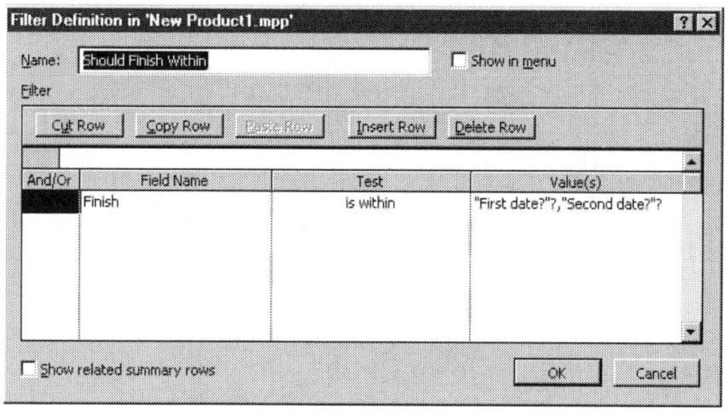

FIG. 22.22

This figure shows an interactive filter asking for input from the user.

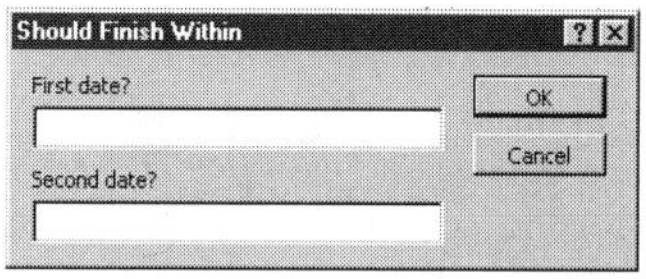

N O T E Notice the use of question marks in interactive filters in Figure 22.21. The first one is part of the prompt to the user. The second one identifies this as a prompt to Microsoft Project.

Creating Calculated Filters

A *calculated filter* compares the value in one field of a task or resource with the value in another field for the same task or resource. For example, tasks that are over budget have in the Baseline Cost field a value that is less than the value in the Cost field (which is the currently scheduled cost field). To filter over budget tasks, the criterion needs to compare the Cost field with the Baseline Cost field (see Figure 22.23).

FIG. 22.23

This figure illustrates a calculated filter that compares two values.

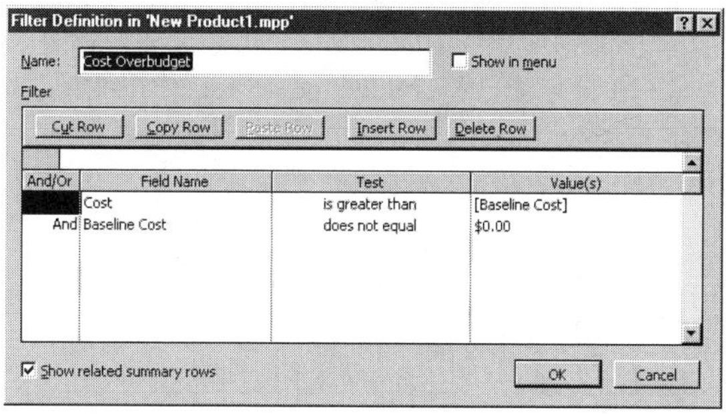

Remember if you are entering a field name in the Value(s) column of the filter definition, the name must be placed in brackets. The drop-down list for the Value(s) column lists all the field names, which Microsoft Project automatically places within brackets.

Creating Multiple Criteria Filters

If more than one test must be used to create the filter, each test is placed on its own row of the filter definition table. The last column (And/Or) is used to designate how each row is to be used with the row that follows it. If it is necessary that the tests on both rows must be satisfied to satisfy the filter, the operator And is placed in the And/Or column. In the calculated filter in the previous example, two criteria had to be met: the Cost had to be greater than the Baseline Cost *and* the Baseline Cost had to be greater than $0 in order to make the comparison.

Another example would be a filter to locate all the critical milestones. This filter would need to test the Milestone field on one row and the Critical field on the next row. Because both requirements must be met, the And operator is placed in the And/Or column (see Figure 22.24). Only tasks that are calculated to be critical *and* specified as milestones will be selected by the filter.

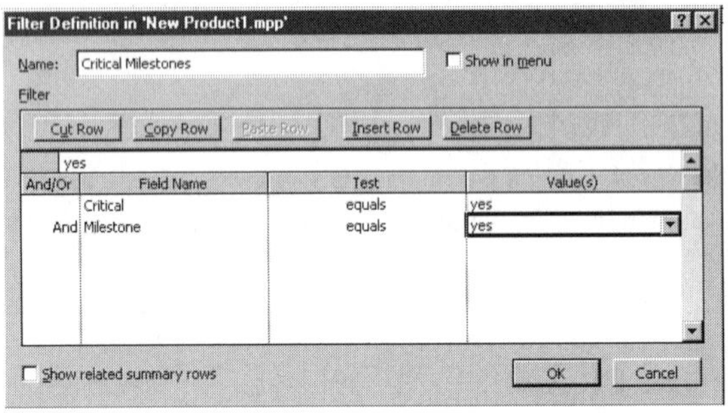

FIG. 22.24

A filter that uses criteria can test for more than one item.

If, however, passing *either* of the tests is sufficient to satisfy the filter, the operator *Or* is placed in the And/Or column. If the Or operator is placed in this column in Figure 22.24, all critical tasks are selected (whether they are milestones or not), and all milestones are selected (whether they are critical tasks or not).

If more than two rows are used to define a filter, the tests are evaluated from the top down. Therefore, the first two rows are evaluated using the operator on the first row, and then the third row test is added using the operator on the second row, and so on—until all rows have been considered. For example, in Figure 22.25, the filter seeks to locate all the critical milestones as well as (or in addition to) all the tasks that include the word "completed."

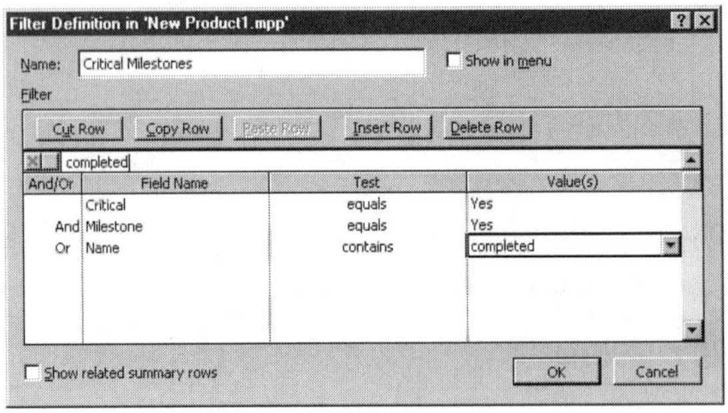

FIG. 22.25

This figure illustrates a filter with more than two tests.

You can also now group multiple criteria together to create more complex filters. For example, the Late/Overbudget Tasks Assigned To filter looks for tasks that are assigned to a resource (whose name is prompted for) and whose baseline has been set, as well as a finish that is later than planned or cost is greater than planned. The first two rows must both be met and then either of the last two rows must be met.

To create a grouped series of criteria, select the And/Or field in a blank row between the two groups, and choose either And or Or and move to the next row without entering any other criteria. Notice the shaded row in Figure 22.26.

FIG. 22.26
This figure illustrates a filter with two grouped series of criteria.

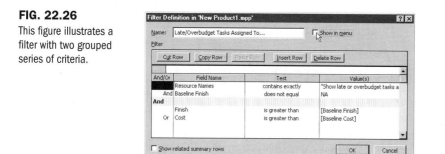

> **N O T E** Other new filters that include this grouping feature are Should Start/Finish By, Slipped/ Late Progress, and Using Resource In Date Range.

Creating Custom Filters with AutoFilter

A very easy way to create a custom filter is by using the Custom option on the AutoFilter list. First, turn on the AutoFilter feature by choosing either the Project, Filtered For, AutoFilter or by clicking the AutoFilter button on the Formatting toolbar. This displays an AutoFilter values drop-down list on each column heading. When you choose any of these, a menu will appear with a number of choices, including Custom. When you choose the Custom option, the dialog box in Figure 22.27 is displayed.

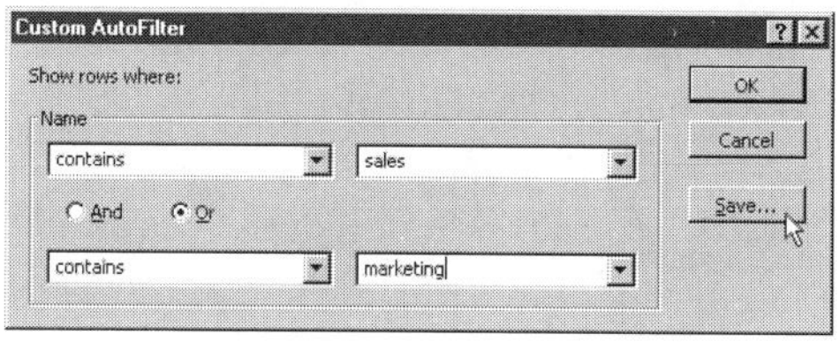

FIG. 22.27
The Custom AutoFilter dialog box helps you create a custom filter.

The first field will be set to whatever column drop-down list you chose, and the test will depend on that field. For example, with a duration, or a start or finish date, the test will be Equals, while the task name field's test would be Contains. The drop-down list to the right of the field has a list of values from which you can choose, or you can type criteria or a prompt as described in earlier sections. If there are multiple criteria, you can enter a second set and use either the And or the Or option. When you choose OK, the filter will be applied. If you want to modify the criteria the next time you access the Custom option from the AutoFilter drop-down list, the previous criteria will still be there.

If the filter you create proves useful for future sessions, you can save it using the Save button in the Custom AutoFilter dialog box. When you choose this button, it takes you to the same Filter Definition dialog box used in earlier sections.

Organizing Views in Project Files

All the customized changes that you make to the views—whether through defining views, tables, filters, or format specifications—are saved as part of the current project file. However, you can choose to make these customized views, tables, and filters available to other project files or to all projects. When they are available to all projects, the view definitions are stored in a global template. In Microsoft Project this file is GLOBAL.MPT. In this version of Microsoft Project, this file can be opened directly.

When you start Microsoft Project, GLOBAL.MPT loads with the project file. When you exit Project, all changes made to the views are only saved with the project file. Customized views created for one project file are not directly available to other project files. If you save the view data to the global file, however, these customized views can be made available across all project files.

To save the view changes to the GLOBAL.MPT file, follow these steps:

1. Choose View menu, More Views and select the Organizer button.

2. The Organizer dialog box has tabs for each set of custom objects that can be copied between project files. The Views tab shows views that are available in the GLOBAL.MPT file on the left of the dialog box, and the customized and modified views (which are available in the current project file) are on the right (see Figure 22.28). The other tabs follow the same format. Choose the tab that contains the customized objects (views, tables, filters, and so on) that you want to copy.

3. Select the view or views in the project file list that should also be in the global file and click the Copy button. This copies these view definitions from the project file over to the global file.

4. The Cancel button changes to Close after the Copy is performed. Click the Close button to close the organizer when you are finished copying the view definitions.

If you save the customized views in the global file, anytime you create a new project those views will be available.

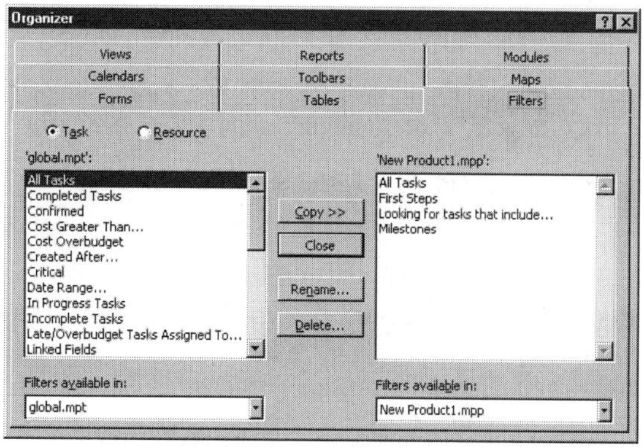

FIG. 22.28

Use the Organizer to manage the storage of your custom views, tables and filters.

> **CAUTION**
>
> When copying custom views to either other files or the GLOBAL.MPT, make sure to copy any custom filters or tables that are part of the custom view.

You can also use the Organizer to rename and delete views from the global or current project files. To delete a view (either customized or standard), perform the following steps:

1. Select the view in the view list from which it should be deleted—either the global file or the current project file.
2. Choose the Delete button.
3. Choose Yes to confirm the deletion or No to cancel the deletion.
4. The view will be gone from either the global file (which will affect all projects that used that view) or from the current project file only—depending on what was selected in step 1.
5. Choose the Close button to complete the Organizer command.

If you don't want to copy a view, table or filter to the GLOBAL.MPT file but you want to use one of those objects in another project file you can copy it from one file to another. First, make sure to open both files. Then, using the Organizer dialog box, choose both files from the drop-down lists at the bottom of the box, one on the left and one on the right. Choose the appropriate tab for the object that you want and copy as specified previously.

If you upgrade Microsoft Project 98 over an earlier version, the customized items in the old GLOBAL.MPT are automatically incorporated into the new template, while retaining any of the new features of the new version of Microsoft Project. The old template does not completely overwrite the old; they are merged.

From Here...

This chapter described most of the customizing features regarding the layout of views and tables. You also learned how to create and customize filters using the various criteria rules.

The following chapters will provide you with some additional formatting and customization techniques:

- Chapter 21, "Formatting Views," discusses the various ways you can format and sort the standard or customized views. Some topics discussed include formatting the text display, formatting timescales, and specific formatting techniques for the commonly used standard views.

- Chapter 24, "Customizing Reports," covers the customization techniques you can use to create and save reports.

- Chapter 27, "Customizing Toolbars, Menus, and Forms," goes into great detail on the ways in which you can customize the layout of the Microsoft Project application window by adding and removing the commands you use most to the toolbars and menus. It also covers the creation and use of custom forms for your project.

CHAPTER 23

Using the Standard Reports

Most of the previous chapters have dealt with working with views. Sometimes, printed views contain all the information you need to document and communicate project information. Reports, however, can provide a different perspective and level of data not available from views. This chapter provides a description of each of the standard reports, along with circumstances when the report might be useful. ■

Learn about Overview reports

Providing a high-level, strategic look at your project, Overview reports display summary data over the life of the project. They are useful for periodic status presentations to management.

Track the progress of your tasks

Current Activities reports provide you with the ability to track the progress of your tasks while the project is underway, enabling you to focus in on the tasks in your project.

When are Cost reports important?

When keeping tabs on project costs is crucial, Cost reports provide a broad range of cost information, including a report that tells you whether you are ahead of or behind schedule based on actual cost incurred.

Assignments reports

Focusing in on resources in your project, Assignments reports help you keep track of which tasks a resource is responsible for working on and which resources are overallocated.

Accessing the Standard Reports

The Reports command on the View menu provides access to the Reports dialog box which lists six groups of report formats: Overview, Current Activities, Costs, Assignments, Workload, and Custom (see Figure 23.1). Together, the first five groups contain 22 predefined summary, calendar, task, resource, and/or crosstab reports that are all set up and ready to print. The last report category, Custom, allows you to customize these reports or create your own reports. Chapter 24, "Customizing Reports," discusses how to tailor reports in Microsoft Project.

FIG. 23.1

Use the 22 predefined reports to keep management and your project team informed of the status of all aspects of the project.

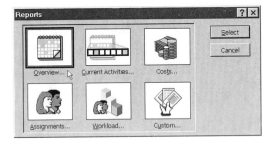

To select one of the report categories, either double-click the category button, or click the button once and choose Select.

After you select one of the category buttons in the Reports dialog box, another dialog box appears showing the actual reports that belong to that category. The Overview Reports category was selected, and the reports available in that category appear in Figure 23.2. To display one of the reports, you can either double-click the desired report button, or click it once and choose the Select button.

FIG. 23.2

The Overview Reports category provides five different kinds of summary reports.

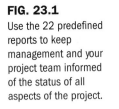
When you select a report to display, you will see the report, based on your active project, in the Print Preview mode. In order to read the text of the report, you need to zoom in on the preview page. Use the magnifying glass button on the toolbar to zoom in, or position your mouse anywhere on the report. The mouse changes to a magnifying glass. Click to zoom in to that part of the report.

Most of the reports have headings at the top of the report. The information displayed comes from the Properties entered in for the project. Choose File, Properties to add or modify this information. Most common in the headings are the Title and Manager fields from the Properties information. Sometimes other fields or a date are also included in the heading.

The Overview Reports Category

There are five different overview reports—Project Summary, Top-Level Tasks, Critical Tasks, Milestones, and Working Days. Together, these reports display summary data over the life of the project. They are useful as documentation for presentations to management after the initial design period has been completed, as well as status reports while the project is underway.

The Project Summary Report

The Project Summary report displays on one page the most significant project information. This report is useful for status meetings with your project team or senior management. Because the Variance and Remaining fields are calculated, this report is a good summary to have at the completion of the preliminary planning for your project, before work on the project actually begins.

There are six sections: Dates, Duration, Work, Costs, Status (both Task and Resource), and Notes (see Figure 23.3). The headings at the top of the report display the Title, Company, and Manager information which was entered into the Properties for the project. The date displayed comes from the Current Date option in the Project Information dialog box. Choose Project, Project Information to display the Project Information dialog box and adjust this date.

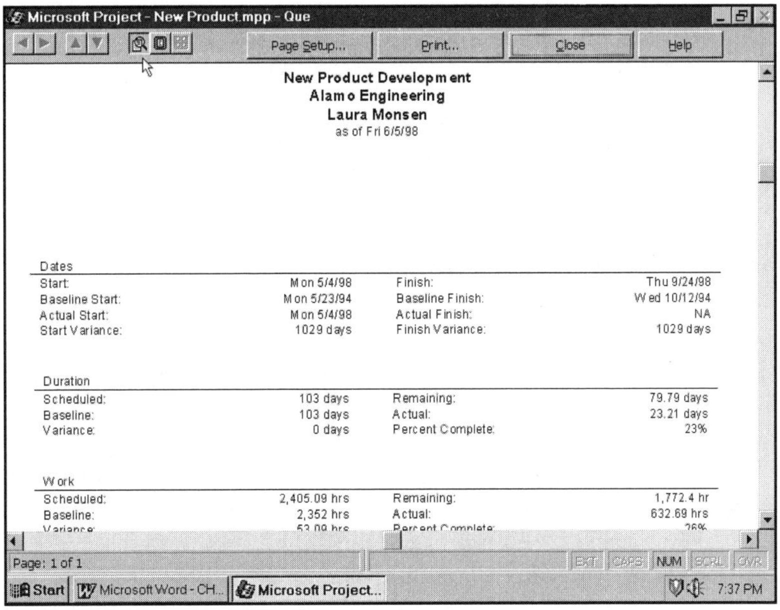

FIG. 23.3

The Project Summary report provides a one-page overview of calculated project information. The top half of the report displays the report headings, the comparison of dates, and durations.

Part
VII

Ch
23

T I P To change the heading for this report, simply change the information stored in the Properties. For example, if you want the name of your company to appear as the first line of the heading, choose File, Properties and then type the company name in the Title field of the Properties dialog box.

Comparisons can be made between what is currently scheduled, what the baseline indicates, and what actually happened.

The Task Status section displays the number of Tasks not yet started, the number of Tasks in progress, and the number of Tasks completed in your project (see Figure 23.4). The number of overallocated resources you have is also given. Comments you enter on the Summary tab under the File, Properties dialog box appear in the Notes section.

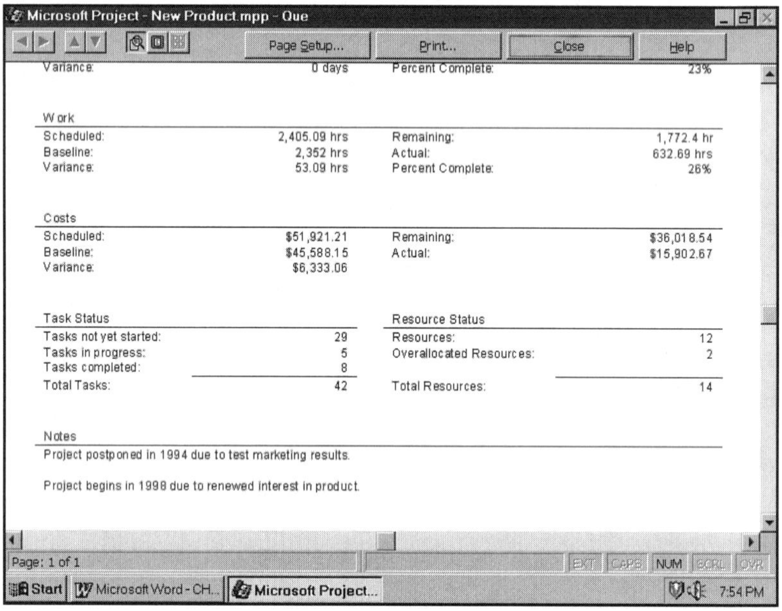

FIG. 23.4

This report provides a consolidated status of your project. The bottom half of the Project Summary report compares Work, Costs, and a status of the Tasks and Resources.

The Top-Level Tasks Report

If you have used the outlining capability to create summary tasks in your project, the Top-Level Tasks report shows the highest level *summary* tasks. This report is used to focus on the major phases of the project, rather than individual tasks. Figure 23.5 shows a sample of this report. For each summary task, there is information about the Duration, Start, Finish, Percent Complete, Cost, and Work. These are rolled up (consolidated) values from the subordinate tasks, similar to the way they appear in the Gantt Chart view. If notes have been added to these summary tasks, they are printed out as well. In Figure 23.5, which shows a zoomed-in view, the mouse pointer—the magnifying glass—is pointing at the notes for the Production Phase summary task.

FIG. 23.5
Summary task information appears in bold in the Top-Level Tasks report.

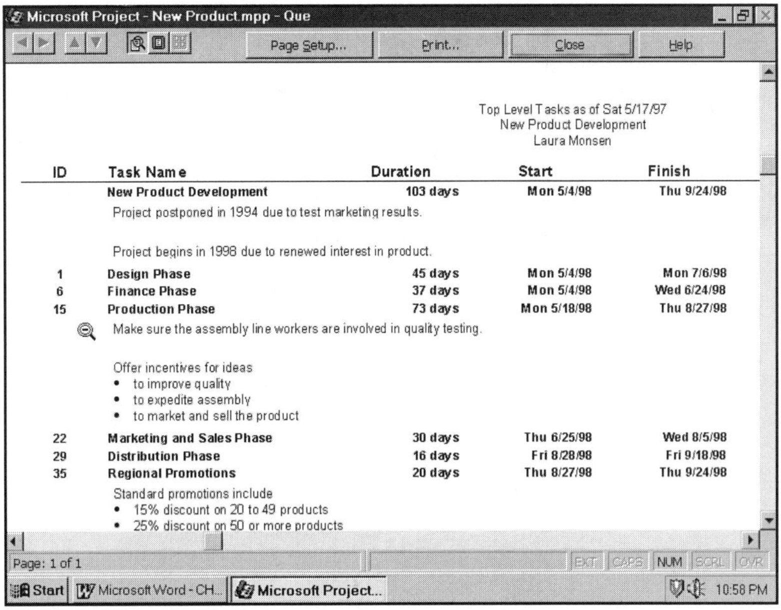

The heading of this report is taken from the Title and Manager fields entered into the Summary tab of the File, Properties dialog box. The date of the printout is also included in the heading.

TIP Make sure if you plan to use this report that you give your top-level summary tasks good descriptive names that clearly describe the tasks or phase they summarize. Otherwise, this report may be meaningless to the people who read it!

The Critical Tasks Report

When you want to make sure your project finishes by a set deadline, you need to focus on the critical tasks. Critical tasks are those tasks which, if delayed, will cause a delay in the finish date of your project. The Critical Tasks Report displays all the critical tasks, categorized under their summary tasks, assuming that outlining (indenting and outdenting) has been used. For each task, there are columns for duration, start, finish, predecessors, and resources. New with this version of Project, the indicators as seen in the table side of the Gantt Chart view are displayed next to the task ID. Refer to Chapter 2, "Learning the Basics of Microsoft Project," for more information on these indicators.

As shown in Figure 23.6, underneath the critical task name is a subchart that displays the successor tasks, along with the type of relationship and any lag or lead. Remember, Project displays leads as a negative number in the lag field. If notes have been added to the tasks, they are printed as well. The heading of the report includes the Title and Manager fields from the Summary tab of the File, Properties dialog box.

FIG. 23.6

Focus on the tasks most important to your deadline with the Critical Tasks Report.

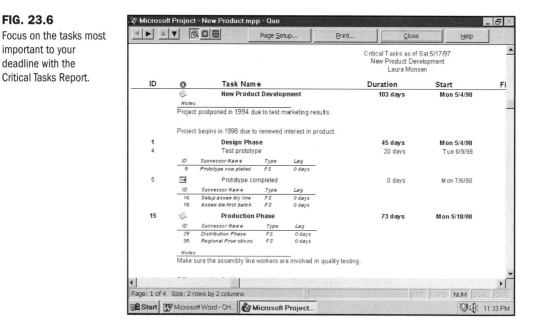

The Milestones Report

Another way of concentrating on the major phases or turning points in the project is to focus on milestones. The Milestones report provides a columnar layout including duration, start, finish, predecessors, and resource names (see Figure 23.7). The indicators have been added to this report, providing additional information about the tasks. Milestones which have been completed are grouped together and listed first. The check mark indicator denotes which tasks have been completed. Those milestones which have not yet been reached are listed next. If notes have been added to the task, they are printed as well.

The Working Days Report

This report provides a list of the working and nonworking times for each base calendar used in your project. Using this report is an excellent way to verify that the appropriate working hours have been established and that the holidays, and other nonworking times, are incorporated into your project. The information for each base calendar is printed on a separate page. Figure 23.8 shows information for the Standard base calendar; the mouse pointer is indicating the name of the base calendar. Figure 23.9 shows information for the Assemblers - AM base calendar; the mouse pointer is indicating the name of the base calendar.

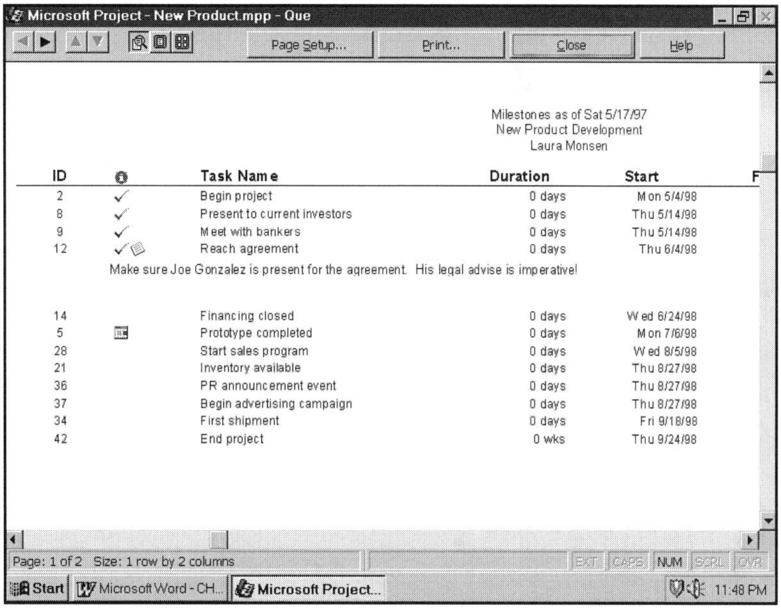

FIG. 23.7

Project does not create milestones to mark the major turning points in the project. You must add milestones to your project; Milestones are tasks with 0 (zero) duration.

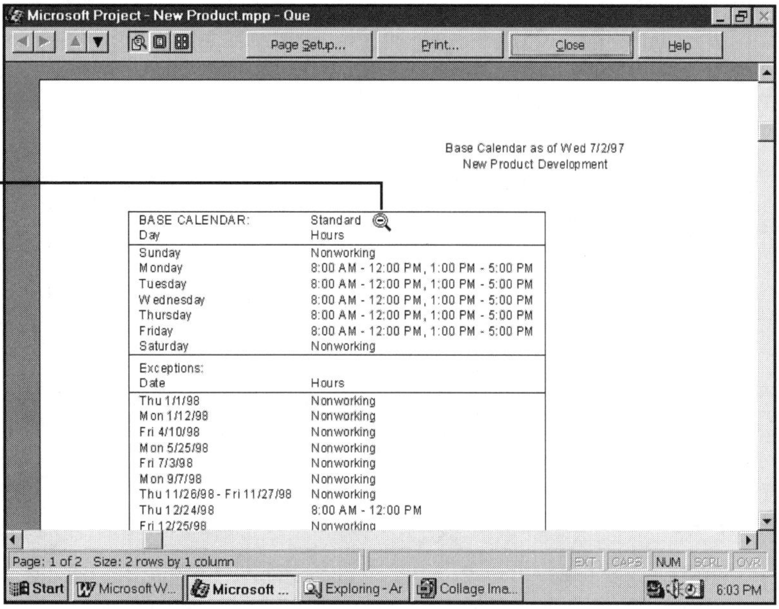

FIG. 23.8

Use this report to verify the base calendars you have created for the project.

Mouse pointer ——————

Part VII
Ch 23

FIG. 23.9

Create base calendars for groups of workers whose hours are significantly different than the normal hours. This figure shows the Assemblers who work a morning shift.

Base Calendar as of Wed 7/2/97
New Product Development

BASE CALENDAR:	Assemblers - AM
Day	Hours
Sunday	Nonworking
Monday	5:00 AM - 9:00 AM, 9:30 AM - 1:00 PM
Tuesday	5:00 AM - 9:00 AM, 9:30 AM - 1:00 PM
Wednesday	5:00 AM - 9:00 AM, 9:30 AM - 1:00 PM
Thursday	5:00 AM - 9:00 AM, 9:30 AM - 1:00 PM
Friday	5:00 AM - 9:00 AM, 9:30 AM - 1:00 PM
Saturday	Nonworking
Exceptions:	
Date	Hours
Thu 1/1/98	Nonworking
Mon 1/12/98	Nonworking
Fri 4/10/98	Nonworking
Mon 5/25/98	Nonworking
Fri 7/3/98	8:00 AM - 12:00 PM, 1:00 PM - 5:00 PM
Mon 9/7/98	Nonworking
Thu 11/26/98 - Fri 11/27/98	Nonworking
Thu 12/24/98	8:00 AM - 12:00 PM
Fri 12/25/98	Nonworking

Page: 2 of 2 Size: 2 rows by 1 column

Mouse pointer

The Current Activity Reports Category

The next major category of reports focuses on tasks and provides you with a comprehensive status of the tasks as the project is underway. There are six reports in this category—Unstarted Tasks, Tasks Starting Soon, Tasks In Progress, Completed Tasks, Should Have Started Tasks, and Slipping Tasks (see Figure 23.10).

FIG. 23.10

The Current Activity reports are useful primarily after your project has started, each focusing on specific groups of tasks.

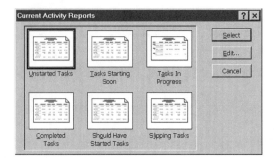

The Unstarted Tasks Report

This report shows tasks for which no actual information has been entered, which means these tasks have not yet started. It specifically looks to see if the actual start date has been entered.

In studying this report, you can focus your attention on tasks that have yet to start, making sure that materials are in place, resources are ready and available, and so on.

The Unstarted Tasks report is a columnar report that includes the following fields—ID, Task Name, Duration, Start, Finish, Predecessors, and Resource Names. In addition, underneath each task name is a subchart that includes the units of each resource assignment, the hours of work, and any delays (see Figure 23.11). If any notes have been added to tasks, they are printed here as well.

FIG. 23.11

The Unstarted Tasks report provides a comprehensive list of tasks which have not begun—flagging those tasks that should have started and are behind schedule, as well as upcoming tasks you can verify are on schedule.

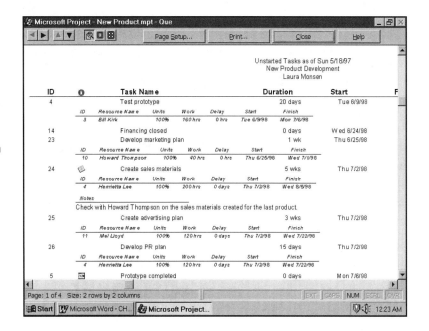

The Tasks Starting Soon Report

This report follows the same format as the Unstarted Tasks report but has an interactive filter as part of the definition of the report (refer to Figure 23.11). Every time the report is run, the Date Range filter prompts you for a range of dates (see Figures 23.12 and 23.13). The tasks must occur within that range of dates in order to be included on the report.

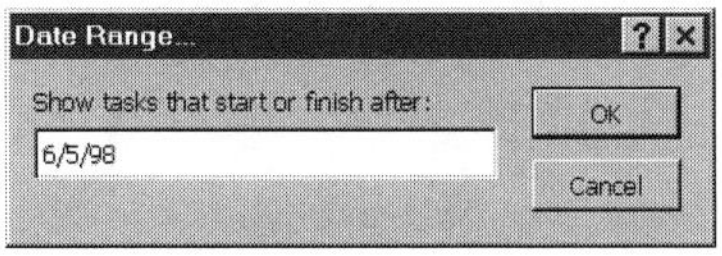

FIG. 23.12

Tasks must be scheduled to start after the date you enter in this prompt to be included in this report.

FIG. 23.13
Tasks must be
scheduled start before
the date you enter in
this prompt to be
included in this report.

Date Range...	? ×
And before:	OK
6/30/98	Cancel

The Tasks In Progress Report

A project manager often needs to know what tasks are currently underway so progress can be checked. The Tasks In Progress report displays all tasks that have a start date entered but no finish date. This is accomplished via the In Progress Tasks filter. The report is displayed in monthly intervals. The format is similar to the other task reports in the Current Activity category (see Figure 23.14). There are columns for ID, Task Name, Duration, Start, Finish, Predecessors, and Resource Names. Under the Task Name is a resource schedule that includes the units of the resource assignment, the hours of work, and any delays.

FIG. 23.14
Only tasks that have
started are included
in this report. The
indicators in the report
are the same indicators
which appear in the
Gantt Chart view. The
monthly intervals make
the report easier to
interpret.

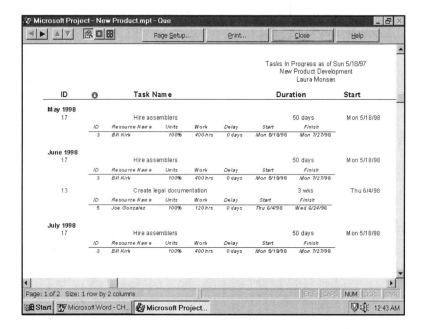

The Completed Tasks Report

A sense of accomplishment is often gained from seeing a list of tasks that have been finished. Using the Completed Tasks filter, this report displays tasks whose Percent complete field has been set to 100 percent. Tasks are listed in monthly intervals with columns Determined by the summary table (see Figure 23.15). The columns included are ID, Task Name, Duration, Start, Finish, Percent Complete, Cost, and Work.

FIG. 23.15
This report lists task by month. If a task starts in one month and finishes in another month, the task will appear in both months.

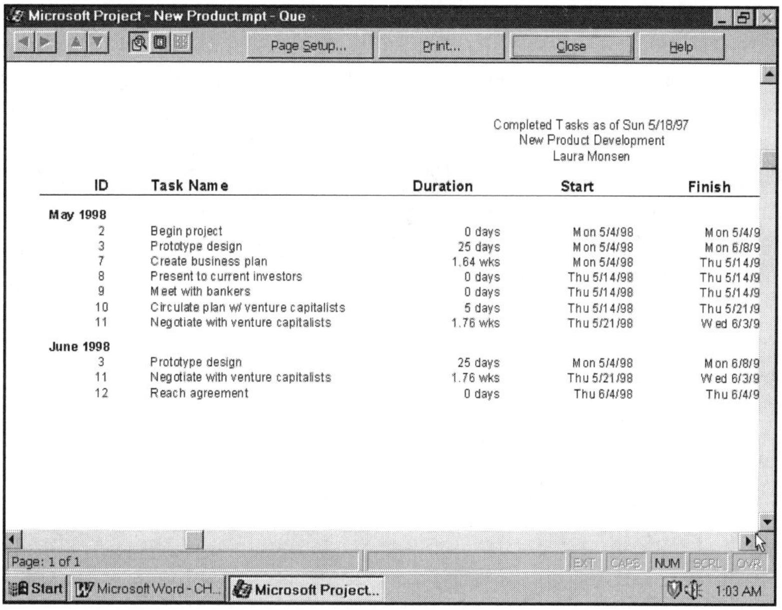

Completed Tasks as of Sun 5/18/97
New Product Development
Laura Monsen

ID	Task Name	Duration	Start	Finish
May 1998				
2	Begin project	0 days	Mon 5/4/98	Mon 5/4/9
3	Prototype design	25 days	Mon 5/4/98	Mon 6/8/9
7	Create business plan	1.64 wks	Mon 5/4/98	Thu 5/14/9
8	Present to current investors	0 days	Thu 5/14/98	Thu 5/14/9
9	Meet with bankers	0 days	Thu 5/14/98	Thu 5/14/9
10	Circulate plan w/ venture capitalists	5 days	Thu 5/14/98	Thu 5/21/9
11	Negotiate with venture capitalists	1.76 wks	Thu 5/21/98	Wed 6/3/9
June 1998				
3	Prototype design	25 days	Mon 5/4/98	Mon 6/8/9
11	Negotiate with venture capitalists	1.76 wks	Thu 5/21/98	Wed 6/3/9
12	Reach agreement	0 days	Thu 6/4/98	Thu 6/4/9

TIP Modify the columns in this report by modifying the Summary table. See Chapter 22, "Customizing Views, Tables, and Filters," for more information on customizing tables.

The Should Have Started Tasks Report

A project manager needs to know at a moment's notice which tasks should have started but haven't. If you have forgotten to update the status of tasks that have begun, the Should Have Started Tasks report will be a good reminder for you. This report uses the Should Start By interactive filter to prompt the user for a date by which the tasks should begin. The date you enter appears in the report title. Tasks that should have started by that date but have not yet started (no actual Start date has been entered) are then displayed (see Figure 23.16). The date you enter is compared to the currently scheduled Start date, not the Baseline Start date.

Summary tasks for each subtask are included with columns determined by the Variance table. Columns include ID, Task Name, Start, Finish, Baseline Start, Baseline Finish, and Variance for Start and Finish. The Variance columns basically tell you how far behind you are for those tasks. Under each Task Name the successor name, relationship type, and any lag or lead is displayed. This way you can see other tasks that are going to be impacted by the delay in starting. If task notes have been added, they are displayed here as well. Since the preview of this report is zoomed in, not all the columns of information are displayed in Figure 23.16.

The Slipping Tasks Report

It is equally important for a project manager to know which tasks have started but are not scheduled to complete on time, or within the duration that was originally planned. Perhaps additional resources or supervision are needed on these tasks. The Slipping Tasks report is based on the Slipping Tasks filter. As determined by this filter, slipping tasks have had a baseline set—the task has started but not finished—and the scheduled finish is later than the baseline (originally planned) finish date. Figure 23.17 shows this report.

FIG. 23.16

Use the Should Have Started report to find those tasks that need immediate attention.

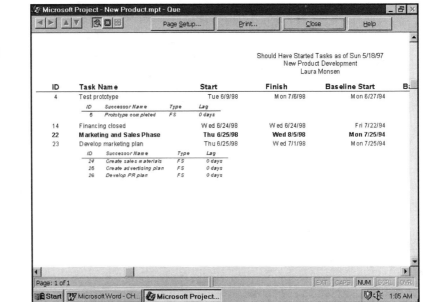

CAUTION

If you have added tasks after first saving the baseline, make sure to update the baseline again for the tasks you added *and* any tasks impacted by adding the new tasks, to make sure that all relevant tasks are displayed in this report. Only those tasks that are included in the baseline will be displayed in the report.

▶ **See** "Capturing the Baseline," **p. 475**

Tasks that meet the criteria of the filter are displayed in a columnar format with their summary tasks. The format is essentially the same as the Should Have Started Tasks report (refer to Figure 23.16). Columns are determined by the Variance table which shows ID, Task Name, Start, Finish, Baseline Start, Baseline Finish, and Variance for Start and Finish. Under each Task Name is a subchart for successor information including the relationship type, and any lag or lead that has been applied. If task notes have been added, they are displayed here as well. Since the preview of this report is zoomed in, not all the columns of information are displayed in Figure 23.17.

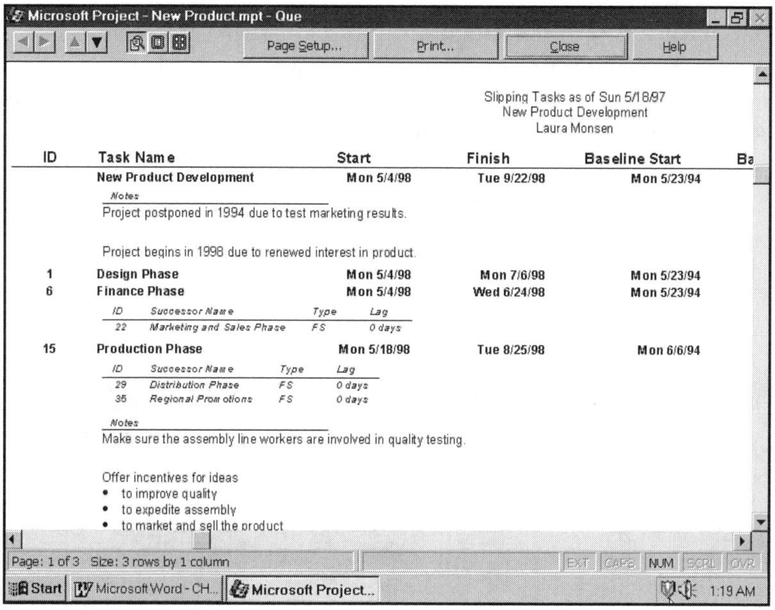

FIG. 23.17

Slipping Tasks are tasks that are behind schedule, where the currently scheduled finish date has slipped beyond the baseline finish date for the tasks.

The Cost Reports Category

There are five reports in the Cost Reports category (see Figure 23.18). These include Cash Flow, Budget, Overbudget Tasks, Overbudget Resources, and Earned Value. These five reports together provide a broad range of cost data which is essential when trying to stay within a budget for a project.

FIG. 23.18

Keeping accurate track of the project budget is a significant concern for most project managers. The reports in the Cost Reports category provide quick access to budget information.

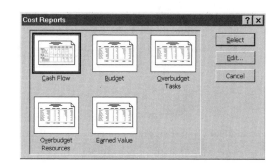

> **TIP**
>
> Most of the reports in this category are based on tables in Project. You can modify the tables to remove any fields that you deem unnecessary for the report you need. Chapter 22, "Customizing Views, Tables, and Filters," provides instructions for removing fields from tables.

The Cash Flow Report

The Cash Flow report can be instrumental in managing how much money is needed and when the money is needed during the life of a project. This is a crosstab type of report, which shows tasks in the first column and weekly periods of time in remaining columns. The subsequent grid or spreadsheet that is created contains cost information (see Figure 23.19). The cost information is derived from resource usage costs and fixed costs associated with tasks. The report displays costs broken down into weekly increments. Tasks are displayed underneath their summary tasks. Each column (week) is totaled and each row (task) is totaled, as well. This allows you to see the total dollars required each week to finance the project, as well as the total cost for each task.

FIG. 23.19

The weekly costs depicted in the Cash Flow report are based on when costs accrue, at the start of the task, the completion of the task, or prorated throughout the duration of the task.

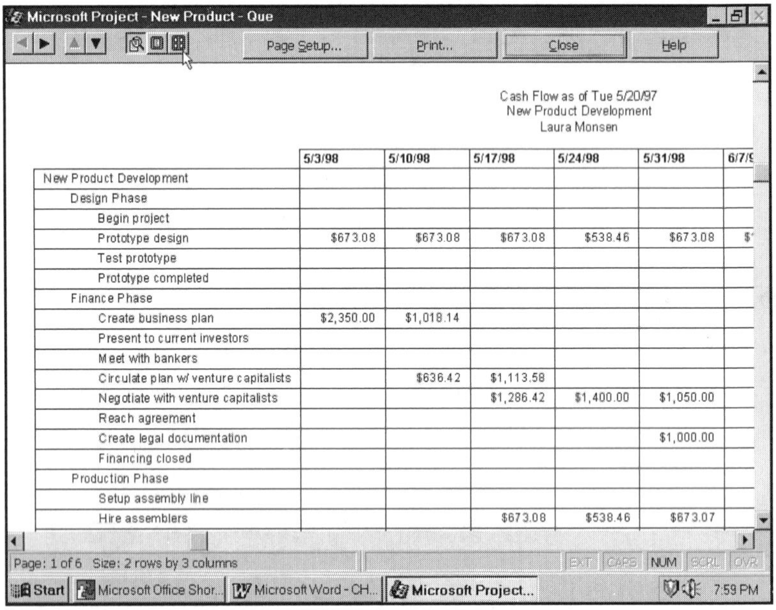

The Budget Report

Using the Budget report, you can see which tasks are most expensive. These tasks will probably need closer management so that they don't go over budget. Secondly, you can see which tasks are going over budget based on actual information that has been entered.

The Budget report also displays a list of all tasks in a columnar format sorted by the total cost for the task, with most expensive tasks first (see Figure 23.20). Columns are determined by the Task Cost table and include ID, Task Name, Fixed Cost, Fixed Cost Accrual, Total Cost, Baseline Cost, Variance, Actual, and Remaining. Each column is then totaled at the bottom so you can see actual totals, variances, and remaining dollars required. Since the preview of this report is zoomed in, not all the columns of information or totals are displayed in Figure 23.20.

FIG. 23.20

Use the Variance column to see which tasks have costs over or under what was planned in the baseline.

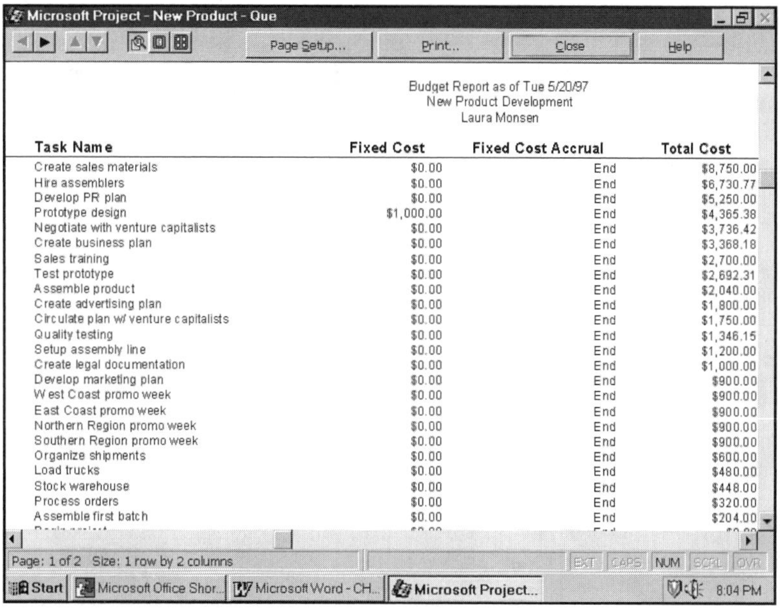

Budget Report as of Tue 5/20/97
New Product Development
Laura Monsen

Task Name	Fixed Cost	Fixed Cost Accrual	Total Cost
Create sales materials	$0.00	End	$8,750.00
Hire assemblers	$0.00	End	$6,730.77
Develop PR plan	$0.00	End	$5,250.00
Prototype design	$1,000.00	End	$4,365.38
Negotiate with venture capitalists	$0.00	End	$3,736.42
Create business plan	$0.00	End	$3,368.18
Sales training	$0.00	End	$2,700.00
Test prototype	$0.00	End	$2,692.31
Assemble product	$0.00	End	$2,040.00
Create advertising plan	$0.00	End	$1,800.00
Circulate plan w/ venture capitalists	$0.00	End	$1,750.00
Quality testing	$0.00	End	$1,346.15
Setup assembly line	$0.00	End	$1,200.00
Create legal documentation	$0.00	End	$1,000.00
Develop marketing plan	$0.00	End	$900.00
West Coast promo week	$0.00	End	$900.00
East Coast promo week	$0.00	End	$900.00
Northern Region promo week	$0.00	End	$900.00
Southern Region promo week	$0.00	End	$900.00
Organize shipments	$0.00	End	$600.00
Load trucks	$0.00	End	$480.00
Stock warehouse	$0.00	End	$448.00
Process orders	$0.00	End	$320.00
Assemble first batch	$0.00	End	$204.00

Page: 1 of 2   Size: 1 row by 2 columns

TIP

Most of the reports in this category are based on the Cost table in Project. You can modify the table to hide the Fixed Cost Accrual field since it is not as crucial as the other fields, especially when presenting status reports to senior management or the project team. Look ahead to Figure 23.21 for an example of this field removed from the Overbudget Tasks report (which is similar to the Budget report).

To hide a field in a table, simply resize the field so that it doesn't show in the Gantt Chart view. When you are finished printing the report, resize the column back to fit the text.

CAUTION

If you select the column and choose Edit, Hide Column, it is the same as *deleting* the column in the table. You will then have to edit the table definition to add the column back.

The Overbudget Tasks Report

The Overbudget Tasks report finds tasks whose Actual, or scheduled, cost is higher than the Baseline Cost. It does this by using the Cost Overbudget filter. Tasks are displayed in order by variance. Tasks that are the most over budget are displayed first (see Figure 23.21). The columnar format is determined by the Task Cost table. Columns include ID, Task Name, Fixed Cost, Fixed Cost Accrual, Total Cost, Baseline Cost, Variance, Actual Cost, and Remaining Cost. Each column is then totaled. Since the preview of this report is zoomed in, not all the columns of information are displayed in Figure 23.21.

Part
VII

Ch
23

FIG. 23.21

The Overbudget Tasks report helps pinpoint tasks that need the project manager's attention; the next step is to determine why the actual cost for a task was more than the budgeted cost.

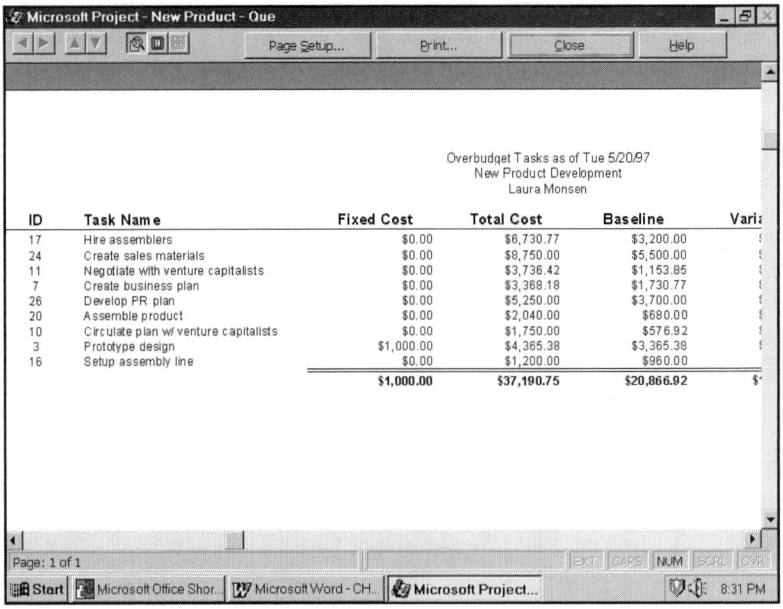

The Overbudget Resources Report

The Overbudget Resources report follows a very similar format to the Overbudget Tasks report, with emphasis on resources rather than tasks (see Figure 23.22). It pinpoints resources whose costs are higher than their baseline cost. The Cost Overbudget filter manages this.

The columnar format is controlled by the Resource Cost table, with ID, Resource Name, Cost, Baseline Cost, Variance, Actual Cost, and Remaining Cost included. Each column is then totaled. The resources that are the most over budget are listed first. Since the preview of this report is zoomed in, not all the columns of information are displayed in Figure 23.22.

The Earned Value Report

This report can be used to examine the accomplishment of tasks in the project. The Earned Value report is a cost comparison tool. It allows you to compare, with regards to cost, what is actually happening on each task in the project to what you expected to happen. The Current Date is used to calculate what costs have incurred and what costs you expected to incur when you originally planned the project. Actual Resource Costs and Fixed Costs are used to calculate the percent complete of each task, rather than what was entered for percentage completed. Then, you can compare if that matches the percentage completed of actual work done. For example, if a task is marked as 25 percent complete, and the actual cost so far is $300, you can calculate whether $300 is equal to 25 percent of the originally planned cost, the cost expected to be incurred by today for this task.

FIG. 23.22

The Overbudget Resources report includes the actual costs incurred for the resources, as well as the costs planned for tasks these resources are assigned to, but have not yet started.

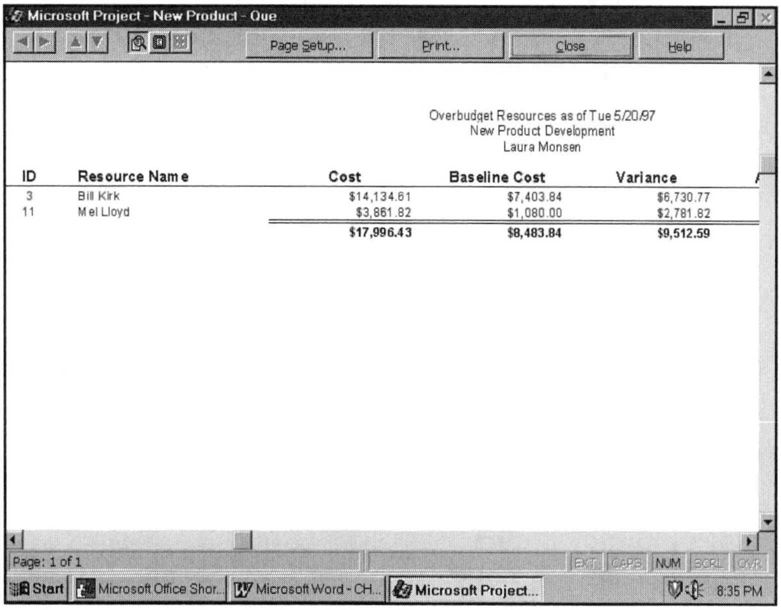

The format of the report is columnar with the columns determined by the <u>E</u>arned Value table (see Figure 23.23). Columns include Budgeted Cost of Work Scheduled (BCWS), Budgeted Cost of Work Performed (BCWP), Actual Cost of Work Performed (ACWP), Schedule Variance (SV), Cost Variance (CV), Budgeted At Completion (BAC), Estimate At Completion (EAC), and Variance At Completion (VAC), which is the difference between the Baseline Cost and the scheduled cost. All normal tasks are displayed, sorted by their ID. Summary tasks are not displayed in this report. Since the preview of this report is zoomed in, not all the columns of information are displayed in Figure 23.23.

A few of the acronyms listed previously are equal to the following:

- BCWP = Planned Percent Complete × Baseline Cost
- BCWS = Planned Percent Complete × Planned Cost
- SV = BCWP minus BCWS
- CV = BCWP minus ACWP

N O T E Critical to the calculation of many of these items is the date used in performing the comparison. By default, Today's Date is used. This is the Current Date setting under the Project Information dialog box (choose <u>P</u>roject, <u>P</u>roject Information). If you prefer to use another date, change the Current Date setting.

FIG. 23.23

The Earned Value report allows you to precisely track progress of resource costs compared to percent of work completed.

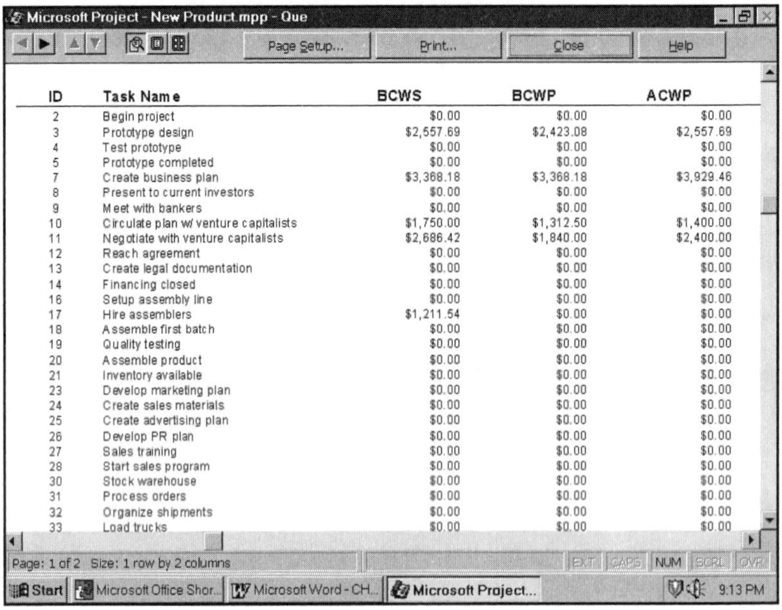

ID	Task Name	BCWS	BCWP	ACWP
2	Begin project	$0.00	$0.00	$0.00
3	Prototype design	$2,557.69	$2,423.08	$2,557.69
4	Test prototype	$0.00	$0.00	$0.00
5	Prototype completed	$0.00	$0.00	$0.00
7	Create business plan	$3,368.18	$3,368.18	$3,929.46
8	Present to current investors	$0.00	$0.00	$0.00
9	Meet with bankers	$0.00	$0.00	$0.00
10	Circulate plan w/ venture capitalists	$1,750.00	$1,312.50	$1,400.00
11	Negotiate with venture capitalists	$2,686.42	$1,840.00	$2,400.00
12	Reach agreement	$0.00	$0.00	$0.00
13	Create legal documentation	$0.00	$0.00	$0.00
14	Financing closed	$0.00	$0.00	$0.00
16	Setup assembly line	$0.00	$0.00	$0.00
17	Hire assemblers	$1,211.54	$0.00	$0.00
18	Assemble first batch	$0.00	$0.00	$0.00
19	Quality testing	$0.00	$0.00	$0.00
20	Assemble product	$0.00	$0.00	$0.00
21	Inventory available	$0.00	$0.00	$0.00
23	Develop marketing plan	$0.00	$0.00	$0.00
24	Create sales materials	$0.00	$0.00	$0.00
25	Create advertising plan	$0.00	$0.00	$0.00
26	Develop PR plan	$0.00	$0.00	$0.00
27	Sales training	$0.00	$0.00	$0.00
28	Start sales program	$0.00	$0.00	$0.00
30	Stock warehouse	$0.00	$0.00	$0.00
31	Process orders	$0.00	$0.00	$0.00
32	Organize shipments	$0.00	$0.00	$0.00
33	Load trucks	$0.00	$0.00	$0.00

The Assignment Reports Category

This category of reports displays information about the assignment of resources to tasks. There are four reports in this category with names that are fairly self-explanatory: Who Does What, Who Does What When, To-do List, and Overallocated Resources (see Figure 23.24).

FIG. 23.24

The Assignment Reports category includes reports that focus on resources and what they are scheduled to do.

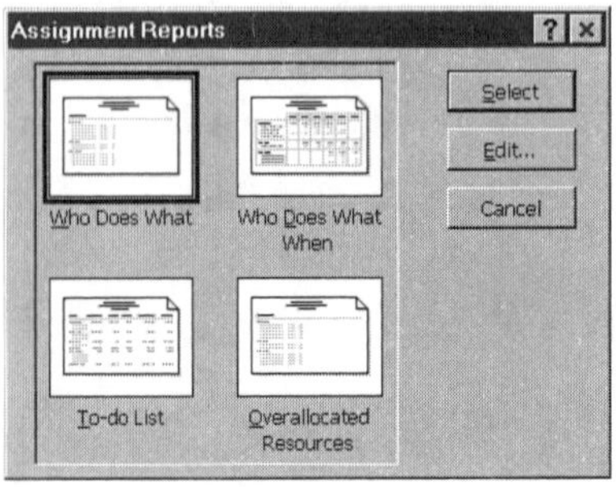

The Who Does What Report

As the title indicates, the Who Does What report provides information about the resources working on your project, and gives a comprehensive list of which tasks they are assigned to. The information in this report is displayed in a columnar format—based on the Usage table—which shows ID, indicators, Resource Name, and the total Work (sometimes referred to as *effort*). See Figure 23.25. Under each resource name is a subchart listing the tasks the resource is scheduled to work on, including the ID and Task Name, Units, Work, Delay, Start date, and Finish date. If task notes have been added, they are displayed here as well.

FIG. 23.25

Indicators, like the resource leveling indicators on Bill Kirk and Henrietta Lee alert you that the resources time is overallocated.

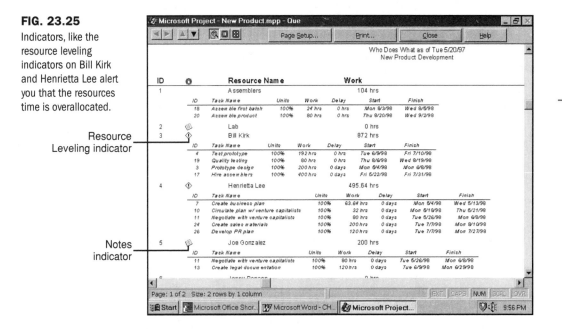

Resource Leveling indicator

Notes indicator

Part
VII

Ch
23

In this figure, the indicator symbols show that there are resource notes for the Lab and Joe Gonzalez. Bill Kirk and Henrietta Lee have resource leveling indicators (shown as an exclamation warning).

The Who Does What When Report

This report takes the Who Does What report one step further and breaks down work assignments by day. Using the Who Does What When report, a project manager would be able to quickly see what everyone is doing at any given time during the project, along with any overallocations. When shifting tasks from one resource to another, you can also see the resources that have time available.

This is a crosstab report that shows resources in the first column with each task that is assigned to them underneath (see Figure 23.26). The remaining columns display each daily time period for the remainder of the project. The resulting grid, or spreadsheet, calculates the hours of work that are assigned each day to each resource, by task.

In this figure, the mouse pointer is located next to the hours for Bill Kirk on 5/22. The total number of hours he is scheduled to work that day is 16—eight hours on Prototype Design and eight hours on Hire Assemblers. This is one instance where his time is overallocated, as noted by the resource leveling (exclamation) indicator in Figure 23.25. Looking at the list of resources, Henrietta Lee, Jenny Benson, and Scott Adams are not working on this project on 5/22, and perhaps can be substituted for Bill Kirk on one of these tasks, resolving his overallocation problem.

FIG. 23.26

The Who Does What When report lists the specific number of hours each day a resource is scheduled to work on the assigned tasks, and the total number of hours each day the resource is working on the project.

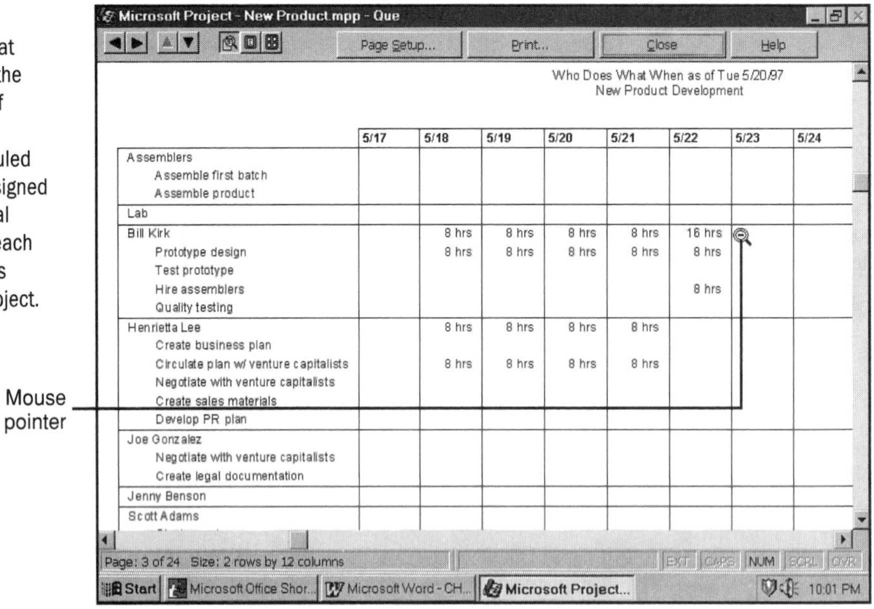

Mouse pointer

The To-Do List Report

The focus of this report is on tasks that are taking place during weekly time periods rather than on resources as in the previous two reports. Each time the report is run, the Using Resource dialog box displays, prompting you to select a resource name (see Figure 23.27).

FIG. 23.27

The To-Do List report is a list of tasks generated for one resource. The Using Resource dialog box is actually a filter prompt where you indicate which resource the To-Do List report is for.

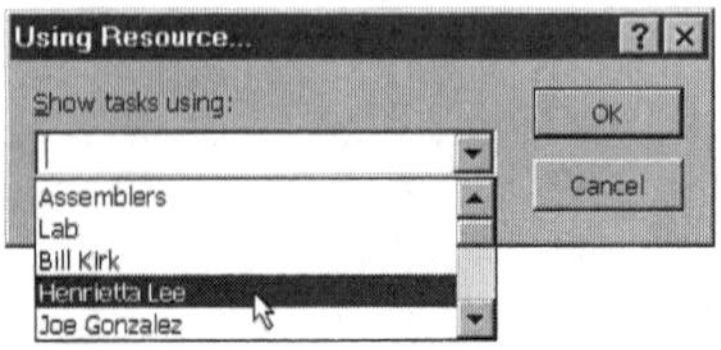

After choosing a resource from the drop-down list in the Using Resource dialog box, the report is run. The report displays only those tasks assigned to that resource (see Figure 23.28). Tasks are listed under a chronological listing of weeks. The columns that are included are determined by the Entry table—ID, indicators, Task Name, Duration, Start, Finish, Predecessors, and Resource Name. Since the preview of this report is zoomed in, not all the columns of information, including Resource Name, are displayed in Figure 23.28.

TIP The title of the report does not indicate the name of the resource, since it appears as the last column in the printed report. To add the resource name to the header or footer of the report, modify the report by selecting the Page Setup button while previewing the report. For more information on print options, see Chapter 13, "Printing Views and Reports."

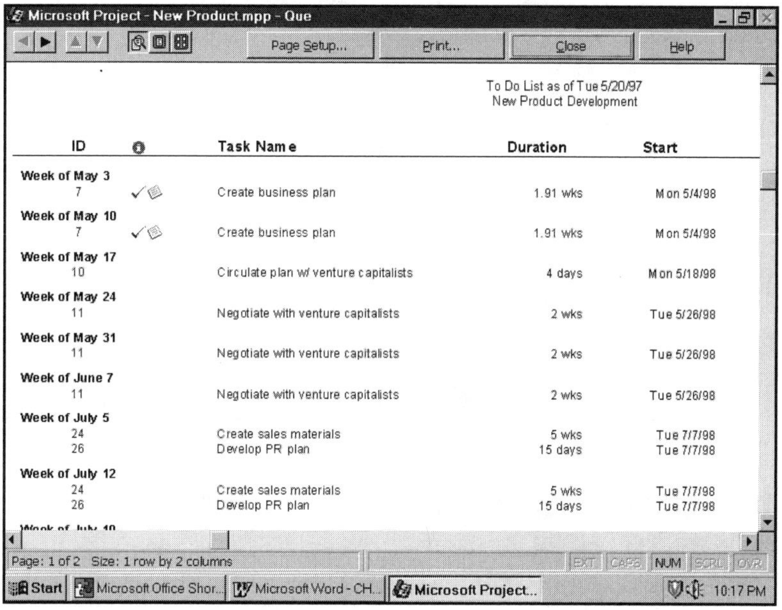

FIG. 23.28
You can print a To-Do List for each of your resources.

Part
VII

Ch
23

> Microsoft Project - New Product.mpp - Que

| Page Setup... | Print... | Close | Help |

To Do List as of Tue 5/20/97
New Product Development

ID	●	Task Name	Duration	Start
Week of May 3				
7	✓	Create business plan	1.91 wks	Mon 5/4/98
Week of May 10				
7	✓	Create business plan	1.91 wks	Mon 5/4/98
Week of May 17				
10		Circulate plan w/ venture capitalists	4 days	Mon 5/18/98
Week of May 24				
11		Negotiate with venture capitalists	2 wks	Tue 5/26/98
Week of May 31				
11		Negotiate with venture capitalists	2 wks	Tue 5/26/98
Week of June 7				
11		Negotiate with venture capitalists	2 wks	Tue 5/26/98
Week of July 5				
24		Create sales materials	5 wks	Tue 7/7/98
26		Develop PR plan	15 days	Tue 7/7/98
Week of July 12				
24		Create sales materials	5 wks	Tue 7/7/98
26		Develop PR plan	15 days	Tue 7/7/98
Week of July 19				

Page: 1 of 2   Size: 1 row by 2 columns   EXT CAPS NUM SCRL OVR

Start | Microsoft Office Shor... | Microsoft Word - CH... | Microsoft Project... | 10:17 PM

The Overallocated Resources Report

During the initial planning stages of the project, it is easy to assign too many tasks to valuable resources. The Overallocated Resources report lists all resources that are assigned to more hours of work than their calendar specifies. Underneath each resource is a subchart list of tasks to which they are assigned, the number of units of that resource that are assigned, the total number of hours of work, any delays that have been imposed, and the start and finish dates of the task (see Figure 23.29).

In this figure, Bill Kirk and Henrietta Lee are listed as the overallocated resources in this project.

With this information, the project manager can make some decisions about how to handle the overallocation: whether to hire additional help for the resource, reassign some tasks to other resources, or modify the resource's calendar.

▶ **See** "Identifying Resource Overallocations," **p. 348**

▶ **See** "Strategies for Eliminating Resource Overallocations: An Overview," **p. 357**

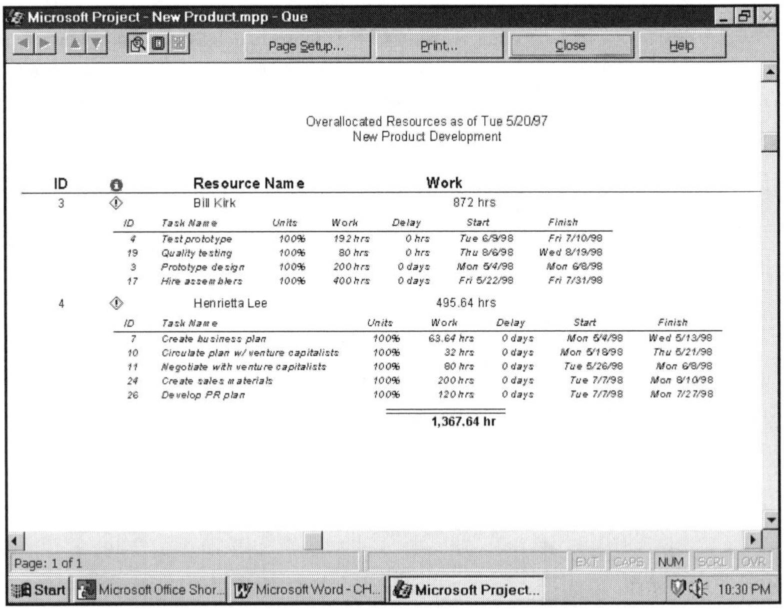

FIG. 23.29

Use the Overallocated Resources report to help make decisions about resolving this resource's work overload.

The Workload Reports Category

The last category of reports contains two crosstab reports that display information about how resources are being used (see Figure 23.30). The only difference between the two is the focus—Task Usage or Resource Usage.

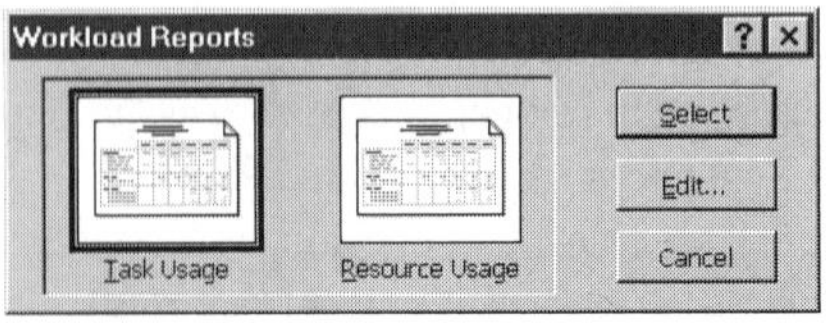

FIG. 23.30

The Workload Reports show how many hours each week a task will be worked on.

The Task Usage Report

This crosstab report lists tasks, broken down by summary task, in the first column with the resources assigned to each task listed underneath. The remaining columns are weekly time increments. The resulting grid, or spreadsheet, format displays the hours of work that each resource is assigned to work that week for that task (see Figure 23.31). Each week's hours are totaled at the bottom of the report; task and resource hours are totaled in the last column at the far right of the report.

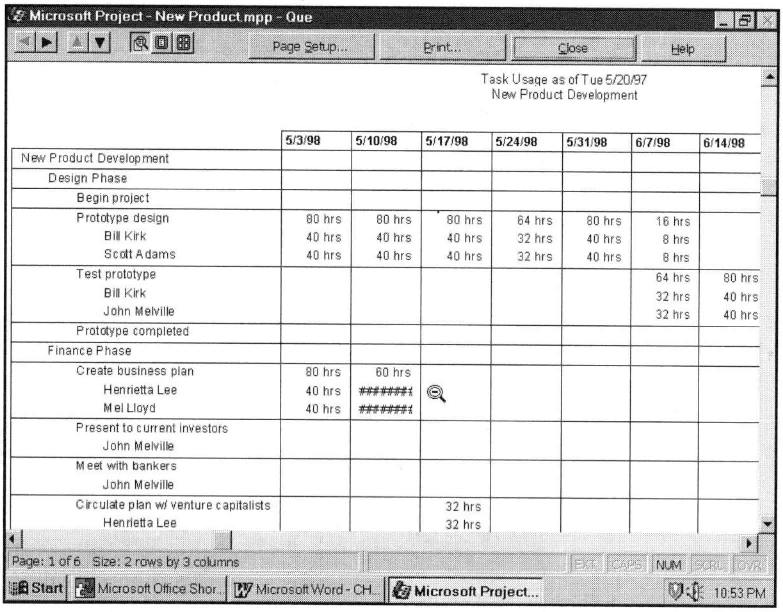

FIG. 23.31

The Task Usage report displays all tasks, not just the subtasks, in a project. The focus of this report is on the hours worked on each task.

Task Usage as of Tue 5/20/97
New Product Development

	5/3/98	5/10/98	5/17/98	5/24/98	5/31/98	6/7/98	6/14/98
New Product Development							
Design Phase							
Begin project							
Prototype design	80 hrs	80 hrs	80 hrs	64 hrs	80 hrs	16 hrs	
Bill Kirk	40 hrs	40 hrs	40 hrs	32 hrs	40 hrs	8 hrs	
Scott Adams	40 hrs	40 hrs	40 hrs	32 hrs	40 hrs	8 hrs	
Test prototype						64 hrs	80 hrs
Bill Kirk						32 hrs	40 hrs
John Melville						32 hrs	40 hrs
Prototype completed							
Finance Phase							
Create business plan	80 hrs	60 hrs					
Henrietta Lee	40 hrs	#######					
Mel Lloyd	40 hrs	#######					
Present to current investors							
John Melville							
Meet with bankers							
John Melville							
Circulate plan w/ venture capitalists			32 hrs				
Henrietta Lee			32 hrs				

Page: 1 of 6   Size: 2 rows by 3 columns

TIP In Figure 23.31, for the week of 5/10/98, the resource hours for the Create Business Plan task are represented by a series of pound (#) symbols, which is the universal Microsoft indicator that the column is not wide enough to display the hours. A simple solution to this problem is to change the format for the dates to a longer format. The column width will change and the hours will display.

To change the date format, click the Close button to close the preview screen. Go back into the Workload category of reports, and click Task Usage report. Choose Edit. In the Crosstab Report dialog box that appears, select the Details tab. Use the Date Format drop-down list box to select a different, longer format (see Figure 23.32). Click OK. Look ahead to Figure 23.33, which shows a similar report where the date format has been changed, allowing the fractional work for Henrietta Lee to be displayed.

The Resource Usage Report

The Resource Usage report is another crosstab report that is very similar to the Task Usage report, except that its focus is on resources rather than tasks. Resources are listed in the first column, with the tasks that they are assigned underneath. The remaining columns are weekly increments during the life of the project. The resulting grid, or spreadsheet, format displays the hours of work assigned to each resource during each week, broken down by task (see Figure 23.33). Each week is totaled at the bottom of the report; resource and task totals appear in the last column on the right of the report. When a project manager is juggling resources to accommodate overallocations or in an attempt to speed up the project, this report can be very useful in identifying resources that are not assigned to their full capacity.

Part
VII
Ch
23

FIG. 23.32

It is sometimes necessary to change the Date Format in crosstab reports in order to see the details of the report.

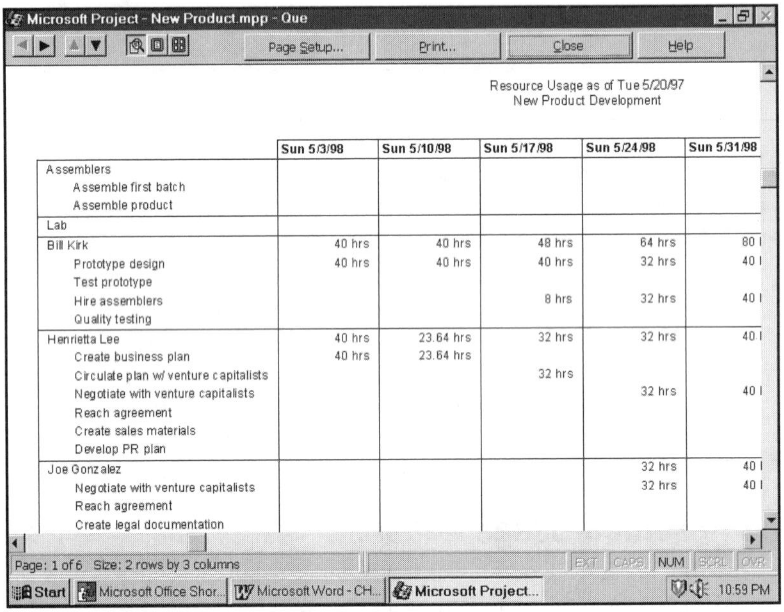

FIG. 23.33

The order of the resources listed in the Resource Usage report is the order they appear in the Resource Sheet view. You can sort the Resource Sheet to display the resources in a different order.

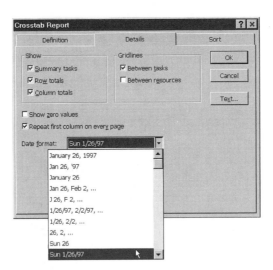

Using the Tip mentioned in the previous section, the Date Format has been changed to show the day of the week. This change was necessary to widen the date columns to display the fractional data for Henrietta Lee. Otherwise, her work information would be showing a series of pound (#) symbols to indicate the column was too narrow for the data.

From Here...

This chapter focused on all the standard reports that are available in Microsoft Project. Most of these reports can be tailored to your specific needs. Additionally, you can design your own reports. It is helpful to learn about customizing other Project items, such as tables and filters, before attempting to customize reports, because many of the reports are based on specific tables or filters.

Refer to the following chapters for help in learning to customize Project:

- Chapter 22, "Customizing Views, Tables, and Filters," guides you through customizing the existing views, tables, and filters, as well as designing your own views, tables, and filters to make working with Microsoft Project more effective.

- Chapter 24, "Customizing Reports," assists you in tailoring the existing reports and creating your own reports from scratch.

Customizing Reports

Customize the predefined reports

Customize any of the 22 standard reports included in Microsoft Project.

Design your own reports

Create new reports based on one of the four report formats: task, resource, crosstab, and monthly calendar.

Share customized reports

Save your custom reports to use with all your project files. Allow other users access to these custom reports.

Chapter 23, "Using the Standard Reports," described the standard reports included with Microsoft Project. Using the View, Reports command, you can access and print any of the 22 predefined standard reports. These reports are divided into five main categories. Customizing has been made easier in this version of Microsoft Project, because you can now edit the content or level of detail to customize some features of the report while you have the report selected. While previewing the report, you can also alter some of the print settings.

There is also a sixth category under View, Reports called Custom, which is another doorway to the range of options available to you to customize any of the existing predefined reports or to create your own reports. This chapter explores the range of options available to those who want to develop customized reports adapted to their project communication needs. ▪

Understanding Report Customization in Microsoft Project

There are varying degrees of report customization available in Microsoft Project. Reports can be customized to change the way they look or the details of the information being presented. You can take an existing report and change the text formatting, layout orientation, or the header and footer. The details of the report can be altered by applying a different table or filter, or by choosing a different sort order for the report.

Most of the predefined reports available to you in Microsoft Project are variations of one of three basic report types: task list, resource list, and crosstab. There is a fourth report type, the monthly calendar report, that you can use for creating new reports but for which there are no predefined examples. There are also two unique predefined reports, the Project Summary report and the Base Calendar report, which are not based on any of the four report types previously mentioned.

The task, resource, and crosstab reports are the primary types used for reports in the Overview, Current Activities, Costs, Assignments, and Workload categories displayed in the Reports dialog box (see Figure 24.1). To access this dialog box, choose View, Reports.

FIG. 24.1

The Reports dialog box lists the five categories of predefined reports and a sixth category for creating or modifying custom reports

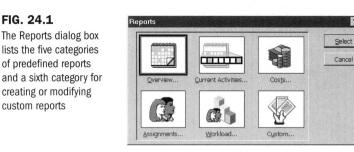

There are 22 predefined reports available in Microsoft Project which can be found in the five categories shown in Figure 24.1. These 22 reports can be accessed through the Custom category as well. The Custom category also includes three generic reports based on the task list, resource list, and crosstab report types that you can use to create custom reports.

In Microsoft Project, you can customize an existing report, create a custom report by making a copy of an existing report and make edit changes to the copy, or create a new report using one of the four report types listed above.

Customizing the Existing Reports

There are two places you can customize an existing report, from within the specific category the report is listed, or from within the Custom category. Chapter 23, "Using the Standard Reports," describes each of the standard, predefined reports if you are not familiar with these reports.

To change a report from within a specific category, double-click the category or click once on the category and choose Select. In Figure 24.2, the Assignments category is selected, and the Overallocated Resources report is selected. In this version of Project, an Edit button within the category listing allows you to edit the contents of the report.

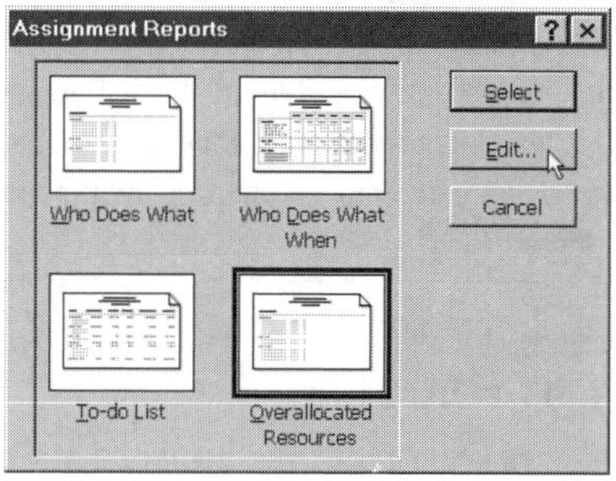

FIG. 24.2

You can now edit the content and level of detail while working in a category of reports.

Part

VII

Ch

24

Selecting the Edit button shown in Figure 24.2 will display a dialog box with the editing changes you are allowed to make. The choices in this dialog box will differ depending on the type of report you are modifying. Figure 24.3 shows a sample dialog box used to make changes.

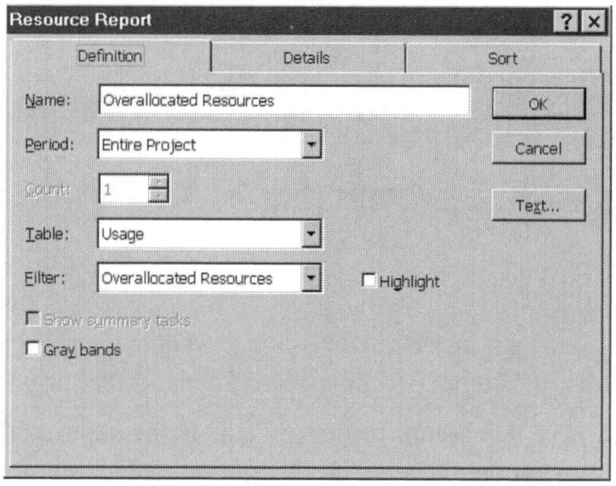

FIG. 24.3

The editing dialog box for the Overallocated Resources report displays choices that will vary depending on the type of report you are editing.

The editing choices listed here are the same that would be available if you were editing the report through the Custom category. Because the steps for editing an existing report are the same as when customizing a report through the Custom category, the steps for editing reports will be addressed later in this chapter.

TIP It is recommended that you do not customize the predefined reports, but instead make a copy of a report, using it as a basis for your new report. This way, the original report is left intact for you to use at a later time.

◆

TROUBLESHOOTING

I've modified one of the existing reports. I want to keep my modified report but also want the
original report available to use later. Access the Custom category of reports through View, Reports.
Using the Copy button in the Custom Reports dialog box, make a copy of the report you modified and
rename it. Next using the Organizer button from the Custom Reports dialog box, access the Global
template. Copy the report *from* the Global template *to* your project file. You now have your modified
report and have reset the original report. For more information on using the Organizer and the Global
template, see Chapter 4, "Working with Project Files."

Using the Custom Category of Reports

The Custom category can be used to make content and level of detail changes to reports. All
reports available within Project can be accessed through this category as shown in Figure 24.4.

FIG. 24.4

Use the Custom Reports
dialog box to select a
report to customize or to
create a new report.

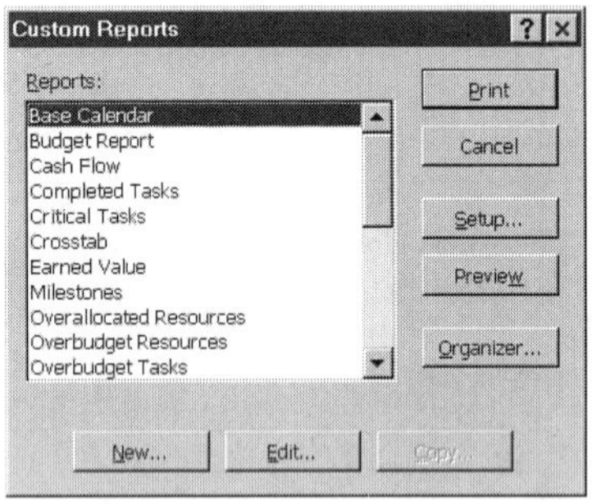

From the Custom category, you can do the following:

- Print one of the reports in the Reports list as the report is currently defined. See Chapter
  13, "Printing Views and Reports," for more information on printing reports.
- Set up the selected report before printing. (This is the same as the Page Setup function,
  which allows you to set up margins, headers, footers, and so forth.)
- Preview one of the reports before printing. With the Print Preview screen activated, you
  have the option of changing Page Setup before sending the report to the printer.
- Access the Organizer to copy customized reports to or from the Global template. This
  Organizer dialog box also allows you to delete reports from your Custom Reports list to
  keep your list current and uncluttered. See Chapter 4, "Working with Project Files," for
  information on using the Organizer.
- Create a New report. The design must follow one of the four report types: task, resource,
  monthly calendar, or crosstab.

■ Edit a report to change the table and filter used and to change the details that are shown (for task and resource reports). You can also edit the column and row information (for crosstab reports), the sort order for presenting the details (for non-calendar reports), the text formatting used for parts of the report, and the use of border lines in the report. These changes become standard features of the named report.

■ Copy an existing report and make modifications in the new report so that you have both the original and the new copy to use when needed.

The New and Copy buttons in the Custom Reports dialog box function almost identically to the Edit button. The only difference is that the end result for both New and Copy is a new report name to be added to the Custom Reports list. Use New to design a report from the ground up. Use Copy to use an existing report as a starting point for a new report. In all cases, the instructions begin at the Custom Reports dialog box.

Once you've modified or created a report, you can print or preview your custom report directly from the Custom Reports dialog box by clicking the Print or Preview buttons.

Part

VII

Ch

24

N O T E   The Copy button is dimmed for the Base Calendar and Project Summary reports, because they can only be edited for simple text formatting changes. ■

Creating Reports

You can create a new report either by copying an existing report and making changes to the copy or by designing an entirely new report from scratch. Regardless of the method you choose to create a new report, once it is created, you will use the same methods for customizing the new report. What follows below are the steps to create the new report. Other sections in this chapter discuss customizing the report once it has been created.

Creating a New Report Based on an Existing Report

One of the best and fastest ways to create a report is to start with one of the predefined Project reports that is similar to a report you need. By making a copy of the existing report, you take advantage of the features of that report, leaving the original report unchanged for use in the future. Modifying a copy of an existing report is quick and convenient.

T I P   It is recommended that you use one of the predefined reports as a basis for your new report, because most of the work in creating the report will have been done already. If none of the predefined reports are similar to what you are looking for, you will have to design a new report.

If you want to copy an existing report, follow these steps:

1. Choose View, Reports.
2. Double-click the Custom category, or click once and choose Select.

3. From the list in the Custom Report dialog box, choose the report you want to copy, and then choose the <u>C</u>opy button.

4. The report definition dialog box for that report will appear. The defined features will be identical to the original report. The only difference will be that the report name will be preceded by "Copy of." For example, the Critical Tasks report would be renamed "Copy of Critical Tasks."

5. In the <u>N</u>ame box, enter a descriptive name for the report.

6. Complete the dialog box for the report type you have chosen to copy. Explicit instructions for making changes to the various types of Project reports are discussed in detail later in this chapter.

Designing a New Report

Another method for creating a report is to design one from scratch. Use this method if none of the existing predefined reports are similar to the report you need. You must use this method if you want to create a monthly calendar report, because there are no predefined examples available for editing.

When you create a new report, you must select one of four report templates: Task, Resource, Monthly Calendar, or Crosstab.

- *Task*. A report that lists all the tasks (or only those selected by a filter) and may include various details about each task. Any of the task fields can be added to this report by basing the report on a task table that includes that field.

- *Resource*. A report that lists all the resources (or only those selected by a filter) and may include various details about each resource. Any of the resource fields can be added to this report by basing the report on a resource table that includes that field.

- *Monthly Calendar*. A monthly calendar similar to the Calendar view. This type of report is not included in the five predefined categories, but can be used to create a new report.

- *Crosstab*. A report in table format that shows cost or work summaries by time period for the project's tasks or for its resources. You choose whether tasks or resources will be listed in the rows; whether columns will cover days, weeks, months, or other time periods; and which cost or work value you want summed for each time period.

To create a new report follow these steps:

1. Choose <u>V</u>iew, <u>R</u>eports.

2. Double-click the C<u>u</u>stom category, or click once and choose <u>S</u>elect.

3. Choose the <u>N</u>ew button.

   You will see the Define New Report dialog box (shown in Figure 24.5) with the four basic types of reports listed. All new reports must be modeled after one of these types.

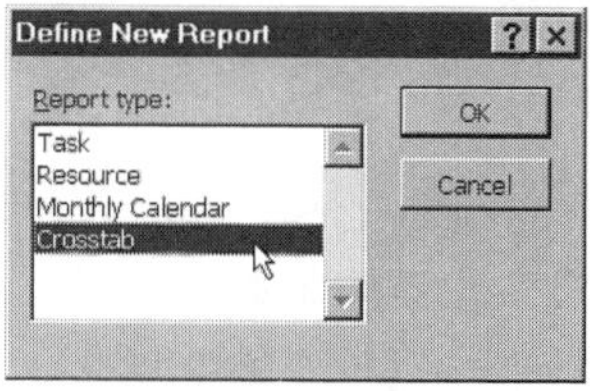

FIG. 24.5

When designing a new report, choose one of these four report types.

4. Choose a type and select OK.

The report definition dialog box for the report type you selected displays with the default settings (see Figure 24.6). A default report name, like Report 1, appears in the Name box.

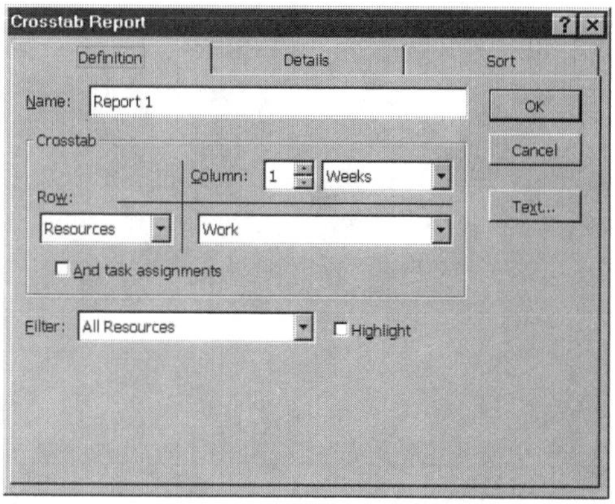

FIG. 24.6

The report options in the definitions dialog box will vary, depending on the type of report selected. The Crosstab definitions dialog box is displayed here.

5. In the Name box, enter a descriptive name for the report.

6. Complete the dialog box for the report type you have chosen. Explicit instructions for customizing the various types of Project reports are discussed in detail later in this chapter.

Using the Common Customization Controls

There are some custom options where the steps to make the changes are the same regardless of whether you are changing an existing predefined report, a copy of a report, or a newly created report. You can change the way reports look by changing the text format, page setup options, or order in which the information is sorted. The following sections describe some of the common custom options.

Controlling Page Breaks in a Report

If your report is based on a particular view, Project will normally reflect the manual page breaks you have inserted in that view (using the Insert, Page Break command). You cannot put page breaks directly into a report.

If you want to print a draft copy of your report on as few pages as possible, you can tell Project to ignore page breaks by clearing the Manual Page Breaks box in the Print dialog box (see Figure 24.7).

FIG. 24.7
Choose File, Print to access the Print dialog box.

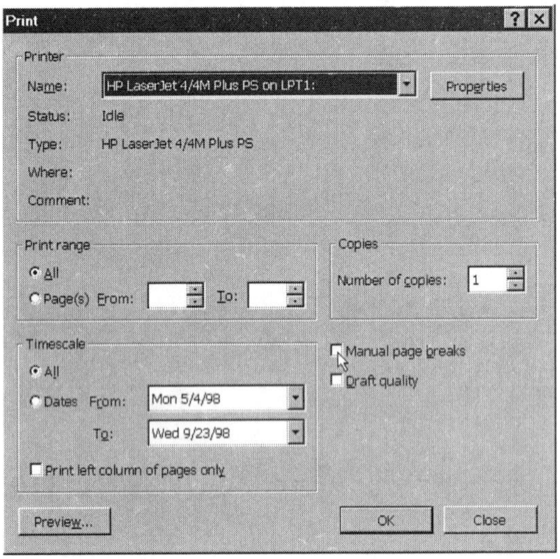

Formatting Text in a Report

Whenever you edit a report or design a new report, you will be presented with the definition dialog box for that report. Although some of the options differ from report type to report type, you can always format the way the text appears in the report. Choose the Text button in the definitions dialog box. If the dialog box has multiple tabs, the Text button appears on each tab. Note that the text styles are automatically displayed when you edit the Project Summary report, because this is the only option you can customize on this report. In Figure 24.8, the Overallocated Resource report is being edited.

FIG. 24.8
Use the Text button to customize the font styles used in a report.

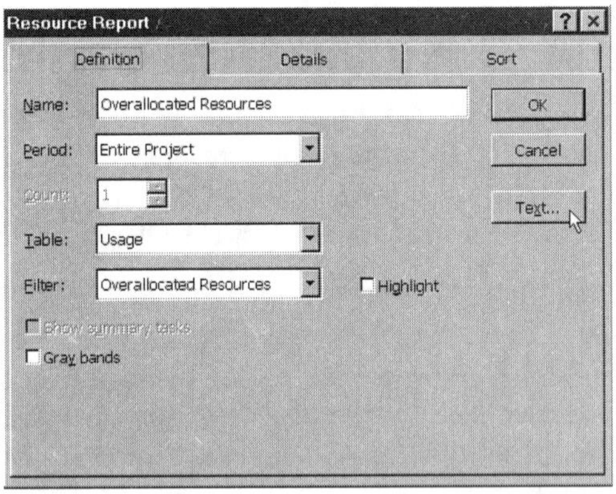

The Text Styles dialog box (see Figure 24.9) appears after selecting the Text button in the definitions dialog box. This dialog box allows you to select special formatting for a category of tasks and resembles the Format, Text Styles dialog box from the main menu. Use the Text Styles dialog box to make certain types of information stand out in your report by changing the size, font, or formatting of categories of text. The default format of each category is 8-point type with no distinguishing characteristics, unless specified in parentheses. By default, all the text will be changed unless you choose a specific type of information (see Figure 24.9). Specific information type choices depend on the type of report you are modifying.

FIG. 24.9
Use the Item to Change drop-down list to choose the text to format.

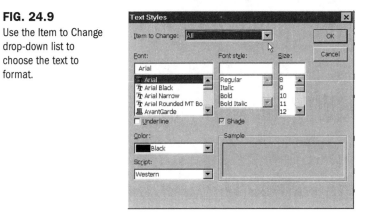

When formatting text in a report, you will need to format the text separately for each individual report and separately from the text format shown in the current view. There is no connection between the text format in the view and the text format in the report. For example, even if summary tasks are shaded in your current Gantt view, they will not appear shaded in a task report unless you specify the Shade option in the Text Styles dialog box.

Choosing the Page Setup Options for a Report

While modifying your report, you may decide you'd prefer it to have different margins or to display a different header. These changes are controlled by the page setup. In order to access the page setup options from the Custom category dialog box, choose the Setup button. If you are previewing the report, choose the Page Setup button at the top of the preview screen. No matter how you access the Page Setup dialog box, the options you have depend on the type of report you are modifying.

▶ **See** "Changing the Page Setup," **p. 420**

Changing the Sort Order for a Report

You can sort the order of the rows in all task, resource, and crosstab reports. From the definitions dialog box, select the Sort tab to access the Sort options for the report. The Sort tab in the Crosstab Report dialog box (shown in Figure 24.10) looks similar to the Sort By dialog box

Part
VII

Ch

24

used with the Project, Sort, Sort By command. The options on the Sort tab allow you to sort by as many as three fields in the report.

When sorting the information in a report, there is no connection between the sort displayed in a view and the sort selected in a report. Therefore, you can print a report sorted by a specific field, such as Priority (for tasks) or Name (for resources), without affecting the task order in your current working view.

FIG. 24.10

Change the sort order of the rows displayed in a report with the controls on the Sort tab.

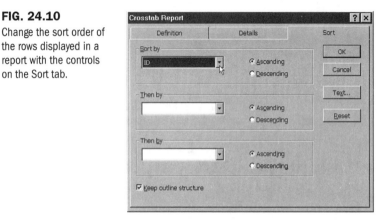

Collapsing Task Detail in a Report

There are two things that affect the level or type of tasks that appear in task, crosstab, or monthly reports—the outline level of the tasks and filters. If the outline is collapsed in the view when you print a report, the subordinate tasks that are hidden will not be displayed in the report. You must expand the outline before you print the report if you want all tasks to be displayed. However, the reports ignore any filter that may have been applied to the current view on-screen. You can select filters within the report definitions to be automatically applied regardless of the filter that may or may not be applied to the active view. Note, however, that subordinate tasks hidden by a collapsed outline at the time the report is printed are not included in a report, even though these tasks usually are selected by the defined filter. Collapsing an outline overrides the filter.

▶ **See** "Collapsing and Expanding the Outline," **p. 162**

▶ **See** "Using Filters," **p. 397**

Customizing Specific Report Types

There are five basic types of reports available in Microsoft Project: task list, resource list, monthly calendar, crosstab, and project summary. Of these reports, the task lists and resource lists have the most options for customization. In each case, you can select the columns of information to be displayed, the filter to be applied, and the amount of supporting detail about the tasks or resources listed. The crosstab reports are also flexible in allowing you to select which task or resource detail you want to examine by given time period. Most of the task, resource, and crosstab reports allow the addition of gridlines or gray bands. (The monthly calendar and Project Summary reports are very specific types of reports; each is addressed separately in sections later in this chapter.)

All reports allow you to use text formatting to further organize the information for easier reading. You can edit reports to change the table and filter used and to change the details that are shown (for task and resource reports), the column and row information (for crosstab reports), the sort order for presenting the details (for non-calendar reports), and the use of border lines in the report.

Customizing the Project Summary Report

The Project Summary report is a specific predefined report listed under the Overview category, and the only one of its kind. This report cannot be copied. The only change you can make to this report is formatting the appearance of the text. Figure 24.11 shows a sample Project Summary report. The project name, company name, and project manager name fields that appear in the header are taken from the Title, Company and Manager fields in the Properties dialog box. Any task notes added to the Project Summary Task or in the Comments field at the bottom of the File Properties dialog box appear at the bottom of the Project Summary report. To enter or change the text for these project values, choose File, Properties, and then choose the Summary tab.

Part

VII

Ch

24

FIG. 24.11
The Project Summary report cannot be customized, beyond changing text fonts. The title rows are enhanced in this example.

Microsoft Project - New Product Development.mpp - Que

| Page Setup... | Print... | Close | Help |

New Product Development
Alamo Enterprises
Laura Monsen
as of Sat 5/24/97

Dates			
Start:	Mon 2/2/98	Finish:	Wed 6/24/98
Baseline Start:	Mon 5/23/94	Baseline Finish:	Wed 10/12/94
Actual Start:	NA	Actual Finish:	NA
Start Variance:	965 days	Finish Variance:	965 days

Duration			
Scheduled:	103 days	Remaining:	103 days
Baseline:	103 days	Actual:	0 days
Variance:	0 days	Percent Complete:	0%

Page: 1 of 1

Start | Microsoft Word - CH... | Microsoft Project...   8.40 PM

To change the formatting of the text for the Project Summary report, choose the report name from the Reports list in the Custom Reports dialog box, and then choose the Edit button. The Report Text dialog box is displayed. Figure 24.12 shows an example of this dialog box. Use the Item to Change drop-down list to choose the text you want to format. Change the formats for the Project Name, Company name, Manager name, and Details. Select the OK button to return to the Custom Reports dialog box. The report in Figure 24.11 was printed with Times New Roman, 14-point text for the project name (New Product Development), 12-point text for the company name, and 10-point text for the project manager name and details.

FIG. 24.12

The Report Text dialog box for the Calendar Report. Use this dialog box to format text styles in your Project reports.

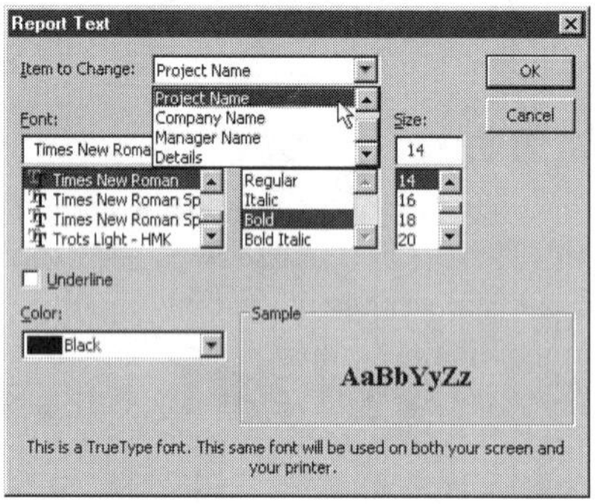

Customizing the Calendar Type Reports

The two calendar reports, as shown below in Table 24.1, are in fact the same report. Normally, a report that is listed under one of the special categories is also listed in the Custom category. However, the Working Days report does not appear in the Custom category. Instead, the Base Calendar report is listed. These reports show the work days, non-working days, and work hours for each base calendar defined for the current file. Each base calendar will be printed on a separate page.

Table 24.1 Predefined Calendar Reports

Report Name	Report Category
Base Calendar	Custom
Working Days	Overview

The only option in the Base Calendar report which can be changed is the text format for the Calendar Name and the Details of the report. To edit the Base Calendar report, choose Base Calendar from the Reports list in the Custom Reports dialog box. Then choose the Edit button. The Report Text dialog box appears as in the illustration for the Project Summary report (refer to Figure 24.12). Use the Item to Change drop-down list to choose the text you would like to format. Select the OK button to return to the Custom Reports dialog box. Then choose Print or

Preview to proceed with printing the report. (See Chapter 13, "Printing Views and Reports" for more information on print options.) The Base Calendar report cannot be copied, nor can you use its format when creating a new report.

Customizing Task Type Reports

The task reports include all reports that are organized around tasks rather than resources and that are not crosstab reports. Table 24.2 lists all the task reports and the report categories from the View Reports group in which they can be found.

Table 24.2   Predefined Task Reports

Report Name	Report Category
Budget	Costs
Completed Tasks	Current Activities
Critical Tasks	Overview
Earned Value	Costs
Milestones	Overview
Overbudget Tasks	Costs
Should Have Started Tasks	Current Activities
Slipping Tasks	Current Activities
Task	(Custom only)
Tasks in Progress	Current Activities
Tasks Starting Soon	Current Activities
Top-Level Tasks	Overview
Unstarted Tasks	Current Activities
To Do List	Assignments

Customizing a report can be accomplished either from the specific category to which the report belongs, or through the Custom category. For purposes of this discussion, we will be accessing the reports from the Custom category list. When you have selected the report you would like to customize, choose Edit. The dialog box that appears is named for the report you selected. For example, if you selected the Task report to edit, the dialog box would be named Task Report (see Figure 24.13). There are three tabs in this dialog box: Definition, Details, and Sort. Though not all options are available for all reports, all the options available on each tab are discussed in the following sections.

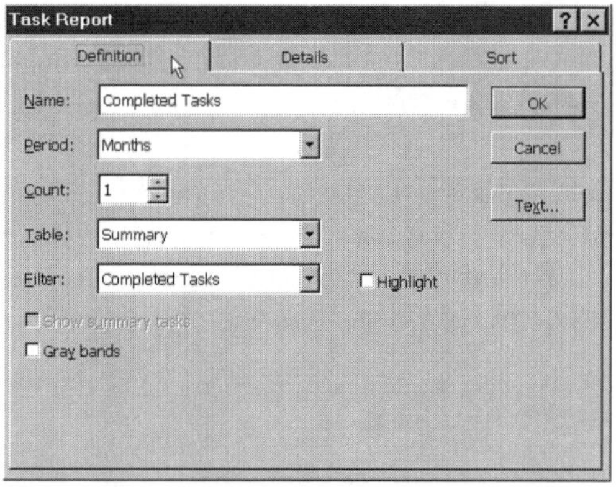

FIG. 24.13

The report editing dialog box is named for the report being edited— here the Task report.

Task Report

| Definition | Details | Sort |

Name: Completed Tasks

Period: Months

Count: 1

Table: Summary

Filter: Completed Tasks   ☐ Highlight

☐ Show summary tasks

☐ Gray bands

OK   Cancel   Text...

Changing the Definitions for a Custom Task Report   Select the Definition tab to see the current settings for the basic content of the report (the table, filter, and timescale). To change the columns of data to be displayed to the right of each task in the report, select the Table box and choose one of the tables from the drop-down list. The Table drop-down list displays all nineteen of the standard task tables, plus any task tables created with the View Tables command. The standard task tables and the fields these tables display are listed in Table 24.3, including the new Hyperlink table.

▶ **See** "Exploring the Standard Tables," **p. 679**

Table 24.3   The Standard Task Tables and the Fields Within Those Tables

Table Name	Fields
Cost	Task Name
	Fixed Cost
	Fixed Cost Accrual
	Total Cost (Scheduled)
	Baseline Cost
	Variance
	Actual Cost (to Date)
	Remaining (Scheduled Cost)
Entry	ID
	Indicators
	Task Name
	Duration

Table Name	Fields
	Start Date
	Finish Date
	Predecessors
	Resource Names
Hyperlink	ID
	Indicators
	Task Name
	Hyperlink
	Address
	SubAddress
Schedule	Task Name
	Scheduled Start and Finish Dates
	Late Start and Finish Dates
	Free Slack
	Total Slack
Summary	Task Name
	Duration
	Scheduled Start and Finish Dates
	Percent Completion (Duration)
	Cost
	Work
Tracking	Task Name
	Actual Start and Finish Dates
	Percent Completion (Duration)
	Actual Duration
	Remaining Duration
	Actual Cost
	Actual Work

Part

VII

Ch

24

continues

Table 24.3 Continued	
Table Name	**Fields**
Usage	ID
	Indicators
	Task Name
	Work
	Duration
	Start
	Finish
Variance	Task Name
	Scheduled Start and Finish Dates
	Baseline Start and Finish Dates
	Start Variance
	Finish Variance
Work	Task Name
	Work
	Baseline (Work)
	Variance
	Actual (Work)
	Remaining (Scheduled Work)
	Percent Work
	Completed

You have the option of grouping tasks by time interval, but the default is to show the entire project with no intervals listed. To change the time period in the report, choose the Period box and choose Years, Quarters, Months, Weeks, or Days. You can also indicate how frequent the interval should be. Use the Count box to indicate if each interval should be displayed every other interval, every third interval, and so on.

For example, by default the Count is 1, which means each interval will display. If you choose Quarters in the Period box, the tasks will be grouped by quarter, with each quarter showing. If you change the Count to 2, you will only see labels for every other quarter (Quarter 1 and Quarter 3). The data for Quarter 2 will be displayed; it just won't have a label indicating when it begins. A better example of how the time grouping might be useful is if the resources are paid every two weeks. In this case, you may want a list of the related task assignments grouped by pay periods. Specifically, you need to set the Period to weeks and also set the Count box to 2. See Figure 24.15 for an example of a biweekly grouping.

Any filter that has been applied to the view has no impact on the filter that is used with the report. To filter the list of tasks, choose the Filter drop-down list and select a filter from the list. Remember that if you want to use a custom filter, you must create it first, using the Project, Filtered For command. If you choose an interactive filter, the interactive prompt appears each time you print or preview the report. (As shown in Figure 24.14, the interactive Using Resource filter has been chosen.)

To use the filter as a highlight filter only, check the Highlight check box. Tasks which meet the filter criteria are shaded. To display only the filtered resources, clear this check box.

Mark the Show Summary Tasks check box if you want to have each detail task shown with its summary tasks. This is useful if the detail task names are general, similar, or are duplicated within the same schedule. Having the detail tasks associated with a more descriptive summary task will explain them more fully for the reader of the report.

Mark the Gray Bands check box if you want gray horizontal lines to separate the time periods.

Figure 24.14 shows the Task Report dialog box with customized Definition options. Figure 24.15 displays the resulting report using the Task Report.

FIG. 24.14

The Task Reports dialog box shown with the Period changed to weekly and a Count of 2. The Using Resource filter has also been chosen.

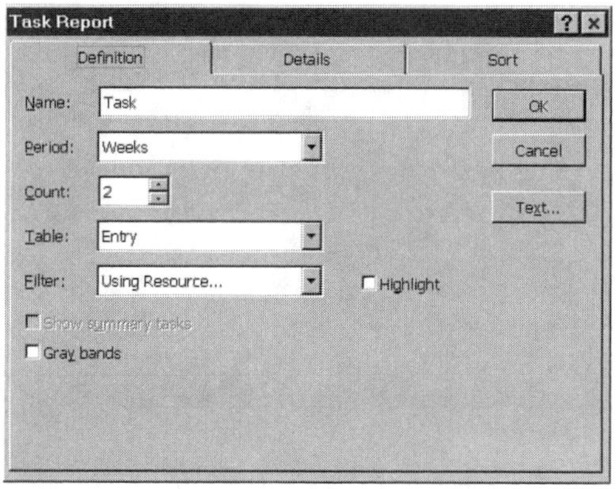

Changing the Details for a Custom Task Report   Some simple keystrokes can lift details about your tasks from your schedule to include in your report. The Details tab of your Task Report definition dialog box (see Figure 24.16) includes several categories of details that can be selected with check boxes. Depending on the Period indicated on the Definitions tab, some of the detail options might not be available. These categories are explained in the following list.

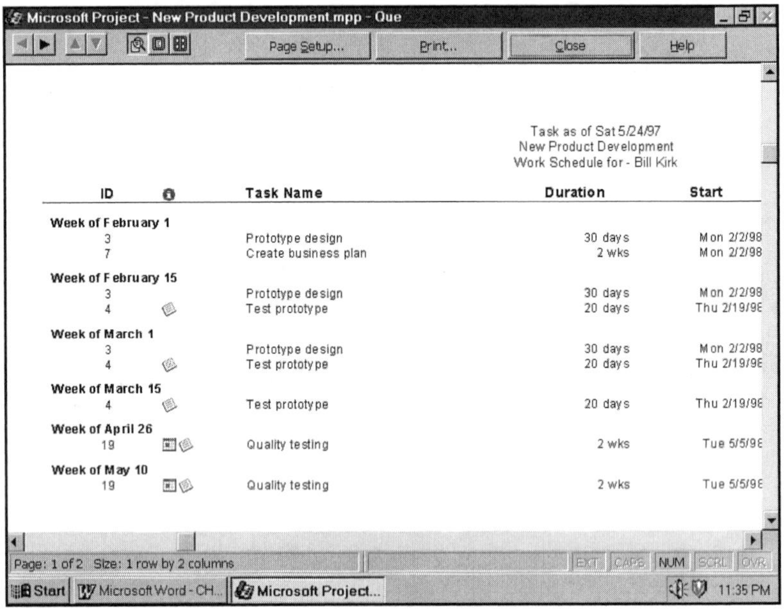

FIG. 24.15

This figure shows a preview of the customized task report, with the settings selected in Figure 24.14.

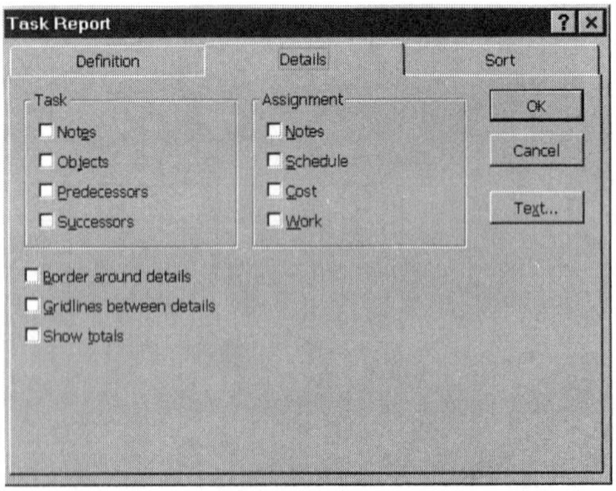

FIG. 24.16

This figure shows the Details tab from the Task Report dialog box. You can include additional information in your report using the options on this tab.

■ Under the Task heading, you can mark any of four boxes, which are described in more detail below:

● Select Notes to include notes you have written for any of your tasks (using the Notes icon on the Standard toolbar).

● Select Objects if you want to include objects you have created using another Windows application, such as Microsoft Word or Excel. An example of an object might be a chart done in Microsoft Excel that shows the costs associated with a group of detail tasks under a summary task (see Figure 24.17).

▶ **See** "Embedding Objects," **p. 654**

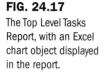

FIG. 24.17

The Top Level Tasks Report, with an Excel chart object displayed in the report.

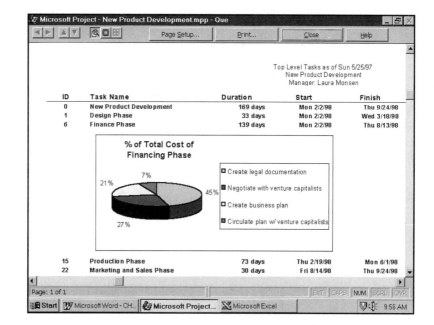

- Select the Predecessors check box if you want to include a list of the predecessor tasks with Type and Lag information under each task.

- Select the Successors check box if you want to include a list of the successor tasks with Type and Lag information under each task.

■ Under the Assignments heading, you can display many kinds of details about each resource by selecting any of the check boxes. Mark the Notes, Schedule, Cost, and Work check boxes to show details of the task assignments for the resource.

Three fields always appear on-screen for the Schedule, Cost, and Work detail sub-chart: Resource ID, Resource Name, and Units (of Resource Assigned). The following list shows the rest of the fields for each sub-chart:

Sub-chart	Fields
Notes	Assignment Notes
Schedule	Work (Scheduled Work)
	Delay
	Start (Scheduled)
	Finish (Scheduled)
Cost	Cost (Scheduled Cost)
	Baseline Cost
	Actual Cost
	Remaining (Scheduled Cost)

continues

continued

Sub-chart	Fields
Work	Work (Scheduled Work)
	Overtime Work
	Baseline Work
	Actual Work
	Remaining Work (Scheduled)

If you choose two or three detail tables, Project will combine the fields into one table if the report has landscape as the orientation in the Setup options. The Work field will not be repeated if the Schedule and Work tables are combined.

- New to Project 98 is the ability to add notes to an assignment to keep track of information specific to that assignment, such as the rate of work or scheduling assumptions. Notes must be added in Task Usage or Resource Usage views. These are a separate set of notes, not related to notes added to tasks or resources.

- If you want the detail sub-chart to be enclosed in border lines, mark the Border Around Details check box.

- If you want to see gridlines between each task, mark the Gridlines Between Details check box.

- Mark the Show Totals check box if you want to show totals at the bottom of the report for all columns in your table containing numeric information.

TIP   It makes the report easier to read if the details are surrounded by a border. Mark the Border Around Details option to display the border.

Figure 24.18 shows the Cost details surrounded by a border for all the tasks in the project.

Changing the Text Formatting in a Task Report   You can access the Text button from any of the tabs in the Task Report dialog box. The Text Styles dialog box (shown in Figure 24.19) allows you to select special formatting for a category of tasks and resembles the Format, Text Styles dialog box from the main menu. Use this dialog box to make certain types of information stand out in your report by changing the size, font, or formatting of categories of text. The default format of each category is 8-point type with no distinguishing characteristics, unless specified in parentheses.

The categories of tasks available for special formatting in Task Reports are as follows:

All (default category)

Noncritical Tasks

Critical Tasks

Milestone Tasks

Summary Tasks (default is bold)

Marked Tasks

Highlighted Tasks (shaded)

Column Titles (default is bold 9-point type)

Task Details (default is italic 7-point type)

Totals

More specific information about formatting text in a report can be found in the section "Formatting Text in a Report," covered earlier in this chapter.

FIG. 24.18

A Task Report customized to show a sub-chart with Cost details. A border encloses the cost information.

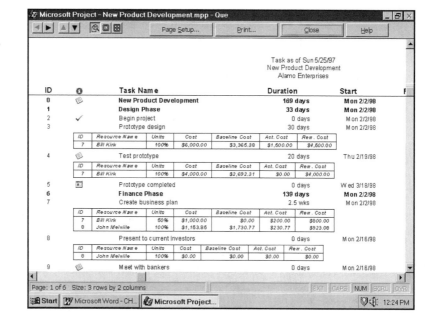

Part VII

Ch 24

FIG. 24.19

Use the Text Styles dialog box to format the text in the report. The Item to Change list box provides several choices of how to enhance the text.

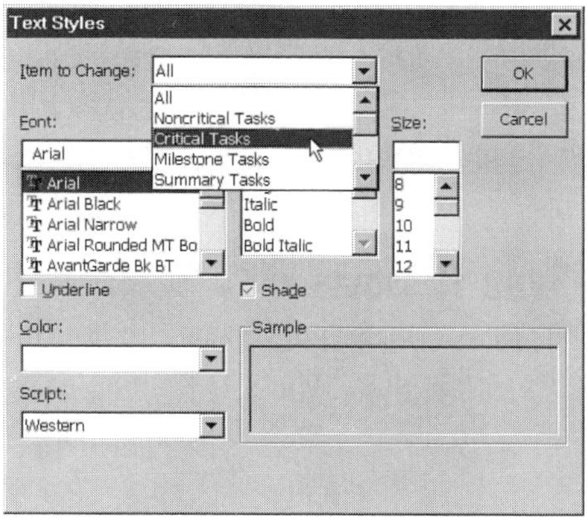

Figure 24.20 displays a task report with Summary Tasks formatted with a slightly larger font, and Milestone Tasks formatted in bold and italics.

FIG. 24.20

Use text fonts to emphasize types of tasks in the report.

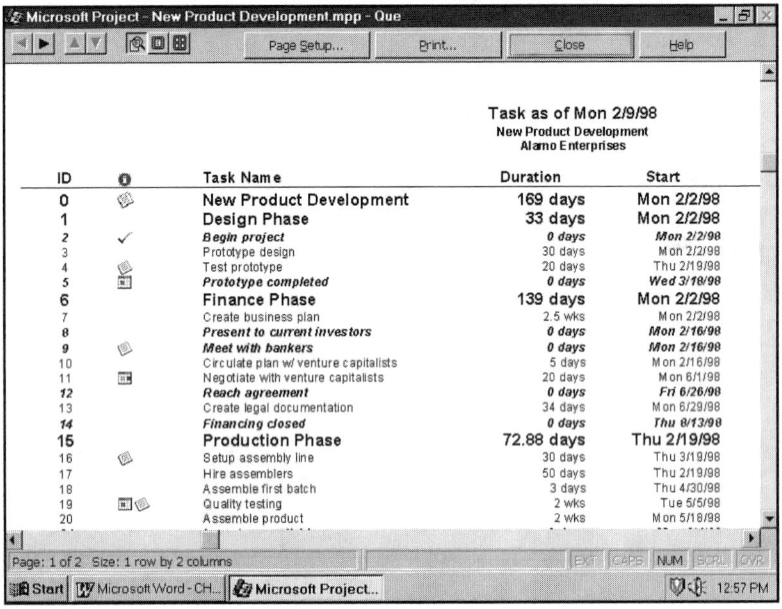

Remember the text formatting you have altered in the view will not show up in the report. You will need to format the text separately for each individual task report and separately from the text format showing in the current view. For example, even if summary tasks are shaded in your current Gantt view, they will not appear shaded in a task report unless you specify the shading in the Text Styles box from the Task Report dialog box for the individual report.

Sorting Tasks in a Task Report   The Sort tab is identical for all custom reports. See the section "Changing the Sort Order for a Report" earlier in this chapter for more information.

Once you have made the custom changes you want, select OK from any of the dialog box's three tabs to return to your Custom Reports dialog box. From there, you can Preview or Print the report.

Customizing Resource Type Reports

The resource reports include all reports that are organized around resources. Table 24.4 lists all of the resource reports and the category from the View Reports dialog box in which they can be found.

Table 24.4   Predefined Resource Reports

Report Name	Category
Resource	Custom
Who Does What	Assignments
Overallocated Resources	Assignments
Overbudget Resources	Costs

N O T E   The Who Does What report is a crosstab report. Customizing Crosstab reports is covered separately, later in this chapter. ▦

Customizing a report can be accomplished either from the specific category the report belongs to or under the Custom category. We will be accessing the reports from the Custom category list in the examples below. When you have selected the report you would like to customize, choose Edit from the Custom dialog box. The Resource Report dialog box appears. There are three tabs in this dialog box: Definitions, Details, and Sort. Though not all options are available for all reports, the options available on each tab are discussed in the following sections.

Changing the Definitions for a Custom Resource Report   The Definition tab on the Resource Reports dialog box (shown in Figure 24.21) is similar to that for the task reports. The Table box lists the standard resource tables, including the new Hyperlink table, plus any custom resource tables created with the View, Tables command. Table 24.5 lists the standard resource tables you might use in a report with the fields they display.

FIG. 24.21

The Definition tab of the Resource Report dialog box, shown with the default settings.

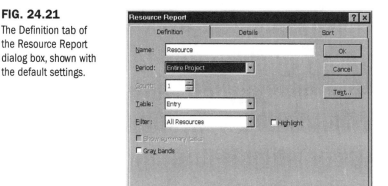

Table 24.5   Standard Resource Tables and Their Fields

Resource Table	Fields
Cost	Cost (Total Scheduled Cost) Baseline Cost Variance Actual Cost (to Date) Remaining (Scheduled Cost)
Earned Value	ID BCWS (Budgeted Cost of Work Scheduled) BCWP (Budgeted Cost of Work Performed) ACWP (Actual Cost of Work Performed) SV (Scheduled Variance) CV (Cost Variance) EAC (Estimate at Completion) BAC (Budgeted at Completion) VAC (Variance at Completion)
Entry	Indicators Resource Name Initials Group Maximum Units Standard Rate Overtime Rate Cost/Use Accrual Method Base Calendar Code
Hyperlink	Indicators Resource Name Hyperlink Address SubAddress
Summary	Resource Name Group Maximum Units Peak Usage Standard Rate Overtime Rate Cost Work
Usage	Indicators Resource Name Work

Resource Table	Fields
Work	Resource Name
	Percent Work Complete
	Work
	Overtime
	Baseline (Work)
	Variance
	Actual (Work)
	Remaining (Work)

You can define a resource filter to use each time you print the report. To filter the list of resources, select the Filter drop-down list and then choose a filter from the list. If you choose an interactive filter, the interactive prompt appears each time you print the report. Remember that if you want to use a custom filter, you must create it first, using the Project, Filtered For command.

Part

VII

Ch

24

To use the filter as a highlight filter only, mark the Highlight check box; tasks which meet the Filter criteria are shaded. To display only the filtered resources, clear this check box.

To change the time period covered in each group in the report, choose the Period box and choose one of these periods:

- Entire Project
- Years
- Half Years
- Quarters
- Months
- Thirds of Months (These are fixed dates on the first, eleventh, and twenty-first of each month.)
- Weeks
- Days

Using the Count box, you can stipulate that each time-period group includes multiple units of the time unit selected. If the resources are paid every two weeks, for example, you may want a list of those resources that worked during each pay period, along with their standard and overtime rates. In this case, you could apply a Custom Entry table, set the Period box to Weeks, and set the Count box to 2 (see Figure 24.22).

If you want to separate time periods with gray bands, mark the Gray Bands box.

Figure 24.22 displays the Resource Report dialog box with customized Definition options. A Custom Entry table, omitting the Resource Initials and Group fields, was used. Figure 24.23 displays the resulting report.

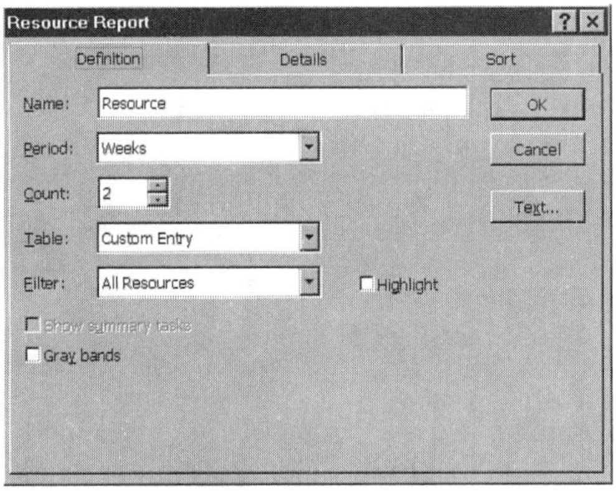

FIG. 24.22

Use the Resource Report dialog box to customize the table, period, or filter used in the report.

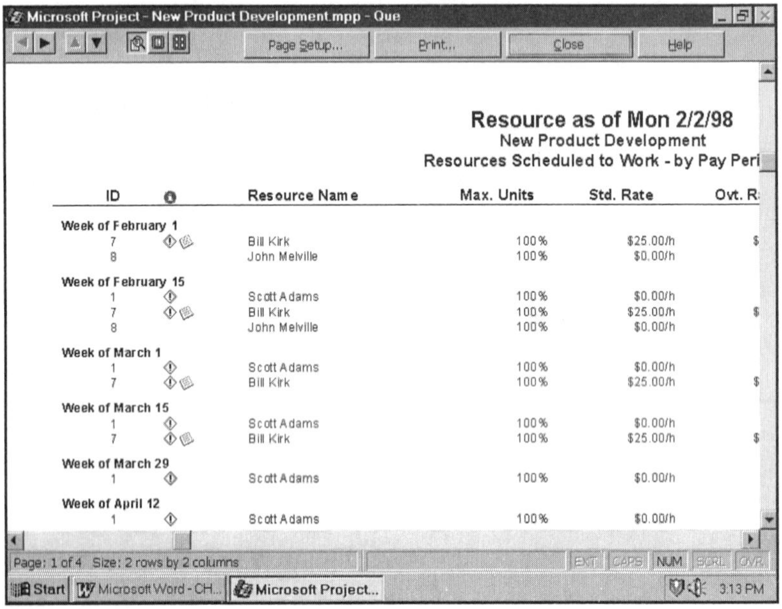

FIG. 24.23

This report shows each resource that is scheduled to work each pay period (every two weeks), along with its rates.

Changing the Details for a Custom Resource Report Changing the details included in a custom resource report is much like changing details in a custom task report. The Details tab of the Resource Report definition dialog box gives you many options. Figure 24.24 shows the Resource Report dialog box with the Details tab selected. You can customize the details described in this list:

N O T E Unless you selected the time period Entire Project on the Definition tab, the following check boxes on the Detail tab will be dimmed: Resource Notes and Objects; Assignment Notes, Cost, and Work; and Show Totals. ■

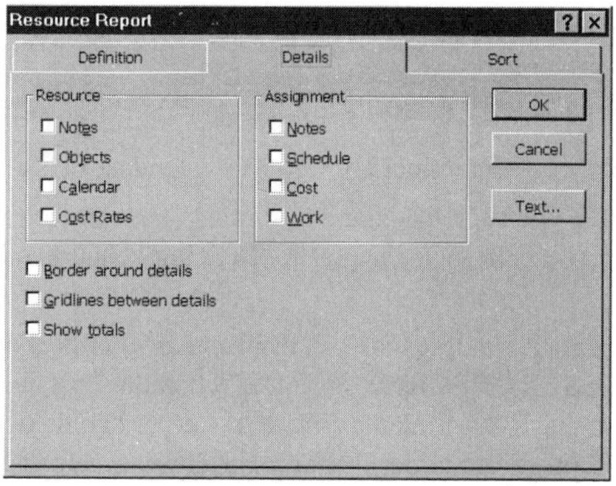

FIG. 24.24

Use the Details tab of the Resource Reports dialog box to select additional information you want to appear in the report.

Part

VII

Ch

24

■ Select the Details tab to select the task and resource details to be included with each task. The options shown on the Details tab for resource reports (see Figure 24.24) vary slightly from those shown for task reports. Figure 24.25 shows a resource report with details information included.

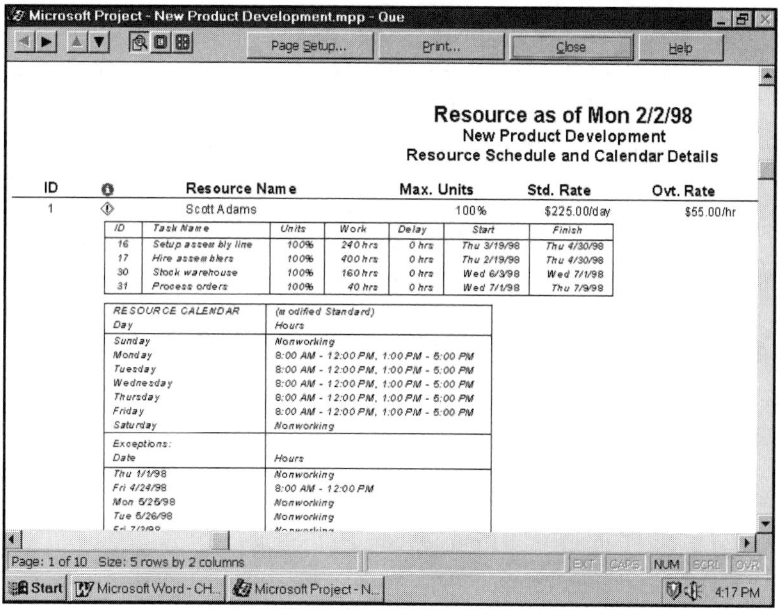

FIG. 24.25

Detail options in a resource report showing calendar and schedule information.

■ Under the Resource heading, you can mark one of four boxes:

Select Notes to include notes you have written for any of your resources (using the Notes button on the Standard toolbar).

Select Objects if you want to represent data you have created using another Windows application, such as Microsoft Word or Excel. An example of an object might be a

Microsoft Excel graph of work hours assigned for a group of resources assigned to a group of tasks.

▶ **See** "Embedding Objects," **p. 654**

Select Ca lendar if you want to include resource calendars in the report.

Select Cost Rates if you want to see the cost rate tables for each resource. Cost Rates are a new feature in Project 98. See Chapter 8, "Defining Resources and Costs," for more information on how they are used.

- Under the Assignment heading, you can display many kinds of details about each resource (see Figure 24.25). Mark the Notes, Schedule, Cost, and Work check boxes to show details of the task assignments for the resource. The fields for each task assigned are the same as those listed under resource details on the Task Reports.

New in Project 98 is the ability to add notes to an assignment to keep track of information specific to that assignment, such as the rate of work or scheduling assumptions. Notes must be added in Task Usage or Resource Usage views. These are a separate set of notes, not related to notes added to tasks or resources.

- If you want the detail tables to be enclosed in border lines, mark the Border Around Details check box.
- To see gridlines separating the resources, mark the Gridlines Between Details box.
- Mark the Show Totals check box if you want to show totals at the bottom of the report for all columns in your table containing numeric information.

Changing the Text Formatting in a Resource Report   You can access the Text button from any of the tabs in the Resource Report dialog box. The Text Styles dialog box allows you to select special formatting for a category of resources and resembles the Format, Text Styles dialog box from the main menu. Use this box to make certain types of information stand out in your report by changing the size, font, or formatting of certain categories of text. The default format of each category is 8-point type with no distinguishing characteristics, unless specified in parentheses below. Categories of resources available for special formatting in Resource Reports are the following:

All (default category)

Allocated Resources

Overallocated Resources

Highlighted Resources (shaded)

Column Titles (default is bold 9-point type)

Resource Details (default is italic 7-point type)

Totals

In the "General Report Customization" section earlier in this chapter, the "Formatting Text in a Report" topic covers specific steps to format the text.

Remember the text formatting you have altered in the view is not related to the text formatting in the report. You will need to format the text separately for each individual task report and separately from the text format showing in the current view. For example, even if overallocated resources are highlighted in your current Resource Sheet view, they will not appear highlighted in a resource report unless you specify the format for highlighted text in the Text Styles dialog box.

Sorting Tasks in a Resource Report   The Sort tab on the Resource Report dialog box is identical for all custom reports. See the section "Changing the Sort Order for a Report" earlier in this chapter for more information.

Once you have made the custom changes you want, select OK from any of the dialog box's three tabs to return to your Custom Reports dialog box. From there, you can Preview or Print the report.

Customizing Crosstab Type Reports

Crosstab reports show cost amounts or work hours by task or resource in a grid format by selected time period. Table 24.6 lists the pre-designed crosstab reports available for customizing.

Table 24.6   Predefined Crosstab Reports

Report Name	Category
Crosstab	Custom
Who Does What When	Assignments
Weekly Cash Flow	Costs
Resource Usage	Workload
Task Usage	Workload

If you would like to customize one of Project's predefined crosstab reports, it is recommended that you make a copy of the report first, then customize the copy. This leaves the standard report intact.

You can customize a report either from the specific category the report belongs to or under the Custom category. From the Custom category list, select the crosstab report you would like to customize and choose Edit. The Crosstab Report dialog box appears. There are three tabs in this dialog box: Definitions, Details, and Sort. Not all options are available for all reports.

Changing the Definitions for a Custom Crosstab Report   Selecting the type of information to be displayed in your crosstab report is done through the Definition tab of the Crosstab Report dialog box. Select the Definition tab to display the Definition box for crosstab reports (see Figure 24.26).

FIG. 24.26
The Definitions tab for
Crosstab provides a
unique way to display
project information.

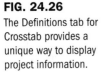

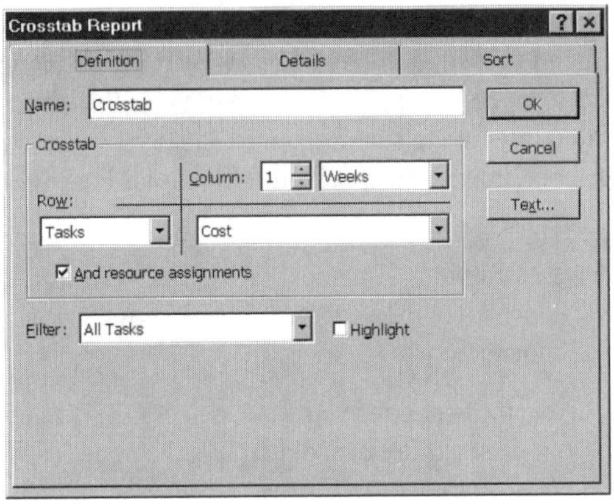

The Definition tab allows you to indicate whether you want to list tasks or resources down your
rows by selecting one of the two in the Row box. The available information to include in the
grid for your row information depends on whether you are working with Tasks or Resources.
Table 24.7 outlines these options.

Table 24.7   Crosstab Row and Column Alternatives

Row Choice	Options
Tasks	Actual Cost
	Actual Overtime Work
	Actual Work
	ACWP (Actual Cost of Work Performed)
	Baseline Cost
	Baseline Work
	BCWP (Budgeted Cost of Work Performed)
	BCWS (Budgeted Cost of Work Scheduled)
	Cost (Scheduled)
	Cumulative Cost (Scheduled, time-phased)
	Cumulative Work (Scheduled, time-phased)
	CV (Cost Variance)
	Fixed Cost
	Overtime Work (Scheduled)
	Regular Work (Scheduled)
	SV (Schedule Variance)
	Work (Scheduled)
Resources	Actual Cost
	Actual Overtime Work
	Actual Work
	ACWP (Actual Cost of Work Performed)
	Availability
	Baseline Cost

Row Choice	Options
	Baseline Work
	BCWS (Budgeted Cost of Work Scheduled)
	Cost (Scheduled)
	Cumulative Cost (Scheduled, time-phased)
	Cumulative Work (Scheduled, time-phased)
	CV (Cost Variance)
	Overallocation
	Overtime Work (Scheduled)
	Peak Units
	Percent Allocation
	Regular Work (Scheduled)
	SV (Schedule Variance)
	Work (Scheduled)

Part VII Ch 24

Once you select the information to appear in the Rows and Columns, you may also select the time period represented by each column in the grid with the Column section. Figure 24.27 shows a crosstab report that lists monthly cumulative work by resources.

FIG. 24.27
This figure represents a Crosstab report showing cumulative work by resources with task assignments.

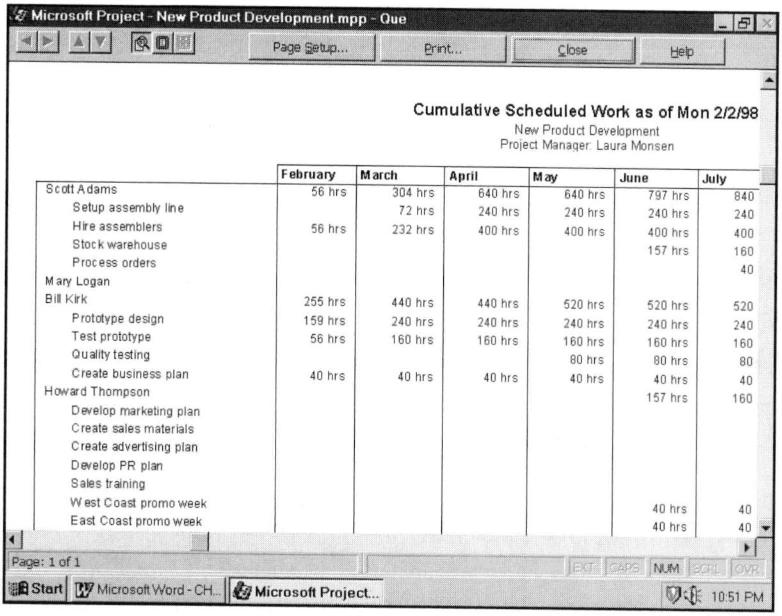

As with resource and task reports, you can select a filter. If you choose to list tasks as your row information, you will be presented with your list of task filters in the Filter box. If you choose to list resources as your row information, you will see your list of resource filters in the Filter box. Remember that if you want to use a custom filter, you must create it first, using the Project, Filtered For command.

▶ **See** "Using the Standard Filters," **p. 686**

If you are listing resources in your rows and want to include details on assigned tasks for each resource, check the And Task Assignments box. The box changes its label to And Resource Assignments if you choose Tasks as your Row information, and it will list all assigned resources for the tasks listed in your report. Figure 24.27 shows monthly cumulative work by resources with task assignments included.

Changing the Details for a Custom Crosstab Report   Adding details to a custom crosstab report is done through the same Details tab available in the custom report dialog box for task and resource reports. However, the details you add to a crosstab report differ somewhat from task and resource reports because the type of information shown in a crosstab report is primarily numeric rather than descriptive. Figure 24.28 shows the Details tab for a crosstab report with all details selected, except gridlines between resources assigned to the same task.

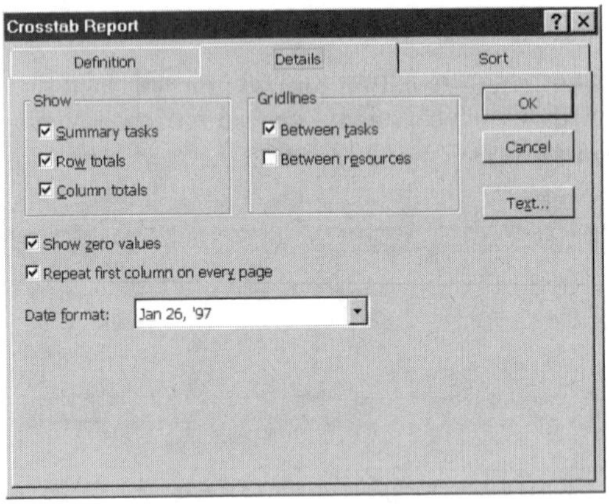

FIG. 24.28
The Details tab of the Crosstab Reports dialog box is notably different from the Task Report and the Resource Report dialog boxes.

The Details options are described in the following list:

- The Show section allows you to print Row totals and Column totals by checking the appropriate boxes. If both boxes are checked, an overall total is printed at the intersection of the Row and Column totals. If you choose to list tasks as your Row information, you have the option of showing Summary Tasks. If you select resources for your Row information, the Summary Task option will be grayed out. Summary task information will include information from all detail tasks even if they are not displayed on the report (see Figure 24.29).

- You may show horizontal gridlines between your tasks or resources by clicking the appropriate box in the Gridlines section.

- The Show Zero Values box allows you to show or suppress 0's for the grid box representing a time period when the time period's value is 0.

- Check the Repeat First Column on Every Page option when your crosstab report extends to more than one page horizontally, and you want the row titles in the first column to repeat on every page.

FIG. 24.29

Task crosstab report showing scheduled weekly Work with most details displayed.

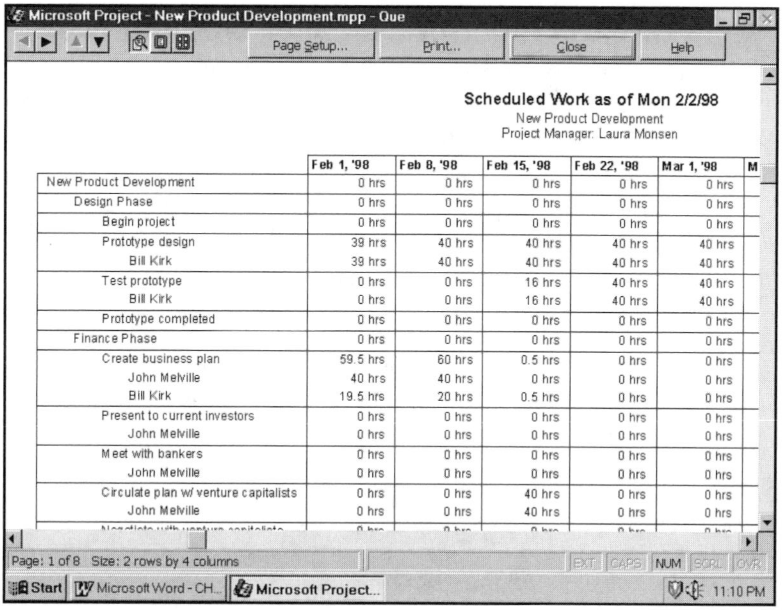

The Microsoft Project screen shows a crosstab report titled "Scheduled Work as of Mon 2/2/98, New Product Development, Project Manager: Laura Monsen":

	Feb 1, '98	Feb 8, '98	Feb 15, '98	Feb 22, '98	Mar 1, '98	M
New Product Development	0 hrs	0 hrs	0 hrs	0 hrs	0 hrs	
Design Phase	0 hrs	0 hrs	0 hrs	0 hrs	0 hrs	
Begin project	0 hrs	0 hrs	0 hrs	0 hrs	0 hrs	
Prototype design	39 hrs	40 hrs	40 hrs	40 hrs	40 hrs	
Bill Kirk	39 hrs	40 hrs	40 hrs	40 hrs	40 hrs	
Test prototype	0 hrs	0 hrs	16 hrs	40 hrs	40 hrs	
Bill Kirk	0 hrs	0 hrs	16 hrs	40 hrs	40 hrs	
Prototype completed	0 hrs	0 hrs	0 hrs	0 hrs	0 hrs	
Finance Phase	0 hrs	0 hrs	0 hrs	0 hrs	0 hrs	
Create business plan	59.5 hrs	60 hrs	0.5 hrs	0 hrs	0 hrs	
John Melville	40 hrs	40 hrs	0 hrs	0 hrs	0 hrs	
Bill Kirk	19.5 hrs	20 hrs	0.5 hrs	0 hrs	0 hrs	
Present to current investors	0 hrs	0 hrs	0 hrs	0 hrs	0 hrs	
John Melville	0 hrs	0 hrs	0 hrs	0 hrs	0 hrs	
Meet with bankers	0 hrs	0 hrs	0 hrs	0 hrs	0 hrs	
John Melville	0 hrs	0 hrs	0 hrs	0 hrs	0 hrs	
Circulate plan w/ venture capitalists	0 hrs	0 hrs	40 hrs	0 hrs	0 hrs	
John Melville	0 hrs	0 hrs	40 hrs	0 hrs	0 hrs	

Page: 1 of 8   Size: 2 rows by 4 columns

■ The Date Format box allows you to specify the date as it will appear along the top of your grid, representing your time period.

Changing the Text Formatting and Sorting in a Crosstab Report You can access the Text button from any of the tabs in the Crosstab Report dialog box. The Text Styles dialog box allows you to select special formatting and resembles the Format, Text Styles dialog box from the main menu. Use formatting to make certain types of information stand out in your report by changing the size, font or formatting of certain categories of text. The default format of each category is 8-point type with no distinguishing characteristics, unless specified in parentheses. Choose Item to Change to select the text you want to format. (In the "General Report Customization" section earlier in this chapter, the "Formatting Text in a Report" topic covers specific steps to format the text.) Remember the text formatting you have altered in the view is not related to the text formatting in the report. You will need to format the text separately for each individual task report and separately from the text format showing in the current view.

The Sort tab for this dialog box is identical for all custom reports. (See the section "Changing the Sort Order for a Report" earlier in this chapter for more information.)

Once you have made the custom changes you want, select OK from any of the dialog box's three tabs to return to your Custom Reports dialog box. From there, you can Preview or Print the report.

Part
VII

Ch
24

Customizing the Monthly Calendar Type Report

Microsoft Project offers the option of a monthly calendar report for those who want to report task information in a calendar format. This is not a report available in any other category but Custom, and must be designed from scratch.

The Monthly Calendar report offers fewer formatting options than the Calendar View, but can be customized to print any individual's resource calendar (something the Calendar View cannot do). The resource calendar for each individual resource can be customized through the Tools, Change Working Time command from the menu.

▶ **See** "Changing Working Times for Resources," **p. 270**

The monthly calendar report is accessed only by clicking the New button from the Custom Reports dialog box. After that, select Monthly Calendar from the Define New Report dialog box, and select OK (see Figure 24.30).

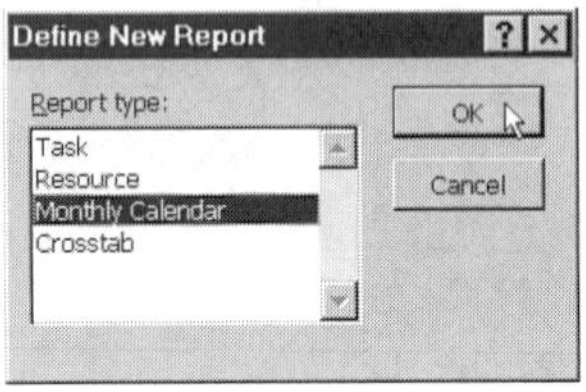

FIG. 24.30

The Define New Report dialog box is the only place you can find the Monthly Calendar report.

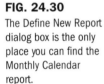

The Monthly Calendar Report Definition dialog box offers you choices for filtering, which base or resource calendar to display, and how to display and label tasks (see Figure 24.31).

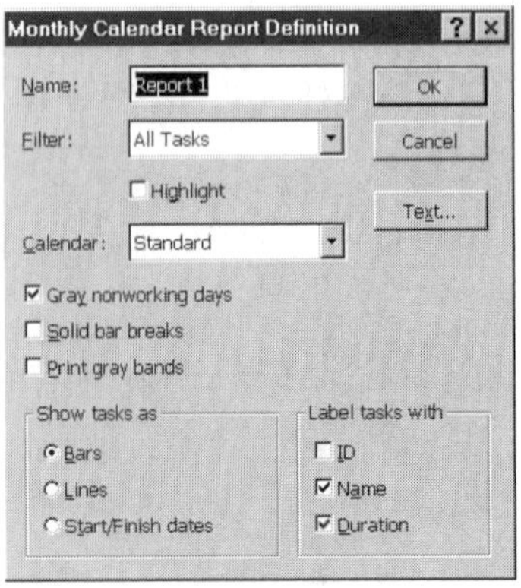

FIG. 24.31

The Monthly Calendar Report Definition dialog box, shown with the default settings.

You can choose any base or resource calendars to use for displaying the working and non-working days on the report. The advantage of this report over the Calendar View is that it prints any individual's resource calendar, reflecting their working and non-working days. To select the calendar to use for the report, choose the Calendar box, and then choose one of the base or resource calendars from the drop-down list.

You can apply one of the filters from the Filter drop-down list to limit the tasks displayed. You might apply the Using Resource filter, for example, to print a calendar to distribute to a certain resource, showing the tasks and dates when the resource is scheduled to work on the project.

To make the filter a highlight filter only, mark the Highlight check box. All tasks will be displayed, but the filtered tasks are displayed with the format chosen for Highlighted Tasks (see the Text choices in the last item in the following list). If you select an interactive filter, the interactive prompt appears each time you preview or print the report.

The remaining options on the Monthly Calendar Report Definition dialog box regulate the display of the data, as shown in the following list:

- To distinguish working and non-working days on the calendar, mark the Gray Nonworking Days check box.
- If you decide to display bars for the tasks, you can choose to display breaks in the bars (from one week or month to the next) with dotted or solid lines at the bar ends. Mark the Solid Bar Breaks check box if you want solid lines. For dotted lines, leave the check box unmarked.
- If you want a gray band to separate the dates in the list, mark the Print Gray Bands check box.
- To show tasks as bars or lines that stretch across the calendar for the duration of the task, mark the Bars or Lines option button. To show the scheduled start and stop dates for tasks on the calendar, mark the Start/Finish Dates option button.
- Mark the check boxes for ID number, Name, and Duration if you want to include these field values in the label for the task. You can use any combination of these three values.
- If more tasks are assigned on a day than will fit on the calendar, an asterisk is displayed beside the day number, and the unprinted tasks appear in a list at the end of the report. The list is sorted by date.
- Choose the Text button to designate different text formats for parts of the report. You can select unique formats for different kinds of tasks (Noncritical, Critical, Milestone, Summary, Marked, and Highlighted) and for the labels in the calendar.

After you finish defining the Monthly Calendar report, select the OK button to return to the Custom Reports dialog box. You then can Print or Preview the report immediately or use the Close button to save the list of reports and print later.

Figure 24.32 shows an example of the settings in the Monthly Calendar Report Definitions dialog box for a Monthly Calendar report filtered to show only the tasks assigned to Henrietta Lee. The report is also defined to use the resource calendar for Henrietta Lee. Figure 24.33 shows the resulting report, previewing the month of May 1998.

Saving and Sharing Your Custom Reports

All the reports are saved with your project file, so remember to save your file if you have customized reports—even if you have not changed your task or resource information. If you want to make your custom reports available to all your project files or to other people sharing the same copy of Microsoft Project, you must copy these reports into the global template file, GLOBAL.MPT, with the Organizer. You can access the Organizer from the Custom Report dialog box. All reports in the GLOBAL.MPT template file are available to all users of Microsoft Project sharing that GLOBAL.MPT file.

▶ **See** "Using the Organizer," **p. 114**

FIG. 24.32

Monthly Calendar Report Definitions dialog box, customized to show a particular resource calendar and filter.

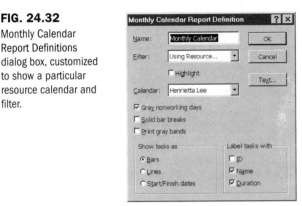

FIG. 24.33

The Monthly Calendar report for an individual resource.

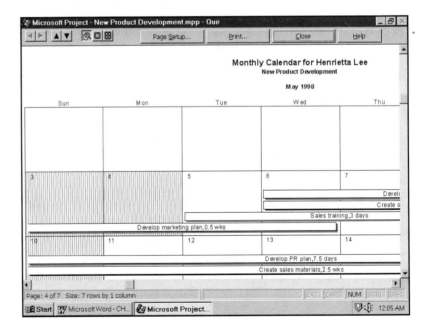

From Here...

In order to take full advantage of customizing reports, it is helpful to be familiar with the existing reports, tables and filters. It is also useful to know how to customize tables and filters. The following chapters will help in learning more:

- Chapter 20, "Using the Standard View, Tables, and Filters," will help you learn more about the existing tables and filters which are used in custom reports.

- Chapter 22, "Customizing Views, Tables, and Filters," assists you in tailoring these items. Once you have designed your own tables and filters, they can then be used in custom reports.

- Chapter 23, "Using the Standard Reports," will acquaint you with the existing, predefined reports. You will learn how to access the reports and when a particular report might be useful. Knowing the reports that already exist will help you tailor you own reports.

Part
VII

Ch
24

Programming and Controlling Microsoft Project 98

25   Using Macros in Microsoft Project   833

26   Using Visual Basic for Applications   849

27   Customizing Toolbars, Menus, and Forms   871

CHAPTER 25

Using Macros in Microsoft Project

Microsoft Project is a very powerful tool, but often your needs are not readily available on the toolbar, View bar, or menu. You often have to perform several complex steps manually. Microsoft Project has a macro feature using the Visual Basic for Applications language to allow you to automate your work. To make it easier to automate your work, the Record Macro feature allows you to capture your keystrokes and mouse actions without having to understand the language.

A Microsoft Project macro is a written instruction to execute a list of Microsoft Project commands, usually commands that emulate the menu commands or your own selecting and typing actions. When you run the macro it executes all of the commands in the list as a group, one after the other. The macro saves you from having to execute each of the commands by hand and from having to remember the correct sequence of commands that are needed. You can execute the macro from the Macro dialog box, a toolbar, or a keystroke.

With Microsoft Project 98, the Visual Basic for Applications language has been updated to match the rest of the Microsoft Office 97 products. For the *Special Edition Using Microsoft Project 98, New Edition*, capturing a macro has been covered separately in this chapter with more complete coverage on Visual Basic for Applications language in Chapter 26, "Using Visual Basic for Applications." ■

Preparing for recording

Before you begin recording your macro, some advance planning is necessary.

Record a simple macro

If you find an action that takes too much of your time, turn on the recorder and walk through the steps to complete the action.

Running the macros

Once the macro is created it is ready for use.

Editing macros

When you capture the macro, you may make a mistake or need to make a change to get the desired result. You can edit the macro without recapturing the entire process.

Planning Your Macro

In the earlier portion of this book, you saw many tools to help you manage your project. As you work on a daily basis, you need to pay attention to those actions you perform every day or more than once a day. These are the actions for which you will want to consider recording macros.

For instance, if accessing a certain report, or adding special formatting is a part of your daily routine, these are good candidates for automation. If you find yourself irritated during a certain step of your setup or management of a project, this is a clear sign that a macro is needed.

Once a process is identified, you need to isolate the steps taken to achieve the desired effect. For this chapter, two processes will be used as examples. The first example involves adding special text formatting and the second simplifies adding heading or outline numbering to your project.

Adding Special Formatting

When you use the text styles to format your text, you can format a group of tasks like summary tasks. Unfortunately, this makes the tasks with no subtasks fade into the background. This means that you may have to format the Summary group of tasks once and then many other individual tasks. Both of these actions can be put in a macro.

During the planning of a macro, you may want to consider walking through the steps (before creating the macro) necessary to achieve the desired effect. To format your summary tasks as Arial Bold 10 pt., you would need to complete the following steps every time:

1. Select Format, Text Style… to open the Text Style dialog box (see Figure 25.1).
2. Select Summary Tasks from the Item to Change drop-down list.
3. Select Arial from the Font list.
4. Select Bold from the Font Style list.
5. Select 10 from the Size list.
6. Select OK.

FIG. 25.1

The Text Style dialog box is used to format a group of tasks.

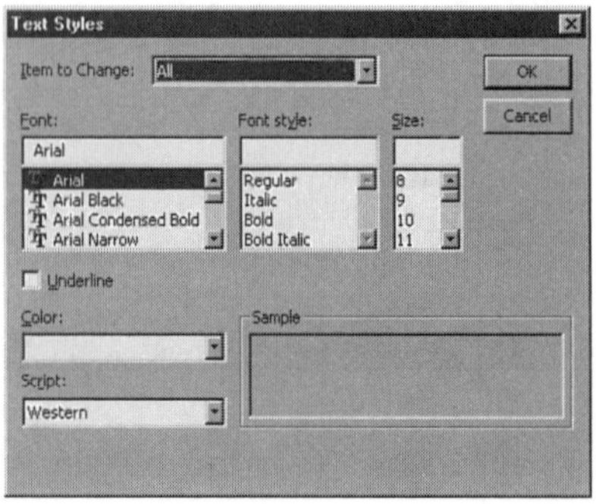

These steps will change the text appearance of the summary tasks. This one series of steps may not look like a candidate for a macro, but notice the problem created by these actions. The size of the columns with the larger text (see Figure 25.2) needs to be wider in many cases. If you were going to create a macro to add this formatting, you would need to clean up the column width problems as well.

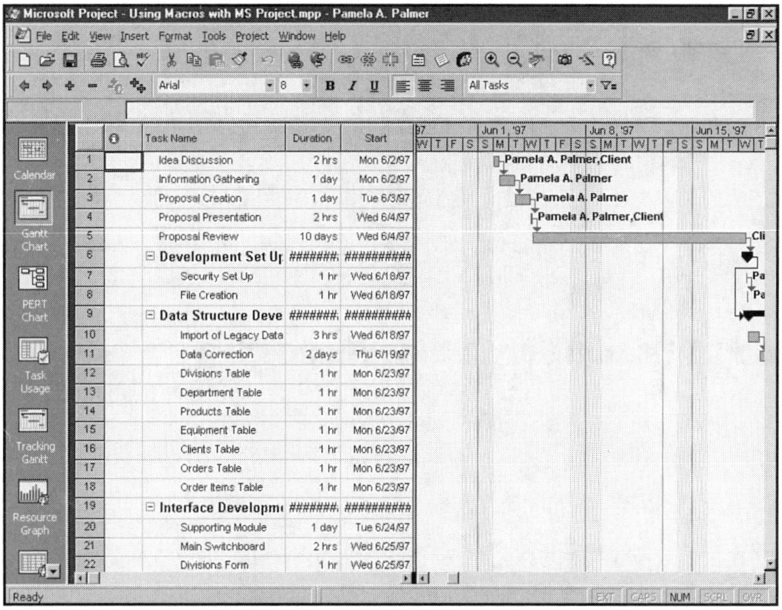

FIG. 25.2

The result of formatting the summary tasks requires some additional work.

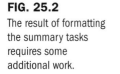

For this example, you would want to double-click the border between the indicator and Task name columns to make the indicator column smaller. You would also want to double-click in between Task Name and Duration, and Duration and Start. Although not visible when viewing the Gantt Chart, you would also need to double-click between Start and Finish, Finish and Predecessors, Predecessors and Resource Names and at the Resource Names to apply the Best Fit to the column width. This adds seven more steps to get the correct look for your task list.

TIP You cannot drag the border of a column when you want to resize it in a macro because the macro cannot assess the distance dragged.

The other type of formatting is for an individual task. With summary tasks, the formatting makes it clear that it is a major item in your project. If there is a task that is a major issue in your project, but isn't a summary task; it may melt into the background without special formatting. The steps to format a task similar to the summary tasks are:

1. Select the task or tasks.

2. Select F<u>o</u>rmat, <u>F</u>ont... to open the Font dialog box (see Figure 25.3).

Part
VIII

Ch

25

3. Select Arial from the Font list.

4. Select Bold from the Font Style list.

5. Select 10 from the Size list.

6. Select OK.

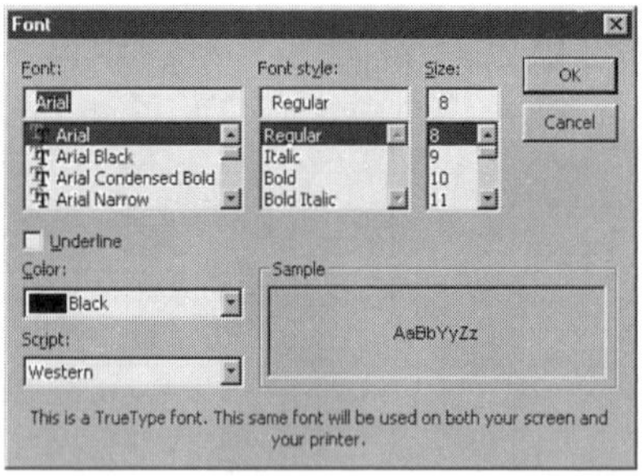

FIG. 25.3

The Font dialog box is used to format individual cells or tasks.

Adding Heading or Outline Numbering

Another type of formatting is the addition of outline or heading numbering to your task list. Outline or heading numbering is a method for numbering each task and subtask for easy reference. This is especially useful when discussing project process in meetings.

To add the numbering, follow these steps:

1. With your project open, select Tools, Options.

2. Select the Show Outline Number check box.

3. Select OK.

The result will add numbers before the task name as shown in Figure 25.4. With the steps for each macro outlined, you are now ready to capture your keystrokes to build the macro.

Creating a Macro

With Project 98, there are two ways to create a macro. You can create the macro by writing the Visual Basic for Applications code or you can record or capture the necessary keystrokes. An easy way to get started is to record the keystrokes.

The first step is to set up the environment. This step can be difficult because you have to determine what should be done prior to recording the macro and what should be included in the macro. For instance, the special formatting macros both work with the task list for the Gantt Chart. To set up the environment, you would want to make sure that the Gantt Chart was the selected view.

To make sure this is the selected view, you could manually select it from the View Bar, or you can plan to include that as one of the steps of the macro. You will need to think about what you are trying to do with the macro and what makes the best sense for the situation. For both of the special formatting macros, trying to run them without a task view visible will cause a run-time error with the macro. For this chapter, you can create the macro without the switch to the Gantt Chart view. Chapter 26, "Using Visual Basic for Applications," discusses how to eliminate this problem.

FIG. 25.4

The Task List with Outline Numbering makes referencing tasks easier.

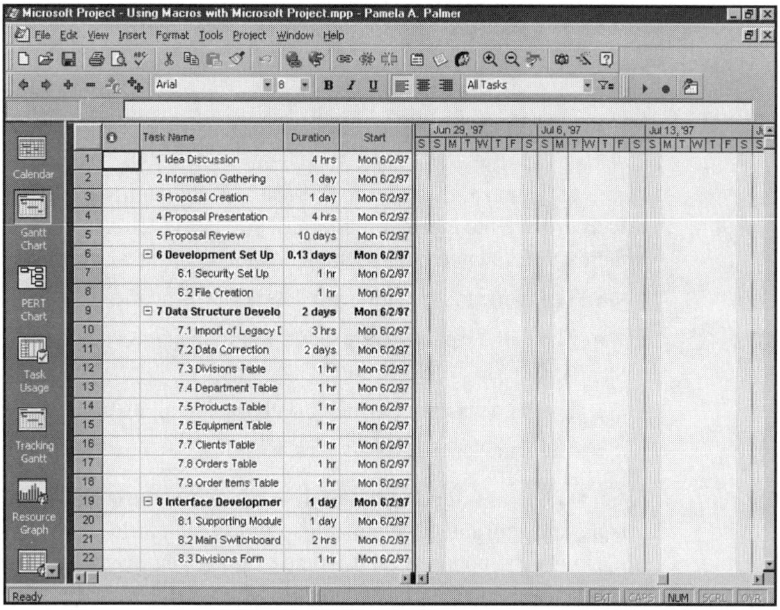

When you want to create a new macro, you will need to complete the following steps:

1. Complete any manual steps necessary to set up the environment for the process you want to automate, like selecting the Gantt Chart view for the formatting macros.

2. If desired, turn on the Visual Basic toolbar (see Figure 25.5) to assist you with the capture process. This will make the recording process easier by providing quicker access to the Macro dialog box and the Record Macro mode.

FIG. 25.5

The Visual Basic toolbar can make it easier to run, record, and edit macros.

3. Select Tools, Record Macro... to display the Record Macro dialog box (see Figure 25.6).

Part

VIII

Ch

25

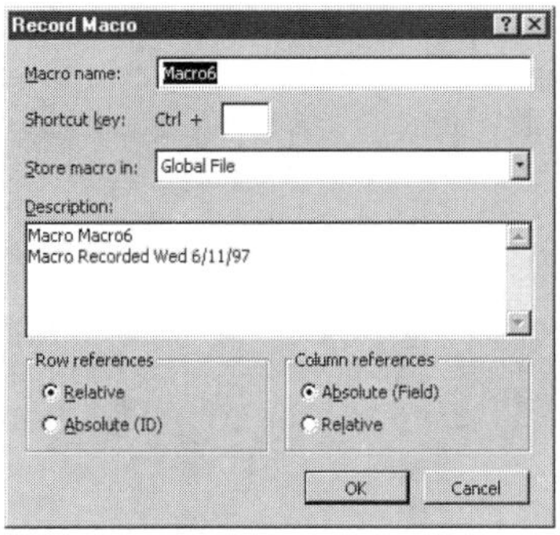

FIG. 25.6

The Record Macro dialog box allows you to name and begin recording the macro.

4. Enter the name of the macro. By default, it will number your macros beginning as Macro1. To make it easier to identify, you can enter a custom name. When naming macros, you will need to use the following naming conventions:

   - The name must begin with a letter.
   - The name can have any letter, number, or special character excluding spaces, period (.), !, @, &, $, and #.
   - The name cannot exceed 255 characters in length.
   - The name cannot be a Visual Basic for Applications reserved word.

   The good news is if you attempt to break any of these rules, Microsoft Project will display an error message indicating the problem. Although Visual Basic doesn't distinguish between upper- and lower-case letters, you may want to consider using a mixed case name to make it more readable.

5. Specify a Shortcut Key if desired.

   The assignment of a shortcut key combination is very valuable for macros you will use frequently, but you do need to use it sparingly. Unlike the other Microsoft applications, Microsoft Project enables the assignment of a shortcut key combination of Ctrl plus a letter.

   Although it appears as though you have up to 26 combinations, you cannot change a combination already used by Microsoft Project like Ctrl+X which is used for Cut. After you eliminate all of the reserved combinations, you are left with eight combinations. You can assign Ctrl plus A, E, J, L, M, Q, T, or Y. If you do not assign a combination, you will have to assign the macro to a button on the toolbar or use the Macro dialog box to access it. With the three macros previously discussed, the formatting of the summary tasks will only need to be run at the start of a project, so it's not necessary to assign a shortcut key combination.

6. Indicate where you want to store your macro.

   When you create a macro, you have a choice as to where you store your macro. You can store the macro with an individual project or place it in the global project. The global project is GLOBAL.MPT. If a macro is placed in the global project, you can share it across projects. For all of the macros for this chapter, the best place for them is the global project because they aren't specific to a particular project, just a particular view.

7. Add a description for the macro. This step is optional. You do not need to enter a description, but it will make it easier to understand the purpose of the macro.

8. Indicate how you want to reference your rows and columns.

   When you are planning your macro, you need to determine if a particular row or column is needed for an operation. For a macro, the positioning can be Absolute—which means that if you are in row 1, it will always run the macro using row 1, or Relative—which means it will look at the row that is selected at the time of execution.

   The same referencing applies with columns. The difference is the default settings. Rows use relative positioning by default, and the columns use absolute positioning as the default. This is because often you are working with a particular field like Task Name for an operation. Then you are ready to begin with the specific steps for your macro.

9. Choose OK.

10. Perform the actions you want to automate.

11. Select Tools, Macros, Stop Recorder.

Capturing the Summary Task Format Macro

The first macro discussed was the macro to change the formatting for the summary tasks to make them stand out a little better. The planning discussion illustrated that this was slightly more complex than it seemed because of the need to clean up the column widths. In the discussion about capturing macros, it was also pointed out that we need to make sure that the Gantt Chart was the selected view to avoid a macro failure known as a runtime error.

TIP

If a macro is one that isn't specific to any one project, you can begin the capture process with any project selected, but you want to make sure that you have saved your project before you begin the process.

This will allow you to close the project without saving the changes made as you walked through the actions with the macro and then re-open the file and test the macro. This is important because the Undo capability in Project is not as robust as it is in Microsoft Word.

To capture the Summary Task Format macro, please complete the following steps:

1. Select Tools, Record Macro... or click the Record Macro button on the Visual Basic toolbar.

2. Enter **SummaryTaskFormat** as the name of the macro.

3. Do not specify a shortcut key because this macro will only need to be run at the start of a project.

4. Select the Global File to store your macro because this macro can be used with any project.

5. Enter **Format the Summary Tasks for Printed Reports** as the description for the macro.

6. Do not adjust the Row and Column references because there isn't a need. The row settings will not be used because this macro is working with a group of tasks. The column reference is already set to absolute referencing which is fine for the resizing actions for this macro.

7. Choose OK to begin recording.

8. Select the Gantt Chart button from the View Bar to make sure the Gantt view is active.

9. Select Format, Text Style to open the Text Style dialog box.

10. Select Summary Tasks from the Item to Change drop-down list.

11. Select Arial from the Font list.

12. Select Bold from the Font Style list.

13. Select 10 from the Size list.

14. Select OK.

15. Double-click between the Indicator and Task Name columns to get the best fit.

16. Double-click between the Task Name and Duration columns.

17. Double-click between the Duration and Start columns.

18. Double-click between the Start and Finish columns.

19. Double-click between the Finish and Predecessors columns.

20. Double-click between the Predecessors and Resource Names columns.

21. Double-click the right edge of the Resource Names column.

22. Select Tools, Macros, Stop Recorder, or select the Stop Recorder button from the Visual Basic toolbar.

After you have captured the macro, you should test it. That is why it is a good idea to save the project before you capture the macro. That will allow you to close the project and then re-open it to test the macro. For this chapter, all of the macros will be tested at once.

Capturing the Special Formatting Macro

The second process that was discussed as a candidate for a macro was the process of formatting an individual task similar to the summary tasks so that it wouldn't get lost in the background. This macro can also be developed for use in any project. To capture this macro, please complete the following:

1. Select Tools, Record Macro or click the Record Macro button on the Visual Basic toolbar.

2. Enter **SpecialTaskFormat** as the name of the macro.

3. Specify Ctrl+A as the shortcut key because this macro will need to be run several times as the project is created and modified. The A is the closest mnemonic given the constraints. It may make it easier to remember as setting attributes for a task.

4. Select the Global File to store your macro because this macro can be used with any project.

5. Enter **Format specific tasks to match the summary tasks for printing** as the description for the macro.

6. Do not adjust the Row and Column references because there isn't a need. The row setting will not need to be adjusted because it is set to Relative. This will allow the macro to work with the active task. The column setting won't affect this macro because the first action is to select the entire task.

7. Choose OK to begin recording.

8. Select the task or tasks.

9. Select Format, Font to open the Font dialog box.

10. Select Arial from the Font list.

11. Select Bold from the Font Style list.

12. Select 10 from the Size list.

13. Select OK to change to the new font settings.

14. Select Tools, Macros, Stop Recorder or select the Stop Recorder button from the Visual Basic toolbar.

This macro will give us a quick way to format individual tasks. However, it is not a fool proof macro because you did not verify that the Gantt Chart view was active. If you choose to run this macro with some of the other views like Calendar or the PERT chart, the macro will not run correctly. Correcting this problem will be addressed in Chapter 26, "Using Visual Basic for Applications."

Capturing the Outline Numbering Macro

The last candidate for a macro is the ability to turn the Outline Numbering on as needed. This macro again will not rely on a particular selection in the view. To create this macro, follow these instructions:

1. Select Tools, Record Macro or click the Record Macro button on the Visual Basic toolbar.

2. Enter **ApplyOutlineNumbering** as the name of the macro.

3. Specify Ctrl+Q as the shortcut key because this macro will need to be run several times as the project is created and modified. The Q is chosen because organizations using a strict quality control policy often use this numbering.

4. Select the Global File to store your macro because this macro can be used with any project.

5. Enter **Turn on Outline Numbering** as the description for the macro.

6. Do not adjust the Row and Column references because there isn't a need. The row and column settings will not need to be adjusted because the macro will not affect individual tasks.

7. Choose OK to begin recording.

Part
VIII

Ch
25

8. With your project open, select Tools, Options.

9. Select the Show Outline Number check box.

10. Select OK to apply numbers.

11. Select Tools, Macros, Stop Recorder... or select the Stop Recorder button from the Visual Basic toolbar.

Now that the necessary macros are created, you are ready to run and test the new macros. This is easier beginning with a clean project. That is why the project was saved prior to beginning of this process.

Running the Macro

Once the macro is completed that isn't the end of the development process. You will want to make sure that the macro works. The first macro developed was the one to format the summary tasks. To test this macro, follow these steps:

1. Close the project.

2. Select No when prompted to save the project.

3. Open the project.

4. Select the PERT Chart view from the View bar.

5. Select Tools, Macro, Macros... or select the Run Macro button from the Visual Basic toolbar to open the Macros dialog box (see Figure 25.7).

6. Select SummaryTaskFormat as the Macro Name.

7. Select the Run button.

FIG. 25.7

The Macros dialog box allows you to run, view, and edit your macros.

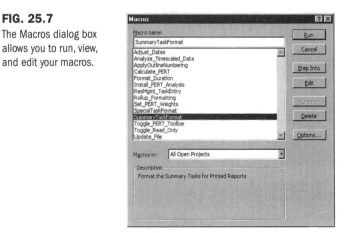

After you select run, you will see the mouse pointer change to an hourglass and the view shift to the Gantt Chart view automatically. After a slight delay, the formatting will change to Arial,

Bold 10 pt. The macro's work is complete. This will cut down on the amount of time needed to set up each project.

Running the Special Formatting Macro

The second macro created was the Special Formatting macro. This macro was designed to format one individual task to match the formatting for the summary tasks. This macro was one that you'll need more frequently than the SummaryTaskFormat macro. You assigned it to the shortcut key combination of Ctrl+A. This makes its execution easier. To run this macro, please complete the following:

1. Place the cell pointer in any task in the active project.
2. Press Ctrl+A.

This macro is more subtle in its operation. After the key combination is pressed, the mouse pointer will change into a hourglass and after a slight delay the task will have the new formatting.

This macro performed well, but it is not foolproof. As discussed above, this macro will run into problems if there is another view selected. For instance, if you press Ctrl+A while the PERT chart is selected, you will get this error message: `Run-time error '1100': The method is not available in this situation`, displayed in the Microsoft Visual Basic error dialog box (see Figure 25.8). It gives you four options. You can choose Continue to execute the macro (which is not available with this macro). You can also choose Debug to enter the Debug mode to track down the problem, or you can End the run of the macro, which is what you should select at this time. The Debug choice is covered in Chapter 26, "Using Visual Basic for Applications." You can also choose Help to get help for the error that has occurred.

Part VIII

Ch 25

FIG. 25.8

The Visual Basic Error dialog box is displayed with the error encountered by the SpecialTaskFormat macro.

Since it is not possible while recording the macro to select the prior view as the first action of this macro, you run the risk of encountering an error. Since you developed the macro, you know why the error occurred and can easily remedy the problem.

However, it is still an extra step for you, and someone else using this macro might panic when this message is displayed. This problem can be eliminated by making a small change to the macro. This task will be completed in Chapter 26, "Using Visual Basic for Applications."

Running the Outline Numbering Macro

The last macro developed was the one to turn on Outline Numbers for the tasks. This was one that you will need less frequently than the special formatting macro so it wasn't assigned a shortcut key combination. This macro can be executed like the first macro.

1. Select Tools, Macro, Macros... or select the Run Macro button from the Visual Basic toolbar to open the Macros dialog box.
2. Select ApplyOutlineNumbering as the Macro Name.
3. Select the Run button.

The mouse pointer will change into the hourglass and after a slight delay each task will have an outline number. This macro does a fine job in changing the display of the outline numbers, but it also has a problem.

The outline numbers take up space at the beginning of the Task Name column. This may mean that you cannot view the entire task name. You may want to turn off the numbers unless you are sending the view to the printer.

If you like the numbers for reporting, but you do not like them while working on the project, you would need a separate macro to turn them off. This can also be accomplished with a little editing.

Editing the Macro

The last two macros work, but they may have some problems. Both situations can be corrected with a little modification to the macros. Before we can correct the problems, you need to understand exactly what you have created as you recorded the macro.

As you stepped through the process for each macro, Microsoft Project was creating a Visual Basic for Applications procedure. Visual Basic for Applications is the universal programming language for all of the Microsoft Office products. It was designed to make it easier to develop applications across products.

Open the Visual Basic Editor

In Microsoft Project, you can view the procedures that were created by selecting the Edit button in the Macros dialog box. When Edit is chosen, it will open the Visual Basic Editor (see Figure 25.9). The Visual Basic Editor is now included as it is with all of the Office 97 applications.

This window will allow you to view all of the macros that have been built for Microsoft Project. The Visual Basic Editor has several windows open for easier access.

Understanding The Project Explorer

There are two windows displayed in the Visual Basic Editor. The first window on the left is the Project Explorer (see Figure 25.10). As a macro is recorded, it is created in a code module. The

Project Explorer allows you to see what modules have been created in the open projects. As you specified the information about the macro before you began recording the steps, you had to indicate whether you wanted to save the macro in the Global project, GLOBAL.MPT, or the open project. The Global Project as well as any open projects will be listed in this window.

FIG. 25.9

The Visual Basic Editor can be used to edit your macro.

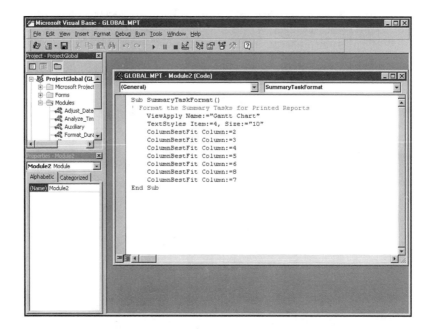

FIG. 25.10

The Project Explorer displays the components of your Visual Basic for Applications project.

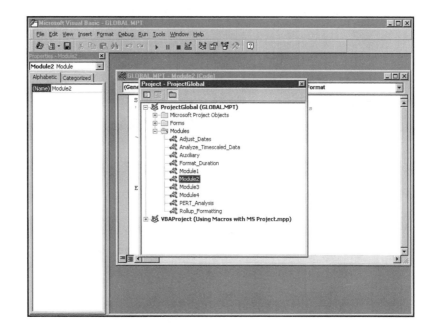

Part
VIII

Ch
25

This allows you to view any of the modules without having to return to the Microsoft Project window and select Tools, Macro, Macros to get to the Edit button.

Understanding the Properties Window

The second window displayed on the left is the Properties window (see Figure 25.11). This window will list the properties for the selected module. In this case, this is a code module so there is one property, which is the name of the module to help you identify it. As you record macros, it numbers the modules beginning with Module1. Renaming the module will make it much easier to identify it later.

FIG. 25.11
The Properties Window allows you to adjust the property settings for your Visual Basic for Applications components.

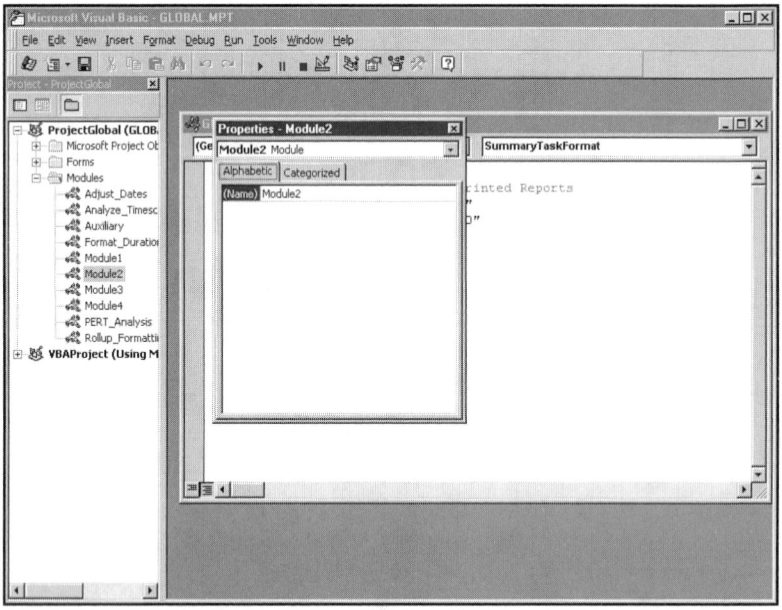

Understanding the Code Window

The macro that was selected in the Macros dialog box before you selected Edit is displayed in the Code window (see Figure 25.12). This window allows you to make any changes to the macro.

For every macro, the Record Macro command creates a subprocedure. That is what is displayed in the Code window.

```
Sub SummaryTaskFormat()
' Format the Summary Tasks for Printed Reports
    ViewApply Name:="Gantt Chart"
    TextStyles Item:=4, Size:="10"
    ColumnBestFit Column:=2
    ColumnBestFit Column:=3
    ColumnBestFit Column:=4
```

```
        ColumnBestFit Column:=5
        ColumnBestFit Column:=6
        ColumnBestFit Column:=8
        ColumnBestFit Column:=7
    End Sub
```

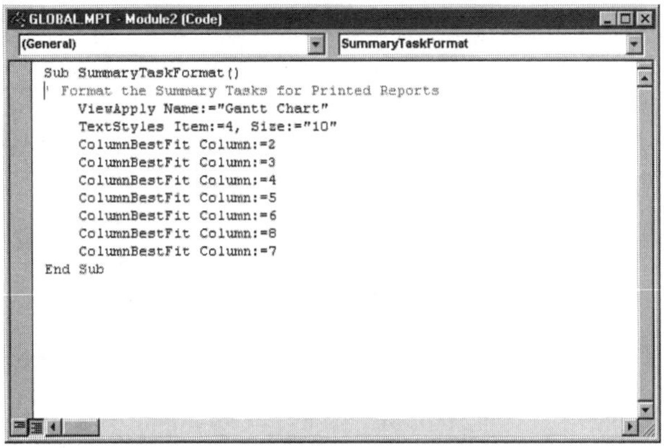

FIG. 25.12

The Code Window is where you can view and make changes to your macro.

```
GLOBAL.MPT - Module2 [Code]
(General)                                    SummaryTaskFormat
    Sub SummaryTaskFormat()
    ' Format the Summary Tasks for Printed Reports
        ViewApply Name:="Gantt Chart"
        TextStyles Item:=4, Size:="10"
        ColumnBestFit Column:=2
        ColumnBestFit Column:=3
        ColumnBestFit Column:=4
        ColumnBestFit Column:=5
        ColumnBestFit Column:=6
        ColumnBestFit Column:=8
        ColumnBestFit Column:=7
    End Sub
```

The subprocedure begins with the Sub keyword followed by the name of the macro. It is also followed by opening and closing parentheses. These can store any arguments needed for a macro.

The description that was entered in the Record Macro dialog box is on the second line preceded by an apostrophe. This lets Visual Basic know that it is a comment line in the code. The next nine lines of code are the actual steps for the macro.

The first line changes the view. This is accomplished with ViewApply. The next line applies a TextStyle to all Item 4's, which are the summary tasks. The next seven lines adjust the column width using ColumnBestFit. The macro ends with the End Sub statement.

The second macro that was created was the special format macro. This macro is stored in another module. You can double-click a module in the Project Explorer to open it in the Code window to see the macro. The same is true for the last macro. Each of these can be viewed and modified with the Visual Basic Editor.

To make modifications to a macro, it is like typing in Microsoft Word. You can add code lines, delete code lines, or modify code lines. A nice feature is that the Editor borrows many of the text navigation features of Microsoft Word. For instance to get to the top of a module, you can press Ctrl+Home.

You can also take advantage of the Clipboard. In the Properties window, you can change the name of the module to make it easier to recognize. You might want to rename Module1 as UsingMacros and then use the Clipboard to move all the other macros created in this chapter to this module to make them easier to find.

Part

VIII

Ch

25

From Here...

In this chapter, you were introduced to the concepts for automating the tasks you use the most. The easiest way to get started is to use the Record Macro command. This will allow you set up the macro and then simply step through the actions.

As illustrated with these examples, you do need to be aware of some potential problems like not having the correct view selected. You can prepare for this by including the selection of a view in the macro. If that isn't possible, recording the macro is not enough. You will need to edit the macro to solve the problem. This will involve the Visual Basic Editor.

When you record a macro, the language is hidden from you because you are selecting actions from the Microsoft Project menus and toolbars. When you need to make changes to a macro, you will need to be familiar with Visual Basic for Applications and the Microsoft Project object collection. See the following chapter for further information:

■ In Chapter 26, "Using Visual Basic for Applications," the Visual Basic for Applications language and the Microsoft Project object collection are discussed in greater detail. As part of that discussion, the two problems with the macros will be corrected.

Using Visual Basic for Applications

Understanding the Project object model

To effectively use VBA with Project, you need to understand the organization of the Project Objects.

Understanding the language

Visual Basic for Applications is a programming language that is very versatile and supportive. You do have to understand what you are looking at.

Using VBA within Project

You can take advantage of VBA to create easier mechanisms to view your project and its associated objects.

In the previous chapter, you were introduced to the method for capturing keystrokes to automate tasks that you do frequently. These sets of captured keystrokes are known as macros. Microsoft Project actually stored these captured keystrokes in a stored procedure in Visual Basic for Applications. Visual Basic for Applications is the shared macro programming language across the Microsoft Office platform.

Visual Basic for Applications allows you to learn one set of base programming components, and then as you need to automate tasks, you will only have to learn the product specific components. These product specific components are referred to as the object model.

This chapter is designed to give you an introduction to the Visual Basic for Applications environment. It will introduce you to some of the basic language components as well as the Microsoft Project 98 object model. This is how you will edit your macros. It allows you to access the tasks, schedules, and resources. ■

The Project Object Model

As you put together your project, you have been taking advantage of many Project objects without realizing it. You create tasks, assign durations, assign resources, and so on. All of these are part of the Microsoft Project Object model. To get a good start on working with and understanding Visual Basic for Applications, this object model is the place to start.

Any object model in the Microsoft family of products consists of four components. Each entity that can be manipulated by the user is referred to as an *object*. If the user can create more than one of these entities they are part of a *collection*. Each object and collection has certain characteristics. These characteristics are known as *properties*. There are also certain actions that can be performed on or to an object. These are known as *methods*. For instance, in Microsoft Project, when a user creates a task, it is an object. It is part of the Tasks collection. When you give the task a name, duration, start date, end date, and so on, these are all properties. In Chapter 25, when we created a macro to format the summary tasks, the ColumnBestFit method was used to format the column widths.

All of the object models for Microsoft products are represented as a hierarchy of objects in their collections. This hierarchy is often represented graphically as shown in Figure 26.1. Here you can see the collections for the objects for access with Visual Basic for Applications.

The *Application* Object

At the top of the model is the Application object. It is the central object for accessing all other Project objects as well as methods and properties. Visual Basic for Applications allows you to access your project from within Microsoft Project or from another application. When you are writing your macros in Microsoft Project the Application object is automatically referenced from inside Project and does not need to be identified in your VBA code.

N O T E   If you are accessing Project from an outside source like Microsoft Access, you will need to declare the Project object type and create an object using its class. If you are creating a VBA function in another application to access a project plan, you would need to include the following lines of code:

```
Dim pjProject as Project
Set pjProject = CreateObject(MSProject.Projects)
```

These lines will only work if you have set your references to the MS Project 8.0 library. To set your references follow these steps:

1. Open the Visual Basic Editor window.
2. Choose Tools, References.
3. Select Microsoft Project 8.0 Object Library.
4. Choose OK. ▓

Under the Application object, you can access the Projects, Windows, Cell, Selection, Assistant, Command Bars, and VBE objects and collections. The Project object is the one you will work with the most because most of the functionality is stored with the Project. The Window collections give you access to adjusting the contents of a particular window as well as the placement of the panes with the Pane object.

FIG. 26.1

The Microsoft Project object model shows the hierarchy of objects for Microsoft Project.

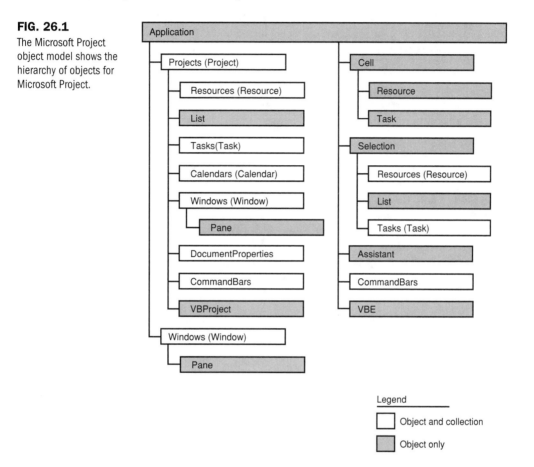

Legend

☐ Object and collection

▨ Object only

The Cell object allows you to determine which cell has the focus. Project is similar to Excel in that each task is stored in a row with the specific fields for that task stored in columns. Each cell will have different objects associated with it, depending on how you are viewing your project.

The Selection object keeps track of what a user has selected in a window. Again, there is a similarity with Excel. The user can place the cell pointer in a single cell or select several rows or columns at a time with the Shift or Ctrl keys. There will be different objects associated with a selection depending on how you are viewing your project.

The last three objects are more generic within the Microsoft family. The Assistant object allows you to get information about the Assistant; the Command Bars object allows you to get information about the command bars in use; and the VBE object gives you access to the different Visual Basic for Applications components in use in your program.

In Chapter 25, "Using Macros in Microsoft Project," one of the decisions was where to store the macro. If it was something you were going to access from several projects, you stored it in the Global.MPP file. The Application object has some properties to make the job of creating a generic macro easier.

When you create a generic macro, you will need to verify what the user is working with when the macro is executed. The Application object has ActiveProject, ActiveWindow, ActiveCell, and ActiveSelection properties to identify the user's location. These are very useful when you are trying to make your code useful for more than one project.

N O T E You may notice that the ActiveProject, ActiveWindow, ActiveCell, and ActiveSelection properties are run together with no spaces between words. This is a common practice in Visual Basic for Applications. It does take some getting used to when writing your Visual Basic for Applications code. ▪

The *Project* Object

The Project object is the object used to access information regarding your project as well as change the settings for a project. Microsoft Project allows you to open more than one project at a time. Each project becomes a member of the Project collection.

Each project has properties that can be used to identify it to the system. Identifying a project is important when you are working with more than one project or accessing it from an outside source.

When you create any type of file in a Microsoft application, you have the opportunity to set up its document properties like you can with all files. The Project object has corresponding properties to access the information stored in the document properties like *Author*, *Title*, *Company*, and *Comments*. To be able to take advantage of these properties in your programming, it does require that they are set in the beginning. This means that you need to do some error handling or force the user to complete the document properties. One simple way to accomplish this is to prompt the user with the document properties as the project is saved. These properties can be set in the Options dialog box on the General Tab.

Another tool for project management is the Project, Project Information command. This command opens the Project Information dialog box. This dialog box allows you to set the beginning or ending date for a project. It also allows the user to view the statistics for a project. These are also available through VBA.

The ProjectStart and ProjectFinish properties are for getting to the beginning and end of the project. The Start and Finish properties retrieve the Planned Start and Finish for a project, and ActualStart and ActualFinish help to track your actual progress.

These multiple starts and finishes are the first level of complexity in Project. Since Project allows you to monitor progress for a project, you will continue to add data as you manage your project. To support time and cost tracking, you will create a project with `ProjectStart` and `ProjectFinish`. When you have completed the plan, you will save a baseline. As tasks are completed you begin to get actual dates and times. These can be compared to evaluate performance. Most of this tracking will be on a task basis rather than on a project basis.

In addition to properties, you have three collections and one object to assist you with your automation tasks. You have a `Resource Object` collection for managing your resources such as people and equipment. The `List` object assists with Project environment management; the `Task` collection stores the project's individual tasks; and the `Calendar` collection controls the schedules used to plan the tasks.

The *Resource* Object

To manage the project resources, the `Resource` object and its collection provide access to the information concerning a resource. There are 38 properties for tracking resources.

There is an ID which is displayed for a resource as well as a UniqueID that will not change as resources are moved and added to the collection. Each resource has a Name and Initials. It can also have a Group to identify its department or division and a Code which could indicate a billing code or any other type of code. There is also an `EmailAddress` property if you are managing via e-mail.

To calculate the task cost, a resource must have an associated Cost. This is often another management issue for a project. Personnel is often strict about releasing pay information. Your corporate policy may prohibit you from using actual cost figures. You may want to invent dummy costs just to give you some figures to work with. It won't be completely accurate, but it will at least give you a framework for your analysis.

In addition to Cost, there are the `CostPerUse`, `AccrueAt`, `MaxUnits` `OvertimeRate`, and `OvertimeWork` properties, to help you with resource availability. To track resource use there are also `Work`, `%WorkComplete`, `WorkVariance`, `BaselineCost`, `BaselineWork`, `ActualCost`, `ActualWork`, `RemainingCost`, `RemainingWork` `CostVariance`, `Peak`, and `OverAllocated` properties.

There is a Notes field for miscellaneous comments, Objects and Linked fields for OLE links, and Text1-5 for additional strings. There is also BaseCalendar to indicate which calendar is used by a resource.

The *List* Object

The `List` object is one that doesn't have an obvious use in Project. It is the object that stores information concerning the Project infrastructure. It contains information about the field identification numbers, field names, resource filters, resource tables, resource views, task filters, task tables, or task views.

Unlike a workbook or a document which both have only one way to view your data, Project allows you to view and analyze your data in many ways. This is accomplished with views like the Gantt Chart, PERT chart, and Calendar. The `List` object gives you access to the different types of views created for a project. This allows you to automate view switching.

The *Task* Object

The Task object is one of the central building blocks for your project. Your objective for your project is broken down into manageable components that are called *tasks*. Each task is stored in the Task collection for the project. The Task object can be used to take action on each task to retrieve information about a task, and to evaluate the progress of the task. The Task object has property values to represent each of the 115 fields available. These properties are very useful for evaluating performance or loading them into another application like Access. They explain what information is tracked in Project.

When you want to automate task management, the first thing to do is to identify the project tasks. This seems easy, but it is a little more difficult depending on which Project options you are utilizing. When you look at the default view, the Gantt chart, the first field is the ID field. The ID field contains an assigned number to identify the tasks visually in the order they are presented. This is useful for managing the project, but it is not a static reference.

For accessing tasks from a macro, you want an ID number that will not change. When a task is created it is assigned a UniqueID. This is an identification number for the task regardless of where it is moved within the project. The Created property tracks the date and time a task was created. There is also a Project property to identify the project of which the task is a part. Another property is WBS, which stands for Work Breakdown Structure. Project supports the use of legal or military numbering for reference purposes. The hierarchy of tasks can be displayed by using the WBS property.

Once a task has been identified, you will want to access information about that task. When you are working with the Gantt chart view, you are only seeing a small portion of the fields available.

When you use Project, the first step is to create a plan. This is often done with the default view. The Gantt Chart shows the ID property along with the Indicators and Name properties. It also indicates a Duration which is the schedule duration for a project, as well as the Start and Finish of a task. These fields are only the beginning of the planning support offered through Project.

The next column is Predecessors. When you are creating a project plan, many tasks are dependent on the completion of other tasks. In Project terminology, this is known as creating a link. If a task is dependent on another task, that other task is its Predecessor and there can be more than one predecessor. If a task has a dependency, it will most likely have a Successor (unless the task is the last task in the project). These are stored in the following properties: Predecessors, UniqueIDPredecessors, Successors, and UniqueIDSuccessors.

If you are not using the default linking, you can set up constraints. By default when a task is linked it has a Finish to Start link. If you need tasks to finish at the same time, you can set up a Finish to Finish link. There are several types of links, but they are all stored in the ConstraintType and ConstraintDate properties.

The last column is ResourceNames. When you add a task, you will assign a resource or several resources to accomplish this task. You can also access the ResourceGroup and

ResourceInitials. When you assign a resource you will indicate whether that resource will affect the Duration by setting the Fixed property.

Behind the scenes, Project takes these settings and calculates some additional field data. There is Work which is the amount of time (effort) resources will spend working on tasks, calculated in minutes and Cost indicating the scheduled cost of the task. FixedCost tracks the fixed portion of a task. The BCWS (Budgeted Cost of Work Scheduled) is also calculated.

There are other properties that you may be unaware of setting as you create your project. As you create your project, you can create subtasks. To create a subtask, you use the Indent button. You are setting the OutlineLevel property for the task and the task above it will become a summary task.

If a task represents a moment in time to evaluate the progress, it is a Milestone. Milestone tasks are created with a duration of 0, and are accessed with the Milestone property. If a task is going to affect the finish of the project, it is considered part of the Critical Path. This is tracked with a Critical property.

Additional information about the tasks is available. You can tell whether subtasks are visible with the RollUp property and whether a task is marked with the Marked property. You can access any notes using the Notes property. You can tell whether a bar is displayed in the Gantt chart with the HideBar property.

If you are managing your project using e-mail, you have properties to assist with that part of the process. There is Contact to identify the e-mail contact, Confirmed to indicate whether it has been accepted by the contact, and UpdateNeeded to determine whether it needs to be updated via e-mail.

Part VIII Ch 26

Once the project is developed, you save the project with a baseline. A baseline is a stored or saved version of the schedule at a particular moment. If you do not lock your project by assigning a baseline, you have no way to compare your performance. When you save your project with a baseline, it takes the Duration, Start, and Finish and posts them to BaselineDuration, BaselineStart, and BaselineFinish. It then calculates the BaselineCost and BaselineWork.

Once the baseline is created, you are then ready to begin monitoring progress. As tasks are completed, actual figures will be entered. There is ActualCost, ActualDuration, ActualFinish, and ActualStart that can be entered for this purpose. These fields and their associated properties give you access to some analysis fields. %Complete, %WorkComplete, and ActualWork will be calculated for you as well as RemainingCost, RemainingDuration, and RemainingWork. There is also DurationVariance between the Baseline and the Actual durations. In addition there are the StartVariance, FinishVariance, CostVariance, and WorkVariance properties as well. BCWP (Budgeted Cost of Work Performed) calculates the cost using the percentage of work completed, CV (Earned Value Cost Variance) compares the baseline cost with the actual cost and SV (Earned Value Schedule Variance) compares the baseline cost with the scheduled cost; these properties will also be calculated for those tasks that are in progress.

Project also anticipates schedule changes. You have the opportunity to resave your baseline. When you do, you can preserve the original baseline by saving it to some special fields. There are 10 of each of these to accommodate schedule changes. There is Cost1-10, Duration1-10, Start1-10, Finish1-10. Another issue that comes up in project management is the overallocation of resources. When this happens, you can manipulate the schedule by adjusting the start and finish dates for tasks.

A task may be able to slide in the process. It may be able to support an `EarlyStart`, `EarlyFinish`, `LateStart`, or `LateFinish`. It may also be suspended by setting `Delay` and `Resume` or `ResumeNoEarlierThan`. These will be tracked with `FreeSlack` and `TotalSlack` properties. Project also has a function called Leveling which uses the settings of these properties to adjust the schedule to tackle allocation issues. If two tasks still overlap, it will use the `Priority` property to see which will be handled first.

Project is designed to be as flexible as possible. There is Flag1-10 to accommodate some additional Boolean factors associated with a task. There is Number1-5 to accommodate any miscellaneous numeric information and Text1-10 for any string information.

There are also `LinkedFields` and `Objects` to indicate whether the task is being used for OLE support. Microsoft Project 98 also has the `HyperLink`, `HyperLinkAddress`, `HyperLinkHREF`, and `HyperLinkSubaddress` to support the inclusion and manipulation of Internet site references.

All of these properties and their corresponding fields are available for use with VBA. You can use them for many task management functions.

The *Calendar* Object

The last object is the `Calendar` object and its associated collection. Calendars indicate working hours, holidays and nonworking time. You can set up a calendar for a project, or for resources or resource groups. The calendars are used to determine the duration of the project.

By default every project and all of its resources use the Base Calendar. You can use the `BaseCalendar` property for the Resource to assign it a different calendar. The Base Calendar uses a standard Monday-Friday work week with 8 a.m. to 12 p.m. and 1 p.m. to 5 p.m. working hours. At the very least, you may want to cut that back to six hours to accommodate miscellaneous tasks such as answering the phone.

Once the calendar is set up, you can access its properties by using the `Calendar` object. It has a `Name` property so that it can be referenced as a BaseCalendar for a resource. It also has a `BaseCalendar` property. When you create a new Calendar, you use one of the base calendars as a model for a special resource calendar. It can be modified with methods like `Weekdays` to complete an action on a particular day of a calendar or with Year to set a holiday for a particular day of a year.

Understanding VBA

In addition to understanding how Visual Basic for Applications views your project through the object model, there is also some basic terminology for Visual Basic for Applications that needs to be understood. When you begin working with Visual Basic for Applications directly, you rely on capturing keystrokes less and less. You need to have some basic knowledge of the language structure. This chapter doesn't offer adequate space for a complete discussion of Visual Basic for Applications. For further information, you may find *Special Edition Using Visual Basic for Applications 5*, published by Que, to be of value.

You will need to understand that you have been creating procedures. You may also want to manage temporary types of information and perform some testing of information in your project file. You may also want to prevent errors. This is the purpose of this section.

Understanding Procedures

To begin with, a macro as referenced in Chapter 25 is actually a Visual Basic for Applications *procedure*. This term is clearly evident when looking at your macro in the Code window in the Visual Basic editor (see Figure 26.2).

FIG. 26.2
The SummaryTask-Format macro clearly indicates what type of procedure it is with the beginning and ending lines.

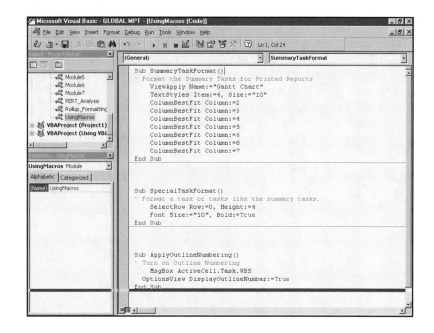

There are three types of procedures that can be created in Visual Basic for Applications. The *subprocedure* is a procedure that executes the steps indicated in the code lines. *Functions* execute a series of steps to return a value. The last type is a *property,* which is used to create a custom property for a custom object and is used in advanced visual basic programming.

For most purposes, you will be creating subprocedures. A subprocedure is also what is created when you capture your keystrokes. To designate the type of procedure created as a subprocedure, the first line starts with the Sub keyword and is followed by the name of the procedure.

The name of the procedure must follow the naming conventions. The name can contain any character excluding the space, period, exclamation, @, &, $, or #. It must begin with a letter and cannot exceed 255 characters. You also have to avoid the names of any language components like properties, methods, and functions. Although not a requirement, it is suggested that you use a mixed-case name to make it more readable.

Following the procedure, there is a set of parentheses for any arguments expected by the procedure. (An argument is some information that is needed for the procedure to work.) Next come the steps or actions for the procedure. Finally, the last line of the procedure is the End Sub line to indicate that the steps are concluded.

Understanding Variables and Constants

As you create more of your Visual Basic for Applications code, there will be times when you need to store information temporarily. This is especially important when comparing values. To allow you to do this in your procedure, Visual Basic for Applications supports the use of *variables*. A variable is technically a location in memory to store information for later use.

When you are creating Visual Basic for Applications code, you will want to take advantage of variables. You can create them by setting a variable equal to a value, but this can make your code harder to understand and can lead to confusion. It is recommended that you declare your variables before using them. This is done with a declarations statement. When you declare your variables, you have several decisions to make. The first is what you will need to access this variable. If its use will be limited to the procedure, you can declare the variable as a local variable. No other procedure will have access to the contents of this variable. This type of variable is declared using the Dim statement.

If you need to access the contents of a variable from more than one procedure, you need to declare the variable differently. You can declare a procedure to be used by all procedures in a *module*. When you edited your macro in Chapter 25, you may have noticed that your macro was stored in a module. You can declare a variable to be accessed by all procedures in a module with the *Private* keyword. You can also make the variable available to all macros. This is accomplished with the *Public* keyword.

After you have determined what type of declaration is needed, you need to determine what type of variable is needed. Visual Basic for Applications supports variables of different types. The type of variable that is chosen will have a direct effect on the kind of information that can be stored in it. Visual Basic for Applications supports the following types of data. You can create a Boolean variable to support True or False information. You can create Byte, Integer, Long, Currency, Decimal, Single, or Double variables to store different sizes of numbers.

The Date type of variable supports information for dates and times. The String variable supports any text information. There is also the Object variable for manipulating objects from the object model. For information concerning the size of the numbers and how much room they take in memory, please refer to Microsoft Projects On-Line Help. To access this information, follow these steps:

1. Select Help, Contents and Index.
2. Select the Index tab.
3. Type in **data types, variables**.
4. Select Data Type Summary from the Topics Found dialog box.

If you fail to specify the data type for your variable, you will get a Variant data type. It will read the data in and then determine which way to store the information. This can result in a lot of wasted space. Each variable takes up room in memory, and the variant type uses more space to accommodate its flexibility.

You should use naming conventions when naming your variables to help you recognize them as you use them. The same rules apply here as they do for naming procedures, but it is recommended that you use a prefix to indicate what type of variable it is. Table 26.1 indicates the recommended prefixes:

Table 26.1   Recommended Variable Prefixes

Data Type	Recommended Prefix
Boolean	bln
Byte	byt
Integer	i
Long	l
Currency	cur
Single	sng
Double	dbl
Date	dt
String	str
Variant	v
Object	obj

Part

VIII

Ch

26

If you needed a string variable for access in one procedure, you could create a local variable with the following line of code:

```
Dim strTaskName as String
```

The other type of data you use as you create a macro procedure is a constant. Unlike variables, the information in a constant doesn't change during the execution of the macro. There are two types of constants you use. There are constants you create yourself and ones that are built into the language. The built-in constants are part of the methods, functions, and statements you use to create your code. Several examples of these are introduced in later sections.

Yet another type is the userdefined constant. The syntax for declaring a constant is similar to that of declaring a variable. The difference is the keyword. To define a constant, you use the Const keyword. For instance, if you need a string constant, the syntax would be:

```
Const strNAME as String = "Your Name"
```

In this way, you can declare and assign a value simultaneously. This is a local constant. If you need a module level or global level constant you add the Private or Public keyword in front of the Const keyword.

Understanding Program Control Mechanisms

Another element of creating Visual Basic for Applications code is the ability to test conditions and take actions based on the result of your test. In programming terminology this is called program control. This will also make your macros more effective. As it was shown in the ApplyOutlineNumbering macro, taking action in a macro is not enough. You often need to see what state the project is in first.

Visual Basic for Applications offers eight program control structures to facilitate the macro processing. The simplest is the If...Then...Else structure. This structure allows you to test an expression and then, based on the result, take various actions. The syntax to use is:

```
If expression then
        statements to execute
Else
        statements to execute
End If
```

This syntax has several forms. It can test a condition and, if it is true, execute steps with nothing specified as the else result. It can also test multiple conditions with the use of the ElseIf keyword. This will be used to solve the problem with the ApplyOutlineNumbering macro mentioned in Chapter 25.

If you need to take different actions based on a range of values, the Select Case structure might be a better choice. It allows for multiple settings for one variable or property. The syntax is:

```
Select Case caseexpression
        Case value1
                statements to execute
        Case value2
                statements to execute
        Case valuen
                statements to execute
End Select
```

This can support many test values. It is great for testing property settings for project objects. Another type of program control supports the need to repeat a series of actions until or while a condition is met or for a certain number of times.

The first loop is the Do...Loop. This can execute actions while a condition is met or until a condition is met, depending upon which keyword is used. The syntax is:

```
Do (While or Until) testexpression
        statements to execute
Loop
```

You can also test after executing the statements once by changing the position of the keyword.

```
Do
        statements to execute
Loop (While or Until) testexpression
```

An older form of these loops is also supported. It is called the While...Wend loop. The While...Wend loop works exactly like the Do While loop. It tests a condition to see if it is true, and if it is, it executes the statements enclosed in the structure. The syntax is:

```
While testexpression
        statements to execute
Wend
```

There is also a counting loop called the For...Next loop. This allows you to repeat an action a certain number of times. The syntax is:

```
For counter = 1 to n
        statements to execute
Next counter
```

There is also a special format of this loop that works with collections. The For Each...Next loop cycles through all of the objects in a collection to allow you to take action on each one. The syntax is:

```
For Each object In group
        statements to execute
Next object
```

The next structure is not a program control structure because it doesn't branch, but it is still useful. If you need to set several properties for an object, you may want to use the With...End With. This can simplify the code and make it more readable. The syntax is:

```
With object
        statements
End With
```

The last structure is the GoTo statement. If you dabbled with Basic programming in the past you might be familiar with this one. It allows you to branch to another location in your code. In Visual Basic for Applications, this is reserved for error handling. Since you do not have line numbers to go to, you need to use line labels. Examples of this are shown in the following section dealing with error handling.

Part

VIII

Ch

26

Understanding Error Handling

As illustrated with the special formatting macro, not all macros are foolproof. If you need to have a specific view selected or be in a particular location, you may have some trouble. In Visual Basic for Applications, you can minimize the time it takes to recover from a problem by implementing error handling.

First of all, be aware that there are two types of errors. The first type of error is the result of a mistake as it is created. This type of problem is often caught when you run through the macro to make sure it works. This is known as debugging. The Visual Basic Editor offers many tools to assist you with debugging. There is the ability to step through your code, set up break points, and watch the values of variables as your code executes. All of these are valuable, but they will not solve all of the problems.

There are problems that are unavoidable like the problem with the SpecialFormatting macro. You can not guarantee that the user will have the correct view selected. This is known as a runtime error. This you cannot debug. You will have to write additional code to tackle this problem. This is known as error trapping. Every time an error occurs with your macro an error code is generated. This code needs to be trapped and dealt with in your code. To trap the error, the On Error statement can be used in conjunction with a special object called Err to trap the error number and take appropriate action.

There are several approaches to tackling errors. You can branch to a central location to solve the problem with the GoTo statement to handle the error in line with code directly following, or in some cases, postpone the error handling until a later time.

If you branch to another location, you also have to determine how to proceed after the resolution. You can accomplish this by using the Resume, Resume Next, or Exit Sub statements. Resume picks up with the line that caused the problem, Resume Next picks up with the line below, and Exit Sub will halt the execution of the macro.

For this chapter, a simple error trap will be set to see what view is used to determine if it is possible to apply the special formatting. All of these concepts will be easier to understand with a little practical application. Let's start by correcting the problems with the macros from Chapter 25.

Correcting the Problem with the Outline Macro

In Chapter 25, "Using Macros in Microsoft Project," the ApplyOutlineNumbering macro did a good job, but it only worked one way. You could turn outline numbering on but you couldn't turn it off with the same macro. This is where working with the Visual Basic Editor can be helpful.

When you look at the ApplyOutlineNumbering macro in the Visual Basic editor, it has one action. It uses the OptionsView method to turn the outline numbering on. The problem with using the OptionsView method is that there isn't a way to test to see whether one of the options is turned on or off. This can make toggling the option difficult, but this isn't the only way to view the outline numbers.

The outline numbers are also stored in the WBS field. You can test whether you are viewing this field and then take appropriate action. The revised macro would resemble the one shown in the following code:

```
Sub ApplyOutlineNumberingRevised()
'   ApplyOutlineNumberingRevised displays the WBS field instead of
'   altering the Options settings
    SelectColumn Column:=2
    If ActiveCell.FieldName = "Indicators" Then
        ColumnDelete
        TableEdit Name:="&Entry", TaskTable:=True, NewName:="", _
            FieldName:="", NewFieldName:="WBS", Title:="", Width:=10, _
            Align:=2, ShowInMenu:=True, LockFirstColumn:=True, _
            DateFormat:=255, RowHeight:=1, ColumnPosition:=0, _
            AlignTitle:=1
        TableApply Name:="&Entry"
        ColumnBestFit Column:=2
    ElseIf ActiveCell.FieldName = "Task Name" Then
        TableEdit Name:="&Entry", TaskTable:=True, NewName:="", _
            FieldName:="", NewFieldName:="WBS", Title:="", Width:=10, _
            Align:=2, ShowInMenu:=True, LockFirstColumn:=True, _
            DateFormat:=255, RowHeight:=1, ColumnPosition:=0, _
            AlignTitle:=1
        TableApply Name:="&Entry"
        ColumnBestFit Column:=2
    ElseIf ActiveCell.FieldName = "WBS" Then
        ColumnDelete
        TableEdit Name:="&Entry", TaskTable:=True, NewName:="", _
            FieldName:="", NewFieldName:="Indicators", Title:="", Width:=10, _
            Align:=2, ShowInMenu:=True, LockFirstColumn:=True, _
            DateFormat:=255, RowHeight:=1, ColumnPosition:=0, _
            AlignTitle:=1
        TableApply Name:="&Entry"
        ColumnBestFit Column:=2
    Else
        Dim lResponse As Long, strMessage As String
        Dim lOptions As Long, strTitle As String
        strMessage = "The first field doesn't match the criteria, "
          strMessage = strMessage & "do you wish to continue?"
        lOptions = vbQuestion + vbYesNo
        strTitle = "Unexpected Field"
        lResponse = MsgBox(strMessage, lOptions, strTitle)
        If lResponse = vbYes Then
            TableEdit Name:="&Entry", TaskTable:=True, NewName:="", _
                FieldName:="", NewFieldName:="Indicators", Title:="", _
                Width:=10, Align:=2, ShowInMenu:=True, _
                LockFirstColumn:=True, DateFormat:=255, _
                RowHeight:=1, ColumnPosition:=0, AlignTitle:=1
            TableApply Name:="&Entry"
            ColumnBestFit Column:=2
        End If
    End If
End Sub
```

This new approach requires more code and involves the use of several methods and properties. It eliminates the single `OptionsView` method and replaces it with code to display the WBS column.

Follow the previous code lines as the rest of this section takes you through each line of code. To begin, you have to select the first selectable column. This is done with the `SelectColumn` method. Most methods need to have specific information to operate. This information is specified with arguments. Visual Basic for Applications supports the use of *named arguments* to make reading the code easier. For instance, the `SelectColumn` method needs to know which column. It is followed by a space and `Column:=2`. The `Column` is the argument, and you are assigning the value 2 to it.

When beginning a macro, you will find it helpful to capture as much of your macro as possible. Capturing the keystrokes for deleting and inserting the new columns will save you quite a bit of typing. If you were to type this line of code instead of capturing the keystrokes, you could get some assistance with argument prompting. Visual Basic for Applications offers argument prompting to assist you with typing in the necessary arguments (see Figure 26.3).

FIG. 26.3

The Argument Prompt can assist you with completing the arguments needed by a method or function.

Argument Prompt

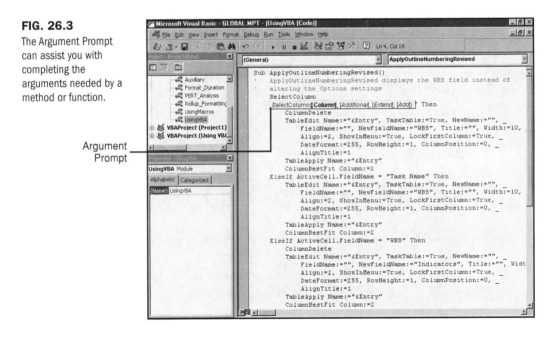

Next, you have to test the `FieldName` property. The testing can be done with the `If...Then... Else` structure. This control structure can support the testing of several values. It gives you an opportunity to take different actions based on the current settings.

The first test allows you to conserve on space. If column 2 is the Indicators field, you may want to delete it with the `ColumnDelete` method. Next, the `TableEdit` method would be needed to set the new column, and the `TableApply` method would be used to display the new arrangement. The last item is to set the column width. This is accomplished with the ColumnBestFit method used in the previous chapter.

With the TableEdit method, you get to see another programming convention. Many of the code lines require many arguments and would be difficult to read on-screen. Visual Basic for Applications allows you to split code lines. At the end of the line you will see a space followed by an underscore. This allows you to break a single line of code into several to make it more readable. A logical place for this separation is after an argument assignment. Each argument is separated from the next with a comma. It makes for a good break.

The next test is to determine whether the Task Name is the second column. In that case, there isn't a need to delete the Indicators column. You can just add the new WBS field. The third test determines whether the WBS field is already displayed. If it is, it is reset to display the Indicators column.

The last part is just a plain Else with no additional expression to test. There are many fields. You do not need to test for all of them. Rather than test for each one, you can ask the user whether to continue. This is accomplished with the MsgBox function. This is a built-in function. You indicate what question you want to ask, what type of box you want and what you want in a title bar. In this case, the arguments can be set up as variables. Notice that the message to the user is split between two lines, but it isn't done with the line continuation. Visual Basic for Applications doesn't like to break string assignments. Here you are adding the first part of the message and then adding the last part to the first part.

The second argument is the type of message box displayed. This is done with built-in constants, vbQuestion and vbYesNo. This indicates the type of graphic to display and the type of buttons to make available for the user to respond.

The result is the display of a common message box (see Figure 26.4) that the user can respond to and indicate a choice. This is tested with another field in the first available column.

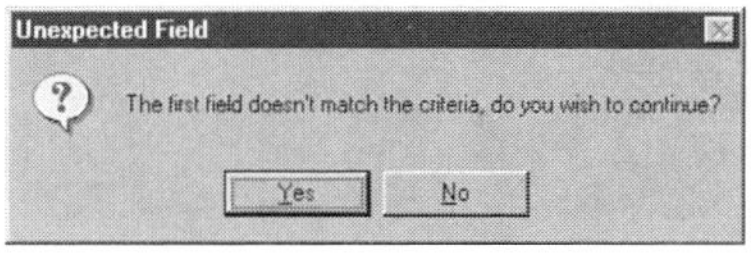

FIG. 26.4
The common message box can be used to communicate with the user and solicit responses.

Correcting the Problem with the Special Formatting Macro

In Chapter 25, "Using Macros in Microsoft Project," the SpecialTaskFormat macro was captured to format a task similar to that of one of the summary tasks so that it wouldn't blend into the background and seem less important. The problem was that if the user did not have a task list selected, the macro would fail. It would display the dialog box (see Figure 26.5) that could land the user in the debug mode for the macro.

FIG. 26.5

The Microsoft Visual Basic Error dialog box can be confusing to some users.

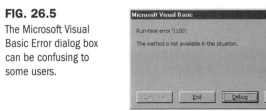

To clean up the performance of the macro, you may want to consider implementing error handling. Rather than allowing Visual Basic to display an error dialog box, you can take advantage of error handling and use the MsgBox to display a slightly less threatening message. The result could resemble the SpecialTaskFormatRevised macro as shown in the following code:

```
Sub SpecialTaskFormatRevised()
' Format a task or tasks like the summary tasks.
    On Error GoTo FormatErr
    SelectRow Row:=0, Height:=4
    Font Size:="10", Bold:=True
    Exit Sub
FormatErr:
    Dim strMessage As String, lOptions As Long, strTitle As String
    If Err.Number = 1100 Then
        strMessage = "You need to be viewing a Task List "
        strMessage = strMessage & "to apply special formatting"
        lOptions = vbInformation + vbOKOnly
        strTitle = "Invalid View"
        MsgBox strMessage, lOptions, strTitle
        Exit Sub
    Else
        strMessage = "Unexpected Error, Error " & Err.Number
        strMessage = strMessage & ", " & Err.Description
        lOptions = vbInformation + vbOKOnly
        strTitle = "Unexpected Error"
        MsgBox strMessage, lOptions, strTitle
    End If
End Sub
```

To add error handling, you can circumvent Visual Basic's handling of any problems. To implement error handling, the first step is to set up the error trap. This is accomplished with the first line of code. The code line, On Error Goto FormatErr, sets up the error trap and indicates that should a problem occur the code should branch to the FormatErr line label.

The next two lines are the original macro. These actually perform the formatting. This is followed by the Exit Sub statement and will end the execution of the macro. This will avoid executing the error handling unless there is a problem.

The next line is the line label for the error handling code. Older versions of BASIC had line numbers, but those are no longer applicable with Visual Basic. Instead, you can branch to a line label. Line labels also have naming conventions like procedures and variables. They must follow all of those rules, but they must also follow some additional rules. You may have noticed that, to make the code easier to read, the code lines have been indented to show the program flow. A line label cannot be indented. It must be flush with the left margin. This puts it in line with the Sub and End Sub lines. It must be followed by a colon.

In the case of the problem encountered by the formatting macro, no action needs to be taken to correct the problem, but the user needs to be notified. The MsgBox can be used as a function, as seen in the previous macro. It will return a value from the user. It can also be used as a statement. This one performs the action of displaying the dialog box, but doesn't return a response.

In this case, you don't want the user to be left in the Visual Basic Editor if they accidentally clicked on the Debug button. Here again the If...Then...Else structure is used. It first tests the Err object to see if the Number property is 1100. This is the number that was displayed with the Visual Basic dialog box. If that is the case, it displays the message dialog box with the Information icon and just an OK button to notify the user that the SpecialTaskFormat macro cannot be used at this time (see Figure 26.6).

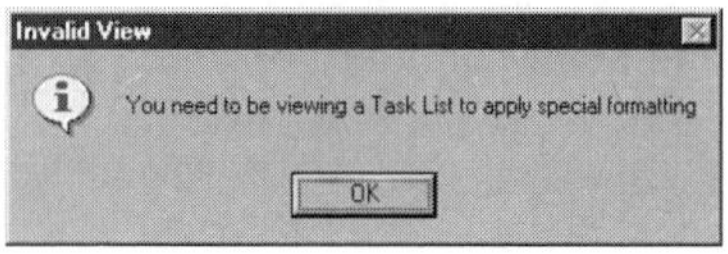

FIG. 26.6
The formatting message box eliminates the possibility that the user will be inadvertently sent to the Visual Basic Editor.

Invalid View
You need to be viewing a Task List to apply special formatting
OK

The Else portion of the error handler is tackling any other error that crops up by displaying the Err object's Number and Description properties. That is just to cover all possibilities. Your macro doesn't operate in a vacuum. It is possible that something else will cause a problem.

It is a good idea to implement error handling with all of your macros. If there is a possibility for something to go wrong during execution, you will want to protect the user from getting into an area for which they aren't prepared. In the ApplyOutlineNumberingRevised macro, it is also possible to be in a view that will not support the action. The same type of change to accommodate error handling would be beneficial.

Part
VIII

Ch

26

Exploring Macro Possibilities

Visual Basic for Applications was added to give you a method for automating the many tasks that you need to accomplish on a daily basis. You can automate selection of views, reporting, and data entry as well as many communication activities. The language is quite extensive. One possible use for macros is to automate reporting.

Automating Summary Reporting Tasks

Project not only offers a variety of views, it also has many reports to display your progress. As with the views, the process for accessing reports can be cumbersome. One task that you may find particularly cumbersome is generating reports for management to bring them up-to-date on a project. There are many steps just to generate one report. For example, it takes seven steps just to get the Project Summary:

1. Select <u>V</u>iew, <u>R</u>eports.
2. Select <u>O</u>verview in the Reports dialog box (see Figure 26.7).
3. Choose <u>S</u>elect.

FIG. 26.7

The Reports dialog box allows you to select a category of reports.

4. Select a specific report like <u>P</u>roject Summary.
5. Choose <u>S</u>elect.
6. Choose <u>P</u>rint.
7. Choose OK.

Step 5 brings up the report for this resource in Print Preview. You still need to select Print, check the settings, and send it to the printer. There are a minimum of seven steps to preview and print this one report.

VBA can provide a solution. There are two methods to give you access to your reports. The first method gives you a way to preview a report. It is `ReportPrintPreview`. It will take a given report and display it in Preview. It can complete all of the steps up to Step 6 of the manual process. The syntax is:

```
[object.]ReportPrintPreview name
```

The other option is to use the `ReportPrint` method. It skips the print preview part of the process. Putting this into a macro can eliminate a lot of work on your part. The syntax for this method is:

```
expression.ReportPrint(Name, FromPage, ToPage, PageBreaks, Draft, Copies,
FromDate, ToDate, Preview, Color)
```

The `Name` argument is the report name in double quotes. The `FromPage` and `ToPage` indicate a page range. The `PageBreaks` argument indicates whether to use manual page breaks or automatically set them. The `Draft` argument indicates the print quality. `ToDate` and `FromDate` allow you to set a date range. The `Preview` argument allows previewing with the method as well and the `Color` argument indicates whether to print in color.

The SummaryReporting macro automates the printing of five reports. This is a macro that you can create quickly by capturing the keystrokes. When you try to capture the printing of reports, the code will use the `ReportPrintPreview` method. It can be easily edited to eliminate the preview portion. If you are using all default settings for the other arguments, they can be omitted.

```
Sub SummaryReporting()
' This sends all reports requested by management once a week
' directly to the printer
    ReportPrint Name:="Project Summary"
    ReportPrint Name:="Top Level Tasks"
    ReportPrint Name:="Unstarted Tasks"
    ReportPrint Name:="Budget Report"
    ReportPrint Name:="Who Does What"
End Sub
```

From Here...

Microsoft Project is a very powerful application. It can assist with the tasks of creating, managing and evaluating performance during the implementation of a project. It is so useful because it offers the user a variety of ways to view and print the data.

The variety and number of ways to view and print the data creates one of the needs for VBA. VBA can be used to save many keystrokes to achieve the same perspective on the data. You can also create macros to change views and print and preview reports.

You can communicate with other applications like Outlook and you can optimize Access to create an archiving and historical analysis tool. Project can assist you with determining where your planning can be improved. For more information about using Visual Basic for Applications, take a look at *Special Edition Using Visual Basic for Applications 5*, published by Que. It offers a complete reference for programming with Visual Basic for Applications. It not only covers the language fundamentals, but it also gives useful insights into using Visual Basic for Applications with the other Microsoft Office products.

Part
VIII

Ch
26

CHAPTER 27

Customizing Toolbars, Menus, and Forms

The toolbars and menus in Microsoft Project provide an efficient means for you to interact with the projects you design. As you have discovered, commands on both the toolbars and menus are organized to group together the tasks you perform most often. You may also have discovered that while most of the toolbars and menus provide you with the commands you need, other commands may be unavailable or buried so deeply on a menu that they aren't convenient to use. Project provides a number of different features that let you customize the user interface to make your work easier and more efficient. With Project 98, often-used commands and macros can be made more readily accessible.

The forms that come installed in Microsoft Project may also need to be customized to allow you to view and edit project data by focusing on those fields of data that are important to *you*. Project enables you to customize these forms to better fit your needs. ∎

Adding or removing tools from toolbars

Learn how to tailor the existing toolbars to display those tools you need. Add new tools that represent commands which do not have a tool or the macros you've created.

Adding or removing commands from the menu bar

Find out how to edit the existing menu bars displayed in Microsoft Project. Once edited, the menu changes are permanent and available in all projects.

Creating new toolbars and menus

Learn how to create new toolbars, which can store the buttons you use most frequently without affecting the buttons on other toolbars. You can create your own custom menu options or menu bar.

Customizing the tool face

To make the tool buttons more useful, you can edit the design on the button, add or change the description, and add or change the ToolTip to the button.

Using and creating custom forms

Learn how to create custom forms and modify existing forms to create the fields of data and information you need.

Creating and Customizing Toolbars

Buttons contained on toolbars provide shortcuts for executing menu commands. The menu commands used most frequently are attached to specific buttons and positioned on toolbars according to the types of tasks they perform. For example, the second button on the Standard toolbar in Microsoft Project displays a picture of a file folder opening. Clicking the button displays the File Open dialog box, from which you choose a file to open. You would get the same result if you chose the Open command from the File menu. Because opening a file is a task you could conceivably perform frequently, Microsoft Project included a button on the Standard toolbar to reduce the number of steps you need to perform.

Microsoft has standardized its toolbars across applications so that those tasks common to all applications remain constant in their presentation on toolbars. As a result, once you become accustomed to using toolbar buttons in one application, you will recognize them in other applications. The Open button, for example, is available on the Standard toolbar of other Microsoft applications.

As you continue to work with Microsoft Project, you will find that some of the buttons on the toolbars are vital to the way you work, while others are rarely used. This is often determined by the type of work you do. In addition, you may find that there are tasks you perform frequently for which there are no toolbar buttons available. You can customize toolbars to remove the buttons you rarely use and replace them with buttons to help perform those tasks you do more frequently.

Each button on a toolbar runs a *macro*—a series of steps designed to perform a task. The example of clicking the Open button to display the File Open dialog box (described earlier) runs a macro that contains the two steps required to perform the same task using the menus. When you create simple macros to perform tasks you do most frequently, you can assign them to toolbar buttons. For example, if you were to create a simple macro designed to turn on the Project Summary task, you can assign a toolbar button to run the macro and include the button on a toolbar. Once it's assigned to a toolbar, all you have to do is click the toolbar button to perform the function.

In previous chapters, you may have created special views, tables, forms, or filters and found that they were stored as part of the project in which you created them. When you needed to use them in another project, you had to copy them into the new project file or to the GLOBAL.MPT. Customizing toolbars and menus is different because toolbars and menus are part of the *application* file rather than a *project* file. As a result, changing them makes them available to all projects you create or edit on your computer. They are stored as part of the GLOBAL.MPT file automatically. You can still copy them from the GLOBAL.MPT file to a project file when you want to include them in a file you are sending to someone else, or when you want to copy them to a different computer. Otherwise, copying them is not necessary.

Reviewing the Built-In Toolbars

Microsoft Project 98 includes 12 built-in toolbars that group tasks by type. Two of these toolbars appear by default when you start Microsoft Project. You may display any of the remaining 10 toolbars as you need them. Of the 12 toolbars, four are new in this version of Microsoft Project—Microsoft Project 95, Web, Analysis, and PERT Analysis.

The two default toolbars are:

- *Standard toolbar*. It provides access to the main Microsoft Project features. Buttons on the left end of this toolbar are found on the Standard toolbars of other Microsoft applications. Buttons on the right end of the toolbar are specific to Microsoft Project.

- *Formatting toolbar*. Buttons on this toolbar give you access to outlining, filters, and text formatting features. Many of the buttons on the right end of this toolbar are found on the Formatting toolbars of other Microsoft applications. Buttons on the left of this toolbar are frequently found on Outlining toolbars of other Microsoft applications.

The 10 additional toolbars included with Microsoft Project are:

- *Custom Forms toolbar*. Contains many of the buttons needed to customize tasks or resource information entry screens.

- *Drawing toolbar*. Provides access to graphic drawing tools for drawing figures and text boxes in the Gantt Chart.

- *Microsoft Project 95 toolbar*. Displays the Standard toolbar from Microsoft Project 95.

- *Resource Management toolbar*. Provides access to tools for resolving resource overallocations.

- *Tracking toolbar*. Provides access to the commands necessary to track progress and reschedule work on uncompleted tasks.

- *Visual Basic toolbar*. Displays buttons for recording, running, and editing macros.

- *Web toolbar*. Displays buttons that activate your World Wide Web browser, keep a list of your favorite Web sites, and assist you in moving through Web pages.

- *Workgroup toolbar*. Provides tools you can use to share project information with others in your workgroup.

- *Analysis toolbar*. Contains tools for adjusting and evaluating your project. Included on the toolbar are the Adjust Dates macro, a tool for activating the PERT Analysis toolbar, and an analysis tool for viewing your timescaled data in Microsoft Excel.

- *PERT Analysis toolbar*. Displays analysis tools for use with the PERT Chart view for indicating best-case, expected, and worst-case scenarios for task durations, start dates, and finish dates.

Many toolbar buttons are easy to identify, and their use is self-explanatory. The purpose of some buttons, however, is difficult to determine. To help identify these buttons, point to the button and pause briefly. The purpose of the button appears in the form of a *ToolTip*. When you

Part
VIII

Ch
27

need a more detailed description of a button, click the What's This command from the Help menu, and then click the button for which you need more information. A definition of the button appears.

Displaying Toolbars

Project enables you to show and hide toolbars using two different procedures. Perhaps the more efficient means is by selecting a toolbar from the Toolbar Shortcut menu. You can use the shortcut menu to select all toolbars except the Microsoft toolbar. Another way to select toolbars is through the Toolbars command. All toolbars are listed in the Toolbars menu. The procedures for displaying toolbars using both approaches are explained in the following sections.

The Toolbar Shortcut menu contains a listing of all toolbars (except the Microsoft toolbar) as well as a command that lets you customize toolbars. To activate the Shortcut menu, position the mouse pointer over one of the toolbars and click the right mouse button (see Figure 27.1). Notice that the Standard and Formatting toolbars have check marks next to them. These check marks indicate that the toolbars are currently displayed or active. Other toolbars do not contain check marks, indicating that they are inactive.

FIG. 27.1

The Toolbar shortcut menu lists all toolbars and identifies the toolbars that are displayed by a check mark. The menu can be used to display or hide individual toolbars.

| ✓ Standard |
| ✓ Formatting |
| Custom Forms |
| Drawing |
| Microsoft Project 95 |
| Resource Management |
| Tracking |
| Visual Basic |
| Web |
| Workgroup |
| Analysis |
| PERT Analysis |
| Customize... |

Choose a toolbar that isn't checked to display the toolbar. If you choose a toolbar that is already active, the check mark disappears, thereby hiding the toolbar.

 While the Shortcut menu provides a quick approach to showing and hiding toolbars, you can also select Toolbars from the View menu. Access to changing your toolbars has been made quicker by changing the Toolbars command to display a submenu instead of a dialog box. The choices are identical to those shown in Figure 27.1.

Positioning Toolbars on the Screen   Most toolbars are set to position themselves at a docking location at the top of the screen. Each toolbar you activate docks below other active toolbars in the order in which you activate them. Once a toolbar is displayed, however, you can move it from the top of the screen to a new position. Toolbars can be *docked* at the sides or bottom of the screen or *floated* in a small window of their own in the middle of the screen. Toolbars that have combination boxes (buttons with a text box and an entry-list arrow) can be floated or docked at the top or bottom of the screen. When docked on the sides of the screen, the combo boxes are not displayed. To reposition a toolbar, click the vertical separator bars that appear on the left edge of the toolbar or any separator bar in the toolbar. As you drag, the outline of the toolbar changes shape to fit the active position. When you have the toolbar placed where you want it, release the mouse button. Figure 27.2 identifies the separator bars and the outline that appears when moving a toolbar.

FIG. 27.2
Toolbars can be positioned on-screen to suit your taste.

Vertical separators (two places)

Gray outline

Docked Tracking toolbar

Floating Analysis toolbar

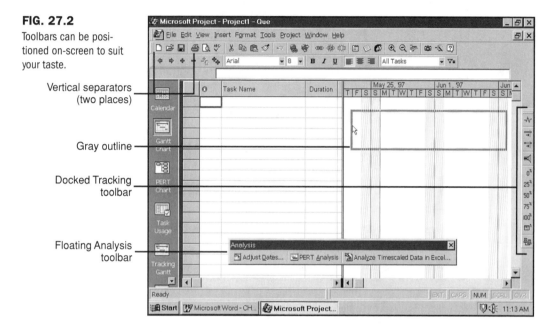

Notice that the floating toolbar has a title bar and a Close button. You can click the Close button to hide a floating toolbar or drag the title bar to dock it.

TIP You also can double-click the toolbar background to make it float as a window in the middle of the screen. Double-click the title of a floating toolbar to return it to its docked position.

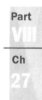

Part
VIII

Ch
27

Using the Customize Dialog Box

Before you can create a new toolbar or customize an existing toolbar, you must display the Customize dialog box (see Figure 27.3). From the Customize dialog box, you can create new toolbars, add or remove buttons from any active toolbar, resize combo boxes, and rearrange the order of the buttons on a toolbar. If you are customizing a toolbar, the toolbar you want to customize must be active.

There are three ways to display the Customize dialog box. Use one of the following:

■ Display the Toolbar Shortcut menu and select Customize.

■ Choose View, Toolbars, Customize.

■ Choose Tools, Customize, and select Toolbars from the cascading menu.

FIG. 27.3
Use the Customize dialog box to create new toolbars, or to change the buttons that appear on the existing toolbars.

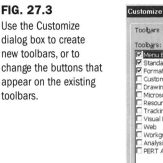

The Customize dialog box displays the custom choices on three tabs:

- *Toolbars.* You can choose to display or hide a toolbar by marking or unmarking the toolbar name. New toolbars can be created, renamed, or deleted, and toolbars you have customized can be reset back to display their original buttons.

- *Commands.* Using the button categories, you can add a tool to a toolbar.

- *Options.* From this tab you can enlarge the tool button size, control what is displayed in the toolbar button ToolTip, and control how the menus are animated.

When the Customize dialog box appears in front of toolbars you want to customize, drag the colored title bar of the Customize dialog box to move it to a different location.

Customizing Toolbars

Most of the toolbars included with Microsoft Project contain the commands you need to complete the most frequently accessed tasks. As discussed earlier in this chapter, however, they are not necessarily designed to contain commands for the tasks *you* perform most often. As a result, it is sometimes necessary to customize a toolbar by removing commands seldom used and adding commands for tasks you use frequently.

Before you can customize a toolbar, the toolbar you want to customize must be activated. The Customize dialog box then needs to be accessed. From the Customize dialog box, choose the Commands tab (see Figure 27.4) to add buttons or remove buttons from any active toolbar.

The Commands tab displays a list of Categories of tools on the left. Whenever you select a category, the corresponding Commands appear in the list box on the right. In Figure 27.4, the File category is selected.

To see the description of a command (which is used as the ToolTip), select a command and choose Description. In Figure 27.5 the [Task/Resource Notes] command from the Project category has been selected. You must click the Description button to see the command description.

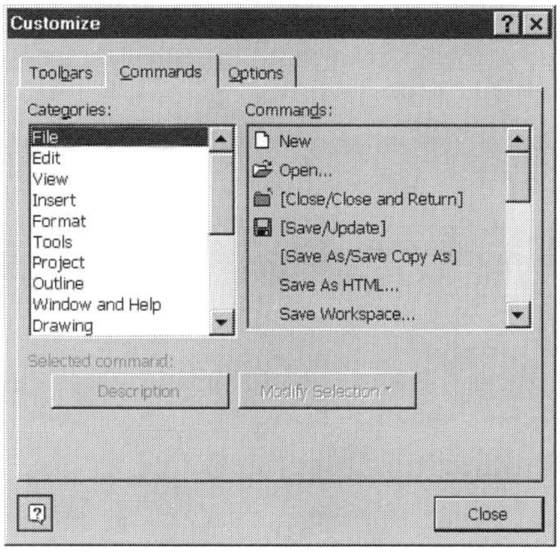

FIG. 27.4

Use the Commands tab in the Customize dialog box to change the buttons that appear on the active toolbars.

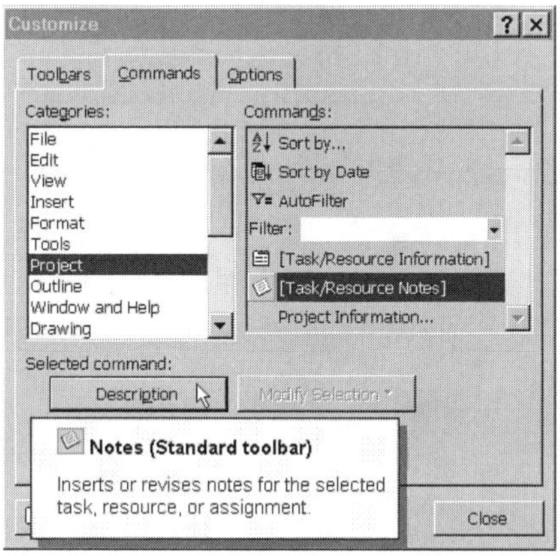

FIG. 27.5

You can find out more about commands by displaying their description.

The Modify Selection button is used to change the command buttons on the toolbars. It is active when you select a command on a toolbar, not when the command is selected in the Commands list box. You can also activate Modify Selection when you right-click a button on a toolbar.

Unlike previous versions of Project, commands you add to the toolbars might or might not have icon buttons. Those that do not have icon buttons will be displayed as text buttons.

Adding and Removing Command Buttons   When you locate the command button you want to add to a toolbar, all you have to do is drag the button from the Commands list onto the desired toolbar. When you position the button between two existing buttons, the button drops into place and existing buttons move to the right to accommodate it. If there are too many buttons on the toolbar, those at the far right end begin to wrap to a new line for the toolbar. To remove a button from a toolbar, simply drag it off its toolbar and release it in the center of the screen away from other toolbars.

To add buttons to a toolbar, follow these steps:

1. Display the toolbar you want to edit.

2. Choose Customize from the Toolbar shortcut menu or choose View, Toolbars, Customize. The Customize dialog box appears.

3. Select the Commands tab.

4. Choose the category containing the desired command.

5. Click the command and drag it into any position on the toolbar. When dragging a command to a toolbar, your mouse pointer changes to the shape of a white arrow with a gray box on the tip of the arrow and an X on the stem of the arrow. When you move the mouse pointer into the toolbar, it becomes a thick capital I.

6. Repeat steps 3-4 until all buttons have been added to the desired toolbars.

   In Figure 27.6, the Close and Properties commands from the File category have been added to the Standard toolbar. A third tool is being added, as can be seen by the mouse pointer shape, as illustrated in Figure 27.6.

7. Close the Customize dialog box.

FIG. 27.6

Commands can be added to any active toolbar. Some appear as icons, while others appear as text.

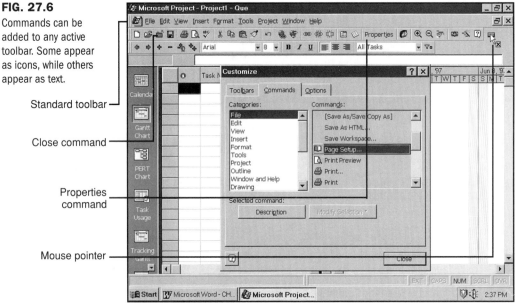

One very nice feature of the toolbars in Project 98 is that if you add more buttons than can be displayed on a single toolbar line, those buttons at the far right end begin to wrap to a new line for the toolbar. The grouping of the buttons determines how many buttons wrap. See the section "Grouping Command Buttons" later in this chapter for more information on setting and changing groups. Naturally, the more toolbars (or lines to a toolbar) displayed, the smaller the viewable area of your screen becomes.

You might find that there are certain command buttons that you never use and decide to re-move them from the toolbar to make room for other buttons. To remove buttons from existing toolbars, follow these steps:

1. Display the toolbar you want to edit.

2. Choose Customize from the Toolbar shortcut menu or choose View, Toolbars, Custom-ize. The Customize dialog box appears.

3. From the toolbar, select the button that you want to remove. A heavy black border indicates which button is selected.

4. Drag the button off the toolbar, being careful to release it away from other existing toolbars. When you drag a command off a toolbar, your mouse pointer changes to the shape of a white arrow with a gray box on the tip of the arrow and an X on the stem of the arrow.

5. Repeat steps 3 and 4 until all desired buttons are removed.

6. Close the Customize dialog box.

Moving Command Buttons   You can rearrange the commands on the toolbar by dragging buttons to different locations. When you select a button to move it, a heavy border indicates the button is selected. As you move the button, the mouse pointer changes to a thick capital I. When rearranging buttons, the Customize dialog box must be active.

When you want to move a button from one toolbar to another, you can remove it from one and add it to the other using procedures described in the previous section. Or, simply drag the button from one toolbar to the other. When moving buttons from one toolbar to another, both toolbars must be displayed, and the Customize dialog box must be active.

Grouping Command Buttons   Command buttons on the toolbars are now organized by groups. Vertical separator bars distinguish one group from another. The Modify Selection button on the Commands tab of the Customize dialog box is new in Project 98, and is used to change the display features of command buttons on the toolbars, including one that allows you to add a separator bar in front of the active command button.

The Modify Selection button is only active when you select a command on a toolbar, not when the command is selected in the Commands list box. Figure 27.7 shows the Properties com-mand selected on the Standard toolbar and the options available in the Modify Selection menu.

TIP   You can also activate the Modify Selection menu when you right-click a command button on a toolbar.

While the Customize dialog box is active, you can add a vertical separator bar in front of the active button, allowing you to group similar commands together. To add a separator bar, select the command button and choose Modify Selection. Click Begin a Group. A check mark appears in front of the option to indicate that a separator bar has been added. You can remove a separa-tor bar from a button by selecting the button and removing the check mark.

FIG. 27.7

The Modify Selection menu allows you to change the display of command buttons on toolbars.

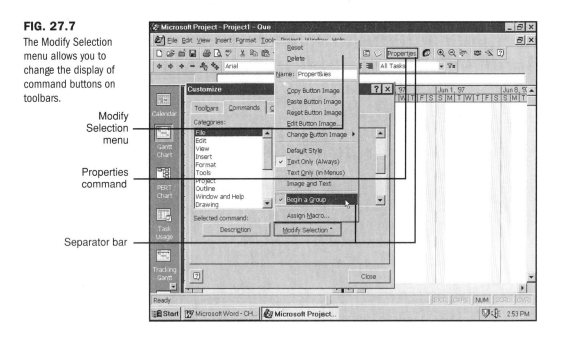

Modify Selection menu

Properties command

Separator bar

Resizing Combo Boxes   Combo boxes are two-part boxes that combine a text box with an entry list arrow that can be used to select valid options. These boxes appear frequently in dialog boxes and on toolbars. For example, on the Formatting toolbar there are combo boxes for Font, Font Size, and Filter. The width of the text box can be changed while the Customize dialog box is active.

To change the width of a combo box, follow these steps:

1. Display the toolbar containing the combo box and the Customize dialog box. You can have any tab in the Customize dialog box active to resize a combo box.

2. Select the combo box in the toolbar. A heavy black border appears around the combo box that is selected.

3. Position the mouse pointer over one side of the combo box. The mouse pointer changes to a two-headed dark arrow (see Figure 27.8).

4. Drag the edge of the combo box to the desired size.

5. Repeat steps 2-4 for each combo box you want to size.

6. Close the Customize dialog box.

Creating New Toolbars

Sometimes the buttons you use most frequently are on several different toolbars. Instead of having four or five toolbars displayed, which reduces the space available on the screen to display the views, you may want to have one or two toolbars that contain most (if not all) of the command buttons you use. At other times, you may want to customize an existing toolbar without affecting the original toolbar. Microsoft Project enables you to create new toolbars on which you can store the buttons you use most frequently without affecting the buttons currently available on other toolbars.

FIG. 27.8

The mouse is set to resize the Filter combo box by dragging the edge of the text box.

Combo box (three times)

Mouse pointer

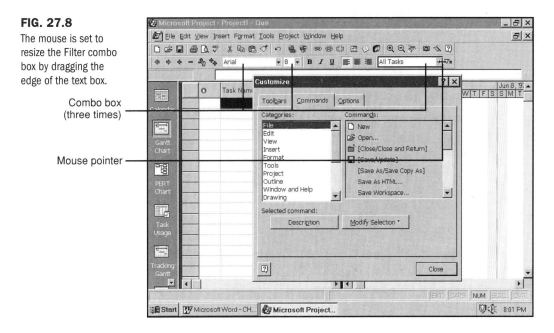

When the toolbar you want to create contains many of the same buttons available on an existing toolbar, you can make a copy of the existing toolbar, give it a unique name, and add the buttons you use most frequently. Alternatively, you can start with a blank toolbar and create a completely new collection of buttons.

If you want to make a copy of an existing toolbar and modify it, you must make the copy in the Organizer before using the Customize dialog box. If you want to create a blank toolbar, you can start from the Customize dialog box.

Creating a Toolbar by Copying an Existing Toolbar When an existing toolbar contains many of the buttons you want to include on your new toolbar, making a copy of the existing toolbar is a good starting point. Copying the existing toolbar reduces the number of buttons you have to place on the new toolbar. You cannot create a copy of a toolbar from within the Customize dialog box. In order to copy a toolbar, you will have to access the Organizer.

To create a copy of a toolbar, follow these steps:

1. From the menu bar choose Tools, Organizer.

2. Select the Toolbars tab in the Organizer. On the left side of the dialog box is the GLOBAL.MPT; on the right side of the dialog box is your active file.

3. Select the name of the toolbar you want to copy from the GLOBAL.MPT, and choose Copy.

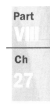

Part

VIII

Ch

27

4. The toolbar name will appear in your active file, listed on the right.

5. Select the toolbar name you just made a copy of on the right (in your active file) and choose Rename. The Rename dialog box will appear.

6. In the Rename dialog box, type in the new name for the copied toolbar and choose OK.

   Make sure the name you type is not a name used by another toolbar. For example, if you copied the Tracking toolbar, rename the copy My Tracking or Custom Tracking to differentiate it from the original Tracking toolbar.

7. Select the toolbar you just renamed (on the right) and choose Copy to place the copy with the new name in the GLOBAL.MPT. This makes the new toolbar available in all of your projects, not just your active project.

8. Select the toolbar on the right (in your active file) and choose Delete. This removes it from the active file. It is not needed there because it is in your GLOBAL.MPT.

9. Close the Organizer.

10. Access the Customize dialog box. Use the techniques outlined in the previous sections to modify the copied toolbar for your needs.

   ▶ **See** "Using the Organizer," **p. 114**

Building a New Toolbar   Creating a new toolbar from scratch creates an empty floating toolbar window that you must fill with the command buttons you want to add to the new toolbar.

To build a new toolbar, follow these steps:

1. Choose Customize from the Toolbar shortcut menu or choose View, Toolbars, Customize. The Customize dialog box appears.

2. From the Toolbars tab, choose New to open the New Toolbar dialog box. Project assigns a generic number sequentially to each new toolbar and identifies the toolbar with a generic name, such as Custom 1.

3. Type the new toolbar name. Toolbar names must be unique and are limited to any combination of 50 characters and spaces.

4. Choose OK.

The new toolbar name appears in the list on the Toolbars tab, while the new empty toolbar appears inside the dialog box (see Figure 27.9). Select the Commands tab and drag command buttons onto the toolbar to create the collection you desire. The toolbar will enlarge as you add command buttons. As is true with all toolbars, you may dock the toolbar or leave it floating.

Deleting a User-Defined Toolbar   Toolbars installed with the Microsoft Project software remain a part of the application even after you customize them. As a result, they can be reset, but they can't be deleted. However, new toolbars you create can be deleted. To delete a user-defined toolbar, follow these steps:

1. Choose Customize from the Toolbar shortcut menu or choose View, Toolbars, Customize. The Customize dialog box appears.

2. From the Toolbars tab, select the toolbar you want to delete.

FIG. 27.9
Drag buttons you want to include on the new custom toolbar.

New custom toolbar ——

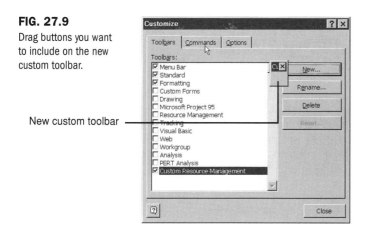

 T I P If the Delete button is not active, you have selected a toolbar that is installed with the Microsoft Project software. These toolbars can be reset, but not deleted.

3. Choose Delete. A warning dialog box appears asking you to confirm the deletion of the toolbar.

4. Choose OK to delete the toolbar.

5. Choose Close to close the Customize dialog box.

Restoring the Built-In Toolbars

Changes you make to toolbars as you customize may become out of date and may not fit every project you create. As a result, you may want to restore the default buttons to a toolbar. Microsoft Project includes a feature that makes restoring toolbars quick and easy. Follow these steps:

1. Select Customize from the Toolbar Shortcut menu or choose View, Toolbars, Customize. The Customize dialog box appears.

2. From the Toolbars tab, select the toolbar you want to restore to its default settings.

3. Choose Reset.

4. Choose OK from the warning box to restore the toolbar.

5. Repeat steps 2-4 for each toolbar you want to restore.

6. Close the Customize dialog box.

Part
VIII

Ch

27

> **CAUTION**
>
> Resetting a toolbar removes *all* customized changes you have made to that toolbar—not just the most recent changes. If you have placed custom buttons on a toolbar that you plan to reset, you lose the custom buttons. Drag the custom buttons to another toolbar if you want to preserve them.

Customizing Command Buttons

Some of the commands available in the Customize dialog box have a blank button image associated with them. When the command is added to a toolbar, only the name of the command is displayed.

Additionally, there will be times when no command button is available for a task you perform frequently, and it may be necessary for you to create a macro to record the steps of such a task. After you have created the macro, the name of the macro is listed on the Commands tab of the Customize dialog box. As with other commands, a blank button image is associated with the macro command. When the command is added to a toolbar, only the name of the macro is displayed.

When you want to add a new command to a toolbar that will perform a custom function, you'll probably want the button image to carry a distinctive design so that you won't confuse it with other buttons on the toolbar. You can change the blank button image to one of the available images, or design your own image for the command button by using the options available with the Modify Selections button.

Using the Modify Selections Button

As mentioned earlier, the Modify Selections button is used to edit the button images. To display the Modify Selection options, choose one of the following methods:

- Display the Customize dialog box. Display the toolbar that contains the command button you want to change. Select the Commands tab and choose the Modify Selection button.

- Display the Customize dialog box. Display the toolbar that contains the command button you want to change. Select the button on the toolbar and right-click it to display the Modify Selection options.

Customizing the Button Face   The Customize dialog box enables you to copy an existing design or access the Editor dialog box so you can customize the button design for blank buttons. If another button carries a design that resembles the one you want to use on the new button, you can copy the design from the button to the Clipboard and then paste it on the blank button. Copying the design does not copy the function of the original button to the new button. After you paste the design on the blank button, you can then modify the design to customize it for the new button.

Changing a Button Image Using an Image from the Library   You can use one of a library of button images to change a blank button image (see Figure 27.10).

To change a button image to one of the existing images, follow these steps:

1. Select Customize from the Toolbar shortcut menu or choose View, Toolbars, Customize. The Customize dialog box appears.

2. If necessary, go to the Toolbars tab and display the toolbar that contains the command to change the button image.

3. Select the button on the toolbar you want to change. A heavy black border indicates that the button is selected.

4. Select the Commands tab and choose Modify Selection.

TIP You can also right-click the command button to display the Modify Selection menu, regardless of the tab you have selected in the Customize dialog box.

5. From the Modify Selection menu, choose Change Button Image. A submenu of button choices appears.

Some of these images are generic, but others may be used by Project or other Microsoft programs.

6. Choose an image from the list.

7. Close the Customize dialog box.

FIG. 27.10

Use the Change Button Image option from the Modify Selection button in the Customize dialog box to add an existing image to a command.

Copying a Button Image   To copy the design of an existing toolbar button to another button, follow these steps:

1. Select Customize from the Toolbar shortcut menu or choose View, Toolbars, Customize. The Customize dialog box appears.

2. Position the mouse pointer over the button on the toolbar containing the design you want to copy and click the right mouse button. The Modify Selection menu appears.

3. Choose Copy Button Image to copy the design to the Clipboard.

4. Point to the button to which you want to apply the design and right-click the mouse.

5. Choose Paste Button Image to place the design on the new button.

6. Close the Customize dialog box.

Designing a New Button Image   When a command has a blank button image, you can design your own image for the command:

1. Display the Customize dialog box and point to the toolbar button you want to edit.

2. Right-click the command button to display the Modify Selection menu. Choose Edit Button Image. The Button Editor dialog box displays.

See the procedures described in the next section for editing an existing image.

Editing the Button Image   After you choose a button image from the library or copy an image from another button, you may want to edit the picture. If the image was copied, changing the picture so that it differs from the design of a button used to perform a different task will help you identify both buttons. To edit the picture you must use the Button Editor dialog box. In Figure 27.11 the design assigned to the Paste button is selected as the design for a new command button (Paste Special), and will be edited so that it isn't confused with the Paste button that appears on the Standard toolbar.

FIG. 27.11

The Paste picture is selected as a template for building a new picture. Use the Button Editor to create or modify button pictures.

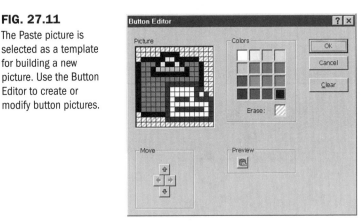

After selecting the design for the button, the Button Editor dialog box is opened so that the selected design may be customized (refer to Figure 27.11). The button design appears enlarged so that individual pixels can be identified in the Picture box. You can then change the location of each pixel in the picture using the mouse to achieve the desired design.

To open the Button Editor, follow these steps:

1. Point to the button you want to edit and right-click it to display the Modify Selection menu.

2. Choose Edit Button Image to open the Button Editor dialog box.

3. Verify that the button you want to customize is selected.

The Colors box is your palette for selecting colored pixels for your design. The Move arrows help you position the picture on the button by moving it one row or column at a time. The Preview area shows you how the current picture appears.

To change the picture, use any of the following techniques:

- To change the color of any pixel, click a color in the Colors box and then click the pixel, or drag the color across the desired pixels.

- To erase or clear pixels, click the erase box and then click all pixels you want to clear, drag the pointer across pixels you want to clear, or click a pixel a second time to clear the existing color.

- To reposition the picture on the button, clear an area along the edge toward which you want to move the design and then click the desired move button.

- To clear the picture canvas, choose <u>C</u>lear.

- To cancel changes and start over, choose Cancel or press Esc.

When you are finished modifying the button, choose OK. The new design now appears on the new button. Figure 27.12 shows the finished picture that will be assigned to the Paste Special button.

FIG. 27.12

This figure shows the finished picture for the Paste Special button.

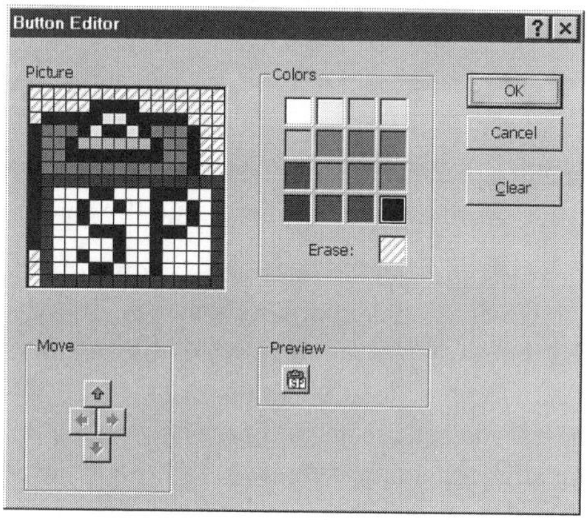

Changing the Attributes of a Button   Once you have added a command button to a toolbar or modified the button image, you may decide to change the command associated with that button. The command that will be executed when the button is clicked is identified in the Command field on the Customize Tool dialog box. A list that identifies all of the Microsoft Project commands you may choose to assign to a button is attached to this field.

For example, to assign a macro to a button, select the macro command that displays the desired macro in double quotes from the Command Entry list. Similarly, to designate the button to activate a custom form, you would choose the Form command that includes the desired form name in double quotes.

In the following example, a macro named ProjectSummary was created and assigned to the new button (see Figure 27.13).

Part

VIII

Ch

27

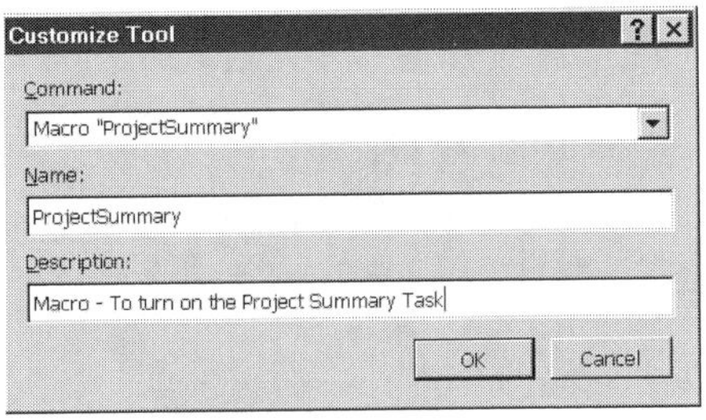

FIG. 27.13

Macros automatically appear in the list of Commands that can be assigned to a button.

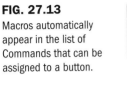

You can access the Customize dialog box directly from the Project window and change the attributes of a toolbar button. Follow these steps:

1. If you need to create a button, see the section "Adding and Removing Command Buttons," earlier in this chapter.

2. Press the Ctrl key and click the button you want to change.

3. Choose the Command drop-down list arrow and scroll through the commands to find the one you need.

4. Choose OK.

   In this example, the Macro Project Summary command is assigned to the new button. Commands are listed in alphabetical order and are grouped by type on the list. As a result, you may have to scroll through the list to find the command you need.

Entering the Description   Descriptions for many commands installed with Microsoft Project automatically appear in the Description field of the Customize Tool dialog box when you choose the command from the list. When you assign a command to a toolbar button, this description is set to appear in the status bar at the bottom of the screen when you use the button. When no description appears, you can create your own description. In addition, you can edit existing descriptions to meet your needs, when necessary. Each description may include up to 80 characters. (Figure 27.13 shows a new description for this macro.)

Managing Toolbars with the Organizer

Toolbars are global objects in Microsoft Project and are attached to the *application* rather than to a specific project. As a result, toolbars are stored as part of the GLOBAL.MPT template and are available for all projects you create, review, or edit. Changes you make to the various toolbars are also stored in the GLOBAL.MPT template. Toolbars not included in the GLOBAL.MPT file are not available for any project. Generally, this is not a problem because the toolbars you create or edit are automatically attached to the GLOBAL.MPT template stored in the computer on which they were created.

However, there may be times when you create a custom toolbar or edit an existing toolbar and want to copy it to another computer system, such as a laptop or a home computer. At other times you may want to include a special toolbar as part of a file you are sending to a coworker.

When you need to include a special toolbar with a particular project file, you can use the Organizer to copy the toolbar. The Organizer also provides options for renaming and deleting toolbars.

To rename a toolbar, follow these steps:

1. Choose Tools, Organizer from the menu bar.

2. The Organizer dialog box appears. Select the Toolbars tab (see Figure 27.14). The GLOBAL.MPT toolbars are listed on the left. The current Project file is shown on the right with no toolbars initially included in it.

FIG. 27.14

The Toolbars tab of the Organizer dialog box shows the named toolbars, which are stored in the GLOBAL.MPT file.

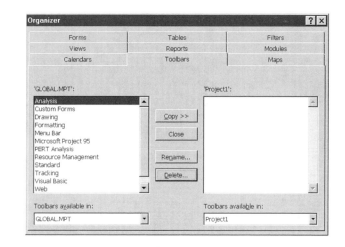

3. Choose the toolbar you want to rename from the list on the left.

4. Choose Rename. The Rename dialog box appears with the name of the selected toolbar in the New Name for Toolbar from GLOBAL.MPT text box.

5. Type the desired name in the New Name for Toolbar from GLOBAL.MPT text box (see Figure 27.15).

6. Choose OK.

Toolbars that are attached to project files can't be displayed directly from the project. When you want to make a toolbar available on a different system, you can copy it to a project and then copy it from the project into the GLOBAL.MPT template on the other system. To copy a toolbar into a project file, follow these steps:

1. Open the project to which you want to copy the toolbar.

2. Choose Tools, Organizer. The Organizer dialog box opens.

3. Select the toolbar you want to copy from those available in the GLOBAL.MPT list on the left. You can select multiple toolbars by dragging the mouse or by pressing the Ctrl key as you click additional toolbars.

Part

VIII

Ch

27

FIG. 27.15

Provide a new name for a toolbar in the Rename dialog box.

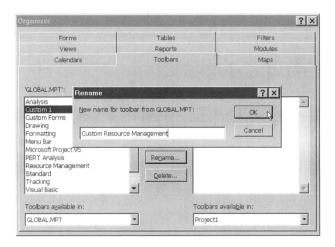

T I P If the project file you want to use doesn't already appear above the box on the right side of the Toolbars tab on the Organizer dialog box, select it from the Toolbars Available In drop-down list.

4. Choose <u>C</u>opy to copy all selected toolbars to the project file.

5. Click the Close button or press Esc to close the Organizer dialog box.

Figure 27.16 shows that a copy of the toolbar Custom Resource Management has been placed in the New Product.mpp project file.

FIG. 27.16

Toolbars copied into a project file can't be displayed, but they can be copied into GLOBAL.MPT templates on other computers.

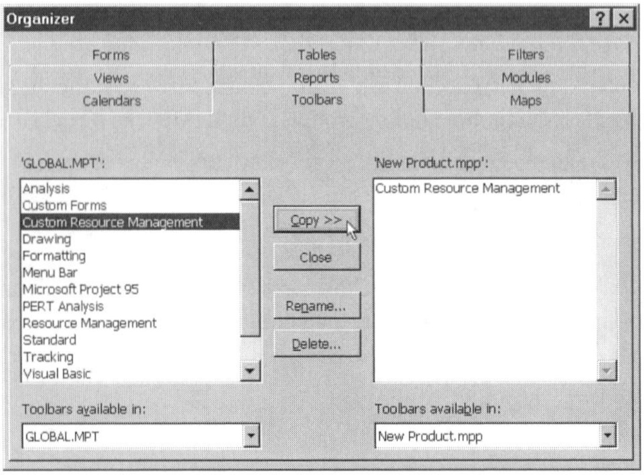

TROUBLESHOOTING

I can't remove a button from the toolbar. Be sure the Customize dialog box is open whether you are adding or removing toolbar buttons. Otherwise, clicking the button automatically performs the commands of the macro that are attached to the button. When the Customize dialog box is open, Project knows you're working with the toolbars rather than issuing commands using the toolbar buttons.

I customized my toolbars at the office, but when I open a project on my system at home the default toolbars appear. The toolbars you customize are attached to the application on the system you were using when you customized them. To install them on your machine at home, you need to copy the GLOBAL.MPT file on your machine at work to a disk and replace the GLOBAL.MPT file on your home system with the one you copied from the office computer.

Customizing the Menu Bar

Customizing toolbars provides an efficient means for accessing the tasks you perform most often. By creating custom toolbars, you can store buttons for the tasks together so that they can be accessed from one toolbar. Customizing menus provides you with another means for creating a storage component for the features and tasks you use most often. As is the case with toolbars, existing menu bars displayed in Microsoft Project can be edited, or you can create your own custom menu bar.

In previous chapters, you learned how to create special views, tables, forms, or filters and found that they are stored as part of the project in which you created them. When you need to use them in another project, you have to copy them into the new project file.

Customizing menus is different because menus are part of the *application* file rather than a *project* file. As a result, changing them makes them available to all projects you create or edit on your computer. They are stored as part of the GLOBAL.MPT file, which is used as a basis for all projects you create or open on your machine. You can still copy them from the GLOBAL.MPT file to a project file when you want to include them in a file you are sending to someone else or when you want to copy them to a different computer. Otherwise, copying them is not necessary.

In Project 98, the menu bar acts very similarly to the toolbars. By default, the menu bar is docked at the top of the screen, but like toolbars, it can be moved and docked at the side or bottom of the screen or left floating in the middle of the screen. The ways in which you customize a menu bar are very similar to the ways you customize toolbars, which are described in the previous sections in this chapter.

In this version of Project, any command that has a pointing triangle is considered a menu. In Figure 27.17, the Edit menu is active. Within the Edit menu there are three other built-in menus—Fill, Clear, and Object.

FIG. 27.17

The Edit menu contains three other built-in menus: Fill, Clear, and Object.

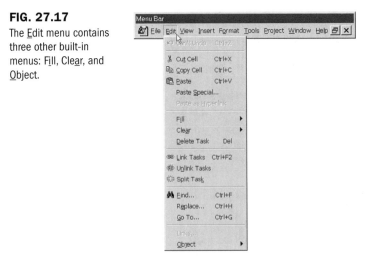

Customizing menus provides you with a wide range of possibilities. You may simply want to attach commands to existing menus. Items such as frequently used views, tables, filters, and macros may be attached to existing menus quite easily. Procedures for adding these features are included in the chapter in which they were created. See Chapter 20, "Using the Standard Views, Tables, and Filters," for information about attaching views to the View menu or View Bar; attaching tables to the View menu; and attaching filters to the Project, Filter For: menu. When you change the name of a menu bar item or create a new menu bar item, you are, in effect, creating a custom menu bar. The next section focuses on creating new menu bars and editing menu bar items for existing menu bars.

Adding a New Command to the Menu Bar

To add a new command to the menu bar, all you have to do is display the Customize dialog box, select the New Menu command, and drag it onto the menu bar. By positioning the command between two existing commands, the new menu drops into place.

To add a new command to the menu bar, follow these steps:

1. Choose Tools, Customize, Toolbars or right-click the menu bar and choose Customize from the shortcut menu. The Customize dialog box appears.
2. Select the Commands tab. (See Figure 27.18.)
3. Choose the New Menu category at the bottom of the Categories list.
4. Click New Menu on the Commands list and drag it into any position on the toolbar. When dragging a command to a toolbar, your mouse pointer changes to the shape of a

white arrow with a gray box on the tip of the arrow and an X on the stem of the arrow. When you move the mouse pointer into the toolbar it becomes a thick capital I.

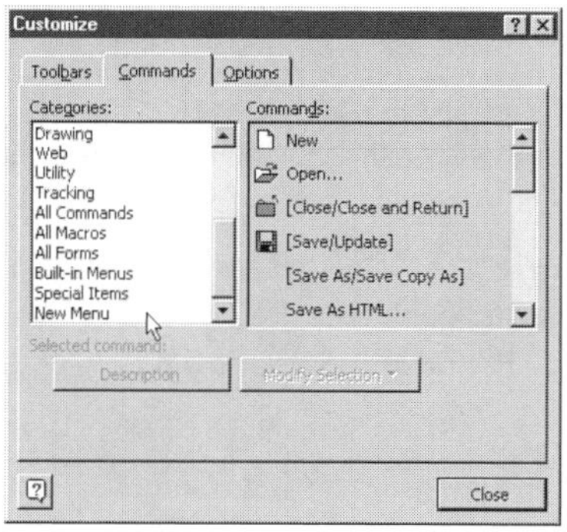

FIG. 27.18
Use the Customize dialog box to modify the menu bar or add menus to toolbars.

5. Repeat steps 3 and 4 until all the new menus have been added. In Figure 27.19, a new menu has been added to the menu bar.

6. Proceed with adding commands to the new menu, as described in the next section.

FIG. 27.19
Adding a new menu command is easy with the New Menu category on the <u>C</u>ommands tab of the Customize dialog box.

Menu bar

New menu

Mouse pointer

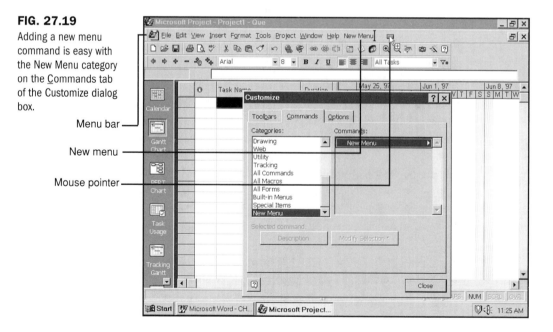

Adding Items to the Menu Bar   You can add commands, other menus, and special items to the existing or new menu bar commands. Adding items to the menu bar is identical to adding buttons to a toolbar. Simply select the category and item you want to add and drag it onto the menu bar. By positioning the command between two existing commands, the new item drops into place.

Part
VIII

Ch
27

The following is a list of several different types of items you can add to a new menu bar:

- *Commands*. Any command can be added to the new menu. Choose the command from either the category in which the command is listed, or from the All Commands category listed toward the bottom of the list. All Commands is an alphabetical listing of every command in Project.

- *Built-in Menus*. Other built-in menus can be added to the new menu. Choose the Built-in Menus category for a complete listing of menus that are installed with Microsoft Project.

- *Special Items*. There are many other items that appear in menus aside from commands and menus. These are often grouped in lists. For example, on the View menu you see lists of different types of views, while in the Window menu, you see a list of your open project files.

See the following list for the Special Items you can add to menus:

- *Task Views*. Only task views marked to display in menus.

- *Resource Views*. Only resource views marked to display in menus.

- *Views*. All views (task and resource) marked to display in menus, identical to the list that appears in the View menu.

- *Tables*. All tables marked to display in menus, identical to the list that appears in the View, Tables menu.

- *Filters*. All filters marked to display in menus, identical to the list that appears in the Project, Filter For menu.

- *Sorts*. All sorts marked to display in menus, identical to the list that appears in the Project, Sort menu.

- *Macros*. All macros, identical to the list that appears in the Tools, Macro, Macros menu.

- *Custom Forms*. All custom forms available from the Custom Forms toolbar.

- *Form View Formats*. All Format Detail options when a form-type view is active. For example, if you split the screen when the Gantt Chart view is displayed, the Task Form view appears in the lower split. You can choose Format, Details to change the information that appears in the form, such as *Resources and Predecessors* or *Resource Work*.

- *Toolbars*. All toolbars, identical to the list that appears in the View, Toolbars menu.

- *Recently Used Files*. The list of files you have worked with recently, identical to the list that appears at the bottom of the File menu. The maximum number of files that can be listed is nine, and is controlled through the General tab under Tools, Options.

- *Windows*. The list of your open files, identical to the list that appears at the bottom of the Window menu.

- *OLE Actions*. A list of actions you can take with objects that have been linked or embedded.

To add a new menu item to the menu bar, follow these steps:

1. Choose Tools, Customize, Toolbars or right-click the menu bar and choose Customize from the shortcut menu. The Customize dialog box appears.

2. Select the Commands tab.

3. Choose the category that contains the command or item you want to add.

4. Select the command or item and drag it into the position on the menu bar. Existing menus expand when the mouse pointer is over them to let you drag the command into the position you want to use.

   When dragging an item, your mouse pointer changes to the shape of a white arrow with a gray box on the tip of the arrow and an X on the stem of the arrow. When you move the mouse pointer onto the desired menu command it becomes a thick capital I, as shown in Figure 27.20.

5. Repeat steps 3-4 until all the items have been added to the menu.

   In Figure 27.21, several items have been added to the menu, including the Close command, the Resource Allocation view, the Tracking built-in menu, and the Adjust Dates and Format Duration macros. A new item, Tables, is being inserted between the Tracking built-in menu and the Adjust Dates macro.

FIG. 27.20

Drag an item from the Commands list to the menu bar.

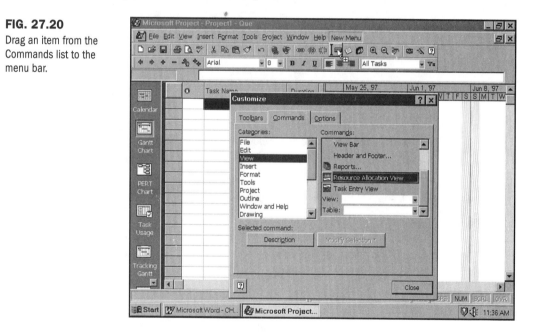

Using the Modify Selections Button

The Modify Selections button is used to edit the new menu bar or the commands on a menu bar. To display the Modify Selection options, choose one of the following:

■ Display the Customize dialog box and select the Commands tab. Select the command on the menu bar that you want to modify and choose the Modify Selection button.

Part

VIII

Ch

27

FIG. 27.21

This figure shows how
you can add other
items to the new menu.

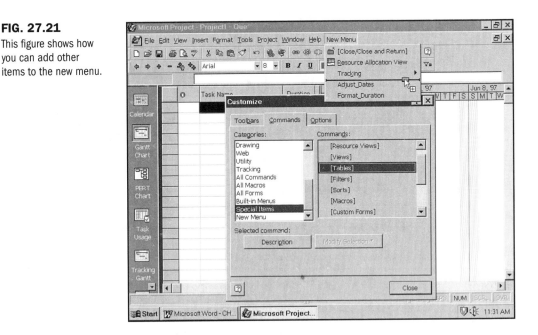

N O T E A heavy black border indicates the command on the menu bar is selected.

Display the Customize dialog box. Select the command on the menu bar and right-click it
to display the Modify Selection options.

Figure 27.22 shows the Modify Selection options, with all the choices available. Depending on
what you select, some of the choices will be grayed out.

Naming the Menu Bar   When you create a new menu bar, you should assign a name to the
menu bar that reflects the special feature(s) attached to it. You can name a menu bar you are
creating or change the name of an existing menu bar through the Modify Selection options.
Follow these steps:

1. Open the Customize dialog box.

2. Select the menu bar command you want to rename. A heavy black border indicates the
    command on the menu bar is selected.

3. Activate the Modify Selection options and choose Name.

4. Type the new menu bar name in the Name text box (see Figure 27.23).

5. Press Enter.

Removing and Restoring Menu Bar Commands   To remove an entire menu or a command
from a particular menu, simply drag it off the menu bar and release it in the center of the
screen away from the menu bar and toolbars.

FIG. 27.22
Use the Modify Selection options to name a menu and group menu commands together.

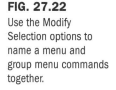

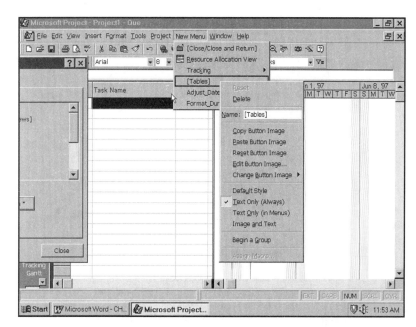

FIG. 27.23
Use the Modify Selection options to rename a menu.

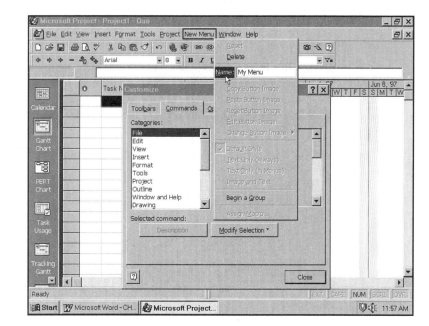

Part
VIII

Ch
27

To remove a menu or a menu command, follow these steps:

1. Display the Customize dialog box.

2. Select the menu or menu command that you want to remove from the menu bar. A heavy black border indicates which item is selected.

3. Drag the menu or command off the menu bar, being careful to release it away from the toolbars. When dragging a command off the menu bar, your mouse pointer changes to the shape of a white arrow with a gray box on the tip of the arrow and an X on the stem of the arrow.

4. Repeat steps 2 and 3 until all desired menus or commands are removed.

5. Close the Customize dialog box.

Once you have removed a menu or command, you can restore standard Project menus or commands by restoring the menu bar.

CAUTION

Restoring the menu bar removes any custom menus you have created.

To restore the menu bar, follow these steps:

1. Display the Customize dialog box.

2. Select the Toolbars tab.

3. Choose Menu Bar from the list of toolbars.

4. Choose Reset. A warning message appears to confirm resetting the menu bar.

5. Choose OK.

6. Close the Customize dialog box.

Moving and Grouping Menu Commands   The order of the menu commands on the menu bar can be rearranged by dragging the menu name to a different location. When you select a menu name to move, a heavy border indicates the menu is selected. As you move the name, the mouse pointer changes to a thick capital I.

You can also reorder the commands within a particular menu. You select the menu name and then the command within the menu you want to reorder. As you drag the command, the mouse pointer changes to a long, thick, black insertion line.

N O T E   When re-arranging the order of the menu commands, the Customize dialog box must be active.

Command items on the menu bar can be ordered in groups. Horizontal separator bars distinguish one group from another. Use the Modify Selection options to add a separator bar between the active menu item. Click Begin a Group. A check mark appears in front of the option to indicate a separator bar has been added. You can remove a separator bar from a menu item by selecting the item and removing the check mark.

Using Custom Forms

Custom forms are pop-up data entry forms that resemble dialog boxes. These forms give you quick access to *fields*—pieces of information—that are not displayed on the current view. Using a custom form enables you to access a field containing the information you need without changing views and to enter the same value into multiple task and resource fields. This section identifies some of the features available for using custom forms and reviews the procedures for accomplishing these tasks.

Project comes equipped with a number of different forms that you can use to perform some of the most common tasks. You can, for example, use the Update Task form when you need to track the progress of a Project task. You may edit built-in forms by moving information around, but you can't add additional fields or delete fields. As a result, you may want to design your own custom forms. The Custom Form Editor, which is one of the server applications in Windows, is used to create custom forms.

Because custom forms are designed for editing and viewing tasks and resources, you attach them to toolbar buttons, to a menu, or to shortcut keys (Ctrl+*letter*). You cannot place a custom form in a pane and then use the form to scroll through the task list or resource list. The task(s) or resource(s) selected when you activate the form are affected by any entries you make. When you select the OK or Cancel button on the form, the form is removed from display.

Because you have to display the form for each new task or resource, these forms are inappropriate as a primary vehicle for original data entry. To provide continued access to fields not included in a standard view, it would be more efficient to create a view that incorporates a custom table. You can then design and display the custom view in the Task or Resource Sheet view. See Chapter 20, "Using the Standard Views, Tables, and Filters," for guidelines in creating custom views.

Reviewing the Forms Supplied with Microsoft Project

Microsoft Project includes eight custom task forms and four custom resource forms. Each of these predefined forms is designed to accomplish a specific task, as described in the following table:

Task Forms	Description
Cost Tracking	Tracks costs for tasks and percent completed and compares costs to the baseline.
Earned Value	Examines calculations of comparative cost variances for tasks, based on the planned, scheduled, and actual duration, as well as work and cost amounts.
Entry	Edits the Task Name, Dates, Duration, and Rollup fields.
PERT Entry	Tracks duration estimates—Optimistic, Expected, and Pessimistic. This information can be displayed in a table.

Part
VIII

Ch
27

continues

continued

Task Forms	Description
Schedule Tracking	Tracks the duration and percentage completed and displays scheduled task dates and variances.
Task Relationships	Displays the list of predecessors and successors for the selected task(s).
Tracking	Tracks the duration and dates for tasks. This is the form that appears when you select the Tracking button on the toolbar.
Work Tracking	Tracks duration and views the calculated Work tracking fields.

Resource Forms	Description
Cost Tracking	Displays total cost for a resource (for all tasks).
Entry	Identifies the resource name, initials, group, rate, and maximum available units.
Summary	Reports the overall cost and Work tracking variances.
Work Tracking	Tracks percent of work completed and compares it to the baseline.

Using Custom Forms

Each custom form that comes with Project is attached to the Tools menu. To make the form more accessible, you may want to attach the form to a toolbar button or a shortcut key. Procedures for using the menus to access a form, and for attaching forms to toolbar buttons and keyboard shortcuts are described in this section.

Using the Menu to Display a Form   When you want to display or edit information for one task or resource, select the task or resource before displaying the form. When you want to display or edit information for multiple tasks or resources, select all tasks and resources before displaying the form. Remember that entries made to the form when multiple tasks or resources are selected affect all selected tasks or resources.

To display a custom form with the menu, follow these steps:

1. Select the task(s) or resource(s) you want to edit.
2. Choose Tools, Customize, Forms. The Custom Forms dialog box appears (see Figure 27.24). If a task is selected, the task forms are listed. If a resource is selected, the resource forms are listed.
3. Select the desired form from the Forms list.
4. Choose Apply.
5. Edit or view field values for selected task(s) or resource(s).
6. Choose OK.

FIG. 27.24
Select a task or
resource form from the
Custom Forms dialog
box.

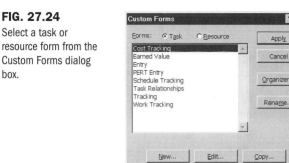

Assigning a Shortcut Key to Display a Form   To make a form you use frequently more accessible, you may want to assign it to a shortcut key. To assign a shortcut key to a custom form, follow these steps:

1. Choose Tools, Customize, Forms to open the Custom Forms dialog box.

2. Select the form you want to assign to a shortcut key from the Forms list.

3. Choose Rename. The Define Custom Form dialog box appears (see Figure 27.25). You can use this dialog box to change the name of the form or to change the shortcut key assignment.

FIG. 27.25
Use the Define Custom
Form dialog box to
rename a form or
assign it a new shortcut
key.

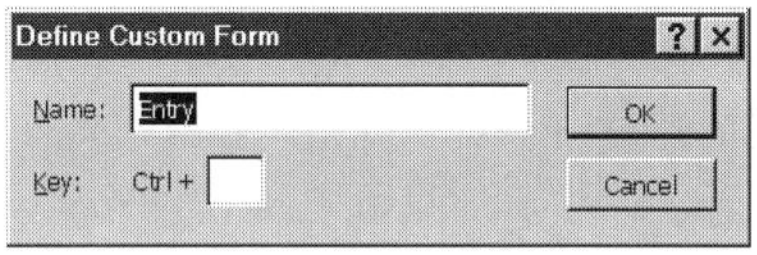

4. Select the Key box and type the letter that you want to use to activate the custom form. Numbers cannot be used. This letter, used with the Ctrl key will display the form.

TIP   The letters are not case-sensitive, so typing an upper- or lowercase letter makes no difference.

CAUTION
Be careful to avoid shortcut keys already assigned to other tasks. The shortcut keys already assigned include: B (Bold), C (Edit, Copy), D (Fill Down), F (Edit, Find), I (Italics), N (File, New), O (File, Open), P (File, Print), S (File, Save), U (Underline), V (Edit, Paste), X (Edit, Cut), and Z (Edit, Undo). You will be warned when you select one of these characters that it's reserved for use with Project and instructed to select a different character.

5. Choose OK to save the key assignment.

Part
VIII

Ch
27

To use the shortcut key, first select the task or resource for which you want to display the form, and then press the shortcut letter while holding down the Ctrl key.

Assigning a Toolbar Button to Display a Form   You can access the Customize dialog box directly from the Project window, without displaying the Customize dialog box, and assign a form to a toolbar button. Follow these steps:

1. If you need to create a button, see the previous section, "Adding and Removing Command Buttons."

2. Press the Ctrl key and click the button you want to display the form.

3. Choose <u>C</u>ommand and type **Form** *form name*, where *form name* is the name that appears in the list of Custom Forms.

 You also can select the drop-down list arrow and scroll the Form commands to find the form name listed.

4. Choose the Description text box and type the description you want to display on the status bar when you click the button.

5. Choose OK to save the button definition.

After you assign a toolbar button to a form, select the task or resource for which you want to view the form and click the assigned button.

Creating a New Custom Form

When the custom forms that come with Microsoft Project do not contain the fields of data and information you need, you can create your own custom form or modify existing forms so that it includes the fields you need. As you found when you created custom toolbars and menu bars, you can create a new custom form by copying an existing form and modifying it to meet your needs, or you can create a new custom form from scratch. The Custom Form Editor enables you to add fields to a custom form and modify the appearance of existing fields by sizing them or repositioning them on the form. You can also use the Custom Form Editor to set the placement of the form on the screen when you activate it.

Many of the procedures you used to create custom toolbars and menu bars can be used to create a custom form. You can assign a name to the form and identify the fields of information you want to include on the form. When you create a form from scratch, the Custom Form Editor (see Figure 27.26) displays a small outline of a dialog box in the center of the screen. Each custom form, by default, includes an OK button and a Cancel button. These buttons are positioned on the right side of the dialog box. You select and add the information to the form that you need.

When you create a new form by customizing a copy of an existing form, the existing form is positioned in the Custom Form Editor screen. Figure 27.27 displays a Copy of Entry form in the Custom Form Editor screen.

FIG. 27.26
The initial form contains only the OK and Cancel buttons. Add text, fields, and group boxes to complete the form.

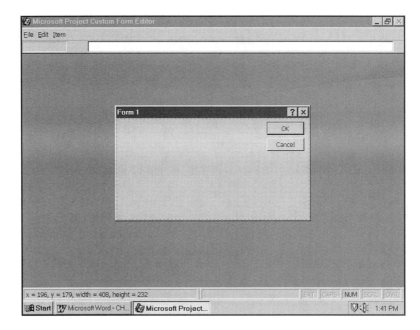

FIG. 27.27
A copy of an existing form can also be used to create a new form. The copy displays the existing form information, which you can edit for the new form.

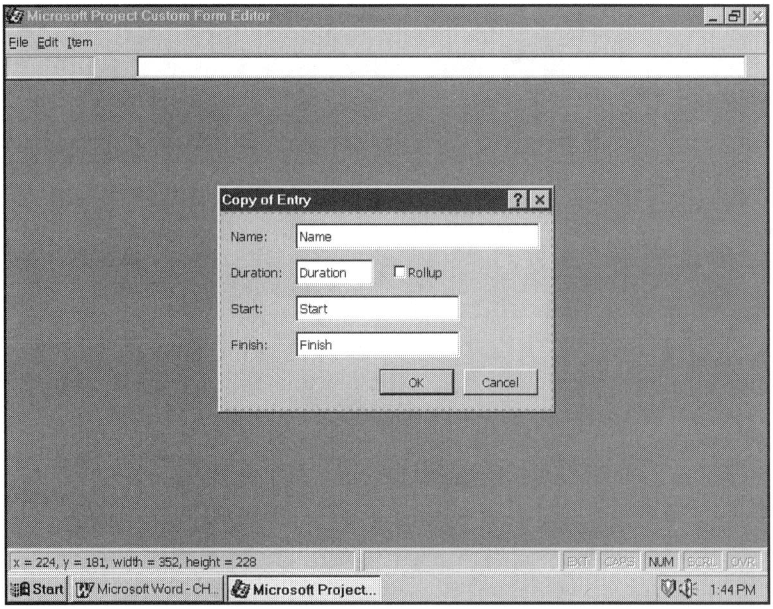

Part

VIII

Ch

27

Opening the Custom Form Editor Regardless of which approach you want to use to create a new custom form, you will need to open the Custom Form Editor. To display the Custom Form Editor, follow these steps:

1. Choose Tools, Customize, Forms. The Custom Forms dialog box appears.

2. Choose New to open the Custom Form Editor, or select a form from the list and choose Copy to base the new form on an existing form.

3. Type a name for the custom form in the Name field of the Define Custom Form dialog box.

4. Assign a shortcut key letter in the Key field, if desired.

5. Choose OK.

Sizing and Positioning the Dialog Box You can use the mouse to resize the Form dialog box using the same procedures as you would to size windows or other dialog boxes. Drag the borders or corners of the box to any desired dimension within the Custom Form Editor window. To reposition the form in the window, drag the title bar until the form is properly positioned. To change the position or size settings for the dialog box, follow these steps:

1. Choose Tools, Customize, Forms to display the Customize Forms dialog box. Select the form you want to edit.

2. Choose Edit to display the Microsoft Custom Form Editor.

3. Select the dialog box outline by clicking once anywhere on the box, or choose Edit, Select Dialog.

4. Double-click the Form dialog box or choose Edit, Info to display the Form Information dialog box (see Figure 27.28).

5. Enter values in the X and Y text boxes if you want to set the horizontal and vertical positions of the dialog box manually.

N O T E The values in the X and Y boxes refer to the resolution values used in the screen display. A value of 1 in the X text box places the box at the left edge of the screen. A value of 100 places the left edge of the box 100 pixels from the left of the screen. If your screen resolution is 800 pixels wide, then a value of 400 would place the left edge of the box at the center of the screen. Similarly, the values in the Y box locate the top edge of the form relative to the top of the screen. Select the Auto check boxes to center the form on the Microsoft Project screen. ▒

6. Enter values in the Width and Height check boxes to set the dimensions of the form.

After you adjust the size of the Form dialog box, you might want to move or re-position existing items on the form. Each item that you place on the form can be positioned and sized by changing the settings in the Item Information dialog box, or you can drag the item to a new position.

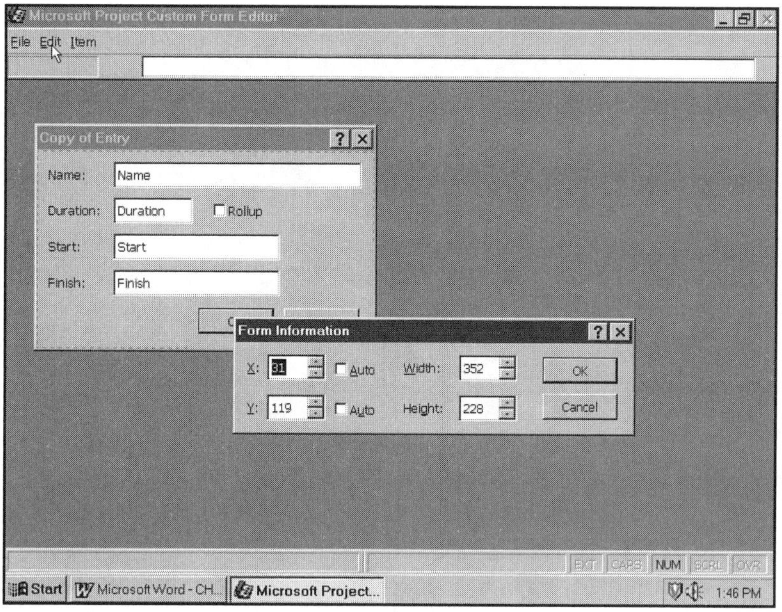

FIG. 27.28

The Form Information dialog box can be used to position or resize the form.

Placing Items on the Form

Fields that contain pieces of information, text, borders, groups, buttons, and check boxes are examples of *items* that you might include on forms. Most forms automatically include OK and Cancel buttons. You can place additional items on forms using commands on the Item menu. As you add each item, you will want to position the item on the form and might need to adjust the size of the form to accommodate all form items. In the following activities, you will add items to the blank form pictured in Figure 27.26.

Placing Text on the Form Text items identify the information contained on a form. For example, to identify a resource name on a custom form, you would include the word "Resource" on the form beside the text box that identifies the resource.

When you add a text item to a form, a text box containing the word "Text" is outlined as a placeholder on the form. To replace the default Text with the information you want to display on the form, select the text and type the desired text. The text placeholder is sized according to the width of the form. As a result, if the text you want to add to the form does not fit into the text placeholder, you will need to adjust the size of the form, re-position items on the form, and drag the text placeholder to accommodate the message. After you complete the text entry, you can reposition, size, or delete the text item. When it is positioned and complete, click a neutral area of the form to deselect the text item.

The position of a selected text item appears in the status bar. You can use these position indicators to position the text item, or you can double-click the text item to display the Item Information dialog box and specify the location of the item. You can also select the text item and then choose Info from the Edit menu.

Part

VIII

Ch

27

Figure 27.29 shows the first text item that was added to the blank form. The mouse pointer displayed can be used to drag the text item to another location.

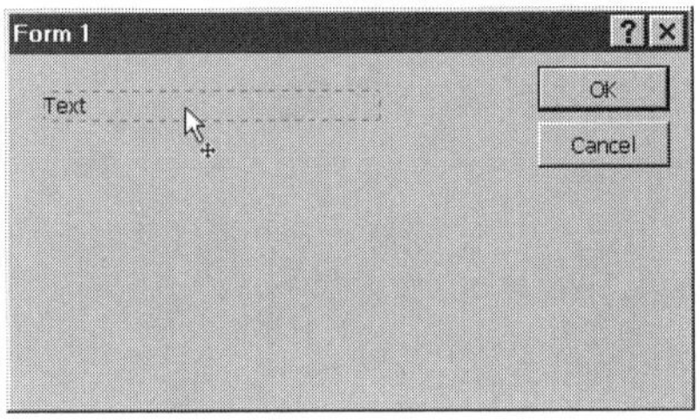

FIG. 27.29

A new text item contains generic text that you can replace with more meaningful text. Then, you can move it to a new location or size it as needed.

To add a text item to a form, follow these steps:

1. Choose Tools, Customize, Forms to display the Customize Forms dialog box and select the form you want to edit.
2. Choose Edit to display the Microsoft Custom Form Editor.
3. Choose Item, Text. A new text placeholder appears on the custom form.
4. Select the default text and type the desired text.
5. Reposition or size the text placeholder to accommodate the text and form.

Placing Field Values on the Form   Custom forms are created to report information about a specific task or resource in an active project. Therefore, they need to be designed to display information from the project file. To do this, you need to add a Field item to the form. Field items access project information and display it in the Custom Form dialog box so that you can review project information. In addition, you may want to allow users to edit information directly to the project file using the custom form. When you want to restrict editing, you can designate that the field be displayed as Read Only so that it can't be edited by selecting and marking the Show as Static Text check box. You can reposition the field item or resize the display of a field item using the same techniques used to reposition and size text items.

To add a field value item to a custom form, follow these steps:

1. Display the form in the Custom Form Editor window.
2. Choose Item, Fields. The Item Information dialog box appears.
3. Select a field from the Field drop-down list. Because the list includes fields of information contained in the project, placing a field in the form will pull the information from the project and report the information for the selected task or resource each time you activate the custom form.
4. Choose Show as Static Text to prevent users from editing the field in the form, if desired.
5. Choose OK. The field item appears on the form as displayed in Figure 27.30. The field item that appears in the example is designed to display the duration of the selected task.
6. Reposition or size the field item as needed.

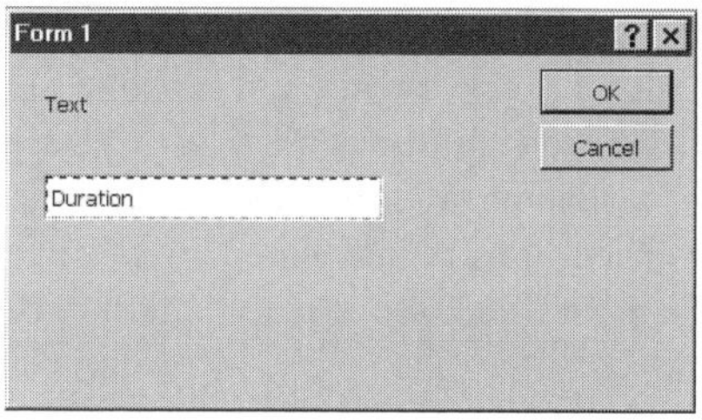

FIG. 27.30

Place a field item on a form to access information from the project.

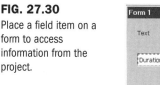

Placing a Group Box on the Form   Group boxes allow you to create sections on a custom form so that you can group related information. A group box provides a boundary line around fields on the form, and you can add fields to a form and place them inside the group box. The same basic procedures are used to add a group box to a form that you used to add a text item to a form. You can then name the group box to summarize the relationship of the fields it contains. Enter the text that you want displayed at the top of the group box while the new group item is still selected, and then use the mouse to position the group box at the desired location. You may need to adjust the size of the form dialog box to accommodate a group box. Positioning it on top of existing items hides other items from view.

To add a group box to a custom form, follow these steps:

1. Display the form in the Custom Form Editor window.

2. Choose Item, Group Box. A new group box placeholder appears on the custom form and displays the default name Group.

3. Press Backspace to remove the default group name and type the desired group name, or double-click the placeholder and type the desired group name in the Text field of the Item Information dialog box.

4. Reposition or size the group box placeholder to accommodate both the information you plan to place in it and the form. Figure 27.31 displays a group box added to the new custom form.

FIG. 27.31

Group boxes are used to provide visual orientation. Place the group item and then move other items into it.

Most items that can be added to a custom form can be included in a group box. To add items to the group box, use these steps:

1. Add a group box to the custom form.

2. Add the desired items to the form and move them into the group box, positioning them as desired.

3. Adjust the size of the group box as required.

Part
VIII

Ch
27

Placing Buttons on the Form   Two different types of buttons may be added to custom forms: the OK button and the Cancel button. Each form may contain only one of each type of button, and these are added by default when you create a custom form. You can delete the buttons if desired, or move them to a new location on the form. If you add a new button that already appears on the form, it simply replaces the original button on the form. Use the same procedures to place a button on the form that you used to place other items on custom forms.

1. Display the form in the Custom Form Editor dialog box.
2. Choose Item, Button.
3. Select the desired button type.
4. Choose OK.
5. Reposition or resize the buttons as desired.

Saving the Form   To save the form and continue working on it, choose Save from the File menu. After the form is complete, choose File, Exit. If unsaved changes exist, you are prompted to save the form again before exiting.

Renaming, Editing, and Copying Custom Forms

Forms you create are attached to the project in which they were created. Therefore, to use a form in another project, you need to copy the form to the project. The Custom Forms dialog box provides access to the Organizer so that you can use the same techniques to copy custom forms to another project that you used to copy toolbars and menu bars to a project. You can also use the Organizer to delete custom forms or rename them. The Custom Forms dialog box can be used to edit an existing form, to make a copy of a custom form, or to rename a form.

Renaming Custom Forms   You can rename a custom form using both the Custom Form dialog box and the Organizer. To change the name of a form using the Custom Form dialog box, use these steps:

1. Choose Tools, Customize, Forms to display the Custom Form dialog box.
2. Select the form you want to rename in the Custom Forms list.
3. Choose Rename.
4. Type the new name for the form in the Name field of the Define Custom Form dialog box.
5. Choose OK to save the form using the new name.

Editing a Custom Form   You can edit an existing custom form when you need to add or remove items but don't want to create a completely new form. Editing an existing form places it in the Custom Form Editor window, and you can use techniques described earlier in this section to add and remove items.

To change the design of a form, follow these steps:

1. Choose Tools, Customize, Forms to display the Custom Form dialog box.
2. Select the form you want to edit in the Custom Forms list.

3. Choose <u>E</u>dit. The Custom Form Editor opens and displays the form for you to edit.

4. Add and remove items following procedures described earlier in this section.

Managing Forms with the Organizer

Custom forms are created and saved in the project file that is active when you create the form. You can use the Organizer to copy a custom form to another project file or to the GLOBAL.MPT template so that it's available for every project. You can also use the Organizer to delete custom forms and to rename them.

To display the Organizer, follow these steps:

1. Choose <u>T</u>ools, <u>C</u>ustomize, <u>F</u>orms to display the Custom Forms dialog box.

2. Choose <u>O</u>rganizer. The Forms tab of the Organizer dialog box is automatically displayed.

You can rename, delete, and copy forms using techniques and procedures described in the earlier sections of this chapter.

TROUBLESHOOTING

When I move an item into a group box, the text box doesn't move with it. Correct. You have to move each piece of data and each item separately into a group box.

I created a custom form but now I can't figure out how to use it. You can display the form from the Customize Form dialog box by selecting the form and choosing <u>A</u>pply. This, however, takes away the advantage of creating the form in the first place. As a result, you will probably want to assign the custom form to a menu, to a shortcut keystroke, or to a toolbar button to make accessing it more efficient.

I created a custom form but when I created a new project, it wasn't there. Correct. Custom forms are stored with the project for which they were created. To use them in other projects, you need to use the Organizer to copy the form to the GLOBAL.MPT so that it's available for all projects.

Part

VIII

Ch

27

From Here...

▨ See Chapter 19, "Exchanging Project Data with Other Applications," to learn more about OLE (Object Linking and Embedding).

▨ See Chapter 22, "Customizing Views, Tables, and Filters," if you are unfamiliar with how to mark these items to display in the menu.

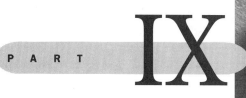

P A R T

IX

Appendixes

A Microsoft Project 98 Shortcut Keys   913

B Glossary   919

C Companion Products for Microsoft Project 98   927

Microsoft Project 98 Shortcut Keys

Most shortcut keys emulate menu commands. They are listed in Table B.1 by the function they perform. In some cases the shortcut key executes a shortened version of the menu command or a special function that is related to the menu command. ■

Table A.1 Shortcut Keys for Microsoft Project 98

Activity/Function	Shortcut Key
Using Menus	
Activate/deactivate the menu and toolbars	Alt or F10
Select next toolbar	Ctrl+Tab
Editing	
Activate entry bar to edit field	F2
Clear or reset contents of selection	Ctrl+Delete
Copy selection	Ctrl+C
Cut selection	Ctrl+X
Delete Task, Resource, or Assignment	Del or Ctrl+ –
Display Assign Resources dialog box	Alt+F10
Display Information dialog box for selected Task, Resource, or Assignment	Shift+F2
Display list in field with list control arrow	Alt+↓
Fill Down	Ctrl+D
Insert Hyperlink	Ctrl+K
Insert Task or Resource	Ins or Ctrl++
Paste	Ctrl+V
Replace	Ctrl+H
Spelling	F7
Undo editing	Ctrl+Z
Linking	
Link Tasks	Ctrl+F2
Unlink Tasks	Ctrl+Shift+F2
Update DDE links	Alt+F9
Calculating	
Calculate Active project	Shift+F9
Calculate All open projects	F9
Turn Auto Calculate On/Off	Ctrl+F9

Formatting

Font (Bold)	Ctrl+B
Font (Italic)	Ctrl+I
Font (Underlined)	Ctrl+U

Outlining

Hide Subtasks	Alt+Shift+–
Indent task in outline	Alt+Shift+→
Outdent task in outline	Alt+Shift+←
Show all tasks	Alt+Shift+*
Show Subtasks	Alt+Shift++

Sorting

Sort again using current sort order	Ctrl+Shift+F3
Sort by ID	Ctrl+F3

Searching

Find	Ctrl+F or Shift+F5
Find Next	Shift+F4
Go to	Ctrl+G
Go to ID number or Date	F5
Go to next resource overallocation	Alt+F5

Filtering

Apply Same filter again	Ctrl+F3
Display all rows (removes filter)	F3

Scrolling Gantt Chart

Timescale one minor time unit left	Alt+←
Timescale one minor time unit right	Alt+→
Timescale one screen left	Alt+Page Up
Timescale one screen right	Alt+Page Down
Timescale to beginning of the project	Alt+Home
Timescale to end of the project	Alt+End

continues

App

A

Table A.1 Continued

Activity/Function	Shortcut Key
Scrolling Gantt Chart	
Timescale to start of current task	Ctrl+Shift+F5
Zoom in	Ctrl+/
Zoom out	Ctrl+*
Selecting Cells in Tables and Usage Views	
Add to selection	Shift+F8
Extend selection mode	F8
Extend selection to first field in a row	Shift+Home
Extend selection to last field in a row	Shift+End
Extend the selection to entire column(s)	Ctrl+spacebar
Extend the selection to entire row(s)	Shift+spacebar
Go to cell in first row	Ctrl+↑
Go to cell in first row, first column	Ctrl+Home
Go to cell in last row	Ctrl+↓
Go to cell in last row, last column	Ctrl+End
Move within a selection down one cell	Enter
Move within a selection left one cell	Shift+Tab
Move within a selection right one cell	Tab
Move within a selection up one cell	Shift+Enter
Reduce selection to a single field	Shift+Backspace
Managing a View	
Display Column Definition dialog box	Alt+F3
Select details area at bottom of Task or Resource Form	Alt+1 (first), Alt+2 (second)
Select next pane or drawing object	F6
Select split bar in multipane view	Shift+F6

File and Windows Operations

Close document window	Ctrl+F4
Close Microsoft Project	Alt+F4
Go to Next Project window	Ctrl+F6
Go to Previous Project window	Ctrl+Shift+F6
New document	Ctrl+N or F11
Open a file	Ctrl+O
Open a new window	Shift+F11 or Alt+Shift+F1
Print	Ctrl+P
Save	Ctrl+S
Save As	F12 or Alt+F2

Macros

Display Visual Basic Editor	Alt+F11
Run macro	Alt+F8

Help

Context-sensitive Help pointer	Shift+F1
Open Help topics	F1

Glossary

The following Glossary contains a short list of common project management terms:

Actual   Actual aspects of the project that have actually happened, as opposed to being planned or scheduled or predicted. Includes recorded dates, duration, work, and/or cost data for tasks and for resource work done on tasks.

AutoFilter   Provides a drop-down menu of all entries found in a column. Click an entry on the menu and the display will be filtered to show only rows that contain that value in the filtered column.

Base calendar   A calendar used as the primary Calendar for the whole project or multiple resources that specifies work and nonwork time.

Baseline   A copy of the scheduled dates, work, and cost data as of a moment in time that's used for comparison purposes when tracking project progress. Usually the final plan just before work begins on the project.

Calculated filter   A filter that compares values in two fields for a task or resource as a basis for selecting the task or resource.

Calendar   A list of time periods during which work can be scheduled. It consists of the normal working days in a week, the normal working hours on those days, and a list of nonworking days and hours that are exceptions to the normal times. See *base calendar* and *resource calendar*.

Collapsed outline   A view of the task outline where the subtasks for one or more of the summary tasks are hidden from view. See *expanded outline*.

Combination view   A view having two panes. The bottom pane view always shows details for the selection in the top pane view.

Consolidated project   A project file that has one or more other projects (see *subprojects*) inserted into it as *summary tasks*.

Constraint   A limitation set on the scheduling of the start or finish of a task. Normally, all tasks are scheduled to start and finish as soon as possible. Constraints can be placed on the start or on the finish of a task. They may be expressed, for example, as Must Start On, Must Finish On, Start No Earlier Than, Finish No Later Than, and so on.

Contour   The name for different patterns of distribution over time of assigned work. The term is derived from the shape that a bar chart would have if you charted the work per period against a timescale. Predefined contour options include flat, back-loaded, front-loaded, late-peak, early-peak, double-peak, bell, and turtle.

Cost   The total scheduled cost for a task, resource, resource assignment, or project. Includes *fixed cost* and *resource cost*.

Cost Rate table   A table that is defined for a resource and that contains the resource's standard cost rates, overtime rates, and per-use rates, with the dates when each set of those rates takes effect. You can define up to five different tables for each resource to represent different types of tasks the resource may be assigned to and for which you want to charge different cost levels.

Criteria   Conditions that must be met in a filter for a task or resource to be selected.

Critical path   A sequence of tasks, each of which must finish on schedule for the project to finish on time.

Critical task   A task which, if its finish date were delayed, would delay the finish of the project.

Cross-Project links   *Dependency relationships* or *links* between tasks that are in different projects. In a project with links to a task in another project, the *external task* is represented by a placeholder copy or surrogate that can be formatted and linked but not edited. See *external tasks*.

App

B

Dependency relationship   General term that describes the relationship between a dependent task and its predecessor. See also *lag time*, *lead time*, and *partial dependency*.

Dependent task   A task whose scheduled start or finish date must be set to coincide with or be linked to the scheduled start or finish date of some other task (its *predecessor*).

Driving resource   One resource among multiple resources that are assigned to a task whose work takes the longest duration to complete. The duration for the task is "driven" by the time needed by this resource to complete its work.

Duration   The number of time units (minutes, hours, days, or weeks) during which at least one resource works on a task.

For example, if resources are scheduled to work six days straight on a task, beginning on a Monday, the duration of the task will be six days, even though two nonworking weekend days occur between the start (Monday) and finish of the task (the following Monday). If one resource is scheduled to work alone on the same task the first four days, and another resource is scheduled to finish the task in the last two days, the duration is still six days because resources worked on the task in six days. See *elapsed duration*.

Effort Driven task   A task whose total work (effort) is reapportioned among all resources when the list of resources assigned to the task is increased or decreased, thus decreasing or increasing the task duration while keeping the total work constant. Tasks are *effort driven* by default. When a resource is added to or removed from the list of assigned resources for a task that is not effort driven, the duration remains the same, and the total work for the task increases or decreases by the amount of the work assigned to the resource.

Elapsed duration   The actual clock time (not the working calendar time) that elapses between the start and finish of a task. This is based on a 24-hour day and a 7-day week.

Expanded outline   An outline view in which all of the subtasks are displayed. See *collapsed outline*.

Export/Import Map   A table showing what data you want to exchange with another application, and which Project fields should be paired with the specific data locations in the other application.

External Task   A placeholder or surrogate copy of a task from another project file that is linked to one or more tasks in the active project file. You can format and link to external tasks, but you must open the project they reside in to edit them.

Field   A data entry point in a table or on a form. All tasks and resources, for example, have a Name field in which you can record a name for the task or resource.

Filter   A criterion or set of criteria that is applied to all tasks or resources to differentiate those that meet the criteria from those that do not. A filter can operate in two ways: It can hide all tasks that fail to match the filter criteria or it can show all tasks but *highlight* those that match the criteria.

Fixed cost   Fixed costs are assigned directly to tasks and remain constant regardless of task duration or work performed (for example, the contracted delivery price for a task supplied by a vendor). See *resource cost.*

Fixed date tasks   Tasks that have constrained dates or that already have a recorded Actual Start Date and cannot be rescheduled by Microsoft Project.

Fixed duration task   A task type for which you can change the duration, but Project will not recalculate the duration when you change the assigned work or units. See *fixed work* and *fixed units tasks.*

Fixed task   Also called *fixed duration task.* A task whose duration will not be affected by increasing or decreasing the quantity of resources assigned to do work on the task. See *resource driven task.*

Fixed units task   A task type (the default task type) for which you can change the assigned units, but Project will not recalculate units if you change the assigned work or the task duration. See *fixed work* and *fixed duration tasks.*

Fixed work task   A task type for which you can change the assigned work, but Project will not recalculate the work when you change the assigned units or the task duration. See *fixed duration* and *fixed units tasks.*

Global template   The GLOBAL.MPT file that contains the defined characteristics of new project files.

Gridlines   Lines that separate rows and columns in a table or timescale view. Also used in graphs to mark value levels against an axis.

Group Resource   A single resource name that refers to a team or group of resource units, such as a group of trucks, or a group of painters.

Interactive filter   A filter that first prompts the user for one or more values that are then used in selecting the tasks or resources to display in a view.

Lag time A delay that must be observed between the scheduling of a task and the scheduled date of its predecessor task. See *dependency relationship*.

Lead time An amount of time by which a dependent task can be scheduled to overlap or anticipate the scheduled start or finish of its predecessor task.

Legend A reference on a graphic image that defines the graphic elements (markers, patterns, colors, shapes, and so on) in terms of the data represented.

Leveling The process of delaying tasks in order to level out the demands on resources so that the resources are no longer overallocated.

Linked tasks Tasks that have a dependency relationship.

List separator character The character that is used to separate items on a list when they are typed on the same line. Defined in the Regional Settings applet of Windows 95 or Windows NT.

Macro An automated list of instructions that you create to replicate an operation or command. Macros are maintained with Visual Basic for Applications.

MAPI Messaging Application Programming Interface is the Microsoft program that coordinates sending user messages from one application to another.

Master project A project that contains one or more tasks that are links to other projects (subprojects) and whose duration, work, and costs are a summary of the entire duration, work, and cost of the subprojects they represent.

Milestone A task whose purpose is to record a significant accomplishment or event in the life of the project—not to schedule work that must be done. If a task is given a duration of zero, it is automatically marked as a milestone. However, any task, even a summary task, can be marked as a milestone.

Node The graphical box used in the PERT Chart to represent a task.

Operator A device used in filters to link multiple criteria. If multiple criteria must all be met to satisfy the filter, the AND operator is used. If meeting any one of the multiple criteria will satisfy the filter, the OR operator is used.

Organizer A tabbed dialog box that allows you to rename, delete, and copy views, tables, filters, reports, calendars, forms, toolbars, export/import maps, and Visual Basic for Applications modules between projects and the GLOBAL.MPT.

Outline A structured presentation in Microsoft Project that allows tasks to be grouped under summary tasks to show functional relationships. Detailed, subordinate subtasks are demoted under their summary tasks to produce a traditional outline appearance.

Overallocation The situation where a resource is assigned more work during a time period than the resource is capable of delivering.

Partial dependency A dependency relationship where two tasks overlap or where there is a specified gap of time between two tasks. See *dependency relationship*.

Percent complete   A measurement of the actual duration or work that has been completed on a task. Measured as the ratio of actual work or duration to scheduled work or duration.

PERT Chart   A network chart used in project management to illustrate the dependency relationships among tasks. Each task is represented by a box (or node) and is connected by a line to each predecessor or successor task to show the sequencing of tasks.

Plan   Technically, the plan is the baseline (the finalized plan, prior to commencing work on the project). The term is sometimes ambiguously (and mistakenly) used to refer to the current schedule.

Predecessor   If the scheduled start or finish of task A is determined by the scheduled start or finish of task B, then B is the predecessor task for task A. *Predecessor* is a misleading term because the term implies chronological precedence, when the important point is that the scheduling of task A is dependent on the scheduled date for task B. See *dependency relationship* and *successor*.

Priority   A task field whose value is used to determine the likelihood of the task being selected as one of the tasks to be delayed during the leveling process. The higher the priority value, the less likely the task will be delayed.

Recurring task   A task that is repeated at regular intervals during all or part of the project.

Reschedule tasks   A Microsoft Project command that you can use when part of the work on a task has been done but the remainder must be rescheduled to a later time.

Resource allocation   The assignment of a resource to do work on a task.

Resource calendar   A list of the working days and hours for a specific resource. It is composed by defining a base calendar as a reference and listing all of the exceptions to the base calendar.

Resource conflict   The conflict that results when a resource is scheduled to do more work in a given time period than the resource is available to deliver.

Resource cost   The sum of all costs for a task that are based on resource assignments. Resource cost includes the product of the hours of work multiplied by the cost rate per hour for the resource (standard and overtime) as well as the cost per use for the resource (if the latter is defined). See *fixed cost*.

Resource driven task   A task whose duration is driven or determined by the number of resource units assigned to work on the task. See *fixed task*.

Resource group   The Group field in the resource database that can be used to enter names of groups to which resources belong. Not to be confused with *group resource*. See *group resource*.

Resource pool   The list of resources that are available for assignment to tasks. A project can have its own resource pool, or it may use the resource pool that is already defined in another project file.

Table | 925

Resource view   A view that displays resources instead of tasks (see *task view*). The standard resource views include the Resource Sheet, Graph, Form, Allocation, and Usage views.

Resources   The people, equipment, facilities, vendors, and suppliers used to complete the work of the project.

Roll up task   To display a marker on a summary task bar in a Gantt Chart to show a date for one of the subtasks.

Schedule   Often called the *current plan*. The current set of actual (already completed) and predicted (yet to be completed) dates, durations, resource assignments, and costs for the project.

Selecting   Before you can use commands on a field or piece of data, you must select it. Selected data is highlighted or marked in some way to show that the data is selected.

Single pane view   A view that uses only the top pane.

Slack   Total slack is the amount of time by which a task can be delayed without delaying the finish of the project. Free slack is even more restrictive: It is the amount of time a task can be delayed without delaying the schedule for any other task.

Slippage   A measure of the amount of time by which a task's schedule is behind its baseline or planned dates.

Split Task   A task whose scheduled work is interrupted by one or more periods of inactivity in order to accommodate other tasks with higher priority.

Subproject   A project file that is inserted as a summary task in a *consolidated* project file. The *consolidated* project file uses the start and finish dates of the subproject as the start and finish dates of the summary task which represents the subproject. The subproject schedule is fitted into the *consolidated* project schedule by linking tasks to the summary task that represents the subproject. See *consolidated project*.

Subtask   A task that is indented under a Summary task.

Successor   In a dependency relationship, the dependent task is often called the *Successor* task, and the task it depends on is called the *Predecessor* task. The tasks may actually overlap in time, however, and you shouldn't assume that the successor task comes after the predecessor task.

Summary task   A task whose sole function is to encompass and summarize the duration, work, and costs of other tasks (called *subtasks*) Can also represent an entire *subproject* that has been inserted into a *consolidated project*.

Table   A table defines the columns that appear in a view of project data that is laid out in columns and rows, like a spreadsheet. The table defines which columns are included in the view, the data field that is to be displayed, the column title, the alignment, and the width of the column. Project provides nineteen predefined tables for tasks, and eight predefined tables for resources.

Task   A normal task is an essential job or operation that must be completed in order for a project to be completed. Milestones and Summary tasks are special types of tasks.

Task view   A view of the project data that is organized around the defined tasks. The standard task views include the Calendar, the Task Sheet, Task Forms, the Gantt Chart, and the PERT Chart.

Timescale   An area in a view that marks chronological dates along the top of the view and shows data for tasks or resources placed in the appropriate time periods.

Variance   The difference between the baseline and currently scheduled data. Variances for tasks usually refer to dates, while those for resources usually refer to work and costs.

View   A screen display of project data. The View command is used to select the display or view that is most appropriate for your work with the project. Project comes with 26 predefined views, but you can easily add your own custom views to the View menu.

Visual Basic for Applications (VBA)   A complete programming language that you can use to automate your work in Microsoft Project, as well as to automate interactions between Microsoft Project and other applications that run under Windows and NT and that have implemented Visual Basic for Applications.

Wild card   In a filter on a text field, a wild card is a symbol (either ? or *) that can be used in Equals and Does Not Equal criteria to take the place of one or more unspecified parts of a search string. For example, if you wanted to find all the task names that begin with a "t" and end with a "p," you would use the filter string **t*p**. When the asterisk ("*") wild card is used, the filter will find entries that have any number of unspecified characters in the position where the asterisk is placed. Thus, the filter **t*p** would find "top," "tp," and "Train supervisors to setup." When the question mark ("?") wild card is used, there must be exactly one character in the position where each question mark is placed, but there are no restrictions on what those characters must be. The filter string **t??p** would select "trip" and "tarp," but it would reject "tip" and "tulip."

Work Breakdown Structure (WBS)   A method of organizing a project by which tasks are grouped into a hierarchical structure featuring major phase groups, with subgroups at many levels. Tasks are assigned a code that identifies the group, subgroups, and individual task within each group. Microsoft Project uses *outlines* to achieve the same organizational objective. See *outline*.

Workgroup   A group composed of a manager and other members who are working on the same project. The manager assigns the other members to work on tasks, and can communicate with the members about assignments in Microsoft Project 98 via e-mail, an intranet, or the World Wide Web.

Working time   The days and hours on a base calendar or a resource calendar during which work on tasks can be scheduled.

Companion Products for Microsoft Project 98

As Microsoft Project has become the leading project management software product in the world, the number of add-on and companion products that extend or enhance Microsoft Project has grown rapidly. Many of the vendors who offer these products are Solution Provider partners with Microsoft.

To introduce you to the wealth of additional functionality that these products offer to Microsoft Project users, a number of the vendors were contacted and offered the opportunity to describe their products and services in this appendix. The text and screen images were provided by the vendors. No warranty, guarantee, or product endorsement is intended by the author or by Que Corporation in including these products. However, we feel confident that you will find merit in each of these products for some, if not all of your project management needs. ■

Product Descriptions and Vendor Information

The products included in this appendix are all designed to be used with Microsoft Project. In most cases, these products rely on Project to do all the scheduling calculations. Some of the companion products provide a front end that guides you in the planning process and helps you reap special advantages from using Microsoft Project. Other products add special features to the Microsoft Project menu and toolbars, such as specialized views and reports, or aids to learning and using Microsoft Project.

Some vendors offer multiple products. The listing is organized alphabetically by vendor, with all products for the vendor listed together.

ABT Corporation

Vendor: ABT Corporation

Address: 361 Broadway
              New York, NY 10013

Phone: 212-219-8945

Fax: 212-219-3597
              1-800-4-PROJEC

Web: **http://www.abtcorp.com**

Project Bridge Modeler   ABT Corporation's Project Bridge Modeler (PBM) is a flexible planning and estimating system designed to work with your firm's best practices and any methodology to produce complete plans for your projects (see Figure C.1). PBM shortens the planning cycle and creates faster, proven defensible project plans that you can insert into Microsoft Project. PBM also has effective Year 2000 Routes that enable you to develop quick and consistent project plans within your millennium conversion effort.

ABT Repository   The ABT Repository (see Figure C.2) is a workgroup management facility that allows project team members, project managers, and project officers and executives to interact with, manage, and report from shared project data. As a central resource pool for facilitating workgroup project management, ABT Repository offers a robust interface to Microsoft Project. With its open, scaleable architecture, Repository serves as an integration environment for business processes and improves organizational reporting and communication by capturing and delivering timely information.

FIG. C.1

A sample process flow diagram in ABT's Project Bridge Modeler.

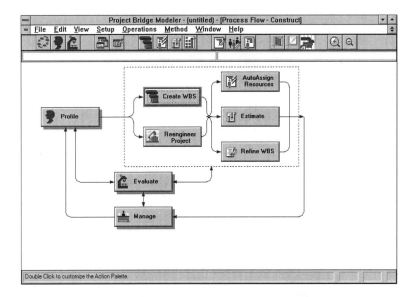

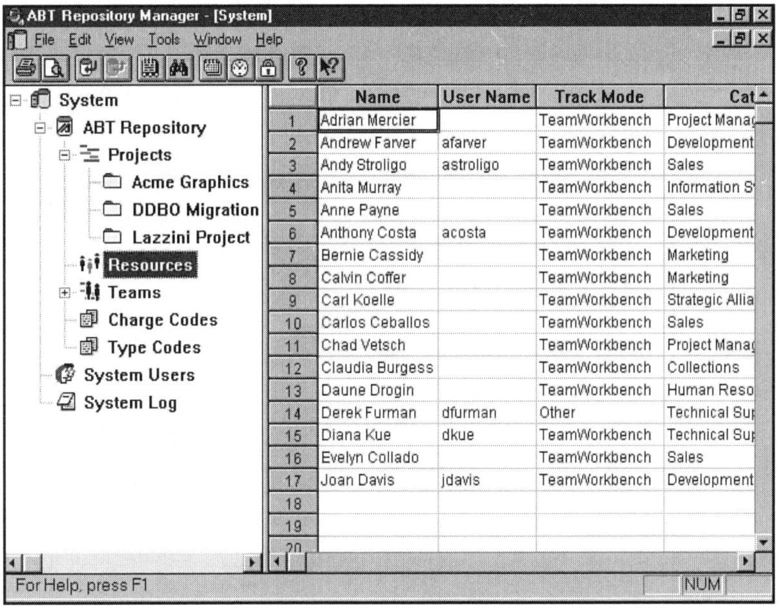

FIG. C.2

A sample Resource listing from ABT Repository.

Critical Tools

Vendor: Critical Tools

Address: 8004 Bottlebrush Drive
            Austin, TX 78750

Phone: 512-342-2232

Fax: 512-342-2234

Web: **http://www.criticaltools.com**

WBS Chart for Project   WBS Chart for Project is a Microsoft Project add-on product that allows you to plan and display your projects using a tree-style diagram known as a *Work Breakdown Structure (WBS) chart*. WBS charts display the structure of a project showing how the project is broken down into summary and detail levels (see Figure C.3). Plan new projects with WBS Chart for Project by using an intuitive "top-down" approach or display existing Microsoft Project plans in an easy-to-understand diagram. WBS Chart for Project is installed directly into Microsoft Project and interacts seamlessly to exchange data. Simply open Microsoft Project, click the WBS Chart for Project toolbar button, and the WBS Chart for Project program is automatically started for you to plan a new project or display an existing Microsoft Project plan.

FIG. C.3

A sample Work Breakdown Structure chart from WBS Chart for Project by Critical Tools.

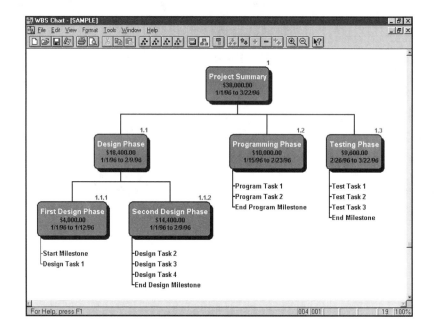

PERT Chart EXPERT   PERT Chart EXPERT is a Microsoft Project add-on product that allows you to create presentation-quality PERT Charts directly from your Microsoft Project plans.

Loaded with features to configure and print many different styles of PERT Chart diagrams, PERT Chart EXPERT contains extensive PERT-charting capabilities unlike those found in Microsoft Project's PERT Chart.

Create timescaled PERT Charts (see Figure C.4), view PERT Charts grouped by Resource, Summary Level or other custom grouping fields, use the Microsoft Project filters to create filtered PERT Charts, automatically hide summary tasks in a PERT Chart, and more. PERT Chart EXPERT is installed directly into Microsoft Project and interacts seamlessly to exchange data. Simply open a project file in Microsoft Project, click the PERT Chart EXPERT toolbar button and a PERT Chart is automatically created.

FIG. C.4
Use PERT Chart EXPERT to place your PERT Chart on a timescale with grouping of tasks by resources.

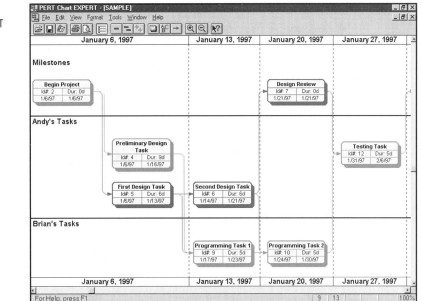

Experience in Software

Vendor: Experience In Software, Inc.

Address: 2000 Hearst Ave.
            Berkeley, CA 94709

Phone: 510-644-0694
            800-678-7008   Orders
            510-649-5923   International

Fax: 510-644-3823

Web: **http://www.experienceware.com**

Project KickStart   Project KickStart makes the intimidating process of planning a project clear and easy. This attractive, easy-to-use program focuses attention on the structure of the project, the goals, resources, risks, and strategic issues critical to the project's success. Your plan is ready in 30 minutes. Project KickStart meets the needs of two types of users:

- Project planners who have small to mid-sized projects which do not involve many resources, budget tracking, and other elements associated with traditional project management. Project KickStart's reports have all the information needed to start these projects.

- Users who manage complex projects using traditional project management software. Though effective once projects are organized, these programs often do not help plan project strategy (that left column in Microsoft Project). Project KickStart easily develops strategy and has expanded capability as a proposal writing tool and business planner (see Figure C.5).

Project KickStart prints seven presentation-ready reports and has direct links with Microsoft Project, Word, Excel, and others.

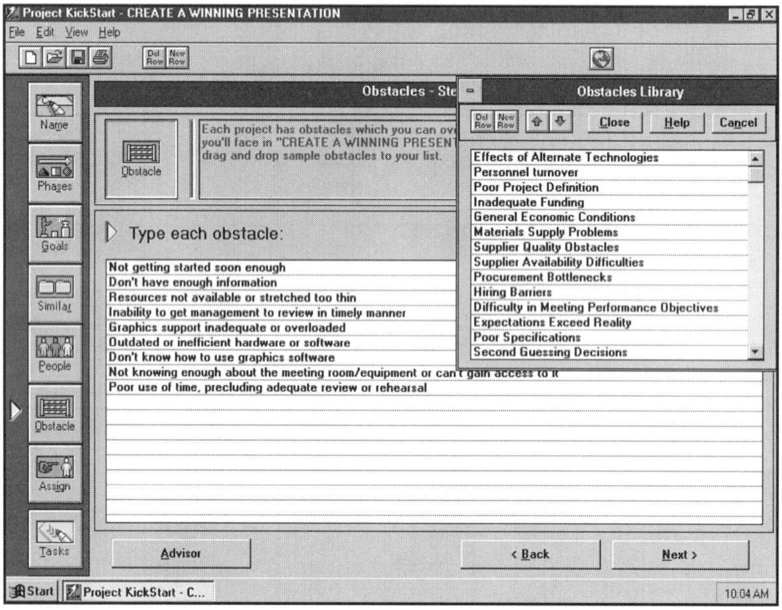

FIG. C.5

Project KickStart helps you build presentations and strategy documents with guidance from experts.

GTW

Vendor: GTW

Address: 500 S. 336th, Suite 204
Federal Way, WA 98003

Phone: 253-874-8884

Fax: 253-838-1798

Web: **http://www.gtwcorp.com**

Project Partner   Project Partner totally transforms Microsoft Project. It does exceptional timescaled logic diagrams, bar charts, cost and resource histograms, S-curves, and spread-sheets. Project Partner's split bar feature allows you to manage by exception just the activities that have a schedule or budget problem. Project Partner also handles fixed costs and adds Earned Value features and overlays. Project Partner can sort, summarize, select, and group your information any way you want.

IMS

The ProjectExchange family of products from IMS provides a completely integrated enterprise, people, project, and time management solution. Microsoft products are combined to provide: senior managers with decision support information, team managers with solutions to allocate, schedule, and track activity information, and team members with solutions to track time, expenses, and activity information.

Vendor: IMS

Address: 549 Columbian Street
           Weymouth, MA 02190

Phone: 617-340-4400

Fax: 617-340-4401

Web: **http://www.imscorp.com**

Portfolio Wizard   Portfolio Wizard is an Executive Information System, providing analysis of information gathered throughout the organization. A user-friendly wizard interface facilitates the organization of information. Portfolio Wizard allows in-depth cost, resource, and activity analysis. It also utilizes familiar Microsoft Excel and Microsoft planning products to display, analyze, and manipulate the organization's information.

TimeXchange   TimeXchange is used to establish project schedules, report actual progress, and analyze information. Team members utilize TimeXchange to record actual progress (see Figure C.6), provide feedback, schedule personal tasks, record expenses, and manage activi-ties from various managers. TimeXchange updates the manager's project file to improve effi-ciency and accuracy.

WebTime   WebTime is a browser-based interactive timesheet, providing the flexibility to report actual progress and receive new or updated assignments via the World Wide Web. Team members report actual hours worked for tasks assigned to them. Managers are automatically updated with actual hours submitted by team members.

TaskClass   TaskClass provides organizations with the ability to define standards and ensure that task-level information is consistent across all project and non-project activities. Teams can easily classify task-level information to provide roll-up capability to organizationally defined

App
C

levels (see Figure C.7). A wizard guides an administrator through the process of defining classification business rules.

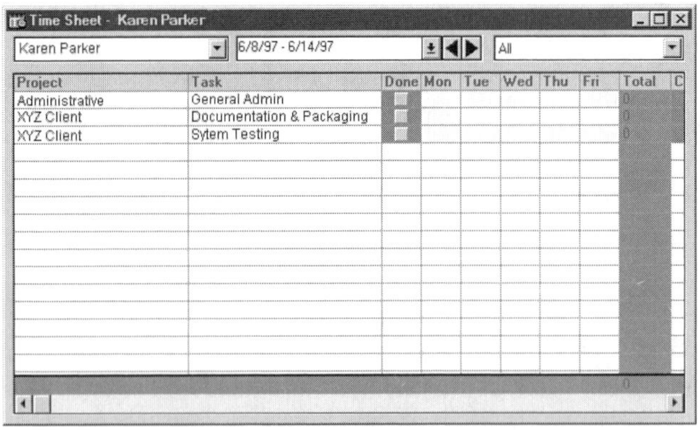

FIG. C.6

A sample time sheet from TimeXchange by IMS.

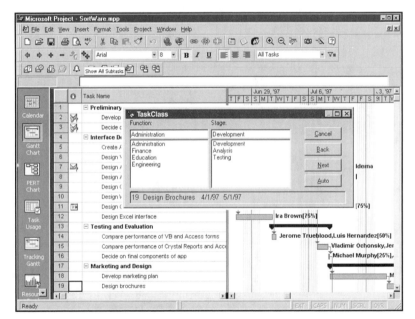

FIG. C.7

TaskClass by IMS is integrated into Microsoft Project to help you classify tasks by defined organization standards.

TimeReview   TimeReview utilizes a three-tier client/server architecture, providing the ability to verify team member compliance with organizational time-reporting standards. Employees may have time automatically validated, while contractors may require a manager to verify reported time. Team members and managers can be notified via electronic mail when updating is delinquent.

DocCheck   DocCheck provides organizations with the ability to classify and store additional project-related information with Microsoft Office documents (see Figure C.8). Whether your organization utilizes an HTML, messaging, or file-based storage method, storing additional information with a Microsoft Office document makes the information easier to retrieve, analyze, and use for collaboration.

FIG. C.8

Link documents to projects and classify them for better reference and retrieval using DocCheck from IMS.

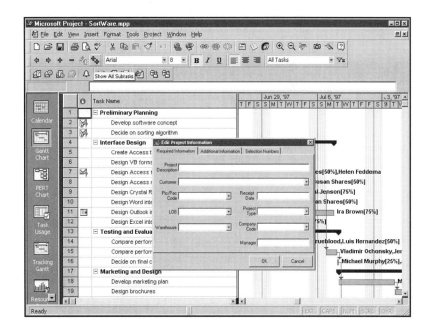

ResourceXchange   ResourceXchange provides organizations with the ability to define a unique Organizational Breakdown Structure (OBS). An outline view of the organizational breakdown structure is available (see Figure C.9) to add, view, and modify an individual's organizational position. In addition to creating and maintaining an OBS, ResourceXchange helps organizations define and maintain resource attributes.

Kalyn Corp.

Vendor: Kalyn Corporation

Address: 876 Lundy Lane
           Los Altos, CA 94024

Phone: 800-595-2596
           415-948-5124

Fax: 415-949-2409

Web: **http://www.kalyn.com**

FIG. C.9
Record your Organizational Breakdown Structure with ResourceXchange from IMS.

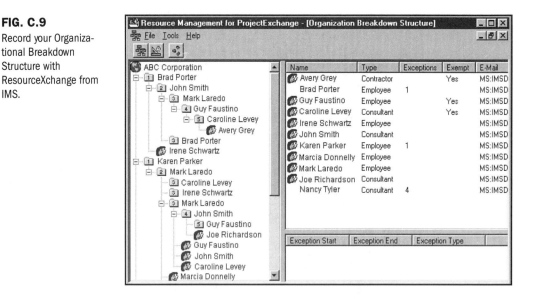

Schedule Insight Schedule Insight helps communicate your Microsoft Project schedules to the non-project managers on your team by providing personalized views of project information without requiring a copy of Microsoft Project. Schedule Insight automatically rolls-up multiple projects and partitions them into simple tables and folders by task, individual, department, project, and company.

Staff members can quickly find their own tasks in a separate folder (see Figure C.10) while managers and executives can see high-level summaries of department and company activities. Includes over 30 built-in reports plus a report writer for custom reports. Runs on Windows 3.x, 95, and NT.

Kalyn Calendar Kalyn Calendar is an intuitive and cost-effective way to let your team view and update their own task assignments. Users log on and see their task assignments on a simple visual calendar (see Figure C.11). Just point and click to update the work performed on a task or double-click to see details for a task, day, week, or month. Kalyn Calendar automatically updates Microsoft Project databases so your schedules always stay current. Security with audit trails keeps your project safe. Available for Windows 95, NT, and as a Java applet for your company's Web intranet.

KIDASA Software, Inc.

Vendor: KIDASA Software, Inc.

Address: 1114 Lost Creek Blvd., Suite 300
Austin, TX 78746

Phone: 512-328-0167 or 800-765-0167

Fax: 512-328-0247

Web: **http://www.kidasa.com**

FIG. C.10
View multiproject summaries of resource assignments with Schedule Insight from Kalyn Corporation.

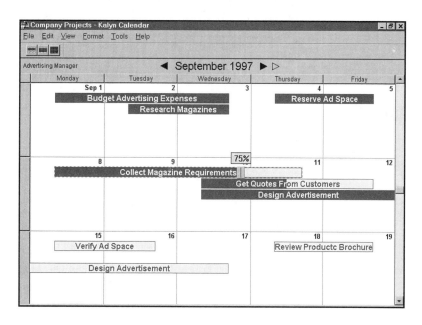

FIG. C.11
Resources view their assignments in the easily understood calendar format and update progress directly from that view with Kalyn Calendar.

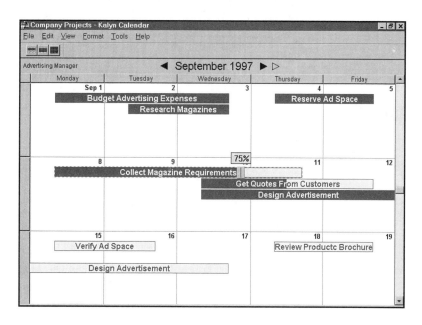

Milestones, Etc.   Milestones, Etc. is an easy and flexible project-scheduling tool which can import and export in MS Project's MPX file format. Use Milestones, Etc. stand-alone or as part of an integrated project management solution. Milestones, Etc. lets you build simple Gantt Charts and detailed milestone schedules (with multiple milestones per task) in minutes (see Figure C.12). Flexible printing and formatting yield presentation-ready results. Schedule setup wizard and built-in starter templates make building new schedules a breeze. Visit their Web page for free demo software, movies, and more!

FIG. C.12

You can use Milestones, Etc. to generate alternative reports of your task data.

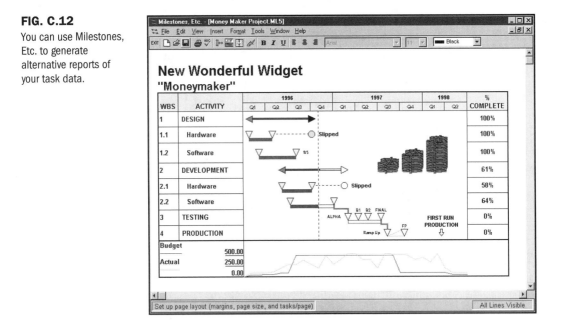

Marin Research

Vendor:	Marin Research
Address:	100 Larkspur Landing Circle, #220
	Larkspur, CA 94939
Phone:	415-461-9784
Fax:	415-461-9788
Web:	**http://www.marinres.com**

Project Gateway   Project Gateway builds multi-project repositories accessible with Notes clients or Internet browsers. The repository contains schedule information from Project (see Figure C.13), team discussions and collaboration, and a secure, accessible container for all of the qualitative project information: for example, specifications, change orders, budgets, deliverables, and so on. It provides bidirectional synchronization with project schedules from

Microsoft Project. A complete timesheet facility is available. The repository generates individual and departmental forecasts of workload for future periods and proactively alerts, via e-mail, people to schedule problems, interproject dependencies, deliverables, and issues. Graphics agents prepare Gantt Charts automatically.

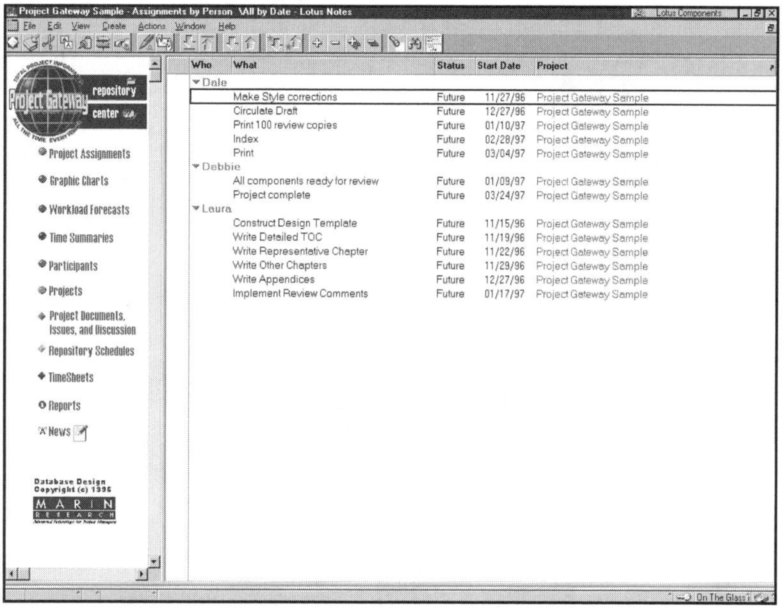

FIG. C.13
Collect and organize project and supporting qualitative information for multiple projects in Project Gateway from Marin Research.

Micro-Frame Technologies

Vendor: Micro-Frame Technologies, Inc.

Address: 430 North Vineyard Avenue, Suite 102
            Ontario, CA 91764

Phone: 909-983-2711

Fax: 909-984-5382

Web: **http://www.microframe.com**

ProjectServer   ProjectServer builds on Microsoft Project, simplifying the creation, upkeep, and management of multiple projects in a central database. ProjectServer complements Microsoft Project by taking individual project data from desktop computers and consolidating it in a central database. ProjectServer generates enterprise-wide project and team status reports and provides quick access to critical information, by project or by resource. It can also be used to forecast project completion dates, highlight resource priority changes, and provide streamlined schedule dates.

TimeServer   TimeServer is an enterprise-wide, mail-enabled timesheet application designed to assist project managers in tracking resource information across multiple projects. TimeServer is used to capture actual hours worked in a time-phased manner. It provides daily resource hours worked and remaining hours on Microsoft Project tasks as well as on user-defined nonproject categories. Now, timesheets can be filled out by project or nonproject personnel. This allows your division or enterprise to utilize a single time-tracking system.

Parsifal Systems

Vendor: Parsifal Systems

Address: 155 N. Craig Street
          Pittsburgh, PA 15213

Phone: 412-682-8080

Fax: 412-682-6291

Web: **http://www.parsifal-systems.com**

Product: BestSchedule   BestSchedule for Projects is a powerful resource scheduling engine that enhances Microsoft Project. It is an easy-to-use, seamless add-on (see Figure C.14) which automatically schedules resources in a superior fashion. It analyzes bottlenecks, available slack, overallocated resources, and due date importances in an iterative process that finds the best solution available.

BestSchedule for Projects V2.0 adds superior automatic task-splitting and task-contouring capability, allowing in many cases for a 20-percent to 30-percent increase in resource utilization, and a corresponding shortening of project completion times. BestSchedule also comes with a number of resource management functions.

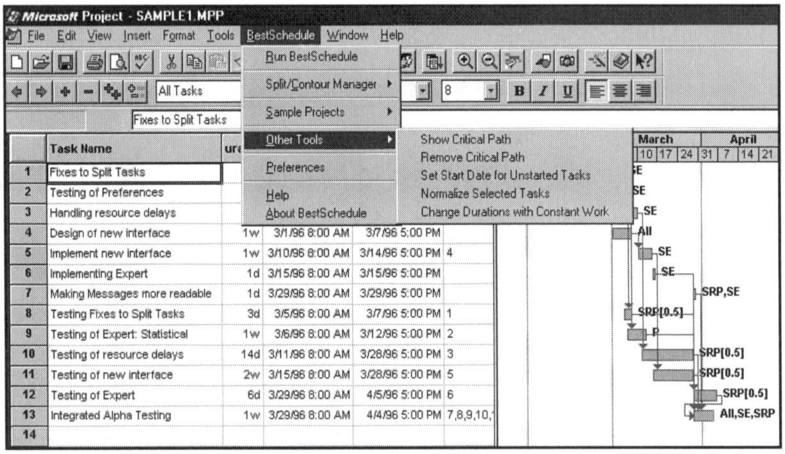

FIG. C.14

BestSchedule is incorporated in the Microsoft Project menu to add seamless new optimization functions.

PMSI

Vendor: Program Management Solutions, Inc

Address: 111 Sepulveda Blvd., Suite 333
Manhattan Beach, CA 90266

Phone: 310-374-0455

Fax: 310-374-2090

Web: **http://www.prog-mgmt.com**

Risk +   Risk + is a comprehensive risk analysis tool that integrates seamlessly with Microsoft Project to quantify the cost and schedule uncertainty associated with your project plans. Precisely predicting how long a project will take or how much it will cost is almost impossible, and single point estimates for task duration and costs can be dangerously misleading. Risk + uses sophisticated Monte Carlo-based simulation techniques to answer questions such as: "What are the chances of completing by 2/28/98?"; "How confident are we that costs will be below $9 Million?"; or "What are the chances that this task will end up on the critical path?" Expensive scheduling systems have provided these tools for years; now, Risk + brings this power to your PC at an affordable price.

Don't worry, it doesn't take a statistical wizard to use Risk + ! They've included Cue Cards that walk you through the risk analysis process, and an extensive user's manual that explains how to interpret each graph and report. As they say, the only thing they left out is the complexity.

Project Assistants, Inc.

Vendor: Project Assistants, Inc.

Address: P.O. Box 7323
Wilmington, DE 19803-0323

Phone: 302-475-8322
800-642-9259   North America Sales

+44 1789 297000   Europe Sales

Fax: 302-529-7035

Web: **http://www.projectassistants.com**

E-mail: **sales@projectassistants.com**

ProjectCommander   You can quickly and easily become a Microsoft Project power user and reduce the learning curve required to master the new features of Microsoft Project 98. ProjectCommander is seamlessly integrated within the familiar Microsoft Project 98 desktop (see Figure C.15). With the powerful new features of Project 98, the complexity of using the sophisticated, more advanced functions can be overwhelming. The logical flow of ProjectCommander will lead you through the process of managing your projects with its

App
C

intuitive planning, tracking, analysis and reporting menus, and automated functions. There's no need to worry about where to double-click, when to secondary click, or how to split the screen, or apply views, tables, and filters to get at your most critical project data. ProjectCommander takes you to the right information at the right time.

FIG. C.15

Use ProjectCommander from Project Assistants, Inc. to guide you through Microsoft Project 98.

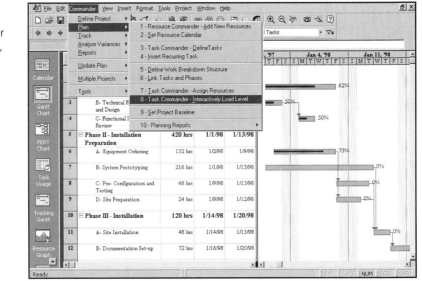

TEAMS (Team Enabled Automated Methodology System)

TEAMS provides all of the benefits of process management while working directly within Microsoft Project. You start by building a customized work plan template in Microsoft Project. Incorporate and automate your organization's methodologies as you easily link tasks to all of the intellectual assets required to perform the task. TEAMS provides detailed methodology steps, Microsoft Word or other document templates, multimedia files such as PowerPoint presentations, hot links to Internet URLs, Excel spreadsheets, Access databases, faxes, and e-mail communications.

As you are executing your project, all of the tools you have built and customized for your particular project are at your fingertips to ensure that control and quality are maintained. TEAMS can be run as a stand-alone field notebook for distributed personnel or controlled from a centralized network environment. The work plans and process templates (assets) are built using the AssetWizard and distributed and deployed using the WorkPlanWizard. An electronic feedback tool is provided to ensure that the process of continuous improvement is fully integrated and easy-to-use. Updates can then be captured and redistributed for replication to the field users who will benefit most from the improvements. All of these functions are launched directly from Microsoft Project. Project Assistants, Inc. can also customize the Project Commander AssetWizard to meet the specific needs of your organization.

Software Made Easy

Vendor: Software Made Easy, Inc.

Address: 1038 Redwood Hwy., Suite B7
Mill Valley, CA 94941

Phone: 415-381-9639

Web: **http://www.smez.com**

Project InVision   Project InVision combines the power of Microsoft Project, Microsoft Office, and Microsoft BackOffice to create a total enterprise project management solution (see Figure C.16). The system consolidates multiple project schedules and related data into a single repository, providing a central point to track all project information via the LAN or intranet.

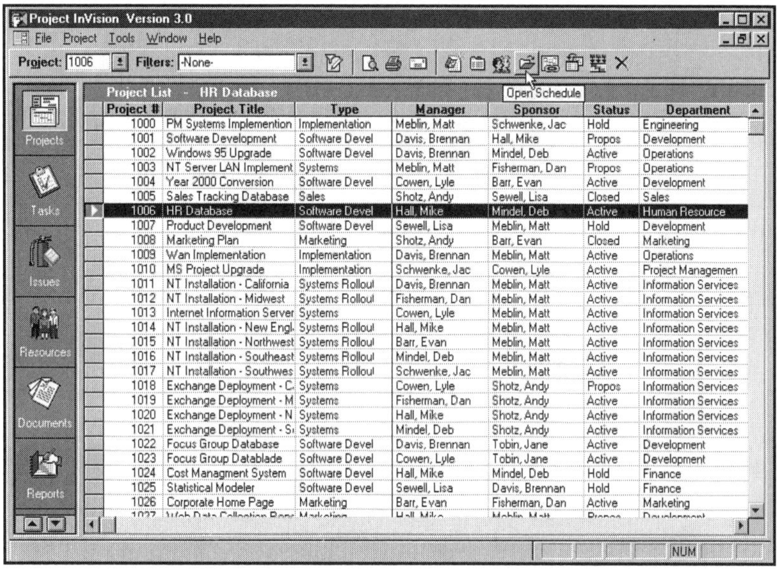

FIG. C.16

Consolidate multiple project files and related documents with Project Control by Software Made Easy.

Index

Symbols

%Complete field, 509
%Work Complete field, 509

A

ABT Corporation, 928
Access (Microsoft) 8.0
  creating import/export
    maps for, 611-620
  databases, creating Web
    pages from, 466
  format
    opening projects, 605-606
    saving projects, 604-606
accessing
  Organizer, 115
  resource calendar, 273-274
  see also opening
accrual of costs, 255
Accrue At field (Resource
  Sheet view), 260-261
active split bar (Gantt Chart
  view), 52
actual aspects, 920
Actual Costs tracking field,
  493-495

Actual Duration tracking
  field, 492
Actual Finish Date tracking
  field, 490-491
Actual Start Date tracking
  field, 490
Actual Work tracking field,
  493-495
ActualFinish property
  (Project object), 852
ActualStart property
  (Project object), 852
ACWP (Actual cost of work
  performed) field, 530
Add Progress Line tool
  button, 523
Adjust Dates macro,
  212-214
Advanced Find dialog box,
  104-107
Aerospace sample template
  file, 113
alarms, setting in Outlook,
  587-588
Analysis toolbar, 873
Analyze Time-Scaled Data
  in Excel tool button,
  530-532

analyzing progress, 508
  Analyze Time-Scale Data in
    Excel tool button, 530-532
  calculating variances,
    509-510
  resource level, 521-522
    Add Progress Line, 523
    Display Progress Lines at
      Recurring Intervals,
      525-526
    Earned Value fields and
      report, 529-530
    Gantt Chart bars, 526-528
    Progress Lines dialog
      box, 523-524
  summary progress informa-
    tion
    cost variances, 512
    date variances, 511
    Project Statistics dialog
      box, 512-514
    Project Summary Report,
      512-514
    work variances, 510
  task level, 514
    cost variances, 519
    date variances, 516-519
    resource assignment
      level variances, 519-521
    work variances, 514-515
  week-to-week trends,
    532-533

Application object (Project Object model), 850-852

applications
copying data, 639-642
exiting, 29
linking data between, 642
deleting links, 646-647
field values to values in
other sources, 643-644
identifying tasks
or resources with
links, 647
refreshing linked data,
645-646
OLE2 compliant, 654-656
pasting objects into, 652-654
Gantt Chart, 649-650
Microsoft Project, 649
Notes Field, 650
Task or Resource
Objects Box, 651-652

applying filters to current view, 690

arguments
Draft, 868
Name, 868

Arrange All command (Window menu), 119-120, 545-546

ASCII Text file format, 597, 637

As Late As Possible (ALAP) constraint, 204-205

As Soon As Possible (ASAP) constraint, 204-205

Assign Resources dialog box, 312-314

Assigned To filter task, 687

Assignment category reports
Overallocated
Resources, 787
To-Do List, 786-787
What Does What, 784-785
What Does What When, 785

Assignment Delay field, 377-378

Assignment Information dialog box
assigning resources, 327-329
selecting cost rate tables,
330-331
selecting predefined
contours, 329-330

assignments
crosstab reports,
adding, 824
delaying to resolve
overallocations, 359, 371,
375-388
fixed contract fees, 337-340
fixed costs, 337-344
leveling to resolve
overallocations, 381
Automatic Leveling, 387
Clear Leveling
command, 387
Level Now command,
385-387
Resource Leveling dialog
box, 381-385
overtime work, 332-333
in fields, 334
with Resource Form, 336
with Task Form, 334-335
resources, 284-285, 311-312
alternate views, 340-343
Assign Resources dialog
box, 312-318
Assignment Information
dialog box, 327-331
Duration with multiple
resources, 296
Effort Driven Tasks,
294-296
fields, 285-287
modifying, 296-305
Task and Task Details
forms, 320-324
Task Information dialog
box, 318-319
task tables, 331-332
task types, 291-294
Task Usage view,
324-327
work formula, 287-291

resource lists, adding, 820
splitting to eliminate
overallocations, 378-381
task lists
adding, 811
notes, 812

Assistant object (Project Object model), 851-852

attaching objects in Gantt Chart view, 240-242

auditing
dependency links in project
plan, 191-197
task links, 197-199

AutoCorrect feature, 130-132

AutoFilter command (Project menu), 692, 763-764, 920

Autolink option, 189-191

Automatic Leveling command, 387

automating reports, 867-869

B

BAC (Budgeted at Completion) field, 530

Back Loaded pattern, 299

backgrounds
color of Web pages,
changing, 451-454
graphics, defining for
templates, 454-455

Bar Rollup view, 663

Bar Styles command (Format menu), 709-710
choosing rows for bars, 712
defining
bar appearance, 710
length of bars, 712
naming bars, 710

placing text in bar charts, 712-713
selecting tasks to display bars, 711-712

Bar Styles dialog box
Calendar View, formatting, 717-719
Resource Graph view, 734-736

Base Calendar
field (Resource Sheet view), 261
property (Calendar object), 856
reports, 794, 804-805

base calendars, 63, 78, 920
creating new, 82-84
printing, 88-90
scheduling dates, 79

baselines, 920
capturing, 475-476
correcting, 477-478
current schedules, 480-481
Cost table, 483
tables, using, 481-482
Task Usage view, 481
Tracking Gantt view, 484-486
Variance table, 482
Work table, 483-484
printing comparison views, 486
saving, 108, 479-480
setting, 474-475
tables, 682
Task object, 855-856
viewing, 476-477

BCWP (Budgeted Cost of Work Performed)
field, 529
Task object, 855

BCWS (Budgeted Cost of Work Scheduled)
field, 529
Task object, 855

Bell pattern, 299

BestSchedule for Projects, 940

BGCOLOR=parameter, 452

borders
placing with Page Setup dialog box, 422
resource lists, adding, 820
task lists, creating, 812

bottom-up approach to creating a task list, 126-127

Box Styles dialog box (PERT Chart view), 720-723

Bring Forward option (Draw button), 238

Bring to Front option (Draw button), 238

browsers (Web), 441

Budget report, 780-781

Budgeted Cost of Work Scheduled, *see* BCWS

built-in
constants, 860
menus, adding to menu bars, 894
toolbars, 873

Button Editor dialog box, 886-887

buttons
attributes, changing, 887-888
command, customizing, 884-888
custom forms, placing on, 908
faces, customizing, 884-885, 888-893
Font, changing text formatting, 426-428
Header and Footer tabs (Page Setup dialog box), 423-424
images
copying, 885
designing, 886
editing, 884-887

New (More Views dialog box), 742-744
Percent Complete, updating tasks, 501
Pool Takes Precedence (Share Resources dialog box), 559-560
Print Preview, 431
Reschedule Work, updating tasks, 503-505
toolbar, 872
adding, 876-879
changing, 877
grouping, 879
identifying purpose, 873, 876
moving, 879
removing, 876-879
Update as Scheduled, 502
View menu (Organizer), 764-765

C

calculated filters, 761, 920

calculating
costs, 252
shortcut keys, 914
work formula, 287-288
applying in new assignments, 288-289
changing existing assignments, 289
driver resource concept, 290-291

Calculation tab (Options dialog box), 498

Calendar
command (View menu), 216
object (Project Object model), 856
view, 216, 660-661
editing in, 222-225
features, 216-217
formatting, 716-719
navigating in, 217-222

calendars, 920
base, 63, 78, 920
Base Calendar report,
customizing, 804-805
copying
Organizer feature, 85-86
to Global template, 86-87
to other projects, 87-88
creating, 82-84, 798
editing in Standard
calendar, 82
Microsoft Project 3.0, 88
preferences, setting, 75-76
printing, 88-90
resource, 78, 924
accessing, 273-274
changing working
times, 273
editing, 273
extending hours
available, 364-365
overallocation of
resources, 348
resource lists adding, 820
standard (default), 78
editing, 79-82
scheduling with, 79
Working Days report,
customizing, 804-805

capturing
baselines, 475-476
keystrokes, 836-842
Outline Numbering
Macro, 841-842
Special Formatting
Macro, 840-841
Summary Task Format
Macro, 839-840

Cash Flow report, 780

**Cell object (Project Object
model), 851**

**cells, double-clicking,
644-645**

Change Working Time
command (Tools menu), 826
dialog box, 79, 274

changing, *see* editing;
modifying

**characters, list separator,
923**

charges, overtime, 332-333

**chart formats, Work
Breakdown Structure, 126**

**checklist for using Microsoft
Project, 21-22**

**circulating items for review
in workgroups, 575-578**
routing slips, 579-582

**Clear command (Edit
menu), 157**

clearing
page breaks before printing,
419-420
tasks from task lists, 156-157

Clipboard, 244

Clippit, *see* Office Assistant

**Close command (File
menu), 120**

closing files, 120
capturing baselines, 475-476
see also exiting

Code
field (Resource Sheet
view), 261
window, editing macros,
846-847

**collapsing outlines,
162-164, 920**
reports, 802
task list outline, 394-395

**colors, hexadecimal
value of, 452**

**Column Definition
dialog box, 752**

columns
crosstab reports,
repeating, 824
inserting into tables,
749-750, 753
removing from tables, 753
widths, 132

**combination views, 660,
746-748, 920**

**combo boxes, sizing,
880-881**

Comma file format, 598

**Command Bars object
(Project Object model),
851-852**

commands
adding new to menu bars,
892-895
buttons, customizing,
884-888
Edit menu
Clear, 157
Delete, 225
Find, 57
Link Tasks, 179-180
Redo, 156
Undo, 156, 225, 647
Unlink Tasks, 194
editing menu bars, 895-898
File menu
Close, 120
Exit, 29
New, 62
Open, 92
Page Setup, 414, 420-421
Print, 414-415, 434
Print Preview, 414,
430-433
Properties, 66, 69, 803
Save, 107
Save As, 108-109,
442-447, 594-595
Save As HTML, 111, 636
Save Workspace,
111-112, 560-561
Send To, 575-582
Format menu
Bar Styles, 709-714,
734-736
Detail Styles, 738
Details, 677, 727-736
Drawing, 241
Font, 247, 700-701, 835
Gantt Chart Wizard,
714-716

Gridlines, 701-702
Layout, 236
Layout Now, 236, 724-727
Text Styles, 685, 698-705,
801, 812, 834, 840
Timescale, 393-394,
704-708
Help menu
Contents and Index,
36, 859
What's This?, 33, 36, 874
Insert menu
Drawing, 237-238
New Task, 223-225
Page Break, 419-420, 799
Project, 548-549
Remove Page Break,
419-420
Project menu
AutoFilter, 763-764
Filtered For, 397-398,
685, 809
More Filters, 395,
754-755
Overallocated Resources,
351-352
Project Information,
62, 852
Sort, 418-419, 696, 802
Sort By, 400-402
Task Information,
147-148
Reschedule tasks, 924
Settings menu
Control Panel, 77
Printers, 415
Start menu, Microsoft
Project, 28
Tools menu
Assign Resources,
312-318
AutoCorrect, 130-132
Change Working Time,
79, 826
Customize, 875
Filtered For, 221-222
Forms, 900
Options, 62, 70,
702-704, 836
Organizer, 86

Progress Lines, 523-524
Project Summary
Task, 510
Record Macro, 837
Resource Leveling,
373-374
Save Baseline,
476-478
Send Schedule Note,
588-590
Set Reminder, 587-588
Share Resources, 559-560
Spelling, 403-404
TeamAssign, 582-583
TeamStatus, 586-587
TeamUpdate, 587
Toolbars, 892-893
Update Project, 501-502
View menu, 926
Calendar, 216
Cost, 483, 512
Customize, 882
Entire project, 393
More Tables, 679
More Views, 54-55, 660,
742-744
Reports, 409-411,
436-437, 768-769,
793, 868
Table, 748-749
Toolbars, 874-875, 878
Tracking, 497-499
Variance, 482, 511
View Bar, 34
Work, 483-484, 510
Zoom, 220-221, 228, 724
Window menu
Arrange All, 119-120,
545-546
Hide, 546
New Window, 546-547
Split, 51, 223, 544, 678
Unhide, 546
**communication options for
workgroups**
e-mail, 567
Internet communication,
575
intranet communication,
567-575

requesting status reports,
586-587
Send Schedule Notes
command (Tools menu),
588-590
sending task updates, 587
setting task reminders,
587-588
submitting status reports,
586-587
TeamAssign, 582-585
**Completed Tasks report,
776-777**
**compressing the timescale,
393-394**
Confirmed filter (Task), 687
**Confirmed Assignments
filter (Resource), 689**
**Confirmed property
(Task object), 855**
conflicts
resolving in task constraints,
208-214
resource, 924
consolidated projects, 920
**constants, VBA
(Visual Basic for
Applications), 860**
Constraint Dates table, 682
constraints, 16, 920
date in Calendar view, 224
scheduling, 23
Start No Earlier Than, 642
tasks
Calendar view, 224
conflict resolution,
208-214
entering, 205-207
hard versus soft, 202-203
removing, 207-208
start and finish task
boxes, 63-64, 152
subtasks in recurring
tasks, 145
Task object, 854
types, 203-205

Contact property (Task object), 855

Contains (filter test option), 757-766

Contains exactly (filter test option), 757

Contents and Index command (Help menu), 36, 859

Contents tab, 39, 67-68

contours, 920
  patterns, 297-300
  predefined, selecting, 329-330

contract fees (fixed), assigning, 337-340

Copy Picture dialog box, 653

copying
  button images, 885
  calendars, 85
    to Global template, 86-87
    to other projects, 87-88
  data
    between application, 639-641
    from other applications, 641-642
    into other applications, 642
  linked copies, 594
  objects
    Clipboard, 244
    Organizer, 85-86, 116-117
  reports
    Base Calendar, 805
    creating, 797-798
    Project Summary report, 803
  static copies, 594
  tasks in task lists, 157-160
  toolbars into project files, 889

correcting baselines, 477-478

cost calculations, 252

Cost command (View menu), 483, 512

Cost Greater Than filter
  Resource, 689
  Task, 687

Cost Overbudget filter, 519
  Resource, 689
  Task, 687

Cost Per Use field (Resource Sheet view), 254, 260

Cost Rate Tables field (Resource Information dialog box), 262

Cost Rates field (Resource Information dialog box), 262

Cost Reports category reports, 410-411, 779
  Budget, 780-781
  Cash Flow, 780
  Earned Value, 782-783
  Overbudget Resources, 782
  Overbudget Tasks, 781

Cost tables
  comparing baselines and current schedules, 483
  Resource, 683
  Task, 681
  viewing in Task Sheet, 262-263

Cost Tracking
  resource form, 900
  task form, 899

costs, 253, 920
  accrual of, 255
  fixed, 337-340, 922
  project
    reducing, 409
    viewing, 398-399
  rates
    resource lists, adding, 820
    tables, 330-331, 920

  resource, 924
  schedules
    reviewing, 408-409
    tasks, 252
  tracking during projects, 486-487
  types, 253, 256-262
    defining, 262-282
    fixed costs, 255
    resource costs, 254-255
  variances
    finding, 519
    reviewing for entire project, 512

crashing the schedule, 407-408

Create Backup File option, 111

Create New Base Calendar dialog box, 82

Created After filter (Task), 687

creating
  calculated filters, 761
  criteria filters, 762-763
  custom filters, 754
    AutoFilter, 763-764
    defining criteria, 756-757
    naming filters, 755
  custom forms, 902, 904
  HTML files, 636-637
  import/export maps for Access and ODBC, 611-620
  interactive filters, 759-761
  macros
    keystrokes, 836-842
    Outline Numbering Macro, 841-842
    Special Formatting Macro, 840-841
    Summary Task Format Macro, 839-840
  resource pools, 263, 558
    Automatically Add New Resources option, 267-268
    filling in resource fields, 268-270

Resource Form view, 265-267
Resource Information dialog box, 270-272
Resource Sheet view, 264-265
tables, 748
  columns, adding, 749-750
  definition, 750-751
  names, 749
  View screen, 751-754
task lists, 126-127
tasks in Gantt Chart view, 128-130
  AutoCorrect feature, 130-132
  column widths, 132
  current task bar, 139-140
  elapsed duration, defining, 135
  height of task rows, 133
  milestones, 140-142
  Multiple Task Information dialog box, 149
  PERT Analysis toolbar, 137-139
  recurring tasks, inserting, 142-147
  task durations, entering, 134-137
  task durations, estimating, 136
  Task Information dialog box, 147-150
tasks with mouse actions, 155-156
template files, 114, 280
text boxes in Gantt Chart view, 246
toolbars, 880, 882
  by copying existing toolbars, 881-882
  deleting user-defined toolbars, 882-883
views, 742-745
  combination views, 746-748
  filter selection, 745
  names, 744, 746

  saving view definition, 746
  screen selection, 744-745
criteria of filters, 756-757, 921-922
  Contains test, 758-766
  entering test values, 757-758
  Not Within test, 758-766
  testing for logical values, 758-766
  wildcard character strings, 759
  Within test, 758-766
Critical filter, 396, 687
critical paths, 921
  Critical Path Method (CPM), 24-25
  identifying, 406-407
  shortening, 405
critical tasks, 24-25, 921
Critical Tasks report, 771-772
Critical Tools, 930-931
cross-project links, 71, 921
Crosstab Report dialog box, 801
crosstabs, 794
  assignments, adding, 824
  columns, repeating, 824
  creating, 798
  customizing, 821-825
  dates, formatting, 825
  filtering, 823
  gridlines, viewing, 824
  sorting, 801-802, 825
  text, formatting, 825
  totals, adding, 824
  zero values, viewing, 824
CSV (comma-separated value) text file format, 637
Ctrl key functions, 120, 219, 225, 229
Current Activity category reports, 774
  Completed Tasks, 776-777
  Should Have Started Tasks, 777

  Slipping Tasks, 777-778
  Tasks In Progress, 776
  Unstarted Tasks, 774-775
Current System Date button (Page Setup dialog box), 423
Current System Time button (Page Setup dialog box), 423
Custom category reports, 796
  copying, 797-798
  crosstab, 821
Custom Form Editor, 902, 904
custom forms, 899
  adding items to menus, 894
  creating new, 902, 904
  Custom Form dialog box, 900
    editing custom forms, 908-909
    naming custom forms, 908
  displaying with menus, 900
  inserting
    buttons, 908
    field values, 906
    group boxes, 907
    text, 905-906
  Organizer, managing with, 909
  predefined forms, 899-900
  saving, 908
  shortcut keys, assigning, 901-902
  toolbar buttons, assigning, 902
Custom Forms toolbar, 873
Custom properties, creating, 69
Custom Reports dialog box, 796, 798, 804
Custom tab (Properties sheet), 68-70
Customize command
  Tools menu, 875
  View menu, 882

Customize dialog box, 875-876, 878
Commands tab, 892
Modify Selections button, 884
button attributes, changing, 887-888
changing button images, 884-885
copying button images, 885
customizing button faces, 884-885, 888-893
designing button images, 886
editing button images, 886-887

Customize Tool dialog box, 888

customizing
command buttons, 884-888
menu bars, 891-892
commands, 892-895
Modify Selections button, 895-898
PERT Chart view, 235-237
reports, 794-796
Base Calendar reports, 804-805
collapsing outlines, 802
crosstabs, 821-825
Custom category, 796-797
formatting text, 800-801
monthly calendars, 826-827
page breaks, 799-800
page setup, 801
Project Summary reports, 803-804
resource lists, 814-821
sorting, 801
task lists, 805-814
Working Days reports, 804-805
toolbars
buttons, 877-879
combo boxes, sizing, 880
Customize dialog box, 875-876

CV (Earned Value Cost Variance)
field, 530
Task object, 855

D

daily recurring tasks, creating, 145-146

data
copying
between applications, 639-641
from other applications, 641-642
into other applications, 642
defining parameters, 21
exporting
to older releases of MS Project, 598-599
to Web pages, 442-447
fields
scrolling, 56, 58
selecting in tables, 57-58
linking between applications, 642
deleting links, 646-647
field values to values in other sources, 643-644
identifying tasks or resources with links, 647
refreshing linked data, 645-646

databases
Open Database Connectivity (ODBC), 107
saving projects in, 599
Microsoft Access 8.0 format, 604-606
MPD (Microsoft Project Database) format, 599-604
ODBC (Open Database Connectivity) format, 606-608

Date Boxes tab (Timescale dialog box), 717

date format, changing in Box Styles dialog box, 723

Date Range filter, 395-396, 754
Resource, 689
Task, 687

Date Shading tab (Timescale dialog box), 717

dates
crosstab reports, formatting, 825
displaying (View page), 77
variables in VBA (Visual Basic for Applications), 859
variances
reviewing for entire project, 511
Start and Finish Date, 516-519

days, defining in options, 72-73

debugging VBA (Visual Basic for Applications), 862

declaration statement variables in VBA (Visual Basic for Applications), 858

Default End Time option, 74

Default Start Time option, 74

defaults
directory, changing, 93-94
displaying external links, 71
duration, 137
legends, 425
new tasks (Effort Driven), 310-311
printers, 415
resource assignments (Units field), 287
standard calendars, 23-24, 78-82
tables (Entry Table), 185-187

tasks (Fixed Units), 291-292, 309-311
view, 30, 50-52

Define Import/Export Map dialog box, 444, 448-450

Define New Report dialog box, 798, 826

Define New View dialog box, 742-744

defining
assignment units, resource, 284-285
calendar
preferences, 75-76
working time, 78
days and weeks, 72-73
Default Start and End Time of Day, 74
elapsed duration in Gantt Chart view, 135
Fiscal Year setting, 74-75
resource pools, 263-264

Delay field
Resource Allocation view, 371-374
resource assignments, 303-305

Delay table, 682

delays
assignments
allowing in schedules, 191-193
entering in Task or Task Details Form, 323-324
resolving overallocations, 371-388
between tasks (lags), 174-175, 923
negative, 381
work on assignments, 359

Delete command (Edit menu), 225

Delete Import/Export Map dialog box, 636

Delete key, 194, 225

deleting
files from Favorites list, 100
icons, 100
links to other sources, 646-647
objects
Gantt Chart view, 246
with Organizer, 118-119
tasks
from task lists, 156-157
in PERT Chart view, 231-232
user-defined toolbars, 882-883
views from files with Organizer, 765

demoting summary tasks, 161-162

dependency links, 173
auditing, 191-193
creating
Autolink option, 189-191
Entry Table, 185-187
menu or toolbar, 180-181
mouse actions, 187-189
Task Form view, 183-185
delays, 174-175, 191-193
inserting, 179-180
relationships, 176
Finish-to-Finish (FF), 178
Finish-to-Start (FS), 177
Start-to-Finish (SF), 178-179
Start-to-Start (SS), 177-178
removing
Entry Table, 194
menu or toolbar, 193-194
mouse actions, 195
Task Form view, 194
Task Information dialog box, 194
successor versus predecessor tasks, 173-176
Task Information dialog box, 181-183

dependency relationships, 23, 921, 923

dependent tasks, 921

Description field (Customize Tool dialog box), 888

designing
button images, 886
reports, 798-799

Detail Gantt, 666-667

details
crosstab reports, customizing, 824-825
resource lists, customizing, 818-820
tasks
linking, 196-197
lists, customizing, 809-812

Details command (Format menu), 677, 727-730, 732
Availability, 733-740
Cost, 733-740
Cumulative Cost, 734
Cumulative Work, 733-740
Overallocation, 733-740
Peak Units, 732-733
Percent Allocation, 733-740
Resource Usage, 736
Work, 733

Details field (Resource Information dialog box), 262

Details Styles command (Format menu), 738

dialog boxes
Advanced Find, 104-107
Assign Resources
adding resource assignments, 312-314
changing names and unit assignments, 316-318
drag-and-drop assignment feature, 314-315
removing resource assignments, 315-316
scheduling resources for work, 314

Assignment Information, 327-331

AutoCorrect, 130

Bar Styles, 709
Calendar View, formatting, 717-719
choosing row for bars, 712
defining bar appearance, 710
defining length of bars, 712
naming the bar, 710
Resource Graph view, 734-736
selecting tasks to display bar, 711-712
Text tab, 712-713

Box Styles, PERT Chart view, 720-723

Button Editor dialog box, 886-887

Change Working Time, 79, 274

Column Definition, 752

Copy Picture, 653

Create New Base Calendar, 82

Crosstab Report, 801

Custom Forms, 900
editing custom forms, 908-909
features, 908
renaming custom forms, 908

Custom Reports, 796, 798, 804

Customize, 875-876, 878
Commands tab, 892
Modify Selections button, 884-888

Customize Tool, Description field, 888

Define Import/Export Map, 444, 448-450

Define New Report, 798, 826

Define New View, 742-744

Delete Import/Export Map, 636

Detail Styles, 738

Export Format, 448

File Open, 92, 872
changing file names display, 95-98
Commands and Settings button options, 98-100
selecting a different location to be searched, 93-95
specifying search criteria, 102

File Properties, 803

File Save, 107-109, 442-447
Create Backup File option, 111
read-only files, 110-121
security options, 109-110

Filter Definition, 395, 754-755

Find, 57

Find Options, 42

Find Setup Wizard, 41

Font, 835, 841

Form, 904

Format Drawing, 241-242
objects disappearing, 248
Size fields, 244

Gantt Chart Gridlines, 701

Gridlines, 701-702

Help button, 36

Layout, 235-237, 713-714, 719

Level Now, 385-387

Links, 645-646

Macro, 837

Microsoft Visual Basic error, 843

Monthly Calendar Report Definition, 826-827

More Tables, 680, 748-749

More Views, 54
combination views, creating, 746-748
creating new views, 742-744

Multiple Task Information, 149

New Window, 546-547

Office Assistant, 38

Open, 67

Options, 70-72
Automatically Add New Resources option, 252, 267-268
Calculation tab, 498
calendar preferences, 75-76
defining days and weeks, 72-73
defining Start and End Time of Day, 74
Fiscal Year setting, 74-75
formatting outlines, 702-704
Outline Options, 164-165
reviewing settings, 76-77
Spelling tab, 404-405

Options (Planning Wizard), 48

Organizer, 796, 923

Page Setup, 421
entering headers and footers, 424-425
Header and Footer tabs, 423-424
Legends tab, 425-426
placing borders, 422
Print Preview button, 436
specifying margins, 422
View tab, 428-430

Paste Special, 643

PERT Chart Layout, 726

Print
Preview button, 436
printing views with timescales, 435-436
quality and number of copies, selecting, 435
selecting pages to print, 434-435

Progress Lines, 523-524, 526

Project Information, 852
Current Date and Status Date text boxes, 64
entering information, 62-63
Project Statistics dialog box, 64-66
Start and Finish Date text boxes, 63-64

Project Statistics, 392, 512-514
Properties, 803
Record Macro, 847
Recurring Task Information, 142
Replace Resource, 317-318
report definition, 798
Report Text, 804
Reports, 436-437, 794, 868
Resource Assignment, 368-369
Resource Information, 257, 357-358
  accessing resource calendars, 273
  changing availability of resources, 360
  changing dates available, 361
  Cost Rate Tables field, 262
  Cost Rates field, 262
  Details, 262
  editing Cost Rate tables, 331
  Email, 261
  Resource field, 261
  resource pools, defining, 270-272
  resources, defining, 268
  Time Stamped, 262-282
  Workgroup, 261
  Working Time tab, 364-365
Resource Leveling, 373-374
  Automatic Leveling, 387
  Clear Leveling command, 387
  setting options, 381-385
Resource Report, 817
Routing Slip, 579
Save Baseline, 477
Save Options, 111-121
Save Search, 106
Send Schedule Note, 588-590
Share Resources, 559-560
Sort, 696

Spelling, 403-404
Table Definition, 749
Task Information, 147-148, 222-223, 663, 669
  assigning resources, 318-319
  creating links, 181-183
  delays and overlaps, 192
  editing information in, 230
  entering data, 148
  inserted projects, 549
  Notes tab, 148
  removing links, 194
  task constraints, 205-206
  Task Type field, 292
Task Report, 805
Tasks Occurring On, 217
Text Styles, 698, 801, 812, 834
  Font scroll bar, 700-705
  Font Style list, 700
  Item to Change drop-down list, 698-699
  Timescale, 704-705
    Calendar View, formatting, 716-717
    definition, completing, 706
    major scales, changing, 705
    minor scales, changing, 706
    Nonworking Time tab, 707-708
Update Tasks, 500-501
Using Resource filter, 692
View Definition, 743-744
Welcome!, 28-29

directories, default, 93-94
discontinuing resource sharing, 561-562
Display Progress Lines at Recurring Intervals, 525-526
displaying
  dates (View page of Options dialog box), 77
  files, 119-120, 595

graphic images on templates, 455-456
money amounts, 77
projects in Calendar view, 216
tasks occuring on specific date, 217
toolbars, 874-875

Do...Loop program control in VBA (Visual Basic for Applications), 861
DocCheck, 935
Double Peak pattern, 299
Down arrow key, 229
Draft argument, 868
drag-and-drop feature
  copying tasks, 159-160
  creating links, 188-189
  moving tasks, 159-160
Drawing command
  Format menu, 241
  Insert menu, 237-238
Drawing toolbar, 237-239, 873
driver resources, 290-291, 921
duration, 921
  elapsed duration, 921
  percent complete, 924
  projects, reducing, 405-408
  tasks
    entering in Gantt Chart view, 134-139
    estimating in Gantt Chart view, 136
Duration field
  multiple resources assigned, 296
  resource assignments, 290-291

E

e-mail
  assigning resources to tasks, 582-585
  communicating with workgroups, 567

hyperlinks, 461-462
requesting status reports, 586-587
sending task updates, 587
submitting status reports, 586-587

EAC (Estimate at Completion) field, 530

Early Peak pattern, 299

Earned Value table, 683-684

Earned Value Cost Variance, *see* **CV**

Earned Value
fields, 529-530
report, 782-783
task form, 899

Edit menu commands
Clear, 157
Delete, 225
Find, 57
Link Tasks, 179-180
Redo, 156
Undo, 156, 225, 647
Unlink Tasks, 194

Edit Points option (Draw button), 238

editing
button images, 886-887
Calendar view
creating links between tasks, 225
deleting tasks, 225
inserting tasks, 223-225
task details, 222-223
custom forms, 908-909
Gantt Chart view
fonts, 247
line and fill style of objects, 244-246
text box properties, 247-248
macros
Code window, 846-847
Project Explorer, 844-846
Properties window, 846
Visual Basic Editor, 844

outlined projects, 164
PERT Chart view
adding tasks, 230-231
changing task data, 229-230
deleting tasks, 231-232
linking tasks, 232-233
moving task nodes, 233-235
printer setup, 415
recurring tasks, 160
reports, 797
resource calendars, 273
shortcut keys, 914
Standard calendar
canceling changes, 85
deleting Working Time text boxes, 82
resetting, 82
saving changes, 85
standard working hours, 81
time formats, 81
working and nonworking days, 79-80
tables, 748
tasks
data in PERT Chart view, 229-230
lists, 156-160
text boxes in Gantt Chart view, 246
see also editing

Effort Driven tasks, 294-296, 310-311, 921

elapsed duration, 135, 371, 921

eliminating resource overallocations, 357
by delaying
assignments, 371, 375-388
tasks, 371-374
by increasing availability of resources, 357-358, 360
changing dates available, 361

extending hours
available, 364-365
scheduling overtime, 361-364
by reducing workload of resource, 359-360, 365
Resource Allocation view, 365
substituting underused resources, 366-370
by splitting
individual assignments, 378-381
tasks, 374-375

Email field (Resource Information dialog box), 261

EmailAddress property (Resource object), 853

embedding objects, 654-656

End key, 229

Enter key, 77

Entire project command (View menu), 393

Entry
bar, 34
resource form, 900
table
creating links, 185-187
entering delays and overlaps, 192
removing links, 194
Resource, 683
Task, 681
task form, 899

Equals (filter test option), 756

Err object, 862

errors
AutoCorrect feature, 130-132
VBA (Visual Basic for Applications)
debugging, 862
error trapping, 862

Outline Macro example, 862-865
runtime errors, 862
Special Formatting Macro example, 865-867

estimating task duration, 136

Event Planning sample template file, 113

Excel 97 (Microsoft) format, 620
exporting data
to PivotTables, 622-628
to worksheets, 620-622
importing data, 629-634

Exit command (File menu), 29

exiting
applications, 29
Microsoft Project, 28-29

expanding outlines, 162-164, 921

Experience In Software, Inc., 931-932

Export filter, 445

Export Format dialog box, 448

export maps, creating, 611-616, 922

Export table, 683-684

exporting data
to Excel
PivotTables, 622-628
worksheets, 620-622
Import/Export map HTML options, 448-450
to Internet, 634-637
to intranets, 634-637
modifying standard HTML template, 450-451
background graphics, defining, 454-455
changing background color, 451-454
formatting text, 457-459

graphic images, displaying, 455-456
hyperlinks, adding, 460-462
title bar text, changing, 456-457
to MS Project, 598-599
projects, 594-598
text file formats, 638-639
to Web pages
saving projects as HTML documents, 442-447
viewing projects as HTML documents, 447

extensions (files), 102-103

external sources, double-clicking cells linked to, 644-645

external tasks, 922

F

facilities for updating tasks, 495-496
mouse in Gantt Chart, 503-505
Percent Complete buttons, 501
Reschedule Work button, 503-505
Task and Task Details Forms, 499-500
Tracking table, 497-499
Update Project command, 501-502
Update Tasks dialog box, 500-501
Usage views, 496-497

Favorites list, adding files to, 100

field values
custom forms, 906
linking to values in other sources, 643-644

fields, 922
%Complete, 509
%Work Complete, 509

ACWP (Actual Cost of Work Performed), 530
Assignment Delay, 377-378
BAC (Budgeted at Completion), 530
BCWP (Budgeted Cost of Work Performed), 529
BCWS (Budgeted Cost of Work Scheduled), 529
changing with Box Styles dialog box, 722
CV (Earned Value Cost Variance), 530
Delay, 371-374
duration, 134-135
EAC (Estimate at Completion), 530
Earned Value, 529-530
resource
Cost Per Use, 254
filling in, 268-270
resource assignment
naming, 285
Units, 285-287
work, 287
Resource Information dialog box
Cost Rate Tables, 262
Cost Rates, 262
Details, 262
Email, 261
Resource, 261
Time Stamped, 262-282
Workgroup, 261
Resource Sheet view
Accrue At, 260-261
Base Calendar, 261
Code, 261
Cost Per Use, 260
Group, 258-259
ID, 257
Indicators, 258
Initials, 258-259
Max Units, 258-259
Name, 258
Overtime Rate, 260
Standard Rate, 259
Resource Usage view, changing, 355-357
SV (Schedule Variance), 530

table definition, 750-751
Task object ID field, 854
tracking
    Actual Costs, 493-495
    Actual Duration, 492
    Actual Finish Date,
      490-491
    Actual Start Date, 490
    Actual Work, 493-495
    Percent Complete,
      491-492
    Remaining Duration,
      492-493
    Scheduled Duration, 493
VAC (Variance at
    Completion), 530

file formats
exchanging parts of projects
    with, 608-609
import/export maps,
    creating for Access and
    ODBC sources, 611-620
Microsoft Excel 97, 638-639
    exporting data to
      PivotTables, 622-628
    exporting data to
      worksheets, 620-622
    importing data from,
      629-634
MPD (Microsoft Project
    Database), 466, 599
    opening projects from
      databases, 603-604
    saving in new databases,
      600-602
    saving projects in,
      600-603
    saving to existing
      databases, 602-603
supported by MS Project 98,
    594-598

File menu commands
Close, 120
Exit, 29
New, 62
Open, 92
Page Setup, 414, 420-421
Print, 414-415, 434
Print Preview, 414, 430-433
Properties, 66, 69, 803

Save, 107
Save As, 108-109, 594-595
Save As HTML, 111,
    442-447, 636
Save Workspace, 111-112,
    560-561
Send To, 575-582

**File Name button
(Page Setup dialog
box), 424**

**File Open dialog box,
92-93, 872**
changing file names display,
    95-98
Commands and Settings
    button options, 98-100
selecting a different location
    to be searched, 93-95
specifying search
    criteria, 102

**File Properties dialog
box, 803**

**File Save dialog box,
107-109, 442-447**
Options button
    Create Backup File, 111
    password protecting,
      109-110
    read-only files, 110-121
    security, 109

files
capturing baselines, 475-476
copying toolbars into, 889
extensions, displaying, 595
formats, *see* file formats
locating, 101
    Advanced Find dialog
      box, 104-107
    ODBC File Open
      option, 107
    searching by characters
      in file names, 103
    searching by date
      saved, 104
    searching for specific
      text, 103-104
    specifying search
      criteria, 102
    specifying type, 102-103

moving tasks, 552
multiple and the Window
    menu, 546-554
names, 107, 109
operations with shortcut
    keys, 917
project, 92
    changing file names
      display, 95-98
    closing, 120
    Commands and Settings
      button options, 98-100
    creating new, 92
    displaying, 119-120
    opening new, 92-93
    selecting a different
      location to be searched,
      93-95
    virus protection, 100-101
saving, 107-108
    capturing baselines,
      475-476
    Create Backup File
      option, 111
    HTML format, 111
    password protecting,
      109-110
    read-only, 110-121
    Read-Only
      Recommended, 111-121
    security options, 109
    Workspace file, 111-112
starting new, 62
templates
    creating new, 114
    Global, 113
    opening, 112-113
    samples, accessing,
      113-114
types, 103
write protecting, 109

**filling in resource fields,
268-270**

**Filter Definition dialog box,
395, 754-755**

Filtered For command
Project menu, 397-398,
    685, 809
Tools menu, 221-222

filtering
  critical tasks, 406-407
  crosstab reports, 823
  monthly calendar
    reports, 827
  resource lists, 395-398, 817
  shortcut keys, 915
  task lists, 395-398, 809

filters, 685, 922
  adding to menus, 894
  applying to current
    view, 690
  calculated, 761, 920
  Cost Overbudget, 519
  creating
    AutoFilter, 763-764
    defining criteria, 756-757
    naming filters, 755
  Critical, 396
  Date Range, 395-396, 754
  Export, 445
  highlight, 397-398
  In Progress Tasks, 754
  interactive, 685, 759-761, 922
  Late/Overbudget Tasks
    Assigned To, 520
  Milestones, 396
  multiple criteria, creating,
    762-763
  operators, 923
  Overallocated, 351-352
  Overallocated Resources,
    278-279
  Resource, 689-690
  resources, 278-279
  selecting for new views, 745
  Should Start By, 535-536
  Standard, 685-686
  Summary Tasks, 396
  Task, 687-689
  Tasks With Fixed Dates,
    396-398
  Using Resource, 396
  wild cards, 926

**final plans, setting,
  474-475**

Find
  command
    Calendar view, 219-220
    Edit menu, 57
  dialog box, 57

  Options dialog box, 42
  tab, 40-43

Find Setup Wizard, 40-41

finding
  current task bar on Gantt
    Chart, 139-140
  project files, 101-103
    Advanced Find dialog
      box, 104-107
    ODBC File Open
      option, 107
    searching by characters
      in file names, 103
    searching by date
      saved, 104
    searching for specific
      text, 103-104
    specifying search
      criteria, 102
  see also searching

**Finish No Earlier Than
  (FNET) constraint,
  204-205**

**Finish No Later Than
  (FNLT) constraint,
  204-205**

**Finish-to-Finish (FF)
  relationship, 178**

**Finish-to-Start (FS)
  relationship, 177**

Fiscal Year setting, 74-75

**fixed contract fees,
  assigning, 337-340**

**Fixed Cost field (Task Sheet
  view), 262-263**

**fixed costs, 252, 255,
  337-340, 922**

**Fixed property
  (Task object), 855**

fixed tasks, 922
  date tasks, 922
  Duration tasks, 291, 309, 922
    contours, assigning, 330
    recurring tasks created
      as, 147
  Units tasks, 291, 309, 922
  Work tasks, 292, 309, 922

Flat pattern, 297-300

**Font button (Page Setup
  dialog box), 423, 426-428**

Font
  command (Format menu),
    247, 700-701, 835
  dialog box, 835, 841

**fonts, changing in Gantt
  Chart view, 247**

**Footer tab (Page Setup
  dialog box), 423-424**

**footers, inserting in page
  setup, 424-425**

**For...Next loop program
  control (VBA), 861**

Form dialog box, 904

form views, 660

**Format Drawing dialog box,
  241-242**
  objects disappearing, 248
  Size fields, 244

Format menu commands
  Bar Styles, 709
    Calendar View, 717-719
    choosing row for
      bars, 712
    defining bar
      appearance, 710
    defining length of
      bars, 712
    naming the bar, 710
    placing text in bar charts,
      712-713
    Resource Graph view,
      734-736
    selecting tasks to display
      bar, 711-712
  Detail Styles, 738
  Details, 677, 727-730, 732
    Availability, 733-740
    Cost, 733-740
    Cumulative Cost, 734
    Cumulative Work,
      733-740
    Overallocation, 733-740
    Peak Units, 732-733
    Percent Allocation,
      733-740

Resource Usage, 736
Work, 733
Drawing, 241
Font, 247, 700-701, 835
Gantt Chart Wizard, 714-716
Gridlines, 701-702, 708
Layout, 236, 713-714, 719
Layout Now, 236, 724-725,
 727
Text Styles, 685, 698, 801,
 812, 834, 840
 Font scroll bar, 700-705
 Font Style list, 700
 Item to Change
  drop-down list, 698-699
Timescale, 393-394, 704-705
 Calendar View, 716-717
 definition,
  completing, 706
 major scales,
  changing, 705
 minor scales,
  changing, 706
 nonworking time,
  changing display,
  707-708
Format menu options, 696
Calendar View, 716
Gantt Chart view, 709
PERT Chart view, 719
**Format Painter button
(Standard toolbar), 700**
formats
HTML (HyperText Markup
 Language), 634-637
text file, 637
 exporting data, 638-639
 importing data, 639
formatting
Calendar View
 Bar Styles dialog box,
  717-719
 Layout dialog box, 719
 Timescale dialog box,
  716-717
dates in crosstab
 reports, 825

Gantt Chart view
 Bar Styles dialog box,
  709-714
 Format menu
  options, 709
 Gantt Chart Wizard,
  714-716
PERT Chart view, 719
 Box Styles dialog box,
  720-723
 Layout Now command
  (Format menu),
  724-726
 Zoom command
  (View menu), 724
Resource Graph view,
 730-732
 Bar Styles dialog box,
  734-736
 selecting values to
  display, 732-734
shortcut keys, 915
Task and Resource Form
 views, 727-730
text
 calendar reports, 804
 crosstab reports, 825
 HTML templates,
  457-459
 macros, 834-836
 Project Summary
  report, 804
 reports, 800-801, 804, 825
 resource lists, 820-821
views
 gridlines, 701-702
 outline options, 702-704
 Resource Usage, 736, 738
 selected text, 700-701
 sorting tasks and
  resources, 696-698
 Task and Resource
  Sheets, 738-739
 Task Usage, 738
 text displays for
  categories, 697-705
 timescales, 704-708
**Formatting toolbar,
 700-701, 873**

forms
scrolling and selecting
 fields, 58
updating tasks, 499-500
**Forms command
 (Tools menu), 900**
**forwarding files with routing
 slips, 581-582**
free slack, 372, 925
**Frequently Asked Questions
 Web site, 48**
Front Loaded pattern, 299

G

**Gantt Chart view, 30-32,
 50-51, 837**
active split bar, 52
adding graphics and text,
 237, 238-239
attaching objects to task
 bars, 240-242
compressing timescale,
 393-394
creating tasks, 128-130
 AutoCorrect feature,
  130-132
 column widths, 132
 height of task rows, 133
deleting objects, 246
editing styles of objects,
 244-246
estimating task
 durations, 136
formatting
 Bar Styles dialog box,
  709-714
 Format menu
  options, 709
Gridlines dialog box, 701
hiding objects, 242
inserting
 delays, 192
 milestones, 140-142
 overlaps, 192
 recurring tasks, 142-147
 tasks, 127-128, 134-139,
  223-224

locating current task bar, 139-140

pasting objects into, 649-650

PERT Analysis, 668

placing free text
  changing text font, 247
  creating text boxes, 246
  editing text boxes, 246

printing timescales, 435

progress bar, 526-528

resizing objects, 243-244

selecting objects, 240

shortcut keys, 915-916

split bar and split box, 54

splitting tasks, 200

Task object, 854

text boxes, changing
  properties, 247-248

Tracking Gantt view, 484-486

updating tasks, 503-505

view, 661-662

Wizard, 662

see also Leveling Gantt

Gantt Chart Wizard command (Format menu), 714-716

General tab (Properties sheet), 67

Getting Started options (Help menu)
  Create Your Project, 43-44
  Microsoft Project 101:Fundamentals, 44
  Quick Preview, 43

global options (Options dialog box), 70

Global template, 922
  copying to, 86-87
  creating new project files, 92
  modifying with Organizer, 116
  opening, 113
  reports, customizing, 796
  storage of toolbars, 888
  views, organizing in project files, 764-765

GLOBAL.MPT file menu bars, customizing, 891-892

GLOBAL.MPT template, see Global template

Go To command (Calendar view), 218-220

Go To Next Overallocation tool, 354-35, 365

goals of projects, 16, 19

GoTo program control in VBA (Visual Basic for Applications), 861-862

graphics
  adding to Gantt Charts, 237
  files, defining background, 454-455
  images, displaying on templates, 455-456
  views, 660

gridlines, 922
  crosstab reports, viewing, 824
  displaying in Box Styles dialog box, 723
  formatting, 701-702
  resource lists, viewing, 820
  task lists, viewing, 812

Gridlines command (Format menu), 701-702, 708

Group field, 258-259

groups
  boxes (custom forms), placing on, 907
  resources, 253, 922

Group... filter (Resource), 689

grouping commands on menu bars, 898

GTW product descriptions, 932-933

H

hard constraints, 202

Header tab (Page Setup dialog box), 423-424

headers
  inserting in page setup, 424-425
  numbering, 836
  text, formatting, 458-459

height of task rows, adjusting in Gantt Chart view, 133

Help menu, 36
  commands
    Contents and Index, 36, 859
    What's This?, 33, 874
  Contents and Index options, 41-43
    Contents tab, 39
    Index tab, 39-40
  Getting Started
    Create Your Project, 43-44
    Microsoft Project 101:Fundamentals, 44
    Quick Preview, 43
  Microsoft on the Web, 45-48
  shortcut keys, 917

hexadecimal value of colors, 452

Hide command (Window menu), 546

HideBar property (Task object), 855

hiding
  objects in Gantt Chart view, 242
  toolbars, 874-875

highlight filters, 397-398

highlighting critical tasks, 406

Home key, 229

Hours Per Day option,
72-73

Hours Per Week option,
72-73

HTML (Hypertext Markup
Language) format, 442
  code
    Customized Project
      HTML Template
      listing, 458, 460
    E-mail Hyperlink
      listing, 461
    Hyperlink to ABC
      Corporation's Home
      Page listing, 461
    Source from a Microsoft
      Word HTML
      Document listing, 453
    Standard Export.html
      File listing, 451-452
  documents, 440-441
  exporting data to Internet or
    intranets, 634-637
  hyperlinks
    adding to tasks or
      resources, 463-464
    deleting for tasks or
      resources, 464
    editing for tasks or
      resources, 464
    managing projects with,
      465-466
    navigating to, 465
  Import/Export map options,
    448-450
  saving
    files in, 111
    projects as, 442-447
  viewing projects as, 447

Hyperlink table, 681, 684

hyperlinks
  adding
    to HTML templates,
      460-462
    to tasks or resources,
      463-464
  deleting, 464

  e-mail, 461-462
  editing, 464
  managing projects with,
    465-466
  navigating to, 441-442, 465

Hypertext file format, 597

I

icons, deleting, 100

ID field
  Resource Sheet view, 257
  Task object, 854

identifying
  critical paths, 406-407
  resource pool links, 562-563

If...Then...Else program
control (VBA), 860

Import/Export maps,
443-447, 608-611,
616-620
  creating for Access and
    ODBC sources, 611-620
  defining HTML options,
    448-450

importing
  data
    from Excel, 629-634
    text file formats, 639
  exporting projects, 594-598
  projects from ODBC
    sources, 607

IMS product descriptions,
933-935

In Progress Assignments
filter (Resource), 689

In Progress Tasks filter
(Task), 687, 754

Incomplete Tasks filter
(Task), 687

indenting tasks, 162

Index tab, 39-40

Indicators field, 258

Initials field, 258-259

Insert menu commands
  Drawing, 237-238
  New Task, 223-225
  Page Break, 419-420, 799
  Project, 548-549
  Remove Page Break,
    419-420

Insert Picture button (Page
Setup dialog box), 424

inserted projects
  accessing information,
    549-551
  creating from large projects,
    551-552
  deleting, 554
  identifying tasks, 553-554
  maintaining and
    naming, 552

inserting
  columns in tables, 753
  milestones in Gantt Chart
    view, 140-142
  recurring tasks in Gantt
    Chart view, 142-147
  task constraints, 205-207
  tasks
    Gantt Chart view,
      127-128
    PERT Chart view, 150
    Task Details view, 154
    Task Entry view, 151-153
    task lists, 156-157
    Task Sheet view, 154-155

installing Personal Web
Server (PWS), 567-568

interactive filters, 685,
759-761, 922

interfaces, Open Database
Connectivity (ODBC), 107

interim schedules, saving,
479-480

Internet
  communicating with
    workgroups, 575
  exporting data to, 634-637

features, 440-441
navigating with hyperlinks, 441-442
publishing Web documents, 467
sample template file, 113

intranets
communicating with workgroups, 567-575
exporting data to, 634-637

Is greater than or equal to (filter test option), 756

Is less than (filter test option), 756

Is less than or equal to (filter test option), 756

Is not within (filter test option), 757

Is within (filter test option), 757

ISO 9000 sample template file, 113

J-K

Kalyn Calendar, 936

Kalyn Corporation, 935-936

keys
Delete, 194, 225
Enter, 77
selection, 228-229

keystrokes, capturing
creating macros, 836-842
Outline Numbering Macro, 841-842
Special Formatting Macro, 840-841
Summary Task Format Macro, 839-840

keywords, VBA (Visual Basic for Applications) variables, 858

KIDASA Software, Inc., 936-938

L

lags, *see* **delays**

Late Peak pattern, 299

Late/Overbudget Tasks filter, Task, 687

Late/Overbudget Tasks Assigned To filter, 520

Layout
command (Format menu), 236, 713-714
dialog box, 235-237, 719

Layout Now command (Format menu)
PERT Chart view, 724-725
arrows and page breaks, 726
linking lines, changing, 725
redrawing the chart, 727
redrawing PERT Chart, 236

leads, *see* **overlaps**

learning aids, 36
Help menu
Contents and Index options, 39-43
Getting Started, 43-44
Microsoft on the Web, 45-48
Office Assistant, 37
accessing, 37-38
changing options, 38-39
Planning Wizard, 48-49

Left arrow key, 229

legends, 425-426, 923

Legends tab (Page Setup dialog box), 425-426

Level Now command, 385-387

leveling, 349, 923
overallocated assignments, 381
Clear Leveling command, 387
Level Now command, 385-387

Resource Leveling dialog box, 381-385, 387
sensitivity setting, 349-350

Leveling Gantt Chart view, 527

Leveling Order drop-down list box, 383-384

Leveling Task object, 856

Line Styles tab (Progress Lines dialog box), 526

Link Tasks command (Edit menu), 179-180

Linked Fields filter
Resource, 689
Task, 688

linking
data between applications, 642
deleting links, 646-647
field values, 643-644
identifying tasks or resources with links, 647
refreshing linked data, 645-646
outlined task lists, 195
detail tasks, 196-197
summary tasks, 195-196
tasks
auditing task links, 197-199
in PERT Chart view, 232-233

links
creating
between tasks in multiple projects, 554-557
Task object, 854
cross-project, 921
dependency, 173, 181-183
auditing, 191-199
creating, 174-176, 180-187, 189-191
entering, 179-180
relationships, 176-179
removing from project plans, 193-195

successor versus
predecessor tasks,
173-175
pasting with mismatched
data, 644
resource pool, identifying,
562-563

Links dialog box, 645-646

List
display, 95-98
object (Project Object
model), 853

listings
HTML Code from
Customized Project HTML
Template, 458, 460
HTML Code from the
Standard Export.html File,
451-452
HTML Code with a
Hyperlink to ABC
Corporation's Home
Page, 461
HTML Code with an E-mail
Hyperlink, 461
HTML Source from a
Microsoft Word HTML
Document, 453

lists
numbering, 402
resource, sorting, 276-278
separator characters, 923

locating, *see* **finding**

**loops, VBA (Visual Basic for
Applications), 861**

M

Macro dialog box, 837

macros, 834-836, 923
Adjust Dates, 212-214
capturing
Outline Numbering
Macro, 841-842
Special Formatting
Macro, 840-841
Summary Task Format
Macro, 839-840

creating
capturing keystrokes,
836-842
Outline Numbering
Macro, 841-842
Special Formatting
Macro, 840-841
Summary Task Format
Macro, 839-840
editing, 844-847
Code window, 846-847
Project Explorer, 844-846
Properties window, 846
Visual Basic Editor, 844
formatting text, 834-836
running, 842-844
Outline Numbering
Macro, 844
Special Formatting
Macro, 843
shortcut keys, 917
see also VBA (Visual Basic
Applications)

**Macros dialog box,
842, 844**

**maintaining inserted
projects, 552**

**major scales (timescales),
changing, 705**

management
projects, preliminary
steps, 22
traditional functions versus
project management, 16
views, shortcut keys, 916

managers
project management
guidelines, 18-20
responsibilities, 17
workgroup, 567

**MAPI (Messaging
Application Programming
Interface), 923**

**margins, specifying
with Page Setup
dialog box, 422**

**Margins tab (Page Setup
dialog box), 422**

Marin Research, 938-939

**Marked property
(Task object), 855**

master projects, 923

**Max Units field (Resource
Sheet view), 258-259**

menus
bar, 33, 891-892
commands, adding,
892-895
Modify Selections
button, 895-898
displaying custom
forms, 900
displaying view name, 746
shortcut keys, 914

methods, 850
OptionsView, 862
ReportPrint, 868
ReportPrintPreview, 868
SelectColumn, 864
TableApply, 864
TableEdit, 865

**Micro-Frame Technologies,
Inc., 939-940**

Microsoft
Access 8.0 format
opening projects saved
in, 605-606
saving projects in,
604-606
Excel formats, 620, 638-639
exporting project data to
worksheets, 620-622
exporting to PivotTables,
622-628
importing data from,
629-634
MDB extension, 596
objects, *see* objects
ODBC data sources
importing projects from,
607-608
saving projects in,
606-607
Project 3.0
calendars, using, 88
files, opening in
Microsoft Project 98,
102

Project 95 toolbar, 873
Project 98, 17-18
Project 101:Fundamentals, 44
Project command
  (Start menu), 28-29
Project Web site, 46
Project window
  components, 29-32
    entry bar, 34
    menu bar, 33
    status bar, 35-36
    toolbars, 33-34
    View Bar, 34-35
  Visual Basic error dialog
    box, 843
  Web site, 441
  XLS extension, 597

**Microsoft on the Web
feature, 45-48**

Milestone
  Date rollup view, 663
  Etc., 938
  filter, Task, 396, 688
  report, 772
  rollup view, 665
  tasks, 855

milestones, 923
  inserting in Gantt Chart
    view, 140-142
  projects, 19

**minor scales (timescales),
changing, 706**

**Modify Selections
button, 884**
  attributes, changing,
    887-888
  face, customizing, 884-885,
    888-893
  editing menu bars, 895-896
    grouping commands, 898
    moving commands, 898
    naming menu bars, 896
    removing commands,
      896-898
  images
    changing, 884-885
    copying, 885
    designing, 886
    editing, 886-887

modifying
  Global templates
    (Organizer), 116
  resource assignments,
    296-297
    contour patterns, 297-300
    overtime to shorten
      tasks, 300-301
    scheduling late starts,
      303-305
    task splitting, 301-302
  see also editing

**money amounts,
displaying, 77**

**Monthly Calendar Report
Definition dialog box,
826-827**

monthly
  calendars
    creating, 798
    customizing, 826-827
    filtering, 827
  recurring tasks,
    creating, 146

**More Filters command
(Project menu), 395,
754-755**

More Tables
  dialog box, 680, 748-749
  command (View menu), 679

More Views
  command (View menu),
    54-55, 660, 742-744
  dialog box, 54
    combination views,
      creating, 746-748
    creating new views,
      742-744

mouse
  actions
    creating links, 187-189
    creating tasks, 155-156
    dragging to create links,
      188-189
    formatting Calendar
      View, 716
    Gantt Chart, updating
      tasks, 503-505

removing links, 195
  setting column
    widths, 753
  pointer, caution, 188

moving
  commands on menu
    bars, 898
  task nodes in PERT Chart
    view, 233-235
  tasks
    in task lists, 157-160
    to create inserted
      projects, 551-552

**MPD (Microsoft Project
Database) format,
599-600**
  opening projects from
    databases, 603-604
  saving
    as databases, 600-603
    projects in, 600-603
  files
    creating from, 466
    updating, 466

**MPX 4.0 (Microsoft Project
Exchange) format, 596,
598-599**

**multiple criteria filters,
creating, 762-763**

multiple projects
  creating links between
    tasks, 554-557
  deleting inserted
    projects, 554
  identifying tasks, 553-554
  Insert menu, Project
    command, 548-551
  maintaining inserted
    projects, 552
  moving tasks to new files,
    551-552
  sharing resources, 558
    creating a pool, 558
    discontinuing sharing,
      561-562
    identifying resource pool
      links, 562-563

resource pools, using,
559-560
saving multiple files,
560-561
Window menu, 544-545
Arrange All command,
545-546
combining tasks from
different files, 546
Hide and Unhide
commands, 546
New Window command,
546-547

**Multiple Task Information
dialog box, 149**

**Must Finish On (MFO)
constraint, 204-205**

**Must Start On (MSO)
constraint, 204-205**

N

Name
argument, 868
field (Resource Sheet
view), 258
property (Calendar
object), 856

naming
files, 107, 109
filters, 755
menu bars, 896
procedures, 858
Project databases, 601
reports, 798
tables, new, 749
variables, VBA (Visual Basic
for Applications), 859
views, new, 744
see also renaming

**navigating Calendar
view, 217**
filters, using, 221-222
Find command, 219-220
Go To command, 218-220
scroll bars, 218
with hyperlinks, 441-442,
465-466
Zoom button, 220-221

negative delays, 381

New
button (More Views dialog
box), 742-744
command (File menu), 62

**New Task commands
(Insert menu), 223-225**

**New Window command
(Window menu), 546-547**

nodes, 923, 723

**non-Project format
tables, 608**

**nonworking and working
days, 78**
editing in the Standard
calendar, 79-80, 85-90

**Nonworking Time tab
(Timescale dialog box),
707-708**

**Not Within test (filter
criteria), 758-766**

notes
resource lists, adding, 819
task lists
adding, 810
assignments, 812

Notes
Field, pasting objects
into, 650
property (Task object), 855
tab (Task Information dialog
box), 148

numbering
headings, 836
lists, 402
outline, 836

O

objectives of projects, 16-17

objects, 850
attaching to task bars or
dates, 240-242
copying
Clipboard, 244
Organizer, 116-117

deleting, 118-119, 246
embedding, 654-656
Err, 862
hiding, 242
methods, 850
naming with Organizer, 118
pasting, 648-649
Gantt Chart, 649-650
into other applications,
649, 652-654
Microsoft Project, 649
Notes Field, 650
Task or Resource
Objects Box, 651-652
Project Object model, 850
Application object,
850-852
Assistant object, 851-852
Calendar object, 856
Cell object, 851
Command Bars object,
851-852
List object, 853
Project object, 852-853
Resource object, 853
Selection object, 851
Task object, 854-856
VBE object, 852
properties, 850, 852
resource lists, 819-820
selecting, 240
sizing, 243-244
styles, changing, 244-246
task lists, 810
variables, VBA (Visual Basic
for Applications), 859

**ODBC (Microsoft) data
sources**
creating import/export
maps for, 611-620
file format, 596
importing projects from, 607
saving projects in, 606-607

Office Assistant, 37
accessing, 37-38
changing options, 38-39
Options dialog box, 38

**OLE (Object Linking
and Embedding)**
actions, 894
error message, 644

OLE2-compliant applications, 654-656

On Error statement, 862

online learning aids, 36
Help menu
Contents and Index options, 39-43
Getting Started, 43-44
Microsoft on the Web, 45-48
Office Assistant, 37
accessing, 37-38
changing options, 38-39
Planning Wizard, 48-49

Online Support Web site, 48

Open command (File menu), 92

Open Database Connectivity (ODBC), 107

Open dialog box (File menu), 67

opening
projects saved in Access databases, 605-606
template files, 112-114

operators, 923

Options command (Tools menu), 62, 70, 836

Options dialog box, 70-72
Automatically Add New Resources option, 252, 267-268
Calculation tab, 498
critical settings
calendar preferences, 75-76
defining days and weeks, 72-73
defining Default Start and End Time of Day, 74
Fiscal Year, 74-75
formatting outlines, 702-704
Office Assistant, 38
Outline Options, 164-165
Planning Wizard, 48-49

reviewing settings, 76-77
Spelling tab, 404-405

OptionsView method, 862

Organizer, 85-86, 114-115
accessing, 115
button (View menu), 764-765
copying
objects, 116-117
to Global template, 86-87
to other projects template, 87-88
custom forms, managing, 909
deleting objects, 118-119
dialog box, 796, 923
Global templates, modifying, 116
naming objects, 118
reports, customizing, 796
toolbars, managing, 888-891

orientation, setting with Page tab, 421

outdenting tasks, 162

Outline Macro, error handling, 862-865

Outline Numbering Macro
capturing, 841-842
testing, 844

OutlineLevel property (Task object), 855

outlines, 923
collapsed, 920
expanded, 921
numbering, adding to macros, 836
options, formatting, 702-704
projects, sorting, 399-402
reports, collapsing, 802
task lists, linking, 195
detail tasks, 196-197
summary tasks, 195-196

outlining
Project plan, 126-127
shortcut keys, 915

task lists, 160-162
collapsing and expanding outlines, 162-164
editing outlined projects, 164
indenting and outdenting tasks, 162
selecting display options, 164-165

Outlook, setting alarms, 587-588

Overallocated field (Resource Sheet), 348-349

Overallocated Resources
filter, 278-279, 689
report, 787

overallocation of resources, 345-346, 923
delaying assignments, 371, 374-388
determining, 346-348
eliminating, 357, 359-360
filtering, 351-352
identifying, 348-351
increase availability of resource, 357-358, 360
changing dates available, 361
extending hours available, 364-365
scheduling overtime, 361-364
Leveling command, 381, 387
Automatic Leveling, 387
Level Now command, 385-387
Resource Leveling dialog box, 381-385
reducing workload of resource, 365
Resource Allocation view, 365
substituting underused resources, 366-370

Resource Usage view, 352-354
  changing fields displayed, 355-357
  Go To Next Overallocation tool, 354-355
  splitting
    individual assignments, 378-381
    tasks, 374-375
  viewing, 351

Overbudget Resources report, 782

Overbudget Tasks report, 781

overlaps between tasks (leads), 174-175, 191-193

Overtime Rate field (Resource Sheet view), 260

overtime work, 358
  assigning, 332, 334
    entering with Resource Form, 336
    entering with Task Form, 334-335
    schedules and charges for overtime, 332-333
    scheduling for resources, 361-364
    shortening tasks with, 300-301
    viewing, 337

Overview category reports, 769
  Critical Tasks, 771-772
  Milestones, 772
  Project Summary, 769-770
  Top-Level Tasks, 770-771
  Working Days, 772-773

Overview Report, 410-411

overwriting existing resources, 641

P

Page Break command (Insert menu), 419-420, 799

page breaks
  displaying and adjusting (PERT Chart view), 726
  formatting, 708
  formatting in views, 708
  reports, controlling, 799-800
  setting and clearing before printing, 419-420

Page Down key, 229

Page Number button (Page Setup dialog box), 423

Page Setup
  command (File menu), 414, 420-421
    printing reports, 796
  dialog box, 421
    entering headers and footers, 424-425
    Header and Footer tabs, 423-424
    Legends tab, 425-426
    placing borders, 422
    Print Preview button, 436
    scaling the printouts, 421-422
    specifying margins, 422
    View tab, selecting options for printing, 428-430

Page tab, setting orientation, 421

Page Up key, 229

pages
  customizing reports, 801
  selecting to print with Print dialog box, 434-435

Parsifal Systems, 940

partial dependency, 923

passwords
  protecting files, 109-110
  write reservation, 110-121

Paste Special dialog box, 643

pasting
  data using Windows Clipboard, 639-641
  links with mismatched data, 644
  objects, 648-649
    Gantt Chart, 649-650
    into other applications, 649, 652-654
    Microsoft Project, 649
    Notes Field, 650
    Task or Resource Objects Box, 651-652
    Start No Earlier Than constraints, 642

patterns (contour), 297-300

Percent Complete, 924
  buttons, updating tasks, 501
  tracking field, 491-492

performance, tracking during projects, 486-487
  facilities for updating tasks, 495-505
  fields for updating tasks, 489-495
  updating tasks, 488-489

Personal Web Server (PWS)
  installing, 567-568
  troubleshooting, 568-569

PERT Analysis
  Gantt Chart, 668
  toolbar, 137-139, 873

PERT Chart, 225, 668-669, 924
  evolution of, 226
  EXPERT, 930-931
  nodes, 923
  redrawing with Layout Now command, 236
  Task, 669
  view, 30, 225
    customizing, 235-237
    editing in, 229-235
    inserting delays and overlaps, 192

inserting tasks, 150
formatting, 719-726
Layout Now command
(Format menu),
725-726
node borders, 226-227
page breaks, 420
redrawing, 727
scrolling and selecting,
228-229
zooming, 227-228

PERT Entry task form, 899

**PivotTable, adjusting layout,
625-626**

placeholders, 905-906

planning, 924
elapsed duration, 135
projects
preliminaries with
software, 21-22
with Microsoft Project
98, 17-18
setting final plans, 474-475
task durations, 134-137
task entries
Gantt Chart view,
127-128
PERT Chart view, 150
Task Details view, 154
Task Entry view, 151-153
Task Sheet view, 154-155
task list creation, 126-127
Gantt Chart view,
128-133
mouse actions, 155-156
task list outlines, 160-165
PERT Analysis toolbar,
137-139
updating plans, 486-487

**Planning Wizard, 29, 36,
48-49**
capturing baselines, 475-476
warning messages
saving baselines, 108
task constraints, 206

**pointer (mouse),
caution, 188**

**Pool Takes Precedence
button (Share Resources
dialog box), 559-560**

**pools, adding names to,
284-285**

Portfolio Wizard, 933

**positioning toolbars,
874-875**

**predecessor tasks,
173-174, 924**
delays and overlaps, 174-175
determining the dependent
task, 175-176
differentiated from
successor tasks, 175
Finish-to-Finish (FF)
relationship, 178
Finish-to-Start (FS)
relationship, 177
Start-to-Finish (SF)
relationship, 178-179
Start-to-Start (SS)
relationship, 177-178
task lists, adding, 811
Task object, 854

**Predecessors tab (Task
Information dialog box),
181-183**

predefined
contours, selecting, 329-330
reports, *see* standard reports

**Preview button (Print dialog
box), 436**

previewing
documents, 436
reports, 796

Print
command (File menu),
414-415, 434
dialog box, 434
Preview button, 436
printing views with
timescales, 435-436
quality and number of
copies, selecting, 435
selecting pages to print,
434-435

Print Preview
button (Page Setup dialog
box), 436
command (File menu), 414

**Printers command (Settings
menu), 415**

printing
baseline comparison
views, 486
calendars, 88-90
printer setup, 415
quality and number of
copies, selecting, 435
reports, 343-344, 796, 800
Resource Sheet view,
280-281
selecting pages with Print
dialog box, 434-435
standard reports, 436-437
summary reports, 409-411
task lists, 166
printing standard task
reports, 167-168
printing the task views,
166-167
views, 416-417
choosing view to print,
417-418
clearing page breaks,
419-420
enhancing text data, 419
page setup, 420-421
setting page breaks,
419-420
sorting display, 418-419
with timescales, 435-436

printouts, scaling, 421-422

priority tasks, 924

**Private keyword variables,
VBA (Visual Basic for
Applications), 858**

**procedures, VBA (Visual
Basic for Applications),
857-858**

product descriptions
ABT Corporation, 928
Critical Tools, 930-931

Experience In Software, Inc., 931-932
GTW, 932-933
IMS, 933-935
Kalyn Corporation, 935-936
KIDASA Software, Inc., 936-938
Marin Research, 938-939
Micro-Frame Technologies, Inc., 939-940
Parsifal Systems, 940
Program Management Solutions, Inc, 941
Project Assistants, Inc., 941-942
Software Made Easy, Inc., 943

Product News Web site, 46

program control, VBA (Visual Basic for Applications), 860-861

Program Management Solutions, Inc, 941

progress
analyzing, 508
Add Progress Line, 523
Analyze Time-Scale Data in Excel tool button, 530-532
calculating variances, 509-510
cost variances, 519
date variances, 516-519
Display Progress Lines at Recurring Intervals, 525-526
Earned Value fields and report, 529-530
Gantt Chart bars, 526-528
Progress Lines dialog box, 523-524
resource assignment level variances, 519-521
reviewing, 510-514, 521-522
week-to-week trends, 532-533
work variances, 514-515
marks, selecting, 723

tracking, 486-487
Actual Costs, 493-495
Actual Duration, 492
Actual Finish Date, 490-491
Actual Start Date, 490
Actual Work, 493-495
facilities for updating tasks, 495-496
fields for updating, 489-490
mouse in Gantt Chart, 503-505
Percent Complete, 491-492, 501
Remaining Duration, 492-493
Reschedule Work button, 503-505
Scheduled Duration, 493
Task and Task Details Forms, 499-500
Tracking table, 497-499
updating tasks, 488-489, 500-502
Usage views, 496-497

Progress Lines dialog box, 523-524, 526

Project
Project 95 toolbar, 873
Assistants, Inc., 941-942
Bridge Modeler, 928
command (Insert menu), 548-549
Control, 943
Explorer, editing macros, 844-846
extension (*.MP*), 102
MPD extension, 595
MPP extension, 595, 596

project files, 92
closing, 120
creating, 92
displaying, 119-120
extensions, 102-103
finding, 101-102
Advanced Find dialog box, 104-107
ODBC File Open option, 107

searching by characters in file names, 103
searching by date saved, 104
searching for specific text, 103-104
specifying search criteria, 102
specifying type, 102-103
opening, 92-93
changing file name display, 95-98
Commands and Settings button, 98-100
selectinging location to search, 93-95
virus protection, 100-101
types, 103

Project Gateway, 938-939

Project Information
command (Project menu), 62, 852
dialog box, 852
Current Date and Status Date text boxes, 64
entering information, 62-63
Project Statistics dialog box, 64-66
Start and Finish Date text boxes, 63-64

Project KickStart, 932

Project Management Institute Web site, 17

Project menu commands
AutoFilter, 763-764
Filtered For, 397-398, 685, 809
More Filters, 395, 754-755
Overallocated Resources, 351-352
Project Information, 62, 852
Sort, 418-419, 696, 802
Sort By, 400-402
Task Information, 147-148

Project Object model, 850, 852-853
Application object, 850-852
Assistant object, 851-852

Calendar object, 856
Cell object, 851
Command Bars object, 851-852
List object, 853
Project object, 852-853
Selection object, 851
Task object, 854-856
    baselines, 855-856
    BCWP (Budgeted Cost of Work Performed), 855
    BCWS (Budgeted Cost of Work Scheduled), 855
    Confirmed property, 855
    constraints, 854
    Contact property, 855
    CV (Earned Value Cost Variance), 855
    Fixed property, 855
    HideBar property, 855
    ID field, 854
    Leveling, 856
    Marked property, 855
    Milestone tasks, 855
    Notes property, 855
    OutlineLevel property, 855
    predecessors, 854
    properties, 854
    resources, 854-855
    RollUp property, 855
    UniqueID, 854
    views, 854
VBE object, 852

Project Partner, 933

project schedules
    auditing task links, 197-199
    dependency links, 173
        auditing, 191-199
        creating in Task Form view, 183-185
        creating with Autolink option, 189-191
        creating with Entry Table, 185-187
        creating with menu or toolbar, 180-181
    creating with mouse actions, 187-189
    delays and overlaps, 174-175, 191-193
    determining the dependent task, 175-176
    entering, 179-180
    removing, 193-195
    successor versus predecessor tasks, 173-174, 175
    Task Information dialog box, 181-183
    types of relationships, 176-179
    factors, 172
    outlined task lists, linking, 195-197
    task constraints
        hard versus soft, 202-203
        types, 203-207
    task splitting, 199-202

Project Statistics dialog box, 64-66, 392, 512-514

Project Summary Report, 512-514, 769-770, 794
    customizing, 803-804
    formatting text, 804

Project Summary Task command (Tools menu), 510

Project Workspace format, 598

ProjectCommander, 941-942

ProjectFinish property (Project object), 852

projects
    consolidated, 920
    cost, 253, 255-282
        accrual of, 255
        defining fixed and total costs, 262-263
        fixed costs, 255, 262-263
        resource costs, 254-255
        tracking, 486-505
        viewing, 398-399
    editing in Calendar view, 222-223
        creating links between tasks, 225
        deleting tasks, 225
        inserting tasks, 223-225
    exchanging with other formats, 608-609
    files, see project files
    inserted projects
        creating from large projects, 551-552
        deleting, 554
        identifying tasks, 553-554
        maintaining, 552
        naming, 552
    management
        constraints, 16
        definition, 17
        goals and objectives, 16-17
        manager guidelines, 17-20
        planning with Microsoft Project 98, 17-18
        scheduling techniques, 23-25
        setting milestones, 19
        temporary nature of, 16
    master projects, 923
    multiple projects
        creating links between tasks, 554-557
        sharing resources, 558-563
        Window menu, 544-546
    performance, 486-487
        facilities for updating tasks, 495-505
        fields for updating tasks, 489-495
        updating tasks, 488-489
    reducing
        duration, 405-408
        schedule, budget, 538-539
        scope to finish on time and on budget, 538
    resources, 253

saving in databases, 599
   Microsoft Access 8.0
     format, 604-606
   MPD (Microsoft Project
     Database) format,
     599-604
   ODBC (Open Database
     Connectivity) format,
     606-608
schedules, *see* project
  schedules
status, 392
   checking spelling,
     403-404
   collapsing task list
     outline, 394-395
   compressing the
     timescale, 393-394
   cost schedules, 408-409
   crashing the schedule,
     407-408
   filtering task or resource
     list, 395-396
   filters, 397-398
   identifying critical path,
     406-407
   printing summary
     reports, 409-411
   shortening critical
     path, 405
   sorting task and resource
     lists, 399-402
   viewing costs, 398-399

ProjectServer, 939

**ProjectStart property
(Project object), 852**

**promoting summary tasks,
161-162**

properties, 850
  adding, 68-69
  Calendar object, 856
  creating Custom, 69
  linking to project fields, 70
  modifying values, 70
  Project object, 852
  Resource object, 853
  Task object, 854
  VBA (Visual Basic for
    Applications), 852

Properties
  command (File menu), 66,
    69, 803
  dialog box, 803
  sheet, 66
    Contents tab, 67-68
    Custom tab, 68-72
    General tab, 67
    Statistics tab, 67
    Summary tab, 66-67
  window, editing macros, 846

**Public keyword variables,
VBA (Visual Basic for
Applications), 858**

**publishing Web
documents, 467**

Q-R

Quick Preview, 43

read-only files, *see also*
write protecting files

**Read-Only Recommended,
111-121**

Record Macro
  command (Tools
    menu), 837
  dialog box, 847

**Recurring Task Information
dialog box, 142**

recurring tasks, 924
  editing, 160
  inserting in Gantt Chart
    view, 142-147

**Redo command
(Edit menu), 156**

**redrawing PERT Chart view,
236, 727**

reducing
  costs of projects, 409
  schedule, budget, 538-539
  scope to finish on time and
    on budget, 538

**refreshing linked data,
645-646**

REGEDIT applet, 93

**relationships, dependency,
176-177**
  Finish-to-Finish (FF), 178
  Finish-to-Start (FS), 177
  Start-to-Finish (SF), 178-179
  Start-to-Start (SS), 177-178

**Remaining Duration
tracking field, 492-493**

**Remove Page Break
command (Insert menu),
419-420**

removing
  columns from tables, 753
  commands from menu bars,
    896-898
  dependency links in project
    plan
     Entry Table, 194
     menu or toolbar, 193-194
     mouse actions, 195
     Task Form view, 194
     Task Information dialog
      box, 194
  task constraints, 207-208

renaming
  custom forms, 908
  objects with Organizer, 118
  projects, 552
  toolbars in Organizer, 889
  views from files with
    Organizer, 765
  see also naming

**Renovation sample template
file, 113**

renumbering, *see*
numbering

**Replace Resource dialog
box, 317-318**

**report definition dialog
box, 798**

Report Text dialog box, 804

ReportPrint method, 868

**ReportPrintPreview
method, 868**

reports
Assignment category, 784
  Overallocated Resources, 787
  To-Do List, 786-787
  Who Does What, 784-785
  Who Does What When, 785
automating, 867-869
Base Calendar report, customizing, 804-805
copying, 797
Cost Reports category, 779
  Budget, 780-781
  Cash Flow, 780
  Earned Value, 782-791
  Overbudget Resources, 782
  Overbudget Tasks, 781
creating, 797-799
crosstabs
  assignments, adding, 824
  creating, 798
  customizing, 821-825
  dates, formatting, 825
  filtering, 823
  formatting text, 825
  gridlines, viewing, 824
  repeating columns, 824
  sorting, 825
  totals, adding, 824
  zero values, viewing, 824
Current Activity category, 774
  Completed Tasks, 776-777
  Should Have Started Tasks, 777
  Slipping Tasks, 777-778
  Tasks In Progress, 776
  Unstarted Tasks, 774-775
customizing, 794, 802-827
  Custom category, 796-797
  existing reports, 794-796
  page setup, 801
  saving, 827-828
editing, 797
monthly calendars
  creating, 798
  customizing, 826-827
  filtering, 827

naming, 798
outlines, collapsing, 802
Overview category, 769
  Critical Tasks, 771-772
  Milestones, 772
  Project Summary, 769-770
  Top-Level Tasks, 770-771
  Working Days, 772-773
page breaks, controlling, 799-800
printing, 343-344, 796
Project Summary, 512-514, 803-804
requesting and submitting status reports, 586-587
resource lists
  assignments, adding, 820
  borders, adding, 820
  calendars, adding, 820
  cost rates, adding, 820
  creating, 798
  customizing, 814-821
  filtering, 817
  formatting text, 820-821
  gridlines, viewing, 820
  notes, adding, 819
  objects, adding, 819-820
  sorting, 821
  time period, changing, 817
  totals, viewing, 820
sorting, 801
standard, accessing, 768-769
task lists
  assignments, adding, 811
  borders, creating, 812
  creating, 798
  customizing, 805-814
  definitions, customizing, 806-809
  filtering, 809
  formatting text, 812-814
  gridlines, viewing, 812
  notes, adding, 810
  objects, adding, 810
  predecessor tasks, adding, 811
  sorting, 814

  successor tasks, adding, 811
  summaries, showing, 809
  time period, changing, 808
  totals, viewing, 812
  text, formatting, 800-801
Working Days report, customizing, 804-805
Workload category, 788
  Resource Usage, 789-790
  Task Usage, 788-789

Reports command (View menu), 409-411, 436-437, 768-769, 793, 868

Reports dialog box, 794, 868

Reschedule tasks command, 924

Reschedule Work button (Tracking toolbar), updating tasks, 503-505

rescheduling
remaining work, 533-535
tasks that haven't started, 535-536
see also schedules

resetting Standard calendar, 82

resizing
objects (Gantt Chart view), 243-244
toolbars, combo boxes, 880

resolving conflicts, 208-214

Resource
Allocation view, 341-342, 679
  Delay field, 371-374
  substituting resources, 365
filters, 689-690
tables, 680, 683-684

Resource Assignment dialog box, substituting resources, 368-369

resource assignments, 284-285
  alternate views, 340
    Resource Allocation, 341-342
    Resource Graph view, 342-343
    Task and Resource Usage, 340-341
  assigning to tasks, 311-312
    Assign Resources dialog box, 312-318
    Assignment Information dialog box, 327-331
    Task and Task Details Forms, 320-324
    Task Information dialog box, 318-319
    task tables, 331-332
    Task Usage view, 324-327
  Duration with multiple resources, 296
  effects of schedules, 25
  Effort Driven tasks, 294-296
  fields, 285
    naming, 285
    Units, 285-287
    work, 287
  modifying, 296-297
    contour patterns, 297-300
    overtime to shorten tasks, 300-301
    scheduling late starts, 303-305
    task splitting, 301-302
  printing reports, 343-344
  task types, selecting, 291-294
  work formula, 287-288
    applying in new assignments, 288-289
    changing existing assignments, 289
    driver resource concept, 290-291
  see also assigments

Resource field (Resource Information dialog box), 261

Resource Form view, 677
  entering overtime, 336
  formatting, 727
    entry field options, 727-730
    options, 727
  resource pools, defining, 265-267
  scheduling overtime, 362-364

Resource Graph view, 342-343, 673
  formatting, 730-732
    Bar Styles dialog box, 734-736
    options, 732
    selecting values to display, 732-734

Resource Group filter, 688

Resource Information dialog box, 257, 357-358
  accessing resource calendars, 273
  changing
    availability of dates, 361
    availability of resources, 360
  editing Cost Rate tables, 331
  fields
    Cost Rate Tables, 262
    Cost Rates, 262
    Details, 262
    Email, 261
    Resource, 261
    Time Stamped, 262-282
    Workgroup, 261
  resource pools, defining, 270-272
  resources, 268
  Working Time tab, 364-365

Resource Leveling
  command (Tools menu), 373-374
  dialog box
    Automatic Leveling, 387
    Clear Leveling command, 387
    setting options, 381-385

Resource Management toolbar, 873

Resource Name Form, 677

Resource object (Project Object model), 853

Resource Objects Box, pasting objects into, 651-652

Resource Range filters, 689

Resource Report dialog box, 817

Resource Sheet view, 30, 348-349, 676
  fields
    Accrue At, 260-261
    Base Calendar, 261
    Code, 261
    Cost Per Use, 260
    Group, 258-259
    ID, 257
    Indicators, 258
    Initials, 258-259
    Max Units, 258-259
    Name, 258
    Overtime Rate, 260
    Standard Rate, 259
  formatting, 738-739
  printing, 280-281
  resource pools, defining, 264-265
  variance analyses, 522

Resource Usage
  view, 340-341, 675-676
    formatting, 736, 738
    overallocation of resources, 352-357
    scheduling overtime, 362
  report, 789-790

Resource view, 894, 925

resources, 253, 925
  allocation, 924
  assignments, *see* resource assignments
  calendars, 78, 924
    accessing, 273-274
    changing working times, 273
    editing, 273

extending hours
available, 364-365
overallocation of
resources, 348
scheduling dates, 79
conflicts, 924
cost, 254-255, 924
creating templates, 280
custom forms
creating new, 902-904
Custom Form dialog box
features, 908-909
displaying with
menus, 900
Organizer, managing
with, 909
placing items on, 905-908
predefined forms,
899-900
shortcut keys, assigning,
901-902
toolbar buttons,
assigning to, 902
discontinuing sharing,
561-562
driven tasks, 924
driving, 921
fields, filling in, 268-270
filters, 278-279
formatting text displays for
categories, 697-698
fonts, 700-705
text style, 700
group, 253, 922, 924
hyperlinks
adding, 463-464
deleting, 464
editing for, 464
managing projects with,
465-466
navigating to, 465
lists, 794
assignments, adding, 820
borders, adding, 820
calendars, adding, 820
cost rates, adding, 820
creating, 798
customizing, 814-821
filtering, 395-397, 817
gridlines, viewing, 820

notes, adding, 819
objects, adding, 819-820
sorting, 399-402,
801-802, 821
text, formatting, 820-821
time period,
changing, 817
totals, viewing, 820
overallocation of,
345-346, 923
determining, 346-348
eliminating, 357-360
filtering, 351-352
identifying, 348-351
increasing availability of
resource, 360-381
leveling, 381-387
Resource Usage view,
352-357
viewing, 351
pools, 253, 263-264, 924
Automatically Add New
Resources option,
267-268
filling in resource fields,
268-270
Resource Form view,
265-267
Resource Information
dialog box, 270-272
Resource Sheet view,
264-265
scheduling tasks based
on, 252
sharing among projects, 558
identifying pool links,
562-563
resource pools, 559-560
saving multiple files,
560-561
sorting
in views, 696-697
lists, 276-278
Task object, 854
task types, 308-311
Resources With
Attachments filter, 689
Resources/Assignments
With Overtime filter, 689

ResourceXchange, 935
restoring
built-in toolbars, 883
commands to menu bars,
896-898
reviewing
cost schedules, 408-409
files with routing slips,
581-582
status of project, 392
checking spelling,
403-404
collapsing task list
outline, 394-395
compressing the
timescale, 393-394
cost schedules, 408-409
crashing the schedule,
407-408
filtering task or resource
list, 395-396
filters, using, 397-398
identifying the critical
path, 406-407
printing summary
reports, 409-411
reducing costs, 409
shortening the critical
path, 405
sorting task and resource
lists, 399-402
viewing costs, 398-399
see also auditing
revising schedules, 508
Analyze Time-Scale Data in
Excel tool button, 530-532
calculating variances,
509-510
progress at resource level,
521-522
Add Progress Line, 523
Display Progress Lines at
Recurring Intervals,
525-526
Earned Value fields and
report, 529-530
Gantt Chart bars, 526-528
Progress Lines dialog
box, 523-524

progress at task level, 514
  cost variances, 519
  date variances, 516-519
  resource assignment
    level variances, 519-521
  work variances, 514-515
summary progress
  information, 510
  cost variances, 512
  date variances, 511
  Project Statistics dialog
    box, 512-514
  Project Summary Report,
    512-514
  work variances, 510
variances, 508
week-to-week trends,
  532-533

Right arrow key, 228

Risk +, 941

roll up tasks, 925

rollup views, 662-663
  Bar, 663
  Milestone, 663, 665

**RollUp property
(Task object), 855**

**Routing Slip dialog
box, 579**

**routing slips to circulate
project files, 579-582**

running macros, 842-844

**runtime errors, VBA
(Visual Basic for
Applications), 862**

S

**sample templates,
accessing, 113-114**

**Save As command (File
menu), 108-109, 594-595**

**Save as HTML command
(File menu), 442-447**

**Save Baseline command
(Tools menu), 476-478**

**Save command (File
menu), 107**

**Save Options dialog box,
111-121**

Save Search dialog box, 106

**Save Workspace command
(File menu), 111-112,
560-561**

saving
  baselines (interim
    schedules), 479-480
  custom forms, 908
  customized reports, 827-828
  files, 107-109
    capturing baselines,
      475-476
    Create Backup File
      option, 111
    HTML format, 111
    password protecting,
      109-110
    read-only, 110-121
    security options, 109
    Workspace, 560-561,
      111-112
  Global template changes,
    764-765
  graphic images (views), 635
  projects, 599
    HTML format, 442-447
    Microsoft Access 8.0
      format, 604-606
    MPD (Microsoft Project
      Database) format,
      599-604
    ODBC (Open Database
      Connectivity) format,
      606-608
  views, 746

scaling printouts, 421-422

Tracking task form, 900

schedules
  baselines, 480-481
    Cost table, 483
    tables, 481-482
    Task Usage view, 481
    Tracking Gantt view,
      484-486

Variance table, 482
Work table, 483-484
conflicts, resolving, 208-214
costs, 408-409
crashing strategies, 407-408
current plan, 925
dependency links, 173
  auditing, 191-199
  creating, 180-191
  delays and overlaps,
    174-175, 191-193
  determining the
    dependent task, 175-176
  entering, 179-180
  relationships, 176-179
  removing, 193-195
  successor/predecessor
    tasks, compared,
    173-175
  Task Information dialog
    box, 181-183
Duration tracking field, 493
evolution, 474-475
Insight, 936
overtime, 332-333
reducing duration, 405
revising, 508
  Add Progress Line, 523
  Analyze Time-Scaled
    Data, 530-532
  calculating variances,
    509-510
  cost variances, 519
  date variances, 516-519
  Earned Value fields and
    report, 529-530
  Gantt Chart bars, 526-528
  progress lines, 523-526
  resource level, 521-522
  summary progress
    information, 510-514
  task level, 514
  variances, 508, 519-521
  week-to-week trends,
    532-533
  work variances, 514-515
saving, 479-480
settings, 172
tables, 681

tasks
    auditing links, 197-199
    resources, 252
    Standard calendar
      (default), 78
    updating, 533-539
    work
      modifying, 326-327
      overallocation, 347-348
      overtime, 358
      percent complete, 924
      resource assignments,
        284-287, 291-305,
        322-324

screens
    components, 29-32
    toolbars, positioning,
      874-875
    views, 744-745, 751-754

ScreenTips, 33

scroll bars, 56
    Calendar view, 218
    fields, selecting, 57-58
    tasks, finding , 57
    timescale, changing, 56

scrolling
    Gantt Chart, 915-916
    PERT Chart view, 228-229

searching
    Advanced Find dialog box,
      104-107
    files
      characters in names, 103
      date saved, 104
      specific text, 103-104
      type, 102-103
    ODBC File Open option, 107
    shortcut keys, 915
    see also finding

**Select Case program
  control, VBA (Visual Basic
  for Applications), 860**

SelectColumn method, 864

selecting, 925
    cells, 916
    keys, 228-229
    nodes, 234-235

objects (Gantt Chart
    view), 240
    tasks, 180-181

**Selection object (Project
  Object model), 851**

**Send Backward option
  (Draw button), 238**

**Send Schedule Note dialog
  box, 588-590**

**Send to Back option
  (Draw button), 238**

**Send To command (File
  menu), 575-582**

**Set Reminder command
  (Tools menu), 587-588**

setting
    baselines, 474-475
    orientation, 421
    page breaks, 419-420
    project goals, 19

Settings menu commands
    Control Panel, 77
    Printers, 415

Share Resources
    command (Tools menu),
      559-560
    dialog box, 559-560

sharing resources, 558
    discontinuing, 561-562
    files, saving, 560-561
    pools, 559-560, 562-563

shortcut keys
    activate, 120
    assigning, 901-902
    calculating, 914
    cells, selecting, 916
    editing, 914
    file operations, 917
    filtering, 915
    Find, 219
    formatting, 915
    Gantt Chart, scrolling,
      915-916
    Help, 917
    macros, 917
    menus, 914

outlining, 915
    searching, 915
    sorting, 915
    views, managing, 916

**Shortcut menu
  (toolbars), 874**

**Should Have Started Tasks
  report, 777**

**Should Start By filter,
  535-536**
    Resource, 690
    Task, 688

**Should Start/Finish By
  filter**
    Resource, 690
    Task, 688

Single pane view, 925

slack time, 372, 925

slippage, 925

Slipped/Late Progress filter
    Resource, 690
    Task, 688

**Slipping Tasks report,
  777-778**

soft constraints, 202

Software Launch file, 113

**Software Made
  Easy, Inc., 943**

**Sort By command (Project
  menu), 400-402**

Sort
    command (Project menu),
      418-419, 696, 802
    dialog box, 696

sorting
    crosstab reports, 825
    file names, 97-98
    reports, 801, 825
    resource lists, 276-278,
      399-402, 821
    shortcut keys, 915
    tasks, 399-402, 418-419,
      696-697, 814

Special Formatting Macro
    capturing, 840-841
    error handling, 865-867
    testing, 843

specific options (Options dialog box), 70

specifying margins in page setup, 422

spell checking, 403-405

Spelling
command (Tools menu), 403-404
dialog box, 403-404
tab (Options dialog box), 404-405

split bar and split box (Gantt Chart view), 54

Split command (Window menu), 223, 544, 678

split tasks, 925

staffing functions, 17

Standard calendar (default), 23-24, 78
editing, 79-82
saving, 85
time formats, 81
working days, 79-80
working hours, 81
Working Time text boxes, deleting, 82
resetting, 82

Standard Export HTML template, 450-451
background color, 451-454
background graphics, 454-455
graphic images, 455-456
hyperlinks, 460-462
title bar text, 456-457
text, 457-459

Standard Rate field (Resource Sheet view), 259

standard reports
accessing, 768-769
printing, 167-168, 436-437

Standard toolbar, 227, 873

Start field (resource assignments), 303-305

Start menu commands (Microsoft Project), 28

Start No Earlier Than (SNET) constraint, 204-205

Start No Later Than (SNLT) constraint, 204-205

Start-to-Finish (SF) relationship, 178-179

Start-to-Start (SS) relationship, 177-178

static copies, 594

Statistics tab (Properties sheet), 67

status bar, 35-36

status (of projects), 392
collapsing task list outline, 394-395
costs, 398-399, 408-409
crashing, 407-408
critical paths, 405-407
filtering, 395-398
reports (TeamStatus), 586-587
sorting, 399-402
spell checking, 403-404
summary reports, printing, 409-411
timescale, compressing, 393-394

string variables, 859

subprocedures, 857-858

subprojects, 925

subtasks, 925

successor tasks, 173-174, 925
delays, 174-175
dependent tasks, 175-176
predecessor tasks, compared, 175
task lists, adding, 811

summaries
reports
automating, 868-869
printing, 409-411

resource forms, 900
tables, 682, 684
tasks, 925
demoting/promoting, 161-162
duration, 136
linking, 195-196
lists, showing, 809

Summary tab (Properties sheet), 66-67

Summary Table view, 398-399

Summary Task Format Macro, 839-840

Summary Tasks filter, 396, 688

SV (Schedule Variance) field, 530

T

Table command (View menu), 748-749

Table Definition dialog box, 749

TableApply method, 864

TableEdit method, 865

tables, 331-332, 925
Baseline, 477
choosing, 745
cells, 916
comparing baselines and current schedules, 481-483
cost rate, 330-331, 920
creating, 748-749
columns, 749-750
definition, completing, 750-751
names, 749
data fields, 57-58
editing, 751-754
export/import maps, 922
non-Project format, 608
Resource, 680, 683-684
Standard, 679
Task, 680-683

Tracking, 497-499
Variance, 482
Work, 483-484

Task Details Form, 320-324, 672
correcting baselines, 477-478
entering tasks, 154, 206-207
updating tasks, 499-500

Task Entry view, 30, 51, 151-153, 678

Task filters, 687-689

Task Form view, 672
creating links, 183-185
entering overtime, 334-335
formatting, 727-730
removing links, 194
task type, selecting, 310
updating tasks, 499-500

Task Information dialog box, 147-148, 222-223, 663, 669
assigning resources, 318-319
creating links, 181-183
editing information in, 230
entering data, 148, 192, 205-206
inserted projects, 549
Notes tab, 148
removing links, 194
Task Type field, 292

task lists, 794
assignments
adding, 811
notes, 812
borders, creating, 812
creating, 126-127, 798
AutoCorrect feature, 130-132
defining elapsed duration, 135
durations, 134-137
Gantt Chart view, 128-133
mouse actions, 155-156
PERT Analysis toolbar, 137-139
customizing, 805-814

editing, 156
clearing, 156-157
copying, 157-160
deleting tasks, 156-157
moving tasks, 157-160
undoing changes, 156
filtering, 395-398, 809
gridlines, viewing, 812
inserting tasks
Gantt Chart view, 127-128
PERT Chart view, 150
recurring tasks, 142-147
Task Details view, 154
Task Entry view, 151-153
Task Sheet view, 154-155
notes, adding, 810
objects, adding, 810
outlining, 160-162
collapsing and expanding outlines, 162-164
detail tasks, 196-197
editing outlined projects, 164
indenting and outdenting tasks, 162
linking, 195-197
selecting display options, 164-165
summary tasks, 195-196
predecessor tasks, adding, 811
printing, 166
standard task reports, 167-168
task views, 166-167
sorting, 399-402, 801-802, 814
successor tasks, adding, 811
summaries, displaying, 809
text, formatting, 812-814
time period, changing, 808
totals, viewing, 812

Task Name Form, 673

Task object (Project Object model), 854-856
baselines, 855-856
BCWP (Budgeted Cost of Work Performed), 855

BCWS (Budgeted Cost of Work Scheduled), 855
Confirmed property, 855
constraints, 854
Contact property, 855
CV (Earned Value Cost Variance), 855
Fixed property, 855
HideBar property, 855
Leveling, 856
Marked property, 855
Milestone tasks, 855
Notes property, 855
OutlineLevel property, 855
predecessors, 854
properties, 854
resources, 854-855
RollUp property, 855
UniqueID, 854
views, 854

Task Objects Box, pasting objects into, 651-652

Task PERT Chart, 669

Task Range filter, 688

Task Relationships task form, 900

Task Report dialog box, 805

Task Sheet view, 670
Cost table, 262-263
formatting, 738-739
inserting tasks, 154-155

Task Usage
report, 788-789
view, 670
assigning resources, 324-326
baseline information, correcting, 478
comparing baselines and current schedules, 481
formatting, 738
modifying work schedules, 326-327

Task view, 926
items to add to menus, 894
resource assignments, 340-341

TaskClass, 933-934

tasks, 926

assigning resources, 311-312
  Assign Resources dialog
    box, 312-318
  Assignment Information
    dialog box, 327-331
  Task and Task Details
    Forms, 320-324
  Task Information dialog
    box, 318-319
  task tables, 331-332
  Task Usage view,
    324-327
  TeamAssign, 582-585
auditing links, 197-199
bars, 57
combining from files,
  546-554
constraints, 203-207
  comparing, 202-203
  inserting, 205-207
  removing, 207-208
  resolving conflicts,
    208-214
creating links between
  separate projects, 554-557
critical, 921
custom forms, 899
  creating, 902-904
  Custom Forms dialog
    box features, 908-909
  displaying with
    menus, 900
  Organizer, managing
    with, 909
  placing items on, 905-908
  predefined forms,
    899-900
  shortcut keys, assigning,
    901-902
  toolbar buttons,
    assigning to, 902
delays (lags), 174-175,
  371-374
dependent, 921
durations
  entering in Gantt Chart
    view, 134, 136-139
  estimating in Gantt Chart
    view, 136

effort driven, 921
external, 922
fixed, 922
formatting text displays for
  categories, 697-698
  fonts, 700-705
  text style, 700
hyperlinks
  adding, 463-464
  deleting, 464
  editing, 464
  managing projects,
    465-466
  navigating, 465
identifying in inserted
  projects, 553-554
linking, 179-180, 923
  auditing links, 197-199
  Autolink option, 189-191
  outlined lists, 195-197
  Task Form view, 183-185
  Task Information dialog
    box, 181-183
  with Entry Table, 185-187
  with menu, 180-181
  with mouse, 187-189
lists, *see* task lists
milestones, 923
moving to create inserted
  projects, 551-552
nodes, PERT Charts,
  233-235, 923
organizing with Work
  Breakdown Structure, 926
overtime, 300-301
predecessor, 924
  Finish-to-Finish (FF)
    relationship, 178
  Finish-to-Start (FS)
    relationship, 177
  Start-to-Finish (SF)
    relationship, 178-179
  Start-to-Start (SS)
    relationship, 177-178
priority, 924
recurring, 924
rescheduling, 535-536
Resource Driven, 924
roll up, 925
rows, adjusting height in
  Gantt Chart view, 133

scheduling
  based on costs, 252
  overallocation of
    resources, 347-348
selecting, 180-181, 291-296,
  711-712
sorting in views, 696
  selecting sort
    operation, 697
  sort keys, 697
split, 925
  assignments, 301-302
  eliminating
    overallocations, 374-375
  splitting feature, 199-202
subtasks, 925
successor, 925
  determining dependent
    tasks, 175-176
  versus predecessor,
    173-175
Summary, 925
tables, 331-332, 680- 683
tracking actual performance
  and costs, 486-487
tracking fields, 489-490
  Actual Costs, 493-495
  Actual Duration, 492
  Actual Finish Date,
    490-491
  Actual Start Date, 490
  Actual Work, 493-495
  Percent Complete,
    491-492
  Remaining Duration,
    492-493
  Scheduled Duration, 493
types, 308-311
updating, 495-496
  during projects, 488-489
  mouse in Gantt Chart,
    503-505
  Percent Complete
    buttons, 501
  Reschedule Work button,
    503-505
  sending updates
    via e-mail
    (TeamUpdate), 587
  Task and Task Details
    Forms, 499-500

Tracking table, 497-499
Update Project
command, 501-502
Update Tasks dialog box,
500-501
Usage views, 496-497
variances, 926

**Tasks In Progress
report, 776**

**Tasks Occurring On dialog
box, 217**

**Tasks With Attachments
filter, 688**

**Tasks With Fixed Dates
filter, 396-398, 688**

**Tasks/Assignments With
Overtime filter, 688**

TeamAssign, 582, 942
feedback to resources,
584-585
responding to requests,
583-584
sending messages, 582-583
TeamStatus messages,
586-587
TeamUpdate messages, 587

TeamInbox, using, 571-575

**TEAMS (Team Enabled
Automated Methodology
System), 582, 942**
feedback to resources,
584-585
responding to requests,
583-584
sending messages, 582-583
TeamStatus messages,
586-587
TeamUpdate messages, 587

**TeamStatus command
(Tools menu), 586-587**

**TeamUpdate command
(Tools menu), 587**

Template file format, 595

templates, 112
creating, 114
Global, 922

customizing reports, 796
modifying with
Organizer, 116
modifying standard HTML
background graphics,
defining, 454-455
formatting text, 457-459
graphic images,
displaying, 455-456
hyperlinks, adding,
460-462
title bar text, changing,
456-457
opening, 112-113
resources, creating, 280
samples, 113-114
Standard Export HTML,
modifying, 450-454

**temporary nature of
projects, 16**

**test options (filter criteria),
756-757**

**Test Style command
(Format menu), 840**

testing
logical values (filter
criteria), 758-766
macros, 842-844
Outline Numbering
Macro, 844
Special Formatting
Macro, 843

text
custom forms, 905-906
displays, formatting for
categories of tasks,
697-705
file formats, 637
exporting data, 638-639
importing data, 639
formatting, 700-701
calendar reports, 804-805
crosstab reports, 825
Font button, 426-428
HTML templates,
457-459
macros, 834-836
resource lists, 820-821
task lists, 812-814

Gantt Charts, 237
placing, 246
Project Summary
report, 804
reports, 800-801
title bar, 456-457

text boxes
creating, 246
Current Date and Status
Date, 64
editing text, 246
properties, changing,
247-248
Start and Finish Date, 63-64
Working Time, deleting in
Standard calendar, 82

Text Styles
command (Format menu),
685, 698, 801, 812, 834
dialog box, 698, 801,
812, 834
Font scroll bar, 700-705
Font Style list, 700
Item to Change
drop-down list,
698-699

**Text tab (Bar Styles dialog
box), 712-713**

time
delays, entering into
schedules, 191-193
formats, editing in the
Standard calendar, 81
lag time, 923
lead time, 923
period
resource lists, 817
task lists, 808
working time, 926
see also timescales

**Time Stamped field
(Resource Information
dialog box), 262-282**

TimeReview, 934

**Timescale command
(Format menu), 393-394,
704-705**
definition, 706
major scales, 705

minor scales, 706
nonworking time, 707-708

Timescale dialog box, 716-717

timescales, 926
compressing, 393-394
contour patterns, 300
formatting, 704-705
definition, 706
major scales, 705
minor scales, 706
nonworking time, 707-708
locating task bars, 57
printing views with timescales, 435-436
Resource Usage view, 355-356
scrolling through, 56

TimeServer, 940

TimeXchange, 933

title bar text, 456-457

To-Do List report, 786-787

Tool menu commands, Options, 702-704

toolbars, 33-34
adding items to menus, 894
Analysis, 873
built-in, 873-874, 883
buttons, 872
adding, 876, 877-879
changing, 877
custom forms, assigning to, 902
grouping, 879
identifying purpose, 873, 876
moving, 879
removing, 876, 877-879
combo boxes, resizing, 880
copying into project files, 889
creating, 880-882
copying existing toolbars, 881-882
deleting user-defined toolbars, 882-883
Custom Forms, 873

customizing, 875-876
displaying, 874-875
Drawing, 873
Formatting toolbar, 873
hiding, 874-875
managing with Organizer, 888-891
naming in Organizer, 889
PERT Analysis, 137-139, 873
positioning, 874-875
Project 95, 873
Project 98, 873
Resource Management, 873
Shortcut menu, 874
Standard toolbar, 873
Tracking, 873
Visual Basic, 873
Web, 873
Workgroup, 873

Toolbars command
Tools menu, 892-893
View menu, 874-875, 878

tools
Go To Next Overallocation, 354-355, 365
Zoom Out, 668

Tools menu, 900

Tools menu commands
Assign Resources, 312-318
AutoCorrect, 130-132
Change Working Time, 79, 826
Customize, 875
Filtered For, 221-222
Forms, 900
Options, 62, 70, 836
Organizer, 86
Progress Lines, 523-524
Project Summary Task, 510
Record Macro, 837
Resource Leveling, 373-374
Save Baseline, 476-478
Send Schedule Note, 588-590
Set Reminder, 587-588
Share Resources, 559-560
Spelling, 403-404
Team Assign, 582-583

TeamStatus, 586-587
TeamUpdate, 587
Toolbars, 892-893
Update Project, 501-502

ToolTips, identifying, 873

Top Level Tasks filter, 688

top-down approach to creating a task list, 126

Top-Level Tasks report, 770-771

Total Cost field (Task Sheet view), 262-263

Total Page Count button (Page Setup dialog box), 423

totals
crosstab reports, adding, 824
resource lists, viewing, 820
slack, 372, 925
task lists, viewing, 812

Tracking
command (View menu), 497-499
table, 497-499, 682
task form, 900
toolbar, 503-505, 873

tracking fields
Actual Costs, 493-495
Actual Duration, 492
Actual Finish Date, 490-491
Actual Start Date, 490
Actual Work, 493-495
Percent Complete, 491-492
Remaining Duration, 492-493
Scheduled Duration, 493

Tracking Gantt view, 484-486, 667

trapping errors
Special Formatting Macro, 866-867
VBA (Visual Basic for Applications), 862

troubleshooting
Personal Web Server (PWS), 568-569

VBA (Visual Basic for Applications), 862

Turtle pattern, 299

typing errors (AutoCorrect feature), 130-132

U

Unconfirmed Assignments filter, 690

Unconfirmed filter, 688

underused resources, substituting, 366-370

Undo command (Edit menu), 156, 225, 647

Unhide command (Window menu), 546

UniqueID (Task object), 854

Units field, resource assignments, 285-287

Unlink Tasks command (Edit menu), 194

Unstarted Assignments filter, 690

Unstarted Tasks
filter, 688
report, 774-775

Up arrow key, 229

Update as Scheduled button, 502

Update Needed filter, 688

Update Project command (Tools menu), 501-502

Update Tasks dialog box, 500-501

updating
projects, 486-487
schedules, 533, 538-539
completing on time and on budget, 536-538
reducing scope, 538
rescheduling remaining tasks/work, 533-536

tasks, facilities for, 495-496
mouse in Gantt Chart, 503-505
Percent Complete buttons, 501
Reschedule Work button, 503-505
Task and Task Details Forms, 499-500
Tracking table, 497-499
Update Project command, 501-502
Update Tasks dialog box, 500-501
Usage views, 496-497

URLs (Uniform Resource Locator), 441

Usage table, 682, 684

Usage view
selecting cells, 916
updating tasks, 496-497

user-defined constants, 860

user-defined toolbars, deleting, 882-883

Using Resource filter, 396, 689, 692

Using Resource in Date filter, 688

V

VAC (Variance at Completion) field, 530

values (filter criteria), 757-758
Resource Graph view, 732
Availability, 733-740
Cost, 733-740
Cumulative Cost, 734
Cumulative Work, 733-740
Overallocation, 733-740
Peak Units, 732-733
Percent Allocation, 733-740
Work, 733

variables, VBA (Visual Basic for Applications), 858-860

dates, 859
declarations statement, 858
keywords, 858
naming, 859
object variables, 859
string variable, 859

Variance
command (View menu), 482, 511
table, 482, 682

variances, 926
analyzing, 508, 522
calculating, 509-510
cost
finding, 519
reviewing for entire project, 512
date
reviewing for entire project, 511
Start and Finish Date, 516-519
work
finding, 514-515
reviewing for entire project, 510

VBA (Visual Basic for Applications), 849, 857
constants, 860
error handling, 862
debugging, 862
error trapping, 862
Outline Macro example, 862-865
runtime errors, 862
Special Formatting Macro example, 865-867
procedures, 857-858
program control, 860-861
Do...Loop, 861
For...Next loop, 861
GoTo statement, 861
If...Then...Else, 860
Select Case, 860
While...Wend loop, 861
Project Object model, 850
Application object, 850-852
Assistant object, 851-852

Calendar object, 856
Cell object, 851
Command Bars object, 851-852
List object, 853
Project object, 852-853
Resource object, 853
Selection object, 851
Task object, 854-856
VBE object, 852
properties, 852
report automating, 867-869
variables, 858-860
dates, 859
declarations statement, 858
keywords, 858
naming, 859
object variables, 859
string variable, 859

VBE object (Project Object model), 852

View Bar, 34-35

View Bar command (View menu), 34

View command, 926

View Definition dialog box, 743-744

View menu
accessing reports, 66
Organizer button, 764-765

View menu commands
Calendar, 216
Cost, 483, 512
Customize, 882
Entire project, 393
More Tables, 679
More Views, 54-55, 660, 742-744
Reports, 409-411, 436-437, 768-769, 793, 868
Table, 748-749
Toolbars, 874-875, 878
Tracking, 497-499
Variance, 482, 511
View Bar, 34
Work, 483-484, 510
Zoom, 220-221, 228, 724

View tab (Options dialog box), 77, 702-704

View tab (Page Setup dialog box), 428-430

View Table menu, 750-751

viewing
baselines, 476-477
files, 119-120
gridlines
crosstab reports, 824
task lists, 812
overtime work, 337
projects as HTML documents, 447
split windows, 223
zero values, crosstab reports, 824

views, 30-32, 926
bar, changing views, 54-55
Calendar, 660-661
changing, 54-55
combination, 660, 920, 746-748
creating, 742-744
choosing a table, 745
displaying name in menu, 746
entering name of view, 744
saving view definition, 746
selecting filters, 745
selecting screens, 744-745
form, 660
formatting
Calendar View, 716-719
Format menu, 696
Gantt Chart Wizard, 714-716
gridlines, 701-702
outline options, 702-704
PERT Chart, 719-727
Resource Graph, 730-736
selected text, 700-701
sorting tasks and resources, 696-698
Task and Resource Form views, 727

text displays for
categories, 697-705
timescales, 704-708
Gantt Chart, 50-52, 661-662
active split bar, 52
adjusting column widths, 132
adjusting height of task rows, 133
creating tasks, 128-132
defining elapsed duration, 135
duration for summary tasks, 136
entering delays and overlaps, 192
entering milestones, 140-142
entering task durations, 134-137
entering tasks, 127-128
estimating task durations, 136
formatting, 709-716
inserting recurring tasks, 142-147
locating current task bar, 139-140
PERT Analysis toolbar, 137-139
printing timescales, 435
progress bar, 526-528
split bar and split box, 54
splitting tasks, 200
graphical, 660
items to add to menus, 894-895
Leveling Gantt Chart, 374-375, 527
List object, 853
managing, 916
organizing in project files, 764-765
PERT Chart
entering delays and overlaps, 192
entering tasks, 150
printing, 166-167, 416-417
choosing view to print, 417-418

enhancing text data, 419
page breaks, 419-420
page setup, 420-421
selecting options, 428-430
sorting display, 418-419
Resource, 925
Resource Allocation, 679
    Delay field, 371-374
    substituting
        resources, 365
Resource Form, 677
    resource pools, defining,
        265-267
    scheduling overtime,
        362-364
Resource Graph, 673
Resource Name Form, 677
Resource Sheet, 676
    printing, 280-281
    resource pools, defining,
        264-265
Resource Sheet fields
    Accrue At, 260-261
    Base Calendar, 261
    Code, 261
    Cost Per Use, 260
    Group, 258-259
    ID, 257
    Indicators, 258
    Initials, 258-259
    Max Units, 258-259
    Name, 258
    Overtime Rate, 260
    Standard Rate, 259
Resource Usage, 675-676
    formatting, 736, 738
    overallocation of
        resources, 352-357
    scheduling overtime, 362
resources, 340
    Resource Allocation
        view, 341-342
    Resource Graph view,
        342-343
    Task and Resource
        Usage, 340-341
rollup, 662-663
    Bar, 663

Milestone, 665
    Milestone Date, 663
saving graphic images
    of, 635
sheet, 660
Single pane, 925
standard, 660
Summary Table, 398-399
Task, 926
Task and Resource Forms
    entry field options,
        727-730
    formatting options, 727
Task and Resource Sheet,
    738-739
Task Details, 154
Task Details Form, 672
    correcting baselines,
        477-478
    entering task constraints,
        206-207
Task Entry, 51, 678, 151-153
Task Form, 672
    creating links, 183-185
    removing links, 194
    task type, selecting, 310
Task Name Form, 673
Task object, 854
Task Sheet, 670
    Cost table, 262-263
    entering tasks, 154-155
Task Usage, 670
    assigning resources,
        324-327
    baseline information,
        correcting, 478
    comparing baselines and
        current schedules, 481
    formatting, 738
Tracking Gantt, 484-486
Usage
    selecting cells (shortcut
        keys), 916
    updating tasks, 496-497
virus protection, 100-101
Visual Basic Editor, editing
    macros, 844

Visual Basic for
    Applications (VBA),
    849, 857
    constants, 860
    error handling, 862
        debugging, 862
        error trapping, 862
        Outline Macro example,
            862-865
        runtime errors, 862
        Special Formatting
            Macro example,
            865-867
    procedures, 857-858
    program control, 860-861
        Do...Loop, 861
        For...Next loop, 861
        GoTo statement, 861
        If...Then...Else, 860
        Select Case, 860
        While...Wend loop, 861
    Project Object model, 850
        Application object,
            850-852
        Assistant object, 851-852
        Calendar object, 856
        Cell object, 851
        Command Bars object,
            851-852
        List object, 853
        Project object, 852-853
        Resource object, 853
        Selection object, 851
        Task object, 854-856
        VBE object, 852
    properties, 852
    report automating, 867-869
    variables, 858-860
        dates, 859
        declarations
            statement, 858
        keywords, 858
        naming, 859
        object variables, 859
        string variable, 859
Visual Basic toolbar,
    837, 873

W-X-Y

warning messages
Planning Wizard, 206
saving baselines, 108
virus protection, 100-101

WBS Chart for Project, 930

Web browsers, 441

Web documents, publishing, 467

Web pages
exporting data to, 442
saving projects as HTML documents, 442-447
viewing projects as HTML documents, 447
modifying stardard HTML template, 450-451
background color, 451-454
background graphics, defining, 454-455
formatting text, 457-459
graphic images, displaying, 455-456
hyperlinks, adding, 460-462
title bar text, changing, 456-457
MPD files
creating from, 466
updating, 466
navigating with hyperlinks, 441-442

Web Publishing Wizard, 467

Web servers for intranets, 567-575

Web sites
Frequently Asked Questions, 48
Microsoft, 441
Microsoft Project, 46
Online Support, 48
Product News, 46
Project Management Institute, 17

Web toolbar, 873

WebInbox, using, 571-575

WebTime, 933

Week Headings tab (Timescale dialog box), 716

week-to-week trends, analyzing, 532-533

weeks, defining in options, 72-73

Welcome! dialog box, 28-29

What's This? command (Help menu), 33, 36, 874

While...Wend loop program control, VBA (Visual Basic for Applications), 861

Who Does What report, 784-785

Who Does What When report, 785

wild cards, 926
character strings (filter criteria), 759-766

Window menu, working with multiple projects, 544-545

Window menu commands
Arrange All, 119-120, 545-546
Hide, 546
New Window, 546, 546-547
Split, 51, 223, 544, 678
Unhide, 546

windows
items to add to menus, 894
splitting view, 223

Windows Clipboard
copying and pasting data, 639-641
moving and copying tasks, 157

Windows operations, 917

Within test (filter criteria), 758-766

work
directory, changing, 93-94
formula, calculating, 287-288, 308
applying in new assignments, 288-289
changing existing assignments, 289
driver resource concept, 290-291
hours, editing in the Standard calendar, 81
overtime, assigning, 332
entering in fields, 334-336
schedules and charges for overtime, 332-333
viewing, 337
resource assignment field, 287
schedules
assigning resources, 322-324
modifying with Task Usage view, 326-327
see also schedules
time, 926
variances
finding, 514-515
reviewing for entire project, 510

Work Breakdown Structure (WBS), 126, 160, 926

Work command (View menu), 483-484, 510

Work Complete filter, 690

Work equation, 293

Work Incomplete filter, 690

Work Overbudget filter
Resource, 690
Task, 689

Work table, 483-484, 682, 684

Work Tracking
resource form, 900
task form, 900

Workgroup
field (Resource Information dialog box), 261
toolbar, 873

workgroups, 926
circulating items for review, 575-576, 578
routing slips, 579-582
communicating, 567
e-mail, 567
Internet communication, 575
intranet communication, 567-575
requesting status reports, 586-587
Send Schedule Notes command (Tools menu), 588-590
sending task updates, 587
setting task reminders, 587-588
submitting status reports, 586-587
Team Assign, 582-585
managers, 567

working and nonworking days, 78
editing in the Standard calendar, 79-80, 85-90

Working Days report, 772-773, 804-805

Working Time
options, 274-276
tab, 364-365
text boxes, 82
times, changing for resource calendars, 273

Workload category reports, 788
Resource Usage, 789-790
Task Usage, 788-789

workspace, saving multiple files, 560-561

Workspace file, saving, 111-112

write protecting files, 109

yearly recurring tasks, creating, 146-147

Z

zero values, viewing crosstab reports, 824

Zoom
button (Calendar view), 220-221
command (View menu), 228, 724

Zoom Out
button (Standard toolbar), 227, 393
tool, 668

zooming, 227-228, 240

Check out Que® Books
on the World Wide Web
http://www.mcp.com/que

As the biggest software release in computer history, Windows 95 continues to redefine the computer industry. Click here for the latest info on our Windows 95 books

Make computing quick and easy with these products designed exclusively for new and casual users

Examine the latest releases in word processing, spreadsheets, operating systems, and suites

The Internet, The World Wide Web, CompuServe®, America Online®, Prodigy® —it's a world of ever-changing information. Don't get left behind!

Find out about new additions to our site, new bestsellers and hot topics

In-depth information on high-end topics: find the best reference books for databases, programming, networking, and client/server technologies

A recent addition to Que, Ziff-Davis Press publishes the highly-successful *How It Works* and *How to Use* series of books, as well as *PC Learning Labs Teaches* and *PC Magazine* series of book/disk packages

Stay on the cutting edge of Macintosh® technologies and visual communications

Find out which titles are making headlines

With 6 separate publishing groups, Que develops products for many specific market segments and areas of computer technology. Explore our Web Site and you'll find information on best-selling titles, newly published titles, upcoming products, authors, and much more.

- Stay informed on the latest industry trends and products available
- Visit our online bookstore for the latest information and editions
- Download software from Que's library of the best shareware and freeware

Complete and Return this Card
for a *FREE* Computer Book Catalog

Thank you for purchasing this book! You have purchased a superior computer book written expressly for your needs. To continue to provide the kind of up-to-date, pertinent coverage you've come to expect from us, we need to hear from you. Please take a minute to complete and return this self-addressed, postage-paid form. In return, we'll send you a free catalog of all our computer books on topics ranging from word processing to programming and the Internet.

Mr. ☐　　Mrs. ☐　　Ms. ☐　　Dr. ☐

Name (first) ☐☐☐☐☐☐☐☐☐☐☐☐　(M.I.) ☐　(last) ☐☐☐☐☐☐☐☐☐☐☐☐☐☐☐☐☐

Address ☐☐☐☐☐☐☐☐☐☐☐☐☐☐☐☐☐☐☐☐☐☐☐☐☐☐☐☐☐☐☐☐

☐☐☐☐☐☐☐☐☐☐☐☐☐☐☐☐☐☐☐☐☐☐☐☐☐☐☐☐☐☐☐☐

City ☐☐☐☐☐☐☐☐☐☐☐☐☐☐☐☐☐☐　State ☐☐　Zip ☐☐☐☐☐ ☐☐☐☐

Phone ☐☐☐ ☐☐☐ ☐☐☐☐　Fax ☐☐☐ ☐☐☐ ☐☐☐☐

Company Name ☐☐☐☐☐☐☐☐☐☐☐☐☐☐☐☐☐☐☐☐☐☐☐☐☐☐☐☐☐☐

E-mail address ☐☐☐☐☐☐☐☐☐☐☐☐☐☐☐☐☐☐☐☐☐☐☐☐☐☐☐☐☐☐

1. Please check at least (3) influencing factors for purchasing this book.

Front or back cover information on book .... ☐
Special approach to the content .... ☐
Completeness of content .... ☐
Author's reputation .... ☐
Publisher's reputation .... ☐
Book cover design or layout .... ☐
Index or table of contents of book .... ☐
Price of book .... ☐
Special effects, graphics, illustrations .... ☐
Other (Please specify): _____ ☐

2. How did you first learn about this book?

Saw in Macmillan Computer Publishing catalog .... ☐
Recommended by store personnel .... ☐
Saw the book on bookshelf at store .... ☐
Recommended by a friend .... ☐
Received advertisement in the mail .... ☐
Saw an advertisement in: _____ ☐
Read book review in: _____ ☐
Other (Please specify): _____ ☐

3. How many computer books have you purchased in the last six months?

This book only .... ☐　　3 to 5 books .... ☐
2 books .... ☐　　More than 5 .... ☐

4. Where did you purchase this book?

Bookstore .... ☐
Computer Store .... ☐
Consumer Electronics Store .... ☐
Department Store .... ☐
Office Club .... ☐
Warehouse Club .... ☐
Mail Order .... ☐
Direct from Publisher .... ☐
Internet site .... ☐
Other (Please specify): _____ ☐

5. How long have you been using a computer?

☐ Less than 6 months　　☐ 6 months to a year
☐ 1 to 3 years　　　　　　☐ More than 3 years

6. What is your level of experience with personal computers and with the subject of this book?

	With PCs	With subject of book
New	☐	☐
Casual	☐	☐
Accomplished	☐	☐
Expert	☐	☐

Source Code ISBN: 0-0000-1252-0

7. Which of the following best describes your job title?

Administrative Assistant .... ☐
Coordinator .... ☐
Manager/Supervisor .... ☐
Director .... ☐
Vice President .... ☐
President/CEO/COO .... ☐
Lawyer/Doctor/Medical Professional .... ☐
Teacher/Educator/Trainer .... ☐
Engineer/Technician .... ☐
Consultant .... ☐
Not employed/Student/Retired .... ☐
Other (Please specify): _____ ☐

8. Which of the following best describes the area of the company your job title falls under?

Accounting .... ☐
Engineering .... ☐
Manufacturing .... ☐
Operations .... ☐
Marketing .... ☐
Sales .... ☐
Other (Please specify): _____ ☐

9. What is your age?

Under 20 .... ☐
21-29 .... ☐
30-39 .... ☐
40-49 .... ☐
50-59 .... ☐
60-over .... ☐

10. Are you:

Male .... ☐
Female .... ☐

11. Which computer publications do you read regularly? (Please list)

_____
_____
_____
_____
_____
_____
_____
_____
_____
_____

Comments: _____
_____
_____

Fold here and tape to mail